The Dynamics of Socio-Economic Development

An Introduction

Why are poor countries poor and rich countries rich? How are wealth and poverty related to changes in nutrition, health, life expectancy, education, population growth and politics? This modern, non-technical introduction to development studies explores the dynamics of socio-economic development and stagnation in developing countries. Taking a quantitative and comparative approach to contemporary debates within their broader context, Szirmai examines historical, institutional, demographic, sociological, political and cultural factors. Key chapters focus on economic growth, technological change, industrialisation and agricultural development, and consider social dimensions such as population growth, health and education. Each chapter contains comparative statistics on trends from a sample of twenty-nine developing countries. This rich statistical database allows students to strengthen their understanding of comparative development experiences. Assuming no prior knowledge of economics, the book is suited for use in interdisciplinary development studies programmes as well as economics courses, and will also interest practitioners pursuing careers in developing countries.

ADAM SZIRMAI is Professor of Technology and Development Studies at Eindhoven University of Technology, the Netherlands, and one of the founders of the Eindhoven Centre for Innovation Studies.

The Dynamics of Socio-Economic Development

An Introduction

Adam Szirmai

CAMBRIDGE
UNIVERSITY PRESS

CAMBRIDGE UNIVERSITY PRESS
Cambridge, New York, Melbourne, Madrid, Cape Town, Singapore, São Paulo,
Delhi, Tokyo, Mexico City

Cambridge University Press
The Edinburgh Building, Cambridge CB2 8RU, UK

Published in the United States of America by Cambridge University Press, New York

www.cambridge.org
Information on this title: www.cambridge.org/9780521520843

First published by Cambridge University Press 2005 as *The Dynamics of Socio-Economic*
Development: an Introduction
© Cambridge University Press 2005

First published 2005
5th printing 2011

Printed in the United Kingdom at the University Press, Cambridge

A catalogue record for this publication is available from the British Library

Library of Congress Cataloging-in-publication Data

Szirmai, Adam, 1946–
Dynamics of socio–economic development: an introduction/by Adam Szirmai.–2nd ed.
  p. cm.
Rev. ed. of: Economic and social development. 1997.
Includes bibliographical references and index.
ISBN 0–521–81763–3 (alk. paper) – ISBN 0–521–52084–3 (pbk. : alk. paper)
1. Economic development.   2. Social change.   I. Szirmai, Adam, 1946– Economic
and social development.   II. Title.

HD75.S97 2004   2004058281
338.9–dc22

ISBN 978-0-521-81763-9 Hardback
ISBN 978-0-521-52084-3 Paperback

Accompanying website: http://www.dynamicsofdevelopment.com

Contents

Figures

Tables

Boxes

Preface

The aim of this book is to provide a general introduction to the dynamics of socio-economic development and to the study of the problems of developing countries. It is a reflection of multidisciplinary courses on 'development', which I have been teaching since 1987 at the University of Groningen and the Eindhoven University of Technology. The book was written for students of universities and other institutions of higher education, who encounter the problems of developing countries in the course of their own disciplinary studies and who are in need of a general introduction to this field. It is also intended for people pursuing a professional career in developing countries and readers with a general interest in development. The text can be read as an introduction by students with no prior knowledge of development. It also can be used at a more advanced level as a handbook, providing an overview of current theoretical and empirical debates and controversies in the field of development studies. The book provides non-economists with a non-technical introduction to economic perspectives on development, while introducing economists to a broader socio-economic view of development.

The central issue in development, as approached in this book, lies in low levels of per capita income and low standards of living among the mass of the population in the so-called developing countries. The key elements in the book are trends in per capita income and changes in standards of living and welfare, and the factors that affect economic development or economic stagnation in the long term. The core of development is thus defined in economic terms. However, the explanatory factors are not limited to economic ones. Historical, institutional, cultural, demographic, political, social and ecological factors are all of great importance for the analysis of economic development. They will receive ample attention in the book.

It needs to be emphasised that the concept of development is much broader than that of economic development alone. Development involves a wide range of changes in a variety of social indicators such as health, education, technology or life expectancy, which are directly or indirectly linked to economic changes, but which need to be studied in their own right. This is reflected in the title of the book, which refers to socio-economic development.

The structure of the book takes the key factors distinguished in economic theories of growth – labour, capital and land and technological change – as its main point of departure. However, in line with the interdisciplinary nature of the book, these factors are interpreted in broad fashion. Technological change lies at the heart of growth and economic development. Two main issues discussed in chapter 4 are the role of technological change in development, and the consequences of accelerating technological change for developing countries. The treatment of the primary production factor 'labour' is couched in terms of a more general discussion of demographic and human factors in development. These include population growth and the interrelationships between population growth and economic development (Chapter 5), topics such as health, disease, mortality and life expectancy (Chapter 6) and education, human capital and literacy (Chapter 7). I argue that health and education are important as independent aspects of development in their own right. But the state of health and levels of education also influence the quality of the labour force, the productivity of labour and the socio-economic dynamics of a country.

Modern economic growth is historically associated with massive capital accumulation in the industrial sector and a structural transformation of agrarian societies into societies in which industry and services become more and more important. Structural change and the shift to industry are discussed in Chapter 8, which also deals with the role of primary exports in these transformations. Capital accumulation is discussed in Chapter 9 in the context of the overall process of industrialisation. This chapter also pays attention to the different industrialisation strategies that developing countries have followed over time, including import substitution, balanced growth, labour intensive export orientation, promotion of the informal sector and technological upgrading.

The discussion of the production factor 'land' is broadened to include the whole issue of agricultural and rural development. The role of the agricultural sector in the wider process of development is examined in Chapter 8, which makes a case for the continued importance of agriculture in developing countries. In Chapter 10, the development of agricultural production and productivity is discussed against the background of social changes in rural communities and rural areas. This chapter also presents data on trends in food consumption and an overview of the recent debates on modern biotechnology.

The discussion of economic development in Chapters 4 to 10, is preceded and followed by chapters which place development in an historical and international perspective. Chapter 2 focuses on the development of the international economic and political order since the fifteenth century. Chapter 3 deals with the theories and empirics of growth and stagnation. The approach in these chapters is historical and comparative. Chapter 11 focuses on the political aspects of development and the interrelations between state formation, democratic rule and economic growth. Chapter 12 introduces the cultural context of development and discusses the dynamic relationships between cultural change and economic development. Changes in the international political and economic order since World War II are reviewed in Chapter 13. In this chapter, attention is paid to the evolution of international institutions and organisations on the one hand, and the implications of the international division of labour and free trade for developing countries on the other. This chapter includes a discussion of developing country debt, the emergence of structural adjustment policies and the recent debates on globalisation and the architecture of the international financial system. The final chapter (Chapter 14) focuses on the role of foreign aid in development. Foreign aid is seen as part of international resource flows. It is discussed in the context of theories of development and the many different factors influencing development in the long run. Every chapter ends with questions for review and suggestions for further readings.

Empirical data have an important place in this book. It is my conviction that a serious debate of development issues should be grounded in sound empirical information. Throughout the book, I present empirical data on long-run economic, social and political trends for a sample of twenty-nine developing countries, representing Asia, Latin America and Africa. These twenty-nine countries represent more than three-quarters of the total population of developing countries in the year 2000. The same set of countries is used throughout the book, providing an empirical basis for the discussion of theories, patterns and trends in development. The book contains over seventy tables, usually covering the period from 1950 to the present and sometimes going back to the pre-war period. The country data are supplemented by aggregate statistics for different regions and continents.

This book is accompanied by a website, which presents the detailed worksheets underlying the tables in the book. These worksheets show how the tables in the book have been put together from a variety of sources. The address of this website is: http:\\www.dynamicsofdevelopment.com. We hope this website will serve as an important didactic tool for the empirical study of development. It will introduce students to the increasing wealth of international comparative statistics on all dimensions of development. More and more data are accessible in electronic form on websites of research institutions and international organisations. Our website will provide links and references to the most important international sources of data on development, serving as a structured portal for statistics on development. A second function of the website is to foster a more critical attitude towards the use of statistics. Statistical tables are constructs, which depend on assumptions, models, concepts, decisions about what data to use, how to combine data from different sources, what years to compare, how to link data for different years in a consistent fashion and so forth. It is important to be clear about how the data have been collected and organised, what assumptions and choices have been made and what sources have been used. If such information is not provided – as is too often the case – the statistics cannot be trusted. Examination of the worksheets on the website will help readers to formulate their own conclusions, which may well differ from those of this author. They will come to understand that tables should be seen as working hypotheses, rather than final statements. Finally, the website allows us to provide more detail than is possible in the tables in the book. It will also allow for updating on a continuous basis, so the statistics remain up to date.

Despite its considerable length this book has no pretensions to completeness. The attempt to synthesise a very wide range of subjects in a single book will inevitably leave specialists on different topics unsatisfied. Also, the book is written as an introduction to the ongoing debate on development, rather than a final summary of our knowledge of all different aspects of it. In the choice of subjects, the emphasis has been on the long-run dynamics of development and the factors that play a role in these dynamics.

This book has a long history. A first version was published in Dutch in 1993. An English translation was published in 1997 by Prentice Hall under the title *Social and Economic Development: Trends. Problems Policies.* However, both the real world and our thinking about development are changing so rapidly that a mere revision was not sufficient. All chapters have been fundamentally rewritten and expanded, the analysis has changed in the light of new insights, new chapters have been added on technology and culture, and new statistics and materials have been incorporated. This has resulted in what amounts to a new textbook, under a new title and with a new publisher. I am grateful to Cambridge University Press for allowing me to undertake this task.

I could not have written this book without the support of numerous colleagues and ex-colleagues. They generously let me profit from their knowledge of and insights into the various aspects of development. I have made extensive use of their advice, their publications, and their empirical research. I have both learned from and enjoyed years of fruitful and intensive discussions with them. I would like to thank the following persons for their advice and stimulating comments on previous drafts of the manuscript: Bart van Ark, Carolina Castaldi, Peter Druijven, Pierre van der Eng, Jacob de Haan, Hal Hill, Niels Hermes, Jojo Jacob, Hans-Paul Klijnsma, Jos Koetsier, Remco Kouwenhoven, Paul Lapperre, Robert Lensink, Angus Maddison, Kees van der Meer, Nanno Mulder, Allessandro Nuvolari, Howard Pack, Dirk Pilat, Gé Prince, Henny Romijn, Johan Schot, Jan Stel, Ida Terluin, Marcel Timmer, Harry van Vianen, Geert Verbong and Bart Verspagen. As always, the responsibility for the book and its shortcomings rests with the author alone. A special word of thanks is due to Paul Lapperre for his help designing the cover and selecting the illustrations.

In preparing the tables, I have been fortunate to enjoy the support of a series of enthusiastic and talented student assistants. At the Eindhoven University of Technology, Dennis Bours, Rick van der Kamp, Herjan Siegers and Rik Luiten have helped collect and organise the statistical materials incorporated in the book. During the last year-and-a-half, Souli Nnafie has provided invaluable help in updating and revising all the tables. I am also thankful for the generous support and encouragement provided by Chris Harrison, Pat Maurice and their colleagues at Cambridge University Press. I gratefully dedicate this book, as previous ones, to my wife Veronika.

Adam Szirmai
Eindhoven   January 2004

Abbreviations

ACER	age-specific enrolment rate
ACP	Asian, Caribbean and Pacific Countries
ADB	Asian Development Bank
ASEAN	Association of South East Asian Nations
BMR	basal metabolic rate
CFCs	chlorofluorocarbons
CGIAR	Consultative Group on International Agricultural Research
CIF	cost, insurance and freight included
CIMMYT	Centro Internacional de Mejoramienta de Maiz y Trigo (International Maize and Wheat Improvement Centre)
CMEA	Council for Mutual Economic Assistance
CPI	Corruption Perceptions Index
DAC	Development Assistance Committee (OECD)
DALYs	disability-adjusted life years
DRS	Debt Reporting System (World Bank)
ECLA	United Nations Economic Commission for Latin America
ECOSOC	Economic and Social Council of the UN
EEC	European Economic Community
EC	European Community
ECLA	United Nations Commission for Latin America
ESAF	Enhanced Structural Fund Facility (IMF)
ESCAP	United Nations Economic and Social Commission for Asia and the Pacific
EU	European Union
EWLP	Experimental World Literacy Programme
FAO	United Nations Food and Agriculture Organisation
FDI	foreign direct investment
FLN	Front de la libération nationale (national liberation front, Algeria)
fob	free on board
GATT	General Agreement on Tariffs and Trade
GDFF	Geographical Distribution of Financial Flows to Developing Countries
GDP	gross domestic product
GFCF	gross fixed capital formation
GGDC	Groningen Growth and Development Centre
GNP	gross national product

GSP	Generalised System of Preferences
HALE	healthy life expectancy
HDR	Human Development Report
HIPCs	heavily indebted poor countries
IADB	Inter-American Development Bank
IBPGR	International Board for Plant Genetic Resources
IBRD	International Bank for Reconstruction and Development (World Bank)
ICC	International Criminal Court
ICRASAT	Research Institute for Crops in the Semi-arid Tropics
ICT	Information and Communication Technology
IDA	International Development Association
IFAD	International Fund for Agricultural Development
IFC	International Finance Corporation
ILO	International Labour Organization
IMF	International Monetary Fund
IPPC	Intergovernmental Panel on Climate Change
IRRI	International Rice Research Institute
ISI	import-substituting industrialisation
ISIC	International Standard Industrial Classification
ITO	International Trade Organisation
LAFTA	Latin American Free Trade Association
LDCs	least developed countries
LEISA	low external input and sustainable agriculture
LMICs	lower-middle-income countries
MICs	moderately indebted countries/middle-income countries
MITI	Ministry of Industry and Trade (Japan)
MNCs	multinational companies
MPS	material product system
N ach	need for achievement
NAFTA	North American Free Trade Association
NATO	North Atlantic Treaty Organisation
NFDI	net foreign direct investment
NGO	Non Governmental Organisation
NICs	newly industrialising countries
NIEO	New International Economic Order
NToD	net transfers on debt
OA	Other Assistance
OAU	Organisation of African Unity
OAS	Organisation of American States
ODA	Official Development Assistance
OECD	Organisation for Economic Cooperation and Development
OEM	original equipment manufacturing
OFID	OPEC Fund for International Development
OPEC	Organisation of Petroleum Exporting Countries

PPPs	purchasing power parities
PRI	Institutional Revolutionary Party
PRS	poverty reduction strategy
QUALYs	quality-adjusted life years
RAUI	'risk aversion causes underinvestment'
R&D	research and development
SAL	Structural Adustment Loan (World Bank)
SAF	Structural Adjustment Facility (IMF)
SECAL	Sectoral Adjustment Loan (World Bank)
SICs	semi-industrialised countries: or severely indebted countries
SNA	System of National Accounts
TNCs	transnational companies
TRIPS	Agreement on Trade-Related Aspects of Intellectual Property Rights
TVEs	township and village enterprises
UIA	Union of International Associations
UMICs	upper-middle-income-countries
UN	United Nations
UNCED	United Nations Conference on Environment and Development
UNCTAD	United Nations Conference on Trade and Development
UNDP	United Nations Development Programme
UNEP	United Nations Environmental Programme
UNEPTA	United Nations Extended Program of Technical Assistance
UNESCO	United Nations Educational, Scientific and Cultural Organisation
UNICEF	United Nations Children Fund
UNIDO	United Nations Industrial Development Organisation
UNITAR	United Nations Institute for Training and Research
UNPF	United Nations Population Fund
USAID	United States Agency for International Development
USSR	Union of Socialist Soviet Republics
WB	World Bank (see IBRD)
WDI	World Development Indicators (World Bank)
WDR	World Development Report (World Bank)
WDT	World Debt Tables (World Bank)
WFP	World Food Programme
WHO	World Health Organization
WIPO	World Intellectual Property Organisation
WRI	World Resources Institute
WT	World Tables (World Bank)
WTO	World Trade Organisation
WWI	World Watch Institute

Acknowledgements

I gratefully acknowledge permission to reproduce the following materials: for Figure 6.1, from 'Relations between Life Expectancy at Birth and National Income per Head for Nations in the 1930s, 1990s and 1960s', scatter diagram in S. Preston, 'The Changing Relation between Mortality and Level of Economic Development, in *Population Studies*, ISSN 9032-4728, 29 (2), 1975, p. 235, Journal of Population Studies, Copyright © Routledge/Taylor Francis; for Table 1.2, from 'Cumulative Percentage of Persons and Incomes/Expenditures', Table 16 in B. Milanovic, 'The World Income Distribution 1988 and 1993. First Calculation Based on Household Surveys Only', *The Economic Journal*, 112, January 2002, pp. 512–92 (published by Blackwell Publishers), Copyright © Blackwell Publishing; for Table 1.3 from 'Population Living Below $1.08 and $2.15 per Day at 1993 PPP by Region', Table 2 in S. Chen and M. Ravallion, 'How Did the World's Poorest Fare in the 1990s?', *Review of Income and Wealth*, 47 (3), September, 2001, p. 290 (published by Blackwell Publishers), Copyright © Blackwell Publishing; for Table 3.7, from 'Gross Value of Foreign Capital Stock in Developing Countries, 1870–1998', Table 3.3 in Angus Maddison, *The World Economy: A Millennial Perspective*, Development Centre Studies, Paris: OECD, 2001, p. 18, Copyright © OECD, Publishing and Editorial Rights Unit; for Table 10.8, from data in top panel of 'Sources of Growth of Crop Production', Table 4.2 in J. Bruinsma (ed.), *World Agriculture towards 2015/2030: An FAO Perspective*, Food and Agriculture Organization (FAO) Rome, London: Earthscan, 2003, p. 126, Copyright © FAO.

'Traditional Junk in Hong Kong', p. 1, reproduced with the permission of the Time Warner Book Group © Time Warner Book Group; 'Paolo Forlani's World Map of 1571', p. 35, reproduced with the permission of the British Library Topographical Image Collection; 'Squatters in Bombay', p. 68, reproduced with the permission of the Ministry of Foreign Affairs, the Netherlands; 'People shopping in Tokyo's main street', p. 141, reproduced with the permission of the Time Warner Book Group © Time Warner Book Group; 'Health Poster', p. 177, reproduced with the permission of UNICEF; 'Education in China', p. 213, reproduced with the permission of UNICEF; 'Polls in South Africa', p. 426, reproduced with the permission of the Time Warner Book Group © Time Warner Book Group; 'UN meeting', p. 515, reproduced with the permission of the Time Warner Book Group © Time Warner Book Group; 'Rice project in Côte d'Ivoire', p. 580, reproduced with the permission of Bussum, Unieboek.

1 Developing countries and the concept of development

This introductory chapter focuses on the concept of development. The low standard of living of the mass of the population in developing countries is singled out as the key issue in development. The development of per capita income over time and the factors that influence economic development or stagnation are important topics in this book. However, the interplay between economic and non-economic factors is of great importance for our understanding of the dynamics of socio-economic development. Economic development cannot be explained by economic factors only, and the concept of development includes more than mere changes in economic indicators.

After a discussion of problems of involvement and detachment in the study of development issues in sections 1.1 and 1.2, we examine the concept of development in sections 1.3 to 1.5. Indicators of growth and development are presented in section 1.6. Section 1.7 highlights the differences between developing countries and the variety of development experiences. The final section addresses the question of what developing countries have in common in spite of all their differences.

1

1.1 Approaches to development

In discussions of development issues two general approaches can be distinguished (see Myint, 1980):

1. *The fight against poverty* This approach focuses on the problems of widespread poverty, hunger and misery in developing countries and on the question of what can be done in order to realise improvements of the situation in the *short term*.
2. *The analysis of long-term economic and social development* This approach concentrates on comparing developments in different countries, regions and historical periods in order to gain a better understanding of the factors that have *long-term* effects on the dynamics of socio-economic development.

One of the characteristics of the first approach is a strong involvement with the problems of developing countries and their inhabitants. Most people who study development issues do so because they feel that present levels of poverty, misery and injustice are simply unacceptable. Their aim is to arrive at concrete recommendations for action. This approach is closely linked with development policies and strategies at international, national, regional or local levels. Some people choose a technocratic interpretation, focusing on policies, instruments and projects, others choose a more radical–political interpretation. The latter argue for political action in order to achieve dramatic changes in the existing order of things.

A potential drawback of strong involvement is a certain trendiness in thinking about development. To illustrate this, one can point to the endless succession of ideas and slogans that have played a role in post-war discussions of development: the idea that large-scale injections of capital are the key to development ('big push'); the 'small is beautiful' movement; human capital as the missing link in development; the green revolution as a technological fix for agricultural development; community development; appropriate technologies; basic needs; integrated rural development; self-reliance; delinking from the world economy; the New International Economic Order; market orientation and deregulation; promotion of the informal sector; structural adjustment policies; or sustainable development.

A common characteristic of these recipes for development is their short-term perspective. Time and again, proposals have been put forward in order to achieve certain goals, preferably within a decade or two (see, for example, Brandt, 1980; 1983; Brundtland, 1987; UNDP, 2003). In the meantime, developments that take place irrespective of the fashion of the day are ignored or disregarded. These fashions often evoke a brief surge of enthusiasm in the world of politics, policy and the development sciences. But when the immediate results are slow in materialising, disenchantment sets in again. The issue disappears from the public eye, and new and more appealing solutions and catch-phrases emerge. The greater the involvement, the harder it is to distinguish between desirability and reality, and the greater the disappointment that follows when the real world proves less manageable than one had hoped (see Elias, 1970). Some of the major mistakes in development policies are a direct consequence of erroneous advice from development advisers and experts. An example is the neglect of the agricultural sector in the drive for industrialisation at all costs in the 1950s.

The long-term approach to development is more detached. One tries to comprehend why, in the long term, such great differences in development have occurred in the different parts of the world (Szirmai, 1993). One tries to identify the factors that may help to explain different patterns of development, such as the accumulation of production factors, the efficiency with which these factors of production are being used, technological changes, external political and economic influences, historical factors, institutions and cultural differences. Economic and social policies figure among these factors, but considering policy as only one of many relevant factors may help to deflate immoderate pretensions and hopes of policy makers, politicians and scientific advisers.

The long-term approach emphasises that economic growth in its modern form is intimately associated with the economic development of the Western countries since the mid-eighteenth century (Landes, 1998; Maddison, 2001). Therefore, the history of the economic development of prosperous European and North American countries will often serve as a point of reference in our comparative discussions of the experiences of developing countries. This is not simply to advocate the copying of Western solutions by developing countries. Rather we hope to gain an insight into the similarities and differences in development processes.

The history of modern economic growth is also associated with industrialisation and a process that Higgins and Higgins (1979: p. 3) have ironically described as 'getting rid of farmers'. Again this historical relationship between industrialisation and economic growth cannot be applied indiscriminately to developing countries. It does, however, serve as another point of reference. Furthermore, comparisons of the historical development of economically advanced countries and developing countries may teach us much about the role of institutions in advancing or impeding economic development. In this context one can think of land tenure relations, intellectual and other property rights, patent institutions, processes of state formation or the emergence of financial institutions.

Finally, the historical study of processes of economic growth reveals the importance of processes of saving and investment in the accumulation of factors of production. Such a study leaves us under no illusion with regard to the human costs of economic growth. In the past, economic growth has always been coupled with an enormous increase in the capital–labour ratio. In order to invest in capital goods a considerable portion of the national income has to be saved. In poor countries, saving means that people living at subsistence levels have to postpone present consumption for the sake of investment in future production. This is not easy. In Western countries such savings have been realised through the ruthless workings of the market mechanism of nineteenth-century capitalism, which kept wages low. In the centrally planned economies of the twentieth century exploitation of people by people through the market was replaced by direct coercion by the state. Both mechanisms have resulted in the transfer of income from consumers to social groups (capitalists, entrepreneurs, government officials) that were both able and willing to save and invest. It is unlikely that such tough choices can be avoided in the future.

An objection to the long-term approach is that it seldom offers neat solutions to the kind of practical problems and choices policy makers, politicians, entrepreneurs or aid workers are inevitably faced with on a day-to-day basis. On the other hand, it is exactly this kind of distance to policy that enables one to analyse problems and developments in a more independent and critical manner. The emphasis on long-term trends can help make us more immune to the fashions and fads of the day and may dramatically alter our perceptions of development.

The choice between the two approaches is not a matter of all or nothing. Both are important. It is perfectly legitimate for politicians, policy makers, engineers, entrepreneurs or aid workers to ask for support and advice from scientific researchers and development experts. Also, strong involvement with the plight of individuals in developing countries does not preclude independent judgement or critical analysis. On the other hand, a long-term approach offers a starting point for a realistic assessment of the effects of national and international development strategies and policies. It provides us with greater insight into the significance and scope of socio-economic policies amidst the many factors that impinge on processes of development.

Central questions that will be tackled in each chapter are: how do the factors discussed influence the development of per capita income, the standard of living and the conditions of life in poor countries? Which are the factors that contribute to socio-economic development? Which are the factors that hamper development? What are the explanations for the observed developments and trends? How can the differences between regions and between historical periods be interpreted and explained?

1.2   The development debate

There are no final answers to the questions mentioned at the end of the previous section. There is no such thing as scientific certainty, especially not in a field as controversial as that of economic and social development. Although the author's views will undoubtedly leave their imprint on this book, it is primarily intended as an introduction to the *debates on issues of development*.

These debates are characterised by numerous clashing perspectives and theories and deep differences of opinion. The results of empirical studies are often contradictory or ambiguous. At times it even seems that empirical research leads to more rather than less uncertainty. This book tries to represent different views and perspectives of development in a balanced fashion, providing the reader with suggestions for further reading. Further, the book provides an overview of trends in thinking about development issues since the end of World War II.

This approach should definitely not result in a non-committal enumeration of points of view, perspectives and approaches, between which no choices need to be made. Though differences of opinion may exist, this doesn't mean that 'everything goes'. It is of great importance for students of development to learn to evaluate statements on development critically and to ascertain to what extent they are consistent with or contradicted by the best empirical evidence available to us at present. Therefore, the exposition is illustrated as much as possible with statistics on development in several countries and regions. The purpose of this material is to introduce readers to international statistics and to stimulate them to distinguish between sense and nonsense in development studies and to find their own way in empirically grounded discussions of the issues of development. Background material to these statistics is presented in a separate website accompanying this book: http://www.dynamicsofdevelopment.com.

By way of example, Box 1.1 presents a number of general statements on development that are no longer tenable as generalisations in the light of the empirical information presently available to us.

Box 1.1 Untenable generalisations about development

- *Developing countries are trapped in a vicious circle of stagnation*; they are condemned to stagnation and poverty. This stereotypical view of developing countries is generally untrue. As will be indicated in Chapter 3, some developing countries exhibit strong economic growth and dynamics, while other countries stagnate. One should also always remember that every economically advanced country was once a developing country.
- *Given the pace of the population growth, food scarcity in developing countries will always be a problem.* This statement, often associated with horrible images of starvation and malnutrition on the African continent, is generally untrue. In the long term, world food production is increasing more rapidly than world population (see Chapter 10). This is the case in most developing countries. However, this does not mean that hunger and malnutrition can be eliminated in the foreseeable future.
- *Agricultural and mining exports cannot contribute to the economic development of a country.* This unfavourable image of agricultural and mining exports originates from the late nineteenth century when tropical developing countries exported agricultural products and industrial countries exported industrial products. Nevertheless, there are many countries where agricultural and mining exports have been the foundation of later economic prosperity. They can also make a positive contribution today.
- *Dependence of developing countries on the advanced economies leads to a net outflow of capital.* This proposition originates from the first half of the twentieth

century, when there was an outflow of resources from colonies to their colonisers. However, during most of the second half of the twentieth century, developing countries have profited from net inflows of capital (see Chapter 13).

- *Rapid population growth is always a threat to economic development.* There is no point in denying that rapid population growth is a problem in many developing countries. However, as will be discussed in Chapter 5, under certain conditions a too low population density may form an obstacle to economic growth. Rapid population growth does not preclude economic growth. Sometimes population growth can be a stimulus to economic development and technological change.

1.3   Growth and development

In the preceding sections, the term 'development' has figured prominently. In common parlance the term is used both frequently and rather casually: development studies, problems of development, developing countries, less developed countries, development cooperation, underdevelopment, development aid, development strategies, development policy and so forth. So what do we mean by 'development'?

Implicit in almost every use of the term 'development' is the notion that some countries and regions of the world are extremely poor, whereas other countries, representing a relatively small fraction of the world population, are very prosperous. The discussion of development is always tied up with basic questions like: why are poor countries poor and rich countries rich? Why do poor countries lag behind rich countries in the development of their standards of living? How can poor countries become more prosperous? How can poor countries catch up with the rich countries? In this sense an important dimension of the concept of 'development' refers to economic growth or more precisely growth of national income per capita.

Development conceived of as economic growth is a quantitative concept and basically means more of the same. Yet, even if we limit ourselves to the economic sphere, it is clear that economic development is more than economic growth alone. Economic development refers to growth accompanied by qualitative changes in the structure of production and employment, generally referred to as *structural change* (Kuznets, 1966). Of particular importance for developing economies are increases in the share of the dynamic industrial sector in national output and employment and a decrease of the share of agriculture. This implies that economic growth could take place without any economic development. An example is provided by those oil-exporting countries, which experienced sharp increases in national income but saw hardly any changes in their economic structure. Another important qualitative change is *technological change*: the ongoing process of change in process and product technologies, resulting in radically new modes of production and new product ranges (Abramovitz, 1989).

In the 1960s the identification of development with economic growth came under increasing criticism. Authors such as Dudley Seers, Gunnar Myrdal, Paul Streeten, Hollis Chenery, Mahbub ul Haq and institutions like the International Labour Organisation (ILO) pointed out that developing countries did not experience much change in the living conditions of the masses of the poor in spite of the impressive growth figures in the post-World War II period (Chenery *et al.*, 1974; ILO, 1976; Myrdal, 1971; Seers, 1979; Streeten, 1972; ul Haq, 1976). They came to the conclusion that development involves more than economic growth and changes in economic structures. Seers formulated three additional requirements for the use of the term development, namely that there should be a decrease in poverty and malnutrition, that income inequality should decline, and that the employment situation should improve (Seers, 1979).

Other critics went even further and challenged the too narrow focus on the economic dimensions of development alone. A country can grow rapidly, but still do badly in terms of literacy, health, life expectancy and nutrition (Sen, 1999). The environmental costs of growth are insufficiently recognised (Mishan, 1967). Economic growth does not necessarily make people more happy or satisfied (Easterlin, 1972). Criticism of growth fetishism led to the emergence of so-called 'social indicators': life expectancy, literacy, levels of education, infant mortality, availability of telephones, hospital beds, licensed doctors, availability of calories, and so forth. Some authors even went so far as to posit an opposition between growth and development. Sri Lanka or the Indian state of Kerala, where growth was not very rapid but where welfare facilities and the level of education were improving, were compared with countries like Brazil where extremely rapid growth had hardly affected poverty levels. Still, most authors reached the conclusion that, especially in the poorest countries, growth is a prerequisite for development, while development involves more than just growth.

Social scientists have stated that development should not be viewed in terms of economics only. One should also pay attention to changes in family structures, attitudes and mentalities, cultural changes, demographic developments, political changes and nationbuilding, the transformation of rural societies and processes of urbanisation.

The Swedish Nobel prize-winner Gunnar Myrdal has argued that discussions of development have implicitly been based on a series of modernisation ideals or values. Opinions may differ on the way in which these ideals should be pursued. Nevertheless, according to Myrdal, there was a widespread consensus on the ultimate objectives of development among the members of political elites in developing countries involved in developmental policy (Myrdal, 1968: pp. 57–69). The broad concept of development therefore involves a change of the entire society in the direction of the modernisation ideals. The modernisation ideals are reproduced in Box 1.2. Compared to the 1960s, the climate of opinion has since changed. Some political leaders in developing countries would now hesitate to use the term modernisation. But the list of modernisation ideals compiled by Myrdal still seems highly relevant.

Box 1.2   Modernisation ideals

- *Rationality* (in policy, in the application of technological knowledge, in structuring social relations, in thinking about objectives and means).
- *Planning for development*; searching for a coherent system of policy measures in order to change situations that are considered undesirable.
- *Increases in production per capita and production per worker*, primarily through industrialisation and increased capital intensity of production.
- *Improvements in the standard of living.*
- *Declines in social and economic inequality.* Development ought to be for the benefit of the people, the masses.
- *More efficient institutions and attitudes* that are conducive to an increase in productivity and to development in general (for example, institutions that allow for mobility, initiative, entrepreneurship, effective competition and equal opportunities; attitudes like efficiency, diligence, orderliness, punctuality, economy, honesty, rationality, openness to change, solidarity and future-orientedness).
- *Consolidation of the national state and national integration.*
- *National independence.*
- *Political democratisation.* The concept of democratisation can be interpreted in various ways of which parliamentary democracy is but one. Democratisation always implies some notion of involving the masses of the population in political decision-making.
- *Increased social discipline.* Developmental goals cannot be attained if governments cannot impose obligations on their citizens.

Source: Myrdal (1968).

Recently, Amartya Sen (1999) has argued for an even broader concept of development focusing on the concept of freedom. He sees development as an integrated process of expansion of substantive freedoms. Economic growth, technological advance and political change are all to be judged in the light of their contributions to the expansion of human freedoms. Among the most important of these freedoms are freedom from famine and malnutrition, freedom from poverty, access to health care and freedom from premature mortality. In a telling empirical example, Sen shows that urban African Americans have lower life expectancies than the average Chinese person or inhabitants of the Indian state of Kerala, in spite of much higher average per capita incomes in the USA.

According to Sen, freedoms are both ends and means. Thus, markets can be an engine for economic growth (means), but – what is sometimes forgotten – they constitute important freedoms in themselves, namely freedoms to exchange or transact. One important area where freedoms have frequently been restricted is the labour market, where slavery, serfdom or other institutional arrangements can restrict the free movement of labour. Political freedoms can contribute to economic dynamism, but are also goals in themselves. Sen argues somewhat optimistically that all freedoms are strongly interconnected and reinforce each other. He also tends to underemphasise clashes between freedoms of different groups of people and the value choices that still need to be made. There is no objective definition of development and there may be basic differences of opinion about the goals of development, even including that of the very goal of freedom, which may not be the ultimate goal from a variety of religious perspectives. Nevertheless, his use of the concept of freedom as a normative yardstick for development is insightful. In his perspective economic growth remains important, but not as a goal in itself. It is important in its potential contribution to a wide range of freedoms. It is not enough in itself. Sometimes changes in other spheres such as education and health can be at least as important in the expansion of freedoms.

At this stage four remarks can be made. First, as Myrdal, Seers and many other authors have noted, development is unavoidably a normative concept involving very basic choices and values. Our normative assumptions should therefore be made explicit. Secondly, though the formulations vary greatly, in practice most writers on development come up with a set of similar developmental goals including reduction of poverty, increased economic welfare, improved health and education, and increased political and social freedom. Development can then be defined as a movement in the direction of these developmental goals. Third, an increase both in productivity and production per head of population in poor countries is an essential ingredient of every definition of 'development'; this is even the case in interpretations of the concept that are critical of a narrow economic approach to 'development'. Economic growth always remains one of the necessary conditions for 'long-term development' and tremendous advances have been made in measuring it in a standardised fashion. It will continue to play a central role in this book. Finally, the fact that there are modernisation ideals or development goals does not mean that all societies ought to develop in the same manner or that they ought to converge to some common standard.

1.4 Are growth and development desirable?

The desirability of economic growth and socio-economic development is not undisputed. Critics have pointed out the drawbacks of growth, development and modernisation. They have pointed to the irreversible disruption of traditional societies and lifestyles, and the spread of a uniform materialistic mass culture, which may lead to cultural shallowness, loss of meaning and spirituality and to the increasing exploitation of people as a result of the spread of capitalist market relations. Sometimes it is suggested that people are happier in traditional societies than in modern societies. They would be more in tune with their natural environment, and their needs and wishes would balance their potentialities. There is a strong Malthusian movement which maintains that continued economic growth will disturb the balance of nature, and will eventually lead to ecological catastrophes (Brundtland *et al.*, 1987; Meadows *et al.*, 1972). The present debates on environmental pollution, global warming and climate change are good examples of this way of thinking (IPCC, 2001; Lindahl-Kiessling and Landberg, 1994; World Bank, 2003).

Some authors see 'development' as a euphemism for Western penetration and domination of the world, involving great misery and exploitation in both past and present (Frank, 1969). An eloquent example of this viewpoint is Stanley Diamond's frontal attack (1974) on a concept associated with development and progress, i.e. 'civilisation'. Diamond argues that processes of civilisation have always involved conquest, violence, coercion and oppression with respect to so-called less civilised peoples. For instance, the Indians have been victims of Western penetration into North America, the slaves have been victims of Western penetration into Africa, and the Eskimos have been victims of the spread of Western culture to Alaska. Yet, Diamond does not restrict himself to the results of Western expansion in the world. Wherever people try to spread their civilisation the fire and the sword are always involved, whether it concerns the expansion of the Greek, the Roman, the Egyptian or the Islamic civilisations.

Such criticism is valuable though at times one-sided. First, it creates an awareness of the costs involved in development. Secondly – and perhaps most important – it brings to our attention the relation between the 'concept of development' and international power relationships. What one understands by 'development' in a particular historical period is strongly influenced by dominant cultures and powers of that period.

On the other hand, it is no coincidence that fiercest criticisms of growth and development are often formulated by members of the elites in the richest countries in the world. When members of traditional tribal societies come in contact with modern consumer goods, their needs turn out to be far from limited. The possession of new goods will be sought for eagerly and widely. If one were to ask poor peasants or residents of urban slums in Africa or Asia whether they would prefer improvement in their productivity and standards of living, an overwhelming majority would respond positively. Only people who have been raised in very affluent societies can afford to have their doubts about the merits of economic growth and material progress.

Criticism of economic growth and development is sometimes inspired by a romantic idealisation of an harmonious and balanced society that may never have existed. And even if isolated and socially and ecologically balanced societies did exist in days gone by, they no longer exist today. The problems developing countries are facing today have much to do with the fact that these countries have already been 'opened up' to trade, investment, colonial domination and partial penetration by the money economy a long time ago (Myint, 1980). If there ever was a choice in whether or not to strive for development, this 'choice' has already been made in the past. Traditional self-sufficient societies have been disrupted. Modern technologies have contributed to a rapid growth of population, the needs of which cannot be met by traditional technologies and methods of production. Contact with the outside world has led to the emergence of modern preferences and needs. Present-day societies have no choice but to strive for socio-economic development. Given the rapid rates of population growth the alternative would be to sink deeper and deeper into a situation of poverty, misery and starvation, which has, for instance, been the case in Bangladesh. Although not all modernisation ideals are supported by all inhabitants of developing countries, almost everybody longs for the socio-economic side of development (Jones, 1988; see Lewis, 1950: Appendix 1; North and Thomas, 1973: pp. 1–2). In turn, socio-economic development is impossible without extensive social modernisation and social changes.

The ambivalence with regard to development is very obvious in the continuing attempts to develop hybrids of the ideals of sustained growth of welfare and productivity and modernisation of social institutions on the one hand, and preservation of valued elements of cultural traditions on the other hand. Examples are African socialism as advocated in the 1960s by political leaders such as Nyerere and Senghor, Indian socialism advocated by Gandhi and Nehru, and the present-day search for an Islamic development model.

Since the mid-1980s, disturbing reports of global warming, climate change, the extinction of rain forests, declining biodiversity and pollution of air and water have revived the discussion concerning the 'limits to growth' (for example, see Bunyard, 1985; Ettinger *et al.*, 1989; IPCC, 2001; World Bank, 1992). In 1987, the influential Brundtland report written for the United Nations introduced the notion of 'sustainable development', that is development that does not diminish the life chances of future generations (Brundtland *et al.*, 1987). However, such ideas have so far tended to have more impact on rhetoric than on practice.

1.5   Development and Westernisation

Apart from such elements as economic growth and productivity, it is difficult to define the concept of development in an objective, abstract and ahistorical manner. The substance and meaning of words like development and modernisation are strongly determined by the international political and economic balance of power. The countries that are economically and technologically advanced and politically and culturally dominant become the models for development in the eyes of their own citizens as well as in the eyes of the peoples trying to break away from their dominance. In the last 400 years the 'West' has emerged as the economic and political centre of the world (Jones, 1988; Landes, 1998). Western countries have become the models for 'modern' societies. This means that present-day 'development' – which has been described above as a change in society in the direction of specific modernisation or developmental ideals – and 'Westernisation' are inevitably entwined. As is illustrated by Myrdal's modernisation ideals, notions of development have been derived from the historical development experiences of the present prosperous Western countries.[1]

This conclusion may shock those who criticise a Western ethnocentric view on issues of development. They may consider it another attempt to project

---

1 Sen (1999) argues that so-called Western notions such as tolerance or human rights are also prominent in ancient Asian traditions, for instance dating back to the third century BC during the reign of King Ashoka in India. But the spread of these ideas in their modern form remains inextricably linked to Western expansion.

the blueprint of Western development on non-Western societies. This is by no means our intention. First, there is no question of Western society being considered 'superior' to other societies. We simply want to note that the explicit or implicit ideals and objectives of development are modelled on the powers that dominate the world economy.

Secondly, the interweaving of development and westernisation does not imply that all countries or societies should or can adopt one and the same development path. Initial conditions and circumstances are so different for each country, region and historical period that previous developmental experiences cannot be blindly copied. Besides, at every stage there are alternative paths and options. Furthermore, we do not say that countries or societies will converge. We only note that the measures for 'developed' or 'less developed' have been highly coloured by the developmental experiences of Western countries.

Thirdly, we nowhere state that the relationship between developmental values and westernisation is a lasting one. As the centre of gravity of economic and political power relationships shifts towards Asia, our understanding of the terms 'modern' and 'less modern', 'developed' and 'less developed' will gradually change. At one time British society was the model of a 'developed' and 'modern' society. In the twentieth century this role has been taken over by the United States. During the 1980s attention started to shift towards Japan as an example of a modern and successful economy that might be imitated. Japanese concepts of quality control, flexible production and management were held up as examples for Western production organisations. In the course of the twenty-first century an emerging China might well become a new model of modernity. Or, to mention yet another example, after the decline of the Soviet empire the world appears to be less attracted to Western ideologies such as Marxism. Planning, which was still high on Myrdal's list of modernisation ideals in the 1960s, is increasingly dropping out of favour.

In summary, it can be concluded that development is a highly value-laden concept. The meaning of this concept is determined by the societies that are considered dominant or advanced at a particular moment in history.

1.6   Indicators of growth and development

Given the centrality of economic growth, the summary indicator most often used to indicate the degree of 'development' of a country is national income per capita. National income can be calculated in three different ways (for example, see Allen, 1980):

1. As the sum of all incomes – wages, profits, interest, dividend and rent – that have been earned by workers, owners of capital and owners of land in a country during the period of one year (the income approach, national income).

2. As the sum of all value added in an economy in a given year (national product).

3. As the sum of all expenditures in a country – consumer spending (*C*) plus investment (*I*), plus government expenditures (*G*) plus the value of exports (*X*) minus expenditures on imports (*I*) – in a given year (national expenditure).

In theory, national income, national product and national expenditure should be equal. In practice, there are statistical discrepancies. An important conceptual distinction is that between gross national product (GNP) and gross domestic product (GDP). The difference between GNP and GDP lies in the net balance of foreign income accruing to nationals of a country, deriving from factors of production abroad and payments to other countries for factors of production within the country, owned by nationals of other countries. This distinction is very important for developing countries. Since a significant part of investment in developing countries is foreign investment, there is a net annual outflow of dividends and profits. Therefore, gross national product (or gross national income or gross national expenditure) will be less than gross domestic product (or gross domestic income or gross domestic expenditure).

There are two kinds of debates on growth indicators such as per capita GNP or per capita GDP. First, there are all sorts of technical objections to the use of per capita GNP as an adequate indicator of the level of economic development of a country. Secondly, there are substantive objections to the use of per capita GNP as an indicator of development. After all, as mentioned in section 1.3, development involves much more than economic growth alone.

The technical objections to the use of per capita GNP as an indicator of economic development are summarised in Box 1.3 (Bauer, 1976: pp. 55–66; Myint, 1980: pp. 8–10).

Box 1.3　Technical problems in the measurement of economic growth

- Principally GNP refers to that part of the national income that is traded via the market for money. In developing countries, however, there is widespread subsistence production. If there is a shift from subsistence production to production for the market in the process of economic development, it seems as if national income is increasing, whereas in reality there is no increase in production.
- GNP does not adequately account for the output of the informal or non-registered sector of the economy.
- GNP does not allow for differences in climate and conditions of life that require different types of clothing, food, transportation and housing.
- Economic growth and industrialisation involve substantial costs that do not occur in pre-industrial societies: the costs of transporting goods and people, the costs of the disposal of waste and the costs of urban living.
- The costs of environmental pollution and depletion of natural resources are not adequately accounted for in the measurement of national income (Hueting and Bosch, 1992; Mishan 1967).
- International comparisons of national incomes are usually made with exchange rates. Dollar incomes of developing countries calculated with exchange rates do not provide

us with realistic estimates of standards of living in these countries. Relative levels of prosperity in developing countries are higher than suggested by official international statistics on national incomes in dollars. One of the reasons for this is that many services and domestically traded goods in developing countries are much cheaper than in prosperous countries (see Kravis, Heston and Summers, 1982).

International comparisons based on purchasing power parities

The technical criticisms have given rise to various improvements in the measurement of economic growth. Modern national accounts make a variety of adjustments for informal sector production or parts of non-market production, such as food produced for own consumption. Poverty lines take the differences in local conditions into account. The newly revised system of national accounts (UN, 1993) includes 'satellite accounts' to account for environmental effects of economic growth.

From an international comparative perspective, one of the important advances in the measurement of national income is the development of purchasing power parities (PPPs). Exchange rates do not provide adequate measures of the purchasing power of currencies because they are based on internationally traded goods only, because they are distorted by policy interventions and influenced by global capital flows. For many years, researchers have been trying to overcome the disadvantages of the use of exchange rates in international comparisons, by calculating measures that explicitly take into account the relative purchasing power of the currencies of the countries being compared (see Kravis *et al.*, 1982; Summers and Heston, 1991). These PPPs are based on price comparisons of a standardised basket of goods and services collected in over 130 countries. By now PPP-based estimates of national income have become available for many countries, though it should be stressed that the quality and reliability of these estimates still varies substantially. In Table 1.1 below (section 1.7), both exchange rate and PPP-based estimates are presented.

The use of purchasing power parities has several important effects. In the first place, the dollar incomes of the poorest countries tend to be two to four times higher than their dollar incomes calculated with exchange rates. PPP-based comparisons provide a more realistic picture of poverty, because they take into account the relative cheapness of services and basic necessities in developing countries. A second effect of the use of PPPs is that the income ranking of countries can change quite substantially, also amongst developing countries themselves. In Table 1.1 a difference in ranking of 10 points or more occurs for 35 of the 138 countries for which we have PPP estimates as well as exchange rate comparisons. Finally, the inequality of average per capita incomes in the world economy is diminished as incomes in the poorest countries tend to be higher, while incomes in the richest countries tend to be lower than estimates based on exchange rates.

Of course, the use of PPPs changes nothing in the underlying reality of poverty and destitution in large parts of the world. It does result in more adequate descriptions and measurements of poverty (and affluence). Therefore, it is likely that PPPs will be used ever more frequently, in spite of all the technical problems involved in their estimation.

Social indicators

Substantive objections to the use of GNP as an indicator of development are all based on the fact that development involves much more than economic growth only. Even from an economic point of view, GNP does not provide us with a good picture of the changes in the life circumstances of the poor masses. Per capita GNP is an average figure. It does not account for the distribution of income and consumption, which is often very unequal. Furthermore, the level of the national income is not directly related to the standard of living. When a considerable part of a country's national income is invested or used for military spending, consumption of the inhabitants of this country may for many years lag far behind the growth of the national income.

Despite increases in national income, living conditions of the very poorest groups in a society may thus deteriorate. In other countries, their situation may improve in spite of a stagnation or slow growth of GNP. From this perspective, it is argued that various other economic and social indicators should be used along with GNP. Such economic and social indicators give a more straightforward picture of developments in a country: the number of people below poverty thresholds, data on malnutrition, employment figures, life expectancy at birth, infant mortality, numbers of doctors, nurses and hospital beds for every thousand inhabitants, energy consumption, the degree of illiteracy, years of education, data on income distribution, miles of roads and railways, access to clean water, equal opportunities for both men and women, human rights, and so forth.

Since 1990 the United Nations Development Programme (UNDP) publishes the *Human Development Report*, which reports on many of these indicators annually. This report has introduced a measure called the *Human Development Index* (HDI). The HDI is a non-weighted average of three variables: an index of per capita gross domestic income, life expectancy at birth and the level of education. In the income index the income categories above the poverty threshold are given progressively lower weights in order to represent the declining marginal utility of higher incomes. The education index is a weighted average of literacy (two-thirds) and the average number of years of schooling (one third) (see UNDP, 1991: pp. 88–91). A country's ranking on the Human Development Index may differ substantially from its ranking in terms of per capita income. For example, in 1999, thirty countries had an HDI ranking that differed more than 20 points from their ranking according to their per capita income in PPP US dollars (UNDP, 2001: p. 141).

These indicators are a valuable addition to the national income data. Still, in practice, they have not yet superseded per capita GNP as a summary indicator of the level of development. First, the quality of many social indicators is often still inadequate for international comparisons of levels and trends between many countries. In contrast, work on standardisation of concepts and measuring techniques with regard to national income has already been continuing for many decades (see UNSO, 1968; UN 1993 (SNA)). Secondly, the weighting of social indicators is rather arbitrary. For instance, if higher incomes get lower weights, one automatically gets a different ranking. Thirdly, in the longer run many social indicators appear to be closely connected with per capita national income trends (Beckerman, 1974; 1993). At any given moment, large discrepancies can be found between the rank order based on income and the rank order based on social indicators for health or life expectancy. These discrepancies provide an interesting indication of policy priorities and institutional influences. However, if per capita national income in a country stagnates over time, this will sooner or later be reflected in a deterioration of the social indicators, while income growth is reflected in improvements in social indicators.

The development of gross domestic product provides an indication of the development of a country's productive potential. How this capacity will be used cannot be known in advance. For example, it may be used for fulfilment of basic needs, health care, education or for military hardware, foreign payments or conspicuous consumption by the elites. This depends very much on the social policies pursued in a country. In any event it is a well-established fact that there can be no long-term improvement of the living conditions of the masses of the population without a corresponding growth of productive capacity. As has been shown in section 1.3, an increase in per capita income is one of the important elements in all definitions of the development concept. This view is also endorsed in the *Human Development Report* (UNDP, 1991: p. 1). The chapters in this book on demography, health care, education and state formation (Chapters 5–7, 11) will pay explicit attention to the interplay of economic growth and social indicators. Long-run trends in a variety of social indicators will be presented separately. No attempt will be made to calculate a single composite index.

1.7   Does the 'third world' exist?

After World War II the term 'Third World' came into vogue as a designation for developing countries (Worsley, 1964). This Third World was contrasted with the First World of the advanced capitalist countries and the Second World of the industrialised socialist countries in Eastern Europe. The use of this term implies that all third world countries have common characteristics and interests, and that a wide and growing gap separates them from the affluent industrialised countries. The same is implied by terms such as 'North' versus 'South'. With regard to these terms, the similarities and differences in circumstances in developing countries will be discussed. In this section the emphasis will be on the diversity of circumstances; similarities will be discussed in section 1.8.

Table 1.1 derived from the *World Development Indicators 2002* (World Bank, 2002) shows a greatly diversified world economy in 2000 with enormous

Table 1.1 *Population, GNP per head and growth in the world economy*

	Country/region	Population 2000 (Millions[a])	2000 (US$)	GNP per capita 2000 PPP estimates (international $)	Average annual GDP growth (%) 1990–2000
	Low-income countries	2,459.8	410	1,980	1.0
	Low-income countries excl. India (GNP per capita < 755 US$)	1,443.9	376	1,686	−0.5
1	Congo, Dem. Rep. (Zaire)	50.9	100[b]	680[b]	−8.1[c]
2	Ethiopia	64.3	100	660	1.5
3	Burundi	6.8	110	580	−3.8
4	Sierra Leone	5.0	130	480	−6.3
5	Eritrea	4.1	170	960	−0.2[g]
6	Malawi	10.3	170	600	1.5
7	Niger	10.8	180	740	−1.5
8	Tajikistan	6.2	180	1,090	−10.6
9	Chad	7.7	200	870	−0.5
10	Burkina Faso	11.3	210	970	2.5
11	Mozambique	17.7	210	800	3.2
12	Rwanda	8.5	230	930	−1.9
13	Mali	10.8	240	780	1.3
14	Nepal	23.0	240	1,370	2.5
15	Madagascar	15.5	250	820	−1.2
16	Cambodia	12.0	260	1,440	2.2
17	Nigeria	126.9	260	800	−0.2
18	Kyrgyz Republic	4.9	270	2,540	−5.1
19	Tanzania	33.7	270	520	0.1
20	Central African Republic	3.7	280	1,160	−0.7
21	Angola	13.1	290	1,180	−2.4
22	Lao PDR	5.3	290	1,540	3.7
23	Togo	4.5	290	1,410	−1.4
24	Uganda	22.2	300	1,210	3.3
25	Zambia	10.1	300	750	−1.9
26	Sudan	31.1	310	1,520	5.2
27	Ghana	19.3	340	1,910	1.8
28	Kenya	30.1	350	1,010	−0.9
29	Uzbekistan	24.8	360	2,360	−2.3
30	Bangladesh	131.1	370	1,590	3.0
31	Benin	6.3	370	980	1.8
32	Mauritania	2.7	370	1,630	1.1
33	Yemen, Rep.	17.5	370	770	1.5
34	Comoros	10.1	380	1,590	−2.4
35	Mongolia	2.4	390	1,760	−1.3
36	Vietnam	78.5	390	2,000	5.6
37	Moldova	4.3	400	2,230	−9.7
38	Nicaragua	5.1	400	2,080	0.4
39	Pakistan	138.1	440	1,860	1.4
40	Guinea	7.4	450	1,930	1.2
41	India	1,015.9	450	2,340	3.6
42	Zimbabwe	12.6	460	2,550	−0.5
43	Senegal	9.5	490	1,480	0.7
44	Haiti	8.0	510	1,470	−2.7
45	Armenia	3.8	520	2,580	−4.5
46	Congo, Rep.	3.0	570	570	−2.7
47	Indonesia	210.4	570	2,830	2.5
48	Cameroon	14.9	580	1,590	−1.1
49	Lesotho	2.0	580	2,590	1.9
50	Azerbaijan	8.0	600	2,740	−6.6
51	Côte d'Ivoire	16.0	600	1,500	−0.5
52	Georgia	5.0	630	2,680	−13.0
53	Ukraine	49.5	700	3,700	−7.6
54	Afghanistan	26.6			
55	Korea, Dem. Rep.	22.3			
56	Liberia	3.1			
57	Myanmar	47.7			
58	Somalia	8.8			
	Middle-income countries	2,694.6	1,970	6,580	2.3

(Continued)

Table 1.1 (*Continued*)

	Country/region	Population 2000 (Millions[a])	2000 (US$)	GNP per capita 2000 PPP estimates (international $)	Average annual GDP growth (%) 1990–2000
	Lower-middle-income countries (GNP per capita between 755 and 2,995 US$)	2,047.6	1,130	4,600	2.3
	Lower-middle-income excl. China	785.1	880	3,077	−0.8
59	Papua New Guinea	5.1	700	2,180	1.9
60	Turkmenistan	5.2	750	3,800	−6.0
61	China	1,262.5	840	3,920	9.0
62	Sri Lanka	19.4	850	3,460	3.9
63	Honduras	6.4	860	2,400	0.4
64	Syrian Arab Republic	16.2	940	3,340	2.7
65	Yugoslavia, Fed. Rep.	10.6	940		1.2[d]
66	Bolivia	8.3	990	2,360	1.4
67	Philippines	75.6	1,040	4,220	0.7
68	Albania	3.4	1,120	3,600	0.7
69	Morocco	28.7	1,180	3,450	0.4
70	Ecuador	12.6	1,210	2,910	−0.3
71	Bosnia and Herzegovina	4.0	1,230		22.8[d]
72	Kazakhstan	14.9	1,260	5,490	−2.7
73	Swaziland	1.0	1,390	4,600	0.1
74	Paraguay	5.5	1,440	4,450	−0.7
75	Egypt, Arab Rep.	64.0	1,490	3,670	2.4
76	Bulgaria	8.2	1,520	5,560	−1.3
77	Algeria	30.4	1,580	5,040	−0.3
78	Russian Federation	145.6	1,660	8,010	−3.9
79	West Bank and Gaza	3.0	1,660		−2.6[e]
80	Romania	22.4	1,670	6,360	−1.5
81	Guatemala	11.4	1,680	3,770	1.4
82	Iran, Islamic Rep.	63.7	1,680	5,910	2.5
83	Jordan	4.9	1,710	3,950	0.6
84	Macedonia, FYR	2.0	1,820	5,020	−1.6
85	El Salvador	6.3	2,000	4,410	2.4
86	Thailand	60.7	2,000	6,320	3.4
87	Colombia	42.3	2,020	6,060	0.8
88	Namibia	1.8	2,030	6,410	1.9
89	Peru	25.7	2,080	4,660	2.2
90	Tunisia	9.6	2,100	6,070	3.1
91	Dominican Republic	8.4	2,130	5,710	4.1
92	Jamaica	2.6	2,610	3,440	0.1
93	Belarus	10.0	2,870	7,550	−1.0
94	Latvia	2.4	2,920	7,070	−3.5
95	Lithuania	3.7	2,930	6,980	−3.7
96	Cuba	11.2			
97	Iraq	23.3			
	Upper-middle-income countries (GNP per capita between 2,996 and 9,265 US$)	647.0	4,640	9,210	2.2
98	South Africa	42.8	3,020	9,160	−0.3
99	Turkey	65.3	3,100	7,030	1.9
100	Gabon	1.2	3,190	5,360	−0.4
101	Panama	2.9	3,260	5,680	2.7
102	Botswana	1.6	3,300	7,170	2.4
103	Malaysia	23.3	3,380	8,330	4.4
104	Brazil	170.4	3,580	7,300	1.3
105	Estonia	1.4	3,580	9,340	−0.1
106	Slovak Republic	5.4	3,700	11,040	0.3
107	Mauritius	1.2	3,750	9,940	4.1
108	Costa Rica	3.8	3,810	7,980	2.9
109	Lebanon	4.3	4,010	4,550	5.3
110	Poland	38.7	4,190	9,000	3.5
111	Venezuela	24.2	4,310	5,740	−0.2
112	Chile	15.2	4,590	9,100	5.0
113	Croatia	4.4	4,620	7,960	−0.6

(*Continued*)

Table 1.1 (*Continued*)

	Country/region	Population 2000 (Millions[a])	2000 (US$)	GNP per capita 2000 PPP estimates (international $)	Average annual GDP growth (%) 1990–2000
114	Hungary	10.0	4,710	11,990	1.1
115	Trinidad and Tobago	1.3	4,930	8,220	2.3
116	Mexico	98.0	5,070	8,790	1.8
117	Czech Republic	10.3	5,250	13,780	0.1
118	Uruguay	3.3	6,000	8,880	2.3
119	Saudi Arabia	20.7	7,230	11,390	−0.5
120	Argentina	37.0	7,460	12,050	3.2
121	Korea, Rep.	47.3	8,910	17,300	5.1
122	Libya	5.3			
123	Oman	2.4			
124	Puerto Rico	3.9			
	Low- and middle-income countries of which:	5,154.4	1,230	3,910	1.8
	Sub-Saharan Africa	658.9	470	1,600	−0.4
	East Asia and the Pacific	1,855.2	1,060	4,130	5.9
	South Asia	1,355.1	440	2,240	3.2
	Europe and Central Asia	474.3	2,010	6,670	−1.8
	Middle East and North Africa	295.2	2,090	5,270	1.1
	Latin America and the Caribbean	515.7	3,670	7,080	1.6
	Highly indebted poor countries	632.2	321		0.8
	High-income countries (GNP per capita > 9266 US$)	902.9	27,680	27,770	1.7
125	Slovenia	2.0	10,050	17,310	1.9
126	Portugal	10.0	11,120	16,990	2.6
127	Greece	10.6	11,960	16,860	1.9
128	New Zealand	3.8	12,990	18,530	1.6
129	Spain	39.5	15,080	19,260	2.4
130	Israel	6.2	16,710	19,330	2.2
131	Kuwait	2.0	18,030	18,690	1.5[f]
132	United Arab Emirates	2.9	18,060[b]	19,410[b]	−2.8[c]
133	Italy	57.7	20,160	23,470	1.4
134	Australia	19.2	20,240	24,970	2.5
135	Canada	30.8	21,130	27,170	1.7
136	Ireland	3.8	22,660	25,520	6.3
137	France	58.9	24,090	24,420	1.4
138	United Kingdom	59.7	24,430	23,550	1.8
139	Belgium	10.3	24,540	27,470	1.8
140	Singapore	4.0	24,740	24,910	4.8
141	Netherlands	15.9	24,970	25,850	2.2
142	Germany	82.2	25,120	24,920	1.3
143	Finland	5.2	25,130	24,570	1.8
144	Austria	8.1	25,220	26,330	1.8
145	Hong Kong, China	6.8	25,920	25,590	2.6
146	Sweden	8.9	27,140	23,970	1.4
147	Denmark	5.3	32,280	27,250	1.9
148	United States	281.6	34,100	34,100	2.0
149	Norway	4.5	34,530	29,630	2.8
150	Japan	126.9	35,620	27,080	1.2
151	Switzerland	7.2	38,140	30,450	0.2
	World	6,057.3	5,170		1.2

Notes:
[a] Countries with more than one million inhabitants.
[b] 1998 instead of 2000.
[c] 1990–1998.
[d] 1995–2000.
[e] 1994–2000.
[f] 1989–2000.
[g] 1992–2000.
Source: World Bank, *World Development Indicators 2002*, CD-ROM.

differences in per capita incomes, and great inequality both between rich and poor countries and among poor countries themselves. In the table countries have primarily been ranked by income per capita. Countries have been divided into three categories: *low-income countries* (sometimes called least-developed countries or LDCs), middle-income countries and high-income countries. The middle-income countries are subdivided into lower-middle-income countries and upper-middle-income countries.

Low-income countries

The category of *low-income countries* consists of fifty-eight countries with a per capita gross national income of less than 755 dollars in 2000. These countries are also called the *least-developed countries* (LDCs). Countries in this category are eligible for aid and loans on more favourable terms than richer developing countries. The total population of the countries in this category is 2.5 billion people, with an average per capita income of 410 dollars in 2000. In the low-income category, we find very many African countries and several countries in South and Southeast Asia. Newcomers to the LDC category are some of the new states in Eastern Europe and Central Asia, which became independent after the break-up of the Soviet Union, such as Armenia, Azerbaijan, Georgia, Moldova, Tajikistan, Turkmenistan, Ukraine or Uzbekistan.

Within the low-income category there is a significant difference between Asian countries with huge populations and high population densities and African countries with small populations and low population densities. Among the low-income countries are three Asian countries – Bangladesh, India and Pakistan – with very large populations and high population densities. The largest is India with 1.2 billion inhabitants and a per capita income of 450 dollars per year, followed by Indonesia with 210 million inhabitants and a per capita income of 570 dollars. Since 1997, giant China with 1,260 million inhabitants and a per capita income of 840 dollars has graduated from the low-income category to the lower-middle-income category (LMIC), owing to its rapid growth in recent years. The low-income category further consists of thirty-four Sub-Saharan African countries, most of which have small populations and relatively low population densities.

Many of the Asian countries are characterised by ancient urban civilisations and age-old experience of centralised political rule and unity. In contrast, most states are new in Sub-Saharan Africa. There have been some tendencies towards larger political entities in African history, but in comparison with Asian countries political centralisation and urban traditions did not develop very far during the precolonial age.

Natural circumstances in Africa (climate, rainfall, quality of the soil, tropical diseases) are relatively unfavourable in comparison with other parts of the world (World Bank, 1989b). Mineral wealth is abundant in African countries. However, up till now these potentialities have not been exploited to the full. Among other things, this is due to poorly developed physical infrastructure (roads, transport, communication). An inadequate infrastructure is a barrier to economic development in this region, in other respects as well.

Since 1965, there has been considerable economic growth in many large poor Asian countries like Indonesia, China, India and Pakistan (with the notorious exception of Bangladesh). Prior to the Asian crisis, Indonesia with 210 million inhabitants showed a respectable growth rate of 5.6 per cent per year. Indonesia is the country most affected by the Asian crisis of 1997. It had graduated to the LMIC class by 1993, but has since fallen back into the LDC category as a result of the crisis and its aftermath. Even so, average growth for the 1990s came to 2.5 per cent. In contrast with Asia, since 1973 there has been stagnation rather than growth in the poor Sub-Saharan African countries (see World Bank, 1989a, 1989b). In no less than ten countries per capita income was lower in 1980 than in 1965. Since 1980, per capita income has decreased in twenty-one of the thirty-seven Sub-Saharan African countries, for which data are included in the World Bank database (World Bank, 2002). In the first half of the 1990s, per capita incomes in most former Soviet states and Eastern European satellites declined dramatically. Though there has been some recovery in the late 1990s, most countries in transition are still well below 1989 income levels.

Lower-middle-income countries

The developing countries that are less poor are described as the *middle-income countries*. In this rather heterogeneous category it is customary to distinguish between the '*lower-middle-income countries*' with an annual per capita income of 755–2,955 dollars and the '*upper-middle-income countries*' with an annual per capita income of 2,966 and 9,265 dollars in 2000.

The distinction between the lower-middle-income countries and the LDCs is somewhat arbitrary. The LMIC category includes several poor countries that are hardly distinguishable from the LDCs. The LMIC category includes several smaller poor countries from Central and South America (Bolivia, Cuba, the Dominican Republic, Ecuador, El Salvador, Jamaica, Guatemala, Panama and Paraguay), and two larger ones (Columbia and Peru). In this category we also find several North African and Middle Eastern countries (Algeria, Egypt, Iraq, Jordan, Morocco, Syria and Tunisia). Finally, this category also includes several countries that used to be part of the Soviet Union (the Russian Federation, Belarus, Kazakhstan, Latvia and Lithuania) and former communist countries such as Bulgaria and Romania. Second and third world, North and South, East and West are all mixed up here.

Most of these countries in the lower-middle-income group experienced sluggish or even negative economic growth in the 1990s. Excluding China, average growth in the 1990s was – 0.8 per cent per year. An exception to this picture of stagnation are the Asian countries China, Thailand and Sri Lanka. The Chinese economy has been growing at some 9 per cent per year. Thailand with 61 million people has been growing rapidly since 1985, though average growth in the 1990s was only 3.4 per cent due to the setback of the Asian crisis in 1997. The other large Asian economy, the Philippines (76 million inhabitants), experienced sluggish growth of less than 1 per cent. The average annual per capita income in the lower-middle-income category is 880 dollars; the total population of these countries is 2,048 million.

Upper-middle-income countries

The category of *upper-middle-income countries* (UMIC) consists of twenty-seven countries with a total of 647 million inhabitants and an annual per capita income 2,996–9,265 dollars. The average annual income is 4,664 dollars. In this category one will find four large and populous Latin American countries: Mexico, Brazil, Argentina and Venezuela and four smaller ones: Chile, Costa Rica, Panama and Uruguay. It is striking that these Latin American countries are among the more prosperous of the developing countries, in spite of their long history of extreme colonial and neocolonial exploitation. The large Latin American countries are characterised by relatively favourable natural circumstances, great natural wealth and a relatively low population density. Often, comparisons are drawn between these Latin American countries and the North American continent; it's an interesting question why Latin America has experienced a less favourable economic development since the nineteenth century in comparison with countries like the USA and Canada.

In the post-war period, many Latin American countries have experienced rapid economic growth. Compared with Asian countries these countries are characterised by an extremely unequal income distribution, as a result of which the poor masses have benefited very little from average increases in welfare. A country like Brazil is often mentioned as an illustration of the fact that large-scale poverty can coexist together with rapid economic growth and a high average income per capita.

In the 1980s growth in Latin America stagnated. Most countries were hit by the debt crisis, which affected their growth performance and their economic prospects negatively. Moreover, countries like Argentina, Brazil and Mexico experienced extremely high inflation. The situation stabilised somewhat in the 1990s, but remains rather uncertain, with periodic crises interrupting growth.

Within the middle-income category one finds several of the more successful former socialist countries like Hungary, Poland, Croatia, the Czech Republic, the Slovak Republic and Estonia. Five countries in this category – Libya, Mexico, Oman, Saudi Arabia and Venezuela – are important oil-exporting countries. Finally, it is interesting to note that in Asia Malaysia is now ranked as an upper-middle-income country, owing to its dynamic economic performance over the last decades.

High-income countries

The category of *high-income countries* consists of twenty-seven countries with a per capita income of over 92,666 dollars and a total population of 900 million. From 1989 onwards, the World Bank no longer distinguishes a separate category of industrialised market economies (the rich Western countries and Japan). In the 1989 *World Development Report* these countries were first categorised together with other affluent countries like Israel, Hong Kong, Singapore, the United Arab Emirates and Kuwait. New entrants to the high-income category include peripheral European economies such as Portugal and Greece, and Asian economies such as Taiwan and South Korea.

Oil-exporting developing countries

The *oil-exporting developing countries* form a separate category. This category cuts across the income classification. Several of these countries belong to the upper-middle-income category (Libya, Saudi Arabia, Oman, Mexico and Venezuela). Iraq and Iran, which used to figure in the UMIC category, have dropped back to the LMIC group owing to political upheavals and wars. Countries like the United Arab Emirates and Kuwait are high-income countries. In spite of their high average incomes they are still considered to be developing countries since their economic structure is extremely one-sided. It depends on a single export product: oil. The oil exporters also include poor countries such as Indonesia and Nigeria.

The central problem for oil-exporting economies is how to realise a *structural transformation* into a more diversified economic structure. Indonesia is one of the countries which has been relatively successful in doing this. The problems involved in structural transformation are not only economic but social as well. Attempts to transform and modernise an economy using oil wealth may evoke great social stress and give rise to social protest movements. To some extent, the rise of Islamic fundamentalism may be viewed in this light.

Newly industrialising countries

Several developing countries – including South Korea, Taiwan, Brazil, India, Mexico, Hong Kong, Singapore and Israel – have experienced impressive industrial growth since World War II. They are called the *Newly Industrialising Countries* (NICs). These countries have succeeded in building up a modern industrial structure in a short period of time. They are a striking illustration of the thesis that developing countries are not condemned to primary production and that industrialisation is a realistic option for developing countries. Some of these countries have built up capital goods industries and have become exporters of capital goods and technology to other developing countries.

Until recently, all of these countries were classified as middle-income countries. Since 1989 Singapore, Hong Kong – reunited with mainland China in 1996 – and Israel have joined the high-income category; South Korea and Taiwan have recently reached this income level. Japan had already succeeded in doing so earlier.

Other countries that have realised a considerable growth of their industrial sector since World War II are Egypt, the Philippines, Colombia, Turkey, former Yugoslavia, Portugal, Spain and Greece. These countries are sometimes referred to as the *semi-industrialised countries* (SICs: see OECD, 1979). In the last quarter of the twentieth century, the so-called second-tier NICs: Indonesia, Thailand, Malaysia, Sri Lanka and China, experienced rapid growth of industrial production and industrial exports, in particular prior to the rude interruption of the Asian crisis of 1997, which temporarily halted growth in Indonesia, Thailand, Malaysia, South Korea and the Philippines.

Former socialist countries in transition

Until 1988, socialist countries in Central and Eastern Europe were considered a separate category in the consecutive editions of the *World Development Report*. However, very few comparable statistics on these countries were available. So it was hard to judge their relative standing. The same applied to centrally planned economies in other parts of the world.

Since 1989, the Eastern European socialist countries are no longer regarded as a separate category. In 1989 the Berlin wall collapsed and in 1991 the Soviet Union disintegrated. Since then the former Eastern European countries, the former Yugoslav republics and the former Soviet republics are in transition to market economies. To the surprise of observers, many of the former Soviet republics in Asia turned out to have much in common with developing countries in other parts of the world. In 2000, no less than eighteen former socialist Central and Eastern European countries and former Soviet republics were categorised as LDCs or LMICs. Yet, the historical path of development of both the former Eastern European socialist economies and the former Soviet republics has been very different from that of other developing countries. Most former socialist countries have experienced very large declines in GDP since 1989. By 2000, only six countries had regained their pre-1989 income levels, namely Czech Republic, Hungary, Poland, Slovakia and Slovenia. Per capita income in Georgia, Tajikistan and Moldova stood at less than a third of pre-transition levels.

Regional differences in poverty, welfare and growth

Table 1.1 also offers a first indication of the regional distribution of wealth and poverty. Poverty is primarily concentrated in Sub-Saharan Africa and Asia, though Asia with its large and dense populations shows much more economic dynamism than sparsely populated Africa, which is characterised by stagnation. Economic stagnation in Africa is compounded by wars, civil wars and political instability, which have much to do with the relatively recent emergence of modern states on the continent (see the discussion in Chapter 11). The implication is that our intuitive association of the problems with Africa conjures up too gloomy a picture of the achievements of developing countries as a whole. Although it is understandable that the media often concentrate on hunger in Africa, by far the greatest number of poor people actually live in East and South Asia (see Table 1.3 on world poverty below). In terms of changes in the life situation of vast numbers of the very poor, one should take into account the developments in the populous Asian countries.

The large Latin American countries are much more affluent and come closer to the levels of prosperity of rich Western countries than most other developing countries. To some extent the Latin America development problem can be characterised as a distributive problem: how can the masses share in the increased average welfare, achieved in the course of the twentieth century? This applies less to poor African and Asian countries where there is not much to distribute in the first place. In the 1980s economic growth in Latin America faltered. At the same time many Asian countries experienced continued growth. Differences in economic policy are among the causes of this contrast in development (see Chapter 13). The resumption of growth in Latin America is hampered by the heavy debt burden. The same applies to several of the poorest African countries. Rapid growth in Asia was interrupted by the unexpected financial crisis of 1997. Since then rapid growth has resumed in some Asian economies such as Korea and Malaysia, while Indonesia and the Philippines are still suffering from the aftermath of the crisis. Large countries such as India and China were less affected by the crisis and continued to grow rapidly.

Dimensions of difference

The discussion above highlights the variety of developmental experiences. This will be elaborated further in Chapter 2, which discusses historical patterns and paths of development. Important dimensions of variation are summarised in Box 1.4. We conclude that the term *Third World* is an unacceptable simplification. It does not do justice to the diversity of circumstances and developmental experiences in different parts of the world. The preferred term in this book is the plural 'developing countries', which emphasises the diversity of development experiences and the dynamic nature of development processes.[2]

Box 1.4 Differences between developing countries

- *Levels of per capita income*
  There are great differences in levels of prosperity amongst developing countries, both between and within income categories (LDCs, LMICs, UMICs).
- *Demographic characteristics*
  Developing countries differ in terms of population size, population density and population growth rates.
- *Natural resources*
  Developing countries differ in climate, soil quality and natural resources. One of the important distinctions is that between oil-exporting developing countries and oil-importing developing countries.
- *Structure of production*
  Developing countries vary in the structure of production. Some developing countries are still predominantly agricultural. Others have developed large industrial sectors. These are referred to as the Newly Industrialised Countries (NICs).
- *Economic regime*
  Developing countries show great variation in their economic regimes and their paths of economic development. One can distinguish inward-looking regimes from outward-looking regimes; centrally planned regimes from market economies. Market economies differ greatly in their degrees of intervention. Many former socialist

---

2 A potential drawback of the term 'developing countries' is that it might suggest that all countries are developing in a 'positive' direction. This is not necessarily the case.

countries are in transition from centrally planned regimes to more market-oriented regimes. These are referred to as economies in transition.
- *Differences in colonial experiences*
  Some developing countries have been colonised at a very early stage, others at a later stage. Some areas have never been colonised at all. There have been great variations in the nature and the intensity of the colonial relationships (see further Chapters 2 and 11).
- *Differences in precolonial history*
  For a full understanding of present-day developments, one has to take into account the precolonial history and the cultural and religious development of the different societies. Of particular importance are the age-old traditions of political centralisation and urbanisation in countries on the Asian continent.
- *Economic dynamism*
  Developing countries are characterised by pronounced differences in economic dynamism, with long periods of growth in some regions and long periods of stagnation in others.
- *Regional characteristics*
  Developmental experiences differ by region. It is useful to distinguish the regional experiences of Sub-Saharan Africa, South Asia, East Asia, North Africa, the Middle East and Latin America.

The gap between rich and poor countries

One of the connotations of the term *Third World* is that of a wide and insurmountable divide between two distinct entities: the developed first world and the poor third world. Let us approach this issue in two ways, first by looking at the degree of income inequality in the world economy, second by looking at the immutability of international income rankings. From the second perspective the question is whether individual developing countries can catch up and bridge the gap separating them from rich countries?

1   How unequal is the world economy?   The degree of inequality in the world economy is very great and it is increasing over time. Table 1.1 shows that – using purchasing power parities as converters – the average per capita income of the twenty-seven richest countries is fourteen times as high as that of the fifty-one poorest countries for which purchasing power parity income estimates are available.[3] The ratio between the richest country in PPP terms, the USA, and the poorest country, Sierra Leone, is no less than 71:1. The gap between rich and poor countries has been increasing dramatically over time. Around 1820, the ratio of per capita incomes of Western countries versus countries in Latin America, Asia and Africa was in the order 2:1 (PPP-based estimates of Maddison, 2001: table 1-9b).

The distribution of world income over households is even more unequal than distribution of the world income over countries, since incomes within countries are also distributed unequally. Furthermore, income inequality in

3 Using exchange rates, the ratio of richest twenty-seven countries to poorest fifty-eight countries is 68:1. This illustrates the vital importance of the choice of converter.

Table 1.2 *Inequality in the world economy*

Cumulative percentage of world population	Cumulative percentage of world income	
	1988	1993
Bottom 10	0.9	0.8
Bottom 20	2.3	2.0
Bottom 50	9.6	8.5
Bottom 75	25.9	22.3
Bottom 85	41.0	37.1
Top 10	46.9	50.8
Top 5	31.2	33.7
Top 1	9.3	9.5

Source: Milanovic (2002).

developing countries is considerably greater than in affluent countries. Berry, Bourguignon and Morrisson (1983) have estimated the distribution of the world income in 124 countries in 1970. They estimate the share of the bottom half of the world population at 8.4 per cent of world income, whereas the share of the top 10 per cent is no less than 49.4 per cent of world income. Recent research by Milanovic (1999) for 91 countries based on household survey data presents a rather similar pattern for the years 1988 and 1993. The results are reproduced in Table 1.2. In this table the bottom 50 per cent of households receives less then 10 per cent of world income and the world income distribution has become more unequal in the five years between 1988 and 1993. Such estimates are subject to many uncertainties. However, they do provide us with a striking illustration of the profoundly unequal distribution of the world incomes. In the following chapters, data will also be presented on inequalities in the social indicators.

2 Can the gap be bridged?   In spite of the huge differences in per capita income, it is not correct to speak of an insurmountable gap between rich and poor countries. The discussion of Table 1.1 shows that the transition from developing countries to affluent countries is a gradual one, rather than a sharp divide. Some countries designated as developing are more affluent than the poorer Western countries or the former socialist countries in Eastern Europe. Countries like Japan, Korea, Singapore and Taiwan, which once used to be considered as developing countries, are now seen as advanced economies. China has graduated from the low-income category to the lower-middle-income category; Malaysia has entered the upper-middle-income category. Also, as world income differentials widen, the speed with which some countries engage in catch-up has accelerated. For instance, growth rates in Asian economies such as China, South Korea or Singapore have been far higher than the historical growth rates of the presently affluent countries. The jump from a very poor to an upper-middle-income country can be realised in the course of one or two generations.

While some countries move upwards, others experience decline and comparative stagnation. Before World War II, Argentina was considered to be a reasonably developed country on the verge of breakthrough to affluence. It is now unmistakably seen as a developing country. The Russian Federation has experienced dramatic declines in its per capita income since 1991, accompanied by declines in its social indicators. The same is true of many of the former Soviet republics. The conclusion is that there is a constant process of change in the ranking of countries rather than a fixed order and an unbridgeable and immutable gap between rich and poor countries (see Reynolds, 1986).

1.8   What do developing countries have in common?

If the third world does not exist, the question arises whether there is a future for development studies. After World War II, development studies and development economics emerged as specific scientific subdisciplines and specialisations (Meier and Stiglitz, 2000). It was felt that the specific economic and social conditions in poor developing countries with institutions that differed greatly from the so-called 'advanced' Western nations, called for specific scientific theories and approaches which could take these circumstances into account. The standard theories and propositions of economics, sociology and the other social sciences would not apply in these very different circumstances. All over the world specialisations emerged in development studies, development economics, development sociology, and so forth.

From the 1980s onwards, there was a counter-tendency to reintegrate development studies into mainstream theorising and research. Though different conditions still had to be taken into account, the theories and approaches were not seen as fundamentally different from those of the mainstream disciplines. Thus, the introduction to the well-known four-volume *Handbook of Development Economics* (Chenery and Srinivasan, 1988) sees development economics as an integral part of the wider discipline of economics. Some authors went even further and called for the abolition of development studies (Lal, 2000).

The position taken in this book is that the reintegration of development studies into the more general disciplines of economics, history, demography or sociology provides a creative and stimulating impulse to the study of developing countries. The focus of development studies on the dynamics of socio-economic development also provides a stimulus to the mainstream disciplines themselves. Nevertheless, there continues to be a need for scientific specialisations focusing on the problems of development, based on intimate knowledge of conditions in developing countries. The specialisation of development studies also has a function in integrating or combining the insights from a wide range of disciplines, which would be lost if too strong a disciplinary focus were taken.

In spite of the diversity of circumstances and developmental experiences discussed in section 1.7, developing countries do have a number of important characteristics and problems in common, which justify a specialised professional focus on development. If we were not able to identify such characteristics, there would not be much sense in writing a book about developing countries. Important common characteristics of developing countries are summarised in Box 1.5.

> **Box 1.5 Common characteristics of developing countries**
> 1. Widespread poverty and malnutrition.
> 2. A relatively large share of agriculture in output and employment.
> 3. Pronounced dualism in economic structure.
> 4. Very rapid growth of population.
> 5. Explosive urbanisation.
> 6. Large-scale underutilisation of labour.
> 7. Political instability, pervasive corruption.
> 8. Environmental degradation.
> 9. Low levels of technological capabilities.

Poverty and malnutrition

As indicated in Table 1.1, in 2000 over 2.5 billion people lived in low-income countries with an average annual per capita income of 410 dollars (or 1,980 PPP dollars). Even this low average income does not offer a correct impression of the incomes of the very poor since the income distribution in most developing countries is heavily skewed. In the 1990s, the share of the total income or total consumer spending of the bottom 20 per cent of the households in the low-income countries ranged from 1.1 per cent to 9.7 per cent. The average share was 5.8 per cent. The average share of the bottom 40 per cent of the population was only 15.5 per cent (World Bank, 2001: table 2.8). Poverty is not restricted to the poorest countries. In developing countries with a higher average income, there are also large numbers of extremely poor people as a result of the unequal distribution of incomes. In the lower-middle-income category the share of the bottom 20 per cent of the households ranges from 1.9 per cent to 11.4 per cent, with an average of 6 per cent. In the upper-middle-income category the share of the bottom 20 per cent averages 6.3 per cent.[4] The greater the income inequality, the higher the incidence of poverty at a given level of average income per capita.

The simplest indicator of poverty is the *head count*, the numbers of people in a given country with incomes or consumption expenditures lower than a given poverty line. A more complex indicator is the *poverty gap*, the amount of money needed to bring people below the poverty line up to the level of the poverty line (Sen, 1981). A recent comprehensive study by Chen and Ravallion (2001) uses two poverty lines, one of 1.08 1993 international dollars and one of 2.15 1993 international dollars.[5] Their results for the head count are reproduced in

---

4 'Data on income distribution should be interpreted with caution' (World Bank, 1995: p. 220). International comparisons of income inequality are not yet very reliable.
5 Poverty is based on household consumption. The 1993 poverty lines are calculated using purchasing power parities for that year. Using national consumer price indices these 1993 poverty lines are

Table 1.3 *World poverty: population living below poverty lines, 1987 and 1998*

| Region | $1.08 per day | | | | $2.15 per day | | | |
| | Headcount index (%) | | Number of poor (millions) | | Headcount index (%) | | Number of poor (millions) | |
	1987	1998	1987	1998	1987	1998	1987	1998
East Asia	26.6	14.7	417.5	267.3	67.0	48.7	1,052.3	885.3
East Asia excluding China	23.9	9.5	114.1	53.9	62.9	44.3	299.9	252.0
Eastern Europe and Central Asia	0.24	3.8	1.0	17.8	3.6	20.7	16.4	98.2
Latin America and Caribbean	15.3	12.1	63.7	60.9	35.5	31.7	147.6	159.1
Middle East and North Africa	4.30	2.1	9.3	6.0	30.0	29.9	65.1	85.3
South Asia	44.9	40.0	474.4	521.8	86.3	83.9	911.0	1,095.0
Sub-Saharan Africa	46.6	48.1	217.2	301.3	76.5	78.0	356.6	488.8
Total	28.3	23.5	1,183.2	1,175.1	61.0	56.1	2,549.0	2,811.7
Total excluding China	28.5	25.6	879.9	961.7	58.2	57.9	1,796.6	2,178.4

Source: Chen and Ravallion, 2001, table 2.
Note: Poverty lines defined at 1993 international dollars using purchasing power parities.

Table 1.3. In 1998, the number of poor people living on an income below the poverty line of 1.08 dollars a day is 1.2 billion; 2.8 billion people have to survive on less than 2.15 dollars a day. Expressed as a percentage of the population, poverty is declining. But the absolute number of people consuming less than 2.15 dollars a day is still on the increase.

One of the most distressing aspects of poverty in developing countries is absolute malnutrition. Estimates of the numbers of undernourished people differ greatly. But the numbers are certainly high. According to estimates by the FAO, 800 million people were undernourished between 1998 and 2000.[6] This comes to 17 per cent of the total population of developing countries.[7] Other sources arrive at even higher estimates than the FAO. For example, the World Bank estimates for the 1980s (World Bank, 1986) are substantially higher than the FAO estimates for the same period. Most studies indicate that the percentage of malnourished people will decline in the long term. However, in view of the enormous population growth, the absolute number of undernourished people will increase. Absolute malnutrition is associated with high death rates, low life expectancy, bad health, impairment of the mental capacities and low productivity.

Large shares of agriculture

In developing countries the share of agricultural production in the total production is much higher than in affluent countries. Labour productivity in

extrapolated to 1987 and 1998. The data set covers 88 developing countries, representing 89 per cent of the population of the developing world.
6 Undernourishment is not limited to developing countries. According to FAO, another 11 million people are undernourished in the developing countries, while 30 million people are undernourished in the transition countries; see Chapter 10, Table 10.9.
7 FAO *State of Food Security in the World 2002,*: ftp://ftp.fao.org/docrep/fao/005/y7352e/y7352e01.pdf

agriculture is much lower than in the industrial sector. The share of the agricultural labour force in the total labour force is therefore even larger than the share of the agricultural production in the total production. This means that in developing countries a much larger proportion of the labour force is active in the agricultural sector than in the affluent countries. Conversely, the share of the industrial sector in production and employment is smaller.

Dualism and inequality

In developing countries there is a wide gap between the modern sector – which includes mining, manufacturing, commercial crop production and modern services – and the traditional sector which uses primitive and low-productivity techniques, e.g. traditional agriculture, in particular food production and the informal sector in the cities and the countryside. The modern sector is an enclave closely linked to the international economy, but isolated from the remainder of the domestic economy. The principal problem of *dualism* is the absence of technological diffusion from the modern technologically advanced sector towards the rest of the economy. Apart from technological dualism, other forms of dualism can also occur such as regional dualism (the traditional and the modern sector have also been divided spatially), cultural dualism and ethnic dualism (some ethnic groups are active in the modern sector, others in the traditional sector). When all dualisms coincide, problems can be quite extreme, and dualism may lead to social conflicts or even to civil wars (Higgins and Higgins, 1979).

Dualism goes hand in hand with very high levels of income inequality. In developing countries, inequality is much higher than in advanced economies and it is on the increase, not in the least in rapid-growth Asian economies such as China. Typically, the share of the top 10 per cent in income is between 26 and 47 per cent. The share of the bottom 10 per cent ranges between 0.5 and 4.0 per cent of total income (World Bank, 2001: table 2).

Rapid population growth

As a result of a decrease in death rates and a continued high level of birth rates, there is a large excess of births over deaths. In the late 1990s, the average rate of population growth in developing countries was 1.6 per cent per year. In low-income countries population was growing at no less than 2 per cent per year (World Bank, 2002).

Rapid urbanisation

Most developing countries experience large-scale migration from rural to urban areas as well as rapid growth of the existing urban population. Urban population growth exceeds the absorption capacity of the urban economy, the urban labour market and the urban infrastructure. Thus, widespread slums and uncontrollable mega-cities come into being; the best-known example of this is Mexico City. In turn the growth of the cities and the relative depopulation of the rural areas reinforce existing dualism. Within urban society, too, there is dualism between the modern formal sector and the small-scale informal sector.

Underutilisation of labour

Open unemployment is relatively low in most developing countries. Given the absence of formal systems of social security few people can afford to be out of work. However, there is widespread underutilisation of labour. Underutilisation of labour means either that only part of available labour is utilised, or that labour is being used so unproductively that labourers can hardly make a living despite working very long hours.

Political instability and pervasive corruption

The nation-state in developing countries is weakly developed. There is a lack of national integration. Feelings of solidarity with a common national culture and society are not fully developed. Loyalties are primarily oriented to a specific area, tribe, ethnic group or family. Many developing countries are racked by ethnic conflicts, which are a threat to national unity. The rule of law is poorly developed. There are insufficient guarantees for human rights. The military play a disproportionately large role in politics. Corruption is rife and transparency of the rules and regulations is limited.

Environmental degradation

The pressure of population on natural resources results in severe environmental degradation. Pollution laws are lax and in countries where industry is growing rapidly, waste water, toxic substances and effluents are indiscriminately dumped into the environment. The concentration of populations in the burgeoning cities with inadequate sewerage and sanitation imposes heavy burdens on the environment, in particular on water resources. Expansion of agricultural land, logging and the use of fuelwood results in rapid deforestation. Environmentally unfriendly types of industrial production and waste disposal are relocated to developing countries. Finally, population pressure, more intensive cultivation and fertilisation frequently result in land degradation, desalination and even desertification in large parts of the developing world (World Bank, 1992).

Though the advanced economies contribute most to global environmental problems, localised environmental degradation is typically concentrated in developing countries. Poverty contributes to environmental degradation – for instance through the use of fuelwood – and the poor are most likely to be victims of environmental pollution (World Bank, 2001).

Low levels of technology capabilities

Improvement of productive capacity in developing countries depends to a considerable extent on technological change, as is the case in the world economy at large (see Chapter 4). Worldwide most technological change is generated in the advanced economies. Developing countries still import much of their technology from abroad. The successful use of imported new technologies depends on the technological efforts and capabilities of individuals and organisations. New technologies have to be selected, adapted, implemented and further developed in mining, manufacturing, agriculture and services. In later stages of development indigenous design and development can substitute for imported technologies. However, many developing countries are presently still handicapped by very low levels of technological capabilities, owing to inadequate schooling, training and experience (Romijn, 1999; Lall, 1990). Low levels of technological capabilities limit the rate of technological change and economic growth and keep developing countries dependent on outside knowledge and expertise.

Together these common characteristics provide a loose characterisation of what constitutes a developing country. Of course, the degree to which these characteristics are present in different developing countries or regions varies. For example, in Tanzania or Ethiopia the share of agriculture in employment is much higher than in Brazil or Argentina; political instability and ethnic tension is more pronounced in Congo or Rwanda than in Brazil or Morocco. Technological capabilities are more developed in Malaysia than in Tanzania. Besides, one should not forget that the differences between developing and economically advanced countries are also differences of degree. Still, the list of common characteristics in Box 1.5 does helps us in identifying the present-day developing countries and their problems, which are the focus of this book.

Questions for review

1. Discuss the relationships between 'economic growth' and 'development'.
2. Is development conceivable without economic growth?
3. Why are Saudi Arabia and Libya still considered to be developing countries?
4. What are the main drawbacks of the use of GNP per capita as an indicator of economic development?
5. What are the most important dimensions along which developing countries differ from each other? Is the use of the term 'third world' justified in the light of these differences?
6. Is the inequality between rich and poor countries increasing or decreasing over time?
7. To what extent is there an insurmountable gap between rich and poor countries in the world economy?
8. What are the most important common problems and characteristics of developing countries?
9. Why is degree of world income inequality measured at purchasing power parities lower than that measured at exchange rates?
10. What are the main trends in global poverty, and how do these trends differ from region to region?

Further reading

Asian Drama by Gunnar Myrdal (1968) provides a useful discussion of the value-laden nature of the concept of development. In his classic study, *The Theory of Economic Growth* (1950), Arthur Lewis gives an excellent early treatment of the desirability of growth and development. An influential article by Dudley Seers on *The Meaning of Development*

(1979) criticises narrow post-war concepts of development. His prerequisites for development include criteria such as poverty reduction, employment creation and equality. In *Development as Freedom*, Amartya Sen (1999) defines development as an expansion of substantive freedoms. Critical perspectives on the concept of development are provided by Peter Bauer in *Dissent on Development* (1976), and Deepak Lal in the *Poverty of Development Economics* (2000).

An important source of information for students of development is the *World Development Report* published every year by the World Bank. Each issue of this report focuses on a different topic, such as population growth, poverty, institution building or human capital. The statistical annex of the WDR presents a wide range of development indicators. Recently the development indicators have been published in electronic form by the World Bank as a CD-Rom with 575 indicators for 225 countries (*World Development Indicators*, 2002). The United Nations Development Programme (UNDP) publishes the annual *Human Development Report*, with a strong focus on social indicators (for instance UNDP, 2003). This report includes the Human Development Index, which ranks countries on a combination of economic and social indicators.

A valuable compendium of original articles on many aspects of development is the four-volume *Handbook of Development Economics* edited by Chenery, Srinivasan and Behrman, published between 1988 and 1995. Important journals on development include *World Development*, the *Journal of Development Economics*, *Economic Development and Social Change*, the *Journal of Development Studies*, *Development and Change*, and *Oxford Development Studies*.

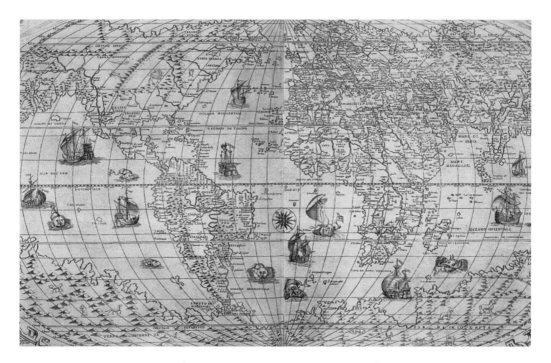

2 Development of the international economic order, 1450–2000

The differences in income levels, which characterise the present-day international economic order, are not self-evident. In the past these differences used to be much smaller. Around 1500 by far the greater part of the world population made its living in agriculture. Although some countries were richer than others, most people in most countries lived close to subsistence levels. The distribution of world income by region was therefore relatively equal (Bairoch, 1980; Cipolla, 1981: p. 220; Maddison, 2001). In contrast in the year 2000, the average income per capita in the twenty-seven richest countries was no less than fourteen times as high as that in the fifty-one poorest countries (see Table 1.1).

How did the present diversity of levels of economic development and welfare in the world economy come about? In order to examine possible answers to this question, this chapter will offer a rough outline of the history of European expansion and the development of the international economic order associated with it.

2.1 International economic order

Instead of presenting a formal definition of the slippery concept of international economic order, Box 2.1 identifies some of its important characteristics (Lewis, 1978b; Maddison, 1985; Maddison, 1989; Streeten, 1984).

Box 2.1 Characteristics of international economic orders

- *Flows of goods* (final products, capital goods, primary products, semi-finished goods) and services.
- *Financial flows* (investments, loans, transfer payments, levies and taxes).
- *Flows of people* (voluntary migration, indentured labour, slave trade, migrant labour).
- *Flows of knowledge* (diffusion of science, knowledge, information and technology).

Other important characteristics of the international economic order include:

- *The intensity of the economic relationships* between the various regions which together form the international economic order. Trade flows, for example, were small until the second half of the nineteenth century (Lewis, 1978b). The different parts of the world economy were not yet closely related.
- *Relations of dependence between countries and regions*. Economic relationships create mutual interdependence. However, in relations of interdependence some areas are more dependent on other areas than vice versa. Dependence on advanced economies is a problem for developing countries.
- *The institutional framework* of the economic and political relations between countries and regions. Is an area under direct political domination as a result of colonial rule or is it being influenced indirectly through foreign economic interests? Is the trade regime characterised by free trade or protectionism? What is the role of international organisations and international treaties?
- *Differential patterns of growth and stagnation* in various parts of the world economy which together make up the international economic order.
- *The size of the income gaps* between countries and regions.

2.2 Economic breakthrough and external expansion from Western Europe

Since the middle of the fifteenth century, Western Europe has experienced a dual process of internal economic growth and external economic and political expansion. This process of development is unique in two respects. First, in a limited part of the world the age-old vicious circle of struggle for survival at near-subsistence level was broken. Secondly, the European expansion led to the formation of a world economy in which all countries and regions in the world are interrelated in networks of interdependence.

Both statements are in need of clarification and qualification. In the first place, economic history prior to the sixteenth century is by no means exclusively a history of stagnation. It is the rule rather than the exception that, in the long run, production increased sufficiently to maintain a slowly growing population (Boserup, 1981; Jones, 1988; Maddison, 1982a). This is referred to as *extensive growth* (Reynolds, 1986: pp. 7–10). There have also been periods in pre-modern history when total production grew faster than population, leading to growth of per capita income (*intensive growth*). This, for example, was the case in China from the ninth century to the thirteenth century.

Nevertheless, economic growth in the Western world since the sixteenth century is distinguished by the long duration of growth and its rapid and accelerating pace.[1] For example, per capita income in the rich capitalist countries is now at least nineteen times as high as in 1820 (Maddison, 2001). Already in the first part of the eighteenth century, on the eve of the Industrial Revolution, the average level of prosperity in countries like England and the Netherlands was substantially higher than in the rest of the world (Landes, 1969; 1998; Maddison, 1983). Per capita incomes in Europe and the European offshoots were twice as high as in the non-European world.[2] Growth in Europe has led to an unprecedented and lasting increase in prosperity for great numbers of people, whereas in pre-modern societies malnutrition and starvation were never far round the corner, even in more prosperous periods and regions. Although economic development in Europe was often attended by impoverishment and disruption, in the long run the masses of the poor also profited from the increases in average per capita income. It is in this sense that one may speak of a breakthrough from the vicious cycle of poverty.

Secondly, the European expansion since the fifteenth century has been preceded by many other processes of political, economic and cultural expansion. To list but a few examples: the formation of the Hellenistic and Roman empires; the spread of the Arab/Islamic sphere of influence under the Umayyad and Abbasid caliphs from 760 to 1100; the Mongolian conquests which stretched from the Pacific to southern India, China, Russia and Central Europe; and the formation of the Ottoman empire. The process of European expansion, however, is different from other processes of expansion in several respects. First, the European process of expansion was characterised by the absence of political centralisation within the core area of Europe. Europe was a multitude of rival nation-states in the making, rather than an integrated empire. Second, the ties between the European countries and the rest of the world were not only political, but also economic (Braudel, 1978; Wallerstein, 1974). The European-based international economic order was not the first international economic order in history. Thus, both the Islamic and the Chinese empires formed the core of large and wide-ranging international trading systems (Abu Lughod, 1989; Isichei, 1997; Klein, 1999). However, the European world system was characterised by a long-run extension and intensification of international economic relationships which in time came to span the whole globe. Third, the process of

---

1 Earlier estimates date the beginning of European growth from the second half of the fifteenth century onwards. According to recent estimates by Maddison (2001), European growth started even earlier, around the eleventh century, with no sharp acceleration around the year 1500. What is new after the fifteenth cenutry, however, is the combination of long-term growth with external expansion.
2 For a dissenting view see Bairoch (1980) who argues that around 1700 developing countries were about as rich as the presently affluent countries at that time. See also Frank (1998).

interweaving the world economy and world society, which was a consequence of the European expansion, is characterised by a certain irreversibility. With the partial exception of the Chinese empire, the history of all ancient empires, processes of expansion and world systems is characterised by rise and fall, centralisation followed by decentralisation, contraction and disintegration. The European expansion from the second half of the fifteenth century onwards, on the other hand, has resulted in a single global economic order of which the constituent parts have become permanently interdependent – for better or worse. They will remain closely interrelated long after the role of the West in the world has come to its term and other leading centres have emerged.[3]

If an early-fourteenth-century observer could have taken a look at the twenty-first century, he would have been very surprised at the present position of Western countries in the world economy. Around the year 1400, little indicated that drastic economic breakthroughs and processes of external expansion would take place especially in Europe. From a military point of view it was by no means obvious that Europe would expand its sphere of influence in the world (Kennedy, 1989). The Moors were not driven out of Spain until 1492. Constantinople fell to the Ottoman Turks in 1453. Towards the end of the fifteenth century the Ottoman empire had occupied Greece, the Ionian Islands, Bosnia, Albania and large parts of the Balkan Peninsula. In 1526, the Ottomans conquered large parts of Hungary; in 1529 they besieged Vienna. In naval technology, European nations gained ascendency in the seventeenth century. But it was not until the late eighteenth and early nineteenth century that military superiority on land was gained over Asian regimes (Fieldhouse, 1982: p. 10; McNeil, 1989).

If our observer had ventured to predict the prospects of economic development in 1400, he would probably have put his money on the ancient and highly developed societies in Asia, the Middle East and, in particular, on China. In the fourteenth century, China was the most advanced society in the world in terms of technology (Boserup, 1981; Castells, 2000; Elvin, 1973; Mokyr, 1990; Needham *et al.*, 1954). China knew firearms, blast furnaces, gunpowder, hydraulic clocks, magnetic compasses, advanced seagoing ships, navigation techniques, the arts of printing and paper-making. Transportation technology was well developed; there were roads and extensive systems of canals and waterways. Money came into circulation at an early stage, along with market relationships. Intensive agriculture was practised, the techniques of which were recorded in handbooks (Perkins, 1969). Complicated irrigation systems were in use. By the twelfth century there was already mass production in manufacturing. Elvin (1973) estimates that in the thirteenth century some 20 per cent of the population lived in towns. There was a highly developed bureaucratic administrative system

3 In his recent book, *Global Economy in the Asian Age*, A.G. Frank has attacked the notion of Western exceptionalism. He reinterprets the period of Western expansion as an intermezzo between an earlier Asian age and the present rise of Asian economies. It is useful to emphasise the continuity between the European period and what has gone before. However, the rates of internal growth in Europe in combination with global expansion remain an historically unique phenomenon. Frank presents no new empirical evidence to contradict this view.

which would much later serve as a model for the British civil service. China was the first country in the world to have a national system of education with comparative examinations providing for entry into positions in the Mandarin bureaucracy. Nevertheless, China was not the first country to experience a major economic breakthrough and nor was it the country from which the rest of the world was penetrated. The penetration of world society started from an insignificant and relatively sparsely populated country in the southwest of Europe: Portugal (Wallerstein, 1974: p. 38 ff).

It is fascinating to note that at the same time as Europeans set out upon their expeditions at the beginning of the fifteenth century, a similar process of expansion was already taking place from China. From 1405 to 1433 the famous eunuch Admiral Cheng Ho undertook a series of expeditions which took the Chinese to the Indian Ocean, Java, Ceylon, Persia and even to the African east coast. However, after Cheng Ho died in 1433, these expeditions were stopped abruptly as a result of changes in Chinese policy. In 1435 shipbuilding was even prohibited by imperial decree. The Chinese fleet was dismantled, and overseas trade was discouraged as much as possible. By 1477 the logs of the naval expeditions were confiscated, hidden or burned. By 1500, the death penalty was imposed for building ships with more than two masts. The empire turned inward (Elvin, 1973; Jones, 1988; Kennedy, 1989; Lin, 1995; McNeil, 1989; Wallerstein, 1974). Traffic along the grand canal connecting North and South China replaced foreign exploration. Scientific and technological development faltered. The empirical and experimental attitude in science and technology was abandoned for a more mystical and comtemplative set of attitudes (Elvin, 1973). The Chinese economy, which had flourished until the middle of the fourteenth century, got caught up in a centuries-long process of stagnation lasting until the communist takeover in 1949. On the other hand, the expansion from Europe continued, filling the vacuum left by the discontinuation of the Chinese expansion. Portugal gave the initial impetus to the European penetration of the world and the gradual formation of a coherent world economy of which the constituent parts would become progressively ever more interrelated in the course of time.

2.3 Why expansion from Europe instead of from China?

These historical developments led Immanuel Wallerstein to pose a series of interesting questions which concern the very essence of the issue of development (Wallerstein, 1974: pp. 36–63): why did the breakthrough of Capitalism and the process of economic growth associated with it, take place in Europe? Why did the Chinese economy stagnate from the fourteenth century onwards despite the initial conditions that seemed so promising? Why was there a process of external European expansion, starting in the fifteenth century? Why did the external expansion of China come to a stop after 1433 and why did China develop in an inward-looking fashion?

Following Max Weber (1920), Wallerstein seeks the answer to such questions in the difference between the centralised Chinese empire and the decentralised feudal system in medieval Europe, which would later generate strong national states and within which capitalist institutions and property rights could develop and flourish. Maintenance of an empire involves a multitude of military and administrative expenses – in the terminology of Kennedy (1989) *imperial overstretch* – which may eventually hinder economic development. In the world economic system that developed in Europe after 1500, economic relations were more important than direct political control radiating from a single administrative centre. The European centre of this 'world system' gave rise to powerful national states in fierce competition with each other. These states offered support to enterprising groups and classes that contributed to internal economic development and external expansion.

Wallerstein seeks the incentives for external European expansion in the crisis of feudalism from the fourteenth century onwards. This crisis offered motivations for expansion to several social groups: the nobility, whose traditional sources of revenue were threatened by the crisis; the rising middle classes; the state apparatus that considered external expansion as a source of revenue and prestige; and members of the new urban semi-proletariat who were available for work as soldiers and sailors.

Incentives for expansion, discussed by Wallerstein, include: the demand for gold, silver and precious metals; spices; food; fuels and raw materials; and the search for new sources of income and employment. Gold was needed for luxury imports from Asia such as jewels and spices. The need for food, fuels and raw materials stimulated expansion to the Mediterranean countries, the Atlantic islands, North and West Africa, Eastern Europe, the Russian steppes and Central Asia. Population growth led to an intensification of agriculture which involved the introduction of cash crops, cattle-breeding and horticulture (see Chapters 5 and 10). There was an increasing demand for corn imports from less densely populated areas. From the fourteenth century onwards England and the Netherlands imported corn from the Baltic and Mediterranean areas. Cultivation of sugar cane was the motivation for expansion towards the eastern Mediterranean and the Atlantic islands. The need for labour for sugar cane processing led to the emergence of the Atlantic slave trade (Klein, 1999). Owing to increasing deforestation, there was a shortage of wood for fuel and for shipbuilding. The textile industry required materials such as pigment and gum.

All these factors played a part in the development of various European States. But a number of factors was specific to Portugal. According to Wallerstein, they may explain why expansion originated from Portugal. He mentions, for example, the absence of alternatives for the Portuguese nobility, Portugal's location by the sea, its previous experience with long-distance trade, the availability of capital from the Italian city-states, and the strength and stability of the state machinery. There was a convergence of interests. The sovereign, the nobility, the commercial middle classes and the urban semi-proletariat that had fled the countryside all benefited from external expansion.

To explain the contrast between Chinese inward-looking development and European expansionism, Wallerstein points to the absence of a convergence of interests in China, the intensification of the food production, and the political characteristics of a centralised Chinese empire.

The absence of converging interests

In China no consensus existed with respect to the benefits of external expansion. The Confucian mandarins in the state bureaucracy opposed the eunuch admirals whose interests lay in expansion. The central bureaucracy had a great dislike for the expense involved in these foreign expeditions. They preferred to invest in major fortifications against invasions from the North and canals. In due course, the emperor sided with the central bureaucracy. The lack of a colonising mission also played a part. In the Chinese world view China was the centre of the world, and the Chinese empire already contained everything of importance in the world. The Chinese were not interested in communication with barbarians, including barbarians from faraway Europe. This world view was to play an important role until the nineteenth century. It is often put forward as an explanation for the half-heartedness of Chinese attempts at modernisation in the face of Western challenges in the nineteenth century.

Intensification of food production

In Europe increasing population density led to a pattern of agriculture in which more densely populated areas concentrated on cattle farming, horticulture and cash crops, while importing corn from less densely populated areas. Compared to crop production, cattle farming is a less efficient way of producing calories. It is only feasible if foodstuffs can be imported from elsewhere (Boserup, 1981). Population growth provided an impulse for external expansion for the purposes of importing corn from less densely populated peripheral regions in the Baltic and Eastern Europe. Subsequently, the availability of animal power in Europe, lacking in China, was a stimulus to further economic development.

In southeastern China an extremely labour-intensive type of agriculture developed causing a shortage of labour (Perkins, 1969). The high level of agricultural and irrigational technology allowed for intensive agriculture – in particular cultivation of rice. The increasing demand for labour was an impediment to external expansion.

Political centralisation

After the fall of the Roman Empire, a highly decentralised feudal system came into being in Europe (Elias, 1969; Maddison, 2001; Wolf, 1982).[4] Money played a relatively small part in this feudal economy, which stagnated economically up and until the eleventh century. Economic entities were highly self-sufficient.

---

4 It may be useful to remind readers that European feudalism was not some sort of primitive initial condition. It came into being after the dissolution of a centralised empire.

The feudal system, with its landowners living on the surplus of the agricultural production, was inimical to the rising groups based on trade and industry. In Europe, capitalism had to struggle to survive, which accounts for its strength in later periods. Capitalist activities were centred in the cities, which managed to preserve their autonomy owing to the decentralised nature of the feudal system. If political pressure became too severe in a particular region, entrepreneurs and merchants could always move to other areas where taxes were lower and economic activities less constrained (McNeil, 1989).

Paradoxically, in the long term the decentralised feudal system gave birth to the highly centralised states of Europe. Some political centres started dominating surrounding regions and, once processes of centralisation were well under way, the feudal mystique was transferred to the central authorities. The mystique surrounding power strengthened the centralising tendencies in the emerging absolute monarchies. We should emphasise here that the tendencies towards centralisation did not result in the rise of another centralised empire, but rather in a multitude of internally highly centralised national-states competing with one another. In this environment the emerging states were also dependent on support offered them by the financial and commercial bourgeoisie, which in turn succeeded in consolidating its position and independence.

Competition between states also contributed to the rapid development of military technology. Technological or organisational innovations were quickly adopted by other states. In the centralised Chinese, Indian and Ottoman empires the rise of firearms and cannons led to the strengthening of central authorities. But the monopolisation of technology by these central authorities hampered further technological development. From the middle of the seventeenth century onwards this would result in an increasing military supremacy of the Western powers in comparison with the Asian empires, initially in naval technology, later in land-based technology (Kennedy, 1989; McNeil, 1989).

Justin Yifu Lin (1995) introduces another interesting explanation of Chinese stagnation, namely the role of classical literary training as prerequisite for entry into the mandarin bureaucracy. This created a disincentive for investments in human capital of the kind required for 'modern' scientific research. As a result, China failed to make the transition from traditional experience-based science and technology to modern mathematically and experimentally based science. 'Therefore, despite her early lead in scientific achievement, China failed to have an indigenous scientific revolution' (Lin, 1995: p. 285).

The Roman empire fell apart in the fifth century in Western Europe in a process of feudalisation. The Chinese empire survived major periods of upheaval and succeeded in maintaining its continuity for over two thousand years (Elvin, 1973). Chinese feudal rulers lived off the land and used serfs as foot soldiers in their military rivalries. Time and again they tried to assert their independence from central authorities. But the central authorities successfully managed to resist decentralising tendencies. Instead of a feudal structure, China developed a *prebendal structure* (Weber, 1920) in which the central authorities appointed a kind of 'officials' to administer far-off regions. These officials did not earn a salary but had to live off revenues collected in their region. Naturally, there were constant tendencies towards feudalisation and autonomy, with officials trying to turn their positions into hereditary ones. These tendencies, however, were countered by the central authorities, who developed a system of regularly transferring officials in order to weaken the ties between them and the regions they had to manage. The emperor and the central authorities succeeded in maintaining a loose form of imperial centralisation.

The instinct of an imperial power is to defend its territory. 'This drains attention, energy and profits which could be invested in capital development' (Wallerstein, 1974: p. 60). In the long term, centralisation will be at the expense of external expansion. All energy is frittered away in the construction of defensive fortifications like the great Chinese Wall. Thus decentralisation was one of the preconditions for expansion in Europe, which was lacking in China. European expansion was furthered by the competition between states. '[W]hen the Turks advanced in the east, there was no emperor to recall the Portuguese expeditions' (Wallerstein, 1974: p. 70). Besides, the degree of centralisation in the Chinese empire was quite low in comparison with the centralisation of the European nation-states in years to come. The absence of a feudal mystique in prebendalism made it easier to resist tendencies towards centralisation around the person of an absolute ruler.

Initially, the contractual nature of prebendalism was conducive to the development of capitalist groups and activities. However, in part because of this, capitalist tendencies in China did not unfold as fully as they did in Europe, where the rising middle classes had to wage a fierce struggle for survival. As opposed to European cities, which developed into independent and autonomous enclaves in feudal society with their own municipal rights, Chinese cities never became completely independent from the central authorities. Capitalist impulses were thus smothered in a non-feudal bureaucratic environment which was initially far from hostile to capitalist impulses. Besides, in centralised empires there was an irresistible tendency to tax and regulate economic activities in order to cover the expenses of the central administrative apparatus (Jones, 1988).

Of course, it is not possible to discuss the voluminous literature on these classical questions adequately in a nutshell.[5] But the very posing of such questions advances our understanding of the sources of development and stagnation in the very long term.

2.4   European expansion in the world

Western expansion in the world proceeded unevenly. Some areas were penetrated very early, others much later; some areas regained their independence long before colonisation even reached other parts of the world.

---

5 An important source for these paragraphs was Wallerstein (1974) who in turn offers an excellent synthesis of the earlier literature on this subject.

In his standard work on the history of European colonisation, Fieldhouse distinguishes between *settlement colonies* and *colonies of occupation* (Fieldhouse, 1982). Settlement colonies involve immigrants from the mother country settling permanently in a colony; these immigrants attempt to build a society resembling as much as possible the society in their country of origin. Settlement colonies can be subdivided into 'pure' settlement colonies, 'mixed' colonies and plantation colonies. In 'pure' settlement colonies such as the United States, Canada and Australia the original inhabitants with pastoral or hunting and gathering modes of production – Indians, Aborigines – were completely crowded out and destroyed by immigrants from Europe who built another European society in the new world. In 'mixed' colonies (for example the Spanish colonies in Mexico and Peru) a substantial minority of European colonists settled in the colony, trying to absorb the local population. In plantation colonies a tiny minority of Europeans settled permanently; they imported slave labour from elsewhere in order to establish a plantation economy (e.g. the Portuguese in Brazil).

Colonies of occupation are characterised by an extremely small elite of foreign colonial officials sent out to rule over native inhabitants with a completely different language and culture.

Finally, apart from settlement colonies and colonies of occupation the Europeans also founded many trading posts all over the world. Types of colonies and phases of expansion and contraction are summarised in Box 2.2.

Box 2.2   Western expansion and contraction
Types of colonisation:
Colonies of settlement

- Pure colonies of settlement (e.g. USA);
- Mixed colonies of settlement (e.g. Mexico);
- Plantation colonies (e.g. Brazil).

Colonies of occupation (e.g. India, Indonesia, Vietnam)
Trading posts

Phases of expansion and contraction:
1400–1815: first wave of expansion

- Colonies of settlement in the Americas;
- Trading posts in Africa and Asia.

1776–1824: first wave of decolonisation in North and South America
1815–1913: second wave of expansion
Colonies of occupation in Africa, Asia and the Middle East.
1930–1980: second wave of decolonisation
The second wave of decolonisation starts in the Middle East in 1930 and accelerates after 1945.

Before the beginning of the nineteenth century, European expansion in Africa and Asia primarily took the form of the establishment of trading posts by the Portuguese, the Dutch and the British. On the American continent the Spanish, the Portuguese, the British, the French and the Dutch founded settlement colonies. Between 1776 and 1824 almost all the colonies in the Americas gained their independence. The second phase of the European expansion started around 1815 after the Napoleonic Wars and was directed towards Asia and later also towards Africa. During this period the colonies that were carved out were mainly colonies of occupation, where alien peoples were dominated by colonial rulers whose prime loyalties lay in their faraway homelands.

2.4.1 Types of international economic orders

Western expansion has led to economic relations between the Western and non-Western world, each of which affected non-Western countries in different ways. Following Maddison, one can distinguish six international economic orders since 1500 (Maddison, 1982b; 1983; 1985; 1989): conquest imperialism; merchant capitalism; free trade imperialism; conflict and autarchy 1913–1950; the post-war golden age; and the economic order since the 1973 oil crisis. Each order is characterised by a specific kind of relationship between the rich Western countries and the developing countries. These orders are ordered in chronological sequence, but different orders can overlap (see Box 2.3). The characteristics of the six orders will only be briefly touched upon here. They will be discussed in more detail later in this chapter and elsewhere in this book.

Box 2.3 Types of international economic orders

1. Conquest imperialism
    1500–1820 Spain in Latin America
2. Merchant capitalism
    1500–1870 Portugal in Brazil
              The Netherlands in Indonesia
              The UK in India
    Beginning of period of capitalist accumulation and development: 1820
3. Free trade imperialism: 1870–1913
4. Defensive autarchy: 1913–1950
5. The golden age of growth: 1950–1973
6. 1973–2004: Differential patterns of growth and stagnation

In *conquest imperialism* the relations between Western countries and the colonies are characterised both by straightforward plundering of the colonised areas' resources and by a transfer of economic surpluses by means of taxation and tribute payments. Such destructive relations existed, for example, between Spain and Mexico from 1500 to 1820.

Merchant capitalism is characterised by the search for monopolistic profits on the production and export of luxury goods from the penetrated areas, by the European powers. Where Western expansion resulted in direct colonial domination, taxation, in addition to monopolistic profits, served to transfer economic surpluses to Western countries. These relations can be found in the areas penetrated by the Portuguese, the French, the Dutch and the British from 1500 to 1870.

The international order of *free trade imperialism* reached maturity in the period 1870–1913 and is characterised by far-reaching liberalisation of international trade. In developing countries such liberalisation was imposed by force or by the threat of force. During this period the typical colonial pattern of international trade emerged, in which developing countries exported primary products to the rich industrialised countries and industrialised countries exported finished manufactured goods to the developing countries.

Between 1913 and 1950 two world wars and an economic depression took place. In this period of *conflict and autarky* free trade was abandoned, and protectionism prevailed. Each country tried to isolate itself from the consequences of the economic crisis at the expense of its trading partners. Partly as a result of this, the volume of world trade fell off, and investment in developing countries decreased dramatically. Economic growth stagnated both in rich countries and the developing countries most involved in international trade. In many colonies, policy attempts to cope with the economic crisis were hampered by colonial constraints.

During the *post-war golden age* from 1950 to 1973 there was an increase in per capita income in rich countries as well as in developing countries. Indeed, per capita income grew more rapidly than ever before. International trade was highly liberalised, though manufacturing sectors in developing countries remained highly protected. The volume of international trade increased sharply, as did international capital flows. The developing countries received a considerable net inflow of capital consisting of direct investments, loans and development aid.

Since the oil crisis in 1973, growth of the world economy as a whole has slowed down and differences between patterns of economic performance in various parts of the world increased. After 1982, economic growth in Latin America stagnated for ten years in the aftermath of the debt crisis. In some developing countries the debt crisis resulted in a substantial net capital outflow to the rich countries. In Sub-Saharan Africa a long period of economic stagnation followed. In major Asian economies growth continued to be rapid and there was substantial catch-up relative to the advanced economies. In 1997 Asian growth was interrupted by a major financial crisis, which dramatically affected real growth rates. The Asian crisis emphasised the vulnerability of developing economies to massive global in- and outflows of capital. Since the Asian crisis, some countries such as China and Korea have recovered, while countries such as Indonesia and the Philippines are still struggling to recover their momentum. In the post-1973 period, there were tendencies towards revival of protectionism but on the whole the principles of free trade have prevailed.

In the following sections the historical developments in international economic relations will be discussed in more detail, combining the discussion of economic orders with that of colonial expansion and contraction.

2.4.2 *The first wave of expansion, 1400–1815*

In the fifteenth and sixteenth centuries Portugal and Spain initiated the first wave of expansion directed towards Africa, Asia and Latin America. The Portuguese were the pioneers. They started to found trading posts and bases along the African west coast from 1415 onwards and along the African east coast in India and the Far East from the late fifteenth century onwards. From these trading posts luxury goods such as gold, ivory, pepper and spices were shipped to Europe. From the second half of the fifteenth century African slaves were transported to sugar plantations on the Atlantic islands and later to plantations in the Caribbean and the American continent. There was no direct colonial rule. Native societies, political systems and the economy were initially left undisturbed. Especially in Asia, the impact of Western penetration would be limited for quite some time. From the beginning of the sixteenth century onwards the Dutch pushed the Portuguese out of the Far East; however, the impact of Dutch presence on local societies was initially also rather weak.

The Spanish colonisation of Latin America from the late fifteenth century onwards was of an extremely destructive nature. Initially, straightforward plunder of gold and silver treasures was predominant. Later, large estates were created for the *conquistadores*, on which the Indians were forced to work. A major part of the economic surplus was transferred to Spain by means of taxation and tribute payments. The ancient Aztec and Inca civilisations were completely erased. Catholicism was imposed by force. The demographic consequences of the Spanish colonisation were disastrous. The Indian population was exposed to new germs against which it had no natural immunity (Diamond, 1998). As a result of wars, heavy labour in mines and on plantations and especially contagious diseases, the original population was decimated (Furtado, 1976).

Present-day Brazil was primarily colonised by the Portuguese after its discovery in 1500 by Cabral.[6] The Portuguese discovered an extremely sparsely populated area. They founded plantations and initiated exports of wood and other primary products. The demand for labour was met by African slave imports. Portuguese colonialism very much focused on making monopolistic profits through trade. In comparison to Spanish colonialism, which was actually a form of organised plunder, Portuguese colonialism was less destructive since new technologies and products were introduced as well. However, neither the slaves nor the original Indian inhabitants benefited much from these new technologies. After an initial increase in per capita production as a result of

---

6 For a short period of time in the seventeenth century, the Dutch also played an important role in Brazil. However, their role had been played out by 1655.

the introduction of a plantation economy based on slave labour into a society of hunters and gatherers, per capita income remained unchanged for three centuries (Maddison, 1985).

Slaves were also imported to Spanish colonies, where the Indian population proved to be unwilling or unsuited to do the heavy work in mines and on plantations. In the nineteenth century the demand for labour in Latin America was also met by the recruitment of indentured labourers from China, India and Java.

The economic history of Latin America is the model for theories of exploitation and underdevelopment; in this model the negative effects of colonialism, neocolonialism and capitalist exploitation account for the backwardness of the poor countries. Not only have economic surpluses been transferred to Europe for centuries, but also regressive social institutions such as landlordism and slavery have been introduced, which were to form an obstacle to economic development long after political independence had been achieved. That exploitation has played an important part in the development of Latin America is beyond dispute. There is, however, a debate on the degree to which present-day economic problems can be explained by adverse colonial experiences and postcolonial foreign influences.

Marxist and radical theorists tend to explain the successful economic development of Western Europe from the perspective of colonial exploitation. It is suggested that gold and silver from Latin America, colonial taxation, monopolistic profits from trade and the revenues of the slave trade figured decisively in the 'original accumulation' which was a prerequisite for the Western European economic breakthrough in later years (Baran, 1957; Williams, 1964). This theory, however, is not very tenable. Domestic savings and a gradual increase in productivity in handicrafts and agriculture have been of more importance to European development than external plunder, taxation and foreign profits (Jones, 1988; Landes, 1969; Maddison, 1982a; 1995; 2001; North and Thomas, 1973). Colonial exploitation certainly contributed to Western prosperity and growth. But the key question is whether economic surpluses and savings could be transformed into productive investments (Wolf, 1982: p. 120). Modern quantitative historical research supports the view of David Landes that 'Western Europe was already rich before the Industrial Revolution – rich by comparison with other parts of the world of that day. This wealth was the product of centuries of slow accumulation, based in turn on investment, the appropriation of extra-European resources and labour, and substantiantal technological progress, not only in the production of material goods but in the organisation and financing of their exchange and distribution' (Landes, 1969: pp. 13–14).[7] Distinctive characteristics of European development include a pattern of political institutional and legal development (property rights) that provided an

---

7 For a dissenting view see Bairoch and Levy-Leboyer (1981). Bairoch and his associates argue that income levels before the industrial revolution are rather similar and that increase in income levels since then is due to exploitation of developing countries.

especially effective basis for the operation of private economic systems. Also of importance were the European receptivity to new technologies and the capacity to assimilate them, a capacity as important as inventiveness itself (Rosenberg, 1982).

It is consistent with this view that the countries that first profited from colonial revenues and plunder – Spain and Portugal – were not capable of converting economic surpluses into productive domestic investments. After the sixteenth century, their role soon came to an end.

In the seventeenth century, economic and political supremacy shifted from southwestern Europe to northwestern Europe. In terms of technological capacity as indicated by per capita income, the Netherlands was the leading economy. For a short period of time the Dutch republic was also the dominant power in world politics (Israel, 1995). The Dutch penetrated Indonesia where they ousted the Portuguese and established trade monopolies. Dutch expansion was of a mercantilistic nature. They did not strive for direct colonial domination but rather for lucrative trade by means of the Dutch East India Company, founded in 1602. The Dutch also penetrated into the western hemisphere. They founded settlement colonies in North and South America and in the Caribbean.

In addition to the Dutch republic, France and England also started colonising North America and the Caribbean in the seventeenth century. In the Caribbean the colonial powers primarily founded plantation economies where sugar was grown with slave labour.

Dutch colonisation in Brazil was not granted a long life. It came to an end in 1665. On the North American continent the Dutch were already ousted by the British in 1667, exchanging New Amsterdam for Surinam. The French and the British continued to compete for control over North America. In the eighteenth century this conflict resulted in a series of Anglo-French wars from which the British arose as the dominant power on the North American continent. At the end of the Seven Years' War in 1763 the role of France in North America had come to an end. Today only Francophone Quebec reminds one of the French expansion in this part of the world.

In the course of the eighteenth century the leading economic and technological position of the Netherlands was taken over by Great Britain. In the second half of the century rapid industrialisation took place in Great Britain, often referred to by the dramatic term 'Industrial Revolution'.[8] In the early nineteenth century the Netherlands were outdistanced by England in terms of per capita production (Maddison, 2001, table B-21). The other Western European countries became the followers of British leadership, profiting from diffusion of technology from the lead country.

In the eighteenth century the British penetration into India gathered momentum. In the seventeenth century the British had already founded trading

---

8 The term 'Industrial Revolution' tends to misrepresent the gradual nature of the long-term increase in economic productivity.

posts and cities along the Indian coastline. Trade was controlled by the British East India Company, founded in 1600. Until the early eighteenth century India was still a powerful Asian empire, somewhat past its prime after a glorious flowering in the sixteenth century under Akbar (1556–1605). In 1757 Bengal was conquered after the battle at Plassey and was henceforth governed by the East India Company as a satrapy. The French, who penetrated into India at the same time as the British, were eclipsed. However, there still was no question of direct colonial control over the entire Indian subcontinent.

From the late eighteenth century onwards Australia was penetrated by the British, starting with the foundation of a penal colony in Sydney in 1788. The convicts were soon followed by voluntary migrants who would eventually turn Australia into a prosperous settlement colony like the United States and Canada, once again at the expense of the indigenous inhabitants.

As can be seen above, the patterns of penetration in various parts of the world differ widely during the first phase of European expansion (Fieldhouse, 1982). In Asia the Europeans were faced with ancient established civilisations that were initially neither technologically nor militarily inferior to the Europeans. The Europeans had the advantage at sea; but on land they were initially not stronger than their opponents. The Europeans were concentrated in enclaves along the coasts. Their influence on the native society was relatively unimportant. On the North American continent the hunting and gathering Indian peoples were totally unable to withstand the European onslaught. The same holds for the large Indian civilisations in Latin America that succumbed to the force of small numbers of determined and unscrupulous Spaniards. European immigrants settled on the American continent. The language and culture of their countries of origin would leave a lasting imprint on the development of colonial and postcolonial society. On the African continent there were initially no permanent settlements with the exception of Cape Colony and Angola. None of the African empires – not even the most developed ones like Benin, Mali or Songhai in West Africa – were militarily a match for the European intruders. However, climate, disease and severe conditions of life were obstacles to permanent European settlement (Isichei, 1997). Trading posts predominated.

2.4.3 The first wave of decolonisation

Decolonisation is not a recent phenomenon. The process of Western expansion would continue in many parts of the world during the nineteenth century, but in other areas direct European political control was on the decline. The British colonies in America declared their independence in 1776 and formed the United States of America. The Napoleonic Wars sounded the death knell for Iberian colonialism. From 1814 to 1824 all Spanish colonies on the American continent became independent. Brazil declared its independence in 1822, although a son of the Portuguese king was crowned as emperor.

The decolonisation of the English-speaking colonies in Australia, Canada, New Zealand and South Africa took place more gradually. Traditionally, English colonies used to have virtual autonomy with respect to their mother country. From the middle of the nineteenth century onwards this autonomy was gradually transformed into a *de facto* independence within the framework of the British Commonwealth. The attainment of formal independence can best be dated *circa* 1931 when a statute was passed stating that dominions were no longer subject to decisions of the British parliament.

2.4.4   *The second phase of European expansion, 1815–1913*

The nineteenth century was the apex of Western expansion and Western political, economic, military and cultural dominance. Per capita production increased sharply (Maddison, 1982a) among others owing to rapid increase in the amount of capital goods per head of population and acceleration of technological progress. The differences in the levels of prosperity between the rich countries and the developing countries increased dramatically. Industrialisation also consolidated the Western military lead. Moreover, formerly powerful empires in Asia and the Middle East were no longer a match for the Western powers. Western expansion progressed more rapidly than ever before. In 1800 Europe, together with its overseas possessions and former colonies, controlled 55 per cent of the surface of the earth. By 1878 this percentage had risen to 67 per cent and by 1914 to 84.4 per cent (Fieldhouse, 1982: p. 178).

The political and economic relationships between the colonial powers and the colonised areas were intensified. In India, Indonesia and other Asian countries indirect influence through commercial relations was transformed into formal political domination of colonies of occupation by the mother countries. The consolidation of colonial domination was attended by a series of military conflicts such as the Indian Mutiny in 1857 and the Diponegoro rebellion on Java (1825–30).

Colonies founded by white migrants in Canada, South Africa, Australia and New Zealand expanded inland at the expense of the native inhabitants. Economic growth in the United States went hand in hand with strong expansionist tendencies. This did not lead to the founding of new colonies, but rather to the annexation of Spanish-speaking areas which became states in the American union. In the mid-nineteenth century tsarist Russia expanded eastward to Central Asia, Siberia and the Far East. France, which had an insignificant colonial empire before the nineteenth century, penetrated into North Africa and Indochina. Algiers was conquered in 1830, and in the fifty years that followed the whole of Algeria was colonised. The French colonisation of Indochina in the second half of the nineteenth century started in 1859 with the occupation of Saigon on the Mekong Delta. Between 1829 and 1914 the far-flung Ottoman empire, heir to the medieval Arab caliphates and the Mameluk empire contracted. The Ottomans had to recognise the southern and southeastern

European Balkan States of Albania, Bulgaria, Greece, Romania and Serbia as independent states. For the better part of the nineteenth century Great Britain was the leading world power both economically, politically and technologically. In Great Britain industrialisation had proceeded furthest and British maritime power was undisputed until the 1890s. As a result of British dominance there were few conflicts between colonial powers. This was the era of *Pax Britannica*.

After 1830, free trade became predominant in the English international trade policy. Tariff rates declined steadily in the course of the century, reaching very low levels after 1870. Colonial monopolies on trade were abolished. Colonies could now also trade with countries other than their mother country. England lowered numerous tariffs on imports from colonies. But it also demanded free access for its industrial exports to both colonial and non-colonial markets. These exports competed with handicraft and beginning industrial production in developing countries and retarded industrialisation outside Europe. The case of the Indian textile industry is frequently mentioned as an example of this.

Establishing free trade involved considerable force and coercion. By means of gunboat diplomacy monarchs and rulers, accustomed to financing their expenditures through royal monopolies on trade, were forced to lower tariffs and to open up their countries to Western exports. Maddison used the term 'free trade imperialism' to describe this economic order (Maddison, 1985). Furthermore, England tried to impede industrialisation in the colonies wherever her influence reached.

Not all colonial powers immediately adopted the policy of free trade. In Java, the Dutch governor Van den Bosch introduced the 'culture system' in 1830. In this system compulsory production of cash crops – for the benefit of the colonial rulers – was the key element. This 'culture system' may be considered as a nineteenth-century continuation of the international economic order of merchant capitalism.

Around 1890 the United States, once a British colony, took the economic and technological lead and has held that position ever since. It innovated in standardised production for mass markets. Western Europe, Australia, Canada, New Zealand and Japan became the followers in the race for technological and economic development. It was not until after World War II that the United States emerged as the dominant power in world politics. However, it did claim the right to intervene in Latin American affairs as early as the nineteenth century. In 1823 the Monroe Doctrine proscribed any intervention by powers other than the United States on the entire American continent.

By the end of the nineteenth century all European powers rushed to obtain new colonies. In doing so, they became more and more entangled in fierce rivalries. Until then, the African continent had hardly been penetrated by whites. Now it was rapidly colonised in what has come to be known as the 'scramble for Africa' (Davidson, 1992). At international conferences the colonial powers drew straight lines on the map in order to demarcate their possessions.

These artificial borders disregarded geographical characteristics and ethnic, cultural and historical dividing lines. Much of the present-day instability of African states has to do with the arbitrariness of these colonial borders (see Chapter 11).

2.4.5   The period 1870–1913

The abolition of forced cash crop production in the Indonesian 'culture system' in 1870 marked the demise of the international economic order based on monopolistic trade relations. Free trade became the predominant characteristic of the international economic order. Since the mid-nineteenth century developing countries had opened their borders to international trade – at times under threat of military force. Also leading countries such as England, France and the Netherlands had lowered their tariff rates on imports.

From 1870 to 1913 economic relations between rich countries and developing countries intensified; this was a new phenomenon. As Arthur Lewis argues convincingly, economic relations between the Western countries and the rest of the world were weak before the second half of the nineteenth century (Lewis, 1978a; 1978b). Initially most of the raw materials needed for industrialisation were available in Europe. The volume of trade between rich industrialised countries and developing countries was negligible. 'Even in 1883 total imports into the United States and Western Europe from Asia, Africa and Tropical Latin America came to only about a dollar per head of the population of the exporting countries' (Lewis, 1978b: p. 5). Improvements in transportation and communication – railways, iron ships, the telegraph – and the opening of the Suez Canal in 1869 changed all this. Both the continuous growth of the population of rich countries and the growth of industrial production caused an increase in the demand for agricultural and mining products. The tropics reacted to this growing demand by greatly increasing the export of primary products (e.g. coffee, tea, palm oil, groundnuts, tropical fruit, jute, sisal, rubber, tobacco, cotton, sugar, mining products). On the one hand, small peasants cultivated surplus land and used part of their surplus labour for the production of cash crops. On the other hand, there were Western investments in plantations and mines (Myint, 1980; Lewis, 1970; 1978b). The revenues from exports created a market for industrial products from industrialised countries. Thus there was a sharp increase in the volume of international trade.

The modern world economy came into being between 1870 and 1913. Western influences were felt everywhere, even in those places where the native lifestyles had remained unaffected until then. The poor countries became involved in the world economy through their exports of agricultural and mining products. They became acquainted with industrial consumer goods that were exported by the industrialised countries. The money economy arose when native inhabitants embarked on the production of commercial crops in addition to the cultivation of food products for their own consumption.[9] Large migration flows established new relationships between the various parts of the world and led to drastic changes in the structure of populations (see section 2.4.6). In many developing countries there was a vast increase in investment by rich countries. These investments focused on plantations, mines and the creation of an infrastructure of railways, roads and harbours for the benefit of exports and imports. Investment flows also increased among the rich countries themselves. According to Lewis (1970; 1978a; 1978b) and Maddison (1989), the 1870–1913 period was a period of increasing per capita income in both developing and rich countries. However, as a result of a complex of factors – among which were colonialism and the overwhelming attractiveness of primary exports – developing countries did not succeed in using the revenues from exports to achieve industrialisation and lasting economic development (Lewis, 1970).

In summary, in the 1870–1913 period an integrated world economy came into being, in which the volume of international trade underwent a sharp increase. International trade was of an asymmetric nature. Poor developing countries exported primary agricultural and mining products. Rich and politically powerful countries exported industrial products. After World War II 'industrialisation' became strongly associated with 'economic development', partly because of the historical experiences during the 1870–1913 period. Dependence on primary exports was more and more seen as a symptom of economic weakness. However, this is not always true, as will be shown in Chapter 8; countries like the United States, Canada and New Zealand benefited very much from agricultural exports at some stage in their development.

2.4.6   Migration flows

Following Arthur Lewis, we have argued that Western economic influence on the rest of the world was limited before the second half of the nineteenth century. Western powers may have had trading posts all over the world. Yet, in many parts of the world native societies continued to exist unchanged alongside European enclaves. Also the volume of international trade was relatively small. Only in the course of the nineteenth century did political penetration intensify and international trade relations become more important.

In at least two respects, however, Lewis's argument may lead to an underestimation of the impact of Western penetration in the world before 1870. First, the enormous impact of former Iberian colonialism in Latin America received insufficient emphasis. Secondly, not enough attention has been paid to the Atlantic slave trade which changed the entire population structure of Latin America and the Caribbean and which has left deep scars on the African continent.

---

9 Both long-distance trade and the use of various kinds of money, of course, preceded European penetration (e.g. Hill, 1986; Isichei, 1997; Klein, 1999; Wolf, 1982). But production for own consumption did play a much greater role in pre-modern economies and monetary transactions tended to be limited to more ceremonial transactions, such as bridewealth.

In this section, we examine migration flows as an important aspect of the international economic order, paying attention to the Atlantic slave trade from 1500 to 1870 and migration flows at the end of the nineteenth century.

The Atlantic slave trade

Tables 2.1 and 2.2 present quantitative estimates of the Atlantic slave trade and its importance for the development of African and Latin American populations. Table 2.1 shows the numbers of slaves imported into different parts of the Americas in different periods. Table 2.2 shows the numbers of slaves exported from Africa by region of origin in different periods.

According to the latest revisions of Curtin's authoritative 1969 estimates (Curtin, 1969; Klein, 1999), in total 11.1 million African slaves were shipped to America between 1500 and 1870.[10] This number does not include the 175,000 slaves who were exported to the Old World in the sixteenth and seventeenth centuries and some 7 million slaves exported to the Islamic world (Klein, 1999). To this should be added widespread slavery within African societies. The slaves for the Atlantic slave trade were collected by African states along the coast through warfare, systematic raiding and tribute. These states prospered thanks to the revenues of the slave trade, which was one of the most important export products along with gold, ivory, hides, pepper, beeswax and gum.

The coastal trade and transportation of slaves to the Americas was completely controlled by white people (first the Portuguese and later also the Dutch, the

Table 2.1 *Slave imports into the Americas, 1451–1870 (thousands)*

	North America[a]	Spanish America[b]	Caribbean[c]	Brazil	The Americas	Old World	Total
Imports 1451–1500						25	25
Population in 1500		9,350	300	1,000	10,650		
Imports 1501–1600		75	0	50	125	116	241
Population in 1600		6,900	200	1,000	8,100		
Imports 1601–1700		293	464	560	1,316	25	1,341
Population in 1700	370	7,600	500	1,250	9,720		
Imports 1701–1800	391	513	3,110	1,700	5,715		5,715
Population in 1800	6,040	10,400	2,000	2,500	20,940		
Imports 1801–70	169	782	247	1,720	2,917		2,917
Population in 1900	23,700	29,600	6,500	18,000	77,800		
Total 1501–1870	560	1,662	3,821	4,030	10,073	142	10,214

Notes:
[a] North America includes Delaware, Georgia, Maryland, North Carolina, South Carolina, Virginia, Kentucky, Mississippi, Alabama, Missouri, Arkansas, Tennessee and Texas. There are no data on Louisiana population. Slave imports into Louisiana have been included in totals for North America.
[b] Spanish America includes Mexico, Central America, Cuba, Peru, Colombia and Venezuela.
[c] The Caribbean includes Jamaica, Barbados, Leeward Islands, St Vincent, St Lucia, Tobago, Dominica, Trinidad, Grenada, the other Leeward Islands, Santo Domingo, Martinique, Guadeloupe, Guyana, the Netherlands Antilles, the Danish West Indies.
Sources: Data on population in McEvedy and Jones, 1978, and Darby Fullart, 1970. Slave imports from Curtin, 1969. Period 1781–1870 revised by Eltis, 1989.

10 Curtin's estimates of the Atlantic slave trade have subsequently been revised and refined by later researchers such as Eltis (1989), Eltis *et al.* (1998), Klein (1999) and Lovejoy (1982), but the overall magnitudes have by and large remained the same. We primarily use the revised estimates reported in Klein (1999).

British, the French and even the Spanish). The expansion of the Atlantic slave trade was highly correlated with the Western conquest of the American hemisphere. The demand for slaves on the American continent increased rapidly. In the fifteenth century 150,000 slaves were shipped to the Americas; in the sixteenth century their number had risen to 1.6 million. The slave trade reached its zenith in the eighteenth century when no fewer than 6.1 million slaves were transported overseas.

In 1807 the British parliament passed a bill prohibiting the slave trade. The holding of slaves in areas controlled by the British was forbidden in 1833. Other nations followed hesitantly, sometimes under British pressure: France in 1848, the Netherlands and the United States in only 1863. In spite of abolition, no less than 3.3 million slaves were transported to America in the course of the nineteenth century, mainly to work on sugar cane and coffee plantations (Hopkins, 1973). Today there are, fortunately, no differences of opinion regarding the ethical repulsiveness of the slave trade. There is, however, a lively academic debate on the effects of the slave trade on economic and demographic development on the African continent. Certainly there has been a considerable demographic bloodletting. The total number of slaves exported over the eighteenth century was no less than 14.4 per cent of the combined population of the exporting regions in the year 1800. Besides, it was young strong males in particular who were sold as slaves. West Africa was the most important slave-exporting region. In the course of the eighteenth century 3.8 million people were forcibly

Table 2.2 *Slave exports from Africa to the Americas, by region of origin, 1500–1870 (thousands)*

| | Exports by region of origin | | | | | |
	West Africa[a]	Western Central Africa[b]	Southeast Africa[c]	Total	Mortality in transit	Arrived in America
Population in 1500	11,000	8,000	7,000	26,000		
Exports 1500–1600		150		150	25	125
Population in 1600	14,000	8,500	8,250	30,750		
Exports 1600–1700[d]	526	1,053		1,579	263	1,316
Population in 1700	18,000	9,000	9,500	36,500		
Exports 1700–1810[e]	3,824	2,242		6,066	351	5,715
Population in 1800	20,000	10,000	12,000	42,000		
Exports 1800–70	1,315	1,598	386	3,299	382	2,917
Population in 1900	27,000	15,000	16,000	58,000		
Total 1500–1870	5,665	5,042	386	11,094	1021	10,073

Notes:
[a] West Africa includes the coastal areas from Senegal to Benin, and Nigeria.
[b] Western Central Africa includes Cameroon, the Central African Republic, Gabon, Democratic Republic of Congo and Angola.
[c] South East Africa includes Uganda, Kenya, Tanzania, Rwanda and Burundi, and Mozambique.
[d] The slave exports to the Old World have not been included. Since most slaves were of Western Central African origin until 1650, we assumed that between 1500 and 1600 Atlantic slaves were exported from Western Central Africa only. It is assumed that in the seventeenth century two-thirds of the slaves were natives of Western Central Africa, and that one third was of West African origin. This rough assumption is borne out by detailed figures for the years 1662–1700 from Klein (1999), appendix table A.1
[e] Discrepancies between exports and arrivals are a rough indication of mortality in mid-passage. However, recent estimates of mortality in passage in the literature are around 7.5 percent (Klein, 1999: p. 130ff). This is lower than the 9.2 per cent calculated from the discrepancies in Table 2.2.
Sources: Population, see Table 2.1; pre-1700 totals of slave exports from Curtin (1969), p. 268. Post-1700, Klein (1999), appendix table A.I.

removed from that region. This amounts to no less than 19 per cent of the West African population in the year 1800. Klein estimates that the population growth rate in areas exposed to the slave trade was reduced from 0.5 to 0.2 per cent per year. Allowing for births forgone, Maddison estimates that population growth in Sub-Saharan Africa would have been three times as high, in the absence of slavery (Maddison, 2001). If one realises that even within West Africa specific regions and ethnic groups were targeted by slave expeditions, then the impact in these regions must have been devastating. Fertile agricultural areas were abandoned by populations subject to slave raids. The increasing demand for slaves fuelled internal warfare, banditry and conflict. Resources were diverted from productive activities to military activity, with negative effects on West African economic development.

On the other hand, authors like Fage and Hopkins (Fage, 1969; 1977; Hopkins, 1973) have pointed out that the annual exports of slaves were less than the natural growth of the population. Even in West Africa there was an absolute increase in the population in the eighteenth century. In the nineteenth century several European countries were faced by even larger out-migrations, than those endured by African societies. These authors emphasise that the European slave trade fits into pre-European patterns of internal slavery and slave exports to the Islamic world (see also Wolf, 1982: chapter 7). They state that several African kingdoms prospered thanks to the Atlantic trade of which the slave trade was a part. Therefore, the effects of the slave trade varied greatly from region to region. On balance, it cannot be denied that the Atlantic slave trade has had a profoundly demoralising impact on African societies and has been one of the obstacles to economic development of Sub-Saharan Africa.

In Latin America the slave trade has transformed the entire structure of the population and thus the entire social structure. Most slaves have been imported into the Caribbean. In 1700 the entire population in the Caribbean was around 0.5 million persons. In the course of the eighteenth century no less than 3.1 million slaves of African descent were added to this total. In Brazil in the eighteenth century, 1.7 million slaves were added to a total population of 1.25 million in the year 1700. In Spanish America the demographic impact of slave imports has been less extreme. Here, the primary demographic impact of Iberian colonial rule consists of the decline in total population. This can be seen by comparing the population figures for 1500 and 1600.

Both demographic data and data on the slave trade are surrounded by many uncertainties. The estimates of the entire Indian population in Latin America in 1492 range between 7.5 million and 100 million (Slicher van Bath, 1989). Slicher van Bath estimates the number of Indian inhabitants at 35 to 40 million. Towards the middle of the seventeenth century he estimates that only 10 per cent of the original inhabitants had survived. If this were true, the negative effects of the Spanish colonisation on the native inhabitants would be much greater than that shown in Table 2.1. In spite of all these uncertainties, the data in Tables 2.1 and 2.2 serve to illustrate the profound demographic significance of the slave trade.

Migration flows from Europe and Asia

During the second half of the nineteenth century two enormous migration flows occurred which were characteristic of the international economic order of 1870–1913. One of these migration flows originated in Europe and was destined for regions with a temperate climate. From 1846 to 1932, 58.6 million people left Europe, of whom one fifth returned home after some time (Palmer and Colton, 1978).[11] Most emigrants – 34 million – left for the United States. Between 1871 and 1915 European emigration amounted to 36 million people, two-thirds of whom emigrated to the United States (Lewis, 1978a: p. 181). Other popular destinies were Argentina, Canada, Brazil, Australia, South Africa and New Zealand.

These 'new worlds' had an abundance of land and were sparsely populated. Everywhere the original inhabitants – Indians, Aborigines, Maoris, Africans – were pushed aside by the immigrants. Tempted, among other things, by the higher wages in these new countries, European migrants left their technologically advanced homelands. Scarcity of labour and the relatively high education of the migrants led to a high capital–labour ratio in the new territories. Therefore productivity of labour was high. Many of the countries where European immigrants arrived were originally exporters of primary products. Today these countries are among the world's richest countries.

The other great migration flow is concerned with those migrants who left very densely populated areas in India, China and Java; they emigrated to tropical areas in the Caribbean, Africa and Asia where they were employed in mines, construction works and on plantations. In the Caribbean, the import of indentured labourers from Asia was an alternative to slavery which had been banned by the British in 1833. Quantitively, however, migration from densely populated areas to sparsely populated areas within Asia was most important.

The estimates of the volume of this second migration flow differ widely. This is also because only some of the migrants settled permanently in a new country. Considerable numbers of people returned to their homeland, whether voluntarily or not, after varying periods of time. Besides, some studies are concerned with migration between countries, whereas other studies also deal with internal migration flows within a particular region. The highest estimate is by Lewis (1978b) who – without mentioning any sources – states that the entire migration flow involved about 50 million people. A frequently quoted source is Kingsley Davis (1951), who calculated the gross migration from India between 1846 and 1937 at more than 30 million people – 6 million of them actually settling abroad permanently. Only a minor part of this migration took place before 1871, and not all migrants were indentured labourers. The most important migration flows went to Burma, Ceylon and Malacca. Migrants from India also ended up in the south and east of Africa where they later came to play an important role in trade and commerce. Between 1880 and 1922 the number of Chinese settling in tropical areas outside China increased by

---

11 This total includes 7 million migrants who left for Asian Russia.

5 million – from 3 million to 8 million. Taking into account remigration, gross migration must have been much greater (Lewis, 1978b: p. 185; see also Baker, 1981). Chinese migrants ended up especially in the Netherlands, East Indies, Thailand, Malacca and other parts of Southeast Asia. Finally, there was also a migration flow from Java, which was densely populated, to several other islands of the Indonesian archipelago. Like slavery, the migration of indentured labour has changed the demographic composition of many Asian, Latin American and African countries.

Breman stresses the involuntary nature of indentured labour (Breman, 1985). Press gangs, deception and coercion played an important role in the recruitment of indentured labourers. Often migrant labour was the only way to pay the taxes imposed by colonial governments and to pay off debts to landlords. Other authors, however, emphasise the appalling conditions of life in the densely populated rural areas of China or India, which provided incentives for voluntary migration. According to Lewis, a salary just above subsistence level was enough to attract an 'unlimited supply of labour' from the densely populated areas (Lewis, 1978b). Migrants made a conscious choice to improve their lot (Emmer, 1986). According to Engerman (1986), the truth lies somewhere in the middle: indentured labour had both voluntary as well as involuntary aspects.

The availability of large numbers of uneducated and cheap labourers has had a negative effect on the development of productivity in mines and on plantations. Western entrepreneurs invested little in schooling and educating their inexpensive raw labour. But little capital was available per worker. According to a well-known theory of Lewis's, the availability of an unlimited labour supply forced down the prices of exports from tropical developing countries. This explains why these countries benefited so little from their primary exports (Lewis, 1954; 1978a; 1978b).

2.4.7 Non-colonised areas

Some countries – China, Tibet, Afghanistan, Korea, Turkey, Iran, Thailand, Mongolia and Japan, to name but a few – were never colonised by the West. With the possible exception of Tibet and Mongolia, the non-colonised countries were, however, also confronted with the Western challenge and the need to respond to it. Using gunboat diplomacy, the British forced Thailand to open up to foreign trade in the treaty of Bowring (1855). In 1853, Japan was faced with the American fleet of Admiral Perry who forced the shogun to open up Japan to foreign trade. The humiliating experience of Western military supremacy has, of course, been one of the reasons for the initiation of a large-scale process of modernisation in Japan which has led to its rapid economic growth. By the end of the nineteenth century Japan already proved capable of joining the Western game of imperialism (Myers and Peattie, 1984). After the Sino-Japanese war (1894–5), Taiwan and part of Manchuria were ceded to Japan. In

1905 Japan defeated Russia. In 1910 Korea was officially colonised, and in 1932 the Japanese puppet state of Manchukuo was set up in Manchuria. It was not until the end of World War II that the period of Japanese imperial expansion in Asia was concluded.

During the nineteenth century a substantially weakened China was penetrated from all sides by colonial powers. From 1840 to 1842 the British waged war against China – in the name of free trade – because the Chinese government refused to allow the import of opium from India. Great Britain thus was one of the first narco states in history. The Chinese were forced to pay the costs of the war and to accept the imports of opium. In addition, they had to cede Hong Kong to the British. After the Opium Wars 'treaty ports' were created along the Chinese coast, where the right of foreigners to trade was guaranteed by treaties. In the treaty ports, Chinese jurisdiction over Western subjects was restricted (extraterritoriality). Towards the end of the nineteenth century several imperial powers, including Great Britain, France, Russia and Japan, had carved out spheres of influence in China. It is mainly owing to colonial rivalry that China was not completely colonised in this period. It is an interesting question as to why Japan reacted to the Western challenge with wholesale modernisation whereas Chinese attempts at modernisation in the face of similar challenges were half-hearted (Boserup, 1981).

2.4.8 Latecomers in the process of economic development

Russia and Japan are well-known latecomers in the process of economic development. During the last quarter of the nineteenth century these two countries began a dramatic modernisation of their economies. In a relatively short time they succeeded in building up a large industrial sector and ranged themselves among the important industrialised nations. Japan, in particular, has emerged as a new industrial superpower in a short period of time.

With regard to the economic development of Russia, Alexander Gershenkron has pointed out the 'advantages of backwardness' (Gershenkron, 1962). A technological leader has to pay all the costs of research and development of new technologies; its followers may copy the newly developed theories at little cost. Under certain circumstances the follower countries can experience a process of rapid catch-up. After 1945 the advantages of backwardness contributed to rapid productivity growth in Japan and Western Europe. More recently, South Korea, Taiwan, Singapore, Hong Kong and China have been experiencing explosive growth and catch-up. The Russian Federation has since fallen behind and is now a relatively poor, lower-income country.

2.4.9 The period 1913–1950

Maddison (1989) describes the international order between 1913 and 1950 as a period of conflict and autarky. The international economic order underwent dramatic changes as a result of two world wars and a deep economic crisis (1929–32). After the Communist Revolution of 1917 the Soviet Union seceded from the world economy and strove for further industrialisation and economic development by means of a centrally planned economy. Attempts to reconstruct the liberal international economic order after World War I did not meet with success.

In many respects the 1913–50 period was the reverse of the economic order of 1870–1913. Economic growth slackened in both rich countries and in developing countries. Investment flows to developing countries dried up. Latin American countries defaulted on their debts, and the international financial system, based on the gold standard, was disrupted. Strong protectionism replaced free trade. Especially after 1929, each country tried to protect its own economy and to saddle other countries with the consequences of the economic crisis. As a result international trade spiralled downwards. The developing countries most involved in international trade from 1870 to 1913 were the most affected. The demand for primary exports of developing countries collapsed; the development of their prices was unfavourable compared with the development of the prices of industrial imports ('deteriorating terms of trade'). In some Latin American countries – Brazil, for example – domestic industries benefited from the fact that industrial imports from the Western countries could no longer be paid for. Moreover, domestic industries were actively stimulated and protected by the government (import substitution).

One of the important ideas rooted in the experiences of developing countries during this period is that of 'export pessimism'. Export pessimists argue that primary exports will not lead to lasting economic development since the global demand for these products is not stable and terms of trade with respect to industrial products tend to decline in the long term. Developing countries ought to isolate themselves more from the international economy and they should strive for industrialisation with the aid of government intervention. These notions will be discussed in more detail in the chapter on industrialisation strategies (Chapter 9).

2.4.10 The period after World War II

From a political point of view the period after World War II marks the end of the process of Western expansion. Rapidly, one colony after the other achieved independence – sometimes through negotiation, sometimes through bloody wars as was the case in Algeria, Vietnam and Indonesia. However, the end of Western supremacy over vast colonial empires did not constitute the end of international relations of dependence. As has already been argued above, Western expansion led to the formation of an integrated world economy with interdependence among its components.

This period also marks the resurgence of industrialisation in part of the developing world. In the nineteenth century moves towards industrialisation were scarce and hesitant (Pollard, 1990). Industrialisation took place in Europe and the USA. Developing countries remained predominantly dependent on agriculture and mining. Only after World War II, after a pause of fifty years, did the industrialisation of developing countries – or some of them – begin in earnest (see Chapter 9).

The period 1950–73 is characterised by growth rates of the national income unprecedented in economic history. In both developing and rich countries there was a strong growth, though not everyone benefited from it to the same degree. One after another, obstacles to international trade were eliminated in rich countries, with the notable exception of agriculture. Liberalisation of international trade resulted in a considerable growth of the volume of international trade. International trade benefited from a stable monetary system based on fixed exchange rates, gold and the dollar. Developing countries used their newly achieved autonomy to systematically pursue economic development. A number of developing countries experienced rapid processes of industrialisation. Some of them even succeeded in producing competitive industrial products for the global market. Almost without exception, industrialisation in developing countries involved protection of the young industrial sector. This constituted an exception to the general trend towards liberalisation of the international economic order. The volume of investment and capital flows increased sharply. Developing countries benefited from a net capital inflow, in contrast to the period before World War II.

The 1973 oil crisis heralded an era of increased uncertainty for both rich and developing countries (Maddison, 1985; 1989). The growth rate of the world economy slackened in comparison with post-war years. Protectionist tendencies re-emerged, though there was no return to pre-war protectionism. Increasingly, economic trends in different parts of the global economy started to diverge. After a period of continued growth in the 1970s, Latin American economic development stagnated for ten years in the wake of the debt crisis of 1982. Most African countries have been experiencing economic declines or at best sluggish growth since 1973. The dissolution of the Soviet Union in 1991 and the transition to the market was accompanied by an economic collapse, with GDP in the Russian Federation dropping to 58 per cent of its 1991 level by 1998 (Maddison, 2001: p. 157). Many of the former Soviet Republics which have become independent show similarities with the poorest developing countries elsewhere in the world. Several countries in South and East Asia, including China, Indonesia, South Korea, Thailand, Taiwan, Malaysia and India, experienced rapid growth and catch-up. They have tended to liberalise their economies, opening up to foreign direct investment, to experience labour-intensive industrial growth. They achieved considerable success in industrial exports to world markets. A distinction is often made between the Asian tigers: South Korea, Taiwan, Singapore and Hong Kong and the late developers such as Malaysia, Thailand, Indonesia, China and India. The Asian resurgence was rudely interrupted by the Asian financial crisis which led to a sudden collapse of economic growth. Some countries recovered rather quickly, while other countries such as the

Philippines and Indonesia are still suffering from the economic and political aftermath of the crisis. Recovery was made more difficult by the world-wide recession of 2001. The post-war period will be discussed in more detail in Chapter 13.

2.5 Two perspectives on developments in the world economy, 1500–2000

The development of the world economy since the sixteenth century can be viewed from two distinctive perspectives, each of which raise different questions. The first perspective is that of the formation and dynamisation of the world economy; the second perspective is that of exploitation and increasing inequality in the world economy.

The perspective of the formation and dynamisation of the world economy

Since 1500 we have seen the first instance of a sustained breakthrough from recurring cycles of poverty in economic history. In most periods in history the majority of the people never lived far above subsistence levels. A bad harvest – as a result of war, drought or flooding – could easily result in famine. The time perspective was short. Most individuals could not even contemplate investing in long-term improvement of their living conditions; their first priority was survival in the short term.

In this respect the process of economic growth, which started in Europe, was a mysterious breakthrough that demands an explanation. This growth, combined with external expansion, challenged peoples and societies in other parts of the world. It induced processes of change everywhere. The example of Western economic development and the threat of Western penetration and domination called forth an almost universal pursuit of development in other parts of the world. There would be no concept of development if the breakthrough had not taken place.

The perspective of exploitation and increasing inequality in the emerging world economy

Around 1450 there were no great differences in the level of prosperity between the various countries and regions of the world. In the subsequent centuries there was a growth of per capita income in Western countries such as the Netherlands, France and Great Britain. At the same time per capita income stagnated in most developing countries such as, for example, China, India, Indonesia and Mexico. The increasing inequalities went hand in hand with exploitation of poor areas by rich – the rich countries appropriating part of the economic wealth of the poor areas they penetrated.

The income differences increased sharply in the nineteenth and twentieth centuries when growth accelerated in Western countries. Even when per capita income in developing countries increased, growth in rich countries was faster, at least until 1973. As a result income differentials between the rich and the poor countries increased further.

From this gloomy point of view, the formation of the world economy involved a truly explosive growth of global income inequality. The gap that divides rich and poor countries has increased. From this perspective, what needs to be explained is the lack of development in developing countries. The emphasis is on understanding centuries of relative economic stagnation and analysing the role of colonial and neocolonial exploitation in such processes of stagnation.

There are important elements of truth in both perspectives. It is neither necessary nor possible to make an absolute choice between them. Advocates of each perspective should realise that there are alternative ways of looking at issues of development and stagnation and that different perspectives raise different kinds of interesting questions.

2.6   Key issues in development

The contrast between the world economy of 2000 and that of 1450 raises several fascinating questions which may help to bring some order in the multitude of schools, theories and approaches concerned with development issues. Three kinds of questions will be distinguished here.

1. *How is it possible that a certain part of the world has experienced an historically unprecedented process of economic growth and development since 1450?*

Two types of explanations can be offered: *internal* explanations and *external* explanations. Internal explanations seek the causes of the Western economic breakthrough in typical factors and conditions which distinguish Western countries from non-Western countries: culture, religion, mentality, institutions, population density, climate, natural circumstances, geographical location and political characteristics. They also devote considerable attention to economic and social policies pursued by governments. External explanations seek the causes of Western prosperity in the success of Western exploitation of other parts of the world. These explanations see the drain of revenues and wealth resulting from colonial penetration and as the decisive factor which put the West and the developing world on different paths of development.

2. *Why have other parts of the world lagged behind the rich Western countries in their economic development since 1450? Why didn't the developing countries experience processes of development similar to those in the West?*

In answering these questions, one can again distinguish *internal* and *external* explanations. Internal explanations focus on the specific factors that have been obstacles to economic development in developing countries: traditional cultural orientations; attitudes towards work, risk, saving or education; institutions that are not conducive to technological progress; patterns of saving and investment; unfavourable natural circumstances such as climate or whether countries are landlocked; characteristics of the political system; misguided or ineffective economic and social policies.

External explanations emphasise the negative effects of Western penetration of the world. The lack of economic growth in developing countries is seen as a result of colonial and neocolonial exploitation or the structure of the world economic order. Moderate versions of this perspective tend to emphasise the disadvantages of backwardness. In a global economy dominated by established economic powers latecomers will find it ever more difficult to initiate successful development.

3. Is it possible for developing countries today to undergo processes of development similar to those experienced by rich countries in the past?

The answers to this last question, of course, depend on the answers to the previous questions. Three types of answers are possible.

1. In principle, developing countries can undergo processes of economic and social development similar to those experienced by the rich countries in the past. This answer was primarily given by the modernisation theorists of the 1950s and 1960s. They emphasised the necessity of breaking through traditional structures, attitudes and institutions that hamper development. Advanced countries may help by providing education, information and financial means for investment in new infrastructures and capital goods.

2. In principle, developing countries cannot pursue the same path as rich countries, since the development of rich countries is based on the (capitalist) exploitation of the rest of the world. Such answers are given by Marxists and radical critics of modernisation theories and orthodox development theories. Underdevelopment of the poor countries is the other side of the coin of development in the West. Only by liberating themselves from the capitalist world economy and by finding their own – different – paths do underdeveloped countries have a chance of attaining development.

3. There is no reason to believe that developing countries are in principle incapable of reaching higher levels of prosperity. However, it is rather unlikely that the path to a higher per capita income will be the same as the path rich countries have followed in the past. Initial conditions for development differ in every historical period and every phase of development of the international economic and political order. Different conditions call for different development paths and strategies. Lessons can be learned from past experiences, but they have to be adapted to new conditions.

Initial conditions have to do with demographic characteristics, the development of the world trade, the nature of international competition in a global economy, technological developments, the international balance of power, and the nature of the relationships with established advanced economies. Latecomers to development may face both major disadvantages and potential advantages. Apart from the differing initial conditions over time, there are also differences in circumstances between various countries and regions. Finally, policy choices made in developing countries themselves are of great importance.

Questions for review

1. List the most important characteristics of the concept of international economic order. Discuss the six types of international economic order which can be distinguished since 1450.
2. Explain the unique features of the Western process of development since the beginning of the sixteenth century, compared to earlier processes of socio-economic development.
3. Why did Chinese economic development stagnate from the fourteenth century onwards, in spite of initial conditions which seemed so promising?
4. Discuss the differences between colonies of settlement and colonies of occupation.
5. What were the characteristics of the international division of labour between rich countries and poor countries which evolved in the period 1870–1913?
6. Discuss the impact of major migration flows on the demographic characteristics of developing countries.
7. Discuss the contrasting perspectives on the role of Western expansion in the formation of the modern world economy.

Further reading

There is a very large literature on the evolution of the international economic order, which includes works by economists, historians, sociologists and anthropologists. The following suggestions are inevitably incomplete. The foundations for the modern quantitative study of growth and development have been laid by Simon Kuznets in a long series of studies, including *Modern Economic Growth: Rate, Structure and Spread* (1966) and *Economic Growth of Nations: Total Output and Production Structure* (1971). A short book by Arthur Lewis on *The Evolution of the International Economic Order* (1987b) gives a brilliant summary of important changes in international order since the nineteenth century. The same topics are dealt with in a more quantitative fashion in his *Growth and Fluctuations, 1870–1913* (1978a).

A source of inspiration for the discussion of the differences between Chinese and European development in this chapter is Immanuel Wallerstein's *The Modern World System* (1974). This is the first of four large volumes on the modern world system from a centre–periphery perspective. China's early technological lead is documented in J. Needham's monumental study, *Science and Civilisation in China* (1954). A well-written overview of Chinese economic development is Mark Elvin's *The Pattern of Chinese Past* (1973). China's agricultural development is documented by Dwight Perkins in *Agricultural Development in China, 1368–1968* (1969). Angus Maddison also analyses the modern economic development of China in historical perspective in his *The Chinese Economic Performance in the Long Run* (1998).

Valuable sources for the historical study of the European breakthrough are David Landes, *The Unbound Prometheus: Technological Changes and Industrial Development in Western Europe from 1750 to the Present* (1969) and his recent provocative and enjoyable study, *The Wealth and Poverty of Nations: Why Some Are So Rich and Some So Poor* (1998). Another study offering a long-run perspective is Ernest Jones's *Growth Recurring: Economic Change in World History* (1988).

An impressive series of quantitative studies by Angus Maddison charts the long-run growth of the Western and non-Western world in comparative perspective. These studies include his *Phases of Capitalist Development* (1982a), his comparative study, *Two Crises: Latin America and Asia, 1929–1938 and 1973–1983* (1985), his *Monitoring the World Economy* (1995) and his latest magnum opus, *The World Economy: A Millennial Perspective* (2001). Maddison makes the case for the early forging ahead of Europe relative to Asia. The opposite view on this issue is argued by Paul Bairoch and M. Levy-Leboyer, in *Disparities in Economic Development since the Industrial Revolution* (1981).

On the Atlantic slave trade, the classic study is Curtin's 1969 book, *The Atlantic Slave Trade*. Curtin's estimates have been revised in an article by Lovejoy, 'The Volume of the Atlantic Slave Trade: A Synthesis' (1982). The various revisions of Curtin's estimates are summarised in H.S. Klein, *The Atlantic Slave Trade* (1999). The quantitative data on the slave trade are now available on CD-Rom (Eltis *et al.*, *The Transatlantic Slave Trade, 1562–1867: A Database CD-Rom* (1998).

A good overview of the political history of European expansion is offered in *The Colonial Empires: A Comparative Survey from the Eighteenth Century* (1982) by Fieldhouse. From an anthropological and historical perspective Eric Wolf's *Europe and the People without History* (1982) provides interesting and sometimes unexpected insights in the relations between European expansion and non-European societies.

For African history, useful studies include: J.D. Fage, *A History of West Africa: An Introductory Survey* (1969); A. G. Hopkins, *An Economic History of West Africa* (1973); and E. Isichei, *A History of African Societies to 1870* (1997). For the economic history of Latin America, a good starting point is Celso Furtado's *Economic Development of Latin America* (1976).

3 Growth and stagnation: Theories and experiences

As discussed in the first chapters of this book, there has been long-run divergence in the world economy. In the fifteenth century disparities in per capita incomes between countries and regions were small. Since then some economies have moved ahead and others have fallen far behind. After 1820, capital accumulation and technological change accelerated. The rate at which income levels diverged increased, resulting in the wide global disparities of the present international economic order. We have also noted that the ranking of countries was not immutable. Former British colonies such as the USA, Canada and New Zealand or Asian economies such as Japan, Singapore and Korea grew so rapidly that they moved far up the income ladder. Other countries such as Argentina, the Ottoman empire or the Russian Federation slipped downward. For a better understanding of development, we are interested in why some countries or societies forge ahead in given periods, while others stagnate or fall behind (Abramovitz, 1989b). We are especially interested in the conditions under which growth and catch-up can be realised in the developing countries of today. Sections 3.1 to 3.5 of this chapter offer a brief introduction to theories of growth and stagnation. Section 3.6 presents theoretically relevant empirical information on long-run economic trends in developing countries.

3.1   What are the basic sources of growth? How do economies grow and societies become more prosperous?

Let us start with the question of what are the basic sources of growth of per capita incomes. In simplified form, these are summarised in Box 3.1.

Box 3.1   Sources of growth of GDP per capita

Economies grow and societies become more prosperous through:

1. *Discovery of riches and natural resources*
   Discovery of natural resources – gas, coal, oil, gold, etc. – can promote growth. However, such growth will not be sustainable unless the revenues from windfall discoveries are transformed into more durable sources of growth.
2. *Effort*
   Working harder, increasing hours worked per year, increasing labour market participation, greater effort and discipline.
3. *Saving and accumulating capital*
   Being sober and abstaining from current consumption in order to save; investing these savings in order to accumulate capital goods, which increase the productivity of labour.
4. *Education*
   Abstaining from current consumption in order to invest in education, training and health and thus improve the productivity of labour.
5. *Theft*
   Appropriating resources from other societies and using these to accumulate capital. If resources are appropriated, but not reinvested, they will have the same non-sustainable effects as windfall discoveries.
6. *Efficiency*
   Becoming more efficient and effective in the use of capital, labour, intermediate inputs and the ways in which these can be combined in production. Efficiency includes the effects of specialisation and international trade, economies of scale, structural change and better utilisation of capacity.
7. *Technological change*
   Developing or acquiring new knowledge about how to produce valued goods and services and applying such knowledge in production.

The factors in Box 3.1 can be represented in the form of a basic production function, which relates output to the so-called *proximate sources of growth* (Denison, 1967; Maddison, 1987; 1988):

$$O = F(K, L, R)^e + A + P$$

In this equation O refers to output. K, L and R refer to the primary factors of production capital, labour and natural resources. The exponent e refers to the efficiency with which the primary factors are used to transform intermediate inputs into final goods and services. The concept of efficiency as used here includes a number of important elements mentioned under points 6 and 7 of

Box 3.1, such as economies of scale, efficient allocation of factors of production within sectors (*appropriate choice of technology*), efficient allocation between economic sectors (*structural change*), efficient allocation between countries (*specialisation and comparative advantage*), utilisation of capacity and, last but not least, technological change which increases output per unit of input. The term A denotes net income from capital investments and labour abroad (net factor income) and P refers to colonial plunder and expropriation (negative) or voluntary transfers and development aid (positive). Several of these proximate factors will be further examined in the coming chapters. Economic historians have made efforts to quantify and measure them. Economists have modelled the relationships between inputs and outputs in a great variety of production functions.

Once we have quantified the proximate sources of growth, we can subsequently explore their links with the wider economic and social sources of growth and development. For instance, one can explore the social, historical and institutional roots of high rates of savings which result in rapid growth of the capital stock in Asia.

Based on the time scale, we can make a distinction between *intermediate sources of growth* and *ultimate sources of growth*. Amongst intermediate sources, we include trends in domestic and international demand, economic and social policies and the distance to the world technological frontier. This distance is an important factor which indicates what opportunities there are for taking over and adapting technologies in order to accelerate growth in a country. This will be further discussed in the next chapter.

Underlying both the proximate and intermediate sources, there are more basic social factors, which we call the ultimate sources of growth. These include long-run trends in scientific and technological knowledge, demographic trends, institutions and institutional change, historical developments, basic social attitudes and capabilities, changes in class structures and relationships between social groups and long-run developments in the international economic and political order and power structures, such as those discussed in Chapter 2. This framework helps us relate and integrate elements from the work of a number of classical and contemporaneous theories of development to be discussed below.

3.2   Classical thinking about growth, development and stagnation

Since the eighteenth century, classical economists and sociologists have concerned themselves with the mystery of breakthrough and economic growth in the capitalist West. Their work is primarily concerned with the ultimate sources of growth and development. Many of their ideas still play a prominent role in topical discussions of problems of development. Without doing justice to the complexities in the thought of the classical authors, we shall briefly touch upon a number of important themes in classical thought, which have retained their relevance for present-day discussions.

3.2.1   Adam Smith

In *The Wealth of Nations* (1776), Adam Smith (1723–90) ranked countries according to their economic performance. The most modern and prosperous country was the Republic of the United Netherlands, followed by England, France, North America, Scotland, China, with Bengal coming in the last place. Smith was interested in how differences between countries had come about and how knowledge about the causes of prosperity could help England improve its relative standing *vis à vis* the Netherlands. Smith attacked traditional obstacles to free trade and free competition, such as guilds and royal monopolies. The more individuals were left free to pursue their own interests, the more the invisible hand of the market would promote collective welfare. In addition, Smith emphasised the importance of the division of labour in the production process, the increase of worker skills owing to the dividing up of tasks, and specialisation and economies of scale. The division of labour within firms and the increase in the scale of production associated with specialisation, trade and expanding markets would lead to dramatic increases in productivity.

3.2.2   The classical economists Ricardo, Malthus and Mill

The classical economists David Ricardo (1792–1823), Thomas Malthus (1766–1834) and John Stuart Mill (1806–73) shared Smith's preference for free markets and laissez-faire policies. The government should intervene as little as possible in the economic process. One might say that the classical economists offered an *institutional explanation* of economic growth. People have an innate tendency to engage in exchange and trade. If social institutions give free play to such tendencies, individual self-interest will stimulate efforts, which contribute to economic growth and increasing prosperity for all.

Compared to Smith, the classical economists placed more emphasis on capital accumulation, the importance of the stock of capital goods used in the production process and on the importance of international trade. Ricardo formulated his famous *law of comparative advantage*. This law states that all countries entering into international trade will profit from such trade if they concentrate on the production of those products in which they are relatively most efficient. This law is still the keystone of modern arguments for liberalisation of international trade and an international division of labour in production.

There are also some pessimistic elements present in the work of the classical authors. Malthus was afraid that food production would not be able to keep up with population growth. In the long run this would result in starvation and widespread famine, which would serve as a check to further population growth. Malthusianism has become the general term for all modern pessimistic perspectives emphasising the limits to economic growth.

Ricardo feared that economic development would stagnate in the long run. As more and more people work in agriculture owing to population growth, less and less fertile soils are taken into production and diminishing returns set in. When the marginal product in agriculture declines, food will become scarce and prices will go up, in turn exerting an upward pressure on wages in industry. Rising food prices are translated into higher wage costs. In due time increasing wages cut into profits and thus into future investment. The engine of economic growth grinds to a halt. Ricardo's theory is a predecessor of modern *two-sector models*, which analyse the relationships between agriculture and industry in economic development (Fei and Ranis, 1964; Lewis, 1954). Ricardo was in favour of abolishing tariffs on food imports, to keep food prices from rising. This would postpone the slowdown of growth.

3.2.3   Friedrich List

Ricardo, Malthus and Mill all lived and wrote at a time when the dominant power in the world economy, England, propagated international free trade. They were convinced of the advantages of free trade. Friedrich List (1789–1846), German by birth and founder of the 'historical school' in economics, was less enthusiastic about the blessings of free trade. According to him, it was the dominant powers which primarily profited from free trade. Latecomers to economic development such as the German states were hindered in their development by competition from economically advanced countries. List argued for tariff protection of newly founded German industries against murderous international competition. This so-called *infant industry argument* would play an important role in the development strategies of developing countries in the twentieth century. List identified stages of development. He was convinced that active government intervention was necessary to build up an industrial sector in late-developing economies and to further the structural transformation of agrarian into industrial societies.

3.2.4   Classical sociologists: Spencer, Tönnies and Durkheim

Like the classical economists, the classical sociologists also focused on the major developmental trends associated with the rise of modern capitalist societies.[1] The classical economists' preference for free markets was mirrored

---

[1] The modern division of labour between the social sciences only emerged in the course of the nineteenth century. Many early authors including Adam Smith combined sociological and economic perspectives in their work.

in the Social Darwinism of Spencer (1820–1903) and his followers. Applying metaphors from biological evolutionism to social evolution, Herbert Spencer argued that societies evolve, adapting to changing environmental conditions.[2] Social evolution is seen as a process of increasing size, differentiation and complexity, but also increasing interaction and integration of differentiated functions. Social regularities emerge as the unanticipated consequences of individual actions and choices. Industrial societies represent later stages of social evolution, militant hierarchical societies represent earlier states. Markets and market exchange emerge as part of the process of social differentiation. Market competition is seen as promoting the survival of the fittest – i.e. the most efficient – firms and thus contributes to further social change and increasing welfare. Governments should abstain from intervening in the markets. Social Darwinism can have some rather crude social implications such as rejection of all welfare systems, minimum wage regulations and imputations of evolutionary superiority of dominant civilisations or ethnic groups. But the analytic elements of variety and selection environments resurface in modern evolutionary economic theories of development.

While the economists primarily focused on the sources and dynamics of growth, many of the classical sociologists focused on the changes in social relationships that accompanied economic growth. Ferdinand Tönnies (1855–1936) highlighted the change from more communal social patterns (*Gemeinschaft*) to more individualistic, specialised and impersonal relationships (*Gesellschaft*). Among others these involved the decline of extended families and communities and the rise of nuclear families which interacted with other nuclear families through markets. While communal relationships based on family, kinship, clan and local community are multistranded and complex, Gesellschaft-type relationships are single-stranded, rational and anonymous. People are bound together by contractual relationships focusing on well-defined exchanges. These polarities will later surface in so-called modernisation theories of development and in many comparisons between 'developing' and 'more developed' societies.

One of the greatest of the classical sociologists, Émile Durkheim (1858–1917) analysed the potentially negative social effects of such social transformations in the course of development. In his early work he distinguished between more communal societies characterised by *mechanical solidarity* (well-integrated local communities rather isolated from each other) and modern societies characterised by *organic solidarity* (extended networks of interdependence and exchange between individuals performing specialised actions). In his later works he pointed to the erosion of common norms (*anomie*) and the rise of divorce rates and suicides in highly individualistic modern societies. The discussion about the disruptive social effects of global economic transformations are still central to all modern debates about development.

---

2 Spencer actually formulated his theories well before Darwin published the *Origin of Species* in 1859.

3.2.5   Karl Marx

Karl Marx (1818–83) focused on the dynamic role of capitalism as an explanation of economic developments in the West. Just like List and other representatives of the historical school of economics, Marx postulated a unilineal theory of stages of development, in which every society sooner or later passes through the same stages. His stages of development were: primitive original communism; slavery; feudalism; capitalism; and socialism, each characterised by a different mode of production and by typical conflicts between the dominant classes, who own the means of production, and the subordinate classes, who do not. Each stage was characterised by internal contradictions between the development of the production forces (the production technology) and the social relations of production (class relationships, the social organisation of production). These internal contradictions were the drivers of socio-economic change.

Each subsequent stage represented a higher level in the development process. In the West the contradictions within feudalism had for the first time led to the overthrow of a feudal economic system based on ownership of land and its replacement by an economic system based on the ownership of capital goods. Sooner or later societies in other parts of the world would inevitably go through the same transition. Such stage theories were the foundation of the negative attitude of many twentieth-century Marxist regimes towards agriculture, which was seen as representing an outmoded stage of development.

In Marxist theories, class contradictions – conflicts of interest between social groups which own the predominant means of production and social groups which do not – play a central role in the explanation of social dynamics. Under capitalism, competition between the owners of the means of production provides the incentive for accumulation of capital and technological progress, on the one hand. But it also leads to an ever-increasing exploitation of the newly created industrial working classes by the capitalist classes. Marx agreed with the classical economists that capitalism had led to a revolutionary increase in productive capacity. The capitalist system was seen as a dynamic and successful system promoting both capital accumulation and technological change. Productive potential was liberated from the shackles of feudalism. In due course, however, these liberating tendencies of capitalism were superseded by repressive tendencies. The capitalist system, in the grip of competitive forces and conjunctural fluctuations, was no longer able to make an efficient use of the newly unchained productive capacities. Competition led to increasing exploitation of workers. Impoverishment of workers led to decreasing purchasing power of the working class. The economic result was overproduction, declining profit margins and ever-deepening economic crises. The social result was pauperisation and increasing revolutionary class consciousness. In the long run, the increased polarisation between the capitalist class and the working class would inevitably lead to revolution and the collapse of capitalism. Marx predicted these revolutions would take place in the most advanced capitalist societies.

According to Marx, the essence of capitalism is production for profit and reinvestment, rather than production for the satisfaction of human needs. Competition forces entrepreneurs to continuously invest in more and qualitatively better means of production. Thus, just as in classical economic thought, accumulation of capital has a central place in Marxist theory. However, in contradiction to the classical economists, Marx did not see capital accumulation and economic growth as an harmonious process leading to increased collective welfare. Economic development is characterised by continuous exploitation, appropriation of surpluses for the purposes of reinvestment, and social conflict. Competing entrepreneurs can only make a profit by paying their workers no more than a subsistence wage, which barely keeps them alive. One of the Marxist ideas which continues to have considerable relevance for modern thinking about economic development is the relationship between appropriation of economic surplus by certain social groups – capitalists, governments – and the process of reinvestment, accumulation of capital and economic growth.

3.2.6   *Imperialism*

Marxist stage theory predicted that socialist revolutions would take place only in the most advanced capitalist countries. These predictions have failed to come true. Where Communist revolutions materialised, they invariably took place in agrarian societies with low levels of industrial development, such as tsarist Russia, China, Vietnam, Cambodia or Cuba. A later generation of theorists (Hilferding, 1877–1943; Luxemburg, 1870–1919; Lenin, 1870–1924; Hobson, 1858–1940) tried to explain the absence of the predicted revolutions in advanced countries with various theories of imperialism. Such theories state that the Western world succeeded in transferring its internal contradictions to the world economy and the developing countries. In the process of imperialist expansion in the second half of the nineteenth century, these countries were colonised and exploited.

Theories of imperialism come in many guises. Some theories explained imperialist expansion by pointing to the lack of investment opportunities in the advanced countries and the search for new investment possibilities in the colonies. Other theories pointed to factors such as the safeguarding of the flow of raw materials as inputs for industrial development or the search for new markets for industrial products which could not be sold in home markets because of overproduction. Theories of imperialism were drawn up at a time when the Western expansion in the world was at its apex. Without exception, these theories stressed the negative effects of imperialism on the development chances of the poor countries.

Today, the empirical evidence for economic explanations of imperialism is considered to be weak (Chirot, 1977; Fieldhouse, 1973; see also Schumpeter,

1976). Nevertheless, these theories have been a source of inspiration for twentieth-century theorists of underdevelopment.

3.2.7   Max Weber and Joseph Schumpeter

To conclude this short excursion through the history of ideas, we will briefly discuss some ideas of two important post-Marxist authors, Max Weber and Joseph Schumpeter. These two authors follow Marx in his emphasis on the importance of class relationships, and the analysis of the dynamics of capitalism. But they also offer fundamental criticisms of the Marxian legacy.

While Marx saw the profit motive as the essential characteristic of the capitalist system, Max Weber (1864–1920) emphasised the principle of rational calculation of means and ends. According to Weber, the development of capitalism was part of a wider long-run social trend of rationalisation and bureaucratisation in Western societies. The profit motive is common to all times; it cannot differentiate capitalism from other systems. New in capitalism is the rational organisation of production for the purposes of sustained profitability, making use of systematic book-keeping methods. The emergence of markets is also part of the long-run rationalisation trend. Production for the market stimulates businesslike rational thinking about means and ends and the calculation of financial costs and benefits, irrespective of the personal relationships involved in the transactions. The rise of bureaucracy was seen by Weber as the rise of a radically new and highly efficient form of organisation, systematically harnessing human capabilities to organisational goals. Not only government bureaucracies, but also big capitalist firms successfully made use of efficient, impersonal bureaucratic forms of organisation.

Weber explicitly posed the question why capitalism had broken through in Western Europe, rather than elsewhere in the world. Marx saw developments in the economic sphere of society, the 'substructure', as determining developments in culture, religion, politics and law (the 'superstructure'). In contradiction to this, Weber sought the explanation of the rise of capitalism in religious influences. He noted that the first capitalist countries were predominantly Protestant. His famous hypothesis – known as the Weber thesis – states that the Protestant ethic favoured economic development. The combination of diligent and disciplined work in one's professional 'calling' and religiously motivated sobriety in consumption promoted high levels of savings and the accumulation of capital (see Chapter 9). The Protestant ethic was the factor which distinguished the Western world from other regions where the breakthrough of capitalism did not take place. Thus the Protestant ethic is the determining factor in the rise of capitalism and process of economic growth in the West (Weber, 1969). Though the Weber thesis has since been heavily criticised for its simple one-directional causality, his emphasis on the attitudinal foundations of economic performance remains of lasting importance.

A third difference in the Marxist tradition lies in the greater importance of the political sphere. According to Marx, developments in the political sphere (part of the superstructure of society) are determined by developments in the economic sphere (the substructure). According to Weber, economic development presupposes the rise of highly centralised state apparatuses, which are able to maintain internal peace and order in a country. Without internal peace, centralisation and standardisation of rules and regulations, markets will never be able to function. If trade is unpredictable, if there are all sorts of capricious local rules, taxes and tithes, if the safety of trade is not guaranteed, a rational weighing of the costs and benefits of long-term investments is impossible. Thus, the formation of stable centralised states precedes the rise of capitalism.

While Weber focused on the origins of the capitalist breakthrough, Schumpeter (1883–1950) was primarily interested in twentieth-century capitalism. From Marx he derived the idea of capitalism as an economic system, riven by deep class conflicts. This system was both destructive and extremely dynamic. However, in contradiction to Marx, Schumpeter did not believe capitalism would be destroyed by its own inefficiencies. In the middle of the Great Depression of the 1930s, Schumpeter correctly predicted a golden age of more than fifty years of economic growth in the Western World (Schumpeter, 1976).

According to Schumpeter, capitalism is characterised by a 'gale of creative destruction'. Old production techniques are continuously becoming obsolescent and are being replaced by new ones. Schumpeter emphasises the importance of technological progress. Long cycles of economic growth were driven by major technological breakthroughs, such as textiles, steam power (1780–1842), railways (1842–97) and chemicals, electrical power and automobiles (1898–1930s). An important role is reserved here for the entrepreneur who realises 'new combinations': new forms of organisation, new production techniques, new products, new markets, new sources of raw materials (Schumpeter, 2000).

Capitalism as a system gives free reign to the entrepreneur and thus creates an ample supply of entrepreneurship. In the long run, Schumpeter thought capitalism would be undermined by its successes rather than its failures. The process of innovation would become routinised. The role of the creative entrepreneur would be taken over by staff departments and research laboratories of large monopolistic enterprises. Gradually and unnoticeably the system would be transformed into something like a socialist planning system, through the planning and administrative procedures of the very large capitalist firms. At the same time, the uncertainties involved in the process of creative destruction would undermine political support for capitalist institutions.

It is not clear whether Schumpeter would consider the present-day Western mixed economies as capitalist or socialist. But the question whether developing countries have a sufficient supply of entrepreneurship is one of the classical questions, which keep cropping up in post-war theorising on development.

A related question is whether developing countries provide a sufficiently stimulating atmosphere for the emergence of entrepreneurial and innovative behaviour.

3.3   Internal and external approaches

The classical discussions were primarily concerned with explanations of the economic breakthrough and growth of the presently prosperous Western countries. Without exception they emphasise the importance of the rise of capitalist institutions, markets and property rights in explaining growth. The post-war discussion of development focuses on the reasons why the poorer countries could not keep up with the richer ones.

At the end of Chapter 2 a distinction was made between internal and external approaches to the problems of development. Both the internal and the external approaches start with the empirical observation that economy and society in developing countries are characterised by *dualism*. The term refers to the existence side by side of a modern and a traditional sector. The modern sector is technologically developed, commercialised and is located in and around urban centres. The traditional sector is characterised by traditional technologies, low productivity, production for own consumption and is predominantly rural. Dualist structures in developing countries came into being at the end of the nineteenth century, when these countries were drawn into international trade. Capitalist enclaves emerged within non-capitalist economic systems.

The main problem of dualism is the economic and social gap between the modern and the traditional sector. The modern sector is oriented to the outside world, rather than to domestic society. There are hardly any linkages between the modern sector and the rest of the economy and society. Thus, a developing country as a whole does not profit much from technological and economic development in the modern sector. Also, a traditional hinterland can form an obstacle to the further development of a modern sector which is relatively small in size.

Internal approaches emphasise the factors within a society which promote or hinder development. Thus, one of the founding fathers of development economics, J.H. Boeke, explained the lack of development of the traditional sector in Indonesia by pointing to the characteristics of oriental man and oriental culture, in which individual economic incentives were not operative. Needs were limited and social needs dominated individual needs (Boeke, 1961). The continuation of a traditional economy alongside the modern enclave was thus explained by cultural and institutional internal characteristics. External approaches try to explain the situation in developing countries by reference to negative influences from outside. Dualistic structures are created by external economic and political penetration and exploitation. These external influences also maintain the dualistic structures. The external and internal perspectives will be discussed in more detail in the following sections.

3.4 Explanations of economic backwardness

Internal approaches to the problems of development draw our attention to unfavourable circumstances and factors within a society, which form an obstacle for development. In the pessimistic perspective of Boeke there is but little chance of overcoming such obstacles. However, most representatives of internal approaches are more optimistic than Boeke. Modernisation theorists of the 1950s and 1960s believed that a long-run process of modernisation has set in, in which all societies gradually move from traditionality in the direction of modernity. Dualism is due to the fact that modernisation has taken place in one part of society, but not yet in society as a whole. The key words are 'not yet'. Less developed countries have a 'lag' compared to more developed countries, just as the less developed traditional sectors lag behind the modern sectors. Once the internal barriers to development have been overcome, the laggards can start overtaking the leaders.

3.4.1 Rostow's theory of the stages of economic growth

One of the most well-known representatives of modernisation theory is W.W. Rostow. In *Stages of Economic Growth* (1960) he sketched a stage theory of growth in which each society sooner or later passes through the same five stages: traditional society, preconditions to take-off, take-off, drive to maturity and mass consumption society. In this development process some countries take the lead, others lag behind. Just as in Marxist theory, however, the path of development is the same for all societies.

In traditional societies (Stage 1) fatalistic patterns of thought predominate, in which people feel at the mercy of external forces of nature, higher powers or political rulers. The production technology is static.

In the precondition stage (Stage 2) the stability of the traditional society is undermined, usually as a result of external threats or challenges. In this stage the idea emerges that people can improve their living conditions or those of their children by their own efforts. A beginning is made with the translation of the insights of modern science into production technologies.

In the economic sphere the conditions for industrialisation are created in this period. The most important condition is an increase in productivity in one of the non-industrial sectors such as agriculture or mining. This creates a surplus above subsistence, which is potentially available for investment in the industrial sector. Especially in agriculture, such an increase in productivity is of the greatest importance. Productivity growth in agriculture frees labour for employment in the industrial sector and fulfils the food requirements of a growing population. Increased earnings in the agrarian sector provide a market for industrial goods, while financial surpluses from agriculture can be invested in industry.

In the precondition stage investments are realised in infrastructure (railways, canals, roads, energy supply, harbours, and so forth), which are a prerequisite for industrialisation. In the social-political sphere, the precondition stage is characterised by the emergence of modernising elites, which consciously strive for development and industrialisation. Socially, the horizon of expectations expands.

The crucial stage is the take-off stage (Stage 3). The analogy is that of an aeroplane which gains sufficient speed on the runway to take off into flight. In the take-off stage the structure of the economy changes very drastically in a short period of ten to twenty years, after which sustained growth can set in. In the take-off stage the level of investment needs to be increased substantially. Echoing earlier publications by Lewis (1950; 1954), Rostow writes that investment should increase from less than 5 per cent to more than 10 per cent of net national income.

In the take-off stage, investment should be directed towards industrial sectors, with the strongest linkages with the rest of the economy. In the past the role of 'leading sector' has been played by the textile industry, the military industry, the railway industry and the chemical industry. Other characteristics of the take-off stage are a sufficient supply of entrepreneurship and a sufficient supply of loanable funds, which can be channelled into the industrial sector voluntarily or involuntarily.

In the subsequent 'drive to maturity' stage, new production techniques spread from the leading sectors to the rest of the economy. In the last stage, mass-consumption society, which looks surprisingly like Rostow's North American society, the whole population benefits from the increased opportunities for consumption.

Parallel with Rostow's primarily economically oriented theories, the 1950s and 1960s witness the rise of various sociological theories of modernisation (Hagen, 1962; Hoselitz, 1960; Inkeles, 1969; Inkeles and Smith; 1974; Lerner, 1958; Moore, 1963). These theories take up themes from classical sociology and chart the social changes which accompany economic growth, including: urbanisation, the transition from extended family structures to nuclear families; increasing division of labour and occupational specialisation; rationalisation in attitudes; increasing social mobility; the transition from ascription to achievement as the determining principle of social stratification[3]; increasing levels of schooling and individualisation. Like Rostovian theory and classical stage theories, modernisation theories usually conceive of development as a unilinear path from a traditional to a modern society. Some sociological modernisation theories focus on the social disruption accompanying rapid technological and economic change. These theories hark back to the classical Durkheimian tradition in sociology, which analyses the increasing normlessness (*anomie*) of modern social life (Durkheim, 1897).

---

3 In an ascriptive society a person's position in the social hierarchy is determined at birth by the position of his or her parents and does not depend on effort, talent or performance.

An important policy recommendation deriving from Rostovian analysis is the requirement of large-scale investment in industry in the take-off stage. Foreign investment, loans and development aid can help compensate for the shortfall in domestic savings, compared to investment needs. Development aid, training and education can also help surmount the traditional obstacles to growth and contribute to the realisation of the preconditions for take-off. From the economic perspective, Rostow represented a wider intellectual climate of the 1950s and 1960s focusing on the need for massive investment, the mobilisation of savings and seeing capital as the missing link in development.

Similar ideas have been formulated by the early development economists Rosenstein-Rodan (1943) and Nurkse (1953), who called for a big push in investment to escape from vicious circles of poverty. The big push approach will be discussed in more detail in the chapter dealing with industrialisation (Chapter 9).

Rostow's theory of stages of development has been severely criticised in the course of time, just like modernisation theory in general. Nevertheless, it is striking how many traces of his theory can be found in the work of later authors.

3.4.2   Kuznets's preconditions for industrialisation

According to Kuznets (1965) it is not possible to distinguish Rostow's stages of growth empirically. The changes in investment and growth rates are more gradual than the dramatic term 'take-off' suggests. The concept of traditional society does not do justice to the great diversity of social and economic circumstances in pre-capitalist societies. Finally, Kuznets, along with many authors, has serious objections to the unilinear concept of development, the idea that every society follows one and the same path of development. It makes a big difference, for instance, whether a country is an early or a late industrialiser, whether industrialisation takes place in a large country with a large domestic market, a small country with a small domestic market, a resource-rich or a resource-poor country (e.g. Chenery *et al.*, 1986). Also, there is nothing inevitable about stages of development. Countries can move backwards as well as forwards (Kuznets, 1965).

Nevertheless, there are also some important similarities between Kuznets and Rostow. Like Rostow, Kuznets emphasises the importance of industrialisation in development. *Changes in the structure of production* are among the main characteristics of modern economic development.[4] Furthermore, Kuznets identifies conditions for industrialisation, which are similar to those mentioned by Rostow: productivity increases in other sectors such as mining, agriculture or

---

4 The importance of structural change is also emphasised by authors such as Lewis and Fei and Ranis, whose work will be discussed in Chapters 8 and 9.

transport, sufficient supply of labour, capital and entrepreneurship and sufficient effective demand for industrial products.

According to Kuznets (1955) industrialisation and urbanisation in developing
countries are accompanied by increasing income inequality. This is caused by
two factors. First, urban/industrial incomes are higher than rural incomes.
Second, urban income inequality is higher than rural income inequality. At
later stages of economic development, the income distribution becomes more
equal as a result of demographic factors, democratisation and the rise of trade
unions and political pressure groups. This is referred to as the *inverted U-curve
hypothesis*, which is still being debated in current international comparative
research.

3.4.3   Advantages of backwardness

Like Rostow, Alexander Gerschenkron emphasises the importance of overcoming traditional obstacles to industrialisation. For nineteenth-century Russia,
such obstacles included serfdom and the absence of a disciplined, reliable
and stable supply of industrial labour. When industrialisation occurs in late-
developing economies, it happens in leaps or in rapid spurts, concentrated in
certain leading sectors of economy (Gerschenkron, 1962). In the post-war period this leaping character of development is reflected in the experiences of
Asian countries such as Korea and Taiwan and currently China.

In two respects Gerschenkron disagrees with Rostow. In the first place there
are important differences between the patterns of industrialisation in different countries and different historical periods. In early processes of industrialisation, self-financing by firms was the most important source of investable
funds. In the economic development of Germany, banks and financial institutions played a far more important role than earlier in England and France.
In Russia, only the government was able to mobilise sufficient amounts of financial capital for massive investment in industry and infrastructure. As time
went by, technological change required investment on an ever larger scale.
This explains why the role of banks, financial institutions and governments
becomes more and more important in late industrialisation. Increasing scale
also explains the explosive nature of industrialisation processes. For industrialisation to succeed in late industrialisation, very many changes in the economy
have to take place simultaneously, in a short period of time. If changes are
only partial or limited, the required scale of investment will not be attained
and the process of industrialisation will stagnate.[5]

In the second place, Gerschenkron argues that the economic development of
a country should be studied in a context of international technology transfer.
In this respect Gerschenkron transcends the limits of internal perspectives. In

---

5 This notion is not incomparable to the Rostovian notion of take-off, but Gerschenkron differs from
Rostow in not making use of a unilinear stage theory.

Gerschenkron's theory, latecomers in economic development have the opportunity to take over technological know-how from economically advanced countries, without having to bear the burden of the costs of research and development of new technologies. Developing countries can choose from a tremendous arsenal of new production techniques, which were not available previously. Thus if the economy and the society is able to absorb new technologies,
latecomers in development can experience faster economic growth than early
developers, because they profit from the *advantages of backwardness*.

Abramovitz (1989b) has further developed the notion of advantages of backwardness. The capacity of developing countries to profit from technologies
developed in the advanced economies depends on the social capabilities of a
developing country and the congruence between technologies developed in the
lead countries and conditions in the follower countries. Social capability refers
to the use a country can make of advanced technology and its capacity to acquire it in the first place. Social capability depends on the technical competence
of a country's people, indicated among others by levels of general education
and the share of population with training in technical subjects. It also is influenced by the degree of experience of managers with large-scale production, the
availability of financial institutions and supporting services and so forth. Once
certain threshold levels of capabilities have been achieved, backward countries
can grow very rapidly as they take over technology from elsewhere. But if they
fail to achieve these threshold levels, gaps will tend to widen.

3.4.4   *Neoclassical theories of growth*

Neoclassical economic theories of growth analyse the relationships between
the growth of inputs (capital, land, labour, technology) and growth of output,
in the form of mathematical models of growth.[6] Compared to the theories
discussed so far, the neoclassical economic theory of growth as formulated by
Solow (1956; 1957) focuses primarily on the proximate sources of growth. It has
little or nothing to say about the more fundamental social mechanisms and
institutions underlying accumulation of capital, technical change and growth.

The Solow model makes use of the so-called Cobb–Douglas function, which
takes the form

$$O = AK^{\alpha}L^{1-\alpha}.$$

Output is a function of the stock of capital and the amount of labour, with
α and $1 - \alpha$ representing the elasticity of output to capital and labour and
A reflecting the state of knowledge (technology). This draws our attention to
the contribution to growth of the accumulation of factors of production and
of changes in the quality of factors of production. It also emphasises the importance of an efficient allocation of factors of production in processes of

---

6 For accessible introductory expositions see Jones, 1998 and Ray, 1998.

economic development. Capital and labour can be substituted for each other. If labour is cheap and abundant, as in many developing countries, then efficient allocation implies a choice for labour-intensive forms of production. Free markets and perfect competition are the mechanisms which make for such efficient allocation.

The Solow model of growth assumes profit-maximising behaviour on the part of economic actors. Firms will continue to use more and more capital and labour in production, as long as the marginal costs of these factors of production are less than their marginal returns. Under competitive conditions and perfect information, this will result in equalisation of marginal costs and marginal returns. The model assumes constant returns to scale, implying, for instance, that if the amount of both capital and labour is doubled, output will also double. If one factor of production is held constant, while the other increases, the marginal returns to the increasing factor will diminish. The model assumes that the growth of labour depends on population growth and is thus given. The growth of the capital stock is determined by the savings rate. The share of savings in national income is assumed constant.

Now, as the savings are used to accumulate more and more capital per worker, labour productivity will go up. But as the marginal returns to capital are declining because of diminishing returns, the rate of increase in labour productivity will decline and productivity growth in the long run will become zero. Then per capita income growth will come to a stop as the economy reaches its steady state. In the steady state output grows at the same rate as population.[7]

The only factor which counterbalances diminishing returns is technological change, the rate of which is determined outside the model and is not explained. Technological change shifts the production function upwards. In the long run, therefore, the growth rate of labour productivity depends on technological change. Technological knowledge is assumed to be freely available to all countries in the world economy. Therefore, in absence of institutions blocking the diffusion of technology, all countries are assumed to have the same rate of technological change.

As developing countries have less capital per worker than rich countries, the marginal productivity of capital should be higher and labour productivity growth will therefore be more rapid than in rich countries. In the long run, per capita incomes in rich and poor countries will tend to converge. This is referred to as the hypothesis of *unconditional convergence*. This tendency towards convergence in the neoclassical theory is strengthened by the assumption that capital moves freely across the world economy. If returns are higher in developing countries, capital will move there, making for convergence. Technology is also conceived of as a public good, which is available to all economies. Therefore in the long run rich and poor countries should converge and their steady

---

7 If savings rates and population growth differ between countries, they will still converge to the same growth rate, but not to the same level of per capita income.

state growth rate of per capita income should be determined by the rate of technological change.

Neoclassical theory does not focus explicitly on developing countries. Implicitly, however, it predicts that, if markets function smoothly and the factors of production can move freely across the world economy, sooner or later rich and poor countries will converge and developing countries will catch up.

As discussed in Chapters 1 and 2, there is no actual convergence to be observed between rich and poor countries in the world economy. On the contrary, world income differentials have been increasing. Within the framework of neoclassical growth theory, the absence of unconditional convergence can be explained by differences in savings rates and population growth rates. If savings rates and population growth rates differ, then the theory states that countries will tend to converge to the same growth rate, but not to the same long-run per capita incomes. Per capita incomes in groups of countries with similar initial savings rates and population growths will tend to converge, countries with lower incomes growing more rapidly than countries with higher initial incomes within a given group. But, convergence within groups can coexist with divergence in the whole world economy.

The hypothesis that countries with similar initial conditions will tend to converge in income level is referred to as the hypothesis of *conditional convergence*. In cross-country regression analyses a wide range of initial conditions have been taken into account, including savings rates, population growth rates, initial levels of capital per worker, educational levels and political variables (see Barro, 1991; Barro and Sala-i-Martin, 1995; Baumol *et al.*, 1989; Mankiw *et al.*, 1992).

Parallel with the rise of neoclassical growth theory, there is the rise of the growth accounting tradition, pioneered by authors such as Abramovitz (1989a), Denison (1967), Jorgenson (1995) and Kendrick (1961). Growth accounting focuses on the empirical measurement and quantification of the contributions of different proximate sources of growth, taking the neoclassical production function framework as an initial point of departure. While growth theory is oriented towards formal modelling, growth accounting has a much stronger empirical orientation. It is more eclectic in its theoretical orientation. Measurement of the proximate sources of growth and their contribution allows one to link up these sources with institutional and historical analysis.

Growth accounting makes a distinction between the growth of inputs (increase in the quantity and quality of capital and labour) and the growth of output per unit of input (see Maddison, 1987). Growth accounting shows that a considerable part of growth cannot be accounted for by increases in the amount of inputs of capital and labour, even after these have been adjusted for increases in quality and education. Growth accounting goes on to explain the growth of output per unit of input (or total factor productivity) by various factors, for example structural shifts from low productivity sectors such as agriculture to high productivity sectors such as manufacturing, economies of scale and technological change. An important part of growth can only be explained by technological advance, which is the interpretation of the residual part of growth which cannot be accounted for by other factors. One of the important debates in recent years is whether rapid growth in some Asian economies is primarily owing to technological change and rapid increases in total factor productivity (World Bank, 1993), or rather, as argued by Young (1995), whether it is primarily due to enormous efforts to accumulate more capital and improve education. The focus of both neoclassical theory and growth accounting on the accumulation of capital, education and technological change places these approaches squarely within the internal tradition in the analysis of backwardness.

New growth theory

The absence of unconditional convergence is one of the points of departure for the so-called new or endogenous theory of growth which has surfaced since the mid-1980s. In the older neoclassical growth models, technological change was conceived of as exogenous. In growth accounting studies it was measured as the residual after the contributions of all other factors were taken into account. New growth theories try to endogenise[8] technological change in two ways (Lucas, 1988; Romer, 1986; 1990; for an overview see Fagerberg, 1994). In the first place it is assumed that technological change (changes in the stock of knowledge) is automatically associated with investment in capital goods and education, through a process of learning by doing. In the second place, one can conceive of investment in a separate sector producing technology and knowledge which becomes available for firms engaged in production of goods and services. The production of various goods and services through the application of increasing amounts of knowledge and technology in production is subject to increasing returns to scale owing to the positive external effects of knowledge in production (spillover effects). The greater the level of initial investment in knowledge and human capital in a country, the greater the returns to further investment. The only limit to unrestricted growth is that the production of knowledge itself is subject to decreasing returns (in other words becomes ever more difficult).

Thus, both strands of new growth theory offer an explanation of the divergence in economic performance between rich and poor countries existing in the world economy. Countries with a head start in accumulation of physical capital, human capital and knowledge will tend to forge ahead. Countries which are backward will tend to stagnate further. On the other hand, new growth theory has great difficulties in accounting for the process of the dramatic catch-up of countries starting at very low levels and moving upwards in world income-ranking in the course of one or two generations. Such processes are better explained by either conditional convergence or theories of the advantages of backwardness.

---

8 Endogenise, i.e. explain something within a model, instead of taking it as exogenous or given outside the model.

Though the ideas contained in new growth theory are stimulating, the empirical verification of these models has run into difficulties (Pack, 1994). It turns out to be almost impossible to discard one model in favour of another, on the basis of statistical tests. Even at a theoretical level, Solow, one of the founding fathers of neoclassical growth theory, has pointed out that neoclassical growth theory can also accommodate divergence (Solow, 1991). He argues that the availability of modern technology does not automatically mean that technological diffusion to less developed economies will indeed take place. In the absence of institutional changes, these economies may simply be unable to assimilate new technologies. This brings the argument back to institutional and structural factors.

3.4.5 Evolutionary theories of economic change

Evolutionary theories of Economic Change refer to a relatively recent strand of theories building on the Schumpeterian tradition. Like Schumpeter, evolutionary theories focus on the central role of technological change and innovation in growth and development (Dosi, 1988; Freeman and Soete, 1997; Nelson and Winter, 1982; Verspagen, 1993; 2001). Investment in new technology is associated with major uncertainties and risks. These uncertainties and risks are not easily dealt with in the neoclassical approaches which assume perfect information, rational profit maximisation and movements towards equilibria and steady states.

Evolutionary theory rejects the notion of rational choice underlying neoclassical theory. Economic agents have to deal with imperfect information. They have to search for information and their decisions are made on the basis of rules of thumb. Evolutionary theory starts with the twin notions of heterogeneity of economic agents and selection environments. Heterogeneity implies that different economic actors faced with uncertainties will use different decision rules and different search strategies, and will arrive at different decisions. Given the selection environment, some choices of some firms turn out to be successful and they and their decision rules are subsequently reinforced. The collective outcomes of these choices and selection processes can put an economy onto a dynamic growth path, which distinguishes it from other economies. This is referred to as path dependence (David, 1975), where relatively small initial differences can be greatly reinforced in the long run. Thus, like new growth theory, evolutionary theory is well equipped to deal with divergence of economic performance in the world economy.

In evolutionary economics, disequilibrium reigns rather than equilibrium. New technological developments, shocks and changes in the environment can make past successful paths irrelevant, and can open new opportunities for dynamic growth for low-income economies. Thus, evolutionary theory can also accommodate processes of catch-up.

Like new growth theory, evolutionary theory suggests that there are increasing returns to investment in technology. Whether or not this leads to increased divergence depends on whether the advanced countries appropriate all the returns to new technology or whether technology diffuses or spills over to developing countries. This depends on the one hand on how intellectual property rights are protected. On the other hand, it depends on the technological capabilities – capabilities to select, absorb and adapt technologies – in developing countries. Developing countries with strong technological capabilities are better placed to profit from the Gerschenkronian advantages of backwardness. But, when technological capabilities are weak and the technology gap separating advanced from developing economies is too wide, then there are insufficient possibilities for diffusion and international spillovers and countries will fall further behind. The concept of technological capabilities emphasises that technology is not freely available, but requires major effort and costs to acquire and master.[9]

3.4.6   North and Thomas: efficient institutions

One of the less satisfactory aspects of modern theories of backwardness discussed so far is how the transition from a traditional to a modern economy takes place. This transition is the central theme of a beautiful study of two economic historians, Douglass C. North and Robert P. Thomas. In *The Rise of the Western World* (1973) they focus on the emergence of efficient institutions. Efficient institutions are defined as institutions which motivate self-interested individuals to act in ways which contribute to collective welfare. Among the efficient institutions discussed by North and Thomas are well-defined property rights, which guarantee that individuals will profit from the fruits of their own exertions. Only under such conditions will individuals be willing to make risky investments in future productive capacity. Protection of intellectual property (patent rights) is one of the conditions for a continuous stream of innovations. The institution of the joint stock company diminishes the risks of large-scale investments for individuals. Land reforms that create well-defined individual rights to land motivate farmers to invest in increased land productivity.

Efficient institutions do not emerge automatically. The rise of efficient institutions depends on the costs and benefits involved in the creation and maintenance of such institutions for different individuals and groups. When population density increased in Europe at the end of the middle ages, this facilitated the development of interregional trade. Production for the market and the money economy become viable alternatives to the traditionally determined exchange relationships of feudal economic systems. Previously these had been more efficient, because the *transaction costs* of market exchanges were too high.

---

9 The tacit nature of much technological knowledge is one of the factors which impedes the effortless adoption of technology by developing countries.

Governments were able to guarantee property rights at lower costs per person than private groups, because the costs could be distributed over larger numbers of people. Also, government intervention avoided the problems of *free ridership*. Therefore the development of individual property rights went hand in hand with the increasing importance of state apparatuses in societies. Not all governments, however, promoted more efficient institutions. Sometimes, government policy was determined by social classes, whose interests lay in the preservation of inefficient institutions. The influence of governments on the development of institutions in its turn was influenced by the power relationships between different classes in society. Thus North and Thomas succeed in an ingenious fashion in combining the neoclassical economic analysis of institutional changes in terms of costs and benefits with the historical study of the power relationships between classes and interest groups.

In more recent publications North (1990; 1993) warns us that efficient institutions do not automatically supplant less efficient institutions. When a society has embarked on a certain institutional path, later developments depend on choices made earlier on in the development process. Such *path dependence* is one of the explanations for the increasing divergence of richer and poor societies in the world economy.

3.4.7   *Myrdal: institutional reforms*

As a last representative of the internal approach to development we now discuss Gunnar Myrdal. Even more than Kuznets and Gerschenkron, Myrdal (1968) emphasises that simple unilinear development schemes are misleading. They do not take into account the important differences in institutional structures in different countries, regions and historical periods. They can give rise to fundamentally mistaken policy recommendations. Myrdal attaches considerable importance to differences in initial conditions. The initial conditions in developing countries – climate, demography, technology, position in the international economic order – are so different from those of the currently rich countries that copying earlier development experiences of Western countries is not a viable option. His approach to initial conditions is much more historical than the a-historical formulations of neoclassical theorists.

In formulations which predate the literature on path dependence, Myrdal formulated the principle of interlocking interdependencies within a process of cumulative causation (1957). This principle states that in the absence of major social, political or policy changes, initial differences in levels of performance tend to increase.

In spite of his criticisms of Rostow and his recognition of the importance of international power relationships, Myrdal should nevertheless be considered as a representative of the internal approach to development. This is because he considers domestic reforms in developing countries among the most important preconditions for development. One of Myrdal's intellectual contributions is the thesis that extreme social inequality is a powerful obstacle to economic development in poor countries. The unequal distribution of rights to land and large landownership hinders the modernisation of agriculture. Poverty and hunger undermine the productivity of workers and peasants. Wealthy unproductive elites consume more than they invest. Both the content and the accessibility of education is geared to the requirements of elites rather than the real developmental needs of societies. Finally, inefficient and ineffective state bureaucracies and widespread corruption (for which Myrdal coined the term *soft state*) form a serious obstacle to all developmental efforts. Without drastic internal reforms, therefore, development will stagnate. According to Myrdal, redistribution of income and productive assets and equalisation of social and political power is an important aspect of such reforms.

3.5   Explanations of underdevelopment

In spite of all their differences of opinion, theorists of backwardness are primarily searching for the internal characteristics of societies that form obstacles to development and for the internal factors and policies that promote development. This is not to say that they are blind to the outside world. Rather they are convinced that it depends on internal characteristics, institutions and policies how a country will respond to external threats, challenges and opportunities.

Proponents of the external perspective on development believe that developments in different countries and regions are mutually interrelated in the context of the international economic and political order. The possibilities for development in poor countries depend in the first place on their relationships with rich countries. These relationships are sometimes conceived of as advantageous; thus the theory of comparative advantage states, for instance, that developing countries profit from entering into international trade. The possibility of taking over technology from advanced countries, discussed above, also belongs to the advantages of international relationships.

A prominent group of development theorists argues, however, that relationships between rich and poor countries are intrinsically detrimental to the developmental chances of the economically and politically weaker parties. The most extreme version of such perspectives is *underdevelopment or dependency theory*.

The choice for the term *underdevelopment* implies that the low level of development in developing countries is the result of active negative influences from outside. One cannot speak of backwardness, because poor countries do not have the chance to follow the same path of development as the currently prosperous countries. Prosperity in the rich countries is even based on past and present exploitation of the developing countries. Poverty in developing countries is the result of such exploitation. The underdevelopment of the non-Western world is thus the other side of the coin of economic development in the West. The internal obstacles to development are seen as the product of negative interaction with advanced countries in the world economy.

The term *dependence* implies that development in poor countries is subordinated to development in affluent countries. A summary of the characteristics of dependent development, derived from Colman and Nixson (1985), is presented in Box 3.2.

Box 3.2 Characteristics of dependent development

1. *Importance of export of primary commodities.* The exports of a dependent economy consist in large part of primary products. The export sector, consisting of mines and plantations, is an enclave within the economy. All its products are exported abroad. Capital equipment is imported from abroad. The infrastructure of a dependent economy is completely oriented towards the interests of the export sector. There are few backward and forward linkages between the export sector and local producers and buyers.
2. *Dependence on imports of manufactured goods.* Most industrial products are imported from the affluent countries. Western-oriented elites consume imported products on a large scale.
3. *Dependence on imports of intermediate goods, capital goods and technology.* Even if a dependent economy succeeds in building up its own consumer goods industry via import substitution, it remains dependent on the advanced countries for imports of intermediate goods, capital goods and technology.
4. The modern sector of the economy is dominated by foreign firms and transnational companies.
5. Surpluses are repatriated abroad, either through direct transfer of profits or through mechanisms of unequal exchange and transfer pricing.
6. Dependence is not limited to the economic sphere. There are also cultural, psychological and political relations of dependence with the advanced nations.

It is clear that from the perspective of underdevelopment the dualistic structure of the economy in developing countries was not the consequence of only Western penetration in the past. It is also maintained by the relationships with the rich Western countries in the present. Dependence does not end with political decolonisation. In the postcolonial period, economic development is still determined by neocolonial influences from abroad. The only chance to realise goals such as development, growth and industrialisation is to withdraw from the global network of dependency relations characterising the capitalist international economic order and to seek alternative paths of development.

Within the underdevelopment theory one can distinguish two partly overlapping theoretical traditions:

1. Neo-Marxist theories of underdevelopment.
2. Structuralism and theories of unequal exchange.

3.5.1 Neo-Marxist theories of underdevelopment

In their criticisms of capitalist relations of exploitation, neo-Marxist theories of underdevelopment build on the Marxist tradition and theories of imperialism.

They analyse class relationships within developing countries in the context of class conflicts in the global economy.

However, classical Marxism was a typical stage theory in which capitalism was considered to be a higher stage than the preceding feudal stage. Therefore, in classical Marxism, Western capitalist penetration in developing countries was considered as a progressive force on the way to the highest stage which would succeed capitalism, namely socialism. This aspect of classical Marxism is rejected by neo-Marxist thinkers. One of the first theorists of underdevelopment, Paul Baran, argues that capitalism in developing economies functions differently from capitalism in the advanced countries. In the advanced countries, capitalism generates an economic surplus which is appropriated by the capitalist class and subsequently reinvested (Baran, 1957). This process of reinvestment promotes economic growth and dynamism. In poor countries, the economic surplus is transferred to rich countries by monopolistic firms or is squandered away in luxurious consumption by wasteful elites. There is a lack of dynamic investment incentives which can fuel domestic economic growth. The absence of a stream of investments and reinvestments in the domestic economy makes for economic stagnation. Only those investments which benefit the rich countries are realised. Thus what development there is, is dependent development.

Capitalist penetration in developing countries thus leads to a distorted form of capitalism: dependent capitalism. Domestic handicraft production is undermined by competition from imported products. Economic surpluses are transferred to rich countries. Simultaneously, a wealthy domestic 'comprador class' is created, which is involved in import and export trade and the interests of which are closely aligned with the interests of the rich capitalist countries. According to Dos Santos (1970) dependence does not refer to only the external economic relations of a country. The class relations within a country are also determined and reinforced by the external dependency relationships. Therefore a country cannot simply withdraw from relations of dependency. This also requires dramatic changes in internal relationships between groups and classes. Domestic reforms, however, can bring about confrontations with rich countries, whose interests are threatened by reform. Latin American history offers many examples of such confrontations.

One of the most developed versions of underdevelopment theory has been put forward by André Gunder Frank (1969; 1971; 1998). Frank analyses a chain of exploitative relationships running from the centre of the world economy to the rural sector in developing economies. He makes a distinction between rich countries at the core or *centre* of the world economy and poor countries at the *periphery*. In between are countries of the semi-periphery. The centre appropriates surplus from the semi-periphery and the peripheral countries. The semi-periphery exploits the periphery. Within dependent peripheral economies, dominant elites emerge whose interests coincide with those of the centre countries. These elites within the modern sector of the economy exploit the peripheral sectors in their own countries. The last link in the chain of exploitation is at the level of the rural sector, where landowners, whose interests coincide with those of members of the urban elites, exploit small peasants and landless rural labourers.

The emphasis on relationships of exploitation within developing countries makes the centre–periphery theory into a theory of regional inequality as well. It offers an alternative explanation of the dualistic structure of developing economies, discussed in section 3.3. From this perspective, the traditional sector is not a lagging sector which has yet to catch up with the modern sector. It comes into being as a result of exploitation by the centre. The so-called traditional sector is artificially maintained as a source of cheap labour, foodstuffs and other products required by the modern sector.

The more a poor country is integrated into the capitalist world economy, the more it becomes underdeveloped. An autonomous process of industrialisation is only possible in periods in which the economic ties with the centre are loosened or in which the rich countries are in economic crisis.

Among the most valuable aspects of Frank's thought is his criticism of the treatment of 'traditional society' in theories of modernisation (Frank, 1969; 1971). Like classical Marxism, modernisation theories conceive of traditional feudal societies as a stage preceding modern economic development. Feudal societies contain various cultural and institutional obstacles to development, which have to be overcome for development to take place. Dualistic structures are explained by the fact that these traditional obstacles and barriers have not yet been transcended in some parts of the economy and society. Frank gives many interesting counterexamples from Latin American history which show that the traditional society, which is called feudal, is in reality the product of Western and capitalist penetration. The Spaniards and Portuguese newly introduced forms of large landownership and serfdom which had not existed before. As we saw in Chapter 2, even the population mix is a product of Western penetration. For instance, almost the whole population of Surinam was imported by the Dutch from Africa and Asia to work on capitalist plantations as slaves or bonded labourers. If one rereads Rostow, after reading Frank, Rostow's use of the term 'traditional society' which precedes higher stages makes a very a-historical impression. The main value of theories of underdevelopment is that they show how 'internal' characteristics and institutions of developing countries have been deeply influenced and shaped by past and present external forces such as colonialism, imperialism, the Cold War and international economic trends and relationships.

The conclusion of neo-Marxists such as Baran and Frank is that the bourgeoisie cannot play the same dynamic role that it played in the earlier development of the currently affluent countries. They argue that socialist revolutions are a necessary condition for development and that developing countries should extricate themselves from international trade and the international division of labour. Similar arguments are advanced by modern exponents of the anti-globalist movement of the late 1990s.

3.5.2   *Structuralism and theories of unequal exchange*

Theories of unequal exchange have been formulated both by neo-Marxists such as Samir Amin and Arghiri Emmanuel and by non-Marxist theorists such as Raúl Prebisch and Hans Singer (Hunt, 1989: chs 5–7; Prebisch, 1950). Theories of unequal exchange reject the orthodox economic proposition that differences in factor endowments in different regions result in mutually advantageous patterns of international trade based on comparative advantage. According to orthodox views, free trade and specialisation in those lines of production in which a country is relatively most efficient will increase all countries' welfare. In the long run free movements of factors of production will also result in a gradual equalisation of returns to the factors of production in rich and poor countries. Theories of unequal exchange, however, state that participation of developing countries in the international division of labour is detrimental to their chances of economic development. Only the rich countries profit from international trade.

These theories emphasise the structural characteristics of the economies of developing countries which hinder the operation of free-market incentives in the domestic economy and comparative advantage in international trade. Therefore these theories are often called *structuralist theories*.

Various arguments are put forward by theorists of unequal exchange to explain why developing countries are at a disadvantage in international trade. In the first place, many developing countries have a comparative advantage in primary products (agricultural products and raw materials). The income elasticity of world demand for these products is low. This means that as per capita incomes in the world economy go up, the demand for primary products will lag behind. (For instance, as people become more prosperous they will buy more manufactured goods and services. But there are limits to how much more bread they can consume.) Prices of primary exports will therefore not keep up with prices of industrial exports for which world demand is much more buoyant. In the second place, high wage levels in the affluent countries stimulate investments in capital and technological development so as to increase labour productivity. In poor countries, the abundance of cheap labour will limit technological advance. The technological gap between rich and poor countries will tend to increase. In the third place, orthodox neo-classical economic theory does not take into account the fact that most investment in developing countries is in foreign hands. Therefore investment behaviour is determined by foreign rather than by national interests. In the fourth place, Prebisch and Singer state that both well-organised trade unions and monopolistic corporations in the rich countries prevent productivity gains in these countries from being passed on to consumers in poor countries in the form of lower export prices. The absence of such institutions in developing countries means that productivity gains in these countries are passed on to consumers in rich countries. For all these reasons the terms of trade between export and import prices of developing countries show a structural decline over time.

An influential version of the theory of the declining terms of trade was formulated by Nobel Prize-winner Arthur Lewis (1954; 1978). He argues that disguised unemployment in the traditional sector of the economy makes for a large flow of cheap labour towards the export sector. This flow of cheap labour has a depressing effect on the export prices of agrarian products from developing countries and the incomes of agrarian workers. In the mining sector high productivity and low wages make for large profits. As mines are mostly foreign-owned, the profits will flow out of the country, which therefore benefits but little from mining exports. According to Lewis, international trade offers poor countries an opportunity to stay poor, as incomes earned in export production remain low. Only if productivity in the traditional food-producing sector goes up will the unlimited supply of extremely cheap labour, with its depressing effects on wages and export prices, come to an end. The evolution of the terms of trade will be discussed further in Chapter 8.

Non-Marxist structuralists draw less radical conclusions than the Marxists with regard to the need for domestic political and economic changes. However, following the classical prescriptions of Friedrich List, they do argue for a development strategy which would make developing countries less dependent on international trade (Sunkel, 1993; Urquidi, 1993). To achieve this, they have to build up and protect a domestic industrial sector which can replace imports of industrial goods by domestic production. This strategy, known as the *import substitution strategy*, has been applied with a certain measure of success in Latin American countries between the 1930s and 1960s, and elswhere in Africa and Asia. After the 1960s this strategy ran out of steam. Asian countries which made an earlier switch towards export orientation performed much better than African and Latin American countries which continued inward-looking import substitution policies (see Chapters 8 and 9).

Structuralists believe that free-market policies will not work in developing countries owing to a variety of structural constraints. These include: the absence of an adequate transport and communications infrastructure; the under-development of the financial system; the limited extent of the market; the lack of market information; the lack of free choice for subordinate classes; and the monopolistic structure of the economy. Both Marxists and Structuralists are in favour of government planning and a leading role of the state in the development process. It is the state that has to break through the structural constraints to development. This recommendation is a corollary of their critique of the workings of capitalism and the free market. Finally, structuralists are among those calling for regulation of international trade and the creation of a new international economic order (NIEO), in which developing countries would have better chances.

In the 1960s and 1970s there was a widespread surge of interest in a new, more regulated international order. This completely disappeared from the agenda in the 1980s and 1990s, when resurgent economic liberalism challenged the tenets of national and international planning and regulation. In rather in-choate form the call for a new international order is now re-emerging at the beginning of the new millennium in the political and academic criticisms of globalisation. The modern critics of globalisation point to financial instability and loss of national independence as negative consequences of participation in the global world economy. The modern debate on globalisation will be taken up again in Chapter 13.

3.5.3   *Underdevelopment theories: a preliminary evaluation*

Theories of underdevelopment have been primarily formulated with reference to the development experiences of Latin America. In the history of this subcon-tinent colonial and neocolonial exploitation by Spaniards, Portuguese, English, Dutch, Americans, and others have played an important role. The artificial cre-ation by Iberian colonists of large landholdings and plantations on the one hand and a poor rural population of landless labourers, serfs and very small farmers on the other hand is prominent in history. The slave trade and the im-port of bonded labourers have changed the total population profile. After the achievement of independence in the early nineteenth century, foreign inter-ests continued to play an important role. Military interventions by the English and later by the Americans occurred frequently and have continued to do so to this very day. The dualist development of the economy went hand in hand with extreme income inequality. Thus, rapid economic growth could coexist with continued widespread poverty.

Theories of underdevelopment have undoubtedly increased our insight into the negative aspects of Western penetration in the world. They form a valuable counterweight to the often a-historic blueprints of modernisation theorists or the bland prescriptions of market enthusiasts. One of the important insights deriving from the underdevelopment tradition is that Western influences can give rise to institutions and constellations of interest groups, which form se-rious obstacles to development in subsequent historical periods. Theories of underdevelopment also help us understand how rapid capitalist growth in Latin America can sometimes coexist with continued poverty of large masses of the population.

Nevertheless, underdevelopment theories also have a number of important shortcomings. The most basic shortcoming is the deterministic nature of many of their propositions. From the perspective of underdevelopment theory it is hard to understand how and why former colonies such as the United States, Canada, Australia or New Zealand have achieved such economic success. Nei-ther do the experiences of dynamic capitalist developments in South Korea, Taiwan, Singapore, Thailand, Hong Kong, Malaysia, Indonesia, China and other newly industrialising countries fit the underdevelopment mould.

Many of the empirical propositions of underdevelopment theory are un-founded. For instance, as we shall see in paragraph 3.6.4, it is simply not true that there is always a net outflow of capital from poor to rich countries. Also, empirical data do not invariably support a law of declining terms of trade for developing countries. Sometimes the terms of trade deteriorate, sometimes they improve. Finally, the proposition that the economic breakthrough in the West should primarily be explained by colonial exploitation and plunder is not supported by empirical historical research, which emphasises the importance of centuries of internal pre-capitalist accumulation and gradual increases in productivity.

In the present economic situation, underdevelopment theory has little to offer in the way of policy recommendations. Socialist central planning of industrial development is increasingly considered a highly inefficient development strategy. There is indeed a renewed debate about the role of industrial and technology policy in Asian economic growth, which some authors refer to as neostructuralist (Sunkel, 1993). But this debate focuses on how developing countries can profit from participation in the international division of labour rather than on how they can extricate themselves from international trade. The disadvantages of extreme import substitution and the related neglect of agriculture are now widely recognised (see Chapters 9 and 13). The advantages of participation in international trade are underlined by the positive development experiences of those developing countries which have shown the strongest export orientation.

Thus, though underdevelopment theory has contributed to our understanding of historical development processes, it has little to offer for the formulation of adequate development strategies in the present. The study of historical questions of guilt and responsibility for underdevelopment cannot substitute for the search for appropriate development strategies in the present.

3.6　Empirical study of development experiences

In this section we discuss empirical data on long-run economic development in poor countries. We will attempt to show how such empirical data are of relevance for some of the theoretical questions raised in the first half of this chapter. The data primarily derive from Angus Maddison's publications, *The World Economy: A Millennial Perspective* (2001) and *Monitoring the World Economy* (1995), supplemented by information from other sources. Here we only present selected economic indicators for the total economy. Information about demography, education, health, nutrition, industrialisation, agricultural development and other aspects of economic and social life will be presented in the following chapters.

Much of the literature on development and development studies is based on examples, case studies or metaphors. It is our conviction that the systematic empirical study of long-term trends in economic and social indicators and systematic comparisons of such trends can contribute to a less ideological and more analytical approach to the emotionally highly charged field of development studies and to a strengthening of its empirical foundations.

The data in this section only refer to a sample of 29 developing countries. Nevertheless the 3.9 billion inhabitants of these 29 countries represent more than three-quarters of total developing country population in 2000. This means that developments in the selected countries do give a picture of changes in the economic circumstances of a large portion of world population.

The choice of countries is primarily determined by the quality and availability of empirical data and by the size of the countries. The sample contains 12 Asian countries, 7 Latin American countries and 10 African countries. For African countries the data can usually not be traced back as far as those for other countries. In many tables developing countries are compared with 16 high-income countries.[10]

We do not want to suggest that the summary data in this section give a complete picture of economic developments in poor countries. Neither do we argue that these data can provide any final answers to the theoretical controversies touched upon in the previous pages. The data themselves should be considered as hypotheses rather than as indisputable facts and are themselves, of course, open to criticism and discussion. The main purpose of presenting these data is to illustrate that discussion of highly politicised theories and propositions can be fruitfully approached in an empirical fashion.

3.6.1 Growth of income per capita: can developing countries grow?

Table 3.1 presents data on the average growth rate of gross domestic product per capita since 1870. This table shows us that average income per head in developing countries has been increasing ever since the beginning of the nineteenth century. This effectively contradicts the myth that growth of per capita income in developing countries is impossible owing to vicious circles of poverty. Several developing countries show considerable economic dynamism. The increase in production per head has been realised in spite of very rapid population growth, particularly since 1950.

The periodisation of the data in Table 3.1 is the same as discussed in Chapter 2. As data for 1870 were very incomplete, a subperiod 1900–13 has also been distinguished. Between 1870 and 1913 there was substantial foreign investment in developing countries and the exports of agriculture and mining products increased rapidly. There was growth in both rich and poor countries, though growth was more rapid in the rich countries. From 1913 to 1950 growth in the world economy stagnated as a result of wars and economic depressions. Developing countries were heavily hit by the economic crisis of 1929, especially the Asian countries. The period between 1950 and 1973 was a golden age of dynamic development, with growth of per capita incomes in the world economy

---

10 These are referred to in shorthand as OECD countries, which is not strictly correct. Developing countries such as Mexico, Turkey and the Republic of Korea are also members of the OECD.

Table 3.1 *Growth of GDP per capita, 1870–2000, annual average compound growth rates (%)*

	1870–1913	1900–13	1913–50	1950–73	1973–2000
Bangladesh	0.5	0.9	−0.4	−0.4	2.1
China	0.1	0.2	−0.6	2.9	5.5
India[a]	0.5	0.9	−0.3	1.4	2.9
Indonesia	0.8	1.6	−0.2	2.6	2.6
Malaysia			1.5	2.2	4.4
Pakistan	0.6	0.9	−0.4	1.7	2.8
Philippines		2.5	0.0	2.7	0.7
South Korea		0.8	−0.4	5.8	6.1
Sri Lanka			0.3	1.9	5.2
Taiwan		0.3	0.6	6.7	5.2
Thailand	0.4	0.3	−0.1	3.7	4.7
Turkey			0.8	3.2	2.1
Argentina	2.5	−0.1	0.7	2.1	0.3
Brazil	0.3	1.4	2.0	3.7	1.4
Chile		2.4	1.0	1.3	2.7
Colombia		1.9	1.5	2.1	1.5
Mexico	2.2	1.8	0.8	3.2	1.5
Peru		1.9	2.1	2.5	−0.3
Venezuela	1.6	2.3	5.3	1.5	−1.0
Congo, Dem. Rep.				1.7	−5.0
Côte d'Ivoire				2.6	−1.3
Egypt		0.0	−0.1	1.5	3.3
Ghana		2.6	1.1	1.0	−0.3
Kenya				1.7	0.2
Morocco			1.6	0.7	1.6
Nigeria				2.7	−0.7
South Africa			1.2	2.2	−0.2
Tanzania				1.4	−0.4
Zambia				2.1	−1.6
Weighted average[b]					
Asian countries	0.3	0.6	−0.2	2.6	4.0
Latin American countries	1.8	1.6	1.4	2.7	1.0
African countries		0.3	1.0	2.0	0.1
Developing countries	0.5	0.8	0.4	2.7	3.0
16 OECD Countries[c]	1.6	1.7	1.2	3.6	2.1

Notes:
[a] India prior to 1950 refers to undivided India, including Bangladesh and Pakistan.
[b] Average of countries in table weighted by their population size.
[c] OECD countries: Australia, Austria, Belgium, Canada, Denmark, Finland, France, Germany, Italy, Japan, Netherlands, Norway, Sweden, Switzerland, UK and USA. Population weighted average.
Sources: 1990 and before: Maddison (2001), supplemented with figures from Maddison (1995); 1991–99: GGDC, *Total Economy Database*, http://www.ggdc.net; 2000: Growth rates 1999/2000 from World Bank, *World Development Report*, 2002.

higher than ever before in economic history. Both rich and poor countries profited from the liberalisation and growth of world trade and the increase in investment and capital flows. After the oil crisis of 1973, there was a slowdown of global growth relative to the period 1950–73 (Maddison, 1989) and many individual countries showed lower growth rates. However, because of dynamic developments in some very populous Asian countries such as China, the total growth rate in developing countries nevertheless accelerated.

For most of the period since 1870 the data in Table 3.1 illustrate that economic developments in rich countries and developing countries tend to run parallel. Otherwise than suggested by theories of underdevelopment, growth in the rich countries is not accompanied by stagnation in developing countries. On the contrary, if the heart of economic growth in the rich countries starts beating at a slower pace, this has negative consequences in other parts of the world economy. If growth in rich countries accelerates, growth in developing countries tends to respond.

This does not mean that the discussion of underdevelopment theses can be concluded. In the first place, Table 3.1 refers to gross domestic product rather than gross national product. It is conceivable that part of gross domestic product of developing countries drains away in the form of factor payments to foreign owners of capital. Not only will national product then be lower than domestic product, but economic growth will also be lower than if all economic surpluses had been reinvested in the domestic economy. In the second place, income per capita is an average figure which disregards the income distribution within a country. Rapid growth usually goes hand in hand with rapidly increasing inequality (see Table 3.10) and can even be accompanied by immiseration of large parts of the population. Even with catch-up the world household income distribution may be becoming more unequal (see e.g. Table 1.2). In the third place, between 1913 and 1950 the development experiences of Latin American countries are not inconsistent with underdevelopment theory. In this period industrial imports from Europe stagnated owing to wars and economic crises. This gave Latin American countries such as Brazil a chance to build up a domestic manufacturing sector.

In order to bring out the effects of three major economic crises: the oil crisis of 1973; the debt crisis of 1982; and the Asian financial crisis of 1997, the post-1973 period is split into three subperiods in Table 3.2: 1973–81, 1981–96 and 1996–2000. After the oil crisis of 1973, growth in the OECD countries slowed down markedly. Latin America experienced slower growth than before 1973, but was able to sustain its growth momentum till around 1981 through highly expansionary fiscal and monetary policies. The average Latin American growth rate for this period was 2.1 per cent. After that, economic development stagnated severely as a result of misguided policies, hyperinflation and the impact of the 1982 debt crisis (Maddison, 1989). Negative growth in Democratic Republic of Congo, Côte d'Ivoire, Ghana, Nigeria, Tanzania, and Zambia reflects the onset of economic stagnation on the African continent after 1973. In contrast, after 1973 growth started accelerating in Asia. The average growth rate of 3.1 per cent was much higher than in the OECD countries or Latin America.

The impact of the 1982 debt crisis was particularly severe in Latin America. Many economies experienced contraction of GDP in the 'lost decade' of the 1980s, only starting an uncertain recovery after 1990 (Hoffman, 1998). African countries also suffered heavily in the wake of the 1982 debt crisis. Between 1981 and 1996 average per capita output declined by 0.4 per cent per year. In contrast, Asian countries' growth surged ahead providing an example of global catch-up relative to the OECD economies.

Table 3.2 *Growth of GDP per capita, 1973–2000, annual average compound growth rates (%)*

	1973–81	1981–96	1996–2000
Bangladesh	1.3	2.1	3.5
China	3.5	6.5	6.0
India	1.7	3.3	4.1
Indonesia	3.3	3.7	−2.7
Malaysia	5.1	4.8	1.2
Pakistan	3.0	3.1	1.2
Philippines	2.5	−0.4	0.9
South Korea	5.3	7.4	3.3
Sri Lanka	3.5	6.4	4.1
Taiwan	5.5	5.5	3.5
Thailand	4.4	6.6	−2.1
Turkey	1.3	2.6	1.9
Argentina	−0.5	0.6	0.7
Brazil	2.8	0.7	1.0
Chile	2.0	3.2	2.4
Colombia	2.5	1.7	−1.3
Mexico	4.1	−0.5	4.0
Peru	1.0	−1.3	0.9
Venezuela	−1.0	−0.9	−1.4
Congo, Dem. Rep.	−3.7	−4.8	−8.4
Côte d'Ivoire	1.4	−3.2	0.6
Egypt	6.2	1.7	3.6
Ghana	−2.5	0.2	2.2
Kenya	0.6	0.3	−1.0
Morocco	3.1	1.4	−0.7
Nigeria	−1.3	−0.4	−0.5
South Africa	0.9	−1.0	0.8
Tanzania	−0.5	−0.9	1.7
Zambia	−1.5	−2.0	−0.3
Weighted average:			
Asian countries	3.1	4.9	3.6
Latin American countries	2.1	0.4	1.2
African countries	0.8	−0.4	0.3
Average developing countries	2.7	3.1	3.6
Average 16 OECD countries	1.8	2.0	2.5

Sources: See Table 3.1.

The euphoria of Asian growth was rudely shaken by the financial crisis of 1997, which dramatically interrupted growth in countries such as Thailand, Indonesia, South Korea and the Philippines. Other Asian countries were less affected, but average growth in the Asian countries declined from 4.9 per cent to 2.8 per cent between 1996 and 2000.

Till 1973, income per capita in rich countries grew more rapidly than in poor countries, so that the gap between rich and poor became ever larger. Since 1973, average growth in our sample of developing countries has been higher than that in OECD countries.[11] This primarily reflected accelerating growth in large Asian economies, including China and India. After 1981, Latin America

---

11 Using population weighted averages gives very different results from the standard practice of examining the unweighted dispersion of per capita incomes. This elementary fact is disregarded in most discussions of development. One should realise that the population of India is about twice as large as the total combined population of Africa.

lost much of its earlier gains, while Asia continued on a catch-up trajectory. After 1973, Africa provided an example of falling behind, with many countries experiencing real declines in per capita GDP over long periods. Thus, from 1973 onwards we see divergent trends in the developing world with catch-up in Asia, stagnation in Africa and a mixed record in Latin America.

Even with higher growth rates in some developing countries, one should realise it takes quite some time for the absolute income gap compared to rich countries to start decreasing. At low levels of income, high growth rates result in modest absolute increases. In the meanwhile, however, some countries such as Taiwan and South Korea will no longer be classified as developing countries in the future. Since 1996 South Korea has been a member of the OECD.

3.6.2   Investment: how important is capital?

One of the important issues in classical and modern theories of economic development has to do with the importance of capital and the rate of capital accumulation. In post-war thinking about development, capital accumulation was seen as the key to growth and development. Lack of savings and capital explained low levels of development.

A well-known theory of Lewis and Rostow, discussed briefly in section 3.4.1, states that sustained economic growth will occur when the rate of investment increases from 5 per cent or less to more than 12 per cent of net national income. The data in Table 3.3 refer to gross investment (i.e. before subtraction of depreciation) rather than net investment. However, one may assume that 5 per cent net roughly corresponds to 8 per cent in gross terms (Maddison, 1989). This implies that most of our developing countries were already investing more than the Lewis–Rostow lower limit of 5 per cent in 1950. Since then most developing economies have succeeded in increasing investment to levels comparable in percentage terms to those of the rich countries. By 1981, the average investment rate in developing countries was higher than in OECD countries. After the 1982 debt crisis, investment rates in six of the seven Latin American and eight of the ten African countries declined sharply. The investment rates in many Asian countries continued to increase, reaching peak levels in the early 1990s (an average of 27.6 per cent of GDP in 1990). By 2000, after the Asian crisis, investment levels had declined somewhat. Average investment levels in OECD and developing countries were at similar levels.

The data in Table 3.3 can be interpreted in two ways. First, it seems clear from a comparison of Table 3.1 and Table 3.3 that, on average, high rates of investment and capital accumulation are associated with rapid economic growth since 1950. Capital is an important source of growth. Yet the causal relationship between investment and growth is not unambiguous. Differences in growth performance between individual countries are not directly related to

Table 3.3 *Gross domestic investment as percentage of GDP (at current market prices)*

	1950	1973	1981	1990	2000
Bangladesh	5.5	12.9	23.5	18.5	23.0
China	10.4[a]	29.4	32.5	34.7	38.0
India	9.9	18.2	23.8	25.2	25.0
Indonesia	11.5	20.8	26.7	30.8	18.0
Malaysia	0	25.5	35.0	33.6	26.0
Pakistan	5.5	12.9	18.8	15.6	15.0
Philippines	15.0	21.8	27.5	24.2	20.0
South Korea	5.7	25.4	29.4	36.9	31.0
Sri Lanka	11.8	13.7	27.8	22.2	27.0
Taiwan	14.5[b]	29.1	29.9	23.1	22.9
Thailand	11.8	27.0	29.7	41.4	22.0
Turkey	11.3	14.7	17.9	24.3	24.0
Argentina	13.3	20.9	22.7	14.0	16.0
Brazil	12.3	23.2	23.1	20.2	23.0
Chile	8.0	10.5	22.7	25.1	22.0
Colombia	16.9	18.3	20.6	18.5	20.0
Mexico	14.1	20.0	27.5	23.1	23.0
Peru	17.1	20.3	34.3	21.1	22.0
Venezuela		31.0	24.4	10.2	14.0
Congo, Dem. Rep.		16.8	10.5	9.0	22.0
Côte d'Ivoire		23.2	25.9	6.7	19.0
Egypt	11.8	13.1	29.5	28.8	24.0
Ghana	15.1	9.0	4.6	14.4	31.0
Kenya		25.8	27.7	24.3	12.0
Morocco		16.9	26.1	25.2	25.0
Nigeria	7.2	22.4	23.3	14.7	22.0
South Africa		27.7	34.2	17.1	15.0
Tanzania		21.4	24.6	22.6	17.0
Zambia		28.9	19.3	17.3	18.0
Average Asian countries	10.3	20.9	26.9	27.6	24.3
Average Latin American countries	15.6	20.6	25.0	18.1	20.0
Average African countries	17.5	20.5	22.6	17.4	20.5
Average developing countries	13.8	20.7	24.9	21.8	22.0
Average 16 OECD countries	21.6	27.2	23.0	23.6	21.2

Notes:
[a] 1952;
[b] 1951.
Sources: 1950: Maddison (1989), table 6.6, except for Egypt, Ghana, Nigeria and Turkey: World Bank, *World Tables 1980*. 1973–90: World Bank, *World Development Indicators*, CD-Rom, 1999, except for Tanzania, 1973–81: *World Tables 1995* and DGBAS, *National Statistics of Taiwan*, republic of China (http://www.stat.gov.tw/main.htm). 2000: from *World Development Report*, 2002.

differences in investment efforts. Similar investment rates can result in very different growth outcomes. Some countries use investments much more effectively and productively than others. Wasteful investment in prestige projects, for instance, results in high investment rates but low growth. The African economies provide ample illustration of the combination of rather high investment rates and low or even negative growth. The 'capacity to absorb investment' is of the greatest importance for the contribution of investment to economic development (Myint, 1980). This capacity depends on a variety of complementary economic, political, cultural and institutional factors.

3.6.3   Export performance

Tables 3.4 and 3.5 give a picture of export performance in developing countries. In Table 3.4 the characteristics of the main phases are clearly distinguishable. Exports were growing at just below five per cent per year from 1900 to 1913. Between 1913 and 1950 growth rates slumped, especially in Asian countries heavily involved in world trade. In four Asian countries export growth was even negative. Between 1950 and 1973 exports from OECD countries grew at 8.6 per cent per year. Average export performance in the developing countries was also higher than in the pre-1913 period, though lower than in the OECD countries. After the 1973 oil crisis, export growth from OECD countries slowed

Table 3.4 *Export performance, 1870–1998*[a] *annual average growth rates (%)*

	1870–1913	1900–13	1913–50	1950–73	1973–98[c]
Bangladesh	2.4	4.2	−1.5	2.0	9.3
China	2.6	4.7	1.1	2.7	11.8
India	2.4	4.2	−1.5	2.5	5.9
Indonesia	4.2	4.0	2.3	6.5	7.3
Malaysia					
Pakistan	2.4	4.2	−1.5	3.6	7.5
Philippines	2.8	2.8	3.7	5.9	9.0
South Korea		8.0	−1.1	20.3	13.9
Sri Lanka					
Taiwan		7.4	2.6	16.3	12.1
Thailand	4.1	5.0	2.3	4.4	11.7
Turkey					
Argentina	5.2	4.2	0.2	3.1	7.1
Brazil	1.9	0.4[b]	1.7	4.7	6.6
Chile	3.4	3.8	1.3	2.6	9.2
Colombia	2.0	7.8	3.9	3.8	5.9
Mexico	5.4	4.6	−0.5	4.3	10.9
Peru	1.7	6.7	2.9	5.8	1.5
Venezuela			5.4	4.0	0.9
Congo, Dem. Rep.					−0.3
Côte d'Ivoire					5.6
Egypt					6.3
Ghana			3.1	2.8	0.4
Morocco					2.7
Kenya					4.7
Nigeria				7.4	1.8
South Africa					2.4
Tanzania				6.3	
Zambia					−0.2
Average Asian countries	3.0	4.9	0.7	7.1	9.8
Average Latin American countries	3.3	4.6	2.1	4.0	6.0
Average African countries				5.5	2.3
Average developing countries	3.1	4.8	1.4	5.7	5.9
Average 16 OECD countries	3.9	4.8	1.1	8.6	5.0

Notes:
[a] Merchandise exports in constant 1990 dollars, except Africa, 1973–97 total exports in 1995 dollars;
[b] 1901–13;
[c] African countries 1973–97 instead of 1973–98.
Sources: Unless otherwise indicated, Maddison (2001); 1900–13 from Maddison (1989) table 6.1; Ghana 1913–50, data made available personally by Maddison; Ghana, Nigeria and Tanzania, 1950–73, World Bank, *World Tables 1980*; Africa, 1993–7, from World Bank, *World Development Indicators* (1999).

Table 3.5 *Manufactured exports as percentage of total merchandise exports*

	1953	1990	2000
Bangladesh	1	77	91
China		72	88
India	48	71	76
Indonesia	0	35	54
Malaysia		54	80
Pakistan	1	79	84
Philippines	8	38	41
Sri Lanka		54	75
South Korea	0	94	91
Taiwan	6	93	95
Thailand	2	63	74
Turkey	1	68	78
Argentina	10	29	32
Brazil	2	52	54
Chile	2	11	17
Colombia	1	25	31
Mexico	8	43	85
Peru	3	18	21
Venezuela	0[a]	10	12
Congo, Dem. Rep.			
Côte d'Ivoire	1[a]		
Egypt	4	42	37
Ghana	10[a]	8	20
Kenya	12[b]	29	23
Morocco		52	49
Nigeria	3[a]	1	1
South Africa			55
Tanzania	13[a]		16
Zambia			
Average Asian countries	7	67	77
Average Latin American countries	4	27	36
Average African countries	7	26	29
Average developing countries	6	47	53
Average 16 OECD countries		72	75

Notes: [a] 1960; [b] 1961.
Sources: 1953: Maddison (1989); Egypt and Turkey derived from Maddison (1970); Venezuela, Côte d'Ivoire, Ghana, Kenya, Nigeria and Tanzania from World Bank, *World Development Report 1983*. 1990: World Bank, *World Development Indicators 2001*; 2000: World Bank, *World Development Report 2002*.

down. The growth of exports from developing countries was somewhat higher than from OECD countries. Asian countries showed exceptionally high growth rates, while exports from African countries grew more slowly. In Nigeria and Zambia the growth rate of exports was close to zero.

Table 3.5 effectively demolishes the stereotype of developing countries as exporters of primary agricultural or mining products. This stereotype derives from the colonial division of labour in the world economy in the period 1870–1913, but is no longer relevant for large parts of the developing world. From 1953 to 2000 the average share of manufactured exports in total merchandise exports increased from 6 per cent to 53 per cent. In Asian developing countries the increase is even more dramatic, from 7 per cent to 77 per cent. This share exceeds that of OECD economies.

3.6.4   External finance: does money flow from poor to rich countries?

Theories of underdevelopment and dependence suggest that there is a permanent drain of resources from poor countries to rich. This net outflow of resources reduces the possibilities for domestic investment, capital accumulation and growth and keeps poor countries poor and dependent. Table 3.6 provides some empirical information about the role of foreign finance in developing countries.

Table 3.6 *External finance as percentage of GDP, 1950–2000 (at current market prices)*

	1950–73	1974–81	1982–90	1991–97	1998–2000
Bangladesh	2.5	6.6	7.9	5.8	5.5
China	0.2[a]	−0.1	0.4	−1.7	−2.5
India	1.8	1.2	2.7	2.5	3.5
Indonesia	3.1[b]	−6.0	−2.3	−1.3	−8.0
Malaysia	−4.1[d]	−3.8	−3.5	0.8	−18.5
Pakistan	4.4	9.2	8.3	3.6	4.5
Philippines	2.1	3.3	1.4	7.1	0.5
South Korea	8.4	5.2	−2.5	1.4	−5.0
Sri Lanka	3.1	7.8	11.4	9.6	7.5
Taiwan	3.1[c]	−0.6	−11.0	−2.4	−2.1
Thailand	1.8	4.4	2.7	4.3	−10.0
Turkey	1.9[d]	4.8	2.7	3.8	5.5
Argentina	0.6	−1.0	−3.5	0.9	1.0
Brazil	1.3	2.2	−3.1	0.2	1.5
Chile	1.3	2.4	−2.5	−0.3	−1.5
Colombia	2.0	−1.1	−1.9	1.0	0.0
Mexico	1.9	2.2	−4.2	1.7	1.5
Peru	2.6	3.0	−0.3	3.3	2.0
Venezuela	−8.6[d]	−3.7	−5.7	−5.9	−9.0
Congo, Dem. Rep.	1.8[d]	2.7	0.5	−1.9	
Côte d'Ivoire	−7.9[d]	−0.5	−5.5	−5.6	−6.0
Egypt	4.0	14.1	12.9	4.9	7.5
Ghana	0.9	0.2	4.3	11.4	16.0
Kenya	0.0[d]	4.9	3.3	1.6	8.0
Morocco	1.4[d]	11.6	7.2	5.4	5.0
Nigeria	4.5[d]	−1.2	−2.2	−5.0	−2.0
South Africa	−2.6[d]	−3.1	−5.4	−2.5	−2.5
Tanzania	3.3[d]	9.4	14.6	24.6[c]	15.0
Zambia	−12.9[d]	0.3	0.5	6.0	19.0
Average Asian countries	2.4	2.7	1.5	2.8	−1.6
Average Latin American countries	0.2	0.6	−3.0	0.1	−0.6
Average African countries	−0.8	3.8	3.0	3.9	6.0
Average developing countries	0.7	2.6	0.9	2.5	1.3

Notes:
[a] 1953–73; [b] 1966–73; [c] 1951–73; [d] 1960–1973; [e] 1990–96.
Sources: 'External finance' is the resource balance (net balance of all exports and imports of goods and non-factor services) divided by GDP, with sign reversed. 1950–81: Maddison (1989), table 6.7 except for countries denoted by footnote d. The data for these countries and data 1981–1997 from World Bank, *World Development Indicators* (1999) (CD-Rom). 1999: from World Bank, *World Development Indicators* (2001), 2000: from World Bank, *World Development Report, 2002*; Tanzania 1960–86, from Tanzania national accounts; Taiwan after 1982 from: DGBAS, National Statistics of Taiwan, http://www.stat.gov.tw/radin.htm

At the beginning of the twentieth century, a typical colony would normally export primary products. It would export more than it imported. The surplus on the trade balance would be compensated by an outflow of profits, interest payments, salaries of colonial officials, gold and reserves to banks in the colonial mother country. This drain limited developing country growth potential, as suggested by dependency theories.

Compared to the pre-war period, one of the salient characteristics of the international economic order since 1950 is that financial flows have been reversed. In most countries and most periods, a net influx of financial capital compensated for deficits in the trade balances and the current account balances. Developing economies were able to import more consumer goods, capital goods and intermediate goods than they could have financed from their export revenues. The capital flows consisted of commercial loans, direct investment, portfolio investment and development aid. Net capital inflows served to finance imports. A part of the net inflow was used to service dividend and interest payments on earlier loans and investments.

Together with imports and exports of goods and services and transfer payments, dividends and interest payments figure on the current account of the balance of payments. Deficits or surpluses on the current account are balanced by capital flows on the capital account or changes in the gold and foreign currency reserves of a country.

In principle, it is more advantageous for a developing country to use net capital inflows to finance imports of goods, especially capital goods, than for the payment of dividends and interest. But dividend and interest payments should not be exclusively interpreted as a detrimental drain of resources. If investments and loans make a positive contribution to the productive potential of a country, then factor payments represent payments for the productive services of foreign capital. Less favourable is the case in which loans have been used for purely consumptive purposes, while new inflows of capital are required to service the debts. Then a country can get caught up in an increasing spiral of indebtedness, without any improvement of its productive potential.

Table 3.6 offers a rough picture of the importance of external finance in developing countries. External finance is defined here as the net balance of exports and imports of goods and non-factor services, with the sign reversed.[12] This concept shows to what extent inflows of capital allowed developing countries to import more goods and services than they were exporting.[13] Between 1950 and 1981 there was an unmistakable net inflow of capital in developing economies, averaging between 0.7 and 2.6 per cent of GDP.[14] This inflow is

---

12 This concept is referred to in World Bank, *World Tables* as resource balance. Factor services refer to the services of the production factors of labour and capital. They include wages for workers working outside their own country, dividends, profits and interest payments.

13 An alternative concept is external finance as the net balance of the current account of the balance of payments with the sign reversed. This concept includes among others payments for factor services. In Table 3.6 the data for 1950–66 from Maddison (1989) refer to this concept of external finance. After 1966 they refer to the resource balance concept.

14 The only exceptions were some typical primary export countries such as Zambia, with a surplus on their balance of payments owing to exports of products such as copper.

inconsistent with underdevelopment theories, which assume that there is a permanent outflow of capital from poor to rich countries.

The debt crisis of 1982 caused the inflow of capital to stagnate, in particular the inflow of private capital. After 1982 an increasing number of developing countries were faced with net outflows of capital, creating the paradoxical situation that poor countries were financing rich ones. The net outflow of capital is most marked in Latin American countries, between 1982 and 1990. The country average for all developing countries in Table 3.6 is still positive in this period, but the inflow of capital is lower than earlier in the post-war period. Outflows from Taiwan and South Korea can be interpreted in a more positive sense. They represent repayment of past debts or new foreign direct investment by rapidly growing economies which have attained surpluses on the balance of payments through export success.

The figures for the period 1991–7 illustrate a resumption of capital flows into most developing countries. But the impact of the Asian financial crisis of 1997 is clearly visible in the most recent figures. For instance there are massive outflows of capital in the hard-hit Asian economies of Indonesia, Malaysia, South Korea and Thailand.

Table 3.7 presents data on the total value of foreign capital in developing countries derived from Maddison (2001). Between 1870 and 1914 investment in developing countries increased rapidly, as foreign direct investment developed harbours, roads and infrastructure to exploit the possibilities of primary exports. The real value of foreign capital in this period increased almost sixfold. After 1914 there was a decline in the stock of foreign capital in developing countries as the world economy slowed down. In real terms the value of capital in 1950 was only 62 per cent of that in 1914. As a proportion of GDP it was down to half its 1870 level. After 1950 we see an explosive increase in the value of foreign capital from 63.2 billion dollars in 1950 to 3,031 billion dollars in 1998.

Table 3.7 *Gross value of foreign capital in developing countries, 1870–1998 ($bn)*

	1870	1914	1950	1973	1998
Total in current prices	4.1	19.2	11.9	172	3,590.2
Total in 1990 prices	40.1	235.4	63.2	495.2	3,030.7
Stock as percentage of Developing Country GDP	8.6	32.4	4.4	10.9	21.7

Note: The gross value of foreign capital refers to foreign direct investment, loans and portfolio equity. GDP at constant 1990 international dollars.
Sources: Maddison (2001), table 3.3.

How to interpret these figures? It is clear that in the long run the stock of foreign capital has increased, indicating net inflows of capital. This contradicts the predictions of dependency theory. However, a negative interpretation of these trends is that the value of foreign capital is a measure of the degree of foreign domination of the economies of developing countries. This domination is increasing. There is an element of truth in this interpretation, especially when domestic economic and political structures are weak and governments are unable to bargain with powerful multinational firms. However, by the same criterion, many European advanced economies are also dominated by foreign capital.

From our macro-perspective the figures can be given a much more positive interpretation. A net inflow of foreign capital provides a positive impulse to the economic development of a country. An inflow of foreign capital can contribute to rapid growth and economic dynamism. Periods when the inflow of capital stagnates, such as the period 1914–50, are usually periods of weak growth performance. Rapid growth in the booming economies in Southeast Asia goes hand in hand with massive foreign investment, which transfers much needed capital, technology and know-how to the receiving economy.[15] Of course, the impact of foreign capital and foreign firms in developing countries needs to be studied in more detail. A positive evaluation of foreign investment does not mean that developing countries should not set conditions for the operation of multinational firms and foreign investors in the domestic economies. The Asian crisis has made us more conscious of the potential drawbacks of extreme openness to foreign capital. This debate will be taken up once more in Chapter 13.

3.6.5   Are developing countries capable of structural change?

Nobel Prize-winner Simon Kuznets has emphasised that modern economic development implies changes in the structure of the economy. In the process of *structural change*, the importance of the agrarian sector declines, while that of the industrial sector increases. The industrial sector offers more scope for accumulation of capital per worker and technological change. Productivity per worker in industry is much higher than in traditional agriculture. Therefore structural change is one of the major forces contributing to productivity growth and economic dynamics in development. At a later stage of development the service sector overtakes the industrial sector and becomes the most important sector in terms of its share in employment and production.

There is an ongoing debate about productivity growth in the service sector. Baumol (1986) suggests that in many service sectors opportunities for productivity growth are constrained, owing to the personal and inherently labour-intensive nature of many services (haircuts, restaurants, tourism, medical services, counselling). Therefore, productivity growth will slow down as the service sector increases in size. However, the service sector is an extremely heterogeneous sector. Some subsectors such as financial services or transport do exhibit substantial technological change and productivity growth.

---

15 South Korea is an interesting exception. Until recently domestic investment predominated.

Table 3.8 presents information on changes in the structure of employment between 1950 and 2000, Table 3.9 on changes in the structure of production between 1950 and 2000. Both tables show that there have been major structural changes in developing countries. The share of agriculture in both employment and value added declined between 1950 and 2000. The shares of industry and services increased. As labour productivity in industry is higher than in agriculture, the share of industry in production is always higher than its share in employment. High labour productivity is one of the reasons why the modern industrial sector in developing countries is unable to provide a rapidly growing population with sufficient employment. This is one of the crucial differences between industrialisation processes in the nineteenth-century and present-day processes of industrialisation.

Table 3.8 illustrates the changes in the structure of employment. The share of agriculture decreased from 64 to 42 per cent between 1950 and 2000s. Nevertheless, agriculture was still by far the largest sector in terms of employment. The share of agriculture was more than ten times as high as that in the OECD countries, indicating that there is still enormous scope for further structural change in developing economies. In countries such as Bangladesh, India, Ghana, Côte d'Ivoire, Kenya, Tanzania, and the Democratic Republic of Congo agrarian employment even accounted for more than 60 per cent of total employment. On average, the share of agriculture in total employment in Latin American countries (22 per cent) was much lower than in the densely populated Asian countries (on average 40 per cent) and the African countries (on average 57 per cent).

For the structure of production, Table 3.9 shows that the share of agriculture in total GDP in developing countries declined from 38 per cent around 1950 to 18 per cent in 2000. Compared to the OECD countries, however, the share of agriculture in developing economies is still nine times as high. The share of industry showed a dramatic increase. In 2000 this share exceeded that of the OECD countries.

It is striking how important the service sector has become in developing countries. Even in the 1950s, services were the largest sectors in terms of value added. Developing countries have not followed the classical sequence of shifts from agriculture to industry, followed by later shifts from industry to services. Rather the service sector developed parallel to the industrial sector, as the shares of agriculture declined. By 2000 the service sector accounted for more than half of total value added and 38 per cent of total employment.

In part the rapid growth of the service sector can be explained by the expansion of the government sector in developing countries. At present there is a lively debate about whether the size and rather low productivity of the government sector in developing countries have become an obstacle to continued economic development.

Table 3.8 *Structure of employment by sector, 1950–2000 (%)*

	1950–1960[a]			1990–2000[b]		
	Agriculture	Industry	Services	Agriculture	Industry	Services
Bangladesh	77	7	16	63	10	25
China	77	7	16	48	22	13
India	72	10	18	67	13	20
Indonesia	75	8	17	45	16	20
Malaysia	63	12	25	18	32	50
Pakistan	77	7	16	47	17	36
Philippines	71	9	20	39	16	45
South Korea	73	3	24	11	28	61
Sri Lanka	56	14	30	42	23	33
Taiwan	57	16	27	10	29	62
Thailand	82	3	15	49	18	33
Turkey	77	8	15	46	21	34
Argentina	25	31	44	12	32	56
Brazil	60	18	22	23	20	57
Chile	36	30	34	14	26	60
Colombia	57	18	25	34	24	42
Mexico	61	17	22	21	25	53
Peru	58	20	22	40	18	42
Venezuela				11	24	65
Congo, Dem. Rep.				68	13	19
Côte d'Ivoire				65	8	27
Egypt	64	12	24	30	22	48
Ghana	62	15	23	62	10	28
Kenya				81	7	12
Morocco				45		
Nigeria				45	7	48
South Africa				14		
Tanzania				84	4	12
Zambia				75	8	17
Average Asia	71	9	20	40	20	36
Average Latin America	50	22	28	22	24	54
Average Africa				57	10	26
Average developing countries	64	13	23	42	18	38
Average 16 OECD countries	25	36	39	4	26	70

Notes:
[a] 1950 except Egypt, South Korea, 1951, China, 1952, Indonesia, Malaysia, and Ghana, 1960.
[b] Data for years between 1995–2000 except Argentina, Colombia, Peru, Ghana, Côte d'Ivoire, Kenya, Morocco, Congo, and Zambia, 1990 Tanzania, 1991 and Nigeria, 1986.
* 'Agriculture' includes agriculture, forestry and fisheries; 'Industry' includes mining, manufacturing, construction, gas, water and electricity. 'Services' include wholesale and retail trading, trade, transport and communication, financial and business services, and community and personal services.
Sources: 1950: Maddison (1989), table C-11 except for Ghana and Egypt from: Mitchell (1982) and Turkey: Maddison (1986). Data for 1990–2000: primarily from ILO (2002), except Argentina, Colombia, Peru, Côte d'Ivoire, Kenya and Nigeria from World Bank, *World Development Report 1995*. Morocco and South Africa: from *World Development Indicators* 1999, CD-Rom.

Table 3.9 *Structure of production, 1950–2000 (value added in agriculture, industry and services as percentage of GDP)*

	1950–60[a]			2000[b]		
	Agriculture	Industry	Services	Agriculture	Industry	Services
Bangladesh	51	21	28	26	25	49
China	39	38	23	16	49	34
India	51	21	28	27	27	46
Indonesia	59	12	29	17	47	36
Malaysia	37	18	45	12	40	48
Pakistan	51	21	28	26	23	50
Philippines	26	28	46	17	30	53
South Korea	46	15	39	5	44	51
Sri Lanka	46	12	42	21	27	52
Taiwan	32	21	46	4	39	57
Thailand	40	19	41	10	40	49
Turkey	46	15	39	16	25	59
Argentina	14	36	50	5	28	68
Brazil	23	30	47	9	32	59
Chile	15	23	62	8	34	57
Colombia	38	22	40	15	29	56
Mexico	20	30	50	4	28	67
Peru	35	23	41	8	38	55
Venezuela	6	43	51	5	47	47
Egypt	30	24	46	17	33	50
Ghana	41	10	49	35	8	56
Côte d'Ivoire	43	14	42	28	29	43
Morocco	69	10	21	13	33	54
Kenya	40	20	40	23	16	60
Nigeria	66	6	27	39	33	28
South Africa	12	40	48	3	31	66
Tanzania	57	11	32	45	15	40
Congo, Dem. Rep.	35	29	36	58	17	25
Zambia				24	25	51
Average Asia	44	20	36	16	35	49
Average Latin America	22	30	49	8	34	58
Average Africa	44	18	38	29	24	47
Average devel. countries	38	22	40	18	31	51
Average 16 OECD countries	15	41	44	2	27	71

Notes:
[a] Data for 1950 except Taiwan, 1951, South Korea and Kenya 1955, Philippines, Thailand, Venezuela, Egypt, Ghana, Côte d'Ivoire, Kenya and Tanzania, 1960, China and Indonesia, 1965, Morocco, 1966.
[b] 2000 except Dem. Rep. Congo, 1999 and Taiwan 1993.
Sources: 1950–60. Unless otherwise specified developing countries from World Bank, *World Tables*, 1980. Taiwan: DGBAS (1994), China 1965: World Bank, *World Development Report 1989*; OECD countries 1950: Maddison (1989); 2000: from World Bank, *World Development Report* (2002), except Congo from World Bank, *World Development Indicators 2001*.

3.6.6   How unequal is the income distribution?

There is widespread consensus that inequality tends to increase in the course of economic development. As discussed in section 3.4, Kuznets has argued that income inequality will tend to increase in the course of industrialisation but then tends to decrease as societies become more prosperous and more modern. This is referred to as the *inverted U-curve of inequality* hypothesis (see Szirmai,

1986: ch. 2). Most economic theories of backwardness emphasise the positive economic functions of inequality, in line with Keynesian economic theories. As the poor consume most of their incomes, while rich people can save part of their income, increasing inequality will increase aggregate savings (see Thirlwall, 1997: ch. 12). Higher saving rates contribute to growth of per capita incomes and, in the longer run, to a reduction of poverty. As income per capita increases, the bargaining power of the poorer sections of the population will increase and income inequality will start to decline. Cross-country research on the relationship between levels of income per capita and the degree of inequality tends to support this hypothesis (Bacha, 1979; Deininger and Squire, 1996), but time series analysis is less conclusive (Deininger and Squire, 1998; Thorbecke and Charumilind, 2002).[16]

Radical and underdevelopment theorists agree that income inequality is increasing, but evaluate this much more negatively. They do not believe that inequality will necessarily lead to higher savings and more growth. They even argue that a combination of increasing average incomes and increasing inequality can lead to impoverishment of the bottom 40 per cent of the population.

The answers to these questions are ultimately empirical rather than ideological and may differ from country to country and region to region. We will return to this debate in subsequent chapters, arguing that on average there is strong evidence that growth of per capita incomes tends to reduce poverty. However, distributional policies can be very important. Similar levels of income per capita can coexist with very different degrees of inequality, poverty and immiseration.

Table 3.10 presents some rough empirical information on income inequality, primarily based on primary household survey data. The table presents information on the Gini index (an index running from zero for complete equality to one for complete inequality),[17] the share in income or consumption of the bottom 40 per cent and the share of the top 10 per cent of the population.

The table provides ample evidence of the high degree of inequality in present-day developing countries. On average, the bottom 40 per cent of the population has less than 16 per cent of total income, while the top 10 per cent has about 35 per cent. The degree of inequality in developing countries is much higher than in the rich OECD countries, which is consistent with the Kuznets hypothesis. Inequality is by far the highest in Latin America, whether measured by the Gini index or by income shares. For our twenty-nine sample countries, the correlation coefficient between income per capita in 2000 and percentage of population earning less than one dollar a day is −0.50.[18] This provides an

---

16 See also F.H.G. Ferreira, 'Inequality and Economic Performance: A Brief Overview to Theories of Growth and Distribution', World Bank Website on Inequality, Poverty and Socio-Economic Performance, http://www.worldbank.org/poverty/inequal/index.htm (accessed 19 June 1999).

17 The Gini index is defined as half of the sum of all possible differences between the incomes of units, divided by the mean income (μ) times the square of the number of units (n^2):

$$G = (\sum_{i=i}^{n} \sum_{j-1}^{n} |y_i - y_j|/(2n^2\mu)$$

18 Income per capita from Table 3.1, percentage of population earning less than $1 a day from World Bank, *World Development Indicators, 2001*, table 2.6.

Table 3.10 *Distribution of income or consumption, 1980–2000*

	1980–90			1990–2000		
	Gini index	bottom 40%	top 10%	Gini index	bottom 40%	top 10%
Bangladesh	25.9	24.0	21.9	33.6	20.7	28.6
China				40.3	16.1	30.4
India	32.1	21.0	26.4	37.8	19.7	33.5
Indonesia				31.7	21.5	26.7
Malaysia				49.2	12.5	38.4
Pakistan	33.4	20.6	27.8	31.2	22.4	27.6
Philippines	41.0	16.6	32.7	46.2	14.2	36.6
South Korea				31.6	20.4	24.3
Sri Lanka	32.5	20.7	26.4	34.4	19.8	28.0
Taiwan	27.7			32.6	20.3	
Thailand	45.2	15.0	35.5	41.4	16.2	32.4
Turkey	43.6	15.7	35.3	41.5	16.0	32.3
Argentina						
Brazil	59.5	8.2	47.3	59.1	8.3	46.7
Chile	56.4	10.0	45.7	57.5	9.7	46.9
Colombia	53.1	10.5	41.2	57.1	9.6	46.1
Mexico	55.1	10.2	44.0	51.9	11.6	41.1
Peru	45.7	14.0	35.5	46.2	13.5	35.4
Venezuela	55.6	9.6	43.5	48.8	12.4	37.6
Congo, Dem. Rep.						
Côte d'Ivoire	41.2	15.8	31.4	36.7	18.3	28.8
Egypt				28.9	23.0	25.0
Ghana	35.4	18.7	27.3	39.6	16.3	29.5
Kenya				44.5	14.7	34.9
Nigeria	38.7	16.4	28.2	50.6	12.6	40.8
Morocco	39.2	17.7	31.8	39.5	17.1	30.9
South Africa				59.3	8.4	45.9
Tanzania				38.2	17.8	30.1
Zambia				52.6	10.9	41.0
Averages						
Asian	42.3	15.6	34.2	42.2	16.1	34.0
Latin American	54.2	10.4	42.9	53.4	10.9	42.3
African	38.6	17.1	29.7	42.2	15.8	33.0
Developing	42.3	15.6	34.2	43.0	15.7	34.6
16 OECD				30.0	21.4	23.6

Sources: 1990–2000: *World Development Indicators 2001*, table 2.8: except for Taiwan: *DG-BAS, National Statistics of Taiwan, the Republic of China* (http://www129.tpg.gov.tw/mbas/doc4/89/book/77.xls); 1980–90: World Bank, *Global Poverty Monitoring website* (http://www.worldbank.org/research/povmonitor/index.htm), except for Taiwan, op cit. The data refer either to inequality of personal income or of consumption. For each period the latest year available has been included in the table. Note that distributional data are notoriously difficult to compare across countries or over time. The Gini index has been multiplied by 100.

indication of the inverse relationship between level of income and poverty on one hand. It also confirms the importance of distributions for poverty, as much of the variation in poverty remains unexplained by average income levels.

Table 3.10 shows no conclusive evidence of increasing inequality in developing countries in the short period covered in the table. The average Gini index for all countries increased marginally from 0.423 in 1980–90 to 0.430 in 1990–2000. It should be noted, however, that distribution data are notoriously difficult to compare across countries and even more so over time. One needs to be very careful in drawing conclusions. Country studies for large countries such as China, Indonesia and India do point to rapidly increasing inequality in recent years.

Questions for review

1. Compare the internal and external explanations of development and stagnation. Is the use of the term 'less developed' associated with internal or external explanations of the situation of development?
2. What are the main elements of classical liberal explanations of growth and development?
3. How do economic theories of imperialism explain economic stagnation in developing countries?
4. Discuss the concept of dualism. Why is dualism an obstacle to development?
5. Which stages of economic growth are distinguished by Rostow and what are their main characteristics?
6. What are the potential advantages of backwardness?
7. How do North and Thomas define efficient institutions? Give examples of institutions which are considered to be efficient.
8. Discuss the characteristics of dependent development, as emphasised by dependency theorists.
9. Discuss André Gunder Frank's criticism of the use of the concept of 'traditional society' in theories of modernisation.
10. Why do neoclassical theories of growth predict convergence of levels of income per capita and why do new growth theories predict divergence of levels of income per capita?
11. What are the main phases of development since 1870 and what are the most important characteristics of the different phases?
12. How do structuralist explanations of development differ from those of liberal and neoclassical theories?

Further reading

One of the most important sources for the empirical study of long-run comparative development is the recent monumental study by Angus Maddison, *The World Economy: A Millennial Perspective* (2001) and its sequel *The World Economy, Historical Statistics* (2003). Other useful sources include, the website of the Groningen Growth and Development Centre (http://www.ggdc.net/) and the website of the Penn World Tables http://www.bized.ac.uk/dataserv/penndata/pennhome.htm. An indispensible source for the comparative study of development is the CD-Rom, *World Development Indicators*, published annually by the world bank. The latest edition of this CD-Rom was published in 2004 (World Bank, 2004). *World Development Indicators* contains time series for around 575 social and economic indicators for 225 countries for the period since 1960. It synthesises data from a variety of international publications such as the annual *World Development Reports*, the *Human Development Reports* and *World Tables*, a publication which was discontinued after 1995.

The literature on development theories is almost impossible to summarise. We selectively mention a few of the older and newer studies which have been consulted in writing this chapter. Everyone interested in development theory can still profit from reading Arthur Lewis's *Theory of Economic Growth* (1950) and his pathbreaking article 'Economic Development with Unlimited Supplies of Labour' (1954). The starting point for the modern debates on multi-sector models lies with Fei and Ranis's book, *Development of the Labour Surplus Economy* (1964). Key publications for modernisation theory and underdevelopment theory respectively are Rostow's, *Stages of Economic Growth* (1960) and André Gunder Frank's *Capitalism and Underdevelopment in Latin America* (1969). For structuralism and unequal exchange an early UN paper entitled *The Economic Development of Latin America and its Principal Problems* by Raúl Prebisch has been very influential (1950). A more recent discussion of structuralism and neostructuralism is found in Sunkel's *Development from Within: Toward a Neostructuralist Approach for Latin America* (1993).

For the potential advantages of backwardness, the work of Gerschenkron and Abramovitz remains as relevant as ever. Useful books are Gerschenkron's *Economic Backwardness in Historical Perspective* (1962), Abramowitz's *Thinking about Growth and Other Essays on Economic Growth and Welfare* (1989a). For evolutionary theory the classic study is Nelson and Winter's *An Evolutionary Theory of Economic Change* (1982). The role of institutions is emphasised in major studies by North and Thomas, *The Rise of the Western World* (1973), North's *Institutions, Institutional Change and Economic Performance* (1990) and Gunnar Myrdal, *Asian Drama* (1968).

Overviews of theories of economic development theory are also found in a variety of recent textbooks, of which we mention Debraj Ray's *Development Economics* (1998), which has a micro-focus on the imperfect functioning of markets in developing countries owing to institutional constraints, Thirlwall's excellent textbook on *Growth and Development* (2003), which has a macro-perspective, and Hunt's overview of development theories in *Economic Theories of Development* (1989). New developments are touched upon in an interesting collection edited by Meier and Stiglitz, *Frontiers of Development Economics: The Future in Perspective* (2000). A delightful older textbook is Hla Myint's *The Economics of the Developing Countries* (1980).

4

Technology and development

In the previous chapter, we discussed a range of development theories. Technological change was identified as one of the important sources of growth and development. This chapter singles out technological change as one of the key issues in the study of development. Two main questions will be raised: (a) to what extent is technological change really one of the driving forces in growth and development? (b) What are the consequences of accelerating global technological change for developing countries? Does technological change constitute a threat to their chances for development? Does technological change offer new opportunities for development?

4.1   The role of technology

Technology refers to the state of knowledge about how to do things, in particular how to produce valued goods and services for the satisfaction of human needs (Evenson and Westphal, 1995). Without offering a formal definition, one may say that technology stands halfway between science (abstract knowledge about the fundamental laws and regularities of the physical environment) and techniques (specific applications of technology in products or processes, singular ways of doing particular things). Prior to the twentieth century many technological advances were not based on scientific knowledge, but on practical experience, on the job tinkering and experimentation. Today more and more technology is science based.

In Chapter 1, we argued that while development is a much broader concept than economic development, growth of income per capita was one of the core dimensions of development. Economic growth refers to increases in the productive capacity of a society. Productive capacity is a potential. It can be wasted for destructive purposes or for conspicuous consumption of elites. It can also be used to improve a broad range of living conditions of the masses of people living in poverty in developing countries. It is one of the necessary conditions for wider socio-economic development.

The concept of productive capacity indicates that socio-economic development is closely connected with technological change. In this sense, technological change is a driving force in development and has been so since the dawn of humanity (see Boserup, 1981; Lapperre, 1992). At the same time it is misleading to see technology as an exogenous force. The term *driving force* suggests technological determinism: technology comes from outside and drives us inexorably in certain directions. Though consistent with the ways in which most people experience technological change, this perspective is incorrect. Technological change is the result of focused human efforts in research laboratories, scientific institutes, small and large firms or inventors' backyards. Societies, organisations and individuals invest in knowledge, schooling and research, just as they invest in physical capital goods. Thus, technological change is driven by human actions and choices. It is not an external phenomenon, which develops in complete autonomy. Whenever we say that technological change is uncontrollable and inevitable, this is just another way of saying that many outcomes of human actions and choices in general are relatively autonomous and hard to control. Technological change is no different from other spheres of human behaviour.

4.2   The technology race

As briefly sketched in Chapter 2, a technological breakthrough occurred in Western Europe after the fifteenth century. This breakthrough resulted in an historically unique process of internal growth and external political, economic and cultural expansion (e.g. Landes, 1998). The European expansion resulted in the formation of an interdependent world economy, characterised by competition between technological leaders and technological followers. This competition involved both dynamic challenges and the creation of new opportunities and a simultaneous increase in global disparities.

The increase of global inequality between rich and poor economies should not be seen as a static process. Technological leadership successively shifted from China to Southern Europe, the Dutch Republic, Great Britain and subsequently to the USA. Since the end of the nineteenth century, dynamic processes of catch-up have taken place in countries such as Japan, Germany, Russia and its successor the Soviet Union, South Korea and Taiwan. Relatively advanced countries or political units such as Argentina, the Ottoman empire and the constituent parts of the former Soviet Union declined. The boundaries between richer and poorer countries are continuously shifting.

Since World War II, the United States has been the undisputable world technological leader. Till the middle of the 1970s, Western Europe and Japan were engaged in a process of catch-up. Large countries in Latin America experienced some catch-up till around 1979, followed by ten years of stagnation during the 'lost decade' following the 1982 debt crisis. Asian NICs such as South Korea, Taiwan, Singapore and Hong Kong developed at breakneck speed. Second-tier Asian NICs such as Indonesia, Thailand, Malaysia and the Philippines grew rapidly prior to the financial crisis of 1997. China forms a case apart. This enormous country has experienced very rapid growth since the liberalisations of 1978, both in agriculture and industry. The other Asian giant, India, showed sluggish growth for a long time. It lagged behind the Asian tigers. But in the 1990s it started liberalising and growth started accelerating. African countries have shown long-run stagnation, since the oil crisis of 1973, even though the initial levels of income around 1950 were very similar to those of the Asian economies (Lal and Myint, 1996). The Soviet Union experienced growth up to 1973. After that stagnation set in. After the collapse of communism in 1989, most former Soviet republics have become caught up in a dramatic process of economic and technological decline, with an accompanying deterioration of social indicators such as health and life expectancy.[1]

Figure 4.1 provides an illustration of the technology race in manufacturing. It presents real output per worker in six Asian and two African economies relative to the United States. The figure shows clear indications of catch-up in Korea and Taiwan. It reveals the acceleration of productivity growth in China, India and Indonesia in the 1990s and shows the deterioration of productivity performance in the two African economies. It is interesting to note that productivity levels in the 1990s were higher in the African economies than in Asia. After 1973, however, productivity levels in Africa showed spectacular long-run decline both in absolute and in relative terms (see Szirmai *et al.*, 2001). Productivity levels in the poor Asian economies kept pace with the USA during most of the period – productivity growth without catch-up – and only started to catch up in the 1990s. The performance of Japan and Australia is rather interesting.

---

[1] The recent history of the Russian Federation and other former Soviet republics provides one of the most powerful examples of the strong correlations between growth and social indicators.

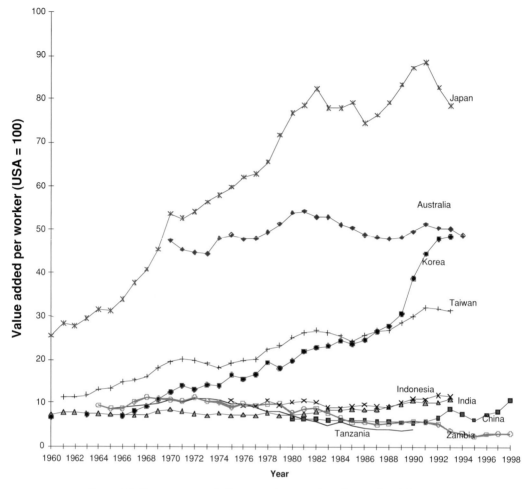

Figure 4.1 Convergence and divergence in manufacturing productivity, 1960–1998.
Sources: Japan, Korea, Taiwan, Indonesia, India and China: Timmer (2000); Australia: Timmer and Szirmai (1997); Tanzania: Szirmai *et al.* (2001).

Japan is one of the famous examples of catch-up in modern economic history but this process came to an end around 1990, when the US economy started forging ahead again, while Japan got caught up in a slump from which it has still not recovered at the time of writing. Australia provides an example of an advanced economy, where the size of the technology gap neither increases nor decreases for quite a long period, because productivity is growing at the same rate as that of the lead country.[2]

---

2 It is sometimes argued that the national state is increasingly losing its relevance as the main unit of analysis. Transnational regions and clusters and groupings of countries are becoming more important. However, Kuznets (1966) and Abramovitz (1989) have made a convincing case for the continued importance of the national setting in studying differences in economic performance.

4.3   Technological change and increases in productive capacity

In the previous section, the technology race was discussed in terms of comparative productivity trends. This perspective on technology will be further elaborated in this section.

To provide for their daily needs, humans need to transform natural resources into goods and services. Labour, capital goods and land – the primary inputs – are used to transform raw materials and semi-fabricated goods – the intermediary inputs – into outputs. The transformation process makes use of the technologies available at a given point in time in given societies. The level of technological capacity of a society is ultimately expressed in the labour productivity per hour worked.

Together with average hours worked per person per year (H/L) and the share of the actually working population in total population (L/P), labour productivity determines gross domestic product per capita as follows:

$$\frac{GDP}{P} = \frac{GDP}{H} \times \frac{H}{L} \times \frac{L}{P}$$

As the equation indicates, productive capacity (and potential welfare) can be increased by working more hours per person, by increasing the proportion of the population that is actively employed or by increasing productivity per hour. In the long run the last factor is the most important, especially as the need for leisure time tends to increase as countries become more prosperous.

GDP per hour is the broadest measure of technological performance.[3] In the remote past and in traditional agriculture, labour is the only factor of production and output per hour is very low. In the broadest sense of the word, technological change has to do with increasing the productive capacity of unskilled, raw labour power. This can be done through the use of simple implements, or complex machines and capital goods, through education and training, through improved production processes, through research and development, through changes in knowledge, information and know-how, through new methods of organisation and the development of new products. Differences in labour productivity are an indication of the size of the technology gap between advanced and developing economies.

4.3.1   *How to increase labour productivity?*

Labour productivity is a crude and summary measure of technological performance. For instance, it makes no difference between the development and implementation of new technological knowledge and the more extensive use

---

3 GDP per hour data are not always available. Therefore, as a first step we frequently use GDP per person engaged as a proxy (see Figure 4.1).

of already existing technologies – more of the same machines or implements per worker. For a better understanding of the role of technological change in development, we try to break down the sources of labour productivity growth into different components. Several of these have already been mentioned in the theoretical overview presented in Chapter 3. They are summarised in Box 4.1.

Box 4.1   Sources of increase in labour productivity

- *Capital accumulation*. Labour productivity is increased by adding implements, machines and capital goods. The amount of capital per worker – capital intensity – increases.
- *Increased scale of production*. Large-scale production of standardised products is usually more productive than small-scale production. Such scale effects can be more easily realised in industry than in spatially dispersed agriculture. This is why industrialisation is important in development.
- *Accumulation of human capital*. Human capital theory suggests that schooling and education makes workers more productive. Accumulation of human capital may take place through formal schooling, but also through on-the-job training, learning by doing and by using new technologies.
- *Increased efficiency*. Increased efficiency covers a wide range of factors such as higher capacity utilisation, better use of technologies, appropriate combinations of labour and capital and other inputs (economic efficiency) and international specialisation according to comparative advantage. Structural change is also an aspect of increased efficiency. Structural change involves shifting resources from sectors with lower productivity to sectors with higher productivity such as manufacturing. One can distinguish micro-economic efficiency (*X-efficiency*), which involves producing more output with given inputs or *allocative efficiency* through better allocation of resources across the economy (specialisation and structural change).
- *Changes in the organisation of production*. This aspect of X-efficiency improvement deserves separate attention. It involves aspects such as the division of labour, flexible production systems, systems of motivation, monitoring systems and changes in the logistic organisation of production.
- *Technological change proper*. Advances in our technological knowledge concerning products and production processes. This involves the development of new production processes, new types of machinery, new forms of organisation, use of new inputs, new products and services, new ways of distributing products and services, new knowledge that can be transferred through education.

Growth accountants try to quantify the impact of different sources of growth. This is of vital importance for our empirical understanding of development (Maddison, 1987; Nadiri, 1972; Pilat, 1994). However, it is also important to realise that many of the sources of productivity growth are complementary and interact with each other in a wider process of technological change, which operates through each of the components (Abramovitz, 1989; Nelson, 1996; Pack and Paxson, 2001).

The factors mentioned in Figure 4.1 contribute to our understanding of the gaps between advanced and developing economies. Thus, we know that the amount of physical capital per worker in developing countries is much lower than in advanced economies. In Chapter 7, we shall show that the amount of schooling per person in developing countries is lower than in advanced economies.

With regard to efficiency, two issues are of special interest. In the first, place owing to a variety of institutional, educational and infrastructural factors, the technical efficiency of production in developing countries is lower than in advanced economies. Even the same machinery, operated with a similar number of workers, will deliver a lower output (Pack, 1987).

A second issue is that of the choice of technology (e.g. Pack, 1987; Stewart, 1972; 1974; 1987). It has often been argued that developing countries with an abundance of cheap labour should choose more labour-intensive technologies. Capital-intensive technologies developed in the advanced economy may not be appropriate to conditions in developing countries and may need to be adapted. Also, it may be easier to transfer mature well-developed technologies to developing countries, rather than the most advanced generations of state-of-the-art technology.

In the long run, however, the key question is whether developing countries can participate in global processes of technological change and close the technological gaps relative to the advanced economies. This involves learning mechanisms which will allow developing countries to move up the technological ladder over time.

4.3.2 Investing in technological change

Just as one can invest in physical capital goods, one can invest in knowledge and technology through Research and Development (R&D). Investments in knowledge, however, have some special characteristics. It is easy to own physical machines and to exclude others from access to these machines in order to appropriate the fruits of investment. It is less easy to appropriate the results of investments in knowledge, even though inventors and investors try to do so through patents, trademarks, secrecy and other strategies. Knowledge is non-rival: use by one person does not diminish the possibilities of use by other people. Knowledge is non-excludable: it is hard to prevent others from using knowledge. Once there, knowledge has a tendency to diffuse or spread ('spillovers'). Other countries, firms and individuals can make use of new knowledge and technology without having to pay for the complete costs of its development. This is what Gerschenkron called the potential 'advantages of backwardness'. Under certain conditions, developing countries can profit from technological investments in the lead countries, without bearing the risks of research and development. Given the right conditions, such technology transfers can result in explosive growth. Examples of catch-up based on such processes in the second half of the twentieth century are provided by Western Europe, Japan and the Asian NICs.

4.3.3 Diffusion of technology and technological and social capabilities

Technological changes seldom occur in isolation. They are interrelated and of a systemic nature (Hughes, 1983; Rosenberg, 1982). Technologies such as steam power, the internal combustion engine, electrification, plastics or information and communication technologies are embedded in far larger systems of complementary technologies, social conditions and infrastructures. Transfer of technology to developing economies frequently fails because the relationships between new technologies and the wider environment in which they are to function are neglected. Technologies have to be appropriate to new settings in the sense that they make use of existing factor proportions (availability of labour, skills, capital or natural resources), market conditions, available infrastructure and climatic conditions. Several authors, using a variety of different terms, have tried to capture this systemic nature of technological change.

Moses Abramovitz has argued that much of modern technology was developed in the context of standardised mass markets in the United States. It cannot automatically be transferred elsewhere where markets are smaller and more fragmented. Abramovitz calls this lack of *technological congruence*.

If problems of technological congruence can be overcome, technological backwardness offers potential advantages and opportunities for accelerated growth (see section 4.4.2). But whether these advantages can be realised depends on what Abramovitz has called the *social capabilities* of a national society (Abramovitz, 1989). Social capability refers to the use a country can make of advanced technology and its capacity to acquire it in the first place. The opportunities offered by technological backwardness can be offset by lack of sufficient social capabilities. Social capability refers to the technical competence of a country's people, indicated by levels of general education and the share of population with training in technical subjects. It also includes the managerial experience of large-scale production, an overlay of supporting legal, financial and commercial services and with availability of adequate infrastructure.

Development economists have formulated a related but somewhat more narrowly defined concept of *technological capabilities* (Lall, 1987; 1992; for an overview see Romijn, 1999). The term 'technological capabilities' refers to the capability to select and acquire appropriate new technologies and capital goods (investment capability), the capability to operate new capital goods (production capability), the capability to adapt and further develop technologies (innovation capabilities). Technological capabilities operate at the micro-level of firms (Biggs *et al.*, 1995), but also at the level of national societies (van Egmond, 2000). The notion of capabilities at a national level has been further developed in the national systems of innovation literature (Freeman, 1987; Lundvall, 1992;

Nelson, 1993). This literature focuses not only on the total levels of techno-logical and educational investment and infrastructure, but also more specifi-cally on creative interactions and networks between innovative actors such as firms, universities, research institutes and governmental organisations. From the macro-perspective, one of the reasons international technology transfer has had disappointing results is because the national systems of innovation of many developing countries are weakly developed.

One of the challenges for development theory is to synthesise the historically oriented literature on social capabilities with the more strictly technologically focused literature on technological capabilities and national innovation sys-tems. Further discussion of technological capabilities and national innovation systems is to be found in sections 4.6.2 and 4.6.3.

An important lesson to be derived from the technological capability literature is that acquisition of technology is neither easy nor free of cost, as suggested by older neoclassical theories of growth. Acquisition of existing technology requires considerable skills, effort and capabilities. The adaptation of interna-tional technology to local conditions requires efforts and capabilities. These capabilities themselves have to develop or be developed through education, training, experience and investment in human capital (see Chapter 7).

In developing countries with fairly well developed social and technological capabilities, there are ample opportunities for catch-up. If such capabilities are weak, then technological gaps will tend to increase and countries will fall behind. The international technology race is thus characterised by two contra-dictory tendencies. On the one hand, lead countries have the most developed technological capabilities and are best placed to profit from new technologi-cal developments. On the other hand, follower countries with adequate and improving capabilities can profit from transfer and acquisition of technolo-gies developed elsewhere and can experience explosive growth. As Abramovitz has emphasised, growth and catch-up themselves can contribute to improving social capabilities in a virtuous circle, which can result in very rapid growth.

4.3.4   *Technology, productivity and competitiveness*

In the modern world economic competitiveness depends more and more on technology and innovation. On the one hand, technological advances in pro-cess technologies contribute immediately to increases in productivity. Along with costs, quality, reliability, speed of delivery and flexibility, productivity is one of the determinants of competitiveness. On the other hand, modern firms in the world economy increasingly compete through innovation itself. Compet-itiveness depends on a continuous flow of new products and services and the emergence of new production processes (James, 2002).

Since the rise of large research laboratories and research and development de-partments in the second half of the nineteenth century, organised research and development has become more and more important as a source of technological change. Knowledge has become one of the important factors of production. This makes it more difficult for latecomers to compete on product markets. Acceleration of technological change in the advanced economies means that developing countries have to grow more rapidly if they are not to fall further behind. For developing countries rapid technological change means that they are shooting at a moving target.

Simultaneously the world economy is becoming more and more interdependent. Between 1960 and 1995 international trade (as the sum of exports and imports) increased from 24 to 42 per cent of world gross domestic product. Multinational enterprises account for one third of global trade (UNDP, 2001). There is a growth of international investment flows, migration flows, tourism and last but not least information flows. Increasing interdependence implies that developing countries are more and more influenced by international technological trends. Even in traditional labour-intensive sectors such as textiles or footwear, developing countries are now faced by technological advances in the advanced economies (Cooper, 2001). At the same time, technologically driven reorganisation of production creates new possibilities for locating part of global production chains in developing countries.

4.4   Economic theories about the role of technological change

Many of the theories of development discussed in Chapter 3, implicitly or explicitly, deal with the role of technological change. Here we zoom in on the role of technology in some of these theories.

4.4.1   Solow

In the 1950s researchers discovered that accumulation of physical and human capital explained less than 50 percent of economic growth in the USA. Robert Solow formulated the famous neoclassical economic model of growth in which, besides labour and capital, technological change turned out to be the driving force in growth (Solow, 1957). In this model technological change was exogenous. Technological change was freely available to any country in the world economy, also for developing countries. Solow assumed perfect information, so that every economy was faced with the same rate of technological change. As mentioned in Chapter 3, his theory – incorrectly – predicted global convergence between advanced and developing economies. He argued that advanced economies had much more capital per worker than developing economies, but that the marginal productivity of capital was higher in developing economies, because they had so little of it. This would make for a flow of investment to developing countries and for accelerated growth. Later criticisms of Solow's theory focused on the exogenous and unexplained nature of technological change, the assumption of perfect information and free availability of technological knowledge.

4.4.2   *Advantages of backwardness*

The economic historian Alexander Gerschenkron formulated his theories about the advantages of backwardness on the basis of the explosive growth of the latecomer countries Russia and Japan since the last quarter of the nineteenth century (Gerschenkron, 1962). These countries were able to profit from copying and taking over technologies developed elsewhere, without bearing the full cost of their development.

To some extent, Gerschenkron makes assumptions similar to those of Solow, namely that technology and knowledge are freely available. However, as an historian, he pays much more attention to the conditions under which certain countries can profit from diffusion of technology. Diffusion is certainly not automatic as in the Solow model. It depends on changes in the social structure and modernisation of society and calls for a greater role of governments and large financial institutions in mobilising resources.

Gerschenkron's theories bear some interesting resemblances to earlier writings of Torstein Veblen on the rise of imperial Germany (1915) and the theories of the Dutch Marxist historian Jan Romein (1937). Romein and Veblen called attention to potential dangers and disadvantages of technological leadership. Lead countries may have invested too heavily in given technologies and their surrounding infrastructure and may be unable to move to new generations of technology. In modern theorising this is referred to as '*technological lock in*'. The loss of technological leadership of the UK since the end of the nineteenth century is explained in these terms.

The combination of the advantages of backwardness and the penalties of leadership can result in rapid catch-up. However, Gerschenkron does not suggest any tendency to global convergence. Rather, he highlights the possibilities of rapid catch-up in individual developing countries.

4.4.3   *Endogenous and evolutionary growth theories*

Of the theories discussed in Chapter 3, both new or endogenous growth theories and evolutionary growth theories focus explicitly on the role of technology in growth. New growth theories pay special attention to investments in knowledge, R&D technology and schooling. The close interactions between capital accumulation and technology, and the positive effects of technology spillovers from firms generating new technologies to other firms, counteract the neoclassical tendency towards diminishing returns to given factors of production. The more advanced an economy is, the better placed are its enterprises to profit from spillovers. Firms in developing economies are not so well prepared to profit from spillovers. Therefore lead countries will tend to extend their lead, while developing countries will fall behind. This theory is consistent with global divergence, but is unable to explain why some developing countries can buck the trend and start catching up.

Evolutionary theories of growth try to combine the contradictory forces of increasing returns in lead countries and the advantages of backwardness. Technologies are primarily developed in the advanced economies and specifically in the lead countries amongst the advanced economies. But technologies can diffuse from lead countries to follower countries and even to developing economies. Whether convergence or divergence takes place depends on the balance between the generation of new technology and increasing returns in lead countries on the one hand and diffusion of technology and spillovers to follower countries on the other (Verspagen, 1993). The outcome of this process is not given in advance. However, the larger the technology gap between leader and follower, the more difficult technology diffusion will become. Beyond some threshold levels, gaps will tend to increase. Developments in Sub-Saharan Africa would seem to illustrate this tendency (see also James, 2002).

An important difference between new growth theory and evolutionary theory is that evolutionary theories also allow room for the penalties of leadership. Technological change is characterised by extreme uncertainties. Once a lead economy has made a choice for a certain technological trajectory, it can get locked into it. When external circumstances change, and new techno-economic paradigms emerge (Freeman and Perez, 1988), they may find it difficult or impossible to profit from them. Follower countries, which have invested less in former generations of technology, may suddenly be better placed to profit from new developments. Thus, there is nothing inevitable about falling behind. Changes in external circumstances and the emergence of new technological paradigms can lead to rather sudden changes in patterns of divergence and convergence, stagnation or catch-up. One of the ongoing changes is the improvement of global communication systems, which can facilitate the international transfer of technology and lower international transaction costs. James (2002) argues that while the changing division of labour in the nineteenth century was driven by changes in transport technologies and transport costs, present-day changes are driven by changes in communication technology and reduction of transaction costs.

One of the interesting similarities between evolutionary and new growth theories is the emphasis on technological effort and learning (see Verspagen, 2001). Technology does not develop automatically or exogenously as in the earlier neoclassical theories. It depends on deliberate efforts, investments in science, R&D, education and training by firms, governments and universities.

4.5   Consequences of the acceleration of technological development for developing countries

4.5.1   *Acceleration of global technological change*

The rate of technological change is increasing very rapidly. For instance the global number of patent applications increased from 1.4 million to 2 million in the four years between 1989 and 1993 (World Bank, 1999). Table 4.1 shows the acceleration of patent applications in the lead country, the USA, since 1870.[4] Since 1870 the number of patents granted in the USA has increased fifteenfold, since 1973, it has increased by a factor 2.5. For the 1990s, the table also documents the marginal role of the developing world in global technological change. Excluding the major innovator amongst the developing countries, South Korea, the share of developing country patents in total patents granted in the USA does not exceed 0.8 per cent. There is a veritable explosion of technological change in information and communication technologies (ICT). These in turn spill over to a great variety of production technologies, through automation, robotisation and computerisation. They also result in rapid changes in the service and communication sectors, including the rise of the World Wide Web. They allow for global dispersal and integration of production activities

Table 4.1 *US patent activity, 1870–2001*

Year	Patent applications	Patents granted	Foreign patents	Developing country patents	Developing countries excl. S.Korea
			Share of patents granted (%)		
1870	19,171	12,157			
1900	39,673	24,656			
1913	68,117	33,915			
1950	67,264	43,039			
1973	103,695	74,139			
1990		99,220	46.6	1.5	0.5
1991		106,842	45.9	1.7	0.5
1992		107,511	45.3	1.8	0.4
1993		109,890	44.3	2.2	0.5
1994		113,704	43.4	2.5	0.5
1995		113,955	43.4	2.8	0.5
1996		121,805	43.0	3.1	0.5
1997		124,146	43.7	3.8	0.6
1998		163,209	44.4	4.7	0.6
1999		169,146	44.4	5.0	0.6
2000		176,084	44.9	4.8	0.7
2001		184,051	46.4	5.2	0.8

Sources: 1870–1973: US Department of Commerce/Patent and Trademark Office (1977), table AI. 1990 and following: United States Patent and Trademark Office (2002).

---

4 As all important innovations tend to be patented in the US, the US data provide an indication of trends in world technological advance. Figures on the number of world patents can be misleading. Important innovations are patented in many countries, resulting in double counting.

by multinational corporations. They create global information networks that increase global interdependence in terms of trade, investment and cultural exchanges (Castells, 2000).

Another area of rapidly accelerating technological change is that of biotechnology with applications in the spheres of health, reproductive practices, agricultural production and food processing. These changes have wide-ranging impacts not only on production, but also on human reproduction and human living conditions.

In the OECD countries the importance of high-tech sectors is rapidly increasing (World Bank, 1999: p. 23). These sectors account for an increasing portion of productivity growth.[5] In some Asian economies such as Malaysia, the ICT sectors have also been important sources of growth and catch-up. Product cycles and time to market become shorter and shorter through a continuous flow of innovations. Production systems become more flexible and have to react very quickly to changes in and diversity of consumer preferences.

4.5.2   Knowledge gaps

In the world economy there is great inequality in technological efforts. An overwhelming proportion of scientific, research and development activities takes place in the advanced economies. Almost all patent applications are concentrated in these countries. The same holds for scientific publications. Large multinational companies take the lead in innovation. Thus the fifty largest multinationals alone account for 26 per cent of all patents in the United States. According to estimates by the World Health Organization, 95 per cent of all medical research focuses on the health problems of the advanced countries (World Bank, 1999).

Developing countries invest a much lower part of GDP in research and development (around 0.5%) than the advanced countries (around 2.0 to 2.5 per cent). Table 4.2 provides some information about R&D efforts of developing countries in the 1990s. This table shows that the technological gaps in terms of R&D per head of population are even greater than in terms of R&D percentages.

The nature of R&D efforts is also very different. Much of R&D in developed countries is directed at technological breakthroughs. R&D in developing countries is more defensive in nature. It functions as an investment in order to keep up with developments elsewhere. In the poorest developing countries the quality of R&D efforts leaves much to be desired (see Bongenaars and Szirmai, 2001). Table 4.3 provides some rough information about differences in technological level in the field of information and communication technologies.

---

5 Mysteriously enough, productivity growth in sectors of manufacturing other than electronics and information and communication technology has slowed down. This is an example of the famous productivity paradox: accelerating technological change, but slower productivity growth (see Tables 3.1 and 3.2)

Table 4.2 *R&D efforts, 1987–97*

	R&D as % of GDP 1987–97[a]	R&D per capita PPP internat. $ 1987–97	Scientists and engineers per 100,000 1987–97
Bangladesh	0.3	2.9	52
China	0.5	13.0	454
India	0.8	9.9	149
Indonesia	0.1	2.8	182
Malaysia	0.3	18.0	93
Pakistan	1.1	9.6	72
Philippines	0.2	6.2	157
South Korea	2.9	285.0	2,193
Sri Lanka	0.2	1.8	191
Taiwan	2.1		544
Thailand	0.1	8.4	103
Turkey	0.4	21.6	291
Argentina	0.4	33.9	660
Brazil	0.7	34.9	168
Chile	0.7	74.9	445
Colombia	0.1	3.7	37
Mexico	0.3	23.4	214
Peru	0.6	24.2	233
Venezuela	0.5	41.2	209
Egypt	0.5	11.1	459
Nigeria	0.1	0.6	15
South Africa	0.7	43.1	1,031
Average Asian countries	0.8	31.6	328.1
Average Latin American countries	0.5	33.7	280.9
Average developing countries	0.6	30.5	336.7
Average OECD countries[a]	2.1	438.2	2,912

Note:
[a] The R&D data from UNESCO are more inclusive than R&D data from the OECD source.
Sources: R&D expenditures for developing countries from UNESCO (1999). GDP and PPP converters from WDI, CD-Rom (1999). Both R&D and R&D as percentage of GDP in OECD (1998). Population from sources mentioned in Table 5.2. Scientists and engineers: from UNDP (2001), except Taiwan: from DGBAS (2002). Data for developing countries refer to the latest year between 1987 and 1997, except Taiwan, 2000, Sri Lanka, 1984, Colombia, 1982. Data for OECD refer to 1995.

Table 4.3 *ICT indicators*

	Telephone mainlines per 1,000 people	Personal computers per 1,000 people	Internet users per 1,000 people
	1995	1995	1996
LICs	25.7	1.6	0.01
LMICs	94.5	10	0.7
UMICs	130.1	24.2	3.5
NIEs	448.4	114.8	12.9
HIEs	546.1	199.3	111

Source: World Development Report, 1999, table 4.2.

4.5.3 *New opportunities offered by technological development*

Rapid technological change offers new opportunities for development. In the area of health, advances in medical technology such as vaccines and antibiotics have contributed to an unprecedentedly rapid decline in death rates and improvements in life expectancy in developing countries (see Chapter 6), irrespective of per capita income.[6] Advances in reproductive technology offer families new opportunities for realising their preferred family size and offer countries new opportunities for birth control and limiting the rate of population growth.

Breakthroughs in agrarian technologies have led to impressive productivity improvements in agriculture and reductions in undernutrition (see Chapter 10). Through technological breakthroughs in plant breeding, fertilisers and pesticides, world cereal yields have doubled since the 1960s.

Information technologies have enhanced the ability of multinational companies (MNCs) to coordinate cross-border activities. Thus, information and communication technologies create new possibilities for relocating parts of global production chains to developing countries, to profit from abundant labour. Surprisingly they also allow multinational companies to decentralise research and development activities, in order to profit from the availability of relatively cheap highly skilled labour in developing countries such as India, Brazil or Korea (James, 2002).

In the field of education, ICT offers new developments in distance learning and multimedia technologies. The declining costs of communication lower the thresholds for diffusion of scientific, technical and statistical information, especially in countries such as India and China, but also in Sub-Saharan Africa. In this respect, ICT technologies contribute to a reduction of international technology and knowledge gaps.

Some technological developments offer possibilities of leapfrogging. For example, mobile telephony can compensate for inadequate fixed communication infrastructure in Tanzania. In India wireless technologies have been developed to connect rural uses with switch exchanges at low costs, thus opening up rural areas. Some developing countries have been able to install new digital telephone networks, where advanced countries have invested heavily in older analogous technologies. India and Brazil have developed new low-cost computers costing 200-400 dollars, with associated savings in software (James, 2002). In developing countries, access to use of ICT facilities is more important than ownership. New institutional arrangements result in rapid improvements in access. For instance, Dar-es-Salaam now has more than fifty internet cafés.

4.5.4   New threats

If a country is unable to keep up in the technology race and is unable to profit from technology transfers, it is threatened with increasing marginalisation in the world economy. The larger the initial knowledge gap, the less adapted or congruent technologies will be to local needs and competences. This makes it ever more difficult to start bridging the gap. This further erodes the capacity to

---

6 The AIDS epidemic in Africa and Asia is now impacting negatively on these positive trends.

compete on international markets and reduces the attractiveness of a country for foreign direct investment.

Another threat is that technology transfer – in so far as it takes place – may lead to increased inequality within developing countries, between groups with access to new technology and groups without access. These problems have been noted in agriculture and in the area of access to communication technologies.

4.6 International technology transfer and technology diffusion

Technological advance in developing countries can take place in two ways: through investments in new technology or through copying new technology. Most R&D takes place in the advanced economies. This R&D results in innovations and in advances at the frontiers of technological knowledge. For most developing countries copying and adapting internationally available technologies is the only realistic path towards technological advance.[7] It should be emphasised, however, that such copying is a form of innovative behaviour that requires considerable efforts on the part of countries, firms and individuals (Evenson and Westphal, 1995). A second point that needs to be made is that international technology transfer has to be complemented by domestic technology diffusion. If new technologies remain completely locked in enclaves of multinational firms and do not diffuse through the economy, the impact of technology transfer will remain limited.

Firms in developing countries can make use of a wide range of channels for international technology transfer. These are summarised in Box 4.2.

Box 4.2 Mechanisms of technology transfer
- Acquisition of technology licences.
- Technology transfer as part of a package of FDI or joint ventures.
- Reverse engineering. Acquisition of technology through imports of new products, which are copied through reverse engineering.
- Competing on export markets. Competing on international export markets and having to meet international quality standards has important learning effects.
- Original equipment manufacturing: producing for foreign firms, according to specifications supplied by these firms.
- Acquisition of technological know-how through the hiring of expatriate experts.
- Sending own personnel abroad for training and schooling. This was the path followed by Japan at the beginning of the twentieth century.

Whether each of these mechanisms actually contributes to reducing international technology gaps depends on a variety of supporting factors. Thus,

---

7 Important exceptions are countries like Brazil, China, India, South Korea and South Africa which engage in innovative R&D activities. As countries develop they can gradually shift their R&D efforts into more innovative channels.

if sending personnel abroad for training and schooling leads to a brain drain because there are no adequate employment prospects, as in many African countries, then efforts to reduce the technology gap will be frustrated. When foreign owners of technology maintain complete control over the technology and prohibit its spread into the domestic economy, the impact of technology transfer will be limited. On the other hand, many developing countries have made very effective and successful use of these transfer mechanisms in the past (Lall, 2000). Examples include Japan, Korea, Taiwan, India and Western Europe. Technology acquisition can lead to explosive growth.

As discussed previously, the success of technology transfer depends both on the conditions under which it is supplied and on the characteristics and policies of the receiving countries, such as education levels, infrastructure, political stability, capabilities of using new technologies and the size of the technology gaps.

In the next paragraphs we discuss some further aspects of diffusion of technology and technology transfer.

4.6.1   Intellectual property rights

Knowledge, technology and information are public goods. They are non-rival and non-excludable. Once knowledge exists, it is difficult to prohibit its use by others. In a market economy, this reduces the incentive for firms and individuals to investment in the development of new knowledge. Throughout economic history, protection of intellectual property rights has proved to be one of the engines of technological change and economic growth. Instruments such as patents allow inventors and investors to profit from the efforts to generate new knowledge and technology.

Protection of intellectual property rights, however, has the potentially negative effect of restricting access to knowledge and slowing down the diffusion of technology. Owners of technology can prohibit the use of technology by others or charge prohibitive fees for its use. In this respect, developing countries are in a potentially vulnerable situation. A second potential disadvantage is that firms and commercial organisations will tend to underinvest in areas where the private returns are less than the social returns. Examples of underinvestment are to be found in the field of research on AIDS, malaria and global warming. Sick people in developing countries cannot afford expensive medicines so that pharmaceutical industries will gear the research to markets in the advanced economies. There has been insufficient investment in agricultural research for semi-arid agriculture in Sub-Saharan Africa. Where there is underinvestment in socially important areas of knowledge and technological change, there is a special task for public support by governments and international organisations.

In recent years the World Trade Organization and international agreements such as the TRIPS agreement have moved towards strengthening the protection of international property rights. There is an ongoing debate on the advantages and disadvantages of such moves (Verspagen 1999). It is important to emphasise that there are not only disadvantages for developing countries. Increasing protection of intellectual property rights can result in increased foreign direct investment and accompanying inflows of technology. Firms will not be willing to risk their advanced technological knowledge base in developing countries without adequate protection. Also a strong case can be made for more effective protection of domestic knowledge (e.g. natural medicines, domestic plant and seed varieties, domestic cultural goods). At present, there is an acute danger of multinational enterprises patenting domestic sources of knowledge and technology such as herbs used in traditional medicines, or local gene varieties, which can only be countered by strengthening the protection of intellectual property rights of the developing countries. Finally, better protection can provide incentives for more research and development efforts in developing countries.

4.6.2   *Technological capabilities*

As emphasised in section 4.3.2, technology transfer requires considerable effort. It does not take place automatically. For instance, it is not enough to import advanced machinery. Much of technological knowledge is implicit and tacit. It exists in the minds of users, and is not captured adequately in blueprints or handbooks. Many of the disappointing effects of development projects in the past stem from disregard of this basic fact.

The success of technology transfer depends among others on technical congruence and technological capabilities. Technological congruence, or technological distance, refers to the degree to which foreign technologies are adapted to conditions in the receiving countries. One can think of differences in the physical environment (temperature, humidity, precipitation, dust, available resources such as water, sunlight, fertile soils, and so forth), the availability of complementary schooling and skills, the organisation of local production, local market size and market conditions. Many modern technologies are tailored to mass markets, which do not always exist in smaller low-income economies.

Technological capabilities include skills, experiences, attitudes and schooling. Technological capabilities are necessary to select and acquire the adequate technologies, to adapt them to local circumstances, to operate them and to develop them further. In cases of successful development, there is a gradual shift from adaptation of imported technology to indigenous development of technology. Japan, Taiwan and Korea are the most well known examples in this respect.

In the capability literature learning is one of the key issues. Learning can be seen as an effort to improve capabilities. Learning refers to formal schooling and professional training on the one hand, and to on-the-job training, experience and internal training on the other hand. Learning by doing (producing capital goods) and learning by using (using capital goods in production) are extremely important (Tunzelmann, 1995). Such learning will not take place if there is no parallel inflow of new capital goods and technologies. This is why investment in human capital alone will have disappointing results (see

Chapter 7). Education and schooling primarily work when they are complementary to technological change.

4.6.3   National innovation systems

Whether a country is able to participate in the technology race depends in part on the characteristics of national systems of innovations. Authors such as Lundvall (1992) and Nelson (1993) have emphasised that the innovativeness of an economy does not simply depend on the sum of innovative actions by separate actors, but also on their interrelationships. For innovation, firms depend not only on their own efforts, but also on their abilities to profit from resources and efforts of other actors: suppliers, competitors, customers, research institutes, government organisation, and so forth. Innovative countries are characterised not only by the volume of their research and development efforts and human capital, but also by strong interrelationships between firms, private and public research institutions, fundamental and applied researchers, and governments. These networks promote the flow of knowledge and diffusion of technology within an economy and contribute to the production of new knowledge.

In spite of all advances in communication, technology flows also have a strongly localised nature (Caniëls, 2000). Technology diffusion within an economy operates more effectively in localised clusters, where people can experience face-to-face interaction and transfer the tacit elements of technology, which are not captured in blueprints and manuals or embodied in machinery.

Many developing countries have made serious efforts to improve their systems of innovation by investing in higher education, research institutes and networks of research and development institutes. However, the diffusion of technology from these systems to the wider economy remains limited.

In Tanzania, for example, a whole set of research and development institutes was set up in order to promote innovation in various sectors of the economy. A detailed study of a research and development institute focusing on industry (Bongenaar and Szirmai, 2001) concluded that some degree of success had been achieved in acquiring, adapting and developing useful small-scale technologies. However, it turned out there was not a single case of successful technology transfer to any enterprise in a period of twenty years. All attention of the institute was focused on generating technology. Little or no attention was paid to early contacts with potential users, needs assessments or market research, which feed into the research effort and increase the chances of successful technology diffusion. Unfortunately, this linear approach is not a-typical for developing countries in general. Rosenberg has emphasised that successful innovation requires combining technical and economic factors and technology push and market pull (Rosenberg, 1990).

In the following two sections, we will discuss the impact of recent developments in biotechnology and information and communication technology in developing countries (see UNDP, 2001).

4.7   Biotechnology

Biotechnological research has contributed to very substantial increases in land productivity in developing countries. Without these increases global food production would not have been able to keep up with global population growth (see Chapter 10). Nevertheless, one always has to ask who profits from technological change. In developing countries, the so-called green revolution has sometimes led to increasing rural inequality. Internationally, technological development has made farmers more dependent on biotechnological multinational enterprises. Intellectual protection of new seed varieties prohibits farmers and peasants from using their own seed. They are required to buy their seed from multinational companies. Sometimes seeds are even genetically manipulated in such a way that they do not produce seed for next year.

We already mentioned the tendency of patenting and appropriating indigenous plant varieties for medicinal purposes by multinational enterprises from the advanced economies. According to the 1989/99 *World Development Report* (World Bank, 1999), 43 billion dollars' worth of medicines are sold annually which are based on plant varieties indigenous to developing countries.

Commercial incentives in agrarian research have resulted in underinvestment in agrarian technologies for semi-arid agriculture in Africa. Here there is an urgent need for new agricultural green revolutions. Realising such breakthroughs requires public investment in research and development, as has been done in the past for rice and wheat.

In the field of medical technology there are similar problems. Quite modest investments can result in radical improvements in health conditions. Think of vaccinations against child diseases, oral rehydration packages for diarrhoea, investments in hygiene and clean water, education about the importance of hygiene.

One of the shortcomings of international research efforts is lack of sufficient research on diseases such as AIDS in their African and Asian context, malaria and river blindness. There is no effective market demand for medicines, because people simply can not afford to pay for them. Here lies a real challenge for guiding international research efforts into socially desirable directions.

4.8   Information and communication technology

The rapid evolution of information and communication technology provides the most telling example of both the opportunities and the challenges of technological change for development (see James 2002; UNDP, 2001).

Thus, new developments in telecommunications provide possibilities for improving both access to and the quality of education. Through distance learning large groups of people can be reached who till now had no access to education. Distance learning is suitable both for school children and for adult education. It is relatively cheap. An example of successful distance learning is provided by the Monterrey Institute of Technology in Mexico. This virtual university has 9,000 students studying for a university degree and 35,000 students enrolled for shorter courses. Other countries investing in distance education include Indonesia and South Africa. Especially where population is geographically dispersed, distance learning can be an excellent solution. The development of the internet improves access to knowledge in developing countries and facilitates international knowledge diffusion and transfer.

Jeffrey James has recently made an interesting analysis of the possibilities and challenges of ICT technology (James, 1999; 2002). His conclusion is in line with the discussion in this chapter that global technological developments lead either to further integration of developing countries into the world economy or to further marginalisation or even exclusion. On the one hand, information and communication technologies lead to geographically dispersed chains of production, both within multinational corporations and in the form of strategic alliances between corporations, including corporations in developing countries (Duijsters and Hagedoorn, 2000). This offers new opportunities for developing countries. On the other hand, countries with insufficient technological capabilities will not be included in and profit from these global production chains. They will be further marginalised.

James distinguishes four categories of developing countries which have profited from technological developments in information and communication technologies: first-generation NICs such as Korea or Taiwan, second-generation NICs such as Malaysia and the Philippines; large developing countries such as India and Brazil with a well-developed scientific and technological infrastructure; and countries localised close to large developed-country markets such as Mexico.

James makes a systematic analysis of the mechanisms through which technology affects developing countries. Negative factors include: an abundance of small-scale enterprises in rural areas; low rates of investment; weak technical capabilities; high labour costs in relation to levels of schooling; the lack of an adequate technological or scientific infrastructure; long distance from advanced markets; and the lack of research competence in the field of information and communication technologies. Countries with these characteristics are being marginalised in the world economy. Their technological and economic backwardness increases. Technological development does not result primarily in a gap between the advanced and developing world, but rather in a parting of the ways amongst developing countries themselves.

4.9   National and international policy

For developing countries, and firms in developing countries, improving technological capabilities is a key priority. Improvements in primary education and in primary and secondary technical education are important in this respect.

Technology policy should focus on the development of capabilities in the key areas where technologies are rapidly changing, namely in information and communication technologies and in biotechnology.

Policy should contribute to the development of more effective national systems of innovation and research systems. The function of R&D is not primarily to contribute to advances at the frontiers of knowledge, but rather as an investment in order to be able to profit from technological developments elsewhere and develop new appropriate adaptations. One of the important issues is strengthening linkages and interaction between publicly funded research institutes and the needs of private and public production units.

A consensus has developed that stronger export orientation contributes to the development of technological capabilities. Competing on international markets requires meeting international technology and quality standards. Some types of foreign direct investment can contribute to the building of technological capabilities, if technology transfer is accompanied by schooling and training efforts and technological knowledge is diffused through the domestic economy. If the foreign investor retains complete and restrictive control of technology, the learning impact will be limited.

The complementarity of technological capabilities and acquisition of new technologies and new capital goods is important. New technologies and imported capital goods will have little impact without appropriate capabilities. But investing in education and technological capabilities will be useless if there is no simultaneous inflow of new technologies in a country.

In the international context, research efforts should be better oriented to the needs and problems of developing countries (UNDP, 2001). Areas which require urgent attention from the international research community include AIDS research for developing countries, malaria research, water management, and agricultural and biotechnological research. Where market incentives result in underinvestment in socially important avenues of research, public research institutes should directly or indirectly try to influence the direction of research efforts.

Questions for review

1. Discuss the main changes in economic and world technological leadership since the seventeenth century.
2. Discuss examples of catch-up in developing countries in the twentieth century.
3. Under which conditions could a developing country profit from international technology transfer?
4. Under which conditions will the acceleration of technological change result in further marginalisation of a developing country?
5. What is a national innovation system? Identify possible weaknesses in the innovation systems of developing countries, which hinder technology change, and the diffusion of technology.
6. Discuss the relationships between technological change, productivity increases and competitiveness.

Further reading

A nice overview of the debates on technology and development is provided by Evenson and Westphal in their article 'Technological Change and Technology Strategy' in Volume IIIA of the *Handbook of Development Economics* (1995). Many of the topics and theories discussed in this chapter are treated in a collection of older and new articles on growth, innovation and technology by Richard Nelson, *The Sources of Economic Growth* (1996) and a volume edited by Kim and Nelson, entitled *Technology, Learning and Innovation: Experiences of Newly Industrializing Economies* (2000). The relationship between technology and productivity is explored in an important study by Howard Pack, *Productivity, Technology and Industrial Development* (1987). This book focuses on the textile industry and is unique in combining economic analysis with engineering information. It presents detailed case studies for textile firms in the Philippines and Kenya. Frances Stewart has written widely on the choice of technology from the perspective of developing countries. We mention the articles 'Choice of Technique in Developing Countries' (1972), 'Technology and Employment in Less Developed Countries' (1974) and an interesting edited volume, *Macropolicies for Appropriate Technology in Developing Countries* (1987). An historical perspective on the choice of technology in textiles in India and Japan is provided in a brilliant study by Otsuka, Ranis and Saxonhouse, *Comparative Technology Choice in Development* (1988). The impact of changes in technological paradigms is explored by Freeman and Perez in 'Structural Crises of Adjustment, Business Cycles and Investment Behaviour' (1988) and Dosi in 'Technological Paradigms and Technological Trajectories' (1988). The concept of national systems of innovation was introduced by Lundvall in *National Systems of Innovation: Towards a Theory of Innovation and Interactive Learning* (1992). Another important source for systems of innovation is a volume edited by Nelson entitled *National Innovation Systems: A Comparative Analysis* (1993). In a series of books and articles Sanjaya Lall has focused on the role of technological capabilities in development. We mention *Learning to Industrialise: The Acquisition of Technological Capabilities in India* (1987), an article in *World Development* on 'Technological Capabilities and Industrialization' (1992) and *Learning from the Asian Tigers: Studies in Technology and Industrial Policy* (1996). Jeffrey James has recently explored the impact of the spread of information technology on the integration or marginalisation of developing countries in the global economy, in *Technology, Globalization and Poverty* (2002). The challenges and opportunities offered by technological change are also explored in the 1989/99 edition of the World Bank, *World Development Report 1989/99, Knowledge for Development* (1999) and the 2001 UNDP *Human Development Report: Making Technologies Work for Development* (2001).

5 Population and development

The following three chapters focus on the various relationships between population and socio-economic development. Chapters 6 and 7 deal with health and education. In this chapter, we discuss the relationships between population growth and economic development.

The chapter opens with a discussion of global demographic trends, which indicates that in the next 150 years world population will increase by a further 4 billion people, before stabilising around 2150. Subsequently, we discuss the economic consequences of population growth and demographic change. We contrast pessimistic Malthusian perspectives which argue that population growth is a threat to sustained economic development, with more optimistic assessments which indicate that technological change has the potential to outpace the growth of population. The second half of the chapter focuses on explanations of why families in developing countries have so many children. These explanations serve as guidelines for the formulation of population policies, which form the topic of the last section of this chapter.

5.1   Introduction

As an introduction to this chapter on population and development, we distinguish eight types of relationships between demographic and economic developments, which are summarised in Box 5.1. Apart from population growth, population size and population density are also important demographic variables. Several countries in Latin America and Africa have rapid population growth, but relatively low population density. Low population density discourages large-scale investment in infrastructure. Population size influences the absolute volume of required investment and the size of domestic markets. Countries with large domestic markets can better afford to follow an inward-looking path of economic development than small countries (Myint, 1980).

Box 5.1   Relationships between population change and economic development

1. Population growth supplies the labour, which is available as an input into economic production. The availability of labour with various qualifications, levels of education and health has considerable influence on the productive potential of a society.
2. The growth of population, on the other hand, also gives rise to employment problems. Can economic development provide a rapidly growing labour force with sufficient productive and paid employment, or does open or disguised unemployment increase?
3. A rapidly growing population can stimulate the growth of production by providing an expanding market for goods and services.
4. The level of consumption in a society depends in part on the relationship between population growth and growth of production. Is the growth of production of goods and services sufficient to provide a growing population with an acceptable standard of living?
5. A growing population creates opportunities for productive investment and can stimulate savings.
6. The size and growth of the labour force is one of the determinants of the need for savings and investment. If investment lags behind the growth of the labour force, then – with given technology – labour productivity will tend to decline and growth of production will not be able to keep up with the growth of population.
7. In the absence of technological change, growth of population increases the pressure on the national environment, especially when combined with increased output per capita.
8. Growth of population and increasing pressure on scarce resources can stimulate technological change.

5.2   Perspectives on population growth

In post-war debates on the population problem Malthusian views predominated up to the 1970s. It was thought that rapid growth of population in developing countries threatened their chances of economic development. Researchers and representatives of international organisations warned about the consequences of the 'population explosion' and pleaded for vigorous family planning programmes (Coale and Hoover, 1958).

Representatives of developing countries countered that an overemphasis on population policy deflected attention from the core of development problems, namely economic underdevelopment. Once economic development accelerated, population growth would automatically slow down, as it had done earlier in the Western countries. In addition, they argued that one quarter of the world population was using more than 80 per cent of global natural resources. The question was not scarcity of world resources, but their unequal distribution (Keating, 1993; Todaro, 1981: ch. 6).

In recent research, there is no firm empirical support for the conclusion that the effects of population growth on economic development are always negative. In some instances, population growth can even have positive effects on factors such as technological change and growth of output (Birdsall, 1988; Kelley, 1988; World Bank, 1984). High population growth rates notwithstanding, some countries have succeeded in substantially raising their per capita incomes. Other countries with rapid population growth show declines in per capita income.

Both in the political debate and in the empirical scientific discussion the contours of a new consensus have become visible: very rapid growth of population can seriously exacerbate existing economic problems in very poor societies. But these economic problems are usually not primarily caused by population growth. Therefore population policy should not be discussed in isolation. Rather it should be integrated into a wider framework of policies aimed at overall economic and social development (Bengtsson and Gunnarsson, 1994; Keating, 1993: ch. 5; UN Population Division, 1994).

5.3   Growth of world population

Table 5.1 presents estimates of world population in the very long run. This table shows that there has always been some measure of global population increase, even in prehistoric times. There was no such thing as a Malthusian equilibrium in which world population remained stable because of the checks of famine and disease. There was *extensive growth*, with increases in production sustaining a growing population. However, the growth of population before 1750 was very slow. After this date there was a dramatic acceleration of growth, which reached its peak between 1950 and 1975. During this period world population increased at 2 per cent per annum. At such a growth rate world population doubles every 35 years.

Figure 5.1 shows that most population growth takes place in developing countries. In the rich countries population has almost stabilised. Between 1995 and 2000 world population increased by some 395 million people. The population of the more developed countries increased by 17.5 million, the population of developing countries by 377.4 million, or around 75 million per year. After 1975, the rate of population growth began to slow down. But growth remained

Table 5.1 *Growth of world population*

Year	Estimated world population (low and high estimates[a] (millions)	Estimated world population (millions)	Average annual growth rate (%)	Population developing countries (millions)	Average annual growth rate developing countries (%)
BC 10,000–8,000	5–10	7.5			
0–14 AD	270–330	300	0.04		
1000	275–345	310	0.00		
1250	350–450	400	0.10		
1500	440–540	490	0.08		
1750	735–805	770	0.18		
1850	1,100–1,300	1,200	0.44		
1900	1,650–1,710	1,680	0.68		
1950		2,519	0.81	1,706	
1970		3,691	1.93	2,683	2.29
1975		4,066	1.95	3,017	2.38
1985		4,825	1.73	3,710	2.09
1990		5,255	1.72	4,106	2.05
1995		5,662	1.50	4,488	1.79
2000		6,057	1.36	4,865	1.63
2005		6,441	1.24	5,240	1.49
2010		6,826	1.17	5,617	1.40
2015		7,207	1.09	5,994	1.30
2020		7,579	1.01	6,362	1.20
2025		7,937	0.93	6,718	1.10
2030		8,270	0.83	7,054	0.98
2050		9,322	0.60	8,141	0.72
2075		9,751	0.18	8,654	0.24
2100		9,898	0.06	8,839	0.08
2125		10,017	0.05	8,962	0.06
2150		10,198	0.07	9,125	0.07

Note:
[a] Durand (1977) presents upper and lower limits of estimates that have the same degree of plausibility. In the second column we have taken the midpoint of the upper and lower boundaries of Durant's indifference ranges.
Sources: BC 10,000–1750 and 1900 AD from Durand (1977); 1850: Cipolla (1978); 1950–2050: United Nations Population Division, *World Population Prospects. Population Data Base*, http://esa.un.org/unpp copyright United Nations. (medium variant); 2050–2150: 2050 extrapolated with growth rates (medium variant) from 2050–2150: United Nations Population Division, *Long-Range World Population Projections: Based on the 1998 Revision: Dataset in Digital Form*: http://www.un.org./esa/population/publications/longrange/longrange.htm.

very high in historical perspective. The projected world population for the year 2050 is 9.3 billion people, of which 87 per cent will be in developing countries. United Nations medium projections (UN, 2002a) suggest that world population will stabilise at around 10.2 billion people in the year 2150. Most of the increase in population will be added between now and 2050. After that, population growth will slow down, both in percentage terms and in absolute numbers.

One should realise that these long-term projections depend heavily on assumptions concerning fertility rates (see section 5.2). Under the assumption that present fertility rates remain unchanged, a world population of 14.5 billion people could already be reached by 2050. Based on low and high assumptions about fertility, population projections for 2150 vary from a mere 3.2 billion to no less than 24.8 billion (United Nations, 2002a). The medium variant

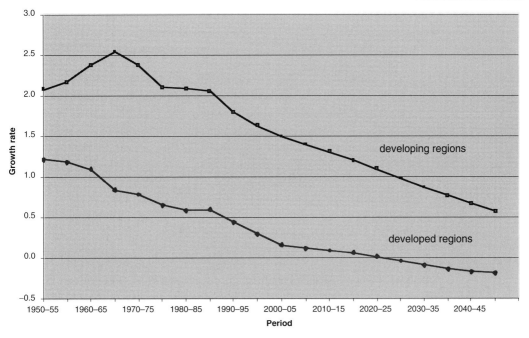

Figure 5.1 Population growth, 1950–2050
Sources: see Table 5.1

reproduced in Table 5.1 assumes that fertility rates continue to decline till the replacement rate is achieved. After that they stabilise. Projections are heavily influenced by developments in the two most populous countries in the world, India and China. When the decline in fertility rates in China was reversed in the late 1980s, projections were revised upwards. In the early 1990s fertility rates dropped again, resulting in lower global projections. The latest projections also incorporate the negative effects of AIDS on mortality and life expectancy.

5.4   The demographic transition

The growth of population is determined by the relation between birth rates and death rates. Acceleration of world population growth is caused by what is optimistically called the demographic transition. Figure 5.2 presents a schematic representation of the demographic transition which has earlier taken place in Europe.

Before the demographic transition both birth rates and death rates were high. The so-called *crude birth rate* – the annual number of births per 1,000 inhabitants – was around 35 per 1,000, the crude death rate – the annual number of deaths per 1,000 inhabitants – was around 25 to 30 per 1,000. The net excess of births over deaths caused a slow increase of population. In the nineteenth century the death rate gradually declined in the presently prosperous

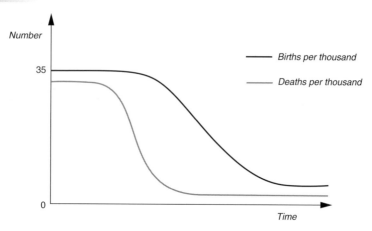

Figure 5.2 The demographic transition

countries, principally as a result of improved nutrition, increases in the overall standard of living and improved hygienic circumstances. As the birth rate
did not decline along with the death rate, the excess of births over deaths
increased. Population growth in Europe accelerated to the hitherto unknown
level of 1 per cent per year. In due course, however, birth rates also started
to decline, under the combined influence of urbanisation, modernisation and
improving standards of living. In the twentieth century a new equilibrium was
reached between low death rates and low birth rates.

A similar process is presently taking place in developing countries, though
even more dramatically. Death rates have declined much faster than they did
in Europe in the nineteenth century, primarily owing to medical progress. Developing country birth rates of around 45 per 1,000 inhabitants in the 1950s
were higher than they were in nineteenth-century Europe. For the time being
birth rates still remain high. The result is an unprecedented rate of population growth. If the earlier pattern of the demographic transition repeats itself,
birth rates in developing countries will decline in the long run and a new
equilibrium between birth and death rates will be achieved at a lower level.

There is evidence that this is happening at the moment, though the characteristics of the demographic transition differ substantially from region to
region (McNicoll, 1994; see also next section). Caldwell (1997) argues that there
is a single global fertility transition which started in nineteenth-century Europe
and which diffused step by step to the rest of the world. Caldwell and Caldwell
(1997) emphasise the importance of the diffusion of the intellectual notion of
birth control in an increasing globally interconnected social system.

In addition to the 'crude birth rate' and the 'crude death rate' two other
concepts are important for an understanding of demographic developments,
namely the *total fertility rate* and *life expectation*.

The total fertility rate is the average number of children a woman will bear in
the course of the fertile period of her life (World Bank, 1984: p. 66). Together

with the age structure of the population, the total fertility rate determines the crude birth rate. A low fertility rate in combination with an age structure comprising many young women in the fertile period of their life could result in the same crude birth rate as a high fertility rate with relatively few women in their fertile years. Rapid population growth in developing countries results in a youthful age structure. This means that population will continue to grow for quite a long time, even if the average number of children per woman has declined to the *replacement level* of two children per woman.

The crude death rate also depends on two factors: life expectation and age structure. Life expectation is the average number of years a child is expected to live from birth onwards. This average is strongly influenced by mortality in the first five years of life. A young population with a high life expectation will make for very low death rates. An old population with high life expectations will have higher death rates. Many affluent countries have an increasing number of elderly people in their population leading to higher death rates in spite of high life expectation.

5.5   Demographic developments in developing countries

Table 5.2 and Table 5.3 offer a picture of demographic developments in developing countries. Table 5.2 presents growth rates for twenty-nine countries, where possible traced back to 1820. These growth rates are compared with those of sixteen OECD countries.[1] Since 1950, population growth in our twenty-nine developing countries is more than twice as high as in the OECD countries, since 1973 three times as high. Since 1973 the rate of growth in developing countries has started to decelerate, but growth is still extremely rapid.

Present rates of growth of total population in developing countries are more than twice as high as population growth rates in the OECD countries in the nineteenth century. We may therefore conclude that the current demographic challenge for developing countries is much greater than that which faced the currently rich countries in the nineteenth century. The acceleration of population growth in the nineteenth century was paralleled by a substantial increase in the demand for industrial labour. Emigration also provided a potential outlet for surplus population.

In developing countries today the industrial sector is unable to provide the massive influx of new entrants to the labour market with sufficient paid employment. On the one hand, the influx is much greater than in the past. On the other hand, increasing capital intensity in production and labour-saving technological change diminishes the demand for labour. Employment will have to be created in other sectors of the economy, such as agriculture, services or the informal sector. Thus, a typical demographic characteristic of many developing

---

1 The term OECD countries is used throughout the book as shorthand for sixteen advanced economies. It is not strictly correct, as a number of developing countries today are also members of the OECD.

Table 5.2 *Population growth in selected developing countries 1820–2000 (%)*

	1820–70	1870–1913[b]	1913–50	1950–73	1973–2000
Bangladesh[a]	0.4	0.4	1.0	2.0	2.2
China	−0.1	0.5	0.6	2.1	1.3
India	0.4	0.4	1.0	2.1	2.1
Indonesia	1.0	1.3	1.2	2.0	2.0
Malaysia	2.1	3.2	2.0	2.6	2.5
Pakistan[a]	0.4	0.4	1.9	2.6	2.5
Philippines	1.7	1.4	2.2	3.0	2.2
South Korea	0.1	0.3	0.7	2.2	1.2
Sri Lanka	1.5	1.3	1.2	2.5	1.3
Taiwan	0.3	0.9	2.2	3.0	1.4
Thailand	0.4	1.0	2.3	3.1	1.5
Turkey	0.3	0.6	0.9	2.6	2.0
Argentina	2.5	3.4	2.2	1.7	1.4
Brazil	1.6	2.1	2.2	2.9	1.9
Chile	1.6	1.4	1.5	2.1	1.6
Colombia	1.4	1.8	2.2	3.0	2.2
Mexico	0.7	1.1	1.8	3.1	2.1
Peru	1.4	1.2	1.5	2.8	2.2
Venezuela	1.7	1.3	1.5	3.8	2.6
Congo, Dem. Rep.		1.1	2.8	2.4	3.0
Côte d'Ivoire		1.0	1.9	3.5	3.5
Egypt	1.2	1.7	1.5	2.3	2.2
Ghana		1.0	2.6	2.6	2.5
Kenya		0.7	2.5	3.2	3.3
Morocco		0.8	2.2	2.6	3.1
Nigeria		1.3	1.6	2.4	2.0
South Africa		2.0	1.8	2.9	2.1
Tanzania		0.2	1.8	2.9	3.0
Zambia				2.6	2.9
Average Asian countries	0.7	1.0	1.4	2.5	1.9
Average Latin American countries	1.5	1.8	1.8	2.8	2.0
Average African countries		1.1	2.1	2.7	2.8
Average developing countries	1.0	1.2	1.7	2.6	2.2
Annual growth total population in developing countries	0.1	0.6	1.0	2.3	1.9
Annual growth total population in 16 OECD countries[c]	0.9	1.1	0.8	1.1	0.6

Notes:
[a] Growth rates of Bangladesh and Pakistan before 1913 equal the Indian growth rate;
[b] All African countries except Egypt 1900–13 instead of 1870–1913;
[c] For developing countries both average growth rates and the growth rate of total population have been calculated. For the OECD countries only the growth rate of total population has been represented;
Sources: 1990 and before: Maddison (2001), supplemented with figures from Maddison (1995); 1991–99: GGDC, *Total Economy Database*, http://www.ggdc.net; 2000: Growth rates 1999/2000: from *World Development Report, 2000/2001*; Egypt 1820–1913: Hansen and Marzouk (1965).

countries is that the absolute size of the rural population is still increasing (see Chapter 10). Emigration on a massive scale is no longer a viable option. For instance, Indonesia has had a large transmigration programme, intended to shift population from the densely populated Java to the outer islands. But the quantitative contribution of such programmes to the population problem is negligible and the resistance to transmigration has been increasing.

Table 5.3 contains a number of important demographic indicators for the post-war period. This table indicates that with the exception of Africa, the developing world is moving into the stage of demographic transition characterised

Table 5.3 *Indicators of demographic changes, 1950–2000, by region*

	Africa	Latin America & Caribbean	Asia[a]	China	India	Developing Countries	More Developed Countries[b]	World
Population (millions)								
1950	221	167	403	555	358	1706	814	2519
1995	704	480	1151	1219	927	4488	1174	5662
2000	794	519	1261	1275	1009	4865	1191	6057
Annual growth rate of population (%)								
1950–55	2.17	2.65	2.08	1.87	2.00	2.06	1.20	1.79
1995–2000	2.41	1.56	1.84	0.90	1.69	1.62	0.30	1.35
Birth rate per 1,000								
1950–55	49.0	42.0	43.7	43.8	45.4	44.6	22.4	37.5
1995–2000	38.7	23.1	26.8	16.2	26.2	25.4	11.2	22.5
Death rate per 1,000								
1950–55	26.8	15.6	23.7	25.0	25.4	24.1	10.3	19.7
1995–2000	14.1	6.5	8.0	7.0	9.0	8.8	10.2	9.0
Fertility rate								
1950–55	6.7	5.9	6.0	6.2	5.9	6.2	2.8	5.0
1995–2000	5.3	2.7	3.3	1.8	3.3	3.1	1.6	2.8
Percentage of urban population								
1950	14.7	41.9	17.4	12.5	17.3	17.8	54.9	29.8
2000	37.9	75.3	43.8	32.1	28.4	39.9	76.0	47.0
Percentage of population under 15 years								
1950	41.9	40.0	38.7	33.5	38.9	37.6	27.3	34.3
2000	42.6	31.5	34.6	24.8	33.5	32.8	18.3	30.0
Percentage of population over 65 years								
1950	3.2	3.7	4.1	4.5	3.3	3.9	7.9	5.2
2000	3.3	5.4	4.5	6.9	5.0	5.1	14.3	6.9

Notes:
[a] Excluding Japan, China and India
[b] Europe, Russian Federation, North America, Japan, Australia and New Zealand
Sources: UN (2001); UN Population Divison, *World Population Prospects: Population Data Base*, http://esa.un.org/unpp; Urban population from UN Population Division, World Urbanization Prospects: The 2001 Revision, http://www.un.org/esa/population/unpop.htm.

by declining fertility rates.[2] Wilson (2001) concludes that a global demographic convergence is taking place.

The demographic transition in developing countries lags some 100 years behind the transition in presently affluent countries. But there are a number of interesting differences between present-day and historical processes of transition (Kelley, 1988; World Bank, 1984).

In the first place, aggregate birth rates in developing countries in the 1950s were substantially higher than they had been in the past. Even at their peak, birth rates in the nineteenth century were never above 40 births per 1,000 inhabitants. Between 1950 and 1955 the birth rate in developing countries was no less on average than 45 per 1,000 inhabitants.

This figure increased further in the 1960s, before declining to 25.4 births per 1,000 by 1995–2000. This birth rate is comparable to that in many European countries in the nineteenth century. Present-day birth rates are lowest in China, which has experienced an astounding decline in birth rates as a result of its harsh birth-control policies. Latin America is in second place. With 39 births per 1,000 inhabitants, the African continent has by far the highest birth rates.

---

2 Even in Africa, there are some indications that fertility rates are starting to decline.

In the second place, death rates in developing countries have been declining much faster than in the past. Historically, death rates declined as a corollary of a general increase in the standard of living, improved nutritional intake, economic growth and modernisation of society. Today death rates are declining in most developing countries, irrespective of their standards of living or economic growth rates. Since 1950, the death rate in developing countries has decreased from 24.1 deaths per 1,000 inhabitants to 8.8 per 1,000, even after accounting for the demographic impact of the AIDS epidemic. It is now lower than in the more developed countries, in part owing to a different age structure. The decline of the death rate proceeded four to five times as fast as in Europe in the nineteenth century (Kelley, 1988; Kuznets, 1980). This decline is not primarily due to an overall improvement in standards of living. Rather, it is explained by medical technical progress – in the treatment of infectious diseases, vaccination, antibiotics, combating animal bearers of diseases (vectors) – and by improvements in curative health care, medical services, education, transport and communication.

In the last quarter of the twentieth century, population growth in developing countries was higher than it had ever been in the presently prosperous countries (cf. Table 5.2). Population growth increased throughout the 1950s and 60s. After the 1960s a decline set in in Asia and Latin America, while growth rates continued to accelerate in Africa. Between 1995 and 2000 the African population was growing at 2.4 per cent per year. Fears that the slowdown in the growth of population in Asia was being reversed (World Bank, 1994) have not materialised. Even a comparison of the period 1990–5 and the period 1995–2000 shows quite marked decreases in population growth rates (United Nations, 2001a). In the period 1995–2000 the growth rates for this in Asia excluding Japan, China and India were 1.84, 0.24 percentage points lower than in 1950–5. In China growth had fallen below the 1 per cent mark.

Between 1973 and 2000, most rapid growth is found in Africa, with growth rates of around 3 per cent per year (extreme cases being Côte d'Ivoire, Kenya, Tanzania, Democratic Republic of Congo and Zambia). Latin America and South Asia come second. Lowest growth is to be found in East and Southeast Asia, in particular in populous China. But even for China, the growth rate of 1.3 per cent since 1973 is higher than peak growth rates of European countries in the nineteenth century.

High fertility and rapid population growth have resulted in a very youthful age structure of the population. At present on average 33 per cent of the population is less than 15 years old. This implies a very high *dependency ratio* – the proportion of the population belonging to age groups that do not make economically productive contributions. The youthful age structure also means that a large proportion of women will be in a reproductive age category in coming years. Thus, even if the fertility rates per woman were to go down, birth rates would continue to be high for quite a long time.

Finally, Table 5.2 also contains information on trends in urbanisation. Latin America is the most urbanised region, with an urban population of 75 per cent, a level similar to that of the developed world. According to Kelley, urbanisation trends in developing countries deviate less from historical patterns than is sometimes suggested. The increase in the share of urban population from 18 to 40 per cent since 1950 is comparable to the speed of urbanisation in earlier historical periods. However, in absolute terms the growth of the size of cities proceeds at a much faster pace. The growth of mega cities such as São Paulo and Mexico City or African capitals such as Dar-es-Salaam confronts policy makers with historically unprecedented challenges in terms of water supply, sanitation and infrastructure. The growth of urban population is caused by not only migration from rural to urban areas, but increasingly growth of the urban population itself (Kelley, 1988). According to UN projections, the level of urbanisation in developing countries is expected to reach 48.6 per cent in 2015 and 54 per cent in 2025 (UN, 2001b).

Demographic characteristics of developing countries are summarised in Box 5.2.

Box 5.2 Demographic characteristics of developing countries

1. Rapid population growth:
   – faster than nineteenth-century growth in the currently rich countries
   – highest in the poorest countries.
2. Very rapid decline in mortality, irrespective of income per capita:
   – faster than in the nineteenth century
   – related to advances in medical technology
   – increased life expectation.
3. High birth rates, high fertility rates:
   – higher than previously in currently rich countries
   – much lower age of marriage than in nineteenth-century Europe
   – beginning decline in some countries, especially in Asia, no decline in Africa.
4. Population growth out of step with the demand for labour.
5. Emigration not an option for excess population.
6. Rapid urbanisation, but also increasing rural population:
   – share of urban population declining. Numbers increasing
   – urbanisation caused both by rural–urban migration and internal population growth.
7. High dependency ratios.

5.6 Socio-economic consequences of population growth

5.6.1 Pessimistic and optimistic perspectives

Since Thomas Malthus wrote his *Essay on the Principles of Population* in 1798, a debate has been raging on the perceived consequences of population growth. Malthusian pessimists believe that population growth threatens human welfare and that there are physical limits to the increase in production, such as availability of land, scarcity of energy and raw materials, and the carrying capacity of the global environment (e.g. Brundtland, 1987; Ehrlich and Ehrlich, 1990; Keating, 1993; IPCC, 2001; Meadows *et al.*, 1972; UN, 1994; World Bank, 2003). Optimists argue that scarcity provides a challenge to human creativity.

In this view, people will always find new technological solutions to the problems of scarcity. For instance, if the prices of raw materials such as oil go up, it
becomes economically feasible to develop alternative sources of energy. Limits
to growth are not fixed, but are shifting all the time. Well-known representatives of the optimistic perspective are Julian Simon, Ester Boserup and Bjørn
Lomborg (Boserup, 1965; 1981; 1983; Lomborg, 2001; Simon, 1982). Optimists
and pessimists differ in not only their analysis of causal mechanisms, but also
their empirical estimates and projections. It is important for the reader to realise that almost every single empirical estimate is hotly debated. This holds
for global warming, greenhouse effects, population projections, or seemingly
incontrovertible facts such as deforestation.

5.6.2   Malthusian analyses

Central to Malthusian thought are two mechanisms, namely the influence of
increasing welfare on population growth on the one hand, and the law of
diminishing marginal returns in food production on the other hand. If the
standard of living improves, people will tend to have more children. If increasing numbers of people have to cultivate limited amounts of land, marginal
returns will have to decline in the longer run. Food production will be unable to keep up with the growth of population. Famines, malnutrition and
epidemics will finally serve as a check on the growth of population.

As we shall show in Chapter 10 (agrarian development), long-run developments clearly contradict Malthusian predictions. In the past there may often
have been major fluctuations in population size in given regions. Also, in
some periods famines and epidemics may have led to depopulation of whole
areas. But at a global level, world population never stabilised at any fixed level.
In Table 5.1, we saw that world population has been growing since prehistoric
times, albeit at a very slow pace (Boserup, 1981: ch. 4). Since the acceleration
of population growth in the nineteenth century, food production has been
increasing even more rapidly than population (van der Meer, 1983; World
Bank, 1984).

The crucial factor generally neglected in Malthusian thought is technical
change. If there were no technical change, it would be correct to assume that
marginal returns to labour in agriculture would decline as the man–land ratio
goes up. But so far, the threat of declining marginal returns has always stimulated people to develop new production techniques.

5.6.3   The neo-Malthusian trap

In the 1950s, Leibenstein and Nelson wrote that developing countries were
in danger of getting caught in an equilibrium at a low level of economic
development (Leibenstein, 1954; Nelson, 1956). This low-level equilibrium,
known as the *neo-Malthusian Trap* is represented in Figure 5.3.

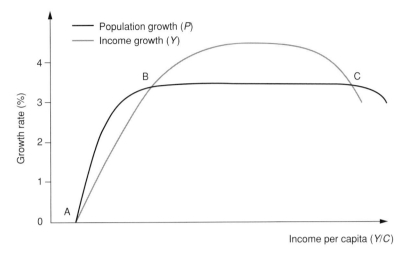

Figure 5.3 The neo-Malthusian trap

The horizontal axis of Figure 5.3 refers to per capita income (Y/C), the vertical axis to growth of population (P) and growth of national income. As per capita income goes up, Malthusian lore states that population growth (P) will increase till the biological maximum of around 3 per cent growth per year is reached. Growth of national income (Y) also depends on per capita income. As people become more prosperous, they are better able to save and invest. Higher investment rates in turn have a positive influence on the rate of growth.

Between points A and B population is growing faster than income. As a result income per capita will decline, till a low-level equilibrium is reached at point A. At this point the economy stagnates at a minimum subsistence level. Beyond the intersection point B, national income grows more rapidly than population. Per capita incomes will tend to increase, with a positive influence on the savings rate and further economic growth. Thus, economic growth becomes self-sustaining. In the very long run, diminishing returns may stabilise per capita incomes at a high-level equilibrium point C. But, in the context of developing economies, we are primarily interested in the trajectory between points A and B. Here we see that a small increase in per capita incomes is not sustainable. The economy will be forced back to its low-level equilibrium point. Only if the whole economy can jump beyond point B, will it be able to realise spontaneous and sustainable economic growth of per capita income. The policy recommendation deriving from this model is that of the 'big push', the attempt to jump over the neo-Malthusian trap by a gigantic investment programme (see Chapter 9).

Just as in classical Malthusianism, the neo-Malthusian model in Figure 5.3 disregards technical change. As production techniques change, line Y will shift upwards. The intersection point B may even disappear (Myint, 1980: p. 90). Furthermore, we have seen in section 5.5 that the relationship between demographic change and income per capita does not obey ahistorical Malthusian laws. On the contrary, the poorest developing countries are those with the highest population growth rates. Birth rates and fertility rates tend to decline rather than increase, as per capita income goes up. These declines are visible in most developing countries, except those in Sub-Saharan Africa. In the post-war period, death rates have been declining irrespective of income levels. This decline can be seen even in the poorest of developing countries.

5.6.4 Growth of national income, growth of per capita income and the dependency ratio

In an arithmetic sense it is obvious that, given the growth rate of national income, a higher figure for population growth implies a lower growth rate of per capita income. If one compares the growth rates of GDP per capita in Table 3.1 with the population growth rates in Table 5.2, it is clear that production in developing countries has grown much more rapidly than production per capita. But one may not conclude automatically that population growth has had a negative effect on the growth of national income per capita. For instance, a growing population may provide incentives to increase production or to work more efficiently. Nevertheless, we may safely assume that the challenges with which developing countries are confronted become greater as population growth becomes higher.

A rapidly growing population is associated with high percentages of young persons in the age structure of the population. Children usually do not contribute fully to production, while they participate in consumption. The higher the so-called *dependency ratio* – the proportion of economically non-active to economically active people – in an economy, the more the active members of the labour force have to produce to attain a given level of welfare.[3] Several theories state that population growth, working through the dependency ratio, has a negative effect on overall economic development.

Conversely, the projected decline in fertility in developing countries may create a window of opportunity for these countries. The slowdown in fertility rates translates into slower population growth and lower dependency ratios, which persist until the aging of the population at a later stage results in increasing dependency rates of a different kind (World Bank, 2003).

5.6.5 Dependency ratio and savings

If there are many small children in a household, the consumptive expenditures of the household will tend to be greater and the proportion of household

[3] Here we interpret the dependency ratio as the ratio of young people in the age category 1–14 years to people in the age category of 15–65 years. Another possible measure is the ratio of all people under 15 or over 65 to the population aged 15 to 65.

income saved will be smaller. A well-known hypothesis states that a high dependency ratio will result in a low savings rate in an economy.

Surprisingly, however, empirical research provides but little support for this hypothesis (Birdsall, 1988; Kelley, 1988; World Bank, 1984). There are several reasons for this. In the first place, the private household is but one of the sources of savings along with firms, financial institutions and government. The savings decisions of firms and financial institutions are not influenced strongly by the dependency ratio. In the second place, the level of financial savings by households is negligible in poor economies. What savings there are, take a physical form, like using family labour to produce tools and implements, clearing land or reserving part of output for feed and seed. These kinds of savings will not show up in statistics. Furthermore, many children in poor families often result in lower consumption, rather than lower savings. Finally, large numbers of children can provide incentives to work harder and to produce more, in order to be able to feed more mouths. Nevertheless the World Bank concludes tentatively that a large family size forms a heavy economic burden for a family and may indirectly have negative effects on its long-run capacity to save (World Bank, 1984). Also, there is ample evidence that the life chances of children from very large families are less favourable than those of children from smaller families (World Bank, 2003).

5.6.6   *Population growth and investment*

Population growth results in an increased number of entrants to the labour market (see section 5.6.8). This can cause a decline in the amount of capital goods available per person engaged (Coale and Hoover, 1958). If one invests a given percentage of national income, while the supply of labour is increasing, the amount of capital per person engaged will decline. In absence of technical change, output per worker will also decline. In such a situation, one has to invest a higher percentage of national income to forestall a decline of the amount of capital goods (implements, machines, and so forth) per worker. In other words, one has to run harder to stay in the same place. A slower rate of population growth would free resources, which could be used for an increase in the investment per worker.

Furthermore, the increasing share of young people in the population structure might create a competition between resources available for investment in capital goods and resources available for investment in schooling and health services (Coale and Hoover, 1958).

Empirical research does not give unequivocal answers to the questions raised here. Theoretically, the effects of population growth on savings and investment depend on numerous assumptions – e.g. assumptions with regard to economies of scale and the degree of substitutability of capital and labour in the production process. According to Birdsall (1988) the effects of population growth on capital accumulation are negligible compared to the effects of the level of national income. Given an investment rate of 18 per cent of national income in 1980, the United States invested $189,000 for every new job. In the same year, Kenya invested 22 per cent of its national income. Per new job this only amounted to $4,700 (World Bank, 1984: p. 87).

Empirical uncertainties notwithstanding, we may nevertheless conclude that rapid population growth places additional burdens on already strained economies by increasing the need for investment.

5.6.7   Population growth, education and health care

A high dependency ratio means that a rapidly increasing youthful population has to be supplied with education. Even if nothing is done to improve the present quality of education, this means more money needs to be spent on education. Once again, developing countries have to run harder just to stay in the same place.

Since World War II, developing countries have succeeded in substantially increasing educational participation, in spite of rapid population growth. At present however, there is a tendency for educational expenditure per student to decline (see Chapter 7). This threatens the quality of education, which is not very high as it is. If the number of pupils were increasing less rapidly, it would be possible to reserve more funds for quality improvement. Also the difficult choices between educational expenditures and investment in physical capital would become less pressing.

Similar dilemmas exist with regard to health care. Rapid population growth means that existing health facilities have to be spread amongst more and more people, creating new dilemmas with regard to government expenditures.

At family level, finally, the negative effects of population growth are clearly discernible. Children from larger families do less well at school and, owing to the pressure on family budgets, have less prospects of enjoying good health (Kelley, 1988; World Bank, 2003).

5.6.8   Employment, income distribution and poverty

With a delay of some 14 to 24 years, births manifest themselves as new entrants onto the labour market. High fertility rates, decreasing infant mortality and a youthful age structure result in rapid increases in the supply of labour. Between 1990 and 1999, the labour force in low-income countries grew at no less than 2.4 per cent per year. The growth rate of the labour force even exceeded the average rate of population growth of 2 per cent per year. In middle-income countries the labour force grew by 1.5 per cent per year (World Bank, 2000, table 3). The influx of large numbers of – unskilled – young people to the labour market depresses wages and increases unemployment, thereby contributing to increased poverty. The modern formal sector (comprising the capital intensive industrial sector, government and commercial services) is unable to supply an ever-growing labour force with sufficient employment.

Unemployment can take two forms: open unemployment and underutilisation of labour. Open unemployment – not being able to find any gainful employment – is not very common in the poorest developing countries, where systems of social security are rudimentary or non-existent. This is especially true in rural areas (World Bank, 1995). We speak of *underutilisation of labour* when people work shorter hours than they would prefer to work or when labour productivity is so low that people can hardly earn enough to survive, in spite of working very long hours.

Labour statistics are notoriously difficult to compare between developing countries, because of differences in concepts, coverage and methods of data collection. Table 5.4 provides some rough estimates of unemployment and informal employment derived from a database of the International Labour Organisation (ILO, 2002). Most ILO data refer to urban areas, where formal unemployment rates tend to be higher than at national levels. Direct estimates of the underutilisation of labour are not available. The table serves to illustrate

Table 5.4 *Unemployment and informal employment in selected countries (%), 1990–2000*

	Informal sector employment	Unemployment
Bangladesh	10.0[a]	2.5
China		3.1[a]
India	44.2[a]	
Indonesia	20.6[b]	6.1
Malaysia		3.4
Pakistan	67.1[ac]	5.9
Philippines	17.0[ad]	10.1
South Korea		4.1
Taiwan		3.0
Thailand	47.6[a]	2.4
Argentina	42.9[a]	12.8[d]
Brazil	37.7[a]	9.6
Chile	32.4[a]	9.9
Colombia	46.9[a]	20.1[a]
Mexico	35.3[a]	2.0
Peru	51.9[a]	8.0[a]
Venezuela	46.6[a]	14.9
Côte d'Ivoire	52.7[ad]	
Egypt		8.2
Ghana	78.5[a]	
Kenya	58.1[e]	21.3
Morocco	28.2[ae]	22.0[a]
Nigeria		3.2
South Africa	17.4[a]	23.3
Tanzania	67.0[d]	3.5
Zambia	80.7	15.0

Notes: [a] urban; [b] manufacturing sector; [c] Punjab/Northwest Pakistan; [d] capital region; [e] excluding agriculture
Source: ILO, (2002). Informal sector employment as percentage of total employment. Unemployment as percentage of the labour force. Latest year between 1990 and 2000. Most unemployment statistics date from the late 1990s.

the extent of informal employment. The informal sector contains a wide variety of economic activities, some of which can be quite dynamic and profitable (Gaillard and Beernink 2001), but by and large the informal sector is a proxy for underutilisation of labour (see further, Chapter 9). Many people are forced to make a living by engaging in low-productive activities in the traditional agrarian sector or in the urban and rural informal sectors of the economy. Thus, the large supply of labour promotes increasing income inequality. In the first place, the abundant labour supply weakens the position of employees *vis à vis* owners of capital. In the second place income inequality between various categories of workers is also increased. Incomes of unskilled labourers in low productivity sectors (in the informal sector or traditional agriculture) lag behind incomes in the formal sector of the economy.

The direct determinants of poverty are twofold:

1. *lack of growth of average per capita income.* This occurs when the rate of growth of national income does not exceed population growth. Other things being equal, growth of per capita income will result in reductions in poverty. Negative growth results in increased poverty. There is overwhelming evidence that growth is important for poverty reduction.
2. *large and increasing income disparities within countries.* The positive effects of growth of average per capita income on poverty may be neutralised by increasing income inequality. As a result, the poor may not share in the benefits of growth. The worst scenario is when economic stagnation goes hand in hand with increasing inequality. There is ample evidence that declines in per capita income do indeed weigh disproportionately on the poor (Ravallion, 2001).

Analytically we saw in sections 5.6.3 and 5.6.4 that rapid population growth can depress per capita income in the absence of technological change, increased effort or increased efficiency. We argued that this was not the inevitable consequence of population growth, but only a possible outcome. The neo-Malthusian scenario presently seems to hold for much of Sub-Saharan Africa.

A second analytical impact of rapid population growth operates indirectly through the labour market. When population grows more rapidly than gainful employment, the share of open and disguised unemployment in the labour force increases. Average income per worker declines and the unemployed and underemployed inflate the ranks of the poor. The influx of labour leads to increased income inequality, further increasing the numbers in poverty and further depressing their incomes.

In Table 1.3, we presented data on the evolution of global poverty using the simplest measure available, the headcount of people living below a given poverty line.[4] In sum, these data do not support the most pessimistic

---

4 The two simplest measures of poverty are: the headcount measure, the number of people living below an absolute poverty line; and the income gap measure, the percentage of GDP required to lift all people above a given poverty line. One should also realise that poverty is a multidimensional concept including not only income, but deprivation in terms of health and education, vulnerability to changes and lack of access to services (World Bank, 2000).

Malthusian predictions. The global percentage of people below the one-dollar-a-day poverty line has declined from 28.3 to 23.5 per cent between 1987 and 1998. The absolute numbers of people in poverty have more or less stabilised. Some regions such as Sub-Saharan Africa or central Asia have experienced increases in poverty. It is interesting to note the substantial absolute decline of poverty in East Asia and the Pacific (including China), in spite of rapid increases in inequality. These are typically regions with marked slowdowns in population growth.

5.6.9 *Population growth and the environment*

Human impacts on the environment include the use and depletion of natural resources and the emissions of pollutants into the ecosphere. The environmental effects of human actions can be decomposed into three elements (UN, 1994: p. 27 ff): quantity of resources consumed and pollution per unit of output (E/GDP); output per capita (GDP/P) and population size (P).

$$E = \left[\frac{E}{GDP} \right] \times \left[\frac{GDP}{P} \right] \times P$$

The first element refers to technology. Technological progress (in resource use, process technology, product technology, environmental technology) reduces the environmental impact per unit of output. Output per capita reflects the affluence effect and population growth the demographic effect. Of course, there is no single indicator for the diversity of environmental effects. But the decomposition technique can be used to analyse various specified environmental effects.

In the prosperous countries the environmental effects of the population factor are limited, as population growth in these countries is by now very slow. The most important factor is the growth of production and consumption per person. The technology factor tends to make for more efficient use of resources. In developing countries the decomposition studies summarised in UN (1994) suggest that one quarter to one third of increases in pollution are owing to population growth. However, the indirect effects of population growth may be even higher and the negative environmental effects tend to weigh disproportionately on the poorest population groups.

In the analysis of environmental effects of population growth and economic development it is useful to distinguish scarcity of natural resources, localised environmental effects and global environmental effects.

Otherwise than predicted by the Club of Rome in 1972 and other neo-Malthusian authors, there is presently no scarcity of raw materials. Where shortages of raw materials occur in the short run, prices are driven up. In the longer run this discourages the use of these raw materials, while making alternative techniques of resource extraction and alternative materials economically more profitable.

It is also not obvious that there is a negative relationship between growth of production per capita in given countries and regions and localised deterioration of the environment. Of course, growth of production implies the emission of various noxious wastes in air and water, which put a severe burden on the environment. On the other hand, however, recent research indicates that pollution of air and surface waters in urban areas of developing countries is far worse than in richer countries (see World Bank, 1992: pp. 44–63). Rich countries can afford to reserve an increasing part of their national income for purposes of environmental protection, provision of clean drinking water, disposal of solid wastes, sewage systems and soil decontamination, which are too expensive for developing countries. Concentrations of solid matter and SO_2 in the air above cities in developed countries are generally declining, as is pollution of surface waters. This has given rise to the notion of the 'environmental Kuznets curve' in which economic growth initially results in increasing local environmental deterioration, followed by environmental improvement at higher income levels (Beckerman 1992; de Bruyn 1997; Ezzati *et al.*, 2001).[5] This is due to changing preferences, policies and changes in the structure of production towards less polluting sectors, processes and products.

In developing countries localised environmental effects are presently very severe and on the increase. 1.2 billion people in developing countries have no access to clean water. 1.7 billion people are not served by adequate sanitary facilities, with tremendous health hazards as consequences. Most urban settlements in developing countries have no sewerage system, while 90 per cent of sewage is discharged without treatment. Air pollution is on the increase (UN, 1994). These localised environmental influences, however disastrous, can be tackled in the long run by technological change and increased investment in pollution abatement, which are positively associated with economic growth.

The latest *World Development Report* (World Bank, 2003) argues that developing countries should not automatically copy the path of 'growing first and cleaning up later', implied by the Kuznets curve. 'Cleaning up later' may be more expensive than taking preventive measures. New technologies have become available which lessen the conflict between growth and environment. Also, some forms of environmental deterioration may be irreversible, which would strengthen the case for simultaneously addressing growth and environmental concerns. Dasgupta, Folke and Mäler (1994) argue that environmental resources should not simply be conceived of as a stock, which can be used or replaced at will. Many environmental processes are non-linear. When the carrying capacity of an ecological system is exceeded it might suddenly and irreversibly flip to a vastly different state.

The debates on this issue continue, but one should realise that it is hard enough to get the engine of economic development moving in low-income

---

5 The environmental Kuznets curve is named after the inverted U-curve hypothesis of Kuznets (1955) which states that income inequality first increases and then decreases in the course of economic development.

countries. It may be asking too much to assume that this can always be done in environmentally friendly ways, however desirable this may be.

Summing up, the prime environmental limits to economic growth and population growth, therefore, do not depend on the availability of natural resources and raw materials or in the lack of solutions for localised environmental problems. The limits primarily lie in the carrying capacity of the global environment (Brundtland *et al.*, 1987; IPPC, 2001; Keating, 1993; UN, 1994). There are ever stronger indications that the growth of world population and the associated growth of world production are beginning to form a threat to the environment at a global level, with consequences which may be irreversible. These indications include:

(a) *Deforestation*

Under the influence of human exploitation, expansion of agricultural land area, logging and acid rain effects, tropical rainforests are rapidly disappearing (see Chapter 10). According to some estimates (World Bank, 1994) 1.1 billion sq km of forest were lost between 1973 and 1988. The most important single cause of deforestation was the expansion of agricultural land area under the influence of increasing population pressure. Other important causes include cutting of trees for fuel wood in poor countries and logging. In the industrial world acid rain contributes to a serious deterioration of the quality of forests. Deforestation contributes to increased CO_2 emissions and declining biodiversity. Land clearing in highland areas leads to land erosion and downstream flooding.

There are indications, however, that deforestation is neither inevitable nor irreversible. According to an interesting study for West Africa by Leach and Fairhead (2000), neo-Malthusians tend to exaggerate the rate of deforestation. In the advanced countries, forest coverage is increasing. Some recent publications suggest that declining demand for croplands may free land for reforestation in the period till 2050 (Waggoner and Ausubel, 2001; see also Chapter 10).

(b) *The greenhouse effect caused by increased emission of CO_2 and other gases*

The greenhouse effect may lead to irreversible climatic changes, such as global warming, the consequences of which for human beings are hard to predict. The third assessment report of Working Group I of the Intergovernmental Panel on Climate Change (IPPC, 2001) estimates that global warming would raise average temperatures by 1.4–5.8°C. Sea levels are projected to rise by between 0.09 and 0.88 metres. There is still a lively scientific debate on whether recent climatic changes are natural fluctuations within the same basic pattern or indications of changes in climatic trends. The greenhouse effect itself is still subject to empirical debate. A second debate rages on whether or not global warming is the result of human behaviour, as against factors such as sun spots or volcano activity. The IPCC (2001: p. 10) concludes that 'there is new and stronger evidence that most of the warming observed over the last 50 years is attributable to human activities'. Critics of Malthusianism such as

Beckerman (1993) and Lomborg (2001) warn that we should balance unknown future effects of climatic changes against the known huge costs of Draconian measures to control CO_2 emissions. On the other hand, the risks of not taking policy measures are so high that governments and international organisations are gradually shifting towards policies aimed at controlling the increase of CO_2 emissions. This is indicated by the adoption of the Framework convention on Climate Change adopted at the international UN conference of world leaders on environment and development in Rio de Janeiro in 1992. In practice, countries have been slow to implement the proposed measures. In 2001, international agreement was reached on a watered-down version of policy measures to reduce greenhouse emissions. But one of the major polluters, the USA, withdrew from the climate convention in 2002.

(c) The dilution of the ozone layer

Dilution of the ozone layer increases the danger of skin cancers and related diseases.

(d) Declining biodiversity

Biodiversity should be seen as a genetic insurance policy against unknown future risks. Declining biodiversity means not only that interesting species are disappearing from the world at an alarming rate but it may also pose a threat towards continued human existence in the longer run.

(e) Land degradation, salination and desertification

It is estimated that in the past 45 years 1.2 billion hectares, almost 11 per cent, of the earth's vegetated surface have suffered moderate to extreme soil degradation (Oldeman, van Engelen and Pulles, 1990, quoted in UN, 1994). Irrigation can lead to salination. Inappropriate agricultural technologies can promote desertification. Land degradation is estimated to cause a loss of 12 million tons of grain output per year, equivalent to half the annual increase in production (Brown and Young, 1990). This is all the more urgent, as a growing world population requires 2 to 3.6 billion tons of additional cereals till 2030 (Birdsall, 1994). The modest impact of land degradation on overall growth tends to obscure the fact that it is the poorest cultivators who are hardest hit by land degradation.

From the preceding it is clear that the global environmental effects pose the most serious limits to unchecked population growth and growth of per capita income. They also provide powerful arguments for a policy mix, which includes effective population policies aimed at reducing growth rates and stabilising world population. Even so, one should not forget that even global environmental effects also depend on the rate of technological change. For instance, land degradation does not have to be irreversible if intensification of land use is accompanied by technological change which maintains or improves the productive capacity of land.

To a considerable extent the global environmental effects – especially those mentioned under b and c – are the consequences of industrial growth in the rich countries. However, if one thinks of the billions of people in developing countries striving to attain standards of living comparable to those in the rich countries, the fundamental threat to the global environment in the absence of technological change is obvious.

It would be incorrect, however, to blame environmental problems exclusively on growth of population and production. Institutions are also important. For instance, desertification and deterioration of agricultural land also have something to do with poorly defined property rights. In many parts of Africa there are still traditionally defined common rights of land use. Where individual property rights do not exist or are not enforced, individual users of land have little incentive to invest in maintaining or improving land quality. As a result farmers may continue to apply inappropriate technologies deriving from historical periods with lower population densities.

In the case of air pollution, water pollution and deforestation, market imperfections also play an important role. In the market the costs of environmental deterioration (external effects) are not charged to producers and consumers. Individual cost–benefit calculations result in outcomes which are socially unacceptable. Changes in market institutions, leading to internalisation of external costs, could contribute to solutions for environmental problems (Birdsall, 1988). Institutions which give voice to the poorest segments of the population can help tackle poverty-related causes of environmental degradation (World Bank, 2003).

Environmental problems are thus not only caused by population growth and economic growth but also by inefficient institutional arrangements. This being said, rapid population growth exacerbates existing environmental problems. It leaves less breathing space in which to search for solutions to environmental problems.

5.6.10   *Population growth and technological progress*

In two books, which have received considerable acclaim – *The Conditions of Agricultural Growth* and *Population and Technology* – Ester Boserup (1965; 1981) has drawn attention to the potentially stimulating effects of population growth on economic and technological development. She argues that increasing *population pressure* is a condition for productivity growth in agriculture and for industrialisation and technological progress in general. In particular in the period before 1750, when transport and communication were not so well developed, there was a strong correlation between the level of technological development and population density. But even today population pressure can exert a positive influence on technological development.

According to Boserup there are two countervailing influences. On the one hand, an increase of population leads to increasing pressure on natural resources. If technology does not change, there are diminishing returns. The economic surpluses available for investment and technological change will decline. On the other hand, population pressure is an incentive to develop new productivity-enhancing technologies (*innovation*) or take them over from elsewhere (*diffusion*).

Especially in agriculture, population pressure has had a stimulating influence, according to Boserup. As long as population is sparse, people can provide for subsistence by hunting, gathering or by very extensive use of land. As population pressure increases, people are forced to switch to settled agriculture and to the ever more intensive use of land. Intensification implies that one has to work ever harder to increase output per hectare, while maintaining land fertility by weed control, fertilisation and water control. The number of harvests per land area also increases gradually from one harvest in fifteen to twenty-five years in forest fallow agriculture, to several harvests per year in areas with high population density. Intensification allows for considerable increase in output per hectare. But it requires so much extra labour input that there is a strong incentive to develop labour-saving and output-increasing production technologies. In a recent neo-Boserupian study, Leach and Fairhead have even shown that in given institutional settings, increasing population density in West Africa can result in reforestation rather than deforestation (Leach and Fairhead, 2000).

Furthermore, without large population size and fairly high population density, it does not pay to invest in agricultural infrastructure. Infrastructural investment in water control and irrigation is a condition for further development of agriculture. Infrastructural investment in transport and communication facilities is even one of the necessary conditions for industrialisation (see Chapter 8) and modern economic growth.

Population size and growth are also preconditions for urbanisation. Prior to the development of modern transport technologies, only regions which were rich in population could afford to maintain and feed urban centres. These urban centres were the breeding grounds for subsequent technical and scientific progress.

Though the interconnections between population and technology have become less tight since the eighteenth century, Boserup is convinced that population pressure can still exert positive effects on development in present times. For instance, she suggests that the economic problems of many African countries are to some extent related to low population pressure. Low population pressure offers an insufficient basis for the necessary renewal and extension of infrastructure. In such a situation Malthusian mechanisms operate, where a growing population, using traditional agricultural technologies, is confronted with diminishing marginal returns.

Boserup's hypotheses are open to criticism. For instance, there are countries where the hypothesised relationships between population and technological development do not obtain. Nevertheless, her most important contribution is the concept of a race between Malthusian mechanisms of diminishing returns, on the one hand and increasing productivity as a result of technological change, on the other hand. These mechanisms are most clearly visible in the agrarian sector (see Chapter 10).

5.6.11 *Consequences of population growth: concluding remarks*

As we have shown, there are different schools of thought with regard to the consequences of population growth. The orthodox view emphasises the dangers of population growth. The 'revisionists' argue that high population growth is not necessarily associated with economic stagnation. They provide empirically founded criticisms of the pessimistic predictions of the Malthusians. Nevertheless, none of the participants in the discussion denies that dramatic population growth provides major challenges to developing countries. Control of population growth is still high on the political agenda, though it is now seen as but one of many aspects of the development problem.

In the final analysis, the exponential growth of world population is the most convincing argument in favour of control of population growth. Many pessimistic predictions concerning the negative consequences of population growth have drawn justifiable criticism. Nevertheless, it is obvious that if we want to provide an ever-growing world population with an adequate standard of living, the carrying capacity of the natural environment will sooner or later be exceeded.

5.7 Why do people in developing countries have so many children?

5.7.1 *Introduction*

In section 5.4, we saw that the high rate of population growth in developing countries can be explained by rapid declines in mortality in combination with continued high birth rates. The high birth rates in turn are determined by the youthful age structure of the population and the high number of births per women (high fertility). For an adequate understanding of the population problems of developing countries, it is important to find out why women in poor countries have so many children, in spite of the fact that large families strain family budgets and reduce the ability of families to invest in their children's health and education (Birdsall, 1994).[6]

In this context, Bongaarts has made a useful distinction between the intermediate determinants of fertility and the underlying economic, social and cultural determinants of fertility (Bongaarts, 1982; Bongaarts and Potter, 1983). The intermediate determinants are factors such as age of marriage, breastfeeding,

---

6 This section has benefited from advice from Harry van Vianen and Bert van Norren.

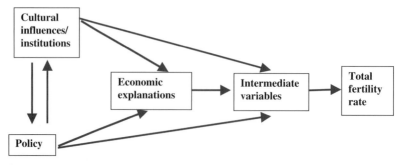

Figure 5.4 Determinants of fertility

contraception or abortion, which exert an immediate influence on the biological processes of reproduction. The more ultimate determinants include factors such as the cultural appreciation of children, sexual attitudes, female–male relationships, institutional arrangements, as well as the conscious or unconscious economic considerations which play a role in determining family size. The ultimate determinants do not affect fertility directly. They always work through the intermediate determinants, which Bongaarts calls '*intermediate fertility variables*'. The relationships are summarised in Figure 5.4. In section 5.7.2 the Bongaarts model of the effects of intermediate fertility variables is discussed. Section 5.7.3 deals with economic explanations of family size. Section 5.7.4 discusses underlying cultural and institutional determinants of fertility.

5.7.2 Intermediate determinants of fertility: the Bongaarts model

The point of departure for the Bongaarts model of fertility is the biological maximum number of childbirths a woman could experience in the course of the fertile period of her life. The intermediate fertility variables determine the extent to which realised fertility deviates from this biological maximum.

Bongaarts distinguishes seven intermediate fertility variables:

1. The percentage of women who, in the fertile period of their lives, are married (or who have a stable sexual relationship).
2. The use and the effectiveness of birth control techniques.
3. The practice of induced abortion.
4. The duration of the infertile period after the birth of a child owing to lactation and *post-partum infecundability*.
5. Frequency of sexual intercourse (*fecundability*).
6. Occurrence of spontaneous intra-uterine abortion.
7. The prevalence of permanent infertility.

Empirical research has shown that the first four variables are by far the most important in explaining variation in fertility.[7] The effects of these

---

7 Bongaarts mentions two criteria for the selection of important factors: (1) variations in a factor should be clearly associated with variation in fertility; (2) factors should vary from society to society. If they do not vary, they will not contribute to explanation of differences in fertility between countries and regions.

four variables are measured in relation to *total fecundity* (TF), which concept measures the combined effects of the last three fertility-inhibiting variables (fecundability, spontaneous abortion and infertility). Total fecundity varies from 13 to 17 births per woman, with an average of 15.3. The Bongaarts model can be summarised in the following equation:

$$TFR = \{C_m \times C_c \times C_a \times C_i\} \times TF$$

Total fertility (TFR, *total fertility rate*) equals the biological maximum of fertility (TF, total fecundity), multiplied by four indexes, varying in value from 0 to 1. If an index has a value of 1, fertility will not deviate from total fecundity owing to this factor. If any of the indices has a value of 0, total fertility will equal 0.

C_m is the *marriage index*. If all women in fertile age groups are married, then the value of this index is 1. If everyone is single, the value is 0. An important determinant of the marriage index is the age of marriage. In nineteenth-century Europe late marriages were the norm, so that substantial numbers of women in fertile age groups remained single. In Sub-Saharan Africa, people marry very young, which contributes to high realised fertility.

C_c is the *contraception index* which measures the use and effectiveness of birth control techniques. If all fertile women and their sexual partners used modern and effective birth control techniques under all circumstances, the index would take the value 0. The total fertility rate would also be 0. If nobody practises birth control, the value of the index would be 1.

C_a is the index for *induced abortion* again running from 1 (abortion is never practised) to 0 (all pregnancies are terminated by abortion).

C_i is the index for the period of infertility after the birth of a child (*post-partum infecundability*). This infertile period lasts a minimum of two months, but can be substantially longer when women breastfeed their children. Also the cultural practice of sexual abstinence after birth of a child can contribute to a lengthening of post-partum infecundability. The index has a value of 1 in case of complete absence of both breastfeeding and sexual abstinence. It takes a value of 0 in case of complete abstinence by women during their whole fertile life.

This Bongaarts model has two important advantages. In the first place it stimulates systematic empirical research concerning the intermediate determinants of fertility in different societies, social classes and historical periods. In the second place, the model structures the investigation of the various underlying economic and cultural variables. These underlying factors can only exert influence on fertility via the intermediate factors. For instance, changes in cultural norms concerning the age of marriage influence the marriage index, which in turn influences fertility. With the help of Bongaarts's analytical model it is possible to analyse, for instance, the extremely high fertility in a country such as Kenya. Here social–cultural changes have led to the disappearance of traditional barriers to high fertility such as lengthy breastfeeding and the practice of sexual abstinence by women after childbirth. The disappearance of traditional obstacles to high fertility is insufficiently compensated by an increase in the use of modern contraceptive techniques.

5.7.3   Economic explanations of fertility

Economic explanations of fertility assume that people to a certain extent weigh the costs and benefits of having children whether consciously or unconsciously. Having and raising children costs parents much time, energy and money. If couples have many children, this means they may have to sacrifice other valued things in life. As most people want to have some children anyway, cost–benefit considerations usually only start playing a role after the birth of a second child.

The following factors can influence in the decision whether or not to have another child (Becker, 1960; Birdsall, 1988; Easterlin, 1978; Schultz, 1997; Willis, 1973; 1994):

1. *The costs of educating children.* Structural changes in the economy require more skilled labour. The longer children have to go to school and the higher the parents' contribution to the costs of schooling, the higher the costs of children.

2. *The contributions of children to household income.* The earlier children start working – for instance by helping their parents in agriculture – the greater their economic advantages. In many African societies women need the help of their children in food production.

3. *Financial sacrifices made by parents.* Mothers especially face high opportunity costs when they are unable to take paid jobs outside the home, because they have to take care of many children. However, if the opportunities for paid work outside the home are scarce, the sacrifices will be correspondingly lower.

4. *Educational opportunities for women.* The greater the educational opportunities for women, the higher the costs of bearing and raising children. Given prevailing male–female relationships, it is difficult for women to participate in education when they have many children. A low level of education in its turn diminishes the chance of a woman finding well-paid work on the labour market.

5. *The distribution of costs and benefits between men and women.* This depends on the nature of relationships between men and women, on family structures and patterns of social organisation. Often the costs of children are not borne by the biological fathers, but by the mothers or by the extended family system. In such situations biological fathers have little incentive to limit family size.

6. *Provisions for old age.* Children function as a provision for old age in societies where publicly guaranteed systems of old age pensions are lacking. Also, the absence of well-developed financial markets and markets for land in many developing societies makes it difficult to save for one's old age. As traditional communities are opened up in the course of development and the geographic mobility of younger generations increases, the value of children as an investment in old age social security may decrease.

7. *Child mortality*. The higher the incidence of child mortality, the more children couples will have in order to ensure a sufficient number of surviving children.

Generalising broadly, one can reach the following conclusions on the basis of an economic analysis of fertility. The higher the household income, the more children as well as other desirable things in life one can afford. In this respect higher incomes make for higher fertility. On the other hand, the higher the level of income and education, the higher the opportunity costs of children become, compared to the costs of other valued goods and services. Usually, the latter effect dominates the former. Members of wealthy and highly educated social classes tend to opt for a smaller number of better-educated children (Birdsall, 1988). At lower income levels and in societies with underdeveloped markets, the advantages of children will be relatively greater and the opportunity costs lower. In such contexts, people tend to choose a large number of children. This implies that large families are related to poverty and that a decline in poverty will contribute towards lower fertility.

According to Caldwell (1976), low-income economies are characterised by an *upward flow of wealth* from younger to older generations. One aspect of the demographic transition is a shift from an upward flow of wealth to a downward flow in which older generations invest in their children.[8]

Of course, the economic analysis of fertility is open to criticism. One may doubt whether parents have sufficient information about costs and benefits. It is far from certain whether they consciously weigh the costs and benefits of children. Nevertheless, the model of economic choice focuses our attention on a number of variables which can be important for population policy. Thus, it seems clear that increasing educational opportunities for women make for lower fertility. Increased educational opportunities for children tend to have the same effects.

5.7.4   *Cultural and institutional explanations of fertility*

The economic model of rational choice can increase our understanding of the considerations affecting family size. However, the model of economic choice is no more than an empty vessel. Decisions and choices are always made within a matrix of institutional constraints and cultural preferences of men and women, which directly or indirectly influence the outcomes of their decision-making processes. With no knowledge of culturally determined preferences, we can say little or nothing about the outcomes of processes of economic choice. To give a very simple example, if the cultural value of children is higher in one society

---

8 Willis (1994) shows that this does not mean that parents in low-income societies are necessarily less altruistic than in high-income societies. The change in the direction of the flow of wealth can also be explained by the relative poverty or affluence of the parents.

than another, then, other things being equal, fertility will be higher in this society.

Cultural factors not only influence choices, they also operate via the intermediate fertility variables. If cultural norms and institutions make for early marriage, fertility will be higher than in societies where late marriage is the rule. If there is a religious taboo on the use of contraceptives, fertility will be higher than in societies where such taboos are absent.

In an interesting review article Caldwell and Caldwell have shown how cultural factors contribute to the extremely high levels of fertility in Sub-Saharan Africa (Caldwell and Caldwell, 1987; see also Caldwell and Caldwell, 1985; McNicoll, 1994). Their central thesis is that traditional belief systems, based on ancestor worship and the continuity of tribe and lineage, continue to be important to the present day in spite of the influences of Christianity and Islam. These cultural systems form a major obstacle to the successful introduction and diffusion of modern birth-control technologies.

Caldwell and Caldwell discuss the following factors:

1. *Ancestor worship*. After their death, the spirits of the deceased have to be tended by their descendants. This guarantees the continued existence of both the spirits and the kinship group. Large numbers of children are among the most important conditions for such continuity.
2. *Social prestige*. High fertility is seen as a reward of higher powers and proof of virtuous behaviour in one's life. The social prestige of women is dependent on having large numbers of children. Infertility is associated with witchcraft, adultery or manifestations of evil. Contraceptive techniques in turn are associated with infertility and are therefore rejected. Fear of infant mortality and concern with the continuity of the lineage form a further legitimisation of large numbers of births.
3. *Respect for elders*. Ancestor worship is associated with respect for elders in lineage groups. Traditional African societies provide a typical example of the upward flow of wealth from younger to older generations. Therefore parents profit from large numbers of children.
4. *Male dominance*. Decisions concerning reproductive behaviour frequently rest with the males, while the burden of upkeep of the children is on the females. This divorce between benefits and costs makes for high fertility.
5. *Kinship relationships*. In several societies, women are not considered to be part of the kinship group of their husbands. Though responsible for the cultivation of the food crops, they have no independent rights to land. Their access to land depends on having children, who can also be used as labour. In this way, women also have an interest in high fertility.
6. *Shared costs of raising children*. Furthermore, in traditional societies the costs of raising children are spread over many relatives in the extended family: aunts, grandmothers, and so forth. Adoption is also a frequent phenomenon. Once again this weakens the links between having children and bearing the costs and responsibilities of their education.

7. *Sexual abstinence.* Lengthy sexual abstinence by women after the birth of a child or grandchild is a traditionally accepted practice. This is sometimes used as a reason for rejecting modern birth control techniques.

According to Caldwell and Caldwell, all these factors together make for high fertility and culturally legitimised opposition to birth control. Cultural barriers explain why birth-control programmes in countries such as Kenya and Ghana have met with so little success. They also explain why governments in African countries are so hesitant to start large-scale birth-control programmes. In another article the same authors argue that the world diffusion of cultural notions of birth control has been an important contributor to the global process of demographic transition.

In the long run cultural factors themselves are in turn also influenced by changes in economic and social conditions and policies. Bengtsson and Gunnarsson (1994) argue that where economic and political institutions provide insufficient basic security for large segments of the population, seemingly 'traditional' fertility patterns and family institutions should be seen as rational responses to extreme uncertainty. Cultural elements and institutions are not autonomous. If equitable economic growth leads to more basic security for large segments of the population, this may be ultimately reflected in institutional changes and choices for smaller families.

Of course, cultural and institutional influences vary from society to society. Nevertheless, we can derive at least four lessons from the studies discussed above.

1. Birth-control programmes which go against the grain of strong culturally determined attitudes, have little chance of success.
2. Cultural factors influence both the intermediate determinants of fertility, and the economic considerations which consciously or unconsciously play a role in determining family size.
3. Culturally buttressed attitudes concerning male–female relationships are of great importance in explaining fertility levels and trends. Conversely, one may say that, whatever the cultural context, improvements in the social position of women – in terms of education, economic and social independence, equality between sexes – contribute to a lowering of birth rates.
4. Cultural factors and institutional arrangements affecting fertility can in turn be seen as responses to risks and uncertainties to which people are exposed over time in stagnant low-income economies.

5.8 Policy

In the 1990s around 5 billion US dollars per year was available for population policies. The bulk of these resources was directly or indirectly devoted to family planning programmes (Bongaarts, 1997). This raises the question of the importance and impact of these and other policies.

In the long run, one may expect fertility rates in developing countries to decline spontaneously under the influence of economic and social development, as has happened in present-day prosperous countries. Indications of declining fertility are now becoming visible in the developing world (see Table 5.3). Improving standards of living, the penetration of the money economy, urbanisation and industrialisation all change the cost–benefit ratios of children and make the advantages of large family size less obvious. Culturally legitimised preferences for high fertility are gradually eroded in the process of development. Such patterns of spontaneous fertility decline manifested themselves in the 1960s in countries such as South Korea, Singapore and Hong Kong (World Bank, 1984: p. 106).

In economic development it is not only the growth of per capita income that is important, but also the distribution of incomes and life chances. Success in combating widespread poverty, improvements in the health situation, increasing life expectations, rising educational levels and declining illiteracy are all conducive to declines in the fertility rate. Thus, between 1965 and 1975 the fertility rate in countries such as Sri Lanka, Thailand and Turkey declined faster than could have been expected on the basis of average economic growth rates.

One may conclude that policies aimed at overall socio-economic development will also contribute to a much-needed decline in fertility, especially if the benefits of development are evenly distributed over the whole population. However, present birth rates are too high for policy makers to wait till spontaneous declines set in. Direct measures aimed at limiting the rate of population growth are still urgently required.

There is an interesting debate about the relative contribution of population policies to past and future fertility declines. Critics such as Pritchett (1994) have argued that the claims of advocates of birth control policies have been overstated. Declines in desired fertility have been more important than catering to unmet demand for contraception through family planning policies. In an overview of this debate, Bongaarts (1997) acknowledges the validity of some of these criticisms. But he concludes that past investments in family planning programmes have nevertheless substantially accelerated fertility declines. As a consequence, world population is expected to stabilise at an earlier date and at a lower level than in older population projections (see section 5.3). Though the future impact of family planning policies will be more modest than in the past, they remain important. The slowdown in population growth rates in the medium projections depends on assumptions concerning continued fertility decline. The medium projections are based on the assumption that programme efforts will be maintained at current levels.

Among the determinants of fertility, the cultural determinants are most resistant to policy influences. At best one can hope that if governments show sufficient conviction in propagating birth control, this may in the long run contribute to a gradual erosion of culturally and religiously founded objections to population control. What policy can do most effectively is change the

Table 5.5 *Government policies and birth control*

Policies and legislation	Government expenditures	Tax programmes
• Minimum marriage age • Promoting breastfeeding • Improving the status of women • Children's education and work • Active encouragement of birth control	• Education • Primary health care • Family planning • Incentives for fertility control • Old-age security	• Family allowances • Tax penalties for larger families

Source: World Bank: (1984: p. 106).

balance of costs and benefits involved in individual choices with regard to family size. Policy can also directly influence the intermediate determinants of fertility.

Table 5.5 summarises the ways in which policy makers can try to influence reproductive behaviour. In this table a distinction is made between: (1) policy and legislation; (2) government expenditures; and (3) tax programmes (World Bank, 1984: p. 106).

Of the policy measures set out in the table, the following primarily affect the intermediate determinants of fertility:

1. Policies or legislation aimed at increasing the minimum age of marriage. Late marriages lead to lower fertility rates.
2. Abortion legislation. Legislation can have a direct influence (positive or negative) on Bongaarts's abortion index.
3. Policies aimed at promoting breastfeeding. Breastfeeding lengthens the period of infertility after childbirth.
4. Government expenditure on and government policy concerning birth control. There is a clear relationship between the use of modern birth-control techniques and family size. Expenditure and policy can increase the availability of modern contraceptives and lower the costs for their users. Such policy is especially effective if there is an unmet demand for birth control. This is the case when many couples have more children than they would prefer to have.

Policy can also aim at influencing the choices parents make. The following areas of policy are of interest in this respect:

1. *Improvement in the socio-economic status of women.* There is a strong correlation between improvement in the social status of women and a decline in fertility rates. Status improvement has to do with both educational opportunities and labour-market opportunities for women and with more equality in relationships between men and women in general.
2. *Improved educational opportunities for children.* Investment in education increases the costs of having children. When educational opportunities are available, parents will tend to opt for a smaller number of more highly educated children.

3. *Regulating or even prohibiting child labour.* This restricts economic activities by children and diminishes their potential economic benefits.
4. *Expenditures for old-age pensions and provisions.* The better old-age provisions are, the less parents will depend on their children for old-age security.
5. *Improved functioning of capital markets.* Capital markets make it possible to set aside savings for old-age provisions.
6. *Educational expenditures.* The greater the educational opportunities for women, the greater the sacrifices they have to make in order to have many children. In addition, education increases knowledge of and receptivity to modern birth-control techniques among both women and men.
7. *Expenditures for primary health care.* Such expenditures contribute to lower child mortality. The higher the child mortality, the more families will tend to insure themselves against the risk of losing children by having many children.
8. *Affordability of contraceptive techniques.* Expenditures for birth control can lower the costs of contraception. This is especially important where there is an unmet need for contraception.
9. *Rewards and sanctions.* One of the most important ways in which governments can influence choices with regard to family size is through material rewards and sanctions. Positive rewards for families with few children can consist of tax cuts, subsidies, better educational opportunities and better housing. Negative sanctions include the loss of tax advantages and subsidies or even tax levies on children. Negative sanctions also include social pressure by local authorities, as in the case of the one-child policy of China.

Rewards and sanctions change the balance between the costs and benefits of children and can stimulate people to have smaller families. But there are all kinds of ethical objections to the too blatant use of rewards and sanctions. In the first place, the sanctions tend to place an additional burden on the children from large families, who will be even worse off than before. In the second place, for very poor people incentives and sanctions can end up as a form of coercion, which violates elementary human freedoms. In the case of China, the pressure for smaller families in combination with the preference for male descendants has led to an increasing imbalance between male and female births. Recent research suggests that this is due to sex-selective abortion (Junhong, 2001). The use of incentives and sanctions to promote irreversible interventions such as sterilisation especially raises fundamental moral issues. This is even more the case if there are insufficient guarantees that participation in birth-control programmes is entirely voluntary, as was sometimes the case in countries such as India and China. Thus the World Population Plan of Action adopted in September 1994 by the United Nations Conference on Population and Development in Cairo, reaffirms the basic right of individuals and couples 'to decide freely and responsibly the number and spacing of their children and to have the information, education and means to do so' (UN Population Division, 1994).

Conversely, population pressure in densely populated countries such as China, India, Bangladesh and Indonesia is so excessively high that a system of incentives can well be defended. Some experts argue for the use of 'deferred incentives' in the form of pension schemes for people with small families. With deferred incentives, the burden of the decision rests on the parents rather than on the children.

Of great importance is the conviction with which governments pursue birth-control policies. In the Middle East and in Africa, government efforts to promote birth control have been half-hearted at best. Cultural and religious factors not only impede the execution of existing policies. They also form obstacles to the formulation of new policies.

In Asian countries, population policy has received greater priority than in Africa and Latin America. Especially in China, a marked decline in fertility has been realised since 1979 in the context of the 'one child per family' programme (Goodstadt, 1982). In this programme extensive use has been made of systems of incentives and sanctions such as those described above.

Questions for review

1. Discuss the concept of the demographic transition.
2. Compare demographic developments in the developing countries with earlier demographic developments in the currently rich countries of Western Europe.
3. Why do families in developing countries frequently have so many children?
4. Is rapid population growth a threat to economic development? Give an overview of the various ways in which population growth could affect the prospects for economic growth.
5. Why is technical change important in assessing the consequences of population growth?
6. Why should rapid population growth result in increasing economic and social inequality?
7. What is the difference between localised and global environmental effects of growth?
8. Summarise the debate on the issue of 'growing first and cleaning up later'.
9. What is the relationship between poverty and fertility?
10. Give examples of how government policies can affect the intermediate determinants of fertility
11. Give examples of how government policies can affect the choices families make with regard to family size.

Further reading

A important source of demographic statistics is the website of the United Nations Population Division, *World Population Prospects: Population Data Base*, http://esa.un.org/unpp. The same organisation is the authoritative source for long-run population projections: *Long-Range World Population Projections: Based on the 1998 Revision. Dataset in Digital Form*: http://www.un.org./esa/population/publications/longrange/longrange.htm Useful summaries of population data are also to be found in Maddison's, *The World Economy Historical Statistics* (2003) and the website of the Groningen Growth and Development Centre http://www. ggdc.net/.

Other relevant statistical publications are: United Nations Population Division, *World Population Prospects: The 1998 revision, Vol. I, Comprehensive Tables* (1999); United Nations Population Division, *World Population Prospects: The 2000 Revision*, Vols. I, II and III (2001);

and United Nations Population Divison, *World Urbanization Prospects: The 2001 Revision,* http://www.un.org/esa/population/unpop.htm

The following three publications provide a comprehensive introduction to the study of the relationships between demography and economic development: Birdsall's article 'Economic Approaches to Population Growth', in the *Handbook of Development Economics,* Vol. I (1988); Kelley's review article 'Economic Consequences of Population Change in the Third World' (1988), in the *Journal of Economic Literature*; and the excellent edition of the World Development Report entitled *Population Change and Development* (1984).

Interesting articles on the demographic transition in developing countries are Caldwell's 1976 article, 'Toward a Restatement of Demographic Transition Theory', his more recent 1997 article 'The Global Fertility Transition: The Need for a Unifying Theory'; and Wilson's article, 'On the Scale of Global Demographic Convergence, 1950–2000' (2001). All these articles have appeared in the *Population and Development Review* which is the most prominent journal for the study of population issues in developing countries. Also of interest is a collection of papers on *The Continuing Demographic Transition* (1997), edited by Jones *et al.*

The term sustainable development was introduced to a wider public in the Brundlandt report, *Our Common Future* (1987). One of the main sources for global warming consists of the reports of the Intergovernmental Panel on Climate Change, such as *Climate Change 2001: The Scientific Basis* (2001). Sustainability is the theme of the 2003 World Development Report, *Sustainable Development in a Dynamic World.*

The anti-Malthusian perspective is represented by Ester Boserup's *Population and Technology* (1981), Julian Simon's *The Ultimate Resource* (1982) and Bjørn Lomborg's, *The Skeptical Environmentalist* (2001).

Intermediate sources of fertility are discussed in the classical article by Bongaarts, 'The Fertility-Inhibiting Effects of the Intermediate Fertility Variables' (1982) and in *Fertility, Biology and Behavior: An Analysis of the Proximate Determinants* (1983) by Bongaarts and Potter. For the economic analysis of fertility one can consult an article, 'Demand for Children in Low Income Countries' (1997), by Theodor Schultz in the *Handbook of Population and Family Economics.* An interesting discussion of the cultural aspects of fertility is provided in the article, 'The Cultural Context of High Fertility in Sub-Sahara Africa' (1987), by Caldwell and Caldwell.

6

Health,
health care
and
development

Health and education are important aspects of development. They belong to the basic needs every development strategy tries to meet (Deolalikar, 1988). Improving the state of health and the level of education also contributes to the realisation of other developmental objectives such as economic development, labour productivity growth, responsiveness to innovation, and future orientedness. From the perspective of economic development investment in education and health care can be regarded as an investment in human capital. In turn, economic growth and development feeds back into improvements and health, education and other indicators of human development (Ranis, Stewart and Ramirez, 2000).

In this chapter the main focus is on the discussion of health-related issues. We document trends in child mortality, average life expectancy, and patterns of morbidity and health. The factors that determine developments in health are identified. In the light of these factors, we pay attention to health policies. In Chapter 7 the focus shifts to education. The following issues will be dealt with: investment in human capital, educational enrolment, literacy and educational policies. Both chapters discuss the interactions between the various aspects of development. For example, education can contribute substantially to improvements in health.

6.1   The state of health in developing countries

6.1.1   Quantitative indicators of the state of health

We can distinguish three main types of indicators of the state of health (Hardiman and Midgley, 1982):

1. *Health service indicators*, such as the number of doctors, medical staff or hospital beds, or financial resources devoted to health and health care.
2. *Morbidity statistics* that chart the prevalence of different types of diseases.
3. *Demographic indicators* such as life expectancy at birth, mortality rates and child mortality rates.

Health service indicators present the least reliable picture of the state of health. These indicators refer to the inputs into health care. They do not provide any information on the functioning or effectiveness of systems of health care. In theory, *indicators of morbidity* (i.e. diseases) offer the most complete picture of the state of health. In practice, however, not enough information on the prevalence of diseases is available. Even in highly developed countries morbidity registration is unreliable; in developing countries the situation is even worse. Here no full medical records of the population are kept. One has to rely on questionnaires in which people subjectively answer questions concerning their past and present health. The data derived from these questionnaires reflect important subjective and culturally determined aspects of illness and health (Strauss and Thomas, 1998). But they are not comparable across countries and regions and they tend to be biased according to age, sex and education. This approach cannot provide us with reliable information about the actual prevalence of different types of diseases in different countries or regions.

Therefore, *demographic indicators* are used most frequently. They are relatively easy to register and they reflect some of the important aspects of health. The drawback of demographic indicators such as the mortality rate and average life expectancy is that they do not tell us very much about the actual state of health of the surviving population. Many diseases in developing countries are chronic. They undermine health and welfare even when they do not result in death.

Demographic indicators also need to be employed with some caution. Data on many developing countries are often incomplete or insufficiently reliable (UN, 1988a; 1988b; Walsh, 1990). Only 74 countries presently have complete coverage of vital mortality statistics (WHO, 2002).

In recent years, demographic indicators have been merged with information about morbidity into indicators measuring *quality-adjusted life years* (QUALYs). One such indicator is years of *healthy life expectancy* (HALE). This indicator deducts average years spent in ill health from average life expectancy (WHO, 2002). A related indicator is *disability-adjusted life years* (DALYs). This indicator measures healthy years of life lost owing to premature mortality or diseases, relative to some reference ideal. Diseases are weighted with a disability weight. Reductions in expected DALYs can be used for policy purposes to measure the benefits of different kinds of interventions (Murray and Acharya, 1997; Murray and Lopez, 1996). These are valuable new indicators. But, the data requirements for the calculation of these indexes are enormous and the choice of standardised weights for different disabilities across the world is highly debatable.

The next sections will pay special attention to the following demographic indicators: infant and child mortality; average life expectancy at birth; patterns of illness as reflected by causes of death.

6.1.2   Infant and child mortality

Mortality is distributed bimodally, with high probabilities of dying in the first years of life (in particular at birth and immediately afterwards) and gradually increasing chances of dying after the age of 30. High mortality among infants and children under the age of 5 is one of the important characteristics of the general state of health in developing countries. This, in turn, affects average life expectancy. For these reasons, the literature on health issues gives prominence to the topic of infant and child mortality.

Table 6.1 presents data on infant and child mortality. Infant mortality is defined as the chance of dying between the age of 0 and 1 per 1,000 births. Child mortality is defined as the chance of dying between the age of 0 and 5 per 1,000 births. In the 1995–2000 period the average infant mortality rate per 1,000 live births in developing countries was 65 as compared to 8 in the more developed countries. The mortality rate for children under the age of 5 was 95 per 1,000 in developing countries and 10 per 1,000 in more developed countries.

It is not just the contrasts between developing and more developed countries that stand out. There are also great differences among developing countries themselves. For example, the infant mortality rate in countries like Pakistan, Côte d'Ivoire, Nigeria, Democratic Republic of Congo, and Zambia is over 85. In countries such as Argentina, Chile, Malaysia, South Korea, Thailand and Venezuela it is between 13 and 31. Africa has by far the highest infant mortality (91). The lowest infant mortality rates are found in Latin America (36) and East Asia (41). The regional distribution of child mortality under the age of 5 shows similar patterns.

Since World War II, infant and child mortality has decreased strongly in developing countries. Even in Africa, which lags behind other developing regions, infant mortality dropped from 181 in 1950–5 to 91 in 1995–2000. During the same period child mortality was halved (see also Vallin, 1989). In other parts of the world, especially in Asia, the decrease was even more dramatic.

In *Global Strategy for Health for All by the Year 2000* (WHO, 1981) one of the stated objectives was that infant mortality in the year 2000 should be no higher than 50. Under-5 mortality should be below 70. For the very poorest countries the

Table 6.1 *Infant and child mortality, 1950–2000 (probability of dying per 1,000 births)*

	1950–5 Probability of dying		1995–2000 Probability of dying	
	Between 0–1 years	Between 0–5 years	Between 0–1 years	Between 0–5 years
Bangladesh	207	312	79	111
China	195	266	41	48
India	190	332	73	99
Indonesia	201	270	48	63
Malaysia	99	147	12	15
Pakistan	181	332	95	144
Philippines	134	178	34	42
South Korea	115	164	8	10
Taiwan			7	8
Sri Lanka	92	151	23	27
Thailand	111	195	25	32
Turkey	233	318	46	60
Argentina	66	84	22	25
Brazil	135	187	42	49
Chile	120	162	13	15
Colombia	123	189	30	39
Mexico	121	193	31	38
Peru	159	268	45	65
Venezuela	106	148	21	25
Congo, Dem. Rep.	166	266	91	151
Côte d'Ivoire	186	350	89	152
Egypt	200	350	51	64
Ghana	149	250	69	112
Kenya	155	254	65	109
Morocco	180	310	52	68
Nigeria	183	345	88	147
South Africa	96	217	58	83
Tanzania	160	270	81	129
Zambia	150	254	94	167
Average 29 developing countries	150	242	49	75
Africa	181	322	91	152
Latin America	126	189	36	45
Asia	182	278	59	80
East Asia excl. Japan	195	267	41	47
Southeast Asia	168	244	48	65
South-central Asia	188	327	76	107
West Asia	190	307	49	62
Developing countries	180	281	65	95
More developed countries	59	73	8	10

Sources: UN Population Division, *World Population Prospects: The 2000 Revision*, Population Data Base, http://esa.un.org/unpp, except Under-5 Mortality Rate 1950–5: United Nations (1988b) and Taiwan: DGBAS (2003).

1990 infant-mortality target was 120 per 1,000. Table 6.1 shows that in Latin America and large parts of Asia the global infant-mortality targets have been met.[1] This is not the case for Africa. In 1995, worldwide 64 per cent of all countries met the under-5 mortality target and 60 per cent met the infant

---

1 Different statistical sources are unanimous with regard to mortality trends, but not with regard to mortality levels. Especially for Asia, the *World Development Indicators* (World Bank, 2002) show much lower levels than the United Nations Population Data Base (UN Population Division, World Population Prospects: Population Data Base, http://esa.un.org/unpp). This is presumably owing to the fact that the World Bank source calculates mortality as a percentage of live births, rather than total births.

mortality target. In WHO projections 94 per cent of all countries are expected to have met these targets by 2025 (WHO, 1998).

Fears that the decrease in infant mortality has been slowing down since the 1980s (Caldwell, 1986; UN, 1984) have so far proved to be unfounded. From year to year, infant and child mortality rates continue to decline. Thus, projected infant mortality in 2000–5 is 59 per 1,000, compared to 77.4 per 1,000 in 1985–90. Projected child mortality for 2000–5 is 86, against 95 in 1995–2000.[2] In African countries hardest hit by AIDS (Malawi, Rwanda, Uganda, Zambia) mortality estimates have being revised upwards (UN, 1994; WHO, 2002). But so far this primarily affects older age groups rather than children.

Despite positive trends, present levels of infant and child mortality in developing countries are still unacceptably high. In relative terms the gap between developing and rich countries has even widened. In 1950, the probability of an infant in a developing country dying before the age of 1 was 3.1 times as high as in rich countries; today the probability is 8.1 times as high. The probability of a child dying before it reaches its fifth birthday in a developing country is almost ten times as high as in more developed countries. Also the gap between the least developed countries and other developing countries seems to be on the increase (UN, 2001; WHO, 1993).[3]

6.1.3 Life expectancy

Table 6.2 and Table 6.3 present data on life expectancy at birth in developing countries. Table 6.2 focuses on our sample of developing countries. Table 6.3 presents aggregate data for regions and compares developing countries with more developed countries.

The increase of life expectancy in developing countries is one of the most marked manifestations of the dynamics of development. On average, a child born at the end of the twentieth century will live 21 years longer than a child born two generations earlier in the 1950s. This is primarily owing to reductions in infant and child mortality. In the twenty-nine countries included in Table 6.2, life expectancy has increased from 45 to 63 years. In the developing world as a whole it has increased from 41 to 63 years. Today, on average, people in economically advanced countries live 12 years longer than people in developing countries (74.9 versus 62.9 years). In 1950, the difference was no less than 25 years. In this important respect, there is a substantial narrowing of the gap between economically advanced countries and developing countries. There are marked differences between regions. Particularly in Africa, life expectancy is still low. In Table 6.2 this is illustrated by the data for countries like

---

2 UN Population Division, *World Population Prospects*: Population Data Base, http://esa.un.org/unpp
3 Between 1985–90 and 2000–2005 infant mortality in the least developed countries increased from 169 per cent to 186 per cent of infant mortality in other LDCs (UN Population Division, *World Population Prospects*, Population Data Base, http://esa.un.org/unpp).

Table 6.2 *Life expectancy at birth in selected developing countries, 1920–2000*[a] *(years)*

	1920	1930	1940	1950	1972	1992	2000
Bangladesh	20[b]	27[c]	32[d]	37	45	56	61
China				41	63	69	70
India		27[e]		39	50	60	63
Indonesia				38	49	63	66
Malaysia				49	63	71	73
Pakistan	20[b]	27[c]	32[d]	41	51	60	63
Philippines				48	58	67	69
South Korea		38	41	48	61	71	73
Sri Lanka				56	65	71	73
Taiwan			43	52[f]	70[g]	74	75
Thailand				52	60	70	69
Turkey				44	58	67	70
Argentina				63	67	72	74
Brazil	37			51	60	66	68
Chile		37	39	55	64	74	76
Colombia		33		51	62	69	72
Mexico			39	51	63	71	73
Peru				44	56	67	69
Venezuela				55	66	72	73
Congo, Dem. Rep.				39	46	52	46
Côte d'Ivoire				36	45	49	46
Egypt			39[h]	42	52	64	68
Ghana				42	50	58	57
Kenya				41	51	57	47
Morocco				43	53	65	68
Nigeria				37	43	50	47
South Africa				45	54	63	48
Tanzania				37	46	49	44
Zambia				38	47	49	38
Average Asian countries				45	58	67	69
Average Latin Am. countries				53	62	70	72
Average African countries				40	49	55	51
Average 29 developing countries	26	32	38	45	56	64	63
Russian Federation				65	70	68	66
Average OECD				69	72	77	78

Notes:
[a] Data for 1950 and before are mostly five-year averages. The figures in the table are simple interpolations.
[b] 1921;
[c] 1931;
[d] 1941;
[e] average 1921–31;
[f] Taiwan, 1950 interpolated with growth rate 1940–60. 1959–60: average from UN (1963);
[g] 1971: the average of male and female life expectancy;
[h] average 1936–8.
Sources: 1920, 1930, 1940: Unless indicated otherwise United Nations (1953); Bangladesh, Pakistan, South Korea: United Nations/ESCAP (1985); 1950: UN Population Division, *World Population Prospects: The 2000 Revision*, Population Data Base, http://esa.un.org/unpp; 1972–2000: World Bank, *World Development Indicators 2002*, except Taiwan, 1972–2000: DGBAS, database: http://www.dgbas.gov.tw/dgbas03/bs2/91chy/catalog.htm, accessed October 2002. Russian Federation, all years: Population Data Base, http://esa.un.org/unpp

Côte d'Ivoire, Kenya, Nigeria, Tanzania and Zambia. In 2000, the average life expectancy was 51.4 years. In South Asian countries average life expectancy is also comparatively low: 61.5 years. In Table 6.2 this region is represented by India, Pakistan and Bangladesh. The highest life expectancy can be discerned in East Asia. In 2000, life expectancy in China was 70 years. Latin American countries also do well in terms of this indicator. Here average life expectancy is 69.3.

Table 6.3 *Life expectancy at birth per region, 1950–2005*

	1950–5	1985–90	1995–2000	2000–5
Africa	37.8	51.7	51.4	51.3
Latin America	51.4	66.6	69.3	70.4
Asia				
East Asia excl. Japan	39.9	67.2	70.0	71.4
Southeast Asia	41.0	61.3	65.3	67.0
South Asia	39.3	57.3	61.5	63.3
West Asia	45.2	65.1	67.9	70.0
Developing countries	41.0	60.4	62.9	64.1
More developed countries	66.2	74.1	74.9	75.6
OECD countries	67.6	75.8	77.8	78.6

Source: *World Population Prospects: The 2000 Revision*, reproduced in Population Data Base, UN Population Division, *World Population Prospects*, Population Data Base, http://esa.un.org/unpp.

The data for the African countries in Table 6.2 reveal the shocking impact of the AIDS epidemic. Since 1992, the trend towards increasing life expectancy in Africa has been reversed. Life expectancy has declined from 55 to 51 years. The most dramatic examples are South Africa where life expectancy decreased from 63 to 48 years and Zambia where life expectancy dropped from 49 to 38. The aggregate figures for all countries in Africa show hardly any decline, but it is clear that the rising trend in life expectancy has come to a halt. The divergence between Africa and other developing countries is increasing.

Table 6.2 also includes a row for the Russian Federation. Here life expectancy has declined drastically by more than four years in the period of economic and political chaos following the dissolution of the Soviet Union. Similar declines have been registered in many other former Soviet republics, especially during the period 1989–95 (Brainerd, 1998; Becker and Hemley, 1998). These reversals in Africa and the Soviet Union provide an illustration of the fragility of developmental gains. There is no unilineal process of everlasting advance and improvement. In a recent estimate the World Health Organization compares life expectancy with and without the impact of AIDS for the year 2000. On average, life expectancy at birth in Sub-Saharan Africa is six years lower than it would have been in the absence of AIDS for males and seven years lower for females (WHO, 2002: table 6). Countries experiencing the most dramatic impacts are Namibia, Botswana, Zambia, Lesotho, Swaziland and Zimbabwe (see also Table 6.5). For instance, the AIDS gap for Namibian females is 21.5 years.

The stated life-expectancy target for 2000 was 60 years (WHO, 1981). In 2000, this target was met in twenty-one of our twenty-nine sample countries. World-wide 86 per cent of all countries had met this target in 1995 (WHO, 1998).

6.1.4   Patterns of disease and health

It is difficult to obtain reliable data on the causes of death in developing countries. There is no complete and systematic registration, and it is often hard to determine the disease a person has died of. Still, some clear patterns can be discerned. In poor developing countries infectious intestinal and respiratory diseases are the most important cause of death. In rich countries neoplasms (cancer), cardiovascular diseases and degenerative diseases rank high among the causes of death (WHO, 1987). Many of these diseases are lifestyle-related, age-related or both. Table 6.4 presents a broad survey of the most important causes of death in different parts of the world for the period 1980–2000. This table indicates that infectious and parasitic diseases caused about 40 per cent of all deaths in developing countries in 1980. Other sources present even higher estimates. According to Hardiman and Midgley (1982), infectious diseases cause 40 per cent to 50 per cent of all deaths in developing countries. In a study by Walsh (1990) the share of infectious and parasitic diseases in 1986 is estimated to be 35.4 per cent and the share of respiratory diseases 26.8 per cent, adding up to a total 62.2 per cent of all deaths. In 1990, WHO statistics indicate that 44.2 per cent of all deaths in developing countries are due to infectious and parasitic diseases. In the year 2000, infectious and parasitic diseases accounted for 39.2 per cent of all deaths.

Infectious and parasitic diseases especially claim the lives of children under the age of 5. Even if these diseases do not result in death, they may permanently impair the development, welfare and general state of health of their victims.

The statistics for 2000 distinguish a special category for AIDS-related mortality. For all developing countries, AIDS accounts for 6.9 per cent of all deaths in 2000, compensating for the declining trend in other infectious diseases. In the African region, AIDS is seen as accounting for no less than 22.6 per cent of total mortality. Including AIDS, infectious diseases account for 63.8 per cent of mortality in Africa.

Table 6.4 shows that cardiovascular diseases, other degenerative diseases, and neoplasms cause over two-thirds of all deaths in the economically more developed countries. Cardiovascular and degenerative diseases cause over 50 per cent of all deaths (see also UN/ESCAP, 1985), and neoplasms (cancer) about 20 per cent. These diseases are very much age-related, that is they gain in importance as the population grows older. Cardiovascular diseases and cancer are also typically Western diseases closely related to lifestyle, stress and eating habits. Between 1980 and 2000 the share of these diseases increased even further to 80 per cent.

These classes of diseases are less important in developing countries than in the more developed countries. The infectious diseases typically characteristic of developing countries manifest themselves primarily amongst children. The diseases characteristic of more developed countries typically occur at more advanced ages. Deaths in these countries are concentrated in the higher age groups.

The difference in patterns of morbidity is one of the explanations for why life expectancy in developing countries is lower than in more developed countries. Moreover, it also explains why the differences in average death rates per 1,000 people are not so pronounced (see Chapter 5, Table 5.3); in more

Table 6.4 Causes of death by region, 1980–2000 (percentages)

Cause of death	Africa		Latin America		South and Southeast Asia		Eastern Mediterranean/ West Asia[a]		East Asia/ Western Pacific[b]		Developing countries			More developed countries[c]		
	1980	2000	1980	2000	1980	2000	1980	2000	1980	2000	1980	1990	2000	1980	1990	2000
Infectious and parasitic diseases	49.7	63.8	31.2	20.6	43.9	34.3	44.4	35.7	27.2	27.4	39.9	44.2	39.2	7.6	4.4	10.6
excluding AIDS		*41.2*		*18.8*		*31.7*		*34.4*		*27.1*			*32.3*			*10.4*
AIDS		*22.6*		*1.8*		*2.6*		*1.3*		*0.3*			*6.9*			*0.3*
Neoplasms	2.9	5.1	8.9	12.4	4.3	8.0	4.0	6.1	8.6	17.2	5.5	7.0	9.7	19.2	21.2	21.9
Cardiovascular (and degenerative) diseases	11.7	14.6	24.5	45.4	15.6	38.4	14.1	38.0	30.0	40.2	19.0	16.9	33.3	53.5	47.5	58.0
Conditions related to the perinatal period	8.5	5.5	8.3	4.3	8.3	7.1	9.8	7.5	4.9	3.1	7.7	9.1	5.6	1.6	0.8	0.7
Injuries and poisoning	3.8	7.1	6.4	12.3	4.3	9.7	4.0	8.4	6.7	11.2	4.9	6.8	9.5	6.5	7.6	7.9
Other causes (ill-defined or unknown)	23.4	3.9	20.7	4.9	23.5	2.5	23.5	4.2	22.5	0.8	23.0	16.1	2.8	11.6	18.6	0.8
Total	100.0	100.0	100.0	100.0	100.0	100.0	100.0	100.0	100.0	100.0	100.0	100.0	100.0	100.0	100.0	100.0
N (× 1,000)	7,180	10,572	3,140	3,097	15,430	14,157	3,960	4,036	9,630	10,238	40,140	38,500	42,100	10,670	11,440	13,594

Notes:
[a] including Libya, Morocco, Somalia, Sudan and Tunisia, excluding former Soviet Asian Republics
[b] excluding Japan, Australia and New Zealand
[c] including former Soviet Republics in Asia
Sources: 1980: WHO, 1987: p. 72; 1990: WHO (1993); 2000: WHO (2001).

developed countries there are more elderly people amongst whom the death rate is obviously much higher than in younger age groups.

Since the 1980s, new trends have become visible in developing countries (WHO, 1993; 1998, 1999). Cardiovascular diseases and cancer are rising rapidly as a proportion of all deaths. By 2000, they accounted for 33 and 10 per cent respectively of all mortality. More than half of all new cancer cases now occur in developing countries. The relative rise of cancer is related to both tobacco use and progress made in tackling other major causes of death. Finally, the AIDS epidemic has emerged as one of the most serious diseases in the developing world, especially but not exclusively in Africa. Nevertheless, non-AIDS infectious and parasitic diseases still remain the most important cause of death in developing countries.

A category of morbidity receiving more attention in recent years is that of mental disorders (WHO, 2001). Worldwide 45 million people are affected by schizophrenia, 29 million people suffer from dementia and 40 million people suffer from different types of epilepsy (WHO, 1997). Depression is one of the major disease burdens. Mental health problems have been underestimated in developing countries, where increasing numbers of adults and children are traumatised by warfare, civil strife, violence and hunger.

6.1.5   Common infectious and parasitic diseases in developing countries

In this section infectious and parasitic diseases have been categorised on the basis of the way they are passed on. Diseases can be transmitted through: (a) contaminated food and drinking water; (b) air; (c) direct physical contact; (d) parasites; and (e) animal bearers of diseases (vectors).

(a)   Diseases transmitted through contaminated water or food

Infectious diseases are often transmitted faecally, through direct contact with faeces or through contaminated food or drinking water. Insects and other animal bearers of infections – *vectors* – cause food to rot or water to be contaminated. Poor hygiene, therefore, is among the most serious pathogenic factors. Infectious diseases that are passed on in these ways include (Hardiman and Midgley, 1982; Maurice and Pearce, 1987; WHO, 1987):

- *Diarrhoea*. Diarrhoea is a collective name for infections of the digestive system. It is one of the most important causes of death among children in developing countries; 23.3 per cent of child mortality in 1990 was caused by diarrhoea (WHO, 1993). In 2000, 2.1 million persons died of this easily preventable disease (WHO, 2001).
- *Bacterial and viral diseases like cholera, poliomyelitis, hepatitis and typhus.* Faecally transmitted diseases like cholera and poliomyelitis are less common as a consequence of vaccination schemes, although they have not been eradicated by far. Cholera reemerged in South America in 1991. It is still prevalent

in at least 80 countries, causing 120,000 deaths a year (WHO, 1996). Polio is now close to eradication (WHO, 1996).

(b) Airborne diseases

Diseases transmitted by air – e.g. pneumonia, tuberculosis, diphtheria, smallpox, meningitis, pertussis (whooping cough) and measles – cause between a quarter and a third of all deaths in developing countries (Hardiman and Midgley, 1982; WHO, 2001: annex table 2). In 1990, 27.6 per cent of total child mortality was caused by acute infections of the respiratory system alone (WHO, 1993). Smallpox was officially eradicated by 1980. The last case was reported in Somalia in 1977 (WHO, 1996). Tuberculosis was once regarded as under control. In recent years it has been making a comeback owing to policy neglect and increased drug resistance. In 1996, TB killed over 3 million people (WHO, 1996; 1997). In 1998, 539 million people were suffering from TB, often in combination with HIV. Most cases are found in Africa (WHO, 1999). There are 100,000 cases of diphtheria a year, causing up to 8,000 deaths annually (WHO, 1996). With these diseases a vicious circle of poverty, undernourishment and infection plays a significant role.

(c) Diseases transmitted through direct physical contact

Other contagious diseases are transmitted through direct physical contact, for example leprosy (10–12 million cases in the 1980s, see Maurice and Pearce, 1987), framboesia and sexually transmissible diseases. Leprosy can easily be treated. Between 1985 and 1996, it has been reduced by 82 per cent worldwide (WHO, 1997).

Within the category of sexually transmitted diseases AIDS has become extremely important. In several countries HIV infections have reached epidemic proportions. The joint United Nations Programme on HIV/AIDS now publishes global estimates of the incidence and impact of AIDS.[4] The dramatic impact of this relatively new disease is amply illustrated by the figures reproduced in Table 6.5.

Globally, some 40 million people are now infected with HIV/AIDS.[5] Of these 40 million cases, no less than 28.5 million occur in Sub-Saharan Africa, the region hardest hit by this disease. Sixteen African countries have the highest incidence of AIDS and in these countries between 5 per cent and 39 per cent of the adult population is infected. In seven countries, the incidence amongst the adult population is above 20 per cent: Botswana, Zimbabwe, Swaziland, Lesotho, Namibia, Zambia and South Africa. Some of these countries have small populations. In terms of absolute numbers, the greatest number of cases is found in South Africa (5 million), India (4 million), Nigeria (3.5 million), Kenya (2.5 million) and Zimbabwe (2.3 million). In 2001, AIDS-related

4 UNAIDS, Report on the Global HIV/AIDS Epidemic, Joint United Nations Programme on HIV/AIDS, http://www.unaids.org/Unaids/EN/Resources/Publications/
5 The estimates are subject to wide margins of error and should still be treated with caution. The UNAIDS report provides low and high estimates which range from 30 to 50 million for the global population.

Table 6.5 *Prevalence of HIV/AIDS in developing countries, 2001*

Region	Number of people with HIV/AIDS	% of total population with HIV/AIDS	% of adult population with HIV/AIDS	AIDS deaths
Sub-Saharan Africa	28,500,000	4.5	9.0	2,200,000
North Africa & Middle East	500,000	0.1	0.3	30,000
Eastern Europe and Central Asia	1,000,000	0.3	0.5	23,000
South and Southeast Asia	5,600,000	0.3	0.6	400,000
East Asia & Pacific	1,000,000	0.1	0.1	35,000
Latin America	1,500,000	0.3	0.5	60,000
Caribbean	420,000	1.3	2.3	40,000
World	40,000,000	0.7	1.2	3,000,000
Countries with 700,000 or more HIV-infected persons ranked by HIV/AIDS as % of adult population				
Botswana	330,000	21.2	38.8	26,000
Zimbabwe	2,300,000	17.9	33.7	200,000
Swaziland	170,000	18.1	33.4	12,000
Lesotho	360,000	17.5	31.0	25,000
Namibia	230,000	12.9	22.5	13,000
Zambia	1,200,000	11.3	21.5	120,000
South Africa	5,000,000	11.4	20.1	360,000
Kenya	2,500,000	8.0	15.0	190,000
Malawi	850,000	7.3	15.0	80,000
Mozambique	1,100,000	5.9	13.0	60,000
Central African Republic	250,000	6.6	12.9	22,000
Cameroun	920,000	6.1	11.8	53,000
Tanzania	1,500,000	4.2	7.8	140,000
Ethiopia	2,100,000	3.3	6.4	160,000
Nigeria	3,500,000	3.0	5.8	170,000
Democratic Republic of Congo	1,300,000	2.5	4.9	120,000
Russian Federation	700,000	0.5	0.9	9,000
India	3,970,000	0.4	0.8	
USA	900,000	0.3	0.6	15,000

Notes: The report provides uncertainty ranges for each estimate. For the world total the range is between 30 and 50 million. For Sub-Saharan Africa the range is from 22 million to 35 million.
Source: UNAIDS, Report on the Global HIV/AIDS Epidemic, Joint United Nations Programme on HIV/AIDS, http://www.unaids.org/Unaids/EN/Resources/Publications/

deaths numbered 3 million, of which 2.2 million occurred in Sub-Saharan Africa. Of HIV infections in adults, 75–85 per cent are transmitted through unprotected sexual intercourse, of which 70 per cent are heterosexual (WHO, 1997).

Many infectious diseases affect children. HIV infections are different. They are most common within the economically most productive age group (25–49). Aids may have serious economic consequences because the most productive and often highly educated segment of the labour force is most seriously affected. There are also fears that agricultural production will be negatively affected. AIDS infections will have negative impacts on child care and care for the elderly. Moreover, the large number of AIDS patients will be an enormous burden on the health care system.

In recent years, AIDS is also being transmitted from mothers to their children. In 1997, no less than 590,000 children under the age of 15 became infected with AIDS. If these trends continue this could reverse some major gains in infant and child mortality (WHO, 1998). But, so far, the impact on infant and child mortality statistics has been modest.

In several African countries, the trend towards declining death rates has been reversed. In other African countries death rates are declining at a substantially lower rate than they would have in the absence of AIDS. In spite of AIDS, population in the African countries studied will continue to grow rapidly, but the rate of growth is slower owing to AIDS.

(d) Parasitic diseases

Parasitic intestinal diseases are also quite common. Approximately one billion people suffer from ascariasis (caused by the roundworm) and ancylostomiasis (caused by hookworms).

(e) Diseases transmitted by animal vectors

Very important are diseases that are transmitted by insects or other animal vectors. These include:

- Malaria (transmitted by the malaria mosquito). In the past, the incidence of malaria had been reduced strongly because of the use of pesticides like DDT and effective treatment. However, in the course of time mosquitoes have become immune to pesticides, DDT is now banned for environmental reasons and the rapid spread of resistance to antimalarial drugs presents a threat to effective treatment. The malaria situation is presently deteriorating worldwide. In the 1980s, the number of malaria cases was estimated to be about 100 million per year (Maurice and Pearce, 1987). By, 1998, no less than 273 million people were suffering from malaria and 1.1 million people died from this disease (WHO, 1999: ch. 4).
- Bilharzia (schistosomiasis, an infectious disease of the intestines and the urinary tract caused by worms). Bilharzia can be found in watery areas and is carried by snails. Between 500 million and 600 million people are exposed to schistosome infection. 200 million are actually infected (Maurice and Pearce, 1987).
- Sleeping sickness (trypanosomiasis). Sleeping sickness occurs in many Sub-Saharan African countries and is passed on by tsetse flies. In thirty-six countries 50 million people are exposed to infection (Maurice and Pearce, 1987) and 16 to 18 million people are actually infected (WHO, 1993).
- Filariasis. Filariasis is a category of parasitic infectious diseases transmitted by mosquitoes, flies, and worms. The most important diseases in this category are lymphatic filariasis (its most serious form being elephantiasis), and river blindness (onchocerciasis). An estimated 905 million people are exposed to lymphatic filariasis and 90 million are actually infected. River blindness is common especially in tropical African countries, where 17 million people were actually infected and 78 million were exposed to infection in the 1980s (Maurice and Pearce, 1987). Substantial progress has

been made in combating onchocerciasis. Large eradication campaigns have been mounted successfully in West Africa and 36 million people have been newly protected since 1974 (WHO, 1997).

- Trachoma (inflammation of the eye membrane). Hundreds of millions of people suffer from this disease, which is passed on by flies and through direct physical contact. Trachoma can result in blindness.

Among infectious diseases, the so-called undernourishment–infection syndrome merits special attention. Infectious diseases interact with undernourishment. Undernourishment increases susceptibility to infection. Infectious diseases, in particular diarrhoea, cause further undernourishment, thus creating a vicious circle. In the end, diseases that are not dangerous in themselves may result in death (Mosley, 1985a; van Norren and van Vianen, 1986). In section 6.2.5 this will be discussed in more detail.

6.1.6 *Epidemiological transition*

The fact that people all over the world live longer today than they did thirty to forty years ago is very much related to the reduction of infectious diseases of the intestines and the respiratory tract. These are diseases that mainly kill young people. In the affluent countries of today infectious diseases have gradually been reduced since the eighteenth century onwards. At present they are no longer very important. Similar trends are emerging in today's developing countries.

Such developments are often discussed in the context of the so-called *epidemiological transition*, which is seen as an integral part of an overall process of economic and social development. The transition involves changes from situations characterised by infectious diseases, high fertility rates, high child mortality rates and low life expectancies to situations characterised by low child mortality rates, few infectious diseases, low fertility rates, high life expectancies and the predominance of cancer and cardiovascular diseases (Frederikson, 1969; Omran, 1971; WHO, 1999). This epidemiological transition is seen as closely interlinked with the wider process of modernisation characterised by increases in prosperity, improvements in nutrition, hygiene and water supply, higher levels of education and improvements in medical technology.

Omran distinguishes three models of the epidemiological transition:

(a) The classical Western model characterised by a gradual decrease of the death rate associated with modernisation, improved nutrition and hygiene. By the beginning of the twentieth century infectious diseases were outstripped by other diseases. The decline in the death rate accelerated.

(b) The accelerated model of epidemiological transition. The difference with the classical model is mainly that the death rate declines more rapidly and that public hygiene, sanitation and medical factors play a more important

role. The pattern of change is similar, however. A typical example of this
model is twentieth-century Japan.

(c) The decelerated epidemiological transition model. This model refers to
today's developing countries and indicates that the transition from older
to newer patterns of disease is still unfinished (Omran, 1971).

Like other modernisation theories that assume a unilinear development from
a traditional to a modern stage, the simple model of epidemiological transition
has proved to be untenable. Changes of patterns of sickness and health never
develop along the same path in different societies and during different historical periods (Frenk *et al.*, 1989). For example, in many developing countries
cardiovascular diseases, cancer, diabetes and other chronic conditions are on
the increase, while infectious diseases continue to remain important (WHO,
1993; 1999). Until recently, lifestyle-related diseases such as cardiovascular diseases and cancer were among the most important causes of death in most
developed countries. However, in Japan cardiovascular diseases have shown a
downward tendency since World War II. They do not rank first among the
causes of death as they do in other rich countries. Also, life expectancy – 81
years – is higher than in other rich countries (World Bank, 2002).

Japan is different in other respects too. In 1900 Japanese life expectancy was
similar to the life expectancy in England whereas per capita income was much
lower. According to Johansson and Mosk (1987), this is explained by the exceptional emphasis on public hygiene in Japan in the late nineteenth century.
Between 1900 and 1940 life expectancy in Japan hardly changed, whereas in
England and in other Western European countries it rose to approximately
60 years. After World War II, Japan embarked on a dramatic process of epidemiological catch-up, which paralleled its economic performance. In health
terms it succeeded in overtaking Western Europe and the US (Johansson and
Mosk, 1987; Vallin, 1989).

Nevertheless, the various patterns of health development have some important elements in common. The share of deaths caused by infectious intestinal and respiratory diseases tends to decrease over time, whether gradually or
rapidly. The share of deaths caused by non-infectious diseases tends to increase.
What comes in the place of infectious diseases can differ, but the decline in
infectious diseases itself is certainly an 'epidemiological transition'.

Table 6.4 provides clear indications that a kind of epidemiological transition is indeed taking place in developing countries today. Non-communicable
diseases, such as diseases of the circulatory system, heart diseases and cancer,
are on the increase. Traditional infectious diseases are declining. Within the
category of infectious diseases, AIDS has exploded into prominence. Finally,
injuries as a result of accidents as well as intentional injuries as a result of
crime, war and civil unrest are on the increase. In 2000, they accounted for
almost 10 per cent of mortality in developing countries.

6.2   Theoretical explanations of changes in health and morbidity

To pursue adequate health-care policies, we need to identify the determinants of health and morbidity. We will discuss this issue from two different points of view. First, we will concentrate on the various factors that may be of importance to the improvement of the state of health. Next, we will consider several important theoretical ideas. Finally, we will attempt a cautious synthesis.

6.2.1   Factors affecting the state of health

The following factors may affect the state of health in a particular country:

1. *Improvements in medical technology.* Improvements in curative medicine and the development of effective medicines make it possible to treat diseases which were previously untreatable. Extremely important are, for example, the antibiotics that are used to combat various infectious diseases. Preventive medicine based on vaccination is also part of medical technology. Several diseases can be eradicated at relatively modest cost by means of large-scale vaccination schemes. For example, vaccination against smallpox has already been very successful. Most countries have schemes for vaccinating children against diphtheria, whooping cough, tetanus, poliomyelitis, measles and tuberculosis (WHO, 1987: p. 76). Still, millions of children continue to die of these diseases, and millions are crippled for life. More vaccinations could have prevented this.

2. *Improvements in water supply, hygiene and sanitary facilities.* Many diseases are passed on through contaminated water, unhygienic treatment of excrements and unhealthy living conditions. In developing countries hundreds of millions of households do not have access to clean drinking water. Facilities for the hygienic treatment of excrements are often woefully inadequate.

3. *Combating animal carriers of diseases (vectors).* An important aspect of health-care policy is controlling vectors that transmit diseases, e.g. flies, mosquitoes, worms, slugs, snails or rats. Chemical substances are often used in combating vectors, although biological methods are applied as well.

4. *Improved nutrition.* According to some theorists, the importance of medical technology is overrated (McKeown, 1976). Nutrition is the most important factor reducing susceptibility to diseases and reinforcing natural resistance against diseases contracted. In this respect, improvement of the state of health primarily depends on overall improvement of the economic situation, standard of living and food supply.

5. *Education.* Other authors like Mosley (1983; 1985a) and Caldwell (1984; 1986) emphasise the importance of education, especially the education of

mothers. Improving educational levels is positively associated with practices favourable to children's chances of survival – both from a preventive
viewpoint, e.g. hygiene, vaccination, food and in a curative sense, e.g. making better use of the possibilities of the health facilities.

6. *Health-care policy*. Countries that make greater efforts with respect to basic
   health care are relatively more successful in combating diseases, reducing
   the child mortality rate and increasing life expectancy. Policy is an important autonomous factor.
7. *Egalitarian patterns of growth*. In developing countries where large segments
   of the population share in the fruits of growth, this is reflected in improvements in health, irrespective of health-care policies (McQuire, 2001).

The first four factors are of a medical–biological nature. They have direct
impacts on processes of disease and treatment. The last three factors are of an
indirect nature. They influence the availability of direct factors and the ways in
which people deal with the direct factors that influence sickness and health.
There are many differences of opinion concerning the relative importance of
these different factors. Some of the most pronounced theories and models will
be discussed in the following section.

6.2.2   *Preston: per capita income and life expectancy*

In a pioneering article published in 1975, Samuel Preston studied the relation
between average per capita income and life expectancy (Preston, 1975; see also
Preston, 1980). At a given moment in time, the level of income and the average
life expectancy are closely related. In poor countries, life expectancy is much
lower than in rich countries. However, in the course of time, life expectancy
in all countries increases regardless of the level of income. This is illustrated
in Figure 6.1 in which the average life expectancy in a country (on the vertical
axis) is set out against per capita income (on the horizontal axis). In this figure
there is a positive relation between per capita income and life expectancy both
in 1930 and in 1960. However, the 1960 curve lies above the 1930 curve. On
the basis of his statistical analysis Preston comes to the conclusion that factors
other than per capita income account for the 75 per cent–90 per cent increase
of global life expectancy. Factors like improved nutrition and a higher level of
education cannot explain the increase in the average life expectancy either.
According to Preston, the rise of life expectancy is explained to a great extent
by improvements in health technology. This includes not only vaccination *technology*, antibiotics, and sulphonamides, but also health policies with respect to
vectors, public hygiene, health education and health facilities for mothers and
their children.

The conclusion often drawn on the basis of Preston's analysis is that a low
level of prosperity does not necessarily hinder improvements in health care
and the state of health by application of modern medical technology (e.g. see

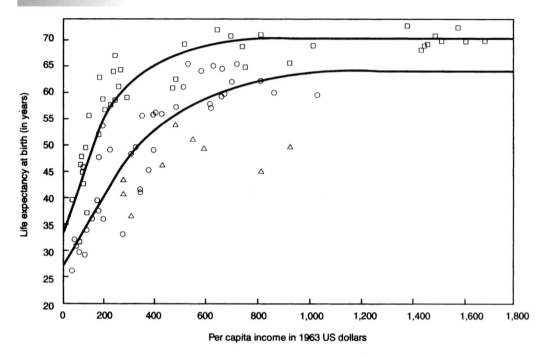

Figure 6.1 Life expectancy at birth, 1900, 1930 and 1960.
Source: Preston (1975).

WHO, 1999; World Bank, 1984: p. 69). However, Preston also stresses the fact
that – after the upward shift of the curve – the relation between per capita
income and life expectancy for the poorest developing countries is even closer
than before. This may be because when life expectancy increases, the diseases
that remain are those most closely related to standard of living – like diarrhoea
and other infectious diseases.

6.2.3   McKeown: the importance of nutrition

In a long series of influential publications, Thomas McKeown comes to radically different conclusions (McKeown, 1976; 1978; 1979; 1988). McKeown concentrates on the history of health and health care in Great Britain in the
eighteenth and nineteenth centuries. He shows that the decreasing number
of deaths owing to diseases preceded important medical breakthroughs in the
treatment of these diseases. This is especially marked in the case of tuberculosis, the leading killer in nineteenth-century Britain. McKeown believes that
nineteenth-century hospitals contributed more to the spread of diseases than
to their effective treatment. He claims that the role of medical technology and
medical progress is highly overrated and that one should look for other possible

sources of the decline in the death rate and the increase of life expectancy. McKeown stresses the importance of nutrition. He argues that the decreasing death rate in Great Britain in the eighteenth and nineteenth centuries was caused to a large extent by increasing immunity from airborne infectious diseases. This immunity was caused by better nutrition.

On the basis of these analyses, McKeown and his followers claim that the state of health in developing countries cannot be improved without overall improvement in the standard of living and levels of nutrition. In other words, economic factors are of crucial importance.

6.2.4   Preston and McKeown

It is by no means easy to make a choice between the incompatible perspectives of Preston and McKeown and their followers. Still, an attempt will be made.

First, McKeown's thesis that only nutrition is of importance can be qualified. Sreter (1988) has convincingly shown that the so-called 'public health movement' in nineteenth-century Great Britain contributed greatly to an improved state of health. This movement focused on the amelioration of hygienic conditions, sewers, supplies of clean drinking water, inspection of food quality and housing conditions and the improvement of preventive medicine. McKeown underestimated the importance of preventive medical technology, in particular vaccination and inoculation. Further, Sreter criticises McKeown for generalising on the basis of the health-care history of a single country. On the basis of further historical statistical analysis, Fogel (1986) concludes that the contributions of improvements in nutritional status can be identified. But they are not overwhelming.

Next, the difference between Preston and McKeown is not as great as it seems (Vallin, 1989). In Preston's data there is also a clear relation between the level of prosperity and life expectancy at a given moment. This relation is especially strong in the case of the poorest developing countries. The economic factor does matter.

One of McKeown's valuable contributions is that he puts the claims of curative medical technology in perspective and stresses the significance of nutrition and undernourishment. The interaction between undernourishment and infectious diseases in particular is very important for a good understanding of the health problems of developing countries. The scepticism about the role of curative medicine may have contributed to the rise of the primary health care movement (see section 6.4).

On the other hand, the conclusion that medical technology and medical progress are unimportant for developing countries is not justified. We should realise that progress of medical knowledge not only encompasses better techniques of curative treatment for diseases contracted, but also the whole complex of preventive health care, better sanitary conditions, knowledge of the causes of diseases, vaccination, vector control and medication.

6.2.5   The Mosley model and the importance of education

Mosley (1983; see also Mosley, 1984; 1985a; 1985b) has made a significant contribution to the debate on the importance of medical versus socio-economic factors. He concentrates on explanations of child mortality. Like the Bongaarts model presented in Chapter 5, Mosley makes a distinction between underlying social and economic determinants and the intermediate (biological) factors that directly influence the chances of contracting disease and dying. The basic principle is the notion that in a well-protected environment 98 per cent of all children under the age of 5 ought to survive, as in the economically advanced countries. The extent to which this survival rate is not realised should be explained systematically.

A decrease in the chances of survival is the result of primary social and economic determinants. These primary determinants, however, operate through intermediate biological mechanisms, which influence the chances of contracting disease and determine the outcomes of processes of illness. In Mosley's model, death is the ultimate result of the multiple episodes of morbidity. It is seldom the result of one isolated instance of illness. The essence of the model is the identification of intermediate variables, in order to analyse how primary determinants influence child mortality through the intermediate variables (see also van Norren and van Vianen, 1986).

Mosley's model consists of the following intermediate variables:

1. *Maternal fertility factors*
    (a) Age of childbearing. When mothers are either too young or too old, the children may be at risk.
    (b) Number of children per woman. Large families reduce the health prospects of children.
    (c) Birth intervals. If intervals between births are short, this may have adverse effects on the state of health. In general, children from large families are more likely to contract diseases than children from small families.
2. *Environmental contamination by infectious agents*
    (a) Contamination of the air.
    (b) Contamination of food, water or fingers.
    (c) Contamination of the skin (caused by soil or mites).
    (d) Contamination by vectors.
3. *Availability of nutrients for foetus and child*
    (a) Calories.
    (b) Proteins.
    (c) Vitamins.
    (d) Minerals.
4. *Injuries*
    (a) Accidents.
    (b) Injuries inflicted intentionally.

5. *Personal disease control factors*
   (a) Personal preventive measures.
   (b) Treatment of illnesses once they are contracted.

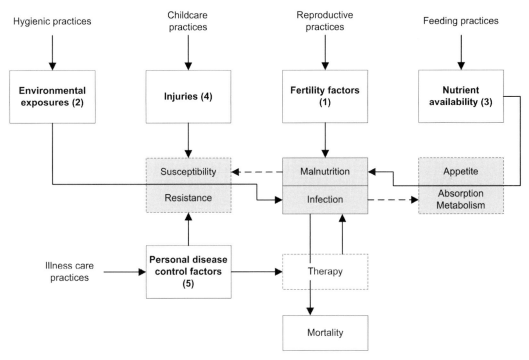

Figure 6.2 Intermediate factors influencing child mortality.
Source: Mosley (1983).

Figure 6.2 summarises the model consisting of five intermediate variables and a set of behavioural practices. The behavioural practices affect health through the intermediate variables. Thus, the availability and distribution of food within the household affects malnutrition of mothers and their children. Hygienic conditions and circumstances affect susceptibility and resistance to diseases. Hygienic conditions in turn are influenced by hygienic practices and policies.

The central element of Figure 6.2 is the malnutrition–infection syndrome. Malnutrition increases susceptibility and decreases resistance to a variety of (infectious) diseases. Infectious diseases result in metabolic changes and in loss of appetite among children. This causes a decreasing capacity to absorb nutrients, which results in further undernourishment. Child mortality is not the result of any one single factor. Most often there has been a long history of illness leading to retardation of growth, undernourishment and undermining of a patient's resistance. At the end of the sequence non-lethal diseases like respiratory infections or diarrhoea may result in death.

Curative health care (therapy) is only one of the many factors in the model. It does not prevent malnutrition or tackle the malnutrition-infection syndrome, but only tries to deal with diseases once they have emerged. Often illnesses are not treated until very near the end of a long sequence of illnesses. Many kinds of medication only affect one specific ailment while several diseases in combination contribute to child mortality. Only if a single disease causes high mortality, can medical treatments have a substantial, demographic influence (this is the case with combating malaria or vaccinating against tetanus). Although Mosley does not take an explicit stand in the debate on the role of medical technology, he tends to play down the importance of treating specific diseases by means of medical interventions. Mosley gives two good examples that may serve to put curative medical interventions into perspective. Vaccination against measles prevents people from contracting it. However, measles is a relatively harmless disease, unless one's resistance has already been affected. Treating diarrhoea by means of 'oral rehydration' may prevent children from dying of diarrhoea. Still, this technique does not halt the gradual deterioration and undermining of a patient's health caused by ever-recurring bouts of diarrhoea.

Mosley's model refers especially to infant and child mortality. Yet, it gives us a more general understanding of the effects of social circumstances on the state of health. De Kadt and Lipton (1988) indicate that health risks are greatest in rural areas. Income in rural areas is very low, food supplies unreliable, especially for those households with insufficient access to land. At the same time the energy requirements for agricultural labour are immense, in particular during peak periods in the agricultural cycle. If the state of health has been undermined by disease, there is a shortage of energy, just in those periods when it is most needed. Chambers (1982) has shown that a shortfall of food supplies most often occurs when the need for food is greatest, i.e. just before harvesting. It is then that food stocks of the previous harvest are depleted, while people need to work hard preparing for the coming harvest. Furthermore, in tropical regions with a wet climate health conditions are extremely unfavourable during the rainy season when much of the agricultural work has to be done. Workers are often exposed to infections, diarrhoea, water-borne parasitic infections, malaria and snakebites (Chambers, 1982). Inhabitants of urban slums are also exposed to serious health risks. In these areas hygienic circumstances in particular are very poor.

On the basis of research in Kenya, Mosley concludes that the prime determinant of child mortality is the level of education of the mother. The level of education operates through several of the behavioural practices and intermediate variables. It positively influences hygienic practices; it affects the distribution of food within the family so that children receive their fair share of food (nutrition practices); it operates through reproductive practices such as birth spacing and birth control; and it affects the way in which preventive and curative medical services are made use of (personal health control factors).

Therefore, a 'primary health care' system should not concentrate merely on medical facilities but rather on the entire complex of nutrition, educational practices, water supply, hygiene, counselling of parents, family planning, and so forth. Mosley's argument should not be considered an attack on health care but rather a plea for considering preventive health care in a broad sense including education and information about health, contraception and nutrition. More attention will be paid to health-care policy in section 6.4.

6.2.6   Caldwell: the importance of health-care policy

In an interesting article published in 1986, Caldwell raises the question why some developing countries have high scores on health indicators despite relatively low levels of prosperity, while other developing countries with relatively high levels of prosperity have relatively low scores on these health indicators (Caldwell, 1986). Caldwell compared the ranking of countries by their average per capita income in 1982 to their ranking by infant mortality per 1,000 live births, and their ranking by average life expectancy.

Caldwell focused on countries whose ranking on health indicators compared favourably with their ranking by per capita income (*superior health achievers*) or unfavourably (*poor health achievers*). Among the superior health achievers Caldwell found four important countries with a Buddhist tradition (Thailand, Vietnam, Sri Lanka and Burma). In the category of *poor health achievers* there was a strikingly large number of Islamic countries. Caldwell associated the health achievements of the Buddhist countries with the positive evaluation of education in Buddhism and the Buddhist concept of 'enlightenment'. According to Caldwell, the poor scores of Islamic countries were closely associated with the low social status of women and the relatively low appreciation of education in general and female education in particular (see also UNDP, 2002).

In general, Caldwell, like Mosley, sets great store by the educational level of women. Education leads to greater openness with respect to preventive health-care measures and a more effective use of existing health services:

> The key factor seems to be that a woman who goes to school is increasingly seen by both herself and others as being part of a global society with an accepted attitude towards bacterial contamination and corresponding hygienic methods, the use of modern medical facilities and persistence in recommended treatments...they are more likely to insist that health centres should provide them with adequate treatment. Educated mothers distribute food within the family in closer accord with needs...they are more likely to behave in accordance with beliefs in bacterial rather than religious pollution. (Caldwell, 1984: p. 108)

Sri Lanka, Costa Rica and the South West Indian state of Kerala are well-known examples of poor societies with relatively good results with respect to health. Caldwell analysed the demographic history of these entities and considered the factors that might explain a lower death rate. The factors he identified as important were: autonomy of women; a positive evaluation of education;

a relatively open political system; and a tradition of political egalitarianism and radicalism. For Caldwell the degree of female autonomy is the central factor in mortality declines in poor but open societies. Female autonomy has very positive effects on the quality of childcare. The combination of education and political radicalism put pressure on the political system to develop and maintain good health-care systems. According to Caldwell, investments in the health-care system and progress in medical technology and medical knowledge have contributed greatly to increases of life expectancy, especially in combination with wider social and economic changes. Centrally planned economies like China, Cuba and Vietnam also score high on health indicators. In their policies high priority is given to the realisation of effective primary health-care systems accessible to large sections of the population.

In Table 6.6, a modified version of Caldwell's method has been applied to recent data for 2000. Caldwell had arranged countries in order of their infant mortality rate and studied those countries whose ranking by infant mortality deviated more than 24 points from their ranking by per capita income. In Table 6.6 the criterion is a rank difference of more than 19 points for either of the two health indicators (infant mortality and life expectancy). Also the new table uses PPP converted national income per capita as the income measure, rather than exchange rate converted national income.[6]

There are several interesting changes in the ranking compared since 1982. China and Costa Rica no longer figure amongst the superior health achievers. This is not because their health performance has deteriorated, but rather because their ranking in PPP converted income is much higher than before. Myanmar is no longer a superior health achiever. Neither is India. Thailand's health rankings are still substantially higher than its income ranking, but it does not pass the 19 rank point difference threshold. In general, the discrepancy between health ranking and income ranking has decreased since the early 1980s.

Quite prominent in the list of superior health achievers in 2000 are a number of former Soviet republics (Tajikistan, Moldova, Azerbaijan, Armenia, Georgia, Ukraine and Uzbekistan). Here, the discrepancy between health and income ranking is caused by the rapid decline of per capita incomes in the wake of the collapse of the Soviet Union.[7]

Among the inferior health achievers of 2000, we find three large Latin American countries where health lags behind relatively high per capita income (Argentina, Brazil and Mexico), four Middle-Eastern Islamic countries (Iran, Iraq, Libya and Saudi Arabia) and a large number of countries from Sub-Saharan Africa, of which South Africa, Namibia, Botswana and Lesotho are the most prominent examples. The main conclusion that can be derived from Caldwell's analysis and from Table 6.6 is that health policy itself is an important

---

6 PPP converted income gives a more realistic idea of real differences in standards of living than exchange rate-converted income.
7 Note that superior health achievement is a relative concept. In absolute terms, a superior health achiever might have quite low health scores.

Table 6.6 *Comparisons of levels of per capita income, infant mortality and life expectancy at birth in 2000*

	Per capita GNP (PPP $)	Infant mortality (per 1,000 live births)	Difference in ranking	Life expectancy at birth (years)	Difference in ranking
Superior health achievements in relation to level of income[a]					
Cuba[c]	1,700	6	72	76	72
Tajikistan	1,090	21	61	69	49
Moldova	2,230	18	42	68	17
Azerbaijan	2,740	13	41	72	32
Armenia	2,580	15	41	74	51
Congo, Rep.	570	68	37	51	26
Georgia	2,680	17	35	73	41
Sri Lanka	3,460	15	32	73	34
Ukraine	3,700	13	31	68	−4
Uzbekistan	2,360	22	30	70	28
Vietnam	2,000	27	28	69	25
Eritrea	960	60	27	52	14
Jamaica	3,440	20	23	75	47
Yemen, Rep.	770	76	23	56	31
Congo, Dem. Rep.[c]	600	85	20	46	12
Albania	3,600	20	20	74	41
Bhutan	1,440	58	19	62	20
Nicaragua	2,080	33	16	69	24
Mongolia	1,760	56	11	67	20
Madagascar	820	88	10	55	25
Panama	5,680	20	3	75	27
Inferior health achievements in relation to level of income[b]					
Belarus	7,550	11	5	68	−32
Estonia	9,340	8	3	71	−22
Kazakhstan	5,490	21	2	65	−26
Hungary	11,990	9	−4	71	−25
Russian Federation	8,010	16	−5	65	−44
Zimbabwe	2,550	69	−16	40	−49
Argentina	12,050	17	−20	74	−6
Saudi Arabia	11,390	18	−20	73	−11
Angola	1,180	128	−21	47	−2
Iran, Islamic Rep.	5,910	33	−23	69	−15
Côte d'Ivoire	1,500	111	−25	46	−16
Mauritania	1,630	101	−26	52	−8
Dominican Republic	5,710	39	−26	67	−23
Guinea	1,930	95	−27	46	−27
Libya[c]	8,900	26	−28	71	−18
Brazil	7,300	32	−30	68	−31
Gabon	5,360	58	−32	53	−45
Turkey	7,030	34	−32	70	−14
Mexico	8,790	29	−33	73	−3
Iraq[c]	2,500	93	−35	61	−7
Lesotho	2,590	91	−35	44	−43
Botswana	7,170	58	−47	39	−91
Namibia	6,410	62	−48	47	−68
South Africa	9,160	63	−65	48	−81

Notes:
[a] 113 middle- and low-income countries have been ranked by income per capita, infant mortality and life expectation. Superior health achievers are countries with a positive rank difference of 20 or more points between the ranking on infant mortality and the ranking on income per capita, and/or between the ranking on life expectation and the ranking on income per capita. The sample of countries excludes countries with fewer than one million inhabitants.
[b] Inferior health achievers are countries with a negative rank difference of 20 or more between the rankings on either of the two health indicators and income per capita.
[c] GDP/capita instead of GNI/capita
Sources: GNI/capita (PPP dollars), infant mortality and life expectancy from *World Development Indicators, 2002.* Income data for Dem. Rep. Congo, Cuba, Iraq, Liberia, Libya and Myanmar from CIA, *The World Fact Book, 2001.*

explanatory factor. Societies giving high priority to the realisation of good health-care systems in the broadest sense were able to achieve excellent results even at low income levels. A given income level is associated with varying levels of health performance. In this respect, McKeown's idea that only the level of prosperity is of importance proves to be incorrect. On the other hand, one should realise that in countries where per capita income shows secular stagnation, sooner or later the economic basis for the maintenance of a good health-care system will inevitably be undermined.

Mosley's thesis that education is more important than medical interventions is also slightly exaggerated. Education – especially education of women – is indeed of great importance. However, the direct effect of education is that the facilities of a health-care system are utilised more effectively. If no health-care facilities are available, education alone will be of less significance.

Underlying factors like religion and culture are highly important since these factors determine attitudes towards education, the status of women, family planning and a scientific approach to health issues. In an interesting article on the relatively unfavourable state of health in Africa, Vallin has paid a great deal of attention to religious and cultural factors as ultimate determinants of the state of health. Unlike Asian and Latin American societies, which were penetrated by great unitary religions like Islam, Christianity or Buddhism, African societies never experienced the predominance of one single religion or civilisation. Rather there is a patchwork of animistic, Islamic and Christian influences. The extreme cultural, religious and ethnic diversity in Sub-Saharan Africa hampers the effective development of health-care services (Vallin, 1989). As adequate knowledge of the cultural backgrounds is lacking, it is difficult to integrate health-care systems into local cultures.

6.2.7   Standards of living, education, medical technology and health-care systems: a synthesis

The 1999 *World Health Report* (WHO, 1999) presents an interesting synthesis of the different perspectives discussed here. In an analysis similar to that of Preston, the report analyses the relationships between infant mortality and per capita income. Cross-section regression analysis shows that at one point in time there is a relationship between GDP per capita (in 1985 PPP dollars) and infant mortality. The higher the income, the lower infant mortality. But between 1952 and 1992 the whole curve shifts downwards. This means that in 1992 the same level of real income as in 1952 is associated with much lower rates of mortality. This shift is due to changes in medical technology and knowledge.

The report cites research by Preker et al. (1999) who have decomposed the changes in mortality and life expectancy between 1960 and 1990 in 115 developing countries. They conclude that 45 per cent of the reduction in under-5 mortality is due to generation and utilisation of new medical knowledge,

38 per cent is due to improved education of adult females and 17 per cent is due to changes in income (standard of living, nutrition). In the case of life expectancy, around 50 per cent of the improvement is due to new knowledge, around 30 per cent is based on the educational level of adult females. Thus the analysis integrates standards of living, education and technological change.

The *World Health Report 1999* concludes that 'typically half the gains in health between 1952 and 1992 result from access to better technology. The remaining gains result from movement along the curve (income improvements and better education)' (WHO, 1999: p. 7).[8]

It is also plausible to argue that compared to past changes, changes in medical technology and its application have become more important. In the nineteenth century there is support for the McKeown thesis that knowledge and tools for improving health have played a limited role in mortality decline. In the twentieth century these technology-related factors have become much more important. The recent history of eradication or reduction of major diseases provides ample examples for the importance of medical technology, especially of a preventive nature. It shows that the use of medical technology is intimately related to health policy. The *1998 World Health Report* (WHO, 1998) provides a summary of progress. Here we mention only a few examples.

By 1995, 80 per cent of the world's children had been immunised against diphtheria, tetanus, whooping cough, polio, measles and tuberculosis, compared to less than 5 per cent in 1974. In India, more than 120 million children were immunised against polio on a single day in 1996 in India (WHO, 1997). Polio is now close to eradication. The use of simple oral rehydration therapies has reduced child mortality that is due to diarrhoea. Onchocerciasis (river blindness) is expected to be eliminated by 2008.

Two cautionary remarks are in order. First, there are no simple technological fixes. Success in combating diseases depends on an integrated approach, where health systems provide access to new technology and knowledge. But health systems and medical technologies interact with improved nutrition, improved sanitation and water supply, and improved education.

Second, in the future existing medical technologies cannot be relied on to the same extent as in the past. New strains of TB, malaria and pneumonia are rapidly becoming drug-resistant and these diseases are re-emerging. Major new diseases such as AIDS are emerging. Finally, the increasing global mobility of people creates new dangers of infection.

The synthesis suggests three main avenues towards improving health: (1) shifting the income–health curve through advances in technology; (2) moving along the curve by increasing income per capita; (3) changing the position relative to the curve by health-care policy and improving the effectiveness of health systems.

---

8 To the extent that education is related to income, education shows up as movement along the curve. However, like health, education can also improve irrespective of income level. Then it will show up in the shift of the curve.

As countries improve their standards of living and levels of education, they will tend to move along the curve. New medical knowledge and its applications will shift the curve downwards (better average health irrespective of average incomes). At the same level of income, some countries will perform worse than average (above the curve), others better (below the curve). Improving health system development should enable countries to join or even exceed the curve. (WHO, 1999: ch. 1). Finally, at the same level of income, a more equal distribution of income will also translate into better health conditions, as the poorer segments of the population share in the fruits of growth. This is illustrated by the experiences of Taiwan and Korea, where health conditions improved in spite of the absence of specific large-scale efforts in health policy (McQuire, 2001).

6.3   Health and economic development

There is a considerable literature on the relationships between investments in health care and economic development (see Baldwin and Weisbrod, 1974; Barlow, 1979; Fogel, 1994; 1997; Keyzer, 1993; Mayer, 2001; Mushkin, 1962; Popkin, 1978; Strauss and Thomas, 1998; Walsh, 1990; WHO, 1999). Health is an important aspect of human capital. Investments and improvements in health are seen as having major positive impacts on economic growth and development.

One can distinguish micro-level and macro-level relationships between health and economic performance. Studies at the micro-level focus on the causal mechanisms through which health affects the economic behaviour and performance of individuals and households. Studies at macro-level analyse the statistical relationships between investments in health, health status and economic development.

The quantification of the relation between improvements in the health situation and changes in economic output is fraught with difficulties. At the macro-level, health interacts with a great variety of other proximate and ultimate determinants of growth. Also, growth itself contributes to better health through factors such as improved nutrition in a circular process. Therefore, it is hard to isolate the specific contribution of health indicators to economic growth. Researchers attempt to quantify the losses in output and productivity caused by illness and reduction of hours worked because of premature death. But, we also know that there is widespread unemployment and underutilisation of labour in most developing countries. Therefore, better health outcomes do not automatically result in higher employment or output. Moreover, workers may compensate for low productivity owing to illness by working longer hours.

At the micro-level, illness undermines the productive capacity of individuals and households. The following relationships can be distinguished:

1. Reduction of labour input. Illness results in a decrease of the number of hours a person is capable of working per year. Absence from work owing to

illness is included under this heading. Downright disablement or invalidity makes it impossible to work.

2. Reduction of labour intensity. Illness and malnutrition often lead to loss of body weight, body length and a decrease in human energy and productivity. Undernourished and unhealthy people become listless, lethargic and passive. Protracted illness and malnutrition in youth can lead to lifelong impairment of mental functions, creativity and learning potential. All this implies direct negative effects on labour productivity and labour income. Thus, in Indonesia men with anaemia were 20 per cent less productive then men without anaemia (Basta *et al.*, 1979). In Tanzania it was shown that schistosomiasis reduced the productivity of sugarcane workers (Strauss and Thomas, 1998). In a study for Ghana and the Côte d'Ivoire, Schultz and Tanzel (1997) found that wages declined significantly for each day of disability. Gallup and Sachs (1998) found a significant negative relationship between the incidence of malaria and economic growth. Lower income in turn affects the ability of households to invest in the future health of their members.

3. A choice of less productive activities, requiring less energy and effort. Illness and malnutrition may force people to choose less productive work and lower incomes (Popkin, 1978).

The so-called *efficiency wage theory* is based on such relationships between health and productivity (Bardhan, 1993; Keyzer, 1993; Leibenstein, 1957). This theory states that it may be inefficient to let market relations determine the minimum wage for labour. The market wage rate in a labour surplus economy may be too low to guarantee sufficient food and health, so that labour productivity is undermined. Thus it may be economically efficient to set minimum wages above free-market rates.

Labour productivity is especially important for households that depend on their own labour for their livelihood. Illness leads to reduced production in subsistence agriculture (Chambers, 1982; de Kadt and Lipton, 1988), lower revenues for the self-employed and lower wage incomes for labourers. It is not hard to imagine the disastrous effects of serious illness on the life chances of a household trying to survive at subsistence level.

At the macro-level, the focus is on the relationships between the state of health of a population and growth and productivity indicators. In historical research, Fogel claims that about one third of economic growth in England in the past 200 years is due to improvements in nutrition and health (Fogel, 1986; 1994; 1997). Mayer (2001) summarises the recent literature on this topic. The percentage of total growth attributed to the various health variables in this literature lies between 26 and 40 per cent.

The following direct and indirect relationships can be distinguished at macro-level:

1. Health improvements result in declining child mortality and increasing life expectancy. In the early stages of the demographic transition (before

the population starts to age) this results in an increase in labour supply and a reduction in the dependency ratio. In East Asia this has contributed to accelerated growth of per capita income. Fogel (1986) estimated that 30 per cent of per capita growth since 1780 in Western countries was due to improvements in heath and nutritional status. These mechanisms, however, only operate if a dynamic economy is also able to provide paid employment for the increased supply of labour (WHO, 1999: ch. 2).

Conversely, high child mortality and a low life expectancy can result in reductions in total labour supply. A short life expectancy implies that the number of years a worker can be active is reduced (UN, 1984: p. 4, WHO, 1999). In the light of widespread underutilisation of labour in many developing countries this does not inevitably lead to reduced growth of production. However, if mortality is highly concentrated in certain occupational groups, there can be negative effects on production. This is clearly the case with AIDS, which hits hardest in the category of young adults with relatively high schooling. AIDS results in a veritable destruction of human capital.

2. High infant and child mortality also leads to *replacement fertility*. This involves a decrease in the productive potential of women during pregnancy and the period of breastfeeding.

3. Low life expectancy is also not conducive to future-oriented attitudes. Increases in life expectancy make for higher rates of collective saving and investment.

4. Illness may lead to a decrease in learning potential. As a result, investments in education and human capital become less attractive. Improvements in infant health and nutrition directly increase the benefits of education (Mayer, 2001). Conversely, investment in education may lead to higher productivity of investment in health care (Mushkin, 1962).

5. The prevalence of diseases such as river blindness (onchocerciasis) may make it impossible or unattractive to open up certain fertile areas for agriculture. Eradication of such diseases can lead to improvements in productive potential in the very short term (Hardiman and Midgley, 1982; WHO, 1999).

Despite the considerable empirical uncertainties mentioned at the beginning of this section, recent research tends to conclude that investments in health care make substantial positive contributions to economic growth and development. The contribution to total growth in different studies varies between 26 per cent and 40 per cent (Mayer, 2001).

6.4   Health-care policy

In building health-care systems after World War II, many developing countries initially copied Western medical institutions. Attention and resources were heavily invested in educating qualified doctors and specialists and in the real-isation of a system of medical faculties, hospitals and curative medicine. The attitude towards native, traditional medicine was negative; it was considered non-scientific (Hardiman and Midgley, 1982; Mosley, 1983). Most hospitals were located in national and provincial capitals and were insufficiently accessible to the rural population and to some extent also to the inhabitants of urban slums. Major urban hospitals and clinics received around two-thirds of the government health budget, while serving just 10 to 20 per cent of the pop-ulation (WHO, 2000). In addition, there were 'vertical' campaigns – outside the hospital system – against particular diseases, e.g. malaria, river blindness, tuberculosis, whooping cough (Netherlands Development Cooperation, 1988). These campaigns focused on combating the vectors of diseases and on preven-tive vaccination. Many of these campaigns were quite successful in the short term. But they were initially not integrated sufficiently into health-care policy as a whole.

There are several objections to a predominantly curative approach to medicine. First, there is too much emphasis on the treatment of diseases (cu-rative medicine) rather than on their prevention. As illustrated by Mosley's model, medical treatment is just one of the many factors influencing dis-ease and death. A second objection is the fact that medical facilities are both expensive and inaccessible to large segments of the population. Medi-cal facilities are heavily concentrated in big cities. Well-trained doctors are seldom willing to work in remote rural areas. Even in urban areas, medical services are predominantly restricted to the more well-to-do sections of society. Paradoxically, there is also an outflow of well-trained doctors to rich coun-tries. Many doctors trained in developing countries are unable or unwilling to find positions in their own country and instead look for jobs in the affluent countries.

In the course of the 1970s there was increasing criticism of the health strate-gies pursued up till then. At a large-scale international conference in Alma Ata in 1978, a plea was made for a system of *primary health care*. At this conference it was stated that health is a basic human right and that health care ought to be accessible, affordable and socially relevant (WHO, 1978).

In the Alma Ata resolutions primary health care is interpreted in a very broad sense – and rightly so, in the light of the theories discussed in section 6.2. It includes health education and information, provision of adequate food supplies and nutritional supplements such as school milk, provision of clean water, measures to promote hygiene (sanitation), health care for mothers and their children, information about birth control, vaccination against infectious diseases, prevention and control of endemic diseases like malaria, treatment of diseases, adequate supply of medicines and the promotion of mental health (WHO, 1978: p. 24).

Furthermore, the primary health-care approach emphasises the reallocation of medical funds to improve the accessibility of medical services. It advocates replacing investments in costly hospitals and medical specialists by investments in cheaper local health care centres and simply trained paramedic personnel. Health-care policy is seen in relation with other aspects of socio-economic policy. Where the benefits of economic development are distributed more equally, the chances of improving primary health care are greater.

Another important aspect is the participation of the local population in the preparation and execution of health-care policies. Thus health-care workers recruited from the local population will function more effectively. Health-care facilities supported and monitored by the local population will tend to be more effective than health-care facilities administered from some inaccessible bureaucratic centre.

For the social relevance and acceptance of primary health care, it is important that health services are adapted to the local culture. Traditional medicine should not simply be eradicated or devalued. It should be merged with newer medical insights. Many people consult both traditional and modern healers. It pays to train traditional healers in order to narrow the gap between various medical approaches. For example, retraining programmes for traditional midwives have been quite successful.

The Alma Ata conference has been extremely influential. In a series of resolutions of international organisations, the recommendations made at the conference have been adopted. National authorities have been urged to implement them. In 1979, the United Nations Assembly endorsed the Alma Ata recommendations. In 1981 the World Health Organization (WHO) adopted the *Global Strategy for Health for All by the Year 2000* (WHO, 1981). Moreover, the WHO makes use of indicators to monitor the degree to which authorities meet their commitments with respect to health policy (see WHO, 1987; 1993; 2000). The commitment to the Alma Ata goals has recently been reaffirmed in the new world health declaration on *Health for All in the 21st Century*, adopted by the World Health Assembly in May 1998.

In detailed evaluations published in 1987, 1993 and in the subsequent editions of the *World Health Report* (e.g. WHO, 1998; 1999), the World Health Organization tried to monitor the degree to which the objectives of the *Global Strategy for Health for All by the Year 2000* were actually being realised. As shown in Tables 6.1, 6.2 and 6.3 of this chapter, there have been substantial declines in infant and child mortality and increases in life expectancy – especially in Asia and Latin America.

The WHO monitoring reports discern slow improvements in the percentage of populations covered by elements of primary healthcare and in the commitment of governments to primary health-care objectives. The availability of safe drinking and sanitary facilities (excreta disposal, waste treatment, sewer systems, and so forth) has improved. Vaccination of children against six targeted diseases (diphtheria, tetanus, measles, poliomyelitis, tuberculosis and whooping cough) has clearly improved. There have been noticeable expansions of local community health services. The numbers of health workers, health volunteers and trained traditional midwives have increased. In some countries there is even an oversupply of medical personnel.

But, the goals of universal access to affordable basic health care have not been realised (WHO, 1999). There are still significant problems. In 1997, there were 10 million deaths of children under 5. Most of these deaths are preventable. Diarrhoea, acute respiratory infections, undernourishment and vaccination-preventable diseases are still the most important causes of death for infants and children (WHO, 1998). In 2000, the probability of dying before the age of 5 is still 95 out of 1,000 births.

Though the percentage-wise availability of elements of primary health care has improved, this does not mean that coordinated systems of primary health care have been developed. Also, owing to population growth the absolute numbers of people without access to health-care facilities are increasing rather than decreasing. In 2000 1.1 billion people still lacked access to clean water supplies and 2.4 billion were living without adequate sanitation.[9] There is an outflow of highly skilled medical personnel to more developed countries. There is a serious maldistribution of health personnel and health resources. It is still exceedingly difficult to get well-qualified doctors to work in rural areas. Semi-skilled medical personnel (community health workers, village counsellors, traditional healers) are paid very poorly. Their motivation is often minimal. Moreover, expectations with respect to briefly trained paramedics were unrealistically high (Netherlands Development Cooperation, 1988).

The ideals of community participation in and democratic control of health services have been insufficiently realised. Local power structures frequently stand in the way of real community participation (Mosley, 1983). The organisation of medical systems is still highly centralised and hierarchical. The efficiency of medical systems is low. The *broad* concept of primary health care – in which health care is integrated into overall economic and social development policy – is more rhetoric than reality. In so far as primary health care services have been established, they remain restricted to medical facilities and services in the *narrow* sense.

Even today insufficient attention is being paid to preventive health care. The emphasis remains – not very surprisingly – on curative medicine. Overall, the availability of medical services is inadequate (WHO, 2000). According to Leisinger, eight out of ten patients in developing countries still consult traditional healers, medicine men or witch doctors (Leisinger, 1989). Moreover, the desired integration of modern and traditional approaches in medicine has usually turned out to be a dead letter in practice.

In addition to the problems mentioned above, health systems in developing countries are challenged by the emergence of new diseases such as AIDS and the re-emergence of old ones such as tuberculosis and malaria, which are becoming drug-resistant.

In the 1980s, the economic crisis and cuts in government expenditures resulting from structural adjustment programmes advocated by the World Bank and

---

9 WHO, *Water Sanitation and Hygiene: Links to Health: Facts and Figures*, http://www.who.int/water_sanitation_health/en/factsfigures04.pdf, updated, March 2004.

the IMF affected health care and education budgets negatively (Cornia, 1984). In the second half of the 1980s, the percentage of national income spent on health showed a slight increase but still remained low. Several developing countries now spend less than 2 per cent of GDP on health, against over 9 per cent in European countries and 14 per cent in the USA. Real educational expenditures per capita declined. Even in a country like Zambia, where health-care expenditures stood at 3 per cent of GDP, per capita health expenditures covered only half the basic package of preventive and curative health of 12 dollars per person (WHO, 1999).

In many post-communist societies, universally accessible collective health-care systems have been dismantled. China has dismantled and partially privatised its rural health-care system. In Sub-Saharan Africa malnutrition is on the increase and AIDS is placing a heavy burden on already overstressed health-care systems. Health indicators show that Sub-Saharan Africa lags further and further behind other regions. Whatever doubts one may have concerning the blessings of economic growth, it is obvious that economic stagnation has deeply unfavourable effects on the state of health.

In the last years of the twentieth century, important new elements emerged in the thinking about health-care policy (WHO, 2000). These can be summarised in three terms: effectiveness, new universalism and balance between public and private efforts. The importance of primary health care is still central to policy thinking. But the new emphasis is on making health care systems more effective. *Effectiveness* implies trying to target diseases with the most negative impacts on health and welfare. It also involves paying increased attention to people's demand for health. In earlier health-care policy, funds were channelled to suppliers of health care based on assumptions about people's needs. Presumed needs may not reflect real demands. The emphasis on effectiveness is mirrored in the emergence of new indicators trying to measure the burden of disease, such as the DALYs discussed in section 6.1.1 of this chapter (Murray and Lopez, 1996). Older ideals of providing everything medically useful to the whole population are being abandoned as unrealistic. Health policy should try to identify diseases that account for large, avoidable burdens of ill health. On the other hand, it should try to identify health and nutrition interventions that have the largest impacts at the lowest cost. This results in a cost-effective package of basic or essential interventions which should be available for everybody. This *new universalism* contrasts with policies focusing on only the poor on one hand and unrealistic older ideals of providing total medical care for everybody on the other (WHO, 2000: ch. 1). The third element of the new policy debate refers to the *balance between private and public health-care provision*. Berman (1998) argues that thinking about health-care systems in the past has overwhelmingly focused on government policies. However, even in a country with a statist tradition such as India, private households account for 75 per cent of health expenditures. Government expenditure accounts for a modest proportion of health expenditure except in the case of preventive primary health care, where government expenditure accounts for 50 per cent. Private expenditures also combine and mix expenditures on 'traditional medicine' and modern 'allopathic' medicine in an interesting fashion. Berman calls for a new balance between private and public provision of medicine. Governments should not try to replace private by public provision but should focus on regulation, health standards, access and combating abuses. This debate is still raging. Proponents of public provision point to the danger that privatised medicine primarily benefits those who can pay. They also point to the effectiveness of collective-based health systems. But the search for a new balance is there to stay.

Several recent reports have pointed to the importance of strengthening the knowledge base for health care and health-care policy. Here, there is a new call for publicly funded medical research directed to the needs of developing countries (WHO, 1999; UNDP, 2001). In the late twentieth century, around US$ 55 billion was invested annually in health research. As research is market-driven, by far the most of this investment is directed towards the health needs of the advanced economies. If poor people cannot afford drugs, there is no market incentive to produce drugs for them. Therefore, research on malaria or the African AIDS epidemic is underfunded. Publicly funded research needs to compensate for this.

Questions for review

1. What are the characteristics of the epidemiological transition? Do the patterns of disease and health change in the same way in all societies, in the course of development?
2. Discuss the relationships between standards of living and nutrition on the one hand and life expectation and child mortality on the other.
3. Do advances in medical technology provide an adequate explanation of the overall decline in death rates and increases in life expectation in developing countries?
4. What is the malnutrition–infection syndrome? How can Mosley's model of this syndrome be used to explain how relatively mild diseases such as diarrhoea can result in death?
5. Why is education considered to be an important factor in combating child mortality?
6. What are the most important differences between preventive health care and curative health care in the context of developing countries?
7. Discuss some of the drawbacks of morbidity indicators.
8. In what ways do investments in health contribute to economic development?

Further reading

Data on indicators such as life expectancy and mortality can be found in the *Population Data Base* of the United Nations Population Division, http://esa.un.org/unpp and in the World Health Organization publication, *World Mortality in 2000: Life Tables for 191 Countries* (2002). Every year the WHO publishes the *World Health Report*, which has an annex with data on health indicators. Two interesting editions of the report are: *Life in the 21st Century – A Vision for All* (1998) and *Making a Difference* (1999). The World Health Reports can be downloaded from the WHO website: http://www.who.int/en/. Quantitative information about the spread of AIDS can be found in *Report on the Global HIV/AIDS Epidemic* of the Joint United Nations Programme on HIV/AIDS (2002). The programme runs a special website on AIDS: http://www.unaids.org/en/default.asp.

Thomas McKeown has written several books arguing the case for the importance of nutrition in health. These include *The Role of Medicine* (1979) and *The Origins of Human*

Disease (1988). Two publications by Simon Preston focus on the role of advances in medical technology: *Mortality Patterns in National Populations* (1976) and an article entitled 'The Changing Relation between Mortality and Level of Economic Development' (1975) in *Population Studies*. Mosley's influential model of the determinants of child mortality is summarised in 'Biological and Socio-Economic Determinants of Child Survival: A Proximate Determinants Framework Integrating Fertility and Mortality Variables' (1985a). An interesting attempt at quantitative synthesis of the different theories and approaches is presented in the 1999 edition of the *World Health Report, Making a Difference*. For the epidemiological transition, two key articles are: 'The Epidemiological Transition: A Theory of the Epidemiology of Population Change' (1971) by Omran and 'Feedbacks in Economic and Demographic Transition' (1969) by Frederikson.

For a discussion of disability adjusted life years (DALYs), see Murray and Lopez, *The Global Burden of Disease. A Comprehensive Assessment of Mortality and Disability from Diseases, Injuries and Risk Factors in 1990 and Projected to 2020* (1996) and Murray and Acharya, 'Understanding DALYs' in *Journal of Health Economics* (1997).

In a stimulating article, 'Routes to Low Mortality in Poor Countries' (1986), Caldwell shows how health-care policy can affect health achievements of countries. The vast literature on the relationships between health and economic development is reviewed in an article by Strauss and Thomas in the *Journal of Economic Literature*, entitled 'Health, Nutrition and Economic Development' (1998). For a discussion of primary health care, see Mosley, 'Will Primary Health Care Reduce Infant and Child Mortality? A Critique of Some Current Strategies, with Special Reference to Africa and Asia' (1985b) and the WHO report, *Primary Health Care: Report of the International Conference on Primary Health Care* (1978). This report was the first of a long series of reports in the Health for All Series published by the WHO.

7 Education and Development

Like health, education is both an end and a means. It is one of the basic human rights and a developmental goal in its own right. But, education also contributes to the realisation of other important developmental goals (UNESCO, 2002). Functions and tasks generally ascribed to education include the following:

1. Promotion of economic growth and development. Investment in the physical capital stock is not sufficient for economic development. Investment in 'human capital' is also required.
2. Modernisation of attitudes and mentalities in society.
3. Contributing to important developmental goals such as increased life expectancy, improved health and reduced fertility. Education of mothers, in particular, makes important contributions to better health of children and reductions in fertility. These are among the important non-economic benefits of education. These relationships have been discussed in the chapters on population and health (Chapters 5 and 6).
4. Political socialisation, promotion of a sense of civic responsibility, contributing to national integration and national political consciousness in developing countries.
5. Reducing social and gender inequality and increasing social mobility.
6. Contributing to personal growth, development and emancipation.

Immediately after World War II, expectations concerning the role of education in development were high. Expansion and improvement of education were generally considered as essential to development. Governments in developing countries were prepared to invest heavily in education. Families saw education as the main way to improve their children's chances in life. International organisations were eager to provide financial and technical support for the construction of new educational systems.

However, since the 1970s, optimism about the contributions of education has been shaken. Not all investment in education proved beneficial to development. Resources were often insufficient and the quality of education was disappointing.

This chapter will present a survey of important debates and theories concerning the role of education in development (section 7.1). It will also discuss the educational performance of developing countries in the post-war period (sections 7.2 and 7.3). Important problems and bottlenecks in education are the subject of section 7.4. Throughout the chapter, special attention will be paid to the role of education in the process of economic development.

7.1   Theories of the contribution of education to economic development

7.1.1   'Human capital' theory

The notion of education as an investment in economic growth arose in the late 1950s in the United States. Economists such as Abramovitz, Solow and Denison found that the growth of national product in economically advanced countries could not be adequately explained by the growth of the physical capital stock and the growth of the labour force. A considerable part of growth remained unaccounted for (Abramovitz, 1956; Denison, 1962; 1967; Kendrick, 1961; Solow, 1957). These authors adjusted the growth of the labour force for increases in labour quality that were due to education. In addition to the growth in physical capital stock, the increase in human capital turned out to be of great importance as well. As people became more and more educated, developed more skills and improved their reading and writing abilities, it was argued they became more productive and they were better able to handle existing and new production techniques. The inclusion of human capital in growth accounting studies substantially reduced the unexplained residual in growth (Maddison, 1987; Pilat, 1994; Timmer, 2000).

Human capital theory developed this line of thought further, particularly at a micro-level (Becker, 1964; Blaug, 1972; 1976; 1990; Mincer, 1974; Schultz, 1961; 1971; 1988). The empirical foundation for this theory was the close relationship observed in many societies between the number of years of education received and a person's income level. The essence of human capital theory was the notion that individuals (supported by their parents) were willing to invest in their own education so that they would be able to earn a higher income in the future. These investments consisted of educational expenses and income forgone by delayed entry into the labour market. The theoretical link between investment in education and the level of income was labour productivity – just as in the macro-approach. Increasing the level of schooling would lead to higher labour productivity. In line with neoclassical economic theory, greater labour productivity would result in higher incomes for the categories of employees concerned.[1]

Not only individuals would benefit from investment in education. Society as a whole would also benefit from an increasing supply of better-educated workers and citizens. *External effects* of education included more rapid technological change, reduced fertility and higher infant health (e.g. Lloyd *et al.*, 2000). Such positive external effects are a justification for public subsidies to education. In almost every country in the world a considerable part of the cost of education is subsidised by the government.

In the mid-1980s and 1990s, these ideas have resurfaced in macro-economics in the context of 'endogenous growth theory' (Barro, 1991; Lucas, 1988; Romer, 1986; see also Chapter 3, section 3.4.4).[2] Endogenous growth theory suggests that investments in technological change, research and development and physical and human capital are subject to increasing returns owing to spillover effects through which firms profit from each others' investments. The more a country has previously invested in technology and in human and physical capital, the more it will profit from additional investment. Such theories thus offer an explanation of increasing divergence of economic performance in the world economy.

Another version of human capital theory is contained in the notion of 'conditional convergence' (Barro, 1991; Mankiw, Romer and Weil, 1992; Wolff and Gittleman, 1993). Given characteristics such as a country's initial investment rate and educational attainment, countries will tend to converge to common productivity levels and growth rates, with countries with lower initial productivity growing more rapidly and countries with higher productivity growing more slowly. However, countries in different convergence groups do not converge on each other. Countries with higher initial levels of education will tend to converge to higher growth rates and levels.

As usual, the econometric literature on the impact of education on growth is not unanimous. Some studies (such as Benhabib and Siegel, 1994; and Pritchett, 2001) do not find significant effects of education. But most recent studies tend to confirm the importance of education as one of the factors with a positive influence on growth, both in advanced and developing economies (for a review see Krueger and Lindahl, 2001). The reasons why it is hard to make unambiguous statements about the impact of education as a factor on its own

---

1 According to neoclassical economic theory, employers will continue to attract labour as long as the marginal returns of additional workers are higher than their gross wages. For the last worker employed, the marginal costs will be equal to the wage rate.
2 The novelty of these ideas has been somewhat exaggerated by the use of the term 'new growth theory'.

will be elaborated on below. But, this does not detract from the importance of education.

Though human capital theory was initially developed in the United States and Europe, it was soon applied to developing countries as well. The idea of furthering development by means of education had already achieved considerable popularity, well before the rise of this theory (Foster, 1965a; Krieger, 1988). Many members of the new elites in developing countries had received their education during the colonial period. It was often via education that they had been exposed to ideas about human rights, nationalism and development. At the same time, colonial educational systems had offered them insufficient opportunities to develop their talents. Independence provided an opportunity for rapid improvements in access to education. Education was also regarded as a modernising force. It would help detach people from traditional cultural influences and social relationships that were seen as obstacles to modernisation.

Human capital theory – both in its micro-economic and its macro-economic guise – provided an additional justification for increased efforts in the field of education. National and international policy makers embraced the theory wholeheartedly.

Human capital theory provides a framework for the systematic evaluation of the costs and benefits of different kinds of education for households. The costs include:

1. School fees, costs of books, teaching materials, school uniforms, and so forth.
2. Income forgone while receiving an education. One of the major costs of formal education is that the entry of a person to the labour market is delayed for years. During this period, the individual or the household not only has to bear the costs of education, but also loses the income which could have been earned in this period.

The benefits consist of the difference between the lifetime income of an individual with a given amount of education and the lifetime income he would receive if he had not had this education. On the basis of the total costs and benefits one can calculate the average annual return on an educational investment, the so-called *rate of return*. In addition to the private rates of return, social rates of return can be calculated for society as a whole. Here the benefits include the positive external effects of educating an individual for society. The social costs refer to the total costs of educating including public subsidies and the production forgone by society because individuals do not produce while being educated.

One of the interesting research findings was the fact that in developing countries the rate of return on investment in education was higher than the rate of return on investment in physical capital (Psacharopoulos, 1985; Psacharopoulos and Patrinos, 2002). The rates of return in developing countries were substantially higher than those in high-income countries. The highest rates were found in the poorest countries. Another interesting finding was that the rates of return for primary education were consistently much higher than those for secondary and higher education (Blaug, 1976; Psacharopoulos, 1985; Psacharopoulos and Patrinos, 2002; Schultz, 1988). On these grounds developing countries should give priority to primary education.

Since governments usually bear the greater part of the costs of education, individual calculations of costs and benefits will differ substantially from social calculations of costs and benefits. Without exception individual rates of return are higher than social rates of return (Coombs, 1985).[3] This is one of the factors contributing to the explosive growth in the demand for secondary and higher education in developing countries.

Prior to a discussion of criticisms of human capital theory, the question should be raised why investment in human capital (education) should lead to higher productivity and economic development. The possible answers to this question are summarised in Box 7.1.

Box 7.1 Education, productivity and economic development

1. *Professional Skills.* Education teaches specific professional skills required for professional practice (for mechanics, plumbers, nurses or doctors).
2. *The three Rs.* Workers who have mastered the three Rs – reading, writing and arithmetic – are more productive than those who have not. Literate employees are able to read instructions, keep records, make calculations, and so on.
3. *Change in Attitudes.* Education and literacy lead to changed attitudes, which indirectly result in higher productivity (Anderson and Bowman, 1976). For example, increased literacy and education changes peoples' perceptions of the alternatives open to them. They will start looking for professions or geographic regions, where the earnings are higher.
4. *Commercial and Financial Aptitudes.* Education and literacy contribute to the development of commercial and financial activities. These activities require people who can work as book-keepers and clerks, who can write letters, file papers, or can manipulate numbers. Literate people are more likely to utilise paper money, hold bank accounts, and use other financial instruments. Literacy is a prerequisite for the development of financial systems and it influences the supply of savings (Sandberg, 1982).
5. *Functioning of market mechanisms.* For market mechanisms to function, people have to be able to acquire information and orient themselves amongst alternatives. Education contributes to this. Effectively functioning markets in turn contribute to the efficient allocation of productive resources and thus to increases in productivity.
6. *Openness to innovation.* Technological development proceeds at an ever-faster pace. It needs well-educated employees to understand and apply the continuous flow of new production techniques. A more educated population is likely to be more innovative, which speeds the adoption of new technology (Nelson and Phelps, 1966). This applies

---

3 The comparison between social and private rates of return is biased because social costs can be measured, while external effects are usually not measured (Psacharopoulos and Patrinos, 2002).

not least to agriculture where new techniques can lead to dramatic increases in productivity (Schultz, 1988).[4]

7. *Dissemination of new ideas and technologies.* In general, literacy has positive effects on the dissemination of new ideas and technologies in a society.

8. *The rate of technological change.* In modern society the rate of technological development itself depends on continued investment in education, research and development (Nelson, 1981). A sufficient supply of scientific and technical personnel is needed to adapt existing technologies from abroad and develop new ones. Highly trained engineers and scientists are essential for R&D (Pavitt, 1980). Technological sophistication of management is needed to make decisions about allocation of resources for R&D and acquisition of technology.

9. *Geographic and occupational mobility.* Education promotes geographic and occupational mobility (Easterlin, 1981; Sandberg, 1982). Some authors consider the loosening of age-old ties to village or ancestral occupation as a prerequisite for modernisation. Geographic and occupational mobility contribute to a more efficient allocation of the production factor labour. Of course, increased mobility also has drawbacks, such as unrestricted migration to urban areas.

7.1.2   Criticisms of human capital theory

Though highly influential, human capital theory has also been severely crit-icised (Blaug, 1976; 1985). The basic points of criticism are summarised in Box 7.2:

Box 7.2   Criticisms of human capital theory

- *Marginal productivity is difficult to measure.* The high correlation between education and personal income does not necessarily mean that education makes workers more productive. Nothing is more difficult to measure than marginal productivity (Blaug, 1990).
- *Difficulty in measuring costs and benefits.* We may have sufficient information on income inequality at a given moment in time. But it is very difficult to draw any conclusions from this concerning the distribution of *lifetime incomes*. Next, it is hard to estimate the income forgone while individuals are being educated. Finally, if we want to calculate the social rate of return of education, we will find the external effects of education difficult to estimate. With so many uncertainties, the whole notion of a cost–benefit analysis of educational investment becomes rather problematic.
- *The benefits of education are not merely economic.* Education also increases one's social status and may lead to greater work satisfaction.
- *Disregard of quality and type of education.* In most cost–benefit analyses of education, only the number of years of education is taken into account. The quality of education and the type of education (e.g. technical education, humanities) is disregarded.
- *Insufficient attention for the ability to pay.* The demand for education does not only depend on costs and benefits, but also on the ability to pay for education.
- *Importance of perceptions of costs and benefits.* It is not just the objective relation between costs and benefits that matters, but also the *perception* of this relation. If

4 This issue is nicely summed up in a quote from *The Economist*: 'What use is modern technology if a poor country's workers cannot read the instructions on a bag of fertiliser?' (Economist, 1996: p. 16).

people believe education will increase their opportunities, they are more likely to make sacrifices for it.

- *Innate abilities and family background may determine rewards.* Education in itself is not important. Individual talents and characteristics of the parental family are the crucial determinants of one's future income. Education merely translates these characteristics into diplomas. Education is rewarded because it is a signal of innate ability (Spence, 1973).
- *Education is not only investment, but also consumption.* Many people study because they find it enjoyable or intrinsically interesting. This makes it difficult to determine causality. Education is both the seed and the flower of economic development. It is difficult to separate the causal effect of education on growth from the increase in demand for education as countries advance economically (Harbison and Myers, 1965).

7.1.3   Screening theory

The most extreme version of the preceding criticisms of human capital theory is contained in *screening theory* (Berg, 1970; Blaug, 1985; Dore, 1976; Spence, 1973). This theory argues that education in itself does not contribute to a person's productivity. The knowledge and skills acquired in educational institutions are not applied in one's later career. The specific skills required in a profession are learned on the job rather than at school.

Why then are higher educated employees paid more than less well-educated employees? Screening theory states that employers find it hard to predict the future performance of job applicants. They use educational qualifications and diplomas as a screening system for ability, achievement motivation, social background, and the right personality traits. Schooling is an indication of trainability itself. Actual training starts when one starts working.

Thus radical versions of the screening theory argue that education merely 're-produces' social inequality from generation to generation (Williamson, 1979). The main function of education for the masses is to teach them discipline, respect for authority, punctuality, obedience, ability to cooperate and concentration (Bowles and Gintis, 1976). Education prepares labourers for inferior-level, routine tasks in productive organisations. People from higher social strata are prepared for top-level positions in the hierarchical structure. Their education develops personal qualities such as self-reliance, self-esteem, autonomy, flexibility, capacity to assume leadership roles, managerial qualities and initiative.

The screening theory suggests that much of education in developing countries is irrelevant. Expanding the educational system merely results in diploma inflation and a scramble for the highest diplomas (*credentialism*). On the labour market, people with higher diplomas displace people with lower educational qualifications without any improvement in productivity. For example, university graduates displace graduates from polytechnics; graduates from polytechnics displace workers with a secondary education. The latter in turn displace people with a primary education. This process is referred to as *bumping down*.

7.1.4   Criticisms of screening theory

Like human capital theory, screening theory is also open to criticism (Blaug, 1985):

1. If screening theory is valid and education does not contribute to productivity, it is hard to explain why self-employed people with a higher education usually have higher earnings than self-employed people with less education (Wolpin, 1977).
2. In screening theory, educational qualifications explain differences in initial earnings. In later stages of a career the relation between education and income should become weaker, as employers gain first-hand experience of an employee's productivity. In fact, however, the correlation between education and income persists throughout people's working lives.
3. If selection is the only real function of the educational system, one might as well use less laborious and less expensive methods of selection and recruitment. Psychological tests would serve just as well to identify the right personality traits. However, in practice, applicants are never selected exclusively on the basis of psychological tests.

7.1.5   An evaluation of the human capital debate

The debate between the proponents and critics of human capital theory is still very much open. In particular the more extreme positions in the debate are based on faith and ideological conviction rather than on empirical evidence.

Since Émile Durkheim, sociologists have emphasised that one of the important functions of education is the transmission of values, standards, attitudes and knowledge to successive generations. In this sense, education has always had a conserving function and will tend to maintain existing structures of inequality. Yet, we also know that education may often lead to change. A well-known example is the colonial educational system, within which members of future nationalist elites received their education. They later rebelled against colonialism in the name of the very political and humanistic ideals transmitted by Western-style education. Education can also be an important means of upward social mobility. Groups with few chances of upward mobility within traditional societies were now offered opportunities to improve their positions by way of education.

It is an interesting empirical question which of these influences – the conserving or the change-oriented – predominated in different societies and historical periods. As we will argue below, the dynamic, change-oriented functions of education predominated in developing countries in the post-war period. Here, we would like to make a preliminary evaluation of the debate between advocates of the human capital theory and those of screening theory.

Screening theory – sometimes also referred to as signalling theory – has drawn our attention to several aspects of education that are also of major importance to developing countries. These are summarised in Box 7.3.

Box 7.3 Key elements of screening theory

- *Learning by doing.* On the job many employees do not use any of the cognitive knowledge they learned in school. Most skills needed in modern industries can be acquired within a few weeks. In this respect 'on-the-job training' and 'learning by doing' are of great importance.
- *Screening.* Screening is one of the social functions of education. Given insufficient information, it is plausible to conclude that educational qualifications serve as an important screening device for job applicants.
- *Diploma inflation.* Expanding the educational system does not always contribute to economic development. Especially the rapid expansion of secondary and higher education may lead to 'diploma inflation'. Of course, it remains perfectly rational for every individual to try to improve his or her life chances by gaining as many educational degrees as possible.

The conclusion of screening theory that education adds 'nothing' to already existing personality traits and thus has no autonomous influence on productivity is not tenable. The most important contribution of education is indeed 'learning to learn'. Reading, writing, and arithmetic are basic requirements for being able to learn later on in life.[5] At higher educational levels, learning to think analytically and evaluate information independently are important preconditions for future learning on the job. On-the-job training is possible in part thanks to the capacity to learn developed in the formal schooling system. Nelson argues that much about semi-conductor design or the production of chemicals cannot be taught at school because the details are too specialised. These details can only be acquired in on-the-job courses, apprenticeships and training programmes, which are usually part of technology-transfer agreements. But at various levels on-the-job training requires prior engineering, scientific and academic training (Nelson, 1981).

Evidently, social background and inherited talents also determine one's educational career. However, inherited talent and high status are not sufficient for success in modern societies. It is the schooling system that translates such factors into qualities that are useful for society. A recent review article suggests that education has an independent impact on earnings and performance, irrespective of innate ability. Education is more than a signalling device (Krueger and Lindahl, 2001). Focusing specifically on studies in developing countries, Glewwe (2002) comes to the same conclusion. Cognitive skills learned at school increase wages and are direct determinants of productivity, irrespective of innate ability.

---

5 Too much emphasis on the insignificance of cognitive skills may lead to the neglect of these essentials, both in developing countries and economically advanced countries.

With regard to developing countries, one may even argue that education to-day is even more important than it used to be in the currently more advanced countries. New production techniques in the industrial and agricultural sector require ever more knowledge and understanding. The pace of technological development is increasing. Only a well-trained labour force can benefit from the opportunities of adopting modern technologies from abroad and adapt-ing these to domestic production processes. Educational investment thus con-tributes to the building of technological capabilities of a country (Evenson and Westphal, 1995; Hobsbawm, 1969).

Though much criticism of human capital theory is justified, we therefore conclude that it is worthwhile for developing countries to invest in further development of their educational systems.

7.1.6   Education as a necessary but not sufficient condition for development

Human capital theory takes neoclassical micro-economics as its point of de-parture and focuses on the costs and benefits of education in a country. An alternative approach is the historical and comparative study of the role of ed-ucation and schooling in the different processes of economic development.

In a classic study based on international comparisons of indicators of liter-acy and economic development, Bowman and Anderson (1963) conclude that economic development can only set in once the level of literacy among the adult male population has reached at least 40 per cent. Analogous to Rostow's theory of the stages of economic growth (see Chapter 3) – which argues that modern economic growth will set in only if physical investment exceeds a cer-tain threshold value – Bowman and Anderson argue that literacy is a *necessary condition* for economic growth. Especially in European and North American his-tory, growth of human capital has been more important than has been hitherto recognised. Education, however, is not a *sufficient* condition for growth and de-velopment. Without investment in physical capital and the rise of institutions that provide positive incentives to productive efforts there will be no economic development.

Once the 40 per cent threshold been reached, further development of literacy has little impact, according to Bowman and Anderson. It is not until literacy ex-ceeds the 70 per cent level that it will have positive effects on further economic development.

As with human capital, an interesting debate developed concerning the Bow-man and Anderson hypothesis (Tortella, 1990). The essential problem is how to determine the direction of causality empirically. It is indisputable that on average more affluent societies are also more literate and have more training per head of the population. However, this may be explained by the fact that people with higher incomes are willing to pay more for education than people at lower income levels. According to Schultz (1988), the income elasticity of education is 1.4. This means that if the national income rises by 1 per cent, expenditure for education goes up 1.4 per cent.

Some authors try to solve this problem by examining the relations between literacy at an earlier moment in time (A) and national income at a later moment in time (B). For Spain Nuñez has estimated that the level of literacy affects provincial per capita income with a 35 years' lag (Nuñez, 1990). Lars Sandberg (1982) even states that for European countries the degree of literacy in 1850 is the best predictor of national income in 1970. In the short run, however, there is no connection between literacy and economic growth.

For Sandberg too, education is only one of the relevant factors in economic development. The volume of investment in physical capital is also of great importance. Sandberg argues that countries will benefit more from physical capital accumulation when their initial level of education is higher. The currently affluent Scandinavian countries, Sweden and Finland, provide examples supporting this proposition. In the nineteenth century these countries were quite poor but at the same time they had high levels of literacy, which were the foundation for their later growth. Japan can also be quoted as an example supporting Sandberg's theory (Hanley, 1990; Pilat, 1994). Around 1869 the Japanese were already highly educated. Since then Japan has continued to invest in education as part of its national development and modernisation strategy. The investment in physical capital, which started after the Meiji Revolution in 1869, enabled Japan to experience rapid economic growth from the late nineteenth century onwards, especially in the period 1950–70. In an excellent analysis of the Japanese catch-up experience, Godo and Hayami (2002) combine the notions of *complementarity* and *threshold*. The early increase in education initially had little impact on growth because capital per worker was growing slowly, so there was little complementarity. After World War II, a threshold level of education had been reached and capital accumulation and slower education advance combined to promote explosive growth. Finally, the rapidly industrialising East and Southeast Asian countries such as China, South Korea, Singapore and Taiwan also achieved high levels of literacy and education at a relatively early stage prior to their economic take-off (World Bank, 1993).

This strand of research is consistent with the notion of 'conditional convergence' discussed in Chapter 3, in which a high level of education is seen as one of the necessary conditions for catch-up (Mankiw, Romer and Weil, 1992).

Other authors object to the notion of education as a necessary condition for development. Mitch argues that the level of literacy is not as essential to agricultural and industrial development as Bowman and Sandberg suppose (Mitch, 1990). Like the critics of the human capital theory, Mitch argues that during the Industrial Revolution it was not important for the working masses to be able to read or write. Literacy only mattered for a limited number of clerks, engineers, book-keepers, managers and foremen. Before the twentieth century literacy did not play a major role in agricultural development either. The development of human capacities is important, but this does not always require a formal education. There are 'functional alternatives' such as working experience, 'on-the-job training,' and 'learning by doing'.

It is also argued that in England and elsewhere the labour force was actually 'deskilled' in the course of the Industrial Revolution. Traditional craftsmanlike skills became obsolete owing to the development of mass production (Nicholas, 1990; Thompson, 1963). The educational level of labourers remained unchanged at best. Nicholas, however, does acknowledge the fact that, on the eve of the Industrial Revolution, England had a high level of education.

In an interesting attempt at synthesis, Sandberg argues that, while education has been an important factor in the history of modern European development, there have always been alternatives to education (Sandberg, 1990). Russia, for example, had an extremely low level of education during the nineteenth century. In part it compensated for this by using highly capital-intensive methods of production, which reduced the need for skilled labour. In a like fashion, the increased role of government in the mobilisation of financial resources compensated for underdeveloped financial markets (Sandberg, 1982).

A recent article by Pack and Paxson confronts the puzzling question why African economies have stagnated in spite of impressive advances in educational performance (Pack and Paxson, 2001). They conclude that investment in education in itself does not promote economic growth. Education will only have major positive impacts if improved education is complemented by inflows of new capital goods and technology which make use of the new skills acquired through education. If such inflows are not forthcoming there will be no learning through experience and people will quickly lose their skills.

This notion of the complementarity of physical, human capital investment and technological is one of the key insights of much modern research on economic growth and technological change discussed in Chapters 3 and 4 (see e.g. Abramovitz, 1989; Godo and Hayami, 2002; Grier, 2002; Kim and Nelson, 2000; Nelson, 1996). Capital accumulation without complementary improvement of capabilities and knowledge will be wasted. Accumulation of human capital without capital accumulation or technological change will be useless. This reads very much like the conclusions arrived at by economic historians such as Sandberg. There are two interesting differences of opinion, however. Sandberg argues that educational investment precedes other types of investment. This implies that even if educational improvement does not lead to economic dynamics in Africa, it may still do so in the future if other complementary factors are forthcoming. Secondly, Sandberg argues that there may be functional alternatives to education. This, however, is increasingly unlikely in the modern global economy in which technological change has become so important.

In this textbook, it is not possible to unravel all these controversies in depth. However, it is interesting to note that there are at least three areas of convergence between the various participants in these debates:

1. Since the mid-nineteenth century education has become increasingly important, as the scientific and technological basis of economic development have become more prominent. In an earlier era, formal schooling may not have been of particular value for learning to master a technology. Now, for many technologies, education is virtually a prerequisite for high-level competence. Investment in education and technology since the late nineteenth century is considered one of the crucial factors in the rise of Germany and Japan as economic powers. Insufficient investment in education in England – particularly in technical and vocational training – is seen as contributing to the relative decline of the former economic leader.
2. In developing countries today education is more important than in Western countries in the past because it increases the potential to adopt and adapt new technologies. The pace of international technological change is much higher than before. In order to develop, developing countries have both the opportunity and the necessity to adopt technological innovations very rapidly in order to develop. Again, we conclude that investment in human capital remains one of the crucial ingredients of a successful development strategy for developing countries today.
3. There are important complementarities between investment in human and physical capital. Only when investments in one type of capital are matched by investments in the other, will they have sustained positive effects on growth.

7.2   Indicators of educational development

Before discussing empirical developments in education in developing countries, the following section will provide a brief discussion of several well-known indicators of educational development (Coombs, 1985; UNESCO, 2000a).

7.2.1   *Indicators of educational enrolment*

The *gross enrolment ratio* is the ratio in a given year of the total enrolment at a given educational level (primary, secondary or tertiary) and the total estimated population in the corresponding age bracket. It is a rather rough criterion, which does not take into account that the numerator includes children outside the relevant age category (e.g. pupils of secondary school age still enrolled in primary education). The gross enrolment ratio, therefore, presents too rosy a picture of primary educational enrolment. Frequently, it even exceeds 100 per cent. Experts suggest that this indicator overestimates actual enrolment by 10 per cent to 30 per cent (Colclough and Al-Samarrai, 2000; Coombs, 1985).

The *net enrolment ratio* is a better criterion of enrolment. This ratio indicates what percentage of each school age group is actually somewhere in the school system. The problem with this concept is that it does not show where in the educational system the pupils actually are. In recent UNESCO publications the definition of net enrolment has been adjusted to take this into account (UNESCO, 2002a). Net enrolment is now defined as the percentage of an age group enrolled in the education level appropriate for that age group. Of course, the new enrolment figure will be lower than the old one because part of the age group is left out of consideration. The change in definition means that it is no longer possible to construct consistent long-run time series of net enrolment.[6]

Indicators of educational enrolment are frequently used. Still, they have several important defects (Coombs, 1985; Hardiman and Midgley, 1982). These are reproduced in Box 7.4.

Box 7.4   Shortcomings of indicators of educational enrolment

1. *Over-reporting*. Enrolment data are inflated since schools have an interest in high enrolment figures in order to receive more subsidies. The same applies to reports on educational enrolment by national ministries of education to UNESCO.
2. *Enrolment versus completion*. Enrolment data do not show how many students actually finish a particular cycle of education. In fact, not more than 60 per cent of all students actually complete the educational cycle in which they are enrolled. Dropping out of school is quite common. Between 20 per cent and 75 per cent of all students do not continue beyond the fourth year of primary school (Coombs, 1985; see also Table 7.3).
3. *Enrolment data provide no information about the quality of education*. At many schools there is substantial absenteeism. Especially in rural areas, school children are expected to work in the fields during agricultural peak periods. Often children are absent for more than one third of the school year. Besides, the data do not tell us anything about the size of school classes, the quality of the teaching materials, and the usually low level of qualification and poor motivation of the teaching staff.
4. *The quality of data of international databases seems to be deteriorating over time*. In recent years less data have been available on secondary and tertiary education.

7.2.2   Educational Attainments

Data on enrolment tell us something about the efforts made by a society to educate its people. However, they provide little information on the outcomes of the educational process by the time people leave school and enter the labour market. A useful alternative indicator is the average number of years of schooling completed by people in different age categories. This indicator provides information on the quantity of human capital per person. Thus, one could look at years of schooling completed for all persons over 15 years of age or all persons over 25 years of age.

Psacharopoulos and Arriagada (1986) have made estimates of years of schooling in the labour force – based on labour-force surveys and population censuses.

---

[6] The old NER indicator resurfaces as Age-Specific Enrolment Rate (ACER), but there are no ACER statistics in the UNESCO publications.

With some justice, they argue that this is one of the best indicators of the stock of human capital. Psacharopoulos and Arriagada weight the percentages of the labour force that have completed a given educational cycle with the cumulative length in years of that educational cycle. They distinguish six phases or cycles: no education, incomplete primary education, complete primary education, incomplete secondary education, complete secondary education and higher education (see Table 7.4).

7.2.3 Financial indicators

Financial indicators give us an idea of the efforts of governments and societies to develop educational systems and the resources available for education. Well-known indicators are:

1. Government educational expenditures as a percentage of the national income;
2. Government educational expenditures as a percentage of total government expenditures;
3. Government expenditure per pupil at different levels of education.

These data refer to government expenditure only. Private expenditure on education is not included. In fact, households are responsible for sizable proportions of educational expenditures. It should be noted that financial indicators are input indicators rather than output indicators. Different countries may achieve very different educational outcomes for similar levels of educational expenditures.

7.2.4 Physical indicators

Physical indicators refer to numbers of teachers, pupil–teacher ratios, numbers of buildings, and so on.

7.2.5 Literacy

Most of the indicators discussed above refer to educational inputs: enrolment; numbers of teachers; amounts of money; years of education. Far less is known about the results of the educational process. Apparently, it is possible to attend school for years without learning to read, write or calculate – even in economically advanced countries.

One of the few indicators of educational outcomes is the degree of literacy. Even here, though, one should be careful. Too often literacy is determined by means of survey questions about literacy to which one can answer yes or no, without any testing of the actual skills themselves. In other estimates of literacy it is assumed that a person is literate when he or she has attended primary school for at least four years. Moreover, literacy itself had been defined in very different ways (Ooijens and van Kampen, 1989; UNESCO, 2002). According to UNESCO a person is functionally literate 'if a person is able to engage in all those activities in which literacy is required for effective functioning of his group and community and for enabling him to continue to use reading, writing and calculation for his own and the community's development' (Ooijens and van Kampen, 1989; p. 2; UNESCO, 2002: p. 60). The functional definition captures the ability of people to use literacy to carry out everyday tasks. But, as common tasks differ across cultures, the comparative measurement of literacy is not easy. The best measures of literacy are based on tests for reading, writing and simple arithmetic calculation. Most often literacy is expressed as a percentage of the population over 15 years of age.[7]

7.3 Educational performance in developing countries

7.3.1 The initial situation after World War II

In most developing countries the state of education after World War II was very poor. Colonial authorities had never invested much in education (Altbach, 1978; 1982; Heinink and Koetsier, 1984). Under colonialism there were two dominant motives for providing education:

1. Religion: missionary work was important in primary education.
2. Educating native elites to fulfil subordinate positions in colonial administration: for members of native elites a limited number of secondary and higher educational institutions were created, modelled on Western educational institutions. The language of education was the colonial 'mother tongue.' The substance of the curriculum was Western-oriented.

The educational system had a dual structure (Heinink and Koetsier, 1984). Primary education in rural areas emphasised practical and moral training under missionary influence. In addition, there was academically oriented primary, secondary and higher education for children of the foreign colonial elites. This education was also open to very restricted numbers of children of native elites. In academically oriented education the emphasis was on preparing pupils for employment in the small modern sector of the economy. It was a weak imitation of Western educational systems. In the curriculum the humanities and, in particular, languages predominated. Little attention was paid to the natural sciences and to native languages and cultures.

Of course, there were differences between the colonial educational systems. More than the British, the French tried to create small elites of assimilated 'coloured French individuals' by means of education (Altbach, 1982). Of all colonising powers, the British paid most attention to education, the Belgians

---

7 Ooijens and van Kampen argue in favour of also including 11- to 15-year-olds in estimates of literacy (Ooijens and van Kampen, 1989).

and the Portuguese the least. At the eve of independence there were hardly any graduates of higher education in Belgian Congo.

In non-colonised countries such as China and Thailand educational opportunities were also rather limited until World War II. In India and in the Islamic world precolonial religiously oriented educational systems persisted alongside colonial education. But their importance tended to decline under colonialism. The most favourable situation was to be found in Latin America where decolonisation had been completed early in the nineteenth century and formal education had been developed furthest. Even here, the level of education in the 1950s was still very low.

In the sections below empirical data will be presented on developments in education since World War II. The educational performance of developing countries should be judged in the light of very poor initial conditions.

7.3.2　*Increases in educational enrolment*

The data on gross enrolment in Table 7.1 indicate that enrolment in developing countries has increased very substantially since 1960. Educational performance in developing countries has been very dynamic. With respect to primary education Asian and Latin American countries in particular seem to be well on the way to achieving the goal of primary education for all. Gross enrolment figures in East Asia and Latin America exceed 100 per cent. On the African continent great progress has been made too, though less than in other regions. Here, enrolment growth declined for ten years after 1980, owing to economic stagnation and budget retrenchments (Colclough and Al-Samarrai, 2000). Enrolment picked up after 1990 reaching 77 per cent in 1999/2000. The data indicate an unambiguous narrowing of the gap between educational levels in developing countries and in more affluent countries. The growth rate of enrolment in secondary and post-secondary education has been far higher than in primary education. Between 1960 and 1980 the number of students enrolled in post-secondary education in developing countries increased by a factor of 5.2, in secondary education by a factor of 3.6 and in primary education by a factor of 1.4 (Coombs, 1985; UNESCO, 1983). For the whole period 1960–2000 these growth rates are 4 per cent, 3 per cent and 0.7 per cent respectively.

Gross enrolment data give a too optimistic picture of primary educational enrolment, as many children over the age of 11 are still in primary school owing to grade repetition or late enrolment. The net enrolment data in Table 7.2 show that the percentage of pupils enrolled for the 6–11 years age bracket is much lower in all regions.[8] The gross enrolment data suggest that by 2000 Latin American and Asian countries have achieved full primary school enrolment. However, the net enrolment data indicate that 18 per cent of all 6–11-year-old

---

8 Recent secondary net enrolment data are not consistent with older ones, as the definition has changed. The new definition refers to the percentage of an age bracket actually enrolled in the school level belonging to that age bracket. The old definition refers to the percentage of an age bracket enrolled somewhere in the school system.

Table 7.1 *Gross enrolment ratios by educational level, country and region, 1960–2000*[a]

Country/region	Primary education		Secondary education		Higher education	
	1960	1999/2000	1960	1999/2000	1960	1999/2000
Bangladesh	47	106	8	54[b]	1	5
China		106	63			7
India	41	101	23	50	2	7[b]
Indonesia	67	108	6	55	1	11[b]
Malaysia	96	101	19	99	1	23
Pakistan	30	96	6	39	1	4[b]
Philippines	95	113	26	76[b]	13	29[b]
South Korea	94	99	27	97	5	72[c]
Sri Lanka	95	106	27	72[b]	1	5[b]
Taiwan		100		99		68[c]
Thailand	136	94	8	79	2	32
Turkey	75	101	14	58	3	15
Argentina	98	119	31	94	11	48
Brazil	95	166	11	103	2	15
Chile	109	107	24	87	4	38
Colombia	77	113	12	71	2	22
Mexico	80	113	11	73	3	20
Peru	83	128	18	81	4	29[b]
Venezuela	100	102	97	59	4	29
Congo, Dem. Rep	60	47	3	18[b]	0.1	1[b]
Côte d'Ivoire	46	77	2	22	0	7[b]
Egypt	66	100	16	84	5	39[b]
Ghana	59	78	3	37[b]	0	2
Kenya	47	91	2	30[b]	0	1
Morocco	47	90	5	39	0.5	9
Nigeria	36	82	3	30[b]	0	4[b]
South Africa	89	119	15	90	3	15[b]
Tanzania	24	63	2	5	0.1	1
Zambia	48	79	1	25	0	2
Average	72	104	16	70	3	19
Developing countries	75.8	100.6	15.7	52.0	2.1	10.0[b]
Africa[d]	40.4	81.2	3.5	26.0	0.3	4.0[b]
Asia[d, b]	85.6	102.9	20.9	57.2	2.6	9.7[b]
East		105.9		66.0		12.0[b]
South		99.8		45.0		6.8[b]
Arab countries	48.3	91.0	10.2	57.0	2.0	15.0[b]
Latin America & Carib.	72.7	114.0[b]	14.6	62.0[b]	3.0	19.0[b]
Developed countries	105.6	102.0	61.1	100.0	13.5	52.0[b]

Notes:
[a] The number of students enrolled per educational level, regardless of their age, as a percentage of the number of persons in the relevant age bracket. The age brackets for educational levels differ per country. Percentages over 100 per cent indicate that persons outside the relevant age bracket are also enrolled.
[b] Data for latest year between 1995 and 1999. In most cases 1998/99 or 1999/2000. For regional totals 1997.
[c] Enrolment in higher education, age bracket 18–21.
[d] Excluding Arab countries, own calculation based on country enrolment weighted by school-age population.
Sources: 1960: UNESCO, *Statistical Yearbook*, 1976 and 1978–99; 1999/2000: UNESCO, Institute of Statistics, Homepage: Global Statistics, Education, Statistical tables, http://portal.unesco.orguis/ev.php; except for Nigeria, and higher education in India, Indonesia, Pakistan and Sri Lanka from *World Development Indicators CD-ROM, 2002*; regions from: UNESCO, *Statistical Yearbook,* 1999 and UNESCO 2002.

children in developing countries did not attend primary school in 2000. The objective of primary education for all has not yet been realised, particularly not in Sub-Saharan Africa. The data for Africa are in line with the conclusion of Colclough and Al-Samarrai (2002) that enrolment levels declined in the 1980s

Table 7.2 *Net enrolment ratios by region, 1960–2000 (Percentage of persons enrolled by age bracket and region)*[a]

Region[b]	6–11 years				12–17 years				18–23 years		
	1960	1987	1992	2000[c]	1960	1987	1992	2000[c]	1960	1987	1992[d]
Africa	29	56	51	57	17	46	41	19	1	9	7
Arab countries	39	73	77	79	18	51	52	55	4	20	20
Asia	53	80	81	85	41	43	47	46	9	14	14
Latin America	58	86	88	96	36	68	68	54	6	25	25
Developing countries	48	76	77	82	35	45	47	45	8	15	14
Developed countries	91	92	92	97	69	87	86	89	15	35	40

Notes:
[a] After 1995 the definition of NER changed. The new definition is the enrolment of the official age group for a given level of education expressed as a percentage of the corresponding population. The 2000 figures are therefore not comparable to the earlier figures.
[b] Africa and Asia exclude the Arab countries. Latin America includes the Caribbean.
[c] 2000: latest year between 1995 and 2000.
[d] UNESCO does not provide more recent data for this age bracket.
Source: 1960, 1987 and 1992: UNESCO, *Statistical Yearbook*, 1989 and 1994.
2000: Homepage UNESCO Statistical Institute (UNESCO, Institute of Statistics, Homepage: http://portal.unesco.org/uis/ev.php, supplemented by data from UNESCO, 1999; 2000b; 2001a; 2001b; 2002c; UN/ESCAP, Sustainable Social Development in a Period of Rapid Globalization, United Nations, Economic and Social Commission for Asia and the Pacific, ch. 11, 'Poverty and Social Equity', http://www.unescap.org/sdd/theme2002/ch2cd.htm. Figures for Asia and Africa 12–17 calculated from country data, using population weights for the age category.

and recovered in the 1990s. For all age categories, the 1992 net enrolment figures are substantially lower than those of 1987. By 2000, primary enrolment had recovered and was just above the 1987 level. The most recent figures in indicate that in Sub-Saharan Africa on average 43 percent of children between the ages of 6 and 11 are not attending primary school. One should realise that even the more realistic net primary enrolment data tend to exaggerate educational performance (see section 7.2.1).[9] For instance, household surveys in Sub-Saharan Africa indicate that the numbers of pupils, who actually attend school are substantially lower than the enrolment figures (UNESCO, 2002: Table 2.6).

Although not all educational objectives have been realised, long-run educational achievements of developing countries have been impressive. Despite considerable population growth they have realised very substantial increases in enrolment since 1960. The educational gap between developing and rich countries has been unmistakably narrowed. As early as 1960 considerable progress had already been made in comparison with the unfavourable initial conditions after World War II. Latin America and East Asia are on course to achieving universal access to primary education. Unfortunately, other regions such as Sub-Saharan Africa are slipping behind (UNESCO, 2002).[10]

9 The dramatic drop in secondary enrolment in Africa is in large part due to the change in the definition of enrolment. The new net enrolment concept is defined as the number of pupils actually enrolled in a given level of education divided by the number of people in the corresponding age bracket. For secondary education this is substantially lower than the old concept, which was defined as the number of pupils of a given age bracket anywhere in the educational system divided by the number of people in that age bracket. For primary education the change of concept does not make much difference.
10 See also UNESCO, Institute of Statistics, Homepage: Global Statistics, Education, Statistical tables, http://portal.unesco.org/uis/ev.php

7.3.3   Education completed

One of the reasons that enrolment data give too rosy a picture of educational performance is that large numbers of students leave school prematurely without a degree. This is illustrated by the data in Table 7.3. For selected years, this table shows what proportion of a given age category has completed primary, secondary or tertiary education. Though the data derive from various years and statistical practices differ from country to country, it is useful to compare these percentages with the gross enrolment data in Table 7.1, which are sometimes even over 100 per cent. The completion data are far lower. An extreme example is provided by India in 1981. In this year, 51.6 per cent of all 15- to 19-year-olds had no education at all; 16.7 per cent had an incomplete primary education. This meant that only 31.7 per cent had successfully completed a primary education. Around that time, the gross enrolment rate in primary education stood at no less than 83 per cent. Other countries with very low completion rates were Bangladesh, Pakistan and Egypt. Completion rates are even lower for the adult population.

Some countries do not distinguish separate categories for completed primary education. The assumption is that all pupils with complete or incomplete secondary education have completed primary education. To increase the comparability between countries, we have calculated the percentage of pupils

Table 7.3a *Highest diploma obtained in selected countries, 1980–2000 (as percentage of 15–19 age bracket)*

Country	No education	Primary education		Secondary education		Higher education	More than primary education
		Incomplete	Complete	Incomplete	Complete		
Bangladesh (1981)	59.8	18.7	–	16.2	5.4	–	21.5
China (1990)	5.3	36.0	–	58.2	–	0.6	58.7
India (1981)	51.6	16.7	–	31.3	–	0.4	31.7
Indonesia (1990)	16.1	45.7	–	38.1	–	0.0	38.2
Malaysia (1980)	6.5	8.1	13.1	68.4	3.1	0.7	72.3
Pakistan (1990)	47.5	19.1	–	17.5	16.9	0.1	33.4
Philippines (1990)	2.4	31.5	–	53.1	–	12.7	66.1
Sri Lanka (1981)	8	32.4	–	59.5	–	0.0	59.6
Thailand (1990)[b]	10.7	69.6	–	13.7	–	5.1	19.7
Turkey (1993)	4.7	2.2	44.8	48.2	–	–	48.3
Argentina (1991)	1.6	9.8	20.7	58.6	–	9.2	67.9
Mexico (1990)	3.8	12.3	19.6	40.7	22	1.6	64.3
Peru (1993)	4.2	23.3	–	51.1	–	19.5	72.5
Venezuela (1990)	12	63.7	–	21.1	–	3	24.3
Côte d'Ivoire (1988)		41.8	–	58.2	–	0.0	58.2
Egypt (1986)	34.5	20.8	–	44.7	–	0.0	44.7
South Africa (1995)	24.6	27.9	6.6	21.3	17.9	1.5	40.9
Zambia (1993)[a]	9.8	67.4		17.6	5.1	0.1	22.8

Notes: The figure in the column to the left of this symbol includes the data for the column(s) in which this symbol appears.
[a] 14–20 years; [b] 6 years and over.
Source: UNESCO, *Statistical Yearbook*, 1997.

Table 7.3b *Highest diploma obtained in selected countries, 1980–2000 (as percentage of 25+ age bracket)*

Country	No education	Primary education		Secondary education		Higher education	More than primary education
		Incomplete	Complete	Incomplete	Complete		
Bangladesh (1981)	70.4	16.7	–	7.4	4.2	1.3	12.9
China (1990)	29.3	34.3	–	34.4	–	2	36.4
India (1981)	57.5	28	–	7.2	–	7.3	14.5
Indonesia (1990)	54.5	26.4	–	16.8	–	2.3	19.1
Malaysia (1980)	16.7	13	20.7	19.4	23.6	6.9	49.6
Pakistan (1990)	73.8	9.7	–	5.8	8.2	2.5	16.5
Philippines (1990)	3.8	20.8	15.1	17.3	21.2	22	60.3
South Korea (1995)	8.7	0.9	17.3	15.7	36.2	21.1	73.1
Sri Lanka (1981)	15.9	48.9	–	34.1	–	1.1	35.2
Taiwan (2001)[c]	4.2	21.3	–	50.0	–	24.5	74.5
Thailand (1990)	20.5	67.3	2.4	4.5	2.3	2.9	9.8
Turkey (1993)[a]	30.6	6.6	40.6	21.9	–	–	22.2
Argentina (1991)	5.7	22.3	34.6	25.3	–	12	37.4
Brazil (1989)[b]	18.7	57	6.9	11.9	5.5	–	17.4
Chile (1992)	5.8	48	–	33.9	–	12.3	46.2
Colombia (1993)	11.9	27.3	18.3	13.3	16.7	10.4	42.5
Mexico (1990)	18.8	28.6	19.9	12.7	10.7	9.2	32.7
Peru (1993)	16.4	34.7	–	27.2	–	20.5	48.9
Venezuela (1990)	21.2	55	–	12	–	11.8	23.8
Congo, Dem. Rep.	52.4	30.3	–	14.6	–	1.3	17.3
Côte d'Ivoire (1988)		48.2	–	43.1	–	8.7	51.8
Egypt (1986)	64.1	16.5	–	14.8	–	4.6	19.4
Kenya (1979)	58.6	32.2	–	7.9	1.3	–	9.2
South Africa (1995)[d]	13	17.1	6.9	26.7	25.7	8.8	63.0
Tanzania (1988)		89.7	–	7.8	0.6	2	10.3
Zambia (1993)	49.8	37	–	5.8	15.5	0.4	22.5

Notes: The figure to the immediate left includes the data for the column(s) in which this symbol appears.
[a] Information on higher education and completed secondary education lacking.
[b] Brazil 10+, no information on higher education.
[c] 15+.
[d] 20+.
Source: UNESCO, *Statistical Yearbook*, 1999; UNESCO, Institute of Statistics, see note 10.

with more than a primary education.[11] Countries that score high in this respect are South Korea, Malaysia, the Philippines, Argentina, Colombia and South Africa. Table 7.3 also shows that the degree of schooling of the 15 to 19 age bracket compares favourably with that of the over-25 age bracket. Younger generations are better schooled than older generations.

7.3.4 *Years of education per member of the labour force*

Table 7.4 shows that the mean number of years of schooling received by members of the labour force in developing countries doubled between 1960 and

---

11 Some countries only publish data on entry into secondary education. These data probably also include those students that have completed primary school but do not continue their education. Other countries distinguish between finishing primary school and enrolment in secondary education. The percentage of people with more than a completed primary school education equals 100 minus the percentage with 'no education', the percentage with 'uncompleted primary education' and the percentage with 'completed primary education'.

Table 7.4 *Mean years of schooling per member of the labour force in fourteen developing countries between 1960 and 1980*

	Percentage with no education			Mean years of schooling		
	around 1960	around 1970	around 1980	around 1960	around 1970	around 1980
China (80)			9.3			8.6
India (61, 81)	89.9		66.7	0.5		1.9
Indonesia (66, 80)	68.1		26.1			4.9
Pakistan (75, 81)		75.8	65.9		1.2	2.5
South Korea (69, 80)		44.9	14.8		3.9	8.0
Thailand (60, 74, 80)	37.4	12.0	10.1	3.3	4.1	4.6
Argentina (60, 80)	7.0		4.7	6.2		7.4
Brazil (60, 80)	48.2		24.7	2.4		5.6
Chile (69, 81)		18.6	4.1		5.9	8.1
Colombia (64, 73, 78)	28.9	16.8	16.3	2.8	4.8	5.0
Mexico (70, 77)		23.6	26.9		4.2	4.5
Peru (61, 81)	31.1		13.5	3.9		7.0
Egypt (60, 76)	63.6		53.2	1.7		3.3
Nigeria (63, 67)	90.0	86.2		0.5	0.8	
Average	49.5	39.7	25.9	2.7	3.6	5.5

Source: Psacharopoulos and Arriagada (1986).

1980 – from 2.7 years to 5.5 years per person employed. However, there was still a large gap compared to affluent countries, where employees have twelve years of schooling on average.

7.3.5   Educational expenditures

The following two tables refer to public expenditures on education. In spite of a host of economic problems, the real expenditures per pupil in primary education in most countries show a modest upward trend in the long run.

Table 7.5 brings out clearly how much more is being spent per student in higher education than in primary education. Extreme cases were Ghana, Kenya, Côte d'Ivoire and Democratic Republic of Congo in 1965. South Korea is the only exception to this skewed pattern for tertiary expenditures. Expenditures in secondary education are also much higher than those in primary education. Over time the skewedness of educational expenditures tends to decline, with expenditures per primary student increasing at the expense of secondary and tertiary levels. By 1990, several countries were spending more per pupil in primary education than per pupil in secondary education. This is consistent with the finding that returns to primary education are higher than those to secondary education and tertiary education (Psacharopoulos and Arriagada 2002; Psacharopoulos and Patrinos, 2002). Educational systems seem to be responding to policy advice in this respect. But expenditures for tertiary education are still far higher than for primary education. Though the comparability of the data leaves much to be desired, the table also highlights the relatively high cost of secondary and tertiary education in African countries.

Table 7.5 *Government expenditure per pupil in selected countries, 1965–1996 (1995$)*

Country	1965			1980			1990			1996		
	Primary education	Secondary education	Tertiary education	Primary education	Secondary education	Tertiary education	Primary education	Secondary education	Tertiary education	Primary education	Secondary education	Tertiary education
Bangladesh	9	15		11	18	102	19	58		17	54	57
China	8			6	102	416				37	75	417
India		47	294	23		190			299	41	68	376
Indonesia								38	121		62	128
Malaysia				274		3,399	326		3,816	426	725	3,624
Pakistan	19	24	323	27	73					46	77	483
Philippines				68	50	161				102	102	159
South Korea	85	118	504	356	315	544	886	731	428	1,804	1,380	637
Sri Lanka	37	95	492							65	101	393
Taiwan				364	690	1,984	1,030	1,835	4,610	2,240	2,945	5,043
Thailand	48	134	852	92	102	671	265			403	317	749
Turkey				126		1,876	238	217		263	175	1,052
Argentina	843	1,648	3,730	385	486	2,463				656	1,231	1,477
Brazil	133			229		2,592				443	1,329	4,340
Chile	40	70	3,313	106		2,682	257	234		466	508	890
Colombia			1,274	140	130	899	132		604	181	242	745
Mexico	81		1,330	186	222	837	111	262	752	373	559	1,461
Peru	232			230	148	907				122	171	367
Venezuela		580	1,793			2,877	83	269	1,240	76	166	
Congo, Dem. Rep.	32		3,482	221		2,313				118	286	927
Côte d'Ivoire	142	419	9,062	158		3,690				126	272	714
Egypt			611	14		359	22					
Ghana	35		7,501	51			47					
Kenya	42		4,542									
Morocco	157	430	1,491	169	593	3,041	212		954	147	587	907
South Africa						1,681	770		3,484	509	746	1,832
Zambia				55						19	42	730

Sources: *World Development Indicators,* 1999. Missing countries 1980: supplemented from Komenan (1987) recalculated to 1995 dollars. 1996 from UNESCO (2000b); National Statistics of Taiwan, Republic of China, Social Indicators 2001, http://www.stat.gov.tw/main.htm

Table 7.6 *Government expenditure as a percentage of gross national product, 1960–2000* [a]

	1960/1	1965	1970	1980	1990	1995	1999/2000[c]
Bangladesh		1.3		1.1	1.5	2.2	2.4
China			1.3	2.5	2.3	2.3	2.1
India	2.3	2.6	2.6	3.0	3.9	3.3	2.9
Indonesia			2.6	1.7	1.0	1.4	1.3
Malaysia			4.2	6.0	5.5	4.7	6.0
Pakistan	0.9	1.5	1.7	2.1	2.7	2.8	2.7
Philippines	2.6	2.7	2.8	1.7	2.9	3.0	4.0
South Korea	3.2	1.8	3.4	3.7	3.5	3.7	3.8
Sri Lanka			4.0	2.7	2.7	3.0	3.1
Taiwan							
Thailand	2.5	3.1	3.2	3.4	3.6	4.1	5.2
Turkey	2.4	3.5	2.1	2.2	2.1	2.2	4.0
Argentina	2.0	3.0	2.5	2.7	3.4	3.8	4.7
Brazil	2.3	1.1	2.9	3.6	4.5	5.1	5.2
Chile	2.7	2.7	5.1	4.6	2.7	3.1	4.3
Colombia	1.8	2.3	1.9	2.4	2.6	4.0	
Mexico	1.3	1.9	2.3	4.7	3.7	4.9	4.6
Peru		5.0	3.3	3.1	2.3	3.9	3.5
Venezuela		3.9	4.1	4.4	3.1	5.2	
Congo, Dem. Rep.				2.6			
Côte d'Ivoire	4.2	5.4	5.3	7.2		5.3	6.4
Egypt	4.9	4.6	4.8	5.7	3.8	4.8	4.1
Ghana	3.4	4.1	4.3	3.1	3.3	4.8	4.2
Kenya		4.6	5.0	6.8	7.1	6.7	6.8
Morocco			3.5	6.1	5.5	5.8	5.2
Nigeria		2.3		3.6	1.0	0.7	0.7
South Africa					6.5	6.8	5.9
Tanzania					3.4		2.1
Zambia	1.8	6.0	4.5	4.5	2.6	2.2	2.5
Africa[b]		2.5	3.4	5.0	4.6	5.1	5.1
Asia[b]		3.5	3.5	3.2	3.2	3.0	3.0
Arab countries and North Africa		4.2	4.7	4.1	4.9	5.0	5.4
Latin America and the Caribbean		3.1		3.9	4.0	4.5	4.6
Developing countries		3.0	3.3	3.8	3.8	3.8	3.9
Developed countries		5.2	5.6	5.1	5.0	5.0	5.1

Notes: [a] Where data for the selected year are lacking, data for the preceding or subsequent year were used, if available (17 observations).
[b] Excluding North Africa and the Arab countries.
[c] For regional averages no data for 1999/2000 available. Instead we used data for 1997.
Sources: UNESCO, *Statistical Yearbook,* 1972; 1976; 1995; 1997; 1999; UNESCO (2000b); Asia: calculated as GNP weighted average for East and South Asia. Country data 1999/2000: UNESCO, Institute of Statistics, Homepage, *Global Statistics, Education, Statistical Tables,* http://portal.unesco.org/uis/.

The financial sacrifices developing countries are willing to make for education are represented in Table 7.6. In 1965, developing countries invested on average 3 per cent of their GNP in education. In 1999–2000 this percentage had increased to 3.9 per cent. In the same year rich countries invested 5.1 per cent of their GNP in education. Since per capita GNP in developing countries is much lower, this of course means that developing countries can spend less on education per head of the population. It is interesting to note that the regions with the lowest primary enrolment figures, Sub-Saharan Africa and North Africa and the Arab states, have the highest proportional public investment in education. This is caused by the fact that declines in GDP growth were greater than declines in educational expenditures. In a comparison of educational expenditures in South Asia and Sub-Saharan Africa, Colclough and Al-Sammarai (2000) conclude that the efficiency of educational expenditures in Africa is low. More could be achieved within the same budgetary constraints.

7.3.6 Non-formal and informal education

All officially registered indicators refer to formal education. However, there are all kinds of education and schooling that fall outside the scope of formal education. For these, terms such as 'non-formal education' and 'informal education' have come into use.

Non-formal education comprises all forms of organised education that are not included in the regular schooling system: adult education; education for dropouts; literacy projects; agricultural extension or information; occupational training; in-firm training programmes; health education; education for family planning, and so on (Coombs and Ahmed, 1974). Advocates of non-formal education believe that it is more suited to practical everyday needs and requirements than formal education. They claim that it offers opportunities to integrate education into wider development strategies.

It is difficult to obtain hard data on non-formal education as it includes such a variety of educational activities financed by various ministries, institutions and private organisations. Still, studies conducted by UNESCO indicate an upward trend in enrolment in non-formal education. In 1985 about 23 million people were enrolled in non-formal education programmes in developing countries (Hallak, 1990: p. 11).

Rapid advances in information and communication technologies have created new opportunities for education in the form of distance learning. Distance-learning techniques range from simple correspondence courses to modern multimedia applications and videoconferencing techniques using the internet. Potentially, distance-learning technology can reach dispersed students in rural areas which cannot adequately be served through traditional formal schooling institutions. In developing countries such as Indonesia, Mexico or South Africa hundreds of thousands of students are involved in distance-learning programmes (Perraton, 2000). Distance learning can supplement the formal educational system, offering the same degrees to the same age groups or supplementing classroom teaching. But there is also a great variety of non-formal programmes which can be combined with work. These include courses for upgrading teacher skills, vocational education, language and literacy programmes, reproductive health, agricultural education, and so forth.

It is well known that schooling and socialisation are not limited to schools. Families, churches, associations, work situations and peer groups can also be very important. *Informal education* refers to the lifelong process of accumulation of knowledge and skills, through experiences in daily life – at play, at work, at home or elsewhere (Coombs, 1985: p. 24; Coombs and Ahmed, 1974). There is no point in considering informal education as part of the educational system. But the rapid rise of new mass media and means of communication, such as newspapers, radio, cinema, television, books and magazines, may be very important. They can serve as mechanisms of information transfer, influence, education or indoctrination. In particular, radio and television provide major opportunities for new modes of education, teaching and dissemination of information.

7.3.7   Summary: comparison with developments in more developed countries

In the post-war period developing countries have given high priority to expanding their educational systems. The increase in schooling and decline in illiteracy proceeded more rapidly than previously in European countries. There primary education expanded very gradually, resulting in universal primary education by the end of the nineteenth century. Developing countries today are on the way to universal primary education. Participation in secondary and higher education today is higher than it was in France, England and Germany in 1950. In Europe democratisation of higher education did not make much headway till after World War II. Before that time entry to higher education was by and large restricted to the offspring of the upper classes.

One of the characteristics of the educational systems in developing countries is that enrolment in secondary and higher education started increasing long before realisation of universal primary education. In this respect, the educational performance of developing countries not only differs from Western development experience, but also from that of the late-developers Japan and the Soviet Union. Both Japan and the Soviet Union experienced an explosive expansion of education from the late nineteenth century onwards. But they gave more priority to universal primary education. After the Bolshevik revolution large-scale literacy campaigns were organised in the Soviet Union and primary education was expanded very rapidly. Secondary education was only developed after universal primary education had been realised. Higher education was expanded at an even later stage (Lind and Johnston, 1986). In developing countries, however, expansion of secondary and higher education received higher priority.

Despite differences in the patterns of educational development one may conclude that developing countries are engaged in a process of educational catchup. They have succeeded in training their own educational staff, in decreasing their dependence on foreign teachers and educators, and developing an educational infrastructure. In the light of the unfavourable initial state of education after World War II, the educational performance of developing countries is quite impressive.

At a meeting in Dakar in 2000, the World Education Forum formulated six major educational goals. The most important goals were: ensuring that all children have access to primary education by 2015; achieving a 50 per cent improvement in levels of adult literacy by 2015; and achieving gender equality in education by 2015.

Monitoring the progress towards these goals, a recent UNESCO report concludes (UNESCO, 2002) major progress is being made: eighty-three countries representing 32.4 per cent of world population will have met these three goals by 2015 or before; forty-three countries representing 35.8 per cent of world population have made major progress and will meet at least two of these three goals. However, twenty-eight developing countries are in serious risk of not achieving any of these goals. These countries include many Sub-Saharan African countries, but also the populous countries of India and Pakistan. This category includes just over 25 per cent of world population.

7.4   Problems

From the mid-1970s onwards important qualitative shortcomings in the educational systems became more and more visible. In their enthusiasm for creating new educational facilities as fast as possible, authorities in developing countries had paid little attention to educational content. The Western-oriented educational systems inherited from the former colonial period were expanded with little or no change; Coombs (1985) calls this a process of 'linear expansion'. In Latin America – where decolonisation had been completed early in the nineteenth century – educational systems were also copies of Western models. As a result, educational systems were in many aspects ill-adapted to the conditions and needs of developing countries. The following section will address some of the most important deficiencies in educational systems.

7.4.1   *Discrepancies between educational needs and financial resources*

Since the late 1970s the pace of growth in educational facilities has declined. The scarcity of financial resources increased as a result of the economic problems of the early 1980s and the cutbacks in government spending in the context of structural adjustment programmes. At the same time the demand for education continued to increase owing to population growth and the youthful age structure of the population (Hallak, 1990; Coombs, 1985). The problems are especially acute in South Asia and Sub-Saharan Africa where growth in numbers of pupils enrolled has outpaced growth of educational expenditures, sometimes leading to declining expenditures per student.

Even without an increase in enrolment, the cost of education tends to rise autonomously. First – if policies are not adjusted – fixed salary structures will lead to increasing salary costs as the teaching staff gets older and as more qualified teachers replace less qualified teachers. Secondly, the costs per student are much higher in secondary and higher education than in primary education. As more students enrol in secondary and higher education, the average expenditure per student increases.

In the coming years, the gap between the demand for education and the available resources is expected to widen even further, before declines in fertility rates result in a drop in the dependency rates and ease the pressures on the schooling system in some ten to fifteen years. In regions where fertility rates have not yet started declining, such as Sub-Saharan Africa, the pressures on the educational system will continue unabated. UNESCO calculates that there is a shortfall of US$ 5.6 billion to meet the external finance requirements to achieve the goals of Education for All by 2015 (UNESCO, 2002). Only 1.2 billion has been pledged by 2002.

Increasing the provision of education, however, is not only a question of more funding. It also has to do with the effectiveness of educational expenditure. Colclough and Al-Samarrai argue that Sub-Saharan Africa has relatively high unit costs compared to other regions and could increase enrolment and improve education by increased effectiveness. Another route to improved education is by private contributions to education, which are becoming important in various developing countries.

7.4.2   The quality of education

The quality of education in developing countries has come under increasing criticism. Classes are very large, with class sizes sometimes even reaching extremes of 70 to 100 pupils. Students are often absent from school, grade repetition and dropout rates are high. In some countries only 10 per cent of all students complete the educational cycle in which they are enrolled. Teachers are underpaid; their training is often insufficient and their motivation is low. Teaching materials are of poor quality, if available at all. Sanitary conditions are frequently unspeakable. Education is very much focused on preparing for examinations and learning by rote. Even when educational cycles are completed, it is not always clear how much the pupils have actually learned. *Educational attainment* does not guarantee *educational achievement*.

The financial problems described in section 7.4.1 may cause the quality of education to deteriorate even further. Educational authorities respond to budget squeezes by increasing the size of classes, using the same buildings more intensively and cutting back on expenditures on educational infrastructure, teaching materials and, where possible, on teachers' salaries. These cutbacks primarily affect primary education, which is – unwisely – given low priority.

After the relative neglect of quality issues in the preceding decades, improving educational quality was included among the six major educational goals formulated for 2015, at the World Education Forum in Dakar in 2000 (UNESCO, 2002).

7.4.3   *Lack of relevance*

Educational systems in developing countries were often set up as copies of Western educational models. The content of education was Western-oriented; textbooks were Western; examination requirements were derived from Western exams. Little attention was paid to the indigenous history, culture and society. In many countries the language of instruction was – and frequently still is – the language of the former colonial power. Education tends to be academically oriented and has little relationship with the life situations of most students.

In the 1970s, radical authors went so far as to characterise Western-oriented education in Africa, Asia and Latin America as an instrument of oppression and alienation (Carnoy, 1974; Freire, 1970; Illich, 1974). At school people learn to look down on their own culture. The more successful their educational career, the more students tend to become alienated from their own social backgrounds (Altbach, 1982).

It is indisputable that education has alienating effects and can contribute to the formation of rootless elites. Still, it is important to realise that education as an instrument of modernisation, technology transfer and social change is always a reflection of the educational systems of the dominant nations in world society.[12] An educational system that is in complete harmony with the requirements of a traditional society would not contribute much to 'development'. A modern educational system cannot but be 'alienating' in a partly traditional society (see the debate on westernisation and modernisation in Chapter 1). The challenge is to develop educational systems that are both relevant to the life situations of people in developing countries and provide meaningful entry into the modern international world of science and technology.

One of the most important shortcomings of education in developing countries is the insufficient attention to agriculture. The majority of students in the least-developed countries will spend the rest of their lives in an agricultural or rural environment. Nevertheless, the educational curriculum is oriented almost exclusively to the modern urban sector of society. Primary education is little adapted to the educational needs of rural young people. In secondary and higher education, courses with agricultural content are rarely taught. Education reinforces the already low status of physical labour and in particular agricultural labour. It contributes to mass migration to urban areas. Almost all authors argue for a more practical orientation of education, with more emphasis on vocational training, work experience and agricultural content.

Most reforms of this nature – however justified – are likely to meet with fierce resistance on the part of students. They rightly consider education as an important means of upward social mobility. This path leads from lower to higher educational levels, which become progressively more academic. In order to gain access to higher educational levels students have to be able to

---

12 In Europe, too, modernisation of educational systems has always been based on foreign models that are considered successful.

pass academically oriented examinations. Lower vocational education is seen as an obstacle to upward educational mobility, though in fact only a minority of students has a realistic chance of entering higher educational levels (Abernethy, 1969; Foster, 1965a, 1965b). Vocationally and practically oriented forms of education are regarded as second-rate by students and their parents, both in developed and developing countries (Psacharopoulos, 1989). The major challenge to educationalists in developing countries is how to make education more relevant for the masses of rural children, who will never go on to higher education, without diminishing the possibilities of upward educational mobility (Hardiman and Midgley, 1982).

It should be noted that actual experiences with vocational education have often been rather disappointing. The specific occupational skills learned at school are hardly applied in later working life (Foster, 1965b; Psacharopoulos, 1989).

An alternative, presently much in prominence, is so-called non-formal education (see section 7.3.6). Among others, non-formal education comprises adult literacy programmes, agricultural extension, on-the-job training programmes, education of school-leavers, health education and education about family planning, and distance learning. Non-formal education offers an opportunity to relate both the form and content of education to the immediate needs and problems of students.

However, it is an illusion to believe that non-formal education could ever replace formal education (Hallak, 1990). Non-formal education supplements and supports formal education rather than providing an alternative to it. The more formal education people have received, the more likely they are to enrol in non-formal programmes and the more likely they are to profit from them. Besides, the costs of non-formal education are by no means lower than those of formal education.

7.4.4   Unequal access to education

Access to educational facilities is distributed very unequally (Coombs, 1985; Hardiman and Midgley, 1982; Ooijens and van Kampen, 1989; Williamson, 1979). In particular, there are great differences between urban and rural areas. In rural areas schools are scarce and of poor quality. Students have to travel great distances to get to school and means of transport are lacking. Both educational participation and the quality of education lag far behind those in urban areas. In the cities there is almost universal primary education. Furthermore, secondary and higher educational institutions are concentrated in urban regions. Rural young people have far less opportunities to follow secondary and higher education than their urban counterparts.

A second significant inequality in educational participation is that between males and females (Coombs, 1985; Fägerlind and Saha, 1989; Schultz, 1988; UNESCO, 2002). In particular, in secondary and higher education female participation lags far behind that of males. In primary education, the *Gender Parity Index* – defined as female enrolment divided by male enrolment ratios – was 0.93 worldwide in 1999. Lowest rates are found in Southwest Asia (0.84), the Arab States (0.88) and Sub-Saharan Africa (0.89). At higher levels of education, gender disparities tend to increase. Disparities at primary level are amplified at secondary and tertiary level. Women are most at a disadvantage in those countries where total enrolment is low. In terms of literacy women are also at a serious disadvantage, especially in Latin America (Ooijens and van Kampen, 1989) and the Arab States. In the Arab States female illiteracy in 1999 was almost double that of male illiteracy (UNDP, 2002).

In the chapters on population (Chapter 5) and health (Chapter 6) we have seen that the education of women was a crucial factor in improving the health situation and in the success of family planning efforts. Research by Nuñez has indicated that education of women is also of importance to economic development. In a study of economic development in Spain, she found that regions where male–female differentials in education were smallest were the regions with most rapid growth of income per capita. Also, improvements in female literacy tended to have more positive effects on economic development than improvements in male literacy (Nuñez, 1990).

Over time the educational status of women has shown substantial improvement. In the past twenty years female participation in all cycles of education has increased. The slowdown in the increase of primary enrolment ratios in the 1990s affected boys more than girls. In developing countries the overall Gender Parity Index increased from 0.86 to 0.92 between 1990 and 1999. Educational disparities at secondary and tertiary levels were also reduced. But gender disparities go beyond the simple numbers (Fägerlind and Saha, 1989; Schultz, 1988; UNESCO, 2002).

A third significant form of educational inequality derives from the socio-economic status of the parental family. As in Western societies, children from upper social strata and income groups or from dominant ethnic groups are significantly more likely to participate in the highest levels of education. However, in the African context, Foster emphasises that access to modern education is relatively open. Education has promoted rather than hampered upward social mobility (Foster, 1980).

7.4.5   Mismatch between education and the labour market

One of the most important points of criticism of education in developing countries is the mismatch between education and the labour market. We already pointed out that agricultural education is almost non-existent in many countries where agriculture provides the main source of employment and livelihood.

Next, secondary and higher educational enrolment has increased more rapidly than the demand for higher educated persons on the labour market

(Blaug, 1979; Gillis *et al.*, 1992). From the 1960s onwards, many countries trained more doctors than nurses, more engineers than mechanics, and so on. People with higher degrees displaced people with lower degrees (see section 7.1.5 on screening theory). As a result many employees were overqualified for their work.

In the 1950s, there were great shortages of well-educated personnel in the civil service, schools and firms. A task of the educational system was to solve these shortages in a brief period of time. Soon, however, shortages turned into surpluses. Today swollen government bureaucracies are no longer able to provide jobs for the growing waves of graduates. Almost all developing countries have extensive academic unemployment. Thus, scarce resources are wasted on a large scale on investment in higher education which could be invested more productively in primary education. Academic unemployment and overqualification can lead to great frustration for students and graduates. Universities are often hotbeds of political turmoil and instability. One of the most paradoxical results of overschooling is the *brain drain*, the exodus of highly qualified doctors, experts and scientists from developing countries to rich countries. Many of the social benefits of educational investment are thus not realised.

Despite widespread unemployment among the educated, there are still severe shortages in specific occupations, especially those requiring technical skills (Psacharopoulos, 1989). Education is still oriented too much to the humanities and social sciences – languages, law, history, sociology, economics – rather than to technical, scientific and agricultural disciplines. In these areas the services of expatriate experts are still often called upon.

To improve the match between education and the labour market, it is often argued that vocational education and on-the-job training should receive more emphasis in educational policy (see section 7.3.6 on non-formal education). However, students still have a clear preference for academically oriented education. Regardless of high-educated unemployment rates, academic education still seems to offer the best career prospects from an individual point of view.

One of the most important recommendations of educationalists is to give higher priority to primary education. Extensive research has shown that both the private and the social returns on investment in primary education are much higher than the returns on investment in secondary and tertiary education (Psacharopoulos and Arriagada, 1992; Psacharopoulos and Patrinos, 2002). In primary education, more could be achieved with less resources. Such a policy switch, however, encounters considerable opposition on the part of politically influential groups, who are defending the educational opportunities of their offspring. Nevertheless, the statistics in Table 7.5 show that primary education is indeed gaining some ground.

Blaug (1979) argues in favour of loosening the ties between educational certificates and paid jobs. Credentialism on the labour market leads to the displacement of people with lower educational qualifications by people with higher qualifications, irrespective of the nature of the jobs involved. It also has very negative effects on the quality of education. All attention is focused on the mechanical preparation for centrally set academic examinations. The content of education is relegated to second place.

7.5   Literacy

In a discussion of education the issue of literacy merits special attention, since it is one of the essential outcomes of the educational process. As noted in section 7.1.6, many authors consider a certain threshold level of literacy as a prerequisite for economic development. In pre-literate societies, families were the main vehicle of transmission of knowledge and skills to successive generations. As the task of transferring knowledge and skills shifts from families to formal educational institutions in ongoing processes of social differentiation, literacy becomes more and more important (Hardiman and Midgley, 1982).

There are several reasons to strive for literacy. Apart from increasing economic productivity, literacy can promote social participation. It can contribute to cultural education, the realisation of humanist goals and to personal awareness.

In the past, religious groups were particularly active in spreading literacy. An important objective of much religiously oriented education was to teach people to read sacred texts. For example, in Scandinavia Protestantism led to widespread literacy as early as the end of the nineteenth century. In developing countries missionaries played an important role. Ideological movements such as communism also set great store by literacy as it would enable people to study Marxist writings.

Since its foundation, UNESCO, the United Nations organisation for education, science and culture, has placed great emphasis on the battle against illiteracy (Jones, 1988). Between 1946 and 1958, one of the main objectives of UNESCO was *fundamental education*. The essence of fundamental education was that every person had a right to learn the three Rs: reading, writing and arithmetic. But fundamental education was not limited to 'literacy' alone; it also included vocational skills, domestic skills, knowledge of hygiene, knowledge of the principles of science, artistic skill, an understanding of one's social environment and the development of personal skills and moral traits. In the early years it was assumed that there were close links between fundamental education and formal schooling.

Within UNESCO there was a lively debate on the scope of educational objectives. Gradually, the notion of fundamental education was broadened to include development in general. Literacy in the narrow sense was seen as one of the instruments for achieving wider developmental objectives. In practice, however, the main emphasis remained on the formal schooling system, which was being rapidly expanded during this period.

Between 1958 and 1966 the concept of fundamental education was dropped altogether from international rhetoric. Education was no longer to be considered a separate issue. It should be integrated into wider development policies. The new catchphrase was *community development*. In this new context formal education became less important. The focus shifted to various kinds of adult education. Literacy was also seen as contributing to community development as a whole.

At the second world conference on adult education in Montreal in 1960 the idea emerged for the first time that illiteracy was a manageable problem and that it could be eliminated within a limited number of years (Jones, 1988). The world conference of education ministers in Tehran in 1965 explicitly adopted the objective of eradicating illiteracy. In 1996, UNESCO launched the Experimental World Literacy Programme (EWLP).

Both at the 1965 conference and in the EWLP the notion of *functional literacy* was paramount. Functional literacy is not just about reading, writing and calculating, but rather about the contribution of these skills to the economic and social welfare of the individual and the community. In contrast to the concept of fundamental education, which relates to individual and social welfare in the broadest sense, functional literacy was given a more limited economic interpretation. Literacy should contribute to the productivity and earning capacity of workers. To realise this, literacy education should be related to work practices and vocational training programmes. It should be aimed at specific groups of urban and rural workers. Pupils should learn skills which would be useful for their work and their future careers. It is clear that non-formal education would receive more emphasis in the context of functional literacy.

Between 1966 and 1974 more than one million students participated in the EWLP in one form or other (Coombs, 1985). On balance, the programme turned out to be a complete failure. The gap between the high-flown rhetoric of international organisations and the intractable problems in the field proved to be too wide. The main problem was the lack of success in integrating literacy projects into economic and social practice. Despite its disappointing results, several noteworthy lessons can be derived from the EWLP (Coombs, 1985; Ooijens and Van Kampen, 1989). These are listed in Box. 7.5. Socialist countries, such as the Soviet Union (in the 1920s), Cuba, Nicaragua, China and Vietnam, have had considerable success with large-scale, politically motivated literacy campaigns. In these programmes the advancement of literacy was closely linked with political mobilisation and ideological propaganda. Adult literacy rates in present-day Cuba and Vietnam are above 90 per cent. The pedagogical

---

Box 7.5   Lessons of the experimental world literacy programme

1. Literacy programmes are most likely to be successful for people who need literacy in their daily life. Literacy is often most effectively learned in the context of acquiring some other skill to which literacy is incidental (Curle, 1964, quoted in Jones, 1988).
2. Literacy requires that reading materials (newspapers, books, information material) continue to be available after completion of the literacy programmes. Maintaining reading skills requires post-literacy programmes either through formal or non-formal education.
3. Teaching materials should be tailored to the students' environments and interests.
4. Literacy should not be taught in isolation from other subjects. Literacy training should be linked with subjects of strong immediate interest and concern to particular learners. The EWLP did not implement these objectives adequately. It made too much use of standardised teaching programmes and teaching materials in a classroom setting.

experiments of Paolo Freire in Latin America are also worth mentioning; Freire linked literacy education to political awareness, political mobilisation and the emancipation of oppressed groups. Most of these literacy campaigns are very much rooted in a particular political and social context. They cannot be used as standard recipes irrespective of time and place. They do illustrate the crucial importance of motivation. If people can be motivated to participate in literacy programmes, impressive results can be achieved in very short periods of time.

Ooijens and van Kampen (1989) rightly point out that the best guarantee for literacy is a well-functioning and accessible system of primary education. This implies that the main function of non-formal education is to maintain literacy after students have left school. Once again, formal and non-formal education are complementary. There is a clear correlation between the expansion of primary education and increases in literacy (UNESCO, 2002: p. 66).

Since 1990, the concepts of literacy have evolved further (UNESCO, 2002: ch. 2). More attention is paid to the varying contexts in which literacy can be used, such as work, personal life, different languages and so forth. Situations can differ substantially in their need for literacy. Literacy is now interpreted as one of many ways of communication. Illiteracy is redefined as the inability to interact adequately with the wider society through reading and writing. All these terminological refinements, however, are not really reflected in indicators. We still measure literacy in terms of whether people are able to read and write.

Despite disappointing results of some literacy programmes, illiteracy shows a clear downward tendency as a joint result of efforts in formal education and non-formal national and international literacy programmes. Since 1946, the percentage of illiterates in the population aged 15 years and over has declined sharply in all countries. The literate share of the adult world population increased from 70 per cent in 1980 to 80 per cent in 2000 (UNESCO, 2002), but the pace of advance is now slackening. In absolute numbers rather than percentages, the results are more modest. Between 1980 and 2000, the total number of illiterates declined by only 10 million, from 870 million to 860 million. Illiteracy is still much more widespread among women. Two-thirds of all illiterates are females (UNESCO, 2002).

In Latin American countries, in particular, the rate of illiteracy has been reduced drastically. In no less than seventeen Latin American countries (including Argentina, Chile, Colombia, Cuba, Costa Rica, Guyana, Mexico, Uruguay, Trinidad and Venezuela) the adult illiteracy rate is below 10 per cent.[13] High rates of literacy have also been achieved in East and Southeast Asia. Much lower levels of literacy are found in the Arab States, South Asia and Sub-Saharan Africa. But even here the declines in illiteracy have been striking. The decline in illiteracy in developing countries is much more rapid than previously in European development (Fägerlind and Saha, 1989: p. 46).

13 UNESCO, Institute of Statistics, Homepage: Global Statistics, Education, Statistical tables, http://portal.unesco.orguis/ev.php

Table 7.7 *Illiterates as a percentage of the population of 15 years and over, 1946–2000*

Countries	1946–55	1956–65	1970	1980	1990	1995	2000
Bangladesh		78.4	75.4	71.1	65.8	62.9	60.0
China			47.1	32.9	21.7	18.1	14.8
India	80.2	72.2	66.9	59.0	50.7	46.7	42.8
Indonesia		84.6	43.9	31.0	20.5	16.5	13.2
Malaysia			41.9	28.8	19.3	15.7	12.6
Pakistan		84.6	79.1	72.2	64.6	60.7	56.8
Philippines	40.0	28.1	18.2	12.2	8.3	6.5	5.1
South Korea	23.2	29.4	13.2	7.1	4.1	3.1	2.2
Sri Lanka			19.5	14.7	11.3	9.8	8.4
Taiwan[a]			0.0	23.7	13.7		8.9
Thailand	48.0	32.3	19.8	12.5	7.6	5.9	4.5
Turkey	68.1	61.9	43.5	31.6	22.1	18.2	15
Argentina	13.6	8.6	7.0	5.6	4.3	3.7	3.2
Brazil[b]	50.6	39.0	31.6	24.0	18.0	15.3	13.1
Chile	19.8	16.4	12.4	8.6	6.0	5.1	4.2
Colombia	37.7	37.7	22.2	16.0	11.6	9.9	8.4
Mexico	43.2	34.6	26.5	18.7	12.7	10.5	8.8
Peru		38.9	28.5	20.6	14.5	12.2	10.1
Venezuela	47.8	36.7	23.7	16.1	11.1	9.1	7.5
Congo, Dem. Rep.			77.2	65.9	52.5	45.4	38.6
Côte d'Ivoire		95.0	79.0	70.5	61.5	56.4	51.4
Egypt	80.1	74.2	68.4	60.7	52.9	48.9	44.7
Ghana		80.6	70.5	56.2	41.5	34.8	28.4
Kenya		80.5	59.4	43.8	29.2	23.0	17.6
Morocco			80.2	71.4	61.3	56.1	51.2
Nigeria		84.6	79.9	67.1	51.3	43.6	36.0
South Africa			30.3	23.9	18.8	16.7	14.8
Tanzania		90.5	64.4	51.0	37.1	30.8	25.0
Zambia			52.3	41.4	31.8	26.7	21.8
Average Asian countries		56.0	42.6	33.1	25.8	24.0	20.4
Average Latin American countries		30.3	21.7	15.7	11.2	9.4	7.9
Average African countries		84.2	66.2	55.2	43.8	38.2	33.0
Average developing countries		55.5	44.7	35.3	27.1	24.1	20.3
Average developed countries[c]			5.5	3.6	2.3	1.8	1.4

Notes: [a] 1999;
[b] 1956–65, 13 years and over;
[c] including former Soviet Asian republics in transition.
Sources: 1946–65: UNESCO, *Statistical Yearbook*, 1994; 1989; 1984 and 1976. Figures refer to the most recent data within each period; 1970 and later: UNESCO Institute of Statistics, Homepage http://portal.unesco.org/uis/ev.php; Taiwan: ADB, 2001. ADB, *Key Indicators 2001: Growth and Change in Asia and the Pacific*, http://www.adb.org

For selected countries Table 7.7 documents the long-run decline in illiteracy. It also shows, however, that the problems of illiteracy are still far from being solved. In many countries, such as India, Pakistan, Egypt, Côte d'Ivoire or Morocco, levels of illiteracy in 2000 are still unacceptably high.

7.6   Nation building

Apart from the economic functions of education, its political functions are also of great importance. After World War II, education was expected to contribute to state formation and the creation of a national identity in developing countries. In many of the newly independent states people identified more with tribe, region, lineage, or ethnic group than with the national state. New political values stood in sharp contrast to traditional ideas about politics. Nationalist leaders fervently hoped that education would contribute to a sense of national awareness and political integration (Fägerlind and Saha, 1989; Hardiman and Midgley, 1982; Krieger, 1988; Psacharopoulos, 1989). Education would further the development of a joint culture and joint political values. Education would familiarise young people with the idea of participation in national political processes. Also, in many countries – particularly those with socialist regimes – education was regarded as a means to achieve political mobilisation and increased social consciousness.

In practice education is often a two-edged sword. Under certain conditions, it can contribute to a sense of national identity. But it can also have very divisive effects. In some states in India education strengthened feelings of regional identification. Unequal access to education for members of different ethnic, cultural or religious groups may lead to political frustrations and conflicts. It may undermine the loyalty of under-represented groups to national institutions. In settings of conflict, different groups can use education to strengthen their own identities and to emphasise their differences. Finally, universities are often hotbeds of political opposition and resistance. Unemployment among the educated in particular is frequently a politically destabilising factor.

In many former colonies in Africa and Asia the choice of language for instruction posed a distinct problem. During the colonial period the language of instruction was the language of the colonial power. In view of national integration and national consciousness it would have been preferable to replace this language with a national language. Yet this often proved to be impossible. In many new states several languages were spoken. To adopt one of these languages as the national language would lead to serious opposition from members of the other language groups. Therefore, English, French or Portuguese were often maintained as the language of instruction, especially in secondary and higher education.

Only in a few multilingual countries was a single language accepted as the national tongue. For the national language one chose trade languages that were acceptable to many groups in society: in Indonesia, Bahasa Indonesia; in Tanzania, Kiswahili.

In the long run education should try to take ethnic, cultural and linguistic diversity into account. This should have more positive results than the forced propagation of a yet weakly developed national culture and identity. An overemphasis on national unity could well have adverse effects. A national political system, which is open to regional diversity, may well achieve more stability. But, of course, this is far from certain. If education does not succeed in creating some sense of national belonging, regional diversity in education, language and culture will end up undermining fragile national unity.

7.7 Policy

During the first few years after World War II educational policy was mainly concerned with the quantitative expansion of educational facilities. Not much thought was given to the content of the educational curriculum. Education was seen as a driving force in economic development. In this respect, the rapid expansion of education was the counterpart of capital accumulation in the industrialisation strategy. In addition, education would contribute to social modernisation and political integration.

The plans to expand the educational system were partly based on the political convictions and ideologies of political leaders in post-war developing countries. But they were also based on various educational planning models. In educational planning three types of analysis have been of importance (Gillis et al., 1992; Hardiman and Midgley, 1982), as follows:

1. planning based on the social demand for education;
2. manpower planning;
3. planning on the basis of cost–benefit analyses.

Planning based on the social demand for education

This type of planning is based on the numbers of students who enrolled in various kinds of education in the past. Past enrolment trends are extrapolated into the future. This kind of planning is the easiest from a political point of view. But it does not always lead to efficient outcomes. The over-expansion of secondary and higher education was to some extent due to planning on the basis of social demand. Members of social elites who want their children to receive a good higher education are more likely to make their voices heard in the political process than powerless rural people who would benefit more from an improvement of primary education.

Manpower planning

Manpower planning tries to determine the social need for employees with different kinds of education. Educational systems are designed to fulfil these needs. For example, estimates are made of the numbers of doctors required. These estimates determine the capacity of medical schools.

In theory this is a valuable approach. In practice, however, the experiences with manpower planning have been very disappointing, both in developing countries and in more developed countries (Gillis et al., 1992). It seems to be impossible to predict the demand for various categories of employees more than two or three years ahead. Since it takes years for changes in the educational system to be realised, the situation may well have changed by the time new graduates come onto the labour market. Moreover, manpower planning doesn't pay any attention to the costs of education.

Cost–benefit analysis of education

In keeping with the recommendations of human capital theory, this form of planning calculates *costs* of different types of education for individuals and the community, and the direct and indirect financial *benefits* deriving from education. This allows one to compare the returns on investment in education to the returns on investment in physical capital stock. One can also determine which kind of educational investment – vocational, general, technical, primary or higher education, and so on – will have the highest returns. Educational planners, of course, are primarily interested in social rather than private costs and benefits.

Since the 1960s, many cost–benefit analyses of education have been performed. Although attractive on theoretical grounds, cost-benefit analysis has some serious drawbacks (see section 7.1.2). First, we know the present remuneration of different categories of employees with different levels of schooling, but we do not know how the structure of earnings will be in the future. Secondly, we cannot be sure that income differentials actually reflect differences in productivity. Thirdly, the indirect benefits of education are very difficult to determine. Finally, cost–benefit analysis usually disregards both the content and the quality of education. Cost–benefit analyses have usually been restricted to comparisons between primary, secondary and higher education. Therefore, in practice cost–benefit analysis does not offer a sound basis for detailed policy making.[14]

Cost–benefit analyses have shown that the returns on investment in education are higher than returns on investment in physical capital goods. The returns are the highest in countries with the lowest per capita incomes (Psacharapoulos, 1993). One of the most important recommendations derived from cost–benefit analyses is that primary education should be given high priority. The returns on primary education are significantly higher than on secondary and tertiary education (Psacharopoulos, 1993). National policy makers have usually disregarded this recommendation. In educational planning social demand and political priorities have predominated. However, in recent years national and international educational policy makers are giving increasing priority to primary education in their policy formulations and their financial incentives.

With regard to vocational education, research indicates that the returns on general secondary education are higher than returns on vocational education (Psacharopoulos, 1993: table 9). This seems to contradict the earlier call for more vocational education. The issue of relevance perhaps depends more on the content of education than on the type of schooling.

Psacharopoulos (1989) pointed out that there is a wide gap between educational planning and educational practice. Often educational plans are

---

14 In recent research, there has been some improvement in this respect. Returns have compared for vocational versus general education and for various disciplines in higher education (see Psacharopoulos, 1985; 1993). But content and quality remain hard to measure.

formulated in a highly abstract manner, disregarding problems of implementation and resource availability. This actually explains why so many educational reforms never get beyond the drawing-board stage. The recent recommendations of the 2000 World Education Forum on Education for All in Dakar have therefore made external finance conditional on the drafting of credible educational plans (UNESCO, 2002).

Since the early 1970s the debate on educational policy has shifted in two directions. On the one hand, as educational performance improved in developing countries increasing attention was paid to achieving education for all. On the other hand, the educational debate increasingly shifted from an emphasis on quantitative expansion to a focus on the content and quality of education.

Following the example of the World Health Organization, the World Conference on Education for All held in Jomtien, Thailand in 1990 formulated the global objective of education for all. In 2000, this was followed by the World Education Forum on Education for All held in Dakar in 2000 (UNESCO, 2000a). This meeting focused on both quantitative and qualitative issues. On the one hand, it specified clear-cut quantitative targets such as Universal Primary Education and a 50 per cent reduction in illiteracy, to be realised by 2015. On the other hand, attention was paid to issues of content and educational quality. Progress towards the goals was monitored in annual monitor reports.

These debates resulted in a series of proposals and recommendations for reform that will dominate the educational agenda in the coming years. In conclusion to this chapter, we will summarise the most important recommendations emerging from the literature and the policy debates.

1. Expansion and improvement of primary education in developing countries is argued for almost unanimously. One of the key goals of international educational policy is the achievement of Universal Primary Education by 2015. The resources to achieve this objective should be transferred from secondary and higher education. National sources should be supplemented by international financial flows. Growth of educational enrolment in secondary and higher education should be limited in order to prevent overschooling and academic unemployment. In higher education students should pay a greater part of the costs of education.
2. Education should be made more relevant to the needs of the labour market.
3. Primary schools in rural areas should pay more attention to subjects that are relevant to the rural population. In secondary and higher education more attention should be paid to agricultural education.
4. In the curriculum more attention should be paid to technical subjects and the natural sciences and less to the humanities and the social sciences.
5. On the labour market educational certificates and diplomas should receive less emphasis. Credentialism results in overschooling.
6. It is no use discussing the content of education without paying attention to the form and content of examinations. Less emphasis in education on the

preparation for academically oriented examinations would have positive effects on educational content and relevance.

7. Quality improvement in (primary) education implies additional (re)training and better payment of the teaching staff. Increasing emphasis should be placed on measuring the outcomes of the educational process rather than focusing on enrolment.
8. Non-formal education should be further developed as a supplement to and in close relationship with formal primary education. Non-formal education can contribute in particular to further training of people who already have jobs and to increased literacy among adults and school-leavers.
9. Reduction of gender inequality has explicitly been adopted as one of the targets of international educational policy. It is one of the key goals for 2015.

Despite the scarcity of financial means, developing countries should try to provide adequately in the increasing need for education in coming years. Scarce resources should be utilised as efficiently as possible, with due regard for costs. Repetition of past mistakes should be avoided. As shown in this chapter, education is no guarantee for development. The high hopes for education have often not been fulfilled. Nevertheless, education is still one of the important links in the process of development. Developing countries are well advised to continue to invest in education.

Questions for review

1. What are the most important problems presently facing educational systems in developing countries?
2. Discuss the non-economic functions of education.
3. Give an overview of human capital theory. Explain the role of productivity in this theory.
4. Why are expenditures in education skewed towards higher education, in spite of the fact that returns on primary education are higher than on tertiary education?
5. Discuss the criticisms of human capital theory put forward by proponents of screening theory.
6. Discuss the most common indicators of educational performance and their strengths and weaknesses.
7. What is non-formal education? To what extent is non-formal education an alternative for formal education?
8. To what extent is investment in education a necessary condition for economic development?
9. What is meant by the complementarities between investment in physical and human capital? Why are these important?
10. Discuss the factors that influence the success or failure of literacy programmes.

Further reading

The main sources of data on comparative educational performance are UNESCO publications and statistics. Many educational statistics and reports can be found on the website of the UNESCO Institute of Statistics, http://www.uis.unesco.org/. Useful statistical publications by UNESCO include the *Statistical Yearbook*, published on an annual basis till

1999, *Education for All. Year 2000 Assessment. Statististical Document* (2000a), and *The 2002 Global Education for All Monitoring Report: Is the World on Track?* (2002).

Seminal publications on human capital theory include Gary Becker's *Human Capital: A Theoretical and Empirical Analysis, with Special Reference to Education* (1964) and Theodor Schultz's *Investment in Human Capital: The Role of Education and Research* (1971). An overview of human capital theory is provided by Schultz in an article in the *Handbook of Development Economics*, 'Education, Investment and Returns' (1988). Marc Blaug has provided an excellent critical evaluation of human capital theory in 'The Empirical Status of Human Capital Theory: A Slightly Jaundiced Survey', published in the *Journal of Economic Literature* in 1976. A more recent evaluation is to be found in his NIAS lecture entitled *The Economic Value of Higher Education* (1990). Empirical estimates of returns to different types of education are provided in a long series of valuable papers by George Psacharopoulos and his associates. These include two World Bank Policy Research papers *Returns to Investment in Education: A Global Update* (1993) and *Returns to Investment in Education: A Further Update* by Psacharopoulos and Patrinos (2002).

Interesting historical publications on the role of education in development are 'Education and Economic Modernization in Historical Perspective' by Anderson and Bowman (1976), 'Human Capital and Economic Modernisation in Historical Perspective' by Bowman and Anderson (1973) and Sandberg's outstanding article, 'Ignorance, Poverty and Economic Backwardness in the Early Stages of European Industrialization: Variations on Alexander Gerschenkron's Grand Theme' (1982).

For a comprehensive overview of educational problems and issues in developing countries a useful, though somewhat dated source is Philip Coombs's book, *The World Crisis in Education: The View from the 1980s* (1985). The current state of the debates on the role of education in economic development is well represented in three recent review articles: Glewwe's 'Schools and Skills in Developing Countries: Education Policies and Socioeconomic Outcomes' (2002), Krueger and Lindahl's 'Education for Growth: Why and for Whom?' (2001) and Pritchett's 'Where Has All the Education Gone?' (2001).

8 Economic development, structural transformation and primary exports

As long as people work with their bare hands, their daily production will remain low. This sets a limit to the attainable level of economic welfare in a traditional agriculture-based economy. Higher standards of living can only be realised if production per worker increases. One of the principal ways to raise labour productivity is by providing workers with tools, implements and machines – in other words through capital accumulation.

Capital accumulation is intimately associated with the emergence of an industrial sector. Therefore, economic development is linked to structural change and industrialisation. This chapter focuses on structural change and the relationships between agriculture and industry in the course of economic development. It provides a setting for the discussion of industrialisation in Chapter 9 and agricultural development in Chapter 10.

The point of departure is the fact that in the process of economic development the share of the agricultural sector in production and employment declines and the share of the industrial sector increases. However, this does not mean that the agricultural sector should be neglected. This chapter argues for a positive view of the contributions of the agricultural sector to the wider process of development. The argument consists of two main elements. First, successful industrialisation processes are usually preceded by increases in agricultural productivity. Second, in later stages of development a stagnating agricultural sector can be an obstacle to further development of the entire economy. Therefore, a balanced approach to agriculture and industry is called for.

Structural transformation can be pursued in different ways. In one strategy, primary exports and international trade provide the resources for structural change and capital accumulation in the industrial sector. In another strategy, resources are transferred directly from one sector to another in the context of a closed economy.

This chapter opens with a brief discussion of capital accumulation and the connections between capital accumulation, structural change and industrialisation (sections 8.1 and 8.2). Sections 8.3 and 8.4 distinguish between the accumulation of capital in the context of closed or open models of the economy. Section 8.5 focuses on open models and discusses the role of primary exports in development. It contrasts the views of optimists, who see trade as an engine of growth, and export pessimists, who focus on the disadvantages of primary exports. The notion of a balance between agriculture and industry in the context of a closed model is discussed in section 8.6.

8.1   Capital accumulation and industrialisation

Physical capital and financial capital

The term 'capital' has two different meanings, one concrete and one financial. The word capital in its concrete sense refers to the physical stock of machines, implements, buildings and devices used in the process of production. Economists usually define capital in this sense as the means of production, with a lifetime of at least one year. The financial meaning of the term 'capital' refers to a hoarded amount of financial means and securities. In explaining economic growth, we are primarily interested in the growth of physical stocks of capital per person employed.

Savings and investment

Capital accumulation in both senses is only possible if people are voluntarily willing or are involuntarily forced to refrain from present consumption in order to free resources for investment in future production. This refraining from consumption is called *saving*.

In a subsistence economy, without a developed financial system of banks, financial institutions and money circulation, there is hardly any difference between saving and investing. If an agricultural household saves part of its harvest as seed, rather than consuming all of it, this represents saving and investment at the same time. A farmer who uses part of his labour to clear new land instead of producing food for consumption is both saving and investing. If a small industrial entrepreneur uses part of his profits to buy new machines and implements rather than consumer goods, his savings equal his investments. The value of his investments is his financial capital. The machines and implements are his physical capital. In early industrialisation processes in Europe much of the finance for investment came directly from within the industrial enterprises themselves.

In a highly developed economy the distance between consumers and producers, saving and investing has become much greater. One of the typical problems of developed economies (and of modern economic theory) is the match between the willingness to save and the willingness to invest. Financial intermediaries play an important role here. Savings are often deposited with financial institutions such as banks, pension funds and investment institutions. Through long and complex chains of financial institutions and financial markets, these savings are finally channelled to investors. Today well-functioning financial institutions and markets are considered to be of major importance for economic development (Hermes and Lensink, 1996; Thirlwall, 1997: ch. 15, World Bank, 1990). The weakness of financial institutions was one of the causes of the disastrous economic crisis of 1997 in Asia (e.g. Hill, 2000).

What is the relationship between capital accumulation and industrialisation?

Capital goods are used in all sectors of the economy. For instance, the agricultural sector makes use of agricultural machinery and invests in irrigation systems (see Chapter 10). The service sector invests in buildings, computers and telecommunications equipment. The transport sector invests in trucks (or ox carts). Nevertheless, in economic history, the increase in the amount of capital per worker was inextricably linked with industrialisation, structural change and the rise of manufacturing. It was the concentrated nature of factory production, which offered and still offers the greatest opportunities for capital accumulation and increases in the scale of production.

The term 'industry' as used here refers not only to manufacturing, but also to the industrial sector in its broadest sense, including mining, construction and utilities (the supply of gas, electricity and water). But within industry, manufacturing is considered to be the most dynamic sector. The dramatic increase in labour productivity and income per capita in the Western capitalist economies since the mid-eighteenth century is primarily the result of processes of capital accumulation and associated processes of technological change in manufacturing. Capital accumulation is a dynamic process, which not only consists of more capital goods, but also of incremental and radical changes in production techniques. Naturally, capital accumulation is not the only way to increase labour productivity. Labour productivity may also increase as a result of more efficient working methods, division of labour, specialisation in production, economies of scale, schooling or investment in improved health of workers. Still, capital accumulation is one of the important means to increase labour productivity in modern economies.[1] The growth of capital stock is the prime explanation for the nineteenfold growth of per capita income in the advanced economies between 1820 and 1998 (see Maddison, 2001).

8.2   Economic development and structural transformation

8.2.1   Definitions of economic sectors

Discussions of dualism, intersectoral relationships and structural change often suffer from a lack of clarity in sectoral demarcations. At least four kinds of sectoral distinctions can be distinguished, as follows:

1.   The primary, secondary and tertiary sectors

The primary sector includes the production of foodstuffs, non-food crops, fishing, hunting, forestry and mining (Lundahl, 1985). The secondary sector uses primary products, which are directly extracted from nature, and converts them into manufactured products. It consists of manufacturing and construction. Utilities, providing gas, water and electricity, are also included in the secondary sector. The tertiary sector consists of a great variety of service activities, including telecommunication services, financial and business services, personal services, hotel, restaurant and tourism services, wholesale and retail distribution, and transport services. While the primary and secondary sectors produce goods, the tertiary sector primarily produces intangibles such as communication, information, movements of goods and people from place to place or financial transactions.[2]

2.   Agriculture versus industry

Besides agriculture proper, the agricultural sector usually also includes hunting, fisheries and forestry. Industry includes mining, manufacturing, construction and utilities (see *ISIC*, 1990). Thus industry equals the secondary sector plus mining. Compared to agriculture, industry is much more capital-intensive. In many two-sector models, the emphasis is on the relationships between agriculture and industry. Services are not explicitly mentioned. However, with respect to capital-intensity the dividing line between industry and services is blurred. Telecommunications, which are part of the service sector, are just as capital-intensive as utilities, which are part of the industrial sector. On the other hand, parts of the service sector such as personal care and personal services are extremely labour-intensive, sometimes even more so than agriculture.

---

1 We abstract here from the complex issue of the distinction between growth of capital stock and technological change.
2 While secondary activities result in goods, services activities result in changes, transformations or movements. For a critical discussion of service-sector definitions see Glasmeier and Howland (1994). The authors note that some modern service activities such as software development result in tangible and permanent outputs.

3.   *The traditional sector versus the modern commercial sector*

The traditional sector includes subsistence agriculture, traditional crafts production and the rural and urban informal sector. The modern sector includes manufacturing, construction and mining, but also commercial agriculture (including plantations). The modern sector is characterised by a monetary economy, production for the market and higher levels of productivity and technological sophistication.

4.   *The rural sector versus the urban sector*

The distinction between the countryside (rural areas) and the urban sector is a spatial one. Cities and towns are locations characterised by higher population densities than rural areas. Industrial activities are more important in the urban sector and agricultural activities more important in the rural sector. In rural areas one finds both subsistence agriculture and commercial agriculture. But the rural sector is not exclusively agricultural (see Chapter 10). In rural areas one also finds rural industries, traditional crafts production, wage labour, sometimes mining, services and a rural informal sector.

The various sectoral distinctions are summarised in Table 8.1. The four distinctions differ considerably. But in the literature on structural change they are often used in a loose and careless manner. For some two-sector models

Table 8.1 *Sectoral distinctions*

Primary sector	*Secondary sector*	*Tertiary sector*
Food production Cash crops Mining Fishery Logging/forestry	Transformation of primary and semi-finished goods Manufacturing Construction Utilities	Services Transport Wholesale and retail trade Communication Finance Tourism Personal services
Agriculture	*Industry*	*Services*
Agriculture Fishery Logging/Forestry	Mining Manufacturing Construction Utilities	See above
Traditional sector		*Modern/Commercial sector*
Subsistence agriculture Informal manufacturing Handicrafts Informal services		Modern industry, incl. Mining Plantations Commercial agriculture
Rural sector		*Urban sector*
Subsistence agriculture Commercial agriculture Rural handicrafts Rural wage labour Rural informal sector Rural industry		Urban industry Formal services/government Urban informal sector

(e.g. the Lewis model of economic development with unlimited supplies to be discussed in the next chapter) the distinction between the traditional sector and the modern commercial sector seems to be the most important one. But, two-sector models also frequently refer to the relationships between agriculture and manufacturing. Other theories focus on the relationships between primary and secondary production. When one is talking about the *urban-industrial bias* (Lipton, 1977), the important distinction is between urban and rural communities. The term *rural development* is also based on the rural–urban distinction. It indicates that the rural community comprises more than agricultural activities only (see Chapter 10).

In sections 8.3, 8.4 and 8.6 of this chapter, the main emphasis is on the distinction between agriculture and manufacturing and the relationships between them in the course of economic development. Agriculture consists of subsistence production and market production of foodstuffs and other agricultural products by both smallholders and large commercial farms and plantations. Forestry and fishing will not be dealt with explicitly, although they also belong to the agricultural sector. In section 8.5, which discusses the role of primary exports in economic development, the focus shifts to the distinction between the primary and the secondary sector. Of course, agricultural exports are important in primary exports and much of the argument in this chapter will focus on agricultural exports, but primary exports also include mining exports.

8.2.2   Structural change

Since the middle of the eighteenth century modern economic growth has been closely associated with industrialisation (Chenery *et al.*, 1986; Kuznets, 1966; Clark, 1940; Maddison, 1991; Syrquin, 1988). In industry it is possible to employ much more capital per worker, so that productivity per person and per hour are much higher than in agriculture. Economies of scale are also of major importance. In the concentrated large-scale mass production processes characteristic of industry, one can produce more efficiently than in the decentralised small-scale production units characteristic of agriculture.

As emphasised in the seminal writings of Colin Clark and Simon Kuznets, economic development involves a *structural transformation* in which factors of production are transferred from the sector with the lowest productivity, agriculture, to the industrial sector where productivity is much higher and the pace of technological change and productivity growth is more rapid.[3] In the course of this process of structural change, the share of agriculture in the total labour force declines, and the share of industry increases. The importance of the agricultural sector also declines in terms of its share in gross domestic product, while the importance of industry increases. Structural transformation

---

3 In discussions of industrialisation, the main emphasis is on the most dynamic sector: manufacturing. The construction sector is quite large, but is usually not seen as a driving force in economic development. The terms structural change and structural transformation are used interchangeably.

involves more than changes in the sector structure alone. It also refers to increases in savings and investment rates, rapid urbanisation, demographic transitions with declining death rates followed by later decline in birth rates, epidemiological transitions, changes in income inequality[4] and changing social institutions, attitudes and beliefs without which modern economic growth would be impossible (Caldwell, 1997; Frederikson, 1969; Kuznets, 1971; Syrquin, 1988).

Apart from the productivity differential, a low income elasticity of the demand for agricultural products also plays an important role in the transformation process. As societies become richer, people tend to spend an ever smaller part of their additional income on agricultural products. There is a limit to the amount of food people can consume. Once the basic need for food has been met, people tend to spend more on manufactured goods as their incomes go up. The share of food consumption in total expenditure will tend to decrease.[5] Thus, structural change is also tied up with changes in the pattern and composition of demand.

Following the rise of the industrial sector, the service sector started to increase. By the 1940s the share of industry in GDP in the advanced economies had reached its peak. It never exceeded 50 per cent of GDP. Since then, the share of services has been on the increase. They now account for more than 70 per cent of GDP and employment in the advanced economies. Modern economies are predominantly service economies. However, the manufacturing sector still plays a key role as the main source of technological change.

The process of structural transformation that took place in the currently rich countries in the past is now taking place in developing countries. Tables 3.8 and 3.9 in Chapter 3 indicate how the share of the agricultural sector has been declining and the share of the industrial sector increasing. According to Kitching (1982), there is an important element of truth – both theoretically and empirically – in the old orthodoxy that economic development goes hand in hand with industrialisation. Benjamin Higgins, one of the early advocates of large-scale industrialisation strategies, writes that 'the basic formula for development...was "getting rid of farmers" (Higgins and Higgins, 1979: p. 12).

In spite of the common trend of a shrinking agricultural sector, it is important to emphasise that there is no standard pattern of structural change that all countries pass through. Developing countries cannot simply copy earlier development experiences. One striking difference with earlier experiences is that service sectors have expanded earlier in developing countries, alongside the growth of the industrial sector. As indicated by Tables 3.8 and 3.9 in Chapter 3, the share of the service sector in developing countries already exceeded those

---

4 The Kuznets hypothesis of the inverted U-curve suggests that income inequality increases in earlier stages of industrialisation and decreases in later stages (Kuznets, 1955). See for further discussion Chapters 3 and 9.

5 This is referred to as Engel's law. The income elasticity of the demand for agricultural products is the percentage increase in the consumption of agricultural products divided by the percentage increase in real income per capita. If income elasticity is less than one, the share of agricultural products in total expenditure will decrease as per capita income rises.

of industry in the 1950s and 1960s. Another crucial difference is that the Western countries were the first to industrialise, while developing countries have to compete as latecomers in a highly competitive world economy dominated by giant industrial corporations and powerful advanced economies.

In a variety of publications Chenery and his co-authors have emphasised the differences in patterns of structural change (Chenery, 1979; Chenery, Robinson and Syrquin, 1986; Chenery and Taylor 1968; Kirkpatrick, 1987; Syrquin, 1988). Thus, in developing countries with an abundance of natural resources the shift away from agriculture and mining will be delayed. As wages in these countries are higher, they are likely to choose more capital-intensive production techniques in manufacturing. They will also focus on resource-processing manufacturing activities. Countries that are unable to export primary products will industrialise earlier and are more likely to concentrate on labour-intensive export production. In small countries the share of trade and capital imports in GDP will tend to be high. These countries will tend to specialise in a few lines of industrial production. In countries with large domestic markets such as China, Brazil, India or Indonesia the pattern of industrialisation will be more diversified. There are greater opportunities for developing domestic intermediate goods and capital goods sectors. The nature of industrial policies also affects the pattern of industrialisation.

Finally, the timing of industrialisation is of importance. Countries such as Brazil, India and Egypt have had at least 60 to 70 years experience with large-scale industry, especially in food processing and textiles. Countries in Sub-Saharan Africa had hardly any experience of industrialisation before World War II. This is one of the reasons why industrialisation in these countries so far has been rather unsuccessful (Szirmai and Lapperre, 2001). The countries with rapid industrial growth in the post-war period all had substantial industrial experience before World War II (Pack, 1988).

In sum, there is no unique pattern of transition from an agrarian to an industrial economy. However, the notion of a global transformation from an agricultural to an industrial society is still undisputed (Syrquin, 1988).

8.2.3   Arguments in favour of industrialisation

There are powerful empirical and theoretical arguments in favour of industrialisation as the main engine of growth in economic development. The arguments are summarised in Box 8.1.

Empirical correlations between industrialisation and economic development
The empirical argument points to the overall correlation between degree of industrialisation and level of economic development. Not only are the advanced economies more industrialised than developing countries, but also the more successful developing countries are invariably those which have been able to industrialise.

> **Box 8.1   Arguments for industrialisation**
> - There is a correlation between industrialisation and economic development.
> - Productivity is higher in the industrial sector than in the agricultural sector. This is referred to as the *structural change bonus*.
> - The industrial sector offers special opportunities for increases in the scale of production, capital accumulation and technological advance.
> - As per capita incomes rise, the share of agricultural expenditures in total expenditures declines and the share of expenditures on manufactured goods increases. This is referred to as *Engels law*.
> - Linkage effects are stronger in manufacturing than in agriculture or mining.

The empirical relationship between industrialisation and development is illustrated in Table 8.2. In this table, the share of manufacturing in the total production of commodities is set out against a country's per capita gross national income in 2000.[6] The correlation between the logarithm of income per capita and the share of manufacturing is 0.79.

In line with the argument in the previous section about different patterns of structural change, the correlation is not a perfect one. Major exceptions among the advanced economies are the primary exporters Norway, Canada and Australia. Among the developing countries, Taiwan, Thailand and Brazil rank higher in terms of industrialisation than in terms of income. But the table illustrates the general point about industrialisation. The poorest countries in the table are clearly those with the lowest share of manufacturing (and the highest share of agriculture). The more prosperous countries are the more industrialised ones.

Structural change bonus

A second argument in favour of industrialisation derives from the fact that labour productivity in agriculture is much lower than labour productivity in industry. A transfer of labour from low-productivity agriculture to high-productivity industry results in an immediate increase in overall productivity and income per capita. This transfer has been a major source of growth in developing countries. It is referred to as the structural change bonus.

Opportunities for capital accumulation and technological change

Furthermore, labour productivity in developing countries tends to increase more rapidly in industry than in agriculture, owing to capital accumulation, economies of scale and technological progress.[7] As explained in the

---

[6] Calculated as the share of manufacturing output in total output of agriculture and industry. The table includes our sample of twenty-nine developing countries and a number of major OECD countries.
[7] In the richest countries of the world, growth of labour productivity in agriculture in the post-war period has been higher than in industry – particularly owing to biotechnological innovation (see Maddison, 1991: pp. 150–1). However, this is an exception to the general pattern. Even in the advanced economies, the level of labour productivity in industry is much higher than in agriculture.

Table 8.2 *Industrialisation and per capita gross national product in 2000*

	Share of manufacturing in total commodity production[a]		GNP per capita (2000 US$)	
	(%)[b]	Ranking		Ranking
Switzerland	72	2	38,140	1
Japan	64	11	35,620	2
Norway	26	40	34,530	3
USA	63	14	34,100	4
Denmark	60	17	32,280	5
Sweden	66	9	27,140	6
Austria	60	16	25,220	7
Finland	66	8	25,130	8
Germany	72	3	25,120	9
Netherlands	58	18	24,970	10
Belgium	69	4	24,540	11
UK	60	15	24,430	12
France	65	10	24,090	13
Canada	56	20	21,130	14
Australia	45	25	20,240	15
Italy	66	7	20,160	16
Taiwan	77	1	14,188	17
South Korea	66	6	8,910	18
Argentina	55	22	7,460	19
Mexico	63	12	5,070	20
Chile	36	32	4,590	21
Venezuela	35	34	4,310	22
Brazil	67	5	3,580	23
Malaysia	58	19	3,380	24
Turkey	36	30	3,100	25
South Africa	55	21	3,020	26
Peru	41	26	2,080	27
Colombia	31	36	2,020	28
Thailand	63	13	2,000	29
Egypt	38	29	1,490	30
Nigeria	38	28	1,180	31
Philippines	48	24	1,040	32
Sri Lanka	36	33	850	33
China	52	23	840	34
Côte d'Ivoire	36	31	600	35
Indonesia	41	27	570	36
India	31	38	450	37
Pakistan	31	37	440	38
Bangladesh	30	39	370	39
Kenya	34	35	350	40
Ghana	15	42	340	41
Zambia	25	41	300	42
Tanzania	12	43	270	43
Morocco	5	45	260	44
Congo, Dem. Rep.	6	44	100	45

Notes: [a] Value added in manufacturing as percentage of total value in commodity production (agriculture, forestry, fisheries, mining, manufacturing, construction and utilities).
[b] Manufacturing share OECD countries, latest year in period 1998–2000.
Sources: GNP per capita and shares from World Bank, *World Development Indicators* CD-Rom, 2002, except: Zaire from World Bank (http://www.worldbank.org/data/countrydata/countrydata.html) Canada, Norway, Sweden, Switzerland, Canada and the USA: calculated with OECD Main Economic Indicators (http://www.oecd.org/EN/document/0, EN-document-7-nodirectorate-no-1-5194-7,00.html) and UNIDO *Industrial Statistics* (http://www.unido.org/Regions.cfm?area=GLO)

introduction to this chapter, the industrial sector offers much better opportunities for capital accumulation, large-scale production and technological progress than agriculture does. In addition, there are important *spillover effects* from the industrial sector to other sectors, such as the service sector. Thus, advances in ICT technologies produced in the manufacturing sector fuel technological change in the service sector.

Some brief remarks need to be made here about the difficulties in unscrambling capital accumulation and technological change (see also Chapter 4). From the perspective of a developing country, the use of more capital goods per worker in itself represents a kind of technological change. The mode of production changes dramatically, and the mastering of new – often imported – technologies requires major innovative efforts on behalf of developing countries and their firms. In this sense, all capital accumulation represents technological change.

But, one should distinguish between the increase in the pure volume of existing capital goods (more of the same) and the shift over time from technologically less sophisticated to technologically more advanced capital goods. This is called *embodied technological change*. Also, in the course of economic development, output per unit of input (total factor productivity) can increase owing to various factors including shifts from one economic sector to another, economies of scale and more efficient allocation of resources within sectors (see Chapter 3 on the proximate sources of growth). One of the most important factors which can cause increases in output per unit of input is so-called *disembodied technological change*. Disembodied technological change refers to general advances in science, technology and the state of knowledge, increased knowledge about products, markets, raw materials, organisation techniques, learning-by-doing effects, and so forth.

In economic growth accounting studies, the contribution of growth of physical capital to growth of output in post-war advanced economies turns out to be less important than previously thought. Other factors such as growth of employment, growth of human capital and disembodied technological change are very important as well (Maddison, 1987; Thirlwall, 1997: ch. 3). However, for developing countries physical capital accumulation still seems to be of great importance, because they start with so much less capital per worker (Hofman, 1993; Nadiri, 1972; Pilat, 1994; Thirlwall, 1997).

The Engels law

The lower the per capita income of a country, the larger the proportion of that income that will be spent on basic agricultural foodstuffs. This is the famous Engels law (Engels, 1857). As per capita incomes increase, the demand for agricultural products will decline and the demand for industrial products will tend to increase. Economic development creates a mass market for industrial products. If a country does not develop its domestic manufacturing industry, it will have to import all of its manufactured goods.

Linkage effects

Another economic argument often put forward in favour of industrialisation is that the *linkage* effects in the manufacturing sector are so much stronger than in agriculture and mining. Investment in one branch of manufacturing can have strong positive effects on other branches of the economy. Thus, industrialisation can contribute to the dynamism of the whole economy. This argument will be elaborated further in Chapter 9.

8.2.4   *The prestige of industrialisation*

The high prestige of industrialisation is not only based on the empirical relationships between per capita income and the degree of industrialisation. It is also grounded in historical experiences. As discussed in Chapter 2, the late nineteenth century saw the rise of the colonial pattern of international trade. Developing countries and colonies exported primary mining and agricultural products, and the rich industrialised Western countries exported manufactured goods. Primary exports came to be associated subjectively with poverty, underdevelopment and dependence. Industry came to be associated with development, power and economic independence.

The unfavourable associations of primary exports were intensified during the 1913–50 period when the terms of trade for primary exports from developing countries deteriorated dramatically. Countries most dependent on primary exports were hardest hit by the great depression (Maddison, 1989). During this period the notion arose – especially in Latin America – that developing countries should develop their own industries in order to become less dependent on the industrialised world (Furtado, 1976).

After World War II, policy makers in developing countries and Western advisers both considered industrialisation to be the royal road to development. Expectations for industrialisation were extremely high. In economic policy, industrialisation was given top priority at the expense of other sectors.

8.3   Accumulation of industrial capital in open and closed models of the economy

8.3.1   *Open and closed models of the economy: early and late stages of development*

Structural change involves changes in the structure of employment and output and transfers of resources from one sector to another. To structure the discussion of industrialisation in the following sections, we make a rough distinction between: (a) earlier and later stages of industrialisation; (b) open and closed models of economic development (Lewis, 1950; 1954; 1978b; Myint, 1975; 1980; Nicholls, 1964; Timmer, 1988).

Earlier and later stages of industrialisation

In order to invest in capital accumulation in the modern sector of the economy, savings need to be mobilised and transferred to the new sector. In this chapter, our main interest is in investment in manufacturing and in the infrastructure of roads, harbours, railways, telecommunications and energy supply.[8] Before the onset of industrialisation the great majority of the population finds its livelihood in agriculture. The agricultural sector is the only domestic sector that can provide labour and savings, which can be used to start industrialisation. The construction of a modern industrial sector inevitably starts with a transfer of productive resources from agriculture to industry.

At later stages of development the agricultural and the industrial sectors exist alongside each other. Strategic choices have to be made with respect to the priority given to either agriculture or industry in economic policy. Now, the question arises of the *appropriate balance between sectors* in the course of structural transformation.

Open and closed models of development and accumulation

The process of capital accumulation in the modern sector of developing countries can be studied in the context of either a closed or an open model of the economy.

In a closed economy there are no economic ties with the outside world. There is no foreign trade. There are no international flows of profits, loans or investments, and there is no international migration. In order to invest in the modern sector of a closed economy, all savings need to be earned and mobilised within the boundaries of the domestic economy. The most extreme example of a closed economy is a subsistence agriculture economy.

In a closed economy, the initial resources for industrialisation can only be forthcoming from the agricultural sector. Closed models of industrialisation, therefore, analyse the different mechanisms for transferring resources from one sector to another. These transfer mechanisms are studied within the framework of so-called *two-sector models* of economic development. These models focus on the interactions and resource flows between agricultural and industrial sectors in different stages of economic development. In closed economy models, an important issue is the *balance* between sectors of the economy. The output of one sector has to be absorbed by another sector. The inputs required by sector have to be produced by the other sectors. Lack of balance may cause bottlenecks. Two-sector models will be discussed further in Chapter 9.

In open-economy models, attention is paid to the relations with the international economy. Some of the interactions between agriculture and industry take place via the outside world. Agricultural exports can earn revenues and foreign exchange, which are potentially available for reinvestment in the industrial sector. Once the mining sector has developed, mineral export revenues

---

8 To a lesser extent we are also interested in investment in mining and construction.

can in turn provide resources for other sectors such as manufacturing. Theories that centre on primary agricultural and mining exports as the engines of growth and transformation are called *theories of primary export-led growth*. These theories will be discussed in section 8.5.

There are also financial flows from and to abroad. Capital accumulation and industrialisation may be speeded up by foreign direct investment, bank loans and aid flows from abroad. But the pace of capital accumulation may also be retarded if resources drain away abroad (Baran, 1957).

An important difference between open and closed models is that there is less need to focus on the *balance between sectors* in open models. If the inputs for a given sector are not produced domestically, they can be imported and can be paid for by the revenues from exported products.

Nevertheless, an open model of structural change also assumes a transfer of resources from agriculture to industry during the initial stages of industrialisation. In this case, export profits from agricultural exports are reinvested in industry. Government policy discriminates against agriculture by taxing exports and transferring funds to other sectors. However, once the industrial sector has started developing, strategic decisions have to be faced in open models just as in closed models. Does policy continue to give priority to industry over agriculture or not?

The distinction between open and closed models can be used as an empirical approximation of reality, but also serves as an indication of the orientation of economic policy. Since the late nineteenth century there have been no completely closed economies. But economies do vary substantially in their degree of openness. In terms of policy orientation, some countries attempt to reduce their dependence on foreign trade and foreign finance through an inward-looking import substitution policy. They still attract foreign finance, investment and capital. But the mental model underlying policy making is a closed one, in which international trade is seen as a threat. Other countries choose specialisation according to comparative advantage, openness to foreign investment and an outward-looking export orientation.

A stylised historical sequence of structural change in developing economies starts with the primacy of agriculture in a relatively closed economy. This is followed by a period dominated by primary agricultural or mining exports, which for developing countries roughly spans the period from 1850 to around 1929. The next phase is that of import-substituting industrialisation, which lasts from the 1930s to the mid-1980s. Since then the emphasis has shifted more in the direction of more outward-looking policies with an emphasis on labour-intensive exports from developing countries.

For an analysis of economic development in developing countries from the mid-nineteenth century to 1929, an open model is most useful. Most developing countries started their modern economic development in the second half of the nineteenth century by exporting primary agricultural and mining products. Export revenues and foreign investment served to finance capital accumulation in infrastructure.

For an understanding of industrialisation strategies from 1930 to 1985 the closed model is more helpful. Export revenues had created an urban market for manufactured imports. Developing countries tried to reduce their dependence on international trade and primary exports and to replace manufactured products imported from Western countries by products manufactured at home (*import substitution*, see Chapter 9). This involved substantial protection of domestic manufacturing industries. Starting in the 1960s, some countries such as Korea and Taiwan pioneered the shift towards labour-intensive industrial exports from developing countries, following the earlier example of Japan. Since the mid-1990s the emphasis has shifted worldwide to more liberalisation and a more open export-oriented policy stance.

8.3.2   Is the agricultural sector a stagnant or a dynamic sector?

In preindustrial societies the majority of the population is active in the agricultural sector. In a closed economy, the means required for developing a domestic industry can only be found in the agricultural sector. In older development theories and strategies the agricultural sector is therefore mainly considered in negative terms as a reservoir of labour, food and savings (financial capital), which can and should be transferred to the industrial sector. The high prestige of industry coincided with a very dismal view of agriculture. The agricultural sector itself was regarded as traditional, stagnant and characterised by low productivity and low potential. The dynamic sector was the industrial sector, which – for this very reason – should be developed as soon as possible. This justified squeezing and exploiting the agricultural sector.

Arthur Lewis's well-known model of 'economic development with unlimited supplies of labour' is an example of this view (Lewis, 1954; see Chapter 9 for a full presentation). This model assumes an extremely low marginal productivity in traditional agriculture. Therefore, labour can very simply be withdrawn from agriculture with little or no loss of food production. This labour can be employed more productively in industry and the construction of infrastructure. Lewis does acknowledge the fact that agriculture needs to grow along with the industrial sector in order to prevent economic development from grinding to a halt. If agricultural production stagnates, food prices will increase and the internal terms of trade (the ratio of agricultural to industrial prices) will turn against the industrial sector.[9] Nevertheless, it cannot be denied that the Lewis model assumes a low agricultural productivity in the initial stages of industrialisation. His assumption is that labour productivity will automatically increase in agriculture when surplus labour is removed. Another example is provided by the famous study of agricultural involution in Java by the economic anthropologist Clifford Geertz (Geertz, 1963). According to Geertz's, in

---

9 When food prices increase, wages in the industrial sector must increase in order to compensate for higher prices; thus, the share of profits in value added will tend to decline.

hindsight mistaken, analysis, Indonesian agriculture was a basket case which should be written off. All energy should be focused on industrialisation.

A more dynamic view of agriculture emphasises that a productive and flourishing agriculture is a precondition for successful industrialisation. Prior to industrialisation, productivity in the agricultural sector must increase sufficiently to produce a surplus over the subsistence needs of the agrarian population. Only when such a surplus is available can processes of transfer to the industrial sector be initiated. Therefore, several authors (development economists, economic historians and agronomists) argue that an increase in labour productivity in agriculture is a necessary condition for industrialisation (Boserup, 1981; Kuznets, 1965; Ranis, 1989; Rostow, 1960; Timmer, 1988).

In an open economy the agricultural sector contributes to economic development through its revenues from agricultural exports, which are available for investment in the industrial sector. As in the closed model, a productive and dynamic agricultural sector produces a surplus over its subsistence needs, which can be utilised for development.

All this implies a more positive view of the role of the agricultural sector even in the early stages of industrialisation. Agriculture is a dynamic sector in its own right, with an important contribution to make to economic development. Prior to industrialisation there has to be an agrarian revolution.[10]

Is there any synthesis possible between these conflicting views – transfer of surpluses from a productive agricultural system or squeezing resources out of a low-productive agricultural sector? In a criticism of negative perspectives on agriculture, Reynolds (1975: p. 14) makes a helpful distinction between transfer of resources from a static agricultural system and transfer of resources from a dynamic agricultural system.

In an economy where agricultural productivity prior to industrialisation is stagnant, there can still be surpluses of labour time, food and savings. These surpluses may be withdrawn from the agricultural sector as part of the industrialisation strategy. Forced transfer of surpluses, however, leads to the impoverishment of the rural population and possibly even to famines. Transfer in a more dynamic context implies that agricultural production and productivity can continue to increase as a result of agricultural investment, technological progress, positive incentives and intensification of production. Part of the increment in agricultural output and agricultural real incomes is available for transfer to industry. But sufficient portions of additional earnings are ploughed back into agriculture to maintain its dynamic momentum.

In the history of European industrialisation, increases in agricultural productivity preceded industrialisation. In developing countries average agricultural output per worker in the 1960s was much lower than in Western countries

---

10 Ester Boserup objects to the term 'agricultural revolution' and emphasises a more gradual nature of long-run processes of productivity increase and intensification of production in the agricultural sector (Boserup, 1981).

between 1810 and 1860 (Bairoch, 1975). Their experiences provide instances of transfer of resources out of relatively static agricultural sectors.[11] Both the stagnation of agricultural development in modern Sub-Saharan Africa and the disappointing outcomes of industrialisation can be interpreted in this perspective (Lapperre, 2001; World Bank, 1989).

8.3.3 *What about the service sector?*

There is considerable debate about the role of the service sector. In classical theories of structural change, the first stage was a shift from agriculture to industry, followed by a later shift from industry to services (Clark, 1940). The image of the service sector was quite negative. This sector could only develop once the industrial sector had been able to supply the population with sufficient physical commodities. According to Veblen (1899), the service and financial sectors were parasitic sectors, which lived off the productive efforts of engineers and workers in industry and manufacturing. Marxists defined the service sector as inherently unproductive. Until recently, the national accounts of communist countries did not even measure the output of much of the service sector.[12] In neoclassical economics, Baumol (1967; 1986) argued that the productivity slowdown of the Western economies was caused by the rise of the service sector (Baumol's law). Hairdressing, restaurants, medical services and government services are inherently labour intensive. There is no way of increasing the productivity of these activities through automation or the use of capital. The bloated government bureaucracies in developing countries can be taken as a case in point. They absorb resources, but contribute little to development.

More recent literature provides a more positive picture of the service sector (Britton, 1990; Daniels, 1989; Glasmeier and Howland, 1994; Riddle, 1986). This sector can also make valuable contributions to the process of industrialisation. It is an important intermediate input for the manufacturing sector. It can be an engine of regional and national growth. Services and manufacturing reinforce each other. At early stages of development, the emergence of communication, transport, trade and financial services is one of the prerequisites for industrialisation. Currently, the financial system is seen as a vital factor in economic development. Weakly developed, shallow, financial systems are an obstacle to development.

---

11 The difference may be explained as follows. In a completely closed economy, transfer from the agricultural sector is only possible when the agricultural sector produces a surplus exceeding subsistence needs in agriculture. This is more or less what happened in eighteenth-century England. In developing countries the foundations for industrialisation were laid in the late nineteenth century, in the context of an open model, with large amounts of foreign investment which subsequently attracted labour from the agricultural sector.
12 The so-called material product system of national accounts (MPS) developed in the Soviet Union excluded most of service output in the calculation of national product. In most former communist countries the MPS has now been completely or partially replaced by the System of National Accounts.

Recent research also points to considerable technological dynamism in parts of the modern service sector, such as telecommunications, banking services, software development, logistics, the explosive development of the internet and so forth (see van Ark *et al.*, 2002; Triplett, 2002). These services are increasingly traded internationally. Though Baumol's law may hold for hairdressers and restaurants, it does not hold for mobile telecommunication, financial services or distance learning.

A different line of argument refers to service sectors such as tourism. Tourism may offer major opportunities of employment creation and develop-ment in some developing countries, especially small island economies where the prospects of industry driven development are dim.

Thus, the service sector is today seen in a more dynamic light (see the col-lection of articles in Bryson and Daniels, 1998). Nevertheless, it remains true that the dramatic expansion of the service industries in advanced economies was preceded by the growth of the industrial sector. In developing countries the historical sequence of industry and services has been reversed. The ser-vice sector expanded at an early stage. There are still good reasons to doubt the developmental dynamism of the service sector in developing countries. Its increased share primarily reflects the expansion of employment in the govern-ment bureaucracies and the public sector. By and large there are good reasons to question the productive contribution of the government sector in devel-oping countries. On the other hand, modern industry, with its high capital intensity, provides insufficient employment for the rapidly increasing labour force. The service industries will inevitably have a more important role in em-ployment creation than was the case in past developmental patterns. More of this employment, however, will have to be generated outside the government sector.

Our conclusion is that for growth of per capita income, the industrial sector still remains a key sector. There is little correlation between the share of the service sector in national income and the level of national income. It is the industrial sector where the opportunities for increases in productivity through capital accumulation and technological change remain the greatest.

8.4 The development of agriculture as a prerequisite for industrialisation

8.4.1 *The role of agriculture in early stages of development*

In the early stages of development one can distinguish the following important contributions of the agricultural sector to the process of economic develop-ment (Boserup, 1981; Johnston, 1970; Johnston and Mellor, 1961; Lewis, 1978b; Nicholls, 1964; Reynolds, 1975; Timmer, 1988): (1) agriculture as a source of food for a growing non-agricultural population; (2) agriculture as a source of industrial labour; (3) agriculture as a source of domestic savings; (4) the agricultural sector as a market for industrial products; (5) agricultural exports as a source of foreign currency.

1. Agriculture as a source of food

In the early stages of development poor countries are characterised by a rapidly increasing demand for food. The rapidly growing population and rising per capita incomes determine the demand for food (Johnston and Mellor, 1961). Poor people tend to spend a large part of their additional income on food.[13] Since the industrial sector withdraws labour from the agricultural sector, the workers remaining in the agricultural sector must meet the growing demand for food.

This will not cause great problems if the agricultural sector is already quite productive before the onset of industrialisation. But if productivity is low and shows no improvement, urban food shortages will push food prices up. High food prices will exert an upward pressure on the costs of labour in the industrial sector, eroding the profitability of the sector.

2. Agriculture as a source of labour

In early stages of development, labour has to be withdrawn from the agricultural sector to create an urban industrial labour force. Labour can also be withdrawn from agriculture for work on infrastructural projects. If productivity is increasing in agriculture, labour can be released more easily than when productivity is stagnant.

3. Agriculture as a source of domestic savings

Until a modern sector has developed, there is no alternative source of domestic savings other than revenues from the sale of agricultural surpluses. The agricultural sector provides the necessary savings for investment in industry and infrastructure.

4. The agricultural sector as a market for industrial products

When a large proportion of the population is active within the agricultural sector, an increase in agricultural incomes will create a market for products of the new industries. However, this function of the agricultural sector as a market conflicts with its function as provider of savings. The more people consume, the less they will be able to save. According to Nicholls (1964), the savings function is more important than the market function in the very early stages of industrialisation. The first manufacturing products are sold on urban rather than rural markets. But urban markets are too small to sustain the expansion of domestic manufacturing.

---

13 In economic terminology the income elasticity of the demand for food is rather high (see footnote 5).

5. Agricultural exports as a source of foreign currency

The above-mentioned functions of agriculture are all typical for a closed model of economic development. The debate on the role of agricultural exports is based on an open model of the economy (Myint, 1975). In the early stages of economic development agricultural exports and other primary exports are the most likely source of foreign exchange earnings. Foreign exchange is needed to finance imports of the capital goods and intermediate goods required for industrialisation.

In theory, an open economy could concentrate on export production. It could meet the demand for food by exporting manufactures, mining products and cash crops, using part of the proceeds to import food (Myint, 1975). Even so, an increase in productivity in domestic food production would lead to considerable savings in scarce foreign exchange, which would otherwise have had to be used for food imports (Nicholls, 1964: p. 12). Agricultural exports will be discussed in more detail in section 8.5.

8.4.2   Historical examples of relationships between agriculture and industry[14]

England and Western Europe

From the eighteenth century onwards a productive agricultural sector provided a sound basis for industrialisation in Western Europe. In the eighteenth century, English agriculture was the most productive in Europe. Farmers switched to more intensive forms of land use, annual harvests and crop rotation, instead of letting part of the land area lie fallow for one or more years. New high-quality food crops like turnips and potatoes were introduced. Farmers switched to intensive cattle breeding. Part of the farmland was used for the systematic production of fodder crops. Animal manure was used to maintain the fertility of the land.[15] Agriculture became commercialised. Till the 1930s, this highly efficient agricultural system was capable of feeding the expanding urban population. There was also a flow of labour from agriculture to the urban centres.

Argentina, Australia, Canada and the USA

The initial conditions in agriculture in sparsely populated countries such as Australia, Canada, the United States and Argentina were extremely favourable. At an early stage these countries were able to realise high labour productivity in agriculture, compensating for the scarcity of labour by employing much capital per worker (Baldwin, 1956). The agricultural sector produced considerable

---

14 This section is primarily based on Nicholls (1964), pp. 16–26.
15 Ester Boserup (1981: pp. 114–17) claims that there was no agricultural revolution in the eighteenth century. Rather, there was a gradual increase in output per hectare due to an increase in population density and a greater use of labour per unit of land. Still, Boserup agrees that British agriculture was the most productive agriculture in Europe.

surpluses of food and other agricultural products, which could be exported. At a later stage, the export revenues were available to finance industrialisation. Immigration and foreign investment were incentives for economic development.

Such countries provide interesting examples of successful primary export-led economic development. But such development does not follow automatically, as can be seen from the disappointing experience of developing countries such as Argentina and Brazil. In these countries inefficient institutions such as large landownership hampered the long-term development of the agricultural sector. Investments in infrastructure and industry were delayed.

Russia

Russia is an example of a country that started its industrialisation under relatively favourable initial conditions. Russian agriculture was potentially one of the most productive systems in the world. However, this potential has never been fully realised. Until 1861, a system of serfdom was maintained under which labour was tied to the land in an unproductive fashion. After the abolition of serfdom in 1861, large capitalist landowners benefited most from the land reforms. They made high profits, but output increased less than it would have if smaller farmers had been allowed to work the lands more intensively. Rural poverty increased rather than decreased. Large landowners invested part of their profits in infrastructure, railways and the industrial sector. The imposition of taxes forced smaller farmers to produce cash crops so that Russia could export wheat.

The Russian pattern of rapid industrialisation and heavy-handed exploitation of the peasantry was continued in the communist Soviet Union. Despite resistance by the rural population, agriculture was collectivised. Coercion was used to force the agricultural sector to provide the growing urban population with cheap food.

From the perspective of industrialisation, the process of transferring resources from agriculture to industry was fairly successful – though it involved immense human sacrifices. Within a short time the Soviet Union succeeded in building an extensive industrial sector. But the overexploitation of the agrarian sector resulted in an agricultural sector performing far below potential to this very day in the Russian Federation and former Soviet Republics such as the Ukraine.

8.4.3   Conclusion

The lesson we can derive from this section is that increases in output and productivity in the agricultural sector at the early stages of development create favourable conditions for industrialisation; a dynamic agriculture, which produces surpluses above subsistence. On the one hand, this helps combat rural poverty. On the other hand, it also creates favourable conditions for the development of industry.

8.5   Open model: are primary exports an engine of growth and structural transformation?

8.5.1   Introduction

As long as we discuss the relationships between agriculture and industry in the context of a closed model, we assume that everything has to be produced within the confines of the domestic economy. However, in an open model, developing countries have the option of exporting primary agricultural and mining products. The revenues from these exports may be reinvested in other sectors. For a proper understanding of the economic history of developing countries an open model is of major importance (Islam, 1989b). The modern economic development of these countries commenced with the export of cash crops and unprocessed mineral products.

8.5.2   Comparative advantage and the role of trade in development

The discussion about the role of primary exports in development should be seen in the context of theories about comparative advantage, the international division of labour and the role of trade in development. According to these theories, countries should specialise in lines of production in which they have a comparative advantage and import products in which other countries have a comparative advantage.

The arguments in favour of international free trade derive from classical economists like Adam Smith and David Ricardo. The basic arguments have remained unchanged in spite of numerous elaborations and refinements. This section provides a very brief summary of these arguments.

Let us assume that there are two countries, A and B, and two goods, for example, food and clothing. For simplicity's sake, we also assume that the production of these two goods only requires labour. This means that the costs of the goods can be expressed in labour hours.[16] When country A can produce food more cheaply than country B and country B can produce clothing more cheaply than country A, it is evident that both countries will benefit from the international trade in food and clothing. The classical economists, however, have shown that the two countries will also benefit from international trade, even when country A produces both products more cheaply than country B. According to the *law of comparative advantage* the two countries should specialise in producing those products in which they are most efficient in relative terms.

The following numerical example illustrates this principle (see Table 8.3). Using one day of labour, country A can produce either one unit of food or

---

[16] This assumption is not essential. It is only used to explain the principle of free trade as briefly as possible.

Table 8.3 *Advantages of international trade*

Labour days required for production of:		
	1 unit of food	1 unit of clothing
Country A	1	2
Country B	3	4
Terms of trade of food and clothing, without international trade		
Country A	1	$1/2$
Country B	1	$3/4$
Terms of trade of food and clothing, with international trade		
Country A	1	$3/4$
Country B	1	$1/2$

Source: Samuelson and Nordhaus, 1989, p. 903.

half a unit of clothing. If the price of the product is expressed in labour units, one unit of food in country A can be traded for half a unit of clothing in the absence of international trade. In country B, one labour day will produce one third of a unit of food and one quarter of a unit of clothing. In the absence of international trade, one unit of food can be traded for three-quarters of a unit of clothing. In this example, country A is more efficient (cheaper) in absolute terms than country B in the production of both goods. However, in relative terms one gets less clothing per unit of food in country A (half a unit of clothing for one unit of food) than in country B (three-quarters of a unit of clothing for one unit of food). This means that country A is relatively more efficient at producing food and country B is relatively more efficient at producing clothing.

The simple example shows that in this case international trade will benefit both countries. If country A specialises in the production of food and exports part of it to country B, one day's work will produce one unit of food, which can be traded for three-quarters of a unit of clothing. This is more than the half a unit of clothing which one can get in absence of international trade. If country B specialises in producing clothing and exports part of it to country A, it will be able to trade one unit of clothing for two units of food. Again, this is more than the one and one third units of food it would get in the absence of international trade. For both countries, therefore, specialisation and international trade is profitable. In addition, specialisation in production often gives rise to economies of scale, which make production even cheaper.

In the twentieth-century version of the theory of comparative advantage, the emphasis is on the proportions of the factors of production capital and labour (see e.g. Kol and Mennes, 1990; Ethier, 1995). Countries with surplus labour and a scarcity of capital will produce labour-intensive products relatively cheaply and will have a comparative advantage in such products. Countries with an abundance of capital and a shortage of labour will have a comparative advantage in capital-intensive products. This theory is also known as the Heckscher-Ohlin-Samuelson theory. The essence of the theory of comparative cost advantage is that international trade is beneficial to all parties involved: it increases total welfare. It is a plea for an international division of labour, international trade and liberalisation.

The theory of comparative advantage includes both static and dynamic arguments. The static version of the theory argues simply that countries will be better off if they specialise according to their comparative advantage. Thus, if developing countries have a comparative advantage in primary goods, they should export these goods and import manufactured goods.

The dynamic version of comparative advantage focuses on the long-run effects of specialisation and trade. There are potential dynamic advantages as well as dynamic disadvantages. The most powerful argument against following comparative advantage is that in the long run it reinforces existing patterns of production and specialisation. If a developing country has a comparative advantage in a limited number of primary products, it may for ever remain dependent on them. The possibility of importing industrial products relatively cheaply from abroad makes it difficult to build up a domestic industrial sector. Thus, a developing country may never industrialise.

A more positive version of dynamic comparative advantage suggests that primary exports can serve as an engine of structural transformation. In early stages of development, the export of cash crops is an alternative to direct processes of resource transfer from agriculture to industry in the closed model. In the first place, agricultural exports result in increases in per capita income. In the second place, the increased earnings of people involved in the export sector create a market for imported industrial consumer goods. In due time this market can be captured by import-substituting domestic industries. In the third place, agricultural exports generate savings, which can be used for investment in industry and infrastructure. Finally, agricultural exports are a means of obtaining foreign exchange, which can be used to finance imports of the capital goods and intermediate inputs required for industrialisation. Like resource transfers in closed models, agricultural exports presume the availability of a surplus over subsistence needs in the agricultural sector, which can potentially be utilised for developmental purposes and structural transformation.

In the following sections we will discuss the role of primary exports in economic development in more detail. The high prestige of industrialisation in the post-war period resulted in an underestimation of the positive role that primary agricultural exports have played in the past and could still play in the future. In the next chapter, the debate about the merits of international trade will be taken up again when we discuss the pros and cons of export-oriented industrialisation versus import-substituting industrialisation.

8.5.3   Primary exports as an engine of growth between 1870 and 1913: vent for surplus

In developing countries agricultural exports have played a crucial part in initiating changes in the economy (Lewis, 1969; 1970; 1978b; Maddison, 1989). By modern standards, the volume of international trade between poor and rich countries before the middle of the nineteenth century was negligible. Prior to the emergence of roads and railways, the interior of developing countries was isolated from the outside world. With the improvement of transport and communication and the growing demand for primary products in industrialised countries, there was an explosive growth of exports of cash crops from developing countries (cotton, oilseeds, cocoa, coffee, tea, bananas, rubber, pineapples, cotton fibres, copra, and so on) between 1870 and 1913.

Following Adam Smith, authors like Myint and Caves (Myint, 1959; Caves, 1965) use the term '*vent for surplus*' to characterise agricultural exports during this period. In a traditional subsistence economy peasants produce food for their own needs. In general, outside the peak periods of sowing and harvesting, they have a good deal of spare time. Not all agricultural land is cultivated intensively. In the absence of market demand and storage facilities, there is little incentive to produce above subsistence. If new opportunities arise, peasants can easily use surplus time and land to cultivate new crops without reducing their subsistence production of food crops. All over the tropics, smallholder peasants started growing cash crops on a large scale. Hence the term 'vent for surplus': unused factors of production are now employed for the first time.

Through agricultural exports money is introduced into traditional subsistence agriculture. In the beginning peasants produce food crops for their own needs and produce additional cash crops in their spare time. They have one leg in the subsistence economy and another in the money economy. The sale of their export crops provides them with money with which to buy imported manufactured goods. Later some peasants specialise in production of export crops and others in food crops, which are sold to those specialising in non-food crops. Thus the money economy penetrates deeper into the traditional peasant economy (Myint, 1980: ch. 2).

Compulsion also played an important role in the expansion of peasant exports. Under colonial rule peasants were sometimes forced to grow cash crops, as under the cultivation system in the Netherlands Indies. Or they had to grow cash crops in order meet their financial tax obligations. Another source of agricultural exports was large-scale plantations owned by colonial expatriates. Unskilled labour was recruited from densely populated areas and set to work on these plantations.

Arthur Lewis has analysed the factors that explain why some countries benefited so much more than others from the new export opportunities (Lewis, 1970). The most important of these factors were the following: (1) establishment of internal law and order; (2) availability of surplus land; (3) access to surplus land; (4) availability of water; (5) government policy.

Internal pacification and the maintenance of law and order are among the most important prerequisites for expansion of trade and markets (see Chapter 11). Second in importance are the availability of sufficient water and land. Peasants will only start producing for export if there is still unused farmland or if they can easily increase the number of crops harvested per acre. Land tenure systems are also important. Latin American countries had abundant land but systems of large landownership restricted the access to land for peasants. Large landowners could also have produced export products on their plantations; but absentee landlords did not always do so. Another factor affecting export growth was government policy. Governments determined who had access to land. Governments were responsible for the construction of infrastructure.

The most rapid expansion of exports was to be found in countries with abundant land and large-scale immigration, such as Malaysia, Brazil and Ceylon, or countries with sufficient land and surplus labour, such as Thailand (Manarungsan, 1989), Burma, Colombia and Ghana. Slowest export growth could be observed in densely populated regions such as India and Java where land was scarce, or in countries where the government left monopolies in landownership unchallenged (Venezuela and the Philippines).

Lewis explicitly excludes differences in entrepreneurial talents and attitudes as an explanation of export performance. Wherever peasants in developing countries had opportunities to improve their economic situation permanently by producing for export, they were eager to take them.

8.5.4   Why disappointing industrialisation?

On balance, the 1870–1913 period was a dynamic period for developing countries, with rapid increases in investment, education and per capita income and the emergence of a modern sector of commercial agriculture and mining (Lewis, 1978a; Maddison, 1989). The conditions for investment in industry and infrastructure seemed to be quite favourable. Nevertheless, industrialisation made surprisingly little headway in this period, in spite of favourable initial conditions. Only a few countries such as Brazil, Ceylon, India and Colombia experienced some measure of industrialisation. How can this lack of structural transformation be explained?

According to Lewis, the most important answer lies in the overwhelming profitability of agricultural exports. The incentive to embark on a difficult process of industrialisation was not very great when agricultural exports were such an easy alternative. Also, foreign trading houses had vested interests in imports and exports and resisted attempts at industrialisation. They were supported by agricultural oligarchies, whose power and influence were threatened by industrialisation. Finally, Lewis believes it takes at least one generation to grow a class of domestic industrial entrepreneurs in a country without an industrial tradition. Industrial entrepreneurship is less easily available than agricultural entrepreneurship. Basically, Lewis argued that comparative advantage locked developing countries into their specialisation in primary exports.

More than Lewis, other authors emphasise the opposition of colonial authorities to industrialisation and the destructive impact of international competition on traditional handicraft industries in such countries as India. Instead of impeding industrialisation, governments could have protected domestic industries and could have invested more in infrastructure and education. In most colonies governments did too little in these areas. In independent Latin American countries industrialisation was hampered by the political influence of groups with interests in agriculture and foreign trade.

All in all, the contributions from agricultural exports to industrialisation were disappointing. Nevertheless, Lewis argues that important improvements were realised in this period in the fields of education, infrastructure and industrialisation. Though more could have been done, he concludes that the foundations of modern economic development in developing countries were laid during this period.

8.5.5   Can primary exports function as the engine of growth?

The vent for surplus theory extends our understanding of the process of economic development in a particular period in history. The vent for surplus theory is a typically classical economic theory focusing on the availability of unutilised factors of production, which may be employed in the process of economic development. Production of cash crops can be expanded, with no loss in food production.

Vent for surplus theories are part of a wider category of theories that emphasise the potentially positive contributions of primary mining and agricultural exports. Because of increasing pressure of population, vent for surplus no longer represents a viable option for most developing countries. Land has become scarce and in most countries available agricultural land has been taken into use. When the factors of production are fully employed, new exports can only be generated by either switching resources from one line of production to another or by increasing the productivity of resources, through investment, increase efficiency or technological change.[17]

Potential benefits of primary exports are summarised in Box 8.2 (Gillis *et al.*, 1992: pp. 421–3; Lord, 1989; Lundahl, 1985; Thoburn, 1977).

Improved utilisation of existing factors of production

Exports result in improved utilisation of existing production factors. If there are surpluses of land or labour, as in the *vent for surplus model*, export demand provides a stimulus to employ the unused production factors. If production factors are already fully utilised, exports may result in a more efficient allocation of production factors as countries specialise in products in which they have a comparative advantage (*static comparative advantage*).

---

17 In contrast to classical theories, neoclassical theories assume that all resources are fully employed and focus on the efficiency of the allocation of resources.

> **Box 8.2 Primary exports as an engine of growth**
> The potential benefits of primary exports include:
> - Improved utilisation of existing factors of production:
>   - Utilising hitherto unused production factors: *vent for surplus*.
>   - More efficient use of available production factors: *static comparative advantage*.
> - Dynamic comparative advantages:
>   - Increased supply of production factors.
>   - Inflow of investment.
>   - Growth of market size.
>   - Increasing returns to scale.
>   - Exposure to international competition.
> - Easing of foreign exchange constraints.
> - Linkages:
>   - Forward and backward linkages.
>   - Consumption linkages.
>   - Fiscal linkages.

Dynamic comparative advantages

Entry into world export markets expands the size of the potential market. The increase in export opportunities for mining and agricultural products encourages an inflow of foreign capital, increases in domestic savings and immigration of skilled and unskilled labour. Thus the stock of production factors expands. Specialisation and larger markets allow countries to profit from increasing economies of scale in production. Competition on world markets contributes to increased productive efficiency. Finally, participation in world trade, investment flows and competition on world markets promote the acquisition of new knowledge. This argument has primarily been used for industry, but also holds for cash crops such as sugar or rubber and for mining.

Easing of foreign exchange constraints

Primary exports are an import source of foreign exchange. This allows a country to import to ease bottlenecks in industrial production by importing productive capital goods and intermediate goods.

Linkages

Primary exports can have positive linkages with other sectors of the economy (Hirschman, 1977). One can distinguish the following linkages:

(a) *Forward and backward linkages*

Primary exports can provide a positive stimulus to the establishment of industries that process primary agricultural and mining products (forward linkages). Examples are food processing, textiles, furniture and plywood industries or oil refining. Backward linkages occur, for example, when agricultural exports call forth investment in railways, roads or harbours or when fishery exports stimulate the building of fishing boats or the production of fishing equipment.

(b) *Consumption linkages*

Incomes earned in export production may be spent in the domestic economy. This can provide a stimulus for other activities. This was the historical sequence in most developing countries. Exports revenues created a market for manufactured imports. Later imports were replaced by domestic industrial production in a process of import substitution (Hirschman, 1977; 1988).

(c) *Fiscal linkages*. Taxes on mining and agricultural exports are an important source of government revenue. These means can be employed to finance development in other areas such as infrastructure, industry, or education.

Examples of countries that have experienced major economic transformations fuelled by primary exports in the nineteenth century include the USA, Australia, Canada and the Scandinavian countries.

8.5.6 Export pessimism

In the 1930s, the developing countries that were most involved in the international economy through primary exports suffered most from the effects of the Great Depression. International trade collapsed and the barter terms of trade of primary exports (the ratio of export prices to import prices) deteriorated considerably. These traumatic historical experiences reinforced negative attitudes towards agriculture and stimulated the pursuit of import-substituting industrialisation. After World War II, several theories were formulated that stated that developing countries did not benefit from primary exports and international trade, contrary to the earlier experience of countries like the United States, Australia, and Canada. The key publications were those by Raúl Prebisch (1950) and Hans Singer (1950), followed by a wide range of other authors (Amin, 1974; Bhagwati, 1958; Emmanuel, 1972; Lewis, 1969; Myrdal, 1957; Nurkse, 1962). Trade was no longer seen as an 'engine of growth'. The dynamic effects of comparative advantage in primary production were seen as negative. Export pessimists give several reasons why dependence on primary exports is bad for developing countries (Meier, 1989). These are summarised in Box 8.3.

Box 8.3 Export pessimist arguments
- Stagnating world demand for primary products.
- Deteriorating terms of trade for developing country primary exports.
- Drain of mining profits to advanced economies.
- Instability of prices and export earnings owing to fluctuations in international trade.
- Weak and ineffective linkages in primary production; the enclave export economy.
- Domestic food production is constrained by production for export.
- Primary exports lead to overvalued exchange rates: the *Dutch disease* effects of primary exports.

Stagnating world demand

The growth of world demand for primary agricultural exports is sluggish. Demand for these exports will not keep up with the growth of per capita income in rich importing countries. As incomes rise, the share of food consumption in expenditure tends to decrease.

With regard to non-food agricultural exports, technological advances result in the substitution of synthetic products for natural products like rubber or cotton. Furthermore, technological progress dramatically reduces the amount of raw materials used per unit of output (Hogendorn, 1996: p. 453).

Deteriorating terms of trade

In the long term, export pessimists believe that prices of primary exports fall relative to prices of imported industrial products. The prospects of a developing country which is too dependent on primary exports are unfavourable (Gillis *et al.*, 1992; Meier, 1968; Prebisch, 1950; Sarkar, 1986; Singer, 1950; Thoburn, 1977). There are several versions of the theory of deteriorating terms of trade:

(a) Net barter terms of trade   The first version of the theory of deteriorating terms of trade refers to changes in the ratio of the prices of exported and imported goods (P_x/P_m).[18] The prime explanation of the deteriorating terms of trade lies in the above-mentioned fact that the demand for agricultural products does not keep up with increases in per capita income in advanced countries, while the demand for manufactured goods tends to increase at higher levels of income.

Also, primary export opportunities in developing countries are limited owing to protectionist measures in rich, economically advanced countries (McBean, 1989). Domestic producers in the European Union and the USA are protected from competition from developing countries by a wide range of tariffs and subsidies. Both consumers in rich countries and producers in developing countries would benefit if agricultural protectionism were reduced.

(b) Income terms of trade   Usually, when the price of a product goes down, more of this product will be bought. When decreasing prices (P_x) are compensated for by an increase in the quantities sold (Q_x), total export revenues will increase. The so-called *income terms of trade* are defined as the changes in the ratio of revenues from exports and prices of imports $(\{P_x \times Q_x\}/P_m)$. Improving income terms of trade signify that total revenues from exports rise more than the prices of imports. Therefore a country can afford more imports on the basis of its exports.

However, when a country has a large share of the world market for a given product, an increase in its production may cause world prices to decrease so strongly that total export revenues decrease. Economists say this country is faced by an 'inelastic demand'. Consequently, this country can import less and

---

18 P_x and P_m are indexes of export and import prices.

less, while exporting more and more. Bhagwati (1958) calls this a process of 'immiserizing growth'.

(c) Factoral terms of trade A third version of the theory of terms of trade refers to the rewards for factors of production – capital and labour – in developing countries and the rewards in the advanced economies. The factoral terms of trade are defined as the ratio of export prices (P_x) to import prices (P_m) multiplied by the productivity of the factors of production (Z_x). When increases in productivity are more than offset by declining barter terms of trade, we say there is a downward trend in the factoral terms of trade ($\{P_x/P_m\} \times Z_x$). In principle, the productivity term can refer both to capital productivity and labour productivity. In practice, the debate focuses on labour productivity. Our main interest is in the real value of labour incomes in a developing country, because this is what affects poverty and welfare. If productivity goes and barter terms of trade remain the same, the real value of imported goods a worker could buy with his or her salary will go up.

Another way of looking at the factoral terms of trade is to ask who benefits from increased productivity in export producing sectors. Is it the producers of exports in the developing countries or the consumers of imports in the advanced countries? Under perfect competition and given demand, technological changes or efficiency gains that increase productivity will result in falling prices for consumers. However, in advanced industrial economies, powerful trade unions succeed in translating increased industrial productivity into higher wages rather than lower prices. Monopolistic manufacturers pass on these increased wages in the form of higher prices charged to the consumers in poor developing countries. In developing countries, the immense surplus of labour keeps wages low. Fierce international competition depresses export prices. Thus, according to authors like Prebisch and Singer (Findlay, 1980; Prebisch, 1950; Singer, 1950) the benefits of increased productivity in export production are passed on to the consumers in the rich countries in the form of lower prices. The real value of wages in the advanced countries will increase relative to wages in the export sector of developing countries. The institutional differences between rich and poor countries (trade unions, powerful monopolistic corporations, the oligopolistic structure of international trade) offer explanations for the deteriorating trend in the factoral terms of trade in developing countries and the improving terms of trade in rich countries. Rich countries benefit more from international trade than poor countries. International exchanges are unequal.

A special version of the theory of unequal exchange was formulated, once again, by Arthur Lewis (Lewis, 1969; 1978a). As long as productivity in the traditional subsistence agriculture sector is low, labour will be available at very low cost for export production. This keeps wages in the export sector down. Lewis's theory of the 'factoral terms of trade' predicts that the incomes of workers in the export sector of developing countries will lag behind labour incomes in the economically advanced countries. Competition on export markets translates low wages into low export prices. Therefore, prices of exports will also lag behind prices of imports. Only when labour productivity in food production increases, will labour incomes in the export sector start to rise.

Although this theory has its weaknesses (e.g. the role of demand in international trade is not mentioned at all), it leads to an interesting conclusion: improvement of export prices requires an increase in productivity in traditional food production. This is the theory of the need for balance between sectors in another guise. Productivity in traditional agriculture has to be increased in order to reverse the declining trend in the factoral terms of trade.

Lewis also observes that developing countries concentrate on a rather limited range of primary export products. They export either products that grow only in tropical conditions or products where low wages compensate for the difference in productivity compared to economically more advanced countries.[19] The resulting overspecialisation in a few export products explains in part why developing countries are so vulnerable to export price instability.

Drain of export profits abroad

A slightly different situation exists with respect to mining exports. In mining, productivity is high and minerals and energy sources are in high demand on world markets. Furthermore, the number of producers in mining is much smaller than in agriculture. Producers are sometimes able to form cartels to keep prices high. Thus, the factoral terms of trade for mining should be more positive than for agriculture.

However, the orthodox theory of international trade pays too little attention to the fact that mining and oil extraction were – and frequently still are – predominantly foreign-owned. Foreign investors were the main beneficiaries of productivity increases and export earnings. A substantial part of these profits was and frequently still is repatriated abroad. Plantations producing export crops for foreign markets were also mainly controlled by foreign interests. Profits again tended to be repatriated abroad.

The wages in mines and plantations remained low, owing to the abundant supplies of labour. Thus domestic workers and the domestic economy profited but little from these primary exports. Even if the factoral terms of trade for mineral exports go up, the domestic population does not profit from this in the form of higher wages. The abundance of low wage labour also provides strong disincentives for providing education and training and upgrading the labour force.

Instability of prices and export earnings

When developing countries export a limited range of primary products, they are vulnerable to the effects of fluctuations in prices on the world market.

---

19 Tobacco and cotton are examples of such products. If there had been no slavery in the USA, with its artificially low remuneration of labour, the South of the USA would not have been able to compete in these products.

Prices of primary products are highly unstable. The resulting instability of export revenues is a threat to the overall development of a country.

Ineffective linkages

The forward and backward linkage effects of export agriculture and mining are limited (Gillis *et al.*, 1992; Hirschman, 1958; Horesh and Joekes, 1985). Mines and plantations often form an enclave economy, isolated from the rest of the economy. The consumption linkages are weak, because incomes of workers in export production are so low. Profit incomes may be higher, but these are often remitted abroad. Fiscal linkages are disappointing, primarily because governments do not employ the revenues from export taxes very productively. Often they use them to finance current deficits on the government budget rather than for additional government investment. Export tax revenues allow politicians to postpone painful choices and decisions.

Stagnating food production

Critics of agricultural exports often claim that the production of cash crops expands at the expense of the production of food crops. Land once used for food production is now used to grow cash crops. Traditional food producers are believed to lose their land to capitalist export farmers. As a result of export production, the local population will become more impoverished.

Boserup (1985) points to the fact that in Africa men concentrate on prestigious cash crops, whereas women are usually responsible for food production. As a result of expansion of export production, women have to use more distant plots of land of inferior quality to cultivate food. They have to travel long distances. Since women are forced to combine food production with housework, food production will suffer in the long run. However, according to Boserup, intensification of agriculture production and investment in agriculture offer possibilities for expanding both food production and the production of cash crops simultaneously. Of course, this requires greater attention to agriculture in government policy.

Overvalued exchange rates

The export of primary products, in particular mining and oil products, may lead to appreciation of the exchange rate. Higher exchange rates make exports more expensive and imports cheaper. Thus the prospects of manufacturing exports are diminished. This is often referred to as the *Dutch disease* effect, named after the economic impact of the discovery of enormous gas reserves in the Netherlands.

In summary, export pessimists claim that participation in international trade contributes little to the economic development of poor countries. Per capita incomes do not increase. No savings are generated. The market for domestic industry is not enlarged. Under such conditions, 'trade gives poor countries an opportunity to stay poor'.

8.5.7   Export pessimism and policy

Export pessimist theories gave a powerful theoretical underpinning to the import-substituting industrialisation policies, to be discussed in Chapter 9. They also contributed to the general policy climate in which industry received preferential treatment and agriculture was completely neglected. Primary exports were taxed heavily, without the government providing any additional means for investment, research and development, and infrastructure. Therefore, it is not surprising that the share of developing countries in world trade of primary products decreased (McBean, 1989).

In the international arena, export pessimism triggered a call for a new international economic order (NIEO) in the 1970s. International commodity agreements and policy measures should stabilise and where possible increase the prices of raw materials and primary exports and improve access to developed country markets, so that developing countries could derive more benefit from international trade (see further Chapter 13).

8.5.8   Finding an appropriate balance between primary exports and industrialisation

As we shall show in the next chapter, the results of import-substituting industrialisation strategies based on closed models were in many respects disappointing. Since the 1970s, this led to a renewed interest in the developmental potential of primary exports (Thoburn, 1977). Though not all the arguments of export pessimists have been refuted, the conclusions regarding primary exports have generally tended to be less negative.

The question of the trends in the terms of trade is an empirical one. It should be investigated systematically for different periods, regions and countries. In an exhaustive survey of the available empirical data, Spraos (1980) comes to the conclusion that authors such as Singer and Prebisch overestimated the deterioration of the terms of trade. From 1870 to 1937 net barter terms of trade of primary exports from developing countries deteriorated. However, this deterioration was not as substantial as Prebisch and Singer suggested. For the whole period 1870–1980 no clear trends can be discerned. Thoburn (1977) also comes to the conclusion that there was a certain deterioration of the terms of trade until the eve of World War II. However, by 1950 the terms of trade were similar to those at the end of the nineteenth century. After World War II, developments in the terms of trade varied from country to country. Till the 1960s, the income terms of trade showed marked improvement.

The estimation of the terms of trade involves a number of thorny problems (Spraos, 1980; Sarkar, 1986). First, if the quality of industrial products increases more rapidly than the quality of primary products, the deterioration of the net barter terms of trade of primary products might be overestimated. Second, shipping freights have declined substantially. As imports of primary goods in industrial countries are valued with cost, insurance and freight included (cif) and exports of industrial products are valued free on board (fob), the deterioration of the terms of trade might be overestimated.[20] Third, it depends very much on which products are included or excluded in the calculation of the terms of trade. Terms of trade will be very different when developing country exports of oil products or industrial products are excluded. The composition of exports differs for each country and during each period of time. Among the most striking characteristics of the post-war period is the growth of the share of industrial products in total developing country exports (see Table 3.5). Also, in the 1980s the advanced economies exported more primary products than developing countries did.

Authors like Thoburn, Spraos, Myint and Lewis have concluded that in the long run there has been no systematic deterioration in the terms of trade of developing countries. In recent years, though, there has been a spate of articles in defence of the original Prebisch–Singer thesis (Gillis *et al.*, 1992; Sapsford, 1985; 1988; Sapsford and Balasubramanyam, 2003; Sapsford and Singer, 1998; Sarkar, 1986; 2001; Thirlwall, 1997; UNCTAD, 2002). Using data sets similar to those of Spraos, Sapsford argues that terms of trade were declining in the pre-war period and in the post-war period. During the war years there was a sudden upward shift in the terms of trade of primary products, after which the downward trend resumed. If one combines the pre-war and post-war series in a single series, it seems as if there is no long-run trend. But if one looks at the two periods separately, the downward trend becomes visible. In a recent paper, Sapsford and Balasubramanyam (2003) emphasise that the poorest countries suffer very serious declines in the long-run terms of trade for their primary exports. They argue that their terms of trade are worsened by increased primary exports from industrialising developing countries.

Sarkar (1986) defends the Prebisch–Singer hypothesis against various critical objections (freight costs, quality changes, etc.) and concludes that declining terms of trade for developing countries are a reality. Sarkar pays special attention to the counter-argument that the terms of trade between developing and developed countries cannot be equated with those between primary exporters and industrial exporters. This argument states that industrialised countries also export primary products and developing countries also export manufactured products. Sarkar convincingly shows that in the trade between developing and industrialised countries, primary exports still predominate in the exports of developing countries and manufactures predominate in the exports of the developed regions. He concludes that, at the aggregate level, the terms of trade between primary and manufactured goods are still representative for the terms of trade between developing and developed countries. However, as the share of manufactures in developing country exports continues to increase, this argument of Sarkar is gradually losing its force.

---

20 The debate on the pre-war terms of trade is primarily based on British data.

Grilli and Maw (1988) take an intermediate position. Their newly constructed indices of price movements from 1900 to 1986 confirm the long-run decline of prices of primary commodities relative to those of manufactures. But they qualify Sarkar's conclusion that the terms of trade of primary versus manufactured exports are representative for the terms of trade of developing versus more developed countries. They estimate the average annual decline of the net barter terms of trade of developing countries at less than one third of the decline in the primary commodity terms of trade. They also emphasise the differences between various primary commodities. Finally, they indicate that the income terms of trade of developing countries in the post-war period have been positive rather than negative.

A serious weakness of the modern proponents of the Prebisch–Singer thesis is their tendency to exclude oil, 'as a special case' (Sarkar, 1986: p. 365). There is nothing special about oil exports other than that their prices rose tremendously in 1973 and 1979 and collapsed thereafter, only to rise again since 2001. Another problem is their exclusive focus on net barter terms of trade. To evaluate the pros and cons of developing countries participating in international trade, the income terms of trade are at least as interesting.

Table 8.4 and Table 8.5 present some rough calculations on the development of the *net barter terms of trade* and the *income terms of trade* since 1950. Figures from the IMF *International Financial Statistics* and the UNCTAD *Handbook of Statistics, 2002* have been used to reconstruct long-run movements in the terms of trade, referring to total export products (including agricultural products, mining products, oil products and manufactures) versus total imports. It should be stressed that these tables do not immediately bear on the debates on the terms of trade of primary versus manufactured exports or on the terms of trade of developing countries versus developed countries. Exports to all countries and imports from all countries are included, irrespective of their sectoral origin. The data do throw some light on the general question whether participation in international trade is beneficial or harmful to developing countries. The main conclusion to be derived from these tables is that few laws or general patterns can be discerned. The barter terms of trade for most developing countries in Table 8.4 show a clear net downward tendency during the 1950–2000 period. However, this does not apply to all countries or all periods. Important exceptions include India, China, Taiwan, Brazil and Morocco, which experienced long-run improvements in their barter terms of trade. The aggregate figures for developing countries show gains between 1960 and 1980, declines between 1980 and 1992 and some improvement between 1992 and 2000. In the long run the aggregate terms of trade for all developing countries show some slight improvement.

The long-term income terms of trade show a sharply increasing trend. Even after 1980 the income terms of trade kept improving for most countries and regions. The income terms fell sharply after 1980 in Africa, the Middle East and the oil-exporting countries, but by 2000 they were close to their 1980 levels. For Asia and Latin America they are a factor three higher.

Table 8.4 *Net barter terms of trade, selected countries, 1950–2000 (1980 = 100)*[a]

Country	1950	1955	1960	1965	1970	1973	1980	1992	1997	2000
Bangladesh							100	72	102	90
China							100	96	108	104
India	137	135	140	128	136	163	100	138	158	139
Indonesia							100	48	56	54
Malaysia		121	92	86	81	71	100	56	51	48
Pakistan					114	135	100	76	86	82
Philippines	254	208	213	187	174	165	100	95	96	109
South Korea				114	134	125	100	119	106	87
Sri Lanka	366	364	281	231	168	132	100	103	111	115
Taiwan							100	132	132	134
Thailand		131	127	129	132	194	100	79	77	67
Turkey					160	175	100	111	106	95
Argentina							100	76	82	82
Brazil			122	133	136	130	100	111	155	136
Chile							100	46	47	41
Colombia			63		75	78	100	67	80	88
Mexico							100	32	32	33
Peru							100	48	52	40
Venezuela				20	18	30	100	45	46	65
Congo, Dem. Rep.							100	115	78	77
Côte d'Ivoire						100	100	80	81	84
Egypt							100	58	50	46
Ghana							100	47	52	49
Kenya		187	149	142	152	120	100	80	113	97
Morocco			91	84	92	81	100	102	105	110
Nigeria							100	36	36	55
South Africa	202	172	156	158	155	150	100	97	103	
Tanzania		144	129	114	106		100	59	60	44
Zambia							100	57	64	50
Developing countries			51	56	52	60	100	63	66	67
Africa	74	67	76	80	83	84	100	57	57	72
Asia				87	103	104	100	66	67	68
Middle East			25	21	20	22	100	51	51	74
L. America and the Caribbean				67	69	102	100	61	68	67
Oil exporting countries				16	12		100	47	48	67
Non-oil developing countries			115	118	121	124	100	79	81	78
Industrial countries (=OECD)	108	108	118	120	123	121	100	113	116	112

Note:
[a] Calculated as the ratio of indices of export and import unit values.
Sources: 1950–73, IMF, *International Financial Statistics Yearbook*, 1986, 1990, 1993, 1995, 1999, 2000. 1980–2002: *UNCTAD Handbook of Statistics, 2002*, except for South Africa and Turkey (1980): IMF (2001).

It would seem that the empirical debate on long-run trends in the terms of trade is still undecided. Much depends on the products included in the analysis, the specific countries selected and the kinds of terms of trade examined. In many countries, particularly the poorest developing countries, the barter terms of trade have declined, while the income terms of trade have at best been stable. As industrial exports become more important in developing countries the relevance of the debate on primary exports diminishes. But for the poorest countries in Sub-Saharan Africa, which remain dependent on primary exports, it is still of importance.

The main objection to the declining terms of trade hypothesis is not so much empirical but rather that it has been used as an ideological justification for the continuation of industrialisation policies that have proved to be ineffective

Table 8.5 *Income terms of trade, selected countries, 1950–2000 (1980 = 100)*

Country	1950	1955	1960	1965	1970	1973	1980	1992	1997	2000
Bangladesh							100	98	373	386
China							100	507	861	1082
India	48	56	56	60	78	112	100	79	116	122
Indonesia							100	127	208	257
Malaysia	29	29	35	37		54	100	269	535	678
Pakistan					54	104	100	82	64	51
Philippines	30	40	56	56	70	91	100	49	134	217
South Korea				3	16	46	100	364	682	903
Sri Lanka	214	266	252	195	140	120	100	67	85	82
Taiwan							100	600	690	752
Thailand	18	21	25	39	46	77	100	305	352	350
Turkey					102	171	100	595	1051	1116
Argentina							100	139	288	314
Brazil	28		27	33	53	76	100	230	397	430
Chile				60	133	60	100	131	213	233
Colombia	25	36	29		49	61	100	139	203	249
Mexico							100	149	335	515
Peru							100	62	115	122
Venezuela				35	39	34	100	63	93	141
Congo, Dem. Rep.							100	47	38	38
Côte d'Ivoire						72	100	91	147	146
Egypt							100	63	66	77
Ghana							100	21	28	28
Kenya	26	38	51	102	130	138	100	128	215	197
Morocco	20	31	38	52	68	81	100	178	307	349
Nigeria							100	18	27	38
South Africa	23	32	24	47	59	80	100	92	121	
Tanzania	56	86	127				100	67	80	76
Zambia							100	34	54	54
Developing countries	13		21	25	41	55	100	139	218	263
Africa	19	29	29	38	51		100	59	74	99
Asia				29	40	61	100	166	256	303
Middle East (including Turkey)			10	14	26	38	100	56	68	99
Latin America and the Caribbean	26		37	40	52	58	100	120	222	284
Oil exporting countries				10	15		100	50	63	91
Non-oil developing countries	18		29	35	57	74	100	254	425	494
Industrialised countries	12	18	27	41	67	85	100	185	264	314

Notes: Index numbers of export values divided by index numbers of import unit values.
Sources: See Table 8.4, plus IMF, 2000.

and sometimes disastrous. The general conclusion that developing countries should not participate in international trade because it is detrimental to their developmental prospects is certainly not justified. We will return to this debate when discussing export-oriented industrialisation in the next chapter.

The focus on the terms of trade has distracted our attention from the fact that the share of developing countries in world trade in primary exports has decreased during the past decades. Between 1961 and 1963 and 1982 and 1984 the share of developing countries in global primary exports fell from 63 per cent to 48 per cent (McBean, 1989; see also Svedberg, 1993). Further declines are noted for Sub-Saharan Africa in the 1990s (Morrissey and Filatotchev, 2001). These declines are in part due to agricultural protectionism in the rich countries. However, they are also caused by the fact that developing countries themselves neglected their agricultural and mining sectors. If governments in developing countries had taxed export production less heavily and had invested more in infrastructure and improvement of production techniques in agriculture and mining, developing countries could have maintained the volume of their exports. For example, the share of farmers in Tanzanian export revenues fell from 70 per cent to 41 per cent as a result of export taxes and payments to 'marketing boards' (McBean, 1989). Tanzanian cashew nut exports dropped from 145,000 tons (30 per cent of world production) in the early 1970s to 17,000 tons in the late 1980s, before recovering somewhat in the 1990s (World Bank, 1994). In Zambia, the volume of copper production declined by 60 per cent between 1973 and 1998 (Yamfwa, 2001: p. 65) owing to sustained neglect. Zambia's share of the world copper market declined substantially.

Myint (1980) makes a powerful case that one should not focus so much on aggregate world demand for agricultural and mining products. From a developing country's perspective it is more interesting to analyse the demand for that country's specific export products. A similar conclusion can be derived from the Grilli and Maw (1988) study. An efficiently producing country may increase its share in the world market for products in which it has a comparative advantage at the expense of its developed country rivals (Lord, 1989; McBean, 1989). Also, the total world demand for various more exotic agricultural products (such as kiwis, mangos or lichees) or mineral products such as vanadium, uranium or tungsten seems to increase rather than decrease with income (Hogendorn, 1996).

For countries which in the past could benefit from vent for surplus exports, more investment in agriculture is essential. Vent for surplus is a once-and-for-all effect. With no changes in technology, unused production factors are brought in to use. Once all production factors are fully employed, export growth will stagnate unless there is investment in improved productivity and technological change.

Just like the closed model of development, the open model of development requires choices between investment alternatives in later stages of development. If primary exports continue to be taxed too heavily in favour of investment in manufacturing, one risks stagnation of primary export growth. The alternative is to reinvest part of export revenues in the primary sector. As long as a developing country succeeds in diversifying its export package and does not remain precariously dependent on one or two primary exports, it may still derive considerable benefit from continued agricultural and mining exports, even today.

More investment in the agricultural sector may also help countries avoid having to choose between food production and production for export. Food crops and export crops are often grown in rotation on one and the same piece of land. According to Boserup, more intensive production techniques may expand both food production and the production of cash crops. But this does require investment in agricultural infrastructure (irrigation, water control) and changes in production techniques (Islam, 1989a). In addition, the option of importing part of food requirements using export revenues from cash crops is, of course, also still available.

Though we have argued that industrialisation and structural change are important goals in the long run, the overwhelming priority given to domestic industrialisation over agricultural and mining exports has not always had positive results. Especially in Sub-Saharan Africa industrialisation did not get off the ground, while the primary export sector languished owing to heavy charges, taxes and price regulations (Lensink, 1995; Szirmai and Lapperre, 2001; Yamfwa, 2001). The World Bank report *Sub-Saharan Africa: From Crisis to Sustainable Growth* (World Bank, 1989) stated that export revenues in Sub-Saharan Africa did not only decrease because of unfavourable developments in the terms of trade but they also decreased owing to a fall in the real volume of exports. The report and subsequent publications (ADB, 2000; World Bank, 1994; 2000), therefore, argued in favour of renewed efforts to expand export production of both agricultural and mining products.

Even though the barter terms of trade may be declining, gaining larger shares of primary export markets could contribute to foreign exchange revenues, which can play a role in overall economic development and structural change. Therefore, present-day policy priorities include reducing domestic disincentives for export production, increased diversification of primary exports to reduce a dangerous dependence on one or two primary products and, last but not least, a reduction of agricultural protection in the advanced economies.

8.6   Closed model: interactions between agriculture and industry in later stages of development and structural change

In the previous section, we focused on the relationships between primary exports and industrialisation in the context of an open model. After the negative experiences of primary exporting developing countries in the 1930s and the subsequent rise of export-pessimist theories, the policy orientation shifted towards more closed models. In the next chapter, we will discuss the dominant post-war industrialisation strategy of import-substituting industrialisation. Here, we focus on the relationships between agriculture and industry in closed models of development. The key issue in the closed economy model is finding an appropriate balance between sectors in the course of structural transformation towards a more industrial economy.

8.6.1   Introduction: import-substituting industrialisation in the closed model

In the initial stages of industrialisation a transfer of resources from agriculture to industry is justified. That the establishment of a new industrial sector should receive priority can also be defended. But once the process of industrialisation is under way, policy makers are inevitably confronted with difficult choices between investments in agriculture or industry. Should all resources continue to be channelled towards the industrial sector, or should the agricultural sector receive more priority? Post-war advocates of large-scale industrialisation and the *Big Push*, like Leibenstein, Higgins and Hirschman (see next chapter), argued that industrialisation must be given top priority. This implied that the transfer of resources from agriculture to industry should be continued in later stages of development. Most developing countries have taken this advice and have given preference to industry over agriculture in the development strategies of the 1950s and the 1960s.

8.6.2 Transfer mechanisms

In the process of resource transfer from agriculture to the industry, government policy played an important role. Imposition of taxes was one of the ways to induce subsistence farmers to start producing for the market. They were forced to earn cash money in order to meet their tax obligations. Moreover, taxes skimmed off a considerable part of productivity increases and thus functioned as a kind of forced saving. Prices were kept low artificially by government intervention, for the benefit of the industrial sector. Often governments made use of 'marketing boards' that bought up the entire agricultural production at prices fixed below market rates. In several countries, including China, compulsory deliveries of rice and food grains were used to secure the supplies of food to the urban population. Deficit finance or increase of the money supply provided governments with funds to invest in the modern sector, while the resulting inflation functioned as a tax on agricultural incomes.

Government expenditure patterns were also biased in favour of industry. Industrial activities were subsidised, protected by tariffs, provided with cheap credit and under-priced inputs. Investment funds for agriculture were relatively scarce and credit facilities expensive and limited.

Resource transfers sometimes also took place in the private sector whenever large landowners reinvested their profits in the industrial sector or in infrastructure, while paying their agriculture labourers low wages.

8.6.3 Towards a balance between agriculture and industry

Since the 1960s, a more balanced approach to agriculture and industry was put forward as an alternative to post-war industrial growth strategies (Mellor, 1976). This approach was called the *balanced growth path* strategy (Myint, 1980: ch. 8).[21] The basic idea of the balanced growth path is that the pace of economic development of a country depends on a balance between the rates of output growth in different sectors. When the growth of one sector lags behind the requirements of other sectors, these other sectors will be affected negatively as well. Thus, economic development in a closed economy is determined by the

---

21 In contrast to the crash industrialisation programmes, which were referred to as *balanced growth strategies*.

growth of the slowest growing sector. If agriculture stagnates as a result of the too heavy burdens imposed upon it, this will also have adverse effects on industrial development. When industrialisation fails to get off the ground, this will act as a constraint for agriculture. Just as within industry, there are numerous linkages and complementarities between agricultural and industrial activities. In a closed model of the economy, successful economic development therefore implies that the growth of production in agriculture and industry should be kept in balance (Myint, 1980: pp. 109–10).[22] In the course of the 1960s, countries such as India, Indonesia and China changed course and started paying more attention to agriculture. In many other developing countries the neglect of the agricultural sector continued, despite some changes in official rhetoric.

In the following section, the various interactions between agriculture and industry in later stages of development will be discussed more systematically.

Contributions of the agricultural sector

1. *Food.* The industrial sector cannot continue to grow, unless the production of food stays in step. If food production falls short, food prices will go up. This causes inflation. Inflation will start off a wage–price spiral, which has negative effects on profits and investment rates in the industrial sector. When food has to be imported to meet urban food requirements, this squanders scarce foreign exchange which could have been used for investment. This occurred in India in the 1960s. In this country the attainment of economic objectives was impeded by recurring food shortages, which necessitated food imports (Bardhan, 1984; Cassen, 1978).

In the absence of positive incentives and technological change, farmers remaining in the countryside will not be willing to work harder to produce additional food for the urban population. They will do so only if they can sell their agricultural surpluses at reasonable prices and have the opportunity of buying industrial goods with the money thus earned.

This is one of the essential points of difference between so-called *classical two-sector models* (Fei and Ranis, 1964; Lewis, 1954) and *neoclassical two-sector models* (Jorgenson, 1961; 1967; 1969). The classical approach states that labour can be withdrawn from the agricultural sector 'free of charge' since this labour is being 'wasted' and has little or no opportunity costs. The neoclassical point of view argues that factors are fully employed. One can never withdraw factors of production from a sector of the economy without some loss in output. This means that a transfer of resources from agriculture to industry involves costs. Amongst others these costs include the rewards needed to motivate those remaining in agriculture to increase their output.

Higher prices for agricultural products can contribute to technological progress and productivity increases in the agricultural sector. In the long term,

---

22 Though Arthur Lewis (1954) is the intellectual father of the notion that production factors can be withdrawn from agriculture at little cost, he elsewhere emphasises the need for balance between agriculture and industry (e.g. Lewis, 1969). We have no satisfactory explanation for this seeming inconsistency in Lewis's thought. In the context of agricultural exports, Lewis also stresses the importance of productivity increases in food production.

the resulting increase in food production will help stabilise food prices. The opposite is true when agricultural prices are kept low artificially. This causes food shortages and upward pressures on food prices. For political reasons (e.g. fear of political turmoil) governments start subsidising food for the urban population. In many countries these subsidies are an increasing burden on government budgets.

Of course, the neoclassical assumption that increasing prices would auto-matically result in increased supplies of food can also be criticised. Markets in developing countries do not function perfectly. There are all sorts of sup-ply constraints such as lack of infrastructure, storage facilities or insufficient information (Helleiner, 1992). Nevertheless, the neoclassical critique of the con-cept of costless development has served as a welcome counterbalance to the post-war neglect of agriculture.

2. *Employment*. In later stages of development, the agricultural sector no longer has to supply labour to the industrial sector as in the early stages. In the urban sector there is widespread unemployment and underemployment and an acute shortage of jobs. A new role for a dynamic agricultural sector is to provide additional employment opportunities. China, for example, has tried to discourage migration to the cities and to create more rural employment – both within agriculture and in other sectors of the rural economy (Rawski, 1979).

3. *Agriculture as a source of savings*. Otherwise than in the very early stages of development, the industrial sector no longer depends exclusively on the agricultural sector for savings. Reinvestment of retained industrial profits and urban savings are important alternative domestic sources of savings. But a dynamic agricultural sector can also be a source of savings in later stages of development, provided that a sufficient part of the savings is available for reinvestment in agriculture itself.

4. *Markets for industrial consumer goods and producer goods*. Newly established industries will find it hard to penetrate international markets. They first have to gain experience on their domestic markets. In countries where the major-ity of the labour force is still in the agricultural sector, the size of the urban market is limited. If industrialisation depends exclusively on the urban mar-ket, the momentum of industrialisation will soon falter. An increase in agri-cultural incomes may create a vast internal market for industrial consumer goods, but also for agricultural machinery, implements, industrially produced fertilisers and chemical inputs. In later stages of development this enlarged market provides an important stimulus to continued growth of the industrial sector. Conversely, stagnating agricultural incomes will have adverse effects on the growth of industrial production by constraining the size of the market. Rural poverty can lead to industrial stagnation.

Proponents of the *balanced growth path strategy* also argue that, in balanced growth, industry will be oriented more to the provision in the basic needs of the rural population than to the luxury needs of urban elites.

5. *Primary inputs for the industrial sector*. There are important complementar-ities between agriculture and industry. Agricultural products such as food, wood, cotton fibres or rubber serve as inputs for the food-processing industry,

the plywood industry, the paper industry, the furniture industry, the textile industry or the rubber industry. The first industries to emerge in developing countries are often food processing, beverages and textiles.

The contributions of agriculture discussed here are similar to those in earlier stages of economic development. But there are a number of important differences in emphasis. In early stages of development, supplies of labour and savings are of prime importance, while rural markets are less prominent. The first markets for industrial products are found in urban enclaves. Even the inputs for new industries are often imported (Hirschman, 1988). In later stages of development the agricultural sector becomes more important as a market for industrial products and as a supplier of inputs to industry. The agricultural sector also generates new employment. Finally, the linkages no longer run only from agriculture to industry. Agricultural development becomes ever more dependent on industrial inputs. The domestic manufacturing sector is a potential supplier of such inputs. It can make important contributions to agricultural development.

Contributions of manufacturing to the agricultural sector

1. *Consumer goods.* Just as agriculture provides food for the industrial labour force and the urban population, the industrial sector provides the agricultural population with consumer goods. The possibility of acquiring industrially produced consumer goods is one of the important positive incentives for the rural population to increase its production. There are complementarities in demand not only within industry, but also between agriculture and industry (Myint, 1980).

2. *Agricultural producer goods.* The agricultural sector has an urgent need for industrial inputs, including farm implements, farming machinery, inorganic fertilisers, water pumps, pesticides, herbicides, electrical energy, irrigation systems and industrially developed seeds. In the absence of inputs from the industrial sector, productivity growth in the agricultural sector will eventually stagnate and food prices will start increasing. This is an example of technical complementarities between the two sectors.

8.6.4   The mix of negative and positive incentives in a balanced growth path

In the preceding section it was assumed that higher prices would motivate farmers to increase production. As already indicated, this thesis is not without its critics. Under certain conditions, higher prices will lead to increased rural consumption rather than to investment in productive agricultural capacity.

When governments do not provide new infrastructure, new inputs, agricultural research and development, agricultural credit and agricultural extension, agricultural production is unlikely to respond strongly to price increases (Islam, 1989a). Research in Sub-Saharan Africa shows that the terms of trade between agricultural and industrial products – the ratio of agricultural prices to prices of manufactured goods – can improve, while agricultural production stagnates. Higher relative prices are in fact caused by shortfalls in agricultural production. These shortfalls in turn are the result of insufficient investment in agricultural infrastructure (Bautista, 1989).

Price increases may also aggravate rural income inequality. Those who benefit most from higher prices are the large, market-oriented farmers. Peasants producing for their own consumption will not profit much. Farm labourers and other rural inhabitants who have to purchase their food on the market will be negatively affected by price increases.

In centrally planned economies, like pre-reform China, the government for a long time took on the task of providing capital goods, machinery, energy, irrigation and inputs. The farmers were compelled to provide the urban population with food.

Proponents of a market-oriented approach to agriculture acknowledge the significance of infrastructural investment. However, they argue with some justification that farmers will only make optimal use of the available infrastructure, technology and institutions if price incentives are positive. Thus, newly developed technologies will diffuse only if price relations make it attractive for farmers to apply them (Islam, 1989a).

Many countries have therefore chosen a mix of negative and positive incentives (Myint, 1980). Negative incentives include taxes and compulsory delivery of part of the output. These are combined with positive incentives such as public investment in infrastructure, investment in agricultural research, education and agricultural extension, provision of new inputs and the right to sell all production exceeding compulsory quotas at free market prices.

Japan in the late nineteenth century (Ohkawa and Rosovsky, 1964) and Taiwan and South Korea during the post-war period provide interesting examples of a policy of 'walking on two legs'. In such a policy, both industrial and agricultural development receive sufficient attention. Tax measures and other negative sanctions ensure that the agricultural labour force does not exclusively appropriate the benefits of agricultural development policy.

In Japan, Korea and Taiwan redistribution of land stimulated small and medium-size farmers to increase their investment. There was intensive research on new seeds and new production techniques. Quite some attention was paid to education and the adequate diffusion of new production techniques to the farmers. At the same time, tax measures skimmed off part of the agricultural surplus. Taiwan maintained the compulsory delivery of a portion of the harvest to the urban population. Part of the taxed surplus was invested in the industrial sector; another part, however, was channelled back into the agricultural sector in the form of expenditures for research, development and irrigation.

After the liberalisation of Chinese agriculture in 1978, the terms of trade of agricultural products to industrial products improved very strongly. Agricultural output and productivity soared (Kalirajan and Wu, 1999). However, some observers feared that the increased revenues of farmers would be consumed and that infrastructural investments would be neglected in the long term (Griffin, 1987). Since the early 1990s, agricultural growth has indeed slowed down and the urban rural divide seems to be growing again under the impact of very rapid industrialisation.

In sum, agricultural development is hampered when the internal terms of trade become too unfavourable to the agricultural sector. In the long run this also affects industrial development adversely. However, if the terms of trade swing too much in favour of agriculture, the urban standards of living and wage levels will come under pressure. The strategy of balanced intersectoral growth therefore requires the search for a delicate dynamic equilibrium between the growth paths of the different sectors. Characteristic of such an approach is that one seeks to make optimal use of the complementarities between sectors and tries to realise parallel increases in output and productivity in both sectors. Intersectoral linkages are most effective when industrial activities are decentralised rather than concentrated in a few large urban centres (Ranis, 1989). China is one of the countries which have made major and quite successful efforts to develop rural industries.

In addition to balanced terms of trade between agriculture and industry, policy should aim at a reasonable balance in the allocation of resources (credit, funds for research and development, subsidies on capital and inputs) to agriculture and industry, and a balance in the imposition of taxes and other burdens.

As will be shown in Chapter 10, relatively cheap investments in the agricultural sector may have high payoffs. In the agricultural sector there are possibilities for land-saving investments, which make use of the abundant supplies of labour. Therefore, a more balanced approach to agriculture and industry would also be desirable from the point of view of employment creation. Further, in countries where agriculture still accounts for a large part of national income and employment, growth of agricultural output and productivity will have major positive effects on income per capita.

In Sub-Saharan Africa, GDP is still very much determined by the agricultural sector. Around 2000, for instance, 45 per cent of GDP and 84 per cent of employment in Tanzania was derived from agriculture (see Tables 3.8 and 3.9). The outcomes of industrialisation have been deeply disappointing (van Engelen et al., 2001; Yamfwa et al., 2002). A revitalisation of agriculture in Sub-Saharan Africa may be one of the prerequisites for an improvement of the region's standard of living (Lensink, 1995).

In the course of economic development the industrial sector gains in relative importance, whereas the agricultural sector becomes relatively less important. But on the road to economic development it is important to maintain and improve agricultural productivity and dynamism. A dynamic agricultural sector will also create new rural employment possibilities outside agriculture and it is conducive to sustainable patterns of industrialisation (Ranis, 1989: p. 43).

8.7   Closed and open models and industrialisation

In this chapter, we have discussed two kinds of structural change, one based on primary exports and the other based on a balanced growth path between sectors in a closed economy model. The discussion served to highlight the importance of the agricultural and mining sectors in the wider pattern of growth and structural change.

At later stages of development, the more open an economy, the more domestic imbalances it can afford. In an open economy countries will concentrate on those lines of production in which they have a comparative advantage. The goods in which a country is relatively unproductive can be imported. For example, a country can export non-food cash crops or certain industrial products and import all of its food. Singapore is an example of such a food-importing economy. Other countries will export both food and labour-intensive manufactured products and import raw materials and capital goods, and so on. The smaller a country and the larger the share of foreign trade in national income, the more appropriate an open model of development will be. For large densely populated countries with enormous internal markets like India and China closed models will be more appropriate, but even here there is enormous scope for specialisation and opening up towards world trade.

In the present chapter, the debate on international trade focused on primary exports. The issue of open and closed models of development will be taken up again in the next chapter, where we discuss import-substituting and export-oriented industrialisation strategies.

Questions for review

1. Why is industrialisation considered to be important for development?
2. Discuss four different kinds of sectoral classifications which are relevant for our understanding of structural change.
3. What are the contributions of agriculture to industrial development in earlier stages of economic development?
4. Why is an agricultural surplus often considered to be a precondition for industrialisation?
5. Why is a balance between the agricultural sector and the industrial sector considered to be advantageous for economic development in later stages of development?
6. How do the relations between agriculture and industry differ between earlier and later stages of development?
7. What are the main characteristics of the vent for surplus model of primary exports?
8. To what extent did primary exports contribute to the economic dynamism of developing countries between 1870 and 1913?
9. Give three definitions of the terms of trade and highlight the differences between them.
10. What are the potential benefits of primary exports to economic development?
11. Assess the arguments of the export-pessimists, who deny that primary exports can serve as an engine of growth.
12. Why has the World Bank argued in favour of expansion of primary exports from Sub-Saharan Africa?
13. Why should agricultural stagnation affect the prospects of industrialisation negatively?

Further reading

Simon Kuznets was one of the pioneers of the quantitative study of structural change in the context of modern economic growth. Amongst his many publications we mention: *Economic Growth and Structure* (1965), *Modern Economic Growth: Rate, Structure and Spread* (1966) and *Economic Growth of Nations: Total Output and Production Structure* (1971). Chenery and his associates have investigated patterns of structural change in developing countries. Interesting publications include Chenery, *Structural Change and Development Policy* (1979); Chenery, Robinson and Syrquin, *Industrialisation and Growth: A Comparative Study*, World Bank (1986) and Chenery and Taylor, 'Development Patterns among Countries and over Time', published in the *Review of Economics and Statistics* (1968).

A classic reference for the contribution of the agricultural sector to economic development is Johnston and Mellor's article, 'The Role of Agriculture in Economic Development' in the *American Economic Review* (1961). The same topic is addressed in an interesting collection of articles edited by Eicher and de Witt, *Agriculture in Development* (1964), as well as in a review article by C.P. Timmer on 'The Agricultural Transformation', in the *Handbook of Development Economics* (1988). Also of interest is a book on *The Primary Sector in Economic Development*, edited by Lundahl (1985). The balance between industry and agriculture is the topic of a collection of articles edited by Nurul Islam, *The Balance between Industry and Agriculture in Economic Development: Factors Influencing Change* (1989a).

For the increasingly relevant question concerning the role of the service sector in development, the reader can consult a three-volume compendium of articles edited by Bryson and Daniels entitled *Service Industries in the Global Economy* (1998).

For the debate about agricultural and mining exports some of the classic references include Caves's article on the vent of surplus '"Vent for Surplus" Models of Trade and Growth' (1965) and the studies by Nobel prize-winner Arthur Lewis, *Tropical Development, 1880–1913* (1970) (an edited volume); *Growth and Fluctuations, 1870–1913* (1978a); and the brilliant overview in *The Evolution of the International Economic Order* (1978b). The key publications representing the export-pessimist perspective on the declining terms of trade are Prebisch's *The Economic Development of Latin America and its Principal Problems* (1950) and Singer's article, 'The Distribution of Gains between Investing and Borrowing Countries', in *The American Economic Review* (1950). Important essays on the terms of trade include Bhagwati's article, 'Immiserizing Growth: A Geometrical Note' (1958); Grilli and Maw, 'Primary Commodity Prices, Manufactured Goods Prices, and the Terms of Trade of Developing Countries: What the Long Run Shows' (1988); Sapsford, 'The Statistical Debate on the Net Barter Terms of Trade between Primary Commodities and Manufactures: A Comment and Some Statistical Evidence' (1985); Sapsford, 'The Debate over Trends in the Terms of Trade' (1988); Sapsford and Singer, 'The IMF, the World Bank and Commodity Prices: A Case of Shifting Sands?' (1998); Sapsford and Balasubramanyam, 'Globalization and the Terms of Trade: The Glass Ceiling Hypothesis', (2003); Sarkar, 'The Singer–Prebisch Hypothesis: A Statistical Evaluation', *Cambridge Journal of Economics* (1986); and Sarkar, 'The Long-term Behaviour of the North-South Terms of Trade: A Review of the Statistical Debate' (2001).

Two international organisations responsible for statistics on international trade are the International Monetary Fund (IMF, http://www.imf.org) and the United Nations Conference on Trade and Development (UNCTAD http://www.unctad.org). Statistical sources include *International Financial Statistics Yearbook* and *World Economic Outlook* published annually by the IMF. IMF also posts statistical series on its website, such as the *World Economic Outlook Database* (http://www.imf.org/external/pubs/ft/weo/2004/01/data/index.htm). UNCTAD publishes the *Unctad Handbook of Statistics*, which provides time series of trade and international finance going back to 1950.

9 Industrial development

This chapter focuses on industrialisation experiences and industrialisation strategies in developing countries, in the period since 1945. The chapter opens with a discussion of the inward-looking industrialisation strategies of the post-war period in section 9.2. The common characteristic of such strategies was the pursuit of comprehensive industrialisation behind protective barriers. These strategies were characterised by large-scale investment, high degrees of protection and a key role for government. The strategies were based on closed conceptions of the economy.

As time passed, the shortcomings of the post-war approaches became more apparent. Section 9.3 provides an overview of the various criticisms of the dominant post-war policies. This paves the way for a discussion of alternative approaches in sections 9.4 to 9.7. These include unbalanced growth policies which provide more scope for the market, the balanced growth path approach which focuses on the relationship between major sectors of the economy, support for the small-scale and informal sector and the most important alternative: export-oriented industrialisation. In the discussion of export-oriented industrialisation, the role of multinational enterprises and the emergence of global production chains receive special attention. In section 9.8 attention is paid to the debates between proponents of neoliberal market strategies and proponents of more interventionist industry and technology policies. Outcomes of industrialisation policies are discussed in section 9.9.

9.1   Introduction

Major technological breakthroughs in textile production and the application of steam power in Great Britain in the second half of the eighteenth century made such a deep impression that in the nineteenth century the term 'industrial revolution' was coined to describe them.[1] The emergence of modern manufacturing would lead to dramatic changes in the structure of the world economy and to sustained increases in the growth of labour productivity and economic welfare. Great Britain became the technological leader in the world economy. It became the exemplar for other countries. The race for industrialisation had begun.

The first industrial followers were European countries such as Belgium, which faithfully copied the English pattern, Switzerland, which country concentrated on technologically advanced products and France (Pollard, 1990; Tunzelmann, 1995). In the nineteenth century, the United States followed a different path towards industrialisation based on primary exports, abundance of land and natural resources, and scarcity of labour. Scarcity of labour encouraged capital-intensive production techniques. Technology was taken over rapidly and creatively from the technological leader Great Britain and there was an inflow of skilled labour from Europe. Technological advance was labour saving. Productivity growth in the US was so rapid that this country would overtake Great Britain by the end of the nineteenth century. The US has retained its technological leadership ever since.

Famous latecomers to the process of industrialisation were Germany, Russia and Japan. As argued convincingly by Alexander Gerschenkron (1962), latecomers can sometimes profit from the availability of modern technologies developed in the leading industrial economies, without bearing all the risks and costs involved in research and development. In modern terminology, they profited from international technology spillovers. Gerschenkron coined the term 'advantages of backwardness'.[2] He reasoned that technological developments had tremendously increased the scale of industrial production. Therefore, late industrialisation would have been of an all-or-nothing character. If the conditions were right, once growth broke through in a late developing country, it would take the form of a leap or a growth spurt. The role of governments and large financial conglomerates in late industrialisation was more important than in early industrialisation. Governments and banks invested directly in industries and railways; they played a crucial role in the mobilisation of resources for investment and they were very active in education and technology

---

1 In some respects the term 'revolution' is misleading. It disregards the gradual nature of increases in productive capacity and the continuity with earlier developments in Northwest Europe, in particular in the low countries (Maddison, 1991). In other respects, it is an apt term.
2 Earlier versions of this idea are to be found in the work of Veblen (1915) on Imperial Germany and the Dutch historian Romein (1937), who both tended to stress the disadvantages of technological leadership and its associated danger of lock-in to technological trajectories that could become obsolete.

acquisition.[3] Development-oriented governments set themselves the task of eliminating historical obstacles to industrialisation.

What about the developing countries? As described by Arthur Lewis (1978a; 1978b), from the middle of the nineteenth century onwards the world economy divided into industrial countries and agricultural countries (see Chapter 2). Colonies and non-colonised countries in the tropics remained predominantly agrarian, while the Western world industrialised. Industrial growth in the West created an increasing demand for primary products from developing countries. Technological advances in transport, infrastructure and communication expanded the opportunities for trade. Thus, the so-called colonial division of labour came into being. Developing countries exported primary agricultural and mining products to the advanced economies. Industrial economies exported their finished manufactured goods to the developing countries. Industrialisation became synonymous with wealth, economic development, technological leadership, political power and international dominance. The very concept of development came to be associated with industrialisation.

In developing countries, moves towards industrialisation were scarce and hesitant. Towards the end of the nineteenth century, one finds such beginnings in Latin American countries, such as Brazil, Argentina, Chile and Mexico, and large Asian countries, such as India and China. But developing countries still remained predominantly dependent on agriculture and mining. The groundswell of world industrialisation, which commenced in Great Britain, washed through Europe and the USA and reached Japan and Russia by the end of the nineteenth century, subsided after 1900 (Pollard, 1990). Only in 1945, after a pause of fifty years, would some developing countries rejoin the industrial race.

Between the two world wars of the twentieth century, the negative experiences of primary exporters reinforced the positive connotations of industrialisation. Exporters of primary products were severely hit by the crisis of the 1930s, and the slowdown in world trade. A few countries such as Argentina, Brazil and South Africa profited from the crisis in Europe to build up their own manufacturing industries, providing early examples of successful import substitution. Manufacturing symbolised economic dynamism, agricultural backwardness and stagnation.

After World War II, leaders of newly independent countries in Asia and Africa had the highest expectations of industrialisation. These expectations were shared by foreign experts and advisers from the Western world, as well as by advisers from the communist countries, with their negative Marxist stereotypes of agriculture as a traditional and stagnant sector, representing an outmoded stage of development. Export-pessimist theories served as a further justification for a drive towards industrialisation. Priority was given to large-scale

---

3 With the wave of mergers of the 1980s and 90s, the role of government in mobilisation of resources has become less important again. The resources of the mega-multinational companies dwarf those of many national states and they are able to mobilise financial resources for gigantic investment projects, without any public support.

industrialisation strategies. Policy makers became almost obsessed with industrialisation.

This chapter provides an overview of industrialisation strategies and industrialisation experiences in developing countries. In spite of serious policy shortcomings, we shall see that major advances have been made in parts of the developing world. In the discussion of industrialisation strategies, we shall once more make use of the distinction between closed and open models of the economy, introduced in the previous chapter. We start with inward-looking large-scale industrialisation strategies associated with the closed model. We then move on to discuss alternative strategies, the most important of which is export-oriented industrialisation, based on labour-intensive manufactures.

9.2   Large-scale industrialisation and balanced growth strategies

In the 1950s, the emphasis was on a transfer of resources from agriculture to the industrial sector and the rapid accumulation of capital in manufacturing. In the following sections, we analyse the characteristics and theoretical foundations of post-war large-scale industrialisation strategies.

9.2.1   Economic development with unlimited supplies of labour

In a famous article 'Economic Development with Unlimited Supplies of Labour' (1954), Arthur Lewis has analysed the process of capital accumulation in a closed two-sector model. We have already referred to this article in the context of the discussion of structural change and the relationships between agriculture and industry in the previous chapter. Here we focus on the implications of the model for the process of industrialisation and capital accumulation.

Lewis opens with the statement that the classical tradition in economics has much to teach us about the process of capital accumulation. Following in the footsteps of classical economists, it was Marx who studied the process of capital accumulation in Europe and who focused attention on the dynamic role of the entrepreneurial bourgeoisie in this process.

According to Marx, capitalists exploited workers and appropriated the surplus value of their production in the form of profits. These profits were then reinvested in capital accumulation, resulting in an enormous growth of productive capacity. Surplus value consisted of the value of production of workers minus a subsistence wage just sufficient for bare survival. Given the abundance of labour on the labour market, competition ensured that wages were never far above subsistence level.[4] According to Lewis, there was a similar surplus

---

4 By now we know that Marx was wrong. Wages did rise under capitalism. In the long run the working classes shared in the increase in prosperity.

of labour in densely populated developing countries. The abundant supply of labour would keep wages at a very low level and would contribute to high profits and a rapid rate of capital accumulation.

The sources of unlimited supplies of labour

In densely populated developing countries, the majority of the population was initially employed in the agricultural sector, where labour productivity was very low. Since too many people worked too little land, Lewis argued that marginal productivity was close to zero.[5] Nevertheless, in rural communities traditional forms of solidarity ensured that all members of society would receive sufficient food to survive at the subsistence level. Further, there was also a reserve army of low-paid, low-productivity workers in the informal sector of urban society: household servants, security guards, shoeshine boys, traders, casual workers, handymen, street vendors and so forth.

As soon as the modern capitalist sector of plantations, mines, cities and manufacturing industries offered wages that slightly exceeded subsistence levels in the traditional sector, there was an enormous flow of cheap labour to the modern sector. Thus, Lewis writes that from the mid-nineteenth century to the 1930s some 50 million people migrated from densely populated regions in China, India and Indonesia to find employment in mines and plantations in the modern sector of the economies of developing countries (Lewis, 1978a; 1978b).

Effects of labour outflow on agricultural production and productivity

The outflow of workers from the agricultural sector does not necessarily result in a decline in food production. After all, the marginal productivity of the departing workers is assumed to be close to zero. In other words, they do not really contribute to agricultural production. When they leave, the average productivity of those left behind will go up and the level of production will remain unchanged. Thus there is actually sufficient surplus food to feed the industrial workers in the cities, while enough is left to fulfil the subsistence needs of the rural population.

Effects of labour inflow into the industrial sector

In the modern industrial sector unlimited supplies of labour cause wages to remain at a low level. Thus huge profits can be made. The income distribution changes in favour of owners of capital. If the profits are reinvested in new capital goods, a rapid accumulation of capital leads to growth of industrial production. A crucial condition of the Lewis model is that high profits are indeed reinvested by a class of private capitalist entrepreneurs or by public managers of state-owned firms. Capital accumulation will falter, if profits are frittered away on luxury consumption by extravagant elites, wasted on wages

---

5 Marginal productivity is the extra contribution to production made by the last worker (or hour) added to the production process. If marginal productivity is zero, the last person employed makes no further contribution to production.

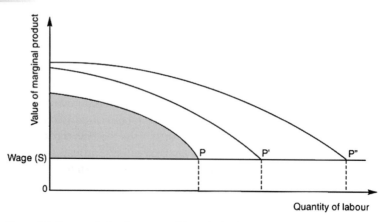

Figure 9.1 Economic development with unlimited supplies of labour.

of non-productive government bureaucrats, used for military purposes or industrial prestige projects, or spent on beautiful temples, churches, palaces or
monuments.

The process of economic development according to Lewis is summarised in
Figure 9.1. At a fixed wage (S), slightly above subsistence level in traditional
agriculture, an unlimited supply of labour is forthcoming.[6] In the initial situation capitalist entrepreneurs will expand production by adding workers to a
given amount of industrial capital goods, until the revenue from the last additional worker (marginal revenue) is equal to the wage level (S). In Figure 9.1,
entrepreneurs will increase production till the equilibrium point P is reached.
Profits – the shaded part in Figure 9.1 – are reinvested in capital goods so that
revenues per worker go up. In the new situation entrepreneurs will increase
production to P'. This process repeats itself until the unlimited supplies of
labour are exhausted and wage levels start to rise. In the phase of unlimited
supplies of labour, capital accumulation and growth in the modern industrial
sector can be very rapid.

There is a second mechanism in the Lewis model, which can be used to accumulate capital. When there is an unlimited supply of labour and a shortage
of capital, labour can be withdrawn from subsistence agriculture at little or
no cost. This labour can directly be set to work to create infrastructure: roads,
viaducts, schools, irrigation works, and so on. An example is Maoist China,
which succeeded in mobilising labour from the rural sector in off-season periods for large infrastructural projects (Rawski, 1979). In the context of 'community development', India tried to mobilise labour during off-season periods for
community projects such as building schools, health centres and digging wells.

According to Lewis, governments can also mobilise funds for investment in
industry by taxing the agricultural sector or fixing prices for food products

---

6 Lewis emphasises the voluntary nature of migration. Other authors argue that coercion also played an
important role (see Chapter 2).

below their market value. Finally, the government may order the central bank to print money to finance its investment expenditures. The resulting inflation works as a tax on agricultural incomes, because the purchasing power of the rural population decreases when prices go up.

The joint element in all these options is the transfer of resources (food, labour, savings) from the agricultural sector to the modern industrial sector. This is inherent in the logic of structural change in the closed model (see Chapter 8). When the great majority of the labour force is employed in agriculture in the early stages of development, the only way to create an industrial sector is to withdraw resources from the agricultural sector and use them to invest in industrialisation.

The key assumptions of the model are that these resources can be transferred at very low cost and that subsistence levels of consumption in traditional agriculture determine wage levels in industry. If agricultural productivity and agricultural incomes were higher, workers would not be prepared to work for the lowest of wages in mines or factories.

9.2.2 Capital–output ratio

An often-quoted passage from Lewis's 1954 article is the following:

> The central problem in the theory of economic development is to understand the process by which a community which was previously saving 4 or 5 per cent or less of its national income, converts itself into an economy where voluntary saving is running at about 12 to 15 per cent of national income or more. (Lewis, 1954, p. 155)

The figures for the required savings rate of 12 to 15 per cent of national income are based on a simple growth model, which relates economic growth to annual investment in the capital stock, assuming a fixed ratio between the capital stock and output (the so-called Harrod–Domar production function). This model assumes that labour cannot be substituted for capital and that capital is the scarce factor of production. As labour is available in abundance in developing countries, the only thing that matters is the rate of investment in the capital stock. The fixed ratio between capital and output is called the *capital–output ratio*. Empirical observation indicates that capital–output ratios are usually somewhere between 3 to 1 and 4 to 1. A ratio of 4 to 1 means that a net investment of $100 (after depreciation) is required to realise a $25 increase in annual output.[7]

The example in Table 9.1 shows that with a capital–output ratio of 3 to 1 and an annual average population growth of 2 per cent – not unusual for developing countries – a savings and investment rate of 6 per cent of net national income is just enough to keep per capital income unchanged. If investment drops to

---

7 One can distinguish between the average capital–output ratio and the incremental or marginal capital–output ratio. Here we assume that incremental capital–output ratio and average capital–output ratio are equal.

Table 9.1 *Capital–output ratios*

	Country A	Country B
National income	1,000	1,000
Savings/investment	60	120
Savings ratio	0.06	0.12
Capital–output ratio	3	3
Increase in output	20	40
Increase in national income	2%	4%
Population growth	2%	2%
Growth of per capita income	0%	2%

5 per cent or less, per capita income will decline. If a country aims at a target growth of per capita income of 2 per cent per year,[8] at least 12 per cent of national income needs to be saved and invested. If the capital–output ratio is more than 3, the percentage of savings has to be over 12 per cent.

9.2.3   Shortage of capital as the key bottleneck in economic development

The pioneering article by Lewis set the tone for the post-war debate on the role of capital in development. Labour in developing countries was believed to be abundant and almost costless (see also Fei and Ranis, 1964). Capital was the scarce factor and therefore the main bottleneck in the process of development. The key policy issue was how to mobilise sufficient resources to accelerate the rate of capital accumulation in manufacturing. In post-war development plans, policy makers made rough estimates of the total amount of savings required to attain target rates of growth, using aggregate capital–output ratios, as illustrated in Table 9.1.

In an economy without much of a modern sector, the agricultural sector is the only possible source of such savings. Therefore, in a closed model the ultimate objective of development policy is to squeeze resources out of the agricultural sector and use them to create a modern industrial sector. Exploitation of the agricultural sector is inherent in the closed model of development.

9.2.4   Does economic development result in increasing income inequality?

The mobilisation of savings for capital accumulation may also have consequences for income inequality. In the closed model of the accumulation process, income inequality increases at the expense of the workers in subsistence

---

8 An increase of per capita income by 2 per cent per year means that per capita income will double in 35 years. A rule of thumb is that a country will double its per capita income in a period roughly equal to 70 divided by the annual average growth rate in percentages.

agriculture and the industrial workers with fixed low wages. The beneficiaries are the entrepreneurs and capitalists in the modern sector, whose incomes derive primarily from profits. The assumption is that people who are trying to survive at subsistence level can hardly afford to save. It is the rich who save out of their profit incomes.[9] The increasing income inequality implies a redistribution of income from poor people, who consume most of their incomes, to rich classes, who are better able to save, thus leading to higher aggregate savings rates.

The increase in savings is not automatic. An ability to save does not necessarily imply an actual willingness to save, which depends on attitudes, culture and the quality of financial institutions. According to Lewis, a prerequisite for an increase in savings is the emergence of a capitalist class of entrepreneurs with a culturally sanctioned drive to save and to invest the savings productively (Lewis, 1954, p. 159). Lewis also notes that governments may perform this function of saving and investing. Then, the socialist government may substitute for the capitalist entrepreneur.

The Lewis model offers a possible explanation for the frequently observed phenomenon of increasing income inequality in the course of economic development. Inequality only starts to decline once labour becomes scarce and wages start increasing in later stages of development.

A similar sequence is sketched in a famous article by Kuznets (1955), which claims that industrialisation and urbanisation initially lead to increases in income inequality, followed by a decline in inequality at later stages of development. Incomes in cities are higher than in the countryside, while the income inequality within urban communities tends to be greater than in rural communities. This implies that a transfer of population to the urban-industrial sector in the early stages of industrialisation automatically results in greater aggregate income inequality. At a later stage of economic development the income distribution becomes more equal as a result of demographic factors, increasing scarcity of labour, democratisation and the rise of trade unions and political lobby groups in the modern sector of the economy. The Kuznets hypothesis, often called the *inverted U-curve hypothesis*, has found support in international comparative research. Many studies find that the income distribution is more equal in rich countries than in middle-income countries and more unequal in middle-income countries than low-income countries (Bacha, 1979; Deininger and Squire, 1996; Paukert, 1973; World Bank, 1985). Whether we may also conclude from such cross-country studies that the U-curve also holds for individual countries over time is contested (Bacha, 1979; Deininger and Squire, 1998; Gillis *et al.*, 1992, pp. 84–98; Rubinson, 1976; Thorbecke and Charumilind, 2002).[10] On the one hand, rapid growth and structural change

9 The standard assumption in economic models is that workers consume all their income and capitalists save all of their profits. In this case, a redistribution of income to the profit-earning classes will increase aggregate savings (see for instance Kaldor, 1956; Sen, 1960; Thirlwall, 1999, ch. 14).
10 F.H.G. Ferreira, Inequality and Economic Performance: A Brief Overview to Theories of Growth and Distribution, World Bank Website on Equality, Poverty and Socio-economic Performance, http://www.worldbank.org/poverty/inequal/index.htm

in low-income countries does seem to be associated with large increases in inequality, as in the case of China, Indonesia or Malaysia since the 1980s. But the relationship between income per capita and inequality tends to differ from country to country. In most advanced economies, income inequality has actually been increasing rather than declining since the 1980s under the influence of globalisation and the pressure on wages levels due to competition from low-wage developing countries.

The proposition that an increase in inequality is a necessary condition for increased saving, economic development and industrialisation has been strongly criticised (Ahluwalia, 1976). The crucial assumption is that the poor do not save and that the rich have a high propensity to save and to invest their savings productively within the domestic economic. However, if profits are deposited in Swiss banks or are frittered away in luxury consumption by extravagant and unproductive elites, then inequality will contribute nothing to economic development but more misery for the poor. In such cases redistribution may even be a necessary condition for increased savings and more productive investments. Several studies indicate that countries with a more equal initial distribution of income grow more rapidly than countries starting with high inequality (Allessina and Rodrik, 1994; Persson and Tabellini, 1994). It has often been noted that the Asian countries that experienced successful industrialisation – e.g. China, Japan, South Korea and Taiwan – were characterised by a rather equal initial distribution of income and large-scale redistribution of land in early stages of development. But in recent years, inequality has been increasing in these countries as well.

9.2.5 The two-gap model of foreign finance: the role of financial flows from abroad

In an open economy, financial flows from abroad are alternative sources of savings. The difference between aggregate savings requirements indicated in national plans and the savings that can actually be mobilised in the domestic economy is the so-called *savings gap*. The savings gap is an indication of the required inflow of foreign capital. This inflow can be supplied either by foreign direct investment, portfolio investment and loans from private banks or by official financial flows, including development aid.

Developing economies not only require foreign finance to supplement domestic savings, they also have an acute shortage of foreign exchange. The capital goods needed to expand manufacturing output are produced in the advanced economies. Foreign exchange is needed to finance the imports of industrial capital goods and imports of semi-finished goods and raw materials that are used as industrial inputs. Foreign exchange can be earned by exports. Typically, however, exports in post-war developing economies are less than imports. The difference between the value of exports and the value of imports is the *trade gap* or foreign exchange gap. This is a second indication of the amount of foreign finance required for growth.

In so-called *two-gap models* (Bruton, 1969; Chenery and Adelman, 1966; Chenery and MacEwan, 1966; Chenery and Strout, 1966), the need for foreign finance is determined by the larger of the two gaps. Two-gap models also provide an important rationale for development aid (see Chapter 14). Given target growth rates, the amount of development aid needed to supplement private capital flows can be calculated.

In the long run, two-gap analysis assumes that the need for foreign finance will become less. If the investment programmes are successful, income per capita will go up and domestic savings will increase. Further, as the economy develops, it will be able to substitute some domestically produced capital goods for imported capital goods and it will start expanding its exports. Thus the foreign exchange gap will also decrease.

Actually two-gap models make reference to a third gap, a *technology gap*. To make productive use of imported capital goods, a developing economy may also need a complementary supply of technical assistance. The capital–output ratio is the inverse of the productivity of capital. As the technological capabilities of a country improve, through investment in human capital, the founding of research and development institutes, learning by doing and technical training, capital productivity will increase and the capital–output ratio will go down. Other things being equal, the amount of investment required for a given growth rate will then tend to diminish. A supply of technical assistance can contribute to increased technological capabilities and a reduction in the technology gap.

9.2.6 Big is beautiful: large-scale investment, government planning and import substitution[11]

Three closely related elements have been prominent in post-World War II industrialisation strategies: a preference for large-scale investment, extensive government planning and intervention, and inward-looking import substitution policies. With regard to scale, it was believed that there was a critical minimum size for the required investment effort. Industrial production is inherently a large-scale activity. Piecemeal industrialisation was destined to fail. If a country was to industrialise successfully, a wide range of industrial activities would have to be undertaken simultaneously, so that all activities would reinforce each other. This was referred to as *balanced growth*. Central planning and regulation by the government was seen as necessary to mobilise sufficient resources for investment and to coordinate all the simultaneous investments in different industrial sectors. Finally, the newly established industries had to be protected

---

11 In *The Economics of the Developing Countries* (1980), Myint has provided an admirable summary of the debate on large-scale industrialisation strategies and balanced growth. The following sections are based on Myint's discussion of these issues.

against competition from powerful international competitors, until they were strong enough to survive. To achieve this, governments erected a panoply of protective policy instruments. The focus of policy was inward-oriented. The aim was to substitute imported manufactured goods on the domestic market, by locally produced goods.

Arguments in favour of large-scale industrialisation

Advocates of industrialisation were convinced that there was a critical minimum size for the investment effort required for successful industrialisation. Several arguments were put forward in favour of large-scale industrialisation.

Rostow (1960) and his followers were of the opinion that sustained economic development could be realised only if investment was increased dramatically within a short period of time (see also Chapter 3). In the 'take-off' phase, an enormous investment boost would set the flywheel of sustained economic development in motion. According to Rostow, historical evidence from the growth experiences of Western countries supported the Lewis hypothesis that investment should increase from less than 5 per cent to more than 12 per cent of net national income in a few decades.

The neo-Malthusian trap, discussed in Chapter 5, also leads to the conclusion that large-scale efforts are required for development (Leibenstein, 1954; Nelson, 1956). This model (see Figure 5.3 in Chapter 5) is based on the notion of a race between population growth and per capita income growth. When the critical minimum level of investment is not reached, an increase in per capita income results in population growth in excess of per capita income growth. As a consequence, income per capita will be forced down, till a low-level equilibrium is reached around subsistence level. Only a big investment push can move a country beyond the point where per capita income growth exceeds the growth of the population. Thus a big push is required for sustained growth.

Important arguments in favour of large-scale industrialisation policies are the so-called *complementarity arguments* (Higgins, 1968; Myint, 1980, ch. 7). The key idea here is that different economic activities will stimulate each other if they are undertaken simultaneously. Government planning and regulation ensures that the various activities are coordinated so that their mutual positive effects are strongest. The emphasis on complementarities in large-scale industrialisation is the main characteristic of *balanced growth* theory (Nurkse, 1953).

In his discussion of *balanced growth*, Myint distinguishes between three types of complementarities: complementarities in demand; complementarities between infrastructure and industry; and complementarities in industrial production.

1. *Complementarities in demand.* In the oldest version of the balanced growth strategy, Rosenstein-Rodan (1943) argued for the simultaneous setting up of a large number of factories for consumer goods. A single factory in an otherwise traditional economy will never be able to survive, as there is no

market for its products. If many factories start operations at the same time, the wages paid to the workers will create sufficient purchasing power. Thus, there will be sufficient demand for the output of all factories together, while a single factory would go bankrupt.

2. *Complementarities with infrastructure.* For industrial production it is essential that there is an uninterrupted supply of raw materials, semi-finished goods, energy and water, and an uninterrupted outflow of the goods produced. Without an adequate infrastructure for transport, communications and energy supply no industry can function properly. Therefore, investment in industry has its complement in investment in infrastructure and social overhead capital. Infrastructural investment is inevitably large-scale in nature. Half a dam will not produce any hydroelectric energy; an uncompleted railway line or highway will not solve any transport problems. Industrialisation, therefore, requires simultaneous investment in a wide range of consumer goods industries and large-scale investments in infrastructure.

3. *Complementarities in production.* Consumers are not the only buyers of industrial output. Industries also supply intermediate inputs to each other. For instance, a car manufacturer needs machines, steel, tyres, spare parts, screws and semi-finished products. Industrial enterprises are dependent on each other via technical input–output relations, the so-called *vertical linkages*. When capital goods industries, intermediate industries and consumer goods industries are set up simultaneously, in the context of a national plan, expansion of output by one industry creates additional demand for inputs from other industries (*backward linkages*). Its output can be used as input by other industries (*forward linkages*). All industries will benefit from one another's demand and the availability of one another's inputs.

The 'Big Push' development strategy

The most comprehensive development strategy within the framework of the balanced growth approach is the *Big Push* strategy (Higgins, 1968; Rosenstein-Rodan, 1957). The big push strategy is a comprehensive industrialisation plan in which large-scale investments in infrastructure, the capital goods sector, the intermediate sector and various consumer goods industries take place simultaneously. All positive 'external effects' can be realised in the form of technical complementarities in the production process, demand complementarities on markets for consumer goods, and complementarities between infrastructure and industrial production.

Arguments in favour of planning and intervention

After World War II there was widespread distrust of the capitalist market economy. Leaders of developing countries associated capitalism with the imperialism and colonialism from which their countries had suffered so painfully. They found inspiration in the experiences of the Soviet Union, which had succeeded in achieving accelerated industrialisation in the twentieth century through central planning. Non-communist developing countries like India also drew up Soviet-style Five-Year Plans and assigned a key role to the government in industrialisation policies.

The basic rationale for planning was that the anarchistic market – where each entrepreneur pursues his private interests and goals – would be unable to coordinate all activities effectively within the framework of large-scale industrialisation. Private entrepreneurs cannot be expected to coordinate their activities with those of others. They are only interested in their own profits, costs and benefits. Whether an investment has positive external effects on the profitability of other industrial activities plays no role in the calculations of a private investor. Thus many investment opportunities would remain underexploited in a market economy. For example, investment in infrastructure is of great importance to economic development as a whole, but not very profitable in itself.

Moreover, it was believed that an active entrepreneurial class had not yet emerged in developing countries – in part owing to the stifling effects of colonialism. Governments had to compensate for the lack of private entrepreneurship. Finally, it was thought that the scale of required investment efforts had become so large that only the government would be able to mobilise sufficient resources for investment.

The conclusion was that the government needed to play a central role in industrialisation, partly by investing itself through parastatal enterprises and partly by coordinating activities of private entrepreneurs through extensive planning, licensing and regulation.

Following the example of the Soviet Union, many developing countries drew up five-year plans. In countries such as China and India, input–output tables were used as a planning tool to set integrated production targets for all sectors of industry, based on their technical interrelationships. The degree of state intervention was highest in the communist economies such as China, Vietnam and Cuba. But, government intervention was also pervasive in developing countries all over the world, in non-communist India, in Latin America, the Middle East and in Sub-Saharan Africa.

In large-scale industrialisation plans, special attention was devoted to the promotion of the capital goods sector and heavy industry. In the history of industrialisation much of technological change in the past centuries has been generated by firms in the capital goods industry, which supply the machinery for industrial production (e.g. Rosenberg, 1982). Development of a domestic capital goods sector was seen as crucial for the supply of capital goods to other sectors and as a source of technological change. Heavy industries such as steel, basic chemicals and cement were seen as key industries, which would provide the intermediate inputs for other industries.

Import-substituting industrialisation and the arguments in favour of protection

The third characteristic element of post-war industrialisation strategies was import substitution. After World War II, there was a strong reaction against the colonial division of labour in international trade, in which developing countries exported primary (unprocessed) agricultural and mining products and imported all manufactured products from the Western countries. By simultaneously investing in infrastructure, capital goods industries, intermediate industries and a whole range of consumer goods industries, it was hoped that developing countries would become more self-reliant. Well-known examples of large countries that have pursued such industrialisation policies include Argentine, Brazil, China, India, Mexico, South Africa and Turkey (Bardhan, 1984; Gereffi, 1990; Kiely, 1998; Maddison, 1992). The underlying goal was to reduce a country's dependence on manufactured imports and international trade.

In order to realise this goal, domestic industries were given as much protection as possible. Imports were restricted by the imposition of high import tariffs, quota and import licensing systems. The effect of these measures is that imports are restricted, domestic prices go up and newly established domestic industries have a chance to survive. Protection also makes it interesting for foreign multinational companies to invest in a country, because they may thus penetrate or even capture a protected domestic market. Protection through tariffs on final products affects the prices of industrial outputs (*nominal protection*). But protection can also aim at making inputs cheaper, either through subsidies to producers or by maintaining overvalued exchange rates. The *effective rate of protection* which takes into account both input and output prices is usually much higher than the nominal rate of protection.[12] Import-substituting industries are also supported by subsidies on investment, preferential access to investment funds, provision of cheap energy, raw materials and other inputs at below market prices, access to cheap credit, various tax benefits and absorption of losses by the central government. Overvalued exchange rates also make imported capital goods and intermediate inputs cheaper. This complex of policy measures is called *import-substituting industrialisation* (ISI). It discriminates in favour of import-substituting industries, discourages imports and discriminates against exporters of industrial and primary goods through taxation and overvalued exchange rates.

Two stages of import substitution can be distinguished: *primary import substitution* and *secondary import substitution*. Primary import substitution focuses on replacing imported consumer goods by domestically produced consumer goods. Secondary import substitution aims at deepening the industrial structure by substituting imported intermediates and capital goods by domestically produced intermediates and capital goods. The first phase is easier than the second one (Furtado, 1976).

Arguments in favour of protection

The chief justification for protection is the *infant industry* argument. Newly established enterprises in developing countries are unable to compete with

---

12 The effective rate of protection ERP is calculated as $ERP = \frac{P_w t_0 - C_w t_i}{P_w - C_w}$, where P_w is the world price of a final good, t_0 the tariff on imports of a final goods, C_w the world price of inputs needed to produce the final good and t_i the tariff on imported inputs.

their powerful and experienced international rivals, whether on international or domestic markets. To prevent the newly established firms and industries from collapsing under international competition, they need to gain experience on protected domestic markets. Through learning by doing and realisation of economies of scale these enterprises will gradually become more efficient and productive, till they become internationally competitive and can dispense with protection (Bruton, 1998). Purposes of protection are summarised in Box 9.1.

Box 9.1 Aims of industrial protection

- Providing newly established firms with time to expand the scale of their production and achieve economies of scale.
- Providing newly established firms with time to become more efficient and productive through learning by doing.
- Allowing for the realisation of external economies and complementarities.
- Promoting diversification of the economy, and making a country less dependent on the – presumed – deterioration of the terms of trade of primary exports.
- Reducing a country's dependence on imports.

There is an important element of validity in the *infant industry* argument. In developing countries import substitution is an essential initial phase in the process of industrialisation. Almost without exception, developing countries that have been successful in developing a substantial industrial sector started out with import substitution. Two well-known examples are Taiwan and South Korea, which started with import substitution policies in the 1950s before moving on to manufactured exports.[13]

In the late nineteenth century, the revenues from primary agricultural and mining exports created a small urban market for industrial consumer goods. These goods were imported from abroad. Once these markets had been established, they could be captured by developing a domestic import-substituting industry and protecting it from foreign competition. Especially the Latin American experiences in the 1930s have been quite significant in this respect. When international trade collapsed as a result of the international economic crisis, countries like Brazil and Argentina managed to develop an impressive domestic manufacturing industry. Other historical examples of successful import substitution include the United States in the early nineteenth century and Germany in the second half of the nineteenth century (Chang, 2002).

9.3   Criticisms of orthodox industrialisation strategies

The orthodox industrialisation strategies described above had a number of characteristics in common: large scale, emphasis on capital as the scarce factor in

---

13 The present rules of the World Trade Organization (WTO) prohibit industrial protection. This may make it difficult for newcomers to embark on industrialisation.

development, priority of industry over agriculture, faith in government planning and regulation, and protection of the domestic market.

All these characteristics were rooted in a coherent industrialisation ideology and strategy. In the meantime, however, the initial enthusiasm for unbridled industrialisation has been tempered (Pack, 1988). In some countries industrialisation never got off the ground. In other countries isolated industrial enclaves developed, claiming disproportionate shares of available resources without contributing much to employment or national welfare. Below, the various assumptions underlying the orthodox industrialisation strategies of the post-World War II era are subjected to critical scrutiny.

9.3.1   Shortcomings of the Lewis model

Can labour be withdrawn from the agricultural sector at no cost?

One of the key assumptions in the Lewis model is that there is disguised unemployment in traditional subsistence agriculture. Therefore, labour can be withdrawn from this sector without any loss of food production. This leads to the optimistic notion of 'costless development', where developing countries can freely utilise their surplus labour for industrialisation.

It is certainly true that there is underemployment in traditional agricultural systems during part of the year, but this is highly seasonal. During peak periods in the agricultural cycle – the brief periods of harvesting and sowing – there are often acute shortages of labour. When too much labour is permanently withdrawn from the agricultural sector, agricultural output will stagnate (Boserup, 1965). This is what occurred in several African countries where young males left the rural areas in search of employment in the modern sector, while women and the elderly were left behind to work the fields.

An agricultural worker may have a low marginal product. But this does not mean that he or she does not contribute anything to agricultural output.[14] Agricultural tasks are shared among all workers.[15] Though the average number of hours worked per person per year may not be that high, total food output will decrease when somebody leaves, unless the people remaining in agriculture start working harder. They will only do this if they can sell their surplus production at reasonable prices on the market and can use the additional income to acquire new industrial products. When there are no economic incentives, peasants will produce only as much as they need for their own subsistence. They have no reason to produce a surplus to feed the urban population.

The industrialisation ideology assumes that agricultural surpluses should be transferred to the urban economy. One can achieve this by taxing agriculture in kind or in money, by keeping food prices artificially low through marketing

---

14 In a later article Lewis actually acknowledges this (Lewis, 1983). Still, he maintains that workers remaining in agriculture can maintain previous levels of production.
15 We abstract here from the division of labour between men and women in agriculture (see Chapter 10).

boards, or by printing money for government investment expenditures, which erodes rural purchasing power through inflation. But if the rural population is exploited too heavily, it will have no motivation at all to produce a food surplus for the urban population voluntarily. Frequently, therefore, coercive measures have been used to ensure food supplies to the urban and industrial sectors. In many countries government policy has included the compulsory delivery of food by farmers to the urban population. If necessary, compliance is achieved by the threat or actual use of terror. This option is well illustrated by the history of both the Soviet Union and China. However, both the human and the economic costs are unacceptably high. Such policies may result in permanent damage to the dynamics of the agricultural sector.

Finally, employing labour in the urban-industrial sector involves all sorts of additional costs for housing, transport, equipment and urban standards of consumption. Wage levels in industry may well be substantially above those in subsistence agriculture.

All in all one may conclude that there is no such thing as a costless withdrawal of labour from the agricultural sector. Lewis's classical notion of an unutilised labour reserve available for development should be amended in a neoclassical direction. The neoclassical perspective in economics assumes that production factors are fully utilised. One can never transfer resources from one activity to another without incurring *opportunity costs* in the form of some loss of output. One has to weigh the costs and benefits of a transfer of resources from one sector to another.

Do wages really remain low in industry?

Contrary to the assumption in Lewis's original model, wages in the modern sector are not always determined by the standard of living in rural areas. In wage determination, political considerations and bargaining with powerful urban trade unions play an important role. As a result urban wages in the formal sector of many countries following an inward-looking industrialisation strategy are relatively high. A small labour elite has emerged, consisting of comparatively well-paid employees in protected industries and government. This elite profits from cheap and subsidised food supplies. Political survival dictates that governments in developing countries do not challenge these privileges.

The combination of high wages and subsidies on investment in capital has resulted in a pattern of investment that typically uses too much capital and too little labour. Owing to the capital-intensive nature of production, the modern sector has proved to be unable to absorb the inflow of labour from the rural sector.[16] Substantial urban unemployment has arisen, and many migrants try to survive in the informal sector of the urban economy (see section 9.6). The expectation embedded in the Lewis model that low wages and a high rate of

---

16 It would be not correct to say that there would be no urban unemployment if more labour-intensive techniques were employed. Technological change has made industrial production generally more capital-intensive. However, an inappropriate choice of techniques certainly worsens employment prospects.

reinvestment would eventually absorb surplus labour has not been realised in most developing countries.[17]

9.3.2 Is capital really so important?

Post-war industrialisation strategies emphasised the shortage of savings and investments. Raising the rate of capital accumulation would automatically result in increases in production. Applying fixed capital–output ratios, the levels of investment, saving and foreign finance required to achieve target growth rates could be calculated.

However, the real state of affairs is more complicated. Not all investments are equally effective or efficient. When an Indian steel plant operates at one third of its capacity, the capital–output ratio will be much higher than when it operates at full capacity. When a Tanzanian airport is built without adequate roads leading to it, its contribution to the economy may be marginal. When workers and managers lack the skills, training and education to operate new machinery and technology, capital productivity will be low. The returns to investment in large-scale prestige projects are often very low. When linkages with the rest of the economy are weak or non-existent, investments will not have very positive effects on growth.

During the post-war period, savings and investment rates have increased in all countries, in accordance with the prescriptions of orthodox industrialisation policies. But, the effects on growth have been mixed. The *capacity to absorb investment* differs widely from country to country (Abramovitz, 1989; Myint, 1980). Countries differ in the efficiency of their governments, degrees of corruption, political stability, macro-economic and monetary stability, the capabilities and skills of the labour force and the managers. The levels of schooling of the labour force and the length of experience with industrialisation are of particular importance (Pack, 1988). Some countries in Southeast Asia have shown a great capacity to absorb investments. In other countries, especially on the African continent, investment efforts have had much less positive effects. Critics argue that industrialisation is primarily constrained not by insufficient savings but by lack of sufficient productive investment opportunities.

9.3.3 How important is the scale of investment?

Several authors have criticised the emphasis on the large scale of investment in orthodox industrialisation policies (e.g. Little, Scitovsky and Scott, 1970). Industrialisation is rarely a question of all or nothing. It is more important to select the most appropriate and profitable investments than to invest in all

---

17 South Korea is one of the few countries where labour surpluses have been successfully absorbed.

sectors simultaneously. Myint (1980) has deftly summarised the criticisms of various versions of balanced growth strategies.

Complementarity in demand. When total demand increases due to the simultaneous setting up of several factories and the payments of wages to their employees, this does not necessarily mean that the sales of a single factory will increase as well. If a new factory does not produce more efficiently than traditional crafts industries, it will never be able to sell its products. Also, part of the increased purchasing power of workers may well leak away to other sectors or abroad via the purchase of imported consumer goods. On the other hand, if a factory can efficiently produce goods which are in high demand, it will be able to make a profit, irrespective of how many other factories are being set up. There is always some demand, even at low levels of industrialisation. Thus, the efficiency of investment is at least as important as the scale of the investment effort.

Infrastructure. There is some validity in the argument that infrastructural investment is inherently large scale. But again, it is not a question of all or nothing. There is always some infrastructure present. One can choose between improving a dirt track and constructing a four-lane highway, between small hydroelectric projects or large dams. It takes many years before large-scale infrastructural projects – such as the Aswan Dam in Egypt or the Three Gorges Dam in China – are completed and start paying off. It is far from easy to coordinate such investments with investments in consumer goods industries. There are many examples of infrastructure projects which have not led to more industrial activities. At each stage of development one is faced with having to choose between more and less efficient investments, including the scale and nature of investment in infrastructure.

Big Push. The advocates of the 'big push' strategy avoided the choices between more and less efficient investments by arguing that everything should be done simultaneously: investing in consumer goods industries, capital goods industries and infrastructure. As a result, this strategy denied the scarcity of resources and the need to choose between alternative options on the basis of their costs and benefits. It disregarded the fact that the sheer size of the investment effort may drive up prices of land, labour and capital. The greater the scale, the greater the risk of expensive mistakes and inefficient investments.

Moreover, the emphasis on government planning in 'big push' strategies placed totally unrealistic demands on the administrative capabilities of weak government systems. If there is a shortage of entrepreneurship in the private sector, why should one expect an abundance of such talents in the public sector?

Thus the idea of a big push proved to be too easy. As illustrated by Tables 3.1 and 3.3, high rates of investment do not automatically lead to sustained economic growth. Among others, growth also requires fundamental changes in institutional structures, attitudes, mentalities, increased levels of skills and education and less hostile relations between the public sector and the business community. The balanced growth approach was too optimistic about the possibilities of rapidly constructing a totally new industrial structure from scratch on the foundations of a traditional economy. At the same time the approach was too pessimistic about the possibilities of gradually replacing traditional crafts production by more productive modern industrial activities (Hirschman, 1988, p. 53).

9.3.4   Protection breeds inefficiency

The shortcomings of ISI are summarised in Box 9.2 and discussed below (see, for example, Kirkpatrick, 1987; Pack, 1988; Thirlwall, 1999). Ideally, protection of domestic industries should be restricted to the early stages of production. Infant industries should be protected only when they are in their infancy. Once an industry has learned to produce efficiently and has started reaping economies of scale, protection should be discontinued. Countries which follow the path of protection too long get saddled with deeply inefficient, wasteful and non-competitive industries. When inputs and outputs of such industries are valued at international prices, their net contribution to national income may even be negative. Examples of such inefficient industries, which are unable to survive in a competitive environment, are found in Latin America, South Asia and in particular in Sub-Saharan Africa (Szirmai and Lapperre, 2001; Yamfwa, 2001).

Box 9.2   Shortcomings of import substitution
- Prolonged protection promotes survival of inefficient firms.
- The goal of reduced import dependence is seldom realised.
- The size of the domestic market is too restricted to achieve sufficient economies of scale.
- Import substitution may create domestic monopolies.
- Tariffs and quotas result in domestic distortions and higher prices for consumers for less goods and services.
- Government's regulatory role creates opportunities and incentives for pervasive corruption.

One of the objectives of import substitution is to reduce dependence on foreign imports. This objective is seldom realised. Usually, one type of dependence is simply exchanged for another. The dependence on imported consumer goods decreases. The dependence on imports of raw materials, semi-manufactured goods, capital goods and technological know-how tends to increase (e.g. Athukorala, 1998a). When developing countries try to build up their capital goods industries, they become more dependent on imports of technology.

A third objection to import substitution is that the size of the domestic market is restricted. In dualistic economies per capita incomes outside the modern sector are too low to create sufficient demand. In smaller countries in particular, import substitution will soon reach its limits, but even in large countries such as Brazil the limited size of the market causes serious problems.

A fourth objection is that import substitution may give rise to domestic monopolies, which may lead to even higher prices and more restricted supply. These domestic monopolies have a vested interest in maintaining protection indefinitely and will exert maximum political pressure to resist change. The possibility of establishing monopolies is one of the reasons why protective barriers attract foreign direct investment.

A fifth objection is that the controls involved in import substitution offer opportunities for corruption and collusion between powerful firms, seeking rents, and government officials. Market distortions result in officials having to make discretionary decisions about allocation of import licences or scarce foreign exchange, which makes them obvious targets for corruption. This is one of the key arguments of the political economy approach to rent-seeking behaviour (Lal and Myint, 1996).

A final objection is that large-scale industrialisation policies and import substitution policies allow economies to postpone the necessary choices between more efficient and less efficient industrial activities. A country should not try to produce 'everything under one roof' but rather concentrate on producing what it is best at.

9.3.5   Urban industrial bias

Since the 1960s, there has been a growing tide of criticism of development strategies that favoured industry over agriculture and cities over the countryside, at all cost. The so-called *urban industrial bias* in policy had numerous adverse effects on both urban and rural areas, and on the economy as a whole. Instead, reducing the dualism between modern and traditional sectors, which the developing countries had inherited from the colonial era, orthodox industrial strategies have often reinforced it (Ranis, 1989). Major characteristics and shortcomings of the urban industrial bias in policy are summarised in Box 9.3.

In a great many developing countries in Africa, Latin America and Asia, protectionist policies and discrimination in favour of industry resulted in excessively large-scale and highly inefficient industrialisation, often dominated by state-owned firms. Vast resources were wasted on unprofitable prestige projects. As protected industries could obtain their capital goods too cheaply, production was too capital-intensive and created insufficient employment. Scant attention was paid to the vast numbers of workers in small-scale industry and the informal sector. A small elite of industrial workers came into being. Industrial workers secured their positions through trade unions and political parties and were paid better wages than the rural population and most workers in the informal sector. Inefficient factories suffered from idle capacity, due to inadequate maintenance, lack of inputs, lack of sales or absence of the work force. At international prices their contribution to national income could even be

Box 9.3 Urban industrial bias
- Preferential treatment and protection of industry by means of:
  - Tariffs, quotas, licensing arrangements.
  - Provision of cheap inputs and raw materials.
  - Overvalued exchange rates.
  - Cheap credit.
  - Preferential allocation of investment resources.
- High wages and capital-intensive choice of technology.
- High degrees of inefficiency, resulting in:
  - Low quality of products and production processes.
  - Low capacity utilisation.
  - High costs of production.
  - Negative contributions to national product when inputs and outputs are valued at world prices (in extreme cases).
- Continued dependence on imported intermediate inputs, capital goods and technology.
- Love of size for the sake of size (gigantomania).
- Production of luxury consumer goods instead of production for basic needs.
- Neglect of the agrarian sector.
- Reinforcement of dualism.

negative (i.e. the value of their inputs at international prices was higher than the value of their outputs). Though the aim of industrialisation was to make developing countries less dependent on the advanced economies, in practice the industrial sector remained dependent on imported intermediates, capital goods and technology.

Agriculture and the rural sector were highly neglected. Most attention was directed to the formal urban sector. The prices paid to farmers were kept low artificially by means of a variety of price controls, compulsory deliveries and marketing boards. Overvalued exchange rates hampered agricultural exports. Moreover, revenues from agricultural and primary exports were heavily taxed in order to finance government expenditures. Credit facilities for the rural population were underdeveloped. Farmers could obtain loans only by borrowing from informal moneylenders at exorbitant interest rates. Government subsidies for agricultural investment were scarce. The bulk of public facilities – schools, health centres, and so forth – were located in the cities.

All these factors together had adverse effects on the agricultural sector and resulted in stagnating agricultural production and productivity. Owing to the systematic neglect of agriculture, many Sub-Saharan African countries that had been self-supporting in food, became dependent on imports of foodstuffs. The same was true in Asia for India and Bangladesh and in Latin America for the former food exporters Argentina and Chile. The lopsided focus on industrialisation reinforced the economic *dualism* between the modern industrial sector and the stagnating rural sector. The stagnation of agriculture acted as a brake on industrial development. From the 1970s onwards, arguments were advanced for a more healthy balance between the agricultural and industrial sectors (Bos, 1984). These arguments have already been touched upon in the previous chapter.

In an interesting paper on the Chinese industrial experience, Lin, Cai and Li (2000) show how the various elements of orthodox industrial strategy hang together. A capital-intensive, heavy-industry-oriented development strategy requires vast amounts of capital, which cannot be raised in a market economy. Distorted macro-policies are required to make heavy-industry projects profitable (which they are not at market rates). These policies include low interest rates, overvalued exchange rates to cheapen imports, a policy of low input prices for energy, raw materials and transportation, and low nominal wage rates for workers.[18] The assumption was that low prices would create profits large enough to repay loans and to reinvest. Private enterprises soon had to be nationalised, because private entrepreneurs would not reinvest on the intended scale. This explains the similarities in industrial practice between communist China and non-communist India. The result is a trinity of a distorted macro-policy environment, a planned allocation mechanism, and a puppet-like micro-management system, where managers follow government directives.

9.3.6   Alternative industrialisation strategies

Since the 1960s a variety of alternatives to the orthodox industrialisation strategies emerged in the theoretical debates and in policy practice. These alternatives include: (a) the strategy of unbalanced growth; (b) the balanced growth path; (c) promotion of small-scale enterprises; (d) labour-intensive export strategies; (e) deregulation, privatisation and liberalisation. These alternatives will be discussed in the following paragraphs.

9.4   Unbalanced growth

9.4.1   The function of dynamic imbalances

The 'big push' approach is a typical example of a development strategy that tries to identify prime movers or crucial bottlenecks in the process of development. When the scarce or missing factor – whether capital, education or technology – is made available, development should follow almost automatically. In *The Strategy of Economic Development*, a book first published in 1958, Albert Hirschman argues that this approach is flawed (Hirschman, 1988). It is impossible to draw up a list of the necessary conditions for growth and development.[19] First, there are alternatives to each prerequisite or factor. Second, the presence of a set of prerequisites does not necessarily result in growth.

---

18 Socialist China was more successful than other developing economies in keeping wages low.
19 For example the growth experience of Japan challenged the notion that a resource-poor nation cannot industrialise and that national resources are a prerequisite for industrialisation.

Hirschman argues that attitudes and value systems favourable to entrepreneurship and economic initiative are of crucial importance in the process of development. But such attitudes should not be seen as static prerequisites for development, which have to be in place before things start moving. Wherever economic opportunities arise, entrepreneurship will sooner or later emerge. There will always be individuals coming forward – members of ethnic minorities or of indigenous populations – who will start exploiting new opportunities. However, where economic opportunities are lacking in a traditional society, entrepreneurship and initiative will remain dormant. Thus, Hirschman rephrases the notion of the vicious circles of underdevelopment. Entrepreneurial initiatives are necessary for economic development, but such initiatives will not be forthcoming in a traditional subsistence economy. When large amounts of capital are poured into a traditional economy, where entrepreneurship is lacking, one should not be surprised that the outcomes are disappointing.

The main challenge in devising a development strategy is not the search for missing factors (savings, capital, education, entrepreneurship, natural resources) or the elimination of obstacles (risk aversion, land tenure systems) but rather the identification of pressures and inducement mechanisms that call forth hidden resources and abilities. In principle there is no serious shortage of savings. In early stages of economic development sufficient savings can easily be mobilised. More important is the development of the capabilities to invest savings productively.

The essence of the theory of *unbalanced growth* is that investments are made in strategic key sectors of the economy. These investments cause dynamic tensions, shortages and imbalances, which call forth entrepreneurship and investment in other sectors. As the modern sector of the economy becomes larger and more dynamic, there will be ever-greater opportunities for new investment. This will elicit new entrepreneurship. Thus, growth sets positive virtuous circles in motion.

9.4.2   *Backward and forward linkages*

Like the advocates of balanced growth, Hirschman assumes the existence of various complementarities between economic activities. First, there are purely technical complementarities. When a factory produces reinforced concrete, it needs steel. More indirect complementarities occur in the construction of office buildings. Empty office buildings create a demand for office furniture. Further, there are complementarities associated with economies of scale in production. When the production of good A increases, the costs will usually decrease. Sector B, which uses product A as an input, will benefit from these lower costs. Another sequence is when the production of good A increases the demand for inputs of good C. This may allow economies of scale to be realised in the production of C. Thus C can also be produced at lower cost.

Hirschman's main thesis is that it is neither possible nor desirable to plan all these activities ahead. If we look at an economy at two different points in time, T_1 and T_2, it seems in retrospect that all activities were related in a process of balanced growth. However, in reality the path from T_1 to T_2 is a dynamic one. Shortages and imbalances at one point in time continuously elicit new activities and investments at a later point in time, which create new shortages and imbalances. A shortage of steel for the production of reinforced concrete or cars will create profitable investment opportunities in the steel sector. As the number of factories increases, the need for an adequate infrastructure will grow stronger, and so on. Development policy should create such dynamic imbalances. It is the movement from imbalance to imbalance which calls forth a stream of entrepreneurship and new investment.

Hirschman distinguishes two different kinds of linkages between economic activities: *forward linkages* and *backward linkages*. Backward linkages occur when an economic activity requires inputs that can be supplied by other domestic enterprises. Often, inputs are initially imported. Later local enterprises may emerge which can produce the imported inputs more efficiently in the domestic economy.

Forward linkages occur when the availability of a product, which is an input into another production process, calls forth investment in this other line of production. For example, the establishment of a basic iron and steel industry may stimulate the rise of fabricated metals industries. The availability of agricultural products may stimulate the rise of food-processing industries. The availability of wood supplies in Indonesia stimulated the rise of an enormous plywood industry, and a furniture industry.

Hirschman also makes a distinction between the *strength* and the *importance* of a linkage. Sometimes a linkage is very strong, but not very important because the new activity has a low value added. For example, there is a strong linkage between the production of car parts and the assembly of these parts. But, the value added of assembly is modest and contributes little to national income.

The relation between infrastructure and industrial production is another example of a forward linkage. Infrastructure may facilitate the rise of industries. It is an important linkage, but not a very strong one. The availability of infrastructure is permissive. It allows for other economic activities, but does not compel them. There are many examples of infrastructural investment that did not result in greatly increased industrial activity. Conversely, investments in industry do have a compelling effect on infrastructure, through backward linkages. It is absolutely essential for a factory to have uninterrupted supplies of energy and means of transport. It will exert all possible pressure on the government to realise improved infrastructure in energy and transport. Such pressures can be observed in the industrialisation experiences of Thailand and Indonesia.

An often-mentioned objection to primary export-led development strategies was that the linkages involved are so weak. Investments in mines, oil wells and plantations have only very limited linkages with the rest of the economy. They result in dualist economies, with small modern enclaves oriented towards the international economy and a traditional sector isolated from the modern sector. One of the advantages of industrialisation is that the linkages involving industrial sectors are so much stronger.

In a country with no industry, industrialisation can only start in consumer goods industries delivering to final demand. In early stages of industrialisation, one will therefore find two kinds of industries: industries transforming domestic or imported primary products into consumer goods, or industries transforming imported semi-manufactured goods into final consumer goods (Hirschman, 1988, ch. 6). The first industrialising European countries had no choice but to take the first road. In developing countries that followed this route, textiles, clothing, food processing and construction materials were of significance.

However, present-day developing countries also have the option of assembling or providing the final touches to almost finished intermediate products imported from abroad. This option is increasingly preferred. Foreign investors make use of surplus labour and low wages to transfer assembly activities to developing countries. Hirschman calls this option 'enclave-import industries' since it initially adds little value to the imported inputs and is completely dependent on imports. In the first stage, the linkages with the domestic economy are as weak as those of primary exports. However, in the course of industrialisation one may gradually work one's way back from these so-called final industries to intermediate industries, basic industries and even capital goods industries. When sufficient consumer goods are being produced domestically, there is a growing market for domestic producers of intermediate goods and capital goods and the strength of linkages will increase.

The notion of linkages offers opportunities to investigate the dynamic effects of investments through the use of input–output tables. Such studies help us identify the key sectors in the economy with the strongest and most important linkages. These are the sectors which should receive priority in an unbalanced growth strategy.

While Hirschman emphasises the importance of the physical flows of inputs and outputs from sector to sector, modern authors focus on the importance of diffusion of technology and technology spillovers from sector to sector. Some sectors such as the capital goods industry or the electronic goods industry are seen as dynamic movers. Technological changes in these sectors diffuse to other sectors, either through new types of machinery or through transfers of knowledge (Fagerberg, 1994; James, 1991; Pack 1994; Rosenberg, 1963a, b; Stewart, 1977). This view is an important complement to the older notion of linkages and has received considerable emphasis in the modern literature on technological change and growth (see Chapter 4).

9.4.3   Shift to the market

The theory of unbalanced growth attributes a different and less central role to government in the process of capital accumulation. It marked the beginning of a shift towards markets in development theory. There is less emphasis on the shortage of capital and more emphasis on entrepreneurship and private initiative. Once dynamic imbalances have been set in motion through investment in the key sectors, it is left to the market to call forth investment in other sectors. The government's role is to maintain and stimulate dynamic imbalances and to identify key sectors for investment. Investment in infrastructure receives a lower priority. It should follow rather than precede other activities. Imports are seen in a more positive light than in balanced growth strategies. They stimulate demand and create the opportunities for later import substitution.

Despite the differences between balanced and unbalanced growth strategies, there are also some interesting similarities. In both strategies, complementarities and linkages between industrial activities are seen as important. Unbalanced growth also assumes that the success of industrialisation depends on large-scale efforts, a wide range of industrial activities and acceleration of the investment process. The most important similarity lies in the high priority given to industrialisation. Both balanced and unbalanced growth policies tend to ignore the importance of the agricultural sector and the interactions between agriculture and industry.

9.5   Balanced growth path

In Chapter 8, we discussed the emergence of the theory of a balanced growth path in the 1960s. Like the theory of unbalanced growth, this theory can also be seen as a response to orthodox balanced growth industrialisation strategies. The novelty of this approach is that it focused on the need for balance between evolving broad sectors of the economy, emphasising the need for an end to the discrimination of the agricultural sector. A healthy and dynamic agricultural sector was now seen as contributing to the success of industrialisation. One of the early examples of a balanced growth path policy was that of Taiwan in the 1950s. The balanced growth path reflected a major shift in policy stance. Important countries such as Indonesia, India and China started paying more attention to agriculture and following a policy of 'walking on two legs'. These policies have been remarkably successful.

An interesting variant of the balanced growth path approach is found in rural industrialisation strategies which try to capitalise on the links between agriculture and rural industry. This policy option will be discussed at more length in Chapter 10.

It is worth noting that the balanced growth path theory is still very much a closed economy approach. It analyses the relationships and balances between broad sectors of the economy, from the perspective that balanced investments should be made across all sectors of the economy. Trade relations with the outside world remain outside the picture.

9.6   Medium and small-scale enterprises and the urban informal sector

The notion of scale in big push industrialisation strategies has two different connotations. The first connotation refers to comprehensiveness of the investment programme. One should invest in all sectors simultaneously. The second refers simply to a preference for large-scale plants, employing thousands of workers per plant.

However, the formal large-scale manufacturing sector in today's developing countries is unable to provide the flow of labour from agriculture with sufficient paid employment. In most developing countries, industrialisation so far has contributed only marginally to solving the problems of unemployment.

One of the alternatives to large-scale crash industrialisation programmes was the promotion and support of smaller enterprises and the search for more appropriate small-scale technologies, which were better adapted to conditions in developing countries (Stewart, 1972; 1974; 1977). As time passed it was discovered that smaller enterprises were often more efficient than the largest ones. They tended to choose more labour-intensive methods of production, more in tune with the abundance of labour in developing countries. Several authors emphasised that medium and small-sized manufacturing firms were a major source of dynamism in both advanced economies and developing economies. In the history of the Western economies, small, skill-intensive workshops, machine tool workshops and capital goods firms have played an important role, alongside larger firms (Rosenberg, 1963a; 1963b). Especially, in developing countries, they could play an important role in developing domestic technological capabilities (Romijn, 1999). Taiwan provides the prime example of successful industrialisation based on relatively small firms (Kiely, 1998). Other authors emphasised the complementarities between large establishments and small-scale subcontractors (e.g. Thee, 1997).

Within small-scale manufacturing, one finds both formal and informal enterprises. Alongside formal employment in industrial establishments, commercial services and government, an *urban informal sector* has emerged, where large numbers of people try to make a living in low-productivity activities. The distinction between small-scale and informal activities is not always easy to make (Breman, 1980; Gaillard and Beernink, 2001). But, it is clear that vast numbers of workers work in the small-scale and informal manufacturing sector. For instance, in Indonesia, in 1986, of the 5.2 million workers in manufacturing, 3.5 million workers were working in establishments engaging less than 20 people (Szirmai, 1994).

Migration to the cities

The expansion of employment in the public sector has not been sufficient to compensate for the slow growth of employment in the formal industrial and commercial sector. Still people continue to migrate to the cities, in spite of insufficient employment opportunities, swelling the ranks of the informally employed and the urban poor. Why is this so?

In his well-known model of labour migration, Todaro (1969) argues that the attractiveness of a job in the modern sector is so great that people will migrate to the city, even though the chances of finding a job in the modern sector are slight. They are willing to stay unemployed for years in the hope of finally finding a position in the modern sector. In the meantime they can depend on traditional forms of solidarity (based on family, ethnic or regional ties) which continue to exist in the city.

In one of his later publications Arthur Lewis recognises the growing levels of urban unemployment. The prime explanation for this is the large gap between formal urban income levels and rural income levels. Further, increasing levels of education create unrealistically high expectations. Education is associated with chances of an urban career. Finally government expenditures on health, education, welfare and development are disproportionately concentrated in urban areas (Lewis, 1983; de Soto, 2000).

The widespread feeling that rural life holds little future for young people also plays a role in migration. When young people come in contact with modern lifestyles through mass communication media, the traditional constraints and hierarchies of rural societies become hard to bear. Also, in many countries the economic prospects in rural areas are so poor that people prefer the risks of urban existence to the certainties of rural squalor.

The informal sector

In a society with no formal systems of social security, people cannot afford to be *openly* unemployed. A large *informal sector* has come into being in which people try to make some kind of a living. The informal sector acts as an employment buffer in the urban economy, providing some minimum of employment for the enormous supply of labour coming from both the countryside and within the cities themselves.

The informal sector includes a wide range of activities. In the informal sector one finds soft drinks vendors, tiny food stalls, small traders, street hawkers, household servants, prostitutes, messenger boys, rickshaw drivers, shoeshine boys, casual workers, car attendants, postcard sellers, repair shops, small garages, photocopying shops, collectors of scrap metals, and so forth. This sector also includes small industrial enterprises such as clothing producers, hand weaving enterprises, potteries, breweries, shoemakers, furniture makers and sawmills, to name but a few.

It is hard to give an unambiguous definition of the rich variety of activities in the informal sector. Frequently mentioned characteristics include: labour-intensive technology, low levels of productivity, preponderance of family labour, irregular working hours, restricted use of capital, lack of legal protection and regulation, little formal schooling, absence of book-keeping procedures, few barriers to entry, personal relations with clients, a small and usually poor clientele, lack of access to credit and lack of government support (Breman, 1980; de Soto, 2000; Gaillard and Beernink, 2001; van Dijk, 1980). One of the most important defining characteristics is that firms are non-registered and therefore have no formal ownership rights, legal status or protection.

The term *informal sector* was first introduced by Hart (1973) and it soon penetrated into official terminology. Initially, the informal sector was defined in a purely negative sense: everything that did not belong to the 'modern sector'. This undifferentiated view of the informal sector as a 'buffer' for surplus labour has been criticised at an early stage by Breman (1980). He points to the heterogeneity of the 'informal sector' and to the links between activities in the rural sector, the modern sector and the informal sector. Activities in the informal sector are dependent on and subordinated to those in the modern sector. The distinction between formal and informal is not clear-cut. Formal activities can easily become informalised when competition becomes fierce, while earnings in some informal activities are higher than in the formal sector (Gaillard and Beernink, 2001). The inflow into the informal sector comes from not only the countryside but also the growing urban population. Entry is not as free as is often assumed. Different ethnic or social groups succeed in monopolising certain economic activities.

The attention paid to the informal sector in government policy is inversely related to its size and importance. While large companies have access to subsidised credit and are supported by the government, small firms cannot borrow any money from formal financial institutions. As they are non-registered, they cannot offer capital, housing or fixed structures as collateral. They are dependent on informal sources of credit, where exorbitant rates of interest are charged, owing to the high risks of default. The informal sector is also deprived in terms of schooling opportunities, access to information and technology and government support. Sometimes entrepreneurs in the informal sector are actively hindered by the government (Tybout, 2000).

It has frequently been suggested that the informal sector could fulfil a dynamic function in the wider economy and that policy ought to give it more priority. Government should help provide cheaper credit, management know-how, upgrading of skills, market information and supply of raw materials. Discriminatory regulations should be repealed (ILO, 1972). Recently, Hernando de Soto (2000) has once more emphasised the developmental potential of the informal sector. In his book *The Mystery of Capital* he celebrates the entrepreneurial dynamics of the informal sector and argues that, in spite of poverty, informal entrepreneurs have accumulated substantial assets in the form of non-registered housing, business premises and so forth. For instance, in one of the poorest countries of the world, Haiti, his estimate of the value of untitled urban and rural assets – mainly housing – comes to no less than US$ 5.2 billion. However, the systematic exclusion of people in the informal sector from formal property rights makes it impossible to capitalise on existing assets for expansion of production. In the words of de Soto, the informal sector is a vibrant but undercapitalised sector. De Soto provides impressive examples of the obstacles facing informal firms. For instance, in an experiment in Lima it took 289 working days to register a one-person garment workshop. The cost of registration was no less than 31 times the monthly minimum wage. De Soto argues passionately for legal reform. When legal systems are reformed so as to protect property rights in the informal sector, its entrepreneurial potential will be unleashed.

There is much to be said for these suggestions. But one should guard against wishful thinking. Much of the small-scale and informal sector consists of very marginal activities of people struggling for bare survival. From the morning till night they try to scratch together a living. There is little economic dynamism involved. Lewis's assumption of a marginal productivity not far from zero seems to apply for many informal-sector workers.

On the other hand, other informal activities like small production or maintenance firms could indeed benefit from cheaper credit, technical and managerial support and access to training. They might be able to provide increasing numbers of workers with gainful and productive employment. So more attention for the developmental potential of the informal sector could be worthwhile.

From the perspective of industrial policy, there is a wide range of options to encourage both formal and informal small-scale enterprises. The most important policy priority is to reduce the discrimination between large-scale activities and small-scale activities. Small enterprises should be provided with better access to credit facilities, business support services, subsidies, inputs such as water and energy, technical expertise, technology and education. Cooperation between firms in the acquisition of inputs and the marketing of products on a larger scale can be encouraged. Obstacles facing informal sector activities such as corruption, explicit harassment and lack of legal protection should be reduced. Very small firms alone will never transform a developing country into an industrialised economy. But they definitely have a role to play.

9.7   Export-oriented industrialisation

9.7.1   The shift from import substitution to export orientation

All the strategies discussed so far focus on the expansion of industrial production within the confines of a domestic economy. The underlying model is a closed-economy model. A major shift towards a more open model of the economy is to relinquish the objective of producing a full range of consumer, intermediate and capital goods within the domestic economy. Instead a country should specialise in those lines of production in which it has a comparative advantage and in which it is internationally competitive. These products can be exported to world markets. Other products can be imported. This strategy is called *export-oriented industrialisation*. It is the most prominent alternative to the orthodox post-war model of *import-substituting industrialisation*.

Table 9.2 *Growth of manufactured exports, 1960–2000 (Constant 1995$)*

Country	1960–73	1973–81	1981–96	1996–2000
Bangladesh		7.4	14.2	14.9
China			14.4	20.4
India		5.0	11.1	5.9
Indonesia		7.4	28.4	7.0
Malaysia	2.3	14.1	23.3	12.9
Pakistan		−0.3	12.0	0.0
Philippines	15.2	16.8	14.8	14.9
South Korea	58.4	15.8	11.8	17.4
Sri Lanka	20.4	17.3	16.6	5.8
Taiwan				
Thailand	26.5	17.6	20.2	13.7
Turkey				8.5
Argentina		14.2	4.0	7.9
Brazil	22.1	19.4	7.6	7.9
Chile	−5.3	28.4	14.5	11.1
Colombia	25.1	2.1	8.6	9.1
Mexico	15.8	−2.7	27.7	15.4
Peru	−1.1	34.0	2.9	15.8
Venezuela		3.3	15.5	−4.7
Congo, Dem. Rep.	30.8	−18.2		
Côte d'Ivoire	26.8	11.1	−0.1	28.2
Egypt	9.5	−12.8	11.2	8.0
Ghana	19.0	−5.8	14.1	
Kenya	6.3	2.2	11.4	−7.7
Morocco	8.6	10.9	10.2	13.0
Nigeria	−0.6	−17.2	16.7	−35.7
South Africa	6.4	−1.4	11.2	3.6
Tanzania				21.5
Zambia		10.5	13.1	
Sub-Saharan Africa			9.9	6.0
Middle East & North Africa				
Latin America & the Caribbean		5.3	11.6	11.1
East Asia & the Pacific			13.7	16.2
South Asia		5.8	11.4	4.3
Developing countries			10.7	10.9
World		8.2	6.1	7.5

Note: Manufactured exports in current dollars, deflated by the price index for total exports. In nine instances data were not available for the exact period specified in the table headings. In those case, growth rates were calculated for the periods for which data were available. *Source: World Development Indicators, 2002.*

Given the abundance of labour, developing countries have a comparative advantage in labour-intensive manufactures. In terms of industrialisation the most successful countries were all countries that turned outwards and followed export-oriented policies at a relatively early stage.

The shift from import substitution to export orientation was pioneered by East Asian economies such as South Korea and Taiwan around 1960. In the 1980s, so-called second-tier NICs such as Thailand, Malaysia, Indonesia and the Philippines followed suit. In the 1990s, giants such as India and China turned outwards. Today almost all countries profess to follow export-oriented policies, though with varying degrees of success. Least success has been achieved in Sub-Saharan Africa (Helleiner, 2002; Morrissey and Filatotchev, 2001).

Table 9.2 provides evidence both of the growth of manufacturing exports and the variety of country experiences in different periods. In the period 1960–73,

Table 9.3 *Manufactured exports as percentage of GDP, 1960–2000*
(at current prices)

Country	1960	1970	1980	1990	2000
Bangladesh			2.92	4.30	10.40*
China		1.19	4.63*	12.53	20.36
India	1.64	1.70	2.75	4.01	6.46*
Indonesia	0.34	0.13	0.64	7.95	23.15
Malaysia	8.52	2.58	9.74	35.93	88.12
Pakistan	2.38*	3.97	5.33	10.99	12.61
Philippines	0.66*	1.18	3.73	6.89	48.80
South Korea	0.18	7.24	25.21	24.07	34.19
Sri Lanka	0.28	0.21	4.92	13.24	22.06*
Taiwan					
Thailand	0.31	0.46	5.06	17.07	42.71
Turkey	0.17	0.29	1.14	5.84	10.80
Argentina	0.43*	0.78	2.41	2.54	2.98
Brazil	0.26	0.86	3.19	3.51	5.41
Chile	0.70	0.59	1.55	3.11	4.18
Colombia	0.28	0.81	2.31	4.22	5.47
Mexico	0.68	1.10	0.96	6.74	24.18
Peru	0.55	0.20	3.18	2.25	2.66
Venezuela	0.36	0.33	0.47	3.73	2.41
Congo, Dem. Rep.	0.29*	1.14*	0.68		
Côte d'Ivoire	0.33	1.93	1.45		6.23
Egypt	1.62	2.69	1.46	2.55	1.48*
Ghana	0.10	0.09	0.26	1.51*	4.75
Kenya	1.20*	1.56	2.08	3.53	3.48
Morocco	1.34	1.19	3.11	8.63	14.26
Nigeria	0.29	0.07	0.13	0.31*	0.10
South Africa	3.73	4.12	5.77	4.60	12.94
Tanzania					0.99
Zambia	0.13*	0.09	5.33	1.17*	

Note: * year other than specified.
Source: World Bank (2002), supplemented by World Bank, *World Tables*, various issues.

there is rapid growth from very low initial levels. In the period 1973–81, high growth rates are found both in Asia and Latin America. After 1981 export growth is most striking in Asia, though growth rates in some countries decline in the wake of the Asian crisis of 1997. Since 1981, the growth rates of manufactured exports in developing countries exceed the growth rate of world manufactured exports, pointing to a global shift towards developing countries.

Export intensities are one of the indicators of outward orientation. The value of manufactured exports expressed as a percentage of Gross Domestic Product is found in Table 9.3. It shows a steady increase in almost all the countries in our sample. With the exception of India, Asian countries have the strongest outward orientation. Latin America has far lower export intensities, with the exception of Mexico.[20] In a schematic view of historical developments, one can interpret the rise of import-substituting industrialisation as a response to traumatic experiences with primary exports and open economy models in the period between the two world wars. In turn, the rise of labour-intensive exports

---

20 In interpreting the percentages one should realise that exports refer to the total value of exports, while GDP refers to value added.

can be seen as a response to the shortcomings and disappointments of large-scale import-substituting industrialisation and the closed economy models of the post-war period.

An export-oriented policy makes it more attractive for firms to focus on the international market. In order to achieve this, overvalued exchange rates have to be devalued to make exports cheaper for foreign customers. Protection of the domestic market should be reduced and imports liberalised so that entrepreneurs have more incentives to look abroad. Reduced protection may also raise the efficiency of firms oriented towards the domestic market, as they are forced to compete with foreign competitors. Finally, exporting industries can be supported in a variety of ways, including preferential access to credit, tax holidays, export zones, pay-back of import tariffs on imported inputs and export subsidies.

The prime models of successful export orientation are South Korea and Taiwan and the city-states of Singapore and Hong Kong. The policies these countries have followed differ substantially, ranging from strong interventionism in South Korea to complete laissez faire in Hong Kong, but the common element has been strong outward orientation (World Bank, 1993a; Kiely, 1998). These countries shifted to export orientation at an early stage. Initially, their export success was based on labour-intensive manufactures, based on abundant supplies of cheap unskilled labour. Later these economies upgraded their workforce and production capabilities, moving into much more sophisticated lines of production such as automobiles, shipbuilding or electronics. Acquisition of technological know-how and design capabilities was a crucial ingredient of this upgrading process.

In a well-known extension of the Lewis model, Fei and Ranis have analysed the experience of Korea and Taiwan (Fei and Ranis, 1964; 1976; Ranis, 1988; see also Cooper, 2001). They identify two crucial turning points. The first turning point is the shift to export substitution. Traditional primary exports are replaced by labour-intensive manufactured exports. This greatly accelerates the absorption of surplus labour. The second turning point is the 'commercialisation point' where cheap unskilled labour starts to become scarce and the economy is forced to start upgrading, at the risk of losing its momentum.

In practice, export orientation seldom means that the economy is completely liberalised or that all forms of protection and regulation are abolished (Amsden, 1989; Kiely, 1998; Verbruggen, 1985; Wade, 1990). South Korea, for instance, has maintained substantial degrees of protection and has pursued active industrial and technology policies. More important is the balance between incentives for production for domestic markets and incentives for exports and the transparency of the regulatory measures. If industries producing for the domestic market are protected or subsidised, export-oriented industries should be subsidised to a similar extent (Helleiner, 1995). Furthermore, support should not be given unconditionally. The efficiency and market conformity of protected industries is monitored. Protection and support of inefficient and loss-making activities will be eventually discontinued. In most – though not all – cases, outward orientation implies increased openness to foreign direct investment by transnational corporations (UNCTAD, 2000). In the past, Korea and Taiwan have tended to restrict FDI, as Japan had done before them (World Bank, 1993). But this strategy is less and less viable today. Transnational firms are of increasing importance in export-oriented industrialisation, especially in the second-tier NICs (Athukorala and Rajapatirana, 2000).

Industrialisation in developing countries has almost invariably started with import substitution. A new manufacturing industry must gain experience in a protected domestic market before venturing abroad onto the world market. In his major study of competitive advantage Porter (1990) emphasises the importance of a strong home base for firms as a foundation for entering export markets. But, as discussed in section 9.3.4, too prolonged protection results in an inefficient allocation of factors of production and technical inefficiency (Little, Scitovsky and Scott, 1970; Pack, 1988). The most successful industrialisers among the developing countries switched from import-substituting industrialisation to export-oriented industrialisation in the 1960s (Verbruggen, 1985). Making use of abundant supplies of cheap labour, they concentrated on labour-intensive exports. Export-oriented activities were supported by a variety of policy measures, including subsidies, tax reduction schemes, access to cheap inputs and foreign exchange and export processing zones to attract foreign direct investment. In those branches of production in which they were competitive, owing to low labour costs, they successfully managed to penetrate international markets. In contrast, Latin American countries such as Mexico and Brazil, which had experienced fifty years of rapid growth based among others on import-substituting industrialisation, ran out of steam and stagnated after 1980, having failed to turn outward in time (Furtado, 1976; Maddison, 1989). Since then, the Latin American economies have also turned outwards. But, with the exception of Mexico, their export intensities are still lower than in many of the Asian economies.

There is an interesting debate about the relationship between growth of manufacturing exports and prior import substitution. Do firms producing for the domestic market simply switch to exports in response to changing incentives after completing their learning curve, or are the exporters new firms? On the basis of statistical research, Athukorala concludes that for Sri Lanka, manufacturing exports emerged *de novo* in response to the creation of new incentives after 1977 (Athukorala, 1998b). The experiences of Sri Lanka are similar to those of Taiwan, Malaysia, Bangladesh and Chile. For Turkey, Colombia, Mexico and Tanzania, Helleiner draws the opposite conclusion (Helleiner, 1995). The position of this textbook is that even when the exporting firms and import-substituting firms are not the same, import substitution does represent a necessary learning stage in the development of a national manufacturing sector.

The main advantage of an export-oriented industrialisation strategy is that economic development is no longer constrained by the limited size of the domestic market. Export-oriented countries also tend to make better use of their abundant labour resources, resulting in more equitable paths of development.

The linkages between industry and the rest of the economy tend to be stronger than in import substitution. The tendency towards dualism tends to be weaker. It turns out that the internal balance between agriculture and industry – initially associated with a closed model – is positively correlated with an open, outward-oriented industrial development (Ranis, 1989).

In East and Southeast Asia, the availability of cheap and relatively well-educated labour has attracted massive flows of foreign direct investment. Competition on world markets has contributed to improved efficiency, improved product quality and the acquisition of modern technology.

Of course, export-oriented policies can also be criticised. They have sometimes attracted so-called footloose industries, which temporarily profit from absurdly low wages, tax holidays and unrestricted profit repatriation. These industries – such as textiles and shoemaking – move on, when conditions are better elsewhere, without making a lasting contribution to economic development. Critics have also pointed to exploitative labour relations, lack of domestic sourcing, environmental damage and political repression. Following the line of reasoning of Cline (1982), a recurrent criticism of industrialisation strategies is whether the world market is large enough to allow other economies to follow the example of the Asian Industrialising Countries (Kiely, 1998). Since Cline wrote his influential paper, several countries have broken through as industrial exporters, including the second-tier NICs, Malaysia, Indonesia, Thailand, Sri Lanka and the Philippines. But the number of industrialised developing countries is still limited and it is a valid question whether all latecomers can follow the same route. By and large only twelve major developing countries – admittedly including very large countries – have succeeded on export markets and have profited from large inflows of foreign direct investment.

On the whole, however, in terms of economic dynamics, the record of export orientation has been exceptionally positive. Countries with a strong export orientation have experienced substantially higher growth rates of industrial production than countries that stuck with import substitution (Krueger, 1978; 1984; 1992; Krueger *et al.*, 1989; Pack, 1988; Westphal, 2002; World Bank, 1993a). Countries that switched to export orientation at an early stage, such as South Korea, Taiwan, Singapore, Hong Kong, and to a lesser extent Thailand and Malaysia, experienced rapid economic growth. Countries that pursued import-substitution policies too long, such as Brazil, Mexico, Argentina and India, experienced relative stagnation (Maddison, 1989). Countries that have opened up their economies and turned outwards since the 1980s, and 1990s, such as Indonesia, India, the Philippines and China, have experienced accelerated growth, at least till the Asian crisis.

The choice between import substitution and export orientation depends to some extent on the size of a country. In very large countries such as India and China the case for balanced growth and import substitution is more compelling, provided one maintains a sufficient degree of competition on the vast domestic market. For the small economies of Singapore, Hong Kong, the Philippines or Taiwan a strong export orientation seems inevitable. But even in the huge economies of China and India the choice for a more outward-looking orientation in the 1990s has led to acceleration of economic growth.

9.7.2   Globalisation, foreign direct investment and the role of multinational companies in development

One of the important issues in late industrialisation is the role of foreign direct investment. Though there were important differences from country to country, on the whole the import-substituting model was rather hostile to private enterprise and foreign direct investment. Foreign direct investment (FDI) was strongly regulated and foreign firms could enter domestic markets as only partners in joint ventures with domestic firms and parastatals.

In some of the first export-oriented Asian NICS, such as Korea, Hong Kong and Taiwan, and earlier Japan, it was the domestic entrepreneurs who started to export. But elsewhere the move towards export orientation was associated with increasing openness to foreign investment and transnational companies. According to recent UNCTAD and UNIDO reports (UNCTAD, 2000; UNIDO, 2002), the increases in developing country exports are driven to a very considerable extent by foreign direct investment and transnational companies.

As the share of services in the advanced economies increased, exports of manufactured goods from developing countries to the advanced economies became more and more important. Transnational companies were a major force in this global relocation of manufacturing production.

Rapid technological change has resulted in sharply falling transportation and communication costs and irreversible trends towards the globalisation of production. In the second half of the 1980s, world merchandise trade has been growing twice as fast as world output; in the 1990s it has been growing three times as fast (Kumar, 1998). One sees the emergence of global production and value chains dominated by transnational companies, which locate different parts of production all across the world (Gereffi, 1990; 1999; Gerreffi and Korzeniewicz, 1994; Morrissey and Filatotchev, 2001). An increasing portion of international trade is between subsidiaries of transnational corporations (TNCs). Competition between firms is increasingly based on design, research and innovation, with production being outsourced. Competition between countries is no longer primarily in terms of competitive advantage for certain goods, but rather in terms of comparative advantages in production activities at certain stages of global chains of production. The rise of global production chains goes hand in hand with an increase in global FDI flows, from an annual 170 billion dollars between 1987 and 1992, annually to 640 billion in 1998 (UNCTAD, 2000). In 1998 there were no less than 60,000 TNCs with 500,000 affiliates and a total turnover of 11 trillion dollars. The share of LDCs in foreign direct investment has been increasing, from 17 per cent in 1985–90 to 26 per cent in 1998.

Most of foreign direct investment in developing countries went to a limited number of countries. In 1998, five countries absorbed most FDI: China 27 per cent, Brazil 17 per cent, Singapore and Thailand 4 per cent, Mexico

Table 9.4 *FDI as percentage of GDP and total fixed capital formation, selected countries, 1960–2000*[a]

Country	FDI as % of GDP					FDI as percentage of Gross Fixed Capital Formation (average)			
	1960	1970	1980	1990	2000[b]	1971–5	1981–5	1991–5	1998–2000
Bangladesh			0.00[c]	0.01	0.38	0.0	0.0	0.1	2.1
China			0.21[c]	0.98	4.34		0.9	10.6	10.8
India		0.01	0.05	0.63		0.3	0.1	1.0	2.3
Indonesia	0.23	0.86	0.24[c]	0.96	−0.78	4.3	0.9	4.5	
Malaysia			3.75	5.30	5.22	13.2	11.9	18.5	9.1
Pakistan		0.23	0.27	0.61	0.84	0.5	1.4	4.0	4.5
Philippines	0.40	−0.43	−0.33	1.20	1.79	0.8	0.7	7.3	12.2
South Korea		0.75	0.11	0.44	1.79	1.9	0.5	0.7	7.9
Sri Lanka			1.07	0.54	1.66	0.1	3.0	4.4	4.3
Taiwan				0.83	0.87	1.4	1.5	2.7	4.4
Thailand	0.07	0.61	0.59	2.86	2.98	2.9	2.5	3.7	23.3
Turkey		0.32	0.03	0.45	0.45	1.5	0.8	2.0	1.9
Argentina		0.27	0.88	1.30	4.50	0.1	2.9	9.2	28.4
Brazil	0.91	0.96	0.81	0.19	4.37	5.3	4.3	2.2	24.1
Chile	0.69	−0.88	0.77	1.95	8.03		6.7	13.5	36.6
Colombia	0.07	0.54	0.47	1.24	3.01	1.7	7.9	7.0	17.4
Mexico	−0.29	0.91	0.94	0.97	2.75	3.6	2.2	9.1	10.6
Peru	0.88	−0.97	0.13	0.16	2.76	2.1	0.1	11.8	14.0
Venezuela	−1.42	−0.17	0.08	0.93	4.36		0.8	8.7	20.1
Congo, Dem. Rep.				0.07	0.03	0.2		0.4	
Côte d'Ivoire		2.12	0.93	0.29	3.14	6.2	2.6	1.2	15.8
Egypt			2.39	1.70		0.0	8.4	7.2	5.0
Ghana	0.32	3.06	0.35	0.25	1.22	9.1	4.8	8.1	5.3
Kenya		0.86	1.09	0.67	0.43	1.2	1.3	0.9	3.3
Morocco			0.47	0.64	1.79	0.6	1.3	5.9	0.1
Nigeria	1.26	1.63	−1.15	2.07	3.21	10.3	8.2	23.3	12.5
South Africa				0.00	1.21			3.2	5.2
Tanzania				−0.07	2.09			3.8	13.5
Zambia		−16.60	1.60	6.17	5.88	3.3	5.3	13.9	34.7

Notes:
[a] Foreign Direct Investment is defined as the flow of investment capital into the reporting economy, including equity capital and reinvested earnings. The FDI figures prior to 1975 are based on an older IMF definition and are not completely consistent with later data.
[b] average 1997–2000.
[c] 1982.
Sources: FDI: 1960–74: IMF, *International Financial Yearbook*, 1988; 1975–2000: IMF, *International Financial Yearbook*, 1995, 2001 and *World Investment Report*, various issues.
GDP at market prices at current dollars: *World Development Indicators*, 2002; Bangladesh, Indonesia 1960: World Bank, *World Development Report 1981* (table 3); Indonesia, 1965, World Bank, *World Development Report 1985*.
FDI as % of GFCF: from World Bank (2002), supplemented by IMF, *World Investment Report*, 1992.

6 per cent. But the impact of FDI was also significant elsewhere (UNCTAD, 2000). Table 9.4 documents the importance of FDI in developing countries. Since 1980, the share of Foreign Direct Investment in GDP and in Gross Fixed Capital Formation (GFCF) has increased dramatically. In the period 1998–2000, FDI accounted for more than 4 per cent of GDP in China, Malaysia, Argentina, Brazil, Chile, Venezuela and Zambia. In thirteen countries from our sample the share of FDI in GFCF exceeded 10 per cent. The highest ratios are found in the Latin American economies. In absolute terms China is the largest recipient of global FDI flows.

It is interesting to note that most FDI took the form of mergers with and acquisitions of existing firms, rather than investment in new plant and equipment (*greenfield investment*). The impact of transnational firms is not limited to foreign direct investment. They also interact with domestic firms through a variety of other mechanisms such as licensing, original equipment manufacturing (OEM), provision of brand names and technology collaboration (Cyhn, 2001). The emergence of global production chains is claimed to represent a new technological paradigm (Freeman and Perez, 1988; Gereffi, 1994). In the past location decisions of transnational companies could be explained by the *product life cycle theory* (Vernon, 1966). According to this theory the production of new products and services is located in the advanced economies. As a product and its associated production technology become mature, markets become saturated and competition increases, production will be shifted to developing countries with an abundance of cheap labour. These countries would start exporting.

With the emergence of the global production chain, the nature of comparative advantage shifts. Rather than only having a comparative advantage in certain products, countries compete for productive activities in certain stages of the global production chain,[21] such as final assembly, software development, research and development, production of components, and so forth. Even traditional sectors such as textiles and clothing are subject to rapid technological change (Abernathy et al., 1999; Cooper, 2001). Therefore, there are no safe niches for developing countries. The competitive challenge is intensifying.

The impact of TNCs on developing countries depends on how international transfers of capital, technology and skills build on and in turn affect the development of local markets, skills and capabilities (Dunning, 1993). The outcomes are determined by the interactions between TNC strategies and developing country policies and characteristics. The extent to which a developing country can profit from activities of transnational companies depends to a considerable extent on domestic capabilities, such as skills and discipline of the workforce, the quality of management, production capabilities, technological effort, macro-economic stability, domestic supply and infrastructure, the development of linkages with domestic firms, and the policies and bargaining capacities of governments.

From the perspective of developing countries, transnational companies have both potential advantages and disadvantages. Advantages include: increased competition, acquisition of technology and know-how, stimulus to local entrepreneurship and domestic supply and access to global markets, sales channels and brand names. Potential disadvantages are decreased domestic competition when too many domestic firms are taken over by transnationals, reduced linkages when transnationals source their activities from abroad, and the stifling of domestic entrepreneurship. Lall (1998) notes that advantages of FDI are highly concentrated in a small number of developing countries. These countries are increasingly integrated in the global economy. Other countries lack the complementary capabilities to attract and profit from FDI and are in danger of becoming marginalised. The least developed countries receive a

---

21 Also referred to as global value chain.

negligible part of global FDI (Kumar, 1998). Nevertheless, a recent UNCTAD report on transnational companies concludes that openness to FDI potentially enhances efficiency, manufacturing growth and economic development in developing countries (UNCTAD, 2000). It rejects a return to the restrictive policies of the import substitution period. The current debate now focuses more on the nature of developing country policies for attracting and effectively absorbing foreign direct investment.

9.8   Liberalisation, deregulation and the debate on industrial policy: neoliberals versus interventionists

One of the main criticisms of orthodox inward-looking industrialisation strategies was the failure of state-led industrialisation, characterised by very high degrees of government control, regulation and intervention in domestic and foreign markets (Lal, 2000). While the apparatus of government in developing countries is still weakly developed, the burdens of planning and intervention are much higher than ever before in the history of the advanced economies. Regulation and planning created distorted economies characterised by massive inefficiencies.

Hand in hand with the liberalisation of international trade and the shift towards an export orientation, there has been a strong move towards the market and towards a more limited role of the state in industrial development. In the influential World Bank study, *The East Asian Miracle* (1993), the conclusion was drawn that the success of the Asian tigers was primarily due to liberalisation, deregulation, outward orientation and market-friendly policies, in combination with prudent macro-economic policies. This is referred to as the *Washington Consensus*: a policy package oriented to macro-economic stability, privatisation of state-owned enterprises, elimination of government intervention in markets, cuts in government expenditures, increased openness to foreign direct investment, reduction of tariffs and quota. It reflected a worldwide change in the policy climate and was backed by powerful financial institutions such as the IMF and the World Bank. All over the developing world, countries engaged in market reforms under both pressure and encouragement from the major international financial institutions such as the IMF and the World Bank, but also under the influence of a changed intellectual climate.

In the wake of the *Asian Miracle* study a vehement and still unresolved debate has erupted over the pros and cons of liberalisation versus interventionism. The opening shot in the debate was fired by Alice Amsden in her study of Korean industrialisation (Amsden, 1989; see also Westphal *et al.*, 1985). Amsden argued that South Korea had followed highly interventionist economic and technology policies, targeting sectors for investment, subsidising exports, promoting the rise of large industrial conglomerates (the *Chaebol*) and stimulating technology acquisition and technological learning. In her view, South Korea followed successful interventionist policies focusing on pursuing dynamic comparative advantage by deliberating 'getting prices wrong' in the short run and working towards a gradual upgrading of technological and economic performance.

The authors of the *East Asian Miracle* admitted that governments in East Asia had intervened systematically and extensively. But they argued that the interventions had basically been either market-following or market-friendly. Policy makers withdrew support from sectors and firms that did not meet export targets or were in decline. Generic interventions were invariably more successful than selective interventions, which frequently backfired on a very large scale. They claimed that governments 'cannot pick winners'. They also warned that East Asian policies could not be copied in African developing countries, because the state was insufficiently isolated from pressure groups and clients. It was unable to pursue similar independent and effective policies.

The authors criticising the neoliberal market orientation (Amsden, 1989; Kiely, 1998; Lall, 1990; 1996; 1998; 2000; Rodrik, 1995; 1999; Wade, 1990; Westphal, 2002) countered with a number of arguments. In the first place, they argued that the neoliberals simply misrepresented how extensive both policy intervention and protection had been in Japan and all the Asian NICS except Hong Kong. Re-reading The *East Asian Miracle*, this argument is quite persuasive. In the second place, they argued that in a global economy, characterised by accelerating technological change, industrial and technology policies were required to acquire and maintain competitiveness. Government policy should target promising sectors, which drove industrialisation and gave opportunities for learning, such as the electronics sector or heavy industries such as steel (Amsden, 1989; Fagerberg, 2000). They should actively promote the acquisition of technological capabilities and technological learning (Lall, 1996). Promising industrial activities should be able to profit from infant industry protection of some kind. For Sub-Saharan Africa, Helleiner (1992) argued that market reforms would fail, if retrenching governments failed to invest enough in the relevant infrastructure. Farmers and firms cannot respond to market incentives and higher prices if there are no roads to transport their products to the markets and the whole transport and communication infrastructure is underdeveloped.

The critics of liberalisation were further strengthened by the eruption of the Asian crisis of 1997. The crisis was basically caused by the increased volatility of international capital flows in an open economy. Loss of confidence, outflows of short-term capital and a collapse of the exchange rate had negative effects on real growth in economies which were growing rapidly before the crisis (Hill, 2000). The Asian crisis deeply affected many of the Asian economies, some of which, such as Indonesia and the Philippines, have still not recovered from the after-effects of the crisis. The outbreak of a deep economic crisis in Argentina in 2002 provided another example of the drawbacks of neoliberal orthodoxies.

In an excellent survey article Westphal (2002, p. 314) concludes: 'interventionist technology strategies, designed to accelerate the realisation of dynamic comparative advantage, were responsible for elevating East Asian performance well beyond the level of moderate achievement'. He argues that the present liberal world economic order prevents other countries in Asia, Latin America or Africa from following similar policies. Though not all countries have the same capacity for effective interventions as the East Asian economies, the present policy climate limits their policy options. It limits their possibilities of protecting and nurturing promising sectors and activities. It is important to note, however, that Westphal is not an opponent of globalisation. He is convinced that participation in world trade through industrial exports has been the motor for economic development in a range of successful countries.

The interventionists have made a powerful and convincing case that intervention and active industrial and technology policy have indeed contributed to the success of export-led growth in several East Asian countries. This calls for a profound rethinking of international policies towards protectionism and industrial policy. However, the case for liberalisation and openness still has much to commend it. In China, liberalisation, deregulation and opening up to foreign investment have resulted in one of the most powerful growth spurts in economic history (Maddison, 1998). In India, liberalisation in the 1990s has ended decades of relatively slow growth and has made the whole economy more dynamic. In Indonesia, liberalisation of trade and progressive deregulation since the 1980s have resulted in astounding industrial growth (Hill, 1996). In Sri Lanka, neoliberal policies have been remarkably successful in promoting industrialisation in export (Athukorala and Rajapatirana, 2000).

In Sub-Saharan Africa, one can only conclude that extensive state intervention in the process of industrialisation has been such an abysmal failure that, for the time being, interventionism should be put on hold. Though liberalisation in the 1990s resulted in a marked decline of the industrial sector in many African countries (Szirmai and Lapperre, 2001; Yamfwa *et al.*, 2002), a reduced role for the government is an inevitable first step in any recovery.

Such a variety of experiences and arguments calls, at the minimum, for pragmatic and non-dogmatic approaches tailored to specific situations. It is very important to note the protagonists on both sides of the debate emphasise the importance of outward orientation and participation in world trade. They do not disagree about globalisation, but they do disagree about the national and international policies needed to allow developing countries to profit from globalisation.

9.9 Outcomes of industrialisation strategies

From 1945, developing countries increased their savings and investment rates. In many cases the recommendations of Lewis and Rostow to invest at least 12 to 15 per cent of net national income were met (see Table 3.2). A substantial part of all investment went to manufacturing. But the results of industrialisation policies varied substantially from country to country and region to region. On balance a rapid process of industrialisation has taken place in the developing world.

Table 9.5 *Growth of manufacturing GDP, 1950–2000 average annual growth rate (%)*

Country	1950–60	1960–70	1970–80	1980–90	1990–2000
Bangladesh		5.7	1.7	2.4	6.9
China[bc]	24.0	5.4	7.9	8.1	10.6
India	6.0	5.2	4.0	7.6	6.1
Indonesia		4.6	14.7	10.1	6.8
Malaysia		12.3	11.6	9.8	10.4
Pakistan		9.9	5.5	7.2	3.8
Philippines		5.8	6.1	0.9	2.6
South Korea	13.2	16.5	15.6	11.2	8.2
Sri Lanka		6.2	2.0	6.2	8.0
Taiwan[ab]		17.2	13.3	7.4	5.2
Thailand		11.6	10.1	9.9	6.8
Turkey		10.9	5.2	7.9	4.4
Argentina		5.6	1.6	−2.1	2.8
Brazil[b]	9.1	6.9	8.7	−0.1	1.7
Chile		5.3	1.1	2.5	4.6
Colombia		5.7	6.0	2.9	−1.4
Mexico	6.8	7.8	6.0	1.8	4.4
Peru		5.8	3.6	−1.7	3.6
Venezuela		6.7	5.4	3.4	1.0
Congo, Dem. Rep.[b]		12.5	−0.9	0.0	−12.4
Côte d'Ivoire		11.6	0.0	1.6	2.6
Egypt		4.8	5.7	6.2	6.2
Ghana[a]		9.6	−1.6	0.9	−2.8
Kenya[a]		5.5	11.7	4.8	1.9
Morocco		0.0	5.6	7.3	6.5
Nigeria		11.9	7.8	2.0	1.6
South Africa		8.6	5.3	0.2	0.7
Tanzania[a]		11.0	5.3	−1.4	1.1
Zambia[a]		15.8	3.3	2.9	−7.3
Average Asia		9.0	8.1	7.4	6.7
Average Latin America		6.3	4.6	1.0	2.4
Average Africa		10.1	4.7	2.5	−0.2
Average developing countries		8.7	6.2	4.1	3.3

Notes:
[a] 1960–70: period other than specified.
[b] 1997–2000: period other than specified.
[c] China: 1950–58 and 1958–60.
Sources: Unless indicated otherwise, World Bank (2002); China, India, Indonesia, South Korea, Taiwan, Brazil, Mexico, Egypt, Morocco, Tanzania, Zambia from GGDC, ICOP industry database, Summary Tables, http://www.ggdc.net; 1960–70: Turkey, Argentina, Egypt, Côte d'Ivoire, from *World Development Report*, 1984; Malaysia, 1960–70 from UNIDO, 1985, page 9; Zaire, 1960–70, UNIDO, 1986; South Africa from van Dijk (2003).

Table 9.5 serves to illustrate the diversity of country experiences. In Africa, there are steadily declining growth rates in manufacturing, with on average negative growth between 1990 and 2000. After rapid growth in the 1960s and 1970s, growth in Latin America slowed dramatically in the lost decade of the 1980s, in the wake of the debt crisis of 1982. There is some recovery after 1990, but growth rates remain modest. Asia shows very high growth rates in all periods, with growth accelerating in some countries and slowing down in others. Average growth rates for 1990–2000 in Asia were influenced by the Asian crisis, which strongly affected countries such as Indonesia, Korea, Thailand and the Philippines. In all regions, average growth rates were highest in the years before the oil crisis of 1973, which resulted in a slowdown of the global economy. Table 9.6 presents aggregate data for developing countries, classified on the basis of their per capita income in 1987.[22] Between 1960 and 1980 there was rapid growth in both industry (including mining, manufacturing, construction and utilities) and in manufacturing proper. Between 1960 and 1970, growth was most rapid in the upper-middle-income countries. Between 1970 and 1980, highest growth was found in the lower-middle-income countries. China registered exceptionally high growth throughout the whole period covered in the table.[23] In the manufacturing sector the increase in production was not restricted to consumer goods. The share of intermediate goods and capital goods also increased over time. For example, between 1963 and 1979, the share of capital goods in manufacturing value added increased from 20.8

Table 9.6 *Aggregate growth in industry and manufacturing, 1960–2000*[a]

Growth of production in industry	1960–70[b]	1970–80	1980–90	1990–2000	1996–2000
Low-income economies	6.6	6.9	7.3	9.9	6.8
Excluding China & India	6.6	6.8	4.7	4.7	0.9
India	5.4	4.0	7.1	5.7	4.8
China	11.2	9.1	9.5	13.6	9.3
Middle-income economies	7.4	6.3	2.7	1.5	3.2
Lower-middle-income	6.2	7.8	2.2	3.1	3.0
Upper-middle-income	9.1	4.1	3.4	−0.1	3.4

Growth of production in manufacturing	1960–70[b]	1970–80	1980–90	1990–2000	1996–2000
Low-income economies	5.5	7.4	8.8	10.5	7.1
Excluding China & India	6.3	7.2	8.7	5.9	1.9
India	4.7	4.0	7.6	5.9	3.8
China	5.4[c]	9.4	9.4	13.2	9.2
Middle-income economies	7.3	6.9	2.8	3.5	4.2
Lower-middle-income	6.5	7.7	1.9	3.5	3.2
Upper-middle-income	8.4	5.4	4.4	3.5	5.4

Share in GDP[d]	Industry			Manufacturing	
	1960	2000		1960	2000
Low-income economies	32.5	41.0		23.3	26.1
Excluding China & India	15.3	33.4		8.1	16.8
India	17.9	24.4		12.8	14.4
China	44.9	50.9		32.6	34.5
Middle-income economies	29.6	30.0		19.2	19.5
Lower-middle-income	27.5	27.7		20.1	18.8
Upper-middle-income	32.7	32.9		16.8	20.5

Notes:
[a] Industry includes mining, manufacturing, construction and public utilities. Countries are classified on the basis of their per capita GDP in 1987.
[b] The source for the period 1960–70 presents the median of growth rates, except for China.
[c] 1958–70.
[d] Where country shares were not available for the selected years, we used data for the adjacent years.
Sources: Weighted Growth Rates 1960–70: *World Development Report*, 1984; 1970–2000: *World Development Indicators CD-Rom* 2002; Chinese manufacturing 1960–70: GGDC website, http://www.ggdc.net; Share: *WDI*, 2002.

22 If one classifies developing countries on the basis of their income in more recent years, the phenomenal growth in some low-income countries is less visible, because they have since become middle-income countries.
23 Official Chinese growth rates tend to be overestimated, but growth is undoubtedly very rapid (Szirmai et al., 2001). Table 9.5 presents downward-adjusted growth rates for China, which are lower than the UNIDO data in Table 9.6.

per cent in 1963 to 31.2 per cent. Between 1980 and 1993, developing countries' share in the world value added in non-electrical machinery, electrical machinery and transport equipment increased from 5.1, 8.3 and 8.2 per cent to 5.7, 12.5 and.10.8 per cent respectively (UNIDO, 1995).

After 1980, the pace of industrial growth in middle-income countries slowed down dramatically. It was influenced by the weak performance of Latin American industrial economies after the debt crisis of 1982. Between 1980 and 1990, the annual growth rate in middle-income countries was only 2.7 per cent for industry and 2.8 per cent for manufacturing. On the other hand, growth in low-income countries accelerated after 1980. Especially China showed rapid growth, followed by India. Excluding the Asian giants, India and China, growth in the low-income economies was lower, especially after the Asian crisis of 1997.

With the exception of the lower-middle-income countries, the share of industry in total GDP between 1960 and 2000 increased in all groups. The share of the manufacturing also increased substantially.

At a major conference of the United Nations Organisation for Industrial Development Organisation (UNIDO) in Lima in 1975, agreement was reached on global targets for industrialisation in developing countries. By 2000, the share of developing countries in total world production of manufactured goods should be at least 25 per cent (Bos, 1984). Table 9.7 indicates that substantial progress has been made towards the realisation of this target. Including China, the share of developing countries in world manufacturing GDP increased from 14.4 per cent in 1980 to 21.9 per cent in 1997. The share of developing

Table 9.7 *Share of developing countries in world manufacturing value added 1960–1996 (%)*[a]

Year	Africa	West Asia	South and East Asia excl. China	China	Latin America	Developing countries[b]
Excluding China (constant 1990$)[c]						
1960[d]	0.8	0.7	1.8		4.9	7.9
1970[d]	0.8	1.3	2.4		6.0	10.5
1980	0.9	1.7	3.7		6.9	13.2
1990	0.9	2.0	6.2		5.5	14.6
1997	1.0	1.8	8.6		5.6	17.0
Including China (constant 1990$)						
1980	0.9	1.7	3.6	1.4	6.8	14.4
1990	0.9	1.9	6.0	2.6	5.4	16.8
1997	0.9	1.7	8.1	5.9	5.3	21.9
Including China (current $)						
1993	0.8	1.7	7.0	4.3	5.8	19.6
1996	0.8	1.6	8.3	5.1	6.2	22.0

Notes:
[a] At exchange rates. Using real output converters, the shares of developing countries could be up to a factor two higher.
[b] Total including Malta and the former republic of Yugoslavia.
[c] Calculated as percentage of total value added excluding China.
[d] Extrapolated using the ratio of the shares of 1960 and 1970 to 1980, at 1980 constant prices.
Sources: 1960: Gosh (1984, p. 351); 1970: UNIDO (1990); 1980–97: UNIDO (1999).

Table 9.8 *Share of developing countries in world manufactured exports, 1963–2000*

	1963	1973	1983	1993	2000
Asia (excl. Developed economies)	2.6	3.9	7.0	14.8	18.9
China				2.6	4.5
India	0.7	0.4	0.4	0.6	0.7
Latin America	0.8	1.6	1.7	2.7	3.6
Brazil	0.05	0.3	0.7	0.8	0.7
Argentina	0.1	0.2	0.1	0.2	0.2
Mexico	0.2	0.3	0.2	1.4	2.9
Africa, incl. S. Africa	1.3	1.2	0.7	0.9	0.9
South Africa[a]	0.6	0.6	0.3	0.4	0.3
Middle East	0.1	0.3	1.2	0.6	0.6
Developing economies[b]	5.9	8.8	14.5	20.5	23.8
Developed economies[c]	75.3	79.0	69.5	75.3	69.3

Notes:
[a] Prior to 1993, South Africa refers to South African Customs Union.
[b] Developing economies excluding former Soviet Asian Republics and Economies in Transition.
[c] Including Turkey
Sources:
WTO(2000). p. 31.
WTO (1997), Vol. II, p. 22.
WDI CD-Rom, 2002.

countries, excluding China, increased from 7.9 per cent in 1970 to 17 per cent in 1997. The share of West Asia almost tripled between 1960 and 1997. The share of South and Southeast Asia increased almost fivefold from 1960, reaching 8.6 per cent in 1997. The Latin American share increased modestly, if one excludes China. On the African continent, the share in total production never exceeded 1 per cent and showed little or no change.

The nineteenth-century division of labour, in which developing countries exported only unprocessed agricultural and mining products and imported manufactured goods, no longer exists. An increasing part of developing countries' exports consists of manufactures. The share of manufactured goods in total commodity exports has increased in all developing countries (see Table 3.4). In some countries, especially in Asia, manufactured goods are by far the most important exports. Most of these manufactures are sold on the markets of the rich Western countries. Worldwide the share of developing countries in total world manufactured exports has increased from 6 per cent in 1963 to 24 per cent in 2000. Most of this increase comes from Asia (see Table 9.8).

Although the aggregate figures thus point to the success of industrialisation in developing countries, progress in manufacturing has been concentrated in a relatively small number of developing countries. These include Brazil, Mexico, Argentina, China, India, South Korea, Taiwan, Singapore, Hong Kong, and Turkey (Lall, 1998; UNCTAD, 2000; UNIDO, 2002). The lion's share of manufactured exports comes from only a few countries, including Hong Kong, Singapore[24], Korea, Taiwan, Brazil, India, Mexico, and in more recent years Malaysia, Thailand, the Philippines and Indonesia.

---

24 Mainly re-exports.

In the course of the 1980s, Latin American industrial economies experienced great difficulties, owing to the debt crisis and the continuation of import substitution and inward-looking policies. In India, the industrial sector suffered from considerable inefficiency and low capacity utilisation. There, liberalisation of the economy in the 1990s brought improvement of performance and acceleration of growth.

With the exception of South Africa and Mauritius, African industrialisation never really got off the ground in spite of the high priority accorded to industrialisation by policy makers. Tanzania provides a representative example of the experiences of many Sub-Saharan African countries (van Engelen *et al.*, 2001). In the post-independence period, industrialisation was high on the policy agenda. From 1961 till 1967, there was rapid growth of manufacturing output, starting from very low initial levels. The driving force for industrial growth was a combination of import substitution, foreign private investment and low levels of regulatory control.

After the famous Arusha declaration of 1967 with its emphasis on 'self-reliance', there was a shift towards nationalisation of private enterprise and a dramatic increase in government regulation and intervention. The fourfold rise in oil prices in the oil crisis of 1973 caused considerable problems for non-oil-producing developing countries such as Tanzania, exposing the structural weaknesses of their economies. The trend towards ever-increasing regulation and state intervention continued, including price controls, import licensing, overvalued exchange rates, high degrees of effective protection and a leading role for parastatal enterprises and the national investment board. Foreign investment virtually disappeared. It was replaced by aid flows as the main source of foreign finance. After 1973, manufacturing growth slowed down. After 1980 real manufacturing output even started to decline in absolute terms (Szirmai *et al.*, 2001).

From the mid-1980s onwards, attempts were made to reform and liberalise the economy. These attempts accelerated in the mid-1990s, when levels of protection were dramatically reduced and parastatals started to be privatised. The initial results of these reforms were disappointing. Once protection was abolished, it turned out that many of the former state-run enterprises were so inefficient that they were simply not viable. Many enterprises had to close and the share of manufacturing in GDP declined in a rapid process of de-industrialisation. At the time of writing, there are some first signs of recovery in the manufacturing sector, growth rates turning positive after 1995. But it is not possible to say whether this recovery is sustainable.

The Tanzanian pattern was repeated with minor variations in many other Sub-Saharan African countries, irrespective of differences in political ideology. Sub-Saharan Africa is in danger of becoming marginalised in a globalised economy. Its share in world manufacturing is low, its share in world exports is negligible, technology gaps are increasing and it is unable to attract foreign direct investment (Helleiner, 1995; Morrisey and Filatotchev, 2001; Wangwe, 1995).

In 1997, East Asia was hit by the Asian crisis, which led to a sudden interruption of economic growth in South Korea, Thailand, Indonesia, the Philippines and other Southeast Asian economies. The large economies of China and India were least affected. Some countries such as South Korea and Malaysia recovered rapidly, reaching pre-crisis levels of output in a few years. Other countries such as Indonesia and the Philippines took longer to recover and were put on to slower growth paths. The crisis affected growth of output and standards of living more than manufactured exports, which continued to grow. One of the manifestations of the crisis was the collapse of exchange rates, which tended to make manufactured exports cheaper.

9.10   Conclusion

In conclusion, developing countries have made substantial progress in industrialisation since 1945. Many developing countries have experienced structural change and the share of developing countries in world manufacturing output and exports has increased.

In the previous sections, we have also highlighted several of the drawbacks of forced industrialisation policies: an uneven development of economy and society, waste of scarce resources and neglect of both the agricultural sector and small-scale informal activities. Also, the benefits of industrialisation have so far been concentrated in a relatively small number of developing countries. Other countries are in serious danger of becoming marginalised. However, this does not mean that industrialisation is no longer important. The old arguments in favour of industrialisation still retain their force. Industrialisation remains high on the policy agenda.

There is a need for more balanced policies which do not neglect other sectors of the economy and which pay more attention to the capacity of a society to absorb industrial investment and new technologies. No one wants a return to the vastly inefficient industrialisation policies of the 1960s and 70s. But there is a need to find a new balance between liberalisation and the role of governments in investment in capability building, learning, infrastructure, and protection and nurturing of potentially viable activities.

Questions for review

1. Does economic development necessarily imply industrialisation? Provide theoretical and empirical justifications for your answer.
2. Discuss the main characteristics of Arthur Lewis's model of economic development with unlimited supplies of labour. What are the most important criticisms levelled against the Lewis model?
3. Provide an overview of the theoretical arguments for large-scale industrialisation in developing countries.
4. Analyse the relationships between large-scale, import substitution and government planning in post-war industrialisation strategies.
5. Summarise the most important criticisms of post-war industrialisation strategies.

6. What is the difference between unbalanced and balanced industrialisation strategies?
7. Why is there less emphasis on the scale of the investment effort in export-oriented industrialisation than in import-substituting industrialisation strategies?
8. To what extent have industrialisation strategies in developing countries been successful in the post-war period?
9. Is import substitution a necessary phase in industrialisation before a country can engage in exports?
10. Discuss the differences between the balanced growth strategy and the balanced growth path strategy.
11. Why is foreign direct investment important for growth of manufacturing in developing countries? What are the potential disadvantages of FDI?

Further reading

One of the key early references for industrialisation in developing countries is Arthur Lewis's article, 'Economic Development with Unlimited Supplies of Labour' (1954). Two-sector models are further elaborated by Fei and Ranis in *Development of the Labor Surplus Economy: Theory and Policy* (1964). The notion of balanced growth was introduced by Rosenstein-Rodan in 'Problems of Industrialisation of East and South-East Europe' (1943), and *'Notes on the Theory of the "Big Push"'* (1957). Other seminal publications on balanced growth and large-scale industrialisation are Nurkse, *Problems of Capital Formation in Underdeveloped Countries* (1953), Nelson, 'A Theory of the Low-Level Equilibrium Trap in Underdeveloped Economies' (1956) and Leibenstein, *Economic Backwardness and Economic Growth: Studies in the Theory of Economic Development* (1957).

The concept of unbalanced growth is analysed in Hirschman, *The Strategy of Economic Development* (1958), which is still very stimulating to read today. Further readings on the small scale and informal sector include Hart, 'Informal Income Opportunities and Urban Employment in Ghana' (1973), Little, Scitovsky and Scott, *Industry and Trade in Some Developing Countries* (1970) and Hernando de Soto's provocative *The Mystery of Capital: Why Capitalism Triumphs in the West and Fails Everywhere Else* (2000).

For an excellent summary and dissection of early theories of industrialisation, we recommend Hla Myint's short textbook, *The Economics of the Developing Countries* (1980), as well as the broad-ranging study, *The Political Economy of Poverty, Equity, and Growth: A Comparative Study* (1996) by Deepak Lal and Hla Myint.

The modern debate on industrialisation in developing countries hinges on the interpretation of the success of East Asian industrialisation. Alice Amsden has emphasised the importance of interventionist policies in her pathbreaking book, *Asia's Next Giant: South Korea and Late Industrialization* (1989). The interventionist interpretation is also found in Wade, *Governing the Market: Economic Theory and the Role of Government in East Asian Industrialization* (1990). In a long series of publications, Sanjaya Lall has emphasised the importance of policies aimed at promoting technological learning and capability building. Here we mention only *Learning from the Asian Tigers: Studies in Technology and Industrial Policy* (1996), and 'Technological Change and Industrialization in the Asian NIEs: Achievements and Challenges' (2000). The liberal interpretation of East Asian success is argued in an interesting study by the World Bank, entitled *The East Asian Miracle. Economic Growth and Public Policy* (1993a). Other references in this debate include: Westphal, Kim and Dahlman, 'Reflections on The Republic of Korea's Acquisition of Technological Capability' (1985); Rodrik's 'Getting Interventions Right: How South Korea and Taiwan Grew Rich' (1995), and *Making Openness Work: The New Global Economy and the Developing Countries* (1999); and Westphal's thoughtful review article 'Technology Strategies for Economic Development in a Fast Changing Global Economy' (2002).

Two interesting publications on the emergence of global value chains are Gereffi, 'Capitalism, Development and Global Commodity Chains' (1994), and Gereffi and Korzeniewicz (eds.), *Commodity Chains and Global Capitalism* (1994). For foreign direct investment, relevant publications include an article by Vernon, 'International Investment and International Trade in the Product Cycle' (1966), Dunning's article, 'Trade, Location of Economic Activity and the Multinational Enterprise: A Search for an Eclectic Approach' (1988), and his book, *The Globalization of Business* (1993). A recent discussion of the impact of foreign direct investment in developing countries is found in the UNCTAD report, *The Competitiveness Challenge: Transnational Corporations and Industrial Restructuring in Developing Countries* (2000), and in the 2002 edition of UNIDO's, *Industrial Development Report: Competing through Innovation and Learning*.

A concise and well-written overview of the modern debates on industrialisation is provided by Kiely in *Industrialisation and Development. A Comparative Analysis* (1998). Broad overviews are also provided by John Weiss in two books, *Industry in Developing Countries: Theory, Policy and Evidence* (1988), and *Industrialisation and Globalisation: Theory and Evidence from Developing Countries* (2002).

UNIDO publishes a variety of industrial statistics, including the *Handbook of Industrial Statistics*, its successor the *International Yearbook of Industrial Statistics* and a CD-Rom with the UNIDO *Industrial Statistics Database* (2003). UNIDO also publishes the *Industrial Development Report* on an annual basis. The homepage of UNIDO is http://www.unido.org/. Statistics on foreign direct investment are presented in the IMF *International Financial Yearbook* and in the *World Investment Reports*, published annually by the IMF. Detailed time series for industrial sectors are found on the website of the Groningen Growth and Development Centre: http://www.ggdc.net.

10 Agricultural development and rural development

Relationships between the agricultural and the industrial sector were discussed in Chapter 8. In the first half of this chapter the focus shifts to the agricultural sector itself. Other sectors are only mentioned in as far as they contribute to agricultural development. In sections 10.1 and 10.2, we analyse long-term trends in agricultural production and identify some of the factors influencing these trends. Theories of agricultural development are also discussed here. Special attention will be paid to the debates on the 'green revolution' and the role of biotechnology. Section 10.3 addresses issues of food consumption and malnutrition. It turns out that food supply is only one side of the equation. Access to food is just as important.

In the second half of this chapter the focus shifts from agriculture to rural development. The concept of rural development is introduced in Section 10.4. Though rural society is characterised by the significance of agricultural activities, rural development is broader than agricultural development. First, various non-agricultural economic activities take place in rural areas. Second, rural development refers to the transformation of rural society as a whole, rather than to only the economic aspects of rural life. Sections 10.5 and 10.6 discuss land reform, agricultural collectivisation and agricultural decollectivisation. In section 10.7, we examine the notion of integrated rural development.

10.1   Is there enough food to feed the world population?

From the eighteenth century to the present day a debate has been raging between Malthusians and anti-Malthusians (Smil, 2000). Malthusians fear that food production will not be able to keep up with population growth, that soils are becoming eroded and degraded as a consequence of new agriculture practices, that biodiversity is declining at an alarming rate (Hogg, 2000), that forests are disappearing and that the world climate is changing for the worse. Technological optimists argue that advances in technology will compensate for diminishing returns, that food production will outpace population and that negative environmental impacts can be mitigated through technological advances. Prominent modern Malthusians include Lester Brown and his co-workers at the Worldwatch Institute (Brown, 1996; WWI, 2001) and researchers of the World Resources Institute (2000). An extreme protagonist of the techno-optimistic perspective is Julian Simon (1996). Recently, the debate took a new turn with the publication of a delightfully controversial book by Bjørn Lomborg, which trashed many of the basic empirical assumptions of the Malthusians (Lomborg, 2000). But one should realise that the debate is conducted at a variety of levels: assessment of empirical trends, evaluation of the seriousness of trends, assessment of risks involved, assessments of the advantages and costs of policy interventions, differences between global and local trends, and so forth. In general, the conclusion of most macro-studies is that food production will be able to keep up with population growth in the next half century (Bruinsma, 2003; Mitchell *et al.*, 1997). But at other levels there is more uncertainty (Hogg, 2000; Smil, 2000).

To set the stage for the discussion of agricultural development, Table 10.1 presents data on world growth of total agricultural production and food production from 1934 to 2002. The data derive from the FAO *Production Yearbooks* and the FAO database.[1] The table distinguishes between food production and total agricultural production, and between production and production per capita.

Table 10.1 illustrates some interesting trends:

- Since 1979–81, the rate of growth of agricultural production, whether in absolute terms or per capita, has been much more rapid in developing countries than in economically more developed countries. The same applies to food production.
- Despite very rapid growth of world population, per capita production of food in developing countries showed a gradual increase. This is contrary to gloomy Malthusian predictions, which state that the production of food will lag behind the growth of population.

1 FAOSTAT, Agriculture Data, Agricultural Production Indices, FAO, http://apps.fao.org/page/

Table 10.1 Indices of agricultural production, 1934–2002 (1979–81 = 100)

	World total[a]		Developed countries total[b]		North America		Western Europe		Eastern Europe		(Former) USSR[c]		Eastern Europe/(Former) USSR[d]		Developing countries total[e]	
	T	PC	T	PC	T	PC	T	PC	T	PC	T	PC	T	PC	T	PC
Total agricultural production																
1934/9	40	82	–	–	40	74	47	63	–	–	–	–	41	55	–	–
1948/52	46	80	–	–	54	84	48	60	–	–	–	–	41	58	–	–
1961	63	90	68	81	64	79	68	76	66	76	75	91	72	83	57	89
1965	70	93	74	84	72	83	73	79	71	79	77	89	75	84	65	92
1970	79	95	83	90	75	82	83	86	79	85	95	104	90	94	76	95
1975	89	97	91	95	88	92	89	91	93	97	98	102	96	100	86	96
1979/81	100	100	100	100	100	100	100	100	100	100	100	100	100	100	100	100
1985	114	105	108	104	108	103	107	106	106	103	109	105	108	104	122	110
1990	127	107	112	104	109	98	110	107	104	100	123	113	117	106	144	117
1995	138	108	104	94	118	101	107	102	89	85	79	72	76	76	174	130
2000	157	115	111	99	134	109	114	108	83	80	75	68	72	72	207	142
2002	160	114	109	97	129	103	112	106	84	81	80	–	–	–	215	144
Food production																
1934/9	39	79	–	–	36	63	47	63	–	–	–	–	41	55	–	–
1948/52	45	77	–	–	50	76	47	60	–	–	–	–	41	58	–	–
1961	62	89	67	80	62	76	68	76	66	76	75	92	72	84	57	88
1965	69	91	72	82	70	81	73	79	70	79	77	88	74	83	64	91
1970	79	95	82	89	74	82	83	86	78	85	96	105	90	94	75	94
1975	89	97	91	95	89	93	89	91	93	97	98	102	96	99	86	95
1979/81	100	100	100	100	100	100	100	100	100	100	100	100	100	100	100	100
1985	114	105	108	104	109	103	107	106	105	103	110	105	108	104	121	110
1990	127	107	112	104	109	99	110	106	105	101	125	115	118	107	144	118
1995	139	109	105	95	118	101	107	102	90	86	81	73	78	77	177	132
2000	160	117	112	100	135	110	114	107	84	81	77	70	74	74	212	146
2002	163	116	111	98	130	104	112	105	85	82	84	–	–	–	221	147

(Continued)

Table 10.1 (continued)

	Africa[f]		Latin America		Near East		Far East[g]		India		Indonesia		China	
	T	PC	T	PC	T	PC	T	PC	T	PC	T	PC	T	PC
Total agricultural production														
1934/9	38	110	33	102	33	84	39	94	–	–	–	–	–	–
1948/52	49	105	40	90	37	81	41	79	–	–	–	–	–	–
1961	67	110	56	91	55	92	56	87	68	104	53	82	49	74
1965	76	114	65	93	63	95	64	88	67	93	57	81	63	87
1970	89	116	74	94	73	96	74	92	81	101	70	87	71	86
1975	95	110	83	94	87	100	85	93	90	100	80	89	83	90
1979/81	100	100	100	100	100	100	100	100	100	100	100	100	100	100
1985	113	98	114	103	117	101	127	113	123	111	128	115	134	125
1990	133	100	125	103	137	103	153	123	145	118	158	130	168	145
1995	151	100	146	110	156	104	192	140	167	125	195	148	227	186
2000	179	105	168	117	178	106	232	156	190	130	194	137	289	226
2002	183	102	179	121	182	104	241	–	187	124	193	133	307	–
Food production														
1934/9	40	114	31	93	32	81	38	90	–	–	–	–	–	–
1948/52	50	108	39	86	36	79	40	78	–	–	–	–	–	–
1961	66	110	53	85	55	91	57	87	68	104	52	80	51	75
1965	75	112	61	88	61	91	63	87	67	93	56	79	63	87
1970	87	115	73	93	71	93	74	91	82	101	69	87	71	86
1975	95	109	83	93	86	98	85	93	91	101	80	90	83	90
1979/81	100	100	100	100	100	100	100	100	100	100	100	100	100	100
1985	114	98	115	104	117	102	126	113	123	111	129	116	132	123
1990	134	101	127	104	139	105	153	123	146	119	160	132	167	144
1995	154	101	152	115	159	106	194	142	169	126	199	152	230	188
2000	183	107	175	122	182	109	237	159	194	132	197	140	296	232
2002	186	103	187	126	187	107	246	–	190	126	197	136	315	–

Notes: T = Total production; PC = Production per capital.

[a] World total until 1961 excluding China.

[b] North America, Europe, Australia, New Zealand, the Former Soviet Union, Israel, Japan and South Africa.

[c] Former USSR includes central Asian developing countries.

[d] FAO weighted averages for these categories not available after 1991. We have calculated our own average using population weights of the two regions.

[e] Excluding Asian republics of the former Soviet Union and excluding South Africa.

[f] Africa excl. South Africa. Pre-1961 data exclude Egypt, Sudan and Libya. These countries included in post 61 series.

[g] The data for the Far East include South Asian, East Asian and Southeast Asian developing countries. The data for 1934–52 exclude what are called the centrally planned Asian economies.

Sources: 1961–2002: FAOSTAT, *Agriculture Data, Agricultural Production Indices,* FAO; 1934–53: *FAO Production Yearbook,* various issues.

http://apps.fao.org/page/ (accessed July 2003)

- Noteworthy is the increase of per capita food production in the densely populated large countries such as China, India and Indonesia. Countries such as Indonesia and India, which were dependent on food imports in the 1960s, have now become self-sufficient in food. As will be explained in section 10.2.2, population growth may provide incentives for technological change and intensification of agricultural production so that total production increases faster than population.
- The only regions where the increase in food production has not kept up with population growth were Africa and the countries of Eastern Europe and the former Soviet Union. In Africa, the race between population growth and growth of production was won by population growth. Output per capita in 2002 was lower than in 1934. After the sudden dissolution of the Soviet Union in 1991 and the abrupt but incomplete transition to the market, agriculture in the transition countries suffered tremendously. In 2000, food production per capita stood at only three-quarters of its 1980 level. The potential for agricultural growth in this region remains enormous, but has not been realised in the past century.

The continued growth of total world food production per capita contrasts with recent indications that the production of cereals per capita is on the decline (Bruinsma, 2003; Lomborg, 2001). In the past, cereal production accounted for some 90 per cent of human demand for food (World Bank, 1992a). The discrepancy between the increase in total food production and the stagnation of cereal production indicates that other types of food such as poultry have been substituted for cereals. The declining trend in cereal production is illustrated by the FAO data reproduced in Figure 10.1.

Since 1986, global cereal production per capita has been declining. Among others this is a consequence of reduced production in the advanced world, as various agricultural protection schemes are very gradually winding down and where average caloric needs are more then being met. Nevertheless, the figure indicates that, until 1996, cereal production in the developing world had been increasing. The enormous productivity gap between developed and developing countries also indicates that there is still ample scope for further productivity improvement in the developing world.

It has often been claimed that expansion of the production of export crops will be at the expense of food production. Dixon (1990), for example, states that the most fertile and best-irrigated lands are often used for growing cash crops and export crops. Moreover, these crops are said to use disproportionate shares of modern inputs, investment and subsidies. In particular when export crops are not food crops[2] and when export crops and domestic food crops compete for scarce land and labour, expansion of cash crops may lead to decreasing food production. An example of this is provided by groundnut production in the East African Sahel (Devereux, 1993). But this is not necessarily the case (see e.g.

2 Rice, for example, is grown as both a food crop and a cash crop.

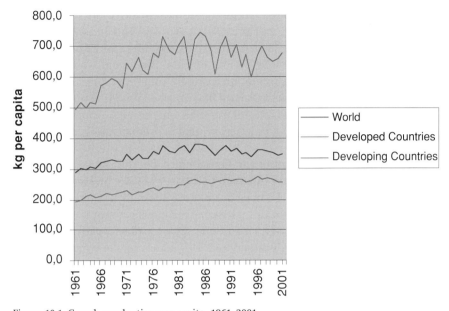

Figure 10.1 Cereals production per capita, 1961–2001
Source: 1961–2002: FAOSTAT, *Agriculture Data, Agricultural Production Indices.*
FAO:http://apps.fao.org/page/ (accessed July 2003).

Braun and Kennedy, 1994; Ravaillon, 1997). In a dynamic agricultural system both food production and non-food production can increase simultaneously.[3] In a less dynamic agricultural system both food production and export production will stagnate. Even if domestic food production does, export revenues from cash crops may be used to import more food than could be produced locally.

From a technical point of view there is no reason to assume that food production cannot continue to grow faster than the population, especially as the growth of world population is slowing down in the course of the twenty-first century (Alexandratos, 1995; Bruinsma, 2003).[4] However, as will be shown in section 10.3, an increase in the average per capita food production or food availability does not necessarily mean that each person will get more food or that the absolute numbers of undernourished people will decline.

A warning is also in order with regard to the reliability of the data in Table 10.1. In her book, *Development Economics on Trial* (1986), the anthropologist Polly Hill severely criticised standardised methods of data collection, such as those applied by the FAO, on the basis of her field experience in West Africa and South India. She elaborates on the shortcomings of the basic data.

---

3 Unfortunately the FAO database does not allow for a comparison of trends in the production of food crops for domestic supply with those for exports. It only distinguishes between food crops and non-food crops such as rubber, cotton or sisal.
4 See also FAOSTAT, *Agriculture Data, Agricultural Production Indices*, FAO, http://apps.fao.org/page/

In West Africa and South India farmers questioned by surveyors seldom know how much land they actually cultivate and how much food and other agricultural products they produce. Farmers often work several scattered plots of land, some of which lie fallow for long periods of time. The amounts produced are hard to assess since many crops are interplanted. Some root crops like cassava are not harvested at once, but rather are dug up when food is actually needed. It is also hard to obtain reliable information on the amount and value of products used for household consumption, that is products not traded on the market.

Usually only the male head of the household is questioned in agricultural surveys. In West Africa, in particular, food production is the preserve of female members of the household. The male head knows little about this subject. Furthermore, farmers are not used to aggregating income flows over longer periods of time, like a month or a year. Finally, the surveyors are usually underpaid, poorly trained and marginally supervised. Hill comes to the conclusion that the margin of error involved in such data is so wide that qualitative statements should be preferred over misleading quantitative data. Her criticisms are supported by an excellent recent study by Wiggins (2000), which claims that systematic analysis of case studies provides a less negative picture of agricultural growth in Sub-Saharan Africa than FAO data. All the indices for this region are dominated by giant Nigeria, a country notorious for the low quality of its agricultural statistics.

These criticisms should be taken seriously. Anyone working with FAO and other international statistics knows how deeply results can be influenced by changes in definitions, coverage and the quality of data collection.[5] Nevertheless, this author completely disagrees with Polly Hill's conclusion. Qualitative verbal statements about trends are quantitative statements in disguise. They are too often based on a limited number of case studies and examples. They are even more difficult to check or verify than statistical time series, the sources and methods of which can be documented with considerable precision. Statistical series should never be regarded as conclusive statements about reality, but rather as working hypotheses, which are to be used until replaced by better estimates. They represent the latest state of our knowledge. Therefore, we should indicate as precisely as possible how these series have been constructed, and should distrust all statistical series where such information is lacking. Furthermore, the striving for aggregation and identification of global trends offers an important counterbalance to the possible biases involved in formulating general statements on the basis of intimate experiences at the micro-level in local settings.[6] Therefore, the statistical working hypotheses contained in Table 10.1

---

5 As more and more data become readily available on international websites, it paradoxically becomes more and more difficult to check the methods of data collection and the consistency of series in terms of concepts and coverage.
6 Lomborg (2001) provides numerous horrendous examples of generalisations based on highly specialised cases. For instance, a UNEP study of land degradation trends in Africa is based on a single case study in South Africa, dating from 1989. See also Waggoner and Ausubel (2001).

and other tables in this chapter will serve as starting points for the discussion of agricultural development.

10.2 What are the sources of growth of agricultural production?

Box 10.1 Three ways to expand agricultural production
1. Expansion of cultivated area.
2. Intensification of land use by shortening the period of fallowing or by harvesting more than one crop per year on the same piece of land (multicropping). Intensification will cause average returns per hectare to increase.
3. Increasing the returns per harvest per hectare:
    (a) When labour is scarce, returns per harvest may be increased by using mechanised equipment. Generally, investment in mechanisation is labour saving.
    (b) When land is scarce, returns per harvest may be increased by making land-substituting investments, like investment in irrigation, organic and chemical fertilisers, and the development of high-productivity seeds. In general, land-substituting investments are land saving and labour intensive.

Expansion of agricultural production can be realised in three different ways (van der Meer, 1983).[7] These are summarised in Box 10.1. In the following sections these means of increasing production will be discussed in further detail.

10.2.1 How much land is still left for cultivation?

Table 10.2 presents information on the expansion of the cultivated area since 1961. This table shows that between 1961 and 2000 cultivated area increased worldwide by 11.2 per cent. The largest percentage-wise expansion can be observed in South America (69.7 per cent), followed by Australia and Oceania (59 per cent) and Africa (32.2 per cent). Since 1990, however, the global expansion of cultivated area has stabilised. Substantial increases in developing countries are balanced by reductions in North America, Europe and the former USSR.

The opportunities for further expansion of the cultivated area are still far from exhausted. Taking Revelle's (1975) estimates of land potentially available for cultivation, currently 56.5 per cent of all potential agricultural land in the world outside the humid tropics is being cultivated. Including potential agricultural land area in humid tropical areas, the figure is 47.5 per cent. Especially in South America, Africa and Oceania only a limited part of all potential agricultural land is presently being cultivated. There is still ample opportunity to increase agricultural production by taking more land into cultivation.

---

7 The format of this section has originally been inspired by articles by C. van der Meer, *Voedselvoorziening en agrarische ontwikkeling* [Food Supply and Agricultural Development] (1983); and P. van der Eng, *Food Supply and Agricultural Development* (1992).

Table 10.2 Cultivated area, potential agricultural land, pastures, woodlands (million ha)[a]

	Cultivated area[b]			Pastures and meadows[c]			Forests and woodlands			Potential Agricultural land		Cultivated area as % of potential area	
										excluding humid areas[c]	including humid areas[c]		
										2000	2000	2000	2000
	1961	1990	2000	1961	1990	2000	1961	1990	2000[e]	I	II	I	II
Africa	155,2	189,6	205,1	898,8	903,4	896,1	735,0	717,3	649,9	620	730	33,1	28,1
Asia[d]	437,1	507,1	511,9	618,5	799,7	853,2	591,2	532,0	527,0	540	620	94,8	82,6
Oceania (incl. Australia)	34,9	53,5	55,5	444,5	430,5	418,9	200,8	201,0	197,6	150	150	37,0	37,0
Europe[d]	151,4	138,5	132,0	89,8	83,5	79,1	142,5	157,6	161,6	170	170	77,6	77,6
North and Central America	259,6	274,6	267,8	373,0	365,4	367,4	840,7	823,9	549,3	450	460	59,5	58,2
South America	68,6	108,5	116,4	418,1	499,9	502,8	950,9	944,9	885,6	370	670	31,4	17,4
(Former) USSR	239,8	228,9	208,8	302,0	327,3	359,4	913,0	941,5	898,4	350	350	59,7	59,7
Total	1.346,5	1.500,8	1.497,4	3.144,7	3.409,6	3.476,9	4.374,2	4.318,1	3.869,5	2.650,0	3.150,0	56,5	47,5

Notes:
[a] Total land area, excluding surface waters, comprises: 1. cultivated area; 2. permanent meadows and pastures; 3. forestry and woodlands, including cleared woodland that has been reforested and 4. other land including roads, cities and wastelands.
[b] Cultivated area comprises 'arable land' (land planted with temporary crops, agricultural land lying fallow, land temporarily used for mowing and pasture, and land used for horticultural crops, incl. cultivation under glass), and 'land under permanent crops' (coffee, cocoa, rubber, fruit trees, nuts).
[c] Potential land for agricultural use, either including or excluding humid tropical land area. 'Humid tropical areas' refer in particular to tropical rainforests. Besides woodland, potential land for agricultural use also includes meadows and pastures.
[d] Excluding (former) USSR in Asia and Europe.
[e] Excluding woodlands.

Sources: FAOSTAT, Agriculture Data, Land Use, updated August 2002, FAO, http://apps.fao.org/page/collections; Forests 2000, from FAO, Global Forest Resources Assessment 2000, Main Report, table 3, FAO, http://www.fao.org/forestry/.

The potential amount of land for agricultural use is determined by such factors as climate, soil conditions and the availability of water (Revelle, 1975). Land has to be frost-free for at least one complete crop cycle. Soil conditions must meet certain standards, like permeability to water and retention of water and nutrients. The land should not be too acidic or too alkaline, neither too steep nor too rocky. On the basis of climatic and soil conditions, potential farmland globally amounts to approximately 3.2 billion hectares. However, water is not equally available in the different parts of the world. Only 30 per cent of the land that is potentially suitable for irrigated agriculture can be actually irrigated. Thus potential farmland is reduced to 2.9 billion hectares. Furthermore, the quality of much agricultural land not yet taken into use is so poor that huge investments are necessary before it can be cultivated.

Even higher estimates of land potentially available for cultivation are found in a recent FAO study (Bruinsma, 2003), which focuses on arable land as a percentage of potential arable land suitable for rain-fed crop production.[8] These estimates are reproduced in Table 10.3. The differences are most probably due to changes in estimates of potential land, and the fact that the table refers to arable land rather than cultivated land. But the conclusions are very similar: Africa and Latin America provide the greatest scope for expansion of cultivated land. Of course, expansion of cultivated area competes with other potential forms of land use, such as forestry and woodlands, pastures for food animals and land used for urban development, construction, roads and recreation. Particularly in humid tropical areas potential farmland consists, to an important extent, of land covered by tropical rainforests. Expansion of agricultural land results in deforestation.

The disappearance of tropical rainforests has two potentially negative effects. Tropical rain forests are the main repositories of biodiversity and forest

Table 10.3 *Arable land in use as percentage of potential arable land, 1997–99*

Sub-Saharan Africa	22
Near East/North Africa	87
Latin America and the Caribbean	19
South Asia	94
South Asia excl. India	162
East Asia	63
East Asia, excl. China	52
Developing countries	34
excl. China	32
excl. India	27
Industrial countries	44
Transition countries	53
World	36

Source: Bruinsma, 2003, p. 133, table 4–7

8 This source does not distinguish between humid and non-humid areas. It focuses on arable land rather than on cultivated area (arable land plus land for permanent crops). It is not quite clear why potential land is defined as land suitable for rain-fed agriculture rather than in terms of both rain-fed and irrigated agriculture.

coverage serves as storage capacity for CO_2. Deforestation may lead to decrease in biodiversity, which can pose an evolutionary threat. Decrease in CO_2 storage capacity can contribute to the greenhouse effect and global warming.

According to Boserup (1990, quoted in Barrow, 1995), 75 per cent of the cereals that have fed growing populations in developing countries between the 1930s and the 1960s came from expansion of cultivated area. Despite the increasing costs of further land reclamation, even in recent years a considerable part of the growth of production in developing countries can be attributed to the expansion of cultivated land area. Between 1960 and 2000, 23 per cent of the growth of total crop production was achieved through expansion of land. According to the projections for the next thirty years, 21 per cent of growth will be realised through continued expansion of cultivated area, especially in Latin America and Sub-Saharan Africa (see Table 10.8).

Competition between agricultural land and forest land

As explained above, the expansion of the cultivated area is an important way of increasing agricultural production in many developing countries (Dixon, 1990). Even in densely populated India, 20 per cent of production growth of cereal products in the 1970s was attributable to the expansion of agricultural land. In some parts of South America and Africa at least 80 per cent of production growth was due to the expansion of agricultural land.

Expansion of cultivated area encroaches on land available for pasture, land available for dwellings, roads and urbanisation, and in particular on forest and woodland area. Though potential agricultural land has not been exhausted, alternative uses, in particular forestry, impose constraints on the unlimited expansion of cultivated area. There is a competition between agricultural and forest land.

Table 10.2 provides a first rough indication of the long-term decline of forest and woodland area on a global scale. Unfortunately, the data for 1990 and 2000 are not strictly comparable. The sources and definitions of forest cover have changed since 1994 and the 2000 data exclude woodlands. Therefore, this table cannot be used to assess deforestation in the 1990s. More consistent data for the 1990s will be presented in Table 10.4. Nevertheless, both statistical and other evidence points to a reduction in forest cover.

Of Africa's 160 million hectares of tropical rainforest an annual 1.3 million hectares were being converted to agricultural land in the 1980s. The situation in the Amazon region was even more extreme: here 18 million hectares of tropical rainforests were cut down every year (Leite and Furley, 1985, quoted in Dixon, 1990).

Of the three main causes of deforestation – logging, collection of fuel wood and expansion of agricultural land – expansion of agricultural land is by far the most important. Given the vital function of the remaining tropical rainforests in preserving biodiversity and a global ecological equilibrium, it is obvious that there are drawbacks to the continued expansion of agricultural land area at the expense of forested area.

Table 10.4 *Deforestation, 1980–2000, regional aggregates and selected developing countries*

Country/area	Land area	Total forest area 2000	Annual average deforestation 1980s		Annual average deforestation 1990s	
		(1000 ha)	(1000 ha)	%	(1000 ha)	%
Africa	**2,978,394**	**649,866**		**−1.4**	**−5,262**	**−0.8**
Cameroon	46,540	23,858	−190	−0.8	−222	−0.9
Nigeria	91,077	13,517	−400	−2.7	−398	−2.6
Zaire/Congo	226,705	135,207	−370	−0.2	−532	−0.4
Asia	**3,084,746**	**547,793**		**−1.0**	**−364**	**−0.1**
Indonesia	181,157	104,986	−920	−0.8	−1,312	−1.2
Malaysia	32,855	19,292	−255	−1.2	−237	−1.2
Philippines	29,817	5,789	−143	−1.5	−89	−1.4
Thailand	51,089	14,762	−397	−2.5	−112	−0.7
Europe	**2,259,957**	**1,039,251**			**881**	**0.1**
North and Central America	**2,136,966**	**549,304**			**−570**	**−0.1**
Oceania	**849,096**	**197,623**			**−365**	**−0.2**
South America	**1,754,741**	**885,618**			**−3,711**	**−0.4**
Bolivia	108,438	53,068	−117	−0.2	−161	−0.3
Brazil	845,651	543,905	−9,050	−1.8	−2,309	−0.4
Colombia	103,871	49,601	−890	−1.7	−190	−0.4
World	**13,063,900**	**3,869,455**			**−9,391**	**−0.2**
Tropical		**1,871,000**			**−12,300**	**−0.63**
Non-tropical		**1,998,000**			**+2,900**	**+0.15**

Note: Forest defined as crown cover of at least 20 per cent in developed countries, and at least 10 per cent in developing countries. Developing country forest area includes plantations.
Source: 1990s: FAO, Global Forest Resources Assessment, 2000, Main Report, FAO, http://www.fao.org/forestry/, Appendix 3, tables 3,4 and 6; 1980s: World Resources Institute (1990), table 19.1, pp. 292–3; these data refer to the early 1980s

Globally, the world has lost around 20 per cent of original forest cover since the dawn of agriculture (Goudie, 1993; Lomborg, 2001). Deforestation has a long history. For instance, Europe has felled most of its forest cover since the Middle Ages, to build the wooden ships that circled the globe, to provide charcoal for iron and steel production and to make way for agriculture. Table 10.4 presents estimates of the rate of deforestation in the 1980s and the 1990s. The data for the 1990s derive from the newest assessments of the FAO, using methodologies such as remote sensing.[9] In the 1990s there was a net annual loss of natural forest of in total 14.2 million hectares in tropical areas. In non-tropical areas there was a net annual gain of 1.7 million hectares. Apart from deforestation, one increasingly important source of loss of natural forest is conversion to forest plantations. Plantations now account for some 5 per cent of global forest cover (FAO, 2001, figure 1.8).[10]

The figures in Table 10.5 refer to total forest cover change, which is the net result of changes in natural forests and plantations. In tropical areas there was a net loss of forest cover of 12.3 million hectares per year, amounting to an annual deforestation rate of 0.63 per cent. In non-tropical areas there was a

9 FAO, Global Resources Assessment 2000, Main Report, htt://www.fao.org.forestry/
10 FAO, Global Resources Assessment 2000, Main Report, http://www.fao.org/forestry/

Table 10.5 *Systems of supply for vegetable food*

System	Description	Frequency of cropping (in %)[a]
Gathering	Wild plants, roots, fruits, and nuts are gathered	0
Forest-fallow	One or two crops followed by 15–25 years' fallow	0–10
Bush-fallow[b]	Two or more crops followed by 8–10 years' fallow	10–40
Short-fallow	One or two crops followed by one or two years' fallow	40–80
Annual cropping	One crop each year with only a few months' fallow	80–100
Multicropping	Two or more crops in the same fields each year without any fallow	200–300

Notes:[a] Frequency of cropping is average annual harvested area as percentage of cultivated plus fallow area.
[b] Bush-fallow is often deceptively referred to as 'shifting cultivation.' In fact, it is a form of sedentary agriculture, where agriculturalists with fixed dwellings alternately work different plots of land (Hill, 1986).
Source: Boserup (1981, table 3.2, p. 19).

net increase in forest cover of 2.9 million hectares, a net afforestation rate of 0.15 per cent. The global rate of total net deforestation is 0.2 per cent per year.

In the 1990s highest rates of deforestation were found in South America and Africa, where most of the world's tropical rainforests are located. In Europe (including the forest-rich Russian Federation), there is some evidence of reforestation. The estimates of the FAO indicate very rapid deforestation in some tropical countries. Among the most extreme cases are Thailand, Indonesia, the Philippines and Malaysia, where rainforests are disappearing at an alarming rate. The deforestation rate in Brazil is 0.4 per cent. Brazil alone accounts for around 30 per cent of the world's rainforests.

Apart from the empirical problems involved, estimates of the pace of deforestation depend on the definitions used (see Jepma, 1993). The FAO and the WRI define deforestation as the complete disappearance of closed or open forests and the use of the land for other purposes (see Table 10.4).[11] Biologists, ecologists and environmentalists employ a broader definition of deforestation, which also includes serious degradation of the quality of forests and woodlands due to forestry, environmental damage and agriculture.

For the 1980s, the estimates of rates of deforestation in tropical rainforests vary from an annual 0.4 per cent (FAO, 1988) to an annual 1.8 per cent (Myers,

---

11 Closed forest is forest where tree crowns cover at least 20 per cent of the land area. In open forests the tree crowns cover 5 per cent to 20 per cent of the land. The recent FAO data take crown cover of 20 per cent in developed countries and 10 per cent in developing countries as the cut-off point for forest cover.

1989). There are also great differences in the estimates of the remaining land areas covered by tropical rainforests.

An important source of disagreement is the estimate of original forest cover. The higher the estimate of original forest cover, the higher the rates of deforestation. In an interesting article based on historical research in West Africa, Leach and Fairhead (2000) have argued that original forest cover has been severely overestimated. Estimates of 'original forest cover' have simply and unrealistically assumed that the whole zone capable of supporting forests was fully forested. Also, through lack of better data, population growth rates have been taken as proxies for the rates of deforestation. The authors conclude that for Benin, Ghana, Côte d'Ivoire, Liberia, Sierra Leone and Togo, deforestation since 1900 may be one third of that suggested by official estimates.

Firm conclusions are difficult to draw. It would seem that earlier estimates of the rate of deforestation in the range of 0.8 per cent per year are too pessimistic. The present estimate of global deforestation is 0.2 per cent per year. But, though the present estimates of worldwide deforestation are lower than earlier ones, the rate of deforestation in tropical countries gives no cause for complacency. One should realise that a deforestation rate of 0.63 per cent per year means that total forest cover will be reduced by more than 12 per cent in twenty years' time.

10.2.2 Intensification of land use

Prior to the nineteenth century, the growth of agricultural production was to a large extent determined by two factors: the expansion of the land area used for agriculture; and intensification of land use (see Boserup, 1965; 1981; 1990). When population increased and further expansion of cultivated area was not possible in a given region, increasing population density resulted in more intensive techniques of land use.

In a series of pioneering publications Ester Boserup criticised the Malthusian notion that the natural environment sets unrelenting limits to the growth of food production. Increasing population density induces changes in agricultural technology, which primarily imply a more intensive use of 'natural' resources.

Boserup distinguishes six major vegetable food supply systems, which can be ranked according to length of fallowing (Boserup 1981: p.19). These are presented in Table 10.5. Box 10.2 summarises the different functions of letting land lie fallow. As population density increases, the period the land can be left fallow becomes shorter. The functions of fallowing increasingly have to be replaced by human operations. The production process becomes more and more labour intensive. Soil fertility is maintained by the application of animal manure and vegetable matter. Parasites or affected plants are removed by hand. Weeds are removed or ploughed under. Seeds are transplanted by hand (e.g. in rice cultivation). Ever more water is required. Water has to be transported to the fields.

> **Box 10.2 Functions of fallowing**
> - Prevention of soil fertility exhaustion. During the period of fallow the soil recovers its fertility. Trees and bushes grow back.
> - Prevention of hillside erosion, by forest fallowing.
> - Controlling weed growth: bushes and trees limit the growth of weeds and grasses.
> - Limiting the spread of plant diseases and pests.

Also, surplus water has to be drained away. For water control and prevention of erosion, land has to be terraced and levelled, and canals and irrigation works dug and maintained. All this makes for increasing inputs of labour per hectare.

Since the nineteenth century, many of these functions can also be fulfilled by industrial inputs: herbicides, pesticides, chemical fertilisers, agricultural machinery, pumps, and so forth. Before the nineteenth century, intensification of land use was the most viable alternative to fallowing in Western countries. In many developing countries this is still the case. The transition from extensive to more intensive forms of cultivation involves an increasing demand for labour in agricultural production. This demand is fulfilled by increasing the number of workers per hectare or by working more hours per person per year. Rawski, for example, calculated that in the Chinese agricultural sector the number of days worked per person increased from 119 per year to 250 per year between 1949 and 1978 (Rawski, 1979). In the process of intensification, returns per hectare increase sharply as fallowing is reduced and cropping intensity increases. However, since the hours worked per person tend to increase, returns per hour worked may well decline (Boserup, 1965).

Boserup also points to the correlation between livestock breeding and population density. Meat and dairy production are inefficient ways of producing calories. Many of the calories consumed by cattle and poultry are lost in the transformation into meat and dairy products. As the population continues to grow and space becomes scarce, the number of cattle per head of the population tends to decrease.

A low population density allows wild game and cattle to thrive in its natural habitat. When land is cultivated more intensively, this becomes more difficult. But land lying fallow can be used systematically as pasture for cattle. The manure from cattle contributes to the fertility of the soil. And cattle can be used as draught animals to work the soil more intensively. When there are annual harvests, farmers have to switch to intensive livestock breeding – part of the land being used for the production of fodder crops, such as maize. Fodder may also be produced industrially or it can be imported from regions with lower population densities. As land is cultivated more intensively, the share of animal food in the diet has tended to decline in pre-modern times.

Boserup (1981, p. 23) combines intensification of animal husbandry and intensification of agriculture in a typology consisting of seven systems of food supply, ranked according to increasing population density:

1. Hunting-gathering systems;
2. (Nomadic) pastoralism;
3. Forest-fallow;
4. Bush-fallow;
5. Short-fallow with domestic animals;
6. Annual harvesting with intensive animal husbandry;
7. Multicropping with little animal food.

This classification by density primarily applies to societies at lower techno-logical levels. After the onset of industrialisation from the eighteenth century onwards, the correlations between population density and systems of food sup-ply became weaker. At higher technological levels, a society has the option of producing fodder industrially or transporting it over long distances. Presently, the demand for animal food is increasing in densely populated countries such as Indonesia or China, as people strive to enrich their diets.

The transition from the first two systems of food supply to sedentary systems of cultivation first took place some 10,000 years ago. It is one of the fundamen-tal technological transitions in the history of mankind (see Diamond, 1998; Goudsblom, 1992). In the agricultural history of preindustrial Europe, England was the technological leader. Between the ninth and the fourteenth centuries the three-course rotation system was introduced. For two consecutive years dif-ferent cereal crops would be grown on one piece of land. In the third year the land would lie fallow. Fallow land was used in common to let domestic cattle graze, the droppings of the cattle serving as manure. The cattle provided an-imal traction for tillage. In the eighteenth century there was a transition to annual harvesting. This is sometimes referred to as the 'agricultural revolution', but this term disregards the gradual nature of the process of intensification. The system of annual harvesting was characterised by crop rotation, the intro-duction of new root crops such as the potato, reserving part of the land for production of cattle fodder and a systematic use of manure.

In the course of the nineteenth century a second agricultural revolution took place, which resulted in farmers applying industrially produced chem-ical inputs and agricultural machinery. For the first time, the inputs came from outside the agricultural sector. Further, there was greater specialisation in agricultural production and foodstuffs were often imported from abroad. This second 'agricultural revolution' falls outside the scope of the process of intensification, analysed by Boserup.

In the course of the intensification process the demand for labour increased in the agricultural sector. The transition to annual harvests also involved a reinforcement of individual rights to land (of ownership or use), and increased investment in agriculture (Hayami and Ruttan, 1985, p. 46). Previously, fal-low land had been in common use for cattle grazing. Intensification, how-ever, demanded a more precise delimitation of ownership rights (c.f. North and Thomas, 1973). The so-called 'enclosure' movement, which took place in England from the second half of the seventeenth century onwards, involved large-scale and fierce social conflicts between villagers who were losing their rights to graze cattle on the commons and (large) landowners who were trying to gain exclusive rights of ownership. Frequently, the acquired ownership titles were used for sheep raising. Currently similar processes are taking place in Africa and Asia where communal rights to land are gradually and slowly being transformed into individual ownership titles. It should be stressed that the transition to more intensive cultivation practices is not uniform. Depending on differences in natural conditions and local circumstances, different systems of cultivation can coexist in one and the same area (Boserup, 1965, ch. 5).

From Boserup's analysis various lessons can be derived that may deepen our understanding of agricultural issues in developing countries. These are summarised in Box 10.3.

Box 10.3 Lessons from the Boserupian analysis

- Intensification of agriculture requires hard work on the part of farmers.
- Much of our 'natural' environment is not natural.
- Intensification of agriculture requires greater inputs of labour.
- The concept of 'disguised unemployment' needs to be re-evaluated.
- Production per hectare may increase sharply as a result of intensification.
- New inputs can contribute to further intensification.
- Food aid can provide disincentives to production in developing countries.
- Low population density may be a disadvantage for agricultural development since a minimum degree of density is required to support infrastructural investment.

Intensification requires hard work

As long as sufficient land is available for more extensive agriculture, this will be the preferred option. Farmers will switch to more intensive methods of agricultural production only when extensive methods become unsustainable owing to increased population density. The sufficient availability of land may, for example, provide an explanation for disappointing results of irrigation projects in Northeast Thailand. Farmers preferred to migrate to other areas, rather than participate in intensive irrigated agriculture (Dixon, 1990; van der Meer, 1981; Wiggins, 2000).

How natural is the natural environment?

The natural environment is the result of centuries of interaction between people and their environments. The characteristics of the natural environment change under the influence of human interventions and actions. These may result in deforestation or reforestation, erosion or land reclamation, the creation of polders below sea level, desertification or irrigation. This approach puts the whole notion of fixed Malthusian limits to production in a different perspective.

Intensification and labour input

Higher labour input can take the form of more persons employed, longer hours worked or both. Intensification also requires increasing investment in infrastructure and water control, which demands further inputs of labour.

Disguised unemployment?

The previous point implies a criticism of the notion of 'disguised unemployment' in agriculture. During peak periods in the agricultural cycle, such as sowing or harvesting, there is often an acute shortage of labour rather than a surplus. This is particularly true for densely populated areas where multicropping and other forms of intensive agriculture are practised. (The assumption of low productivity per hour worked still seems to be justified.)

Intensification as a source of agricultural growth

The shift from extensive to intensive systems of agriculture is an important source of agricultural growth.

New inputs can result in further intensification

Nowadays, inputs from outside the agricultural sector, such as new seeds, chemical fertilisers, pesticides or herbicides are available. These inputs, together with investments in water control and agricultural infrastructure may contribute to further intensification of agriculture.

Food aid can provide disincentives for production

Subsidised food imports from economically advanced regions such as the European Union or the United States have negative effects on the development of agricultural production and productivity in developing countries. They form a powerful disincentive for agricultural development in developing countries and allow developing countries to postpone the difficult and backbreaking process of agricultural intensification (Boserup, 1983).

Disadvantages of low population density

Without infrastructural investment, e.g. in water control or land preparation, it is hard to intensify agriculture. If there is rapid population growth in countries with low initial population densities, farmers may continue to use extensive methods of agriculture in spite of diminishing supplies of land. Fallow periods are too short to allow the land to regenerate. The continuation of extensive agricultural practices may thus result in land degradation. A vicious circle arises in which the increase in agricultural production lags behind population growth. Circumstances like this seem to apply in several countries in Sub-Saharan Africa.

Cropping intensity

Intensification of agriculture manifests itself in increasing cropping intensities. Table 10.6 presents empirical data on cropping intensity by region. A cropping intensity of one means that there is one harvest per year on any given plot of land. Table 10.6 illustrates the huge differences in cropping intensity between irrigated and non-irrigated land. Irrigation allows for far higher cropping intensities. Cropping intensity in Asia is much higher than in Sub-Saharan Africa and Latin America, both for irrigated and non-irrigated areas. Highest cropping intensities are found in East (and Southeast) Asia, and in particular in China. Over time, cropping intensities have been increasing in all regions. FAO projections up till 2030 indicate that there is ample scope for still further intensification.

10.2.3   *Increasing yields per harvest*

The third and most important source of agricultural growth lies in increased yields per harvested crop. Increased returns can be generated through labour-saving mechanisation, which reduces crop losses through efficiency gains or allows for closer planting. But the most important sources of yield improvement are increased irrigation, the use of chemical and organic fertilisers, the use of chemical and other scientific methods of pest control, and the development of new seeds with higher productivity. We will discuss increases in yields in more detail in the sections on the Green Revolution (10.2.5) and biotechnology (10.2.6). Here, we focus on the contributions of irrigation.

Table 10.6 *Cropping intensity in developing countries, 1974–2030*[a]

	Non-Irrigated				Irrigated				Total	
	1974–6	1982–4	1997–9	2030	1974–6	1982-4	1997–9	2030	1997-9	2030
Sub-Saharan Africa	0.51	0.54	0.67	0.75	1.03	0.84	0.86	1.02	0.68	0.76
Near East/North Africa	0.56	0.62	0.72	0.78	0.82	0.98	1.02	1.12	0.81	0.90
Latin America and the Caribbean	0.59	0.59	0.60	0.68	0.92	1.02	0.86	1.00	0.63	0.71
Far East total			1.13	1.16			1.38	1.52	1.21	1.30
South Asia			1.03	1.09			1.24	1.37	1.11	1.21
India			1.06	1.06			1.29	1.40	1.14	1.21
East Asia			1.20	1.22			1.54	1.69	1.30	1.39
China			1.40	1.58			1.65	1.83	1.54	1.67
Far East, excl. China	1.02	1.00	1.01	1.03	1.18	1.29	1.24	1.36	1.06	1.16
Total Developing countries excl. China	0.70	0.71	0.76	0.81	1.07	1.18	1.14	1.27	0.83	0.90
Total Developing countries			0.83	0.87			1.27	1.41	0.93	0.99

Note:
[a] Ratio of the annually harvested area to total arable land area in use.
Sources: 1974–6, FAO (1981), annex table 9 (ninety developing countries, excluding China); 1982–4: Alexandratos (1988), p. 130: ninety-three developing countries excluding China; 1997–2030: Bruinsma (2003), p. 135, table 4.8, including projections for 2030.

Irrigation

Irrigation contributes both to increased frequency of cropping (see Table 10.6) and to increased returns per crop. In some areas irrigation allows crops to grow in areas, where there is insufficient rainfall for rain-fed crop production. In other areas irrigation makes it possible to have more than one harvest per year, for example in rice production. Irrigation also contributes to higher yields. Without a well-regulated water supply new varieties with higher returns per harvest cannot flourish.

Table 10.7 provides information on irrigation intensity. The table shows that there is a steady growth of irrigation intensity in all regions. The only exception is China, where irrigation intensity declined after 1980 because total cultivated area grew more rapidly than irrigated area. The table also illustrates the large differences between low irrigation intensities in Africa and Latin America, and high irrigation intensities in Asia. In the Far East irrigation intensity reached 35 per cent in 2000, in Sub-Saharan Africa it stood at 2.5 per cent. In 2000, a total of 204 million hectares was irrigated of which 42 million hectares consists of arid or hyperacid land, which could not have been cultivated in the absence of irrigation (Bruinsma, 2003: p. 138). In 2000, 24 per cent of all agricultural land in developing countries was irrigated. But contribution of irrigated land to agricultural growth is far greater than indicated by its share of land.

There are great differences in the quality of irrigation systems, which are not reflected in the FAO statistics. Irrigation systems vary from simple traditional techniques to large-scale modern systems (van der Eng, 1993, ch. 3). The percentage of irrigated land also depends on the definitions used. For the 1980s, Dixon (1990) presents much lower figures than the FAO. He gives an estimate of 112 million hectares of irrigated land in developing countries, 14 per cent

Table 10.7 *Irrigated area in developing countries*

	Irrigated area (1000 ha)					Irrigated area (%)*				
	1961	1970	1980	1990	2000	1961	1970	1980	1990	2000
Sub-Saharan Africa	1,901	2,107	2,852	3,595	3,678	1.8	1.8	2.2	2.7	2.5
South Africa	808	1,000	1,128	1,290	1,498	6.3	7.6	8.5	9.0	9.5
Latin America and the Caribbean	8,260	10,190	13,807	16,786	18,624	8.1	8.7	10.0	11.2	11.7
North Africa/Near East	16,073	18,124	19,782	26,810	29,603	16.7	17.8	19.2	24.4	26.0
South Asia	36,275	45,048	55,798	66,529	78,917	19.1	22.8	27.6	32.6	38.5
India	24,685	30,440	38,478	45,144	54,800	15.3	18.4	22.9	26.6	32.3
East and Southeast Asia	40,115	48,908	59,722	65,624	74,251	22.6	27.3	32.5	28.8	31.9
China	30,411	38,121	45,470	47,967	54,402	28.9	37.2	45.4	36.5	40.1
Far East total	76,390	93,956	115,520	132,153	153,168	20.8	24.9	29.9	30.6	35.0
Developing countries Total	101,953	123,753	151,290	178,690	204,625	15.1	17.3	20.0	21.6	23.9

Note:
*Irrigated area as percentage of cultivated area.
Sources: FAOSTAT, Agriculture Data, Land Use, updated August 2002, FAO, http://apps.fao.org/page/collections.

of the entire area cultivated. In spite of these substantial differences, it is clear that the potential to expand irrigation has not yet been exhausted.

Unequal availability of water does set a limit to continued expansion of irrigation. Dixon rightly remarks that locations most suited to irrigation, like river deltas, are already irrigated (Dixon, 1990; Alexandratos, 1988). Further expansion is technically possible, but it is not always economically profitable to do so. Many farmers in developing countries will remain dependent on rain-fed agriculture. Also, part of existing irrigated area is lost because of salinisation, waterlogging and inadequate maintenance of irrigation facilities (Ruttan, 2002).

Today, around 50 per cent of land with irrigation potential in developing countries (estimated at 403 million ha) is irrigated in some form or other (Bruinsma, 2003: p. 138, table 4.9). The irrigated area in developing countries is projected to increase by some 40 million ha in the next thirty years, which means that the rate of expansion of irrigated area is slowing down compared to the past thirty years.

One of the pressing concerns of recent years is whether there is enough water supply on a global scale. Fresh water in use for irrigation may compete with other uses such as drinking, hygiene or sanitation. Countries with the least rainfall are also the countries in greatest need of irrigation. Countries where irrigation withdraws more than 20 per cent of water resources are considered to be in danger of water scarcity. By 2025, regions from North China, East Asia to North Africa and Northern Sub-Saharan Africa may experience absolute or severe water scarcity (Ruttan, 2002). One of the ways to defer the advent of water scarcity is to increase irrigation efficiency.

Desertification and land degradation

The extent to which potential agricultural land can be cultivated is affected negatively by processes of soil degradation and desertification (Barrow, 1995, ch. 6). Soil degradation can be among the unintended consequences of intensification of cultivation and attempts to increase yields through fertilisation and irrigation.

Desertification is a rather ill-defined catchphrase referring to dry land and semi-arid land degradation. As the end result is 'desert like' it is called desertification, but Barrow warns that one should not think of deserts spreading outwards. Desertification is the result of combined effects of climatic conditions and human actions, which reduce the carrying capacity of soils. Human causes of desertification include increasing population density in combination with unchanged agricultural technologies, overgrazing, deforestation and fuel wood collection. Desertification is on the increase, but the estimates vary considerably. UNEP (1993, quoted in Barrow, 1995) estimates that some 7–9 per cent of world land surface may have become desertified. However, other observers suggest that desertification may have been overestimated by a factor of 3.

Soil degradation refers to the decline of soil fertility and erosion, the loss of soil organic matter. It is a component of desertification, but is not limited to dry lands and does not always result in desert-like conditions. Causes of soil degradation include pollution, use of inappropriate agricultural machinery, overuse of fertiliser and deforestation (Barrow, 1995). Irrigation can also lead to soil degradation through salinisation. One assessment (Harrison, 1992, quoted in Barrow, 1995) suggests that between 1945 and 1990, 12.2 million sq km of agricultural land suffered serious loss of productivity due to soil degradation.

According to estimates based on a world soil degradation map discussed in Lomborg (2001, p. 104 ff), 17 per cent of all land is degraded to some extent. But only 0.07 per cent is severely degraded. Of agricultural land some 38 per cent is affected, 20 per cent moderately, 6 per cent strongly. Lomborg estimates that degradation results in a total cumulative loss of agricultural production of 5 per cent in forty-five years. This amounts to 0.1 per cent per year. Compared with the annual productivity increase of 1 per cent to 2 per cent per year, he concludes that the effect of land degradation on growth of production is limited.[12] However, in certain regions such as Sub-Saharan Africa, soil degradation can be a serious problem and can form an obstacle to growth of output. Preventing soil degradation and erosion can require substantial additional efforts and investments by farmers.

As will be emphasised in the following sections, land degradation is not necessarily irreversible. A switch to appropriate agricultural techniques and soil conservation policies can reclaim degraded soils, though sometimes at considerable cost.

10.2.4　*Models of agricultural development*

In their authoritative study *Agricultural Development. An International Perspective* (1971, 1985), Hayami and Ruttan distinguish five models of agricultural development: the resource exploitation model; the conservation model; the urban-industrial impact model; the diffusion model; and the high-payoff input model. Three of these models – the resource exploitation model; the conservation model and the high-payoff input model – are directly related to the three ways of expanding agricultural output discussed in the previous section: expansion of land, crop intensification and increased yields per harvest. But the models place more emphasis on the mechanisms operating in agricultural growth and development. They also clarify the distinction between the increase in returns per harvested crop and more traditional ways of expanding production.

The resource exploitation model
The resource exploitation model corresponds to the process of expanding the cultivated agricultural area as described in section 10.2.1. During most of agricultural history, expansion of cultivated area was the prime method of expanding total production. In *frontier societies* like the United States, the frontier

---

12 Similar conclusions are drawn by Ruttan (2002).

of the cultivated area expanded westwards at the expense of Indian hunters and gatherers, and nomadic pastoralists. Hayami and Ruttan also include the vent for surplus model – discussed in Chapter 8 – under the heading 'resource exploitation'. According to the vent for surplus model, farmers have reacted to the increasing demand for primary products since the middle of the nineteenth century by taking hitherto uncultivated land into use. As explained above, this route to growth of production has not yet been exhausted, but in different parts of the world the limits to further expansion of cultivated area are becoming visible.

A drawback of the resource exploitation model is that it makes a too absolute distinction between cultivated and not cultivated area. In section 10.2.2 it was emphasised that there was a gradual increase in cropping intensity. From a Boserupian perspective even land harvested only once every twenty years is being cultivated. When fallow land is disregarded, cultivated land as a percentage of potential cultivated area will be overestimated.

The conservation model

In the transition to annual crops in eighteenth-century England, animal manure and organic wastes came to play an important role in maintaining soil fertility. The inputs into the agricultural system were all supplied from within the agricultural sector.

From the basis of this agricultural system in England, German agronomists in particular developed the concept of soil exhaustion. In the conservation model the development of agricultural production involves a struggle to maintain the fertility of the soils. Whatever is taken out of the soil has to be put back in later on. If one continues to add other production factors to limited amounts of land without soil conservation, agriculture will sooner or later run into diminishing returns.

This is a rather static perspective in which nature sets limits to agricultural production. However, the theory of Boserup indicates that soil fertility and conservation can also be seen in a more dynamic perspective. By more intensive cultivation of the land, increasing returns per hectare may be realised without any loss of soil fertility. Nevertheless, Hayami and Ruttan include Boserup in the conservation model because the inputs into agriculture are forthcoming from within the agricultural sector itself in a self-sustaining system. The provision of agricultural inputs by the industrial sector dates from after the 'second agricultural revolution' in the nineteenth century.

The urban-industrial impact model

The urban-industrial impact model in its modern form was formulated by Theodor W. Schultz (1953). Schultz argued that productivity, agricultural incomes and growth of production are highest close to urban centres. This is because product markets and markets for factors of production function better in the vicinity of areas with rapid urban and industrial development. This leads to a more efficient allocation of production factors in agriculture.

Hayami and Ruttan consider the empirical evidence for this relationship to be inconclusive and its relevance for poorer developing countries rather limited.[13] A possible policy implication for developing countries would be to spread urbanisation and industry as much as possible over an entire country. This would be preferable to the growth of mega-cities. Decentralisation of urbanisation and rural industrialisation would intensify the linkages between agriculture and industry, which are positive for agricultural growth. This issue will be addressed further in the section on integrated rural development (section 10.7).

Irrespective of whether the distance to urban centres is really important, the degree to which agricultural markets contribute to efficient allocation is of obvious significance to agricultural development (Ellis, 1988: p. 75). With respect to West Africa, Hill argues that in some regions rural markets actually function quite well. One should not confuse production for the market with urbanisation (Hill, 1986). Lal and Myint (1996) speak of institutional underdevelopment, when lack of transport infrastructure, lack of information and inadequate channels of distribution isolate farmers from wider markets and stifle incentives to increase productivity. The Chinese agricultural reforms after 1978 provide a prime example of how improved functioning of agricultural markets contributed to very rapid growth of output and productivity between 1978 and 1985 (Huang, 1998).[14]

The diffusion model

There are huge differences in agricultural technology and productivity between countries, but also within countries, regions and even between different farmers in the same village. The diffusion model takes such differences as its point of departure. International and national diffusion of most advanced technologies can help narrow the gap between 'best practice' and the average farmer. *Inter alia*, the possibilities of transfer to developing countries of agricultural technologies developed in Western countries are featured.

The policy implications of this model include a strong emphasis on the construction of systems of agricultural extension and education. In many economically advanced countries (e.g. the Netherlands and the United States) there are highly developed networks of agricultural education and extension, which allow for very rapid diffusion of new agricultural technologies. In many developing countries substantial efforts have been made to build up systems of agricultural extension. There is widespread agreement on the fact that agricultural extension is one of the important building blocks of successful agricultural development.

Nevertheless, the diffusion model can also be criticised. An important assumption of the diffusion model is that the reason why farmers do not adopt

---

13 However, see Wiggins (2000) who argues on the basis of case studies that proximity to large urban centres provides market access and contributes to agricultural development.
14 After 1985, agricultural growth slowed down to a respectable 3.8 per cent per year, down from 7.4 per cent in the earlier period. New debates arose between proponents of further market reforms and proponents of reimposition of central planning.

new production technologies is that they are ignorant or ill-informed. This assumption is by no means justified. Farmers in developing countries are often better informed about local economic, ecological and social conditions than the extension workers sent out to educate them. According to Schultz (1964), farmers work quite efficiently and rationally, given the difficult conditions of their existence. They are poor but efficient.

Often, new seeds and agricultural techniques that perform well in laboratories or model farms turn out to be less successful in the field. They are insufficiently adapted to local conditions. This is especially the case when technologies and seeds developed in Western countries are transferred to developing countries. Farmers are justified in treating innovations with a healthy degree of suspicion.

With the introduction of new varieties, numerous 'secondary functions' of existing varieties – provision of hay, fodder, building materials, fuel, and so forth – are often forgotten. Also, traditional agricultural practices tend to minimise risk, which is of great importance to the survival of small farmers. In recent years, it is argued that agricultural innovation should try to build on existing local practices.

High-payoff input model

The high-payoff input model finds its inspiration in the work of Theodor Schultz (1964; 1968). As mentioned, Schultz maintained that traditional farmers act rationally. Given the conditions in which they have to operate, they allocate their resources optimally. Within the constraints of a traditional economy there are not many opportunities to realise increases in output and productivity.

Schultz therefore argued for new inputs coming from outside the agricultural sector to be made available to farmers with government support and subsidies. In this approach the emphasis was on stimulating technological progress which was adapted to local circumstances, the development of high-yielding varieties of maize, wheat and rice with high returns per harvest, and the search for the optimal conditions under which the new varieties would flourish. These conditions included the application of chemical fertilisers, chemical pesticides, irrigation and water control.

Schultz and his numerous followers argued in favour of investment in the following areas:

1. *Agricultural research centres* producing new, well-adapted, technical knowledge.
2. *Industrial activities oriented towards agriculture.* The industrial sector should develop and produce new agricultural inputs and supply them to farmers.
3. *Agricultural education and extension activities*, which help farmers to apply the technologies and use the new inputs.

The high-payoff input model incorporates the preceding three models – conservation, urban-industrial impact, and diffusion. The new inputs contribute to maintaining soil fertility when land use is intensified. Well-functioning factor and product markets are a prerequisite for the adequate utilisation of new inputs and technologies. Where small peasants have insufficient access to new inputs due to market imperfections, cheap agricultural credit should be made available. Attention should also be paid to transport infrastructure and the development of market systems through which agricultural surpluses can be traded. Schooling and agricultural extension are explicitly included in the high-payoff input approach, as in the diffusion model. However, in the high-payoff input model, there is much more emphasis on adapting new technologies to local conditions. The name of the model, finally, refers to the positive relationship between investments in agricultural research, schooling and extension and the high returns of the new inputs. According to Schultz, the returns to agricultural investment in research, development and extension are even higher than returns to investment in industry.

The theory of induced technological development

According to Hayami and Ruttan, even Schultz's high-payoff input model has its limitations. Insufficient attention is paid to the direction of technological development and the process of institutional change. Technological development does not happen in a vacuum. Its course is influenced, among others, by the relative scarcity of factors of production. If market prices of production factors reflect their relative scarcity, farmers will prefer technologies that economise on the most scarce production factors. If agricultural research institutions are responsive to farmers' needs and preferences and there are effective interactions between farmers, research institutions and industrial producers of agricultural inputs, farmers' preferences for certain types of technological development will be translated into research programmes and in production plans of suppliers of agricultural inputs. The responsiveness of research and development institutions to local farmers' needs is an institutional characteristic.

Where research institutions are responsive to producers' needs, a relative scarcity of labour will induce labour-saving technological development. This has been the path followed in the United States and also in England since the late nineteenth century. Where labour is plentiful and land is scarce, technological development in a responsive research environment will be directed towards land saving. Land-saving technology includes:

1. Biological technology, in particular selective breeding of plants, development of new varieties. In the past fifteen years, genetic modification techniques have been added to the arsenal of biotechnology.
2. Chemical technology, including organic and inorganic fertilisers that add nutrients for plant growth to the soil, and pesticides and herbicides.
3. Development of land and water control.

Examples of the land-saving path of technological development include the Netherlands, Denmark, late nineteenth-century Japan, and Taiwan between 1900 and 1940.

If the research system is closed, hierarchical and inflexible, induced technological development will be less influenced by the relative scarcity of production factors and the needs of producers. This may easily lead to technological developments that are insufficiently adapted to local conditions in developing countries. Thus the process of institutional development in the field of research, development and agricultural extension is also an important determinant of the nature of technological development.

Hayami and Ruttan point to the fact that the process of induced technological change is not a gradual process – even under the best of conditions – but rather a succession of dynamic disequilibria. It is comparable to the process of 'unbalanced growth' analysed by Hirschman and discussed in Chapter 9. Changes in relative scarcity and changes in technology can also induce changes in agricultural institutions, such as large landownership, communal ownership, tenure relationships, market characteristics, credit institutions and the organisation of research and extension.

The theory of induced technological development links up economic analysis with the analysis of institutions. Nevertheless, Hogg (2000) has recently criticised this theory from an evolutionary perspective. The theory states that if institutions are open and flexible the scarcity of different factors of production will influence the direction of research. Hogg argues that this neglects the historical context of path dependence. Once a research system evolves in a certain direction, it gets locked into this path and change will be difficult. Hogg argues that there are environmentally more sustainable alternatives to the present emphasis on yield improvement through biotechnological change which are not sufficiently explored because of lock-in.

10.2.5   The green revolution: increase in yields per harvest

The high-payoff input model is closely related to the third way of increasing agricultural production mentioned in section 9.2: increasing returns per harvested crop.[15] This model is often also called the 'green revolution'. The green revolution refers to breakthroughs in research into new varieties of maize, wheat and rice, which – together with a set of complementary inputs – may result in dramatic increases in the yields per harvest. When new varieties shorten the crop cycle from sowing to harvesting, the green revolution also allows for more crops per year and thus contributes to further intensification of agriculture and increase of output per unit of land. The characteristics of the green revolution are summarised in Box 10.4. The complementarities between all these so-called non-conventional inputs form one of the most basic characteristics of the green revolution. When some

---

15 Diffusion of technology, more intensive production and more efficient allocation can also take place within more traditional agricultural systems. These 'models' are not necessarily associated with recent technological breakthroughs in agriculture.

Box 10.4   Characteristics of the green revolution

- The development of new plant varieties with high yields that have been adjusted to local conditions, for example Mexican wheat varieties that are highly sensitive to fertiliser use, not very sensitive to sunlight, more resistant to diseases, and with short stems. The dwarf varieties introduced in India in 1965 had yields of 4,450 kg per hectare on experimental plots, compared to yields of 1,200 kg per hectare for older varieties. Outside experimental stations' yields of 3,200 kg per hectare were also quite impressive (Dixon, 1990).
- Use of industrially manufactured fertilisers, pesticides and herbicides.
- Land-saving innovations.
- Increased volume of – relatively cheap – investments in agricultural research; a positive attitude towards science-based agriculture.
- The organisation of an effective system of agricultural extension.
- Investments in irrigation and water control.
- The development of delivery systems for new seeds and inputs.
- The development of credit institutions and facilities, which enable farmers to purchase the new inputs.
- Complementarities between the different inputs: research, new seeds, industrial inputs, irrigation, education and extension, delivery and credit facilities.

elements of the package are lacking, the potential increases in yields will not be realised.

The green revolution is associated with two well-known institutes for agricultural research: the International Rice Research Institute (IRRI) founded in 1960 in Los Banos in the Philippines and the International Maize and Wheat Improvement Centre (Centro Internacional de Mejoramiento de Maiz y Trigo) CIMMYT in Mexico. In the 1950s, the CIMMYT developed high-productive varieties of maize and wheat. The success of wheat research promoted research into rice varieties. In the 1960s, new varieties of rice were developed at the IRRI. The work at these institutes was initially financed by the Rockefeller Foundation. Since 1971 it has been financed and supervised by the CGIAR (Consultative Group on International Agricultural Research). Today the CGIAR supervises the work of an international network of sixteen agricultural research institutes (Colman and Nixson, 1986, p. 217; Oasa, 1987).

The initial technological breakthroughs led to dramatically increased yields per crop. Also the rapid maturing of dwarf varieties allowed for more harvests per year. The enthusiasm about these breakthroughs was translated into political rhetoric by the term 'green revolution'. This term suggests that technological breakthroughs might lessen the need for fundamental social reorganisation and prevent the rise of revolutionary movements.

In rice production there were green revolutions long before the 1950s and 1960s: in medieval China, in Japan between 1881 and 1920, Taiwan between 1900 and 1940, and Korea in the 1920s. The early varieties developed by IRRI were based on genetic materials drawn from China, Taiwan, Japan and Indonesia. Semi-dwarf wheat originated in Japan in the 1800s (Parayil, 1992). In their famous article, 'The Role of Agriculture in Economic Development',

Johnston and Mellor (1961) analysed the rapid increase in agricultural production and productivity in Japanese agriculture between 1881 and 1920. According to their estimates, production increased by 77 per cent, while the area of land used for agriculture was expanded by only 21 per cent. The yields per hectare increased by 46 per cent, per capita food production by 20 per cent. The Japanese example shows how technological developments of a mainly biological nature can lead to substantial increases in yields per hectare and per head of the population in a densely populated area (van der Meer and Yamada, 1990, p. 73 ff). Nevertheless, the sudden increases in productivity achieved in the research institutes in the 1950s and 60s had the character of a technological breakthrough.

In India new wheat seeds were introduced in 1965, of which the yields per hectare were far in excess of the yields of traditional varieties. New rice varieties were introduced in the Philippines in 1966 and spread rapidly to different Asian countries. By 1970 the new strains were being cultivated over an area of 10 million hectares. Within a few years Pakistan ceased to be dependent on food imports from the United States and India became self-sufficient in food.

The success of the green revolution in the 1960s and the euphoria that followed gave rise to a wave of criticism. Part of this criticism concerned technical matters. Outside the experimental fields and laboratory conditions yields of newly developed varieties were often disappointing. The seeds performed poorly under less than optimum conditions (Griffin, 1976; Pearse, 1977; Glaeser, 1987). The new varieties were susceptible to diseases, pests and weather conditions. They were not sufficiently adjusted to local conditions. Chambers (1983) argued that often valuable local knowledge and insights were lost, owing to international research programmes and their recommendations. Dixon gives an interesting example of the rejection by farmers of a new, fast-growing variety of sorghum in Ethiopia. The new variety grew faster but had less stem and leaves than existing varieties. Stems and leaves were traditionally used as roofing material and fodder. Agricultural researchers had neglected the secondary functions of sorghum (Dixon, 1990, p. 97). Furthermore, critics pointed to the dangers of the loss in genetic diversity due to the introduction of several standardised varieties (*genetic erosion*). Diversity acts as an insurance policy against natural calamities, climatic influences and plant diseases. The new production techniques turned out to have various environmental hazards (Barrow, 1995). Topsoils were eroded as a result of intensive use. The use of nitrogenous fertilisers resulted in eutrophication of freshwater streams and lakes. Pesticides created health problems and pests were increasingly becoming resistant. Applications of fertiliser ran into diminishing returns (Glaeser, 1987; Oasa, 1987). Finally, it was claimed that the nutritional value of new varieties, particularly of rice, was lower than that of traditional varieties and food crops.

Technical problems and criticisms gave rise to the search for technical solutions: developing disease-resistant plants, better adjustment to local conditions, setting up gene banks, biological pest control, integrated pest management, improved nitrogen absorption of new varieties, and so forth. In response to criticisms, new agricultural research institutes were founded, focusing on specific crops, climatic conditions or problems. According to Oasa (1987) there was a shift from the search for new breakthroughs to a second generation of research of a more incremental nature. The new approach tried to achieve better integration of technological change with social factors and environmental constraints.

The most fundamental criticisms of the green revolution are of a political-economy nature (Glaeser, 1987; Griffin, 1976; 1981; Pearse, 1977; Pinstrup-Anderson, 1982; Pinstrup-Anderson and Hazell, 1985). These criticisms state that the introduction of the green revolution leads to increased rural inequality, increased landlessness and to impoverishment of the rural masses. The criticisms include the following elements:

1. Large farmers have better access to new inputs than small peasants. The green revolution therefore makes for more inequality. First, large farmers have financial reserves, which they can use to purchase expensive new inputs. Second, they have relationships and contacts with government officials and agricultural extension institutions. They have easier access to cheap loans, information and water supplies. For example, this applies to India and Bangladesh, where coalitions between medium-sized and large farmers and government officials have emerged (Bol, 1983; Cassen, 1978).
2. The position of small peasants is threatened by the increasing cost of inputs. To purchase new inputs they are forced to contract loans and go into debt. They become more and more dependent on the sale of their surplus production on the market. When yields or prices are disappointing in a given year they may be forced to sell their land. Peasants have less access to land, capital, new seeds and complementary inputs such as water and fertiliser. In many countries they are also dependent on large landowners for credit. Thus, the green revolution increases rural inequality and landlessness. Sometimes poor peasants are not dispossessed of land, but are forced to lease out their lands to rich farmers and work on these lands as farm labourers.
3. When prices fall because of increases in total production, small peasants who were unable to apply the new technologies will be worse off. This is also conducive to inequality.
4. Because of their economic power large landowners pay too little for their production factors, land and capital. For example, they have access to subsidised credit so they will use too capital-intensive methods. Large farmers tend to employ less farm labour and try to get out from under traditional sharecropping arrangements. All these factors together make for increasing landlessness, concentration of landownership and rural unemployment (for example in India; see Singh, 1982). Also, the total volume of production may be lower than is the case when production factors are allocated more efficiently.

5. Farmers in developing countries become more and more dependent on a few agricultural multinationals, which have a monopoly on the provision of new seed varieties.

6. Production for export may have negative effects on women's allocation of time and energy. The best plots of land are reserved for cash crops, which are often cultivated by males. Food production is shifted to land of marginal quality, often located far from the household dwelling. In many African countries food production is the preserve of women. Their position can be affected negatively by the shift to export crops. In addition to their household duties, they have to travel long distances to cultivate their fields.

7. The green revolution involves increasing production for the market and exports. According to the critics, it is conceivable that an increase in production per hectare goes hand in hand with decreased availability of food in a given region, especially when the landless labourers have insufficient means to buy food. Thus, the green revolution may be lead to impoverishment and malnutrition.

These criticisms contain some valuable elements. Introduction of technological changes, with no regard for power relationships, class structures and institutions, may result in reinforced dualism and increasing inequality. However, in some cases the initially even-handed critical analysis of the green revolution by authors like Griffin was replaced by outright ideological rejection in the 1970s and 1980s. The green revolution came to be seen as an international conspiracy of the capitalist agribusiness, at the expense of human values and food requirements in developing countries.

In reply to the often one-sided criticisms of the green revolution, numerous counter-arguments have been put forward (see, for example, Ellis, 1988; Hayami and Ruttan, 1985; Pinstrup-Anderson, 1985).

First, the argumentation of critics is often fragmentary, based on case studies rather than aggregates. There is a tendency, especially amongst anthropologists, to idealise traditional agricultural systems. Second, technological change is an absolute must when population is increasing rapidly. If technology does not change and population increases rapidly, marginal returns to agricultural efforts will decrease. This inevitably results in a decrease in food availability per head of the population.

Critics like Griffin remarked that there are no significant differences in production trends before and after the introduction of new varieties. Therefore they concluded that the outcomes of the new technologies were rather disappointing. Hayami and Ruttan (1985), however, note that this argumentation contains serious logical flaws. One should not compare the situation before and after the introduction of new varieties, since population density is changing over time. What one should compare is the productivity trend with a growing population *without* technological change and the productivity trend with population growth *with* technological change. In the absence of new technologies, per capita production and production per hectare would have been much lower, than is presently the case.

It is true that larger farmers introduce new varieties sooner than small peasants. After some years, however, there is usually a diffusion of the new technologies to other categories of farmers. Small farmers and peasants also start to adopt the new varieties and apply the new technologies. There is nothing intrinsically capital-intensive about the green revolution (Hayami and Ruttan, 1985). It can be applied just as well on small as on large farms. The above-mentioned example of Japan illustrates the labour-intensive potential of the new techniques. In post-war Indonesia and China technological innovation also appears to contribute to expansion of employment in agriculture. In these countries, the relatively equal distribution of land is also a positive factor in this respect.

Finally, growth of agricultural production may result in lower prices for food. As production for own consumption becomes less important, an increasing part of the rural population of developing countries is dependent on the purchase of foodstuffs on the market. The poor thus benefit from lower food prices, in both urban and rural areas.

In conclusion one may say that increases in productivity and technological change in agriculture are absolutely essential to feed a growing world population. Today, this is no longer disputed, even by critics of the green revolution (Glaeser, 1987). In particular in Sub-Saharan Africa there is great need for technological advances in semi-arid agriculture, which may contribute to agricultural growth as happened previously in Asia and Latin America. More research in this field is urgently needed. Moreover, older research focused primarily on maize, wheat and rice, while in many developing countries other food crops provide the basic foodstuffs (tuberous crops like cassavas, sweet potatoes, potatoes, yams, taro and tree crops like sago palm, plantain and breadfruit). Research into these crops is still highly underdeveloped.

The critical debate on the green revolution continues, but international research has also to some extent – at least on paper – responded to the earlier criticisms (Oasa, 1987).[16] There is more emphasis on the ecological consequences of new technologies, and new approaches such as the *farming systems approach* try to integrate ecological, social and technological factors. Attempts are made to adapt existing traditional technologies and practices to present-day requirements. Since 1972 there has been a specialised research institute for crops in the semi-arid tropics (ICRASAT) in Hyderabad, India. In 1976, the International Centre for Agricultural Research in Dry Areas was founded in Beirut. Since 1974, the International Board for Plant Genetic Resources (IBPGR) has focused on genetic diversity. For various crops and kinds of livestock there are specialised research institutes located in different parts of the world.[17] Also, in

---

16 According to Oasa, who represents the critical strand in the literature, the response is real but insufficient. It does not tackle the fundamental political economic contradictions.
17 These institutes include the International Potato Centre in Peru, the International Livestock Centre for Africa in Ethiopia and the West African Rice Development Association in Monrovia, Liberia.

the international research effort, there are attempts to focus on technologies which are useful and feasible for smaller resource-poor farmers.

In the introduction of technological innovations, an increase in rural inequality in some stages of the process of agricultural development is probably inevitable, as wealthy and less risk-averse farmers will tend to adopt new highly productive technologies at an earlier stage than poor, risk-vulnerable small farmers and peasants. In the light of the political economic criticisms discussed above, however, more attention should be paid to the institutional and political aspects of technological change. Institutions should be designed to promote technological developments which are more in line with factor proportions. When labour is abundant, labour-intensive technological improvements should be sought. Small farmers should get easier access to credit facilities. Subsidised credit to wealthy farmers should be abolished. Land reforms could help improve the position of peasants and landless rural workers. Policy should ensure that not only the urban population, but also people in rural areas benefit from lower prices for food.

10.2.6   The green revolution continued: biotechnology and genetically modified crops

The original technological breakthroughs of the green revolution were based on selective plant breeding. However, since the 1960s, the pace of biotechnological change has accelerated dramatically. Advances in gene splicing, tissue culture and genetic manipulation have created new possibilities for developing new strains of plants more rapidly and equipping them with desired features. Along with the emergence of new opportunities, the fears of unintended social and technological consequences of genetic manipulation have also been magnified. The debates on the green revolution are being refought with a new intensity at the start of the twenty-first century.

Gene splicing allows for the industrial production of seeds with desirable characteristics. A drawback of these seeds and older hybrid seeds is that they do not reproduce. Farmers in developing countries cannot replant part of their harvest. They have to buy seeds every year. This makes farmers in developing countries more and more dependent on the large profit-oriented agricultural multinationals.

Genetic manipulation not only allows for a more rapid development of new strains, it even allows for transgenic modification of plants by adding genes from other plants or even animals (e.g. genes from frogs added to tomatoes). In agriculture, GM foods have advanced at an astounding rate since 1995 in the USA, Canada, Argentina and China. Though commercial applications of Genetically Modified Crops were only released for production in the mid-1990s, by 2000 they accounted for 54 per cent of soybean production, 72 per cent of cotton production and 33 per cent of corn production in the USA (Paarlberg,

2001). The USA has followed a permissive approach to genetically modified crops, arguing that genetic modification does not differ essentially from traditional selective breeding. Europe and Japan, on the other hand, have taken a precautionary stance. They argue that as long as the risks of GM crops are unknown, one should be careful in introducing them. Developing countries are caught in the middle of this transatlantic trade debate. As potential exporters to European countries and potential recipients of European aid, they have been reluctant to introduce GM crops.

Here, we provide a brief summary of the relevant issues in the modern debates on biotechnology. The critics of biotechnological advances emphasise the following points, many of which echo the debates about the green revolution (see Bruinsma, 2003, ch. 11; Hogg, 2000; Ruttan, 2002):

- *Loss of genetic diversity.* The increased reliance on a few standardised strains of food crops creates large evolutionary risks. Genetic diversity peaked in the nineteenth century, and has since declined. There is increasing risk of catastrophic losses due to epidemics, against which variety would provide a defence.
- *Increasing danger of soil degradation, erosion and waterlogging* as a result of the high-input strategies and intensification strategies, requiring more fertilisers, more pesticides and more water.
- *Increased dependence of farmers in poor countries on monopolistic seed producers in the advanced countries.* Patenting of gene sequences has made farmers more dependent on the large biotechnology firms.[18] The strengthening of intellectual property rights protection may have speeded up innovation, but it reduces the spread of innovation in agriculture.
- *Threats to bio-safety from genetic manipulation.* There are risks of gene leakage with unintended consequences, such as the spread of pest resistance to weeds, creating super weeds, harmful competition with desirable species, unwanted resistance of pests to pesticides and the creation of new strains of viral pathogens.
- *Threats to consumer health through the spread of new allergens.*
- *The neglect of research on environmentally friendly alternatives to specialisation and high-input agriculture.* Both Hogg (2000) and Bruinsma (2003, ch. 11) argue that Low External Input and Sustainable Agriculture (LEISA) alternatives, such as biodynamic farming, integrated pest management and polycultures, can be surprisingly productive and show substantial productivity gains. But the bulk of ongoing research continues to go into high-input avenues of research.

The proponents of modern biotechnological research argue that the differences between modern biotechnology and traditional breeding practices have

---

18 While the research leading to the green revolution was predominantly publicly funded, modern biotechnological research is dominated by a small number of private companies (Byerlee and Fischer, 2002).

been exaggerated. Genetically modified plants have a number of important potential advantages for farmers in developing countries:

- *Increased yields.* Biotechnological research can contribute to the continued increase in yields per harvest, which are necessary to sustain food supply in excess of population.
- *Lower fertiliser needs.* Genetically modified varieties have lower fertiliser needs, as they are more efficient in absorbing nutrients. This is environmentally advantageous.
- *Pest resistance.* Genetic modification can produce pest-resistant varieties which require less pesticides, resulting in less pollution and health risks. Reduction of crop losses due to pests and plant diseases will be an important avenue for production increases once biological limits of further yield increases are approached.
- *Disease resistance.* Disease-resistant varieties, such as new strains of sweet potatoes, can substantially reduce the cost of labour and the cost of chemical inputs.
- *Efficiency.* Genetic modification is more efficient than traditional breeding techniques because it can focus on specialised traits.

Gale Johnson (2002) argues that opposition to genetically modified crops on the part of Europe and non-governmental organisations is harmful to developing countries, and forms a threat towards their prospects of improved productivity and nutrition.

While the green revolution spread very rapidly from its introduction onwards, the spread of genetically modified crops in developing countries has so far been retarded. Only China has introduced new genetically modified cotton varieties on a reasonable scale. Other countries with strong biotechnological research capabilities, such as Brazil and India, have been hesitant to introduce these new crops so far because of opposition from many developed countries.

One might expect that, once the dust of the debate has settled, the further spread of new varieties in developing countries will pick up again. The need for technological advances is great and the potential of new technologies is large. But given the rate of technological change, and the potential risks and unknown factors, the present debate on the pros and cons of genetic modification and possible alternatives to high-input agriculture serves a positive function.

10.2.7   Summary and prospects

Table 10.8 summarises the effects of expansion of the agricultural area and increases in yields per unit of land since 1961. The increase in yields per hectare incorporates the effects of increased cropping frequency and higher yields per crop. During the past forty years, no less than 23 per cent of the increase in total crop production in developing countries can be explained by the expansion

Table 10.8 *Sources of growth of crop production, 1961–2030*

| | Production Growth Attributable to (%) | | | | | |
| | Expansion of arable land | | Increases in cropping intensity | | Increases in yield per harvest | |
	1961–99	1997/9–2030	1961-99	1997/9–2030	1961–99	1997/9–2030
All developing countries	23	21	6	12	71	67
excl. China	23	24	13	13	64	63
excl. China and India	29	28	16	16	55	56
Sub-Saharan Africa	35	27	31	12	34	61
Near East/North Africa	14	13	14	19	72	68
Latin America and the Caribbean	46	33	−1	21	55	46
South Asia	6	6	14	13	80	81
East Asia	26	5	−5	14	79	81
World	15		7		78	

Source: Bruinsma (2003: p. 126, table 4.2).

of cultivated area.[19] In the same period increases in cropping intensity account for 8 per cent of agricultural growth, with increases in yields accounting for the lion's share of 71 per cent. The FAO projections up till 2030 suggest that expansion of area continues to be an important source of agricultural growth (21 per cent), with cropping intensity (12 per cent) and yield increases (67 per cent) accounting for the remainder. Yield increases are thus by far the most important sources of agricultural growth. This highlights the continued importance of biotechnological research and development. Without this, agricultural development will grind to a halt.

For land-abundant regions of Africa and Latin America, the projected contributions of area expansion are much higher than the developing country averages (27 and 33 per cent respectively). As these regions harbour most of the world's tropical rainforests, this indicates that increases in agricultural production in these regions may conflict with the preservation of tropical forests and woodlands. On the other hand, intensification of production and increasing yields per harvest may also threaten the environment, since intensification involves the use of increasing amounts of chemical fertilisers, pesticides and herbicides which pollute the soil and ground water (Barrow, 1995, p. 194 ff; World Bank, 1992a, p. 134). According to the World Bank, the greatest challenge for agricultural policy is to increase production and at the same time to protect the natural environment. When population increases to an estimated 9.3 billion people in 2050, cereal production – which accounts for 90 per cent of the world demand for food – should be increased by a factor 1.7. This is a difficult task in the light of the various constraints to expansion of area, intensification of production and yield increase discussed above. But, given sufficient investment in agricultural research and development in developing countries and advanced economies, it is not an impossible task (Bruinsma, 2003; Ruttan, 2002).

19 Similar figures are found for the period 1961–1988 by Gillin and Krane (1989). With respect to cereals the contribution of area expansion is much lower than for total food production: 8 per cent between 1961 and 1990; see World Bank (1992).

Summarising, we observe that agricultural production increased in the long run due to expansion of cultivated area, increases in cropping frequency and improved yields per crop. In the history of agriculture the most important factors were expansion of cultivated area, and increases in cropping frequency and intensification of land use by applying more labour per unit of land. In many developing regions these avenues of production expansion have not yet been exhausted. But as the limits to labour intensification are being reached (e.g. in Asian countries like Indonesia and China), the emphasis will increasingly shift to the increase of yields per crop by means of biotechnological innovation. Technological innovation in turn may lead to further intensification of production, for example in glasshouse production of vegetables and intensive cattle- and poultry-breeding. There is no reason why technological change in future years should not continue to allow food production to expand more rapidly than population. Still, there are numerous economic, institutional, biological and environmental barriers to production growth. There is a continued need for agricultural research on new agricultural technologies that are well adapted to local conditions and which minimise negative environmental impacts.

10.3   Food consumption and nutrition

In section 10.1, we showed that world food production exceeds the growth of world population. With the exception of Sub-Saharan Africa, this also holds for food production in developing countries. However, this does not mean that the appalling problems of malnutrition and starvation in developing countries are in any way close to a solution.

In his famous study, *Poverty and Famines* (1981), Amartya Sen argues that the occurrence of starvation and malnutrition depends not only on food production and food availability, but also on people's actual *entitlements* to food. These entitlements may be based on one's own labour (a family producing for its own needs), on landownership (the owner of land is entitled to part of the harvest), on purchasing power (money that has been earned is used to purchase food) and on legislation or government measures (e.g. food rationing, food distribution, social security). Analysing two notorious famines (the Bengal famine from 1942 to 1944, and the famine in Ethiopia, 1972–4), Sen shows that the famine was not primarily due to insufficient production of food per head of population. In both famines, a slight shortfall in production led to widespread speculation, food hoarding and skyrocketing of prices. Food distribution systems failed in moving food surpluses to deficit areas. Consumers lacked the financial means to buy food at its inflated prices. If governments had imported limited amounts of food and taken the responsibility for its distribution, prices could have been brought under control and famines could have been averted. Since independence in 1947, India has pursued such policies. Unlike what has happened in China between 1958 and 1960, there have been no large-scale famines in India in the post-war period (Sen, 1982). A relatively open society and timely identification of food shortages are the prerequisites for success of a policy aimed at preventing famines. Sen's exposition illustrates the importance of prices. Poor people may profit greatly from price decreases due to production growth (see section 10.2.5).

One should distinguish between *malnutrition* and *starvation* (van de Meer, 1983). Malnutrition refers to a situation where, during longer periods of time, the diet is insufficient for people to lead a healthy and productive life. Starvation is a situation in which people die because of an acute shortage of food. *Malnutrition* typically occurs in rural areas prior to the harvesting season. In sparsely populated areas, with no scarcity of land, undernourishment results from shortfalls in production in terms of quantity or quality. In densely populated areas, social inequality and unequal access to the means of production play a more important role. Even when the volume of food production is sufficient, the poor and landless may have too little purchasing power to realise their entitlements to food. Thus, in some areas undernourishment may increase while production is growing. *Famines* are mainly caused by crop failures, natural disasters, wars, civil wars and social disruption. Again, it is not always the absolute shortage of food at an aggregate level that causes famine. Rather, famines are associated with situations in which people in given areas are unable to effectuate their entitlements to food.

In the twentieth century great famines occurred primarily in China, the USSR and India (Arnold, 1988). In 1920–1 a famine in China led to 0.5 million casualties. In 1943 the Chinese province of Honan was struck by a famine resulting in 2 million to 3 million casualties. The latest great Chinese famine took place from 1958 to 1961. The estimates of number of casualties during this period vary from 16 to 30 million. Between 1942 and 1944 a famine killed 3 million people in Bengal, part of former British India. In 1921 a famine claimed 1 million to 3 million lives in the Soviet Union. Between 1932 and 1934 5 million people died, owing to famines that resulted from Stalin's forced agricultural collectivisation. A famine hit Bangladesh in 1974; here the number of deaths was estimated to be between 300,000 and 1 million. The Ethiopian famine in 1984–5 led to over 1 million casualties.

In sparsely populated areas, famines are also caused by shortcomings in infrastructure. When there are local shortages of food due to crop failures, poor infrastructure and malfunctioning distribution systems will hamper the transport of food from surplus areas or other countries. In densely populated areas infrastructure is usually better. These areas can import food whenever there are shortages. In such conditions famines are primarily caused by social disruption, government policy failures, civil wars, rebellions and international wars. Countries where social disruption resulted in famine include Burundi, Cambodia, Bangladesh, Biafra, Ethiopia, Rwanda, Somalia and the Sudan.

The degree of openness of a society is also of the greatest importance for the prevention of famine. In China massive famines could occur between 1958 and 1961 without any knowledge of them reaching the outside world and the international community. In India, on the other hand, imminent famines rapidly led to mobilisation of national and international relief actions (Sen, 1982). Because of improved medical facilities, better infrastructure, better communication facilities, and international relief organisations, the number of deaths due to famines since 1950 has declined in comparison with the first half of the twentieth century. The exception is the hermetically closed society of North Korea, where reportedly millions of people died of famine between 1994 and 1998.[20]

Table 10.9 and Table 10.10 present rough trends in availability of food in developing countries. Average food availability is calculated as the sum of domestic food production (in calories) plus food imports and minus food exports, divided by total population. Table 10.9 shows that the average amount of calories available per person in developing countries increased from 89 per cent of average requirements in 1964 to 116 per cent of average requirements in 1998–2000.[21] In absolute numbers, average kilocalories available per person increased worldwide from 2,360 in 1964 to 2,800 in 2000. In developing countries they increased from 2,050 to 2,700. Especially in Asia and the Near East, the availability of food calories improved considerably. In Sub-Saharan Africa the food supply situation is much less favourable. Though there was some improvement in

Table 10.9 *Average availability of calories, 1964–2015*[a]

	Kilocalories per person per day					as % of average requirements				
	1964/6	1974/6	1984/6	1997/9	2015[c]	1964/6	1974/6	1984/6	1997/9	2015[c]
Sub-Saharan Africa	2,058	2,079	2,057	2,195	2,360	88.3	89.2	88.3	94.2	101.3
Latin America and the Caribbean	2,393	2,546	2,689	2,824	2,980	99.3	105.7	111.6	117.2	123.7
Near East/North Africa	2,290	2,591	2,953	3,006	3,090	93.4	105.7	120.5	122.6	126.1
South Asia	2,017	1,986	2,205	2,403	2,700	88.2	86.9	96.5	105.1	118.1
East Asia	1,957	2,105	2,559	2,921	3,060	85.6	92.1	112.0	127.8	133.9
Industrial countries[b]	2,947	3,065	3,206	3,380	3,440	115.4	120.0	125.5	132.4	134.7
Transition countries[b]	3,222	3,385	3,379	2,906	3,060	125.5	131.9	131.6	113.2	119.2
Developing countries	2,054	2,152	2,450	2,681	2,850	88.7	92.9	105.8	115.8	123.1
World	2,358	2,435	2,655	2,803	2,940	98.9	102.1	111.3	117.5	123.3

Notes:
[a] The average caloric requirement differs from country to country. It depends on average height, age and sex distribution of the population, climactic conditions and average requirement of physical effort. The harder the effort, the more calories required. The average caloric requirement in this table is the number of calories required for normal productive functioning in society.
[b] Industrial countries, formerly called developed market economies. Transition countries: former Soviet Union and Eastern European countries.
[c] FAO projections.
*Sources:*Kcal per day from 1964 onwards from: Bruinsma (2003), p. 30, table 2.1; 1961/63 from: FAO, *Production Yearbook*, 1988 and 1992. Average caloric requirements calculated from FAO (1975), *State of Food and Agriculture 1975*, p. 76. The average caloric requirements for the Far East (South Asia, East and Southeast Asia) were calculated as the average of the older categories centrally planned economies and market economies.

20 Andrew Natsios, The Politics of Famine in North Korea, Special Report, United States Institute of Peace, Washington, DC, http://www.usip.org/events/
21 Using average requirements as calculated in FAO (1975). In reality average requirements may increase over time as populations grow older and body height and weight increases.

Table 10.10 *Undernourishment in developing countries, 1969–2000*[a]

	Number of undernourished persons (millions)			Undernourished persons as % of the population			
	1979–81	1990–2	1998–2000	1969–71	1979–81	1990–2	1998–2000
Sub Saharan Africa	125.4	166.4	195.9	35.0	36.5	35.1	33.3
Near East/North Africa	21.5	26.0	40.0	24.0	9.1	8.1	10.4
Asia and the Pacific, of which	727.3	567.3	508.1		31.6	20.2	16.1
East and Southeast Asia	396.1	274.7	191.9		28.0	16.3	10.4
East Asia	307.7	198.2	128.4	44.0	29.0	16.0	9.6
China	303.8	193.0	119.0		30.4	16.5	9.4
Southeast Asia	88.4	76.5	63.5		24.9	17.2	12.5
South Asia	330.5	291.6	314.9	34.0	37.3	26.0	24.1
India	261.5	215.6	233.3		38.0	25.0	23.5
Latin American and the Caribbean	45.9	58.8	54.8	19.0	12.9	13.3	10.9
Developing Countries [b]	920.1	818.5	798.8	36.0	28.0	20.0	17.0
Transition countries			30.2				7.0
Developed countries			11.0				
World			840.0				

Notes:
[a] Alexandratos (1995) defines undernourishment thresholds in relation to the basal metabolism rate (BMR). The BMR is the energy requirement of a person who is fasting and inactive in a warm environment. It varies according to age, weight and climate and ranges from 1,760 kcal per day for Asia to 1,985 for Latin America. Malnourished persons consume insufficient food to perform light activities and maintain their body weight. The threshold value is set at 1.54 BMR. Recent FAO sources do not provide the threshold values for undernourishment. We assumed they are the same as those of Alexandratos.
[b] 69–71: 93 developing countries, from 1979 onwards 99 countries.
Sources: FAO, *State of Food Insecurity in the World 2002*, http://www.fao.org/ p.9 and p. 31 table 1; 1969–71 from Alexandratos (1995), p. 50.

the 1990s, only 95 per cent of the average caloric requirements were being met in 1998–2000. It should be stressed that these figures are averages. When one considers separate countries, it turns out that during the 1990s the per capita food availability decreased in no less than 27 of the 95 developing countries for which data were available (Bruinsma, 2003, Table A2). Fifteen of the countries experiencing a decline were in Sub-Saharan Africa, six in the Near East and three in Latin America and the Caribbean. There are currently 30 countries with less than 2,200 kcal per person per day. On the other hand, there are 33 developing countries with more than 2,600 calories per head of the population at the end of the 1990s.

It is important that much of the improvements took place in six large countries with more than 100 million inhabitants (e.g. Brazil, China, India, Indonesia, Nigeria and Pakistan). Of the largest developing countries, only Bangladesh remained at low levels of per capita availability.

Sufficient availability of food does not mean that there is no undernourishment. Access to food is very unequally distributed, not only amongst regions within a country, amongst households and even amongst the members of a single household (men versus women, adults versus children). As explained above, not all individuals are equally capable of effectuating their entitlements to food. Availability of calories does not equal consumption, not even at aggregate levels (Alexandratos, 1988, p. 57).[22] If the variation in nutrition is large enough, sufficient average availability in a country can coexist with widespread undernutrition. Within households young children in particular are likely to be exposed to malnutrition. Further, part of the available food is lost, owing to problems of transport or storage. Thus, a sufficient average availability of food does not necessarily preclude widespread malnutrition and hunger.

Table 10.10 contains data on numbers and percentages of undernourished people in ninety-nine developing countries. When caloric intake is less than 80 per cent of average caloric requirements, there are serious health hazards and dangers of arrested growth. When caloric intake is between 80 per cent and 90 per cent of average requirements, there are no direct health risks, but the calories consumed are insufficient to lead an 'active working life' (van der Eng, 1992; World Bank, 1986a). This definition is used in Table 10.10. As in the case of health, there is a clear-cut relation between nutritional status and economic productivity. Undernourished people are less productive and are less able to earn a decent living. Improving nutritional import therefore contributes in a wider fashion to poverty reduction and economic performance.

Table 10.10 shows that marked progress has been made in reducing malnutrition. In the 30 years since 1969, the percentage of undernourished people in developing countries has declined by more than 50 per cent from 36 per cent to 17 per cent. In absolute terms the number of undernourished people declined from 920 million in 1979 to 800 million in 1998–2000. The declines have been especially marked in East and Southeast Asia. Highest rates of malnutrition are found in Sub-Saharan Africa. Here the numbers of undernourished people have swelled substantially, while the percentages show hardly any change.

In spite of progress, the numbers of undernourished people are still vast. In 1998, there were in total 840 million undernourished persons, of which 34 million were in countries of the former Soviet Bloc, where malnutrition has been on the increase since 1991.

The majority of undernourished people is found in South Asia (Bangladesh, India, Pakistan and Nepal), East and Southeast Asia and Sub-Saharan Africa. In Asia the absolute numbers are influenced by the vast population figures. Yet, on this continent, the proportions of undernourished persons are declining rapidly. In sub-Saharan Africa the number of undernourished people has increased rapidly and the proportions remain high, in spite of some marginal improvement.

The World Food Summit held in Rome in 1996 set a target for the reduction of undernourishment by 2015 (FAO, 1996). Undernourishment was to be reduced to 50 per cent of the base year level of 1990–92. Present projections of the

22 Alexandratos writes that the estimated availability of calories for developing countries as a whole is higher than what would appear to be realistic on the basis of evolution of per capita incomes.

FAO (Bruinsma, 2003)[23] suggest that undernourishment will indeed continue to decline. But the rate of improvement is slowing down. If present trends continue, the reductions in malnutrition will fall far short of the targets agreed in 1996.

Concluding remarks on agricultural policy

The above data illustrate the urgency of further improvements in the world food situation. Since the 1970s the climate of opinion with respect to the potential contributions of agriculture to development has gradually become more positive. In several countries, increasing attention has been paid to the agricultural sector in development policy. Attempts have been made to counter the 'urban-industrial bias'.

The examples of India, China and Indonesia illustrate that it pays for developing economies to pay more attention to agriculture. In these densely populated countries it proved possible to realise substantial increases in agricultural production per hectare and per head by combining new inputs, infrastructural investment, institutional changes and better incentives. Earlier pessimistic predictions about agricultural involution and the negative prospects for agricultural growth (Geertz, 1963a) have proved to be unfounded.

On the production side, price policies should provide positive incentives for farmers to increase their production and productivity. In addition, policy should focus on maintenance and improvement of agricultural infrastructure with respect to water control, land development and storage and distribution. Finally, investments in agricultural research and extension remain of considerable importance.

In the international arena, economically advanced countries should provide less protection to their agricultural sector and reduce subsidies on agricultural exports to developing countries. Such exports are dumped on developing country markets at prices far below world market prices. They provide strong disincentives to agricultural producers in developing countries and have negative effects on agricultural development. Some progress has been made towards reducing protectionism in the US and the European Union. But levels of protection are still unacceptably high.

On the consumption side, entitlements to food should be extended. This can be done among others by improving access to land or by stimulating off-farm employment in the rural sector for those who can no longer find employment in agriculture. This subject will be taken up again in the following sections on rural development. In times of temporary food shortages, national governments and the international community should intervene in the market to prevent prices from soaring, disequilibria from getting out of hand and famines breaking out. But permanent intervention in the form of subsidised food for the urban population should be phased out.

---

23 FAO, The State of Food Security in the World, http://www.fao.org/

10.4   Rural development versus agricultural development

Rural development is a broader concept than agricultural development in two senses. First, rural development refers not only to economic changes, but also to transformations and changes in wider rural societies. A multidisciplinary approach is therefore called for. It is especially interesting to combine economic studies of agricultural development with anthropological and sociological studies of processes of socio-economic change in rural areas. Second, rural development indicates that economic activities in rural areas are not limited to agriculture. Though agriculture is the defining characteristic of rural areas, rural populations have always been involved in other economic activities such as trade, handicraft production and services. More recently public services and rural industries have also been established in rural areas. Non-agricultural activities are becoming more and more important. The interrelationships between these various activities are studied in the context of rural development. Without claiming to be comprehensive, the following sections provide an introduction to some interesting aspects of changes in rural communities.

The study of rural development is interesting for quite a few reasons. Table 10.11 shows that the share of agriculture in the total labour force is still quite high, though it has been declining over the years. The share is highest in Asian and African countries. A much lower share is found in Latin America. The share of the rural population in the total population is even higher than that of agriculture in the labour force. In 2000, 60 per cent of the total population of developing countries lived in rural areas.

The absolute numbers of inhabitants of rural areas in developing countries have increased from 1.4 billion in 1950 to 2.9 billion in 1995. Only in exceptional cases does the absolute number of rural inhabitants show a decline (e.g. Argentina, Brazil, South Korea, Turkey). Presently, the growth of rural population is slowing down. But in spite of rapid urbanisation, the rural population of developing countries is still expected to grow by around 0.2 per cent per year till it reaches a peak in 2025 (UN, 2002). Apart from the demographic importance of the rural sector, the study of rural development is also very important because rural–urban income differentials are increasing and so much of global poverty is concentrated in rural areas.

Table 10.10 also shows that the share of agricultural production in national income is much lower than the share of agriculture in the total labour force. There are two explanations for this. First, labour productivity in the agricultural sector is lower than in other sectors. Second, many persons who are registered as employed in agriculture are also active in other sectors of the economy. For example, 10 per cent to 20 per cent of the male agricultural labour force also has some part-time employment in the rural-industrial sector (UNDP, 1988). Especially in Asian and African countries, the rural population share is much higher than the agricultural labour force share.[24] Again this is

---

24 With the strange exception of Turkey, 2000.

Table 10.11 *Share of rural population, agricultural labour force and agricultural production, 1950–2000*

Country/region	Share of rural population (%)				Share of agricultural labour force (%)			Share of agriculture in GDP (%)				Rural population (mn)			
	1950	1970	1985	2000	1960	1980	1990–2000[a]	1960	1965	1980	2000	1950	1970	1985	2000[c]
Bangladesh	95.8	92.4	82.5	75.0	86.0	72.6	62.1	57.5	52.8	49.6	24.6	40,009	61,247	79,736	98,943
China	87.5	82.6	77.0	64.2	83.2	74.2	47.5	22.3	37.9	30.1	15.9	485,232	686,138	824,088	857,210
India	82.7	80.2	75.7	72.3	74.3	69.5	66.7	45.2	43.7	38.6	24.9	295,867	445,294	578,385	727,401
Indonesia	87.6	82.9	73.9	59.0	74.8	57.8	45.0	51.5	56.0	24.0	16.9	69,675	99,512	122,767	124,359
Malaysia	79.6	66.5	54.1	42.6	63.3	40.8	18.4	34.3	28.8	22.6	11.1	4,886	7,222	8,480	9,913
Pakistan	82.5	75.1	70.7	66.9	60.8	59.8	47.3	46.2	40.2	29.5	26.3	32,710	46,449	67,246	86,990
Philippines	72.9	67.0	57.0	41.5	63.6	52.3	39.1	25.7	25.9	25.1	15.9	14,570	24,497	30,905	31,290
South Korea	78.6	59.3	35.1	18.1	61.3	37.1	11.6	36.4	37.8	14.8	4.6	14,831	18,927	14,328	8,557
Sri Lanka	85.6	78.1	78.6	77.2	56.6	51.9	41.6	31.7	28.2	27.6	19.5	6,405	9,606	12,270	14,790
Thailand	89.5	86.7	82.1	80.2	83.7	70.9	48.5	36.4	31.9	23.2	10.5	17,570	31,443	41,577	47,611
Turkey	78.7	61.6	47.5	34.2	78.7	60.3	45.8	41.0	34.0	26.4	16.2	16,898	22,296	24,656	22,824
Argentina	34.7	21.6	15.2	11.8	20.6	13.0	12.2	17.0	12.9	6.4	4.8	5,944	5,178	4,611	3,925
Brazil	63.5	43.5	29.1	18.8	52.1	36.7	23.4	20.6	18.7	11.0	7.4	34,267	41,741	39,424	31,866
Chile	41.6	24.8	17.4	14.2	30.5	20.9	14.4	9.4	8.7	7.3	10.5	2,529	2,352	2,093	2,343
Colombia	57.9	43.4	34.8	25.0	50.2	40.5	22.2	34.0	29.3	19.9	13.8	7,276	9,793	11,031	10,617
Mexico	57.3	41.0	30.4	25.6	55.1	36.3	21.0	16.0	13.7	9.0	4.4	15,906	20,733	22,977	25,079
Peru	64.5	42.6	33.1	27.2	52.3	40.3	35.7	19.6	16.5	8.6	7.9	4,922	5,619	6,467	6,980
Venezuela	53.2	28.4	18.1	13.1	33.4	14.6	10.8	4.8	5.3	4.8	5.0	2,709	3,048	3,095	3,045
Congo, Dem. Rep.	80.9	69.7	72.1	69.7	79.3	71.6	67.8		20.1	25.3		9,856	14,360	23,159	35,511
Côte d'Ivoire	86.8	72.6	62.5	56.4	83.9	64.8	59.9	47.9	39.6	25.9	29.2	2,410	4,008	6,540	8,583

(*Continued*)

Table 10.11 (Continued)

Country/region	Share of rural population (%)				Share of agricultural labour force (%)			Share of agriculture in GDP (%)				Rural population (mln)			
	1950	1970	1985	2000	1960	1980	1990–2000ᵃ	1960	1965	1980	2000	1950	1970	1985	2000ᶜ
Egypt	68.1	57.8	56.1	57.3	58.1	57.1	29.8	30.0	28.6	18.3	16.6	14,863	20,392	27,871	35,059
Ghana	85.5	71.0	67.7	63.9	63.3	61.5	62.2	40.8	43.5	57.9	35.3	4,191	6,125	8,945	11,892
Kenya	94.4	89.7	80.2	66.6	87.9	82.2	79.5	38.2	35.3	32.6	19.9	5,915	10,199	15,852	20,132
Morocco	73.8	65.4	55.2	44.5	65.7	56.0	44.7		23.5	18.4	13.5	6,606	10,012	12,140	12,601
Nigeria	89.9	80.0	69.3	55.9	73.2	54.0	43.0	63.9	54.9	20.6	29.5	26,769	38,401	51,284	71,070
South Africa	56.9	52.2	51.7	43.1	37.5	17.3	13.5	11.2	9.2	6.2	3.2	7,785	11,826	17,050	19,260
Tanzania	96.2	93.3	82.4	67.7	92.6	85.8	84.4	57.0	46.0	45.0	45.1	7,587	12,836	18,255	24,329
Zambia	91.1	69.8	60.3	60.4	84.6	76.1	74.6	11.0	15.6	15.1	27.3	2,224	2,952	4,243	5,599
Africaᵇ	85.3	76.9	70.4	62.8	79.7	68.9	63.2	0.0	26.3	16.6	16.1	188,769	274,679	381,583	496,812
Latin America and the Caribbean	58.1	42.4	31.9	24.6	49.0	34.2	17.0	0.0	17.0	10.3	7.1	97,093	120,870	127,888	125,327
Asia	82.6	76.6	70.6	62.5	78.2	68.6	64.2	30.5	37.0	20.8	15.7	1,113,199	1,611,493	2,009,012	-2,290,990
Developing countries	82.2	74.9	67.9	59.6	76.1	65.6	45.9		27.6	18.5	11.6	1,401,516	2,010,377	2,523,020	-2,909,816

Notes:
ᵃ Most recent year for which data are available between 1990 and 2000.
ᵇ Including South Africa.
ᶜ No data for regions and total in 2000. 1995 figures extrapolated, using weighted average growth rates for the countries in the region, 1995–2000.
Sources: Share and absolute size of rural population from United Nations Population Division (2003) and World Urbanization Prospects: The 2001 Revision, http://esa.un.org/unpp, accessed July 2003; Rural population 2000, from World Development Indicators, 2002.
Share of agricultural labour force in total labour force, 1960–90: WDI CD-Rom, 1999; 1991–2000: WDI CD-Rom, 2002; Bangladesh 2000 and regional totals 1960–80: ILO, LABORSTA, (http://laborsta.ilo.org), July 2003.
Share of agriculture in GDP: World Bank, World Development Indicators, 2002, supplemented by World Development Report various issues.

due to the fact that so many rural people primarily depend on some kind of off-farm employment for their livelihood.[25] For example, the United Nations organisation UNDP has estimated that as early as the 1980s 25 per cent of primary employment in rural areas consisted of non-agricultural activities (UNDP, 1988).

10.4.1 Changes in rural societies

In the course of economic and social development, societies in which agriculture predominates change into societies in which industry and services become more important. While in the past most people used to live in rural conditions, more and more people come to live in an urban environment. The share of agriculture in national output and employment tends to decline.

The shifts from the countryside to the city and from agricultural to other economic activities are not the only transformations. Rural societies themselves undergo change. Rural areas are increasingly less isolated from the outside world, owing to improved transport, trade, mobility, communications and the emergence of new media. As the money economy expands, the importance of commercial production for both local and national markets increases at the expense of non-market production for own consumption needs. In many rural areas, mobility increases as a result of migration and migrant labour. Traditional redistributive arrangements and institutions within village communities come under pressure, owing to commercial production for the market. Social relationships within households, between villagers, and between social groups and classes undergo change. Traditional diffuse patterns of rights and obligations between powerful patrons and their rural clients become more businesslike with the expansion of the money economy. The division of labour between men and women within households changes when new opportunities and challenges emerge (Doss, 2001).

Both increasing population density and commercialisation of agriculture put great pressure on traditional farming systems, traditional communal rights to the use of land and other land-tenure arrangements. When extensive agricultural practices are maintained unchanged, increasing population density results in erosion and impoverishment of the soils. Agricultural investment and technological advances require clearer definitions of property rights to land. Processes of social differentiation take place, resulting in more unequal distribution of the access to land and rising landlessness. Non-agricultural activities such as rural industries, trade and services gain in importance. The central authority of the national state penetrates ever deeper into rural communities through regulation and taxation.

Thus, rural development refers to the whole complex of economic, social and cultural changes taking place in rural societies. Long (1977, p. 4) defines rural

---

[25] In addition, demographic factors, such as the number of dependents per member of the labour force, may also play a role.

development as 'the processes by which rural populations of the Third World are drawn into the wider national and international economy and with the accompanying social transformations and local-level responses'.

10.4.2   Three perspectives on rural development

In the social sciences one can distinguish three important theoretical approaches to rural development (Druijven, 1990; Long, 1977):

1. The modernisation approach, which emphasises cultural obstacles to development.
2. The incorporation approach, which stresses the changes that take place in traditional rural communities under the influence of penetration of (capitalist) market relations.
3. The transactionalist approach, which concentrates on the ways in which individuals in various circumstances respond to the challenges and changes they are faced with.

Modernisation theories

Modernisation theory was the predominant approach in the 1950s and 1960s (see also Chapter 3). Modernisation theories interpret rural development as a transformation process from a traditional to a modern community, under the influence of economic and technical developments (Moore, 1963). Driving forces for change are: technological development; commercialisation of agriculture; the rise of cash crops and agricultural wage labour; industrialisation and urbanisation.

From this theoretical perspective, modernisation implies a process of differentiation and specialisation. Diffuse, multifunctional, personal social relationships are replaced by specialised, one-stranded, anonymous social relationships. Extended families make way for nuclear families. The family loses many of its functions with regard to education and socialisation to specialised educational institutions. Consumption and production, which were integrated in the extended household, are gradually separated. Families' activities become more focused on emotional gratification. A social hierarchy based on ascription (class, family of origin, social background) changes into a hierarchy based on achievement criteria. Specialised political and religious institutions are established. The need arises for new mechanisms of integration within the context of national societies, such as political parties, unions, bureaucracies, and so forth. When integration does not keep up with differentiation, social strains and tensions are the result.

Though modernisation theory contains useful insights, the prime weakness of this view is the implicit unilinear path running from a traditional pole to a modern pole, which is assumed to be the same for all societies. This unilinear perspective does not do sufficient justice to the diversity of circumstances and developmental paths in societies, lumped together under the heading 'traditional'. It also underemphasises the amount of individual ingenuity, creativity and entrepreneurship to be found in a great variety of cultural contexts. Further, there are also numerous examples of modern economic developments that contribute to the preservation of traditional cultural and social arrangements rather than to their disruption (see Kuper, 1984). Some modernisation theorists such as Eisenstadt (1970) try to distinguish different traditional settings and different paths of modernisation, but the bipolarity of traditional versus modern continues to be the framework of analysis.

At present it is hard to find unequivocal supporters of unabashed modernisation theory. Nevertheless, the question whether there are 'cultural barriers' to development, which derives from modernisation theory, remains of interest. In a series of publications in the 1960s, the anthropologist Foster (1965; 1975) defended the thesis that the concept of *limited goods* functions as a cultural barrier to economic and social change in traditional societies. The external reality is seen as something, that human beings are unable to control. People find it hard to imagine that total welfare could increase as the result of individual efforts. The total amount of goods and welfare is seen as limited. This implies a zero-sum game in which the success of one person is a threat to the welfare of other individuals. According to Foster, there is little solidarity within such traditional village communities. Cooperation is riddled with mutual mistrust because it may result in claims to authority by some of the participants. Economic success gives rise to jealousy. It sets off redistributive mechanisms such as the obligation to organise social festivities or to support relatives. Thus, the idea that the total amount of goods is limited makes for conservatism and forms a barrier to entrepreneurship.

The main problem with this theory is a tendency towards overgeneralisation. It is conceivable that, under certain conditions of uncertainty or risk, the notion of a limited store of goods crystallises into a powerful cultural element which inhibits change. But, as Long points out, there are also many instances where traditional cultural elements are quite compatible with modern economic behaviour. Economists like Myint (1980) and Higgins (1959) and anthropologists such as Geertz (1963b) have pointed out that entrepreneurship emerges all over the world, whenever there are new opportunities for trade due to improvements in transport, communication and infrastructure.

Incorporation theories

Incorporation theories are much more historical in nature than modernisation theories. They study the effects of the penetration of a capitalist market economy in various non-capitalist agrarian societies in different historical periods (see Dixon, 1990; Druijven, 1990; Frank, 1969; Long, 1977). The term '*incorporation*' refers to the ways in which non-capitalist or pre-capitalist societies become involved in international market relationships.

Dixon (1990, p. 39 ff) presents an interesting overview of different processes of incorporation. Incorporation took place through the establishment of plantation economies by colonists using native or imported slave and contract labour to cultivate export crops. In countries such as South Africa, Kenya, Zimbabwe and Algeria, settlement colonies (see Chapter 2) were created, where white settlers appropriated the most fertile lands. The indigenous population was resettled on 'native' reserves, which were overcrowded and had infertile lands. The dispossessed native population served as a labour reserve for settler farming activities.

The example of export production on plantations was frequently followed by smallholder peasants who also started to cultivate export crops. Opinions differ as to whether or not this occurred voluntarily. According to incorporation theory, colonial tax levies in cash in effect forced smallholders to cultivate cash crops. Also, colonial authorities often imposed obligations on peasants to supply labour to plantations or to deliver a quota of export crops in kind (e.g. sugar). More positive incentives were provided by the availability of new consumer goods and new agricultural inputs, which could only be acquired by means of money.

In post-war Africa, mines and new industries attracted a flow of migrant labour. Able-bodied young males travelled long distances to find work in these new sectors, leaving women, children and the elderly to cope with food production in the rural areas.

The incorporation theories, mainly of a neo-Marxist bent, emphasise the negative aspects of the penetration of the market economy in pre-capitalist societies. Survival strategies, which offered protection against crop failures and other risks in traditional societies, are disrupted. Aspects of traditional societies that are incompatible with the market economy are undermined. Behavioural patterns, which can be made subservient to the market economy, are preserved. For example, land scarcity in Latin American *minifundia* (peasants) simply forces peasants to offer their labour cheaply to large landowners.

Modernisation theories are primarily concerned with social relations within the village community. Incorporation theory focuses on the chains of dependence and exploitation, which extend far outside the village community. After colonies gained their independence, foreign-owned plantations were often nationalised – but dependence remained. Dependency theories argued that a few multinational agribusinesses had a monopoly on the processing, distribution and marketing of agricultural export crops and the supply of new seeds, fertilisers, machinery and other inputs.

Like modernisation theories, incorporation theories suffer from a tendency to overgeneralisation. The emphasis on the disruptive effects of the market economy goes hand in hand with an idealisation of harmonious pre-capitalist relationships. In reality, production for the market sometimes provides small farmers with an escape from traditional constraints and power relationships. Also, insufficient justice is done to examples of successful agricultural development in different periods and countries. For example, during the late colonial period cocoa exports had very positive effects on the economic development of Ghana. More generally, primary exports from tropical countries provided a stimulus to economic development in the late nineteenth century (see Chapter 8). Rice production in Indonesia provides an example of very successful agricultural development, despite the gloomy predictions of the 1960s (see Geertz, 1963a). In recent years, several Asian countries have become self-sufficient in fertilisers. Finally, incorporation theories share some of the unilinear biases of modernisation theories. Rural development is not a simple transition of subsistence production to market production. There were extensive agricultural markets in many pre-modern societies. Also, in countries undergoing civil turmoil in present-day Africa, there is frequently a partial return to subsistence production as markets cease to function.

Transactionalist and decision-making theories

Long criticises both modernisation theories and incorporation theories for their tendency to depict rural populations as helpless victims, whether of traditional cultural obstacles or of external exploitation (Long, 1977; see also Druijven, 1990). He calls for an analysis of the differential responses to change shown by individuals and social categories within a population. As a third perspective on rural development, he distinguishes the *transactionalist approach*, which analyses the active strategies of the poorest, the less poor and the rich. In this approach special attention is paid to entrepreneurship and the manipulation of networks of clients and middlemen. This approach provides a more active picture of the rural population.

Anthropological studies of entrepreneurship in 'traditional' societies, such as Hill's study of Ghanaian cocoa farmers (Hill, 1986), also give a much more dynamic image of rural communities and a more realistic assessment of potential resources of entrepreneurship and creativity. Simultaneously, more insight is gained into inequality and diversity within rural communities. Some individuals follow more effective strategies than others. There are both winners and losers.

The emphasis in transactionalist approaches is on survival strategies, in which farmers are flexible with regard to the use of their labour and can seek alternative sources of employment outside the agricultural sector, in trade, services and crafts production. Ceremonial obligations, which were primarily interpreted as redistributive mechanisms by modernisation theorists, are reinterpreted here as investments in social relations and networks. These social investments are made in order to achieve certain goals in the future. The transactionalist approach in anthropology (see Barth 1966; Boissevain, 1974) provides a valuable bridge to micro-economic models of decision-making in rural households (e.g. Ray, 2000). However, analysis of micro-decisions and strategies is most interesting when they are studied against the backdrop of wider changes, challenges and trends taking place at macro-level.

10.4.3   The peasant economy and peasant households

In the discussion of rural development peasants play an important role. The study of peasant economies allows for a combination of transactionalist analysis of household behaviour and macro-analysis of major changes in rural societies.

As early as the 1920s the Russian agronomist Chayanov drew attention to interesting differences between the economic behaviour of large, commercial farmers producing for the market and small peasants producing mainly for their own consumption (Chayanov, 1966; see also Kitching, 1982). In his publications Chayanov defended Russian peasants against the communist reproach that they were capitalist farmers (*kulaks*). He did so by stressing the differences between capitalist farms and peasant agriculture. On such grounds, Chayanov rejected the collectivisation of agriculture.

A profit-maximising commercial farmer will expand employment, up to the point where the additional financial returns to the last agricultural worker equal the wage rate. The wage rate is in part determined by wages being paid outside the agricultural sector. Russian peasants at the start of this century, however, did not produce for the market, but for their own subsistence. They used their own and their family's labour power, rather than wage labour. There were hardly any opportunities for full-time paid employment outside agriculture, so no implicit wage could be determined.

According to Chayanov, under such circumstances financial returns and wages have little meaning for a peasant household. The peasant does not weigh financial returns against the financial cost of labour. Rather, he looks at the amounts of food needed to feed the family and the amounts of backbreaking physical labour required to produce this food. Since labour of the peasant and his family does not 'cost' any money, he will continue to work until he can provide sufficiently for the subsistence of his household. Equilibrium is reached when the disutility of additional drudgery equals the utility of additional family consumption. At this point the peasant will stop increasing his labour input. The labour input per hectare depends on family size and in particular on the number of dependents in the household (children and the elderly). The more mouths to be fed, the more work will be done. Labour input per hectare is also determined by the availability of land and the possibilities of part-time paid employment outside agriculture.

Other things being equal, the Chayanov model implies that a small self-supporting peasant will use more labour per unit of land and will realise a greater production per unit of land than a commercial farmer producing for the market. He will not stop working when the value of his output is less than his implicit wage. He will continue to work till he has produced enough to feed his family. Of course, other things are hardly ever equal, in particular with respect to the amount of capital and the kind of technology employed. Nevertheless, it is a common finding that yields per hectare on small and medium-sized farms are generally higher than on large farms. This does not hold for very small farms, with too little land to farm efficiently.

In a study, incorporating data on a large number of countries, Berry and Cline (1979) found that both financial returns per hectare and real production per hectare are inversely related to the land area available to a farmer. The authors concluded (p. 29) that redistribution of land from larger to smaller farmers would lead to an increase of total agricultural output and employment. Redistribution would reduce underutilisation of labour on tiny plots of land. Also there would be an increased demand for the labour services of the landless rural workers. Land reform will be discussed in more detail in section 10.5.

Characteristics of peasant economies

Inspired in part by Chayanov's work, a group of authors associated with the *Journal of Peasant Studies* has tried to identify general characteristics of the peasant economy which call for a specific theoretical analysis (Shanin, 1971; 1973; 1974; see also Wolf, 1966).

Peasants are small farmers, producing primarily for own consumption with the use of family labour. The peasant family is a unit of both production and consumption. There is a relatively low level of occupational specialisation, although there is a division of labour between age groups and sexes. Peasants work with little capital. Ownership of land is not individualised. Households have rights of access to communal land on the basis of their membership in a village community. Access to communal land is allocated by the village authorities (Scott, 1976). A portion of agricultural surpluses is reserved for ceremonial obligations like feasts, religious rituals, payment of bride money, burials, and so forth. Credit is hard to obtain, markets are underdeveloped, and risks are high for households living close to subsistence levels. Security, therefore, is valued higher than innovativeness.

Peasants live in relatively closed village communities. Nevertheless, there are at least two kinds of links with the outside world. In the first place, there is always some contact with the world outside the village through kinship ties and rural market places. Second, there are always relationships with powerful outsiders who appropriate part of the agricultural surpluses, whether in kind, money or labour. These outsiders can be feudal or prebendal landlords, colonial administrators, large landowners or modern tax collectors and bureaucrats. Peasant societies are to be found in both pre-industrial Europe and present-day developing countries.

According to Wolf (1966), 'peasant economies' stand midway between isolated tribal communities of primitive agriculturalists, hunters and gatherers, and fully integrated market economies. Many studies of changes in rural societies focus on the transformations of peasant economies. How do peasant economies respond when confronted with the rise of centralised state power and the penetration of market relationships (Ellis, 1988; Moore, 1966; Popkin, 1979; Scott, 1976; Wolf, 1966)?

Ellis (1988, p. 3) estimates – without any mention of sources – that over a billion people belong to peasant households, most of these in developing countries. On the basis of a survey of the literature, he distinguishes the following characteristics of the *peasant society*:

- Peasant society represents a transition from relatively dispersed, isolated and self-sufficient communities of farmers or pastoralists to fully integrated market economies.
- Although relatively isolated, peasant society is part of a larger economic and political system. Peasants are exposed in some degree to market influences. They stand in relations of subordination to powerful political outsiders (Wolf, 1966).
- Internal differentiation. Within peasant communities there are numerous differences in social and economic status. In particular there are important differences between men and women.
- Peasants obtain their livelihood from the land, mainly by the cultivation of crops. This distinguishes them from landless labourers, pastoralists or nomads.
- A peasant household is both a unit of production and a unit of consumption. Households are, at least to some extent, self-sufficient. The degree of self-sufficiency varies strongly. Production for own consumption does not preclude part of the harvest being traded on the market.
- The primary source of labour is family labour. This characteristic distinguishes peasant households from capitalist farms employing wage labour. But this does not rule out the use of some hired labour in peak periods.
- In some way or other peasants have access to land to provide in their livelihood. This distinguishes them from landless agricultural workers and industrial labourers. Land is allocated on the basis of non-market criteria. Allocation depends on the social status of the household within the village community.
- Peasants are partially integrated into markets for products and factors of production. They stand with one leg in the non-market village economy and one leg in a market economy. The markets on which peasants are active are imperfectly functioning markets. This has to do with poor infrastructure (transport, communications), insufficient information and power relationships that constrain peasants' freedom of choice. This implies that the supply of agricultural products responds only weakly to changes in price levels. In this context Lal and Myint (1996) use the term *institutional underdevelopment*.[26]
- Partial integration into markets implies that non-market criteria of reciprocity still play an important part in transactions between peasant households.

---

[26] They argue for expansion of agricultural exports since this tends to diminish institutional underdevelopment.

According to Ellis, partial integration into imperfectly functioning markets is the principal characteristic of peasant economies. It distinguishes peasants from commercially oriented family farmers who trade their entire product and purchase all their inputs on the market. On the other hand, access to the production-factor land distinguishes peasants from landless agricultural labourers. In rural societies, peasants function alongside the commercial family farmers, who are more closely integrated into markets, and labourers working for wages on plantations or lands of large landowners. Also, as mentioned, agriculture is not the only source of livelihood in rural areas, though this is somewhat underemphasised in the literature on peasants.

Diversity of conditions

In generalisations about rural development, there is – in spite of all qualifications and denials – a tendency to think in terms of a traditional–modern polarity. On the one side, one distinguishes the traditional self-supporting pre-capitalist agricultural society, with communal rights to land and redistributive institutions within villages. On the other side, one distinguishes a modern money and market economy in which farmers produce commercially for the market.[27] This schematic conception is present both in modernisation theories, which stress the institutional and cultural obstacles to change, and in the radical and Marxist literatures on peasant societies which analyse the penetration of money economy into traditional peasant societies and the associated processes of disruption.

In her book *Development Economics on Trial* (1986) the anthropologist Polly Hill launches a ferocious and delightful attack on universal developmental generalisations such as the transition from self-sufficiency to production for the market, the penetration of the money economy, increasing inequality, migration from rural to urban areas, the transition from communal land rights to private ownership of land, Boserupian intensification of land use, or the thesis of Theodor Schultz that traditional peasants are efficient. Such generalisations do insufficient justice to the rich diversity of agricultural circumstances in developing countries and the dynamic entrepreneurship, which can often be found among members of so-called traditional societies. Often the generalisations are not only wrong, they may even be harmful when they lead to inadequate policy recommendations which do not take the variations in local conditions into account.

Development economists and agricultural economists generalise because this is how they have been trained. They were nurtured on 'universal generalisations' and 'development schemes'. In as much as they do any empirical research at all, Hill argues they base themselves on deplorably unreliable statistics (see section 10.1) and make little attempt to become intimately familiar with the rural societies about which they are writing.

---

27 Our brief summary of trends of change in rural societies could also be easily misunderstood as a sketch of the transition from 'traditional' to 'modern'.

For example, Hill demonstrates that in some regions farmers have already been involved in market production for many centuries. Both in West Africa and in South India money has played an important role in economic transactions far back in history. Rural marketplaces in the Sudan date back to the fourteenth century. The subsistence economy is a myth. So-called 'traditional' rural societies in the past have always known numerous non-agricultural activities – in trade, services and handicraft production. Extensive and intensive agricultural activities can coexist side by side in one and the same region.[28] In West Africa, rural markets developed earlier than urban-oriented markets. It is incorrect to state that the market economy penetrated rural areas from urban centres. Migration from one rural area to another is at least as important as rural–urban migration. Some rural societies have communal rights to land. In others there has long been private ownership of land, and land has long been freely saleable. These two types of land use can coexist.

In rural societies one finds a great variety of farmers: farmers who have rights to cultivate communal land owned by the village, clan or tribe; agricultural labourers who receive wages to work on land that is owned by others; predominantly self-sufficient family farmers who rent or own their land; commercial family farms producing for the market; large commercial farms and plantations using hired wage labour. The distinctions between these categories are rather vague and indistinct. Self-sufficient farmers or their relatives, for example, often also work as hired workers on land owned by others. Both rich and poor farmers participate in non-agricultural activities, like trade and crafts. Rich farmers do so because non-agricultural activities are so profitable, poor farmers because they cannot survive on agriculture alone. The richest farmers enjoy the greatest trading advantages. Further, there are great differences in the amounts of land available to different farmers, and there is a great variety of land-tenure institutions: individual ownership; rights of use; sharecropping arrangements; lease relations; and so forth.

Hill argues that the use of the term *peasant economy* as a blanket term for all these different types of agricultural activities is inappropriate and misleading. It denies significant intra-village inequalities in power, wealth, income and status. It disregards the differences between cattle-raising societies and crop-raising societies, between irrigated agriculture and rain-fed agriculture, and differences in natural circumstances and climatic conditions.

Next, the focus on peasant economies also neglects the differentiation between males and females within village communities and households in Africa, Asia and Latin America. For example, in much of Africa there are generally two separate economic spheres for males and females. Women are responsible for subsistence food production to feed the household. On the side they often engage in trade. Men are responsible for the raising of high prestige cash crops

---

28 In her polemic sharpness, Hill does not always do justice to her opponents. For example, as early as 1965 Boserup explicitly pointed out that different intensities of land use can coexist in the same region, owing to differences in soil quality and natural circumstances (Boserup, 1965, p.57 ff).

and cattle-breeding. Women tend to have less secure access to land, less access to inputs, finance and new technologies (Boserup, 1970; Doss, 2001).

Hill prefers terms such as country people, farmers, cultivators to 'peasant'. The connotations of the term *peasant* are derogatory. It does not do justice to the inventiveness, creativity and entrepreneurial spirit which Hill observed in her empirical research among country people. In this respect, Polly Hill comes very close to the positions of development economists such as Schultz, Lewis and Myint whom she elsewhere criticises so fiercely.

Hill's polemic is refreshing. It encourages readers to take into account the variety of local conditions in rural communities. Generalisations should relate to specific agrarian systems, e.g. dry-grain farming in densely populated regions. However, Hill has a tendency to misrepresent the positions she is attacking and to exaggerate the differences of opinion. Like Hill, Schultz – one of Hill's black sheep – pointed to entrepreneurial qualities and creativity among farmers. Boserup (1970) was one of the first authors to analyse the role of women within rural communities. Marxist studies also emphasise rural inequalities.

Finally, there is a risk that Hill's love for anthropological detail may end up in no more than ethnographic description and a rejection of all attempts to generalise and to formulate hypotheses on rural development. In our opinion, Ellis's synthesis of the characteristics of peasant societies, described earlier, meets most of Hill's objections. The characteristics of peasant societies are no longer defined in absolute terms but leave scope for variation. For example, the transition from self-sufficiency to production for the market is seen as a continuum. The use of family labour does not exclude the hiring of wage labour, nor family members themselves working as paid labourers on other farms. The existence of off-farm employment is acknowledged, as are the differences between households. Finally, Ellis admits that the peasant household is only one of many types of rural households, albeit an important one. Provided they are applied carefully, the characteristics of the peasant economy may contribute to a better understanding of processes of rural change.

10.4.4   Rationality, risk and survival strategies in peasant societies

Increases in agricultural production and productivity are prerequisites for improvements in living conditions in rural areas. Production may be raised through expansion of the amounts of production factors (land, labour, agricultural equipment), more efficient use of existing means of production, or introduction of new techniques of production. A crucial question is to what degree peasant societies are willing and able to increase efficiency and introduce new technologies. Ever since Boeke (1955) pointed to the 'limited needs' in Indonesian society, there is a tradition that stresses the cultural obstacles to increases in efficiency, to entrepreneurship and to innovation. We have come across this view in the discussion of the diffusion model and modernisation theories.

In his pioneering work, *Transforming Traditional Agriculture*, Theodor Schultz (1964), later awarded the Nobel prize in economics, objected to this point of view. On the basis of fieldwork conducted by other researchers, he concluded that, given their circumstances, 'traditional farmers' use their production factors efficiently. According to the neoclassical economic theory, 'efficient' means that the marginal returns to the factors of production equal their marginal costs. The implication is that there are no cultural barriers to efficiency. Traditional farmers know exactly what they are doing and use their available factors of production in a rational fashion. They have a profound knowledge of the possibilities of traditional agriculture. Within the constraints of traditional economy, society and technology there are few opportunities to increase efficiency and productivity. Productivity is very low, but they are doing the best they can. Peasants live close to subsistence. They are unable to make large investments in new agricultural technologies (seeds, fertilisers, pesticides, irrigation, and so on). In Schultz's words, farmers are 'poor but efficient'.

Schultz sees an important role for government in stimulating the development of new, highly productive technologies and making them available to farmers in traditional agriculture. There is sufficient entrepreneurship among farmers to ensure that new technologies will be adopted if they are likely to pay off. But economic incentives for the use of new technologies have to be created and negative incentives like inadequate access to credit or too low prices for agricultural products should be eliminated (Schultz, 1978).

Schultz's view has been severely criticised by anthropologists such as Adams (1986) and the aforementioned Polly Hill. Schultz bases himself on a limited number of ethnographical studies, which are not very representative; what is more, he does not always interpret them correctly. Adams's most serious objection is that Schultz pays no attention to the cultural context in rural societies, to values and attitudes, and to social stratification. Peasants may act rationally, but their efficiency depends on their culturally determined perceptions of reality and their informedness about technology, credit and price movements of products and inputs. Character traits and motivation are also of great importance. In daily practice, there are great differences in performance and efficiency between different farmers in the same village. According to Adams, Schultz also pays too little attention to the significance of production for own needs – analysed by Chayanov – and the significance of risk in poor rural societies.

Cultural factors are stressed in James C. Scott's study, *The Moral Economy of the Peasant* (1976). Scott belongs to the so-called *substantivist* tradition in anthropology (Polyani, 1957), which stresses reciprocity in exchange, relationships and the differences between traditional multifunctional relationships and modern impersonal single-stranded relationships in a capitalist economy, in which rational calculation of costs and benefits prevails.

Unlike modernisation theorists, Scott places little emphasis on obstacles to modernisation. He stresses the positive survival functions of traditional institutions in Southeast Asia. Peasants live at the margin of subsistence. Crop failures are an immediate threat to their bare survival. In their choice of production techniques, the essential criterion is safety and minimisation of risk rather than maximum output. This is why they cultivate different crops, on scattered strips of land. They prefer to cultivate food crops rather than cash crops, the returns to which may fluctuate with market conditions.

The social institutions of rural communities were traditionally oriented to stability and the assurance of a minimum standard of living to the inhabitants. There were communal lands, which were periodically redistributed amongst the cultivators. The village community also allocated taxes and levies imposed by royal rulers, governments or landlords. There were obligations for villagers to support each other with labour when this was needed (work sharing). Norms of reciprocity were very important. There were redistributive social obligations for the richer villagers. They were expected to be charitable, sponsor ceremonial celebrations and festivities, donate to shrines and help indigent kin.[29] Decision-making within village communities was aimed at reaching consensus.

Subsistence insurance was not confined to the village. Tenancy and share-cropping relations between peasants and powerful landlords also had survival aspects. Traditionally the rent consisted of a fixed share of the harvest. This meant lower rents when harvests were bad and higher rents when they were good. Furthermore, in times of need rich patrons had certain obligations to provide food to their starving tenants or to forgo the collection of rent. In exchange, peasants had obligations to their patrons, such as showing respect, providing corvée labour and political support.

Scott writes that a *moral economy* and a *subsistence ethic* had developed in Southeast Asia, in which survival was a central element. This subsistence ethic provided guidelines for individual actions. Though there was considerable in-equality within the village and between villagers and external elites, there was also a moral claim to a guaranteed minimum income. According to Scott, this 'moral' survival economy was undermined by two tendencies: political centralisation and penetration of the market economy. Political centralisation involved the imposition of fixed taxes on land, which did not vary with harvest returns. The risk of output fluctuations was shifted onto the peasants. Com-mercialisation introduced the uncertainties of fluctuating market prices. Local crafts and services, which provided alternative sources of income in bad times, were disrupted because of increased competition from without. Where possi-ble, influential groups tried to reduce common use of communal land and introduced individualised ownership. Finally, traditional paternalistic relation-ships between patrons and peasants became more impersonal and contractual. Guarantees for survival were undermined. Risks were shifted to the peasants. According to Scott, it was not the increase in inequality in itself, but rather the weakening of traditional guarantees for survival, which provided an expla-nation for the large-scale peasant uprisings in Southeast Asia during the first

---

29 Scott does not idealise the traditional village community to the extent his critics suggest. He believes the redistributive obligations are enforced through expressions of envy, gossip and social control. Dependence on community support entails loss of status.

part of the present century. (For a more general formulation of this perspective, see Barrington Moore, 1966.) Peasants revolt when their traditional moral expectations of support by fellow-villagers and patrons in times of need are violated.

Scott's view has been fiercely criticised by Samuel Popkin in his study, *The Rational Peasant* (1979). Popkin accuses authors like Scott, Wolf and other substantivists of idealising traditional peasant societies and traditional power structures. For them, capitalist penetration was the main culprit, disrupting traditionally harmonious relationships and survival arrangements.

Popkin, on the contrary, argues that 'traditional' peasants in Vietnam – just as individuals elsewhere – are constantly engaged in the rational pursuit of their interests. They try to increase their welfare through short-term and long-term investments, including investments in social relations and social networks. Popkin's political economy approach is an example of the so-called *formalist* tradition in anthropology. This tradition insists that peasant societies can be analysed with the same analytic tools as social relations in Western societies. Popkin's work can be seen as one possible elaboration of the transactionalist approach introduced above.

Within villages there are continuous conflicts and feelings of mutual distrust. As in every social setting, some villages try to profit from communal arrangements as 'free riders', without making any contribution of their own. Traditional savings institutions are constantly threatened by the suspicion that some may benefit more than others. Also every village community has its outsiders who are denied access to communal land. In sum, the moral economy approach seriously underestimates the extent of inequality, exploitation, competition and conflict within village communities.

Popkin interprets the often paternalistic relationships between patrons and clients not as a result of cultural or moral factors, but rather as relations of dependence. In these relations landlords have succeeded in monopolising all external relations of peasants – with regard to credit, purchase of inputs, marketing of surpluses, processing of agricultural products. The guarantees they offer peasants in times of need serve to maintain their dependence. The penetration of market relations offers peasants a chance to escape the monopoly power of local landlords. Often rich farmers and landlords try to block peasants' access to markets, fearing the peasants' increasing independence.

Popkin agrees that risk avoidance is a predominant feature of peasant society. However, he interprets it more as an individual survival strategy. Peasants are risk-averse. But this does not necessarily mean that they will never invest or make a gamble. If the potential loss is small, and there is a chance of a big outcome, peasants are quite willing to gamble. Penetration of the money economy and the centralised state, therefore, is not always perceived as a threat. Sometimes it offers new opportunities and escape from traditional relations of subordination.

Popkin's criticism is supported by empirical research by Haggis *et al.* (1986) into peasant revolts in Asia. These authors conclude that peasant revolts did not start as a reaction to the disappearance of the moral economy. It was not necessarily the poorest peasants who revolted. Often richer farmers, who felt their opportunities were being restricted, played an important role. Much political turmoil was not directed towards the restoration of traditional 'moral' relations. Class struggle and nationalist elements also played a role. Haggis *et al.* (1986) also come to the conclusion that Scott gives too rosy a view of the 'moral economy' of traditional relations of dependence and subordination.

By stressing the calculating aspects of peasant behaviour, Popkin narrows the gap between the thought of economists and anthropologists. Starting from pure neoclassical principles of utility maximisation, the economist Lipton arrived at an analysis of risk aversion very similar to that of Popkin (Lipton, 1966). In many developing countries, the large variability of rainfall makes it impossible to predict the volume of production. Many peasants live close to subsistence levels. A crop failure may force them to borrow money for food and result in loss of land or even starvation. New inputs and technologies demand large investments, while returns vary from year to year. Though these investments might result in higher average returns, they may cause severe indebtedness in years of bad harvests. Therefore, the calculating behaviour of peasants is determined by a risk-averse *survival algorithm*. Traditional varieties with low but stable yields are preferred over newer varieties involving more uncertainty. Peasants also prefer to pay interest in kind rather than in money. Even if this costs them more, they are insured against sudden falls in the price of grains. Finally, Lipton points to the inequality relations, due to which peasants have less access to water, seeds, fertiliser, herbicides and pesticides which are all required to achieve higher yields. All in all there is no contradiction between highly risk-averse behaviour and an extremely rational consideration of costs and benefits. This is also referred to as the RAUI hypothesis: risk aversion causes under investment (see Wharton, 1970).

The lesson that can be derived from risk-aversion analysis is that policy measures that reduce peasants' risks, like cheap credit or buffer food stocks, will increase their willingness to innovate.

However, Roumasset warns against easy generalisations about risk aversion. Under suboptimal conditions, the recommended use of fertilisers may be objectively inefficient. The decision not to adopt new technologies is then based on considerations of efficiency rather than risk aversion (Roumasset, 1976; David and Roumasset, 2000).

We feel that the more individualistic approach to peasant institutions and behaviour is rather convincing. If one considers changes in agriculture since the end of the nineteenth century, it seems obvious that peasants all over the world have responded dynamically, innovatively and rationally whenever they were offered new opportunities. Still, it would not be wise to neglect cultural constraints altogether, as most economists tend to do. Behaviour, which is a rational response to challenges in a given situation, tends to crystallise and harden into cultural patterns, patterns of behaviour, and institutions. These in turn influence future responses and choices. Individual behaviour is also determined by internalised norms, which are culturally transmitted. One should also not forget that cultural norms and institutions within societies are often maintained by means of powerful social sanctions. The very perception of the alternatives between which one has to choose is partly determined by culture and institutions (North, 1993). Also, the options and alternatives themselves are institutionally determined. If market institutions have not developed, peasants will not be able to respond to modern economic incentives. The cultural and the individualistic approaches are not so opposed as would seem to be the case on first sight.

10.5   Land reform

Access to land is one of the central themes in the study of rural development. In many developing countries landownership and access to land is distributed very unequally. Inequality tends to increase in the course of time and the number of landless people in rural areas is on the rise (Ghai and Radwan, 1985, for African countries; Griffin, 1981; Singh, 1982, for Southeast Asia). A more equal distribution of land could contribute to a decrease in rural poverty since improved access to land would enable the poor to support themselves (Kanbur and Lustig, 1999).

Moreover, redistribution of land may also contribute to increased productivity and efficiency (de Janvry et al., 2001). In section 10.4.3 we noted that smaller farmers generally cultivate their fields more efficiently than larger farmers and realise higher yields per hectare. A survey article by Binswanger and associates concludes: 'Most of the work on the relationship between farm size and productivity strongly suggests that farms that rely mostly on family labour have higher productivity levels than large farms operated primarily with hired labour' (Binswanger et al., 1995, pp. 26–64). Unlike manufacturing, the agricultural sector has relatively few economies of scale. Therefore, large-scale agriculture is not more productive than small-scale agriculture. Besides, many large absentee landowners do not employ their production factors very efficiently. They often live in urban areas and are not personally involved in agricultural production. They are characterised by highly consumptive lifestyles. Frequently, ownership of land is no more than a safe investment. Peasants employ more labour per hectare than large landowners, have higher cropping frequencies and higher yields per crop. Improved access to land can also allow landless households to utilise family labour that cannot otherwise be put to use through the market (de Janvry et al., 2001).

In sum, most researchers believe that redistribution of land and other land reforms may not only contribute to a more equitable distribution of income, but also to reductions of poverty, and to increases in productivity and agricultural development (Alexandratos, 1988; Binswanger et al., 1995; de Janvry et al., 2001; Dorner, 1972). In countries where access to land has been distributed more equally – such as China, Japan, Korea and Taiwan – agricultural development has been more successful than in countries where there is a wide gap between large landowners with modern farm management and small peasants who cannot afford new inputs. In this context, Johnston and Kilby (1975) refer to a unimodal versus a bimodal agricultural development strategy. They warn, however, that there is no question of a simple policy choice between one kind of agricultural policy or another. Countries that have pursued a unimodal agricultural strategy benefited from initial conditions which were the outcome of unique historical circumstances.

There is no complete consensus that the effects of redistribution of land are positive under all circumstances. Myint (1980) argues, for instance, that larger, modern-oriented farmers are often the bearers of agricultural innovation. He believes one has to accept the associated inequalities. In a series of publications based on research in the Philippines, Roumasset fiercely criticises the general assumption that land reform will necessarily increase efficiency and productivity (David and Roumasset, 2000; Roumasset, 1995). Increasing landlessness can also be a consequence of productivity improvements in agriculture, which call for a shift of surplus labour to other sectors of the economy.

When referring to land reform, redistribution of land from large to smaller landowners is the first thing that comes to mind. However, land reform comes in many forms, depending on the kind of land-tenure relationships in a country (see Box 10.5). In addition to land redistribution, land reforms can include: cadastral reforms in which land rights are more clearly defined; improvements in the status of sharecroppers; bringing new land into cultivation; improved contractual arrangements; collectivisation and decollectivisation. Some types

---

Box 10.5   Varieties of land reform
Differences in initial conditions
Sub-Saharan Africa
- Common rights to land cultivation.
- Land is not tradable.

Latin America
- Large landownership with land cultivated by hired labour.
- *Minifundia* cultivated by small peasants.

Asia
- Less inequality in access to land and size of farms.
- More sharecropping and tenant farmers.

Varieties of land reform
- Consolidation of plots.
- Registration of individual titles to land.
- Bringing new land into cultivation.
- Redistribution of landownership.
- Improvements in legal status of sharecroppers and tenant farmers.
- Decrease in land rents or payments in kind.
- Collectivisation of agriculture.
- Decollectivisation of agriculture.

of land reform such as titling are aimed at counteracting environmentally unfriendly practices by poor farmers, by providing incentives to invest in maintaining soil quality (Fearnside, 2001). Communal access to land under conditions of increasing population density can result in what is called the tragedy of the commons: land degradation through overuse or overgrazing.

In several Sub-Saharan African countries there is a tradition of common rights to land use.[30] Land is not for sale. Rights to cultivate land are in principle allocated to members of the community by chiefs of clans, village elders, and so forth. Such land-tenure relations date back to the time when population density was low, land was abundant and agriculture was extensive. When cultivation becomes more intensive and land becomes scarce, common rights to land form a disincentive for individual investment in maintenance or improvement of soil fertility. The value of land goes up, and conflicts break out over land rights (van Hekken and Thoden van Velzen, 1972). There is a pressure for institutional change. Gradually more individualised property rights to land begin to emerge (Boserup, 1965; Feeny, 1982; 1987; North, 1990; North and Thomas, 1973).

During the colonial period, the authorities tried to introduce *cadastral land reform*, that is registration of individual ownership titles and consolidation of scattered plots of land. In addition, new land was brought into cultivation. Private property of land was to the advantage of colonists and plantation owners, who successfully laid claim to the most fertile lands in countries such as Kenya, Zambia, Zimbabwe and South Africa. But attempts were also made to register ownership titles on behalf of native farmers. This type of land reform was continued after independence. It is interesting to note, though, that traditional practices of land allocation continued to function long after the formal legal relationships had changed (e.g. Firmin-Sellers and Sellers, 1999).

In the post-World War II period, the significance of foreign-owned plantations declined. Many plantations were *expropriated*. Expropriated land was taken into collective use or was allocated to individual cultivators. Where possible, new land was brought under cultivation, as in the pre-war period. Allocation of newly cultivated and expropriated lands among African farmers sometimes led to an increase in rural inequality rather than its decline (Ghai and Radwan, 1985). An example is the 'million acre scheme' in Kenya, which primarily benefited large farmers.

Many Latin American countries are characterised by an extremely unequal distribution of landownership (see Dorner, 1972; Furtado, 1976; Maddison *et al.*, 1992), which has its origin in the pattern of Spanish and Portuguese colonisation in the sixteenth century. On the one hand, there are vast estates owned by large landowners (*latifundia*). On the other hand, there are tiny plots of land owned by peasants (*minifundia*). These are too small to provide a decent

---

30 Hill (1986), however, points out that in parts of West Africa some land is freely traded. Where white settlers have practised agriculture, as in Zimbabwe, Kenya or South Africa there are also large agricultural estates.

living for peasant households. Therefore, peasants are forced to offer their labour to the large landowners. The large landowners have their land cultivated or their cattle grazed by agricultural labourers. Sometimes the agricultural labourers are even allocated small plots of land to cultivate for their own use in exchange for their labour services.

On the large estates cultivation of land is extensive, and relatively capital-intensive. The available reserves of labour are underutilised. Output per unit of land is not very high. At the same time, the smallest farms are so tiny that their productivity is also low. Under such circumstances, a radical *redistribution* of landownership creating more small and medium-sized farm holdings of viable size could contribute to an improvement in the living standards of the poor and increased production per unit of land.

Mexico is the best-known example of a Latin American country where radical land reforms have taken place and large estates have been expropriated. The 1915 Land Reform Act gave rise to a type of communal landownership by the village community, the *ejido*. The *ejido* gave villagers rights to cultivate land, while pastures and woodlands remained in common use. In Mexico, the inequality of access to land is now less marked than in other large Latin American countries. In addition to the *ejidos*, however, there is also private landownership. Lands of the highest quality are usually owned by individuals. Other countries where land reforms have been implemented are Bolivia, Cuba, Chile (under Allende), El Salvador and Nicaragua.

In many South and Southeast Asian countries, colonial practices and administrative centralisation have long ago resulted in a diminishing importance of traditional communal rights to land. Except in communist countries, most land is in private hands. Despite inequality of landownership, actual access to land is less unequal than in Latin America. Much land is rented out in some form to peasants who cultivate the land on their own account. The peasants pay rent in money or in kind, as a share of the crop. Under such circumstances land reforms are especially concerned with improvements in the *legal status of tenant farmers* and the reduction of the rent or the crop share owed to the landowner. When the position of tenant farmers is legally precarious or when a large portion of every increase in production automatically goes to the landowner, tenant farmers will have no incentive to invest in increased productivity and technological innovation.[31]

In Asia, the most radical land reforms were implemented in China after the revolution of 1949. In the process of land reform an estimated 900,000 farmers – justly or unjustly classified as large farmers or *Kulaks* – lost their lives. Initially, expropriated land was reallocated to individual farmers. But in the 1950s agricultural cooperatives were established. In 1958 the agricultural

---

31 In the post-war literature, tenant relations were considered to be less efficient than cultivation of the land by its owner. However, in particular in areas where markets for producers and production factors are quite underdeveloped, lease proportions may divide risks among the tenant farmer and his/her landlord (see de Janvry *et al.*, 2001; Hayami and Ruttan, 1985, p. 391 ff.).

sector was completely collectivised and large communes were established, sometimes including over a million people. After 1978, a reverse process operated, with communes being gradually dismantled and family units being reinstated.

With respect to the *redistribution of land*, Dorner (1972) and Hayami and Ruttan (1985) warn against inflated expectations. It is true that, other things being equal, peasants can realise higher yields per hectare, by cultivating the land more intensively, than large farmers can. But like the 'vent for surplus' effects, the effects of land redistribution are once and for all. If new inputs and the means to purchase and use them are not made available to the peasants, agricultural development will stagnate after land reform. As was already noted, larger farmers are more likely than peasants to employ new techniques. For land redistribution to succeed, the total institutional structure has to be adjusted, so that small peasants and farmers can gain access to credit, schooling, agricultural extension, new inputs and water without being faced with unacceptable risks.

During the past twenty years, great emphasis has been put on the expansion of credit facilities for small farmers and increasing their access to new inputs, with good reason. Nevertheless, time and again larger farmers succeed in getting a disproportionate part of the available credits and resources, owing to their good political contacts, their social standing and power, their higher creditworthiness and their better education (Bol, 1983). The risks involved in granting credit to small peasants are so high that financial institutions mainly focus on larger, creditworthy farmers. In the end the net effect of many credit programmes is the granting of subsidised credit to the wealthier farmers, which makes for capital-intensive agriculture rather than the opposite. Following the success of the Grameen bank in Bangladesh, many developing countries in recent years have attempted to set up micro-credit schemes, where grass roots mechanisms of social control ensure repayment of loans (Bornstein, 1996).

Although many developing countries in Africa, Asia and Latin America profess to pursue a policy of equalising access to land, not much redistribution has occurred in practice. Almost everywhere, the close political ties between large landowners, representatives of the government and dominant political movements prevent the realisation of land reform. This holds for countries such as India (Cassen, 1978; Frankel, 1978), the Philippines, Brazil, Argentina, Kenya and Zambia. Attempts at gradual reform through legislation are sabotaged effectively.

There are instances of sweeping redistribution of land: China in 1949 (Hsu, 1982), Taiwan and Korea after World War II (Griffin, 1976), Mexico after the Mexican revolution, and Japan in the Meiji reforms after 1867 and again during the initial years of World War II. Such radical land reforms all took place in exceptional periods in history, when the whole social fabric was in turmoil. In revolutionary countries, the new regimes implemented land reforms with the use of widespread coercion and physical violence. In other cases, societies had been seriously disrupted as a result of wars, occupations or external threats, all circumstances in which the resistance of powerful landed elites could be overcome. Yet, one should realise the high cost of these changes in terms of human life and human suffering.

Since the 1970s, large-scale state-led expropriative land distribution and other radical approaches to land reform are off the agenda (de Janvry *et al.*, 2001). The exception is Zimbabwe where violent expropriation of large land holdings of white farmers by the Mugabe regime has led to economic collapse and widespread food shortages. But, according to a recent collection of studies in de Janvry *et al.* (2001), more gradual approaches to land reform are very much back on the agenda for the twenty-first century. The authors argue for an incremental and eclectic approach. Individual ownership titles are not a universal panacea and efforts to introduce individual titling do not always succeed (Firmin-Sellers and Sellers, 1999). Access to land can also be improved through improved rental contracts, tenure reform and a reliance on a variety of informal tenure arrangements. Instead of a sharp dichotomy between communal and individual landownership, Deininger and Binswanger (2001) argue for increased effectiveness of individual property rights under existing arrangements. With regard to redistribution of land, countries such as Brazil, Colombia and South Africa are now trying to implement a gradualistic model of 'negotiated land reform'.

It is now widely accepted that land reform policies should be comprehensive. It is not enough that access to land be changed. There is need for a wide range of complementary policies with regard to infrastructure, transport training and availability of finance and inputs, and improved functioning of land and product markets.

10.6　Collectivisation and decollectivisation

Both collectivisation and decollectivisation are very important varieties of land reform. We stated above that there are few economies of scale in agriculture. This does not mean there are none. Some crops such as sugar and bananas have economies of scale in processing and distribution. These products have to be processed or shipped within hours of harvesting, to avoid deterioration. Therefore plantation production of such products continues to be of importance (Binswanger *et al.*, 1995). Certain activities and investments exceed the financial capacity of smaller individual farmers. These may include the construction of irrigation systems or the purchase of capital goods such as tractors and farm machinery. Finally, there may be important economies of scale with respect to the marketing of output and the purchase of inputs.

Such arguments provide the theoretical justification for the formation of agricultural cooperatives. When many small farmers cooperate, they will be able to purchase inputs more cheaply and sell their products at better prices. They can profit from common investment in agricultural machinery, land improvement and water control.

In centrally planned economies like the Soviet Union, China and Vietnam the foundation of cooperatives was merely a step on the way to complete collectivisation of agriculture. In the Soviet Union and Romania, authorities believed in the creation of a collectivised industrial agricultural system, in which economies of scale could be achieved through massive infusions of capital goods and large-scale production. Like other post-war industrialisation strategies and development theories, Marxist theory was pervaded with negative evaluations of 'backward' agriculture and a glorification of the industrial sector. In China one of the considerations for collectivisation was the fact that extremely large-scale infrastructural works and irrigation systems were required, which could only be realised by a massive mobilisation of labour. Consequently, communes were established which at their apex included more than one million people per commune (Hsu, 1982). With regard to the infrastructural aspects, some degree of success of this policy cannot be denied.

However attractive collectivisation of agriculture may be in theory, the problems of worker motivation and efficient allocation turned out to be insuperable in practice. In the Chinese communes the links between efforts and rewards were completely severed. Other than fear and political mobilisation, there was no incentive to work. The work points, which were the basis of rewards, were allocated according to political criteria. The forced introduction of communes during the Great Leap Forward in 1958–60 resulted in widespread famine in which, according to some estimates, as many as 30 million people died of hunger (Ashton et al., 1984).

After 1960, Chinese agriculture was gradually decentralised. The introduction of a 'household responsibility system' in 1978 led to a period of explosive growth of agricultural output until the mid-1980s. Total output grew by no less than 7.4 per cent per year (Huang, 1998). Under the responsibility system Chinese farmers were allowed to sell the surpluses that remained after fulfilment of obligatory delivery quotas, at market prices. This provided them with strong incentives to increase their production. In addition, state procurement prices were increased. Further market reforms were introduced in 1985 and 1991. As yet land remains in public ownership, but individual farmers acquired the right to cultivate well-defined plots of land for periods of up to fifteen years. However, the lack of clear-cut private titles to land discouraged farmer investment after 1985 and growth in agriculture started to slow down, albeit to a still respectable rate of around 3.8 per cent per year.

The absence of a clear relationship between effort and reward is the main problem in all large-scale collectivised agriculture, both in developing countries like Cuba and Tanzania, and in former socialist countries in Eastern Europe. It is one of the main diseconomies of scale. In former socialist countries in Eastern Europe, for example, the small plots of land that were privately cultivated had vastly higher productivity than collectivised agriculture. In agriculture, the family farm, whether or not supplemented by hired labour, has generally proved to be the most efficient form of organisation, both in comparison with large-scale collectivised agriculture and with large landownership (Deininger and Binswanger, 2001, p. 412). There is, however, still a valid case for voluntary cooperation and cooperatives in developing countries. In agrarian development projects, attempts are currently being made to build on existing traditional informal forms of cooperation, like credit cooperatives and grain banks. Also, in settings of low population density individual cultivation can be combined with a variety of communal tenure arrangements.

After 1989, decollectivisation of agriculture also took place in Eastern Europe and many former Soviet Republics. Here the experiences were less positive than in China and East Asia (see Table 10.1). There was a large decline in per capita agricultural production. In part, this was due to a long period of uncertainty about land ownership. In many countries, such as Uzbekistan, decollectivisation was half-hearted and hesitant (Pomfret, 2000). In the Soviet Union, the experience of almost three-quarters of a century of collective agriculture left farmers badly prepared for privatisation. Finally, all forms of land reform and changes in patterns of land tenure, including decollectivisation, require complementary policies. When these are not forthcoming, the results of reform will be disappointing.

10.7 Non-agrarian activities and integrated rural development

In this final section we return to the topic of non-agricultural activities in rural communities (see, for example, Dixon, 1990; Druijven, 1983; Druijven, 1990; Hogg, 1984; Teszler, 1984). One can distinguish between *off-farm employment* and *non-farm employment*. Off-farm employment refers to all activities of members of farming households outside their own household, including paid work within the agricultural sector. Non-farm employment refers to employment outside the agricultural sector, whether as side employment or as primary activity.

Non-agricultural activity in itself is not a recent phenomenon. In the past there has always been a wide range of non-agricultural activities in rural societies, like trade, transport, services and traditional crafts (Alexander *et al.*, 1991). Still, several important changes can be discerned in the post-war period.

First, there are technical changes. Traditional methods of craft production change under the influence of new technical possibilities. For example, tailors can use pedal sewing machines or even electrically driven ones. The range of goods supplied in the informal sector undergoes change. For instance, waste products like old tyres are reworked into sandals (Teszler, 1984). Existing traditional craft activities are replaced by rural industries.

Second, the importance of non-agricultural employment increases over time. According to an estimate by Eicher and Staatz (1984), between 30 per cent and

50 per cent of the rural population in developing countries is dependent on industrial and other non-agricultural activities as a primary or secondary source of employment. New lines of activity are emerging, such as maintenance of motorcycles, bicycles and cars, and putting-out arrangements, where some stages of industrial production – e.g. sewing of clothing or shoemaking – are performed in homes. New sources of employment include, among others, public works road construction, construction of communal facilities, irrigation and other infrastructural works. These often offer temporary employment outside agricultural peak periods. In services there are numerous activities in the informal sector. Furthermore, jobs are also being created in health care, education, administration and agricultural extension. Finally, employment in rural industry is growing. In part, this has to do with traditional production in small brickyards, carpenters, furniture making or potteries. But there are also small-scale rural factories. These factories are often established in smaller cities, but provide employment for the rural population.

Finally, as part of the ongoing division of labour, the numbers of rural people who depend on non-agricultural activities as their primary means of support are increasing.

Integrated rural development policy focuses on the whole scale of activities existing in rural areas. Proponents of an integrated rural development argue that government policies should transcend sectoral limits. A sectoral approach implies that the Department of Agriculture is responsible for the agricultural policy, the Department of Education for the education policy, the Department of Health for healthcare policy, and the Department of Industry for industrial policy. In the integrated approach, policy makers try to coordinate all activities undertaken within a given region. Rural industrialisation requires better education of employees and improved infrastructure and energy supply. Public services contribute to employment. At local levels, the positive interactions and linkages between agriculture and industry can be exploited to the full (Hogg, 1984). Rural industries are especially suited to local production of goods needed in rural areas: products meeting basic needs (processed food, shoes, clothing, building materials, basic medicines, bicycles, household utensils) or agricultural inputs (simple agricultural implements, pumps, chemical fertilisers). Precisely because the distance to the market is smaller, production is more easily adjusted to local needs. In addition, rural industries often use locally produced inputs, like food, textile fibres, wood, clay, raw materials. Rural industrialisation offers opportunities of realising balanced growth path objectives, in which the relationships between economic sectors are optimised (see Chapter 9).

China is one of the countries that paid considerable attention to the promotion of rural industries (Druijven, 1983). The underlying notion of the central planners was that this might help limit migration to the cities and narrow the gap between rural and urban areas. Some of the rural industries were even located within communes. Others functioned as autonomous rural industries, producing steel, machinery, cement and energy. Especially during the Great Leap Forward between 1958 and 1960, numerous small-scale steel factories were established. The steel manufactured in these so-called backyard factories turned out to be of such inferior quality that most of these plants were sooner or later forced to close down. Attempts to decentralise industry were also not always in line with comparative cost advantages and locational advantages of different regions.

In the 1990s, rural industrialisation in China received a boost with the spectacular expansion of township and village enterprises (TVEs). In recent years, TVEs have been amongst the most dynamic enterprises in the expanding manufacturing sector (Szirmai *et al.*, 2001). Nevertheless, the bulk of industrial production in China remains concentrated in urbanised coastal regions and urban–rural gaps are again on the increase.

In theory an integrated rural development policy seems to have nothing but advantages. However, as with all development strategies, one should not be misled by the sirens of 'development rhetoric'. In practice it turns out to be exceedingly difficult to transcend sectoral policy boundaries. The pursuit of an integrated policy can easily result in immense bureaucratic coordination problems exceeding the available administrative capabilities.

Questions for review

1. To what extent has the Malthusian prediction that food production cannot keep up with population growth been validated in the course of the twentieth century?
2. To what extent does an increase in food production in a country imply that the consumption of food is also increasing and that undernourishment and malnutrition are on the decrease?
3. Discuss the three ways in which agricultural output can be increased. What were the most common routes to growth of output in the past? What is the most applicable route in the present?
4. Discuss Ester Boserup's theory of the impact of increasing population density on changes in agricultural technology. What lessons can be derived from Boserup's analysis?
5. Discuss the five models of agricultural development of Hayami and Ruttan.
6. What is the relationship between balanced growth path theory and rural industrialisation?
7. Why are farmers farming smaller plots often more efficiently than large landowners?
8. What are the defining characteristics of the 'Green Revolution'? Provide a summary of the debate on the advantages and disadvantages of the green revolution.
9. What is the difference between rural development and agricultural development?
10. Discuss the differences between the three approaches to rural development: the modernisation approach; the incorporation approach; and the transactionalist approach.
11. What are the characteristics of a peasant economy? Summarise the debate on the advantages and disadvantages of the use of the concept of peasant economy.
12. Why do small farmers in developing countries generally prefer to minimise risks rather than maximise output? What kind of strategies do they pursue in order to minimise risks?

13. What is integrated rural development?
14. What are risks and potential advantages of genetic manipulation as a source of agricultural growth in developing countries?

Further Reading

An indispensable overview of theories and issues in agricultural development is provided by Hayami and Ruttan in *Agricultural Development: An International Perspective* (1985). Other influential publications include Eicher and Staatz (eds.), *Agricultural Development in the Third World* (1984), Mellor, *The Economics of Agricultural Development* (1966) and Schultz, *Transforming Traditional Agriculture* (1964). The process of agricultural intensification is analysed by Ester Boserup in two brilliant books: *The Conditions of Agricultural Growth* (1965); and *Population and Technology* (1981). Boserup was also one of the first authors to analyse the role of women in agriculture in *Women's Role in Economic Development* (1970). In a trendsetting book, *Poverty and Famines* (1981), Amartya Sen shows that producing enough food is not always sufficient to avert famines. This book develops the entitlements approach.

Two useful textbooks on rural development are Dixon, *Rural Development in the Third World* (1990) and Ellis, *Peasant Economics: Farm Households and Agrarian Development* (1988). Key publications on rural development include Chambers, *Rural Development. Putting the Last First* (1983); Lipton, 'The Theory of the Optimizing Peasant' (1966); Popkin, *The Rational Peasant: The Political Economy of Rural Society in Vietnam* (1979); and Scott, *The Moral Economy of the Peasant, Rebellion and Subsistence in South East Asia* (1976). *Development Economics on Trial* by the anthropologist Polly Hill is a lively polemic against economists' tendencies to generalise about agricultural growth and rural development on the basis of insufficient evidence. She also provides a trenchant criticism of statistics on agricultural growth.

Three books published by the Food and Agricultural Organisation (FAO) provide a wealth of statistical data as well as comprehensive discussions of theories of agricultural development, policy options, prospects and environmental issues. They are: Alexandratos, *World Agriculture towards 2000* (1988); Alexandratos (ed.), *World Agriculture: Towards 2010* (1995); and Bruinsma (ed.), *World Agriculture towards 2015/2030: An FAO Perspective* (2003).

Other publications on trends in agriculture and food production include Brown, *Tough Choices. Facing the Challenge of Food Scarcity* (1996); Mitchell et al., *The World Food Outlook* (1997); Smil, *Feeding the World: The Challenge for the Twenty-First Century* (2000); and an article by Ruttan in the *Journal of Economic Perspectives*: 'Productivity Growth in World Agriculture: Sources and Constraints' (2002). For a criticism of doomsday prophecies and Malthusian pessimism, students are advised to read Bjørn Lomborg, *The Skeptical Environmentalist: Measuring the Real State of the World* (2001).

Keith Griffin has written an early critical analysisis of the green revolution in *The Political Economy of Agrarian Change* (1976). Other interesting books about the green revolution, technological change and biotechnology include: Glaeser (ed.), *The Green Revolution Revisited: Critique and Alternatives* (1987); Pinstrup-Anderson, *Agricultural Research and Technology in Economic Development* (1982); Pinstrup-Anderson and Hazell, 'The Impact of the Green Revolution and Prospects for the Future' (1985); Hogg, *Technological Change in Agriculture: Locking in to Genetic Uniformity* (2000); and Paarlberg, *The Politics of Precaution: Genetically Modified Crops in Developing Countries* (2001).

For land reform one can consult the article by Binswanger, Deininger and Feder, 'Power, Distortions, Revolt and Reform in Agricultural Land Relations', in the *Handbook of Development Economics* (1995) and an article by Deininger and Binswanger on the 'Evolution of the World Bank's Land Policy' (2001).

The Food and Agriculture Organisation (FAO) publishes a wide range of statistics on agriculture, fisheries, forestry and the environment. These include: the FAO *Production*

Yearbooks, the FAO annual reports on *The State of Food and Agriculture; The Sixth World Food Survey* (1996); the *Global Forest Resources Assessment 2000* (2001); and *The State of Food Insecurity in the World 2002* (2002). Many reports and statistics can be assessed via the FAO website: http://www.fao.org/ and the FAO statistical database FAOSTAT (http://faostat.fao.org/).

11

State formation and political aspects of development

This chapter focuses on the processes of state formation in developing countries. Until recently most economists ignored the relationships between state formation and economic development. Nevertheless, political and economic developments are closely interconnected. For example, it is of little use to discuss the economic development of Nicaragua in the 1980s without taking the war with the USA into consideration. Also, it is not much use analysing the economic development of African countries, if one does not realise that many countries on the African continent are in a state of open or latent civil strife or international conflict. At the moment of writing (2003), this applies for instance to countries such as Burundi, Congo, Côte d'Ivoire, Liberia, Nigeria, Rwanda, Sierra Leone, Somalia, the Sudan and Zimbabwe (Marshall and Gurr, 2003).

   The political aspects of development will be discussed from two perspectives with which the reader will by now be familiar. In the first place, the interactions between state formation and economic development will be analysed. In this context an interesting paradox comes to the fore. The tasks and demands nowadays facing the government apparatus in developing countries are heavier and more comprehensive than ever before in economic history. At the same time, the apparatus of government is less well-equipped to fulfil these tasks.

In the second place, the characteristics of state formation and political development will be discussed as important independent aspects of development in their own right. In Chapter 1 we argued that 'development' is much more than economic change alone. Themes like national independence, effectiveness of government policy, political democratisation, and political participation are all included in a broader conception of development.

In this chapter the following themes and topics will be discussed: concepts of state and nation (section 11.1); classical perspectives on the relationships between the state and the economy (section 11.2); state formation as a prerequisite for economic development: European patterns of development (section 11.3); specific characteristics and problems of state formation in developing countries (section 11.4); the role of the state in economic development and industrialisation (section 11.5); interactions between political and economic developments (section 11.6); the predatory state as a potential obstacle to economic development in Sub-Saharan Africa (section 11.7).

11.1   Concepts

In *Social Change in the Twentieth Century* (1977, pp. 11–15) Daniel Chirot provides useful definitions of concepts such as 'state' and 'nation'. Following Max Weber, Chirot defines the *state* as a social system with a set of *rules* enforced by a *permanent administrative body* (the apparatus of government). This body is the highest source of authority in the wider social system. It claims the right to make collective decisions and to enforce them. A similar definition can be found in van den Hoogen (1992), according to whom the distinguishing characteristics of a state include a territory, a population and a sovereign authority that can impose rules and decisions on its own citizens. In the international political system *states* are the most important political actors.[1]

A *nation* is a group of people who feel they have so much in common that they should have their own state. The joint element may be religion, culture, language, common descent or shared historical experiences (see also Kellas, 1991). The important thing is the subjective feeling that people share common descent or history, from which they derive their claim to statehood. Van den Berghe (1981) defines a nation as a politically conscious ethnic group.

The term *society* may have many different meanings. In the context of state formation and nation building the term 'society' refers to the population that

---

1 There is some conceptual confusion about the distinction between 'state' and 'state apparatus'. The term state as used in the text above (e.g. the Dutch state or the Chinese state) refers to the wider social system or society, the common rules of which are established in the political process. These rules are implemented and enforced by a permanent administrative body (the 'state apparatus'). However, elsewhere, for instance in the Marxist literature the 'state', is also used to refer to the 'apparatus of government' (which includes the civil service, the army, the police and such political institutions as the political executive, the head of state, the judiciary, parliament and other representative organs). When we discuss processes of state formation in this chapter, we are referring to the wider concept of state. When we discuss the role of the state in the process of economic development, we are referring to the apparatus of government.

is controlled by a state apparatus or the population that forms a nation or both. A *country* refers to a well-defined geographical territory which is effectively controlled by a state apparatus. Effective control is the usual criterion for international diplomatic recognition of a country.

The term *nation-state* refers to the overlap of the population that is controlled by a state, and the population with shared feelings of belonging. This overlap is by no means self-evident. Nationalism – the idea that each nation should have its own independent state – is a relatively recent phenomenon, dating – in its modern form – from the nineteenth century. Prior to the nineteenth century most people used to identify more with village, region or kin than with larger territorial political units. In many developing countries today they still do so. In pre-nineteenth century Europe politics were mainly dominated by royal and noble elites. Kinship relationships within these elites played an important role in politics.

We do not mean to say that there were no nationalist sentiments or movements prior to the nineteenth century. Examples which immediately come to mind are the French popular resistance to British domination in the fifteenth century, inspired by Joan of Arc, the Dutch revolt against Spanish rule in the sixteenth and seventeenth centuries, and French nationalism following the French Revolution in the eighteenth century. Still, important defining characteristics of modern nationalism were lacking, like the use of modern means of communication and organisation to mobilise large numbers of people into mass movements and the underpinning of mass movements by nationalist ideologies.

There are nations without their own state, like the Jews before the establishment of the state of Israel, the Kurds and the Palestinians. There are also movements that seek to unite larger groups with an appeal to their common identity, such as Pan-Slavism or Pan-Arabism. There are also *multinational states* in which several national groups with a distinctive 'we feeling' coexist within a territory controlled by a single state apparatus. Well-known examples are the Habsburg monarchy till 1918, the Ottoman empire till 1918, the former Yugoslavia, the former Soviet Union and present-day India.

Finally, there are also examples of *multi-ethnic states*. These states comprise various ethnic groups that are characterised by ethnic 'we feelings', but do not claim their own separate states (see van den Berghe, 1981, p. 61). The Frisians in the Netherlands or the Welsh in Great Britain are examples of such a group. Often countries like the United States and Brazil are also called multi-ethnic states. Most Western societies have become more multi-ethnic since World War II as a result of massive immigration.

All these concepts represent sliding scales rather than absolutes. Within multi-ethnic states nationalist sentiments may develop, which may give rise to separatist movements. On the other hand, in processes of state formation separate groups may also develop common national identities. Although the term nation sometimes has biological undertones of common descent or kinship, national awareness often develops as a result of shared historical experiences. In *The Embarrassment of Riches* Simon Schama (1988) has impressively shown how Dutch national feelings were cultivated in the seventeenth century, resulting in the emergence of a Dutch national identity. The struggle for independence contributed to the emergence of national awareness in many former colonies.

Chirot makes a distinction between core societies and peripheral societies, which is of relevance for an understanding of state formation processes in developing countries.[2] In countries in the core of world society, state, nation, society and geographical boundaries tend to coincide. Examples of highly integrated nation-states are Denmark, France, Japan, the Netherlands, the United Kingdom and the United States. The main characteristic of such nation-states is a relatively high degree of political autonomy in national decision-making,[3] strong cultural integration and associated feelings of cultural self-confidence, at times bordering on complacency and feelings of superiority. Such 'strong states' are also characterised by effective government institutions (Thomas, 1987). From an economic point of view, core states are generally rich, highly industrialised and have a diversified economy.

On the periphery of world society, states and nations coincide to a far lesser extent. Many states are multi-ethnic or multinational. Country borders cut across ethnic boundaries. People are more likely to relate to tribe, village or region than to a far-off national state or national government. Separatist movements, religious conflict, civil wars and external interference constantly threaten the unity of the national state. The capacity of the state apparatus to make and implement collective decisions and rules is weakly developed. There is greater dependence on external influences than in core countries. Internally, there is a large degree of cultural heterogeneity. Externally, one is confronted with the cultural challenge of the West and penetration by Western cultural influences. Van den Hoogen points out that attempts to establish a strong, central authority in developing countries may actually become a source of conflict, violence and repression (van den Hoogen, 1992). There is resistance not only to authoritarian government, but also to the very notion of nation building itself. In economic terms, peripheral states are poorer, less industrialised and less diversified in their economic structure.

In recent years, we have become more aware of the fragility of nation-states, even in core states of the world economy. In almost all Western countries the unity of the nation-state has become less self-evident. Movements for regional

---

2 The terms 'core' and 'periphery' derive from theories of dependence in which conditions in developing countries are primarily explained by external influences (see section 3.5). The use of these terms, however, does not necessarily imply acceptance of these theories.
3 Since national states are part of networks of international interdependence, autonomy in national decision-making is always a matter of degree. For example, the national autonomy of European countries is constrained by supranational institutions such as the European Union. The latitude for national economic policies in small countries such as the Netherlands or Belgium is determined in by developments in the international economy.

autonomy and separatist movements have gained in strength and importance. Examples include Scotland, Wales, the Basque Provinces and Catalonia in Spain, Corsica and Brittany in France, Flanders and the Walloon provinces in Belgium, Northern Italy, Southern Tyrol and Quebec. In the United States, Australia and Western Europe cultural integration has weakened and identification with the dominant national culture has declined among members of so-called ethnic minorities. This holds both for peoples who have been living in a country for ages like Indians and Spanish Americans, Australian Aborigines and African Americans, and more recent immigrants. In particular in Western Europe, cultural heterogeneity increased rapidly during the post-war period, owing to migration flows from former colonies and other regions. Not only does the nation-state become less self-evident due to increased internal cultural and ethnic diversity, but the latitude for independent national policy also diminishes, owing to supranational economic and political influences in an increasingly interdependent world socio-economic system.

In several former communist states a destructive and, until recently, unthinkable process of national disintegration unfolded from 1989. The Soviet Union, Czechoslovakia and Yugoslavia broke up into smaller states. Within these new political entities ethnic groups struggled for ascendancy or claimed their own autonomy. In Yugoslavia this resulted in a bloody civil war in which various groups of Slavic descent (including Catholic Croats, Orthodox Serbs and Islamic Serbs) fought each other ferociously and applied ethnic cleansing in an attempt to create smaller ethnically homogeneous nation-states. Similar processes took place in Georgia, Tajikistan, Azerbaijan and Chechnya.

The demographer Keyfitz argues that the formation of smaller, ethnically homogeneous states is nothing but a continuation of the worldwide process of decolonisation and breakdown of empires (Keyfitz, 1991). The borders of the present existing states are accidental. Some nations like the Kurds, the Tamils and the Kashmiris had the bad luck that the process of state formation was consolidated before they were granted states of their own.

This is a dangerous notion. It ignores the fact that most regions in the world are ethnically mixed. The smaller the political entities claiming national independence, the sharper and more murderous the conflicts between the various 'nations' within the borders of the 'state'. The ultimate consequence of Keyfitz's perspective is the acceptance of ethnic cleansing by victors in ethnic struggles.

Presently, many developing countries are faced with separatist movements and potential challenges to their survival as an integrated national entity. These countries include India, Indonesia, China, Iraq, the Philippines, Sudan and Nigeria.

Many of these developments are taking place as this text is being written and it is not clear what their outcomes will be. They illustrate once again the fruitlessness of simple dichotomies: opposing highly developed and less developed political units and the tendency to think of development as a process of irreversible change from 'less developed' to 'more developed'.

11.2   Marxist and Weberian perspectives on the state

Classical Marxist and Weberian writings provide important insights into the process of state formation in developing countries and the role of the state in the overall process of development.

In the Marxist tradition, class relationships – the contradictions and conflicts between social groups and categories that have objective economic interests in common – are the central focus. Together with technological change (the forces of production), class relationships form the substructure of society. The dynamics of class relationships and class conflicts ultimately determine what happens in the superstructure of society: culture, religion, law and the state.[4] Reduced to its bare bones, this view implies that at a given moment in time the activities of the members of the state apparatus are completely determined by the interests of the ruling class. For instance, the state in capitalist society is said to be no more than the executive committee of the ruling class of capitalists and the bourgeoisie. In a feudal society the state represents the interests of the landed gentry and feudal landlords. After a socialist revolution, class contradictions would be abolished and the state would finally wither away (Marx, 1955).

This short summary does no justice to the discussions and polemics within the Marxist tradition concerning the interactions between the state and class relationships. Several neo-Marxist writings point in particular to the *relative autonomy* of the state apparatus. This implies that the state apparatus has a margin of freedom in relation to other social institutions. Political decisions and government actions have an independent measure of influence on the course of social and economic development (see, for example, Skocpol, 1979).

In addition, both Marxists and neo-Marxists stress the fact that government officials may be regarded as a separate 'class' with its own interests. Government actions and policies are in part determined by this interest group (Bardhan, 1984; Dahrendorf, 1963; Skocpol, 1979). In his analysis of communist states, Djilas even used the term 'the new class' for politicians and bureaucrats who function within the state apparatus. Their position in government was the basis for their social and material privileges (Djilas, 1957; Lane, 1971). Nevertheless, one may safely conclude that in the Marxist and neo-Marxist tradition the functioning of the state is ultimately primarily determined by the interests of dominant groups and classes in the economic sphere.

The Marxist perspective provides a useful counterbalance to the notion that the state is a neutral institution, standing above social parties, which produces rules and decisions more or less in a social vacuum, with the goal of improving social welfare.[5] The Marxist perspective is a source of inspiration for the empirical study of the social constraints within which governments must

---

4 State in this section refers to the 'state apparatus': government and political institutions (see footnote 1).
5 This notion of the state as a neutral arbiter is part of the intellectual tradition of post-war social democracy in Western Europe.

operate and the influence of classes, interest groups and pressure groups on government actions and policies (Alavi, 1979). The idea of the state as an arena for contending economic and social interest groups, including interest groups from within the state apparatus itself, has found wide acceptance. It is now also the prevailing perspective among non-Marxist political scientists and political economists. However, the simple Marxist class categories have been left behind. In their place, we see, both within and outside the apparatus of government, a multitude of interest groups, lobbies and pressure groups, whose influence can be analysed (Buchanan and Tullock, 1962; Frey, 1978; Olson, 1965; Tullock, 1965).[6] One of the non-Marxist founders of this 'new political economy' was Joseph Schumpeter in his study *Capitalism, Socialism and Democracy* (1946).

Another important source of inspiration for present-day studies of the state is the work of Max Weber (1922). Unlike Marx, Weber emphasised that political power is not a mere reflection of economic power. The political sphere has an autonomy of its own in relation to the economic sphere.[7] There is no question of the state withering away. On the contrary, Weber predicted correctly that the state would become increasingly important within the context of a long-term process of bureaucratisation and rationalisation. The general tendency towards bureaucratisation would be reinforced in countries where socialist revolutions would take place.

Although Weber was very concerned about the social consequences of continued bureaucratisation and rationalisation, 'bureaucracy' itself does not have a negative connotation in his work. On the contrary, 'bureaucracy' represents a newer and vastly more efficient form of organisation in which the activities of large numbers of people are coordinated in a network of specialised functions. In a bureaucracy decisions are made on the basis of formal rules and precedents rather than on the basis of the fancies and favours of royal sovereigns or personal obligations and ties between patrons and clients. Job qualifications are defined as objectively as possible, and functions are ordered in a hierarchical structure. Recruitment for functions is based on objective meritocratic criteria such as competence, education and experience, irrespective of personal relationships and ties. In theory, personal connections, relationships of kin and social background play no role. There is a complete separation between the bureaucratic office and the personal sphere of the functionary. Finally, fulfilling a function in a bureaucracy is a full-time and fully-paid professional activity. According to Weber, the bureaucratic form of organisation was more rational (i.e. non-arbitrary) than previous forms of organisation. Both in the political and in the economic domain, bureaucracy was superior to other forms of organisation. It made for greater effectiveness and predictability. Bureaucratic

---

6 A potential drawback of this interesting strand of literature is that everything is reduced to interest groups and their supposedly rational calculations. The constraining role of institutions tends to be underemphasised (Evans, 1995).

7 In this respect, modern neo-Marxist authors were inspired not only by Marx, but also by his intellectual opponent Weber.

organisation was a characteristic of not only the modern state apparatus, but also large modern rationally organised capitalist enterprises. Bureaucratisation, thus, was an aspect of successful economic and political development.

Again in contrast to Marx, Weber considered state formation as one of the important *prerequisites* for economic development. State formation in Europe involved centralisation of power and rule making, and the pacification of the territory within the borders of the national state in the making. Political centralisation implied the abolition of all sorts of local legislation, toll barriers, privileges, tariffs and rules that hampered the emergence of national markets and the growth of trade. Local currencies were abolished and replaced by national currencies. The right to impose taxes became the monopoly of national authorities. Pacification implied that incessant conflicts and wars between local rulers gradually made way for a central power that acquired a monopoly on the use of violence. Only the army and the police had the legitimate right to apply violence on behalf of the central authority.

It is clear that pacification within a larger territory is an essential prerequisite for an expansion of trade and markets, an increase in investment and for economic growth in general. Where there are wars, conflicts and sporadic violence, no one's property is safe. Few people will be prepared to take the risks involved in long-term investments. Trade can only flourish when the transport of goods is not obstructed and when people can be sure that their property rights will be respected. Entrepreneurship will only make its appearance if people have some guarantee that future benefits of risky investments in the present accrue to those who have taken the risks.

Political centralisation, uniformity of regulation at the national level and the development of a well-functioning government bureaucracy increase the predictability, which is a prerequisite for rational calculations of costs and benefits in a market economy. Legal protection of individual ownership rights by central rules, sanctioned by the central apparatus of violence, contributes to entrepreneurship and investment in capital goods and technical innovation. In the long term these lead to an increase in collective welfare (North and Thomas, 1973).

11.3　Processes of state formation in Europe

In *Über den Prozess der Zivilisation* (1969) Norbert Elias – building on the insights of Max Weber and historians like Bloch, Lefèbre and Pirenne – presents an analysis of century-long processes of centralisation and state formation in Europe and in particular in what is now known as France. In this chapter, these processes serve as a basis for comparison with more recent processes of state formation in developing countries.

The European states developed out of the highly decentralised feudal system that had emerged in Europe after the fall of the Roman empire. The linchpin of this system consisted of local feudal landlords. They lived off agricultural surpluses produced in their territory and provided their serfs and dependants with some form of military protection against the depredations of other lords, robber barons and overseas raiders. The peasants farmed primarily for their own consumption and were obliged to transfer part of their agricultural surpluses to their feudal landlord and his household. Although there was some trade, the small feudal domains were largely self-sufficient. The lords in turn were in vassalage to superior liege lords and sovereigns whom they owed military support in times of war; lords would then mobilise their serfs to serve as foot soldiers. The feudal value system had mystical elements, which at a later stage could be called upon by monarchs to legitimise strong central authority in emergent national states (Wallerstein, 1974).

Feudal landlords continually strove to make their rights to land hereditary and to increase their autonomy from their liege lords. At the same time they tried to expand their own spheres of influence and to subject others to their authority. For many centuries, the European feudal systems fluctuated between centralisation and decentralisation. Sometimes local rulers would succeed in gaining military superiority and expanded the territory under their control in processes of centralisation. However, these processes of centralisation were rather precarious. Military expansion required funds and people which had to be withdrawn from the local economy. This perpetually threatened to undermine the economic basis of political expansion (cf. Elvin, 1973 for China). The centralised rule over larger areas also involved considerable costs such as the support of a centralised administrative apparatus, and the maintenance of systems of transport and communication. These costs could easily exceed the carrying capacity of the economic base.[8]

Feudal lords who supported a sovereign in his expansionist campaigns were frequently granted part of the conquered lands as a fief. The sovereign claimed the supreme authority over these lands. His vassals, however, continuously strove to make their rights to land hereditary and to increase their independence from central authority. For such reasons, processes of centralisation alternated with processes of decentralisation and disintegration. A telling example of the difficulty of maintaining a central apparatus of government is the way in which early rulers like Charlemagne had to travel around the country with their courts. Agricultural surpluses were simply insufficient to support a large, permanent court in a central seat of government. The sovereign and his court were fed from the yields of the lands of the vassals who received the honour of a royal visit. Similar patterns were found in many of the older African states and empires (Isichei, 1997).

Centralisation

From the twelfth century onwards the scales tipped in favour of centralisation. Certain royal dynasties gradually succeeded in establishing their authority over

---

8 The tension between productive capacity and the costs of political expansion in feudal society is also found in much greater empires. It has been well analysed by authors such as Paul Kennedy (1989), Marc Elvin (1973), and Immanuel Wallerstein (1974). Kennedy uses the term 'imperial overstretch'.

other feudal lords, subjecting more and more regions to their rule. For example, the Duchy of the Île de France eventually became the nucleus of the later kingdom of France; London would become the centre of a British kingdom and Madrid of a Spanish kingdom. The new national kingdoms that came into being were much smaller than the ancient empires of Rome or China. But, they were more strongly centralised and were administered more effectively (Wallerstein, 1974; see also Chapter 2).

In the process of centralisation relations, the balance of power between social classes underwent great changes. In a feudal society one can distinguish: (1) the landed classes (the nobility and the clergy)[9]; (2) the serfs who worked the land, transferred parts of their agricultural surpluses to the landlords, and provided them with various labour services; (3) the sovereign and his court, and (4) the rising classes of traders, financiers, artisans and urban citizens.

Especially alliances between bourgeois groupings and the royal courts have been of decisive importance in processes of centralisation. Financial support by merchant bankers and taxes on urban economic activities provided the sovereign with independent means and increased his power *vis à vis* the nobility. The possibility of funding standing mercenary armies made it less necessary to appeal to feudal loyalties for military manpower and support. This also worked in favour of centralising tendencies.

Between the twelfth and the seventeenth centuries centralising tendencies prevailed, and feudalism was converted into centralised royal absolutist states, which were the forerunners of modern national states. These processes of centralisation involved struggles for two important monopolies: the *monopoly of violence* and the *tax monopoly*. The military pacification of larger areas involved the establishment of a monopoly of violence. Only the military and the police had the right to exercise violence on behalf of central authorities. Attempts were made to curb the use of violence by individuals, groups and local rulers (see, for example, Tilly, 1975, p. 27 ff). As the power of the central authorities increased, they increasingly claimed the exclusive right to impose taxes on their subjects. Step by step the rights of taxation of local feudal rulers and urban authorities were gradually curtailed or were integrated into a national system. Sovereigns who succeeded in setting up effective central bureaucracy had a head start in the battle for the tax monopoly.

Changes in the balance of power between classes

For complex reasons – including demographic fluctuations and the gradual emergence of an economy based on trade, crafts and manufacturing centring on towns – the influence of the feudal landed nobility started to wane from the late Middle Ages onwards. The fourteenth century in particular was a

---

9 Elias does not pay much attention to the role of the clergy in processes of state formation, nor to the protracted conflicts between 'secular' and 'religious' powers. The clergy based part of its social influence on its religious functions. But the clergy also lived off the revenues of its estates and as such can be seen as belonging to the landed classes.

century of crisis in the feudal system. At the same time the influence of commercial middle classes was growing. By the time the power and influence of these two competing social categories were more or less in balance, the central sovereign could act as the supreme arbiter. His power and latitude increased dramatically.

Members of the feudal nobility were losing out in the economic sphere, but their social standing was still very high. They spent part of their time at the king's court, cultivating an exclusive and refined lifestyle (Elias, 1979). The commercial bourgeoisie became more powerful economically, but its members were not yet taken seriously socially. The monarchy could play off these rival classes against each other.

In the sixteenth and seventeenth centuries centralisation trends culminated in royal absolutism. The seemingly unlimited power of the crown reached its peak in France under the Sun King, Louis XIV. Here the contending classes were most evenly balanced. All over Europe there were similar processes of centralisation and concentration of power. However, in countries where either the bourgeoisie (as in England or in the Low Countries) or the landed nobility (as in German states) had more influence, the position of the central monarch was correspondingly weaker (see Barrington Moore, 1967; Elias, 1969, Vol. II, p. 229 ff).

Once a central authority with an effective monopoly of violence and a tax monopoly had been established, a *process of democratisation of power* got under way, in which the absolute power of the crown was gradually circumscribed. Bourgeois groupings, which had to raise most of the taxes, played a significant role in this process. The sovereign increasingly came to be answerable to institutions in which taxpayers were represented. Democratisation was also furthered by the continuing social ascent of bourgeois groups and the continuing decline of the landed nobility. The sovereign was no longer able to play these two groups off against each other. At later stages other social classes, such as the emerging industrial working classes, also participated in the process of democratisation.

The process of democratisation also involved a gradual separation of the private and public functions of the crown. Initially, there was not much difference between public funds and the private fortune of the sovereign. Later, however, a distinction developed between the sovereign's personal finances and the finances of the state, for which the sovereign was accountable to representative bodies.[10] The central administrative apparatus also became more independent from the central sovereign. From a loose collection of people with personal ties and obligations to the sovereign, it was transformed into a professional bureaucracy. Democratisation in the nineteenth century took the form of the rise of political mass movements. Ever larger groups participated in the political process and the struggle for universal suffrage began.

---

10 A similar differentiation developed in the economic sphere between the private property of the entrepreneur and the assets of the firm.

The rise of nationalism

From the mid-eighteenth century onwards *nationalist movements* and *ideologies* arose, emphasising the connection between a people (nation) and a state. This type of nationalism came to replace earlier feelings of identification with region, village or town. Nationalist sentiments also come to predominate among members of political elites, between whom there had previously been more feelings of supranational loyalty based on kinship, social class and personal relationships.

In the nineteenth century, nationalism was one of the driving forces in colonial expansion. In the twentieth century, modern nationalism – the idea that all peoples or nations are entitled to their own independent states – was to be an important force in the colonial struggles for independence from Western colonisers.

European processes of state formation have a number of specific characteristics which distinguish them from processes of state formation in other parts of the world. First, centralisation did not emanate from one single centre, but from various focal points within Europe. Second, centralisation never led to the establishment of an all-embracing European empire. Parallel processes of centralisation resulted in a multitude of national states, competing with each other for technological advance, military supremacy, and economic and political expansion. Third, the resulting European states were strong and effectively centralised compared to larger but more loosely organised political entities, such as the Chinese empire. Finally, rising bourgeois groups, who were the bearers of a money and market economy, had a relatively independent position. They were never completely subordinated to a central political authority, as was the case in the great empires of the past. In the competition between states, political leaders actually depended in part on the support of their entrepreneurial classes. These classes supported the new strong states in their financial needs and their competition with other states. The states in turn supported their entrepreneurial groups in their urge for external economic expansion. Initially, the European expansion in the world was economic rather than political in nature.

In *Social Origins of Dictatorship and Democracy* (1967) Barrington Moore analyses differences in state formation processes in France, Germany and England, which are closely associated with differences in the balance of power between social classes and groups. In France, the French Revolution led to a dramatic overthrow of the *ancien régime* by a popular movement led by bourgeois groupings whose social ascent and emancipation had been blocked. In England this process was more gradual and less violent. The bourgeoisie and the nobility intermixed. The nobility participated in the modern market economy and the bourgeois classes underwent the cultural influences of the upper classes. In Germany the process of state formation was altogether different. In part as a result of the Thirty Years' War (1618–48), the degree of political centralisation had lagged behind and political unity was not achieved until 1870. The landed nobility retained much of its influence, and the middle classes were weakly developed. When Germany achieved political integration in the second half of the nineteenth century under Prussian leadership, and strove for rapid economic development, a kind of coalition was formed between the landed nobility (the Junkers) and the rising working classes. Partly bypassing the middle classes, there was a policy of radical economic modernisation and industrialisation 'from the top down'.

In Great Britain and France, the development of capitalism, industrialisation and the rise of the middle classes in France and England were associated with the rise of parliamentary democracy. According to Barrington Moore, the insecure position of the middle classes in Germany weakened democratic tendencies and contributed to the later rise of fascism. There are interesting parallels between German and Japanese economic and political development. Both countries were latecomers to industrial development. In both cases modernisation was initiated from above by groups originating in old feudal elites. In both cases there was a reactive kind of nationalism in response to external challenges and the examples of established and economically successful nation-states.

Modernising authoritarian regimes in Latin America and Asia show interesting similarities with the German and Japanese patterns of development, not least with regard to the weak development of the middle classes. The wider relevance of Barrington Moore's study for developing countries is that it focuses our attention on the interplay between changes in the class structure, processes of state formation and economic development.

11.4   State formation in developing countries

In section 11.3 we paid attention to the notion, deriving from Max Weber, that state formation – characterised by pacification, centralisation and the development of a monopoly of violence, a tax monopoly and effective government institutions – is a prerequisite for economic development (see also Righart *et al.*, 1991; Chapters 2 and 3).

In many developing countries since 1945 the state has not been completely consolidated and the national territory not fully pacified. In several Latin American, African and Asian countries the tax monopoly is underdeveloped, especially with respect to income taxes. The fiscal basis of the state is often weak (O'Connor, 1973). Wealthy citizens pay little or no income tax. Government revenues are highly dependent on taxes on land and agricultural production, tariffs on exports and imports, and, in some cases, financial aid from abroad. A potential source of government revenue is monetary financing of expenditures. This form of financing is passed on to citizens in the form of inflation tax or *seigniorage* (see de Haan *et al.*, 1993). According to Myrdal (1968), many newly independent states were '*soft states*', by which he meant that governments did not have effective means to implement policy intentions and to impose binding obligations on their citizens so as to harness efforts and resources for development. Myrdal referred in particular to non-communist states in South and Southeast Asia, though his analyses are also relevant for an understanding of state formation in Latin America and Africa.

In the following sections attention will be paid to the specific characteristics and problems of state formation processes in developing countries. Here it can already be stated that political instability, malfunctioning of government, war and civil strife are at least as important as purely economic factors in explaining economic stagnation in developing countries. The interactions between processes of state formation and economic development will be discussed in more detail in section 11.6.

11.4.1   The importance of external penetration in processes of state formation

In Western Europe the nation-state was the outcome of centuries-long processes of decentralisation and centralisation from within, with modern political national institutions gradually evolving out of local traditions. With the exception of a limited number of countries such as China, Ethiopia, Iran, Japan, Thailand and Turkey, this is not the way states were formed in developing countries.[11] Usually the impetus for modern state formation in developing countries was *colonial penetration* by a foreign ethnic group (Goldthorpe, 1979, ch. 12; Sandbrook and Barker, 1985; van Benthem van den Bergh, 1980). The current borders of many developing countries have been decisively influenced by colonialism (Davidson, 1992) and the institutions of the modern state have been imposed from outside.

Within their borders, the new states often contain a multiplicity of ethnic groups that hardly identify with the national institutions (Nettle, 2002). Furthermore, ethnic tensions and divisions have been exacerbated by classical divide-and-rule policies of colonial regimes. In some respects the ethnic and tribal divisions are even the product of modern influences (Davidson, 1992). Traditional ethnic ties were used by various colonial and post-colonial elites for the purposes of modern political mass mobilisation.

The legitimacy of the new state institutions is often weak. The internal pacification of the territory has not yet been completed, the tax monopoly is poorly developed, and the effectiveness of national state institutions is limited. Moreover, especially in Africa, the colonial intermezzo has been brief. In this respect, also, modern state institutions have had relatively little time to take root (Sandbrook and Barker, 1985).

The following examples illustrate the significance of external penetration in state formation. Before the colonial period India was a hotchpotch of principalities. In the fifteenth and sixteenth centuries there had been a powerful Muslim

---

11 Van den Berghe (1981) rightly points out that European states did not develop out of stateless societies. Almost all European states developed out of the fragmentation or decentralisation of older political entities or empires, or the merging of existing, smaller political entities. That is why we have emphasised processes of both decentralisation and centralisation. Of course there are also European examples of states whose borders have been determined by external forces, like former Yugoslavia and former Czechoslovakia.

empire in the centre and north of India, the Mogul empire, which reached its peak under Akbar (1556–1605). This empire might have been the potential core of a future Indian nation-state. However, after the arrival of the English, it disintegrated into a multitude of smaller kingdoms and principalities. Initially, British influence was concentrated in Bengal. In the nineteenth century British India was centralised as a colonial empire. This empire included the territory of present-day India, Pakistan, Bangladesh and Burma. After decolonisation Burma became an independent state. Religious differences between Muslims and Hindus resulted in a bloody division of the rest of British India into India and Pakistan. After a civil war combined with a war with India in 1971, Pakistan broke up into two parts: Bangladesh and present-day Pakistan.

The current unitary state of Indonesia came into existence in a similar way as a result of Dutch colonial centralising impulses in the nineteenth century. A multitude of 'native' principalities, which had been politically independent until then, were united under colonial rule in a process that involved numerous wars and uprisings (Ricklefs, 1981). The last of these wars was the Aceh war at the end of the nineteenth century. During and after the struggle for independence nationalist leaders took the colonial borders as their point of departure for postcolonial state formation. Even the annexation of Dutch New Guinea by Indonesia in 1963 was justified by Sukarno with reference to the fact that New Guinea had been part of the Dutch colonial empire. It should therefore be part of the new state of Indonesia. The bloody occupation and annexation of East Timor in 1976 was also justified by the idea that the borders of the Indonesian state should coincide with the areas formerly ruled by Europeans (including in this case the Portuguese who ruled East Timor as a colony till 1975).[12]

In Indochina, the modern borders of states like Vietnam, Laos and Cambodia were determined by the brief period of French rule from the mid-nineteenth century onwards. Here, too, national boundaries and ethnic dividing lines do not always coincide. Nevertheless, it is important to note that in Asia, powerful and well-established states existed prior to Western colonisation. There was long experience with centralised political rule.

In Latin America the present-day states came into existence after the disintegration of the Spanish and Portuguese colonial empires during the first decades of the nineteenth century. The Spanish colonisers had extirpated all vestiges of the earlier Inca and Aztec empires. Brazil had never known any form of centralised rule prior to Western colonisation. Thus, in Latin America, there was little or no precolonial political heritage as a source for modern nation building.

The former viceroyalty of New Granada broke up into Colombia, Ecuador and Venezuela. The viceroyalty of Peru was divided into Peru, Chile and Bolivia. Attempts by Simon Bolivar, the leader of the struggle for independence, to

---

12 East Timor became independent in 2002. In Aceh, a separatist movement is presently fighting for independence from Indonesia.

form a Greater Colombian republic uniting New Granada and Peru, failed. In 1903 Panama broke away from Colombia, partly at the instigation of and with the support of the USA.

Mexico evolved out of the viceroyalty of New Spain, which had included Central America, the Spanish West Indies and, for some time, Venezuela. Here, too, attempts to maintain larger political units failed. The Central American states broke away from Mexico between 1820 and 1830. In a war between 1845 and 1848 Mexico lost half of its territory to the United States (Texas, New Mexico, California, Arizona, Nevada and Utah). Argentina, Paraguay and Uruguay developed out of the viceroyalty of Rio de la Plata. Brazil gained its independence from Portugal in 1822. Dom Pedro, the son of the last Portuguese king, became the first emperor of independent Brazil.

In each Latin American country the political scene was initially dominated by descendants of white colonists and immigrants. For a very long time descendants of the original Indian population, imported slaves and contract labourers hardly participated in the political process. To this very day they are under-represented in politics.[13] Since independence the military have played an important role in politics in most countries. There has been widespread political instability. In the nineteenth and twentieth centuries, foreign powers frequently intervened in order to safeguard their economic and political interests. There have also been numerous internal wars and conflicts that led to adjustments of national borders. Nevertheless, it is clear that modern processes of state formation in Latin America commenced at an earlier stage than in Africa and Asia. Despite the considerable ethnic diversity in Latin America, most territorial borders of the countries in this region are not in question. From the mid-1980s onwards, several countries in Latin America have experienced a process of democratisation, with military regimes gradually making place for civilian rule. It remains a problem that the legitimacy of national institutions is limited.

The consequences of external penetration for the process of state formation have been most extreme in Africa and the Middle East. In Africa borders were determined both by military conquest and by diplomatic negotiations between the European powers, which started with the Berlin conference of 1884/1885 (see Ake, 1996; Jackson and Rosberg, 1986, p. 6). In a brief period in the late nineteenth century the whole of Africa was colonised in the 'Scramble for Africa'. This process was completed by 1900. By 1914 only two countries in Africa remained independent: Abyssinia and Liberia. In the Middle East, the European powers entered the vacuum left after the fall of the Ottoman Empire, and established a multitude of colonies and protectorates. Both in Africa and in the Middle East, the present borders are often straight lines that ignore geographic circumstances or ethnic composition. These lines were drawn on maps with rulers by representatives of the great colonial powers. In their

---

13 The election of Luiz Inacio Lula da Silva (Lulu) as president of Brazil in 2002 formed a significant break with this tradition.

land-hunger, military rivalry and mutual competition, the great powers divided up the land amongst themselves. In particular, countries with few colonies, like Germany and France, were eager to get a stake.

One of the presumed distinguishing characteristics of African history, in comparison with Asia, is the absence of a tradition of centralised states prior to European colonisation. This view is manifestly incorrect. Egypt and Ethiopia are very ancient states and the Maghreb in Northwest Africa has a long history of centralised rule. In Sub-Saharan Africa there has been a rich diversity of ancient states, empires and confederations (Davidson, 1992; Isichei, 1997; Sandbrook and Barker, 1985; Schoenmakers, 1992). We mention but a few: the medieval realms in the savannas of Ghana and Mali; the Songhai empire centred on Timbuktu from the second half of the fifteenth century to the end of the sixteenth century; the ancient kingdoms of Nubia and Ethiopia; the seventeenth-century kingdom of Buganda in present-day Uganda; the Asante kingdom in Ghana, founded at the end of the seventeenth century; the nineteenth-century Lozi kingdom in present-day Zambia; the great kingdom of Benin from the twelfth century to the nineteenth century; the Kaabu empire from the sixteenth to the nineteenth century in the region of Guinea Bissau; the Zulu empire in Southern Africa in the nineteenth century; and many more.

However, absence of the written word outside the Arabic-Islamic sphere of influence restricted the strength of most African states. Writing is a prerequisite for the emergence of permanent, centralised systems of book-keeping and administration, which are essential ingredients of strong states. Except for warfare, conquest and the taking of slaves, the impact of precolonial African states on everyday life in agricultural and nomadic societies was much more limited than that of modern state-formations or precolonial states in other parts of the world. Even in the 'great states' most people lived in villages or scattered hamlets and usually central government impinged very little on their lives (Isichei, 1997). The territorial size of precolonial states was also usually rather small. Precolonial political formations might possibly have formed a basis for political centralisation from within. But they were unable to resist the colonial penetration from Europe, from the second half of the nineteenth century onwards.

Apart from kingdoms, empires, and tribal confederations, many African peoples lived in decentralised tribal configurations with no central political leadership: so-called *acephalous* political units (Mair, 1967). Their loyalty was to village, lineage, region or tribe rather than to remote and unfamiliar concepts such as empires or national states. Nomadic and acephalous societies were the main sources of slaves. They were preyed upon by the more centralised states, which gained part of their revenues from the sale of slaves to Western and Arabic slave traders (Hopkins, 1973; Klein, 1999).

In the colonial period, bureaucracies in Africa were tiny and were far removed from local communities. The borders of the colonies cut across a rich variety of traditional political institutions, confederations and tribal communities. In the process of decolonisation in the decades following World War II, these extremely heterogeneous societies were transformed into independent national states, with inexperienced bureaucracies and imported political institutions such as parliaments or judiciaries. Soon after independence, these states quickly degenerated into one-party states and personal regimes (see section 11.7).

Linguistically, external influences on the process of state formation have also been of importance. In the process of gradual political centralisation in Europe, the local dialect of the dominant centre usually developed into a national language over the centuries. However, in many former colonies there was no linguistic unity. A great variety of languages was spoken. For want of a national language, the language of the colonial rulers was used as a common means of communication. This situation continued after independence. After all, a choice for the language of one of the principal ethnic or cultural groups could easily spark off feelings of resentment among other ethnic groups. Thus, English became a national language in India, Pakistan, and former British colonies in Africa like Ghana, Nigeria and Zimbabwe. French became the national language of the former West African colonies of France. Portuguese is now the national language in Brazil, Spanish in the rest of Latin America.

In Indonesia, the nationalist movement deliberately chose Bahasa Indonesia – a variant of Malay, used as a trade language – as the national tongue as early as 1928. Both Dutch and Javanese, the language of the dominant ethnic group in Indonesia, were rejected as the national language. By now Dutch has almost disappeared in Indonesia, except among people of 55 years and older. As the internationally oriented language, it has been replaced by English. In this respect, Indonesia is a unique example of successful cultural decolonisation. In a somewhat similar fashion, Israel succeeded in establishing modern Hebrew as the national language for Jewish immigrants coming from all over the world.

It is interesting to note that in their fight against Western colonialism, independence movements took colonial borders as given. The pursuit of 'national' independence was strongly influenced by Western ideas about nationalism and national states. It was based on the assumption that the population of a colony was a nation (van Benthem van den Bergh, 1980).

11.4.2   Internal political instability

In the former colonies, nationalist resistance against foreign rule created a sense of national solidarity. However, when the tangible oppressor disappeared with the departure of the colonial rulers, contradictions between different ethnic groups and 'nations' within the borders of the newly independent states usually intensified (Ake, 1996). This was, and still is, an important and continuing source of political instability. Central authorities often regard expressions of ethnic, tribal, religious, cultural and linguistic individuality as a threat to the political unity of the national state. These expressions, therefore, are suppressed, frequently by force. This may lead to an intensification of political conflicts and to the rise of new nationalist separatist movements. Thus the very process of state formation itself can become a new source of political conflict and instability (van den Hoogen, 1992).

The instability of new states is augmented by the contradiction between what O'Connor calls the 'accumulation function' and the 'legitimation function' of the state. According to O'Connor (1973), governments have to choose between conflicting objectives: the use of state power in support of capital accumulation by entrepreneurial classes on the one hand, and maintenance of social harmony and legitimacy by means of redistributive and welfare-oriented government expenditures, on the other hand. In developing countries, this contradiction can result in a permanent fiscal crisis and political crisis. A related contradiction is found in states characterised by personal rule. Here, the ruler uses state resources to distribute favours to client groups at the expense of accumulation and growth (see further section 11.7).

The greater the role of the government in the economy, the deeper the tension between these two functions. The legitimation function of the state implies that the government should not take any measures that will lastingly alienate politically important groups of the population. Maintaining social harmony may, however, require policies that hamper economic growth, such as food and energy subsidies, creation of employment in the government sector and subsidies to urban industry. Such measures lead to an overextended public sector, large fiscal deficits and inflation. In the long term these factors have negative effects on economic growth (e.g. in Brazil and Mexico, see Maddison *et al.*, 1992). The implementation of a policy of structural adjustment aimed at limiting the role of the government, restricting fiscal deficits, cutting subsidies and liberalising the economy, jeopardises the very political survival of regimes in many countries. All over the developing world, implementation of World Bank and IMF recommendations goes hand in hand with increasing social unrest.

In her pioneering study *States and Social Revolutions* Theda Skocpol (1979) discerns a similar tension between the necessity of levying taxes for purposes of warfare, putting government finances on a sound basis and economic modernisation on the one hand, and maintaining the support of crucial sections of the population on the other hand. She explains the sudden and seemingly inexplicable fall of regimes in the French and Russian revolutions and the 1911 revolution in China by the fact that governments were forced to implement unpopular economic reforms in order to cope with external challenges. These reforms conflicted with the specific interests of those groups that had been the most loyal allies of the ruling regime up till then. Thus, at a crucial juncture, a regime would suddenly lose the support of these groups. It would become more vulnerable to the political opposition of other groups and classes. The meltdown of communism in 1989 provides a vivid example of the operation of such mechanisms in recent times.

11.4.3 External political interference as a destabilising factor

Not only is the political unification of many developing countries the result of colonisation, but also after decolonisation, processes of state formation continue to be influenced by external intervention and interference. Radical authors have even coined the term 'neocolonial relations of dependence'. External interference may be of an economic or a political nature. Economic interference may be the result of factors such as the operations of multinational enterprises, foreign investors or conditions imposed by international economic institutions such as the IMF, the World Bank, the World Trade Organisation or the large trade blocs of the rich countries (OECD, EU).

In this paragraph, we focus on political and military interference. Internal political instability invites political interference from without. External interference augments internal political instability. Initially minor differences between ethnic groups within a country may easily acquire geopolitical or regional dimensions.

The Cold War between East and West from 1945 to 1989 found its counterpart in conflicts between the 'clients' of the two blocs. These clients were often recruited on an ethnic basis in the pursuit of geopolitical objectives. Regional powers such as South Africa, Vietnam, India, Libya, Iraq, Iran and Syria also tried to widen their spheres of influence. Their interventions in internal political conflicts in other countries exacerbated ethnic conflicts. Simultaneously, political leaders of ethnic groups solicited external military and political support in their struggles for control over the new national institutions. External interference made internal conflicts bloodier, less manageable and longer.

The list of developing countries in which external interference since World War II played a role in processes of state formation or national disintegration is long, Box 11.1 provides examples of external interference during this period (Banks *et al.*, 1998; Marshall, 2003; Marshall and Gurr, 2003; Sivard, 1991; for Africa, see for example, David, 1987; Gavshon, 1981). This list – by no means complete – illustrates the importance of both the East–West competition and regional tensions in exacerbating conflicts within and between new states in Asia, Africa and the Middle East and older states in Latin America. For the Cold War superpowers, their mutual rivalry was more important than the question whether the regimes or movements they supported were in any way worthy of their support.

Box 11.1 State formation and external political interference

- *The Korean War.* In Korea, the USA and several Western allies fought a full-scale war against the Chinese in 1950–52. This war eventually resulted in the division of the former Japanese colony of Korea, into present-day North and South Korea.
- *Secessionist movements in Zaire.* In 1960, France, England and Belgium first supported the secessionist movement of Moise Tshombe in Katanga, an area rich in minerals,

while the USA and the Soviet Union supported the Democratic Republic under the first president Patrice Lumumba. Later the USA collaborated in the overthrow of the Lumumba regime, when it oriented itself more towards the Soviet Union. The USA supported a takeover by Mobutu. In 1977/8 there was another secessionist movement in Katanga, initiated by Angolan exiles. This uprising was suppressed by Mobutu with the help of Moroccan troops and French logistic support. A second invasion from Katanga in 1978 was suppressed with the assistance of French and Belgian troops and American logistic support. Zaire, since renamed Democratic Republic of Congo, has remained unstable ever since. Cold War intervention has been replaced by regional interventions by Rwanda, Zimbabwe and Uganda each supporting their own factions and ethnic groups in a bloody civil war.

- *The Vietnamese War.* After the defeat of French Forces by the independence movement led by Ho Chi Minh, Americans and American-supported regimes fought the nationalist independence movements and communist revolutionary movements, supported by China and the Soviet Union from 1945 to 1973. In 1973, Vietnam was reunified under communist rule.
- *Cambodia.* In Cambodia the Americans, the Chinese and the Vietnamese tried to exert their influence in changing coalitions during different periods during much of the post-war period.
- *The war between Somalia and Ethiopia over the Ogaden in 1977/8.* Until 1977 the Americans offered military support to Ethiopia, and the Soviet Union to Somalia. After the Somalian invasion of the Ogaden in 1977, the Soviet Union and Cuba supported Ethiopia by means of military supplies, advisers and Cuban soldiers. The US ended their support to Ethiopia and in time started to support Somalia. Eventually, the invasion of the Ogaden was repulsed and millions of ethnic Somalis fled across the Somalian border. In Somalia politics degenerated into clan warfare, which persists to this very day. The national state has ceased to exist.
- *The struggle for the secession of Eritrea from Ethiopia from 1962 to 1992.* Until 1974 Haile Selassie received large-scale US support. Since 1977, Eritrean resistance against the communist regime of Haile Mariam Mengistu was supported by the Islamic countries and indirectly by the USA. After the fall of the communist regime in Ethiopia, Eritrea seceded peacefully in 1992. But full-scale trench warfare erupted between 1998 and 2000 and an uneasy peace has only recently been concluded.
- *The Angolan civil war after the fall of the Portuguese regime in 1974.* The MPLA government of Agostinho Neto and Dos Santos received large-scale military support from the Soviet Union and Cuba. The opposition of Holden Roberto's FNLA and Jonas Savimbi's UNITA was supported by South Africa and the USA. For a while the FNLA was also supported by China. South African support even took the form of a military invasion. Large numbers of Cuban soldiers fought on the government side. A peace agreement was finally signed in 1994, but implementation of the peace accords was slow and was only realised after the death of Savimbi in 2002.
- *The secession of Biafra from Nigeria.* During the Nigerian Civil War (1967–70) about the secession of Biafra, the USA offered some military support, albeit covertly, to the secessionist movement, whereas the UK and the Soviet Union supported the regime in Lagos. The unity of Nigeria was maintained.
- *Nicaragua, Cuba, Chile, the Dominican Republic, Panama and Granada.* In these countries the USA tried to prevent the establishment of communist regimes by means of either open or covert military and political intervention. In the case of Nicaragua a complete army of Contras was organised and funded by the USA for the violent overthrow of the Sandinist regime.

- *Lebanon.* In Lebanon interference by Syria, Iran, the Palestinians and Israel caused the fragile balance between various ethnic and religious groups to be destroyed, resulting in a protracted and destructive civil war lasting from 1975 to 1991.
- *The conflict over mineral-rich Western Sahara.* Since 1973, the Polisario independence movement struggles for independence from Morocco, with the support of Algeria. A peace treaty was concluded in 1991, but has not yet been implemented.
- *Mozambique.* After independence, the South Africans and the Rhodesians gave military support to the opposition movement RENAMO. Cuba and several Eastern European countries supported the government of Samora Machel. The civil war lasted from 1975 to 1992.
- *The Kurdish struggle for autonomy or independence in Turkey, Iran and Iraq.* In their mutual conflicts the Turkish, Iranian and Iraqi regimes constantly supported separatist movements in the other countries with a view to weakening their opponents. Internally, even the peaceful pursuit of Kurdish autonomy was suppressed, for it was regarded as a threat to national unity. Kurdish autonomy in Iraq was supported by the international community, to keep up the pressure on the Baghdad regime of Saddam Hussein. After the war in Iraq in 2003 and the overthrow of the regime, the Iraqi Kurds were promised autonomy, but not independence, by the American and British occupiers of Iraq. It remains to be seen what measure of autonomy will be realised in a new Iraqi constitution after the handover of power to the Iraqi interim government in 2004.
- *Military interventions in Afghanistan.* In Afghanistan, the Soviet Union intervened militarily in favour of a communist government. Islamic and Western countries supported various oppositional groups and factions, resulting in the withdrawal of Soviet troops in 1989. After a period of instability and warlordism, the Taliban established a fundamentalist Muslim regime with the support of Pakistan in 1995/6. This regime was overthrown by an American-led coalition in the Afghan war of 2001.
- *Chad.* In Chad factions supported by the French and the Libyans fought for control for thirty years, till an unstable peace was achieved in 1990.
- *The war between Iran and Iraq.* In the Iran–Iraq war of 1980–88, the Western countries initially supported the Iraqis in their war against the deeply anti-American Muslim-fundamentalist regime of the Ayatollah Khomeini in Iran. Later in the Gulf War in 1991 an international coalition under the leadership of the USA violently put an end to the sudden Iraqi annexation of the oil-rich sheikdom of Kuwait.
- *Sri Lanka.* Since the mid-1980s Tamil separatists in the North have fought for independence from the Sinhalese majority. Tamils from the Indian federal state of Tamil Nadu supported the struggle for independence of the Tamil minority, originating in India. The Indian government, however, later sided with the central Sri-Lankan authorities and was even briefly involved in an unsuccessful attempt at peace enforcement in Sri Lanka. The struggle for secession continues to this very day, though peace negotiations were intermittently held in 2003.
- *Kashmir.* In Kashmir, the claims of Pakistan and India and Muslims and Hindus clashed, in both the Pakistan-ruled part of Kashmir and the Indian-ruled part of Kashmir. India and Pakistan fought a short war in 1971, which resulted in the Independence of Bangladesh. They were on the brink of a nuclear confrontation in 2002. The conflict contributes to internal violence and instability in both countries.

Table 11.1 provides rough figures on internal and external conflicts in developing countries and the numbers of victims involved. Between 1945 and 2000, 29.3 million people were killed in internal and external conflict: 18.4 million

Table 11.1 *Wars and war casualties, 1945–2003*

	Civil wars		International wars	
	Number of years	Number of casualties	Number of years	Number of casualties
Latin America		*666,000*		*8,500*
Argentina	5	23,000	1	1,000
Bolivia	2	3,000		
Brazil	1	1,000		
Colombia	32	301,000		
Costa Rica	2	3,000		
Cuba	2	5,000		
El Salvador	13	75,000		
Guatemala	31	151,000		
Honduras	20	1,000	2	5,500
Jamaica	1	1,000		
Mexico	3	1,000		
Nicaragua	10	70,000	1	500
Panama			1	1,000
Paraguay	1	1,000		
Peru	15	30,000	1	500
Middle East		*449,000*		*781,000*
Cyprus	5	2,000	1	5,000
Egypt	8	3,000	1	3,000
Iran	18	93,000	9	500,500
Iraq	48	181,000	7	116,500
Israel	37	18,000	1	4,000
Israel–Arabian conflict			5	101,000
Jordan	1	10,000		
Lebanon	1	2,000	1	55,000
Oman	5	3,000		
Syria	1	25,000	1	1,000
Turkey	25	53,000		
Yemen	15	59,000		
South Asia		*1,245,700*		*2,043,500*
Afghanistan			24	1,010,000
Bangladesh	17	25,000	1	1,000,000
India	38	1,097,700	8	33,500
Pakistan	20	18,000		
Sri Lanka	20	105,000		
Far East		*7,207,500*		*5,935,000*
Cambodia	15	1,655,000	14	76,000
China	42	3,189,000	7	104,500
Indonesia	18	576,500	8	214,500
Korea South	2	2,000		
Korea War			3	3,000,000
Laos	28	35,000		
Malaysia	13	28,500		
Myanmar	54	102,000		
Philippines	33	1,590,000		
Taiwan	2	10,000	1	5,000
Thailand	1	2,500		
Vietnam	1	15,000	30	2,535,000
Sub-Saharan Africa		*8,770,100*		*1,067,500*
Angola	27	1,000,000	15	51,000
Burundi	13	218,000		
Cameroon	0		5	30,000
Central African Republic	1	600		
Chad	29	75,000		
Congo-Brazzaville	4	12,500		
Côte d'Ivoire	2	2,500		
Djibouti	3	1,000		
Ethiopia	3	12,000	19	850,000
Ghana	2	2,000		

(continued)

Table 11.1 (*Continued*)

	Civil wars		International wars	
	Number of years	Number of casualties	Number of years	Number of casualties
Guinea Bissau	1	6,000	12	15,000
Kenya	2	2,000	9	20,000
Lesotho	1	1,000		
Liberia	10	46,000		
Madagascar			1	40,000
Mali	1	1,000		
Mauritania			1	500
Mozambique	11	1,000,000	10	30,000
Namibia			25	25,000
Niger	7	1,000		
Nigeria	16	2,024,000		
Rwanda	18	607,500		
Senegal	8	3,000		
Sierra Leone	20	25,000		
Somalia	14	100,000	1	1,000
South Africa	14	21,000		
Sudan	25	1,500,000		
Uganda	29	364,000	1	3,000
Congo, Dem. Rep.	22	1,621,000	1	1,000
Zambia	1	1,000		
Zimbabwe	11	23,000		
North Africa		*78,000*		*1,007,500*
Algeria	12	62,000	9	1,000,500
Morocco	14	15,000	5	4,000
Tunisia	1	1,000	2	3,000
Total		*18,416,300*		*10,843,000*

Sources: Marshall, *Major Episodes of Political Violence, 1946–2002* (2003), with adjustments by the author.
Supplementary sources: Sivard (1991), Small and Singer (1982), White (2003), Kidron and Smith (1983), and Smith (1997).

in internal conflicts and 10.9 million in external warfare. In some countries (including Algeria, Angola, Guinea-Bissau, Indonesia, Cameroon, Kenya, Mozambique, Morocco, Tunisia and Vietnam) the majority of casualties occurred in the fight for independence against colonial rulers. One of the most striking features of Table 11.1 is the large number of victims of internal conflicts in Sub-Saharan Africa (almost 9 million) in relation to absolute population size. Casualties were also high relative to population in the Middle East, mainly owing to external wars. In absolute terms, the highest numbers of casualties of combined internal and external conflicts are found in East Asia. About half of these casualties were caused by international wars.[14] Finally, though Latin America is generally perceived to be a violent continent, the number of casualties here is relatively low.

At the end of the 1980s, it was widely expected that the thaw in East–West relations and the end of the Cold War would contribute to a pacification of internal conflicts within and wars between developing countries. So far this

---

14 From the preceding discussion, it should by now be clear that it is difficult to make unambiguous distinctions between external warfare and internal conflicts (see Small and Singer, 1982).

expectation has not yet materialised. In retrospect it turned out that the East–West conflict not only exacerbated conflicts and tensions, but also had some important stabilising functions. With the disappearance of the East–West opposition and the sudden collapse of the Soviet empire, regional conflicts and internal ethnic, cultural and religious tensions increased rather than decreased. This is manifest in the continued fighting in Angola in the early 1990s, in the failed attempt by Saddam Hussein of Iraq to annex Kuwait in 1991, in the ethnic conflicts preceding the first free elections in South Africa, in the continued civil war in Afghanistan, in the secessionist movements in India (in the Punjab), Sri Lanka (the Tamils) and Indonesia (Aceh), in civil wars in Liberia, Sierra Leone, Somalia, the Sudan and Congo and many of the former Soviet Asian republics, in wholesale ethnic slaughter in Rwanda and Burundi and the brutal Ethiopian–Eritrean War of 1998–2000.

In India the differences between Muslims and Hindus have deepened since 1991 owing to the rise of Hindu-fundamentalist movements. In North Africa and the Middle East tensions between fundamentalist Muslim movements – which to some extent can be interpreted as a cultural response to Western penetration – and nationalist regimes have increased, for example in Algeria, Tunisia and Egypt. In Algeria this degenerated into a bloody civil war, which has still not been resolved at the time of writing.

The resurgence of nationalist sentiments led to the disintegration of the Soviet Union, Yugoslavia and Czechoslovakia, and to intensified social tensions within almost all of the new smaller political entities in Europe and Asia. The smaller the new nation, the more hostile it seems to be to its minorities. The civil war in former Yugoslavia between 1991 and 1995 is said to have claimed between 200,000 and 300,000 victims. Worldwide the total number of refugees fleeing across national borders increased from 2.5 million in 1970 to 23 million in 1997. In addition, in the 1990s some 30 million people were internally displaced (WHO, 2002, p. 225). In the developing world the number of people fleeing from areas of civil strife in one year peaked in 1991 at 36 million (WHO, 2002, table 8.1).[15]

An increasing number of conflicts across the globe appears to have a religious dimension involving Islam. This includes secessionist movements in Xinjiang in China, Chechnya in Russia, Aceh in Indonesia, tensions between North and South Nigeria, civil war between Christians and Muslims in the Sudan and on the Moluccan Islands of Indonesia, civil wars in Bosnia and Algeria, tensions between India and Pakistan, and the Afghanistan war of 2001.

On the other hand, there are also countries where the improvement in East–West relations allowed for breakthroughs in long-standing ethnic and political conflicts. Examples include the recent movements towards pacification in Cambodia, Angola, Rwanda and Mozambique, the election of a multiracial government in Namibia and the abolition of the apartheid regime in South Africa. The ending of the Cold War has also provided new opportunities for moves towards democratisation in Africa and Asia.

---

15 Including both internally displaced persons and cross-border refugees.

Researchers argue whether the number of violent conflicts in developing countries shows a long-run declining trend in the course of time (Kende, 1972; Marshall and Gurr, 2003; Starr and Most, 1985). Starr and Most come to the conclusion that no long-term increase or decrease can be discerned. Rather there is a cyclical trend with a peak between 1965 and 1968. In the period covered by their research, the locus of conflicts has unmistakably shifted from Europe to developing countries, and the importance of internal conflicts has increased in comparison to classical wars between countries. According to a more recent quantitative estimate by Marshall and Gurr (2003), the index of the total magnitude of global armed conflict peaked around 1985 and subsequently declined to half its peak level by 2002, indicating a declining trend in violent conflict since the end of the Cold War.[16]

Thus, there are two diametrically opposed trends. On the one hand, the weakening of East–West tensions since 1989 has led to a strengthening of centrifugal forces and a strong resurgence of nationalism, cultural contradictions and separatist movements. The scope for outside intervention has increased rather than decreased, now that regional powers are less dependent on the international superpowers. On the other hand, the decline of East–West tensions has contributed elsewhere to processes of pacification. This is the case in regions and countries where superpowers had backed different countries, parties or factions in their attempts to expand their spheres of influence. It is too early to say what the net outcome of these trends will be. In any event, the examples discussed above provide an indication of the overwhelming importance of external political and military interference and its impact on state formation processes in developing countries.

11.4.4 The role of the military in politics

During the past fifty years, the military have played very prominent roles in the political processes of many developing countries, even when they were not formally in power (Clapham and Philip, 1985; Finer, 1988; Goldthorpe, 1979).[17] The prominence of the military was especially pronounced in the 1970s and 1980s. The importance of the military in the post-war period is illustrated by the figures on political regimes in developing countries in 11.2.

For 1982 and 1995, Table 11.2 distinguishes between one-party states, military regimes, personal rule by a sovereign or an absolute ruler, restricted parliamentarism and multi-party systems. The table is based on a survey for 1982 by Kidron and Smith (1983), updated with a variety of sources.

In 1982, no less than thirty developing countries had a military regime; sixteen of these were in Africa, eight in Latin America. Twenty-six countries had a one-party system; fourteen of these were located in Africa. In eighteen

---

16 The index of the magnitude of armed conflict not only refers to casualties, but also to the comprehensive effects on the states affected by the warfare, including numbers of combatants, size of affected area, dislocated population and extent of infrastructural damage.

17 This section has been inspired by Goldthorpe's (1979) excellent chapter on political characteristics of states in the poor countries and by the literature quoted in Goldthorpe's chapter.

Table 11.2 *Political regime in developing countries*[a]

	One-party state	Military regime	Personal rule	Total authoritarian rule		Restricted parliamentary system		Multiparty democracy		Non-classif.	Total[b]
	no.	no.	no.	no.	(%)	no.	(%)	no.	(%)	no.	no.
1982											
Africa	14	16	6	36	78	3	7	5	11	2	46
Asia	8	4	2	14	67	3	14	4	19	0	21
Latin America	1	8	1	10	45	5	23	7	32	0	22
Middle East	3	2	9	14	88	1	6	1	6	0	16
Total	26	30	18	74	70	12	11	17	16	2	105
1995											
Africa	1	10	3	14	30	7	15	21	46	4	46
Asia	3	1	2	6	29	1	5	13	62	1	21
Latin America	1			1	5			21	95		22
Middle East	2		7	9	60	4	27	2	13		15
Total	7	11	12	30	29	12	12	57	55	5	104
2000											
Africa				14	30	11	24	21	46		46
Asia				8	38	2	10	11	52		21
Latin America				1	5	1	5	20	91		22
Middle East				9	60	5	33	1	7		15
Total				32	31	19	18	53	51		104

Notes:
[a] Excluding countries with less than 1 million inhabitants.
[b] Number of countries declines because of reunification of Yemen.
Sources: 1982: Kidron and Smith (1983); 1995: CIA, *World Fact Book* (1995); 2000: Freedom House, *Democracy's Century* (2000),
http://www.freedomhouse.org/reports/century.html with adjustments by the author

countries there was a system of personal rule; nine of these were in the Middle East and six in Africa. One should note that military influence is not restricted to countries with a purely military regime. In one-party states and in systems of personal rule, the military usually also play an important role behind the scenes. Even in some of the countries with a parliamentary system, the military wield considerable influence, for instance in a country like Turkey.

In a later survey for 1991, Kidron and Smith (1991) distinguish between military regimes, regimes dominated by the military and other regimes. A regime dominated by the military is a regime in which civilian institutions are formally restored, but in which real power still lies with the military. Although the subdivisions in the two sources are hard to compare, the number of purely military regimes has clearly decreased since 1982. In 1990 there were only eleven countries with a military regime, compared to thirty in 1982. However, another twenty-six countries had a regime that was indirectly dominated by the military. The data for 1995 confirm the decline in purely military regimes. As in 1991, eleven countries have military regimes. These data do not indicate the number of military-dominated regimes. But compared to 1982, the total number of authoritarian regimes has declined from seventy to around thirty in 1995. A similar figure is found for 2000.

The data in Table 11.2 need to be interpreted with utmost caution, owing to a host of empirical problems with regard to the comparability of data from different sources. Nevertheless, they do tentatively suggest that the role of the military in politics in developing countries is becoming less important than in the past (see further section 11.4.6).

Explanations for the important role of the military in developing countries in the post-war period are of two kinds, having to do with: (1) characteristics of societies and political systems; (2) characteristics of the military system.

The role of the military and characteristics of societies and political systems

In advanced industrial societies the complexity of economic and political institutions and structures functions as a constraint to military intervention in politics. The lower degree of institutional complexity in many developing countries and the weaker development of other national political institutions allow a greater involvement of the military in politics (Finer, 1988). The unstable nature of political systems and their inability to accommodate sectional interests peacefully creates a political climate in which military intervention becomes conceivable. However, as societies and economies become more complex and differentiated in the course of their development, government by the military becomes more and more difficult. The trend towards restoration of civilian governments in Latin America since the mid-1980s seems to fit this line of reasoning. Military regimes in countries such as Brazil and Argentina proved unable to pursue effective economic policies in an increasingly complex economic environment. They ended up relinquishing their power to civilian regimes.

The role of the military and characteristics of military institutions

The second category of explanatory factors refers to characteristics of military institutions themselves. First, the military has control over the means of violence. Potentially this allows it to play a political role. Secondly, the military is a subsector of society, which is, in certain respects, more 'modern' than other subsectors (Bienen, 1971; Finer, 1988; Janowitz, 1981; Shils, 1964). For example, in Latin America in the 1920s, military officers had higher levels of education than comparable groups in civilian society (Philip, 1985). The military has access to modern technologies, modern means of communication and transport. It has a modern bureaucratic, hierarchical and centralised organisation structure, a tradition of internal discipline and a strong corporate spirit.

The self-image of military officer classes is one of standing above the daily wear and tear of politics, political parties and interest groups. All over the developing world, the military sees itself as the ultimate safeguard of national interests. The military outlook involves elements of puritanism and contempt for the corruption, indecisiveness and decadence which the military associate with civilian rule (Janowitz, 1981). Thus the military comes to see itself as a factor contributing to the modernisation of society and to economic development (Bienen, 1971). Such attitudes can be found, for example, amongst military elites in Argentina, Brazil, China, Chile, Indonesia, Myanmar, Pakistan, South Korea, Thailand and Turkey.

The takeover of power by the military often takes the form of a *coup d'etat* against the civilian government. To justify its intervention in politics, the military can appeal to deep-seated popular feelings of resentment about widespread corruption and ineffectiveness in politics. In Latin America the alleged or real threat of left-wing revolutionary movements often served as a justification for military takeovers. A third motive for intervention is the protection of the autonomy of the army against interference by civilian politicians (Philip, 1985). Sometimes, the military reacted to cuts in military expenditures, sometimes to attempts to politicise the military forces, and sometimes, to attempts to introduce political patronage by controlling the recruitment of officers. Finally, factions in civilian politics sometimes actively seek the support of the military in their rivalry with other factions and parties.

In Latin America the military has played an important role in politics since 1822. During the first years of political independence, *caudillos* competed for power, frequently leading informal armies. Later the officers' corps was professionalised through the establishment of military academies. Politicians hoped that professionalisation would contribute to a more neutral army. Compulsory military service was introduced for the recruitment of common soldiers. Officers originated from the class of landowners, and formed an internally homogeneous and highly united group of professionals. Professionalisation helped differentiate military institutions from civilian institutions and society. According to Philip (1985), by 1920 the military was one of the best-organised forces in society. It was highly trained and felt isolated from and superior to civilians.

Between 1922 and 1932, there was a wave of military *coups d'etat* in South America, partially as a result of the collapse of civilian governments during the Great Depression. Vargas came to power in Brazil, Peron in Argentina, Benavides in Peru, Terra in Uruguay. Even in Chile, with its tradition of civilian government, Ibanez became the military president from 1927 to 1932. Sometimes with interruptions, elsewhere continuously, military regimes ruled Latin America until the 1980s. The longest period of military rule was in Argentina where regimes controlled by the military stayed in power from 1930 until the inauguration of Alphonsin as president in 1983. Some military regimes – like that of Juan Peron – pursued populist policies with which they tried to win the support of the trade unions and the urban poor.

Military coups, however, do not lead to more stable governments. Once the legitimacy of civilian government has been eroded, the first military coup may give rise to a succession of coups. Many military governments are just as much affected by corruption as the civilian governments, they replace. Again and again dissatisfied groups emerge, often from the lower military ranks, attempting to take over power by force.

Coups have played a prominent role in political processes since 1945. Luttwak (1979) presents an overview of the total number of military coups in developing countries from 1945 to 1977. All in all, he registers 271 attempted coups, of which 147 were successful, while 124 were unsuccessful. In Africa there

Table 11.3 *Successful coups in developing countries, 1945–2002*

	1945–77	1978–90	1990–2002	1945–2002
Africa	64	26	13	103
Asia	28	7	4	39
Latin America	76	14	2	92
Middle East	30	1	0	31
Total	198	48	19	265

Sources: 1945–1990: de Haan and Siermann (1993); original sources: Luttwak (1979), Taylor and Hudson (1972), Taylor and Jodice (1983), Banks (various issues) and Steinberg (various issues). 1990–2002: Banks *et al.* (1998), p. 389; Wikipedia, *The Free Encyclopedia*, http://en.wikipedia.org/wiki/Coup_d'%e9tat, and McGowan (2003), p. 351.

were ninety-eight attempted coups, of which forty-four were successful. In Latin America ninety-five coup attempts took place, of which fifty-seven were successful.

Another estimate by Finer (1988) for the period between 1962 and 1980 comes to a total of 152 coups. In 1980, there were thirty-seven countries in which the government had come to power through a *coup d'etat*. Twenty-five per cent of all independent states had a military government. Military regimes ruled over 55 per cent of the Latin American population and almost two-thirds of the population of the Arab states in North Africa and the Middle East. Similar percentages obtain for Sub-Saharan Africa (Finer, 1988).[18] Ghana tops the list with no less than five successful coups, six attempted coups and thirteen political conspiracies, between 1965 and 1985 (Fosu, 1992).

Table 11.3 presents estimates of the number of successful coups between 1945 and 2002. Unsuccessful coup attempts are not included here. Owing to differences in definitions, the number of successful coups for the period until 1977 is higher than those in Luttwak (198 versus 147). In this table, too, political instability is highest in Africa and Latin America. The average number of coups per year is significantly lower in the second period than in the first (2.8 per year versus 6.2 per year).

11.4.5   One-party states

Another characteristic of political systems in developing countries is the frequent emergence of one-party states in the post-war period. In 1982 there were twenty-six one-party states throughout the world, fourteen of which were in Africa (see Table 11.1). In a one-party state the ruling party professes to be the personification of national aspirations and tries to channel all political activity within the party. Thus, the party integrates opposition parties, trade unions, youth movements, women's movements, employers' associations and so on.

---

18 These figures exclude regimes which only survive thanks to military backing as in Jordan and Morocco, or regimes where the military have temporarily withdrawn from politics as in Guatemala and the Dominican Republic.

Communist countries like China, Vietnam, Laos and Cuba are good examples of one-party states. In such political systems the military is subordinate to the primacy of politics, even when individual military personal fulfil important political functions. The party organisation penetrates all sections of the military organisation. The line between one-party systems and multi-party democracies is not always easy to draw. For instance, India has had a well-functioning parliamentary system of government since independence. Nevertheless, the Congress Party stayed in power continuously from 1947 to the early 1990s. In Mexico, the Institutional Revolutionary Party (PRI) stayed in power from 1910 to 2000.

The rapid rise of one-party states in Africa after independence is quite striking. Initially, Western-style parliamentary institutions were introduced in most countries after the proclamation of independence. However, before long all power was taken over by a single party, usually under the leadership of a charismatic leader who had played an important role in the struggle for independence. Other parties were forbidden or were absorbed into the dominant party. It is interesting to note that the transition from parliamentary systems to one-party states was not restricted to countries that became independent in the immediate post-war period, but also took place in countries which gained their independence in the late 1970s like Angola, Mozambique and Zimbabwe.

Several of the possible explanations for the rise of one-party states in Africa are summarised in Box 11.2 (Ake, 1996; Coleman and Rosberg, 1964; Zolberg, 1966). One-party states do not provide for a peaceful transfer of power by means of elections. As a result, the initial idealism of nationalist movements often degenerated into monopolisation of power by one ethnic group or even absolute rule by a strong man (see section 11.7). The one-party state became increasingly dependent on military support, or it was overthrown in a military coup. The state itself was increasingly at stake in conflicts between ethnic groups, struggling for control of the state apparatus.

Box 11.2   Explanations for the emergence of One-Party Rule in Africa
- The legacy of centralised, bureaucratic and authoritarian colonial rule.
- The tribal and ethnic heterogeneity of many of the new states. In the absence of traditions of national identification, political party organisation often followed ethnic dividing lines. Political opposition was regarded as a threat to the unity of the state.
- Strong one-party states were considered indispensable for the realisation of national integration between regional and tribal groupings and the creation of bonds between new national political elites and an electorate with little sense of national identification.
- In the struggle for independence one movement usually emerged as the most powerful or influential. This movement would obtain an 'aura of legitimacy' for its contributions in the struggle for independence (Coleman and Rosberg, 1964, p. 658). As political movements were generally weakly developed, the first nationalist movements would acquire a decisive head start. At an early stage they were recognised as discussion partners by colonial rulers, in search of representatives of the population with whom they could negotiate (Zolberg, 1966).
- With respect to ideology, there were strong socialist and communist influences on the new political movements. There was a generalised distrust of Western economic and

political institutions. This is hardly surprising since both markets and Western political institutions were associated with colonial oppression. Communist ideology in particular provided a powerful underpinning to the notion of a one-party state.

- In many countries leaders genuinely felt that they needed to find alternatives to Western capitalist solutions and that they had to search for a new synthesis between traditional African political institutions and modern political institutions. Sometimes attempts were made to anchor the dominant political party in village meetings, urban district meetings or other base-level groupings (youth groups, women's groups) who sent delegates to higher branches of the party. Worsley interprets the 'African socialism' of leaders like Julius Nyerere in Tanzania, Léopold Senghor in Senegal and Sékou Touré in Guinea as a variant of 'populist ideologies' of rural populations threatened by the penetration of industrial and financial capital (Worsley, 1967, p.118 ff).
- Internal instability and external political interference reinforced the tendency towards the establishment of one-party states.

11.4.6   Is there a resurgence of democracy in developing countries?

As indicated above, there has been a tendency towards restoration of civilian governments and a (re)introduction of multi-party systems since the 1980s. In most cases this trend was the result of the inability of one-party states and military regimes to cope adequately with the economic and political challenges facing them, combined with outside pressure from the Western World. In Latin America this trend is unmistakable, in Africa more uncertain.

The data in Table 11.2 suggest that there is indeed a certain trend towards more democratic regimes.[19] The number of authoritarian regimes in developing countries has declined from seventy in 1982 to thirty-two in 2000. The number of countries with multi-party elections increased from 16 to 51. The reduced role of the military and the decline of one-party states raises the question whether there is a resurgence of democracy in developing countries? How genuine are these trends?

This debate was fuelled by the publication of Samuel Huntington's study *The Third Wave, Democratisation in the Late Twentieth Century* (Huntington, 1991). Samuel Huntington identified three waves of democratisation. The first wave lasted from the beginning of the nineteenth century till 1926. The second wave occurred during the period 1943–1962. The third wave started in 1974 with the overthrow of dictatorship in Portugal and affected countries in Southern Europe, Latin America and East Asia. It continued in the 1990s spreading to Eastern Europe, Central America and Sub-Saharan Africa (Ake, 1996; Bratton and van de Walle, 1997; Doorenspleet, 2000; Lijphart, 2000; Widner, 1994). The

---

19 It is not clear whether the classification criteria of the data for 2000 and 1995 are identical to those of 1982. So, any conclusions from this table can only be tentative. The 2000 data no longer allow us to distinguish military regimes, personal rule and one-party states. Another problem is the classification of countries as restricted parliamentary systems versus fully democratic systems. A fully democratic system allows for not only competitive elections, but also full freedom of speech and organisation for opposition parties.

only region where democratisation has not taken further hold is the Middle East, where authoritarian regimes continue to dominate.

In the mid-1970s, dictatorships in Greece, Portugal and Spain collapsed. In Latin America, Brazil began *abertura* or opening in 1974, and completed its transition to civilian rule by 1985. New civilian regimes emerged in Ecuador in 1979, Peru in 1980 (later temporarily reversed), Bolivia in 1982, Uruguay in 1984 and Chile in 1989. Nineteen eighty-nine was the year of the fall of the Berlin War and the dissolution of the Soviet Bloc. In 1991, the Soviet Union fell apart into fifteen independent republics. In Sub-Saharan Africa, the wave of democratisation began with popular protests in Benin in 1989, eventually resulting in a new constitution and multi-party elections. After that events evolved very rapidly. In the five years prior to 1989 only nine Sub-Saharan African countries had had competitive multi-party elections: Botswana, Gambia, Mauritius, Senegal and Zimbabwe. Another four countries had competitive elections, which were, however, severely flawed by electoral malpractice: Liberia, Madagascar, South Africa and Sudan. This record changed dramatically after 1990 (Bratton and van de Walle, 1997). In five years, thirty-eight out of forty-seven countries held competitive legislative elections. In many cases, these elections resulted in leadership turnover. By 1994 not a single *de jure* one-party state remained. Democratisation was fuelled by a combination of internal protests and increased international pressure by donor nations after the end of the Cold War.

Bratton and van de Walle (1997) provide an excellent institutional analysis of political changes in Sub-Saharan Africa. The authoritarian political regimes in Africa were so-called neopatrimonial regimes with a strongly personalistic nature. These regimes will be discussed in more detail in section 11.7. They can be contrasted with authoritarian regimes of a more bureaucratic nature. Neopatrimonial rulers use state revenues to maintain their personal power in such a manner that in due course the potential for economic development is undermined. This creates hardship, dissatisfaction and opposition amongst people excluded from political power. At the same time, as a result of economic stagnation, the rulers are no long able to pay off all their clients, supporters and civil servants, creating dissatisfaction within the elites (Bates, 1994). Multi-party elections are organised as an ultimate measure to diffuse political protest.

Bratton and van de Walle sound a cautionary note about the prospects of democracy in Sub-Saharan Africa. The new regimes are often disappointingly similar in their behaviour to the old ones. The institutional characteristics of neopatrimonial regimes do not suddenly disappear, once elections have been held. Though there are instances of new leaders coming to power through elections, the political actors are often the same ones as in the old system. There is institutional continuity and the appropriation of public resources to maintain power is deeply embedded in the political system. Thus, the statistical trends in Africa and elsewhere most likely suggest too optimistic a picture. Multi-party elections in developing countries are often anything but fair and free, corruption and electoral manipulation are widespread and the military continue to be an important force behind the scenes. Freedom of speech for opposition parties is under pressure and democratic elections can be followed by a return to authoritarian rule.

The dominant parties of the post-war period find it very hard to give up power. They have usually made use of their hold on the government bureaucracy and the means of mass communication to gain an advantage in the electoral process. In other countries, election results have been falsified and violence has been applied to intimidate opposition parties as in the Zimbabwean elections of 2002.

Nevertheless, the data do point to an interesting development. They suggest an unmistakable decline in the legitimacy of various forms of authoritarian rule such as one-party systems and military dictatorships.

11.4.7   Rapid growth of the public sector since 1945

In all developing countries the size of the apparatus of government has increased substantially since independence. Much of the rapid growth of the share of services in employment (see Table 3.8) is due to the expansion of government employment. This has much to do with the building up of a social infrastructure of education, agricultural extension and medical care and with the increasing role of the government in the economy in the post-war period.

The new educational systems produced an increased outflow of graduates, with firm expectations of a guaranteed job in the public sector. The fear of political turmoil was one of the motives for governments to continue to employ many of these graduates. A government job was also considered as a reward for political loyalty and political services. As the legitimacy of one-party rule and military regimes declined, public employment became an important source of political patronage. This aspect of government would become a serious impediment to the effective functioning of the public sector. It is only since the 1990s that structural adjustment programmes and cuts in government spending have put limits on the further expansion of the public sector in developing countries.

11.4.8   'Soft states' and the political economy of rent seeking

The debate on the 'soft state' was opened by Nobel prize-winner Gunnar Myrdal in his study *Asian Drama: An Inquiry into the Poverty of Nations* (1968), dealing with India in particular and Southeast Asian states in general. The term 'soft state' implies that the government does not have the effective instruments to translate policy intentions into actual policy, and to impose binding obligations on its citizens. Among others, this is caused by a lack of legitimacy of political institutions and by the underdeveloped administrative capabilities of the state apparatus.

Powerful interest groups (large landowners, civil servants, trade unions, foreign enterprises, members of the high castes, parastatal enterprises) manage to emasculate any policy that runs counter to their interests. For example, in India the legislation on land reform has never really been implemented, in part because at local levels the dominant Congress Party was controlled by landed interests. Further, the richer segments of the population in Latin America and Asia pay little or no income taxes, as there is no effective system of taxation. For its revenues, the government depends on taxes that are easily collected, like taxes on land, agricultural production, or exports and imports. The tax base is small and taxes are typically paid by the poor. Because of the underdeveloped income tax system, government is continuously threatened by a *fiscal crisis* (O'Connor, 1973). For their financial requirements, governments depend on deficit finance, monetary financing of governmental expenditures and sometimes an inflow of foreign aid. This makes for inflation and economic instability.

There are few feelings of loyalty to the government or the state among the masses of the population. Therefore, it is hard for governments to mobilise the efforts of large groups of people for infrastructural works, community development or other collective goals. Myrdal had a distinct preference for stronger states, like communist China, which seemed to be more capable of mobilising their citizens for developmental purposes. But Myrdal had little regard for the potentially disastrous consequences of flawed policies in strong states. One only has to recall the casualties of the 'great leap forward' in China between 1958 to 1960 when tens of millions of people died, owing to forced industrialisation and collectivisation of the agricultural sector (see Ashton, 1984; Bannister, 1984), or the horrors of the Cultural Revolution between 1966 and 1969 when the Chinese regime persecuted millions of its educated citizens and intellectuals (see Chang, 1991; Leys, 1978).

An interesting characteristic of 'soft states' is the abundance of regulatory instruments in the economic sphere. Myrdal aptly describes how one set of regulations calls forth further regulations. When a government starts restricting imports and controlling financial transactions with foreign countries – as a result of a shortage of foreign exchange – it is forced to develop a licensing system for the establishment of new enterprises, the expansion of existing ones or access to credit. When government plans determine the prices of inputs and final products, governments are also forced to draft rules to ration and allocate inputs and outputs to enterprises. Subsidising of some economic enterprises implies that other enterprises do not receive any subsidy. This means that government officials have to spend part of their time impeding the activities of new enterprises, in favour of enterprises that are already being subsidised.

Since it is difficult to devise detailed rules for every conceivable situation, the rules leave considerable latitude for discretionary decisions by officials. This can easily result in arbitrariness and corruption. Large domestic and foreign firms and interest groups will try to influence key decisions to their own advantage. Since public officials are often underpaid, they are vulnerable to bribery.

In many developing countries with mixed economies, there was, until very recently, a marked degree of animosity and distrust between the large collective sector and the private sector – e.g. in Peru, Argentina, Mexico and India. This led to further attempts at regulation of the economy in the name of public interest. At the same time, private enterprises did their best to evade public regulations or to influence them to their advantage. In India the large enterprises were most successful in safeguarding their interests under this regulatory regime – whether by corruption or by other means. One of the explicit objectives of government policy in India was to prevent the rise of monopolies in the private sector. Nevertheless, the concentration ratios in the private sector (i.e. the shares of the largest enterprises in total output) tended to increase. Often the largest enterprises obtained monopolies through their access to licences.

Corruption

The combination of extensive intervention in the economy, low levels of payment of civil servants, the absence of a tradition of impartial public service and the absence of checks and balances has made corruption endemic (Jain, 2001). In many developing countries corruption is the rule rather than the exception, both at the top of the political system and at lower levels of the bureaucracy and state apparatus. In turn, corruption reduces the effectiveness of the government. It further undermines civilian faith in government, legal security and the rule of law and promotes further corruption. From high to low people turn to patron–client relationships, in which people render each other services and favours, rather than appealing to formal legal rights or procedures. The predictability of government behaviour declines and bureaucracy is replaced by a 'personalist system' in which networks of personal relationships are the determining factor. One of the most extreme examples of a corrupt machinery of government was the system of *cronyism* in the Philippines under the regime of Ferdinand Marcos, where huge amounts of public funds and development aid disappeared in private pockets. Other well-known examples include Indonesia under the Suharto regime, Nigeria and Zaire (the Democratic Republic of Congo) under Mobutu sese Soko. Zaire is an example of a state where the whole apparatus of government has been made subservient to the survival and enrichment of the ruling clique.

One of the key problems with pervasive corruption is its unpredictability. As long as corruption is predictable, it functions like an informal tax. But, it may not be enough to bribe officials at the top of political hierarchies. One might encounter unorganised and anarchistic corruption at all levels of the political system. Where this is the case, corruption may actually kill off all productive activity (Mauro, 1995; 2000).

The modern literature on rent-seeking behaviour goes beyond the analysis of corruption to look at the very nature of economic policy formation (e.g. Jain, 2001). Corruption does not only refer to bribes. Rent-seeking behaviour refers to activities by interest groups and firms to acquire monopolistic profits through manipulation of the political system. This involves not only manipulating specific decisions in the favour of a firm or an interest group, but also influencing the direction of policy formation. Thus, in sub-Saharan Africa, urban interest groups impose tax burdens on rural farmers or exporters, loss-making state-owned firms are subsidised in China and macro-economic stabilisation policies are not implemented when they run counter to major interests in many Latin American countries.

11.5   The role of government in economic development

With regard to the economic role of the government in development, there is an interesting paradox of a *weak state with disproportionately heavy tasks*. In the economically advanced countries of today, the role of the state in economic development in the nineteenth century was relatively restricted. The main tasks of government were the maintenance of law and order, the defence of private property and external defence (the so-called night-watch state). In comparison, the role of the state in the economic process in developing countries since 1950 has been much greater. The demands on the functioning of the state apparatus were much higher. At the same time, the apparatus of government was less well-equipped to fulfil these heavier demands.

It is indisputable that the role of government in the economic process has increased, in both poor and in rich countries (Evans, 1995; Gerschenkron, 1962; Maddison, 1986; Myint, 1980; White, 1984). In *Economic Backwardness in Historical Perspective* (1962) Alexander Gerschenkron offers an interesting explanation for this phenomenon. As a result of technological development, the required scale of investment is becoming ever larger. The time span between the moment of committing financial resources and the moment an investment starts to yield a return grows longer. Thus it becomes more difficult and risky for individual private enterprises to mobilise the necessary funds for investment. During the Industrial Revolution in eighteenth-century England, self-financing by firms was the main source of investment. In nineteenth-century Germany, large banks and financial conglomerates (*das Finanzkapital*) together with the government were the institutions which mobilised the necessary funds for investment (see Tilly, 1986). In late nineteenth-century Russia the risks of huge investments in railways and industry had become so large that they were mainly borne by government in cooperation with foreign investors. In Japan the government also played a crucial role in initiating processes of capital accumulation in the industrial sector. Thus in late development the task of the government is not only to create a favourable environment for private economic activities (legal security, predictability, pacification) but also to help mobilise savings and to act as an investor itself, where private investment is insufficient. In recent years, the nature of international competition has changed further. Modern competition is increasingly based on innovation and technological advance. One of the tasks of modern governments is to create or nurture the conditions under which a country's enterprises can keep up in the modern technology race.[20]

In developing countries, there are some additional considerations. First, it was believed that there was a shortage of entrepreneurship in the private sector. Entrepreneurial classes were weakly developed. There were no groups in the domestic private sector which would generate sufficient investment. The state had to compensate for the shortage of entrepreneurship by acting as an investor itself. Second, there were enormous backlogs with respect to infrastructure, education and health care. Improvements in these fields required additional government efforts. Third, there was a policy goal of accelerated development in order to narrow the gap between rich and poor countries. This also called for a more active role on the part of government. In the Latin American context, this role is sometimes referred to as *developmentalism* (Urquidi, 1993). Notions concerning external effects and complementarities, discussed in Chapter 9, play a central role in this approach.

There were also subjective considerations. On the basis of their historical experiences, newly independent countries associated capitalism, market mechanisms and international trade with colonialism and foreign oppression. There was a deep distrust of the free market and a search for alternative paths of development. In the post-war years the Soviet Union served as a model of a poor and backward country that had succeeded in industrialising rapidly by means of socialist planning. This model provided a further ideological justification for extensive state intervention in the economy.

During the past fifteen years, the climate of opinion has shifted in the direction of a modest role of the state in economic development. But, looking at the period since 1945 as a whole, it is safe to conclude that this was a heavily interventionist period in developing countries.

11.5.1   *The role of the state in economic development: five examples*

This section provides illustrations of the pervasive role of the state in economic development in a discussion of the developmental experiences of Japan, China, Brazil, South Korea and India.

Japan

The government played an extremely important role in the economic development of Japan after the Meiji restoration in 1868 (Maddison, 1969; Pilat, 1994). The feudal system based on landownership by samurai, daimyo and the shogun was abolished (the shogun alone owned about one quarter of all land). The large landowners were compensated with government obligations and were stimulated to invest their financial resources in industry. Land was redistributed to

---

20 In the modern global economy, the great multinational enterprises command resources which dwarf those of smaller national states. Their role in the mobilisation of capital has increased, relative to the period discussed so astutely by Gerschenkron.

the actual cultivators, on whom land taxes were imposed. The financial system was reformed, and compulsory education was introduced in 1872.

The government played a decisive role in the process of industrialisation with investments in the military industry, shipbuilding and heavy industry. The government share in total investment was high. A pattern developed in which the government took the initiative for large-scale investments in industry. Once these industries started to function, they were sold off to the private sector. Large-scale investments were also made in the Japanese colonies (Korea, Taiwan, Manchuria). The government stimulated the growth of modern, very large industrial conglomerates (*zaibatsu*) that maintained strong ties with the government. At an early stage government policy started promoting industrial exports and giving firms with export success preferential treatment.

The Japanese government pursued an active policy of research and development. Foreign investments were impeded, but Japan managed to obtain technological know-how by systematically inviting foreign scientists and technical specialists and by organising study tours to Western countries.

Traditionally, the government paid a great deal of attention to schooling, education and technological development. Both agricultural growth and participation in international trade were promoted at an early stage. In agriculture, much attention was paid to the linkages between agricultural and industrial development. During recent decades overprotection of agriculture, however, has led to increasing inefficiencies in this sector (van der Meer and Yamada, 1990).

In the Japanese model of industrialisation, it is not quite clear whether government sets the course for private enterprise, or whether private enterprise determines the direction of public policy. Rather, there was an intensive interaction between public and private sector. The government actively pursued an industrialisation policy in which key industries with bright prospects were identified and supported. 'Sunset' industries were drastically cut back.

The Japanese industrial sector has a dual structure with small labour-intensive, market-oriented firms acting as subcontractors for large, capital intensive firms pursuing long-term strategic objectives. Until recently these large companies offered their employees *lifetime employment*. In such a dual structure many of the risks of economic fluctuations are shifted to the small labour-intensive enterprises operating on the market.

The rapid economic and industrial development of Japan is an example of industrialisation and modernisation imposed from above (Barrington Moore, 1967). Members of the feudal class of samurai took control of the state apparatus during the Meiji reforms and took the initiative in transforming and modernising the entire economy and society. In this process the commercial middle classes played a less important role than they did earlier in European history.

As Japan drew closer to the technological frontier, its catch-up processes slowed down. The system, which was so successful in assimilating and further developing international technology, was less suited to the requirements of innovation. Since the 1990s, the economy has been in a state of semi-stagnation. The system of intensive interaction of the state, large-scale industry interaction and the financial system is now being re-examined in the light of new challenges.

China

In China the role of the government in industrialisation and economic development was even greater than in Japan (Maddison, 1998). In the years following the communist revolution of 1949, all industrial enterprises were brought under public ownership. Large-scale land reforms were implemented. The land of large landowners was nationalised without compensation and redistributed among the peasants. After that, the agricultural sector was collectivised step by step, starting with voluntary cooperatives in the early 1950s and ending with the establishment of immense communes, sometimes involving over a million people in 1958–60 (Hsu, 1982). Initially, economic policy followed the example of the Soviet Union. The emphasis was on the development of heavy industries. In the Marxist terminology this branch was referred to as 'Sector I': the production of machines to produce machines.

National Five-Year Plans were introduced in which the physical production goals for all industries were laid down and industries were allocated predetermined amounts of inputs. These plans had been based on input–output models with fixed technical coefficients and a complete elimination of price mechanisms. Just like Japan, China succeeded in realising a high level of savings. All investment was done via the public sector. Lin *et al.* (2000) explain brilliantly how the choice for heavy industry and the key role of the state interact, in China and elsewhere. Heavy industries require investment with long gestation periods, imported capital goods and large lump-sum investments. In a predominantly agricultural economy, capital is scarce, market interest rates are high, foreign exchange is scarce and the economic surplus is small. In order to make large-scale industrial enterprises profitable, one needs distorted macro-economic policies (cheap energy prices, low interest rates, low wages, overvalued exchange rates), which require government intervention. Private entrepreneurs were not willing to invest in heavy industry where the market prospects of profitability were low, so nationalisation became more or less inevitable. This resulted in what Lin *et al.* call the holy trinity of a distorted macro-policy environment, a planned allocation mechanism, and a puppet-like micro-management system. This was found irrespective of ideology in other countries pursuing heavy industry-oriented development such as India or Brazil.

A difference with Soviet Russian development is that China paid more attention to agriculture. To be sure, agriculture was allocated a relatively modest part of total investment compared to heavy industry (Kitching, 1982). Still the rural population was successfully mobilised for large-scale infrastructural works like the land reclamation, terracing, road construction and irrigation works (see Rawski, 1979; Hsu, 1982).

Although the land reforms initially provided the communist regime with a degree of legitimacy amongst the peasant population, the collectivisation of agriculture eventually turned out to be a great failure. Links between effort and reward were completely severed. After 1978, a liberalisation of the agricultural sector commenced which led to an explosive growth in agricultural production. Simultaneously, inefficiency in the industrial sector was on the increase.

It seems possible – albeit often at great human and economic cost[21] – to build up a basic industrial sector by means of central planning and collective mobilisation of savings. At later stages of industrial development, however, the planning system seems to be too inflexible to respond to differentiated and varying consumer needs.

Since the mid-1980s, market reforms have been gradually introduced in the industrial sector as well (Lin *et al.*, 2000; Sachs and Woo, 1997). This is not done by privatising existing large public enterprises, but rather by permitting the rise of new market-oriented enterprises, stimulating foreign investment, encouraging exports and opening up the economy. The share of private enterprises, semi-private enterprises such as village and township enterprises and foreign enterprises has increased dramatically. The past decade has seen very rapid growth of industrial production and explosive growth of exports (Szirmai *et al.*, 2001; Szirmai and Ren 2000). The performance of the state-owned enterprises is still lagging behind. Attempts are made to shed redundant labour on a large scale, but the authorities fear to privatise this sector of the economy because of fear of the employment consequences of privatisation. In contrast to the disappointments of Big Bang liberalisation in the former Soviet Union, China has opted for a policy of gradual liberalisation, which appears to be remarkably successful. Compared to the period before 1980, the role of the state has been reduced substantially, but it still remains pervasive.[22]

Brazil

Brazil is a well-known example of a country that pursued a strong policy of import-substituting industrialisation (Maddison, 1992; Furtado, 1976; Evans, 1995). Brazilian economic policy has sometimes been characterised as *state capitalism*.

Since the mid-nineteenth century revenues from agricultural exports, in particular coffee, created a domestic market for industrial consumer goods. But political power was controlled by agricultural oligarchies to whom industrialisation was of little interest. Nineteen thirty saw the beginning of a new phase of economic development when Getulio Vargas came to power after a military *coup d'état*. During this period export prices of primary products fell, and the flow of imports from Europe dried up. The government chose to

---

21 Sometimes disastrous mistakes were made, like the attempt at forced industrialisation during the Great Leap Forward, between 1958 and 1960.
22 There is a very interesting debate on the Soviet Union–China comparison. Jeffrey Sachs and Wing Thye Woo (1997) argue that China could liberalise more gradually because it was less industrialised than the Soviet Union and could start with agricultural liberalisation. The Soviet Union was over-industrialised and had no option but to follow sudden liberalisation policies.

pursue a strong policy of import substitution which protected Brazilian industries against foreign competition. This was realised by means of exchange-rate
policy, rationing and the allocation of foreign currencies, import tariffs on
consumer goods and subsidies on investment. Just like in Japan, private and
public interests were entwined, with the government itself acting either as an
investor or as a partner in joint ventures. A characteristic of Brazilian economic
policy is its relative openness to foreign investment. Foreign investors often
formed *joint ventures* with domestic private companies and public enterprises.
Many of these joint ventures acquired monopolies on the protected domestic
market.

A populist industrialisation strategy was pursued in which the political elites
maintained ties with organised labour. Industrial workers got preferential treatment over the rural population. Workers were organised into a kind of corporative state union, which served among others to control the production factor
labour.

There was some degree of planning of economic activity and a high degree
of state participation in investment. There were large government investments
in the mining sector. Macro-economic policy was highly expansionary. Growth
was given precedence over macro-economic stability and controlling inflation.

Between 1929 and 1980 Brazil (together with Mexico) ranked among the
fastest growing economies in the world. Within a relatively brief period of
time, Brazil succeeded in establishing a diversified industrial sector. Because of
the great income inequality the poor benefited but little from the economic
growth. But even critics of the Brazilian economic miracle must admit that
the poor suffered more from the economic stagnation of the 1980s, than from
the unequally distributed growth in earlier decades.

After 1980 the shortcomings of Brazilian economic policy became manifest.
Prolonged protection of domestic industry had resulted in great inefficiencies,
inflexibilities and low levels of capacity utilisation. The industrial sector was
too inward-looking and had not succeeded in penetrating foreign markets.
Macro-economic instability increased, inflation reached astronomic levels and
Brazil proved to be incapable of servicing its debt. The inflow of new capital
stagnated. After 1980, Brazil experienced a decade of stagnation.

In the 1990s, Brazil belatedly followed the world trend of deregulation, privatisation of the large public-owned sector and further export promotion. It
succeeded in stabilising its economy and growth has gradually been picking
up, though Brazil remains vulnerable to external shocks. Its problems of transition are comparable to those of the former centrally planned economies in
Eastern Europe.

South Korea

South Korea is another example of an economy where the state played
a large role in the process of industrialisation and capital accumulation
(Amsden, 1989; Evans, 1995; Kiely, 1998; Pilat, 1994). According to Amsden
and Pilat, government policy has been of crucial importance in the process of

accelerated growth that took place in South Korea after 1953. In many respects, the role of the government in Korea has been similar to that in Brazil and Japan. The government actively participated in planning industrial activities through subsidies, credit facilities, protectionist tariffs, price controls and public investment. The government taxed the middle classes, without offering much in the way of social services for broad groups in the population. This provided the government with abundant financial means for investment. It encouraged the establishment of very large industrial conglomerates (*chaebol*).

Like Brazil, South Korea had a period of import substitution during which the domestic industry was protected against foreign competition. The difference with Brazil is that the Korean government started to support and subsidise export-oriented activities as early as the 1960s. Government policy stopped discriminating in favour of firms that produced for the domestic market. Another difference is the far greater degree of discipline involved in subsidising private companies. The government consistently refused to bail out large companies in financial difficulties. Weakly performing sectors of industry were forced to restructure. Subsidies and other kinds of government support were made dependent on performance criteria in terms of production growth, increase in productivity and penetration into export markets. Until recently Korea had an authoritarian political regime. Though the political system was not free from corruption, an effective bureaucracy succeeded in isolating itself from undue influence of pressure groups and was thus able to enforce performance criteria on the firms in the private sector (Booth, 1999).

According to Amsden's interpretation the government succeeded in identifying potentially successful branches of activity and supported these by means of subsidies and price policies. The government pursued a policy of 'getting prices wrong' in order to stimulate investments which would be profitable in the long run. This meant that short-term prices deviated from free-market prices. In the long term the policy was market-oriented, because only efficiently producing enterprises would receive continued support. Monopolistic price-fixing by large conglomerates was not allowed. The outward orientation of industrial policy meant that Korean products had to be competitive on international markets. Amsden points to a possible relationship between the authoritarian nature of the 'strong' Korean state and the success of its economic policy. However, she sees no reason why a 'strong' state could not be compatible with political democracy (Amsden, 1989, p. 18).

In 1997, Korea was severely hit by the Asian crisis which exposed weaknesses in the hitherto so successful economic system. These weaknesses included weaknesses in the banking system with non-performing loans, insufficient reserve requirements and an obligation to finance industrial activities in line with government policies. The close interaction between the Chaebols and the government departments, once seen as one of the strengths of the Korean system, now came to be seen as a source of inflexibility. However, the recovery from crisis was very rapid, which reduced the pressure for reform.

India

After the attainment of independence in 1947 India pursued economic development in accordance with a model referred to as *Indian socialism* (Bardhan, 1984; Cassen, 1978; Maddison, 1974). This model had some typical characteristics. On the one hand, it emphasised the development of traditional crafts like spinning, weaving and small-scale industry in the tradition of Mahatma Gandhi. In this respect policy tried to build on traditional Indian patterns of craft production. Homespun clothing even became the symbol of the Indian struggle for independence. On the other hand, Jawaharlal Nehru strove to establish heavy industry along the lines of the Soviet planning model. Physical production objectives were laid down in a series of Five-Year Plans. Socialism was to be realised by means of huge government investments in heavy industry. It was believed that the required volume of investment exceeded the capabilities of the private sector. Especially in the second Five-Year Plan from 1956–61, heavy industries were given high priority. The private sector was allowed to continue its operations. But a rapidly expanding apparatus of government tried to control and regulate private economic activities. The role of foreign investment was restricted.

One of the explicit objectives of regulation was to prevent monopolisation and the domination of the Indian economy by large foreign investors and large domestic enterprises. Paradoxically, though, the largest companies profited most from government regulation. Through their contacts within the bureaucracy and through corruption, they often succeeded in establishing monopolies or acquiring licences. The degree of concentration in the economy increased substantially. Smaller companies were not able to make their way through the red tape and the intricacies of government bureaucracies. There were long-standing complaints from the private sector that private entrepreneurs were bound hand and foot by government regulations. Nevertheless, the pressure for change was not very strong, as the largest companies benefited from the niches and monopolies which were the inadvertent consequence of government regulation.

The Indian industrialisation model can also not be denied a certain measure of success. India succeeded in building up a diversified industrial infrastructure with a large share of capital goods and intermediate goods in total output. In addition, there were substantial investments in education, research and development. After the mid-1960s, more attention was also paid to agricultural development.

Just as in China, the establishment of basic industries like steel plants or power stations proves to be possible by means of central planning. In later stages of industrial development, however, the planning model in India turned out to be too inflexible. Since the 1970s industrial development in India has stagnated. Production was plagued by industrial unrest, logistic problems and insufficient utilisation of capacity. Protectionism was conducive to inefficiency.

The emphasis on the capital goods industry required high levels of production in other sectors of the economy in order to generate sufficient demand for capital goods. But domestic purchasing-power was insufficient to create a growing market for consumer goods industries, in part owing to low income levels in the agricultural sector. Indian industries were not sufficiently competitive for international markets. The protection of the traditional craft production also involved great waste, as these activities were not viable without protection. Furthermore, distrust of foreign investors reduced the inflow of foreign capital. In comparison with other Asian countries, growth of the Indian economy in the post-war period has been sluggish.

According to Bardhan (1984), the economic problems were especially caused by the fact that government policy was insufficiently insulated from the influence of powerful interest groups, as the legitimacy of government acquired in the struggle for independence was gradually eroded. Political contradictions between agricultural interests, the interests of professionals within the civil service and the interests of industrial capital paralysed government policy. They channelled government spending into wasteful direct and indirect subsidies that had to keep the different interest groups satisfied. The mobilisation of investable financial resources – in itself fairly successful – led to government consumption rather than more government investment. Bardhan sees declining public investment as an important explanation for the slowdown in industrial growth in the 1960s and 70s.

Another characteristic of Indian socialism was the strong emphasis on equality and land reform. The rhetoric of egalitarianism, however, had few consequences in practice. Through their hold on the Congress Party at local levels, powerful landed interests succeeded in frustrating the implementation of land-reform measures. Despite a policy of preferential recruitment of untouchables and other underprivileged groups, the highly inegalitarian caste system remained extremely influential. In India there has been much talk about 'democratic planning' from the bottom up. In practice, however, there was little participation of the population in the process of economic planning.

Since the mid-1980s, India has also participated in the worldwide trend towards deregulation, strengthening of market incentives and a reduction of the role of the government in the economy. The tensions between the public sector and the private sector are increasingly regarded as one of the impediments to economic development and an increased inflow of foreign investment. Many observers attribute the relatively slow economic growth in India, compared to other Asian economies such as Korea, Malaysia, Thailand, Indonesia and Taiwan, to the negative influences of a cumbersome and ineffective apparatus of government, with great discretionary powers and a considerable degree of corruption.[23] In the 1990s, the trend towards liberalisation of domestic

---

23 Bardhan (1984) gives a similar critical analysis of the role of the government in relative stagnation. However, his conclusions are different. He does not argue in favour of liberalisation. Rather he pleads for a more efficient government and an increase in public investment. Bardhan still defends the leading role of government in late industrial development. In his opinion, India should model its behaviour on South Korea and should try to insulate government policy from manipulation by interest groups.

markets and international trade accelerated. India became more open to foreign investment. The private sector became more important and the share of exports and imports in GDP increased. New sectors emerged, such as software and telecommunications. Economic growth accelerated substantially, though not reaching the rates of China.

These five examples illustrate that the role of the government in processes of late industrialisation has been larger than previously in economic history – irrespective of political system or ideology. They also illustrate that overprotection of domestic production, inward orientation and the elimination of economic incentives for efficient production and allocation result in economic stagnation.

A consensus has emerged that the role of state intervention in the economy should be reduced in developing countries, that economies should be deregulated, and that economies should be more exposed to national and international competition. The elements of the new consensus are the following:

1. In comparison with the practice of the period 1950–90, reduction of the dominant role of the state in the economic process in developing countries seems advisable. Regulation of the private sector, which gives rise to misallocation of scarce resources, should be diminished.
2. The effectiveness of the apparatus of government should be increased. Structural adjustment is not only an economic recipe. It also involves reorganisation and restructuring of the political and administrative system. The government should take on less economic tasks and execute a more limited range of tasks more effectively (World Bank, 1997). Where corruption impedes the normal execution of government functions, privatisation of these functions should be considered. Key functions of government are increasing political stability, preservation of internal peace and order, and increasing the predictability of the economic processes. Stability and predictability are preconditions for increased investment and capital accumulation in the private sector. The success and failure of government intervention does not only depend on economic arguments. It also depends on the quality and capabilities of the administrative system. The lower the quality and the weaker the capabilities, the stronger the case for deregulation.
3. Following the example of East Asian states, developing country governments should not protect inefficient enterprises indefinitely. Government policies should be more in conformity with market success. They should stimulate those activities in the private sector, which are successful on national or international markets.
4. Nevertheless, the role of the state in the economic process will be larger than previously in earlier periods of economic history. Even the critics of interventionist political systems in developing countries are agreed on this. The state retains essential tasks with respect to investment in education, infrastructure, health care, environmental protection, promotion of agricultural research and development, organisation of agricultural education,

promotion of industrial research and development – also for the benefit of small-scale industries – and improvement of the urban infrastructure. In addition, the state still has a role in mobilising investment and functioning as a negotiating partner for powerful foreign investors.

The debate on the exact scope and mode of government intervention continues (Evans, 1995). In the past ten years, developing countries all over the world have tended to reduce the role of government and have liberalised their economies. In countries such as China, Sri Lanka, India and Brazil this has had a positive impact on economic dynamics. Elsewhere, liberalisation, transition to the markets and structural adjustment have frequently had disappointing results, whether in Africa, Latin America or in the former Soviet Union. Some authors blame this on liberalisation and an excessive belief in the blessings of the market. Others argue that liberalisation is still incomplete and has not yet gone far enough to contribute to economic dynamics. As discussed in Chapter 9, authors like Amsden, Westphal, Lall and Bardhan point to South Korea and Taiwan to illustrate the fact that governments can indeed act in a proactive manner and can promote efficient and dynamic economic behaviour. They argue that government policy can and should contribute to the creation of dynamic comparative advantage. Other authors argue for decentralisation of government rather than automatic transmission of government functions to the market (Bardhan, 2002).

11.6   Interactions between political and economic developments

In this section we will discuss four aspects of the relationships between economic and political developments in developing countries: the effects of political instability on economic growth; the effects of economic growth on political instability; the relationships between authoritarian rule, democracy and economic development; and the role of good governance.

11.6.1   Political instability as a source of economic stagnation

In section 11.2 we pointed to the importance of internal pacification as a prerequisite for economic development. The absence of violence within a state is one of the principal aspects of political stability. Kuznets (1966, p. 451) stresses that a minimum degree of political stability is required for entrepreneurial individuals to be assured of a stable relation between their efforts and their rewards. Only then will they be prepared to invest in future production. Political instability, social unrest and abuse of civil rights hamper long-run capital accumulation. It results in capital flight and a brain drain, with the most skilled and best-educated members of the labour force emigrating in search of better economic opportunities (Alesina *et al.*, 1966; 1989; de Haan and Siermann, 1993; Fosu, 1992). Political instability, whether in the form of political turmoil, ethnic tensions or unpredictable changes in regimes and governments, causes economic stagnation.

It is not hard to come up with examples of political conflicts and political instability resulting in economic stagnation: the famines in Ethiopia and Somalia in the aftermath of the Ethiopian–Somalian wars, the total collapse of the economy of Uganda under Idi Amin and recently of Zimbabwe under Robert Mugabe, or the economic stagnation in countries like Cambodia, Angola and Somalia. In quantitative, comparative studies many researchers observe a negative relationship between indicators of political instability and economic growth. For example, McGowan and Johnson (1984) find a negative correlation between an index of political instability and growth of per capita income in 39 countries in Sub-Saharan Africa. Fosu (1992) distinguishes between countries with relatively high political stability and countries with relatively low political stability in Sub-Saharan Africa. He comes to the conclusion that, other things being equal, annual economic growth is at least 1 per cent lower in the 'high political instability' countries. De Haan and Siermann (1993) also note a negative correlation between political instability (represented by the frequency of changes of government) and economic growth in Sub-Saharan Africa. With respect to Asian countries there is an indirect negative relationship between instability and growth via an investment variable. For Latin America, Grier (2002) finds strong support for the argument that political instability negatively affects the stock of physical capital. He argues that increases in uncertainty result in negative effects on investment and growth. Also, war and civil war destroys the capital stock.

There is also an interesting body of literature on the negative relationship between ethnic diversity, linguistic fragmentation and economic growth (Easterly, 2001; Easterly and Levine, 1997; Nettle, 2000). Nettle (2000) finds evidence of an inverse relationship between linguistic heterogeneity (measured as the percentage of the national population who are native speakers of the most widespread language) and economic development. The absence of a shared language may obstruct economic development, among others because it is an obstacle for widening the scale of markets and economic activities. But the causality is complex. Economic development itself leads to increases in communication and fosters the emergence of standardised national and even international languages (such as English in the present world economy). This was the case in European history.

Easterly and Levine (1997) argue that ethnic diversity in Africa has important indirect negative effects on growth and development. Ethnically polarised societies are more prone to competitive rent seeking by different groups, which will have more difficulty in agreeing on public goods and effective public policies. Easterly and Levine present cross-country regression analyses relating ethnic fractionalism to growth and a variety of other indicators. There are significant negative relationships between ethnic diversity and school attainment, quality of infrastructure, black market premiums, distorted foreign exchange markets and underdeveloped financial systems. The authors conclude that ethnic diversity encourages poor public policies, with significant indirect negative effects on growth.

Interestingly enough, Easterly and Levine find little or no direct relationships between ethnic diversity and political instability. Whether ethnic diversity results in political instability depends very much on the quality of institutional arrangements, which can or cannot mitigate the effects of ethnic conflict. Ethnic diversity has a much more adverse effect on policy and growth when legal and political institutions are weak (Easterly, 2001).

11.6.2   Economic development and political stability

Just as political stability is a prerequisite for economic development, economic development is one of the prerequisites for political stability. Only when there is economic growth, capital accumulation and an increase in productivity can an effective government administration be financed and the government play a mediating role in conflicts between social groups and classes. If there is no growth, standards of living will stagnate or even decline, creating widespread dissatisfaction and a potential for political protest and opposition. In economic stagnation, the government is threatened by fiscal crisis and is forced to take sides in clashes of interest between social classes. This may manifest itself in increased repression of workers, unions, peasants and oppositional movements (Anglade and Fortin, 1985). It may also manifest itself in attempts at economic reform, which sometimes alienate the very groups on which a regime relies for support (Skocpol, 1979). The potential for instability is especially marked when periods of rapid growth and rising expectations are followed by slower growth or stagnation.

Surprisingly, under certain circumstances even economic growth may also give rise to political instability (Terhal, 1992). In accordance with Kuznets's well-known U-curve-hypothesis, income inequality tends to increase during the early stages of industrialisation (Kuznets, 1955). As an explanation of the tendency towards increased inequality in early stages of industrialisation, Ahluwalia (1976) points to the emergence of a new production factor, capital, with an extremely high productivity. Ownership of and access to this new production factor has a skewed distribution. Thus, economic growth leads to increasing inequality between those groups who benefit from the increase in productivity associated with the new factors of production and the groups who do not. Thus growth and industrialisation can give rise to political tensions and conflicts, as for instance in Iran under the regime of the Shah. In the long term, Ahluwalia suggests, such political tensions may result in a certain redistribution of the access to the new production factors and to decreasing inequality.

Terhal emphasises that such redistribution does not occur automatically. Rapidly increasing inequality may just as well result in escalating political conflict and lasting political instability. Terhal identifies the following two groups as crucial in processes of social conflict.[24]

1. *The mobile but unsatisfied group.* This group includes people whose position has improved economically, but who remain unsatisfied;
2. *The stagnating immobile group.* This includes a considerable group of poor people whose economic position remains more or less stagnant.

The groups that experience economic improvement in absolute and relative terms may still be dissatisfied if their aspirations to achieve equal footing with older ruling elites are frustrated. The groups whose economic situation remains unchanged in absolute terms may accept increasing inequality for quite a long time. They hope that sooner or later they will enjoy the same social and economic improvements which they can see other groups are enjoying at present.[25] However, if such expectations remain unfulfilled for too long, a dramatic switch may take place in which acquiescence and hope are replaced by extreme frustration (Hirschman, 1973). When both these types of frustration and dissatisfaction occur simultaneously, a politically explosive situation can arise, especially when economic dividing lines coincide with ethnic or geographic divisions. This explosive combination of growth in combination with rapidly increasing inequality can be found in many developing countries, such as China, India, Brazil and Indonesia.

According to Terhal, political elites can try to mitigate social tensions by co-opting the economically rising groups and improving their access to political power and social status. At the same time a regime can increase its legitimacy amongst the poor masses, which are not profiting much from economic growth, by a process of political democratisation. Terhal quite rightly remarks, by the way, that the political tensions associated with economic growth will be even more pronounced in conditions of economic stagnation.

In conclusion, it can be stated that political instability may result from economic growth as well as from economic stagnation. In the literature on social conflict there is no consensus on the question whether political instability is greatest under circumstances of rapid growth, declines in the rate of growth or straightforward economic stagnation (see Szirmai, 1988, ch. 9). Under present circumstances, continued economic stagnation would seem to be the most important threat to political stability in many developing countries. In many countries, where the promise of growth and development has failed to materialise in the past decennia, there is a tremendous reservoir of frustration and disillusionment that can be tapped by extremist political and religious movements.

---

24 In total Terhal identifies four groups: the disadvantaged and impoverishing; the stagnating immobile, the mobile satisfied and the mobile but unsatisfied.
25 Hirschman (1973) calls this the 'tunnel effect'. He draws an analogy with car drivers in a traffic jam before a tunnel; if they see cars moving in the other lane, they hope and expect that cars in their own lane will also start moving sooner or later.

11.6.3   Is there a relationship between democracy and economic development?

With the exception of colonial Hong Kong, the Asian tigers Singapore, Korea and Taiwan had dictatorial regimes during their take-off and high-growth phases. These regimes had admittedly tolerated a number of civil, religious and especially economic freedoms but were restrictive and repressive with regard to political freedoms such as the right of association and assembly or freedom of speech. These experiences gave rise to a painful question, whether democracy is compatible with rapid economic development in late-developing countries.

In 1959, the political scientist Seymour M. Lipset noted that average per capita income in democratic countries was much higher than in non-democratic countries. He concluded that economic development promoted democracy. But the causality of this relationship remains problematic.

In the debate on the relationship between democratic regimes and economic growth three perspectives can be identified (Barro, 1996; Helliwell, 1994; Scully, 1988; Sirowy and Inkeles, 1990). One perspective states that there is a degree of tension between democratic institutions and the requirements of economic development in developing countries, especially in the case of late industrialisation. A policy aimed at capital accumulation and rapid economic growth cannot be too democratic since accumulation and a sober macro-economic policy require sacrifices a poor population can hardly be expected to make voluntarily. Long-term economic growth can only be achieved if the political system can be insulated from the short-term wishes of the people. Examples of countries with more or less autocratic regimes that achieved high economic growth rates include Brazil, China, Indonesia, Malaysia, Taiwan, Thailand and South Korea. Bardhan (1984) blames slow economic growth in India on the political regime's incapacity to insulate itself sufficiently from the influences of interest groups. O'Donnell (1979) has argued that bureaucratic authoritarian regimes are most capable of meeting the challenges of late industrialisation. These challenges include, among other things, building up intermediate and capital goods industries, achieving political predictability and stability, and pursuing sober macro-economic policies. A different strand of (neoliberal) argument states that democracies can impose a reduction in growth rates, through distributive and distortive interventions and too great scope for political interest groups (Barro, 1996; Olson, 1982). From these perspectives, one should focus on economic development as a route to later democratisation rather than the other way round. Democratisation is not the first priority.

Other authors defend the thesis that political democratisation, civilian freedoms and economic growth have reinforced each other in history. Political pluralism is a prerequisite for economic pluralism and the flowering of entrepreneurship – in developing countries as well as advanced economies. Scully (1988) states that between 1960 and 1980 open societies with political, civilian and economic freedoms grew three times as fast as societies in which these freedoms were restricted. There are many examples of authoritarian regimes that continued to pursue ineffective or harmful economic policies, in part owing to the absence of democratic checks, balances and controls. We will return to this theme in our discussion of predatory states in section 11.7. The more authoritarian a regime, the greater chance of a dictator stealing or squandering a country's wealth (Barro, 1996).[26] From this perspective, democratisation is seen as contributing to economic development. This assumption is embedded in present foreign policies of Western countries and international institutions, when they include political democratisation and improved observance of human rights as conditions for financial support and trade advantages.[27]

Quantitative empirical research has not yet resulted in any consensus about these questions. Studies contradict each other, depending on the definitions used, the time span covered, the sample of countries included and the research methods employed. The complexity of the debate is increased by the fact that protection of private property and a market economy (indicators of economic freedoms) may well coexist with the absence of any form of political democracy. In a review article Sirowy and Inkeles (1990) conclude that there is no support for the hypothesis that political democracy as such leads to more rapid economic growth. There are just as many studies claiming that there is no significant relation between democracy and growth as there are those claiming that there is a negative relationship between these two factors.

Helliwell (1994) has refined the argument by distinguishing direct and indirect effects of democracy on growth, in cross-country statistical studies. Helliwell starts by reaffirming the correlation between per capita income and measures of democracy. Democracy takes root and survives where levels of economic development are high. He interprets these results as suggesting that democracy has an intrinsic value that is increasingly sought after as populations become better off and better educated.

With regard to the effects of democracy on growth, the indirect effects are positive. The adoption of democracy has a positive effect on schooling and investment, which in turn contribute to growth. The direct effect of democracy on growth is negative. More democratic societies have slower growth. The net result of negative direct and positive indirect effects is positive, but very small. The best conclusion to be derived from the results is that there is no significant relationship between democracy and growth. The same conclusion was reached by Sirowy and Inkeles in their review article.

This debate, however interesting, does not do sufficient justice to the fact that democratisation and the observance of human rights are of major importance as intrinsic objectives of development, irrespective of their economic

---

26 In this respect it is useful to distinguish different types of autocratic regimes. Some autocratic regimes pursue effective development policies. Other autocratic regimes function as predatory states, which destroy the very basis of economic development. Such essential distinctions are not easily captured in cross-country regression studies.

27 Foreign policies of the Western countries show little consistency in this respect. Sometimes, human rights are emphasised. At others, they are played down when the economic interests of the countries involved are threatened, e.g. in recent relations between the USA and China in 1995.

significance. The optimistic conclusion of Helliwell is that democracy, intrinsically valuable, is available at little economic cost. It is not realistic to expect that introducing democracy is likely to accelerate growth. But, there is no empirical support for the notion that continued growth is incompatible with democracy.

11.6.4   Good governance and economic development

A key political condition for economic development is good governance (Ndulu and O'Connell, 1999). Good governance has a wide range of connotations, including the effectiveness of government bureaucracies, prudent macro-economic policies, the transparency and predictability of public decision-making, the existence of checks and balances to control the abuse of political power, the insulation of the bureaucracy from undue influences from pressure groups, the rule of law and the impartial and independent functioning of the judicial system.

As the example of Singapore shows, good governance in the economic sphere is conceivable without full democracy. The Singapore political system is not democratic and even has a pervasive system of censorship. Nevertheless, it has an efficient, modern and non-corrupt system of administration and a severe but open and independent administration of justice.

One of the important dimensions of good governance is a low degree of corruption. Corruption can take many forms. The most obvious one is that of bribery. But corruption also includes nepotism, official theft, fraud, patronage and extortion (Jain, 2001; Johnston, 2001).

Some authors have argued that corruption is the inevitable grease for the wheels of commerce, in a world stifled by bad governance. From the point of view of the individual firm this may well be true. But, Tanzi and Davoodi (2001) argue that this view is not correct from a collective perspective. There are no social benefits associated with corruption (Jain, 2001). Bribes are usually not paid by the most efficient individuals, but by rent-seeking individuals. There are strong negative correlations between indexes of corruption and levels and growth rates of GDP per capita across the world. Tanzi and Davoodi summarise an increasing volume of recent empirical research showing that corruption has negative influences on economic growth (*inter alia* Azfar and Lee, 2001; Booth, 1999; Easterly, 2001; Ehrlich and Lui, 1999; Mauro, 1995; 2000; Wei, 1997a; 1997b; World Bank, 1997). This research correlates indexes of corruption with indicators of economic performance. Corruption indexes are usually based on surveys of perceptions of the degree and cost of corruption amongst business people.[28]

---

28 One of the widely used indexes is the *Corruption Perceptions Index* (*CPI*) of Transparency International (*www.transparency.org/documents/cpi*). Johnston (2001) provides an useful discussion of the strengths and weaknesses of various indicators of corruption. While acknowledging the usefulness of existing measures, he argues for a broader more institutional approach to corruption.

The negative effects of corruption on growth include the following. Corruption acts as a tax on investment, and substantially reduces the rate of investment and therefore of growth. It reduces the rates of return to capital. The more unpredictable corruption is, the more negative the effects on investment and growth. If unpredictability becomes too great, this can choke off all private investment.

Corruption reduces the rates of return to capital for small firms more than for large firms. Large firms find it easier to circumvent regulations and to protect themselves from corrupt petty officials. Larger firms use their political power to realise economic rents. Their corruption is of a cost-reducing kind, allowing them to enjoy monopoly profits and scale economies. New start-ups and small firms are more vulnerable to corruption. For them corruption acts as an additional cost-increasing tax on their activities. Thus, corruption will impede the entry of small-scale firms which can make important contributions to innovation and employment growth.

A somewhat unexpected effect of corruption is that it is likely to increase the rate of investment in public infrastructure, while decreasing its quality and productivity. The often noted paradox that developing countries prefer investment in new infrastructural projects, rather than maintaining existing infrastructure, becomes more understandable. Thus, corruption contributes to the decay of existing infrastructure.

Finally, corruption and rent seeking may have negative impacts on growth if they create incentives for highly talented individuals to engage in rent seeking and other unproductive activities (Baumol, 1990; Murphy, Shleifer and Vishny 1991).

That corruption has negative influences on the rate of growth does not mean that corrupt societies cannot experience rapid growth. Much depends on the ways in which the proceeds of corruption are applied. In some societies such as the Philippines under Marcos, or Nigeria under Abacha, the fruits of corruption are siphoned off into totally unproductive channels such as golden shoes or Swiss banks. In other societies, the proceeds of corruption are reinvested in new economic activity, contributing indirectly to economic dynamics. Thus, both China and Indonesia are countries that have combined pervasive corruption with rapid economic growth. But the experience of Indonesia in the Asian crisis of 1997 illustrates that corruption can reach such levels that a regime becomes totally incapable of responding adequately to economic challenges.

Reducing the extent of corruption is a difficult task, as corruption is deeply embedded in the nature of political systems. But, as the historical record indicates, it is not impossible. There are a variety of measures that can contribute to reduced corruption. The most important of these include introducing checks and balances into the political system, guaranteeing the effectiveness and independence of the judicial system, increasing accountability of officials towards the community and the public, continued national and international monitoring of the extent of corruption, international legislation penalising multinational companies for participating in bribery, and reducing the discretionary power of officials, replacing arbitrary rules by standardised ones.

In this section, we have briefly discussed the relationships between good governance and economic development. But it is important to emphasise that good governance is vitally important from the perspective of human rights. Protection of individuals against arbitrary actions of the state and its officials is one of the key elements of a wider perspective on development.

11.7   The predatory state as an obstacle to economic development in Sub-Saharan Africa

In previous sections we saw that the role of the government in developing countries may be more important today than previously in history. Also, several issues have been raised with regard to the functioning of the apparatus of government and the political process in developing countries. This section takes a closer look at the position of a number of authors (Ake, 1996; Bratton and van de Walle, 1997; Jackson and Rosberg, 1982; Ndulu and O'Connell, 1999; Sandbrook, 1986; Sandbrook and Barker, 1985; van de Walle, 1994) who claim that in Sub-Saharan Africa the state itself has become an obstacle to economic development. In this literature, African states are characterised as extreme examples of *Predatory States*. Predatory States are states that extract wealth from the citizens at the expense of society. Through their actions they undercut the dynamics of development (Evans, 1995; Lal, 1984).[29]

According to Sandbrook, Jackson and Rosberg, many African states are characterised by a system of *personal rule*. Personal rule is the answer of the political leaders to the question how to rule predominantly rural populations, only marginally integrated into national markets and national societies, under conditions in which national political institutions have little legitimacy (see also Jackson and Rosberg, 1986). The various ethnic groups have little feelings of loyalty towards the central state apparatus. National borders cut across ethnic and cultural dividing lines. Often the effective control of the state over its territory only exists in name. Under such circumstances, it is hardly surprising that parliamentary institutions and multi-party systems never took root. The state adapted itself to the particularist norms of a multi-ethnic society.

In the colonial period bureaucracies were very small and had limited tasks. The higher positions in the administration were all filled by European expatriates. Middle positions in the civil service, commerce, trade and industry were predominantly occupied by members of minorities: Lebanese, Syrians and Indians. After the achievement of independence, government bureaucracies were rapidly Africanised and simultaneously expanded, in spite of the initially

---

29 Evans contrasts predatory states with developmental states, which through their actions and policies contribute positively to capital accumulation and socio-economic dynamics.

inadequate supply of trained and experienced officials. Bureaucratic character-istics of the civil service were soon diluted and replaced by networks of per-sonal relations, which Sandbrook, Jackson and Rosberg, and Bratton and van de Walle (1997) refer to as *neopatrimonialism*[30] or *personal rule*. The administration was commercialised. Officials exploited their positions for financial returns. Political leaders used public funds for private purposes and for those of friends, family and clients. The political classes lived in relative luxury, financed among others by bribes from foreign companies in return for trading concessions. According to Rosberg and Jackson, Mobutu, lifetime head of state of Zaire, used 150 million dollars from the central bank for private ends between Jan-uary 1977 and March 1979. Between 1979 and 1983, under Shehu Shagari's democratically elected government of Nigeria, 5 billion to 7 billion dollars were appropriated by government officials (Jackson and Rosberg, 1986, p. 23). According to Bates and Collier (1993), Kenneth Kaunda controlled 40,000 pa-tronage positions in Lusaka alone. Characteristics of personal rule are sum-marised in Box 11.3.

Box 11.3   Characteristics of personal rule

- *A strong man* (the ruler, often the lifetime president). The person of the ruler is identified with the nation. All strategic positions within the political system, the government bureaucracy, the police force and the military are occupied by individuals who are personally loyal to the ruler. These individuals are usually recruited from the ethnic group of the political ruler.
- *Patron–client relationships.* Patron–client relationships pervade the entire apparatus of government, from top to bottom. At all levels individuals maintain and strengthen their positions by granting personal favours to loyal clients in the form of jobs, use of government funds and opportunities for corruption and enrichment. In return for political favours, the private sector is expected to reciprocate.
- *Armed forces that are personally loyal to the political ruler.*

Owing to personal rule, newly established African states have lacked the capabilities to create the conditions for capital accumulation. The economic rationality of state actions is low. The government administration and the pub-lic enterprises (*parastatals*) are characterised by mismanagement, inefficiency and widespread corruption. An impersonal, predictable and bureaucratically rational functioning of the state apparatus becomes impossible.

Public means are squandered and entrepreneurial efficiency is discouraged. Easy profits can be made by political manipulation. Much human creativity and entrepreneurial talent is directed at manipulating the political system in order to obtain subsidies, licences and market monopolies. Rent-seeking behaviour

---

30 The term 'patrimonialism' derives from Max Weber (1922) and refers to a form of traditional authority in which one owes obedience to the person of the ruler rather than to rules, principles or procedures. Tradition is the prime source of legitimacy and circumscribes the power of the ruler. The term 'patrimonial' refers to the fact that members of the administrative apparatus are recruited from amongst the ruler's family, kin or tribe. Another characteristic is the absence of a distinction between the personal and the public sphere. Neopatrimonialism or personal rule is a political system in which patrimonial rulers have no constitutional or traditional legitimacy.

comes in the place of economic efficiency and the search for economically productive investment opportunities. Foreign companies make their investments
dependent on government-guaranteed monopolies.

Personal rule is usually an unstable form of political organisation. Mostly
the ruler depends on a single ethnic group to maintain his power. This group
profits from the control of the apparatus of government to the exclusion of
other groups. Other groups are prone to resort to violent opposition. *Coups
d'état* and military revolts are quite common. The strong men seek military and
financial support from foreign powers. Their opponents do the same, soliciting
support from competing foreign powers to the further detriment of political
stability.

The state is in an almost permanent fiscal crisis. The need for revenues to
maintain the system of patronage is high. Wealthy citizens succeed in evading
income taxes. For their financial requirements, governments are forced to impose heavy taxes on peasants, primary production, exports and imports. The
agricultural marketing boards – discussed in Chapter 10 – are also used for
such purposes. In some countries (e.g. Uganda under Idi Amin; Zaire under
Mobutu), the financial burdens imposed on the peasants were so heavy that
they withdrew from the official market economy, started trading on parallel
black markets or even moved back to subsistence production. This eroded the
tax base even further.

According to Sandbrook, personal rule prevailed in most African countries
in the early 1980s. The major exceptions were militant socialist states such as
Angola or Tanzania, where socialist ideology provided a degree of legitimacy.
Sandbrook stresses the fact that political systems in Africa, as elsewhere, also
show considerable variation. There are relatively strong states – Botswana, the
Côte d'Ivoire, Cameroon, Kenya, Malawi and Senegal – and extremely weak
states – Chad, Ghana, Nigeria, Somalia and Zaire.[31] Moreover, he emphasises
quite rightly (especially in Sandbrook and Barker, 1985) that the roots of the
economic crisis in Sub-Saharan Africa are manifold and not limited to politics.
Factors contributing to economic problems include the unfavourable international economic environment, the scarcity of natural resources, poor soil
conditions, sustained droughts and rapid population growth. These factors interact with state formation processes. Economic stagnation leads to greater
malfunctioning of government institutions. Characteristics of the state apparatus may result in further economic stagnation, resulting in a downward
spiral.

Given the characteristics of state and politics in Sub-Saharan Africa, Sandbrook argues in favour of a more limited role of the public sector in the economy. This would leave more scope for a healthy development of the private
sector. The government should concentrate on a selected number of key issues

---

31 Uganda, which was high on Sandbrook's list of weak states in the early 1980s, has since then made a
remarkable political and economic recovery. Zimbabwe, on the other hand, has recently degenerated into
total chaos under the personal rule of the aged dictator Mugabe.

only. Reducing the size of the public sector is not enough.[32] The effectiveness of the smaller government apparatus has to be increased if the state is to contribute to the conditions for successful capital accumulation. Further, the government and the political system should try to regain some legitimacy in the eyes of the people. The very recent trend towards more multi-party elections (see Table 11.2) should be seen in this light.

The key question remains, however, whether the political conditions are ripe for reform and whether there is a real political will to move from systems of neopatrimonial personal rule to systems of impersonal bureaucratic management and effectively functioning administration. We have seen that several African states have introduced democratic reforms in the past decade. Also, in several countries there has been a marked shift towards less intervention in the economy and a privatisation (or closure) of parastatal enterprises. Nevertheless, the institutions of neopatrimonialism and personal rule show remarkable persistence. The challenges of a policy of sustainable political reform are just as great as those of economic reform.

11.8   Concluding remarks

This chapter has emphasised the importance of state formation and nation building in the process of development. The emergence of stable and effective states with good governance is important both from the perspective of economic development and from the wider perspective of the quality of life of individuals within these states. In many parts of the developing world, the political problems of the establishment of internal peace take precedence over economic problems and issues.

With regard to the economic role of the state, the analysis points to an interesting paradox between the weaknesses of the state apparatus on the one hand, and the wide range of tasks imposed on the state apparatus in many countries since 1950. Though the debate on the exact role and scope of the state in the economy is far from resolved, there is a shift in development strategy towards a more limited economic role for the state, which should be performed more effectively. Good governance is not limited to the economic tasks of governments, but also refers to the establishment of the rule of law and the respect for basic human rights of a country's citizens.

Questions for review

1. Provide definitions of the concepts of state, nation, society and nation-state. Give examples of states which are not nation-states and nations which are not nation-states.
2. Discuss the differences between the Marxist and the Weberian perspectives on the role of the state in socio-economic development.

---

32 According to Sandbrook, the share of the government in the national income in Sub-Saharan Africa is not exceptionally large in comparison with other developing countries and with affluent countries. What is rather more crucial in this respect is the regulating nature of government activities.

3. Why does Max Weber interpret the emergence of bureaucracy as a positive factor in economic development?
4. Analyse the mutual interrelationships between economic growth and political stability or instability.
5. Analyse typical characteristics of state formation in developing countries. What are the most important differences between processes of state formation in developing countries and earlier processes of state formation in Western Europe?
6. Provide an analysis of the economic effects of corruption in developing countries.
7. Why has the military played such a prominent role in politics in many developing countries?
8. Why is the role of the state in economic development in present-day developing countries greater than the role of the state in the development of Western countries in the eighteenth and nineteenth centuries? To what extent is the increased importance of the state a stimulus for or an obstacle to economic development?
9. What kind of relationships can be identified between democracy and economic development? To what extent is democratic rule compatible with rapid economic development?
10. What are the characteristics of neopatrimonial rule and why do these characteristics form an obstacle to economic development in Africa?
11. What are the main sources of political instability in developing countries?

Further reading

For the broad comparative study of state formation a good point of departure is Barrington Moore's *Social Origins of Dictatorship and Democracy: Lord and Peasant in the Making of the Modern World* (1967). From the extensive literature on state formation in developing countries in Africa, we mention: Coleman and Rosberg (eds.), *Political Parties and National Integration in Tropical Africa* (1964); Davidson, *The Black Man's Burden: Africa and the Curse of the Nation-State* (1992); Ake, *Democracy and Development in Africa* (1996); and Sandbrook and Barker, *The Politics of Africa's Economic Stagnation* (1985).

For an analysis of the neopatrimonial state in Africa, two interesting references are Richard Sandbrook's article in *World Development*, 'The State as an Obstacle to Development', *World Development* (1986), and an interesting article by van de Walle on 'Neopatrimonialism and Democracy in Africa', with an Illustration from Cameroun (1994).

Two references for the role of the military in politics are Finer's excellent study, *The Man on Horseback* (1988) and a volume edited by Janowitz, *Civil–Military Regimes: Regional Perspectives* (1981). A key reference for *coup d'états* is Luttwak's, *Coup d'Etat: A Practical Handbook* (1979 and various editions). There is a large econometric literature examining the consequences of ethnic and linguistic diversity in developing countries. Interesting samples of this literature are: Easterly, 'Can Institutions Resolve Ethnic Conflict?' (2001); Easterly and Levine, 'Africa's Growth Tragedy: Policies and Ethnic Divisions' (1997); and Nettle, 'Linguistic Fragmentation and the Wealth of Nations: The Fishman–Pool Hypothesis Reexamined' (2000).

For trends in civil and international conflicts one can consult Small and Singer, *Resort to Arms, International and Civil Wars, 1816–1980* (1982), Starr and Most, 'Patterns of Conflict: Quantitative Analysis and the Comparative Lessons of Third World Wars' (1985) and Marshall and Gurr, *Peace and Conflict, 2003* (2003). There is a useful overview of armed conflicts by Marshall on the internet: *Major Episodes of Political Violence, 1946–2002* (http://members.aol.com/cspmgm/warlist.htm). Other sources of information include Smith, *The State of War and Peace Atlas* (1997 and various other issues), WHO, *World Report on Violence and Health* (2002) and Sivard, *World Military and Social Expenditures* (1991 and various issues).

A volume edited by Jain on *The Political Economy of Corruption* (2001) gives a good impression of ongoing research on this topic. Frequently cited references include: two articles by Mauro, 'Corruption and Growth' (1995) and 'The Effects of Corruption on Growth, Investment and Government Expenditure' (2000). A *Corruption*

Perceptions Index (CPI), is published on the website of Transparency International: www.transparency.org/.

For the debates on the role of the state in economic development, the reader is referred to Chapter 9, Further Reading. An important additional reference is Evans's study, *Embedded Autonomy: States and Industrial Transformation* (1995).

An early publication on the relationship between democracy and development is an article by Seymour Lipset, published in the *American Political Science Review* of 1959: 'Some Social Prerequisites of Democracy, Economic Development and Political Legitimacy'. A more recent reference is Huntington, *The Third Wave, Democratisation in the Late Twentieth Century* (1991). Two review articles on the statistical debate on the relationship between democracy and development are Sirowy and Inkeles, 'The Effects of Democracy on Economic Growth and Inequality: A Review' (1990) and Helliwell, 'Empirical Linkages between Democracy and Economic Growth' (1994). For analysis of democratisation in Africa, see Bratton and van de Walle, *Democratic Experiments in Africa: Regime Transitions in Comparative Perspective* (1997). Useful sources of data on political regimes include Freedom House, *Democracy's Century. A Survey of Global Political Change in the Twentieth Century* (2000), http://www.freedomhouse.org/reports/century.html, and Banks *et al.*, *Political Handbook of the World: Governments and Intergovernmental Organizations* (1998 and other issues).

12

Cultural dimensions of development

In the discussion of the concept of development in Chapter 1, we emphasised that development is not limited to the economic sphere. It also involves a broad range of social changes. An important dimension of development is cultural change. We cannot study economic developments in isolation, but also have to take into account cultural aspects such as attitudes, religious precepts, lifestyles, identities and values. Culture as a dimension of development is extremely important. It is also a somewhat slippery concept, as almost anything can be classified under the heading of culture: culture as art, identity, religion, language, nationalism, attitudes, institutions, material artefacts, and so forth.

A full treatment of cultural change is not possible in the context of a single chapter. This chapter will have an exploratory and open character, focusing primarily on the interrelationships and interconnections between culture and economic development. It will be more reflective and open-ended than other chapters. Its aim is not to summarise the literature or to develop general hypotheses or firm conclusions about the role of culture, but rather to make the reader aware of and sensitive to the possible importance of cultural elements in the broader process of development. The chapter addresses the following issues: the role of religion in economic development; the notion of efficient institutions; traditional versus modern culture; cultural obstacles to development; cultural consequences of and reactions to Western penetration in the non-Western world; the pros and cons of cultural mapping for development projects and policies.

12.1   Introduction

12.1.1   Concepts

We will not attempt a formal definition of culture. We do make a distinction between so-called high culture (art, music and literature, and so on) and the broader anthropological concept of culture, which refers to the complete lifestyle of a society, that is transmitted through education and socialisation and is passed on from generation to generation. It includes attitudes, expectations, knowledge, norms, values, habits, religion, ideology, notions of what is beautiful or ugly, traditions and standard solutions to the problems of social interaction. It is this anthropological concept that we will refer to in this chapter.

In this sense, culture primarily refers to characteristic mental maps and values shared by members of a group or society. It excludes the material objects and artefacts that are produced by members of a culture (material culture). On the other hand, it also excludes institutions which structure human behaviour. We agree with Huntington that too broad a conception of culture becomes scientifically useless, because it then explains everything and therefore nothing (cf. Huntington, 2000, p. xv).[1]

There is a tendency to think of cultures as homogeneous patterns. But one should keep in mind that there are contradictions and conflicts within every culture. There are cultural universals, which apply to all members of a social community, and cultural alternatives, which do not. There are cultural specialities, elements that are specific to certain subgroups in a community. In every society, there are a variety of groups with their own subcultures. Some of these are dominant insider groups, others are outsiders. Elements of cultural patterns may even be in conflict with each other. One of the interesting cultural contradictions in advanced capitalist societies is the contradiction between the need for a disciplined work ethic on the one hand and a culture of hedonistic consumerism on the other, as analysed by Daniel Bell, in the 1960s, in 'The Cultural Contradictions of Capitalism' (1971).

12.1.2   How important is culture?

Can cultural differences explain differences in socio-economic dynamics, or does culture simply adapt to changes in the economic and the social sphere? One can contrast a *structuralist approach* to culture and *an idealist approach*. An example of the structuralist perspective is Marxist theory, which sees culture as determined by economic interests. When interests and power relationships

---

1 We shall also steer clear of concepts such as postmodernism and deconstructionism, which abound in modern cultural studies, but which are so fuzzy that they do not serve to clarify any of the developmental issues we are discussing in this book.

change, cultural change will follow. The opposite view is the idealist perspective, which sees cultural traits as determining behaviour, economic activity and economic development. From this perspective cultural differences explain differences in economic performance.

The debate between these polar positions is fruitless. One can analyse the social genesis of different cultural patterns and show how the structural patterns of relationships between individuals and groups crystallise into cultural patterns that influence their subsequent behaviour (e.g. Elias, 1969). But, once a cultural pattern has emerged and hardened, it will have a certain persistence of its own and will play an independent role in channelling and regulating behaviour for long periods of time. Of course, cultural elements can gradually change under the influence of structural changes, such as the emergence of global markets, changes in the balance of power between interest groups, or the impact of mass media. But, that does not warrant the conclusion that culture has no influence on development, as an independent variable. Our very perceptions of our interests and our identifications with interest groups are culturally influenced. So, even if one prefers the structuralist perspective on cultural change, as this author does, it is important and interesting to analyse cultural aspects of development. Culture does matter.

On the other hand, one should not make the mistake of assuming that culture is immutable. It is subject to change when the social conditions change. One of the first development economists, J. Boeke (1930; 1947), posited the notion of an oriental culture which was supposed to be inconsistent with modern rational market behaviour. Boeke's *oriental culture* included an emphasis on social rather than economic values, a short time span, a tendency to stop working when immediate needs were fulfilled (the hypothesis of the *backward bending supply curve of labour*, which states that workers will work less if they receive higher wages). We now know that such a culture is a long-term adaptation of individuals to a real lack of economic opportunities for peasants in colonial and precolonial societies. When the opportunities improve, a rational and entrepreneurial spirit can emerge among peasants. They start to plant new cash crops for domestic and international markets and to employ new technologies. For instance, this occurred on a large scale at the end of the nineteenth century and effectively debunked the myth that peasants and farmers in developing countries have a culturally determined lack of entrepreneurial spirit.

But one should also realise that cultural change can be very slow. Attitudes and expectations that have evolved over centuries do not disappear overnight, apart from the fact that powerful groups in society may also have strong interests in maintaining traditional cultural elements. It is not easy to tinker with culture.

Once one concludes that culture matters for socio-economic development (Harrison and Huntington, 2000), the next question is how important are cultural factors in the explanation of socio-economic development. What weight do they have compared to other factors, such as technological change, economic cycles, natural resources or power and dependence relationships in the international order?

Structuralist authors such as Jeffrey Sachs and Jared Diamond argue that in the very long run geography, location, climate and natural resources rather than differences in culture determine economic success (Diamond, 1998; Sachs, 2000). For instance, it is well known that almost all economically advanced nations lie in moderate climatic zones. But these ecological explanations cannot explain why in similar environmental conditions some societies develop and others do not. Many authors have tried to explain lack of development or underdevelopment on the basis of the history of colonialism, exploitation, availability of resources, the terms of trade or the structure of the world economy. But, again, these explanations fail to explain why some former colonies develop into advanced economies, while others stagnate. Cultural differences are at least part of the story.

12.2   The Protestant ethic and the rise of capitalism

A useful starting point for the discussion of the role of culture in development is Max Weber's classic article 'Die Protestantische Ethik und der Geist des Kapitalismus', 1905. This article can be seen as a response to the Marxist disregard of culture as an independent force in development. Weber's core question was: why did capitalist economic development break through in Northwest Europe, and why not elsewhere in the world (see the discussion in Chapter 3)? What was the role of religion in this breakthrough?

Weber argued that many of the preconditions for capitalist growth could also be found in non-Western parts of the world and in other historical periods. The profit motive, the use of money, the emergence of markets, urbanisation or individualism are not unique to the West. Innovation and technological advance have occurred in many societies. Mass manufacturing had already emerged in China in the twelfth century. But capitalism had not broken through. What was lacking in these societies, according to Weber, was the key notion of 'rentability'. Rentability refers to the systematic and rational planning for a sustainable flow of future profits. This notion of rentability was linked to religion.

Weber noted that all the countries where capitalism broke through in the sixteenth and seventeenth centuries were Protestant countries and more particularly Calvinist countries: the Netherlands, England, Scotland, the East Coast of the USA and Switzerland. The Protestant religion was what differentiated them decisively from other countries and societies. In Europe, Protestants were also strongly over-represented amongst capitalists, traders and entrepreneurs. Therefore, Weber argued, Protestantism must have played an important role in the breakthrough of capitalism. This led Weber to a systematic comparison of the economic values (*Wirtschaftsethik*) embedded in the main world religions: Catholicism, Judaism, Islam, Hinduism, Buddhism and Confucianism (Weber, 1920).

Puritan Protestantism had a number of crucial elements, which differed from all other religions. These are listed in Box 12.1.

Box 12.1   Characteristics of the Protestant ethic
- The ideal of disciplined pursuit of one's profession in society (*Innerweltliche Askese*) versus the ideal of ascetic withdrawal from society in convents, monasteries or contemplation (*Ausserweltliche Askese*). In world religions such as Hinduism, Catholicism and Buddhism the religious ideals include withdrawal from the humdrum affairs of the world, in order to focus on religious contemplation, by monks, mystics or sages. According to Weber, Protestantism was unique in the notion that one could follow one's religious calling in the daily world of work and profession.
- The individual responsibility of the believer versus the submission to hierarchy characteristic of, for instance, Catholicism. Among others, this manifested itself in the translation of the scriptures into the vernacular, so that everyone could read them. Protestantism provided a major impetus to literacy.
- The search for a rational conduct of life and religious practice versus submission to tradition and fate. The high value placed on a rational conduct translated into the economic sphere, where the rational organisation of production and a rational approach to investment in the search for sustained profit became the rule. Rationalisation also resulted in the emergence of bureaucracy as the dominant form of organisation.
- The belief in predestination for eternal salvation or damnation. The belief in predestination creates a tremendous psychic anxiety amongst individuals and an urgent search for signs of election. These signs include social and economic success in this world. This creates a strong unconscious motivation for economic effort, disciplined performance and a powerful work ethic.
- A high value placed on sobriety and discipline. Consumption and luxury were perceived as sinful and corrupt. The combination of the work ethic and sobriety had the unintended consequence of a high rate of savings and rapid capital accumulation.

The Weber thesis gave rise to a fascinating ongoing polemic, which continues to this very day. Opponents of the Weber thesis argued that empirical foundations were shaky (e.g. Tawney, 1926; Trevor Roper, 1972). For instance, many entrepreneurs in the Protestant Low Countries turned out to be of Catholic origin and Catholic cities such as Antwerp were major centres of dynamic capitalist activities. The critics emphasised the role of migrants from Catholic to Protestant areas. In the sixteenth and seventeenth centuries, in the Low Countries, people fled to the Calvinist-controlled areas to escape the turmoil of the counter-Reformation. They became successful as entrepreneurs and many of them later adopted Protestantism as their religion. If this is correct, Protestantism does not explain the capitalist breakthrough, but rather capitalist entrepreneurs adopted a religion that was congenial to them.

Other critics have pointed to the entrepreneurial success of migrant groups with very different religious backgrounds: the Chinese in Southeast Asia and the Indians in East Africa. It was the marginal position of these migrant groups in their societies, not religion, that was the driving force for entrepreneurial success. The same holds for the prominent position of Jews in the history of West European capitalism.

Later observers pointed to the economic success of Japan and the East Asian economies in the twentieth century. These societies were predominantly Confucian in tradition. This was completely at odds with the Weber thesis about the importance of Protestantism, and the presumed negative economic impact of Confucian religious beliefs. These experiences have resulted in a whole new set of studies arguing that Confucian values are especially conducive to growth in the late twentieth century and that a *Confucian Ethic* was one of the explanations of modern economic success (Dore, 1987; Goodell, 1995/6; Hofstede, 2001; Hofstede and Bond, 1988; Pye, 2000; Senghaas, 1984).

Weber may well have overstated the uniqueness of Protestantism in relation to economic activity. But, in spite of justified criticisms of the Weber thesis, the consequences of religious and cultural traits for economic performance have remained on the agenda ever since. One cannot but note that all economically successful societies are characterised by a powerful work ethic and entrepreneurial drive, by social discipline, sobriety and a high value placed on savings and future orientation. Probably, the role of Calvinism is not unique, but a puritan work ethic, future orientation and entrepreneurial and innovative attitudes seem to be important ingredients in individual and collective economic success all over the world.

12.3   Efficient institutions

In Chapter 3, we introduced the concept of efficient institutions. Like culture, institutions raise endless problems of definition, which we will not go into too deeply. Institutions can be loosely characterised as standardised patterns of social interaction for the solution of core problems people face in social life. They are a complex of ideas, norms, rules and socially sanctioned, standardised patterns of behaviour with regard to the key questions of social life. Family institutions regulate interactions between men and women and their children, as well as issues of sex and procreation; military institutions regulate the use of violence; economic institutions, such as markets or planning systems, regulate how people provide for their livelihood. Political institutions regulate the access to positions of power and the ways in which collective decisions are arrived at.

Economically efficient institutions are institutions that motivate self-interested individuals to act in ways that contribute to collective welfare and economic development (North, 1990; North and Thomas, 1973). Key economic institutions in the history of Western capitalist countries include clearly defined property rights, the rise of joint-stock companies, protection of intellectual property rights, book-keeping and financial accounting and interest. Well-defined property rights assigned the fruits of efforts to those who made investments in future returns. The rise of the joint-stock company allowed individuals to cooperate in raising capital and limited the risks by isolating personal wealth from the specific assets invested in the company. Protection of intellectual property rights provided a spur to invention, innovation and technological change, by allowing the owners of intellectual property rights to charge fees for the use of their inventions. Book-keeping, financial accounting and interest were key institutional ingredients of the pursuit of sustainable profit through productive activity, with systematic reinvestment of part of the current profits. The notion of rentability contrasted with other types of search for profit such as piracy, rent seeking or maximisation of short-term speculative profits at the expense of long-run profitability. Medieval Catholicism (and traditional and modern Islam) prohibited the charging of interest on loans as an immoral activity (Lewis and Algouid, 2001). This worked as a barrier to the rise of modern capital markets, capital accumulation and a rational attitude towards investment. Protestantism and Judaism had no such prohibitions.

What is economically efficient or inefficient varies in time and place. Institutions that are efficient in one phase of development may become inefficient at a later stage. North and Thomas (1973) have shown how feudal institutions were efficient in medieval Europe, given the prevailing conditions. They became inefficient when the conditions changed, owing to improvements in transport, technology and the emergence of extended markets. Deepak Lal (1988) has argued in a similar fashion that given the circumstances in pre-modern India, the Hindu caste system has been relatively efficient for 2,000 years. Much of the literature on efficient institutions suggests that in the modern world, markets, individual property rights, and family farms are economically superior to other types of economic institutions. But the characteristics of economic breakthroughs and processes of catch-up vary from one historical period to another. Different conditions may require different efficient economic institutions.

It does seem clear that in a modern economy institutions that restrict the optimal use and allocation of human talents are economically less efficient. For instance, the Hindu caste system assigns people to given economic categories by birth rather than ability. The son of a sweeper has to be a sweeper, the son of a Brahmin intellectual has to be a priest or engage in intellectual activities. Many religious belief systems restrict the access of women to education and the labour market. Today this is clearly the case in many Islamic countries (UNDP, 2002), though of course with considerable variation from country to country.

Institutions are buttressed by culture, which provides the – often unconscious – norms, values, expectations, roles and mental maps that help regulate behaviour.[2] So, one of the ways in which culture affects economic development is through the shaping of institutions.[3] But institutions are also important as such. It is not enough to have appropriate culturally determined attitudes or mental maps, such as a work ethic, if the institutions, policies and mode of

---

2 Weisner (2000) warns against too rigid a conception of cultural traits. They are not simply fixed patterns that determine institutions and behaviour. They are also tools for adaptation in the course of one's life.
3 Above, we excluded institutions from our informal definition of culture. Nevertheless, we do discuss institutions in this chapter – albeit briefly – because one of the ways in which culture affects development is through the shaping of institutions.

governance of a society provide the wrong kind of incentives (Landes, 2000). Actual behaviour is influenced by a mix of culturally determined attitudes and structural and institutional constraints, which interact with each other in a process of change.[4]

12.4 Traditional versus modern cultures

12.4.1 *Modernisation theory*

Max Weber put forward a set of historical hypotheses about the cultural causes of the breakthrough of capitalism in the West. After World War II, modernisation theorists developed this theory into a theory of cultural obstacles to development, both generalising and simplifying the Weber thesis.

Modernisation theorists posited a dichotomy between traditional and modern societies. The economic core of modernisation is industrialisation, which requires a measure of congruence between economic developments and their social and cultural environment. This was the position taken by Clark Kerr in *Industrialism and Industrial Man* (1962).

The dichotomy between traditional and modern societies involves changes in a number of cultural and institutional dimensions. Some of the most frequently mentioned dichotomies are listed in Box 12.2 below. If industrialisation involves congruence between economic and social change, modernisation theories imply that industrialisation will not take off in societies with strong traditional cultures, collectivist orientations, fatalist attitudes, weak work ethics and social discipline, negative attitudes towards risk and entrepreneurship, and inefficient institutions. The cultural obstacles to economic change and development will be too strong.

> **Box 12.2 Modernisation theory: dichotomies between modern and traditional societies**
> - *Achievement versus ascription*. In modern societies social positions are assigned to individuals on the basis of achievement and meritocratic criteria. In traditional societies social positions are assigned on the basis of birth, social origin and other ascriptive criteria.
> - *Mobility versus hierarchy*. Modern societies are characterised by increased upward and downward social mobility in comparison with traditional static hierarchical societies.
> - *Rational versus traditional behaviour*. Modern society is characterised by rational thinking about ends and means. In pre-modern societies traditionally defined patterns of behaviour predominate.
> - *Future orientation versus fatalism*. In modern societies, people believe that their actions influence their future. They are willing to make long-term investments for a

---

4 An interesting example of these interactions is provided by Patterson (2000) in his analysis of the emergence of fatherless households and parental abandonment in African-American communities, which are rooted in the legacies of slavery.

better future for themselves and their children. Traditional societies are characterised by fatalism and a short-term horizon.

- *Nuclear families versus extended families.* It is argued that extended families and kinship relationships act as a break on economic development, because the strong pressure towards redistribution within the extended family impedes capital accumulation (Bauer and Yamey, 1957). Modernisation involves the breakdown of extended families and the emergence of nuclear families.
- *Political democratisation versus authoritarian rule.*
- *Increased role for civil society.* Modernisation implies increased roles for union, parties, political pressure groups and other associations of civil society.
- *Single-stranded versus multi-stranded social relationships.* Many transactions in modern markets and modern bureaucracies are anonymous and specialised (single-stranded). In traditional societies, relationships are more personal and involve many dimensions (a variety of economic and financial exchanges, relationships of kin and tribe, friendship, relationships of authority and dependence).
- *Universalistic versus particularistic relationships.* Modern societies define rules in formal and abstract ways, and try to apply them in social relationships irrespective of the people in question. In traditional societies, the personal ties between participants in a social relationship are more important than the formal rules.
- *Affectivity versus affective neutrality in group relationships.*
- *Individualist orientation versus collectivist or communal orientation.* In traditional societies, social obligations are more important than in modern societies, where people feel free to pursue their individual interests.

One of the most extreme formulations of the modernisation approach was that of David McClelland in *The Achieving Society* (1961). McClelland emphasised the importance of entrepreneurship in economic development. Entrepreneurial attitudes are acquired through an educational process, which instils the need for achievement (N ach) in children. McClelland analysed the values emphasised in children's books to see which societies implanted the need for achievement in their younger generations. In modern societies, these books emphasised the value of hard work, openness to influences from the environment (against orientation towards tradition), control of one's own impulses and behaviour, control of one's natural environment.

Similar ideas are found in the study, *Becoming Modern*, by Inkeles and Smith (1974). Inkeles and Smith developed an index of modernity. Elements of modernity included: confidence in the possibilities of finding solutions to problems with the help of science and technology; a sense of efficacy and goal-orientedness; positive attitudes towards innovation and innovativeness; concern for planning and control of time; and respect for subordinates.

The practical recipe derived from these studies is that one should try to change traditional cultures and mentalities through education, information, schooling and seminars. Among others this involved the setting up of courses and workshops in entrepreneurship. This points to a rather simplistic belief in the short-term mutability of attitudes. It was not surprising that the results of such development strategies were disappointing. Attitudes are not easily changed by social tinkering. Strangely enough, Chinese communism manifested a not completely dissimilar attitude towards cultural change. The Communist regime used massive political mobilisation and indoctrination as an instrument of thought change and modernisation of traditional mentalities.

12.4.2 Towards a more differentiated approach to the opposition between traditional and modern

In hindsight, modernisation theory now seems hopelessly dated, naive and ethnocentric. It was ethnocentric in the sense that modernisation was conceived of as 'becoming more like the West'. Every society was assumed to converge to the Western cultural pattern. Modernisation theory disregarded the enormous varieties of 'traditional societies' in different parts of the world. It assumed a one-dimensional movement along the axis from traditional to modern. The positive connotations of the modern pole of the axis tended to draw attention away from urgent social problems and shortcomings in the so-called advanced societies (Schech and Haggis, 2000; Sen, 1999).

As explained in Chapter 3, modernisation theory paid insufficient attention to differences in patterns of modes of economic development in different historical periods. In the eighteenth century a number of European countries pioneered industrialisation in a world economy without industry. Latecomers were in a very different position. They had to face established industrial giants. It is therefore not surprising that the economic and social development of Japan, Korea, Singapore, Hong Kong, Taiwan and China proceeded and proceed along very different paths and patterns to those of Western Europe in the past.

Modernisation theory also had unrealistic expectations of the role of education in changing mentalities. Finally, the opposition between modern and tradition draws our attention away from the negative impacts of external penetration and colonisation. It tends to obscure the fact that many societies started to change in response to external challenges and threats.

Other strands of anthropological and sociological research argued for a more refined perspective on the opposition between traditional versus modern cultures. Implicitly or explicitly most of these authors do accept that there are some cultural imperatives deriving from economic development and industrialisation. But the simple opposition between 'traditional' and 'modern' needs to be replaced by a more differentiated and empirically realistic approach.

In a classic study of entrepreneurship in two Indonesian cities, Clifford Geertz (1963) showed how various elements of presumably traditional societies and religions can contribute to modern economic development and innovative entrepreneurship. In the town of Modjokuto in Java, he showed how Bazaar-type trade networks were in a process of transition into modern firms. The key innovators were a group of traders of Reformist Islamic persuasion. They were deeply religious and far stricter in their religious observances than other inhabitants of the city. Geertz shows that in many ways they shared some of the characteristics of the Protestant ethic: a strong work ethic, discipline and sobriety, and an orientation towards the world of work. This goes against the stereotypical view of Islam as a traditional value system that forms an obstacle to development. In Tabanan, on the Hindu Island of Bali, the role of modern entrepreneur was taken up by members of the traditional aristocracy who had been displaced by the colonial rulers and were struggling to maintain or regain their social pre-eminence through economic success. They used their social standing in a traditional agrarian society to mobilise people and resources for the construction of large-scale modern manufacturing enterprises. Geertz concludes that a wide range of cultures is capable of generating economic development, if the favourable factors are used and the unfavourable factors are suppressed. Development policies should take these local differences into account and should try to capitalise on them. For Geertz, industrialisation and modern economic development does require changes in culture, but the sources of change can be found in supposedly traditional cultures.

A second example of a more complex perspective on the opposition between traditional and modern is Kuper's discussion of the relationships between traditional African family institutions and the modern institution of migrant labour in Southern Africa (Kuper, 1984). Traditional African economic institutions commonly distinguish between a so-called *subsistence mode* (which includes the cultivation of food crops, horticulture and gathering activities), and an *investment mode* (which is more future-oriented and includes cash crops, cattle and hunting). The division of labour between these activities depends on status, age, ethnic group and in particular gender. The women are responsible for food production and other activities in the labour-intensive subsistence mode. The males monopolise activities in the more capital-intensive investment sector. In traditional African cultures, women supply the labour for the labour-intensive sector. Males will invest the returns from the investment sector as bride wealth to acquire partners in polygamous relationships.

In the course of the twentieth century, migrant labour emerged as an important phenomenon, especially in areas where there was insufficient scope for animal husbandry and local cash crop production. Males went off to work in mines, plantations and the modern urban sector. From a comparison of Lesotho and Botswana, Kuper concludes that the 'modern' phenomenon of migrant labour served to buttress traditional family institutions and practices. In Lesotho, the proceeds of migrant labour were invested in bride wealth and the continuation of traditional or neotraditional extended family relationships. In Botswana, where there was less migrant labour, the traditional extended family and traditional practices were in decline. Thus, in Lesotho traditional institutions do not impede modern developments and modernisation reinforces traditional family relationships.

A third example of the complexity of the relationship between traditional and modern culture and institutions refers to the economic implications of extended family institutions in China, the Middle East and Africa. In the older literature it has been argued that the extended family acts as a major brake on entrepreneurship and economic development (e.g. Levy and Shih, 1949). It imposes redistributive obligations on its more successful members, which act as an obstacle to capital accumulation. It reduces the incentives for innovative behaviour and risk taking. Also, strong family ties may result in nepotism, clientelism and corruption.

While admitting the potential economic dysfunctions of the extended family system, the modern literature also points to positive functions of the extended family, especially in the Asian context. Perkins (2000) argues that the reliance on personal and kinship-type relationships in Asia has provided an alternative to the rule of law in the Western world. Personal relationships provide an element of security, which is essential for commercial activities. Families and personal networks are collectively responsible for the enforcement of contracts. Networks and network obligations are more important than contracts. Family ties have played a very important role in the emergence of large business conglomerates and proved to be one of the means of mobilising large amounts of capital, both in East Asia and in Southeast Asian countries where Chinese minorities play such an important role in the economy. Perkins argues persuasively that this system served East and Southeast Asia well in the past thirty years. He also argues that the reliance on kinship relationships is now becoming an increasing liability for further economic development, as corruption spirals out of control and the expectation that the network will bail out the individual firm creates moral hazard. The Asian crisis of 1997 is a manifestation of these underlying problems, as is the stagnation of the once so dynamic Japanese economy between 1990 and 2000. In addition, it is interesting to note that Asian societies are currently experiencing an erosion of extended family relationships and the rise of nuclear families, as suggested by original modernisation theory.

12.5 Are there cultural obstacles to economic development?

Today, there are few explicit adherents of modernisation theory in its simple and schematic form. However, if we drop the generalising and causal approach of modernisation theory, we can start re-examining the question whether certain elements of culture act as obstacles to economic growth and development in the modern globalised economic order, while other elements act as a stimulus. In the introduction to a World Bank-sponsored conference on culture, Salim (1994) notes that we live in an interdependent world within which each society must strive to keep pace with scientific and technological progress. It is a challenge to find a synergy between technological change and cultural values. Modernisation theory turns out to be less dead than we thought.[5]

---

5 Three interesting collections of recent articles (Clague and Grossbard-Shechtman, 2001; Harrison and Huntington, 2000; and Serageldin and J. Taboroff, 1994) were among the sources of inspiration for this

The debate about cultural obstacles to development is fraught with difficulties. In the first place, it assumes that people across the world agree on the content and goals of development. In Chapter 1 we have argued that development is inevitably a highly value-laden concept, but that one can indeed identify the contours of a development concept, including increased welfare, productivity, health, education and an extension of political and social freedoms. However, different societies may have different preferences and priorities. In the second place, the notion of cultural obstacles assumes that one can evaluate cultures against some universal yardstick, which goes against a deeply ingrained habit of cultural relativism which states that each culture can only be judged in terms of its own values.

In an impassioned and thought-provoking criticism of the platitudes of older and newer modernisation theorists, the anthropologist Richard Shweder (2000) argues that there are a great many valued social goals which cannot be achieved at the same time (justice, autonomy, liberty, beneficence, care for the elderly, and so forth). Every culture involves painful trade-offs between the valued things in life. Different cultures make different trade-offs. Cultural diversity is a fact of life. This is not a choice for the radical cultural relativism. All cultures contain indefensible practices which can be criticised. But on the other hand, it should also be obvious that there is no one single way to lead a decent, rational and fulfilling life. Not everyone needs to become like a Western Protestant.

The position taken in this book is that one has to be very careful in evaluating cultures in terms of superior or inferior. Nevertheless, there are some inconsistencies in Shweder's stance. Criticising indefensible practices such as ethnic genocide, cronyism and corruption, torture or the stoning of unfaithful women inevitably assumes some universal criterion of human dignity, which sets limits to cultural relativism. Also, from a perspective of socio-economic dynamics and progress, cultural patterns can be judged to the extent that they empirically contribute to such dynamics. If people in a society value economic dynamism highly, this may require certain kinds of cultural change. Though a variety of cultural arrangements may be compatible with economic development, this does not preclude the fact that some elements of a culture may act as obstacles to modern economic development. This is especially marked if one looks at the dynamics of socio-economic development from a macro-perspective and notes the differences in dynamics in different parts of the world. Selected examples of the possible impacts of culture on development follow below.

12.5.1   The caste system

In Hinduistic societies such as India, the caste system acts as an obstacle to the most efficient use of human capabilities and talents in the economic process

chapter. Some of the articles in these collections revive the stark dichotomies of modernisation theory. Other contributions reflect the more differentiated perspective which informs the present chapter.

(Maddison, 1974). The caste system defines a religiously legitimised hierarchy of social estates, which are restricted in their interactions with each other. At the top of the caste hierarchy are the Brahmins, specialising in religious and intellectual activities, followed by Kshatriyas (warriors and aristocrats), Vaisyas (merchants) and Sudras (workers). Quite at the bottom are the untouchables, who perform the most menial tasks, such as leather working and sweeping. Within this wider framework of the *varnas*, there is a great variation of region-specific subcastes (*jatis*) or endogamous kinship and occupational groups. The interaction between groups and castes is restricted by rules and prohibitions of ritual pollution. The groups also differ in political influence, landholding. and so forth (Adams 2001).

A person's caste position is determined at birth (ascription). Each caste and subcaste specialises in given occupational, social and political activities, which are proscribed for members of other castes. In the caste system, physical labour is a typically low-caste activity, with corresponding low status. Merchants and economic activities also stand relatively low on the social scale.

Though caste has now been rejected as an organising system in modern India, it still is deeply embedded in social life (Lal, 1988).[6] Lal himself denies that the caste system itself is the prime cause of slow economic growth in post-independence India. In his view, the slow rate of growth between 1950 and 1990 (sometimes called the Hindu rate of growth) is primarily due to inappropriate government policies. But the Indian distrust of markets, the heavy tax burden and the high degrees of intervention are all continuations and manifestations of the low status of economic activity in the caste system. While there may be many causes of slow growth, it is clear that discrimination and inefficient allocation of labour are one of the cultural and institutional obstacles to more rapid economic development.

12.5.2   The low status of physical work and effort

In many cultures there are negative attitudes towards physical labour and effort. In African societies, the heaviest physical work in food production is usually left to the women, while men engage in activities with higher status. The negative stereotypes of physical effort have been further reinforced by agricultural extension workers and Western-oriented education, with its emphasis on cognitive and academic performance (Dumont, 1962).

Along with emergence of entrepreneurship, a work ethic involving the ability and willingness to work long, hard and in a disciplined fashion would seem to be one of the ingredients of successful economic performance.[7] The work

[6] To some degree, elements of caste and estate are to be found in all societies, even societies that profess to be completely meritocratic.
[7] We do not claim that a work ethic is a 'cause' of development. For many centuries, an exploited Chinese peasantry has engaged in backbreaking labour in rice production, without much evidence of economic dynamism. But a work ethic does seem to be a developmental resource, which can be tapped when a country starts industrialising.

ethic also makes it possible to subject an originally rural labour force to the disciplines and time-driven schedules of modern factories and organisations.

The work ethos was present in Japan, as well as among Chinese peasant populations. It is less frequently found on the African continent, where cultural attitudes to work tend to be different and where social obligations tend to absorb a large amount of time and energy. It has been suggested that the work ethic is a cultural adaptation to high population densities in Asian rice-producing societies such as China and Japan. Intensive rice production requires enormous efforts on behalf of the peasants to produce sufficient food. On the contrary, sub-Saharan Africa has always had low population density and was able to support its populations at relatively low levels of effort (Boserup, 1981).

An interesting example of differences in work ethic is provided by Malaysia. The indigenous Malay population tends to look down on physical labour as something suitable for Chinese 'coolie' labourers who were imported in the nineteenth century to work in mines and plantations. The Malaysians of Chinese origin have developed not only more entrepreneurial attitudes, but also a strong work ethic. They have been extraordinarily successful in business, manufacturing and economic life, much more so than the indigenous population. The same holds for most economies in Southeast Asia.

12.5.3   Social obligations in African cultures

Many observers have remarked on the importance of social obligations in African cultures, where self-reliance and self-interest are subordinated to ethnicity and group loyalty (e.g. Dia, 1994; Nyang, 1994; Rao, 2001). The value of economic behaviour is measured in terms of its effects on group reinforcement. The extended family is always present and imposes itself on its members in a variety of ways, including ceremonial obligations. Workers in modern African manufacturing enterprises are frequently absent from work for burials, marriage ceremonies and other festivities, which might last for days or even weeks. Excess income of individuals leads to more lavish consumption and a widening of the circle of those benefiting from income redistribution.

From the perspective of individual entrepreneurship, the ability to save and accumulate capital and the successful operation of modern economic organisations, these social obligations may function as major obstacles to economic development and economic success. However, these social network obligations have important economic functions. Festivals and marriages are arenas where reputations are built, networks maintained and status achieved (Rao, 2001). They enhance relative positions in society and build social cohesion and capacity for collective action, which is important for people's survival. The high value attached to leisure reflects the importance of reinforcing social bonds. Rather than calling for an emancipation from social obligations, Dia (1994) argues for the development of new management practices which try to reconcile traditional practices with the requirements of economic efficiency and accumulation. Whether this is really feasible is the question. Perhaps economic efficiency is really inconsistent with such heavy social obligations. But the Chinese example discussed in section 12.4.2 indicates that the use of kinship networks for capital accumulation is not impossible.

12.5.4   Gender discrimination

Inequality between the sexes and discrimination against women is embedded to different degrees in most world religions and cultures. Like caste systems, occupational discrimination by sex is a potential obstacle to the optimal use and allocation of human talents. In a great many societies, women have less access to paid jobs, health services and in particular education. In some of the most orthodox Islamic societies, women are prohibited from engaging in education and paid work outside the house. In several of the preceding chapters, we have shown that improved access to education and the labour market for women has positive impacts on spontaneous fertility decline and improved health of families and children. In addition, in many societies females have potentially important roles in trading and entrepreneurship, but are hampered by inadequate access to capital and support services.

12.5.5   The importance of trust in market relationships

Many observers have remarked that trust is one of the cultural prerequisites for the functioning of modern impersonal market relationships and market exchanges. Trust is an element of culture, which implies that in principle people expect that contracts should and will be fairly observed. If there is no trust, market transactions will simply break down. One has to believe that parties will fulfil their obligations; otherwise every rationally calculating individual has a short-term incentive to default on his own obligations. Thus, relations of trust complement the individual search for advantage via markets.

Where personalistic relations dominate, anonymous market relations will not function well because the basis of trust is lacking. People turn to other mechanisms such as clientelism, nepotism, family ties or corruption to pursue their interests. Trust is a nice example of how cultural elements emerge from experiences with previous interactions and feed back into future interactions. A culture of trust evolves from a history of experiences with successful exchanges, and solidifies into a system of expectations which structures further market relationships. It can also break down when too many individuals exhibit free ridership and opportunistic behaviour. One of the characteristics of the culture of poverty is the complete absence of trust, weak participation in networks and associations and the belief that everybody is out to cheat each other, as documented in the classic study of Banfield (1958).

12.5.6   The mysterious role of ethnic minorities in economic development

One of the famous puzzles of development is the important economic role of ethnic minorities. The Chinese have been extremely successful as entrepreneurs all across East and Southeast Asia, and likewise the Palestinians in the Arab world. Indians and Pakistanis dominate business activities in East Africa. In European history, Jews have played a prominent role in finance, business and also in culture and the intellectual pursuits. The interesting thing about these successful minorities is that they often originated from rather traditional cultures and from societies that had long been economically stagnant. In spite of their economic success or perhaps because of it, all these groups have usually been discriminated against. In the case of the Chinese in Asia and the Asians in Africa, the forefathers of the present inhabitants were imported as contract labourers by the colonial authorities, but later received preferential treatment as middle men in the context of divide-and-rule colonial policies.

Explanations for the extraordinary economic role of ethnic minorities are interesting from the point of view of the role of culture. It is argued that migration frees migrants from the cultural and institutional constraints of the country of origin. Also, it is usually the most dynamic individuals and groups who are willing to migrate in search of new opportunities and to escape the constraints of their own societies. Joseph Schumpeter, who saw the entrepreneur as the key driver of economic development, argued that entrepreneurs are typically marginal people (Schumpeter, 1943). Their very marginality enables them to be innovative and entrepreneurial, terms which for Schumpeter were almost synonymous. In the case of migrants, they are not only freed from the cultural constraints of their country of origin, they are also marginal in their newly chosen country of settlement.

12.5.7   Cultural differences between North and Latin America

Some authors point to cultural differences as contributing factors to the different paths followed by North America and Latin America (e.g. Harrison, 1985; Hartz, 1964; Hoetink, 1984). In the nineteenth century there were many similarities in conditions and levels of economic development between North America and Latin America. Both regions were thinly populated areas, with mass immigration from Europe. Both areas were endowed with mineral riches. In both areas, independence was achieved at an early stage. Both areas had a history of slavery and contract labour. Both areas were predominantly agrarian, dependent on primary exports and imports of manufactures from Europe.

Nevertheless, economic development proceeded rapidly in North America, which had already overtaken Great Britain as technological leader by 1890, while Latin America stagnated and is now seen as part of the developing world.

Hartz and Hoetink have emphasised the cultural differences as one of the factors contributing to the divergences of the two regions.

North America was characterised by an immigrant population of which a large portion originated in the Protestant countries of Northwest Europe with a strong work ethic, an emphasis on effort, discipline and the optimal utilisation of opportunities. Latin America was colonised by Catholic migrants from the Iberian Peninsula. Culturally, it had an aristocratic ethic, with an emphasis on honour, status, bravery and submission to fate. These cultural differences influenced the subsequent economic development of the Americas.

According to the historian Hartz, the cultural differences can be linked to the cultural origins of the dominant colonists. The characteristic ethos of societies such as Australia, Canada, the USA and Latin America can be understood only if we connect this to the mood of their respective mother countries at the time of their founding. Latin America was influenced by the hierarchic and corporative traditions of Iberian Europe, with a tradition of absolute leadership, Machiavellian power politics and a corporate state financed by taxes on land and agriculture. The USA was influenced by the protestant culture of Northwest Europe and its entrepreneurial spirit.

Hartz argued that the transfer of cultural elements by migrants to new worlds resulted in magnification of the cultural traits of the society of origin. The checks and constraints operating in the region of origin were absent in the newly colonised areas. Therefore, it turns out to be vitally important that colonists imported a feudal-type culture from the Iberian Peninsula to Latin America, which did not exist in northwestern Europe, from which the original colonisers of North America originated.

12.5.8   *The Soviet legacy*

All across the countries that made up the former Soviet Union, the legacy of seventy-five years of communism, preceded by a long period of royal absolutism under the Czars, has implanted and frozen anti-entrepreneurial attitudes, which persist after the collapse of the communist regimes (Landes, 2000; Putnam 1994). After 1989, it was hoped that the introduction of market reforms and political liberalisation would usher in a period of rapid growth. For a variety of reasons, including cultural ones, this hope has proved to be false. Standards of living have declined dramatically. People remained oriented towards the state and dynamic private entrepreneurship was not readily available.

12.5.9   *Asian values and the Confucian ethic*

In the course of the twentieth century a number of East and Southeast Asian countries embarked on a remarkable process of development and catch-up. The pioneer was Japan, which commenced its catch-up process in the late nineteenth century. Japan was remarkably successful in acquiring and assimilating modern Western technology, while maintaining vital elements of traditional Japanese culture and social relationships. Among others this resulted in totally new management practices such as quality circles and just-in-time production, which spread from Japan to other parts of the world. Another new element was the close ties between the Ministry of Industry and Trade (MITI) and the large private conglomerates, which were the pillars of Japanese industrialisation.

After World War II, the example of Japan was followed by Korea, Taiwan, Singapore and Hong Kong, followed later by rapid growth and industrialisation in a second generation of countries such as Thailand, Malaysia, Indonesia, China and today Vietnam. In one way or another, these countries have all been influenced by Chinese culture. Taiwan, Singapore and Hong Kong are Chinese societies. Chinese minorities play a vital role in the economic development of Thailand, Malaysia and Indonesia. Japan, Vietnam and Korea have been influenced by Chinese culture and the Confucian tradition for over a thousand years.

Some researchers have started to wonder whether the economic dynamism of the region cannot in some ways be explained by common cultural elements, more in particular by what they refer to as the *Confucian Ethic* (e.g. Dore, 1987; Hofstede, 2001; Hofstede and Bond, 1988). Important Confucian principles include: the notion that stability of society is based on unequal relations between people, characterised by respect and obedience and a sense of mutual obligations. The family is seen as the prototype of social and political organisation. The harmony of family-type relations is seen as vitally important. Individuals learn to subject their individuality to maintain harmonious social relations. The Confucian tradition also emphasises virtuous behaviour, benevolence and acquisition of skills, hard work and moderation.

On the basis of cross-cultural survey research, Hofstede (2001) has identified five basic dimensions of national culture, which contribute to differences in social behaviour. These dimensions are:

1. *power distance*, the extent to which less powerful members of organisations and institutions accept and expect that power is distributed unequally;
2. *uncertainty avoidance*, the extent to which a culture programmes its members to feel uncomfortable or comfortable in unstructured situations;
3. *individualism versus collectivism*, the degree to which individuals are supposed to look after themselves or remain integrated in groups, usually around the family (see also Ball, 2001);
4. *masculinity versus femininity*, the distribution of emotional roles between the sexes. Masculine societies are societies where the values of men and women differ most. In typically masculine societies, males focus on masculine work goals such as money, careers, while females focus on caring, social goals, helping others. In more feminine societies the differences between male and female values were less marked;

5. Long-term versus short-term orientation, also referred to as the dimension of Confucian dynamism.

This fifth dimension was added to the first four on the basis of later survey research in China (Hofstede and Bond, 1988). The long-term orientation is characterised by values such as persistence (perseverance), ordering relationships by status and observing this order, thrift, and having a sense of shame. The opposite pole of short-term orientation characterised by values such as personal steadiness and stability, protecting 'face', respect for tradition and reciprocation of greetings, favours and gifts.

An interesting aspect of the Confucian dimension is that both the positive and negative poles derive from the Confucian tradition. Hofstede recognises this explicitly when he writes: 'The correlation between *certain* Confucian values and economic growth over the past decades is a surprising, even a sensational finding' (Hofstede, 2001, p. 167).[8]

Since 1980, Hofstede's research has generated a vast amount of cross-cultural research on national value systems. This research has contributed to our knowledge and understanding of differences in national cultures and the ways in which they score on different dimensions. It has been less successful in demonstrating causal links between elements of culture and subsequent economic development. The argument is loose and impressionistic. Hofstede has more to say about measuring differences in cultural traits and dimensions than about the systematic relationship between these traits and economic development.

Based on more anecdotal evidence for Korea, Taiwan, Singapore and Hong Kong, Goodell (1995/6) identifies characteristics of the Asian values system, resulting in some paradoxical cultural combinations. In business life, eccentric individualism is combined with strong group bonding. On the one hand there is cut-throat competition and a search for material advance through self-sacrifice. On the other hand there is organisational efficiency based on ritual and a deep respect for traditional authority. Many observers emphasise the importance of personal relationships. In the classical bureaucratic paradigm officials and businessmen must deal with each other impersonally, through standardised procedures. But in Asian societies, personal bonding is extremely important as manifested by lavish partying and getting drunk together.

People develop privatised, personal networks. Capital does not flow through public channels, but through clan-like networks. Similar networks exist between government bureaucrats and private enterprises. There are strong outsider–insider perceptions. One has strong obligations to insiders, while it is permissible to defraud outsiders. Time and again observers point to the mistrust of formal law and a reliance on family networks (Perkins, 2000). Many observers point to the emphasis on hard work and high savings, and a strong

---

8 In an interesting criticism of the Confucian dimension, Fang (2003) argues that Chinese people would find it hard to distinguish the two poles of the dimension. For the Chinese, the values at the two ends of long-term orientation are not contrasting or opposing values, but rather closely interrelated with one another.

achievement drive which are also to be found in the Puritan ethic. The dynamic Asian societies seem to differ in these characteristics from developing countries that are less dynamic.

Much of this interesting literature remains highly speculative. It is still a puzzle as to why Chinese culture has coexisted with economic stagnation in China from the fourteenth century to 1950, suddenly becoming a dynamic force in development in the second half of the twentieth century (Pye, 2000).

One interesting hypothesis is that elements of East Asian culture have been especially conducive to growth in the specific conditions of late industrialisation and catch-up in a globalised economy. This is the position taken by the famous China scholar Dwight Perkins. He argues that the family- and network-based way of doing business has served Asia well for the past three decades, but that its limitations are now becoming more manifest since the Asian crisis of 1997 and the slowdown of economic dynamism in Japan. There is an increasing need for strengthening the rule of law, reaching decisions more impartially, scaling down the conglomerates, reducing the vulnerability of banks and financial institutes, tackling rampant corruption and loosening the ties between government bureaucracies and private enterprise. An even stronger position is taken by Lucian Pye who argues that Confucian values such as unlimited patience, insensitivity to monotony, controlled politeness, and capacity for unlimited hard work are not the qualities which produce capitalism, but they are ideally suited for emulating capitalist and industrial practices in a process of catch-up.

The debate about Asian values and growth serves to illustrate the potentially important links between culture and economic development. It also illustrates the limitations of cultural explanations. The same cultural values operating in different circumstances and institutional and policy environments can have different results and outcomes. Both individualist and collective orientations can be compatible with growth and entrepreneurship (Ball, 2001). Cultures are complex and can have many different contradictory values[9] and in different periods different combinations of these values are selected.

12.6   Civic culture

In an interesting study of the sources of differences in institutional performance in North and South Italian regions, the political scientist Robert Putnam pointed to the importance of civic culture (Putnam, 1993; 1994). Though this study focused on a European country, it has wider implications for our understanding of the role of culture in development.

In 1970, Italy introduced political decentralisation creating twenty regional governments. Putnam found that, in spite of similar political structures, northern regions systematically scored higher on an index of institutional

---

9 For instance, traditional Confucianism scorned hard work and physical exertion.

performance (based on indicators such as cabinet stability, timely presenta-tion of budgets, statistical and information services, quality of legislation, day care centres, family clinics, housing and urban performance, bureaucratic re-sponsiveness, and so forth).

The most important explanatory factor for these differences turned out to be not, as expected, the level of socio-economic development, but socio-cultural factors such as civic engagement, active participation in public affairs, partic-ipation in voluntary associations, political equality, solidarity, trust and tol-erance, and political equality (measured by an index of civic community). To quote Putnam (1994, p. 56):

> Many theorists have associated the civic community with small, close-knit premodern societies, quite unlike our modern world – the civic community is the world we have lost. In its place arise large, modern agglomerations, technologically advanced but dehumanizing, which induce civic passivity and self-seeking individualism. Moder-nity, it is said, is the enemy of civility. Quite the contrary, our studies suggest. The least civic areas of Italy are precisely the traditional southern villages. Life in much of traditional Italy is marked by hierarchy and exploitation, not by share and share alike. The most civic regions of Italy...include some of the most modern towns and cities of the peninsula.

Putnam explains these differences by tracing historical developments since the twelfth century, contrasting feudal monarchies in the South with the commu-nal republics and city-states in the North. One of the most exciting results of the statistical analysis in this study is the strong correlation between indexes of civic traditions in the nineteenth century and those of the late twentieth century. Controlling for civic traditions, economic variables such as levels of economic development do not explain differences in modern institutional per-formance. Even more important: civic traditions seem to explain differences in levels of socio-economic development better than indicators of past socio-economic performance.

Putnam's conclusions are relevant for the study of development in general. Institutional reforms will not work without a civic foundation and these cul-tural foundations take a very long time to develop. Putnam explicitly refers to the disappointing outcomes of institutional reforms in the former Soviet Union as a case in point. As far as policy conclusions can be deduced from this analysis, policies of cultural change should try to promote civic culture and participation, but this inevitably takes a very long time.

12.7 Cultural consequences of and reactions to Western penetration

12.7.1 *Cultural consequences*

As discussed in Chapter 3, one of the shortcomings of post-war modernisation theories is their neglect of the historically important phenomenon of Western colonisation and penetration of the non-Western world. As Western countries have been dominant economic, political and technological actors in the world system during the past four hundred years, our very conceptions of modernity have become entangled with Westernisation.[10]

The Western expansion has disrupted indigenous societies across the globe and has set in motion processes of change, for the better or for the worse. There has never been one single route towards modernity. But different societies have been confronted with a common Western cultural and technological challenge. Their different reactions to this challenge become embedded in their own cultural traditions.

Western penetration proceeded along three lines: traders, missionaries and soldiers. All three routes led to disruptions in existing cultures and societies. In the nineteenth century, an international racist hierarchy emerged with white people as the dominant group and their culture as the dominant culture. In traditional societies, this created identity crises, self-deprecation and negative images of self and society. It also gave rise to deep feelings of ambivalence with regard to Western cultures, Western imperialism and Western dominance. On the one hand, the technologically advanced countries were admired as models of modernity and success. On the other hand, they were rejected as oppressive, foreign and dominating. In the twentieth century, advances in transport technology and the rise of mass communication media increased the exposure of indigenous cultures to Western influences.

In all developing countries, members of the elites started to be educated in Western-oriented education systems. They adopted European languages as their preferred modes of communication and came to see Western societies as more advanced than their own societies. In the process, they became partly alienated from their own societies. The fact that the social mobility of these elites was blocked by the racial discrimination characteristic of colonial societies became an important motivating force for nationalist, anticolonial movements and deep-seated feelings of resentment.

The disruptions set in motion in the nineteenth century accelerated in the twentieth under the influence of continued globalisation, interdependence and mass communications. Traditional communities and cultures are subjected to an accelerated rate of change, in particular affecting the poor. Box 12.3 provides an overview of the changes affecting traditional communities (see Serageldin, 1994, p. 21).

12.7.2   Reactions to Western penetration and cultural disruption

Reactions to Western cultural dominance and to modernisation and economic change in general took a variety of forms, including: traditional opposition

---

10 There is nothing unique about such an entanglement. It has occurred many times in the past. Thus, the Roman empire at its peak served as a model for other civilisations, China was the centre of modernity and civilisation for the countries under its sway, and in medieval times the Arabic–Islam world formed a focus of civilisation and modernity.

> **Box 12.3   Changes affecting traditional communities and cultures**
> - The accelerated rate of change implicit in the development process.
> - Demographic growth, urbanisation, education and marginalisation of traditional economic activities.
> - The breakup of traditional units of community such as village and extended family.
> - The overwhelming impact of Western culture, which is frequently transferred only in the rudimentary form of consumption-oriented behaviour and technology.
> - The impact of mass communications, especially through radio and television.
> - Homogenising efforts at building national identity through mass media, political organisations and the school system, which conflict with geographic, tribal and kinship lines of affiliation.
> - Inadequate adaptation of education and training to the opportunities of employment and the needs of self-employment.
> - Rapid loss of authentic traditional cultural legacies, which are primarily orally transmitted, due to increased mobility and perceived lack of short-term relevance for the young.

movements; messianistic movements; modern nationalist movements; Marxist and social movements; and the revival of political Islam.

Traditionalist opposition movements sought to restore the precolonial status quo. Examples of such revolts were the revolt against the Dutch in Java, led by Prince Diponegoro from 1825 to 1830, or the Indian mutiny of 1857. These movements were frequently led by representatives of the former ruling classes who had been displaced by the colonial rulers.

A second type of reactions consisted of the emergence of *messianistic movements*, cargo cults, and so forth, which sometimes combined elements of Christianity with elements of traditional cultures. Examples of these include the dance mania that swept across North American Indian tribes between 1870 and 1890, the cargo cults of New Guinea and Melanesia (Worsley, 1957) and messianistic movements in Africa. The cargo cults involved beliefs that ancestors would arrive on ships bringing material wealth in the form of Western goods, such as canned salmon. Other examples of reactive protest movements with strong messianic characteristics were the Boxer revolution in China in 1900, and the Tai Ping revolt based on Nanjing from 1850 to 1864, which may have claimed as many as 25 million casualties.

A third and crucial type of reaction consists of the *modern nationalist movements*, which drew on Western humanitarian values and ideals such as equality, democracy and human rights as intellectual sources for the rejection of colonial oppression and imperialist practices. These nationalist movements played a crucial role in the struggle for independence in most of the former colonies. The Meiji reformation in Japan in 1868 can also be interpreted as a nationalist response to Western challenges (Barrington Moore, 1966). The Meiji regime not only drew upon Western science and technology to radically modernise Japanese society but it also showed itself eager to copy Western imperialist practices, creating an empire of its own in East Asia between 1894 and 1946.

A fourth and related type of reaction consists of *Marxist and Socialist movements*, which emerged in parallel with the nationalist movements. These movements had a powerful appeal for elites in developing countries after 1945 and many countries embarked on socialist experiments. Like nationalism, the intellectual sources for these movements were found in a Western ideology, Marxism, which was adapted to local circumstances, especially by Mao Zedong.[11] An interesting element of many ideological movements which emerged in response to the Western penetration was an attempt to synthesise Western socialist ideologies with presumed communal practices derived from traditional (village) societies and cultures. Examples of this are the Indian Socialism of Nehru, the African Socialism of Leopold Senghor, the Ujamaa programme of Julius Nyerere, and Burmese Socialism.

Both Marxism and Nationalism have now run out of steam. In China, Marxist rulers are engaging in capitalist experiments on a vast scale. Former socialist countries such as India and Tanzania are liberalising their economies. Communism has collapsed in the former Soviet Union and, with few exceptions, no longer serves as a source of inspiration for movements in developing countries. Nationalist regimes in North African and Middle Eastern countries such as Egypt, Jordan, Syria, Algeria or former Iraq have degenerated into autocracies, which have not been able to deliver on their promises of development and have lost all legitimacy in the eyes of their populations.

Though one should beware of overgeneralisation, it would seem that the rise of political Islam in the last quarter of the twentieth century fills the oppositional vacuum left by the collapse of communism and nationalism. Islamic movements, whether in power or in opposition, present a radical alternative to and rejection of Western cultural, technological, military and economic dominance in the present-day world economy. This is evident in societies such as Egypt or Algeria, which have so far not been able to realise catch-up and major improvements in their standards of living, but also in Iran, where modernisation and economic development under the autocratic rule of the Shah gave birth to a radical Islamist reaction under Ayatollah Khomeiny. However, it is interesting to note that political Islam itself also involves ambivalence towards elements of Western culture and modern technological advance. With the possible exception of the former Taliban regime in Afghanistan, Islamic regimes and movements strive for economic development, technological advance, improved health-care systems and military progress including access to nuclear technology. All of these involve intense interactions with Western systems of knowledge.[12] In the economic sphere, Islamic countries are attempting to devise new institutions, which are compatible with the world of modern economics and finance and at the same time respect religious injunctions against interest. Thus, in *Islamic banking* Lewis and Algaoud (2001) explain how

---

11 The forcible removal and subsequent mass starvation of Cambodians from the cities to the countryside under the Khmer Rouge in Cambodia between 1975 and 1978 was inspired by a doctoral thesis on rural development defended in Paris in 1950 by one of the Khmer Rouge leaders, Khieu Samphan.
12 Some of the ambivalences of the Islamic world are well documented by the novelist V.S. Naipaul in *Among the Believers* (1982).

new systems of profit (and loss) sharing by banks and depositors replace the payment of interest on loans and deposits.

12.8   Interactions between culture, technology and economics at micro-level

A different strand of analysis focuses on the role of culture at micro-level. Here the emphasis is on understanding the cultural constraints within which development projects or economic projects have to function. Technology does have cultural implications, and when introducing new technologies one needs to take cultural values of a specific society into account. Many development projects have failed because the cultural environment was not conducive to success (Salim, 1994).

Kottak (1986) presents an interesting metaphor derived from evolutionary biology. The legs of amphibious animals have evolved from fins of fish. The evolutionary value of legs initially lay not in escaping water to walk on land, but rather to be able to search for pools of water when water levels declined. In the same way, poor peasants will not voluntarily cooperate in projects which involve radical changes in the way they pursue their daily lives. The risks of innovation are too high for persons trying to survive close to subsistence levels. The chances of project success are greatest if a new project can guarantee peasants that they will produce at least as much as at present. Changes are oriented to avoiding deterioriation of their economic positions.

Kottak concludes that over-innovation should be rejected. Innovations and projects should be embedded in and consistent with local cultures, institutions and practices (Kottak 1991). Thus irrigation projects that build upon systems that have been developed locally have greater chances of success. A second example consists of land reforms, which allow small farmers to farm the same amounts of land as before, but with higher output. A well-known example of an institutional innovation that fitted in well with local culture was the successful Grameen bank in Bangladesh. The Grameen bank provided micro-credit to the poor in rural areas. The bank was financed from deposits by local depositors. The responsibility for repayment was placed in the hands of local networks and groups, In general cooperative movements and projects have greater chances of success if they are embedded in existing local institutions.

An example of over-innovation is the forced resettlement of nomadic pastoralists in Tanzania in villages, in the context of the Ujamaa village-isation programme. The failure of this programme had major negative effects on agricultural development in Tanzania. A second example of over-innovation was the introduction of potentially valuable cash crops such as pepper in South Asia. The project failed because the harvest period of the new crops coincided with that of the major food crop, rice.

On the basis of such theories, some anthropologists (e.g. Cochrane, 1979; Schönhut, 1991) argue for systematic cultural mapping preceding the design of development projects. They see cultural mapping as a precondition for the choice of appropriate technologies, projects and institutions.

Several of the authors contributing to a major World Bank conference on Culture and Development (Serageldin and Taboroff, 1994) emphasise both the urgency of the need for cultural change in Africa and the fact that cultural changes have to take indigenous culture as the point of departure. As agricultural innovation has to take into account local soils and conditions, cultural change has to take existing preferences and cultures into account. If this is not done, there is the danger of a total breakdown of the social fabric.

Development as creative destruction

It is one thing to say that it is important to take culture into account in projects and policies. It is a different thing to show how this can be done successfully. In a provocative article, Klitgaard (1994) argues that the anthropologists and social scientists have done better at showing that culture is important than showing how understanding of culture can lead to improved projects and policies. He writes: 'the legacy of sociology and anthropology in this century might be described as the promise of application in search of a how' (p. 85). According to Klitgaard, cultural mapping and cultural checklists have not helped to make development projects more successful. There is no relationship between costly social soundness analysis and eventual project success. In virtually every case where claims have been made for social soundness analysis, the project's success can be explained in economic terms. Rather than focus on projects, cultural studies should focus on knowledge of culture that can be incorporated in policy making and management practices, and also in policy making oriented towards cultural change.

The anthropological literature on culture and development is saturated with a romantic longing to maintain traditional cultures in the face of economic and technological change. However, as Schumpeter has so convincingly written, throughout history economic development has always been a matter of creative destruction. Old practices and handicrafts are destroyed and are replaced by radically new ones. It may be an illusion to think that one can profit from the fruits of economic development without experiencing creative destruction, including the wrenching experience of cultural change. As early as 1967, Albert Hirschman, one of the founding fathers of development economics, made a distinction between *trait-taking* and *trait-making* in development projects (Hirschman, 1967). Trait-taking takes existing cultures and conditions as given and tries to adapt projects and policies to these existing conditions, thereby accepting a built-in conservatism. Trait-making involves confronting and changing existing cultural traits in a process of creative destruction. Cultural checklists may help provoke thought, but do not help in the trade-off between trait-taking and trait-making (Klitgaard, 1994).

What this chapter has hopefully made clearer is that in different societies and settings there do exist cultural and institutional barriers to economic development and socio-economic dynamics. It is important to increase our knowledge and understanding of culture and cultural backgrounds in different settings, regions and countries. But it is not enough to draw up lists of cultural traits which have to be taken into account or deferred to. We need a more analytic approach, which shows us how cultural elements interact with incentive structures, opportunities, policies and institutions to produce development or stagnation and help us identify those elements which obstruct desired changes.

Questions for review

1. Discuss theories about the role of religion in economic development. What are some of the main criticisms levelled against these theories?
2. What role do cultural factors play in explanations of the divergent developments in North America and Latin America? How important do you think cultural factors are in comparison with other determinants of economic development?
3. Discuss the different types of political movements which evolved in response to the Western colonisation of developing countries.
4. Discuss four of the often-mentioned differences between so-called traditional and so-called modern societies.
5. Provide an analysis of the extent to which traditional cultural elements form an obstacle to economic development.
6. Discuss the role of ethnic minorities in economic development.
7. Provide a critical discussion of the concept of efficient institutions. Give examples of efficient and inefficient institutions.

Further reading

The following three collections of articles provide a good introduction to the topic of culture and development. They are: *Culture and Development: International Perspectives*, edited by Clague and Grossbard-Shechtman (2001), *Culture Matters: How Values Shape Human Progress* edited by Harrison and Huntington (2000), and *Culture and Development in Africa*, edited by Serageldin and Taboroff (1994). Recent books from the perspective of economic anthropology include: Plattner (ed.), *Economic Anthropology* (1989); Wilk, *Economies and Cultures: Foundations of Economic Anthropology* (1996); and Evers and Schraders (eds.), *The Moral Economy of Trade: Ethnicity and Developing Markets* (1994).

For comparative empirical research on dimensions of culture, the work of Geert Hofstede is of importance. Here we mention Hofstede, *Culture's Consequences: Comparing Values, Behaviors, Institutions and Organizations Across Nations* (2001; first edition 1980), Hofstede, *Cultures and Organisations: Software of the Mind* (1991) and an article in *Organization Dynamics* by Hofstede and Bond, 'The Confucius Connection: From Cultural Roots to Economic Growth' (1988).

The starting point for the debate on the role of religion in economic development is Max Weber's 1905 article, 'Die Protestantische Ethik und der Geist des Kapitalismus' (1969). It is still worth reading. Another classic study is Clifford Geertz's thoughtful analysis of the complexities of modernisation in *Peddlers and Princes: Social Change and Economic Modernization in Two Indonesian Towns* (1963). Two articles criticising simple contrasts between traditional and modern cultures are Kuper, 'African Culture and African Development' (1984) and Shweder, 'Moral Maps, "First World" Conceits and the New Evangelists' (2000).

Edward Banfield has analysed the absence of trust in traditional societies in another key publication, *The Moral Basis of a Backward Society* (1958). The political scientist Roger Putnam has highlighted the importance of an active civil society for socio-economic development in a comparative study of Italian regions. This study has considerable relevance for the wider analysis of the role of culture in development. Publications about this topic include: Putnam (with Leonardi and Nanetti), *Making Democracy Work: Civic Traditions in Modern Italy* (1993) and Putnam, 'Democracy, Development and the Civic Community. Evidence from an Italian Experiment' (1994). For an analysis of the economic functions of the caste system in India, we recommend Deepak Lal's study, *The Hindu Equilibrium*, Vol. I: *Cultural Stability and Economic Stagnation: India, c. 1500 BC–AD, 1980* (1988).

The cultural anthropologist Kottak has argued for cultural mapping of development projects in 'Dimensions of Culture in Development' (1986) and 'When People Don't Come First: Some Sociological Lessons from Completed Projects' (1991). The cultural mapping approach has been criticised by Klitgaard in 'Taking Culture into Account: From "Let's" to "How"' (1994).

13 The international economic and political order since 1945

Chapter 2 introduced the concept of an international economic order. International economic orders are characterised by typical patterns of flows of goods and services, financial capital, people and knowledge. Other characteristics include the intensity of relationships between economies and the institutional structure of these relationships. In this chapter, we discuss developments in the international order and their significance for developing countries since 1945. In addition to the economic aspects of the post-war international economic order, we deal extensively with political and institutional aspects such as the international balance of power, the role of international organisations such as the United Nations, the World Bank and the IMF, and important international conventions and treaties.

This chapter identifies four stages in the development of international economic relationships. These stages are characterised by typical patterns of regional and global growth and by dominant policy orientations. Each period ends with a major system shock, which affects not only patterns of economic development, but also theoretical and practical thinking about economic policies and development strategies. The periods are: the period of liberalisation of world trade (1944–73), the rise and eclipse of the policy goal of a New International Economic Order (1960–82), the period of debt crisis and structural adjustment (1982–97) and the period since 1997, which is characterised by a revival of the intellectual debates on globalisation and liberalisation. The three major system shocks are the oil crisis of 1973, the debt crisis of 1982 and the Asian crisis of 1997, each of which affected growth trajectories and resulted in a fundamental rethinking of development strategies.

The chapter is structured as follows. Important economic and political characteristics of post-war international order are discussed in section 13.1. A chronological outline of the development of important international organisations and institutions is given in section 13.2. The second half of the chapter provides an analytic discussion of the evolution of the international order. Section 13.3 summarises the early criticisms of the liberal economic order and the debates on a New International Economic Order. The debt crisis and its consequences are discussed in section 13.4. This section contains empirical data on debt and international financial flows. Section 13.5 focuses on structural adjustment. Section 13.6 discusses the renewed debate of the advantages and disadvantages of globalisation in the wake of the Asian crisis.

13.1   Characteristics of international relations since 1945

13.1.1   Economic aspects

Important characteristics of the international economic order since 1945 are summarised in Box 13.1 (Bhagwati, 1988; Dicken, 2003; Grassman and Lundberg, 1981; Krueger, 1990; Maddison, 1985; Maddison, 1989).

Box 13.1   Characteristics of the post-war economic order
- Rapid growth of the volume of international trade.
- Breaking the mould of the colonial pattern of international trade: the emergence of industrial exports from developing countries.
- A modest share of developing countries in international trade.
- Financial flows from the developed countries to developing countries.
- Liberalisation of international trade.
- Liberalisation of capital flows; increase in the volume of capital flows.
- The emergence of global production chains and the increased importance of intra-firm trade.
- Acceleration of growth of per capita national income in both rich and poor countries in the period 1950–73, followed by divergent growth trends.
- Increased financial instability, especially from the 1990s onwards.

Rapid growth of international trade

Between 1950 and 1973 the volume of international trade increased very rapidly (Bhagwati, 1988; Maddison, 1989). This increase went hand in hand with the liberalisation of international trade and substantial reductions in restrictions for industrial exports to the advanced capitalist economies. In developing countries, which were building up their industrial sectors, industrial protectionism remained the rule.

With respect to agriculture, the advanced economies continued to follow highly protectionist policies. Expensive agrarian production by domestic farmers was protected against foreign competition; agricultural exports were massively subsidised. Since the mid-1970s, there has been some revival of industrial protectionism in the advanced economies, particularly through non-tariff restrictions on imports. However, there is no question of a return to the protectionism of the pre-war period.

The period of rapid growth of international trade and per capita incomes between 1950 and 1973 came to an end with the first oil crisis in 1973. After 1973, the growth of world trade slowed down (Table 13.1). A second dramatic hike in oil prices in 1979 contributed to the retardation of the growth of the world economy and world trade, along with the negative effects of the debt crisis of 1982. After 1985, the world export growth picked up again, accelerating towards the end of the 1990s, in spite of the negative effects of the Asian crisis of 1997. Taking the post-war period as a whole, the growth of trade exceeds the growth of production, pointing to increasing interdependence in the world economy.

Table 13.1 *Growth rate of world exports (%)*

1720–1820	0.9
1820–70	4.2
1870–1913	3.4
1913–1950	0.9
1950–73	7.9
1973–85	*3.6*
1985–96	*6.6*
1996–2000	*7.0*
1973–2000	5.3

Sources: 1720–1820: Maddison (1982), p. 254. 1820–70, Maddison (1995), p. 74; 1870–1973: Maddison (2001), p. 362; 1973–2000: IMF (2001); 2000: UNCTAD (2002).

Breaking the mould of the colonial division of labour

The colonial pattern of international trade established between 1870 and 1913 involved a clear-cut international division of labour. Developing countries exclusively exported primary products and economically advanced countries exported manufactured products. In the post-war period, the share of industrial products in the total exports of developing countries increased strongly, as indicated in Tables 3.5 and 9.3 in this book. Some developing countries, particularly in Asia, were successful in penetrating European and US markets for industrial products and became major industrial exporters (OECD, 1979; ch. 9; UNCTAD 2000; UNIDO, 2002). This involved a major restructuring of the pattern of international production and trade. On the other hand, this trend is still primarily restricted to about twelve major developing countries. In the poorest developing countries, in Sub-Saharan Africa and elsewhere, the share of primary exports in total exports still remains high.

A modest share of developing countries in international trade

In spite of the rapid growth of exports, the share of developing countries in world trade still remains quite modest. The expansion of international trade till 1973 was mainly accounted for by the advanced industrial countries (Bhagwati, 1988; Thoburn, 1977). In 1966, the share of these countries in total world exports was no less than 71 per cent. The share of the poorest countries in international trade was low and declined even further between 1960 and 1977 (Lewis, 1978; Streeten, 1984). After 1973, developing country shares started picking up. Between 1973 and 1986, the exports of Latin American and Asian developing countries increased faster than those of OECD countries (Bhagwati, 1988; Maddison, 1989; World Bank, 1987).

From the 1970s onwards, the aggregate share of developing countries in world merchandise exports recovered to almost 30 per cent. This increase was mainly driven by the export performance of the East Asian countries.[1] The secular decline of the share of African developing countries continued. In the 1950s, the share of African countries in world commodity exports stood at 5 per cent. By 1998, it had declined to no more than 2 per cent. Latin America's shares in world exports also halved between 1950 and 1998. It is interesting to note that the increase in the aggregate share of developing countries since the mid-1970s is in part due to increased trade amongst developing countries themselves. The shares of developing countries in total exports are lower than for commodity exports, as the advanced economies dominate the trade in services.

Financial flows from rich to poor countries

In a reversal of earlier patterns between 1913 and 1950, there was a substantial net inflow of capital to developing countries, between 1950 and 1982 (see Chapter 3, Table 3.6). This meant that developing countries could afford to import more than they exported. Financial inflows can contribute to the expansion of the productive potential, especially if these resources are used for productive investments in infrastructure and capital goods, or imports of intermediate goods. However, the use of net capital inflows for consumptive purposes or defence expenditures is less conducive to future growth. The pattern of net capital inflows was temporarily interrupted after 1982 – as will be shown later

---

1 UNCTAD, Back to Basics: Market Access Issues in the Doha Agenda, United Nations, E.03.II.D.4, New York and Geneva, http://www.unctad.org/

on in this chapter. In the years following the debt crisis of 1982, there was a net outflow of financial resources from poor to rich countries, especially from Latin America. In the 1990s, net inflows resumed, till the outbreak of the Asian crisis of 1997. After 1997, several large Asian countries suffered from very serious outflows of resources.

In aggregate terms, there is a dramatic shift from loans to foreign direct investment. In 1970 net transfers on long-term debt were three times as high as net FDI flows. In 2001, substantial negative transfers on long-term debt are more than compensated for by net inflows of foreign direct investment (see Table 13.3).

Liberalisation of international trade and capital flows

The post-war economic order was characterised by a high degree of freedom in the trade of goods and services, and in movements of capital. In successive trade rounds, barriers to the free movement of goods and services were progressively reduced, with the notable exception of agriculture. Initially, less priority was given to full liberalisation of capital flows. In the 1990s, capital flows were also liberalised, leading to increased mobility of capital. Most of the financial flows are flows between the advanced economies rather than between advanced economies and developing countries. The increased mobility of capital manifested itself in increases in long-term capital flows and foreign direct investment, but also in more volatile short-term flows, including portfolio investment, short-term loans and currency speculation. According to Tobin (2000), the value of foreign exchange transactions per business day amounts to 1.5 trillion dollars. Nine-tenths of these transactions are reversed within a week, 40 per cent within a day. Compared to goods, services and capital, there have been continued attempts to restrict the mobility of labour and people. In spite of these restrictions, there have been substantial increases of immigration from developing countries in Africa, the Middle East, Asia and Latin America to the advanced economies.

The emergence of global production chains

The international order of 1870–1913 was characterised by increased trade in final goods and services. An interesting characteristic of the post-war economic order is the greatly increased importance of intra-firm trade and the emergence of global production chains. The increasing volume of foreign direct investment is dominated by large transnational companies. Some 60,000 TNCs dominate some 500,000–700,000 foreign affiliates (Dicken, 2003; UNCTAD, 2000). Production processes become fragmented, with different parts of the production process located in different regions including developing countries, depending on the availability of factors of production, national resources, investment climate and the proximity of markets (Dunning, 1988; Helleiner 1989). A substantial part of international trade takes place within the global production chains and within the transnational companies. The intensity of global interdependence increases due to functional integration.

Per capita national income trends in rich and poor countries

Between 1950 and 1973, national income and income per head increased rapidly in both rich and poor countries. Per capita income in the richer countries increased faster than in poorer countries, so that international disparities increased. Between 1973 and 1982 the growth of per capita incomes decelerated, particularly in the economically advanced countries which pursued contractionary economic policies after the oil crisis. In Asia and Latin America, economic growth continued. In Sub-Saharan Africa it stagnated. If oil-rich Nigeria is left out of consideration, average per capita income in Africa declined in this period (Toye, 1993).

After 1982, growth trends in different parts of the world diverged (see Table 3.2). In the advanced economies there was a modest economic recovery, although the growth rates of per capita income remained lower than before 1973. Several large Asian economies experienced extremely rapid economic growth (World Bank, 1993). Latin America experienced economic stagnation in the aftermath of the debt crisis. In countries such as Argentina and Venezuela per capita incomes decreased on average by 2.5 per cent per year between 1980 and 1989. In Brazil real per capita income was the same at the end of the period as at the beginning (Hofman, 1993). Sub-Saharan Africa experienced long-term stagnation (World Bank, 1989). On average per capita income here decreased by 1.6 per cent per year (Elbadawi *et al.*, 1992, p. 35). For Africa and Latin America the 1980s are often seen as a 'lost decade'.

In the 1990s, Asian growth continued to be very rapid, especially in China and the East and Southeast Asian NICs, but also in India. Growth in the USA and the European countries also recovered, though it did not reach the peak rates of the golden age. There was some recovery in Latin America, but it was shaky and interspersed with recurrent crises. Stagnation in Africa continued, though some African countries bottomed out in the mid-1990s. After the collapse of communism in 1989, many of the former Soviet republics experienced deep economic stagnation with output and standards of living plummeting. Only a few of the former communist countries in 2000 had GDP levels exceeding those of a decade earlier, including Hungary, Poland, Slovakia and Slovenia. In 2000, Russia's GDP was two-thirds of that in 1989. In Moldova it was approximately one third, in the Ukraine 43 per cent (Maddison, 2003; Stiglitz, 2002).

In 1997, the Asian growth path was rudely interrupted by the financial crisis of that year. The crisis deeply affected Thailand, the Philippines, South Korea, Indonesia and Malaysia, which till then had been doing extremely well. Exchange rates collapsed, exposing weaknesses in the banking system and bankrupting many firms whose debts were denominated in dollars. There was massive capital flight and production contracted at alarming rates, calling into doubt the wisdom of liberalising capital markets and short-term capital flows (Stiglitz, 2002). The worst hit was Indonesia, where real output contracted by 13 per cent in one year. Most of the countries recovered fairly quickly, with the notable exception of Indonesia where political instability inhibited sustained recovery (Hill, 1999). The larger Asian countries such as India and China, with more closed capital accounts, were less affected by the crisis and continued their rapid growth. On the whole, the Asian region outperformed the Western countries in the 1990s, providing an example of global catch-up.

Growing financial instability

Since 1982, the international order has been characterised by increased vulnerability to major financial crises. In 1982, a debt crisis was triggered by the decision of Mexico to defer payment of its debt service. The debt crisis ushered in a decade of stagnation in Latin America and put the stability of the international financial system in question. Since 1994, there has been a series of major financial crises in developing countries, which have deeply affected their growth and development patterns. In 1994, Mexico had to turn to the IMF for massive balance-of-payments support, owing to capital flight and the collapse of the peso. The Asian crisis erupted in 1997. In 1998, the financial crisis spread to Russia and Brazil, in 2000 to Turkey. In 2001 and 2002, a financial crisis all but destroyed the Argentine economy, while Brazil experienced further financial turmoil in 2001/2. In short, the international order seems to be characterised by increasing financial instability (Adelman, 2000; Citrin and Fischer, 2000; Fischer, 2003; Soros, 2002; Stiglitz, 2000; 2002; Tobin, 2000).

13.1.2 Political aspects

Decolonisation

From a political point of view, decolonisation was one of the main characteristics of the period since World War II (Emmer, 1992; Grimal, 1978; Morris-Jones and Fischer, 1980). Between 1945 and 1976, the Asian and African colonies of Great Britain, Belgium, the Netherlands, France and Portugal achieved their independence. In the Middle East, decolonisation mainly took place in the interwar period. Before 1919, regions like Syria, Lebanon, Iraq, Palestine, Kuwait and Jordan had been part of the Ottoman empire. After World War I, they were ruled as mandates by Great Britain and France in the name of the League of Nations (e.g. Lebanon, Syria). Between 1930 and 1947, these mandate territories were granted independence: Iraq in 1930; Syria and Lebanon in 1946; Jordan and Israel in 1947.

The decolonisation of Asia took place between 1947 and 1957. India and Pakistan became independent in 1947, Burma in 1948 and Malaysia in 1957. Ho Chi Minh proclaimed the independence of Vietnam in 1945, in the wake of the departure of the Japanese. France, however, was loath to relinquish its colonial authority to a communist-oriented nationalist movement. It waged war against the Viet Minh until it was decisively defeated at Dien Bien Phu in 1954. In 1954, Vietnam was partitioned into North and South Vietnam and the question of unification was deferred to the future. The French colonies of Laos and Cambodia also became independent in 1954. In South Vietnam, after 1954, an anticommunist government was strongly supported by the United

States. The United States waged a full-scale but unsuccessful war to prevent a communist takeover of South Vietnam. The US withdrew from Vietnam after the Paris peace agreements of 1973. In 1976, North and South Vietnam were reunited under a communist regime.

On the African continent, decolonisation commenced with the independence of Ghana in 1957. Between 1957 and 1980, all African colonies, with the exception of the South African mandate area of Namibia, became independent, sometimes after bloody conflicts. The Portuguese colonies were among the last to gain their independence. The independence of Mozambique, Guinea-Bissau and Angola was not recognised until 1976. Namibia became independent in 1990.

Rhodesia (former Southern Rhodesia) is a special case. Here white settlers unilaterally proclaimed their independence in 1965, in order to prevent power from passing to representatives of the black majority. In 1980, internal resistance and external pressure resulted in a transfer of power to a government under the leadership of Robert Mugabe and the declaration of the independence of the republic of Zimbabwe.

South Africa gained its *de facto* independence from Great Britain in 1931, but was ruled by representatives of the white minority till 1994. Racial oppression was formalised in the apartheid-regime erected from the 1960s onwards. Apartheid was abolished in the early 1990s in a series of negotiations between President Botha and the African National Congress and its charismatic president, Nelson Mandela. After elections in April 1994, Mandela was inaugurated as the first black president of a multiracial South Africa on 10 May 1994.

Many processes of decolonisation involved bitter struggles. These were often the consequence of the presence of large numbers of European settlers who fiercely resisted independence. Such was the case, for example, in Algeria, Mozambique, Angola, Rhodesia, Kenya and South Africa. A second reason for wars of decolonisation was when the former colonial powers were unable to transfer power to their preferred political successors. This was the case in Vietnam, Malacca and the Dutch East Indies (Emmer, 1992).

Some million people of European descent had settled in French Algeria. These settlers, initially together with the French government, opposed the independence movement FLN in a bloody war between 1954 and 1962. Over 800,000 Europeans had settled in the Portuguese colonies in Africa. They strove to maintain political ties with Portugal. In general, the decolonisation of the British colonies in Africa involved less bloodshed than that of the colonies of other countries. Amongst the British colonies, Kenya was the exception. Between 1952 and 1955 there was violent resistance to British rule on the part of the Mau-Mau movement, in the course of which the British interned 50,000 Kikuyus in detention camps (Grimal, 1978). British policy was aimed not so much at preventing the independence of Kenya, but rather at safeguarding the privileges of the European settlers.

In Vietnam, the French and later the Americans resisted the transfer of power to the communist-oriented nationalist movement, Viet Minh. In Burma and Malacca the British government also resisted independence movements, for fear of the establishment of communist regimes. In Malacca independence was not granted until 1957, after the threat of communism had subsided. Sukarno proclaimed the independence of the Dutch East Indies on 17 August 1945, on the eve of Japanese capitulation. The Dutch wars against Indonesian independence were partly inspired by the wish to restore pre-war colonial relations, but also in part by differences of opinion with regard to the political constitution of the future independent state (a federalist solution preferred by the Dutch versus the strong unified state claimed by the leaders of the independence movement). Indonesian military resistance and growing international pressure, especially by the United States, finally resulted in Dutch recognition of the independence of Indonesia in 1949.

According to Emmer (1992), decolonisation is generally the result of three factors: increasing resistance to foreign rule within the colonies; decreasing willingness to rule colonies in the home countries; and increasing international pressure. In the period immediately following World War II, not only the Soviet Union but also the United States actively supported the process of decolonisation. Later, however, fear of the emergence of communist regimes in the newly independent states came to play a significant role in US foreign policy. The United States shifted to a more colonial stance, as in the case of the Vietnam War. The delayed decolonisation of the Portuguese colonies in Africa was explained by not only the dictatorship of Salazar in Portugal, but also US fears of an expansion of the communist sphere of influence in Africa.

Initially, in the years after World War II, it was assumed that colonial rule was one of the main sources of economic and social underdevelopment. It was widely hoped and expected that decolonisation would lead to rapid economic development (Franck and Munangsangu, 1982; Meier, 1984). When this did not materialise quickly, some observers blamed this on neocolonial relations of economic dependence. Disappointing economic outcomes also led to a call for a new and more just international economic order.

In the 1980s the climate of opinion changed. The quality of domestic economic policies in developing countries received more emphasis. This shift of opinion has been influenced by the remarkable differences in economic performance between developing countries in different parts of the world.

Interdependence and the emergence of international institutions

Another important characteristic of international relationships in the post-war period is the great increase in the number of international intergovernmental organisations and international treaties. In 1939 there were 80 international organisations, in 1990 there were 293 (Baehr, 1992). For 1999/2000, the *Yearbook of International Organizations* lists more than 5,000 international intergovernmental organisations (UIA, 2003/4).

National states found international organisations to pursue common objectives and to improve international coordination. With the exception of the European Union, most of these organisations are not supranational. The participating states retain their sovereignty. The coordinating potential of international organisations is limited because of the absence of binding regulatory powers. Their effective functioning depends on the voluntary cooperation of sovereign states, in particular economically, politically and militarily powerful ones.

From an analytical point of view, an important characteristic of the international order is the combination of increasing interdependence of people, societies and states on the one hand and a poorly developed capability for international political coordination on the other (Streeten, 1984). International trade has increased strongly. The economies of poor countries have become highly dependent on those of the rich countries. The disappearance of rainforests, global warming due to the emission of CO_2 gases, damage to the ozone layer by CFCs, radiation risks associated with nuclear power stations and nuclear wastes all indicate that the ecological consequences of economic activities have now become global. As a result of improved transport, international mobility is increasing strongly. As a result of improved communications, the dissemination of new ideas and technologies proceeds more rapidly and cultures are ever more subject to influences from other cultures.

Given this increased interdependence, the capability of international institutions to fulfil a coordinating and regulating role has lagged behind. The creation of a patchwork of international organisations, international institutions and treaties may be regarded as an – incomplete – first step in the direction of international coordination.

One can make a comparison with the formation of national states, as analysed in Chapter 11. In processes of state formation, political power is centralised by means of internal consolidation or external penetration. Centralisation results in a monopoly of the means of violence and, in due time, in some measure of democratisation of the control over the state apparatus. There is a process of standardisation in which a national legal system replaces a diversity of local customs and regulations. Laws and regulations are enforced by the state through its monopoly of violence. The state finances its expenditures through its monopoly on taxation.

In a world order consisting of competing nation states there is no comparable process of international centralisation and pacification. Perhaps the *Pax Britannica* of the nineteenth century came closest to some kind of international centralisation. At that time British economic, military, technical and cultural hegemony in the world resulted in a long period of relative international and national pacification.

The United States has been the dominant power of the period since World War II, but has so far not achieved a degree of pacification similar to that of the *Pax Britannica*. First, until 1991 the Soviet Union was a major rival centre of power. The period 1945–91 is characterised by the rise and subsequent decline of the Soviet power bloc and the Soviet sphere of influence, by tensions between rich countries in the northern hemisphere and poor countries in the southern hemisphere, and by tensions between poor countries themselves. Only the direct conflicts between East and West were more or less pacified as a result of the threat of mutual nuclear destruction.

Secondly, decolonisation led to a proliferation of independent states in a non-pacified world. Wars mainly occurred in developing countries. Between 1945 and 1976 there have been no less than 104 wars. From 1945 till 2003, there have been more than 29 million casualties in wars and internal conflicts (see Chapter 11). Prior to 1991, most of the international conflicts had an East–West dimension. The superpowers fought wars by proxy within and between developing countries.

Besides the East–West dimension, a factor of importance in post-war international political relations was the emergence and subsequent decline of the group of non-aligned developing countries as a coherent political force. The movement of non-aligned countries was founded at the Bandung conference of 1955. This movement received a new impetus when China joined it after its rift with the Soviet Union in 1960. After 1966, this movement organised itself in the international arena as the 'Group of 77'. The formation of this bloc was stimulated by the initial success of the cartel of oil-producing countries in 1973.

Since the 1970s, however, the bloc of developing countries has broken up again into a diversity of groups with differing interests (van Dam, 1984). These include oil-exporting countries, oil-importing countries, newly industrialised countries or regional blocs like the ASEAN, the organisation of American States (OAS), the Latin American Free Trade Association (LAFTA) and the ACP countries associated with the European Union through the Lomé agreements. The political relevance of developing countries as a united bloc declined substantially in the 1980s and 90s. The joint position taken by China, Brazil and India in 2003 in the trade negations of the Doha round at Cancun perhaps marks a reversal of this trend, but it is still too early to say.

After the disintegration of the Soviet Union in 1991, the USA is the only remaining superpower. Quantitative estimates by Marshall and Gurr (2003), discussed in Chapter 11, suggest that the level of global armed conflict has indeed declined substantially from a peak level attained in 1985. Nevertheless, at least for the time being, this has not resulted in a pacified international order. The nature of conflicts has changed. In addition to ethnic violence, civil wars and interstate wars, new forms of warfare involving non-state groups and terrorist actions have become more prominent, as witnessed by the dramatic terrorist attacks on the World Trade Centre in New York on 11 September 2001. These conflicts are sometimes referred to as asymmetric warfare, to indicate the immense difference between the means of violence at the disposal of states, and the use of instruments of terror and suicide attacks against civilians by non-governmental networks.

Despite the lack of an international monopoly of violence, the post-war period has seen several initiatives towards the creation of an international political and legal order. The most recent step in this direction is the setting up of the International Criminal Court (ICC) in The Hague in July 2002. Per November 2003, there were 139 signatories to the Rome Statute setting up the Court. But such initiatives have been hard to sustain, precisely because there is no centralised monopoly of violence and there are no independent sources of finance for international institutions. The international legal order depends almost entirely on voluntary agreements between sovereign states. They may negotiate international treaties and agree to implement them with the help of the organs of the national state. For example, a European agreement to reduce overfishing is implemented by national governments with respect to their own fishermen. In the case of the ICC, the most powerful nation, the USA, has refused to ratify the agreement and is claiming exemption from its clauses.

Apart from concluding international treaties and conventions, states may also found international organisations and institutions. In some cases they may voluntarily transfer some of their prerogatives to these institutions, for instance in the case of the European Union. Finally, states may voluntarily agree to submit their disputes to international arbitration. Such procedures can crystallise into international common law (Franck and Munansangu, 1982).

The development of an international legal order depends on the voluntary cooperation of national states. If the most powerful states are not willing to cooperate, international organisations will be paralysed. If one of the parties involved in a conflict is unwilling to bring this conflict before the International Court of Justice in The Hague, the Court is powerless. A further problem is the fact that international institutions do not have the independent means to implement their decisions. International organisations are also powerless against large-scale violations of human rights. Only if coalitions of powerful states are prepared to sanction violations of international norms and resolutions and other powerful states do not oppose them actively, can some decisions of international bodies actually be enforced.

In recent years, important steps have been taken to create international legal institutions for the supranational adjudication of war crimes and crimes against humanity. Thus, the United Nations has set up international war crime tribunals for the Balkan Wars, the Rwandan Genocide and crimes committed in the Sierra Leone civil wars. In addition, the former dictator Pinochet of Chile has been accused of war crimes, in a British court. With the legal cases against Pinochet in the UK, Milosevic in The Hague and most recently Saddam Hussein in Iraq, the immunity of heads of state and senior politicians is no longer self-evident.

13.2 Institutions and institutional change since 1945: a chronological overview

This section presents a chronological overview of international organisations, treaties, conventions, events and meetings defining the institutional characteristics of the international order since 1945. They are summarised in Box 13.2. The subsequent sections will provide a more analytical discussion of the different phases of the post-war order.

Box 13.2　Important international organisations, treaties and conferences, 1944–2002

1944	Bretton Woods Conference:
	● IMF (International Monetary Fund);
	● IBRD (International Bank for Reconstruction and Development) (World Bank).
1945	Founding of the United Nations at the San Francisco conference:
	● General Assembly;
	● Security Council;
	● ECOSOC (Economic and Social Council).
1947	General Agreement on Tariffs and Trade (GATT) signed in Geneva.
1947–8	Drawing up of the Havana Charter for the International Trade Organisation (ITO).
1948	Founding of the Organisation of American States (OAS).
1949	Founding of the North Atlantic Treaty Organisation (NATO).
1949	Second round of GATT negotiations on tariff reductions (Annecy).
1951	Third round of GATT negotiations on tariff reductions (Torquay).
1955	Founding of the movement of non-aligned countries at Bandung.
1955	GATT gets a permanent status.
1955	Founding of the Warsaw Pact.
1956	Fourth round of GATT negotiations on tariff reductions (Geneva).
1956	Founding of the International Finance Corporation (IFC), a subsidiary of the World Bank, for the stimulation of private foreign investment in developing countries.
1957	Signing of the treaty of Rome: founding of the European Economic Community (EEC) by six states: Belgium, the Federal Republic of Germany, France, Italy, Luxembourg and the Netherlands.
1960	Founding of the International Development Association (IDA), a subsidiary organisation of the World Bank. This organisation issues soft loans to developing countries.
1960–1	GATT: Dillon Round.
1961	Founding of the Organisation for Economic Cooperation and Development (OECD), with Western European countries, the USA, Canada and Japan as its members.
1961	The UN proclaims the First Development Decade.
1963	Founding of the Organisation of African Unity (OAU).
1964	UNCTAD I (United Nations Conference on Trade and Development). First UNCTAD Conference in Geneva. Establishment of the group of 77 non-aligned countries within the UN. Raúl Prebisch, Secretary-General of the ECLAC, pleads for a new international economic order.
1964–7	GATT: Kennedy Round. With respect to GATT negotiation rounds up to and including the Kennedy Round, it is generally assumed that tariff reductions for products from developing countries were lower than for other products. During the Kennedy Round the largest tariff reductions were negotiated for advanced technologies and capital-intensive products.
1965	Founding of the UNDP (United Nations Development Programme) which centred on technical assistance to developing countries and the financing of development projects.
1965	Addition of a new chapter 'Trade and Development' to the GATT agreements. The requirement of reciprocity was abandoned for developing countries.

Box 13.2   continued

1968	Second UNCTAD conference in New Delhi.
1971	Collapse of the Bretton Woods fixed exchange rate system.
1971	Lima declaration of ministers of the G7 on targets for industrial production. Objective: by the year 2000, 25 per cent of world industrial production should be produced in developing countries.
1971–6	GATT: gradual introduction of the Generalised System of Preferences (GSP) to facilitate the exports of industrial products from developing countries to the industrialised countries.
1972	Third UNCTAD conference in Santiago de Chile.
1973	Oil crisis.
1973	In a speech in Nairobi the President of the World Bank, Robert McNamara, calls attention to the basic needs of millions of people living in absolute poverty.
1973–9	GATT negotiations: Tokyo Round. Tariffs reduced by 30 per cent.
1974	Sixth special meeting of the General Assembly of the UN. Acceptance of a resolution on a New International Economic Order. A 'Charter of the Economic Rights and Duties of States' is formulated.
1974	Multi-fibre Arrangement. 'Voluntary' quantitative import restrictions for textile exports from developing countries.
1975	Lomé Convention signed in February 1975 by the EEC and 63 ACP countries (former European colonies in Africa, the Caribbean and the Pacific). The agreement includes a series of non-reciprocal trade concessions by the EEC and the setting up of two funds for the stabilisation of export revenues of developing countries.
1975	UN resolution on 'Development and International Economic Cooperation'.
1976	UNCTAD IV in Nairobi.
1976	World employment conference by the ILO in Geneva calls for an emphasis on basic needs in development policy.
1979	UNCTAD V in Manila.
1979	Second oil crisis.
1979	World Bank introduces Structural Adjustment Loans (SALs).
1980	Treaty on an Integrated Programme for Commodities. The treaty has not yet been ratified by the required 90 states and therefore is still not being implemented.
1980	Publication of the Brandt report: *North-South, A Programme for Survival*. Emphasis on mutual interests of rich countries and developing countries.
1980	Prime minister Michael Manley of Jamaica refuses to meet IMF conditions for further financial support. First political conflict about 'conditionality'.
1981	World Bank introduces Sectoral Adjustment Loans (SECALs).
1982	Signing of a comprehensive treaty on maritime law, in Jamaica in December 1982. Among others, this treaty deals with the common exploitation of natural resources on the seabed outside territorial waters. This agreement has not been signed by the US, the United Kingdom and the Federal Republic of Germany. It has not been implemented.
1982	Mexico postpones payments of its debt service. Start of the debt crisis. Since 1982 the IMF and the World Bank increasingly emphasise 'structural adjustment policies' as a condition for obtaining new loans.
1983	Third ACP–EEC treaty signed in Lomé.

Box 13.2 continued

1985	Baker Plan introduced in Seoul: *A Programme for Sustained Growth*. The Plan argues for renewed capital flows to developing countries. Recognition of the fact that a solution of the debt crisis depends on resumption of economic growth.
1986–93	GATT: Uruguay Round on liberalisation of international trade. Completed 15 December 1993. Agricultural products and services are included in the agreements for the first time. Agreement on the creation of the World Trade Organisation.
1986	IMF: Structural Fund Facility (SAF) to finance structural adjustment programmes.
1987	IMF: Extended Structural Fund Facility (ESAF) to finance sectoral structural adjustment programmes.
1989	Fall of the Berlin Wall.
1989	Fourth ACP–EEC agreement signed in Lomé.
1989	Brady Plan launched in March 1989. First step towards voluntary debt reduction as a contribution to the resumption of economic growth.
1991	Disintegration of the Soviet Union.
1992	9 May: Adoption of the text of the Framework Convention of Climate Change at the UN Headquarters in New York.
1992	United National Conference on Environment and Development (UNCED) in Rio de Janeiro. At this conference resolutions are passed on pressing global environmental issues such as reduction of CO_2 emissions, CFCs and deforestation. The Framework convention is opened to signature.
1993	Mexico, the US and Canada agree on a North American free trade treaty (NAFTA).
1993	Treaty of Maastricht. The European Economic Community is transformed into the European Union. Agreement on the introduction of a common European currency by 1999.
1994	World Population Plan of Action adopted by the United Nations Conference on Population and Development in Cairo, September 1994.
1994	15 April 1994: signing of the Agreement on Trade-Related Aspects of Intellectual Property Rights (TRIPS) at Marrakesh, Morocco. Signature of the WTO agreements based on the Uruguay Round.
1995	Start of the World Trade Organisation in Geneva.
1995	Second Mexican Debt Crisis.
1996	The World Bank and the IMF launch the debt initiative for Heavily Indebted Countries, focusing on debt relief. HIPC initiative further amended at the G8 summit of June 1999.
1997–2001	Kyoto Protocol. On 11 December 1997: the Kyoto Protocol, for practical implementation of the Convention for Climate Change, was adopted in Kyoto, Japan. The Protocol focuses on reductions of emissions of carbon dioxide. 1997–2001 further negotiations on Kyoto Protocol resulting in an agreement, which has been ratified by 120 countries per November 2003, but not by the USA and Russia.
1997	The Asian Crisis, sparked by devaluation of the Thai baht.
1999	Anti-globalisation protests at the Seattle meeting of WTO in 1999.
2000	June: Lomé V convention between the European Union and 71 ACP countries for the period 2000–2007.

Box 13.2   continued

2001	November. Start of the Doha Round of trade liberalisation. This round is called the Development Round and is explicitly intended to improve the positions of developing countries in international trade and to address agricultural protection by the advanced economies. In spite of some progress at a meeting in Cancun, Mexico in September 2003 representatives of developing countries and advanced economies failed to reach agreement. The talks have stalled.
2001	11 December. China joins the WTO after 15 years of negotiations.
2002	1 July: Rome Statute on International Criminal Court in The Hague enters into force.
2002	18–22 March: United Nations International Conference on Financing for Development at Monterrey, Mexico. Renewed commitment to the additional financing of development aid, US $12 billion.

Sources: Johnson (1967), Meier (1984); Fey (1985); Schrijver (1985); Bhagwati (1988); Teunissen (1990); Hermes (1992); Singer (2001); Raffer and Singer (2001).

Many new international organisations were founded in the post-war period. In this context it is meaningful to distinguish between a cluster of specialised financial institutions dominated by the rich countries, and the United Nations and its numerous specialised daughter organisations, in which decisions are reached by majority vote and developing countries have much more influence on policy (Schrijver, 1985).

The UN family includes the FAO (Food and Agriculture Organisation), UNIDO (United Nations Industrial Development Organisation), UNCTAD (United Nations Conference on Trade and Development), UNDP (United Nations Development Programme), UNESCO (Educational, Scientific and Cultural Organisation), UNICEF (the children's emergency fund), the WHO (the World Health Organization), the UNEP (the United Nations Environmental Programme), UNITAR (Institute for Training and Research), the ILO (International Labour Organisation), and many more.[2] In theory, all specialised UN organisations fall within the compass of the responsibility of the Economic and Social Council of the UN. They have to submit annual reports to the council. In practice, however, they are largely independent (Nerfin, 1985).

The financial institutions dominated by the rich countries include the institutions of General Agreement on Tariffs and Trade (GATT) and its successor the World Trade Organisation (WTO), the International Monetary Fund (IMF), the World Bank and its subsidiaries, the Asian Development Bank (ADB), the African Development Bank, the Inter-American Development Bank (IADB), the International Development Association (IDA) and the International Finance Corporation (IFC), the OECD and the periodic meetings of the leaders of the seven largest industrialised countries (the G7).[3] As specialised UN organisations, the

---

[2] Among others: the International Civil Aviation Organization, the Universal Postal Union, the International Telecommunication Union, the International Maritime Organisation, the World Meteorological Organisation, the World Organization for Intellectual Property.
[3] Since 1994, Russia has joined these meetings, which are now referred to as G8 meetings.

International Monetary Fund and the World Bank are accountable to the Economic and Social Council of the UN. But the number of votes in these organisations depends on financial contributions provided by member countries. This means that the policies of these organisations are determined by the rich countries. The founding of these organisations actually preceded the founding of the United Nations.

13.2.1 *Free trade versus international regulation*

A recurrent theme in the succession of international conferences, resolutions and treaties in Box 13.2 is the debate between advocates of a liberal international order based on free trade and proponents of a new international order based on some measure of international regulation. The institutions dominated by the affluent countries championed free trade and argued that free trade and an outward orientation would benefit developing countries as well as the advanced economies. United Nations organisations and meetings dominated by developing countries called for a new, more just international economic order, which offered a better deal for developing countries. The World Bank, the IMF and the GATT responded to these claims with new policies aimed at improving developing country access to the developed country markets (cf. Schrijver, 1985). In the late 1980s, developing countries started to realise that participation in the international economy and the opening up of the domestic economy to international competition had some advantages. At the same time, strangely enough, protectionist tendencies seemed to be on the increase in the economically advanced countries (Krueger, 1990). This prompted renewed criticisms of the international order in the 1990s.

13.2.2 *The financial institutions*

The foundations for the institutional structure of the post-war liberal international economic order were laid at a conference in Bretton Woods in 1944 (Burk, 1990). Forty-four countries were represented at this conference, among which were twenty-one developing countries. These played only a very minor role in the debates. At the conference, agreements were reached on a system of stable exchange rates, with the dollar as the base currency and with currencies convertible to gold at fixed rates. The International Monetary Fund was set up to safeguard international financial stability. The IMF provided financial support to countries faced with sudden deficits in their balance of payments. The initial task of the new International Bank for Reconstruction and Development (World Bank) was to provide funding for economic reconstruction of war damages. The Bank started operations in 1946 and gradually shifted its focus of attention to developing countries after 1950. The Bank concentrated mainly on investment in infrastructure. By 1981 the total of outstanding loans was over 5 billion dollars (Meier, 1984). Voting power in institutions like the IMF and the World Bank depends on the amount of financial resources contributed by the member countries.

With the IMF and the World Bank, the General Agreement on Tariffs and Trade (GATT) became the third pillar of the liberal international economic order. In the GATT treaty signed in Geneva in October 1947, 123 separate trade agreements between twenty-three advanced economies were combined into a single agreement (Fey, 1985). Important principles underlying this agreement are summarised in Box 13.3.

Box 13.3   GATT principles
- Governments should refrain from interference in international trade. They may only impose tariffs on imports.
- Quantitative restrictions and trade barriers are permitted under only specified conditions.
- Reciprocity: tariff reductions have to be reciprocal.
- Non-discrimination: trade advantages granted to one country have to be granted to all other countries. This is referred to as the 'most-favoured-nation clause.'

The GATT agreement was meant to be a temporary arrangement in anticipation of the founding of an International Trade Organisation (ITO) with broader responsibilities. From November 1947 to March 1948 a charter for this organisation was negotiated in Havana. In these discussions representatives of developing countries played a more prominent role than in the GATT negotiations. The concept for the ITO charter, therefore, also included a chapter on 'Economic Development and Recovery', which paid attention to foreign direct investment and to the protection of infant industries. In another chapter, the subject of agreements to stabilise commodity prices was broached. The Havana conference ended in a conflict between developing countries and economically advanced countries. The ITO did not get off the ground. Therefore, in 1955 the GATT institutions, originally intended as temporary, received a semi-permanent status.

Including the Uruguay Round concluded in December 1993, GATT negotiations took place in eight rounds. Between 1947 and 1979, the first seven rounds led to a reduction in the average import tariffs by no less than 92 per cent (Bhagwati, 1988). Until the Uruguay Round agricultural products were excluded from the negotiations. Tariff reductions referred mainly to industrial products. The GATT agreements also included procedures to solve trade disputes between participating countries. The reduction of trade barriers mainly affected exports to the rich countries. Developing countries continued to protect their industrial sectors.

The reductions of tariffs continued beyond 1979, but they were increasingly offset by the growth of non-tariff barriers to imports to rich countries. Non-tariff barriers include 'voluntary agreements on the restriction of exports', appeals to 'anti-dumping clauses' of the GATT and imposition of restrictive quality and environmental requirements. However, according to Bhagwati (1988), there has been no relapse into the protectionism of the interwar period. The liberalisation of the 1950s and 1960s has not been undone. But the further reductions of import tariffs have been balanced by increases in other forms of protection.

In part due to tariff reductions, trade between economically advanced countries increased twice as fast as their real output. The growth of trade was also spurred by the decreasing costs of transport and communication. Major exceptions to the liberalisation of international trade were agriculture and textiles. Until recently, the US and European policy with respect to agricultural products was highly protectionist, which especially hurt the growth prospects of poorest developing countries dependent on primary exports. Attempts were made to protect the textile industry in the rich countries against imports from low-wage countries by means of the so-called Multi-fibre Arrangement of 1974, and its predecessors. In practice, developing countries were quite successful in evading these import restrictions in the 1980s. Exports of textiles and clothing from developing countries to the OECD countries increased annually by 13 per cent and 20 per cent respectively (Krueger, 1990).

The eighth GATT round of negotiations – the Uruguay Round – took place between 1986 and 1993. It contained provisions for the setting up of a permanent world trade organisation (WTO). The pressure on developing countries to open up their economies and abolish restrictions to trade and foreign investment increased. Among the provisions of the Uruguay Round was an agreement on Trade-Related Intellectual Property Rights (TRIPS), which is generally seen as protecting the interests of the advanced economies and the large transnational corporations engaging in R&D (see Chapter 4). Another new element was the inclusion of agricultural protection in the trade negotiations, but little progress was made in this area. The multi-fibre agreement was to be phased out by 2005.

The World Trade Organisation (WTO) was set up in 1995. China finally joined the WTO after protracted negotiations lasting fifteen years, achieving automatic most-favoured-nation status under the terms of the WTO. With some justification, developing countries claim that the WTO imposes import liberalisation on developing countries, making them vulnerable to competition from the advanced economies, prohibiting protection of promising infant industries and reducing the scope for industrial policy (Westphal, 2002). At the same time the advanced economies have continued to restrict trade in textiles, agricultural products and other products. They have also used environmental, health, labour and quality regulations to restrict imports. They do not practise what they preach.

The Doha Round of trade negotiations – starting in 2001 – was meant to repair some of the shortcomings of the Uruguay Round, for the first time giving priority to reduction of agricultural protection by the US and the EU and targeting anti-dumping provisions and non-tariff barriers in the rich countries. At a meeting in Cancun, in 2003, the developing countries led by China, Brazil and India refused to agree to the terms offered by the advanced economies, which were deemed inadequate. At the time of writing the Doha talks are stalled.

13.2.3 The UN family of institutions and the call for a new international economic order

The United Nations was founded in 1945 at a conference in San Francisco. Initially, its main objective was to safeguard international peace and security. It had fifty-one member states. Only four developing countries in Africa and Asia were represented. Between 1945 and 1965, sixty-five former colonies became independent and joined the UN as sovereign member states. More and more, the focus of UN attention shifted to problems of development. By 1992, 152 of the 180 UN member states were developing countries (UN, 1993a; 1993b). Per 2003, the UN has 191 member states. Box 13.4 summarises the principal organs of the United Nations.

> **Box 13.4 Principal organs of the United Nations**
> - *The General Assembly.* Each member state has one vote in the general assembly.
> - *The Security Council.* The Security Council has 15 members. The victors of World War II (the USA, France, Great Britain, the Soviet Union and China) are permanent members with the power of veto. Ten other members are elected for two-year periods by the general assembly.
> - *The Economic and Social Council (ECOSOC).* In principle, ECOSOC coordinates the work of the numerous specialised UN organisations. The council has 54 members. These are elected for three-year periods by the general assembly.

The rich countries provide most of the funds for the work of the UN organisations. This provides them with considerable leverage. Still, on the basis of the 'one country, one vote' principle, developing countries have a great deal of influence within UN organisations, both with respect to policy making and staff recruitment. Through specialised organisations like the United Nations Conference on Trade and Development (UNCTAD) and through the General Assembly of the UN, developing countries can make themselves heard and can express their criticisms of the liberal international economic order.

At the first UNCTAD conference in Geneva in 1964, a bloc of seventy-seven non-aligned developing countries was formed. With Raúl Prebisch as one of their main spokesmen, they called for a new international economic order. In this new order, the position of developing countries in the system of international trade would be strengthened and their access to markets in developed countries would improve. The call for a new international economic order (NIEO) became stronger and stronger at subsequent UNCTAD conferences. The pursuit of the NIEO received a substantial boost when a cartel of petroleum-exporting countries (OPEC) managed to raise oil prices dramatically in 1973. In 1974, the General Assembly of the UN accepted a resolution on the formation of a new international economic order. One of the important demands included in this resolution was more voting power for developing countries in the financial institutions dominated by the rich countries. Another aim was the stabilisation or even improvement of the terms of trade of primary exports, through the establishment of buffer funds and commodity agreements.

13.2.4   *Responses to the new international economic order*

The demand for more votes in financial institutions was never met by the rich countries. But in several other ways the international institutions did respond to the pressure for change. As early as 1955, it was accepted that developing countries could temporarily protect their domestic industries while trade barriers in the rich countries were being reduced. The justification for this exception was the 'infant industry' argument. In 1965 an additional chapter was added to the GATT agreements, in which the reciprocity requirement was dropped for developing countries. Developing countries do not have to reciprocate tariff reductions in rich countries. Between 1971 and 1976 a system of Generalised Preferences was developed, in which industrial exports from developing countries were given a measure of preferential access to markets in rich countries. However, the effects of these measures on export growth in the poorest countries were disappointing.

The World Bank increasingly turned into a real development bank. It not only financed infrastructural projects, but also increasingly supported agricultural, industrial and educational projects. In 1956, the International Finance Corporation (IFC) was established as a separate subsidiary, to promote private investment in developing countries. The year 1960 saw the founding of the International Development Association (IDA), which issued soft loans to developing countries on favourable conditions. From 1973 the policy emphasis shifted, at least in theory, to poverty alleviation (Chenery *et al.*, 1974; van Dam, 1989). This change was heralded in a speech by the President of the World Bank, Robert McNamara, in October 1973. McNamara argued for policies to increase the productivity and the employment chances of the very poor. From the late 1960s till the late 1970s the share of infrastructural projects in World Bank lending decreased from 60 per cent to 33 per cent. By 1980, 50 per cent of all World Bank loans were being used to finance rural development, education, population projects, urbanisation, water supply and nutrition (Meier, 1984).

The tasks of the IMF were initially restricted to monetary stabilisation in case of balance-of-payments problems. Developing countries received no special attention. Later the IMF also started focusing on the economic problems of developing countries. Separate facilities were created to assist developing countries with balance-of-payments problems and to compensate for shortfalls in export revenues. In recent years, the bulk of IMF loans has been going to developing countries.

Among the responses to the call for a new international economic order, one should mention a series of agreements between the EEC and former European colonies in Africa, the Caribbean and the Pacific (the ACP countries). In the so-called Lomé agreements, an attempt was made to provide a framework for policy dialogue between developing countries and rich European countries. Special funds were established to help stabilise export revenues from agricultural and mining exports of developing countries (STABEX and SYSMIN).[4] Exports from ACP countries were granted preferential access to European markets and the resources for financing development projects were expanded. Unfortunately, these measures have had little impact. The share of the ACP countries on the European markets have declined, even in comparison to those of other developing countries excluded from the Lomé agreements (Fitzpatrick, 1983).

The pursuit of an NIEO reached its high point in the signing of an agreement on an Integrated Programme for Commodities in 1980 and an agreement on the joint exploitation of the natural resources of the seabed in 1982. The integrated programme was meant to stabilise prices of primary exports at a high level through the creation of buffer stocks.

Neither this programme nor the treaty on the exploitation of the seabed has ever been implemented. The reasons for this are manifold. In the first place, it is an illusion that developing countries have joint interests. The interests of oil-exporting countries, oil-importing countries, newly industrialising countries and agricultural exporters, richer and poorer countries show considerable divergence. This prevented developing countries from presenting a united front to rich countries in international negotiations. Secondly, there was resistance on the part of the rich countries, and in particular the United States and Great Britain (Johnson, 1967). The United States, for example, refused to sign the maritime treaty on the joint exploitation of the resources of the seabed. This treaty would have provided the UN with independent sources of income, and would have rendered the organisation less dependent on its rich sponsors. In the third place, there was increasing criticism of the contents of the NIEO proposals themselves (see section 13.3.3). Finally, NIEO disappeared from the international agenda as a result of the debt crisis that broke out in 1982.

13.2.5   The debt crisis and the rise of the Washington consensus

After 1982 all attention went to the debt crisis, which threatened world financial stability. The inflow of private financial capital to developing countries temporarily came to an end. Since that time, debt has become one of the major issues in the international order. There have been a variety of initiatives to reduce debt burdens of the poorest countries, which will be further discussed in section 13.4.4. The latest of these initiatives is the initiative for heavily indebted poor countries (HIPC) launched in 1996 (Neumayer, 2002).

---

4 STABEX refers to a fund for Stabilisation of Export Earnings; SYSMIN refers to a fund for Stabilisation for Mining Exports. See section 13.3.2.

From the 1980s onwards, international financial institutions like the IMF and the World Bank increasingly started attaching conditions to the provision of new credit. These conditions implied that developing countries had to pursue 'structural adjustment policies', which were aimed at improving their balance of payments, reducing the role of government, deregulating the economy and stimulating an export-orientation. The 1980s were completely dominated by the debate on structural adjustment policy (see Lensink, 1995; Mosley *et al.*, 1995). The intellectual justification for this policy was provided by the remarkable economic success of several Asian countries, where sober macro-economic policies had been followed and export-orientation had been encouraged. Structural adjustment policies are consistent with the resurgence of liberal perspectives on both national and international economic policy.

Krueger (1990; 1993) and later Stiglitz (2000; 2002) rightly point to the paradoxical situation that developing countries are turning to the market under the pressure from international financial institutions, while there is a simultaneous revival of protectionist tendencies in the rich countries that stood at the cradle of the post-war liberal economic order. Until 1979, subsequent GATT negotiation rounds had managed to reduce average import tariffs on manufactured goods to 5 per cent (Fey, 1985). At the same time, protectionist tendencies resurfaced along with the slowdown of economic growth in the rich countries after 1973. Apart from excluding agriculture and services, the GATT agreements included numerous clauses of exception to which the protectionist interests could appeal. One of the clauses referred to the right to take countermeasures in case of 'dumping' by another country. 'Dumping' is a very elastic concept. Between 1980 and 1985 the EEC countries, the USA and six other advanced economies appealed to antidumping provisions 1,155 times in order to restrict imports from other countries. There were another 425 appeals to anti-subsidy provisions (Bhagwati, 1988). Another exception to free trade is provided by situations in which there is the danger of 'serious injury to domestic producers'. In such cases, temporary relaxation of GATT and WTO rules is possible. With this clause as a fallback, rich countries can blackmail developing countries into signing 'voluntary' agreements on export quotas. Another threat to the liberal international order is the rise of trade blocs with internal free trade and intensified protectionism at the outside borders (Krueger, 1993).

Although the fear of revived protectionism is not without grounds, Bhagwati interprets recent protectionist measures differently. He sees them as a peace offering by free trade-oriented governments to domestic pressure groups, rather than as a fundamental break with a free-trade regime. Developing countries have been quite successful in evading protectionist measures. In spite of the deceleration of the growth of world trade after 1973, world trade between 1973 and 1983 increased faster than world production. The increase in non-tariff restrictions did, however, compensate for the further reduction of import tariffs which was realised in GATT negotiations after 1973.

At the formal level, liberalisation of trade received a further impetus from the successful completion of the protracted negotiations of the GATT Uruguay

Round in December 1993. For the first time, agriculture was also included in the packet of tariff reductions. Agreement was reached on the phasing out of the multi-fibre agreements. Trade in services has also been liberalised. Finally, agreement has been reached on the establishment of a World Trade Organisation (WTO), originally scheduled for 1948. The WTO started operations on 1 January 1995.

From the mid-1980s onwards, the international agenda has been dominated by what has come to be called the *Washington Consensus*. The ideas of the Washington consensus were based on the negative experiences of state-led inward-looking development in Latin America and the success of export orientation in East Asia. This approach recommends the pursuit of macro-economic stability by controlling inflation and reducing fiscal deficits, the opening up of economies to the rest of the world through trade liberalisation and capital account liberalisation, and the liberalisation of domestic product and factor markets through structural adjustment policies. The policy package includes import liberalisation, competitive exchange rates, tax reform, openness to FDI, privatisation, deregulation, protection of intellectual property rights, and public expenditure priorities in education and health (Fischer, 2003; Gore, 2000; Williamson, 1990; 1993; 1997). We will discuss these proposals in more detail in the section on structural adjustment.

13.2.6   The Asian crisis and the debate on the architecture of the international order

The late 1990s are characterised by a fierce debate on the international financial institutions. On the one hand, publications such as the Meltzer report (2000) called for a reduced role for the IMF and the World Bank. These institutions are seen as having outlived their usefulness. Much of their work could be taken over by private financial institutions. The Meltzer report proposes to replace loans by a smaller volume of outright grants which are tied more strongly to prior economic performance and liberal economic reforms. On the other hand, there was a mounting wave of criticism of the liberal Washington consensus, sparked by the Asian crisis and increasing financial instability in the global economy. This resulted in a variety of proposals for a new architecture of the global financial system (Adelman 2000; Soros 2002; Stiglitz, 2002; Tobin, 2000). Key issues include the dangers of liberalisation of international capital markets, the negative impacts of full trade liberalisation on the industrial prospects of developing countries, the perceived inflexibility and dogmatism of the IMF and the need to reduce the debt burdens of the poorest countries. Anti-globalisation protesters meeting vociferously at the margin of international meetings since the WTO meeting in Seattle 1997 reject the international division of labour altogether. Most of the academic critics of the international order are in favour of continued openness and export orientation, but call for changes in the rules of the game. These issues will be discussed further in section 13.6.

13.2.7   *Environment*

A final trend in the evolution of the international order is the emergence of a series of conferences and treaties on the environment, based on increasing fears of global warming due to CO_2 emissions. In 1992, the text of a Framework Convention on Climate Change was adopted at the UN and opened for signature. Between 1997 and 2001, there were intensive negotiations on the implementation of measures to reduced greenhouse gas emissions. These resulted in the Kyoto Protocol on greenhouse gas emissions, which has now been signed by over 120 countries. The United States has refused to sign the protocol and Russia is still deliberating at the time of writing.

13.3   The call for a new international order in the 1960s and 1970s

13.3.1   *Criticisms of the liberal international order*

The principles underlying free trade have been discussed in Chapter 8. The basic arguments have remained unchanged since Adam Smith sang the virtues of free trade in the eighteenth century. Participation in international trade, specialisation and an international division of labour will increase the welfare of all parties, whether developing countries or advanced economies. There is strong theoretical and empirical support for the general argument that free trade is beneficial for growth and that those developing countries which have participated most in international trade have developed more rapidly than those which have not.

   Nevertheless, free trade has always had its critics. Despite the rapid growth of the world trade and per capita incomes in the 1950–1973 period, there was increasing dissatisfaction with the liberal international economic order on the part of developing countries (see Brandt *et al.*, 1980; Johnson, 1967; Lewis, 1978; Schrijver, 1985; Seers, 1979; Streeten, 1984). The essence of their criticisms was the argument, deriving from Friedrich List, that powerful countries with a highly developed economy benefit more from international free trade than poor countries trying to catch up. Developing countries had profited insufficiently from the growth of the world economy. Within developing countries growth had largely bypassed the poorest classes of the population. The international order should be restructured in such a way that the masses of the population in poor developing countries could profit from international trade. Exports should provide developing countries with the financial resources needed for development. This would make them less dependent on development aid ('trade, not aid'). The main arguments of the critics of the liberal economic are summarised in Box 13.5.

Box 13.5 Criticisms of the liberal international order in the 1960s

- In the post-war period, neither decolonisation nor development aid resulted in sufficient economic growth in developing countries. Although most countries had achieved their formal political independence, economically they felt just as dependent on the dominant rich countries as before. There was widespread disappointment about development aid. On the one hand, the amount of aid fell far short of the original target of 0.7 per cent of the gross national product of the donor countries. On the other hand, countries became increasingly irritated with the paternalism and meddling in internal affairs that seems inextricably connected with aid.
- Economic growth in developing countries did not result in much decrease in poverty owing to the extremely unequal distribution of incomes.
- The share of the poorest developing countries in world exports decreased. Excluding oil-exporting countries, the share of the low-income countries in world trade decreased from 3.6 per cent in 1960 to 1.5 per cent in 1977.[5]
- Most prices of primary exports of developing countries showed downward trends, both in absolute terms and relative to prices of imported manufactured goods.
- Prices of primary exports of developing countries fluctuated strongly in the short run so that export revenues were very unstable.
- International income inequality increased since per capita incomes in the rich countries increased faster than those in the poor countries.
- Large multinational enterprises contributed to a drain of resources. They tend to repatriate their profits abroad, they contribute little to the domestic economy and they reinforce the economic dependence of the developing countries on the advanced economies.

Sources: Bhagwati (1977); Corden (1979); Myint (1980); Streeten (1984); Ul Haq (1976).

As an alternative to the liberal international economic order, a New International Economic Order (NIEO) was launched at the first meeting of the UNCTAD in 1964. The NIEO consisted of a comprehensive set of measures formulated by Raúl Prebisch, the Secretary-General of the Economic Commission for Latin America (ECLA) and representatives of the group of seventy-seven non-aligned countries. The NIEO was further elaborated at successive UNCTAD conferences. The call for a new international order was strengthened by the short-lived but spectacular success of the OPEC oil cartel, which managed to increase oil prices drastically in 1973 and 1979. Important elements of the NIEO proposals are summarised in Box 13.6.

Box 13.6 Elements of the new international economic order

- *Commodity agreements for primary exports of developing countries.*
  - (a) The creation of *buffer stocks* of important commodities. When world prices fall below critical levels, the commodities are bought up at guaranteed minimum prices. If prices go up again, the buffer stocks are sold on the market.

---

5 As indicated in section 13.1.1, the share of the poorest countries in world trade has continued to decline since the 1970s (UNCTAD, http://www.unctad.org/).

(b) The provision of *compensatory finance* in case of wildly fluctuating export revenues. If export revenues of a country drop below given limits, the programme will compensate for the shortfalls. When revenues are high, payments are made to the compensatory fund.

(c) The provision of *financial resources* for the setting up of primary resource processing industries in developing countries, to reduce countries' dependence on primary exports.

(d) The *indexing of export prices* of developing countries to the prices of their imports, to avoid deterioration of the terms of trade.

The overall objective of commodity agreements is to stabilise primary export prices and export revenues in the short term and to improve the terms of trade for developing countries in the long term.

- *Reducing protectionism on the part of the advanced industrial economies.*
- *Preferential and non-reciprocal access to developed country markets for manufactured exports from developing countries.*

The developing countries retain the right to protect their domestic industries. The goal of these measures is to increase the share of developing countries in world manufacturing production and manufactured exports.

- *Producer cartels.*

Recognition of the right of developing countries to establish producer cartels in order to raise the prices of their primary export products. The model for such cartels was the Organisation of Petroleum-Exporting Countries (OPEC).

- *Nationalisation of foreign enterprises.*

Recognition of the right of developing countries to exploit their own natural resources such as oil and minerals; This includes the right to nationalise foreign enterprises.

- *Increased shares of developing countries in world transport.*
- *Formulation of a code of conduct for multinational enterprises.*

A code of conduct should be formulated for multinational enterprises, including requirements such as the reinvestment of part of their profits, training of local employees, transfer of technology, respect for local rules and laws, cooperation with local entrepreneurs and subcontractors and domestic sourcing. The aim of the code is to increase the contributions of multinationals to the domestic economy.

- *Increased financial resources for development.*

Increasing the volume of international financial resources available for development programmes of international organisations such as the World Bank and the IMF.

- *Debt relief for the poorest developing countries.*
- *More voting rights for developing countries in the IMF and other international financial institutions.*
- *Independent sources of funding for international organisations.*

Independent sources of funding for the United Nations and other international organisations would make them less dependent on financial contributions from the advanced economies. One of the proposals is to use the proceeds of the joint exploitation of the natural resources of the seabed for such funding.

- *Increasing South–South trade.*

Increasing trade flows between developing countries.

These proposals were eventually incorporated in a resolution on the New International Economic Order accepted by the UN General Assembly in 1974. The commodity agreements have been worked out in the 1980 draft treaty for an Integrated Programme for Commodities and a 1982 draft treaty on the exploitation of natural resources of the seabed. Neither of these treaties has been implemented.

13.3.2   Lomé agreements

In 1975, the first of a series of agreements between the European Community and the former European colonies in Africa, the Caribbean and the Pacific (the ACP countries) was concluded in Lomé. These agreements tried to realise some of the ideas of the new international economic order. The Lomé agreements developed out of a dialogue between rich countries and developing countries. Among others, they comprise a European development fund for developmental projects; a fund for the stabilisation of revenues from primary agricultural exports from developing countries (STABEX); and a fund for the stabilisation of revenues from mining exports (SYSMIN). In addition, agreements were reached on preferential access to European markets for manufactured exports from the ACP countries.

Despite high hopes and initial enthusiasm, the results of these Lomé agreements have been highly disappointing. The stabilisation funds were soon exhausted, as more and more claims were made, while no money was ever paid back as originally intended. Also, the funds were paid out to governments rather than to producers, so that there were no incentives to increase production or to improve productivity. Moreover, the funds functioned automatically. There were no conditions with regard to macro-economic policies.

In the most recent Lomé agreements of 2000 between the European Union and seventy-seven ACP countries, STABEX and SYSMIN were abolished. Despite preferential access to European markets, market shares of the ACP countries have declined. At the same time, Asian developing countries excluded from the Lomé agreements, succeeded in improving their market shares. Some critics point to European protectionism as a possible cause of the disappointing outcomes, but over time the theoretical framework underlying the new international economic order itself came to be criticised. In recent years, the preferential access of the ACP countries increasingly conflicts with the provisions of the WTO, which demands equality of access for all developing countries. The preferential access for ACP countries to EU markets is very gradually being phased out in the context of a more general reduction of trade barriers.

13.3.3   Criticisms of the new international order

In the late 1970s, there was a turning point in the debates on economic development. There was increasing criticism of the market-distorting impacts of government planning in developing countries and of attempts to regulate international trade in the context of the NIEO.

First, there was criticism of the export-pessimist assumptions underlying the proposals. Some critics denied that there is a systematic deterioration of the terms of trade of exports from developing countries (Grilli and Maw, 1988; Johnson, 1967; Myint, 1980; Spraos, 1980). The debate on the terms of trade continues (Sapsford, 1985; 1988; Sapsford and Balasubramanyam 2003; Sarkar, 1986; 2001). There is recent evidence pointing to declines in the terms of trade of the poorest primary exporters. However, we concluded in Chapter 8 that no systematic law-like patterns can be discerned. The terms of trade vary from period to period, country to country and product to product. Countries with a flexible production structure and a diversified export package are less affected by price movements than countries with inflexible production structures and dependence on a single export product (monocultures). According to Myint, export pessimists have made too much of the low income elasticity of the demand for primary products.[6] Western demand for some exotic agricultural products (e.g. mangoes, kiwi fruit, lichis) actually increases as incomes go up. Moreover, price elasticity (the relation between changes in quantities demanded of a product and changes in its price) may be more important for a developing country than aggregate income elasticity. The prices of primary exports turn out to be no more unstable than those of manufactured goods or capital goods. One should also not forget that many developing countries no longer exclusively export primary products.

Even more important is the fact that export pessimism was used to prolong inward-looking and interventionist import-substitution policies, which in retrospect have turned out to be very unsuccessful. The countries that turned outward at an early stage – many East Asian economies – performed much better than Latin American and African economies, which continued to follow inward-looking policies. They achieved export success without any changes in the international order.

Next, experience has shown that attempts to stabilise commodity prices above their market levels through commodity agreements or price cartels are hardly ever successful in the long run. If prices are higher than free-market equilibrium prices, extra supply is elicited till the commodity fund is exhausted or prices collapse. This happened with oil. Attempts to stabilise the prices of commodities such as tin, cocoa or coffee also failed dismally.

The Lomé agreements demonstrate that preferential access to advanced country markets does not guarantee successful export performance. Efficient low-cost industrial producers in Asian countries were able to compete on European markets, while producers in ACP countries were not. Emphasising the right of developing countries to continue to protect their domestic industries indefinitely was seen as prolonging the existence of non-viable industries in Latin America and Africa.

Attempts to increase the voting power of developing countries in international financial institutions have met with fierce resistance from the countries

---

6 A low income elasticity implies that the demand for primary products does not increase in proportion to the increase in average per capita incomes.

which provide the funds of these institutions. More votes for developing countries conflicts with ever-stricter conditions the IMF and the World Bank attach to the provision of financial support. Finally, the demise of the new international economic order was also furthered by the increasing heterogeneity of developing countries. Attempts to legislate a comprehensive framework for the international order clashes with the diversity of interests and circumstances in developing countries (van Dam, 1984). The bloc of developing countries does not speak with one voice.

Foreign direct investment

One of the issues about which the climate of opinion has changed dramatically is foreign direct investment. In the 1970s, multinationals and foreign investors were regarded with suspicion. Developing countries feared foreign domination of the economy and the drain on domestic resources through profit repatriation and transfer pricing. The right to nationalise foreign enterprises was included in the resolutions on the new international order. There was also a call for a code of conduct for multinationals.

At present, developing countries are vying with each other to attract foreign direct investment, including formerly closed economies such as China and India. Foreign direct investment can bring financial resources into a country without increasing the volume of debt. Net foreign direct investment has replaced net capital flows as the prime source of financial resources for developing countries, even in Africa (see Tables 13.3 and 13.4 below). Foreign direct investment comprises more than financial flows alone. It includes a complete package of finance, management experience, transfer of technology and skills, marketing expertise and access to world brand names and world markets (Dunning, 1988; Gillis *et al.*, 1992; Helleiner, 1989; UNCTAD, 2000).

The right to nationalise multinational enterprises emphasised in the NIEO increasingly clashed with the new goal of attracting more and more foreign direct investment. The very threat of nationalisation had adverse effects on the behaviour of multinationals. When the political future is uncertain, multinational enterprises will charge an 'uncertainty premium' and go for maximum short-term profits, which will be repatriated as soon as possible. Enterprises will display a less 'predatory' behaviour if their long-term prospects in a country are more secure.

Since the 1970s, progress has been achieved in drawing up codes of conduct for multinational enterprises. Such codes specify the obligations of multinationals, such as training local staff, reinvesting part of their profits, respecting domestic legislation, subcontracting, using local intermediate goods and entering into joint ventures with domestic investors. The codes also offer more certainty to foreign investors.

This is not to say that foreign direct investment does not raise a number of major problems. Some multinationals raise all their capital on domestic markets, while repatriating part of their profits. A sizeable minority of foreign investment projects costs more in terms of the opportunity cost of the resources

used than the earnings generated (Helleiner, 1989). In some sectors, multinationals enter the economy in search of low-cost labour, but leave it just as
quickly when wages elsewhere are lower. The distribution of benefits between
the multinational and the host country still depends in part on the bargaining
power of the host country. Once a multinational has committed its resources
and the host country has gained more experience, the latter's bargaining position can improve. But many national governments are in a weak position
vis à vis giant foreign companies (Vernon, 1977). Clear delineation of the rights
and obligations of multinational companies and governments continues to be
an objective of negotiations within the UN Centre for Transnational Corporations.

In recent years, restrictions on foreign direct investment have been reduced
in many developing countries, including local content requirements and obligations to engage in joint ventures. This has contributed to a further increase
in the inflow of foreign direct investment, especially in Asia, though the danger of footloose capital in low-wage sectors such as textiles and shoemaking
remains a serious problem for developing countries.

In the post-war period, the importance of foreign direct investment fluctuated. Its share in net capital flows to developing countries was quite high in the
1950s and 1960s. It reached a low point in 1980 and recovered after that. The
debt crisis created new interest in direct foreign investment. In 1980, net FDI
was 5.2 per cent of net total capital flows. By 1987, FDI had increased to 34 per
cent of net capital flows. From 1996 onwards, net FDI was higher than net capital flows. By 2002, the net value of FDI amounted to 143 billion dollars, more
than twenty times as high as net total capital flows (see Table 13.3). New relationships with international firms have also developed, such as joint ventures,
licensing agreements, Original Equipment Manufacturing (OEM), franchising,
management contracts and subcontracting.

The increased importance of FDI and multinational companies is part and
parcel of the emergence of global production chains. According to Vernon's
product life-cycle theory (Perez and Soete, 1988; Vernon, 1966; 1974) new products and processes will be located in advanced economies. As mass markets are
penetrated and the technologies become more mature, production is relocated
to developing countries with an advantage in cheap labour, for instance in
textiles, shoemaking or to countries with abundant resources such as wood or
rubber. However, in recent years, several developing countries have succeeded
in upgrading their production processes, attracting investment not only in traditional industries such as textiles, but also in software, R&D and electronics.
Global production chains are increasingly dispersed, offering new opportunities for some developing countries. Developing countries may attempt to 'un-
package' the total direct investment package in order to select those aspects
that are most to their advantage.

The eclectic theory of multinational investment (Dunning, 1988) gives three
explanations for foreign direct investment. First there are unique firm-specific
characteristics, which explain the foreign firms' advantages over domestic

firms. These include intangible factors such as technologies and management skills, economies of scale, servicing networks and access to markets. A second set of factors refers to locational advantages as determined by labour costs, transport costs, availability of natural resources, tariff protection, tax burdens and other government policies in the host country. The third set of factors, which Dunning calls internalisation advantages, is very interesting. A foreign firm has to choose between selling its firm-specific advantages to local firms or setting up lines of production itself. In a nutshell, Dunning argues that the uncertainties of markets lead foreign firms to prefer the internal hierarchy of the multinational organisation to market transactions between independent firms. The very attempt to internalise market uncertainties and imperfections again indicates that there is considerable leeway for bargaining.

We may conclude that the climate of opinion with regard to the new international order shifted radically in the 1980s. We shall see, however, that some of its proposals will resurface again after the Asian crisis.

13.4   The debt crisis

In 1982, Mexico suspended the payment of its debt service, owing to insufficient foreign exchange. Other developing countries and countries in Eastern Europe also turned out to be unable to keep up payments on debt. Private banks responded by a sudden reduction in the supply of new credit. The debt crisis was a fact (Hermes, 1992). There were two aspects to this crisis: a threat to the stability of the global financial system, and a threat to the economic development of poor countries. After 1982, all attention was focused on coping with the consequences of the debt crisis. The urgency of the crisis effectively ended the faltering debate on the new international economic order. Though the threat to the global financial system has subsided, the problems of indebtedness for developing countries are as acute as ever. High debt is one of the potential obstacles to development.

13.4.1   What is wrong with debt?

For most people debt has negative connotations. In some stages of economic development, however, it is quite normal to incur debts. The accumulation of a stock of capital goods and the building up of industry and infrastructure in developing countries is facilitated by a substantial inflow of capital from abroad. This inflow may take the form of foreign direct investment, development aid or loans from governments, international financial institutions or private banks. Unlike foreign direct investment, loans result in increasing foreign indebtedness. As long as the borrowed funds are invested economically, debt causes few problems. Productive investment of loans implies that the borrowed resources contribute more to the growth of national income than they cost in terms of interest payments. Interest payments can be financed from the increase in national income. According to Lewis (1978), the absolute volume of debt is of no significance. As long as loans are invested economically, the more debt the better.

Lewis distinguishes four stages of the *debt cycle* (see also Hermes, 1992, p. 29; World Bank, 1985). During the first stage new borrowing exceeds debt service payments, so that interest payments, principal repayments and additional investment can all be financed from new loans.[7] The country imports more goods and services than it exports. During the second stage new borrowing exceeds repayments of outstanding loans, but it is less than total debt service. The volume of foreign debt is still increasing. In the third stage there is a surplus on the current account of the balance of payments and the volume of foreign debt starts to decrease. In the final stage of the debt cycle a country becomes a net creditor.

Debts only become a problem when loans are used unproductively (e.g. for consumptive purposes, for the financing of wasteful government bureaucracies or for investments with dubious returns). Debts become even more of a problem when they only serve to finance debt service payments on previous debts. Then the volume of debt continues to increase, while no new financial resources become available for investment in future production. When all earnings from additional productive efforts are swallowed up by debt service payments, this creates a major disincentive for further economic development.

During most of the post-war period developing countries were at the first stage of the debt cycle. Tables 3.6, 13.3 and 13.4 in this book point to a steady influx of capital to developing countries and sustained deficits on their trade balance of goods and services. Until 1977, the relationship between foreign finance and development was a positive one. Around 1977, this situation changed for many Latin American and African countries. Economic growth faltered and a perverse situation arose. Developing countries had to go ever deeper into debt to finance debt service payments on outstanding debt, while their export revenues were shrinking and their economies were stagnating. They suffered from a situation of *debt overhang*.

13.4.2　What caused the 1982 debt crisis?

The debt crisis was the result of a complex of internal and external causes (Buiter and Srinivasan, 1987; Griffin, 1988; Hermes, 1992; Lensink, 1993: ch. 2; Maddison, 1985; Wood, 1985). After 1973, the growth of world economy and world trade slowed down. Increased oil prices fuelled inflation. The Western countries responded to inflation by pursuing restrictive fiscal and monetary policies at the expense of growth and employment. Developing countries were faced with declining export revenues, deteriorating terms of trade for their export products and, except for the oil-exporting countries, rising energy bills.

---

7 Debt service is the sum of repayments of principal and interest payments in a given period.

Nevertheless many developing countries, in particular in Latin America, responded differently to the slowdown than the Western countries. In anticipation of a recovery of world economic growth, they tried to stimulate their economies through expansionary Keynesian fiscal and monetary policies. Deficits on the current account of the balance of payments were increasingly financed by short-term loans from the private banking sector. Compared to the 1950s and 1960s, the share of foreign direct investment – which does not increase foreign indebtedness – in the capital flows to developing countries declined strongly. Initially this was compensated for by loans from official financial institutions and governments (Lensink, 1993). But the volume of finance supplied from these public sources fell far short of financial requirements. Private borrowing increased. By borrowing from private banks, developing countries were able to evade the increasingly strict conditions imposed by the World Bank and the IMF (Wood, 1985).

Private banks were eager to provide loans to developing countries. They had accumulated huge amounts of petrodollars, which were being 'recycled' into the banking system by the oil-exporting countries. Private banks even pursued aggressive marketing strategies to expand their credit to developing countries. Owing to high inflation, real interest rates were low, sometimes even negative. The loans usually consisted of short-term credits with variable interest rates.

Until 1979, expansionary macro-economic policies in Latin America appeared to be quite successful. Latin American countries managed to keep up the momentum of economic growth, though at the price of high inflation. But the anticipated recovery of the world economy failed to materialise, especially in 1979 when oil prices again quadrupled and a new and even more serious depression followed (Maddison, 1985). Under the influence of the restrictive monetary policies of the Reagan administration, real interest rates suddenly soared. Since many loans were short-term and interest rates variable, the debt service suddenly went up. More and more loans had to be contracted just to meet debt-service obligations.

As debt problems cumulated, the Latin American economic policies of the 1970s turned out to be less successful than initially assumed. There had been economic mismanagement on a vast scale. Many of the funds borrowed had been squandered on inefficient subsidies or non-profitable government projects.[8] In addition, financial resources were used to maintain systems of political patronage, clientelism and corruption. Owing to huge government deficits and loose monetary policies, inflation increased sharply. High inflation disrupted domestic markets, discouraged the inflow of new foreign direct investment and stimulated capital flight. Unlike Southeast Asia, where outward-oriented policies had long been pursued, the protection of inefficient domestic industries in Latin America had been continued for far too long. Domestic economic structures had become rigid and attempts to penetrate export markets

---

8 Contrary to what is generally assumed, a considerable part of the loans was used to keep up investment (Hermes, 1992). However, this says nothing about the efficiency of investments.

met with little success. Insufficient revenues from exports made it inevitable to finance debt service with new loans.

In the debates on the debt crisis, Latin American countries play a central role. It was their inability to meet their debt-service payments that triggered the debt crisis. In Africa, private lending was of little importance. For foreign finance, African countries depended primarily on loans from foreign governments and international institutions. In absolute terms, the volume of debt was much smaller than in Latin American countries. Nevertheless, economic problems on the African continent had been mounting since 1975. A combination of poor economic policies – with respect to agriculture as well as industry and international trade – unfavourable natural circumstances, and an unfriendly international economic climate resulted in a protracted period of economic stagnation and mounting debt.

13.4.3   Quantitative data on debt and financial flows in developing countries

Debt indicators

Tables 13.2 to 13.4 give the reader an idea of the magnitude of the debt problems of developing countries since 1982. Table 13.2 presents data on trends in debt burdens in twenty-three heavily indebted countries between 1982 and 2001. The sixteen countries in the upper panel of the table are classified as 'severely indebted' in the World Bank publication *Global Development Finance*, 2003. Severely indebted countries (SICs) are countries where the present value of total debt service is over 80 per cent of GNP and/or over 220 per cent of the value of exports.[9] *Debt service* comprises annual repayments of long-term and short-term debt (including IMF credit), interest on long-term debt, charges for IMF credit and interest on short-term debt.

Debt is a persistent problem. Of the sixteen severely indebted countries included in Table 13.1, eight countries were already classified as 'heavily indebted' (HICs) in 1982.[10] But, there are also dramatic changes in levels of indebtedness. In 1982, eight countries in the table – Argentina, Brazil, Ecuador, Nicaragua, Peru, Angola, Côte d'Ivoire and Sudan – were not yet classified as heavily indebted. In these countries the debt situation has since deteriorated. In the bottom panel of Table 13.1 one finds seven countries that were considered heavily indebted in 1982, which are no longer classified as severely indebted in 2001. The debt situation in these countries has improved.

---

9 The present value of debt service is the sum of all debt service due during the lifetime of a loan, discounted to current dollar values using the interest rates of the loans. Excluding Yugoslavia and Moldova, there were forty-five SICs in 2001. The top panel of Table 13.1 includes the sixteen severely indebted developing countries with the largest absolute volume of debt. These countries account for 88 per cent of the total debt of the forty-five severely indebted countries and 97 per cent of their total debt service. The data in the table are annual data, rather than discounted present values.

10 The definitions for 1982 and 2001 are unfortunately not identical. The 'heavily indebted countries' of 1982 also include countries classified as 'moderately indebted countries' (MICs) in 2001. In 1982, four criteria of indebtedness were used. The 1982 criteria refer to the value of debt service in a given year rather than to the discounted value of debt service, as in 2001.

Table 13.2 Developing countries with heavy debt burdens, 1982–2001

	Total external debt (million current US$)			Total debt service (million current US$)			Debt as % of GNP			Debt service as % of exports		
	1982	1990	2001	1982	1990	2001	1982	1990	2001	1982	1990	2001
Severely indebted countries (SICs) 2001[a]												
Indonesia[b]	25,133	69,872	135,704	3,856	9,946	15,530	27.9	64.0	97.2	16.1	33.3	23.6
Lebanon[b]	721	1,779	12,450	117	99	1,457		51.4	70.5		3.3	50.9
Pakistan[b]	11,704	20,663	32,020	877	1,902	2,958	38.5	52.9	55.4	28.7	23.0	25.8
Syrian Arab Republic[b]	6,184	17,259	21,305	500	1,189	266	36.9	144.4	113.5	21.6	21.8	3.4
Jordan[b]	2,752	8,333	7,480	294	628	669	55.9	219.0	84.6	15.5	20.4	10.7
Argentina	43,634	62,233	136,709	4,876	6,158	24,254	55.1	46.0	52.5	63.6	37.0	66.3
Brazil	93,932	119,964	226,362	19,215	8,172	54,322	35.2	26.5	46.9	89.6	22.2	75.4
Ecuador	7,705	12,107	13,910	2,144	1,084	1,550	60.1	127.8	85.8	73.5	321.7	21.4
Nicaragua	2,936	10,745	6,391	201	16	337	127.9	1087.6	302.9	51.4	4.0	26.2
Peru	10,709	20,064	27,512	2,036	476	2,190	45.0	78.7	52.1	49.7	10.8	22.0
Uruguay[b]	2,647	4,415	9,706	513	987	1,489	29.6	49.3	52.9	39.2	40.8	36.3
Angola	447	8,594	9,600	11	326	1,865	7.6	104.6	122.1	0.5	8.1	26.5
Cote d'Ivoire	8,961	17,251	11,582	1,540	1,262	618	127.5	187.3	118.4	55.9	35.4	13.5
Nigeria[b]	11,972	33,439	31,119	2,087	3,336	2,562	24.6	130.7	81.4	25.7	22.6	12.0
Sudan	7,169	14,762	15,348	296	50	56	81.0	119.2	137.5	32.2	8.7	2.3
Congo, Dem. Rep.[b]	5,078	10,259	11,392	222	348	18	38.6	119.6	162.0	13.4	13.5	1.7
Subtotal	241,684	431,739	708,590	38,785	35,979	110,141	39	50	62	46	26	42
Total all 45 SICs[a]	270,102	494,650	777,776	43,547	43,163	113,422	41	53	64	45	28	39
Developing countries	809,293	2,188,763	2,352,106	121,730	299,062	378,675	27	35	39	19	19	19
Heavily indebted in 1982, but not severely indebted in 2001												
Egypt	27,332	33,016	29,234	1,714	3,073	1,932	115	79	29	25	22	9
Mexico	86,081	104,442	158,290	15,684	11,313	48,300	47	41	26	52	21	26
Morocco	12,090	24,458	16,962	1,721	1,793	2,628	80	98	51	58	22	18
Portugal	13,598						61			29		
Romania	10,003	1,140	11,653	2,910	18	2,607		3	30		0.3	19
South Korea	37,330	34,968	110,109	6,348	8,274	26,040	51	14	26	25	11	14
Tanzania[c]	6,201	6,456	6,676	152	179	152	51	158.5	71.9	30	32.9	10.3

Notes:
[a] Excluding Federal Republic of Yugoslavia, which was severely indebted in 2001 with a debt $ 11,740 US$ and Moldova with a debt of 1214 US$ in 2001
[b] Severely indebted in 2001, but not heavily indebted in 1982
[c] Highly indebted in 1982, moderately indebted in 2001
Sources: 1990–2001 *Global Development Finance: Striving for Stability in Development Finance*, World Bank (2003).

The countries in the bottom panel illustrate the important point that one should not worry about the volume of foreign debt as such. One should consider debt in relation to other key variables such as national income or exports. Thus, South Korea and Mexico had foreign debt stocks of respectively 110 and 158 billion dollars in 2001. Nevertheless, they are no longer regarded as severely indebted countries. In a dynamic economy such as the South Korean one, *debt service* (interest payments and repayment of debts) does not cause great problems. Debts are only a problem when debt-service obligations become an impediment to resumption of economic growth and development. In a situation of *debt overhang* there is little incentive to work at improving the economic situation, as all the fruits of growth accrue to foreign financial institutions.

The case of Mexico is also interesting. Mexico triggered the debt crisis in 1982. By 2001, it had accumulated a huge foreign debt of 158 billion dollars. Nevertheless, it was no longer listed as a severely indebted country according to the World Bank criteria.

In the last six columns of Table 13.2, foreign debt is expressed as a percentage of Gross National Income, and annual debt service as a proportion of export earnings. The data illustrate that debt servicing may absorb a considerable proportion of export earnings in developing countries. For all the SICs combined, the debt service to exports ratio was no less than 39 per cent. For all developing countries it was 19 per cent.

In terms of the debt service to exports ratio, Brazil tops the list in 2001 with 75 per cent, followed by Argentina (66 per cent) and Lebanon (51 per cent). Brazil's debt situation has worsened dramatically since 1990, when it seemed well on its way towards a more sustainable debt burden. The same holds for Argentina, where the debt service–export ratio has almost doubled since 1990, in spite of Argentina's faithful adherence to IMF policy advice. The Argentine economy collapsed in 2001 and has temporarily defaulted on its debt obligations. It is only now starting to recover from a very deep crisis.

There are several countries in the table with high debt–GNP ratios and relatively low debt service–export ratios. These include Syria, Nicaragua, Côte d'Ivoire, Sudan and Democratic Republic of Congo. Their low debt service–export ratios reflect either some form of debt default or agreements with international financial institutions, deferring debt service payments to some future date. Another factor of importance is the restructuring of debt, with an increasing share of official loans with low interest rates.

Of the sixteen severely indebted countries in the top panel of Table 13.2, six are Latin American and six are African. Severely indebted countries include both oil-exporting countries like Nigeria and Indonesia and oil-importing countries. Until 1991, oil-exporting Mexico was also severely indebted. In the oil-importing countries, the increase in oil prices in 1973 and 1979 was one of the factors contributing to the debt crisis of 1982. In the oil-exporting countries the debt problems were triggered by the huge debts they had incurred before 1982 and the subsequent collapse of oil prices during the 1980s.

In terms of absolute volume, debts are highest in the three largest Latin American countries: Brazil, Mexico and Argentina. Compared to most developing countries, average per capita incomes are relatively high in these countries, making them less eligible for debt relief. Debt–GNP ratios are by far the highest in African countries such as Democratic Republic of Congo, Sudan, Angola and Côte d'Ivoire. The highest ratio is found for Nicaragua.

Between 1982 and 1990, the debt service as a percentage of export earnings declined in twelve of the twenty-three countries included in Table 13.1, while it worsened in only four countries. For the sixteen countries with the highest debts, the ratio declined from 46 to 26 per cent. For the 45 SICs, the ratio declined from 45 to 28 per cent. This suggests a certain measure of success of the economic stabilisation programmes implemented after 1982, aimed at restoring the equilibrium on the balance of payments in the short term (see section 13.5). But debt default or deferment of debt service payments also contributed to the declining ratios. Between 1990 and 2001, the ratios worsened again, reaching aggregate levels almost as high as those of 1982.

Since 1982, debts as a percentage of GNP have increased substantially in fourteen of the sixteen countries in the top panel of Table 13.2. The same holds for all developing countries combined. The ratio of debt to GNP is steadily increasing.

Net financial flows

For most of the post-war period, there was a net inflow of financial resources into developing countries, which increased the resources potentially available for investment in growth and development. However, in the mid-1980s a perverse situation arose, in which there were net capital outflows from developing countries to rich countries. This switch is illustrated in Tables 13.3 and 13.4. Table 13.3 presents an overview of aggregate financial flows to developing countries between 1970 and 2002. Table 13.4 presents similar data for selected developing countries.

Debts are subdivided into *long-term debts* with a maturity of more than one year and *short-term debts* with a maturity of less than one year. Table 13.4 provides data on only long-term debt and foreign direct investment (FDI). Table 13.3 provides more comprehensive data, including short-term debts and IMF credits and profit remittances on FDI. The stock of total debt including short-term debt is much higher than that of long-term debt only, but the general trends for the two indicators are comparable. Table 13.3 also distinguishes between net capital flows on debt and net transfers on debt. *Net capital flows* (or net flows on debt) refer solely to the balance of new loans disbursed and principal repayments of old loans. Interest payments are left out of consideration. *Net transfers on debt* equal net capital flows minus interest payments on existing loans. There are several years in which net capital flows are positive, while net transfers on debt are negative. The table also contains data on foreign direct investment, portfolio investment, grants and profit remittances out of foreign investment. The net balance of all flows is found in the lines

Table 13.3 *Debts, foreign investment and financial flows in developing countries, 1970–2002 ($ bn)*[a]

	1970	1975	1980	1982	1985	1987	1990	1996	1997	1998	1999	2000	2001	2002
Long-term debts														
Total long-term debts	61	162	433	561	809	1,128	1,155	1,668	1,723	1,947	1,999	1,968	1,908	1,943
New loans[b]	13	44	104	116	96	120	122	246	279	287	262	257	249	218
of which private[b]	8	29	76	83	62	71	71	110	133	136	130	118	128	105
Total debt service	8	24	72	96	114	142	132	239	268	272	322	340	350	307
repayments[c]	6	15	41	48	58	84	80	161	185	180	224	238	248	220
of which, private[b]	4		34		45	0	55	108	134	136	180	189	204	167
Interest payments	2	9	31	48	56	58	53	78	83	92	97	102	103	87
Net capital flows[d]	7	29	63	68	38	36	43	85	94	107	38	19	0	−1
Net transfers on debt[e]	*4*	*21*	*32*	*20*	*−18*	*−21*	*−10*	*7*	*11*	*15*	*−60*	*−83*	*−103*	*−88*
Net foreign direct investment	2		5	11	11	15	24	128	169	174	179	161	172	143
Net Portfolio investment	0		0		16	1	5	34	27	7	15	26	6	9
Grants	2		13			17	28	28	27	28	29	30	30	33
Profit remittances on FDI	1		19			13	18	47	55	57	60	75	77	66
Aggregate net transfers	*10*		*62*			*56*	*82*	*227*	*261*	*260*	*201*	*161*	*130*	*118*
Long- and short-term debts														
Total long- and short-term debt stocks[c]	70	196	580	809	1,036	1,369	1,422	2,126	2,189	2,395	2,427	2,363	2,332	2,384
Net flows on long- and short-term debt	6		96		45	44	58	114	102	57	14	−1	3	7
Net transfers on long- and short-term debt			50		−27	−29	−10	15	−3	−52	−103	−124	−116	−96
Aggregate net transfers, incl. short term			**49**				**29**	**157**	**164**	**100**	**61**	**18**	**15**	**24**

Notes:
[a] This table contains data for 138 developing countries reporting to the World Bank. The data for 1975 and 1982 refer to 111 developing countries, the data for 1985 to 116 countries, with the exception of the items net FDI, net portfolio investment and total long-term and short-term debt stocks which refer to 157 countries, including tiny ones.
[b] Including publicly guaranteed loans from private creditors.
[c] Including IMF credit, and short-term debt.
[d] Balance of new loans disbursed and principal repayments (also referred to as net flows on debt).
[e] Net capital flows minus interest payments (discrepancies due to rounding errors).
Sources:
1970, 1980, 1990–2002: World Bank, *Global Development Finance*, 2003; 1987: *World Debt Tables, 1988–89* (1989). 1975: *World Debt Tables 1994–95* (1995). 1982: *World Debt Tables 1989–1990* (1990); 1985: *World Debt Tables 1992–1993* (1993), except the items of foreign direct investment, net portfolio investment and total long- and short-term debt stocks for 1975, 1982 and 1985, which derive from *WDI 2002*, CD-Rom, 2002. The WDI data refer to 157 countries including tiny countries, which hardly affect the totals.

Table 13.4 *Net transfers with respect to foreign debt and foreign investment selected countries, 1970–2001 ($ million)*

		1970	1980	1982	1986	1990	1995	1997	1998	1999	2000	2001
Bangladesh	NToD		553	518	806	718	56	64	177	199	203	490
	NFDI		9	0	2	3	2	159	190	180	280	78
China	NToD			−6	4,213	3,813	7,748	5,640	−2,115	−2,078	−5,201	−4,211
	NFDI			430	1,875	3,487	35,849	44,237	43,751	38,753	38,399	44,241
India	NToD	388	1,191	1,182	2,653	161	−4,146	−3,782	−613	−4,009	−130	−4,997
	NFDI	46	79	72	118	237	2,144	3,577	2,635	2,169	2,315	3,403
Indonesia	NToD	471	431	914	−833	800	−1,503	1,298	−6,184	−8,232	−8,956	−8,156
	NFDI	83	180	225	258	1,093	4,346	4,677	−356	−2,745	−4,550	−3,278
Malaysia	NToD	−24	774		−1,035	−2,481	2,903	2,939	1,306	165	−401	1,147
	NFDI	94	934	1,397	489	2,333	4,178	5,137	2,163	3,895	3,788	554
Pakistan	NToD	341	458	816	121	326	294	1,079	510	−558	−804	−244
	NFDI	23	64	64	105	245	723	716	506	532	308	383
Philippines	NToD	113	733	678	−653	−529	−1,730	1,522	−1,090	2,252	−2,124	−2,843
	NFDI	−25	−106	16	127	530	1,478	1,222	2,287	573	1,241	1,792
South Korea	NToD	195	790	−16	−4,363	−1,643	4,775	14,083	−1,327	−19,510	−6,000	−7,907
	NFDI	66	6	69	435	788	1,776	2,844	5,412	9,333	9,283	3,198
Sri Lanka	NToD	24	188		234	196	255	343	414	−97	76	53
	NFDI	0.0	43	64	30	43	56	430	193	176	173	172
Thailand	NToD	57	1,349	608	−1,237	232	3,671	2,654	−4,110	−9,036	−8,723	−9,449
	NFDI	43	190	191	263	2,444	2,068	3,895	7,315	6,213	3,366	3,820
Turkey	NToD	156	1,373	−263	261	−1,609	−3,846	13	−1,963	3,595	5,275	−6,170
	NFDI	58	18	55	125	684	885	805	940	783	982	3,266
Argentina	NToD	−203	1,518	3,325	−3,064	−3,803	1,565	2,962	6,298	224	−5,107	−1,5412
	NFDI	90	678	227	574	1,836	5,610	9,160	7,291	23,988	11,657	3,214
Brazil	NToD	1,106	−1,814	−1,400	−6,286	−3,089	483	3,981	12,163	−26,714	−14,600	−14,541
	NFDI	421	1,911	2,910	320	989	4,859	19,650	31,913	28,576	32,779	22,636
Chile	NToD	343	1,171	−515	−588	118	−662	2,290	3,113	1,027	−1,032	−451
	NFDI	−79	213	401	116	661	2,957	5,277	4,808	8,988	3,639	4,476
Colombia	NToD	118	501	551	657	−1,753	147	2,081	−1,254	1,142	−1,129	−19
	NFDI	43	157	366	674	500	968	5,562	2,829	1,468	2,281	2,328
Mexico	NToD	75	2,241	199	−7,123	3,427	7,774	−8,087	2,461	2,822	−10,406	−9,090
	NFDI	323	2,090	1,655	1,523	2,549	9,526	12,831	11,897	12,478	14,192	24,731
Peru	NToD	−108	−382	731	84	32	−124	159	37	−628	−94	−142
	NFDI	−70	27	48	22	41	2,558	2,140	1,644	1,939	662	1,064
Venezuela	NToD	162	312	−1,331	−3,764	−2,516	−2,656	−843	1,972	−1,548	−3,018	−4,079
	NFDI	−23	55	257	16	451	985	5,536	4,495	3,290	4,465	3,448

(Continued)

Table 13.4 (Continued)

Congo Dem. Rep.	NToD	−3	67	0	37	178	0	0	0	8	0	0
	NFDI	6	110	−2	6	−15	−22	−44	61	11	23	32
Côte d'Ivoire	NToD	39	427	953	−689	78	−186	−993	−840	−1,121	−756	−504
	NFDI	31	95	48	71	48	212	415	380	324	235	246
Egypt	NToD	−91	1,988	3,167	604	−760	−1,517	−809	−914	−1,297	−1,120	187
	NFDI	1	548	294	1,217	734	598	891	1,076	1,065	1,235	510
Ghana	NToD	16	112	27	249	235	346	290	199	−12	3	353
	NFDI	68	16	16	4	15	107	83	56	63	110	89
Kenya	NToD	32	261	60	131	59	−126	−352	−339	−344	−32	−152
	NFDI	14	79	13	33	57	33	20	11	14	111	5
Morocco	NToD	121	743		145	172	−1,543	−1,868	−1,192	−1,506	−943	−1,437
	NFDI	20	89	80	1	165	438	1,079	333	850	201	2,658
Nigeria	NToD	−14	981	2,010	−421	−2,377	−1,344	−1,069	−1,018	−848	−1,628	−2,452
	NFDI	205	−739	433	167	588	1,079	1,593	1,051	1,005	930	1,104
South Africa	NToD						623	−901	−1,288	−926	260	−429
	NFDI						1,248	3,811	550	1,503	969	7,162
Tanzania	NToD	49	270	259	168	157	52	121	14	80	39	40
	NFDI	3	5	17	−8	0	120	158	172	183	194	224
Zambia	NToD	302	273	160	254	−9	−15	42	−103	115	83	138
	NFDI	−297	62	39	28	203	97	207	198	162	122	72
Total 11 Asian countries	NToD	1,721	7,840	4,431	167	−16	8,477	25,833	−14,995	−37,309	−26,785	−42,287
	NFDI	388	1,417	2,583	3,827	11,887	53,505	67,679	65,036	59,862	55,585	57,629
Total 7 Latin American countries	NToD	1,493	3,547	1,560	−20,084	−7,584	6,527	2,543	24,790	−23,675	−35,386	−43,734
	NFDI	705	5,131	5,864	3,245	7,027	27,463	60,156	64,877	80,727	69,675	61,897
Total 10 African countries	NToD	451	5,122	6,636	478	−2,267	−3,710	−5,539	−5,481	−5,851	−4,094	−4,256
	NFDI	51	265	938	1,519	1,795	3,910	8,213	3,888	5,180	4,130	12,102
Total 28 countries	NToD	3,665	16,509	12,627	−19,439	−9,867	11,294	22,857	4,314	−66,835	−66,265	−90,277
	NFDI	1,144	6,813	9,385	8,591	20,709	84,878	1,36,048	1,33,801	1,45,769	1,29,390	1,31,628

Note: NToD (Net Transfers on Debt) equals net transfers on long-term capital flows minus interest payments on long-term debts (or new loans minus principal repayments and interest payments). NFDI: refers to Net Foreign Direct Investment. Foreign direct investment is defined as investment that is made to acquire a lasting management in an enterprise operating in a country other than that of the investor.

Sources:

1970–80, 1990–2001: World Bank, *Global Development Finance*, 2003;
1982: NToD: World Bank, *World Debt Tables* 1992–3; NFDI: *WDI CD-Rom*, 2002;
1986: World Bank, *World Debt Tables* 1994–1995 (1995).

referring to *aggregate net transfers*. Aggregate transfers can be calculated excluding or including short-term debt. The concept including short-term debt provides the best indication of net financial flows into or out of developing countries.

The total volume of long-term debts of the 138 developing countries reporting to the World Bank increased from 61 billion dollars in 1970 to 561 billion dollars in 1982. By 2002 the total long-term debt had increased further to 1,943 billion dollars. Including short-term debts, the 2002 debt stock amounted to 2,384 billion dollars.[11] Of course, the nominal volume of debt also depends on the exchange rate. If the value of the dollar drops, as in 1985–7, 1990, 1995 or 2003, the nominal dollar value of debt contracted in foreign currencies other than the dollar will go up. Another vital consideration is the exchange rate of the borrowing country. If the currency of a country suddenly depreciates against the dollar, as in the Asian crisis, the value of a country's debt in national currency can soar, increasing the burden of debt tremendously.

Table 13.3 reveals that the increase in the share of private credit from 1970 onwards came to an end in 1982. After 1982, private financial institutions were no longer willing to provide additional credit. The share of private credit declined from 72 per cent in 1982 to 48 per cent in 2002. Most of the loans provided in the 1980s served to finance the repayment of earlier loans. The balance of not publicly guaranteed private loans – a category not included separately in Table 13.3 – even turned negative for a time.

It is interesting to note the differences between net capital flows and net transfers on debt. Net capital flows remained positive during the entire period 1970–2000. The volume of new loans exceeded the sum of repayment of earlier loans and the outflow of capital to other countries. The net long-term capital inflow decreased from 68 billion dollars in 1982 to 36 billion dollars in 1987. After that it picked up again, increasing in nominal terms to 107 billion dollars by 1998. Hermes (1992) has calculated that, expressed in constant 1988 dollars, the real value of capital inflows between 1981 and 1989 halved. After 1998, net capital flows dried up in the wake of the Asian crisis, reaching zero in 2001.

The picture is different for net transfers on debt, which include interest payments on debt. Net transfers turned negative after 1984. Instead of a net flow of resources from rich to poor countries, characteristic of the post-war economic order, there was an outflow of resources from poor to rich countries. This net outflow reached its peak in 1988. Since then there has been a recovery. Between 1992 and 1998 the net transfers on debt became positive again. After 1997, there was once again a dramatic downturn. Suddenly, net transfers on debt took vast negative proportions. If we include short-term debt, net transfers on total debt were continuously negative in all years between 1985 and 2002.

---

11 One hundred and thirty-eight developing countries participate in the World Bank Debt Reporting System. Developing countries that were part of the former Soviet Union are also included. For earlier years' data refer to smaller numbers of countries.

Increasing role for foreign direct investment

The picture of a permanent and massive outflow of financial resources based on statistics on loans and interest payments on loans is somewhat misleading. One of the most striking trends emerging from Table 13.3 is the increasing importance of foreign direct investment compared to loans. One of the advantages of FDI is that it is a non-debt-creating inflow.[12] The increase in the inflow of foreign direct investment more than compensated for the decline in net capital flows. Long-term net aggregate transfers remained positive in all years for which we have data. Even including short-term debt, net aggregate transfers were positive in all years since 1989. The havoc wrought by the Asian crisis is clearly visible in the downward trends since 1997, but even in this period the net balance remains positive. Our earlier conclusion in section 13.1.1 that the post-war economic order is characterised by net inflows of financial resources to developing countries is borne out by the data of Table 13.3. But, the table also serves to illustrate the amplitude and severity of the financial crises affecting developing countries.

Country data

Table 13.4 presents data for twenty-eight selected countries for two of the key variables – net transfers on long-term debt and net foreign direct investment. The regional differences are striking. The outflow of resources in the 1980s hit Latin American and African countries far harder than Asian countries. Latin America suffered very heavily between 1984 and 1990. As illustrated by the data for 1986, negative transfers on debt were not compensated for by increased flows of foreign direct investment. Mexico, for example, was faced by an enormous capital flight between 1982 and 1986. Though there was some recovery after 1990, the situation in Latin America continues to be very volatile. When economic prospects improve, flight capital can return to a country, but it is also quick to leave again. In Asia, net transfers on debt were hardly ever negative and were more than compensated for by increases in foreign direct investment.

The negative net transfers on debt in Chile and South Korea in the 1980s have different connotations than in the other countries. In the late 1980s, favourable economic developments formed the basis for repayment of part of foreign debts. For South Korea, the declining ratio of debt to national income is also clearly visible in Table 13.2.

For the 1990s, we must distinguish between the first and second halves of the decade. With the exception of the African countries, developing countries experienced positive net inflows of capital in the first half of the decade. After the Asian crisis these flows turned deeply negative. The effects of the crisis are clearly visible in the entries for the Asian countries most hit by the crisis: Indonesia, the Philippines, South Korea, Thailand and Malaysia. In Latin America,

---

12 From a nationalist perspective, one of the potential disadvantages is the increasing control of the domestic economy by foreign capital.

Argentina and Brazil experienced the great difficulties. But, again it is interesting to note that in most countries net FDI flows compensated for the drying up of long-term loans. The only exception to this rule is Indonesia, where political instability also contributed to negative net foreign direct investment.

13.4.4   How to deal with debt?

One of the immediate consequences of the debt crisis of 1982 was a sudden drop in the flow of private loans to developing countries. When new loans were forthcoming, they served mainly to finance existing debt service. Finance for new investments or imports of indispensable intermediate inputs was scarce. Thus the debt crisis contributed to the stagnation of economic growth in many African and Latin American developing countries. The debt crisis also threatened the stability of the international banking system and consequently the entire international financial system. Many private banks, especially in the USA, had pursued reckless credit policies. Their existence was jeopardised when countries in Latin America and Eastern Europe suspended debt-service payments following the Mexican example.

During the first years after 1982, therefore, international efforts were aimed mainly at preventing the imminent collapse of the financial system. Later, attention shifted to the consequences of the debt crisis for developing countries. The International Monetary Fund played a prominent role in the prevention of an international financial crisis. It imposed rigorous changes in domestic economic policy as conditions for balance-of-payments support, new loans and agreements on debt rescheduling. Since private capital flows had dried up, developing countries could no longer get around the 'conditionality' of official financial institutions. The World Bank had formerly operated independently of the IMF and had focused on long-term investment projects. Now it also made its loans conditional on acceptance of IMF policy recommendations. These recommendations are generally referred to as *structural adjustment policies*. Their short-term aim is to improve the balance of payments and reduce government deficits (*stabilisation*). The long-term objective is to achieve a more dynamic and flexible economic structure (*structural adjustment*).

In the short term, the goal was to cut back on developing country imports in order to reduce deficits in the balance of payments. This would decrease the need for external finance. Between 1982 and 1985 these policies have been fairly successful (Hermes, 1992). Deficits in the balance of payments were indeed reduced, not so much by growth of exports but by a decline in imports. Private banks that had over-exposed themselves during the 1970s, increased their reserves for non-repayable debts. By 1985, it was clear that a collapse of the international financial system had been averted. Between 1985 and 1990, debt service as a percentage of export revenues also started to go down (see Table 13.2).

The consequences of stabilisation policies were less positive for developing countries. The restrictions on imports of semi-finished goods and capital goods led to a slowdown in industrial production. In some Latin American countries and most countries in Sub-Saharan Africa per capita incomes fell sharply. Economic stagnation triggered a debate on how to mitigate or avoid the negative consequences of the debt crisis for developing countries through debt relief, which continues to this very day. In this debate two conflicting points of view can be distinguished: that of debt forgiveness and that of moral hazard (e.g. Buiter and Srinivasan, 1987; Griffin, 1988; Neumayer, 2002; Raffer and Singer, 2001; Sanford, 2002; Stiglitz, 2002; Wood, 1985).

Debt relief versus moral hazard

Authors such as Griffin, Singer and recently Stiglitz argued that the debt crisis and economic stagnation were very much the result of external factors such as slower growth of the world economy, deteriorating terms of trade, protectionism by advanced and irresponsible policies of private banks and international institutions. Since the enormous debt service hinders all attempts to revive economic growth, debt relief or debt forgiveness is essential. Debt overhang reduces all incentives for economic development. Therefore debt relief should have the highest priority.

Buiter and Srinivasan (1987) have sharply criticised this point of view. They represent the moral hazard point of view, which argues that debt forgiveness rewards bad economic policies and profligate behaviour (for a recent overview of the arguments see Neumayer, 2002). According to Buiter and Srinivasan, the main causes of economic stagnation and rising debt in Latin America were bad economic management and profligate economic policies. These countries had high budget deficits and pursued inefficient protectionist policies, which resulted in inflexible economic structures. Major debtors such as Brazil, Argentina and Mexico were much richer than the poor Asian countries, which pursued more prudent and effective macro-economic policies. Their financial problems were caused in part by capital flight. Debt relief would mean rewarding economic mismanagement and punishing countries that pursued more effective policies and paid their debts. In Latin American countries, structural adjustment policies were needed to restore the confidence of international financial institutions. Financial inflows would then resume and capital flight would be reversed.

Buiter and Srinivasan agreed that financial aid flows to very poor African countries should be increased. But they regarded debt restructuring in Latin America as a disguised subsidy to the American banking system. Moral hazard refers to not only the policies of developing countries, but also to behaviour of private financial institutions. Interestingly the same argument is used by recent critics of the international financial institutions (e.g. Stiglitz, 2000; 2002). They argue that debt problems have been in part caused by actions of irresponsible financial institutions in the rich countries, which should bear part of the costs of their own risky behaviour. Stiglitz argues with considerable force that bankruptcy laws in developing countries should be tightened. Inefficient firms and banks should be allowed to go bankrupt, so their assets can be bought up and recapitalised by new owners who can restart operations. International banks that have provided loans to inefficient or corrupt organisations, in the conviction that they would be bailed out in any event by the international financial institutions, should be forced to pay the price for their own decisions. Even the former vice-president of the IMF, Stanley Fischer, concedes this point. He argues that if private banks are in part responsible for financial crises, they should contribute to a recovery by providing new sources of finance (Citrin and Fischer, 2000). Empirical research throws some doubt on whether debt forgiveness contributes to improved policies and performance and thus provides evidence in support of the moral hazard reasoning. Easterly (2000; 2001a) argues that past forgiveness efforts have had perverse incentive effects and have contributed little to increased productive potential. Knack (2001) argues that aid flows to countries with weak governance further weaken the quality of governance.

Both parties in the debate acknowledge that resumption of economic growth in the poorest developing countries requires renewed net transfers of resources. However, one point of view stresses outright cancellation or reduction of debts; the other point of view emphasises the implementation of programmes of structural adjustment and improvements in domestic policies as a condition for new loans or the restructuring of earlier ones. As time has passed, the notion of debt relief for the poorest developing countries has been gaining ground.

Debt relief

Three plans have been of major importance in the international responses to debt and the debt crisis:

1. The Baker Plan in 1985 (*A Programme for Sustained Growth*);
2. The Brady Plan for voluntary debt reduction in 1989;
3. The Heavily Indebted Poor Countries initiative of 1996 (HIPC initiative).

1. The Baker plan   This plan was put forward by the American Secretary of the Treasury, Baker. It assumes that revival of economic growth is only possible if the net inflow of financial resources to developing countries is resumed. The plan argues for cooperation between the IMF, the World Bank and private banking institutions. Private institutions are encouraged to grant new loans. A precondition for the expansion of credit is the pursuit of adjustment policies. The aim is resumption of net capital inflows. At this stage, debt reduction is not yet on the cards. The adjustment policies in the Baker Plan are not limited to short-term stabilisation, as was the case between 1982 and 1985. The plan also strives to improve the functioning of markets in the long term, by reducing protection and opening up the economy to foreign investment and foreign competition.

The Baker Plan has been only moderately successful. Private banks have been reluctant to cooperate voluntarily and the recommendations for structural adjustment have been only partly realised. Most of the funds went to just three large countries: Brazil, Mexico and Argentina. Moreover, the renewed net inflow of capital was still modest.

In the meantime, it was realised that debt reduction should also be considered. In the poor African countries the debt burden was so heavy that the problems could not be solved without outside help. A beginning was made with debt relief and cancellation of part of the debt stock. As official financial institutions had supplied almost all loans, policy in this area was not dependent on the cooperation of the private banking system. Similar policies were proposed with respect to severely indebted Eastern European countries such as Poland and Bulgaria. Further, private banks realised they were better off with repayment of a portion of outstanding debts than default on total debt. They started participating in plans and measures for voluntary debt reduction.

2. The Brady plan   The Brady Plan of 1989 focuses on voluntary debt reduction in a country-by-country approach. The IMF and the World Bank reserved financial resources for this purpose. Private banks were persuaded to write down the value of risky outstanding loans. The main argument for debt reduction is a decrease in the so-called *debt overhang*. If a country has an excessive foreign debt, all benefits of domestic policy reforms accrue to foreign creditors. This undermines the political will to implement painful adjustment measures. Debt reduction may increase the willingness and capability to meet part of future debt service obligations. Another advantage is that more financial means are available for investment. The creditors themselves benefit more from partial repayment of debt in the future than from no repayment at all. Several techniques for the reduction of debt have been developed. They include buying back outstanding debts at a reduced prices, selling debt on the second-hand market for debts, debt-for-equity swaps in which loans are exchanged for equity shares, cancelling debt in exchange for environmental protection (debt-for-nature swaps), and replacing short-term debt by long-term debt with lower interest rates. The willingness to implement structural adjustment packages negotiated with the IMF remains a precondition for all types of debt-reduction deals.

Between 1985 and 1990, debt reduction totalled 25 billion dollars. In relation to the total volume of debt, this is merely a drop in the ocean – 2.4 per cent of the average long-term debt stock. Nevertheless, there were some countries where economic growth resumed, so that debt service became less of a problem, in spite of the high volume of debt. In the second half of the 1980s, capital flows to many developing countries resumed as discussed above. By the early 1990s, even in Africa the net total resources flows had turned positive again (see also Lensink, 1995).

3. The Heavily Indebted Poor Countries initiative of 1996   During the second half of the 1990s, the debt situation of developing countries worsened again and new initiatives were taken to reduce the debt burdens of the poorest developing countries, in addition to existing mechanisms for debt rescheduling and debt reduction. In 1996, the IMF and the World Bank adopted the initiative for Debt Relief for Heavily Indebted Poor Countries (HIPC). The main argument was that even with sound economic policies and the full use of all existing mechanisms for debt rescheduling, debt reduction and concessional finance, poor countries would not be able to reach sustainable levels of debt within a reasonable time period (Boote and Thugge, 1997).

Countries eligible for the HIPC initiative are the severely indebted countries with the lowest per capita incomes. The conditions for eligibility for debt relief include an unsustainable debt burden and a strong record of policy reform under IMF/World Bank-supported structural adjustment programmes. An interesting new condition for debt relief is the drafting of a poverty reduction strategy. The resources that come free through the reduction of debt service obligations should primarily be devoted to health, education, social services and poverty reduction. Some thirty-seven countries are potentially eligible, the great majority of them in Africa. The total cost of the initiative is estimated at $50 billion in net present value terms, though not all the resources have yet been assembled IDA/IMF, 2003.[13] Once the conditions have been met, debt is actually cancelled.

The initiative distinguishes between an initial three-year first stage during which debts are rescheduled. If countries fulfil the policy conditions during these three years, a second three-year stage of support begins in which negative flows on debt are reduced. If the country meets the policy conditions of the second stage, a completion point is reached after which the total stock of debt is reduced. Up to 80 per cent of the present value of the debt stock can be cancelled, depending on the country's circumstances. Debt sustainability is considered to be reached when a country is able to meet its current and future debt-service obligations in full, without recourse to further rescheduling. By September 2003, some twenty-seven countries had received some form of HIPC relief, twenty-three of them in Africa. Seven countries have reached their completion points, including Bolivia, Burkina Faso, Mali, Mauritania, Mozambique and Uganda.

A characteristic element of the new programme is the shift from providing finance on the basis of agreements about future policies to the providing of finance on the basis of positive evaluations of past policies. At each stage, past performance is assessed before reaching a decision on debt reduction in the next stage. Thus, if the evaluation of past policies is positive at the completion point, debt relief is provided unconditionally. If the evaluation is not positive, debt relief will not be provided, at least in theory.

Grants versus loans

Even if sustainable levels of debt can be reached, the poorest developing countries will continue to be dependent on concessional finance. One of the current

---

13 IMF, *Factsheet – Debt Relief under the Heavily Indebted Countries (HIPC) Initiative,* http://www.imf.org/external/np/exr/facts/hipc.htm

elements in the debate is whether loans should be replaced by grants, as advocated by the Meltzer report (2000). Grants would provide development finance, without increasing the debt burdens of poor. Opponents of these proposals, however, argue that the conversion of loans to grants involves a secret agenda for reduction of the total volume of aid (Sanford, 2002). If the total volume of aid remains unchanged, the shift to grants implies a reduction in the size of actual financial flows. Also, the provision of grants will increasingly depend on evaluations of past performance rather than on agreements about future policies. This increases the power and leverage of the international financial institutions.

13.5   Structural adjustment policies

13.5.1   Neoliberalism versus structuralism

The five main objectives of structural adjustment policy are summarised in Box 13.7.

Box 13.7   Objectives of structural adjustment policies

1. Improvement of the external balance between imports and exports. This goal is pursued by reductions in expenditures, depreciation of overvalued exchange rates and shifts in expenditure to domestically produced goods and services.
2. Rationalisation of the public sector and cuts in government expenditures, in particular expenditures on loss-making public enterprises.
3. Structural adjustments in the production structure aimed at a more efficient allocation of production factors, greater flexibility and sustained growth.
4. Stable incentives for private enterprise, liberalisation of the economy and reinforcement of market mechanisms.
5. Opening up of the economy to international competition.

Source: Selowsky (1987).

Structural adjustment policy stands in sharp contrast to the central ideas underlying development strategies from 1950 to 1980. In these strategies government was assigned a critical role in initiating development and industrialisation. The state acted as a large-scale investor itself and tried to coordinate private sector investment by means of planning. It provided protection to the industrial sector against cut-throat international competition, in order to give domestic industries time to mature.

The preference for government intervention was based on a *structuralist interpretation* of the economic conditions in poor countries (Sunkel 1993; Sunkel and Zulefa, 1990; Urquidi, 1993; see also Chapter 3). Structuralist theories assume that the conditions for a beneficial functioning of the market mechanism are absent in developing countries, because there are so many restrictions, bottlenecks and market imperfections. For instance, there is insufficient infrastructure, insufficient education for productive participation in the modern economy, lack of information and a lack of entrepreneurship. Underdeveloped financial markets cannot supply potential entrepreneurs with sufficient finance. The risks of traditional agriculture restrict the opportunities for innovation. Under such circumstances, a free-market economy will not motivate people to engage in new productive activities. Rather, it will cause their situation to deteriorate. Structuralist policies aim at the supply side of the economy. But from the structuralist perspective, reinforcement of the supply side in developing countries requires government intervention to compensate for market imperfections (Mosley, 1991; Toye, 1993). Structuralist notions thus justify extensive government intervention in the economy.

Structural adjustment policy is a frontal neoliberal attack on post-war structuralist policies. Advocates of structural adjustment believe that many African and Latin American governments pursued policies which gave rise to increasing economic imbalances and market distortions. In some developing countries the interventionist state itself had become an obstacle to economic dynamism. Although the debate on the role of the government is far from concluded, previous chapters have shown that such criticisms are far from unfounded.

In the explanations of economic stagnation in the 1980s, less importance is ascribed to external causes, such as decreasing export prices or the stagnation of the world economy. The emphasis is mainly on internal factors such as corruption, rent seeking and misguided domestic policies. It is emphasised that several Asian developing economies performed very well during the 1980s in spite of unfavourable external circumstances. It is argued that countries that converted from *inward-looking* to *outward-looking* development strategies at an early stage did much better economically than countries that continued to pursue inward-looking import substitution policies (see Chapter 9).

It is interesting to note that the advocates of structural adjustment policy also use structuralist-type arguments, in spite of their preference for free markets; hence the term 'structural' adjustment. They agree with the older structuralists that the supply side of the economy in developing countries does not function properly, owing to bottlenecks, constraints and market imperfections. Economic institutions do not provide sufficient incentives for productive behaviour. Therefore, countries must explicitly pursue a structural policy aimed at increasing their productive capacities and the efficiency of the production structure. But in this case, government policies, parastatals, excessive regulation and intervention in the market are identified as the prime causes of structural inflexibility. The traditional structuralist argument is thus stood on its head (Toye, 1993). Liberalisation is the instrument for structural reform.

13.5.2   *Structural adjustment, IMF and the World Bank*

The discussion of structural adjustment predates the debt crisis (Lensink, 1995). As early as 1979 the World Bank introduced the financial instrument of Structural Adjustment Loans (SALs). At the time, the World Bank was deeply dissatisfied with its project-related financial flows. Too many funds were allocated to large-scale capital-intensive projects of dubious effectiveness (Toye, 1993). Far from all projects were completed. After official completion, sometimes insufficient means were available to continue the projects. Developing countries were not so much in need of new project aid, but rather of additional resources for the completion, upkeep and maintenance of existing infrastructural projects. As prices did not reflect real scarcity relations due to distorted markets, it was almost impossible to formulate good projects and to weigh their costs and benefits.

The structural adjustment loans were designed to make new, non-project-related funds available and, at the same time, to formulate conditions with respect to reinforcement of market mechanisms, strengthening economic incentives, improving macro-economic policies and liberalising the economy.

After the debt crisis, the pressures to implement structural adjustment policies increased. The roles of the World Bank and the IMF converged. Initially, the World Bank had focused on medium- and long-term project aid and the IMF on short-run financial support for countries with balance-of-payments difficulties. Now the World Bank moved from project to programme lending and the IMF created instruments for medium-term structural adjustment (Lensink, 1995). The World Bank and the IMF coordinated their actions and both set structural adjustment as a condition for the provision of new loans. First, a country had to turn to the IMF for a stand-by arrangement through which means are made available to finance deficits in the balance of payments. Only after IMF conditions had been met, could a country apply for adjustment loans from the World Bank aimed at long-term restructuring of the economy. Between 1979 and 1991, 99 developing countries received structural adjustment loans from the World Bank. The reforms developed into a coherent package which was referred to as the *Washington Consensus* and which consisted of policies aimed at short-term stabilisation and long-term liberalisation and market reform (Williamson, 1990).

13.5.3   Stabilisation and structural adjustment

Although the term 'structural adjustment' is frequently used to refer to both *economic stabilisation policy* and *structural adjustment policy* in a more restricted sense, it is useful to distinguish clearly between these two kinds of policy (Hermes, 1992; Lensink, 1993; Mosley, 1991).

The aims of stabilisation policies are to restore the external balance on the balance of payments and to reduce inflation in the short term. Imports should be restricted and exports should be promoted. Financial means, which were employed to finance imports, thus become available for debt servicing. Stabilisation is realised by means of measures that influence the demand side of the economy. Demand is restricted by measures such as tax increases, reduction of government deficits and government expenditures, abolition of government subsidies, higher prices for government services, lower wages, tight monetary policies, increases in interest rates and, especially, depreciation of overvalued exchange rates. Depreciation makes imports more expensive and exports cheaper, contributing to a recovery of the external balance. Stabilisation measures are summarised in Box 13.8.

Box 13.8 Stabilisation measures
- Devaluation of overvalued exchange rates.
- Reduction of budget deficits; raising taxes; cutting expenditure, reforming tax system.
- Restructuring foreign debts.
- Financing government debts on capital markets instead of through monetary financing.
- Increasing interest rates (financial liberalisation); increasing food prices; increasing prices of public services.
- Controlling wages.

Structural adjustment measures are measures directed towards long-run improvements in the supply side of the economy, so that production can increase and economic subjects can respond better to economic incentives. Structural adjustment packages usually include stabilisation measures, but their scope is wider. The long-run aim is to reduce the role of the state and liberalise the whole economy, so that prices actually reflect scarcity and promote more efficient economic behaviour. Discrimination against agriculture in favour of the industrial sector should be ended. Restrictions on trade and capital flows should be phased out. Protection of domestic industry by means of tariffs and quotas should be reduced. Domestic firms should be exposed more to foreign competition and should try to penetrate export markets. Exports should follow the lines of comparative advantage.

Of course, stabilisation programmes and structural adjustment programmes are complementary. The imbalances in the economy that result in financial crisis in the short term are partly due to the inadequacy of domestic supply with respect to domestic demand. This causes inflation and deficits on the current account of the balance of payments. In the long-term removal of structural impediments and increased flexibility of the production structure are the best way to prevent financial crisis from recurring (Husain, 1993).

Structural adjustment policy measures

In negotiations with the IMF and the World Bank a set of economic reform measures is drawn up for each specific country. The provision of new loans and development finance is made dependent on the wholehearted acceptance of the package of reforms. Ideally the concrete package differs from country to country, depending on the circumstances. But the IMF is increasingly accused of a cookbook approach to structurally imposing a uniform set of measures on all countries, with little regard for their differences and specific conditions

(Stiglitz, 2002). A list of frequently used measures is reproduced in Box 13.9 (Doroodian, 1993; Greenaway and Morrisey, 1993; Lensink, 1995; Mosley, 1991; Mosley, Harrigan and Toye, 1991; Selowsky, 1987; Toye, 1993).

Box 13.9 Structural adjustment policy measures
Liberalisation of domestic markets
- Abolition of price controls and liberalisation of price policies; an end to the practice of indexing wages to inflation, abolition of minimum wage regulations.
Trade policy
- Depreciation of overvalued exchange rates. A cheaper currency makes imports more expensive and exports cheaper. Import-substituting domestic production becomes more profitable.
- Liberalisation of trade policy by abolishing import quotas; import tariff systems are made more transparent and tariffs themselves are reduced. When exchange rates are determined by market forces, growth of imports will lead to depreciation of the exchange rate. This in turn makes for recovery of the external balance. Liberalisation of imports also undermines monopoly positions of traders who profited from import licensing under a protectionist regime. Former domestic monopolists are exposed to the discipline of international competition.
- Striking a balance between incentives for import-substituting production and incentives for export production, so as to promote a stronger outward orientation.
The public sector, fiscal policy, government expenditures, public enterprises
- Reforms of the budgetary and fiscal system, aimed at better control of government expenditure and more effective collection of taxes.
- Reducing government expenditures and government deficits.
- Restructuring the priorities in government investment. More priority to investment in the agricultural sector.
- Increasing the government's capacity to formulate and execute government investment programmes; increasing the general efficiency of government.
- Increasing the output and efficiency of loss-making public enterprises (*parastatals*).
- Privatisation of public enterprises and public activities.
- Reducing subsidies for energy and food. Increasing taxes on consumer goods.
Capital market
- Liberalisation of domestic and foreign capital markets.
- Deregulation of interest rates. Higher interest rates elicit higher domestic savings. Higher interest costs lead to a more efficient use of capital in the production process.
- Creating new financial institutions; privatisation or restructuring of government-controlled banks.
Agricultural policy
- Increasing agricultural prices in order to stimulate agricultural production.
- Abolishing or limiting the role of state marketing boards that used to have a monopoly on the trade in food and export products. Liberalisation of agricultural trade.
- Reducing subsidies for agricultural inputs.
Industrial policy
- Intensifying incentives for efficient production in the industrial sector, among others by refusing to bail out unprofitable firms and investment projects.
Energy policy
- Increasing the domestic prices of energy to relieve the government budget; promoting the domestic supply and efficient use of energy.

13.5.4   The effectiveness of structural adjustment programmes

Since 1979, over 150 countries have received World Bank loans in the context of structural adjustment programmes (Easterly, 2001b). While short-run stabilisation policies have been fairly effective, the long-run success of structural adjustment policies has been fiercely debated for years. Two central questions in this debate are: (1) how acceptable are the social consequences of adjustment policies? (2) to what degree does structural adjustment contribute to economic recovery? Unfortunately, it is hard to provide unambiguous empirical answers to these questions. First, by no means all adjustment measures agreed upon are actually implemented; next there are countries which do not receive adjustment loans but nevertheless implement their own adjustment policies (e.g. India). Third, circumstances and the initial conditions differ from country to country. Fourth, policy is only one of the many factors impinging on economic and social development.

Factors affecting the success of adjustment policies

In the literature the following factors are identified as important for the success of adjustment policies (Edwards, 1990; Greenaway and Morrisey, 1993; Lensink, 1995; Mosley, 1991; Mosley, Harrigan and Toye, 1991).

1. *Implementation.* Is a government really prepared to implement painful measures? Isn't the drawing up of an SAP just a feint to obtain new loans? On average only 60 per cent of all reform measures agreed upon are actually implemented (Mosley, 1991). In the nine countries studied by Mosley, Harrigan and Toye (1991), the implementation percentages vary from 25 per cent to 90 per cent. Stabilisation measures are generally easier to implement than structural reform measures, which often meet with resistance from powerful interest groups whose 'rents' are threatened. In recent years, the emphasis is shifting from conditionality, to the provision of further development finance on the basis of evaluations of past performance (Meltzer, 2000).

2. *Credibility of government policy.* Is the government able to convince private entrepreneurs that it will continue to carry out adjustment policies in spite of their unpopularity? If credibility is lacking, positive responses from the private sector are very unlikely. Frequent changes in policy have negative effects on economic development.

3. *The sequencing of adjustment measures.* If policies are implemented in the wrong order, they may actually harm rather than aid the economy (Greenaway and Morrissey, 1993). This is illustrated by the following examples. Abolishing controls over capital flows before reforming domestic financial markets can result in capital flight. Without prior reduction of budget deficits, liberalisation of financial markets will lead to inflation. A sudden increase in interest rates may also increase government expenditures. Without prior macro-economic stabilisation, liberalisation of trade leads to a

deterioration of the economic situation. Liberalisation of trade without depreciation of the currency leads to increasing deficits on the balance of payments. Sooner or later these will force the government to intervene again.

In the literature the following sequence is suggested as most fruitful (Edwards 1990; Greenaway and Morrissey, 1993; Lensink, 1995, p. 228 ff; Tobin, 2000; Toye, 1994).

1. Reform policies start with macro-economic stabilisation, depreciation of exchange rates, tackling inflation and reducing government deficits. Almost all authors stress the importance of reducing budget deficits and depreciating the currency as the first step in any process of reform.
2. Liberalisation of the domestic real economy: liberalisation of prices and liberalisation of labour markets.
3. Liberalisation of foreign trade. Once the domestic economy has been liberalised, the stage has been set for liberalisation of foreign trade.
4. Reform of domestic financial markets. If financial markets are liberalised before step 2, financial resources may be wasted on unproductive activities. Most authors argue that financial liberalisation should come after trade liberalisation, to avoid resources being squandered on import substitution. According to some authors, efficient allocation of production factors only takes place if the financial system is already well developed. This argues for financial liberalisation preceding trade liberalisation. Thus the sequence of steps 3 and 4 is still disputed. In practice, trade liberalisation tends to precede financial liberalisation. It should be emphasised that the liberalisation of financial markets requires increased regulation, oversight and transparency of the financial system, without which financial liberalisation contributes to corruption and risky investment behaviour.
5. The last stage involves liberalisation of international capital flows. If one does this before domestic financial markets have been liberalised, there will be capital flight because domestic interest rates are still too low due to interest and credit ceilings. Liberalisation of international flows comes in two steps: liberalisation of long-term investment flows and liberalisation of short-term capital flows and full exchange-rate convertibility (Eichengreen, 2000). Liberal authors claim that full liberalisation of international capital markets is the ultimate goal for all countries. An increasing number of critics argue that the full liberalisation of short-term capital movements is extremely destructive for developing countries (see section 13.6).

Social consequences of adjustment policies

In 1987, Cornia, Jolly and Stewart published their study *Adjustment with a Human Face*. In this study they criticised the social consequences of adjustment programmes. Cutbacks in government expenditures were realised at the expense of education and health-care expenditures. Abolition of subsidies and increased prices of food and energy subsidies hurt the poor. Thus structural adjustment policy led to not only further impoverishment, but also to insufficient investment in human capital, which endangers the opportunities of future economic growth. The authors pleaded for a more gradual implementation of structural adjustment policy and for compensatory finance to deal with the social consequences of expenditure cuts. Their call has to some extent been heeded by UN organisations like UNICEF and the Economic Commission for Africa. In the design of new adjustment programmes the World Bank today also pays more attention to the consequences for poverty, at least on paper. Thus, the formulation of *Poverty Reduction Strategies* is now one of the conditions for debt relief.

A counter-argument is that subsidies, educational facilities and health-care services in developing countries are usually not accessible to the poorest anyway. Because of the urban–industrial bias, urban inhabitants and relatively privileged people like students, civil servants or industrial employees are the main beneficiaries of public services and subsidies. An adjustment policy that cuts back on subsidies may raise the price of agricultural products and improve the terms of trade for the rural areas. This would actually improve the situation of some of the poor who depend on agriculture for their livelihood.

The question is not really whether structural adjustment policies have negative social consequences. In the short term, it is certain that they do. More important is the question whether or not adjustment policies lead to an improvement in economic dynamics in the long term (Gunning, 1988). If this is the case, then short-term suffering may be justified. The worst case is a situation in which adjustment policy takes its toll of the poor without the prospects of resumption of economic growth and development. This is what occurred in the Russian Federation and other former Soviet republics after their flawed transition from a centrally planned economy to a market economy after 1991 (Menshikov, 1993).

Does structural adjustment policy achieve its goals?

With respect to the effects of the structural adjustment policy, opinions in the literature vary from rather favourable to extremely critical (Cornia, Jolly, Stewart, 1987; Cornia, van der Hoeven and Mkandawire, 1992; Elbadawi, 1992; Elbadawi, Ghura and Uwugaren, 1992; Husain, 1993; Stiglitz, 2002; van der Hoeven and Taylor, 2000; World Bank and UNDP, 1989).

Before discussing the pros and cons of structural adjustment, it is important to note that countries may not have a choice whether or not to follow adjustment policies. Any country that is faced with external shocks and soaring deficits on its balance of payments will sooner or later be forced to implement or undergo some kind of economic adjustment, whether or not it formally negotiates a structural adjustment package with international financial institutions such as the IMF or the World Bank. So the most interesting questions focus more on the kind of adjustment policies to be implemented rather than on whether or not adjustment policies should be followed.

In a large-scale evaluation study for the 1980s, Mosley, Harrigan and Toye (1991) conclude that countries that have implemented far-reaching structural adjustment policies are generally more successful in terms of economic growth and balance of payments. The effects on export performance are not all that clear (Greenaway and Morrissey, 1993).

Of the ninety-nine structural adjustment programmes, forty-four were drawn up for extremely poor countries in Sub-Saharan Africa. The results in this region are definitely disappointing. It is true that African countries that have implemented more drastic adjustment programmes do not perform as poorly as other countries, but the trends of economic stagnation have by no means been reversed. An earlier optimistic World Bank report on the success of structural adjustment policies in Africa (World Bank and UNDP, 1989) has been severely criticised (Mosley and Weeks, 1992). A later article by Mosley and his associates (Mosley *et al.*, 1995) concludes that there is no statistical support for the assertion that structural adjustment promotes growth in Sub-Saharan Africa. Only seven of the eighteen countries following adjustment programmes showed improved growth performance, while fourteen suffered declines in investment.

In a review of studies on structural adjustment in Africa, Lensink (1995) concludes that there are modest positive effects on GDP growth, mixed results with respect to export growth and disappointing effects on savings and investments. But the methodological problems of ascertaining the impacts of structural adjustment remain great. In addition to economic policy, numerous other factors also play an important role in this region, like constant political turmoil, ethnic conflicts, droughts and an unfavourable international economic climate. A recent study by Easterly[14] for the period 1980–1999 finds no systematic relationship between structural adjustment lending and growth. Loans do tend to mitigate the negative impact of economic contraction on poverty, while reducing the positive effects of growth on poverty reduction, thus smoothing the overall effects of growth on poverty.

It is worrisome that many studies conclude that there are adverse effects of structural adjustment programmes on investment levels. The explanation for this is that reductions in government expenditures of course also affect government investment. Contrary to what was anticipated, this was not compensated for in the short term by increases in private investment. In the long term, a decline in investment rates is incompatible with the goals of increasing productive capacity. At the same time the decline in investment is also interpreted by some as the result of stricter criteria being applied to unprofitable projects.

For Latin America, the results of structural adjustment are also mixed (Dijkstra, 2000). Almost all Latin American countries have followed structural adjustment policies, but these have so far not resulted in stable and sustained growth in most of these countries. While trade liberalisation contributed to static efficiency and export growth, Latin America experienced a decline in

---

14 W. Easterly, *IMF and World Bank Structural Adjustment Programs and Poverty*, World Bank http://www.nber.org/~confer/2001/ccdf/easterly.pdf

its technological capabilities and decline in many of the more advanced and high-tech branches of manufacturing, including capital goods sectors, which suffered from increased competition from imports.

Structural adjustment and infrastructural investment in Africa

Mosley (1991) presents a useful distinction between adjustment programmes in middle-income countries and adjustment programmes in the poorest African countries with a stagnating economy. In middle-income countries, structural reforms may help transform a too inward-looking economy into a more export-oriented economy. In this respect, structural adjustment programmes in Turkey and the Philippines have been fairly successful. In countries like Chile, Mexico, pre-1997 Indonesia and at an earlier stage in South Korea, adjustment policies also met with positive outcomes.

In the poorest developing countries the inward-oriented strategy may not be the main problem. Rather the problem lies in the fact that the agricultural infrastructure, the transport system and the capital stock have been neglected. In Sub-Saharan Africa the cutbacks in government expenditure have been re-alised at the expense of essential investments in agricultural infrastructure, schooling and agricultural education. If prices of food and export crops are no longer controlled and state marketing boards are abolished, farmers will not necessarily respond by increasing their production. Farmers' ability to respond to market incentives is restricted by factors such as a sparse and scattered population, bad roads, poor transport and communication, insufficient agricultural schooling and education, insufficient agricultural research and poor possibilities for marketing (Helleiner, 1982a). Helleiner is convinced that invest-ment in infrastructure is at least as important as higher prices. Both Mosley and Weeks (1992) and Helleiner (1992a; 1992b) conclude that African countries that liberalised agricultural prices without simultaneously increasing govern-ment investment in infrastructure performed worse economically than other African countries.

When price liberalisation is combined with increased investment in the rural infrastructure and agricultural services, it may lead to remarkably positive results. An example of this was provided by Nigeria between 1986 and 1991 (Husain, 1993). During this period the value of food imports decreased from 2.5 million dollars to 300–400 million dollars per year, owing to increased agricultural self-sufficiency.

According to Mosley, structural adjustment in the poor countries in Sub-Saharan Africa does not require reduced government intervention. He and other authors of this school actually argue for an increased role for govern-ment and more investment in education, schooling and infrastructure. Pro-vided governments can be made more efficient, government intervention is what is needed to combat market imperfections associated with poor infras-tructure, an inadequate and dated capital stock and insufficient education to guarantee participation in economic life. The traditional structuralist argu-ments are still alive and kicking here.

The argument for more infrastructural investment is quite convincing. What is less convincing is the faith in an increased role of government in the economic process in Africa. It is not enough to say that governments should be more efficient than in the past. In the light of the criticism on the functioning of the state apparatus in Sub-Saharan Africa in Chapter 11, it is open to serious doubt whether present African governments can fulfil the dynamic role suggested by Mosley and Helleiner.

In sum, the recent empirical and statistical literature is increasingly sceptical about the beneficial effects of structural adjustment loans and programmes. Before rejecting the whole notion of structural adjustment, as some critics are now tempted to do, it is useful to reflect on country experiences. In doing so, the emphasis is not so much on measuring the effects of structural adjustment loans and conditions, but rather on wider policy strategies and economic performance. Authors such as Easterly argue that many of the failures of structural adjustment are due to the fact that loans have been forthcoming, while the policy reforms have not really been implemented (Easterly, 2001). In a variety of developing countries a combination of fiscal discipline, economic liberalisation and export promotion have contributed positively to growth, development and poverty reduction. Examples include Ghana, Mauritius and Uganda in Africa (Dijkstra and van Donge, 2001; Easterly, 2001a), China, India, pre-1997 Indonesia and Sri Lanka in Asia, and Chile in Latin America. Thus, while the effects of structural adjustment programmes as such are now predominantly seen as disappointing, the experiences with liberalisation and economic reform in a number of important developing countries are more positive.

With the eruption of the Asian crisis in 1997, the debate on the international economic order took a new turn. As happened before with the debt crisis, received wisdom came to be questioned. The advantages of continued globalisation came under fire.

13.6   The Asian crisis and the renewed debate on globalisation

In 1997, the Asian crisis erupted after the devaluation of the Thai baht. One after another, the currencies of Asian countries went into free fall and short-term capital was withdrawn from these countries at an alarming rate. The collapse of the currencies increased the debt burdens on companies and banks whose foreign liabilities were denominated in dollars or other international currencies. The fragility of the banking systems in countries such as Indonesia, Thailand and Korea due to hidden non-performing loans, pervasive corruption and undercapitalisation was exposed. The financial crisis quickly translated into a crisis in the real economy, which had been booming up till then. A number of Asian economies experienced unprecedented declines in real output, as documented in Table 13.5.

Table 13.5 *The Asian crisis: GDP growth 1995–2001*

	Korea	Malaysia	Thailand	Indonesia	Philippines
1995	8.9	9.8	9.2	8.2	4.7
1996	6.8	10.0	5.9	8.0	5.8
1997	5.0	7.3	−1.4	4.5	5.2
1998	−6.7	−7.4	−10.5	−13.1	−0.6
1999	10.9	6.1	4.4	0.8	3.4
2000	9.3	8.3	4.6	4.8	4.4
2001	3.1	0.5	1.8	3.3	3.2

Source: Maddison (2003).

The Asian crisis most severely hit five countries – Thailand, the Philippines, Malaysia, Korea and Indonesia – which up till that moment were seen as paragons of economic success. These countries were characterised by fiscal discipline, macro-economic balance, low inflation, modest deficits in government spending, export success, rapid growth of output and productivity, and technological upgrading (Athukorala, 2001; Hill, 1999; Woo *et al.*, 2000). Admittedly countries like the Philippines, Indonesia and Thailand were plagued by extensive corruption, but so far this had not stood in the way of their growth dynamics. Financial instability spread across the global economy, with Russia and Brazil suffering major financial crises in 1998, Turkey in 2001, Argentina in 2001 and Brazil in 2001/2. In the meanwhile the growth of the global economy slowed down dramatically.

The IMF response to the Asian crisis has been severely criticised as contributing to a further worsening of the crisis by imposing deeply contractionary policies on countries that were not suffering from macro-economic imbalances. The criticism of the IMF was that it imposed standard conditions on countries irrespective of their actual circumstances. Of the Asian countries, Malaysia refused to follow IMF policies. It introduced restrictions on short-term capital movements to provide itself with a breathing space for a more expansionary response to the crisis (Athukorala, 2001; Stiglitz, 2002). With South Korea, Malaysia was the first country to resume growth after the crisis, though in fact all countries recovered rather quickly with the exception of Indonesia. Malaysia's recovery can be seen as an argument against IMF policies. But the rapid recovery of other countries is also used as an argument in defence of these policies.

After the Asian crisis a renewed debate broke out on the advantages and disadvantages of liberalisation and globalisation. Starting with the WTO meeting at Seattle in 1999, almost every international meeting was accompanied by vociferous and sometimes violent demonstrations against globalisation. These demonstrations brought together a wide range of activists: Marxists, environmentalists, feminists, trade unions, anticapitalists, critics of the international division of labour, activists opposed to the spread of Western products such as coca cola and hamburgers, proponents of debt forgiveness. These demonstrations were primarily sound and fury, with little in the way of substance or content, but they did serve to reopen the debate on globalisation.

Parallel to these protest movements various strands of academic criticism emerged which targeted different aspects of the Washington consensus and the liberal international order as promoted by the powerful financial institutions (e.g. Adelman, 2000; Caballero, 2003; Eichengreen, 2000; Gore, 2000; Soros, 2000; Stiglitz, 2000; 2002; Tobin, 2000). One of the most influential critics was Nobel prize-winner in economics and former World Bank vice-president Joseph Stiglitz who published a furious tract entitled *Globalisation and its Discontents* (2002). This book reflects the various strands of intellectual disenchantment with globalisation and the prevailing intellectual climate. It makes a powerful case for reform of international policies. Stiglitz argues that since the mid-1990s market fundamentalism has contributed to financial instability, crises and increased poverty in many developing countries in Latin America, Asia and the former Soviet Union and that the international financial institutions bear a major part of the blame.[15]

Most of the modern critics believe that globalisation of international trade remains the key to development. However, the present architecture of the international order does not deliver on the promise of globalisation. On the contrary, it harms many developing regions. The criticisms can be summarised in three key points[16]:

1. Complete capital account liberalisation is harmful to growth and stability in developing countries. Full capital account convertibility and the free movement of short-term capital flows in and out of developing countries create a tremendous degree of financial instability. This manifests itself in a succession of financial crises, which harm developing countries. The Asian crisis was preceded by a vast speculative inflow of hot money (short-term loans, portfolio investment, currency speculation), followed by sudden capital flight. Some form of regulation of international capital flows is urgently needed (Adelman and Yeldan, 2000; Caballero, 2003; Eichengreen, 2000; Tobin 2000). Countries that continued to control capital flows such as China and India were not affected by the Asian crisis. Malaysia, which imposed capital controls in spite of IMF pressure, recovered most rapidly from the crisis. Tobin (2000) has argued that a very modest tax of 0.1 or 0.2 per cent on short-term capital transactions will not affect long-term capital flows, but will seriously slow down short-term speculative flows. Malaysia was rather successful in devising effective capital controls – first restrictions on repatriation of short-term investments, later an exit tax for short-term capital flows – which left long-term foreign direct investment unaffected (Athukorala, 2001).

2. Radical liberalisation of international trade favours the advanced economies more than the developing countries. The new rules of the WTO

---

15 At times Stiglitz gets carried away by his own rhetoric and one-sidedly assigns the blame for all economic woes to the IMF and its policies.

16 The full list of criticisms and proposals for change is much longer. Many of them echo the debates on the New International Order such as more attention to poverty and inequality, debt relief, increases in financial resources for development and voting power for developing countries in the international financial institutions.

prohibit industrial policies and technology policies in developing countries, which nurture promising industrial activities, protect them for a time from international competition and promote industrial upgrading. The critics do not call for a return to the inward-looking protectionist policies of the immediate post-war policies. They are in favour of export promotion and participation in world trade. The importance of fiscal discipline and control of inflation is fully recognised (e.g. Sunkel, 1993). However, they argue with considerable force that the export success of the Asian NICs was characterised by active policy interventions of government – both through export subsidies and through protection, which are now being denied to developing countries (Westphal, 2002). In a review article on the rise and fall of the Washington Consensus, Gore (2000, p. 796) writes: 'The process of growth and structural change is best achieved through the "strategic integration" of the national economy into the international economy, rather than either de-linking from the rest of the world or rapid across-the-board opening up of the economy to imports and external capital.' Strategic integration in world trade requires active industrial and technology policies by governments, including export subsidies and the use of instruments of protection. Also, the critics argue that the advanced economies do not practise what they preach. They continue to protect their agricultural systems and use dumping provisions against manufactured exports from developing countries. Where the international system is becoming more liberal – as in the trade in services and in the protection of intellectual property rights – it favours the advanced economic powers rather than the developing countries.

3. The international financial organisations have been too rigid and dogmatic in their stabilisation policies and their imposition of rapid market reforms. The IMF does not take local conditions into account when responding to financial crises. Its procedures are secretive and lack transparency. It imposes a standard package of contractionary measures on all countries. This goes against the Keynesian theories which prevailed when the IMF was set up, which called for expansionary finance in the context of a crisis (Stiglitz, 2002). In the Asian crisis, the IMF insistence on contractionary measures and liberalisation of capital accounts has contributed to a worsening of the economic conditions. In the former Soviet Union the rapid and imperfect transition from central planning to the market has led to the theft of state property by mafia-type oligarchs. Market reforms created a kind of monopolistic klepto-capitalism, which has resulted in years of economic stagnation and hardship (Menshikov, 1993). Russia compares unfavourably with China, which followed a more gradual path of reform.[17] Stiglitz argues that privatisation needs to be preceded by competition policies and

---

17 Sachs and Woo (1997; Woo et al., 2000), however, point to the differences between the Soviet Union and China. China was a predominantly agricultural economy. In 1978, reform started in the agricultural sector and gradually spread to other sectors. The Soviet Union was an overindustrialised economy, where reform inevitably led to cut backs in industrial output, as inefficient activities were discontinued.

institutional and legal changes which create a viable framework for market reforms. Stiglitz criticises the rapidity of market reforms – the big bang approach – calling for a more incremental approach.

As was the case with earlier system shocks, the Asian crisis has forced policy makers, politicians and academics to start rethinking their policies with regard to the international order. The interesting thing about the present process of rethinking is that the lessons of the past are not being forgotten. There is no call for a return to the inefficient inward-looking development strategies of an earlier period. The lesson that interventionist policies by corrupt and inefficient governments can result in rent-seeking behaviour and complete economic stagnation is still with us. Most – though not all – of the critics still believe that markets function better than planning systems, that market reforms can bring benefits, that export orientation is crucial to development, that foreign investment can bring benefits to developing countries and that globalisation can be a force for the good. However, there is a renewed realisation that national and international markets are imperfect, that government policies should try to compensate for market imperfections and that rapid across-the-board liberalisation can also harm the prospects of developing countries. Policies should take differences in initial conditions, institutions and government capabilities into account. Public investment in education, health and infrastructure is essential. Import liberalisation should be more gradual. Tariffs should be complemented by special policy measures to promote strategic exports.

We do not mean to suggest that there is a consensus on new policies. Some authors one-sidedly put all the blame on the international institutions; other authors emphasise developing countries' failure to reform their domestic institutions. But, increasingly the opponents in the debates do focus on the same common issues and problems. There is an ongoing and interesting search for a new balance in policies with regard to the international order.

Questions for review

1. Discuss the characteristics and institutions of the liberal international order, devised at the Bretton Woods conference in 1944. What were the tasks assigned to the IMF and what were the tasks assigned to the World Bank?
2. What were the main criticisms of the liberal international economic order on the part of the advocates of a new international economic order in the 1960s and 1970s?
3. What were the most important policy proposals for a new international economic order?
4. To what extent have policy proposals for a new international economic order so far been implemented? What are the main reasons for non-implementation of some of the important policy proposals of the NIEO?
5. What are the primary objectives of structural adjustment policies? Compare structural adjustment policy proposals with the characteristics of orthodox post-war development strategies.
6. What are the differences between structural adjustment policies and economic stabilisation policies? Are there also similarities between the two?

7. How effective have structural adjustment policies been? Summarise the debate on the (positive or negative) consequences of structural adjustment policies in different parts of the developing world.
8. Discuss some of the important indicators of indebtedness.
9. Under which circumstances are debts a threat to the development of a country?
10. Is debt relief an appropriate response to excessive debt burdens in developing countries? What are the main arguments in favour of debt relief? What are the arguments against debt relief?
11. Discuss the main initiatives for reducing debt burdens of developing countries since 1982.
12. What are the most important differences between the characteristics of globalisation in the period 1870–1913 and globalisation since the 1980s?
13. What are the most important criticisms of the international economic order since the Asian crisis? To what extent do the critics want to return to the economic policies of the 1960s and 1970s?
14. What are the similarities in the diagnosis of the main problems facing developing countries offered by structuralists and neoliberals?
15. Discuss some of the shortcomings of the Uruguay Round of trade negotiations from the perspective of developing countries.
16. Why did the outbreak of the Asian crisis come as a shock to most students of development? What are the potential lessons to be derived from the Asian crisis?

Further reading

Characteristics of the post-war international order are documented in a series of important studies by Angus Maddison. Here we mention: *Two Crises: Latin America and Asia 1929–38 and 1973–83* (1985), *The World Economy in the Twentieth Century* (1989) and *Monitoring the World Economy* (1995). Another reference to the international order is a volume edited by Grassman and Lundberg, *The World Economic Order: Past and Present* (1981). Two useful publications about decolonisation are Grimal, *Decolonization: The British, French, Dutch and Belgian Empires, 1919–1963* (1978) and Morris-Jones and Fischer, *Decolonisation and After: The British and French Experience* (1980). Gerald Meier describes the emergences of the post-war international institutions in *Emerging from Poverty: The Economics that Really Matters* (1984).

For the debates on the new international economic order, the interested reader can consult Paul Streeten, 'Approaches to a New International Economic Order' (1984), Corden, *The NIEO Proposals: A Cool Look* (1979) and a recent book by Raffer and Singer, *The Economic North–South Divide: Six Decades of Unequal Development* (2001). The liberal policy recommendations which emerged in the wake of the debt crisis of 1982 are discussed in a number of often-cited publications by Jeffrey Williamson: 'What Washington Means by Policy Reform' (1990), 'Democracy and the Washington Consensus' (1993) and 'The Washington Consensus Revisited' (1997).

An older article by Buiter and Srinivasan in *World Development*, 'Rewarding the Profligate and Punishing the Prudent and Poor: Some Recent Proposals for Debt Relief' (1987), provides a good introduction to the debates about debt relief. Two recent articles in *World Development* give the reader a taste of current debates on this topic: Neumayer, 'Is Good Governance Rewarded? A Cross-National Analysis of Debt Forgiveness' (2002) and Sanford, 'World Bank: IDA Loans or IDA Grants' (2002). The IDA/IMF publication, *Heavily Indebted Poor Countries (HIPC) Initiative – Statistical Update* (2003), provides statistical information on debt relief under the HIPC initiative.

Lensink, *Structural Adjustment in Sub-Saharan Africa* (1995) provides an accessible introduction to the vast literature on structural adjustment. Overviews are also provided by Mosley in 'Structural Adjustment: A General Overview 1980–89' (1991) and Tarp in *Stabilization and Structural Adjustment: Macro-economic Frameworks for Analysing the Crisis in Sub-Saharan Africa* (1993). The liberal perspective on structural adjustment is represented by Krueger, *Economic Policy Reform in Developing Countries* (1992) and Krueger and Duncan, *The Political Economy of Controls: Complexity* (1993). An influential publication criticising the negative social consequences of structural adjustment is Cornia, Jolly and Stewart (eds.), *Adjustment with a Human Face* (1987). Recent contributions to the debate include a special issue of the *Journal of Development Studies* on Structural Adjustment and the Labour Market, edited by Van der Hoeven and Taylor (2000), an interesting article by Dijkstra and van Donge, 'What Does the "Show Case" Show? Evidence of and Lessons from Adjustment in Uganda' (2001) and a paper by Easterly, *IMF and World Bank Structural Adjustment Programs and Poverty* (2001) http://www.nber.org/~confer/2001/ccdf/easterly.pdf

Two polar authors in the debates on globalisation and the architecture of the international financial system are Joseph Stiglitz and Stanley Fischer. Stiglitz has severely criticised the functioning of the IMF and the World Bank in his book *Globalization and Its Discontents* (2002). Fischer takes a more positive view of their performance, though he also acknowledges the need for reforms. Of his publications we mention his co-authored article, Citrin and Fischer, 'Strengthening the International Financial System: Key Issues' (2000) and his article in the *American Economic Review*, Fischer, 'Globalization and its Challenges' (2003). An excellent collection of articles is published in a special issue of *World Development* on the 'Architecture of Global Financial Systems' (2000). Among others, this issue, edited by Irma Adelman, contains an interesting article by Tobin, 'Financial Globalization', defending a tax on international capital flows (the Tobin tax). An important report on the future of international financial institutions is the so-called Meltzer report, *Report of the International Financial Institution Advisory Commission* (2000).

Statistics on debt and international financial flows are to be found in the publications of the IMF, the World Bank and the OECD. These include the annual IMF publications *International Financial Statistics Yearbook* and *World Economic Outlook*, and the World Bank publication, *World Debt Tables* and its successor *Global Development Finance: Striving for Stability in Development Finance* (2003). The IMF publishes a fact sheet on the Heavily Indebted Poor Countries initiative on the web: http://www.imf.org/external/np/exr/facts/hipc.htm. The OECD publishes a CD-Rom entitled *International Development Statistics*, which contains a variety of datasets on debt, aid and financial flows to developing countries.

14 Foreign aid and development

In this concluding chapter, we discuss the role of foreign aid in development. The central question is whether aid works. To what extent and under which conditions does aid make a positive contribution to socio-economic development?[1]

The decision to discuss foreign aid at the end of this book is a deliberate one. After all, socio-economic development is determined by a complex of factors, including proximate sources of growth, historical experiences, natural circumstances, demographic factors, power structures and processes of state formation, institutions, attitudes and aptitudes, international economic relations and economic policies. Foreign aid is just one of many factors. At best, its contribution can be only modest. The original theories of economic aid formulated in the 1950s and the 1960s by authors such as Chenery and Strout, Rostow and Rosenstein-Rodan, recognise this explicitly. They state that under certain conditions foreign aid may contribute to an acceleration of growth and development, but it cannot transform processes of stagnation into dynamic processes of development. In the debates between the supporters and opponents of foreign aid this tends to be forgotten.

Until the 1990s, the desirability of development aid was not questioned in the political debate. In the 1980s, all donors together granted approximately 60 billion

1 In this chapter the terms development aid, development assistance and foreign aid are used interchangeably.

580

dollars per year in official development assistance. Despite the substantial resources involved, the budgets for foreign aid were exempted from expenditure cuts in most countries until the late 1980s. Although there has been a lively debate on the effectiveness of aid flows, development aid was supported by political parties across the political spectrum and by the general public. It was not until the early 1990s that this consensus started to unravel. This manifested itself in a substantial decline in the real value of aid flows between 1991 and 2000 and a renewed urgency of the debates on the desirability and effectiveness of foreign aid in its different guises.

This chapter is structured as follows. Section 14.1 examines the motives for granting foreign aid. Section 14.2 presents a brief outline of the history of development aid. Different sources and types of aid are distinguished in section 14.3. Quantitative data on aid flows are presented in section 14.4. Section 14.5 concentrates on the objectives and expected outcomes of aid. Underlying development aid are theories of socio-economic development which identify different constraints and bottlenecks in the development process. Implicitly or explicitly these theories provide justifications for different kinds of aid. In the final section the debates between supporters and opponents of development aid are summarised. Attention is paid to radical criticisms, which interpret foreign aid as an instrument to prolong the dependence of poor countries and to keep them subordinated to the interests of the rich countries. Subsequently, attention is paid to the criticisms of proponents of the free market who see development aid as one of the obstacles to development. The central question in these debates is whether development aid, in spite of its stated aims of reducing poverty and misery and increasing the autonomy of people in developing countries, does not in fact contribute to continued dependence. Finally, this section presents a review of the empirical literature on aid effectiveness and the mainstream responses to criticisms from the radical left and the neo-liberal right. The mainstream claim is that, in spite of many shortcomings, aid on balance does make a positive contribution to development.

14.1 Why foreign aid?

The debate on development aid has been complicated by a failure to distinguish clearly between the principles and moral motives underlying aid and the assessments of its effects and results (Riddell, 1987, chs 2, 3, and 4). A statement to the effect that, given the urgency of the poverty issue and the enormous income gap between rich and poor countries, governments have a moral obligation to provide aid implicitly assumes that the effects of aid are positive. For if foreign aid was thought to have negative effects on development, the moral case for aid would automatically become invalid.

If the contributions of aid to development are disappointing, we have to ask whether this is due to inherent shortcomings of aid or whether this depends on the specific ways in which aid is provided. For instance, a topical issue is whether aid from governments to governments is the most suitable way of providing aid. In sum, our judgements concerning the desirability of aid also depend on our perspectives on the empirical reality of which aid is a constituent part. Here we will first discuss the different motives underlying foreign aid. In section 14.6, we will discuss empirical research on the effectiveness of aid.

The following kinds of motives for development aid can be distinguished: moral motives; references to mutual interests; commercial motives; and political and strategic motives (Dollar and Pritchett, 1998; Hoebink, 1988; 1990a; 1990b; Lumsdaine, 1993; Maizels and Nissanke, 1984; Riddell, 1987; Stem, 2002).

Moral motives

Moral motives for development aid include:

- *Humanitarian motives.* Given widespread poverty, malnutrition and unacceptable living conditions in many developing countries, there is a moral obligation to provide aid. These motives take some criterion of absolute human needs as their point of departure.
- *Egalitarian motives.* From an egalitarian point of view, the extreme inequalities between rich and poor countries, and rich and poor people, and the widening gaps between rich and poor in the world economy are morally unacceptable. The rich have a moral duty to help the poor. Development aid is seen as an equalising transfer payment.
- *International solidarity.* It is not self-evident that criteria of need and egalitarian justice should be applied on a global scale. It can be argued that the main task of a state is to provide for the welfare of its own citizens, according to the criteria of justice within the society. The moral argument for development aid includes the proposition that moral obligations transcend the borders of national societies. In its most extreme version this argument states that we are all members of a new global society.
- *Reparation of past wrongs.* In the past, rich Western countries have exploited poor countries and have harmed their chances of development through colonialism and external intervention. As the Western world is responsible for the underdevelopment of poor countries, Western countries have a moral obligation to repay past debts. From this perspective, development aid is a kind of compensation payment.

Mutual interests

Poor countries and rich countries are mutually interdependent in a global society. Economic and social development in poor countries is not only in the interest of the citizens of these countries. It is also in the interest of rich countries and their citizens (see Brandt *et al.*, 1980; 1983). The mutual interest motive is expressed in different modalities, as follows:

- *Interdependence.* The world economy is increasingly an interdependent whole. Economic development and increasing per capita incomes in poor countries create new markets for exports from rich countries. Economic stagnation in poor countries has negative effects on economic growth in rich countries.

- *Global environmental problems.* Global environmental problems caused by pollution, depletion of resources, population growth and economic growth threaten the welfare and development prospects of both rich and poor countries. Protection of the global environment and sustainable development are common interests (e.g. the Brundtland report, *Our Common Future*, 1987).
- *Avoiding international conflicts.* The enormous gaps in income levels in the world economy may lead to destructive conflicts between the rich countries in the North and the poor countries and their inhabitants in the South. Avoiding such conflicts by promoting economic development in poor countries is also in the interest of rich countries.
- *Immigration.* A special version of the mutual interest motive is the prevention of massive immigration from developing countries to the economically advanced countries. This line of reasoning states that in the modern global economy extreme deprivation in the developing countries will spill over into the rich countries (World Bank, 2002a). If economic conditions in developing countries improve owing to development aid and other efforts, migration flows to the rich countries, which are experienced as threatening, will come to an end.

Commercial motives

Development aid is seen as an instrument of export promotion. Development aid is used to support firms exporting to developing countries, and to help develop new export markets. It is hard to draw the boundary between commercial motives and mutual interests. Sometimes the only motive is blatant self-interest, with firms in rich countries lobbying for support and foreign aid functioning as a form of export credit in disguise. Sometimes there is a genuine conviction that the promotion of economic development in a developing country is compatible with an expansion of exports to this country.

Political and strategic motives

Foreign aid is frequently an instrument of foreign policy aimed at cementing the political ties between donors and client countries (e.g. Maizels and Nissanke, 1984; Schraeder *et al.*, 1998; Alesina and Dollar, 2000). Former European colonial powers tried to maintain or reinforce their political, economic and cultural ties with their former colonies through development aid. For the United States, preventing countries from falling within the communist sphere of influence was clearly an important motive for foreign aid during the Cold War. In the 1950s and 1960s, most of US foreign aid went to South Korea, South Vietnam and Taiwan. In the 1970s, the lion's share of aid was provided to Egypt and Israel. Foreign aid was one of the main instruments of US foreign policy in the Middle East. Eighty per cent of aid from the former Soviet Union was allocated to Cuba, Mongolia and Vietnam. Most French development aid went to its former colonies in Africa. In the early period of Dutch development aid, a large proportion was reserved for (former) colonies. Japanese aid went to countries that voted along with Japan in the United Nations (Alesina and Dollar, 2000). For a public justification of their aid policies, governments tend to appeal primarily to moral motives. But in practice, all the motives mentioned above play a role in maintaining broad political and social support of foreign aid policy.

In a lucid analysis of the ethical and moral arguments for foreign aid, Riddell (1987, pp. 12–16) identifies seven propositions which together constitute the argument that there is a moral obligation for governments to provide foreign aid to developing countries. These are summarised in Box 14. Each of these propositions can be challenged. The criticism of the moral motives for aid has been formulated by contract theorists such as Nozick, Bauer and Hayek, applying procedural theories of justice. From this perspective, all inequalities in outcomes and rewards obtained by individual effort and according to just procedures are justified. Redistribution of outcomes on the basis of needs or egalitarian criteria is rejected as unjust. Only when inequality is the result of unjust acquisition in the past, may there be a basis for compensation in the present. However, here the debate shifts to the empirical domain. The critics of egalitarian and needs-based criteria are convinced that differences in economic development are empirically explained by differences in skills, talents, efforts, institutions and policies, and not by past exploitation.

Box 14.1   The case for foreign aid

1. On the basis of comparisons between domestic standards of living in rich countries and those in developing countries, potential donors accept that there are problems in developing countries which provide a moral basis for action.
2. Direct intervention can help solve such problems.
3. External financial and/or technical assistance contributes to a development strategy aimed at solving these problems.
4. Aid flows from government to government contribute to the solution of problems.
5. There is a moral obligation to give aid to defined categories of countries, and – through the governments of these countries – to defined groups within these countries.
6. The moral obligation to provide aid to identified countries is so strong, that the use of funds for foreign aid is justified in the light of other legitimate claims on a government's financial resources.
7. The resources furnished by means of foreign aid actually help promote development or have the potential of doing so in the future, based on the learning experiences of past mistakes.

Source: Riddell (1987).

A second line of criticism is that governments are responsible for only their own citizens and have no obligations to citizens of other countries. A third category of arguments, formulated in particular by Peter Bauer, refers to the fact the aid is provided on a government-to-government basis. Even if one subscribes to the moral argument in favour of aid, which Bauer certainly does not, there may still be good reasons to be opposed to intergovernmental aid flows.

In practice, according to Bauer, aid means that poor people in rich countries are taxed in order to subsidise rich people and members of political elites in poor countries. Once again, the discussion about principles of justice is mixed with discussion about empirical realities.

Without doing sufficient justice to the interesting debate on the moral foundations of development aid – well summarised by Riddell – we will take the moral arguments for development aid as our point of departure. In the rest of the chapter our focus will be on the empirical discussions about the effects of aid on development. This means that less attention will be paid to other motives underlying foreign aid. These will only enter the discussion when they have negative effects on the realisation of the primary objectives of development aid: that is, contributing to an improvement in the living conditions and socio-economic dynamics in developing countries.

14.2   The emergence of foreign aid

In the period immediately after World War II, the first priority was the reconstruction of war damage in Europe. The United States provided massive support to Western European countries by means of the Marshall Plan. The success of the Marshall Plan created a positive climate with regard to the role of international financial flows in economic development (Krueger *et al.*, 1989, ch. 1). The differences between the reparation of war damages in economically advanced areas and the transformation of economic structures in poor countries were hardly taken into consideration.

The official involvement of the United States in development aid dates back to January 1949 when President Harry S. Truman gave his inaugural address. In the fourth point of his address Truman announced a new programme for making the benefits of scientific and industrial progress in the affluent countries available to developing countries. The emphasis was on technical assistance. This so-called Point Four programme was later enacted in legislation, although the budgeted resources remained much lower than those set aside for the Marshall Plan. In 1950 Congress allocated $34.5 million to technical assistance. It was not until about 1960 that resource transfers to developing countries reached levels approximating the Marshall Plan.

The United States was not alone in starting foreign aid in 1950. In the same year the World Bank issued its first development loan to Colombia, and the Expanded Programme of Technical Assistance (UNEPTA) of the UN was launched. Later this programme would be replaced by the United Nations Development Programme (UNDP).

In January 1950, Great Britain and the Commonwealth members Australia, Canada and New Zealand committed themselves to providing foreign aid by signing the Colombo Plan. Aid was especially intended for the countries that used to be part of former British India. India, in particular, became a testing ground for foreign aid and theories of development.

Other (ex)colonial powers in Europe, like France, Belgium and the Netherlands, also started to provide foreign aid. After some time their example was followed by the countries defeated in World War II – Germany, Japan and Italy. In these countries, foreign aid commenced once their economies had recovered from the damage caused by the war.

By 1960, multilateral institutions like the World Bank, the International Finance Corporation and the International Development Association (IDA) had become important sources of external financial flows to developing countries. Around 1960, the United States were responsible for more than half of all bilateral and multilateral development aid. Most of the rest was supplied by four former colonial European powers: France, England, Belgium and the Netherlands.

Prince (1976) stresses the continuity between the post-war development aid of European countries and the pre-war colonial policies, particularly in the field of technical assistance. In France and the United Kingdom, development aid was closely tied in with decolonisation and the objectives of decolonisation policy. An important goal of pre-war French colonial policies had been the assimilation of colonised peoples into French culture. In the postcolonial period French foreign aid flows concentrated on Francophone Africa. Elements of assimilation policy resurfaced in aid policies. There was a strong emphasis on the spread of French language and culture, on education by French experts and on maintaining the economic ties with France. Until 1993, the currencies of French West African countries were directly linked to the French franc. According to research by Alesina and Dollar (2000), French aid is exceptional in the degree to which strategic political objectives dominate all other aid objectives.

The long-term objective of British colonial policies in the twentieth century was the association of former colonies in a Commonwealth of English-speaking countries. The system of colonial administration was based on *indirect rule*. In comparison with France, Great Britain intervened less in the internal political and social affairs of its colonies. Foreign aid was seen as a continuation of gradual preparations for independence in the context of the Commonwealth during the pre-war period. Therefore, aid flows were strongly centred on Commonwealth countries.

In the case of the Netherlands, there was a sudden rift with Indonesia in 1949 after the so-called police actions of 1947–49. The Netherlands attempted to restore its damaged international prestige by participating on a large scale in multilateral technical assistance, which was beginning at that time. The Netherlands had a reservoir of experience in the form of colonial training programmes, unemployed colonial civil servants and experts. It was successful in finding employment for its experts in multilateral aid programmes (Teszler, 1978; van Soest, 1975). As small countries, the Netherlands and the Scandinavian countries used development aid as defining characteristics of their foreign policies.

Reasons for the United States to expand its bilateral aid in the 1950s and 1960s included, among others, the fear of Chinese communist expansion in Asia and the influence of the Cuban revolution in Latin America. Because of the Cold War, large amounts of aid were provided to countries on the periphery of the communist bloc, such as Greece, Turkey, South Korea, Taiwan, South Vietnam and Laos. In 1960 President John Kennedy launched the *Alliance for Progress*, a programme for economic development and cooperation in Latin America. The same year saw the foundation of the Peace Corps, an initiative that would soon be copied by other countries.

In 1960, development aid from the OECD countries was institutionalised in the Development Assistance Committee (DAC). The DAC coordinated and recorded aid-related efforts by the OECD countries. More and more OECD countries started to provide foreign aid, while the US share in total aid flows gradually declined. In 1960 the share of the USA in total OECD foreign aid was 57.5 per cent. By 1987 it had dropped to 21.5 per cent. As a percentage of gross national income US aid in 1987 was only 0.2 per cent, the lowest percentage of all OECD countries, except Austria and Portugal (Krueger, *et al.*, 1989, p. 35). In 2001, the share of the United Sates in total DAC aid was 21.8 per cent, but as share of GNP it had declined to 0.11 per cent (OECD, 2003a). In 2001, three-quarters of total ODA was accounted for by six countries, the USA, Japan, Germany, UK, France and the Netherlands.

According to van der Hoeven (2001, p. 110), the international economic climate of the 1980s forced many countries to adjust their economies in order to accommodate to external shocks. This led to a shift from project aid to programme aid in the form of structural adjustment programmes and conditionality. Conditionality was inspired by liberal theories of development, which focused on the importance of market reforms and the elimination of state-imposed distortions. The end of the Cold War at the end of the 1980s ushered in a new phase in development cooperation (Dijkstra and White, 2003; Doornbos, 2001). The strategic motives for aid became less important. The links between aid and policy reform, and aid and good governance become more prominent. In the economic sphere, conditionality initially focused on macro-economic policy and structural adjustment. But aid also increasingly came to be linked with issues such as democratic reform, elections, human rights, and the effective functioning of government bureaucracies and social service delivery. Alesina and Dollar (2000) showed that countries that introduced democratic reforms tended to receive substantial increases in aid.

In the 1990s, the donor community became increasingly disenchanted with the effectiveness of structural adjustment and conditionality (e.g. Meltzer, 2000). There was a shift from *conditionality* to *selectivity*. Under conditionality, aid had been supplied to countries that had agreed to implement reforms in the future. Under selectivity, the allocation of aid and debt relief was increasingly guided by assessments of policy reforms that developing countries had already implemented in the past. Policy reforms were conceived of broadly, including democratic reforms, improvement in the effectiveness of government institutions, the protection of property rights and the rule of law, and effective macro-economic policies. Criteria for the allocation of aid also came to include poverty-reduction strategies, this in response to earlier criticisms that the international agencies had neglected poverty issues. In the current debates on aid, however, selectivity has also come under fire in the light of broader criticisms of the neoliberal perspectives on aid, which underlie both conditionality and selectivity. We will return to these issues in section 14.6.

14.3   Development aid: sources and categories

Since 1977, the Development Assistance Committee (DAC) of the Organisation for Economic Cooperation and Development (OECD) presents an annual survey of aid flows to developing countries in the *Geographical Distribution of Financial Flows to Developing Countries* (*GDFF*). This publication is now available in electronic format, with complete data for the whole period 1960–2001 (OECD, 2003a). In this publication official development assistance (ODA) is defined as: financial flows to developing countries provided by official agencies, with the objective of promoting the economic development and welfare of developing countries and with a grant element of at least 25 per cent. The *sources* of development aid are summarised in Box 14.2.

Box 14.2   Sources of development aid

- *Aid provided by advanced economies united in the OECD*. This aid is coordinated by the Development Assistance Committee (DAC). This includes official development assistance (ODA) and other aid flows that meet the criteria of ODA: Other Assistance (OA).
- *Aid provided by Arab oil-producing countries*. These aid flows increased in the 1970s when oil prices were raised. In the 1980s these flows declined again. At present only three countries are specifically listed in the *GDFF* (OECD, 2003a) as bilateral donors: Saudi Arabia, Kuwait and the United Arab Emirates. But there are also multilateral flows from the Arab countries.
- *Aid from the formerly centrally planned countries united in the CMEA* (Council for Mutual Economic Assistance). The amounts were quite modest. Eighty per cent of aid offered by the former Soviet Union was allocated to just three countries: Cuba, Vietnam, and Mongolia. Within the former Soviet Union there were several republics and regions, which were comparable to developing countries. In hindsight, the expenditures of the former Soviet Union included flows that were comparable to development aid but have not been registered as such in international statistics. These aid flows dried up in the mid-1980s and were discontinued after 1989. They have since been replaced by aid flows from DAC countries to the newly independent states in Asia and by Other Assistance (OA) flows to newly independent states in Europe.
- *Aid provided by voluntary development organisations (non-governmental organisations; NGOs)*. These flows can be quite substantial. In the Netherlands voluntary organisations annually provide aid to the equivalent of 5 to 10 per cent of official development aid (Kruyt and Koonings, 1988).[2]

---

2 The distinction between official aid flows and voluntary aid flows is not always clear-cut. Some aid organisations are entirely funded by voluntary donations from the public. Other non-governmental aid organisations are heavily subsidised by governments. In the Netherlands, four of the largest NGOs receive about three-quarters of their revenues from the government.

DAC statistics on development assistance primarily refer to aid provided by OECD member countries of the DAC and Arab countries. Aid offered with other than developmental objectives (e.g. military assistance) is excluded. Aid flows include both outright grants (in money or kind) and soft loans with a grant element of at least 25 per cent. Loans without this grant element, like export credits, are not classified as part of official development assistance. The concessionality of a loan – the softness or grant element – is the difference between the costs of a loan (depending on the maturity of the loan, the grace period before first repayment and the annual interest) and the costs a borrower would have to pay at market rates. For practical purposes, the reference interest rate for commercial loans is set at 10 per cent. The grant element in development assistance differs from country to country, but it is quite high. In 2001 the average grant element was 82 per cent (OECD, 2003a). Aid is not always financial. Sometimes it consists of goods (food, machines, fertilisers) or services (technical experts, teachers). In such cases, the value of the goods and services is included in the statistics.

The OECD records both *bilateral aid*, which is provided directly on a country-to-country basis, and *multilateral aid* through international organisations. Important sources of multilateral aid are the World Bank; the International Development Association (IDA), a subsidiary organisation of the World Bank, which issues soft loans for development objectives; the regional development banks; the World Health Organization (WHO); the International Fund for Agricultural Development (IFAD); and the European Development Fund. Multilaterally funded technical aid is offered by the United Nations Development Programme (UNDP) and the Food and Agriculture Organisation (FAO). There are also specific Arab-financed multilateral agencies such as the OPEC Fund for International Development (OFID). In 2001, multilateral aid was 31 per cent of total ODA (OECD, 2003a).

In general, governments find it easier to put their stamp on aid policy in bilateral aid relations than via aid provided through multilateral agencies. Bilateral aid also offers more opportunities for support of domestic producers and exporters in the donor country. The distinction between bilateral and multilateral aid is not absolute, however. Much bilateral aid is coordinated on a recipient-country basis via international donor consortia. The European Development Fund is also a mixture of bilateral and multilateral aid.

The following four categories of aid can be distinguished (Cassen, 1986; Dijkstra and White, 2003): project aid; programme aid; food aid; technical co-operation.

Project aid

Under the heading of project aid, support is provided for a consistent set of activities with a specified duration and a well-defined objective. Project aid makes available specific capital assets or packages of technical assistance. An important component of project aid consists of infrastructural works, such as roads, harbours, dams, irrigation projects, energy projects or telecommunications projects. In addition there are projects in large- and small-scale agriculture, integrated rural development, education, population, health, women's emancipation, and so forth.

Programme aid

In the case of programme aid, financial support is provided to governments in the form of financial grants or concessional loans in support of economic policy programmes. Programme aid may be provided for the benefit of the entire economy or for specific sectors. In the latter case, the developing country receives financial resources to execute certain policies in one specific sector – education, agriculture, small-scale industry, and so on. Programme aid comes in the form of balance-of-payments support, budget support or debt relief. Programme aid leaves more to the discretion of the recipient than project aid does. It is easier to disburse quickly, which makes it a more flexible instrument. It is usually linked to policy dialogue with the donors.

Food aid

Food aid is concerned with the provision of food in kind from the agricultural surpluses of rich countries. This food is provided either free of charge or at low price. Apart from emergency aid in case of natural disasters and famines, food aid is also offered when the food production in a country fails to meet the demand for food. Food may also be provided to people in exchange for work on roads, infrastructure or municipal facilities (*Food for Work*). In recent years, food aid is sometimes provided in cash, allowing developing countries to buy food in their own or neighbouring countries to supply it to food deficit regions.

Technical cooperation

Technical cooperation is defined as activities the primary purpose of which is to augment the level of knowledge, skills and technical know-how in developing countries. It involves providing technical services of experts, volunteers and teachers and actions targeted at education, training and advice. The boundary between technical cooperation and project aid is not quite clear since elements of technical cooperation are included in almost all projects. However, project aid mainly finances physical capital goods which are supplied in kind or for which money is provided. Technical aid refers to 'experts' who contribute to engineering design and construction of capital projects, the transfer of knowledge, education and educational institution building, institutional development or technology transfer. Scholarships, short training programmes and education services of international educational institutions in donor countries are also considered part of technical cooperation.

In principal, programme aid could also be used to pay for services of technical experts or for investments in education. Most often, however, technical aid is provided in the form of payment of the salaries of experts posted in developing countries. If programme aid targets the educational sector, it will be supplied as budget support to ministries of education.

The distinction between project aid and programme aid is a matter of the form in which aid is provided. Food aid and technical cooperation are mentioned separately because of their specific substantive characteristics and because of the fact that most donor countries have separate programmes and statistics for these kinds of aid.

14.4 Quantitative data on aid flows

As an empirical background for the debates on aid, this section provides quantitative data on the magnitude, allocation and sources of aid flows, as well as data on the relative importance of aid for different countries.

14.4.1 *Long-term trends in the magnitude and geographical distribution of aid flows*

Table 14.1 presents data on the total volume of official development assistance from OECD and OPEC countries. Aid flows from voluntary organisations have not been included in the table. At constant 2000 dollars, the value of the total aid flows doubled between 1960 and 1990. As mentioned above, the share of the largest donor, the USA, decreased strongly during this period. The number of countries providing aid increased, as did the volume of aid per country. The 1970s were characterised primarily by a strong growth of aid flows from oil-exporting countries. Aid from the Soviet Union and former socialist countries in Eastern Europe has always been modest in volume and was discontinued after the collapse of the Soviet Union. After 1991, the growth of aid came to an end. In 2000, aid in real terms was 21 per cent lower than in 1991, with an upturn in 2001.

Most aid goes to low-income countries. Aid flows to the least developed countries increased strongly between 1970 and 1990. The regional data show a dramatic threefold increase in the volume of aid to African countries between 1960 and 1990. After that aid declined to the levels prevailing in the late 1970s. Aid flows to Asia peaked in 1980, especially due to high aid levels in the Middle East. In the 1990s, they shrank to the levels of around 1960. The only region that has experienced a sustained increase in aid inflows was Latin America.

Since 1991, there have been increasing aid flows to several of the newly independent states of the former Soviet Union and to former communist countries in Eastern Europe. The aid flows to the Asian republics of the former Soviet Union are included in the totals for Asia in Tables 14.1, 14.2 and 14.3. These flows amounted to 1.5 billion dollars in 2001. Aid flows to European countries in transition and more advanced developing countries are recorded separately

Table 14.1 Net receipts of development assistance by income level and region, 1960–2001[a] ($bn, at constant 2000 prices and exchange rates)

	1960	1965	1970	1975	1980	1985	1990	1991	1995	1997	1999	2000	2001
All developing countries	29.7	39.1	35.3	50.5	56.3	59.5	62.1	63.7	51.6	46.5	50.4	50.3	53.6
Income category[b][c]													
Low-income countries	12.7	21.0	17.5	23.2	25.3	27.9	29.8	30.7	27.1	22.6	24.8	24.4	27.7
Least developed countries	2.8	5.5	4.4	11.8	14.7	17.5	18.0	17.1	14.9	12.4	11.8	12.4	13.9
Lower-middle-income countries	7.5	7.7	7.0	15.3	14.3	14.3	16.3	16.3	11.3	11.4	12.6	11.7	12.6
Upper-middle-income countries	2.1	4.1	3.6	2.6	3.7	2.7	3.9	3.9	2.2	1.5	1.4	1.7	1.9
Unallocated	3.2	3.2	4.6	6.4	10.1	9.7	9.6	10.1	9.6	10.3	10.9	12.5	11.6
Region													
Total Africa	7.7	9.5	8.7	17.6	17.5	22.7	27.3	26.0	18.9	17.2	15.3	15.7	17.0
Sub-Saharan Africa	2.4	6.3	5.9	9.5	12.7	16.7	19.2	18.2	15.9	13.6	12.2	12.7	14.0
North Africa	5.4	3.0	2.6	8.0	4.6	5.3	7.7	7.2	2.6	2.8	2.6	2.2	2.4
Total Asia	16.2	19.6	17.2	21.8	22.9	21.6	19.5	21.2	16.2	13.6	16.9	16.1	17.4
Low-income countries in Asia	14.2	17.7	15.4	16.8	14.8	15.9	13.6	15.7	11.8	9.8	12.7	12.1	13.5
The Middle East	2.1	1.7	2.4	6.2	9.0	7.3	5.1	5.5	2.5	2.4	2.3	2.3	2.5
Latin America	1.7	5.5	5.3	4.0	3.8	6.3	5.7	6.1	5.6	5.3	5.8	5.0	6.2
Oceania	0.2	0.9	1.4	1.7	1.7	1.7	1.5	1.4	1.6	1.5	1.4	0.8	0.8
Europe	2.9	2.3	0.9	0.4	2.0	0.8	1.5	2.3	2.0	1.7	3.5	3.7	3.5
Not specified by region	1.0	1.3	1.8	4.8	8.4	6.5	6.5	6.7	7.3	7.2	7.5	9.0	8.8
All developing countries (current US $)	4.0	6.2	6.9	17.8	33.5	32.3	57.9	61.8	59.8	48.7	52.7	50.3	51.7

Notes:
[a] New grants and loans minus repayment of outstanding loans for 152 developing countries. Net ODA receipts are total net ODA flows from DAC countries, multilateral organisations and non-DAC countries. ODA excludes official aid (OA) to European countries in transition and 14 more advanced developing countries and territories, including Taiwan, Korea, Singapore and Hong Kong. Between 1990 and 2001: average official aid is around 6.2 billion dollars per year.
[b] Countries have been classified on the basis of their 1998 GNI/capita. Within the low-income category, forty-nine countries are classified as Least Developed Countries.
[c] Not all aid has been registered per income category. Even including the unallocated row the sum of subcategories is less than the total, especially for the earlier years.
Sources: OECD, *Geographical Distribution of Financial Flows to Aid Recipients, 1960–2001*, International Development Statistics CD-Rom, 2003a.

Table 14.2 *Distribution of net official development assistance from OECD countries by region*[a]

Region	Regional share in aid receipts (%)					Population share in 2000 (%)	Net aid ($ bn) 1998	Net aid ($ bn) 2001[b]
	1975–6	1985–6	1995–6	1997–8	2000–01			
Sub-Saharan Africa	26.0	31.1	33.8	34.7	33.1	13.2	13.1	13.5
Asia and Oceania	40.0	35.5	35.2	35.9	35.7	68.8	14.9	17.5
Asia	34.0	33.0	31.7	32.0		68.6	13.3	16.7
Oceania	6.0	2.5	3.5	3.9		0.2	1.6	0.8
North Africa and Middle East	18.0	19.5	14.4	13.4	10.2	5.9	5.1	4.8
Latin America	14.0	12.5	12.5	12.1	13.1	10.2	4.6	6.0
Europe	1.0	1.4	4.1	4.0	7.9	1.9	1.6	3.3
Total	139.0	136	135	136	100	100.0	39.3	45.2

Notes:
[a]Net Official Development Assistance from DAC members (OECD countries except for Mexico, Greece, Iceland, Korea and Turkey) and DAC member-financed multilateral organisations. The table excludes amounts not allocated by country and amounts unspecified by region. Therefore, the totals are much lower than those in Table 14.1.
[b]For 2000/1, Net ODA receipts include receipts from DAC countries as well as non-DAC countries. All other data in the table exclude ODA from non-DAC countries.
Sources: 1975–6 from OECD, *Financing and External debt 1985* (table III.5), Paris, 1986;
1985–6 from OECD, *Development Co-operation 1997* (table 39), Paris, 1998;
1997–8 from OECD, *Development Co-operation 1999* (table 28), Paris, 2000;
1995–6 and 2000–01 from OECD, *Statistical Annex of the 2002 Development Co-operation Report* (table 28), International Development Statistics (IDS) CD-Rom, 2003b.

Table 14.3 *Country contributions to aid, 1985–2001*

	Country shares in total DAC ODA					Net Aid as % of GNP (current prices and exchange rates)				
	1985–6 average	1990–1 average[a]	1999	2000	2001	1985–6 average	1990–1 average[a]	1999	2000	2001
Japan	14.6	18.3	27.2	25.1	18.8	0.29	0.32	0.34	0.28	0.23
United States	29.4	20.7	16.2	18.5	21.8	0.23	0.20	0.10	0.10	0.11
Germany	10.5	12.0	9.8	9.4	9.5	0.45	0.40	0.26	0.27	0.27
United Kingdom	5.1	5.3	6.1	8.4	8.7	0.32	0.30	0.24	0.32	0.32
France	11.1	13.3	10.0	7.6	8.0	0.58	0.61	0.39	0.32	0.32
Netherlands	4.5	4.6	5.6	5.8	6.1	0.97	0.90	0.79	0.84	0.82
Sweden	3.0	3.8	2.9	3.3	3.2	0.85	0.90	0.70	0.80	0.81
Canada	5.1	4.6	3.0	3.2	2.9	0.49	0.45	0.28	0.25	0.22
Denmark	1.8	2.2	3.1	3.1	3.1	0.85	0.95	1.01	1.06	1.03
Italy	5.4	6.2	3.2	2.6	3.1	0.34	0.30	0.15	0.13	0.15
Norway	2.1	2.2	2.4	2.4	2.6	1.10	1.15	0.90	0.80	0.83
Other DAC	7.5	10.1	10.6	10.5	12.1					
TOTAL DAC	100.0	100.0	100.0	100.0	100.0	0.33	0.33	0.24	0.22	0.22

Notes:
[a]Including debt forgiveness of non-ODA claims in 1990 and 1991, except for total DAC.
Source: OECD, *Development Co-operation Report, 2002: Statistical Annex,* CD-Rom, International Development Statistics (IDS), 2003b.

as Official Aid (OA). These flows are not included in the totals of Tables 14.1, 14.2 and 14.3, but they are of increasing importance, amounting on average to 6.2 billion dollars a year in the 1990s (OECD, 200a). If Official Aid is taken to into account, total aid flows have remained stable since 1990, but many countries on the OA list do not really qualify as developing countries.[3] Therefore, from the

---

3 Official Aid (OA) meets the same criteria as Official Development Assistance (ODA). Countries receiving OA include the three Baltic Republics, the Czech Republic, the Slovak Republic, Poland, Russia, Belarus,

perspective of developing countries, the conclusion that real aid flows declined in the 1990s is justified.

Table 14.2 presents further information on the distribution of aid over different regions. This table is not directly comparable to Table 14.1 as it refers to aid from only OECD countries and excludes unallocated amounts. Compared to their shares in developing country population, two regions are heavily over-represented in the aid flows: Sub-Saharan Africa, and North Africa and the Middle East. The share of these regions in annual aid flows is two to three times as high as their share in population. For the Middle East, this is explained by the strategic importance of the region. Foreign political considerations determine the magnitude of aid flows to Israel, Jordan and Egypt. The over-representation of Sub-Saharan Africa has to do with the deep economic problems and the extent of poverty in this region. In proportion to its share in population, Asia is highly under-represented in aid flows. Also striking are the over-representation of developing countries in Oceania and Europe. For Europe, this is due to the increase in financial flows to the Balkan countries in the wake of the Balkan wars.

Table 14.3 provides information about country contributions to total aid, bilateral as well as multilateral. Six countries – the USA, Japan, Germany, the United Kingdom, France and the Netherlands – provide three-quarters of all aid provided by all the DAC countries together. For most of the post-war period, the USA provided the largest share of aid, but in the late 1990s it was temporarily overtaken by Japan. Net aid as a percentage of national income fell far short of the target of 0.7 per cent of GNP agreed upon in the 1960s. Only the Nordic countries and the Netherlands met these targets. For all DAC countries, the share of aid to GNP fell sharply from 0.33 per cent in 1990/1 to only 0.22 per cent in 2000 and 2001, providing an indication of aid fatigue in this period. For the United States, aid as a percentage of national income declined from 0.23 per cent in 1985/6 to 0.11 per cent in 2001. However, in 2001, it was still the largest donor in absolute terms, making it a dominant force in shaping multilateral aid efforts. During much of the post-war period, the US has targeted one third of its bilateral assistance to Egypt and Israel. France has given overwhelmingly to former colonies. Japan is highly correlated with UN voting patterns in line with Japanese preferences (Alesina and Dollar, 2000). The share of multilateral aid in total aid flows showed a steady increase from almost nothing in 1960 to 30.5 per cent in 2001 (OECD, 2003a).

14.4.2   Development aid in proportion to total resource flows

Aid is part of the wider flow of financial resources to and from developing countries. Table 14.4 contains information on the share of net development

Hungary, Moldova, Romania and Bulgaria. In addition, OA goes to some richer countries such as Libya, Korea, Hong Kong, Taiwan, Israel and several tiny island countries such as the Falklands, Bermuda or the Netherlands Antilles. Before 1996 most countries in the second group were on the ODA list. In the late 1990s they received around 1.2 billion dollars per year in OA.

Table 14.4 *Net development aid as a percentage of the total net inflow of financial resources by income and region, 1960–2001 (current $US)*[a]

	1960	1970	1975–6	1980	1985	1990	1991	1996	1999	2000	2001
All developing countries	56.1	44.7	30.5	29.2	44.1	43.2	44.2	23.0	23.2	24.1	28.0
Income category[b]											
Low-income countries			71.3	70.2	55.7	56.9	65.1	26.0	37.4	30.4	38.0
Least-developed countries			80.4	75.0	89.3	86.4	97.4	84.1	63.4	74.0	68.9
Other-low-income countries								15.1	27.3	18.9	26.2
Lower-middle-income countries					44.0	36.3	34.8	29.7	30.5	40.2	30.5
Upper-middle-income countries					15.0	13.5	11.2	2.2	1.3	1.7	2.4
Region											
Total Africa				67.6	60.2	84.5	98.0	86.3	53.3	68.8	59.8
Sub-Saharan Africa			47.7	59.2	60.5	85.7	92.5	89.8	47.3	62.1	59.0
North Africa								63.8	84.8	92.0	53.3
Total Asia and the Pacific			47.6	41.7	37.4	25.8	26.6	17.0	25.2	21.1	25.0
of which: Low-income countries					36.0	31.0	42.5	16.4	33.4	20.9	28.3
North Africa and the Middle East[c]			49.1	56.9	68.8	97.5	131.9	193.8	168.6	76.7	48.5
Latin America and Caribbean			10.6	6.8	16.4	23.3	19.8	7.7	5.6	5.5	7.5

Notes:
[a] Net total resource flows include ODA, other official flows and net private capital flows, including guaranteed export credits, foreign direct investment, portfolio investment and private bank loans. Not all ODA is specified by region or income category. Therefore the subcategory percentages underestimate the share of aid. This is not the case for the totals. North Africa has been included in the total for Africa; the Middle East has been included in the total for Asia and the Pacific.
[b] 1960–1991: Countries have been classified by their 1991 GNP per capita. 1996–2001: countries have been classified by their 1998 income per capita.
[c] Percentages above 100 indicate that net non-ODA capital flows are negative.
Sources: ODA:1960 from Krueger *et al.* (1989, p. 36); 1970 from OECD (1993b); 1975–80 from OECD, *Financing and External Debt of Developing Countries 1985*, Paris, 1986; 1985–91: from OECD, *Financing and External Debt of Developing Countries 1992*, Paris, 1993a; 1996–2001: ODA from OECD (2003a).
Net resource flows (long-term): from World Bank (2003). The World Bank categories have been readjusted to the GGDF categories, for regions and income groups.

aid in total net financial flows to developing countries. This share fluctuates considerably. In the 1970s, the relative importance of development aid decreased when private banks increased their lending to developing countries. Between 1980 and 1986, the share of development aid rose to 56 per cent of the net resource flow. This was primarily caused by the curtailment of private lending and foreign direct investment after the debt crisis. Subsequently, the trend reversed and the share of aid in net total resource flows declined again. In 2001 it stood at 28 per cent, reflecting the greatly increased role of net private flows to developing countries, including in particular foreign direct investment.

Regardless of these trends, Table 14.4 shows that development aid accounts for a substantial part of the total inflow of financial resources into developing countries. The Least Developed Countries and African countries are not able to attract much private investment, due to their narrow markets and lack of dynamism. In these categories, development aid accounts for the greater part of the total net resource inflow. In North Africa and the Middle East, in some years the share was far in excess of 100 per cent. This means that the net aid flow was higher than the net total resource flow. The balance of the other financial flows (other official financial flows and private flows) was negative in those years.

Tables 14.5 and 14.6 present similar data for 29 selected developing countries. Table 14.5 contains the absolute figures on net aid flows and net total resource flows. In Table 14.6 net aid flows are expressed as a percentage of the total resource flows. Unfortunately, the country data on the total resource flows in Table 14.5 from the *Geographical Distribution of Financial Flows to Developing Countries* (OECD, 2003a) are not consistent with those from *Global Development Finance* (World Bank, 2003), used for the aggregates in Table 14.4. Owing to differences in the definitions, the aggregate private resource flows in the first source are much lower than in the second.[4] Therefore, the shares of development aid in total flows in Tables 14.5 and 14.6 are higher than in Table 14.4. Still, these two tables are interesting since they provide the country detail lacking in the other sources and illustrate how much the share of aid in total resource flows can vary from country to country and from year to year.

Several countries in Table 14.5 have net outflows of resources in certain years. In such years the outflow of financial resources is caused by either debt-service obligations or capital transfers to other countries. Examples of countries with a substantial net outflow of financial resources are Mexico and Nigeria in 1990, Malaysia, Thailand and Nigeria in 2000. Capital flight is a response to uncertain economic prospects. (Non-registered capital flight is not even taken into account.)

In Table 14.6 net aid flows have been expressed as a percentage of net total resource flows. What immediately meets the eye are the extremely large shares of aid in the total resource flows for African countries like Egypt, Ghana, Côte d'Ivoire, Kenya, Tanzania, Democratic Republic of Congo and Zambia, and in Asia for Bangladesh. These countries depend almost exclusively on foreign aid for an inflow of foreign financial resources.

In Asia we note a strong decrease in the share of aid in Taiwan and Thailand. In countries like Taiwan and South Korea, which were successful in their economic development, the share of development aid has become very small and in some years even negative, when earlier aid loans are being repaid. India and Pakistan both show a pattern of decreases in the share of aid flows, followed by some recovery. Such fluctuations illustrate the short-run volatility of capital flows. The aid shares have to be examined in conjunction with the absolute figures in Table 14.5.

The negative signs in Table 14.6 require some explanation. The sign may be negative when the net aid flow is negative and the net total resource flow positive (see note[b]). The percentages are usually low. The sign may also be negative when the net total resource flow is negative and the aid flow is positive. In these instances, the negative percentages refer to the reduction of net resource outflow in percentage terms, due to inflows of aid (see note[c]).

Dollar and Pritchett (1998, p. 8) conclude that private capital flows are heavily concentrated in a few developing countries and these flows are very volatile.

---

4 The second source did not contain the required country data.

Table 14.5 Net official development assistance and net total resource flows in selected countries, 1960–2001 ($US million)[a]

	1960 ODA	1960 Total	1970 ODA	1970 Total	1980 ODA	1980 Total	1990 ODA	1990 Total	1995 ODA	1995 Total	2000 ODA	2000 Total	2001 ODA	2001 Total
Bangladesh					1,281	1,290	2,095	2,167	1,292	873	1,171	1,250	1,024	637
China				574	66	324	2,084	4,850	3,531	13,489	1,733	734	1,460	6,394
India	730	781	825	842	2,192	2,453	1,407	4,185	1,739	1,959	1,485	2,203	1,705	2,324
Indonesia	83	83	465	625	946	1,775	1,743	3,535	1,391	8,049	1,731	2,511	1,501	1,531
Malaysia	13	15	27	90	135	689	469	1,630	109	4,123	45	−441	27	1,701
Pakistan	254	262	421	495	1,183	1,421	1,129	1,718	824	1,999	703	227	1,938	1,801
Philippines	52	53	46	318	300	971	1,277	2,009	890	3,376	578	1,509	577	1,344
South Korea	251	251	275	411	139	818	52	1,082	57	7,242				
Sri Lanka	11	14	49	59	390	427	730	738	555	648	276	398	330	162
Taiwan[b]	104	106	10	191	−4	439	36	452	0	438				
Thailand	44	51	74	200	418	1,114	797	2,808	859	7,727	641	−1,316	281	1,753
Turkey	137	135	176	237	953	1,871	1,219	2,054	307	111	325	8,064	167	2,584
Argentina	29	22	10	235	21	2,776	170	−673	144	7,971	76	7,909	151	7,036
Brazil	24	34	189	937	85	4,484	156	−1,884	273	9,190	322	20,842	349	10,565
Chile	13	18	73	157	−10	409	104	936	157	743	49	176	58	3,630
Colombia	−11	−6	160	276	90	833	90	404	171	1,678	187	427	380	819
Mexico	−2	17	80	324	56	4,462	159	−1,154	385	3,556	−54	919	75	3,789
Peru	−12	−11	57	35	203	628	400	−89	373	1,409	401	660	451	993
Venezuela	−8	−5	10	162	15	1,303	78	−3,770	44	573	77	2,387	45	2,276
Congo, Dem. Rep.	82	90	89	133	428	742	897	1,411	196	241	184	198	251	251
Côte d'Ivoire	0	0	53	116	210	918	688	796	1,213	1,129	352	733	187	144
Egypt	178	209	172	403	1,385	2,352	5,438	3,311	2,015	2,441	1,328	3,242	1,255	2,800
Ghana	3	2	59	29	192	227	563	730	651	806	609	533	652	614
Kenya	21	21	58	95	397	557	1,186	1,484	734	537	512	854	453	515
Morocco	60	60	86	152	899	1,318	1,049	1,620	495	617	419	586	517	377
Nigeria	33	40	108	200	36	1,201	258	105	212	−486	185	−1,985	185	798
South Africa									389	3,082	488	−838	428	795
Tanzania	10	10	51	59	679	864	1,173	1,128	877	881	1,022	1,160	1,233	1,242
Zambia	1	1	13	27	318	376	480	583	2,034	2,014	795	703	374	397
Total 29 countries	2,099	2,252	3,636	6,808	13,002	37,043	25,926	32,164	21,916	86,417	15,641	53,643	16,053	57,271

Notes:
[a] Net total resource flow: ODA, other official flows and private capital flows.
[b] After 1997 Taiwan no long receives ODA, though it still receives small amounts of other assistance (OA).
Sources:
OECD, Geographical Distribution of Financial Flows to Aid Recipients, 1960–2001, International Development Statistics (IDS) CD-Rom, 2003a.

Table 14.6 *Net official development assistance as a percentage of net total resource flows in selected developing countries, 1960–2001 ($US)*

	1960	1970	1980	1990	1995	2000	2001
Bangladesh		100.0[a]	99.2	96.7	148.0	93.7	160.6
China			20.4	43.0	26.2	236.2	22.8
India	93.4	98.0	89.4	33.6	88.7	67.4	73.4
Indonesia	100.0	74.4	53.3	49.3	17.3	68.9	98.0
Malaysia	88.7	29.5	19.6	28.8	2.6	−9.3[c]	1.6
Pakistan	96.7	85.1	83.2	65.7	41.2	310.2	107.6
Philippines	98.1	14.5	30.9	63.6	26.4	38.3	42.9
Sri Lanka	80.4	83.2	91.3	98.9	85.7	69.4	204.2
South Korea	100.0	66.8	17.0	4.8	0.8		
Taiwan[d]	98.1	5.0	−0.8	8.0	0.0		
Thailand	85.9	37.2	37.6	28.4	11.1	−32.7[c]	16.0
Turkey	102.1	74.3	50.9	59.3	276.6	4.0	6.5
Argentina	130.6	4.0	0.7	−20.1[c]	1.8	1.0	2.2
Brazil	70.5	20.1	1.9	−7.6[c]	3.0	1.5	3.3
Chile	70.7	46.5	−2.4	11.1	21.2	27.9	1.6
Colombia	193.2	58.1	10.8	22.2	10.2	43.8	46.4
Mexico	−13.3[b]	24.8	1.3	−12.1[c]	10.8	−5.9[a]	2.0
Peru	109.3	161.7	32.3	−81.7[c]	26.5	60.7	45.4
Venezuela	166.7	6.2	1.2	−2.0[c]	7.6	3.2	2.0
Egypt	85.4	42.7	58.9	164.2	82.5	41.0	44.8
Ghana	152.6	201.7	84.6	77.1	80.8	114.3	106.2
Côte d'Ivoire	100.0	45.6	22.9	86.4	107.5	48.0	130.0
Kenya	101.0	60.9	71.2	79.9	136.8	60.0	87.9
Morocco	99.8	56.4	68.2	64.7	80.3	71.6	136.9
Nigeria	82.1	53.8	3.0	245.7	−30.4[c]	−8.5[c]	23.2
South Africa					12.6	−36.8[c]	53.9
Tanzania	104.0	86.9	78.5	104.0	99.6	88.1	99.3
Congo, Dem. Rep.	91.4	67.3	57.6	63.6	81.1	92.8	100.2
Zambia	100.0	49.6	84.6	82.4	101.0	113.1	94.0
Subtotal	93.2	53.4	35.1	80.6	25.4	29.2	28.0

Notes:
[a] Bangladesh, 1971 instead of 1970.
[b] Net ODA is negative. When net total receipts are positive the sign is negative.
[c] ODA is positive, net total resource flows are negative. The negative figure in the table now refers to the reduction of the net outflow in percentage terms due to ODA.
[d] After 1 January 1997 Taiwan gets OA instead of ODA.
Sources: Calculated from the absolute figures in Table 14.5.

In a typical low-income country, foreign aid remains the primary source of external finance. Aid does matter here.

14.4.3   Net development assistance as a percentage of gross domestic product

In Table 14.7 the inflow of aid has been related to gross domestic product. In nineteen of the twenty-nine countries in the table, the share of foreign aid in GDP in 2000 was below 1 per cent of GDP; in another four countries it was between 1 and 1.5 per cent. In the large Latin American countries the role of foreign aid has always been marginal. In Asian countries, the share of aid in GDP has tended to decline since the late 1970s, reflecting the increasing

Table 14.7 *Net development assistance as a percentage of gross domestic product in selected developing countries, 1960–2000*

	1960	1970	1980	1990	1992	1994	1998	2000
Bangladesh[a]		0.2	7.3	7.0	5.7	5.2	2.6	2.5
China			0.0	0.6	0.7	0.6	0.3	0.2
India	2.0	1.3	1.2	0.4	0.9	0.7	0.4	0.3
Indonesia	0.9	4.8	1.2	1.5	1.5	0.9	1.4	1.1
Malaysia	0.5	0.6	0.5	1.1	0.3	0.1	0.3	0.1
Pakistan	6.8	4.2	5.0	2.8	2.1	3.1	1.7	1.1
Philippines	0.7	0.7	0.9	2.9	3.2	1.7	1.0	0.8
Sri Lanka	6.0	0.6	0.6	0.3	0.2	0.1	0.1	0.1
South Korea	16.7	12.0	3.5	0.7		−1.0	−0.3	0.0
Taiwan[a]	6.5	0.2	0.0	0.0	0.0	0.0	0.0	0.0
Thailand	1.6	1.0	1.3	0.9	0.7	0.4	0.6	0.5
Turkey	4.0	1.0	1.4	0.8	0.2	0.1	0.0	0.2
Argentina[a]	0.16	0.03	0.03	0.12	0.12	0.06	0.03	0.03
Brazil	0.2	0.4	0.0	0.0	−0.1	0.0	0.0	0.1
Chile	0.3	0.8	0.0	0.3	0.3	0.3	0.1	0.1
Colombia	−0.3	2.2	0.3	0.2	0.5	0.1	0.2	0.2
Mexico	0.0	0.2	0.0	0.1	0.1	0.1	0.0	0.0
Peru	−0.5	0.8	1.0	1.5	1.1	0.7	0.9	0.8
Venezuela	−0.1	0.1	0.0	0.2	0.1	0.0	0.0	0.1
Congo, Dem. Rep.	1.3	0.0	3.0	9.6	3.3	4.2	2.2	
Côte d'Ivoire	0.02	3.6	2.1	6.4	6.8	20.8	8.4	3.8
Egypt	4.3	2.2	6.0	12.6	8.6	5.2	2.4	1.3
Ghana	0.2	2.7	4.3	9.6	9.6	10.1	9.4	11.7
Kenya	2.7	3.6	5.5	13.9	11.1	9.5	3.6	4.9
Morocco	2.9	2.2	4.8	4.1	3.3	2.1	1.5	1.3
Nigeria	0.8	0.9	0.1	0.9	0.8	0.8	0.6	0.4
South Africa						0.2	0.4	0.4
Tanzania[a]	1.7	4.0	13.2	27.5	29.1	21.4	11.6	11.3
Zambia	0.1	0.7	8.2	14.6	32.5	21.5	10.8	27.3

Notes:
[a] Taiwan 1961 instead of 1960, Argentina, 1962 instead of 1960, Bangladesh, 1971 instead of 1970.
Sources: ODA from OECD (2003).
GDP at current market prices from World Bank, *World Development Indicators, 2002*, CD-Rom, World Bank (2002b), except for Taiwan: The Central Bank of China (http://www.cbc.gov.tw/EngHome/economic/statistics/Annual.htm); Indonesia 1960: current values from World Bank, *WDI 2002*, CD-Rom (2002b) converted with exchange rates from *World Tables, 1980*; Turkey, 1960, Tanzania, 1960 and 1970: from *World Tables, 1980*; Tanzania, 1980: from *World Tables, 1995*.

importance of private capital flows and foreign direct investment. Only in Bangladesh does the share of aid remain high at 2.5 per cent in 2000.

In contrast, the significance of foreign aid in the African countries included in the table is considerable. Between 1990 and 2000 several African countries had shares above 10 per cent of GDP. In 2000, the share for Zambia reached the astounding figure of 27.3 per cent. Tanzania had a share of 29.1 per cent in 1992, though it declined rapidly thereafter. Where aid-to-GDP ratios are so high, it is clear that most government expenditures and investments will be financed by foreign aid flows.

According to Lensink and White (2001), the early 1990s were a period of high aid inflows. In 1970, only eight developing countries had aid inflows above 20 per cent of GDP. By the first half of the 1990s, fourteen developing countries had aid ratios of 20 per cent to 30 per cent (including Burundi, Mauritania, Tanzania and Malawi), eight countries had ratios of more than 30 per cent (including Zambia, Rwanda, Guyana, Nicaragua) and four countries had ratios of over 50 per cent (Sao Tome, Mozambique, Somalia and Guinea-Bissau).[5] Country examples may be misleading, however. For all developing countries together, aid flows as a proportion of GDP were less than 1 per cent (van der Hoeven, 2001, p. 110).

14.4.4   Reduction of the real value of aid by tying

A part of bilateral foreign aid is 'tied' aid. The recipient of tied aid is obliged to spend it on the purchase of goods and services in the donor country. This means that development aid functions as an export credit for the donor country. Tying reduces the total value of aid, because the recipient is not free to use the financial resources provided to buy the cheapest and best goods and services available on international or domestic markets. Often the prices of imports from the donor country will be 20 per cent to 30 per cent above world market prices. Moreover, it is very likely that the recipients of aid are forced to buy goods that are not optimally suited to their needs and local circumstances. Furthermore, a country may end up with many different and incompatible brands of the same product from different countries. Estimates of the percentage by which tying reduces the value of aid vary. Sometimes developing countries use foreign aid to finance goods they would have imported anyway. The resources saved can then freely be used for other purposes, so the negative effects of tying are diminished (Jepma, 1992).

Jay and Michalopoulos (1989, p. 74) conclude that on average 45 per cent of all official development assistance from OECD countries (both bilateral and multilateral) could be classified as tied in 1985–1986. Jepma (1992, p. 7) estimates that in 1988, 50 to 55 per cent of all bilateral aid from European Community countries was tied aid. In addition, donors may influence expenditure patterns of developing countries by providing aid for specific sectors in which their own industry or expertise is well represented. Thus, it is very likely that Dutch aid for dredging projects finds its way back to the Netherlands even if it is formally untied. Sending out 'experts' from donor countries also automatically means that a large portion of project costs consists of the salaries of citizens of the donor country itself. Hancock (1991) estimates that there were some 80,000 highly paid expatriate experts working in Africa in the 1980s, more than in the colonial period. Worldwide, a total of 150,000 expatriates were employed.

The proportion of foreign aid that thus flows back to the donor country (the 'flow-back percentage') may exceed the tying percentage. Hoebink, for example, estimates that the flow-back percentage for West German and British aid was 60 to 75 per cent in the 1980s. With respect to Dutch aid in the early 1970s, this used to be about 90 per cent. Since the 1980s, the Dutch flow-back percentage

---

5 Lensink and White present data on aid as a percentage of GNP, rather than GDP which gives somewhat higher percentages. The high-aid countries include several tiny island economies.

has been reduced to 55 per cent, owing to an increased willingness to finance local costs and local personnel in developing countries (Hoebink, 1988, pp. 235 and 330). Dollar and Pritchett (1998) suggest that tying reduces the value of aid by about 25 per cent. Among OECD countries there has been a clear trend away from tied aid. In 1995 it accounted for about a fifth of all aid.

14.4.5   Conclusion: the volume of aid is not negligible

Although foreign aid flows represent a very modest percentage of the national income of the donor countries, the quantitative survey presented above indicates that aid flows are not without importance in international economic relations. Foreign aid forms a substantial part of the total capital flows between rich countries and developing countries.

In most large Latin American and Asian countries the role of foreign aid as a percentage of GDP is limited. Yet, especially in the poorest African countries, the inflow of aid represents a considerable percentage of GDP. Aid is not a marginal phenomenon here. It represents one of the central facts of economic life. The debate on the quality and the effects of aid is not just an academic debate. It touches on the economic prospects of the poorest African countries.

14.5   Theories of development and objectives of aid

Discussions of foreign aid are implicitly or explicitly based on theories of socio-economic development, in which aid flows can fulfil certain functions (Bauer, 1981; Bruton, 1969; Bos, 1990; Cassen, 1986; Dijkstra and White, 2003; Hermes and Lensink, 2001b; Krueger *et al.*, 1989; Lensink, 1993a; Riddell, 1987). Together with normative considerations, these theories determine the specific goals and objectives one hopes to realise by means of development aid. Aid has a variety of objectives including: self-sustaining growth, poverty reduction, environmental sustainability of economic development, improving the position of women and good governance and democratisation (Lensink and White, 2001; World Bank, 2002a). In keeping with the main focus of this book, we primarily consider the first two goals, though the other objectives will be discussed incidentally.

14.5.1   Aid as a source of investment, capital accumulation and growth

The foundations of theories of the role of foreign aid in development were laid in the 1950s and 1960s. As sketched in the chapter on industrialisation strategies (Chapter 9), the prevailing assumption was that developing countries were caught in vicious cycles of poverty. Because of low per capita incomes, savings were low. Because of low savings rates, investment was low, so that there were few prospects for future growth of national income and development of the industrial sector.

Capital was seen as the scarce factor in development. What was required was a large-scale investment programme in industry and infrastructure, which would help economies break out of their vicious circles (Millikan and Rostow, 1957; Rosenstein-Rodan, 1961; Rostow, 1971).

From this perspective, an influx of foreign capital and foreign aid could contribute to increased investment, without the necessity of a simultaneous decline in domestic consumption. Aid would come in two forms: finance for capital goods and industrial inputs; and technical aid to promote the transfer of complementary knowledge and skills. Starting from growth targets established in national plans, the required levels of savings and investments were calculated by means of fixed capital–output ratios (see Chapter 9). Given the domestic savings ratios, the need for foreign capital could be determined. Development aid would have to provide part of the required foreign capital flows. It was assumed that private capital markets would be unable to meet all the foreign finance requirements of developing countries. Distrust of markets dominated development strategies. This formed a justification for government intervention and financial aid flows from governments to governments.

The two-gap model of Chenery and Strout

The most complete formulation of the line of thinking described above is Chenery and Strout's (1966) *two-gap model* (see also Chenery and Adelman, 1966; Chenery and MacEwan, 1966; Bruton, 1969; Chenery, 1979). Transformation of the economic structure requires a large inflow of external financial resources in a short period of time. In poor developing countries private capital flows may be insufficient to provide for the need for foreign finance. Foreign aid can contribute to the acceleration of economic growth and structural transformation by relieving crucial bottlenecks in the process of development. This would increase the efficiency of the use of domestic economic resources.

Chenery and Strout distinguish two gaps: *the savings gap* and *the foreign exchange gap*. As mentioned above, economic growth requires large investments in industry and infrastructure. Domestic savings are insufficient to meet investment requirements. This is Chenery and Strout's first gap. The inflow of foreign financial resources, of which foreign aid is part, can compensate for the shortage of domestic savings. In this respect, the crucial assumption is that the inflow of aid will result in increased investment and does not result in a decline in domestic savings (see Bruton, 1969). If domestic savings do decline, the inflow of development aid will result in an increase in domestic consumption, but the investment and growth objectives will not be realised. In 1979, Chenery adjusted his model to allow for the possibility that part of the inflow of resources is consumed, so that the increase of total investment is less than the additional inflow of resources from abroad (Chenery, 1979).

Chenery and Strout's second gap refers to the shortage of foreign exchange. In a developing country where a new industrial sector and infrastructure is being built from scratch, most of the machines, capital goods, raw materials and intermediates have to be imported from abroad. This requires foreign exchange. Even when sufficient levels of domestic savings have been realised, exports from a developing country may yield insufficient foreign exchange to finance these imports. In this line of reasoning, foreign finance is necessary to finance the import of the required goods (and services and technical assistance) from economically advanced countries. The larger of the two gaps determines the aggregate need for foreign finance.

In the *two-gap model* there is a strong emphasis on the amounts of capital needed and the scale of investment required.[6] The question of the efficiency and effectiveness of investment is hardly raised. It should be stressed that the role of development aid in the total strategy is a fairly limited one. Foreign aid is part of total capital flows to developing countries. Under certain favourable conditions, it may contribute to an acceleration of growth and development by relieving specific bottlenecks. The idea was that both the large-scale investment push and development aid should be of relatively short duration (some ten to fifteen years). As per capita incomes go up, domestic savings will increase and the savings gap will shrink. As the industrial sector develops, it will start exporting manufactured goods, reducing the need for foreign exchange. Once sustained growth has been achieved, there would be no need for further aid flows. The private capital market would be able to meet the financial requirements of developing countries.

Gap analysis is now seen as somewhat dated. It is based on an unrealistic production function – the Harrod–Domar production function – with a one-sided focus on capital. A wider production is required including capital, education, knowledge transfer, capacity building and the policy framework, and their interactions. Gap analysis pays insufficient attention to the absorptive capacity, and the institutions and policies of the receiving country. According to gap models, the amounts of aid supplied to Zambia should have financed rapid growth that would have pushed per capita income to about 20,000 dollars. In reality per capita income stagnated at around 600 dollars (Easterly, 1997). Aid may be substituted for domestic savings rather than finance additional investment. In the past, aid has been provided to countries which have simultaneously restricted the inflow of private capital to the detriment of investment (Bauer, 1984). Tanzania is a prominent example of this phenomenon. Dijkstra and White (2003) argue that one should focus on the marginal impact of aid flows rather than on the size of gaps.

Although the assumptions of the Chenery and Strout model have been strongly criticised, some kind of 'gap analysis' still underlies modern debates on the financial requirements of developing countries (Lensink, 1993a). When the World Bank calls for a doubling of real aid flows to achieve the developmental

---

6 As explained in Chapter 9, Chenery and Strout also argue in favour of technical aid as a complement to aid for capital accumulation. The shortage of human capital could actually be seen as the third gap of the Chenery–Strout model.

targets of the Millennium Development Goals by 2015, this implicitly assumes the existence of financial gaps (World Bank, 2002a).[7]

14.5.2   Aid, growth and poverty reduction

One of the important objectives of development aid is the improvement of the living conditions of the poor in developing countries. Initially, theories of economic development assumed that economic growth would sooner or later automatically lead to a reduction of poverty. It was seen as inevitable that income inequality would increase in the early stages of development. Economic growth and industrialisation require increased savings rates and increased savings rates imply shifts in income shares from poor classes, who consume all their income, to rich classes, who are able to save and invest (e.g. Lewis, 1954; Sen, 1960). But as economic growth got under way and per capita incomes started increasing, the advantages of growth would *trickle down* to large sections of the population, as had happened in nineteenth-century Western Europe. Also, the income distribution tended to become more equal at later stages of development (Kuznets, 1955; see also Szirmai, 1988, chs 2 and 6).

In the 1960s and 1970s, the *trickle-down* theory was fiercely criticised. It was believed that even in countries that experienced rapid growth the poorer sections of the population profited little, owing to increasing income inequality. Power structures and vested interests stood in the way of the benefits of growth trickling down automatically. The assumption that only the rich save, while the poor workers consume all their income, also came in for criticism. Poor people are eager to invest in increasing their productivity; the rich elites are sometimes characterised by wasteful, consumptive lifestyles. A too-high degree of inequality may become an obstacle to growth because it inhibits the increase in productive capacity of the mass of the poor population and constrains the growth of domestic market demand. Redistribution of incomes and productive resources may contribute to growth.

On the basis of this theoretical analysis, a strategy of growth and redistribution was proposed in which production factors were to be reallocated to poor sections of the population (Chenery *et al.*, 1974; ILO, 1976;). Key phrases were 'redistribution with growth' and 'basic needs strategy'. More credit for small peasants and better access to land would increase agricultural output and productivity. More credit and technological support for small enterprises in the informal sector would have favourable employment consequences. Better education and better systems of health care for the poor – investments in human capital – would result in increased labour productivity of the working population. Redistribution and growth were thus considered as complementary rather

---

7 The Millennium Development Goals 1990–2015 were adopted at a meeting of heads of state in 2000. Among others they include the halving of the proportions of people living on less than a dollar a day by 2015. The financial implications of the Millennium Development Goals were spelled out at the Monterrey Conference on Financing for Development in March 2002 (World Bank, 2002a; UNDP, 2003).

than conflicting objectives. Development aid should not only contribute to economic growth, it should explicitly aim at reducing poverty and inequality.

Since the early 1970s, policy statements on development aid concentrated increasingly on direct poverty reduction and on reaching target groups of the poor. In practice, only a limited part of funds targeted to the poor actually reached their destination. In Dutch aid policy, poverty reduction was the prime goal of aid policy between 1973 and 1977. Nevertheless, Hoebink (1988) estimates that only some 6 to 7 per cent of aid to Sri Lanka (a focus of Dutch aid) actually reached the designated poverty groups. In other countries these percentages were even lower.

The empirical foundations for this debate were rather weak. It was primarily an ideological debate, in which preoccupations existing within the rich countries were projected onto the developing countries (van Dam, 1978). It is now clear that growth remains the key to poverty reduction. Progress in health, education and nutrition depends to an important, though not exclusive, extent on the acceleration of economic growth (Dollar and Pritchett, 1998; World Bank, 2002a).[8] When growth in Latin America stagnated in the 1980s or in Asia during the Asian crisis of 1997, the poorest segments of the population were the principal victims of economic stagnation. Their situation was much worse than it had been in periods of growth and economic dynamism, despite the unequal distribution of the benefits of growth. When growth collapsed in the former Soviet Union, the impact of economic decline on the social indicators was catastrophic. As the cases of China and Indonesia illustrate, growth can lift millions of people out of poverty, in spite of increasing inequality. Economic growth remains one of the keys to poverty reduction.

This being said, it is undoubtedly true that the impact of growth on poverty would be much greater if the same rates of growth could be achieved with a more equitable distribution of income. Next, the examples of East Asian growth in China, Taiwan and South Korea confirm the positive effects of a more equal initial distribution of incomes and productive resources on subsequent growth. There is also validity in the arguments for increasing the resources of the poor in developing countries. In the chapters on health, education and agricultural development, we argued that investments in human capital of the poorer segments of the population can increase productivity and contribute to growth. The same holds for investment in the human capital of women and reductions in gender inequality. What is being questioned, here, is the independent scope for aid policy in poverty reduction and the associated tendency to play down the benefits of growth. It is unlikely that any direct attack on poverty will be effective in the absence of adequate macro- and micro-economic policies.

The search for effective poverty-alleviation policies in developing countries continues. One of the most recent developments is that aid flows and debt relief are provided on the condition that a country formulates a poverty reduction

---

8 Bruno, Ravallion and Squire (1998) estimate that on average a 1 per cent increase in per capita income in developing countries reduces poverty by 2 per cent.

strategy (PRS) as a part of its wider development strategies (see Chapter 13). Here, the emphasis shifts from the direct effects of aid flows on poverty to a wider policy dialogue.

14.5.3   Technical assistance, human capital theory and growth

In the 1950s and 1960s, there was a debate between the proponents of capital transfers and the proponents of technical assistance (Krueger *et al.*, 1989). The supporters of capital transfers emphasised the required size of the investment effort. They focused on increasing the investment rate and increasing the availability of physical capital goods and intermediate inputs. Supporters of technical assistance pointed to the importance of the transfer of knowledge and technical know-how. They argued that output would increase through knowledge of new methods of production and more adequate and efficient use of existing means of production. Theoretically speaking they emphasised the role of learning, technology transfer, technical efficiency and technological development in growth of output.

In practice, it is obvious that capital transfers and technical assistance are complementary. It is useless to provide capital goods without training and schooling on how to use them effectively. It is also useless to increase levels of knowledge and proficiency when there are no physical means of production to which such knowledge can be applied (Pack and Paxson, 2001). Development projects, therefore, often included combinations of capital transfers and technical assistance.

In the course of time, technical assistance was reinterpreted, in a broader sense, as an *investment in human capital*. It was not limited to the transfer of existing Western technologies by sending Western experts abroad. Rather it involved support for increases in levels of education in the broadest possible sense, so that the capabilities to absorb new technologies and insights would be increased (see Chapter 7). Specific training and transfer of know-how are of little value in the absence of prior investment in the general levels of schooling. Investment in human capital would also make it easier to adapt imported technologies to local circumstances in developing countries. In response to these insights, the World Bank and national aid agencies increased the priority of funding for the development of the educational systems in developing countries.

Technical assistance is also provided in the form of doctors, nurses and family planning workers. Especially if this kind of technical assistance also involves the sustained training of domestic health personnel and other experts, it can also be considered as another aspect of investment in human capital. As explained in Chapter 6, investments in the health of adults and children can contribute to economic dynamism and increased productivity.

The formulation of the theory of human capital has been influenced by *theories of agricultural development* inspired by the work of the Nobel Prize-winner Theodor Schultz (1964; see also Chapter 10). Schultz emphasised the importance of so-called 'non-conventional' inputs into the agricultural sector. What he considered most important was not an increased supply of capital goods, but rather investment in agricultural education, extension and agricultural research. Following Schultz, it was realised that an expansion in agricultural research capacity in and for the benefit of developing countries could lead to breakthroughs in agricultural productivity (Hayami and Ruttan, 1985). In this context, it is important that agricultural technologies should be well adapted to local circumstances. According to Schultz, investment in human capital is a broad concept. It involves informing farmers about new techniques, training agricultural extension workers, setting up educational and research institutions which are closely linked to extension networks. Investment in human capital then shades into investment in *institution building*. Schultz and his followers have shown that such investments in human capital and institution building can have very high returns. Subsidies and contributions to agricultural research and development, diffusion of technology and institution building have been amongst the success stories of development aid.

In modern theories of innovation and growth, human capital and technological change are seen as core elements of both growth and catch-up (see Chapter 4). From the perspective of theories of aid, this involves support in improvement of technological capabilities. The notion of institution building discussed in the context of agriculture can be extended into the development of national systems of innovation (Lundvall, 1992).

14.5.4 *Policy dialogue and programme aid: policy reform and improvements in governance and institutions*

Since the early 1980s, policy makers have realised that it does not make much sense to consider only the effects of a series of isolated development projects. Any positive impacts of development projects are nullified if bad macro-economic policies are being pursued, or if institutions at the micro-level are hostile to entrepreneurship, investment or growth of production and productivity. For example, it is not much use to provide capital to a country where inflation is running so high and expectations are so uncertain that entrepreneurs and financiers try to move all their resources out of the country. It is pointless to finance costly investments in irrigation if the prices of agricultural products are kept so low that there are no incentives for farmers to increase their production. If prices do not reflect scarcity relations, it also becomes impossible to make decent cost–benefit evaluations of projects.

As has been indicated in Chapter 13, many developing countries, in particular in Latin America and Africa, have pursued ineffective macro-economic policies. Excessive protection of domestic industries and overvalued exchange rates led to non-viable industries and an inability to compete on international markets. Preferential treatment of manufacturing and artificially low prices for agricultural products hampered the development of the agricultural sector. Too much government intervention, a poorly functioning administrative apparatus, huge deficits on government budgets, and loose monetary policies were conducive to macro-economic instability. As stressed by authors like Krueger (1978), Balassa (1978), Bhagwati (1985a) and Sachs and Warner (1995), countries that started exporting early, pursued sober macro-economic policies and depreciated their exchange rates performed much better economically than other countries.

Since the early 1980s, foreign aid, therefore, is increasingly linked with a 'policy dialogue' aimed at improvement of macro-economic policy and institutional reform (OECD, 1985). In this context, there has been a shift from project aid to programme aid (Cassen, 1986). The dialogue element in programme aid is considered of great importance, as the success of policy reforms requires the active commitment and involvement of policy makers in developing countries. Financial support is provided to governments for the implementation of structural adjustment programmes aimed at macro-economic stabilisation and deregulation of the economy. A restoration of market mechanisms and a reduced role for government is part of almost all reform programmes (Williamson, 1990).

Development aid may have three different functions within the context of policy dialogue. First, the traditional objectives of development projects are more likely to be realised if developing countries pursue better policies. Second, foreign aid and other financial flows are used to put pressure on policy makers in developing countries to engage in policy reform. This is referred to by the term *conditionality*. Third, programme aid may help mitigate the adverse effects of structural adjustment policies (Riddell, 1987). For instance, balance-of-payments support may allow firms to import the inputs they need so that production will not needlessly stagnate. As shown in the previous chapter, the need for aid is probably the greatest in the poorest countries where the adaptive capacity of the economy is the least developed.

Part of aid flows may be used for consumptive purposes or to maintain educational and health services which would otherwise be subject to expenditure cuts. At the same time, some critics of policy dialogue argue that the availability of financial support diminishes the pressure to restore the health of government finances in developing countries (Knack, 2001). If the apparatus of government itself is an obstacle to development (see Chapter 11), providing more programme aid may not be of much help.

The intensification of policy dialogue does not mean that the debate on the role of governments and markets in economic development is concluded. On the contrary, the late 1990s have seen a resurgence of the debates concerning the role of market liberalisation in development policy (e.g. Hermes and Lensink, 2001b).

On the one hand, the neoliberal critics of aid argue for ever-stronger links between policy reform and aid flows. Conditionality is seen as insufficient because developing countries can make promises of reform on which they later renege once the aid funds have been disbursed. Reforms should be 'owned' by developing countries rather than being imposed by donors from outside. In this context, there is a shift in the aid debate from *conditionality* to *selectivity* (Dollar and Pritchett, 1998; Meltzer, 2000). Under selectivity, aid and debt relief is provided to countries that have already implemented reforms in policies, institutions and governance. The content of reform is broadened beyond macro-economic policy to include more effective bureaucratic governance, the rule of law, transparency and the reduction of corruption and political reforms (see below, section 14.6.4).

On the other hand, there is a growing surge of criticism of the content of the proposed reforms, of which Nobel Prize-winner Joseph Stiglitz is one of the most prominent exponents. These critics believe that dogmatic imposition of free-market reforms by the international institutions, especially with regard to the free movement of capital, threatens the growth prospects of developing countries. It is the international institutions themselves which are in need of reform (van der Hoeven, 2001). In spite of these debates, one may conclude that the connection between aid flows, debt relief and policy dialogue is stronger than ever at the beginning of the twenty-first century.

14.6 Does aid work? Different perspectives on the effectiveness of development aid

14.6.1 *Does aid contribute to welfare and socio-economic dynamism?*

The basic idea underlying development aid is that it contributes to building up the productive potential and the institutional structure of a country, in order to promote the self-reliance of that country. This immediately brings us to the central dilemma involving all aid relations: the tension between dependence and self-reliance. The debate on the pros and cons of development aid boils down to the following issue: does aid ultimately contribute to social welfare and economic dynamism in developing countries, or does it ultimately result in a permanent dependence of the aid recipient, which forms an obstacle to autonomous social and economic dynamics?

Basically, three positions can be distinguished in the debate on aid[9]:

1. The orthodox view that development aid on balance contributes to economic and social development and to the solution of socio-economic problems in developing countries.
2. The radical left-wing view that development aid promotes the penetration of capitalist market relationships in developing countries and consequently leads to the sustained dependence and underdevelopment of these countries.

---

9 See Riddell's excellent summary of the debate in *Foreign Aid Reconsidered* (1987).

3. The neoliberal view that development aid hinders economic growth and development, since it maintains inefficient government intervention and obstructs the unfolding of dynamic market relationships.

The orthodox or mainstream attitude is prevalent among governments in donor countries, governments in aid-receiving countries, officials in national and international development organisations and development bureaucracies, aid workers, young idealist intellectuals and students, and – until very recently – the general public in the rich countries. Until recently there was a widespread consensus on the desirability of development aid. This consensus was partly maintained by intensive publicity campaigns funded from budgets for development aid. The political support for aid was not based on its proven effectiveness. Rather, it was based on the moral need to do something about the problems of abject poverty, hunger, malnutrition, disease and inequality in world society.

In the orthodox approach there are two central ideas. First, aid provides additional resources that would otherwise not have been available for development. Second, it contributes to the mobilisation of latent resources in developing countries. Within the mainstream, however, there is a great variety of opinions and points of view. Some people favour project aid, others programme aid. Some are supporters of poverty alleviation, others of investment in infrastructure. Some would like to provide aid without conditions, others prefer to increase conditionality and selectivity.

Even within the mainstream there has been growing criticism of ineffectiveness, inefficiency, and waste in development aid (e.g. Cracknell, 2000; Jepma, 1988; Meltzer, 2000).[10] Some critics argue that under a smoke screen of idealistic motives, rich countries do nothing but pursue their national strategic interests. Other authors criticise the lack of coordination and coherence in aid policies. Often the ill-adaptedness of aid to local economic, social, and cultural circumstances is singled out for criticism. The organisational structure of development organisations and the relations between developmental bureaucracies are increasingly subjected to critical analysis (Meltzer, 2000; Quarles van Ufford et al., 1988; Raffer and Singer, 2001; Stiglitz, 2002).

Representatives of developing countries complain about the paternalist or even neocolonialist nature of foreign aid. They argue that aid should be made available to governments, organisations and individuals with no strings or demeaning conditions attached. Developing countries should determine their own priorities. Also, some of the conditions being imposed are seen as harmful for the development prospects of these countries.

On the other hand, for quite some time, the notion has been gaining ground that aid is only of use within the framework of an effective economic and social

---

10 For the Netherlands see Berlage and Renard, 1993; Bol, 1983; Breman, 1986; 1989b; Emmerij, 1984; Haan, 1989; Hoebink, 1988; Jepma, 1984; 1988; Kruyt and Vellinga, 1983; Lensink, 1993b; Quarles van Ufford et al., 1988; Roth, 1993; Tims, 1985; 1989; van Dam, 1989a; Vingerhoets, 1986; Zoomers, 1992. The debate in the Netherlands is interesting, because this is one of the countries where public support for foreign aid was strongest. But similar literatures exist for other countries, e.g. Dijkstra and White (2003) for Sweden.

government policy. If the policy framework is not right, a string of separate projects can never be very successful. This line of reasoning leads to more and more conditions being attached to aid. This is referred to as 'conditionality', 'policy dialogue' or 'selectivity'. We have already noted above that there has been a shift from project aid to programme aid, and that programme aid is increasingly provided on certain conditions. These conditions refer primarily, though not exclusively, to economic policy. The observation of human rights and democratic principles by governments may also be a condition for aid, but Western policy in this respect is very erratic.

A common characteristic of these mainstream approaches is that the desirability of aid as such is not questioned. The critics concentrate on the reform, reorganisation or change of specific aspects of aid policy.

More fundamental are the criticisms by representatives of left-wing radical and right-wing neoliberal perspectives on development aid. From both perspectives, foreign aid is explicitly considered as an obstacle to development. The critics are not concerned with reforming aid but rather with abolishing it. Besides important differences, there are some interesting similarities between the radical and the liberal criticisms of foreign aid. Both point to the perpetuation of dependence as a central characteristic of aid relations. Thus, the debate on aid shows interesting parallels with the left- and right-wing criticisms of the Western European welfare states which surfaced in the 1980s.

The criticism from the left reached its peak in the 1970s in the context of a general radicalisation of the intellectual climate. The neoliberal criticism became more strident during the 1980s and 1990s. At present, criticism by market liberals is the most fundamental challenge to the development establishment. But there was also a resurgence of criticism of market ideologies in the late 1990s. The following sections present an overview of this debate. Section 14.6.2 discusses the arguments of the left-wing radical critics; section 14.6.3 pays attention to the criticism by neoliberals. Section 14.6.4 focuses on criticisms of aid projects and programmes. Section 14.6.5 deals with responses from the mainstream to its radical and neoliberal critics. In this section attention is also paid to the results of empirical research into the effectiveness of foreign aid.[11]

14.6.2   Radical criticisms of development aid

The criticisms of development aid from the radical left (Griffin, 1970; 1987; Griffin and Enos, 1970; Griffin and Gurley, 1985; Hayter, 1971; 1981; 1989; Hayter and Watson, 1985; Lappé, Collins and McKinley, 1980; Mende, 1973; Zeylstra, 1975) were formulated mainly in the 1970s. These criticisms should be seen against the backdrop of the emergence of theories of underdevelopment

---

11 The classification of authors in schools is fraught with difficulties. Many of the empirically oriented studies contain conclusions which are in keeping either with radical left-wing or liberal right-wing criticisms. But an author is usually not classified as such unless he or she explicitly concludes that aid is an obstacle to development.

and dependence discussed in Chapters 2 and 3. In these theories, poverty and social disintegration in developing countries are seen as the consequences of Western economic and political expansion. In contrast to the Western countries, the spread of the capitalist market relations only leads to further impoverishment in developing countries. Tiny, wealthy elites in business and government benefit from capitalist penetration. They ally themselves with foreign interests and help maintain the chains of exploitation in developing countries. From this perspective, foreign aid is one of the many ways in which developing countries are made subject to the Western capitalist sphere of influence. Foreign aid helps maintain repressive regimes that exploit their own people. Foreign aid primarily serves to promote the further penetration of capitalist market relations in developing countries from which only the rich countries can benefit. It also maintains the dependence of the poor on the rich and of poor countries on rich countries.

The radical leftist criticism also contains a range of more specific objections to development aid and its workings in practice. Lappé *et al.* (1980) argue that aid does not reach the kind of people for whom it is officially intended. Official aid is provided by governments to governments. Aid flows channelled via powerful elites will never reach the powerless. Credit meant for poor peasants is provided to rich farmers. Most benefits of irrigation works go to large landowners. Funds for development end up in the bank accounts of politicians. Ultimately, aid results in a reinforcement of the positions of the more powerful at all levels of society. According to the radicals, only a drastic revolutionary change in the power structure could create a situation in which aid also has positive effects for the poor.

The thesis of Lappé *et al.*, that development aid provided through governments and ruling elites hardly ever reaches the poor, finds support in numerous less ideologically pronounced empirical studies. Bol (1983) has shown for Bangladesh and Hoebink (1988) for Tanzania and Sri Lanka how little aid actually reaches the poor, even when this is one of the main objectives of aid policy. In part this can be explained by the interests of Western donors, who use foreign aid as an instrument of export policy. It also has to do with the nature of power and inequality structures in developing countries. To implement a development project successfully one needs the cooperation of powerful and influential key figures at national, regional and local levels. But their interests are usually not served by improvements in the conditions of the poorest groups. This, by the way, also applies to other aspects of domestic policy in developing countries (Frankel, 1978; Myrdal, 1971).

In *Aid as Imperialism* Hayter (1971) argued that development aid in Latin America was one of the means to impose capitalist market relations on developing countries. She was one of the first to note that aid was provided on condition that Western policy prescriptions were followed. Countries that tried to pursue alternative policies focusing on the needs of the poor, like Cuba, Chile or Nicaragua, were cut off from aid, boycotted economically and attacked militarily.

For Mende (1973), the key to economic development lies in the domestic mobilisation of resources for investment. Only then can a truly autonomous and dynamic process of economic development start. Alienated ruling elites in developing countries, however, lack the capacity to start the process of internal mobilisation of people and financial resources. In order to maintain their positions, they depend on foreign aid and support from abroad. Mende concludes that development aid hardly ever has any positive effects. It merely helps maintain the status quo. Foreign aid thus weakens the capacity for domestic mobilisation of savings and self-reliant development.

Lappé *et al.* mention food aid as an example of aid that discourages domestic production. The provision of large quantities of cheap food to developing countries relieves affluent countries of their agricultural surpluses. However, this makes production of food in developing countries unprofitable. Thus, developing countries become permanently dependent on food imports. This criticism of food aid is echoed by numerous later studies (e.g. Boserup, 1983; Jackson, 1982).

Griffin (1970; see also Griffin and Enos, 1970) launched an explicit attack on orthodox theories of aid, in which expansion of the resources available for investment is a central element (see section 14.5). On the basis of a cross-section analysis, he concludes that there is a negative correlation between the inflow of development aid and the volume of domestic savings. His data also point to an absence of positive correlations between the magnitude of aid flows on the one hand and investment rates and economic growth on the other hand.

In a more recent publication Griffin (1987) concludes that in twelve African countries foreign aid crowds out domestic savings. Development aid is spent by governments, partly for consumptive purposes, partly on defence expenditures, partly on wages. When aid is earmarked for investment, domestic means which come free are used for consumption (see the discussion of *fungibility* below). Even in those cases where investment does increase slightly as a result of aid flows, this has no positive consequences for economic growth. This is because donors have a distinct preference for large-scale capital-intensive prestige projects that are ill adapted to local circumstances. These projects have high capital–output ratios and contribute little to growth of output. Thus development aid encourages an inefficient use of resources in the economy. According to Griffin, recipients of large aid flows, such as Bangladesh, Ethiopia, Democratic Republic of Congo, Haiti and the Sudan, grow more slowly than countries that receive less aid.

Like many other critics, Griffin observes that aid does not reach the poor in spite of all developmental rhetoric. Aid helps to maintain corrupt and repressive regimes. In their economic policies these regimes have tended to neglect agriculture, the sector in which most of the poor people have to eke out a living. Developing countries would benefit more from less aid and more independence, better access for their exports to the protected markets of rich countries, and stronger governments, which would have better chances of mobilising domestic savings.

In recent years, there has been a resurgence of radical criticisms of the international order which argue that the whole structure of this order is weighted against the developing countries (e.g. Hertz, 2001; Klein, 1999; Raffer and Singer, 2001; see also Chapter 13). According to these critics, the IMF, the World Bank and the World Trade Organisation force developing countries to open up their economies to unrestricted competition from the advanced economies. They urge developing countries to liberalise their capital accounts, so that multinational enterprises can take over control of the domestic economies. The TRIPS agreement for trade-related intellectual property rights protects the property rights of firms from the advanced economies. Aid is seen as one of the tools used to blackmail developing countries into submission. At the same time the international organisations condone continued agricultural and industrial protectionism by the USA, Japan and the countries of the European Union. This issue of protectionism is a very valid point of criticism.

14.6.3   Neoliberal criticism of development aid

Just like radical leftist criticism of development aid, neoliberal criticism is part of a more comprehensive perspective on society, the economy and economic development. From this perspective, the main engine of growth and development consists of the efforts from creative and enterprising individuals on free markets. Intervention in the market discourages individual entrepreneurship and an efficient allocation of resources. Development aid is one of the guises of interventionism. Therefore, it is one of the obstacles to economic growth.

The neoliberal perspective on economic development goes back to the work of the economists Friedrich Hayek and Milton Friedman. In the 1980s it was specifically elaborated with regard to development aid. The main authors of this school are Bauer and Yamey (1981; 1986), Krauss (1983a; 1983b) and Lal (1978; 1983; 2000). In the 1990s, otherwise than in the 1970s, neoliberal criticism was the main challenge to foreign aid. This is partly due to the disintegration of the communist bloc and the loss of credibility of centralised planning as a development strategy (Fukuyama, 1992).

The most influential representative of this movement is Peter Bauer who criticised the assumptions of foreign aid in a long series of publications (Bauer, 1976; 1981; 1984; 1988; Bauer and Yamey, 1981; 1986). Bauer's point of view is characterised by the following quotation: 'Aid promotes the delusion that a society can progress from indigence to prosperity without the intermediate stage of economic effort and achievement' (1981, p. 107). According to Bauer, all countries that experienced economic growth did so without foreign aid. They realised economic growth because they had the right skills, attitudes, motivations and institutions at their disposal. Foreign aid cannot help create such capabilities, but it can form an obstacle to their development. According to Bauer, the market is the bearer of economic growth. Development aid reinforces the positions of interventionist governments who have hostile attitudes towards the market.

Bauer presents a sharp, humorous, though not systematically empirically grounded, criticism of almost all aspects of development aid. His criticisms, which are representative of the entire range of neoliberal attacks on aid, can be summarised in the following five points:

1. Savings are not a bottleneck for economic development

Bauer argues that there is no shortage of savings in developing countries. Rather, there is an insufficient capacity to absorb investment. If there are sufficient opportunities for economically productive investment, domestic and foreign entrepreneurs and suppliers of capital will mobilise the resources needed. For example, if an investment in infrastructure contributes to increased productivity in the long run, the government can easily borrow money on the capital market and finance interest and repayments from future increases in tax receipts. Even under the most favourable circumstances, the positive impact of development aid is therefore restricted. It saves some of the costs of loans for investments, which would have been undertaken anyway in the absence of aid.

However, the fact that aid is 'free' increases the chances of waste and inefficient use of financial resources. In the modern economic terminology, aid is characterised by *moral hazard*. Aid stimulates investment in unprofitable projects, which do not contribute to the growth of the economic potential of a country, while increasing the indebtedness of a country (if aid is not provided as a grant).

Together with the left-wing critics, Bauer is of the opinion that considerable portions of aid are used for consumptive purposes, the upkeep of patron–client relationships, payments of civil servant salaries, or for investments in unrealistic, prestige projects.

2. Development aid does not contribute to poverty alleviation

Official development assistance is provided to governments rather than to individuals. For governments in developing countries the interests of the poor seldom have high priority. For example, the European aid flows provided in compensation for shortfalls in agricultural export revenues did not end up in the hands of the farmers themselves. It was the governments that profited. According to Bauer, foreign aid means taxing the poor in rich countries for the benefit of the rich in poor countries. If foreign aid has to be provided at all, Bauer prefers to channel it through non-governmental organisations (NGOs). They are less dependent on the cooperation of governmental institutions in developing countries. There is a greater chance that some of the money reaches the people it is intended for. However, non-governmental organisations sometimes show the same failings as governmental aid organisations – waste, bureaucracy, dependence on powerful intermediaries, and so forth (see for example, Kruyt, 1988).

3. Foreign aid strengthens the position of regimes guilty of large-scale violations of human rights

Development is provided to regimes in total disregard of their respect of human rights and tolerance of political opposition. Thus the regimes of Papa Doc in Haiti and Mobutu in Zaire have been large-scale recipients of aid. Not infrequently the recipient governments are also hostile to the most entrepreneurial and economically successful ethnic groups in their country, which are discriminated against and are sometimes even deported *en masse*.[12] Examples that come to mind are the position of the Chinese in Indonesia, Malaysia and Thailand, and the position of Asian minorities in East Africa.

4. Foreign aid reinforces the position of governments pursuing anti-market policies harmful to economic development

Governments receiving aid have pursued policies discriminating against the agrarian sector. They have protected inefficient and unviable industries by means of import-substitution policies. They have intervened in markets through extensive regulation, licensing or support of poorly run parastatals. They have been hostile to private entrepreneurs and foreign investors. They pursued inadequate macro-economic policies characterised by huge government deficits, high inflation and overvalued exchange rates. And finally, they have used aid as an instrument to safeguard their personal privileges and to secure their hold on power.

5. Development aid stimulates the politicisation of the whole society in developing countries

According to Bauer, this is the most fundamental objection to aid. Aid causes resources to be channelled to the government. Creative individuals are tempted to use all their talents to acquire subsidies and manipulate public resources, licences and regulations to their own benefit. This causes conflicts between ethnic groups that have access to the machinery of government and ethnic groups that do not. Thus aid can contribute to political instability. For instance, Michael Maren (1997) has documented how large-scale aid methodically undermined civil society in Somalia in the 1980s, contributing ultimately to the total collapse of the Somali nation-state.

Economic entrepreneurship aimed at seeking new opportunities for productive activity in the private sector is discouraged. 'Rent seeking', the search for monopoly profits through governmental licences and regulations, becomes the norm for entrepreneurial behaviour. Foreign aid can also weaken the state bureaucracies of recipient governments. It siphons scarce talent away from the civil service, as donor organisations pay so much better (Knack, 2001).

It is interesting to see how many elements the criticisms from the left and from the right have in common. According to both schools of thought: aid

---

12 A well-known example is the deportation of 50,000 people of Indian descent from Uganda by dictator Idi Amin.

never reaches the poor; aid crowds out domestic savings; aid helps maintain repressive regimes; aid contributes to indebtedness; and aid preserves the dependence of poor countries on rich countries. The crucial difference between the two perspectives, however, lies in their evaluation of the market. Left-wing critics regard aid as the handmaiden of exploitative capitalist market relationships in developing countries. Neoliberal critics believe profoundly in the beneficial workings of the market economy. Foreign aid is seen as an obstacle to the unfolding of the market mechanism.

The main shortcoming of both perspectives is that if one does not subscribe fully to *a priori* notions about the market – capitalist market relations frustrate development, all government intervention in markets is detrimental to development – the argumentation is not convincing. On the basis of impressionistic and selectively chosen examples, advocates of both perspectives come to very far-reaching general conclusions about aid, which do not stand up to closer empirical analysis.

14.6.4 *Criticism of development projects*

A useful contribution to the debate is the fierce attack on the practice of development aid by the journalist Graham Hancock in *Lords of Poverty* (1991). This book contains a horrifying catalogue of the things that can go wrong in development projects. Some examples are listed in Box 14.3. Hancock shows convincingly that these are not incidental mistakes. They occur with great

---

Box 14.3 Examples of project shortcomings
- repeated shipments of food aid consisting of food stocks unfit for human or animal consumption;
- a shipment of polystyrene igloos to tropical regions in Africa;
- shipments of electric blankets to tropical Africa under the terms of emergency aid;
- supply of medicines for which the expiry dates had been exceeded by more than fifteen years;
- large dams in river basins that caused the flooding of the dwellings of hundreds of thousands of people, displaced millions of people, severely damaged the environment and silted up within a short period of time;
- unsuccessful transmigration projects that caused deforestation and erosion without offering migrants much chance of making an acceptable living;
- large shipments of trucks to Africa, of which 95 per cent were out of operation within a few months;
- large-scale energy projects which are ill adapted to the local circumstances;
- capital-intensive fishing projects in regions where cheap labour was easily available;
- roads constructed without the necessary bridges across rivers;
- experts whose expertise was based solely on the colour of their skin;
- the construction of a nuclear plant on a geological fault line in an earthquake-prone area in the Philippines (George, 1988);
- Defence procurement in the donor country as a condition for aid.

regularity all over the world. His book also provides a wealth of concrete examples to illustrate that much financial aid is spent on salaries of expatriate experts living a life of relative luxury in developing countries, on imports of luxury consumer goods from Western countries, or is appropriated by members of the elites in developing countries. Hancock, too, stresses how little aid actually reaches the poor. Finally, he presents numerous examples of corrupt and totally inefficient regimes that have been supported liberally by means of development aid, including Mobutu in Zaire, Bokassa in the Central African Republic, Ferdinand Marcos in the Philippines and Papa Doc in Haiti. Often these regimes were also guilty of large-scale violations of human rights.

Like other authors discussed above, Hancock comes to the conclusion that development aid mainly serves the interests of donor governments, Western businesses and members of development bureaucracies and governmental organisations in both rich countries and developing countries. Other studies provide further examples of what can go wrong in development projects. For instance, in Tanzania, donors poured a colossal 2 billion dollars into building roads over a period of twenty years. There was no improvement of the road network for a lack of maintenance meant roads often deteriorated faster than they could be built (Dollar and Pritchett: 1998). On the basis of cross-country evidence, Knack (2001) concludes that in ethnically divided countries, aid is significantly correlated with increases in levels of corruption.

14.6.5   Empirical debates about aid effectiveness and proposals for reform

Since the 1980s, the international aid establishment has started paying more and more attention to the quality and effectiveness of aid flows in response to the growing stream of criticisms (Cracknell, 2000). The World Bank and national development organisations have commissioned thousands of evaluation studies and have set up research projects to examine the effectiveness of aid. In the 1980s, three authoritative studies in the mainstream tradition deal extensively with all the criticisms of foreign aid and try to formulate recommendations for its improved effectiveness. The studies are: *Does Aid Work?*, by R.A. Cassen (1986); *Foreign Aid Reconsidered*, by R.C. Riddell (1987); and *Aid and Development*, by A.O. Krueger, C. Michalopoulos and V.W. Ruttan (1989). Recently, the Meltzer commission in the US has formulated far-reaching recommendations for the reform of international organisations (Meltzer, 2000). In 1998, Dollar and Pritchett published an interesting study for the World Bank – *Assessing Aid: What Works, What Doesn't and Why* – which responded explicitly to earlier criticisms of aid effectiveness with detailed proposals for reform. These proposals have had a major impact on aid policies. In 2002, the World Bank published *A Case for Aid: Building a Consensus for Development Assistance*, which presented a rather slick defence of aid efforts and lacked the intellectual depth of the earlier analyses. All these studies subscribe to many of the criticisms of development aid. Yet, on balance, their final conclusions about the effectiveness of aid are more positive.

Riddell rightly emphasises that in the past expectations concerning aid have been unrealistic. Development aid in itself cannot create economic growth; nor can it reverse patterns of economic stagnation. As one of the many factors impinging on development, foreign aid may – under favourable circumstances – contribute to some acceleration of economic development. At the micro-level, evaluation studies suggest that the majority of development projects do contribute positively to development. At the macro-economic level, the results of a spate of older and newer empirical studies are contradictory. There is no consensus about the hypothesis of a positive correlation between aid and economic growth. However, there is also little evidence for the opposite conclusion that aid is detrimental to economic development. In countries implementing effective economic policies, the net contribution of foreign aid seems positive, but the econometric analysis underlying this conclusion has been attacked (Hermes and Lensink, 2001a). According to authors such as Riddell, Cassen and Krueger, critical analysis of foreign aid can help us to learn from past mistakes and past failures, but also from past successes. The notion that development aid cannot be reformed or improved is rejected outright.

The effectiveness of development projects

Project evaluation In his review of a large number of evaluation studies, Cassen (1986; 1988) concludes that about two-thirds of all development projects evaluated have been more or less successful in the light of the originally stated objectives.[13] Cost–benefit analyses often show returns of 10 per cent and higher. For instance, 80 per cent of all evaluated projects, funded by the International Development Agency, proved to have returns of over 10 per cent. Of the examined samples of loans provided by the Asian Development Bank and the Inter American Development Bank, 60 per cent met their objectives and another 30 per cent met them partially. In the *Case for Aid*, the World Bank (2002a, p. 45), claims that the economic rate of return to project aid was 16 per cent in the 1980s, rising to 25 per cent in the 1990s.

In general, formal evaluations and cost–benefit analyses give a more positive picture of projects than qualitative assessments by eye-witnesses and participants (*cf.* Roth, 1993). It is hard to reach definitive conclusions. It almost seems as if the publications are coming from two completely different planets. It is even more confusing when critics such as Hancock freely quote from evaluations by international organisations when it suits their argument, but reach completely different conclusions from those of the organisations themselves. The Meltzer report also quotes World Bank sources to reach conclusions

---

13 In the fifteen years preceding 1987 the DAC recorded over 9,000 project evaluations (Riddell, 1987, p.185).

opposite to those of the World Bank itself. It states that according to the World Bank's own criteria, 59 per cent of investment programmes failed between 1990 and 1999 (Meltzer, 2000, table 3.8). It also criticises evaluation procedures of the World Bank as totally inadequate, because they use vague criteria of success and do not return to assess the sustainability of projects in the years after their completion.

The moral outrage of critical observers like Hancock or Susan George does not always contribute to the clarity of the argument. As Schumpeter wrote, the process of economic development is a process of creative destruction, with both 'winners' and 'losers'. When pros and cons are not dispassionately weighed, an extremely negative picture easily emerges. For example, Hancock (1991) criticises structural adjustment programmes in general, because they result in declining real incomes in the short term. This misses the point. Even the most successful adjustment programmes will cause problems in the short term.

On the other hand, cost–benefit analysis also has some serious limitations, especially in conditions in which the price mechanism does not function properly. The use of arbitrary 'shadow prices' offers ample opportunities to calculate oneself into economic success (see, for example, Bol, 1983 for a criticism of cost–benefit analysis of development projects). Riddell (1987) points out that the objectives of projects are often poorly defined, or even mutually contradictory. In such circumstances it is hard to say whether a project is a success or a failure. He also estimates that not more than 10 per cent of all development projects has been evaluated. How representative are the evaluated projects is not known.

Often the long-run effects of projects are hard to determine. Some projects have unintended positive results and learning effects that were not foreseen in the project design. For instance, a project may not reach the very poor as intended, but can contribute to economic dynamics, technology transfer or learning in other ways.

Fungibility   One of the reasons why reliable evaluations of aid projects and programmes are so difficult is the so-called fungibility of money. According to the *fungibility thesis* aid does not really finance the high priority investments it ostensibly pays for. These would have been carried out anyway. Rather, development aid finances more marginal investments or consumption, using the funds released from high-priority projects.

Cassen (1986) rejects the fungibility thesis. First, the number of investment projects in a developing country is not static. As investment increases, new investment opportunities continue to arise. Some worthwhile investment projects would not even exist in absence of aid. For instance, complicated irrigation or hydroelectric projects could not be realised without technical cooperation with foreign donors. In the second place, even if there is some replacement of investment, the notion that the recipient country has sufficient resources to finance all high-priority projects is evidently not correct. Many authors besides Cassen stress that national and international capital markets are far from perfect. The fact that there are very profitable investment projects does not mean that private finance will be automatically forthcoming. In the third place, there are complementarities between investments (see Chapter 9). Investment projects financed by foreign aid may make other investments in the private sector more profitable. Finally, it is no great problem if some part of financial aid is used for expansion of consumption in a very poor country, as long as a substantial part of the aid flow is available for additional investment.

In the more recent literature, fungibility is taken for granted (Burnside and Dollar, 1997; 2000; Dollar and Pritchett, 1998; World Bank, 2002a). There is simply no way of controlling what governments do with the resources that have been freed through aid. They may use these to increase the salaries of civil service employees, reduce budget deficits or lower taxes so that people can consume more. However, they may also top up aid funds and actually spend more on a given line of activities than budgeted. This is referred to as the so-called *flypaper effect* (Pack and Pack, 1993). The interesting implication that Dollar and Pritchett derive from fungibility is that aid donors should pay more attention to the overall quality of policy in a country. If policy and governance are effective, then there is more reason to believe that funds will be used effectively, even if they are diverted from their original purposes.

Reasons for project failure   Reasons for project failure include lack of coordination, conflicting objectives, imperfections in project design, expenditure deadlines, insufficient attention to maintenance and insufficient feedback and learning from past mistakes.

A common problem is the lack of coordination between donors and a lack of coordination capabilities in the recipient country. In some of the poorest developing countries, such as Burkina Faso or Tanzania, aid workers from different donor countries and international organisations stumble over each other. The projects from different countries are not integrated and heavy burdens are imposed on the scarce administrative capabilities of the receiving countries. A second reason for project failure is conflicting objectives. All authors agree that the pursuit of commercial objectives or foreign policy objectives has a negative effect on the chances of success of development projects. But environmental objectives and economic objectives may also conflict in a fashion fatal for the project. Many projects fail, owing to technical imperfections in the project design and the neglect of local circumstances (*cf.* Cochrane, 1979). Far too often projects make insufficient use of local expertise and knowledge.

Another cause of project failures is the pressure on donor organisations to spend their allocated budgets before the budgetary period runs out. This pressure to spend makes for built-in waste and inefficiency. It is a characteristic of all aid programmes that specify that certain sums have to be disbursed by certain dates. In the early years of Dutch development policy, the available funds grew more rapidly than the numbers of civil servants responsible for foreign aid. In combination with expenditure targets, this was later identified as an important source of inefficiencies.

In the recent literature, one of the reasons for project failure is that money is supplied to the providers of outputs and services rather than to the users (Meltzer, 2000). If the funds were made available to the final users and paid to the suppliers on effective delivery of the service or product, this would improve the incentives for project success.

A major shortcoming is that development aid focuses too much on new projects and too little on the continuation and upkeep of existing projects. Thus there is a systematic tendency to reserve insufficient funds for maintenance, spare parts, energy costs and the costs of local personnel. Donors expect the local costs of projects to be funded from the budgets of the aid recipients. But these budgets are inadequate for such purposes, especially when governments are forced to cut back on expenditure under the terms of structural adjustment programmes. Thus, newly built roads soon become impassable owing to a lack of maintenance, and newly constructed energy facilities operate at a fraction of their capacity. At the recipients' end, the shortage of administrative capacity is identified as a problem, especially in combination with a preference for large-scale prestige projects.

Finally, critics point to lack of sufficient feedback and learning effects from past experience. Not enough lessons are learned from past mistakes (see also Burki and Ayres, 1986; OECD, 1985). There is too little feedback from evaluation studies to new project design. There is almost no exchange of information between different national and international organisations concerned with development aid. Krueger and her co-authors (1989) are slightly more positive about the learning effects in project aid. Much of the criticisms – especially with respect to the excessively large-scale nature of industrial and infrastructural projects – refer primarily to projects from the early years of development aid. In more recent projects, the criticisms have been taken more to heart.

Examples of success   To keep a balanced perspective on aid it is important to emphasise that there have been important successes in aid as well as major failures. The mainstream literature identifies several areas in which development aid has been relatively successful. One of them is agricultural development. In many developing countries in Asia and Latin America, the growth of the agricultural production exceeded the growth of the population (see Chapter 10). This was realised in part through investments in agricultural research, education, extension, irrigation and land improvement financed by development aid. Agricultural research financed from international aid flows made a major contribution to the advances of the green revolution and to the growth of agricultural production and productivity.

Positive results have also been achieved in the field of infrastructure – in spite of many disappointments. Infrastructural investment in roads, harbours, telecommunications systems, dams and energy supply are an essential component of all development strategies. These investments can seldom be financed via private capital markets.

Another area where aid has made a worthwhile contribution is education. A substantial proportion of all World Bank loans goes to education and educational projects. The World Bank is the world's largest external funder of education, having provided a cumulative 30 billion dollars for education projects over the years (World Bank, 2002a). The rapid expansion of the educational systems in developing countries since World War II (as described in Chapter 7) was facilitated by foreign aid flows. Despite many disappointments, it is clear that education in developing countries benefited from technical and educational assistance. In a country such as India, success has been achieved in building up an independent research infrastructure of high quality. Aid flows have also contributed to literacy campaigns which have been instrumental in improving literacy.

A fourth area of relative success is that of family planning and health-care policy. Though population growth in many countries is still much too high, this does not mean that the resources invested in family planning have been wasted. The dramatic decreases in death rates discussed in Chapter 5 are in part the result of a multitude of projects which contributed to the transfer of medical technologies and the spread of new knowledge about disease and health care. The eradication of diseases such as river blindness in West Africa are cited as an instance of success.

Riddell examines the criticisms of food aid (Riddell, 1987, pp. 228–36). Besides many failures, there have also been examples of success. According to Riddell, these are not restricted to emergency aid but also include other food aid programmes and projects. He recognises the danger of food aid acting as a disincentive to domestic food production. He concludes that the way in which food aid is provided may be more important than the question whether food aid should or should not be provided. One of the more recent innovations is to supply money rather than food in kind, so that food can be bought in the country or the region.

On the other hand, even the mainstream defenders of project aid also admit that there are many areas in which the results of project aid have been very disappointing. There has been a marked lack of success in integrated rural development programmes (Ruttan, 1989a; 1989b), due to the difficulties of coordinating activities of various government organisations and departments. Special problems were encountered in the extension of small-scale pilot projects into general practice on a regional or national scale. There were also negative experiences with credit programmes aimed at small farmers. These projects often failed to appreciate the role of traditional credit institutions. The resources hardly ever reached the intended target groups. A final area of project failure is found in cattle-breeding projects.

Regionally, the success rate of projects has been highest in South and Southeast Asia. Project aid in Sub-Saharan Africa has been significantly less successful than in other areas of the world.

Development as a process of trial and error   In arriving at a considered judgement of the effectiveness of aid projects, one should not forget how often major investment projects are unsuccessful in Western countries and in the private sector. Major multinational electronics, telecommunication or automotive companies regularly write off hundreds of millions or even billions of dollars in risky investments in new technologies, that have failed. Governments in Western Europe have invested billions of euros in failed attempts to shore up sunset industries such as shipbuilding, airlines or steel production. Nevertheless, no one dreams of suggesting that firms discontinue investing in innovation or that governments discontinue investing in major infrastructural projects. It sometimes seems as if development aid is judged by different and stricter standards than those of the private sector or Western governments. This is unfair. Socio-economic development and aid policy is a process of 'trial and error' in which 'learning by doing' is essential. In this process, failures and disappointments are inevitable. They are part and parcel of the learning process.

Macro-economic effects of development aid

At the macro-level, it is useful to consider foreign aid as part of the aggregate inflow of financial resources to developing countries, characterising the postwar international economic order (see Tables 3.6, 13.3 and 14.4). This net inflow is one of the differences between the post-war period and the period between 1913 and 1950 when there were capital outflows from many colonies to the rich countries (Maddison, 1989). Potentially, a net resource inflow offers developing countries the opportunity of importing new means of production and adopting new technologies. In the post-war period the net inflow of financial resources, of which aid flows were a part, contributed to an economic climate that was favourable to growth and dynamism.

As regards the specific contribution of development aid, the macro-economic debate focuses on the relationships between the amounts of aid a country receives and its savings, investments and economic growth. Both the older and newer econometric studies in this field are deeply contradictory (see Riddell, 1987, pp.102–27). Griffin (1970) and Griffin and Enos (1970) observe a negative relationship between aid and domestic savings, and aid and economic growth. Papanek (1972; 1973) finds a positive relation, just as Heller (1975). Rana and Dowling (1988; 1990) note modest but positive effects of development aid. In 1980, Mosley found no statistically significant relationships for all developing countries together. For the thirty poorest countries in his sample, however, there was a positive relation between aid and growth. In a later study Mosley (1987) found no significant relations at all. A negative relationship between aid and savings rates is reported by Gupta and Islam (1983). In a summary of the literature of the seventies, Jepma (1997) concludes that foreign aid has crowded out private saving, has supported public consumption and has had no significant positive impacts on macro-economic policies and growth.

The debate about selectivity   In the more recent literature, using more sophis-ticated econometric techniques, some of the findings are more positive. Two groups of studies can be distinguished. The first group focuses on the interac-tions between aid and effective policies. The second group of studies criticises the assumptions of the first group and comes to more positive conclusions about the independent contributions of aid.

The first group of studies concludes that there is no significant overall rela-tionship between aid flows and growth. However, if one includes an interaction term between aid and good governance in the regressions, the coefficient of aid becomes highly significant (Burnside and Dollar, 1997; 2000; Dollar and Pritchett, 1998). On the basis of these findings, the World Bank report by Dol-lar and Pritchett (1998) concludes that aid is very effective if it is provided to poor countries with effective macro-economic policies, effective institutions and good governance. By effective macro-economic policies the study refers to low levels of inflation, modest government deficits, the introduction of market reforms and an outward orientation. Good governance also involves the effec-tiveness of government bureaucracies. The report advocates a reorientation of aid flows to poor developing countries with good governance. Donors should be willing to cut back financing to countries with persistently low-quality pub-lic sectors and policies. This report has been very influential for a number of reasons.

In the first place, it builds on the conclusions of an older generation of aid evaluations by Cassen, Riddell and Krueger, discussed above. These stud-ies all concluded that the success of foreign aid depends to an important extent on the *development policies* pursued in the countries receiving aid. At the macro-level, policies should aim at macro-economic stability getting gov-ernment finances under control, deregulation of the economy and a change from an inward-orientation to more export-oriented development (see Chapter 13). At the micro-level, the goal should be the development of institutions and policies that provide positive incentives to the economic efforts of individuals. If there are no changes in policy, development projects – regardless of their individual merits – will not contribute much to a change in the underlying economic dynamics. If foreign aid contributes to a reorientation of policy, its impact should be judged to be positive, irrespective of the returns to specific development programmes. If, on the other hand, foreign aid provides policy makers with only the means to postpone painful measures of reform, its net effects will be negative.

In the second place, the 1998 World Bank report (Dollar and Pritchett, 1998) reaches similar conclusions to those of the Meltzer commission on the future of international financial institutions in 2000. Together with many other authors, the Meltzer report (2000) concluded that the older notion of conditionality, which linked aid and debt relief to agreement on policies of stabilisation and structural adjustment, had by and large failed. Promises of future reforms were insufficient, because developing countries that did not wholeheartedly support reform would renege on the implementation of reforms when the going got rough. Like the World Bank, Meltzer made a strong case for a shift from conditionality to selectivity. Rather than supply funds on the basis of agreement on structural adjustment policy, aid should be provided on the basis of past performance and past implementation of reform. This would guarantee that the developing country governments wholeheartedly supported the reforms, which is referred to as 'ownership of reforms'. The Meltzer report also called for a substantial increase in development finance in the new context of selectivity. Grants should replace concessional loans to avoid increasing indebtedness of developing countries. For countries that had met the criteria of good governance and policy reform, debts should be forgiven without further conditions. The call for additional aid flows was picked up at the Monterrey Conference on Financing Development of 2002 and the 2002 World Bank report on aid which called for a doubling of development finance to achieve the Millennium Goals for 2015 (World Bank, 2002a).

Though not all recommendations of the World Bank and the Meltzer report have been adopted, they have had a major influence on aid policies in recent years.[14] Many donor countries and donor agencies have shifted towards selectivity. For instance, the Dutch government reduced the number of countries receiving bilateral aid from more than one hundred to some seventeen countries.

The second group of studies comes to different conclusions, in two important respects. In the first place, they argue that the econometric evidence on which Burnside, Dollar and Pritchett base their conclusions is extremely shaky. Using the same dataset as Burnside and Dollar (2000), Dalgaard and Hansen (2001) show that, if five deleted observations are reinserted into the sample of observations, the crucial coefficient for the interaction term between policy variables and aid flows becomes non-significant. Other econometric studies in the collection edited by Hermes and Lensink (2001b) all conclude that the interaction term is non-significant. They argue that the far-reaching policy conclusions with regard to selectivity drawn by the World Bank are not supported by the evidence.

A second important conclusion of this set of studies (Dalgaard and Hansen, 2001; Guillaumont and Chauvet, 2001; Hansen and Tarp, 2000a; 2000b; Lensink, 1993a; 1993b; Lensink and White, 2001) is that there is a significant positive relationship between aid and economic growth, after all. A third very important finding is that there tend to be diminishing returns to aid. The higher the share of aid in national income, the less effective additional aid becomes. Beyond a certain point, the impact of aid turns negative, because a country is unable to absorb more aid. However, according to the paper by Lensink and White (2001), the turning point is very high, beyond 50 per cent of national income.

---

14 For instance, the proposal that all loans be converted into grants has run into strong opposition from European donors. They fear that this conversion will result in a reduction of the overall volume of aid flows. They also point to the fact that a very substantial part of aid flows already consists of grants.

The authors of the second set of studies do not deny the importance of policy reform. Good policies and improved governance do have significant effects on growth in developing countries. What they criticise is the empirical basis for the very strong conclusions about the interaction between aid and policy. Policy reform is important in its own right. However, if aid has an independent effect on growth irrespective of policy, the case for being very selective in the allocation in aid becomes weaker.

The empirical problems are compounded by theoretical ones. There is no full agreement on the content of policy reform. As we saw in the previous chapter, some aspects of market reforms in developing countries are increasingly being criticised. The critics argue that developing countries should have the right to subsidise and protect promising economic activities and that full capital account liberalisation is a threat to the prospects of developing countries, as evidenced by the Asian crisis. They criticise the international financial agencies for arrogantly imposing a uniform reform agenda on all developing countries, while injustices in the international order are not addressed. Most critics remain sympathetic to the overall idea of liberalisation. More open and liberalised economies have performed better than closed interventionist ones. But they call for a less dogmatic approach to policy reform. Market reforms need to be complemented by government policies and extreme liberalisation is not the answer to all problems. Countries at different levels of development require different reform packages (Dijkstra and White, 2003; Doornbos, 2001). Developing countries should be able to develop their own reform programmes, based on the specific conditions in each country. These reform programmes could be submitted to international donor agencies for discussion.

An alternative way to assess the impacts of aid is to look at country experiences. Defenders of aid point to a number of countries where massive infusions of aid have contributed to economic development. In the 1950s, South Korea and Taiwan profited from large inflows of aid, which contributed to their later growth. In the period 1966–1997, Indonesia experienced rapid growth and reduction of poverty. It profited from large inflows of aid, while engaging in an ongoing policy dialogue with international advisers. Other examples of positive impacts are provided by countries such as Lesotho, Botswana, Malawi and Bangladesh, which initially could not have survived as independent states without outside help. For recent years, Ethiopia, Uganda, Mozambique, China, Vietnam, India and Poland are cited as examples where policy and institutional reforms sparked an acceleration in economic growth and where aid flows contributed to the overall process of reform.

There are also many counter-examples of countries that received large amounts of aid, with little or no impact on development. These include countries such as Zambia, Tanzania, Kenya, Haiti, Democratic Republic of Congo, Somalia, Burkina Faso or Surinam. Also, none of the examples of success is undisputed. For instance, some observers believe that in South Korea large-scale development aid in the 1950s and 1960s contributed to the build-up of infrastructure and the educational system, which were prerequisites for later economic growth. Other observers argue that the economic development of South Korea did not take off till after 1960, when the United States curtailed financial aid. It was the prospect of the end of aid flows which forced South Korea to pursue more effective economic policies.

We conclude that neither the claims of the critics of aid, nor those of the unabashed supporters of aid can be substantiated unequivocally. First, in most developing countries development aid is modest in proportion to national income and other financial flows. Other economic and non-economic factors are far more important. It is very difficult to isolate the independent effects of aid. Second, one of the reasons for providing aid is that some countries are in great economic difficulties. A large amount of aid flows to the poorest African countries with the most intractable economic problems. Of course, one may not conclude from this that there is an inverse relationship between aid and economic stagnation. Rather, the magnitude of aid flows is influenced by the intractability of the economic problems.

We agree with Riddell who calls for a balanced approach to development aid, in which the effects of aid are analysed country by country and from period to period. Aid cannot set economic growth in motion. At best, it can help accelerate growth and assist directly or indirectly in some alleviation of poverty. Though the econometric evidence is contested, it is consistent with the analysis in this whole book that aid flows should be seen in relation to overall effectiveness of policies and institutions in different countries. In this respect, we find ourselves in sympathy with the shift towards the new more selective approach championed by the international institutions. However, selectivity calls for an undogmatic approach to what constitutes good policy and effective governance in the context of a given country.

14.6.6 Epilogue: an attempt at evaluation

Above, a small part of the extensive literature on the pros and cons of development aid has been discussed. The empirical results and theoretical analyses are so contradictory that it is illusory to expect to arrive at unambiguous conclusions. The final choices are inevitably value-laden. Nevertheless, in order to avoid being too non-committal, we have chosen to specify the reasoned conclusions we have derived from these important debates. They can be summarised in the following points:

1. There are strong moral considerations to provide development aid. The considerations gain in strength if aid, on balance, makes positive contributions to development and the solution of concrete problems in developing countries.

2. The fact that large amounts of aid are wasted is in itself not an argument against aid. Considering the urgency of developmental problems, a considerable degree of waste is acceptable, as long as aid realises some part of its developmental objectives (see also point 5 below). Development is a risky process of trial and error, which inevitably involves mistakes. Of course, one should always try to increase the effectiveness of aid and in particular the ability to learn from past mistakes.

3. The fact that development aid also serves the interests of the donor countries is not an important argument against aid, provided that aid, on balance, contributes to the realisation of developmental objectives. However, when the strategic interests of the donor countries seriously conflict with the effectiveness of aid, aid programmes should be discontinued.

4. The fact that aid does not immediately reach the poor is no reason to discontinue aid as long it contributes on balance to the economic dynamism of the recipient countries. An important proposition in this whole book is that in the long run a dynamic economy is the main prerequisite for reducing poverty.

5. Development aid should be discontinued if it can be shown to be an obstacle to development. This may be the case when foreign aid is directly responsible for the continuation of regimes violating basic human rights or pursuing disastrous economic and social policies resulting in economic stagnation and widespread human suffering. Furthermore, especially in countries which pursue very inadequate economic policies and where government expenditures are overwhelmingly financed by aid flows, there is a clear relationship between foreign aid and policy failure. In such cases, reductions in the volume of aid or even discontinuation of the aid relationship should be considered.

6. If the provision of goods as part of aid is a disincentive to the production of these goods in the developing countries themselves, these kinds of aid should be discontinued. In this context we refer mainly to food aid in other than emergency situations.

7. There are diminishing returns to aid. Countries where net foreign aid flows exceed 10 per cent of gross domestic product are in danger of becoming too dependent on aid. When human talents are exclusively oriented towards aid flows and their use, aid itself turns into a long-run obstacle to autonomous socio-economic development. Reduction of aid flows to below critical levels should be seriously considered, though the choice of the specific level beyond which aid becomes an obstacle remains arbitrary.

8. Western countries bear part of the responsibility for situations in which many people in developing countries have become dependent on aid flows. Countries engaging in policy reform should therefore be able to rely on continued support for longer periods of time, even if the long-run goal is a reduction of aid flows. Aid flows should not be discontinued from

one day to another (with the possible exception of extreme situations mentioned under point 5). Rather, aid should be used to encourage reform. In these cases, however, policy reform should include the objective of reducing the dependence on foreign aid flows in the longer run.

9. Even when government-to-government aid flows are discontinued, continuation of direct aid to poverty groups by non-governmental organisations can be defended. Non-governmental agencies are usually more effective at channelling the aid to the groups for which it is intended, but this certainly does not mean they should be excluded from critical scrutiny.

10. There is a strong humanitarian case for emergency aid in case of disasters, floods or famines. Again, a condition is that a reasonable part of aid meets its objectives and reaches the target groups for which it is intended (see point 2). Also the availability of aid should not undermine incentives for production (see point 5).

11. On balance one may conclude that aid flows have made positive contributions to development in several countries. It is more worthwhile to devote our energy to improving the effectiveness of aid than to argue for its discontinuation.

12. Nevertheless, the criticisms discussed in this chapter have shown that aid relations between donor countries and developing countries leave much to be desired. Part of development aid flows back to the rich donor countries. Much aid is of questionable effectiveness. Given these circumstances, improving the effectiveness of foreign aid has a higher priority than maintaining or increasing the volume of aid flows.

13. Development aid can never be a decisive factor in economic growth and development. Economic development can only be achieved through the efforts and policies of individuals and their governments. In the context of effective national and international policies, foreign aid may also make a positive contribution to development.

Questions for review

1. Discuss the different motives for providing foreign aid to developing countries.
2. How does the Two-Gap model of Chenery and Strout provide a theoretical justification for providing foreign aid to developing countries?
3. Discuss some of the shortcomings of gap analysis as a justification for aid.
4. Should aid be targeted directly at groups living in poverty?
5. Discuss the importance of foreign aid as a proportion of total financial flows to developing countries and as a percentage of Gross Domestic Product in different developing countries and regions.
6. Summarise the main characteristics of the radical left-wing and neoliberal criticisms of foreign aid. Discuss some of the similarities between the two sets of criticisms.
7. What are some of the potential disadvantages of food aid?
8. What is the relationship between programme aid and policy dialogue?
9. Discuss the fungibility thesis. What are the implications of fungibility for the evaluation of development projects? What are the implications for aid policies?

10. What are the main points of the orthodox argument in defence of foreign aid?
11. To what extent does the empirical literature conclude that there is a relationship between aid and growth?
12. To what extent does the effectiveness of aid depend on development policies and development strategies in the countries receiving aid?
13. Discusses the differences between conditionality and selectivity.

Further reading

One of the most thoughtful books on aid is still Riddell's *Foreign Aid Reconsidered* (1987). It provides a balanced overview of the ethical, theoretical and empirical issues in the debate on aid and a fair treatment of different schools of thought. A prominent liberal critic of aid is Peter Bauer. Two of his books, *Dissent on Development* (1976) and *Equality, the Third World and Economic Delusion* (1981), have influenced the course of the debate on aid. Radical critics of aid include Hayter and Lappé. Here we mention: Hayter, *Aid as Imperialism* (1971), Hayter and Watson, *Aid: Rhetoric and Reality* (1985), and Lappé *et al.*, *Aid as Obstacle: Twenty Questions about our Foreign Aid and the Hungry* (1980). Interesting examples of the shortcomings of aid projects and aid policies are provided in two journalistic books: *Lords of Poverty* (1991) by George Hancock and *The Road to Hell: The Ravaging Effects of Foreign Aid and International Charity* (1997) by Michael Maren. Mainstream discussions of aid and its effectiveness are to be found in Krueger, Michalopoulos and Ruttan, *Aid and Development* (1989) and a World Bank evaluation study by Cassen, *Does Aid Work?* (1986).

The macro-economic rationale for aid is set out in a classic article by Chenery and Strout in the *American Economic Review*: 'Foreign Assistance and Economic Development' (1966). Aid flows are linked to shortfalls in savings and foreign exchange. There is a large set of empirical studies assessing the impact of aid on growth and economic development. These studies are of two kinds: cross-country econometric studies; and studies of effectiveness of aid policies in given countries. An influential article in the econometric vein is Burnside and Dollar, 'Aid, Policies and Growth', published in the *American Economic Review* in 2000 (an earlier version of this article was published in 1997). Burnside and Dollar argue that there is a positive relation between aid and growth, but only in countries with good governance. The conclusions of the Burnside–Dollar study have been criticised in other econometric work, for instance in 'Changing the Conditions for Development Aid: A New Paradigm?', a special issue of the *Journal of Development Studies* edited by Hermes and Lensink (2001a). The empirical debate on the relationship between aid and growth is not yet concluded. Interesting selections from the literature include (in chronological order): Griffin and Enos, 'Foreign Assistance: Objectives and Consequences' (1970); White, 'The Macroeconomic Impact of Development Aid: A Critical Survey' (1992); Schraeder *et al.*, 'Clarifying the Foreign Aid Puzzle: A Comparison of American, Japanese, French and Swedish Aid Flows' (1998); Alesina and Dollar, 'Who Gives Foreign Aid to Whom and Why?' (2000); Hansen and Tarp, 'Aid Effectiveness Disputed' (2000a); Tarp and Hjertholm (eds.), *Foreign Aid and Development* (2000); and Knack, 'Aid Dependence and The Quality of Governance: A Cross-Country Empirical Analysis' (2001). A recent volume edited by Dijkstra and White, *Programme Aid and Development: Beyond Conditionality* (2003), examines the effectiveness of aid in a series of country studies.

Two interesting policy reports argue in favour of linking aid to good governance in the recipient country. The first report is an influential World Bank report based on the econometric study by Burnside and Dollar quoted above: David Dollar and Lance Pritchett, *Assessing Aid: What Works, What Doesn't and Why* (1998). The second report is a report of a US commission chaired by Allan Meltzer on the future of international financial institutions, entitled *Report of the International Financial Institutions Advisory Commission* (2000). Both reports suggest making the provision of aid conditional on liberalisation and policy reform. Nobel prize-winner and former World Bank vice-president Joseph

Stiglitz criticises the liberal policy prescriptions in 'The World Bank at the Millennium' (1999) and his very readable and disturbing book *Globalization and Its Discontents* (2002).

The primary source of empirical data on aid flows is the OECD. This organisation publishes a variety of statistics, including OECD, *Financing and External Debt of Developing Countries* (various issues), OECD, *Development Cooperation* (various issues) and OECD, *Geographical Distribution of Financial Flows to Developing Countries 1989–1993* (1995, and various earlier issues). In 2003, OECD brought out a CD-Rom entitled *International Development Statistics*. This CD-Rom includes the 2002 OECD *Development Cooperation Reports* and the dataset, *Geographical Distribution of Financial Flows to Aid Recipients, 1960–2001*.

Bibliography

Chapter 1 Developing countries and the concept of development

Abramovitz, M. (1989) 'Thinking about Growth', in M. Abramovitz, *Thinking about Growth and Other Essays on Economic Growth and Welfare*, Cambridge University Press, pp. 3–79.

Allen, R.D.G. (1980) *An Introduction to National Accounts Statistics*, London: Macmillan.

Bauer, P.T. (1976) *Dissent on Development*, London: Weidenfeld and Nicolson.

Beckerman, W. (1974) *In Defense of Economic Growth*, London: Jonathan Cape.

Beckerman, W. (1993) 'Is Economic Growth Still Desirable?', in A. Szirmai, B. van Ark and D. Pilat (eds.), *Explaining Economic Growth: Essays in Honour of Angus Maddison*, Amsterdam: North Holland, pp. 77–100.

Behrman, H. and T. N. Srinivasan (eds.) (1995a) *Handbook of Development Economics*, vol. IIIA, Amsterdam: Elsevier.

Behrman, J. and T.N. Srinivasan (eds.) (1995b) *Handbook of Development Economics*, vol. IIIB, Amsterdam: Elsevier.

Berry, A., F. Bourguignon and C. Morrisson (1983) 'The Level of World Inequality: How Much Can One Say?', *The Review of Income and Wealth*, 3 September, pp. 217–42.

Brandt, W. *et al.* (1980) *North–South: A Programme for Survival*, London: Pan Books.

Brandt, W. *et al.* (1983) *Common Crisis: North–South Cooperation for World Recovery*, London: Pan Books.

Brundtland, G.H. *et al.* (1987) *Our Common Future*, The World Commission on Environment and Development, Oxford University Press.

Bunyard, P. (1985) 'World Climate and Tropical Forest Destruction', *The Ecologist*, 15, pp. 125–36.

Chen, S. and M. Ravallion (2001) 'How Did the World's Poorest Fare in the 1990s?', *Review of Income and Wealth*, 47(3), September, pp. 283–300.

Chenery, H., M.S. Ahluwalia, C.L.G. Bell, J.H. Duloy and R. Jolly (1974) *Redistribution with Growth*, New York: Oxford University Press.

Chenery, H. and T.N. Srinivasan (1988) 'Introduction', in H. Chenery and T.N. Srinivasan (eds.), *Handbook of Development Economics*, Vol. I, Amsterdam: North Holland, pp. 1–8.

Chenery, H. and T.N. Srinivasan (eds.) (1989) *Handbook of Development Economics*, Vol. II, Amsterdam: North Holland.

Diamond, S. (1974) *In Search of the Primitive: A Critique of Civilization*, New York: Transaction Books.

Easterlin, R.A. (1972) 'Does Economic Growth Improve the Human Lot', in P.A. David and M.W. Reder (eds.), *Nations and Households in Economic Growth: Essays in Honor of Moses Abramovitz*, Stanford University Press.

Elias, N. (1970) 'Problemen van distantie en betrokkenheid' [Problems of Detachment and Involvement], in N. Elias, *Sociologie en geschiedenis en andere essays*, Amsterdam: Van Gennep.

Ettinger, J. van, T.H. Jansen and C.J. Jepma (1989) 'Climate, Environment and Development', Paper for the International Steering Committee for the preparation of the Ministerial Conference on Atmospheric Pollution, November.

Frank, A.G. (1969) *Capitalism and Underdevelopment in Latin America*, rev. edn, New York: Monthly Review Press.

Higgins, B. and J.D. Higgins (1979) *Economic Development of a Small Planet*, New York: Norton and Co.

Hueting, R., P. Bosch and B. de Boer (1992) *Methodology for the Calculation of Sustainable National Income*, The Hague: Sdu Uitgeverij/CBS-publikaties.

ILO (1976) *Employment Growth and Basic Needs: A One World Problem*, Geneva: ILO.

IPCC (Intergovernmental Panel on Climate Change) (2001) *Climate Change 2001: The Scientific Basis*, Contribution of Working Group I to the Third Assessment Report of the IPCC, Cambridge University Press.

Jones, E.L. (1988) *Growth Recurring: Economic Change in World History*, Oxford: Clarendon Press.

Kravis, I.B., A. Heston and R. Summers (1982) *World Product and Income*, Baltimore: Johns Hopkins University Press.

Kuznets, S. (1966) *Modern Economic Growth, Rate, Structure and Spread*, New Haven, CT: Yale University Press.

Lal, D. (2000) *The Poverty of Development Economics*, 2nd, rev. and exp. US edn, Cambridge, MA/London, England: The MIT Press.

Lall, S. (1990) *Building Industrial Competitiveness in Developing Countries*, Paris: OECD.

Landes, D.S. (1998) *The Wealth and Poverty of Nations: Why Some Are So Rich and Some So Poor*, New York/London: Norton and Co.

Lewis, A. (1950) *The Theory of Economic Growth*, London: Allen and Unwin.

Lindahl-Kiessling, K. and H. Landberg (eds.) (1994) *Population, Economic Development and the Environment*, Oxford and New York: Oxford University Press.

Maddison, A. (2001) *The World Economy: A Millennial Perspective*, Development Centre Studies, Paris: OECD.

Meadows, D.H., D.L. Meadows, J. Randers and W.W. Behrens (1972) *The Limits to Growth*, New York: Universe Books.

Meier, G. M. and J. E. Stiglitz (eds.) (2000) *Frontiers of Development Economics: The Future in Perspective*, Washington, DC, The World Bank/New York: Oxford University Press.

Milanovic, B. (2002) 'The World Income Distribution, 1988 and 1993: First Calculation Based on Household Surveys Only', *The Economic Journal*, 112 (January), pp. 512–92.

Mishan, E.J. (1967) *The Costs of Economic Growth*, New York, Praeger.

Myint, H. (1980) *The Economics of the Developing Countries*, 5th edn, London: Hutchinson.

Myrdal, G. (1968) *Asian Drama: An Inquiry into the Poverty of Nations*, Harmondsworth: Penguin Books.

Myrdal, G. (1971) *The Challenge of World Poverty*, New York: Vintage Books.

North, D.C. and R.P. Thomas (1973) *The Rise of the Western World*, Cambridge University Press.

OECD (1979) *The Impact of the Newly Industrializing Countries*, Paris: OECD.

Reynolds, L.G. (1986) *Economic Growth in the Third World*, New Haven, CT: Yale University Press.

Romijn, H. (1999) *Acquisition of Technological Capabilities in Small Firms in Developing Countries*, London: Macmillan.

Seers, D. (1979) 'The Meaning of Development', in D. Lehman (ed.), *Development Theory: Four Critical Studies*, London: Frank Cass, pp. 9–30.

Sen, A. (1981) *Poverty and Famines*, Oxford: Clarendon Press.

Sen, A.K. (1999) *Development as Freedom*, New York: Anchor Books.

Streeten, P. (1972) *The Frontiers of Development Studies*, London: Macmillan.

Summers, R. and A. Heston (1991) 'The Penn World Table, Mark 5: An Expanded Set of International Comparisons, 1955–1988', *Quarterly Journal of Economics*, May.

Szirmai, A. (1993) 'Introduction', in A. Szirmai, B. van Ark and D. Pilat (eds.), *Explaining Economic Growth: Essays in Honour of Angus Maddison*, Amsterdam: North Holland, pp. 1–34.

ul Haq, M. (1976) *The Poverty Curtain: Choices for the Third World*, New York: Columbia University Press.

UNDP (1991) *Human Development Report 1991*, New York/Oxford: Oxford University Press.

UNDP (2001) *Human Development Report 2001: Making New Technologies Work for Human Development*, New York/Oxford: Oxford University Press.

UNDP (2003) *Human Development Report 2003, Millennium Development Goals: A Compact among Nations to End Human Poverty*, New York: Oxford University Press.

United Nations (1993) *A System of National Accounts*, Brussels and Luxembourg, New York, Paris, Washington DC: Commission of the European Communities/IMF/OECD/UN/World Bank.

UNSO (United Nations Statistical Office) (1968) *A System of National Accounts*, Studies in Methods, series F, No. 2, rev. 3, New York UNSO.

World Bank (1986) *World Development Report 1986*, Oxford and New York: Oxford University Press.

World Bank (1989a) *World Development Report 1989*, Oxford/New York: Oxford University Press.

World Bank (1989b) *Sub-Saharan Africa: From Crisis to Sustainable Growth*, Washington, DC: World Bank.

World Bank (1992) *World Bank Development Report 1992: Development and the Environment*, Oxford and New York: Oxford University Press.

World Bank (1993), *World Development Report 1993*, Oxford/New York: Oxford University Press.

World Bank (1995) *World Development Report 1995: Workers in an Integrating World*, Oxford/New York: Oxford University Press.

World Bank (2001), *World Development Indicators, 2001*, Washington DC: The International Bank for Reconstruction and Development.

World Bank (2002a) *World Development Indicators 2002*: CD-Rom, Washington, DC: World Bank.

World Bank (2002b) *World Development Report 2002. Building Institutions for Markets*, Oxford and New York: Oxford University Press.

World Bank (2003), *World Development Report 2003: Sustainable Development in a Dynamic World*, New York: The World Bank/Oxford University Press.

Worsley, P. (1964) *The Third World*, London: Weidenfeld and Nicolson.

Chapter 2   Development of the International Economic Order, 1450–2000

Abu-Lughod, J.L. (1989) *Before European Hegemony: The World System A.D. 1250–1350*, New York/Oxford: Oxford University.

Bairoch, P. (1980) 'Le bilan économique du colonialisme: mythes et réalités', in L. Blussé, H.L. Wesseling and G.D. Winius (eds.) (1980) *History and Underdevelopment: Essays on Underdevelopment and European Expansion in Asia and Africa*, Paris: Editions de la Maison des sciences de l'homme, pp. 29–41.

Bairoch, P. and M. Levy-Leboyer (1981) *Disparities in Economic Development since the Industrial Revolution*, London, Macmillan.

Baker, C. (1981) 'Economic Organization and Slump in South and South East Asia', in *Comparative Studies in Society and History*, 23, pp. 325–49.

Baran, P. (1957) *The Political Economy of Growth*, New York: Monthly Review Press.

Boserup, E. (1981) *Population and Technology*, University of Chicago Press.

Braudel, F. (1978) 'Expansion of Europe and the Longue Durée', in H.L. Wesseling (ed.), *Expansion and Reaction*, Leiden University Press.

Breman, J. (1985) *Arbeidsmigratie en transformatie in koloniaal Azie* [Labour migration and Transformation in Colonial Asia], series of working documents 7, Rotterdam: CASP.

Castells, M. (2000) *The Information Age: Economy, Society and Culture*, Vol. I, *The Rise of the Network Society* 2nd edn, Oxford: Blackwell.

Cipolla, C.M. (1981) *Before the Industrial Revolution: European Society and Economy, 1000–1700*, 2nd end, London: Methuen.

Curtin, P. D. (1969) *The Atlantic Slave Trade: A Census*, Madison: University of Wisconsin Press.

Darby, H.C. and H. Fullart (1970) *The New Cambridge Modern History Atlas*, Cambridge University Press.

Davidson, B. (1992) *The Black Man's Burden – Africa and the Curse of the Nation State*, London: James Currey.

Davis, K. (1951) *The Population of India and Pakistan*, Cambridge, MA: University of Princeton Press.

Diamond, J. (1998) *Guns, Germs and Steel: A Short History of Everybody for the Last 13,000 Years*, London: Vintage.

Elias, N. (1969) *Über den Prozess der Zivilisation* [The Civilising Process], Vol. II, 2nd edn, Bern: Franke Verlag.

Eltis, D. (1989) *Economic Growth and the Ending of the Transatlantic Slave Trade*, New York: Oxford University Press.

Eltis, D., S.D. Behrend, D. Richardson and H.S. Klein (1998) *The Transatlantic Slave Trade, 1562–1867: A Database CD-Rom*, Cambridge University Press.

Elvin, M. (1973) *The Pattern of Chinese Past*, Stanford University Press.

Emmer, P.C. (1986) 'The Meek Hindu: The Recruitment of Indian Indentured Labourers for Service Overseas, 1870–1916', in P.C. Emmer (ed.), *Colonialism and Migration: Indentured Labour before and after Slavery*, Dordrecht: Nijhoff, pp. 3–18.

Engerman, S.L. (1986) 'Servants to Slaves to Servants: Contract Labour and European Expansion', in Emmer (ed.), *Colonialism and Migration*, pp. 263–94.

Fage, J.D. (1969) *A History of West Africa: An Introductory Survey*, 4th edn, Cambridge University Press.

Fage, J.D. (1977) 'Slavery and the Slave Trade in the Context of West African History', in Z.A. Konczacki and J.M. Konczacki (eds.), *An Economic History of Tropical Africa*, Vol. I: *The Pre-Colonial Period*, London: Frank Cass, pp. 166–78.

Fieldhouse, D.K. (1982) *The Colonial Empires: A Comparative Survey from the Eighteenth Century*, 2nd edn, London: Macmillan.

Frank, A.G. (1998) *ReOrient: Global Economy in the Asian Age*, Berkeley: University of California Press.

Furtado, C. (1976) *Economic Development of Latin America*, 2nd edn, Cambridge University Press.

Gerschenkron, A. (1962) *Economic Backwardness in Historical Perspective*, Cambridge, MA: Harvard University Press.

Hill, P. (1986) *Development Economics on Trial: The Anthropological Case for a Prosecution*, Cambridge University Press.

Hopkins, A.G. (1973) *An Economic History of West Africa*, London: Longman.

Isichei, E. (1997) *A History of African Societies to 1870*, Cambridge University Press.

Israel, J. (1995) *The Dutch Republic: Its Rise, Greatness and Fall, 1477–1806*, Oxford: Clarendon Press.

Jones, E.L. (1988) *Growth Recurring. Economic Change in World History*, Oxford: Clarendon Press.

Kennedy, P. (1989) *The Rise and Fall of Great Powers*, New York: Vintage Books.

Klein, H.S. (1999) *The Atlantic Slave Trade*, Cambridge University Press.

Kuznets, S. (1966) *Modern Economic Growth: Rate, Structure and Spread*, New Haven CT: Yale University Press.

Kuznets, S. (1971) *Economic Growth of Nations: Total Output and Production Structure*, Cambridge, MA: Harvard University Press.

Landes, D. (1969) *The Unbound Prometheus: Technological Changes and Industrial Development in Western Europe from 1750 to the Present*, Cambridge University Press.

Landes, D. S. (1998) *The Wealth and Poverty of Nations: Why Some Are So Rich and Some So Poor*, New York/London: Norton and Co.

Lewis, A. (1954) 'Economic Development with Unlimited Supplies of Labour', *The Manchester School of Economic and Social Studies*, 22, pp. 139–91.

Lewis, W.A. (ed.) (1970) *Tropical Development 1880–1913*, London: Allen and Unwin.

Lewis, W.A. (1978a) *Growth and Fluctuations 1870–1913*, London: Allen and Unwin.

Lewis, W.A. (1978b) *The Evolution of the International Economic Order*, Princeton University Press.

Lin, J.Y. (1995) 'The Needham Puzzle: Why the Industrial Revolution Did Not Originate in China', *Economic Development and Cultural Change*, 43(2), January, pp. 269–92.

Lovejoy, P.E. (1982) 'The Volume of the Atlantic Slave Trade: A Synthesis', *Journal of African History*, 33, pp. 473–501.

McEvedy, C. and R. Jones (1978) *Atlas of World Population History*, Harmondsworth: Penguin.

McNeil, W.H. (1989) 'European Expansion and Warfare since 1500', in J.A. de Moor and H.L. Wesseling (eds.), *Imperialism and War*, London: Brill.

Maddison, A. (1982a) *Phases of Capitalist Development*, Oxford University Press.

Maddison, A. (1982b) 'International Economic Orders Past and Present: The West and the Rest since 1500', in: *Syllabus Leergang Ontwikkelingsproblematiek*, mimeograph, Groningen, pp. 23–38.

Maddison, A. (1983) 'A Comparison of Levels of GDP per Capita in Developed and Developing Countries, 1700–1980', *Journal of Economic History*, 43(1), March, pp. 27–41.

Maddison, A. (1985) *Two Crises: Latin America and Asia, 1929–1938 and 1973–1983*, Paris: OECD.

Maddison, A. (1989) *The World Economy in the 20th Century*, Paris: OECD.

Maddison, A. (1995) *Monitoring the World Economy*, OECD Development Centre Studies Paris: OECD.

Maddison, A. (1998) *The Chinese Economy in the Long Run*, OECD Development Centre Studies, Paris: OECD.

Maddison, A. (2001) *The World Economy: A Millennial Perspective*, OECD Development Centre Studies, Paris: OECD.

Mokyr, J. (1990) *The Lever of Riches: Technological Creativity and Economic Progress*, New York: Oxford University Press.

Myers, R.H. and M.R. Peattie (1984) *The Japanese Colonial Empire, 1895–1945*, Princeton University Press.

Myint, H. (1980) *The Economics of the Developing Countries*, 5th edn, London: Hutchinson.

Needham, J. *et al.* (1954) *Science and Civilisation in China*, Cambridge University Press.

North, D.C. and R.P. Thomas (1973). *The Rise of the Western World*, Cambridge University Press.

Palmer, R.R. and J. Colton (1978), *A History of the Modern World*, 5th edn, New York: Knopf.

Perkins, D.H. (1969) *Agricultural Development in China, 1368–1968*, Edinburgh University Press.

Pollard, S. (1990) *Typology of Industrialization Processes in the Nineteenth Century*, Harwood: Academic Publishers.

Reynolds, L.G. (1986) *Economic Growth in the Third World: An Introduction*, New Haven, CT: Yale University Press.

Richardson, D. (1989) 'Slave Exports from West and West-Central Africa, 1700–1810: New Estimates of Volume and Distribution', *Journal of African History*, 30(1), pp. 1–22.

Rosenberg, N. (1982) *Inside the Black Box: Technology and Economics*, Cambridge University Press.

Slicher van Bath, B.H. (1989) *Indianen en Spanjaarden: Een ontmoeting tussen twee werelden, Latijns-Amerika, 1500–1800* [Indians and Spaniards: A Meeting between Two Worlds, Latin America, 1500–1800], Amsterdam: Bakker.

Streeten, P. (1984) 'Approaches to a New International Order', C. K. Wilber (ed.), *The Political Economy of Development and Underdevelopment*, 3rd edn, New York: Random House, pp. 473–97.

Wallerstein, E. (1974) *The Modern World System*, New York: Academic Press.

Weber, M. (1920) 'Confuzianismus und Taoismus [Confucianism and Taoism]', in *Gesammelte Aufsätze zur Religions-soziologie* [Collected Essays in the Sociology of Religion], Vol. I, Tübingen: Mohr.

Williams, E. (1964) *Capitalism and Slavery*, 2nd edn, London: Deutsch.

Wolf, E.R. (1982) *Europe and the People without History*, Berkeley: University of California Press.

Chapter 3   Growth and stagnation: Theories and experiences

Abramovitz, M. (1989a) 'Resource and Output Trends in the United States since 1870', in *American Economic Review*, May 1956, 46(2), pp. 5–23, repr. in M. Abramovitz, *Thinking about Growth and Other Essays on Economic Growth and Welfare*, Cambridge University Press.

Abramovitz, M. (1989b) 'Thinking about Growth', in M. Abramovitz, *Thinking about Growth*, pp. 3–79.

Bacha, E.L. (1979) 'The Kuznets Curve and Beyond: Growth and Changes in Inequality', in E. Malinvaud (ed.), *Economic Growth and Resources*, Vol. I, London: Macmillan.

Baran, P. (1957) *The Political Economy of Growth*, New York: Monthly Review Press.

Barro, R. (1991) 'Economic Growth in a Cross Section of Countries', *Quarterly Journal of Economics*, 106, May, pp. 407–44.

Barro, R. and X. Sala-i-Martin (1995), *Economic Growth*, New York: McGraw-Hill.

Baumol, W.J., S.A.B. Blackman and E.N. Wolff (1989) *Productivity and American Leadership*, Cambridge, MA: MIT Press.

Baumol, W.J. (1986) 'Productivity Growth, Convergence and Welfare: What the Long-Run Data Show', *American Economic Review*, 76(5), December, pp. 1072–86.

Boeke, J.H. (1930/1961) 'Dualistische Economie 1930', repr. in Boeke, J.H., *Indonesian Economics: The Concept of Dualism in Theory and Practice*, The Hague: Van Hoeve.

Chenery, H., S. Robinson and M. Syrquin (1986) *Industrialisation and Growth: A Comparative Study*, World Bank, Oxford University Press.

Chirot, D. (1977) *Social Change in the Twentieth Century*, New York: Harcourt, Brace and Jovanovich.

Colman, D. and F. Nixson (1985), *Economics of Change in Less Developed Countries*, 2nd edn, Oxford: Phillip Allen, Totowa, NJ: Barnes and Noble Books.

David, P.A. (1975) *Technical Choice, Innovation and Growth*, Cambridge University Press.

Deininger, K. and L. Squire (1996) 'A New Data Set Measuring Income Inequality', *World Bank Economic Review*, 10, September, pp. 565–91.

Deininger, K. and L. Squire (1998), 'New Ways of Looking at Old Issues', *Journal of Development Economics*, 57, pp. 259–87.

Denison, E.F. (1967) *Why Growth Rates Differ*, Washington, DC: Brookings Institution.

DGBAS (1994) Executive Yuan, *National Income in Taiwan Area of the Republic of China*, Taipeh: DGBAS.

Dos Santos, T. (1970) 'The Structure of Dependence', *American Economic Review*, 60(2), May, pp. 231–6.

Dosi, G., C. Freeman and R. Nelson (eds.) (1998) *Technical Change and Economic Theory*, London: Pinter.

Durkheim, E. (1973) *Le Suicide*, Paris: Press Universitaires de France (first edn 1897).

Fagerberg, J. (1994) 'Technology and International Differences in Growth Rates', *Journal of Economic Literature*, 32, September, pp. 1147–75.

Fei, J.C.H. and G. Ranis (1964) *Development of the Labor Surplus Economy: Theory and Policy*, Homewood, IL: Irwin.

Fieldhouse, D.K. (1973) *Economics and Empire, 1830–1914*, Ithaca: Cornell University Press.

Frank, A.G. (1969) *Capitalism and Underdevelopment in Latin America*, rev. edn, New York: Monthly Review Press.

Frank, A.G. (1971) *The Sociology of Underdevelopment and the Underdevelopment of Sociology*, London: Pluto Press.

Frank, A.G. (1998) *ReOrient: Global Economy in the Asian Age*, Berkeley: University of California Press.

Freeman C. and L. Soete (1997) *The Economics of Industrial Innovation*, 3rd edn, London and Washington: Pinter.

Gerschenkron, A. (1962) *Economic Backwardness in Historical Perspective*, Cambridge, MA: Harvard University Press.

Hagen E.E. (1962) *On the Theory of Social Change: How Economic Growth Begins*, New York, NY: Feffer & Simons.

Hofman, A. (1998) 'Latin American Development: A Causal Analysis in Historical Perspective', Groningen.

Hoselitz, B.F. (1960) *Sociological Aspects of Economic Growth*, New York: The Free Press.

Hunt, D. (1989) *Economic Theories of Development: An Analysis of Competing Paradigms*, New York: Harvester.

ILO (2002) *Key Indicators of the Labour Market, 2001–2002*, Geneva: International Labour Organisation.

Inkeles, A. (1969) 'Making Men Modern: On the Causes and Consequences of Individual Change in Developing Countries', *American Journal of Sociology*, 75(2), September, pp. 208–25.

Inkeles, A. and D. Smith (1974) *Becoming Modern*, Harvard, MA: Harvard University Press.

Jones, C.I. (1998) *Introduction to Economic Growth*, New York: Norton.

Jorgenson, D.W. (1995) *Productivity*, Cambridge, MA: MIT Press, 2 vols.

Kendrick, J.W. (1961) *Productivity Trends in the United States*, New York: NBER; Princeton University Press.

Kuznets, S. (1955) 'Economic Growth and Income Inequality', *American Economics Review*, 45(1), pp. 1–28.

Kuznets, S. (1965) *Economic Growth and Structure*, London: Heinemann.

Lerner, D. (1958) *The Passing of Traditional Society: Modernizing the Middle East*, Glenco, IL: The Free Press.

Lewis, W.A. (1950) *Theory of Economic Growth*, London: Allen and Unwin.

Lewis, W.A. (1954) 'Economic Development with Unlimited Supplies of Labour', *The Manchester School of Economic and Social Studies*, 22, pp. 139–91.

Lewis, W.A. (1978) *Evolution of the International Economic Order*, Princeton University Press.

Lucas, R.E. (1988) 'On the Mechanics of Economic Development', *Journal of Monetary Economics*, 22, July, pp. 3–42.

Maddison, A. (1970) *Economic Progress and Policy in Developing Countries*, New York: Norton.

Maddison, A. (1986) *Notes on Developing Country Performance*, mimeograph, Groningen.

Maddison, A. (1987) 'Growth and Slowdown in Advanced Capitalist Economies', *Journal of Economic Literature*, 25, June, pp. 649–98.

Maddison, A. (1988) 'Ultimate and Proximate Growth Causality: A Critique of Mancur Olson on the Rise and Decline of Nations', *Scandinavian History Review*, 2, pp. 25–29.

Maddison, A. (1989) *The World Economy in the Twentieth Century*, Paris: OECD.

Maddison, A. (1995) *Monitoring the World Economy*, OECD Development Centre Studies, Paris: OECD.

Maddison, A. (2001) *The World Economy: A Millennial Perspective*, OECD Development Centre Studies, Paris: OECD.

Maddison, A. (2003) *The World Economy: Historical Statistics*, OECD Development Centre Studies, Paris: OECD.

Mankiw, N.G., P. Romer and D.Weil (1992) 'A Contribution to the Empirics of Economic Growth', *Quarterly Journal of Economics*, 107, May, pp. 407–38.

Meier, G.M. and J.E. Stiglitz (eds.) (2000) *Frontiers of Development Economics: The Future in Perspective*, Washington, DC: The World Bank/New York: Oxford University Press.

Mitchell, B.R. (1982) *International Historical Statistics: The Americas and Australasia*, London: Macmillan.

Moore, W.E. (1963) *Social Change*, Englewood Cliffs, NJ: Prentice Hall.

Myint, H. (1980) *The Economics of the Developing Countries*, 5th edn, London: Hutchinson.

Myrdal, G. (1957) *Economic Theory and Underdeveloped Regions*, London: Duckworth and Co.

Myrdal, G. (1968) *Asian Drama: An Inquiry into the Poverty of Nations*, Harmondsworth: Penguin Books.

Nelson, R.N. and S. Winter (1982) *An Evolutionary Theory of Economic Change*, Cambridge, MA: Harvard University Press.

North, D.C. (1990) *Institutions, Institutional Change and Economic Performance*, Cambridge University Press.

North, D.C. (1993) 'The Ultimate Causes of Growth', in A. Szirmai, B. van Ark and D. Pilat(eds.), *Explaining Economic Growth: Essays in Honour of Angus Maddison*, Amsterdam: North Holland, pp. 65–75.

North, D.C. and R.P. Thomas (1973) *The Rise of the Western World: A New Economic History*, Cambridge University Press.

Nurkse, R. (1953) *Problems of Capital Formation in Underdeveloped Countries*, New York: Oxford University Press.

Pack, H. (1994) 'Endogenous Growth Theory, Intellectual Appeal and Empirical Short-comings', *Journal of Economic Perspectives*, 8(1), pp. 55–72.

Prebisch, R. (1950) *The Economic Development of Latin America and its Principal Problems*, Department of Economic Affairs, New York: UN.

Ray, D. (1998) *Development Economics*, Princeton University Press.

Romer, P. (1986) 'Increasing Returns and Long-Run Growth', *Journal of Political Economy*, 94(5), (1990), pp. 1002–37.

Romer, P. (1990) 'Endogenous Technological Change, *Journal of Political Economy*, 95(5), October, pp. S71–102.

Rosenstein-Rodan, P. (1943) 'Problems of Industrialisation of East and South-East Europe', *Economic Journal*, June–September, pp. 201–11.

Rostow, W.W. (ed.) (1965) *The Economics of Take-Off into Sustained Growth*, London: Macmillan.

Rostow, W.W. (1960) *The Stages of Economic Growth*, Cambridge University Press.

Schumpeter, J.A. (1976) *Capitalism, Socialism and Democracy*, London, Allen and Unwin, (first edn 1943).

Schumpeter, J.A. (2000) *The Theory of Economic Development*, New Brunswick/London: Transaction Publishers (first published in 1912 as *Theorie der Wirtschaftlichen Entwicklung*).

Smith, A. (1961) *An Inquiry into the Nature and Causes of the Wealth of Nations*, ed. E. Cannan, London: Methuen (first edn 1776).

Solow, R.M. (1956) 'A Contribution to the Theory of Economic Growth', *Quarterly Journal of Economics*, 70(1), February, pp. 65–94.

Solow, R.M. (1957) 'Technical Change and the Aggregate Production Function', *Review of Economics and Statistics*, 39(3), August, pp. 312–20.

Solow, R.M. (1991) 'New Directions in Growth Theory', in B. Gahlen, H. Hesse, H.J. Ramser and G. Bombach (eds.), *Wachstumstheorie und Wachstumspolitik: Ein neuer Anlauf*, Tübingen: Mohr/Siebeck, pp. 3–17.

Sunkel, O. (1993) *Development from Within: Toward a Neostructuralist Approach for Latin America*, Boulder, CO: Lynne Reiner Publishers.

Szirmai, A. (1986) *Inequality Observed*, Aldershot: Avebury.

Szirmai, A., B. van Ark and D. Pilat (eds.) (1993) *Explaining Economic Growth: Essays in Honour of Angus Maddison*, Amsterdam: North Holland.

Thirlwall, A.P. (1997) *Growth and Development, with Special Reference to Developing Economies*, 6th edn, London: Macmillan.

Thirlwall, A.P. (2003) *Growth and Development, with Special Reference to Developing Economies*, 7th edn, London: Palgrave.

Thorbecke, E. and C. Charumilind (2002) 'Economic Inequality and Its Socioeconomic Impact', *World Development*, 30(9), pp. 1477–95.

Urquidi, V. (1993) 'The Developmentalist View', in A. Szirmai *et al.*, *op. cit.*, pp. 447–66.

Verspagen, B. (1993) *Uneven Growth between Interdependent Economies: An Evolutionary View on Technology Gaps, Trade and Growth*, Aldershot: Avebury.

Verspagen, B. (2001) *Economic Growth and Technological Change: An Evolutionary Interpretation*, OECD, STI Working Papers, No. 1, 2001, Paris OECD.

Weber, M. (1969) *Die Protestantische Ethik*, ed. J. Winckelmann, Munich: Siebenstern (first edn 1905).

World Bank (1993) *The East Asian Miracle: Economic Growth and Public Policy*, New York: Oxford University Press.

World Bank (2002) *World Development Report 2002*, Oxford/New York: Oxford University Press, and various issues.

World Bank (1980) *World Tables*, Baltimore and London: Johns Hopkins University Press, and various issues.

World Bank (1999) *World Development Indicators [WDI]*, CD-Rom, Washington, DC: World Bank.

World Bank (2001) *Word Development Indicators 2001*, 5th edn, Washington DC: World Bank.

World Bank, CD-Rom (2004) *World Development Indicators 2004*, Washington, DC: World Bank.

Young, A. (1995) 'The Tyranny of Numbers: Confronting the Statistical Realities of the East Asian Growth Experience', *Quarterly Journal of Economics*, 110(3), 1995, pp. 641–80.

Chapter 4   Technology and development

Abramovitz, M. (1989), *Thinking about Growth and Other Essays on Economic Growth and Welfare*, Cambridge University Press.

Biggs, T., M. Shah and P. Srivastava (1995) *Technological Capabilities and Learning in African Enterprises*, World Bank, Technical Paper, No. 288, Africa Technical Department Series, Washington, DC: World Bank.

Bongenaar, B. and A. Szirmai (1999) *The Role of a Research and Development Institute in the Development and Diffusion of Technology*, ECIS Working Paper, 09–1999.

Bongenaar, B. and A. Szirmai (2001) 'Development and Diffusion of Technology: The Case of TIRDO' in A. Szirmai and P. Lapperre (eds.), *The Industrial Experience of Tanzania*, Basingstoke: Palgrave Press, pp. 171–93.

Boserup, E. (1981) *Population and Technology*, Oxford: Blackwell.

Caniëls, M.C.J. (2000) *Regional Growth Differentials, The Impact of Locally Bounded Knowledge Spillovers*, Cheltenham: Elgar.

Castells, M. (2000) *The Rise of the Network Society*, Vol. I, *The Information Age*, 2nd edn, Oxford: Blackwell, 3 vols.

Cooper, C. (2001) 'The Role of Technological Factors in the Early Stages of Industrial Exports: A Note', in A. Szirmai and P. Lapperre (eds.), *The Industrial Experience of Tanzania*, Basingstoke: Palgrave, pp. 114–32.

DGBAS, Republic of China (Taiwan) (2002) Directorate General of Budget Accounting and Statistics, *China Statistical Yearbook 2002*, Taipeh (http://www.stat.gov.tw/bs2/ Year-Book.htm).

Dosi, G. (1988) 'Technological Paradigms and Technological Trajectories', *Research Policy*, 11, pp. 147–62.

Duijsters, G. and J. Hagedoorn (2000) 'International Technological Collaboration: Implications for Newly Industrialising Economies', in L. Kim and R.R. Nelson (eds.), *Technology, Learning and Innovation: Experiences of Newly Industrializing Economies*, Cambridge University Press, pp. 193–215.

Evenson, R.E. and L.E. Westphal (1995) 'Technological Change and Technology Strategy', in H. Behrman and T. N. Srinivasan (eds.), *Handbook of Development Economics*, Vol. IIIA. Amsterdam: Elsevier, pp. 2211–99.

Freeman, C. (1987) *Technology and Economic Performance, Lessons from Japan*, London: Pinter.

Freeman, C. and C. Perez (1988), 'Structural Crises of Adjustment, Business Cycles and Investment Behaviour, in: G. Dosi, *et al.* (eds.), *Technical Change and Economic Theory*, London/New York: Pinter, pp. 38–65.

Gerschenkron, A. (1962) *Economic Backwardness in Historical Perspective*, Cambridge, MA: Harvard University Press.

Hughes, T.P. (1983) *Networks of Power: Electrification in Western Society 1880–1930*, Baltimore: Johns Hopkins.

James, J. (1999) 'Information Technology, Globalization and Marginalization', in: A.S. Bhalla (ed.), *Globalization, Growth and Marginalization*, Basingstoke: Macmillan.

James, J. (2002) *Technology, Globalization and Poverty*, Cheltenham: Elgar.

Kim, L. and R.R. Nelson (eds.) (2000) *Technology, Learning and Innovation: Experiences of Newly Industrializing Economies*, Cambridge University Press.

Kuznets, S. (1966) *Modern Economic Growth: Rate, Structure and Spread*, New Haven, CT: Yale University Press.

Lal, D. and H. Myint (1966) *The Political Economy of Poverty, Equity and Growth: A Comparative Study*, Oxford University Press.

Lall, S. (1987) *Learning to Industrialise: The Acquisition of Technological Capabilities in India*, London: Macmillan.

Lall, S. (1992) 'Technological Capabilities and Industrialization', *World Development*, 20(2), pp. 165–86.

Lall, S. (1994) 'Technological Capabilities and Industrialization', *World Development*, 22(4), pp. 635–44.

Lall, S. (1996) *Learning from the Asian Tigers: Studies in Technology and Industrial Policy*, London: Macmillan.

Lall, S. (2000) 'Technological Change and Industrialization in the Asian NIEs: Achievements and Challenges', in L. Kim and R.R. Nelson (eds.), *Technology, Learning and Innovation: Experiences of Newly Industrializing Economies*, Cambridge University Press, pp. 13–68.

Landes, D.S. (1998) *The Wealth and Poverty of Nations: Why Some Are So Rich and Some So Poor*, New York/London: Norton & Co.

Lapperre, P. (1992) 'Man, Technology, Society and Development', dissertation, Eindhoven University of Technology.

Lundvall, B.A. (1992) *National Systems of Innovation: Towards a Theory of Innovation and Interactive Learning*, London: Pinter.

Maddison, A. (1987) 'Growth and Slowdown in Advanced Capitalist Economies', *Journal of Economic Literature*, 25, June, pp. 649–98.

Maddison, A. (1991) *Dynamic Forces in Capitalist Development*, Oxford University Press.

Mankiw, F., D. Romer and D. Weil (1992) 'A Contribution to the Empirics of Economic Growth', *Quarterly Journal of Economics*, 107(2), May, pp. 407–38.

Nadiri, M. (1972) 'International Studies of Factor Inputs and Total Factor Productivity: A Brief Survey', *Review of Income and Wealth*, June.

Nelson, R. (ed.) (1993) *National Innovation Systems. A Comparative Analysis*, Oxford University Press.

Nelson, R.R. (1996) *The Sources of Economic Growth*, Cambridge, MA: Harvard University Press.

OECD (1998) *Science, Technology and Industry Outlook 1998*, Paris: OECD.

Otsuka, K., G. Ranis and G. Saxonhouse (1988) *Comparative Technology Choice in Development*, London: Macmillan.

Pack, H. (1987) *Productivity, Technology and Industrial Development*, New York: Oxford University Press.

Pack, H. and C. Paxson (2001) 'Is African Manufacturing Skill Constrained?', in: A. Szirmai and P. Lapperre (eds.), *The Industrial Experience of Tanzania*, Basingstoke: Palgrave, pp. 50–72.

Pilat, D. (1994) *The Economics of Rapid Growth: The Experience of Japan and Korea*, Aldershot: Elgar.

Romein, J. (1937) 'De dialectiek van de vooruitgang: bijdrage tot het ontwikkelingsbegrip in de geschiedenis' [The Dialectics of Progress: A Contribution to the Concept of Development in History], in: J. Romein, *Het onvoltooid verleden; cultuur-historische studies*, Amsterdam: Querido.

Romer, D. 'Increasing Returns and Long-Run Growth', *Journal of Political Economy*, 94, October 1986, pp. 1002–37.

Romijn, H. A. (1999) *Acquisition of Technological Capability in Small Firms in Developing Countries*, London and New York: Macmillan and St. Martin's Press.

Rosenberg, N. (1982) *Inside the Black Box: Technology and Economics*, Cambridge University Press.

Rosenberg, N. (1990) 'Science and Technology Policy for the Asian NICs: Lessons from Economic History', in R.E. Evenson and G. Ranis (eds.), *Science and Technology: Lessons for Development Policy*, Boulder, Co, and San Francisco: Westview Press, pp. 135–55.

Solow, R.M. (1957) 'Technical Change and the Aggregate Production Function', *Review of Economics and Statistics*, 39(3), August, pp. 312–20.

Stewart, F. (1972) 'Choice of Technique in Developing Countries', *Journal of Development Studies*, 9(1), October, 99–121.

Stewart, F. (1974) 'Technology and Employment in Less Developed Countries', *World Development*, 2(3), March, pp. 17–46.

Stewart, F. (ed.) (1987) *Macro-policies for Appropriate Technology in Developing Countries*, Boulder, CO: and London: Westview Press in cooperation with Appropriate Technology International, Washington, DC.

Szirmai, A., M. Prins and W. Schulte (2001), 'Measuring Manufacturing Performance in Tanzania', in A. Szirmai and P. Lapperre (eds.), *The Industrial Experience of Tanzania*, Basingstoke: Palgrave Press, pp. 73–113.

Timmer, M.P. (2000) *The Dynamics of Asian Manufacturing: A Comparative Perspective, 1963–1993*, Cheltenham: Edward Elgar.

Timmer, M.P. and A. Szirmai (1997) 'Australian Manufacturing Performance in Asian Perspective', mimeograph, Eindhoven.

Tunzelman, N. von (1995) *Technology and Industrial Progress*, Cheltenham: Edward Elgar.

UNDP (2001) *Human Development Report, 2001: Making Technologies Work for Development*, New York/Oxford: Oxford University Press.

UNESCO (1999) *Statistical Yearbook 1999*, Paris: UNESCO.

US Department of Commerce, Patent and Trademark Office (1977), *Technology Assessment and Forecast*, 7th Report, Washington, DC: March.

US, Patent and Trademark Office, Technology Assessment and Forecast Office (2002), *Special report, All Patents, January 1977– December 2001*, Washington, DC.

van Egmond, E. (2000) 'Technology Mapping for Technology Management', Ph.D thesis, Technical University of Delft, 410 pp.

Veblen, T. (1915) *Imperial Germany and the Industrial Revolution*, New York: Macmillan.

Verspagen, B. (1993) *Uneven Growth between Interdependent Economies: An Evolutionary View on Technology Gaps, Trade and Growth*, Aldershot: Avebury.

Verspagen, B. (2001) *Economic Growth and Technological Change: An Evolutionary Interpretation*, OECD, STI Working Papers, 1, Paris: OECD.

Verspagen, H.H.G. (1999) 'Intellectual Property Rights in the World Economy', Merit Working Paper, 99–17 Maastricht.

World Bank (1999) *World Development Report 1989/99: Knowledge for Development*, World Bank/Oxford University Press.

Chapter 5   Population and development

Becker, G.S. (1960) 'An Economic Analysis of Fertility', in National Bureau for Economic Research (ed.), *Demographic and Economic Change in Developed Countries*, Princeton University Press.

Beckerman, W. (1992) 'Economic Growth and the Environment: Whose Growth? Whose Environment?', *World Development*, 20(4), pp. 481–96.

Beckerman, W. (1993) 'Is Economic Growth Still Desirable?', in A. Szirmai, B. van Ark and D. Pilat (eds.), *Explaining Economic Growth: Essays in Honour of Angus Maddison*, Amsterdam: North Holland, pp. 77–100.

Bengtsson, T. and C. Gunnarsson (1994), 'Population Development and Institutional Change: Summary and Analysis', in K. Lindahl-Kiessling and H. Landberg (eds.), *Population, Economic Development and the Environment*, Oxford and New York: Oxford University Press, pp. 1–24.

Birdsall, N. (1988) 'Economic Approaches to Population Growth', in H. Chenery and T.N. Srinivasan (eds.), *Handbook of Development Economics*, Vol. I, Amsterdam: Elsevier/North Holland, pp. 477–542.

Birdsall, N. (1994) 'Government, Population and Poverty: A Win-Win Tale', in K. Lindahl-Kiessling and H. Landberg (eds.), *Population, Economic Development and the Environment*, Oxford and New York: Oxford University Press, pp. 173–98.

Bongaarts, J. (1982) 'The Fertility-Inhibiting Effects of the Intermediate Fertility Variables', *Studies in Family Planning*, 13(6/7), June/July, pp. 179–89.

Bongaarts, J. (1997) 'The Role of Family Planning Programmes in Contemporary Fertility Transitions' in G. W. Jones, R.M. Douglas, J.C. Caldwell and R.M. Souza (eds.), *The Continuing Demographic Transition*, Oxford: Clarendon Press, pp. 422–43.

Bongaarts, J. and R.G. Potter (1983) *Fertility, Biology and Behavior: An Analysis of the Proximate Determinants*, New York: Academic Press.

Boserup, E. (1965) *The Conditions of Agricultural Growth*, London: Allen and Unwin.

Boserup, E. (1981) *Population and Technology*, Oxford: Basil Blackwell.

Boserup, E. (1983) 'The Impact of Scarcity and Plenty on Development', *Journal of Interdisciplinary History*, 14(2), pp. 383–407.

Brown, L.R. and H.E. Young (1990) 'Feeding the World in the Nineties', in L.R. Brown and L. Starke (eds.), *State of the World 1990*, World Watch Institute Report, New York: Norton.

Brundtland, G.H. *et al.* (1987) *Our Common Future*, The World Commission on Environment and Development, Oxford University Press.

Bruyn, S. de (1997), 'Explaining the Environmental Kuznets Curve: Structural Change and International Agreements in Reducing Sulfur Emissions', *Environment and Development Economics*, 2, pp. 485–503.

Caldwell, J.C. (1976) 'Toward a Restatement of Demographic Transition Theory', *Population and Development Review*, 2, pp. 321–66.

Caldwell, J.C. (1997) 'The Global Fertility Transition: The Need for a Unifying Theory', *Population and Development Review*, 23(4) December, pp. 803–12.

Caldwell, J.C. and P. Caldwell (1985) 'Cultural Forces Tending to Sustain High Fertility in Tropical Africa', *PHN Technical Note*, 85–6, Population, Health and Nutrition Department, Washington, DC: World Bank.

Caldwell, J.C. and P. Caldwell (1987) 'The Cultural Context of High Fertility in Sub-Sahara Africa', *Population and Development Review*, 13(3), September, pp. 409–36.

Caldwell, J.C and P. Caldwell (1997) 'What do We Now Know about Fertility Transition?', in G.W. Jones, R.M. Douglas, J.C. Caldwell and R.M. Souza (eds.), *The Continuing Demographic Transition*, Oxford: Clarendon Press, pp. 15–25.

Cipolla, C.M. (1978) *An Economic History of World Population*, 7th edn, Harmondsworth: Penguin.

Coale, A.J. and E.M. Hoover (1958) *Population Growth and Economic Development in Low-Income Countries*, Princeton University Press.

Dasgupta, P., C. Folke and K-G. Mäler (1994) 'The Environmental Resource Base and Human Welfare', in K. Lindahl-Kiessling and H. Landberg (eds.), *Population, Economic Development and the Environment*, Oxford and New York: Oxford University Press, pp. 25–50.

Durand, J.D. (1997) 'Historical Estimates of World Population: An Evaluation', *Population and Development Review*, 3(3), pp. 253–95.

Easterlin, R.A. (1978) 'The Economics and Sociology of Fertility: A Synthesis', in C. Tilley (ed.), *Historical Studies of Changing Fertility*, Princeton University Press.

Ehrlich, P.R. and A.H. Ehrlich (1990) *The Population Explosion*, New York: Simon and Schuster.

Ezzati, M., B.H. Singer and D.M. Kammen (2001) 'Towards an Integrated Framework for Development and Environmental Policy: The Dynamics of Environmental Kuznets Curves', *World Development*, 29(8), pp. 1421–34.

Gaillard, H and A. Beernink (2001) 'The Urban Informal Sector in Tanzania', in: A. Szirmai and P. Lapperre (eds.), *The Industrial Experience of Tanzania*, Basingstoke: Palgrave, pp. 318–40.

Goodstadt, L. (1982) 'China's One Child Family', *Population and Development Review*, 8, pp. 37–50.

Hansen, B. and G.A. Marzouk (1965) *Development and Economic Policy in the U.A.R. (Egypt)*, Amsterdam: North Holland.

ILO (2002) *Key Indicators of the Labour Market 2001–2002*, Geneva: ILO.

Intergovernmental Panel on Climate Change (IPCC) (2001) *Climate Change 2001: The Scientific Basis*, Contribution of Working Group I to the Third Assessment Report of the IPCC, New York: IPCC.

Jones, G.W., R.M. Douglas, J.C. Caldwell and R.M. Souza (eds.) (1997) *The Continuing Demographic Transition*, Oxford: Clarendon Press.

Junhong, C. (2001) 'Prenatal Sex Determination and Sex-Selective Abortion in Rural Central China', *Population and Development Review*, 27(2), pp. 259–81.

Keating, M. (1993) *Agenda for Change: A Plain Language Version of Agenda 21 and the Other Rio Agreements*, Geneva: Centre for Our Common Future.

Kelley, A.C. (1988) 'Economic Consequences of Population Change in the Third World', *Journal of Economic Literature*, 26, December, pp. 1685–1728.

Kirsten, E., E.W. Buchholtz and W. Köllman (1956) *Raum und Bevolkerung in der Weltgeschichte* [Space and Population in World History], Würzburg: Ploetz, 1956.

Kuznets, S. (1955) 'Economic Growth and Income Inequality', *American Economic Review*, 45(1), pp. 1–28.

Kuznets, S. (1980) 'Recent Population Trends in Less Developed Countries and Implications for Internal Income Inequality', in R. A. Easterlin (ed.), *Population and Economic Change in Developing Countries*, University of Chicago Press, pp. 471–515.

Leach, M. and J. Fairhead (2000) 'Challenging Neo-Malthusian Deforestation Analyses in West Africa's Dynamic Forest Landscapes', *Population and Development Review*, 26(1), March, pp. 17–43.

Leibenstein, H. (1954) *A Theory of Economic Demographic Development*, Princeton University Press.

Lomborg, B. (2001) *The Skeptical Environmentalist*, Cambridge University Press.

McNicoll, G. (1994) 'Institutional Analysis of Fertility', in K. Lindahl-Kiessling and H. Landberg (eds.), *Population, Economic Development and the Environment*, Oxford and New York: Oxford University Press, pp. 199–230.

Maddison, A. (1989) *The World Economy in the Twentieth Century*, Paris: OECD.

Maddison, A. (1995) *Monitoring the World Economy*, Paris: OECD Development Centre.

Maddison, A. (2001) *The World Economy: A Millennial Perspective*, Development Centre Studies, Paris: OECD.

Maddison, A. (2003) *The World Economy, Historical Statistics*, OECD Development Centre Studies, Paris: OECD.

Meadows, D.H., D.L. Meadows, J. Randers and W.W. Behrens (1972) *Limits to Growth*, New York: Universe Books.

Myint, H. (1980) *The Economics of the Developing Countries*, 5th edn, London: Hutchinson.

Nelson, R. (1956) 'A Theory of the Low Level Equilibrium Trap in Underdeveloped Economics', *American Economic Review*, 46, pp. 894–908.

Oldeman, L.R., V.W.P van Engelen and J.H.M. Pulles (1990) 'The Extent of Human-Induced Soil Degradation', in L.R. Oldeman, R.T.A. Hakkeling and W.G. Sombroek (eds.), *World Map of the Status of Human-Induced Soil Degradation: An Explanatory Note*, 2nd rev. edn, Wageningen: International Soil Reference and Information Centre.

Pritchett, L. (1994) 'Derived Fertility and the Impact of Population Policies', *Population and Development Review*, 20(3), pp. 1–55.

Ravallion, M. (2001) 'Growth, Inequality and Poverty: Looking beyond Averages', *World Development*, 29(11), pp. 1803–15.

Schultz, T.P. (1997) 'Demand for Children in Low Income Countries', in M. Rosenzweig and O. Stark (eds.), *Handbook of Population and Family Economics*, Amsterdam: North Holland.

Simon, J. (1982) *The Ultimate Resource*, Princeton University Press.

Szeresewski, R. (1965) *Structural Changes in the Economy of Ghana, 1891–1911*, London: Weidenfeld and Nicolson.

Todaro, M.P. (1981) *Economic Development in the Third World*, 2nd edn, New York: Longman.

United Nations (1994) *Population, Environment and Development*, New York: UN.

United Nations Population Division (1994) *World Population Plan of Action*, Dept. for Economic and Social Information and Policy Analysis, New York: UN.

United Nations Population Division (1999) *World Population Prospects: The 1998 revision, Vol. I, Comprehensive Tables*, United Nations Publication, Sales No. E. 99. XIII.9, New York: United Nations.

United Nations Population Division (2001) *World Population Prospects: The 2000 Revision*, Vols. I, II and III, New York: United Nations.

van der Meer, C.L.J. (1983) 'Voedselvoorziening en Agrarische Ontwikkeling [Food Supply and Agricultural Development]', in C.L.J. van der Meer (ed.), *Landbouw en Ontwikkeling*, The Hague, VUGA, pp. 177–206.

Waggoner, P.E. and J.H. Ausubel (2001) 'How Much Will Feeding More and Wealthier People Encroach on Forests?', *Population and Development Review*, 27(2), pp. 239–57,

Willis, R. (1973) 'A New Approach to the Economic Theory of Fertility', *Journal of Political Economy*, March/April, S14–S64.

Willis, R. (1994) 'Economic Analysis of Fertility: Micro-Foundations and Aggregate Implications', in K. Lindahl-Kiessling and H. Landberg (eds), *Population, Economic Development and the Environment*, pp. 139–72.

Wilson, C. (2001) 'On the Scale of Global Demographic Convergence, 1950–2000', *Population and Development Review*, 27(1), pp. 155–71.

World Bank (1984) *World Development Report 1984, Part 2: Population Change and Development*, Oxford/New York: Oxford University Press.

World Bank (1992) *World Development Report 1992: Development and the Environment*, Oxford/New York: Oxford University Press.

World Bank (1994) *World Population Projections 1994–95*, Baltimore/London: Johns Hopkins University Press.

World Bank (1995) *World Development Report, 1995: Workers in an Integrating World*, New York: World Bank/Oxford University Press.

World Bank (2000) *World Development Report, 2000/2001: Attacking Poverty*, New York: World Bank/Oxford University Press.

World Bank (2002) *World Development Report, 2002: Building Institutions for Markets*, New York: The World Bank/Oxford University Press.

World Bank (2003) *World Development Report 2003: Sustainable Development in a Dynamic World*, New York: The World Bank/Oxford University Press.

Chapter 6   Health, health care and development

Baldwin, R.E. and B.A. Weisbrod (1974) 'Disease and Labor Productivity', *Economic Development and Cultural Change*, 22(3), pp. 414–35.

Bardhan, P. (1993) 'Economics of Development and the Development of Economics', *Journal of Economic Perspectives*, 7(2), Spring, pp. 129–42.

Barlow, R. (1979) 'Health and Economic Development: A Theoretical and Empirical Review', *Human Capital and Development*, 1, pp. 45–75.

Basta, S. et al. (1979) 'Iron Deficiency Anemia and Productivity of Adult Males in Indonesia', *American Journal of Clinical Nutrition*, 32(4), April, pp. 916–25.

Becker, C.M. and D.D. Hemley (1998) 'Demographic Change in the Former Soviet Union during the Transition Period', *World Development*, 26(11), pp. 1957–97.

Berman, P.A. (1998) 'Rethinking Health Care Systems: Private Health Care Provision in India', *World Development*, 26(8), pp. 1463–79.

Brainerd, E. (1998) 'Market Reform and Mortality in Transition Economies', *World Development*, 26(11), pp. 2013–27.

Caldwell, J.C. (1984) 'Introductory Remarks on Interactions between Health, Mortality and Development', in United Nations, *Mortality and Health Policy, Proceedings of the Expert Group on Mortality and Health Policy*, International Conference on Population, New York: United Nations, pp. 106–11.

Caldwell, J.C. (1986) 'Routes to Low Mortality in Poor Countries', *Population and Development Review*, 12(2), pp. 171–221.

Chambers, R. (1982) 'Health, Agriculture and Rural Poverty: Why Seasons Matter', *Journal of Development Studies*, 18(2).

CIA (2001) *World Factbook*, Washington, DC: CIA.

Cornia, G.A. (1984) 'A Summary and Interpretation of the Evidence', *World Development*, 12(3), pp. 381–91.

de Kadt, E. and M. Lipton (1988) *Agriculture–Health Linkages*, WHO Offset Publication No. 104, Geneva: WHO.

Deolalikar, A.B. (1988) 'Do Health and Nutrition Influence Labor Productivity in Agriculture? Econometric Estimates for South India', *Review of Economics and Statistics*, 70(2), May (2002).

DGBAS (2003) Republic of China (Taiwan), Directorate General of Budget Accounting and Statistics, *China Statistical Yearbook 2003*, Taipeh, http://www.stat.gov.tw/bs2/2003YearBook.pdf.

Fogel, R.W. (1986) 'Nutrition and the Decline in Mortality since 1700: Some Preliminary Findings', in S.L. Engerman and R.E. Gallman, (eds.), *Long Term Factors in American Economic Growth*, NBER, University of Chicago Press, pp. 439–555.

Fogel, R.W. (1994) 'The Relevance of Malthus for the Study of Mortality Today: Long Run Influences on Health and Mortality, Labour Force Participation and Population Growth', in L. Lindahl-Kiessling and H. Landsberg (eds.), *Population, Economic Development and the Environment*, Oxford and New York: Oxford University Press, pp. 231–84.

Fogel, R.W. (1997) 'New Findings on Seculary Trends in Nutrition and Mortality: Some Implications for Population Theory', in M.S. Rosenzweig and O. Starke (eds.), *Handbook of Population and Family Economics*, Vol I.A, Amsterdam: Elsevier Science, pp. 433–81.

Frederikson, H. (1969) 'Feedbacks in Economic and Demographic Transition', *Science*, 166, 1969.

Frenk, J., T. Frejka, J.L. Bobadilla, C. Stern, J. Sepulveda and M. José (1989) 'The Epidemiologic Transition in Latin America', *International Population Conference*, New Delhi, Vol. I, Liège: IUSSP, pp. 419–32.

Gallup, J. and J. Sachs (1998) 'Development and Poverty in a Global Age: Location, Geography and Economic Development', *Harvard International Review*, 21(1), pp. 56–61.

Hardiman, M. and J. Midgley (1982) *The Social Dimension of Development: Social Policy and Planning in the Third World*, Chichester: Wiley.

Johansson, S.R. and K. Mosk (1987) 'Exposure, Resistance and Life Expectancy: Disease and Death during the Economic Development of Japan, 1900–1960', *Population Studies*, 41(2), July, 1987, pp. 207–36.

Keyzer, M.A. (1993) '*Welfare Assessment of the Efficiency Wage Argument*, Unpublished, development economics seminar paper No. 93–3/13, Institute of Social Studies, November.

Leibenstein, H. (1957) *Economic Backwardness and Economic Growth: Studies in the Theory of Economic Development*, New York: Wiley.

Leisinger, K.M. (1989) *Poverty, Sickness and Medicines: An Unholy Alliance? Development Policy, Health and the Role of the Pharmaceutical Industry in the Third World*, Geneva: Féderation International de l'Industrie du Medicament.

McKeown, T. (1976) *The Modern Rise of Population*, London: Arnold.

McKeown, T. (1978) 'Fertility, Mortality and Causes of Death: An Examination of Issues Related to the Modern Rise of Population', *Population Studies*, 32(3), pp. 535–42.

McKeown, T. (1979) *The Role of Medicine*, Oxford: Basil Blackwell.

McKeown, T. (1988) *The Origins of Human Disease*, Oxford: Basil Blackwell.

McQuire, J.W. (2001) 'Social Policy and Mortality Decline in East Asia and Latin America', *World Development*, 29(10), pp. 1673–97.

Maurice, J. and A.M. Pearce (eds.) (1987) *Tropical Disease Research: A Global Partnership*, Geneva: WHO.

Mayer, D. (2001) 'The Long-Term Impact of Health on Economic Growth in Latin America', *World Development*, 29(6), pp. 1025–33.

Mosley, W.H. (1983) 'Primary Care: Rhetoric and Reality', *Populi*, 10(3), 41–54.

Mosley, W.H. (1984) 'Child Survival: Research and Policy', *Population and Development Review*, 10, Supplement, pp. 3–23.

Mosley, W.H. (1985a) 'Biological and Socio-Economic Determinants of Child Survival: A Proximate Determinants Framework Integrating Fertility and Mortality Variables', in Mosley, *Congrès International de la Population, Florence 1985*, Liège: Ordina Editions, pp. 189–208.

Mosley, W.H. (1985b) 'Will Primary Health Care Reduce Infant and Child Mortality? A Critique of Some Current Strategies, with Special Reference to Africa and Asia', in J. Vallin and A.D. Lopez (eds.), *Health Policy, Social Policy and Mortality Prospects*, Liège: Ordina Editions, pp. 103–38.

Murray, C.J.L. and A.D. Lopez (1996) *The Global Burden of Disease. A Comprehensive Assessment of Mortality and Disability from Diseases, Injuries and Risk Factors in 1990 and Projected to 2020*, Cambridge, MA: Harvard University Press.

Murray, C. J. L., and A. K. Acharya (1997) 'Understanding DALYs', *Journal of Health Economics*, 16(6), pp. 703–30.

Mushkin, S. (1962) 'Health as an Investment', *Journal of Political Economy*, 70(5), October pp. 129–57.

Netherlands Development Cooperation (1988), *Primary Health Care: Evaluation of Dutch-Supported Activities in the Field of Extramural Health Care since 1975*, Ministry of Foreign Affairs, The Hague: DGIS.

Omran, A.R. (1971) 'The Epidemiologic Transition: A Theory of the Epidemiology of Population Change', *Millbank Memorial Fund Quarterly*, 49, pp. 509–38.

Popkin, B.M. (1978) 'Nutrition and Labor Productivity', *Social Science and Medicine*, 12C (3/4), pp. 117–25.

Preker, A., E. Bos, J. Wang, J. Peabody and D.T. Jamison, (1999) *Measuring Country Performance on Health: Selected Indicators for 115 countries*, Washington, DC: World Bank.

Preston, S.H. (1975) 'The Changing Relation between Mortality and Level of Economic Development', *Population Studies*, 29(2), pp. 231–48.

Preston, S.H. (1976) *Mortality Patterns in National Populations*, New York: Academic Press.

Preston, S.H. (1980) 'Causes and Consequences of Mortality Declines in Less Developed Countries in the 20th Century', in R.A. Easterlin (ed.), *Population and Economic Change in Developing Countries*, University of Chicago Press, pp. 289–341.

Ranis, G., F. Stewart and A. Ramirez (2000) 'Economic Growth and Human Development', *World Development*, 28(2), pp. 197–219.

Schultz, T.P. and A. Tansel (1997) 'Wage and Labor Supply Effects of Illness in Côte d'Ivoire and Ghana', *Journal of Development Economics*, 53(2), August, pp. 251–86.

Sreter, S. (1988) 'The Importance of Social Intervention in Britain's Mortality Decline *c.* 1850–1914: A Re-interpretation of the Role of Public Health', *Social History of Medicine*, 1(1), April, pp. 1–38.

Strauss, J and D. Thomas (1998) 'Health, Nutrition and Economic Development', *Journal of Economic Literature*, 36(2), pp. 766–817.

UNDP (2001) *Human Development Report, 2001, Making Technologies Work for Development*, New York/Oxford: Oxford University Press.

UNDP (2002) *Arab Human Development Report 2002. Creating Opportunities for Future Generations*, New York: UNDP.

United Nations, (1953) *Demographic Yearbook*, New York: UN.

United Nations (1963) *Demographic Yearbook*, New York: UN.

United Nations (1984) *Mortality and Health Policy*, Proceedings of the Expert Group on Mortality and Health Policy, International Conference on Population, United Nations, Department of International Economic and Social Affairs, New York: UN.

United Nations/ESCAP (1985) *Mortality and Health Issues*, New York: UN.

United Nations (1985), *World Population Trends, Population and Development, Interrelations and Population Policies: 1983 Monitoring Report*, Vol. I, New York: UN.

United Nations (1986) *World Population Prospects: Estimates and Projections as Assessed in 1984*, New York: UN.

United Nations (1988a) *World Population: Trends and Policies, 1987*, Monitoring Report, New York: UN.

United Nations (1988b) *Mortality of Children under Age 5: World Estimates and Projections, 1950–2025*, Population studies, No. 105, New York: UN.

United Nations (1993a) *World Population Prospects: The 1992 Revision*, New York: UN.

United Nations (1993b) *World Urbanization Prospects. The 1992 Revision*, New York: UN.

United Nations (1994) Department for Economic and Social Information and Policy Analysis, *Aids and the Demography of Africa*, New York: UN.

United Nations Population Division (2001) *World Population Prospects: The 2000 Revision*, Vols. I, II and III, United Nations.

Vallin, J. (1989) 'Conclusion. Théorie(s) de la baisse de la mortalité et situation Africaine [Theories of Mortality Decline and the African Condition]', in G. Pison, E. van de Walle and M. Sala-Diakanda, *Mortalité et Société en Afrique au Sud du Sahara, Travaux et Documents* [Mortality and Society in Sub-Saharan Africa], Cahier No. 124, Paris: Presses Universitaires de France, pp. 399–431.

van Norren, B. and H.A.W. van Vianen (1986) *The Malnutrition–Infections Syndrome and its Demographic Outcome in Developing Countries*, Programming Committee for Demographic Research, publication No. 4, The Hague.

Walsh, J.A. (1990) 'Estimating the Burden of Illness in the Tropics', in: K.S. Warren and A.F. Mahmoud (eds.), *Tropical and Geographical Medicine*, 2nd edn, New York: McGraw-Hill, pp. 185–96.

WHO (World Health Organization) (1978), *Primary Health Care: Report of the International Conference on Primary Health Care*, Health for All Series, No. 1, Geneva: WHO.

WHO (1981) *Global Strategy for Health for All by the Year 2000*, Health for All Series, No. 3, Geneva: WHO, pp. 74–6.

WHO (1987) *Evaluation of the Strategy for Health for All by the Year 2000*, Seventh Report on the World Health Situation, Vol. I, *Global Review*, Geneva: WHO.

WHO (1993) *Implementation of the Global Strategy for Health for All by the Year 2000: Second Evaluation*, Eighth Report on the World Health Situation, Vol. 1. *Global Review*, Geneva: WHO.

WHO (1996) *World Health Report 1996*, Geneva: WHO.

WHO (1997) *World Health Report 1997*, Geneva: WHO.

WHO (1998) *World Health Report 1998 Life in the 21st Century – A Vision for All*, Geneva: WHO.

WHO (1999) *World Health Report 1999: Making a Difference*, Geneva: WHO.

WHO (2000) *World Health Report 2000: Health Systems: Improving Performance*, Geneva: WHO.

WHO (2001) *World Health Report 2001, Mental Health: New Understanding, New Hope*, Geneva: WHO.

WHO (2002) *World Mortality in 2000: Life Tables for 191 Countries*, Geneva: WHO.

World Bank (1983) *World Tables 1983*, Baltimore/London: Johns Hopkins University Press.

World Bank (1984) *World Development Report, 1984: Population Change and Development*, Oxford University Press.

World Bank (1990) *World Development Report 1990*, Oxford/NewYork: Oxford University Press.

World Bank (1992) *World Development Report 1992*, Oxford/New York: Oxford University Press.

World Bank (1994a) *World Development Report 1994*, Oxford/New York: Oxford University Press.

World Bank (1994b) *World Population Projections 1994–95*, Baltimore: Johns Hopkins University Press.

World Bank (2002) *World Development Indicators, 2002* CD-Rom, Washington, DC: World Bank.

Chapter 7   Education and development

Abernethy, D. (1969) *The Political Dilemma of Popular Education: An African Case*, Stanford University Press.

Abramovitz, M. (1956) 'Resource and Output Trends in the United States since 1870', *American Economic Review*, Papers and Proceedings, May, pp. 5–23.

Abramovitz, M. (1989) 'Thinking about Growth', in M. Abramovitz, *Thinking about Growth and Other Essays on Economic Growth and Welfare*, Cambridge University Press, pp. 3–79.

Altbach, P. G. (1982) 'Servitude of the Mind? Education, Dependency and Neocolonialism', in P. G. Altbach, R.F. Arnove and G.P. Kelly (eds.), *Comparative Education*, New York: Macmillan, pp. 469–84.

Altbach, P.G. and G.P. Kelly (1978) *Education and Colonialism*, New York/London: Longman.

Anderson, C.A. and M.J. Bowman (1976), 'Education and Economic Modernization in Historical Perspective', in L. Stone (ed.), *Schooling and Societies: Studies in the History of Education*, Baltimore: Johns Hopkins University Press.

Barro, R.J. (1991) 'Economic Growth in a Cross Section of Countries', *The Quarterly Journal of Economics*, 106, May, pp. 407–33.

Becker, G.S. (1964) *Human Capital: A Theoretical and Empirical Analysis, with Special Reference to Education*, New York/London: Columbia University Press.

Benhabib, J. and M. Spiegel (1994) 'The Role of Human Capital in Economic Development: Evidence from Aggregate Cross-Country Data', *Journal of Monetary Economics* 34, October, pp. 143–79.

Berg, I. (1970) *Education and Jobs: The Great Training Robbery*, New York: Praeger.

Blaug, M. (1972) *The Economics of Education*, Harmondsworth: Penguin.

Blaug, M. (1976) 'The Empirical Status of Human Capital Theory: A Slightly Jaundiced Survey', *Journal of Economic Literature*, September, 14, pp. 827–56.

Blaug, M. (1979) 'Economics of Education in Developing Countries: Current Trends and New Priorities', *Third World Quarterly*, January, pp. 73–83.

Blaug, M. (1985) 'Where Are We Now in the Economics of Education?', *Economics of Education Review*, 4(1), pp. 17–28.

Blaug, M. (1990) *The Economic Value of Higher Education*, Netherlands Institute of Advanced Studies, Ühlenbeck Lecture VIII, Wassenaar: NIAS.

Blaug, M., R. Layard and M. Woodhall (1969) *Causes of Graduate Unemployment in India*, London: Allen Lane, Penguin Press.

Bowles, S. and H. Gintis (1976) *Schooling in Capitalist America*, New York: Basic Books.

Bowman, M.J. and C.A. Anderson (1963) 'Concerning the Role of Education in Development', in C. Geertz (ed.), *Old Societies and New States: The Quest for Modernity in Africa and Asia*, Glencoe, IL: The Free Press.

Bowman, M.J. and C.A. Anderson (1973) 'Human Capital and Economic Modernisation in Historical Perspective', in F.C. Lane (ed.), *Proceedings of the Fourth International Conference of Economic History*, 1968, Paris: Mouton.

Carnoy, M. (1974) *Education as Cultural Imperialism*, New York: David McKay.

Colclough, C. and S. Al-Samarrai (2000) 'Achieving Schooling for All: Budgetary Expenditures on Education in Sub-Saharan Africa and South Asia', *World Development*, 28(11), pp. 1927–44.

Coombs, P. (1985) *The World Crisis in Education: The View from the 1980s*, New York/Oxford: Oxford University Press.

Coombs, P. and M. Ahmed (1974) *Attacking Rural Poverty: How Nonformal Education Can Help*, Baltimore, Johns Hopkins University Press.

Curle, A. (1964) *World Campaign for Universal Literacy: Comment and Proposal*, Occasional Papers in Education and Development, Cambridge, MA: Graduate School of Education, Harvard University.

Denison, E.F. (1962) *The Sources of Economic Growth and the Alternatives Before Us*, New York: Committee for Economic Development.

Denison, E.F. (1967) *Why Growth Rates Differ*, Washington, DC, Brookings Institution.

Dore, R. (1976) *The Diploma Disease: Education, Qualification and Development*, London: Allen & Unwin.

Easterlin, R.A. (1981) 'Why Isn't the Whole World Developed?', *Journal of Economic History*, 41.

Economist (1996) 'The Mystery of Growth', *The Economist*, 25 May, p. 16ff.

Evenson, R.E. and L.E. Westphal (1995) 'Technological Change and Technology Strategy', in H. Behrman and T. N. Srinivasan (eds.), *Handbook of Development Economics*, Vol. IIIA, Amsterdam: Elsevier, pp. 2211–99.

Fägerlind, I. and L.J. Saha (1989) *Education and National Development: A Comparative Perspective*, 2nd edn, Oxford: Pergamon.

Foster, P. (1965a) *Education and Social Change in Ghana*, London: Routledge and Kegan Paul.

Foster, P. (1965b) 'The Vocational School Fallacy in Development Planning', in C.A. Anderson and M.J. Bowman (eds.), *Education and Economic Development*, Chicago: Aldine, pp. 142–6.

Foster, P. (1980) 'Education and Social Inequality in Sub-Saharan Africa', *Journal of Modern African Studies*, 18(2), pp. 201–36.

Freire, P. (1970) *Pedagogy of the Oppressed*, New York: Seabury Press.

Gillis, M., D.H. Perkins, M. Roemer and D.R. Snodgrass (1992) *Economics of Development*, 3rd edn, New York/London: W.W. Norton and Co., Chapter 9: 'Education', pp. 217–39.

Glewwe, P. (2002) 'Schools and Skills in Developing Countries: Education Policies and Socioeconomic Outcomes', *Journal of Economic Literature*, 40, June, pp. 436–82.

Godo, Y. and Y. Hayami (2002) 'Catching Up in Education in the Economic Catch-up of Japan with the United States, 1890–1990', *Economic Development and Cultural Change*, 50(4), July, pp. 961–78.

Grier, R.M. (2002) 'On the Interaction of Human and Physical Capital in Latin America', *Economic Development and Cultural Change*, 50(4), July, pp. 891–913.

Hallak, J. (1990) *Investing in the Future: Setting Education Priorities in the Developing World*, UNESCO/International Institute for Education Planning, Paris/Oxford: UNDP.

Hanley, S.B. (1990) 'The Relationship of Education and Economic Growth: The Case of Japan', in G. Tortella, *Education and Economic Development*.

Harbison. F. and C. Myers (eds.) (1965) *Manpower and Education*, New York: McGraw-Hill.

Hardiman, M. and J. Midgley (1982) *The Social Dimensions of Development: Social Policy and Planning in the Third World*, Chichester: Wiley, Chapter 7, pp. 182–210.

Heinink, A.L. and J.M.B. Koetsier (1984), 'Onderwijs in de derde wereld. Hefboom voor ontwikkeling? [Education in the Third World. The driving force of development?]' *INFO*, Informatiebladen van het Instituut voor Onderwijskunde, 15(2), March, pp. 73–86.

Hobsbawm, E. (1969) *Industry and Empire*, London: Penguin.

Illich, I. (1974) *Deschooling Society*, New York: Harper and Row.

Jones, P.W. (1988) *International Policies for Third World Education: UNESCO, Literacy and Development*, London/New York: UNESCO.

Kendrick, J.W. (1961) *Productivity Trends in the United States*, Princeton University Press.

Kim, L. and R.R. Nelson (eds.) (2000) *Technology, Learning and Innovation: Experiences of Newly Industrializing Economies*, Cambridge University Press, pp. 193–215.

Komenan, A.G. (1987) *Improving the Efficiency of Education in Developing Countries*, Washington, DC: World Bank, Annex: World Education Indicators.

Krieger, M. (1988) 'African Policy Linking Education and Development: Standard Criticisms and a New Departure', *International Review of Education*, 34 (3), pp. 293–311.

Krueger, A.B. and M. Lindahl (2001) 'Education for Growth: Why and for Whom?', *The Journal of Economic Literature*, 39(4), December, pp. 1101–37.

Lind, A. and A. Johnston (1986) *Adult Literacy in the Third World: A Review of Objectives and Strategies*, Education Division Documents, No. 32, Stockholm: SIDA.

Lloyd, C.B., C. E. Kaufman and P. Hewett (2000) 'The Spread of Primary Schooling in Sub-Saharan Africa: Implications for Fertility Change', *Population and Development Review*, 26(3), September, pp. 483–515.

Lucas, R.E. (1988) 'On the Mechanics of Economic Development', *Journal of Monetary Economics*, 22, July, pp. 3–42.

Maddison, A. (1987) 'Growth and Slowdown in Advanced Capitalist Economies', *Journal of Economic Literature*, 25, June, pp. 649–98.

Mankiw, T., D. Romer and D. Weil (1992), 'A Contribution to the Empirics of Economic Growth', *Quarterly Journal of Economics*, 107 (May), pp. 407–38.

Mincer, J. (1974) *Schooling, Earnings and Experience*, New York: Columbia University Press.

Mitch, D. (1990) 'Education and Economic Growth', in Tortella, *Education and Economic Development*.

Naik, J.P. (1975) *Equality, Quality and Quantity: The Elusive Triangle in Indian Education*, Bombay: Allied Publishers.

Nelson, R. (1981) 'Research on Productivity Growth and Productivity Differences: Dead Ends and New Departures', *Journal of Economic Literature*, 19, September, pp. 1029–64.

Nelson R. and E.S. Phelps (1966) 'Investment in Humans, Technological Diffusion and Economic Growth', *AER*, 56, March, pp. 69–75.

Nicholas, S. (1990) 'Literacy and the Industrial Revolution', in Tortella (1990) *Education and Economic Development*.

Nuñez, C. (1990) 'Literacy and Economic Growth in Spain, 1860–1977', in Tortella. *Education and Economic Development*.

Ooijens, J. and P. van Kampen (1989) *Analfabetisme en alfabetisering in Latijns Amerika en het Caribisch gebied* [Illiteracy and Literacy Education in Latin America and the Caribbean], CESO, Verhandelingen, No. 46, December, The Hague: CESO.

Pack, H. and C. Paxson (2001) 'Is African Manufacturing Skill Constrained?', in: A. Szirmai and P. Lapperre (eds.), *The Industrial Experience of Tanzania*, Basingstoke: Palgrave, pp. 50–72.

Pavitt, K. (ed.) (1980) *Technical Innovation and British Economic Performance*, London: Macmillan.

Perraton, H.D. (2000) *Open and Distance Learning in the Developing World*, London: Routledge.

Pilat, D. (1994) *The Economics of Rapid Growth: The Experience of Japan and Korea*, Aldershot: Edward Elgar.

Pritchett, L. (2001) 'Where Has All the Education Gone?', *World Bank Economic Review*, 15(3), pp. 367–93.

Psacharopoulos, G. (1985) 'Returns to Education: A Further International Update and Implications', *Journal of Human Resources*, 20 (4), pp. 583–604.

Psacharopoulos, G. (1989) 'Why Education Reforms Fail: A Comparative Analysis', *International Review of Education*, 35, pp. 179–95.

Psacharopoulos, G. (1993) *Returns to Investment in Education: A Global Update*, World Bank, Policy Research Working Papers in Education and Development, WPS, 1067, Washington, DC: World Bank.

Psacharopoulos, G., and A.H. Arriagada (1986) 'The Educational Composition of the Labour Force', *International Labour Review*, 125 (5), pp. 561–74.

Psacharopoulos, G. and A.M. Arriagada (2002) 'The Educational Composition of the Labor Force: An International Update', *Journal of Educational Planning and Administration* 6(2), pp. 141–59.

Psacharopoulos G. and H. A. Patrinos (2002) *Returns to Investment in Education: A Further Update*, World Bank Policy Research Working Paper, 2881, Washington, DC: World Bank September.

Romer, P. (1986) 'Increasing Returns and Long-Run Growth', *Journal of Political Economy*, 94 (5), pp. 1002–37.

Sandberg, L.G. (1982) 'Ignorance, Poverty and Economic Backwardness in the Early Stages of European Industrialization. Variations on Alexander Gerschenkron's Grand Theme', *Journal of European Economic History*, 11, pp. 675–98.

Sandberg, L.G. (1990) 'Education and Economic Growth: Voices from Valencia', in Tortella, *Education and Economic Development*.

Schultz, T.W. (1961) 'Investment in Human Capital', *American Economic Review*, 51, January, p. 17 ff.

Schultz, T.W. (1971) *Investment in Human Capital: The Role of Education and Research*, New York: The Free Press.

Schultz, T.W. (1988) 'Education, Investment and Returns', in H. Chenery and T.N. Srinivasan (eds.), *Handbook of Development Economics*, Vol. I., Amsterdam: North Holland, Chapter 13, pp. 543–630.

Solow, R.M. (1957) 'Technical Change and the Aggregate Production Function', *Review of Economics and Statistics*, 39, August, pp. 312–20.

Spence, M.A. (1973) 'Job Market Signaling', *Quarterly Journal of Economics*, 87 (3), pp. 355–74.

Thompson, E.P. (1963) *The Making of the English Working Class*, New York: Vintage.

Timmer, M.P. (2000) *The Dynamics of Asian Manufacturing: A Comparative Perspective, 1963–1993*, Aldershot: Edward Elgar.

Tortella, G. (ed.) (1990) *Education and Economic Development since the Industrial Revolution*, València: Generalitat Valenciana.

UNDP (2000) *Arab Human Development Report* 2002, New York: UNDP.

UNESCO (1983) *Trends and Projections of Enrolment, 1960–2000 (as Assessed in 1982)*, UNESCO, Division of Statistics on Education, Office of Statistics, March, Paris: UNESCO.

UNESCO (1976) *Statistical Yearbook*, Paris: UNESCO, and various volumes.

UNESCO (1997) *Statistical Yearbook 1997*, Paris, UNESCO.

UNESCO (1998) *Statistical Yearbook 1998*, Paris: UNESCO.

UNESCO (1999) *Statistical Yearbook 1999*, Paris UNESCO.

UNESCO (2000a) *Education for All: Year 2000 Assessment: Statististical Document*, Nîmes: UNESCO Institute for Statistics.

UNESCO (2000b) *World Education Report 2000*, Paris: UNESCO.

UNESCO (2001a) *Education Statistics, 2001: Regional Report on Latin America*, Paris: UNESCO.

UNESCO (2001b) *Education Statistics, 2001, Regional Report on Africa*, Paris: UNESCO.

UNESCO (2002) *The 2002 Global Education for All Monitoring Report: Is the World on Track?*, Paris: UNESCO.

Williamson, B. (1979) *Education, Social Structure and Development: A Comparative Analysis*, London: Macmillan.

Wolff, E. and M. Gittleman (1993) 'The Role of Education in Productivity Convergence: Does Higher Education Matter?, in A. Szirmai, B. van Ark and D. Pilat (eds.), *Explaining Economic Growth. Essays in Honour of Angus Maddison*, Amsterdam: North Holland.

Wolpin, K. (1977) 'Education and Screening', *American Economic Review*, 67(5), pp. 949–58.

World Bank (1993) *The East Asian Miracle: Economic Growth and Public Policy*, New York: Oxford University Press.

World Bank (2002) *World Development Indicators 2002*, CD-Rom, Washington, DC: World Bank.

Chapter 8   Economic development, structural transformation and primary exports

ADB (African Development Bank) (2000) *African Development Report 2000*, New York: Oxford University Press.

Amin, S. (1974) *Accumulation on a World Scale*, New York: Monthly Review Press.

Ark, B. van, R. Inklaar and R. H. McGuckin (2002) ' "Changing Gear": Productivity, ICT and Service Industries: Europe and the United States', Paper for Som/TEG Conference: The Empirical Implications of Technology Based Growth Theories, Groningen, Mimeo, August.

Bairoch, P. (1975) *The Economic Development of the Third World since 1900*, Berkeley: University of California Press.

Baldwin, R.E. (1956) 'Patterns of Development in Newly Settled Regions', *Manchester School of Economic and Social Studies*, May.

Baran, P. (1957) *The Political Economy of Growth*, New York: Monthly Review Press.

Bardhan, P. (1984) *The Political Economy of Development in India*, New Delhi: Oxford University Press.

Baumol, W.J. (1967) 'Macroeconomics of Unbalanced Growth: The Anatomy of Urban Crises', *American Economic Review*, 57 (3), June, pp. 415–26.

Baumol, W.J. (1986) 'Productivity Growth, Convergence and Welfare: What the Long Run Data Show', *American Economic Review*, 76(5), December, pp. 1072–86.

Bautista, R.M. (1989) 'Domestic Terms of Trade and Agricultural Growth in Developing Countries', in Islam, N. (ed.), *The Balance between Industry and Agriculture in Economic Development: Factors Influencing Change*, Proceedings of the Eighth World Congress of the International Economic Association, Vol. V, Basingstoke: Macmillan Press.

Bhagwati, J. (1958) 'Immiserizing Growth: A Geometrical Note', *Review of Economic Studies*, 25, pp. 201–5.

Boserup, E. (1981) *Population and Technology*, Oxford: Basil Blackwell.

Boserup, E. (1985) 'The Primary Sector in African Development', in M. Lundahl (ed.), *The Primary Sector in Economic Development*, London: Croom Helm.

Britton, S. (1990) 'The Role of Services in Production', *Progress in Human Geography*, 14(4), December, pp. 529–46 (reproduced in H.R. Bryson and P.W. Daniels (eds.), *Service Industries in the Global Economy, Volume II, Services, Globalization and Economic Development*, Cheltenham: Edward Elgar, 1998).

Bryson, H.R. and P.W. Daniels (eds.) (1998) *Service Industries in the Global Economy, Volume II, Services, Globalization and Economic Development*, Cheltenham: Edward Elgar.

Cassen, R.H. (1978) *India, Population, Economy, Society*, London: Macmillan.

Caldwell, J.C. (1997) 'The Global Fertility Transition: The Need for a Unifying Theory', *Population and Development Review*, 23(4) December, pp. 803–12.

Caves, R.E. (1965) '"Vent for Surplus" Models of Trade and Growth', in R.E. Baldwin *et al.* (eds.), *Trade, Growth and the Balance of Payments*, Chicago: Rand McNally.

Chenery, H. (1979) *Structural Change and Development Policy*, New York: Oxford University Press.

Chenery, H.B. (1986) *Structural Transformation: A Program of Research*, Harvard Institute for International Development, Discussion Paper No. 232.

Chenery, H., S. Robinson and M. Syrquin (1986) *Industrialisation and Growth: A Comparative Study, World Bank*, Oxford University Press.

Chenery H. B., and L. Taylor (1968) 'Development Patterns among Countries and over Time', *Review of Economics and Statistics*, 50, pp. 391–416.

Clark, C. (1940) *The Conditions of Economic Progress*, London: Macmillan.

Daniels, P.W. (1989) 'Some Perspectives on the Geography Services', Progress in Human Geography, 13(3), September, pp. 427–37 (reproduced in J.R. Bryson and P.W. Daniels (eds.), *Service Industries in the Global Economy*, Vol. II, 1998).

Eicher, C.K. and L.W. de Witt (eds.) (1964) *Agriculture in Development*, New York: McGraw-Hill.

Emmanuel, A. (1972) *Unequal Exchange: A Study of the Imperialism of Trade*, New York: Monthly Review Press.

Engels, E. (1857) 'Die Produktions- und Consumptionsverhältnisse des Königreichs Sachsen' [Production and Consumption Relations in the Kingdom of Saxony], *Zeitschrift des Statistichen Bureaus des Koniglich Sächsischen Ministeriums des Innern*, November.

Ethier, W.J. (1995) *Modern International Economics*, 3rd edn, New York/London: Norton.

Fei, J.C.H. and G. Ranis (1964) *Development of the Labor Surplus Economy: Theory and Policy*, Homewood, IL: Irwin.

Findlay, R. (1980) "The Terms of Trade and Equilibrium Growth in the World Economy", *American Economic Review*, 70 (3), pp. 291–9.

Frederikson, H. (1969) 'Feedbacks in Economic and Demographic Transition', *Science*, 166.

Furtado, C. (1976) *Economic Development of Latin America*, Cambridge University Press.

Geertz, C. (1963) *Agricultural Involution: The Processes of Ecological Change in Indonesia*, Berkeley: University of California Press.

Gillis, M., D.H. Perkins, M. Roemer and D.R. Snodgrass (1992) *Economics of Development*, 3rd edn, New York: W.W. Norton and Co.

Glassmeier, A. and M. Howland (1994) 'Service-Led Rural Development: Definitions, Theories and Empirical Evidence', *International Regional Science Review*, 16(1&2), pp. 197–229. (Reproduced in J.R. Bryson and P.W. Daniels (eds.), *Service Industries in the Global Economy*, Vol. II, 1998.)

Griffin, K. (1987) *World Hunger and the World Economy*, London: Macmillan.

Grilli, E.R. and Maw, Chen Yang (1998) 'Primary Commodity Prices, Manufactured Goods Prices, and the Terms of Trade of Developing Countries: What the Long Run Shows', *The World Bank Economic Review*, 2(1), pp. 1–47.

Helleiner, G.K. (1992) 'Structural Adjustment and Long-Term Development in Sub-Saharan Africa', in F. Stewart, S. Lall and S. Wangwe (eds.), *Alternative Development Strategies in Sub-Saharan Africa*, Basingstoke: Macmillan Press.

Hermes, N. and R. Lensink (eds.) (1996) *Financial Development and Economic Growth: Theory and Experiences from Developing Countries*, London: Routledge.

Higgins, B. and J.D. Higgins (1979) *Economic Development of a Small Planet*, New York: Norton and Co.

Hill, H. (2000) 'Indonesia: The Strange and Sudden Death of a Tiger Economy', *Oxford Development Studies*, 28(2), pp. 117–39.

Hirschman, A.O. (1977) 'A Generalized Linkage Approach to Economic Development, with Special Reference to Staples', in Manning Nash (ed.), *Essays on Economic Development and Cultural Change in Honor of Bert F. Hoselitz*, Special Issue, *Economic Development and Cultural Change*, Supplement, 25, 1977.

Hirschman, A.O. (1988) *The Strategy of Economic Development*, New Haven, CT: Yale University Press (first edn 1958).

Hofman, A. (1993) 'Economic Development in Latin America in the 20th Century – A Comparative Perspective', in A. Szirmai, B. van Ark and D. Pilat (eds.), *Explaining Economic Growth, Essays in Honour of Angus Maddison*, Amsterdam: North Holland.

Hogendorn, J.S. (1996) *Economic Development*, 3rd edn, New York: Harper Collins Publishers.

Horesh, E. and S. Joekes (1985) 'The Impact of Primary Exports on the Ghanaian Economy', in M. Lundahl (ed.), *The Primary Sector in Economic Development*, London: Croom Helm.

IMF (2001) *International Financial Statistics Yearbook*, Washington, DC, and various volumes.

ISIC (1990), *International Standard Industrial Classification of All Economic Activities: Third Revision*, Statistical Office of the United Nations, Statistical Papers, Series M, No. 4, rev. 3, New York: United Nations.

Islam, N. (ed.) (1989a) *The Balance between Industry and Agriculture in Economic Development: Factors Influencing Change*, Proceedings of the Eighth World Congress of the International Economic Association, Vol. V, Basingstoke: Macmillan Press.

Islam, N. (1989b) 'Introduction to Part I, Relative Price Changes in Agriculture and Industry', in N. Islam, *The Balance between Industry and Agriculture* 1989.

Johnston, B.F. (1970) 'Agriculture and Structural Transformation in Developing Countries: A Survey of Research', *Journal of Economic Literature*, 3, pp. 369–404.

Johnston, B.F. and J.W. Mellor (1961) 'The Role of Agriculture in Economic Development', *American Economic Review*, 51, pp. 566–94.

Jorgenson, D.W. (1961) 'The Development of a Dual Economy', *Economic Journal*, June, pp. 309–34.

Jorgenson, D.W. (1967) 'Surplus Agricultural Labour and the Development of a Dual Economy', *Oxford Economic Papers*, 19, November, pp. 288–312.

Jorgenson, D.W. (1969) 'The Role of Agriculture in Economic Development: Classical versus Neoclassical Models of Growth', in: C. Wharton (ed.), *Subsistence Agriculture and Economic Development*, Chicago: Aldine.

Kalirajan, H.P. and Y. Wu (eds.) (1999) *Productivity and Growth in Chinese Agriculture*, Basingstoke: Macmillan Press.

Kirkpatrick, C. (1987) 'Trade Policy and Industrialization in LDCs', in N. Gemmell (ed.), *Surveys in Development Economics*, Oxford: Basil Blackwell.

Kitching, G. (1982) *Development and Underdevelopment in Historical Perspective*, London: Methuen.

Kol, J. and B.M.M. Mennes, (1990) 'Internationale handel-theorie en beleid [International Trade Theory and Policy]', *Economische en Statistische Berichten*, 21 November, pp. 1088–93.

Kuznets, S. (1955) 'Economic Growth and Income Inequality', *American Economic Review*, 45(1), pp. 1–28.

Kuznets, S. (1965) *Economic Growth and Structure*, London: Heinemann.

Kuznets, S. (1966) *Modern Economic Growth: Rate, Structure and Spread*, New Haven, CT: Yale University Press.

Kuznets, S. (1971) *Economic Growth of Nations: Total Output and Production Structure*, Cambridge, MA: Harvard University Press.

Lapperre, P.E. (2001) 'Industrialisation in Tanzania: Can Tanzania Learn from European History?', in A. Szirmai and P.E. Lapperre (eds.), *The Industrial Experience of Tanzania*, Basingstoke: Palgrave, pp. 283–300.

Lensink, R. (1995) *Structural Adjustment in Sub-Saharan Africa*, London: Longman.

Lewis, A. (1950) *The Theory of Economic Growth*, London: Allen and Unwin.

Lewis, W.A. (1954) 'Economic Development with Unlimited Supplies of Labour', *The Manchester School of Economic and Social Studies*, 22, pp. 139–91.

Lewis, W.A. (1969) *Aspects of Tropical Trade, 1883–1965*, Stockholm: Almquist and Wicksell.

Lewis, W.A. (ed.) (1970) *Tropical Development, 1880–1913*, London: Allen and Unwin.

Lewis, W.A. (1978a) *Growth and Fluctuations, 1870–1913*, London: Allen and Unwin.

Lewis, W.A. (1978b) *The Evolution of the International Economic Order*, Princeton University Press.

Lipton, M. (1977) *Why Poor People Stay Poor: Urban Bias in World Development*, London: Temple Smith.

Lord, M.J. (1989) 'Primary Commodities as an Engine for Export Growth in Latin America', in N. Islam (1989a), *The Balance between Industry and Agriculture*.

Lundahl, M. (ed.) (1985) *The Primary Sector in Economic Development*, London: Croom Helm.

McBean, A.I. (1989) 'Agricultural Exports of Developing Countries: Market Conditions and National Policies', in N. Islam (1989a).

Maddison, A. (1987) 'Growth and Slowdown in Advanced Capitalist Economies', *Journal of Economic Literature*, 25, June, pp. 649–98.

Maddison, A. (1991) *Dynamic Forces in Capitalist Development*, Oxford University Press.

Maddison, A. (1989) *The World Economy in the Twentieth Century*, Paris: OECD.

Maddison, A. (2001) *The World Economy: A Millennial Perspective*, OECD Development Centre Studies, Paris: OECD.

Manarungsan, S. (1989) 'Economic Development of Thailand, 1850–1950, Response to the Challenge of the World Economy', University of Groningen, Dissertation.

Meier, G.M. (1968) *The International Economics of Development*, New York: Harper.

Meier, G.M. (1989) 'The Old and New Export Pessimism: A Critical Survey', in N. Islam (ed.) (1989a) *The Balance between Industry and Agriculture*.

Mellor, J.W. (1976) *The New Economics of Growth*, Ithaca: Cornell University Press.

Morrissey, O. and I. Filatotchev (2001) 'Globalisation and Trade: The Implications for Exports from Marginalised Countries', in O. Morrissey and I. Filatotchev (eds.), *Globalisation and Trade*, London: Frank Cass.

Myint, H. (1959) 'The "Classical Theory" of International Trade and the Underdeveloped Countries', *Economic Journal*, 68, pp. 317–37.

Myint, H. (1975) 'Agriculture and Economic Development in the Open Economy', in L.G. Reynolds (ed.), *Agriculture in Development Theory*, New Haven, CT: Yale University Press.

Myint, H. (1980) *The Economics of the Developing Countries*, 5th edn, London: Hutchinson.

Myrdal, G. (1957) *Economic Theory and Underdeveloped Regions*, London: Duckworth.

Nadiri, M. (1972) 'International Studies of Factor Inputs and Total Factor Productivity: A Brief Survey', *Review of Income and Wealth*, 18, June.

Nicholls, W.H. (1964) 'The Place of Agriculture in Economic Development', in C.K. Eicher and L.W. de Witt (eds.) (1964), *Agriculture in Development*.

Nurkse, R. (1962) *Patterns of Trade and Development*, The 1959 Wicksell Lectures Oxford: Basil Blackwell.

Ohkawa, K. and H. Rosovsky (1964) 'The Role of Agriculture in Modern Japanese Economic Development', in: C. Eicher and L.W. de Witt (eds.) (1964) *Agriculture in Development*, pp. 45–68.

Pack, H. (1988) 'Industrialization and Trade', in H. Chenery and T.N. Srinivasan, *Handbook of Development Economics*, Vol. I, Amsterdam: North Holland, ch. 9, pp. 334–80.

Pilat, D. (1994) *The Economics of Rapid Growth: The Experience of Japan and Korea*, Aldershot: Edward Elgar.

Prebisch, R. (1950) *The Economic Development of Latin America and its Principal Problems*, UN, Department of Economic Affairs.

Ranis, G. (1989) 'Macro Policies, the Terms of Trade and the Spatial Dimension of Balanced Growth', in N. Islam (ed.) (1989a) *The Balance between Industry and Agriculture*.

Rawski, T. G. (1979) *Economic Growth and Employment in China*, World Bank, New York/ Oxford: Oxford University Press.

Reynolds, L.G. (1975) *Agriculture in Development Theory*, New Haven, CT: Yale University Press.

Riddle, D.I. (1986) *Service-Led Growth: The Role of the Service Sector in World Development*, New York: Praeger.

Rostow, W.W. (1960) *The Stages of Economic Growth*, Cambridge University Press.

Samuelson, P. and W.D. (1989) Nordhaus, *Economics*, 13th edn, New York: McGraw-Hill.

Sapsford, D. (1985) 'The Statistical Debate on the Net Barter Terms of Trade between Primary Commodities and Manufactures: A Comment and Some Statistical Evidence', *The Economic Journal*, 95, September, pp. 781–8.

Sapsford, D. (1988) 'The Debate over Trends in the Terms of Trade', in D. Greenaway (ed.), *Economic Development and International Trade*, London: Macmillan, pp. 117–30.

Sapsford, D. and H. Singer (1998) 'The IMF, the World Bank and Commodity Prices: A Case of Shifting Sands?', *World Development*, 26(9), pp. 1653–60.

Sapsford, D. and V. N. Balasubramanyam (2003) 'Globalization and the Terms of Trade: the Glass Ceiling Hypothesis', in: H. Bloch (ed.), *Growth and Development in the Global Economy*, Cheltenham: Edward Elgar, pp. 157–69.

Sarkar, P. (1986) 'The Singer-Prebisch Hypothesis: A Statistical Evaluation', *Cambridge Journal of Economics*, 10, pp. 355–71.

Sarkar, P. (2001) 'The Long-term Behaviour of the North–South Terms of Trade: A Review of the Statistical Debate', *Progress in Development Studies*, 1(3), 2001, pp. 309–27.

Singer, H.W. (1950) 'The Distribution of Gains between Investing and Borrowing Countries', *The American Economic Review*, 41, pp. 473–86.

Spraos, J. (1980) 'The Statistical Debate on the Net Barter Terms of Trade between Primary Commodities and Manufactures', *The Economic Journal*, 90, March, pp. 107–28.

Svedberg, P. (1993) 'Trade Compression and Economic Decline in Sub-Saharan Africa, in M. Blomström and M. Lundahl, *Economic Crisis in Africa: Perspectives on Policy Responses*, London/New York: Routledge.

Syrquin, M. (1988) 'Patterns of Structural Change', in H. Chenery and T.N. Srinivasan (eds.), *Handbook of Development Economics*, Chapter 7, pp. 205–73.

Szirmai, A. and P.E. Lapperre (eds.) (2001) *The Industrial Experience of Tanzania*, Basingstoke: Palgrave.

Thirlwall, A.P. (1997) *Growth and Development with Special Reference to Developing Economies*, 6th edn, London: Macmillan.

Thoburn, J.T. (1977) *Primary Commodity Exports and Economic Development. Theory, Evidence and a Study of Malaysia*, London: Wiley and Sons.

Timmer, C.P. (1988) 'The Agricultural Transformation', in H. Chenery and T.N. Srinivasan, (eds.), *Handbook of Development Economics*, Vol. I, Chapter 8, pp. 276–331.

Triplett, J.E. (2002) ' "Baumol's Disease" Has Been Cured: IT and Multifactor Productivity in U.S. Services Industries', Paper, Som/TEG Conference: The Empirical Implications of Technology Based Growth Theories, Mimeograph, Groningen, August.

Tybout, J.R. (2002) 'Manufacturing Firms in Developing Countries: How Well Do They Do, and Why?', *Journal of Economic Literature*, 38(March), p. 11–44.

UNCTAD (2002a) *Least Developed Countries 2001 Report*, Geneva: United Nations.

UNCTAD (2002b) *Unctad Handbook of Statistics*, New York/Geneva: UNCTAD.

van Engelen, D., A. Szirmai and P. Lapperre (2001) 'Public Policy and the Industrial Development of Tanzania, 1961–1995', in A. Szirmai and P. Lapperre (eds.) (2001) *The Industrial Experience of Tanzania*, pp. 11–49.

Veblen, T. (1989) *The Theory of the Leisure Class*, New York: Macmillan.

World Bank (1989) *Sub-Saharan Africa: From Crisis to Sustainable Growth*, Washington, DC: World Bank.

World Bank (1994) *Adjustment in Africa: Reforms, Results and the Road Ahead, A World Bank Policy Research Report*, New York: Oxford University Press.

World Bank (1990) *World Development Report 1990*, Oxford and New York: Oxford University Press.

World Bank (2000) *World Development Report, 1999/2000: Entering the 21st Century*, New York: Oxford University Press (Chapter 2, 'The World Trading System: The Road Ahead').

World Bank (2002) *World Development Indicators CD-Rom*, Washington, DC: World Bank.

Yamfwa, F.K. (2001) Improving Manufacturing Performance: The Case of Zambia', Dissertation, Eindhoven Centre for Innovation Studies, October.

Yamfwa, F.K., A. Szirmai and C. Lwamba (2002), *Zambian Manufacturing in Comparative Perspective*, Eindhoven, Eindhoven Centre for Studies Working Paper, 02–21, 2002.

Chapter 9   Industrial development

Abernathy, F.H. *et al.* (1999) *A Stitch in Time: Lean Retailing and the Transformation of Manufacturing: Lessons from the Apparel and Textile Industries*, New York: Oxford University Press.

Abramovitz, M. (1989) 'Thinking about Growth', in M. Abramovitz, *Thinking about Growth and Other Essays on Economic Growth and Welfare*, Cambridge University Press, pp. 3–79.

Ahluwalia, M.S. (1976) 'Inequality, Poverty and Development', *Journal of Development Economics*, 3, September, pp. 307–42.

Allesina, A. and D. Rodrik (1994), 'Distributive Politics and Economic Growth', *The Quarterly Journal of Economics*, 109, pp. 465–89.

Amsden, A. (1989) *Asia's Next Giant: South Korea and Late Industrialization*, New York/Oxford: Oxford University Press.

Athukorala, P. (1998a) *Trade Policy Issues in Asian Development*, London/New York: Routledge.

Athukorala, P. (1998b) 'Export Response to Liberalisation: The Sri Lankan Experience', *Hitotsubashi Journal of Economics*, 39, 49–65.

Athukorala, P. and S. Rajapatirana (2000) 'Liberalization and Industrial Transformation: Lessons from the Sri Lankan Experience', *Economic Development and Cultural Change* 48(3), pp. 543–72.

Bacha, E.L. (1979) 'The Kuznets Curve and Beyond: Growth and Changes in Inequalities', in E. Malinvaud (ed.), *Economic Growth and Resources*, Vol. I, London: Macmillan.

Bardhan, P. (1984) *The Political Economy of Development in India*, New Delhi: Oxford University Press.

Bos, H.C. (1984) 'The Role of Industry and Industrial Policies in the Third Development Decade', in P.K. Gosh (ed.), *Industrialization and Development*, Westport, CT: Greenwood Press.

Boserup, E. (1965) *The Conditions of Agricultural Growth*, New York: Aldine.

Breman, J. (1980) *The Informal Sector in Research: Theory and Practice*, Rotterdam: CASP.

Bruton, H.J. (1969) 'The Two-Gap Approach to Aid and Development: Comment', *American Economic Review*, 59, June, pp. 439–46.

Bruton, H.J. (1998) 'A Reconsideration of Import Substitution', *Journal of Economic Literature*, 36(2), pp. 903–36.

Bureau of Statistics, Tanzania (1995) *Selected Statistical Series, 1991–1994*, Dar-es-Salaam: Bureau of Statistics.

Chang, H.-J. (2002) *Kicking away the Ladder: Development Strategy in Historical Perspective*, London: Anthem Press.

Chenery, H. and I. Adelman (1966) 'Foreign Aid and Economic Development: The Case of Greece', *Review of Economics and Statistics*, February.

Chenery, H. and A. MacEwan (1966) 'Optimal Patterns of Growth and Aid: The Case of Pakistan', *Pakistan Development Review*, Summer.

Chenery, H. and A. Strout (1966) 'Foreign Assistance and Economic Development', *American Economic Review*, 56, pp. 679–733.

Cline, W.R. (1982) 'Can the East Asian Model of Development be Generalized?', *World Development*, 10(2), pp. 81–90.

Cooper, C. (2001) 'The Role of Technological Factors in the Early Stages of Industrial Exports: A Note', in A. Szirmai and P. Lapperre (eds.), *The Industrial Experience of Tanzania*, Basingstoke: Palgrave, pp. 114–32.

Cyhn, J. (2001) *Technology Transfer and International Production: The Development of the Electronics Industry in Korea*, Cheltenham: Elgar.

Deininger, K. and L. Squire (1996) 'A New Data Set Measuring Income Inequality', *World Bank Economic Review*, 10, pp. 565–91.

Deininger, K. and L. Squire (1998) 'New Ways of Looking at Old Issues', *Journal of Development Economics*, 57, pp. 259–87.

de Soto, H., *The Mystery of Capital: Why Capitalism Triumphs in the West and Fails Everywhere Else*, New York: Basic Books, 2000.

Dunning, J.H. (1993) *The Globalization of Business*, London: Routledge.

Dunning, J. (1988) 'Trade, Location of Economic Activity and the Multinational Enterprise: A search for an Eclectic Approach', in J. Dunning, *Explaining International Production*, London: Unwin Hyman, pp. 13–40.

Fagerberg, J. (1994) 'Technology and International Differences in Growth Rates', *Journal of Economic Literature*, 32, September, pp. 1147–75.

Fagerberg, J. (2000) 'Technological Progress, Structural Change and Productivity Growth: A Comparative Study', *Structural Change and Economic Dynamics*, 11, pp. 393–411.

Fei, J.C.H. and G. Ranis (1964) *Development of the Labor Surplus Economy: Theory and Policy*, Homewood, IL: Irwin.

Fei, J.C.H. and G. Ranis (1976) 'A Model of Growth in the Open Dualistic Economy: The case of Korea and Taiwan', *Journal of Development Studies*, May.

Freeman, C. and C. Perez (1988) 'Structural Crises of Adjustment, Business Cycles and Investment Behaviour', in G. Dosi, C. Freeman, R. Nelson, G. Silverberg and L. Soete (eds.), *Technical Change and Economic Theory*, London: Pinter.

Furtado, C. (1976) *Economic Development of Latin America*, 2nd edn, Cambridge University Press.

Gaillard, H. and A. Beernink (2001) 'The Urban Informal Manufacturing Sector in Tanzania: Neglected Opportunities for Socioeconomic Development', in Szirmai and Lapperre (eds.), *The Industrial Experience of Tanzania*, pp. 318–40.

Gereffi, G. (1990) 'Paths of Industrialization: An Overview', in G. Gereffi and D. Wyman (eds.), *Manufacturing Miracles*, Princeton University Press.

Gereffi, G. (1994) 'Capitalism, Development and Global Commodity Chains, in L. Sklair (ed.), *Capitalism and Development*, London: Routledge.

Gereffi, G. (1999) 'International Trade and Industrial Upgrading in the Apparel Commodity Chain, *Journal of International Economics*, 48(1), pp. 37–70.

Gereffi, G. and M. Korzeniewicz (eds.), (1994) *Commodity Chains and Global Capitalism*, Westport, CT: Prager.

Gerschenkron, A. (1962) *Economic Backwardness in Historical Perspective*, Cambridge, MA: Harvard University Press.

Gillis, M., D.H. Perkins, M. Roemer and D.R. Snodgrass (1992) *Economics of Development*, 3rd edn, New York: W.W. Norton and Co.

Gosh, P.L. (1984) *Industrialization and Development*, Westport, CT: Greenwood Press.

Hart, K. (1973) 'Informal Income Opportunities and Urban Employment in Ghana', in R. Jolly, E. de Kadt and F. Wilson (eds.), *Third World Employment: Problems and Strategy*, Harmondsworth: Penguin.

Helleiner, G.K. (1992) 'Structural Adjustment and Long-Term Development in Sub-Saharan Africa', in F. Stewart, S. Lall and S. Wangwe (eds.), *Alternative Development Strategies in Sub-Saharan Africa*, Basingstoke: Macmillan Press.

Helleiner, G.K. (ed.) (1995) *Manufacturing for Export in the Developing World: Problems and Possibilities*, London: Routledge.

Helleiner, G. K. (ed.) (2002) *Non-Traditional Export Promotion in Africa: Experience and Issues*, Basingstoke: Palgrave.

Higgins, B. (1968) *Economic Development*, New York: Norton and Co. (first edn 1959).

Hill, H. (1996) *The Indonesian Economy since 1966: Southeast Asia's Emerging Giant*, Cambridge University Press.

Hill, H. (2000) 'Indonesia: The Strange and Sudden Death of a Tiger Economy', *Oxford Development Studies*, 28(2), pp. 117–39.

Hirschman, A.O. (1988) *The Strategy of Economic Development*, Boulder and London: Westview Press (first edn 1958).

ILO (1972) *Employment, Income and Equality: A Strategy for Increasing Productive Employment in Kenya*, Geneva: ILO.

IMF (1998) *International Financial Yearbook*, Washington, DC: IMF, and various issues.

IMF (1992) *World Investment Report*, Washington, DC: IMF, and various issues.

James, D. (1991) 'Capital Goods Production and Technological Learning: The Case of Mexico', *Journal of Economics Issues*, 25(4), pp. 977–91.

Kaldor, N. (1956) 'Alternative Theories of Distribution', *Review of Economic Studies*, 2(2), pp. 83–100.

Kiely, R. (1998) *Industrialisation and Development: A Comparative Analysis*, London: UCL Press.

Kirkpatrick, C. (1987) 'Trade Policy and Industrialization in LDCs', in N. Gemmell (ed.), *Surveys in Development Economics*, Oxford: Basil Blackwell.

Krueger, A.O. (1978) *Foreign Trade Regimes and Economic Development*, Cambridge, MA.: Ballinger.

Krueger, A.O. (1984) 'The Newly Industrializing Countries: Experience and Lessons', in M. Dutta (ed.), *Studies in United States–Asia Economic Relations*, Durham, NC: Acorn Press, pp. 253–74.

Krueger, A.O. (1992) *Economic Policy Reform in Developing Countries*, Oxford: Basil Blackwell.

Krueger, A.O., C. Michalopoulos and V.W. Ruttan (1989) *Aid and Development*, Baltimore/London: Johns Hopkins University Press.

Kumar, N., 'Introduction', in: N. Kumar (ed.), *Globalization, Foreign Direct Investment and Technology Transfers: Impacts and Prospects for Developing Countries*, London/New York: Routledge.

Kuznets, S. (1955) 'Economic Growth and Income Inequality', *American Economic Review*, 45(1), pp. 1–28.

Lal, D. (2000) *The Poverty of 'Development Economics'*, 2nd rev. and expanded US edn, Cambridge, MA/London: The MIT Press.

Lal, D. and H. Myint (1996) *The Political Economy of Poverty, Equity, and Growth: A Comparative Study*, Oxford: Clarendon.

Lall, S. (1990) *Building Industrial Competitiveness in Developing Countries*, Paris: OECD.

Lall, S. (1996) *Learning from the Asian Tigers: Studies in Technology and Industrial Policy*, London: Macmillan.

Lall, S. (1998) 'Exports of Manufactures by Developing Countries: Emerging Patterns of Trade and Location', *Oxford Review of Economic Policy*, 14(2), pp. 54–73.

Lall, S. (2000) 'Technological Change and Industrialization in the Asian NIEs: Achievements and Challenges', in L. Kim and R.R. Nelson (eds.), *Technology, Learning and Innovation: Experiences of Newly Industrializing Economies*, Cambridge University Press, pp. 13–68.

Leibenstein, H. (1957) *Economic Backwardness and Economic Growth: Studies in the Theory of Economic Development*, New York: Wiley.

Leibenstein, H. (1954) *A Theory of Economic Demographic Development*, Princeton University Press.

Lewis, W.A. (1954) 'Economic Development with Unlimited Supplies of Labour', *Manchester School of Economic and Social Studies*, 22, pp. 139–91.

Lewis, W.A. (1978a) *Growth and Fluctuations 1870–1913*, London: Allen and Unwin.

Lewis, W.A. (1978b) *The Evolution of the International Economic Order*, Princeton University Press.

Lewis, W.A. (1983) 'Reflections on Unlimited Labor', in M. Gersowitz (ed.), *Selected Writings of Sir W.A. Lewis*, New York: New York University Press, pp. 421–43 (original publication in 1967).

Lin, J.Y., F. Cai, and Z. Li (2000) 'The Lessons of China's Transition to a Market Economy, Paper for APSEM/ANU/World Bank conference, Achieving High Growth, Experience of Transitional Economies in East Asia, Canberra, 6/7 September.

Little, I.M.D., T. Scitovsky and M. Scott (1970) *Industry and Trade in Some Developing Countries*, New York: Oxford University Press.

Maddison, A. (1989) *The World Economy in the Twentieth Century*, Paris: OECD.

Maddison, A. (1991) *Dynamics of Capitalist Development*, Oxford University Press.

Maddison, A. and associates (1992) *The Political Economy of Poverty, Equity and Growth: Brazil and Mexico*, New York: Oxford University Press.

Maddison, A. (1998) *The Chinese Economy in the Long Run*, OECD Development Centre, Paris: OECD.

Morrissey, O. and I. Filatotchev (2001) 'Globalisation and Trade: The Implications for Exports from Marginalised Economies', in O. Morrissey and I. Filatotchev (eds.), *Globalisation and Trade: Implications for Exports from Marginalised Economies*, London: Frank Cass, pp. 1–12.

Myint, H. (1980) *The Economics of the Developing Countries*, 5th edn, London: Hutchinson and Co.

Nelson, R. (1956) 'A Theory of the Low-Level Equilibrium Trap in Underdeveloped Economies', *American Economic Review*, 46, pp. 894–908.

Nurkse, R. (1953) *Problems of Capital Formation in Underdeveloped Countries*, New York: Oxford University Press.

Pack, H. (1988) 'Industrialization and Trade', in H. Chenery and T.N. Srinivasan (eds.), *Handbook of Development Economics*, Vol. I, Amsterdam, North Holland, Ch. 9, pp. 334–80.

Pack, H. (1994) 'Endogenous Growth Theory: Intellectual Appeal and Empirical Shortcomings', *Journal of Economic Perspectives*, 8(1), pp. 55–72.

Paukert, F. (1973) 'Income Distribution at Different Levels of Development: A Survey of the Evidence', *International Labour Review*, 108, pp. 97–125.

Persson, T. and G. Tabellini (1994) 'Is Inequality Harmful for Growth? Theory and Evidence', *American Economic Review*, 84(3), pp. 600–21.

Pollard, S. (1990) *Typology of Industrialization Processes in the Nineteenth Century*, New York: Harwood Academic Publishers.

Porter, M. E. (1990) *The Competitive Advantage of Nations*, New York: The Free Press.

Ranis, G. (1988) 'Analytics of Development', in Chenery and Srinivasan (eds.), *Handbook of Development Economics*, Vol. I.

Ranis, G. (1989) 'Macro-Policies, the Terms of Trade and the Spatial Dimension of Balanced Growth', in N. Islam (ed.), *The Balance between Industry and Agriculture in Economic Development: Factors Influencing Change*, Proceedings of the Eighth World Congress of the International Economic Association, Vol. 5, Basingstoke: Macmillan Press.

Rawski, T.G. (1979) *Economic Growth and Employment in China*, World Bank, New York/Oxford, Oxford University Press.

Rodrik, D. (1995) 'Getting Interventions Right: How South Korea and Taiwan Grew Rich, *Economic Policy*, 20, pp. 53–97.

Rodrik, D. (1999) *Making Openness Work: The New Global Economy and the Developing Countries*, Overseas Development Council, Washington, DC.

Romijn, H. (1999) *Acquisition of Technological Capabilities in Small Firms in Developing Countries*, London: Macmillan, January.

Romein, J. (1937) 'De dialectiek van de vooruitgang: bijdrage tot het ontwikkelingsbegrip in de geschiedenis' [The Dialectics of Progress: A Contribution to the Concept of Development in History], in: J. Romein, *Het onvoltooid verleden: cultuur-historische studies*, Amsterdam: Querido (first published 1935).

Rosenberg, N. (1963a) 'Capital Goods, Technology, and Economic Growth', *Oxford Economic Papers*, November, pp. 217–27.

Rosenberg, N. (1963b) 'Technological Change in the Machine Tool Industry, 1840–1910', *Journal of Economic History*, December, pp. 414–43.

Rosenberg, N. (1982) *Inside the Black Box: Technology and Economics*, Cambridge University Press.

Rosenstein-Rodan, P. (1943) 'Problems of Industrialisation of East and South-East Europe', *Economic Journal*, June–September, pp. 201–11.

Rosenstein-Rodan, P. (1957) *Notes on the Theory of the 'Big Push'*, Cambridge, MA: MIT, CIS, March.

Rostow, W.W. (1960) *The Stages of Economic Growth*, 2nd edn, Cambridge University Press, 1971.

Rubinson, R. (1976) 'The World Economy and the Distribution of Income within States: A Cross National Study', *American Sociological Review*, 41, August, pp. 611–23.

Sen, A.K. (1960) *Choice of Techniques*, Oxford: Basil Blackwell.

Stewart, F. (1972) 'Choice of Technique in Developing Countries', *Journal of Development Studies*, 9(1) October, pp. 99–121.

Stewart, F. (1974) 'Technology and Employment in Less Developed Countries', *World Development*, 2(3), March, pp. 17–46.

Stewart, F. (1977) *Technology and Underdevelopment*, Basingstoke: Macmillan.

Szirmai, A. (1994) 'Real Output and Labour Productivity in Indonesian Manufacturing, 1975–1990', *Bulletin of Indonesian Economic Studies*, No. 3, August, pp. 49–90.

Szirmai, A., M. Bai and R. Ren (2001) *Labour Productivity Trends in Chinese Manufacturing, 1980–99*, ECIS Working Paper, 2001 10, October.

Szirmai, A. and P.E. Lapperre (eds.) (2001) *The Industrial Experience of Tanzania*, Basingstoke: Palgrave.

Szirmai, A., M. Prins and W. Schulte (2001), Measuring Manufacturing Performance in Tanzania', in: A. Szirmai and P. Lapperre (eds.), *The Industrial Experience of Taiwan*, pp. 73–113.

Thee, K.W. (1997) 'The Development of the Motor Cycle Industry in Indonesia', in M.E. Pangestu and Y. Sato (eds.), *Waves of Change in Indonesia's Manufacturing Industry*, Tokyo: Institute of Developing Economies, pp. 95–135.

Thirlwall, A.P. (1999) *Growth and Development with Special Reference to Developing Economies*, 6th edn, London: Macmillan.

Thorbecke, E. and C. Charumilind (2002) 'Economic Inequality and Its Socioeconomic Impact', *World Development*, 30(9), pp. 1477–95.

Todaro, M. (1969) 'A Model of Labor Migration and Urban Unemployment in Less Developed Countries', *American Economic Review*, 59(1), March, pp. 138–48.

Tybout, J.R. (2000) 'Manufacturing Firms in Developing Countries: How Well Do They Do, and Why?', *Journal of Economic Literature*, 38(March), pp. 11–44.

UNCTAD (2000) *The Competitiveness Challenge: Transnational Corporations and Industrial Restructuring in Developing Countries*, New York/Geneva: UNCTAD.

UNIDO (1985) *Industrial Development Review, Series Malaysia*, Vienna: UNIDO, July.

UNIDO (1986) *Industrial Development Review, Series Zaire*, Vienna: UNIDO, July.

UNIDO (1990) *Handbook of Industrial Statistics 1990*, Vienna: UNIDO.

UNIDO (1995) *International Yearbook of Industrial Statistics 1995*, Vienna: UNIDO.

UNIDO (1999) *International Yearbook of Industrial Statistics 1999*, Vienna: UNIDO.

UNIDO (2002) *Industrial Development Report, 2002/3: Competing through Innovation and Learning*, Vienna: UNIDO.

UNIDO (2003) *Industrial Statistics Database, 2003* at the 3-Digit Level of ISIC (Revision 2), CD-Rom, Vienna: UNIDO.

van Dijk, M. (2003) 'South African Manufacturing Performance in a Comparative Perspective, 1970–99', *South African Journal of Economics*, 71(1), pp. 119–42.

van Dijk, M.P. (1980) 'De informele sector van Ouagadougou en Dakar: De ontwikkelingsmogelijkheden van kleine bedrijven in twee Westafrikaanse hoofdsteden' [The Informal Sector of Ouagadougou and Dakar: The Development Opportunities of Small Enterprises in two West African Capitals], Dissertation, Free University of Amsterdam.

van Engelen, D., A. Szirmai and P.E. Lapperre (2001) 'Public Policy and the Industrial Development of Tanzania, 1961–1995', in A. Szirmai and P. Lapperre (eds.), *The Industrial Experience of Tanzania*, pp. 11–49.

Veblen, T. (1915) *Imperial Germany and the Industrial Revolution*, New York: Macmillan.

Verbruggen, H. (1985) 'Gains from Export-Oriented Industrialization with Special Reference to South East Asia', Amsterdam, Dissertation, Free University.

Vernon, R. (1996) 'International Investment and International Trade in the Product Cycle' *Quarterly Journal of Economics*, 80(2), May, pp. 190–207.

von Tunzelman, N. (1995). *Technology and Industrial Progress*, Aldershot: Elgar.

Wade, R. (1990) *Governing the Market: Economic Theory and the Role of Government in East Asian Industrialization*, Princeton University Press.

Wangwe, S.M. (ed.) (1995) *Exporting Africa, Technology, Trade and Industrialisation in Sub-Saharan Africa*, UN/INTECH, London and New York: Routledge and Kegan Paul.

Weiss, J. (1988) *Industry in Developing Countries: Theory, Policy and Evidence*, London: Croom Helm.

Weiss, J. (2002) *Industrialisation and Globalisation: Theory and Evidence from Developing Countries*, London: Routledge.

Westphal, L.E. (2002) 'Technology Strategies for Economic Development in a Fast Changing Global Economy', *Economics of Innovation and New Technology*, 11(4/5), August/October, pp. 275–320.

Westphal, L.E., L. Kim and C.J. Dahlman (1985) 'Reflections on The Republic of Korea's Acquisition of Technological Capability', in N. Rosenberg and C. Frischtak (eds.), *International Technology Transfer: Concepts Measures, and Comparisons*, New York: Praeger, pp. 167–221.

World Bank (1993a) *The East Asian Miracle: Economic Growth and Public Policy*, New York: Oxford University Press.

World Bank (1984) *World Development Report*, Oxford/New York: Oxford University Press, and various issues.

World Bank (1985) *World Development Report 1985*, Oxford University Press.

World Bank (1993b), *World Tables 1993*, Baltimore, Johns Hopkins University Press, and various issues.

World Bank (2002) *World Development Indicators 2002*, CD-Rom.

WTO (2001) *International Trade Statistics 2001*, Geneva: World Trade Organisation.

WTO (1997) *Annual Report 1997*, Vol. II, Geneva: World Trade Organisation.

Yamfwa, F.K. (2001) 'Improving Manufacturing Performance: The Case of Zambia', Dissertation, Eindhoven University of Technology, October.

Yamfwa, F.K. (2002) Adam Szirmai and Chibwe Lwamba, *Zambian Manufacturing Performance in Comparative Perspective*, ECIS working paper, 02–21, December (also published as Groningen Growth and Development Centre Working Paper, GD 53).

Chapter 10 Agricultural development and rural development

Adams, J. (1986) 'Peasant Rationality: Individuals, Groups, Cultures', *World Development*, 14(2), pp. 273–82.

Alexander, P., P. Boomgaard and B. White (eds.) (1991) *In the Shadow of Agriculture: Non-farm Activities in the Javanese Economy, Past and Present*, Amsterdam: Royal Tropical Institute.

Alexandratos, N. (1988) *World Agriculture towards 2000*, London: Belhaven for FAO.

Alexandratos, N. (ed.) (1995) *World Agriculture: Towards 2010*, Chicester: John Wiley and Sons for FAO.

Arnold, D., *Famine: Social Crisis and Historical Change*, Oxford: Basil Blackwell.

Ashton, B., K. Hill, A. Piazza and R. Zeitz (1984) 'Famine in China, 1958–61', *Population Development Review*, 10(4), pp. 613–45.

Barth, F. (1966) *Models of Social Organisation*, London: Royal Anthropological Institute.

Barrow, C.J. (1995) *Developing the Environment: Problems and Management*, London: Longman.

Berry, R. and W.R. Cline (1979) *Agrarian Structure and Productivity in Developing Countries*, Baltimore: Johns Hopkins University Press.

Binswanger, H.P., K. Deininger, G. Feder (1995) 'Power, Distortions, Revolt and Reform in Agricultural Land Relations', in J. Behrman and T.N. Srinivasan (eds.), *Handbook of Development Economics*, Vol. 3B, Amsterdam: North Holland, pp. 2659–772.

Boeke, J.L. (1955) *Economie van Indonesië*, Haarlem: Tjeenk Willink.

Boissevain, J. (1974) *Friends of Friends: Networks, Manipulators and Coalitions*, Oxford: Basil Blackwell.

Bol, D. (1983) *Economen en armoede: Moedwil en misverstand in de ontwikkelingshulp* [Economists and Poverty: Bad Faith and Misunderstandings in Development Aid], Amsterdam: Van Gennep.

Bornstein, D. (1996) *The Price of a Dream: The Story of the Grameen Bank and the Idea that is Helping the Poor Change their Lives*, New York: Simon and Schuster.

Boserup, E. (1965) *The Conditions of Agricultural Growth*, New York: Aldine.

Boserup, E. (1970) *Women's Role in Economic Development*, New York: St. Martin's.

Boserup, E. (1981) *Population and Technology*, Oxford: Basil Blackwell.

Boserup, E. (1983) 'The Impact of Scarcity and Plenty on Development', *Journal of Interdisciplinary History*, 14(2), pp. 383–407.

Boserup, E. (1990) *Economic and Demographic Relationships in Development*. Essays Selected and Introduced by T. Paul Schultz, Baltimore and London: Johns Hopkins University Press.

Braun, J. von, and E. Kennedy (eds.) (1994) *Agricultural Commercialisation, Economic Development and Nutrition*, Baltimore: Johns Hopkins University Press.

Brown, L. (1996) *Tough Choices: Facing the Challenge of Food Scarcity*, New York: Norton.

Bruinsma, J. (ed.) (2003) *World Agriculture towards 2015/2030: An FAO Perspective*, Food and Agriculture Organisation (FAO) Rome, London: Earthscan.

Byerlee, D. and K. Fischer (2002), 'Acccessing Modern Science: Policy and Institutional Options for Agricultural Biotechnology in Developing Countries', *World Development*, 30(6), pp. 931–48.

Cassen, R.H. (1978) *India, Population, Economy, Society*, London: Macmillan.

Chambers, R. (1983) *Rural Development. Putting the Last First*, Harlow: Longman Scientific and Technical.

Chayanov, A.V. (1966) 'On the Theory of Non-Capitalist Economic Systems', in D. Thorner, B. Kerblay and R.F. Smith, *The Theory of Peasant Economy*, Homewood, IL: Richard Irwin, pp. 1–28.

Colman, D. and F. Nixson (1986) *Economics of Change in Less Developed Countries*, 2nd edn, Oxford: Philip Allan.

David C. and J. Roumasset (2000) 'The Microeconomics of Agricultural Development in the Philippines', Paper presented at the conference The Philippine Economy: On the Way to Sustained Growth?, ANU, November 2–3.

Deininger, K. and H. Binswanger (2001) 'Evolution of the World Bank's Land Policy', in A. de Janvry, J.-P. Platteau, G. Gordillo and E. Sadoulet (eds.), *Access to Land, Rural Poverty and Public Action*, Oxford University Press, pp. 406–40.

Devereux, S. (1993) *Theories of Famine*, New York: Harvester Wheatsheaf.

Diamond, J. (1998) *Guns, Germs and Steel: A Short History of Everybody for the Last 13,000 Years*, London: Vintage.

Dixon, C. (1990) *Rural Development in the Third World*, London and New York: Routledge.

Dorner, P. (1972) *Land Reform and Economic Development*, Harmondsworth: Penguin Books.

Doss, C.R. (2001) 'Designing Agricultural Technology for African Women Farmers: Lessons from 25 Years of Experience', *World Development*, 29(12), pp. 2075–92.

Druijven, P.C.J. (1983) 'Rurale industrialisatie in de Volksrepubliek China' [Rural industrialisation in the Peoples' Republic of China], Free University of Amsterdam, Geografisch en Planologisch Instituut, Bijdragen tot de Sociale Geografie en Planologie, No. 6, Amsterdam.

Druijven, P.C.J. (1990) 'Mandenvlechters en Mezcalstokers in Mexico' [Basket weavers and Mescal distillers in Mexico], Dissertation, Free University, Amsterdam.

Eicher, C.K. and J.M. Staatz (eds.) (1984) *Agricultural Development in the Third World*, Baltimore and London: Johns Hopkins University Press.

Eisenstadt, S.N. (1970) 'Social Change and Development', in S.N. Eisenstadt (ed.), *Readings in Social Evolution and Development*, Oxford and London: Pergamon.

Ellis, F. (1988) *Peasant Economics: Farm Households and Agrarian Development*, Cambridge University Press.

FAO (1981) *Agriculture Towards 2000*, Rome: FAO.

FAO (1988) *An Interim Report on the State of Forest Resources in the Developing Countries*, Rome: FAO.

FAO (1988) *Production Yearbook*, Rome: FAO and various volumes.

FAO (1975) *State of Food and Agriculture, 1975*, Rome: FAO.

FAO (1989) *State of Food and Agriculture, 1989*, FAO, Rome, 1989.

FAO, *State of Food and Agriculture, 1990*, FAO, Rome, 1990.

FAO, *Production Yearbook*, Vol. 44, *1990*, Rome, 1991.

FAO, *State of Food and Agriculture, 1991*, FAO, Rome, 1991.

FAO, *Production Yearbook*, Vol. 46, *1992*, Rome, 1993.

FAO, *State of Food and Agriculture, 1993*, FAO, Rome, 1993.

FAO, *Production Yearbook*, Vol. 48, *1994*, Rome, 1995.

FAO (1996) *The Sixth World Food Survey*, Rome: FAO.

Fearnside, P.M. (2001) 'Land-Tenure Issues as Factors in Environmental Destruction in Brazilian Amazonia: the Case of Southern Pará', *World Development*, 29(8), pp. 1361–2001.

Feeny, D. (1982) *The Political Economy of Productivity: Thai Agricultural Development 1880–1975*, Vancouver and London: University of British Columbia Press.

Feeny, D. (1987) 'The Development of Property Rights in Land: A Comparative Study', in: R.H. Bates (ed.), *Toward a Political Economy of Development: A Rationalist Perspective*, Berkeley: University of California Press, 1987.

Firmin-Sellers, K. and P. Sellers (1999) 'Expected Failures and Unexpected Successes of Land Titling in Africa', *World Development*, 27(7), pp. 1115–38.

Foster, G. (1965) 'Peasant Society and the Image of Limited Good', *American Anthropologist*, 67(April), pp. 293–315.

Foster, G. (1975) *Traditional Cultures and the Impact of Technological Change*, New York: Harper and Row.

Frank, A.G. (1969) *Capitalism and Underdevelopment in Latin America*, rev. edn, New York: Monthly Review Press.

Frankel, F.R. (1978) *India's Political Economy, 1947–1977*, Princeton University Press.

Furtado, C. (1976) *Economic Development of Latin America*, Cambridge University Press.

Geertz, C. (1963a) *Agricultural Involution: The Processes of Ecological Change in Indonesia*, Berkeley: University of California Press.

Geertz, C. (1963b) *Peddlars and Princes: Social Change and Economic Modernization in Two Indonesian Towns*, University of Chicago Press.

Ghai, D. and S. Radwan (eds.) (1985) *Agrarian Policies and Rural Poverty in Africa*, ILO: Geneva.

Gillin E.D. and J. Krane (1989) 'Where does the Increase in Crop Production Come From?', *FAO Quarterly Bulletin of Statistics*, 2(4), pp. iii–iv.

Glaeser, B. (1987) 'Agriculture between the Green Revolution and Ecodevelopment: Which Way to Go?' in B. Glaeser (ed.), *The Green Revolution Revisited: Critique and Alternatives*, London: Allen and Unwin, pp. 1–9.

Goudie, A. (1993) *The Human Impact on the Natural Environment*, Oxford: Basil Blackwell.

Goudsblom, J. (1992) *Vuur en beschaving* [Fire and Civilisation], Amsterdam: Meulenhof.

Griffin, K. (1976) *The Political Economy of Agrarian Change*, London: Macmillan.

Griffin, K. (1981) *Land Concentration and Rural Poverty*, 2nd edn, London: Macmillan Press.

Haggis, J., S. Jarret, D. Taylor and P. Mayer (1986) 'By the Skin of their Teeth: A Critical Examination of James Scott's The Moral Economy of the Peasant', *World Development*, 14(12), pp. 1435–55.

Harrison, P. (1992) *The Third Revolution: Population, Environment and a Sustainable World*, Harmondsworth: Penguin.

Hayami, Y. and V.W. Ruttan (1971) *Agricultural Development: An International Perspective*, Baltimore: Johns Hopkins University Press.

Hayami, Y. and R.W. Ruttan (1985) *Agricultural Development: An International Perspective*, rev. edn, Baltimore: Johns Hopkins University Press.

Helleiner, G.K. (1992) 'Structural Adjustment and Long-Term Development in Sub-Saharan Africa', in F. Stewart, S. Lall and S. Wangwe (eds.), *Alternative Development Strategies in Sub-Saharan Africa*, Basingstoke: The Macmillan Press.

Higgins, B. (1959) *Economic Development Problems, Principles and Policies*, New York: Norton.

Hill, P. (1986) *Development Economics on Trial: The Anthropological Case for a Prosecution*, Cambridge University Press.

Hogg, D. (2000) *Technological Change in Agriculture: Locking in to Genetic Uniformity*, London: Macmillan.

Hogg, M.V. (1984) 'Industrialization and Rural Development: An Analysis of Basic Issues', in P.K. Gosh (ed.), *Industrialization and Development*, Westport, CT: Greenwood Press, pp. 153–83.

Hsu, R.C. (1982) *Food for One Billion: China's Agriculture since 1949*, Boulder, CO: Westview Press.

Huang, Y. (1998) *Agricultural Reform in China*, Cambridge University Press.

Janvry, A. de, J.-P. Platteau, G. Gordillo and E. Sadoulet (2001) 'Access to Land and Land Policy Reforms, in A. de Janvry, J.-P. Platteau, G. Gordillo and E. Sadoulet (eds.), *Access to Land: Rural Poverty and Public Action*, Oxford University Press.

Jepma, C.J. (1993) *Deforestation in the Humid Tropics: A Socio-economic Approach*, Groningen: Stichting International Development Economics, February.

Johnson, D. Gale (2002) 'Biotechnology Issues for Developing Countries', *Economic Development and Cultural Change*, 51(1), October, pp. 1–2.

Johnston, B.F. and P. Kilby (1975) *Agriculture and Structural Transformation: Economic Strategies in Late-Developing Countries*, New York: Oxford University Press.

Johnston, B.F. and J.W. Mellor (1961) 'The Role of Agriculture in Economic Development', *American Economic Review*, 51, pp. 566–94.

Kanbur, R. and N. Lustig (1999) *Why Is Inequality Back on the Agenda*, Annual Conference on Development Economics, Washington: World Bank.

Kitching, G. (1982) *Development and Underdevelopment in Historical Perspective*, London: Methuen.

Kuper, A.J. (1984) 'African Culture and African Development', in C.A.O. van Nieuwenhuijze (ed.), *Development Regardless of Culture*, Leiden: Brill.

Lal, D. and H. Myint (1996) *The Political Economy of Poverty, Equity and Growth*, Oxford University Press.

Leach, M. and J. Fairhead (2000) 'Challenging Neo-Malthusian Deforestation Analyses in West Africa's Dynamic Forest Landscapes', *Population and Development Review*, 26(1), March, pp. 17–43.

Leite, L.L. and P.A. Furley (1985) 'Land Development in the Brazilian Amazon' in J. Hemming (ed.), *Change in the Amazon Basin II*, Manchester University Press.

Lipton, M. (1966) 'The Theory of the Optimizing Peasant', *Journal of Development Studies*, 4, pp. 327–51.

Lomborg, B. (2001) *The Skeptical Environmentalist: Measuring the Real State of the World*, Cambridge University Press.

Long, N. (1977) *An Introduction to the Sociology of Rural Development*, London: Tavistock.

Maddison, A. (1989) *The World Economy in the Twentieth Century*, Paris: OECD.

Maddison, A. and Associates (1992) *The Political Economy of Poverty, Equity and Growth. Brazil and Mexico*, Oxford University Press.

Mellor, J.W. (1966) *The Economics of Agricultural Development*, Ithaca and New York: Cornell University Press.

Mitchell, D.O., M.D. Ingco and R.C. Duncan (1997) *The World Food Outlook*, Cambridge University Press.

Moore, B., Jr (1966) *Social Origins of Democracy and Dictatorship*, Harmondsworth: Penguin.

Moore, W.E. (1963) *Social Change*, Englewood Cliffs, NJ: Prentice Hall.

Myers, N. (1989) *Deforestation Rates in Tropical Forests and their Climatic Implications*, London: Friends of the Earth.

Myint, H. (1980) *The Economics of the Developing Countries*, 5th edn, London: Hutchinson.

Natsios, A. (1999) *The Politics of Famine in North Korea*, Special Report, United States Institute of Peace, Washington, August (www.usip.org/events/).

North, D.C. (1990) *Institutions, Institutional Change and Economic Performance*, Cambridge University Press.

North, D.C. (1993) 'The Ultimate Sources of Economic Growth', in A. Szirmai, B. van Ark and D. Pilat (eds.), *Explaining Economic Growth: Essays in Honour of Angus Maddison*, Amsterdam: North Holland.

North, D.C. and R.P. Thomas (1973) *The Rise of the Western World: A New Economic History*, Cambridge University Press, pp. 65–76.

Oasa, E.K. (1987) 'The Political Economy of International Agricultural Research: A Review of CGIAR's Response to Criticisms of the "Green Revolution"', in B. Glaeser (ed.), *The Green Revolution Revisited: Critique and Alternatives*, London: Allen and Unwin, pp. 13–55.

Paarlberg, R.L. (2001) *The Politics of Precaution: Genetically Modified Crops in Developing Countries*, Baltimore: Johns Hopkins University Press.

Parayil, G. (1992) 'The Green Revolution in India: A Case Study of Technological Change', *Technology and Culture*, 33, pp. 737–56.

Pearse, A. (1977) 'Technology and Peasant Production: Reflections on a Global Study', *Development and Change*, 8.

Pinstrup-Anderson, P. (1982) *Agricultural Research and Technology in Economic Development*, London/New York: Longman.

Pinstrup-Anderson, P. and P.B.R. Hazell (1985) 'The Impact of the Green Revolution and Prospects for the Future', *Food Review International*, 1(1), pp. 1–25.

Polyani, K. (1957) *The Great Transformation*, Boston: Beacon Press.

Pomfret, R. (2000) 'Agrarian Reform in Uzbekistan: Why the Chinese Model has Failed to Deliver?', *Economic Development and Cultural Change*, 48(2), January, pp. 269–84.

Popkin, S.L. (1979) *The Rational Peasant: The Political Economy of Rural Society in Vietnam*, Berkeley: University of California Press.

Ravallion, M. (1997) 'Famines and Economics', *Journal of Economic Literature*, 35 (September), pp. 1205–42.

Rawski, T.G., *Economic Growth and Employment in China*, World Bank, New York/Oxford: Oxford University Press.

Ray, D. (2000) *Development Economics*, Princeton University Press.

Revelle, R. (1975) 'Will the Earth's Land and Water Resources Be Sufficient for Future Populations?, in UN, *The Population Debate: Dimensions and Perspectives. Papers of the World Population Conference*, Bucharest, 1974, Vol. II, New York: UN,' pp. 3–14.

Roumasset, J. (1976) *Rice and Risk: Decision-Making among Low-Income Farmers in Theory and Practice*, Amsterdam: North Holland.

Roumasset, J. (1995) 'The Nature of the Agriculture Firm', *Journal of Economic Behaviour and Organization*, 27, pp. 171–7.

Ruttan, V.W. (2002) 'Productivity Growth in World Agriculture: Sources and Constraints', *Journal of Economic Perspectives*, 16(4), Fall, pp. 161–84.

Schultz, T.W. (1953) *The Economic Organisation of Agriculture*, New York: McGraw-Hill.

Schultz, T.W. (1964) *Transforming Traditional Agriculture*, New Haven and London: Yale University Press.

Schultz, T.W. (1968) *Economic Growth and Agriculture*, New York: McGraw-Hill.

Schultz, T.W. (1978) 'On Economics and Politics of Agriculture', in T.W. Schultz (ed.), *Distortions and Agricultural Incentives*, Bloomington: Indiana University Press, pp. 1–23.

Scott, J.C. (1976) *The Moral Economy of the Peasant, Rebellion and Subsistence in South East Asia*, New Haven, CT: Yale University Press.

Sen, A. (1981) *Poverty and Famines*, Oxford: Clarendon Press.

Sen, A. (1982) 'How Is India Doing?', *New York Review of Books*, 16 December, pp. 41–5.

Shanin, T. (ed.) (1971) *Peasants and Peasant Societies*, Harmondsworth: Penguin.

Shanin, T. (1973) 'The Nature and the Logic of the Peasant Economy, Part I: A General-ization', *Journal of Peasant Studies*, 1(1), October, pp. 63–80.

Shanin, T. (1974) 'The Nature and the Logic of the Peasant Economy, Part II: Diversity and Change, Part III: Policy and Intervention', *Journal of Peasant Studies*, 1(2), January, pp. 186–206.

Simon, J. (1996) *The Ultimate Resource*, 2nd edn, Princeton University Press (first published 1981).

Singh, I. (1982) 'The Landless Poor in South Asia', Proceedings of the 18th Conference of the International Association of Agricultural Economists, mimeograph Jakarta.

Smil, V. (2000) *Feeding the World: The Challenge for the Twenty-First Century*, Cambridge MA: MIT Press.

Szirmai, A., M. Bai and Ren R. (2001) *Labour Productivity Trends in Chinese Manufacturing, 1980–99*, ECIS Working Paper, 2001.10.

Teszler, R. (1984) 'Blotevoetenindustrie en plattelandsontwikkeling [Infant industry and rural development]', *Internationale Spectator*, 38(12), December, pp. 702–12.

UN (1989) *Prospects of World Urbanization*, New York: United Nations.

UN, *World Urbanization Prospects: The 1992 Revision*, New York: United Nations 1993.

UN (2002) *World Urbanization Prospects: The 2001 Revision*, New York: United Nations.

United Nations Population Division (2003) *World Population Prospects: The 2002 Revision*, New York: United Nations.

UNDP (1988) *Development of Rural Small Industrial Enterprise: Lessons from Experience*, Joint Study by UNDP, Government of the Netherlands, Vienna: ILO/UNIDO.

UNDP (1988) *Development of Rural Small Industrial Enterprise: Lessons from experience*, Joint Study by UNDP/Government of the Netherlands, Vienna: ILO/UNIDO.

UNEP (1993) *Ecoforum*, 17(1/2), UNEP 17–5–1993, p. 12.

van der Eng, P. (1992) 'Food Supply and Agricultural Development', in W.P.M.F. Ivens (ed.), *World Food Production Textbook*, Vol. I, Heerlen: Open University, pp. 89–116.

van der Eng, P. 'Agricultural Growth in Indonesia since 1880', Dissertation, Groningen.

van Hekken, P.M. and H.U.E. Thoden van Velzen (1972) *Land Scarcity and Rural Inequality in Tanzania*, The Hague: Mouton.

van der Meer, C.L.J. (1981) 'Rural Development in Northern Thailand', Dissertation, Groningen.

van der Meer, C.L.J. (1983) 'Voedselvoorziening en agrarische ontwikkeling [Food supply and agricultural development]', in C.L.J. van der Meer (ed.), *Landbouw en ontwikkeling* [Agriculture and development], The Hague: Vuga, pp. 177–205.

van der Meer, C.L.J. and S. Yamada (1990) *Japanese Agriculture: An Economic Comparative Analysis*, London: Gower.

Waggoner, P.E. and J.H. Ausubel (2001) 'How Much Will Feeding More and Wealth-ier People Encroach on Forests?', *Population and Development Review*, 27(2), pp. 239–57.

Wharton, C.R. (ed.) (1970) *Subsistence Agriculture and Economic Development*, Chicago: Aldine.

Wiggins, S. (2000) 'Interpreting Changes from the 1970s to the 1990s in African Agricul-ture through Village Studies', *World Development*, 28(4), pp. 631–62.

Wolf, E. R. (1966) *Peasants*, Englewood Cliffs, NY. Prentice Hall.

World Bank, *World Development Report 1992*, Oxford University Press, 1992a.

World Bank (1992c) *World Tables 1992*, Baltimore/London: Johns Hopkins University Press 1992c.

World Bank (2002) *World Development Indicators 2002*, CD-Rom.

WWI (Worldwatch Institute) (2001) *The State of the World 2001*, ed. L. Brown et al., New York: Norton.

World Resources Institute (1990) *World Resources 1990–1991*, Oxford University Press.

World Resources Institute (2000) *World Resources 2000–2001: People and Econosystems: The Fraying Web of Life*, New York, WRI in collaboration with UNEP, UNDP and the World Bank, Oxford University Press.

Chapter 11   State formation and political aspects of development

Ahluwalia, M.S. (1976) 'Inequality, Poverty and Development', *Journal of Development Economics*, 3(4), pp. 307–42.

Ake, C. (1996) *Democracy and Development in Africa*, Washington, DC: Brookings Institution.

Alesina, A. and G. Tabellini (1989) 'External Debt, Capital Flight and Political Risk', *Journal of International Economics*, 37, pp. 199–220.

Alesina, A., S. Ozler, N. Roubine and P. Swage (1996) 'Political Instability and Economic Growth' *Journal of Economic Growth*, 1, pp. 189–211.

Ashton, B., K. Hill, A. Piazza and R. Zeitz (1984), 'Famine in China, 1958–61', *Population Development Review*, 10(4), pp. 613–45.

Alavi, H. (1979) 'The State in Post-Colonial Societies: Pakistan and Bangladesh', in H. Goulborne (ed.), *Politics and the State in the Third World*, London: Macmillan, pp. 38–70.

Amsden, A. (1989) *Asia's Next Giant: South Korea and Late Industrialization*, New York: Oxford University Press.

Anglade, C. and C. Fortin (1985) 'The State and Capital Accumulation in Latin America: A Conceptual and Historical Introduction', in C. Anglade and C. Fortin (eds.), *The State and Capital Accumulation in Latin America*, Vol. I, University of Pittsburgh Press.

Azfar, O. and Y. Lee (2001) 'The Causes and Consequences of Corruption', *The Annals of the American Academy of Political and Social Science*, 573, 1, pp. 42–57.

Banks, A.S., A.J. Day and T.C. Muller (eds.) (1998) *Political Handbook of the World*, New York: McGraw-Hill, and various volumes.

Banks A.S., W. Overstreet and T.C. Muller (eds.) (1998) *Political Handbook of the World: Governments and Intergovernmental Organizations*, London: McGraw-Hill.

Bannister, J. (1984) 'Analysis of Recent Data on the Population of China', *Population and Development Review*, X, pp. 241–71.

Bardhan, P. (1984) *The Political Economy of Development in India*, Oxford: Basil Blackwell.

Bardhan, P. (2002) 'Decentralization of Governance and Development', *Journal of Economic Perspectives*, 16, (4), Fall, pp. 185–205.

Barro, R.J. (1996) *Getting It Right: Markets and Choices in a Free Society*, Cambridge, MA: MIT Press.

Bates, R.H. (1994) 'The Impulse to Reform in Africa, in J.A. Widner (ed.), *Economic Change and Political Liberalisation in Sub-Saharan Africa*, Baltimore and London: Johns Hopkins University Press, pp. 13–28.

Bates R.H. and P. Collier (1993) 'The Politics and Economics of Policy Reform in Zambia', in: R.H. Bates and A.O. Krueger (eds.), *Political and Economic Interactions in Economic Policy Reform in Zambia*, Oxford: Basil Blackwell, p. 391 ff.

Baumol, W.J. (1990) 'Entrepreneurship, Productive, Unproductive and Destructive', *Journal of Political Economy*, 98, pp. 893–921.

Benthem van den Bergh, G. van (1980) *On the Dynamics of Development of Contemporary States: An Approach to Comparative Politics*, ISS Occasional Paper, The Hague: November.

Berghe, P.L. van den (1981) *The Ethnic Phenomenon*, New York/Oxford: Elsevier.

Bienen, H. (1971) *The Military and Modernization*, Chicago: Aldine/Atherton.

Booth, A. (1999) 'Initial Conditions and Miraculous Growth: Why is South East Asia Different from Taiwan and South Korea?', *World Development*, 27(2), February, pp. 301–21.

Bratton, M. and N. van de Walle (1997) *Democratic Experiments in Africa: Regime Transitions in Comparative Perspective*, Cambridge University Press.

Buchanan, J. and Tullock, G. (1962) *The Calculus of Consent: Logical Foundations of Constitutional Democracy*, Ann Arbor: Michigan University Press.

Cassen, R.H. (1978) *India: Population, Economy, Society*, London: Macmillan.

Chang, J. (1991) *Wild Swans: Three Daughters of China*, Doubleday: New York.

Chirot, D. (1977) *Social Change in the Twentieth Century*, New York: Harcourt, Brace and Jovanovich.

CIA, *World Factbook,* various issues, Online edition: http://www.cia.gov/cia/publications/factbook/index.html

Clapham, C. and G. Philip (eds.) (1985) *The Political Dilemmas of Military Regimes*, London: Croom Helm.

Coleman, J.S. and C.B. Rosberg Jr (eds.) (1964) *Political Parties and National Integration in Tropical Africa*, Berkeley: University of California Press.

Dahrendorf, R. (1963) *Class and Class Conflict in Industrial Society*, London: Routledge and Kegan Paul, 1963.

David, S.R. (1987) 'The Use of Proxy Forces by Major Powers in the Third World', in S.G. Neuman and R.E. Harkavy (eds.), *The Lessons of Recent Wars in the Third World*, Lexington: Heath.

Davidson, B. (1992) *The Black Man's Burden: Africa and the Curse of the Nation-State*, London: Currey.

Djilas, M. (1957) *The New Class: An Analysis of the Communist System*, New York: Praeger.

Doorenspleet, R. (2000) 'Reassessing the Three Waves of Democratization', *World Politics*, 52(3), April, pp. 384–406.

Easterly, W. (2001) 'Can Institutions Resolve Ethnic Conflict?', *Economic Development and Cultural Change*, 49(4), July, pp. 687–706.

Easterly, W. and R. Levine (1997) 'Africa's Growth Tragedy: Policies and Ethnic Divisions, *The Quarterly Journal of Economics*, November, No. 4, pp. 1203–49.

Ehrlich, I. and F.T. Lui (1999), 'Bureaucratic Corruption and Endogenous Growth', *Journal of Political Economy*, 107, pp. 270–93.

Elias, N. (1969) *Über den Prozess der Zivilisation*, 2nd edn, Bern: Franke Verlag, 1969.

Elias, N. (1979) *Die höfische Gesellschaft*, 4th edn, Darmstadt and Neuwied: Luchterhand.

Elvin, M. (1973) *The Pattern of Chinese Past*, Stanford University Press.

Evans, P. (1995) *Embedded Autonomy: States and Industrial Transformation*, Princeton University Press.

Finer, S.E. (1988) *The Man on Horseback*, 2nd enlarged edn, Boulder: Westview Press.

Fosu, A.K. (1992) 'Political Instability and Economic Growth: Evidence from Sub-Saharan Africa', *Economic Development and Cultural Change*, 40, July, pp. 829–41.

Freedom House, *Democracy's Century: A Survey of Global Political Change in the Twentieth Century*, 2000, http://www.freedomhouse.org/reports/century.html

Frey, B.D. (1978) *Modern Political Economy*, Oxford: Martin Robertson.

Furtado, C. (1976) *The Economic Development of Latin America*, Cambridge University Press.

Gavshon, A. (1981) *Crisis in Africa: Battleground of East and West*, Boulder, CO: Westview Press.

Gerschenkron, A. (1962) *Economic Backwardness in Historical Perspective*, Cambridge, MA: Harvard University Press.

Goldthorpe, J. (1979) *De derde wereld* [The Third World], The Hague: Vuga, pp. 257–79.

Grier, R.M. (2002) 'On the Interaction of Human and Physical Capital in Latin America', *Economic Development and Cultural Change*, 50(4), pp. 891–913.

Haan, J. de and C.L.J. Sierman (1993) 'Political Instability, Freedom and Economic Growth: Some Further Evidence', rev. version, Groningen, mimeograph, September.

Haan, J. de, D. Zelhorst and O. Roukens (1993) 'Seignorage in Developing Countries', *Applied Financial Economics*, 3, pp. 307–14.

Helliwell, J.F. (1994) 'Empirical Linkages between Democracy and Economic Growth', *British Journal of Political Science*, 24, pp. 225–48.

Hirschman, A. (1973) 'The Changing Tolerance for Income Inequality in the Course of Economic Development', *World Development*, 1(12), December, pp. 29–36.

Hoogen, T.J. van den (1992) 'Security and Third World States: A Conceptual Analysis', *Development and Security*, No. 38, Centre for Development Studies, University of Groningen, December.

Hopkins, A.G. (1973) *An Economic History of West Africa*, London: Longman.

Hsu, R.C. (1982) *Food for One Billion: China's Agriculture since 1949*, Boulder, CO: Westview Press.

Huntington, S.P. (1991) *The Third Wave, Democratisation in the Late Twentieth Century*, Tulsa, OK: University of Oklahoma Press.

Isichei, E. (1997) *A History of African Societies to 1870*, Cambridge University Press.

Jackson, R. and C. Rosberg (1982) *Personal Rule in Black Africa*, Berkeley: University of California Press.

Jackson, R. and C. Rosberg (1986) 'Sovereignty and Underdevelopment: Juridical State-hood in the African Crisis', *The Journal of Modern African Studies*, 24(1), pp. 1–31.

Jain, A.K. (ed.) (2001) *The Political Economy of Corruption*, London and New York: Routledge.

Janowitz, M. (ed.) (1981) *Civil-Military Regimes: Regional Perspectives*, London: Sage.

Johnston, M. (2001) 'Measuring Corruption: Numbers versus Knowledge versus Under-standing' in Jain (ed.), *Political Economy of Corruption*, pp. 157–79.

Kellas, J.G. (1991) *The Politics of Nationalism and Ethnicity*, London: Macmillan.

Kende, I. (1972) *Local Wars in Asia, Africa and Latin America, 1945–1969*, Center for Afro- Asian Research, Studies of Developing Countries, No. 60, Budapest.

Kennedy, P. (1989) *The Rise and Fall of the Great Powers*, New York: Vintage Books.

Keyfitz, N. (1991) *The Demography of the Fission of Empires*, Population Research Centre, Groningen, November.

Kidron, M. and D. Smith (1983) *The War Atlas: Armed Conflict – Armed Peace*, London: Heinemann.

Kidron, M. and D. Smith (1991) *The New State of War and Peace*, New York: Simon and Schuster, 1991.

Kiely, R. (1998) *Industrialisation and Development: A Comparative Analysis*, London: UCL Press.

Kitching, G. (1982) *Development and Underdevelopment in Historical Perspective*, London: Methuen.

Klein, H.S. (1999) *The Atlantic Slave Trade*, Cambridge University Press.

Kuznets, S. (1995) 'Economic Growth and Income Inequality', *American Economic Review*, 45(1), pp. 1–28.

Kuznets, S. (1966) *Modern Economic Growth: Rate, Structure and Spread*, New Haven, CT: Yale University Press.

Lal, D. (1984) *The Political Economy of the Predatory State*, Development Research Papers, No. 105, Washington, DC: World Bank.

Lane, D. (1971) *The End of Inequality? Stratification under State Socialism*, Harmondsworth: Penguin.

Leys, S. (1978) *Ombres Chinois* [Chinese Shadows], Paris: Laffont.

Lijphart, A. (2000) *Democracy in the Twenty-First Century: Can We Be Optimistic?*', Uhlenbeck Lecture 18, Wassenaar: NIAS.

Lin, J.Y., F. Cai and Z. Li (2000) 'The Lessons of China's Transition to a Market Economy', paper for APSEM/ANU/World Bank conference, Achieving High Growth, experience of Transitional Economies in East Asia, Canberra, 6/7 September.

Lipset, S.M. (1959) 'Some Social Prerequisites of Democracy, Economic Development and Political Legitimacy' *American Political Science Review*, 53, pp. 69–105.

Luttwak, E. (1979) *Coup d'Etat. A Practical Handbook*, London: Wildwood House.

McGowan, P.J. (2003) 'African Military Coups d'Etat, 1956–2001: Frequency, Trends and Distribution', *Journal of Modern African Studies*, 41(30), pp. 339–70.

McGowan, P.J. and T.H. Johnson (1984) 'African Military Coups d'Etat and Under-development: A Quantitative Historical Analysis', *Journal of Modern African Studies*, 22(4), pp. 633–66.

Maddison, A. (1969) *Economic Growth in Japan and the USSR*, New York: Norton.

Maddison, A. (1974) *Class Structure and Economic Growth in India and Pakistan*, London: Allen and Unwin.

Maddison, A. (1986) 'Marx and Bismarck; Capitalism and Government, 1883–1953', in H.J. Wagener and J.W. Drukker (eds.), *The Economic Law of Motion of Modern Society: A Marx, Keynes, Schumpeter Centennial*, Cambridge University Press.

Maddison, A., *The Chinese Economy in the Long Run*, Paris, OECD Development Centre, 1998.

Maddison, A. and Associates (1992) *Brazil and Mexico, The Political Economy of Poverty, Equity and Growth*, A World Bank Comparative Study, Oxford University Press.

Mair, L. (1967) *Primitive Government*, Harmondsworth: Penguin Books.

Marshall, M.G. (2003) *Major Episodes of Political Violence, 1946–2002*, Centre for Systemic Peace, University of Maryland, http://members.aol.com/cspmgm/warlist.htm, updated 25 May.

Marshall, M.G. and T.R. Gurr (2003) *Peace and Conflict, 2003: A Global Survey of Armed Conflicts, Self-Determination Movements and Democracy*, Centre for International Development and Conflict Resolution, University of Maryland.

Marx, K. (1848) *The Communist Manifesto*, New York: Appleton Century Cross, 1955.

Mauro, P. (1995) 'Corruption and Growth', *Quarterly Journal of Economics*, 110(3), August 1995, pp. 681–712.

Mauro, P. (2000) 'The Effects of Corruption on Growth, Investment and Government Expenditure', in: A.J. Heidenheimer and M. Johnston (eds.), *Political Corruption*, New Brunswick, NJ: Transaction.

Meer, C.L.J. van der and S. Yamada (1990) *Japanese Agriculture: An Economic Comparative Analysis*, London: Gower.

Moore, B. Jr. (1967) *Social Origins of Dictatorship and Democracy: Lord and Peasant in the Making of the Modern World*, Harmondsworth: The Penguin Press.

Murphy, K., Shleifer, A. and R. Vishny (1991) 'The Allocation of Talent: Implications for Growth', *Quarterly Journal of Economics*, 106, May, pp. 503–30.

Myint, H. (1980) *The Economics of the Developing Countries*, 5th edn, London: Hutchinson.

Myrdal, G. (1968) *Asian Drama: An Inquiry into the Poverty of Nations*, Harmondsworth: Penguin.

Ndulu, B. and S.A. O'Connell (1999) 'Governance and Growth in Sub-Saharan Africa', *Journal of Economic Perspectives*, 13(3), Summer, pp. 41–66.

Nettle, D. (2000) 'Linguistic Fragmentation and the Wealth of Nations: The Fishman–Pool Hypothesis Reexamined', *Economic Development and Cultural Change*, 48(2), January, pp. 335–48.

North, D.C. and R.P. Thomas (1973) *The Rise of the Western World: A New Economic History*, Cambridge University Press.

O'Connor, J. (1973) *The Fiscal Crisis of the State*, New York: St. Martin's Press.

O'Donnell, G. (1979) *Modernization and Bureaucratic-Authoritarianism in South American Politics*, Berkeley: University of California Press.

Olson, M. (1965) *The Logic of Collective Action*, Cambridge, MA: Harvard University Press.

Olson, M. (1982) *The Rise and Decline of Nations*, New Haven and London: Yale University Press.

Philip, G. (1985) 'Military Rule in South America: The Dilemmas of Authoritarianism', in C. Clapham and G. Philip (eds.), *The Political Dilemmas of Military Regimes*, London: Croom Helm.

Pilat, D. (1994) *The Economics of Rapid Growth: The Experience of Japan and Korea*, Aldershot: Edward Elgar.

Rawski, T.G. (1979) *Economic Growth and Employment in China*, World Bank, New York/Oxford: Oxford University Press.

Ricklefs, M.C. (1981) *A History of Modern Indonesia*, London: Macmillan.

Righart, H. et al., *De trage revolutie: Over de wording van industriële samenlevingen* [The Slow Revolution: On the Origin of Industrial Societies], Boom: Open University.

Sachs, J.D. and W.T. Woo (1997) 'Understanding China's Economic Performance', Harvard Institute for International Development/University of California, Mimeograph, May.

Sandbrook, R. (1986) 'The State as an Obstacle to Development', *World Development*, 14(3), pp. 309–22.

Sandbrook, R. and J. Barker (1985) *The Politics of Africa's Economic Stagnation*, Cambridge University Press.

Schama, S. (1988) *The Embarrassment of Riches*, New York: Fontana Press.

Schoenmakers, H. (1992) 'Staatsvorming, Rurale Ontwikkeling en boeren in Guinée Bissau' [State Formation, Rural Development and Peasants in Guinea Bissau], Dissertation, Catholic University Nijmegen.

Schumpeter, J. (1946) *Capitalism, Socialism and Democracy*, London: Allen and Unwin.

Scully, G.W. (1988) 'The Institutional Framework and Economic Development', *Journal of Political Economy*, 96(October), pp. 652–62.

Shils, E. (1964) 'The Military in the Political Development of New States', in J. Johnson (ed.), *The Military and Society in Latin America*, Palo Alto, CA: Stanford University Press, pp. 7–67.

Sirowy, L. and A. Inkeles (1990), 'The Effects of Democracy on Economic Growth and Inequality: A Review', *Studies in Comparative International Development*, 25(1), Spring, pp. 126–57.

Sivard, R. (1991) *World Military and Social Expenditures*, Washington, DC: World Priorities.

Skocpol, T. (1979) *States and Social Revolutions*, Cambridge, MA: Cambridge University Press.

Small, M. and J.D. Singer (1982) *Resort to Arms: International and Civil Wars, 1816–1980*, Beverly Hills: Sage.

Smith, D. (1997) *The State of War and Peace Atlas*, International Peace Research Institute, Oslo, London: Penguin.

Starr, H. and B.A. Most (1985) 'Patterns of Conflict: Quantitative Analysis and the Comparative Lessons of Third World Wars', in R.E. Harkavy and S.G. Neuman (eds.), *The Lessons of Recent Wars in the Third World*, Vol. I, Lexington: Lexington Books, pp. 33–52.

Szirmai, A. (1988) *Inequality Observed: A Study of Attitudes towards Income Inequality*, Aldershot: Avebury Press.

Szirmai, A, B. van Ark and D. Pilat (eds.) (1993) *Explaining Economic Growth: Essays in Honour of Angus Maddison*, Amsterdam: North Holland.

Szirmai, A. and R. Ren (2000) 'Comparative Performance in Chinese Manufacturing, 1980–92', *China Economic Review*, 11(1), pp. 16–53.

Szirmai, A., M. Bai and R. Ren (2001) *Labour Productivity Trends in Chinese Manufacturing, 1980–99*, Eindhoven Centre for Innovation Studies Working Paper, 2001, No. 10, Eindhoven, October.

Tanzi, V. and H. Davoodi (2001) 'Corruption, Growth and Public Finances', in A.K. Jain (ed.), *The Political Economy of Corruption*, pp. 89–110.

Taylor, C.L. and M.C. Hudson (1972) *World Handbook of Political and Social Indicators*, New York: Yale University Press.

Taylor, C.L. and D.A. Jodice (1983) *World Handbook of Political and Social Indicators*, New Haven: Yale University Press.

Terhal, P. (1992) 'Economic Growth and Political Insecurity: Towards a Multidisciplinary Approach', Development and Security, No. 36, August 1992, Centre for Development Studies, Groningen.

Thomas, C. (1987) *In Search of Security: The Third World in International Relations*, Boulder CO: Lynne Rienner.

Tilly, C. (ed.) (1975) *The Formation of National States in Western Europe*, Princeton University Press.

Tilly, R. (1986) 'Financing Industrial Enterprise in Great Britain and Germany in the Nineteenth Century: Testing Grounds for Marxist and Schumpeterian Theories?', in H.J. Wagener and J.W. Drukker, *The Economic Law of Motion of Modern Society*.

Transparancy International, *Corruption Perceptions Index (CPI)*, www.transparency.org/documents/cpi

Tullock, G. (1965) *The Politics of Bureaucracy*, Washington, DC, Public Affairs Press.

Urquidi, V. (1993) 'The Developmentalist Perspective', in Szirmai, van Ark and Pilat (1993).

Wagener, H.J. and J.W. Drukker (eds.) (1986) *The Economic Law of Motion of Modern Society: A Marx, Keynes, Schumpeter Centennial*, Cambridge University Press.

Walle, N. van de (1994) 'Neopatrimonialism and Democracy in Africa, with an Illustration from Cameroun' in J. Widner (ed.), *Economic Change and Political Liberalization in Sub-Saharan African*, Baltimore: Johns Hopkins University Press.

Wallerstein, I. (1974) *The Modern World System*, New York: Academic Press.

Weber, M. (1922) *Wirtschaft und Gesellschaft*, Tübingen: Mohr.

Wei, S. (1997a) *How Taxing is Corruption on International Investors?*, NBER Working Paper no. 6030, Cambridge, MA: National Bureau of Economic Research.

Wei, S. (1997b) *Why is Corruption So Much More Taxing than Tax?*, NBER Working Paper no. 2048, Cambridge, MA: National Bureau of Economic Research.

White, G. (1984) 'Developmental States and Socialist Industrialisation in the Third World', *Journal of Development Studies*, 20, pp. 97–120.

White, M. (2003) *Death Tolls for the Major Wars and Atrocities of the Twentieth Century* (http://users.erols.com/mwhite28/warstats.htm), last update January.

WHO (2002) *World Report on Violence and Health*, Geneva: WHO.

Widner, J.A. (ed.) (1994) *Economic Change and Political Liberalisation in Sub-Saharan Africa*, Baltimore and London: Johns Hopkins University Press.

World Bank (1997) *World Development Report 1997: The State in a Changing World*, New York: Oxford University Press.

Worsley, P. (1967) *The Third World*, 2nd edn, London: Weidenfeld and Nicolson.

Zolberg, A.R. (1966) *Creating Political Order: The Party States of West Africa*, Chicago: Rand McNally.

Chapter 12   Cultural dimensions of development

Adams, J. (2001) 'Culture and Economic Development in South Asia', in C. Clague and S. Grossbard-Shechtman (eds.), *Culture and Development: International Perspectives, Special Issue of the Annals of the American Academy of Political and Social Science*, 573 (January), pp. 152–73.

Ball, R., 'Individualism, Collectivism and Economic Development', in Clague and Grossbard-Shechtman (eds.), *Culture and Development*, pp. 57–84.

Banfield, E.C. (1958) *The Moral Basis of a Backward Society*, New York: Free Press.

Bauer, P. and B.S. Yamey (1957) *The Economics of Under-developed Countries*, University of Chicago Press.

Bell, D. (1971) 'The Cultural Contradictions of Capitalism', in D. Bell, and I. Kristol (eds.), *Capitalism Today*, New York: Basic Books.

Boeke, J.H. (1947) *Oriental Economics*, New York, Institute of Pacific Relations.

Boeke, J.H. (1961) 'Dualistische Economie 1930', reprinted in J.H. Boeke, *Indonesian Economics: The Concept of Dualism in Theory and Practice*, The Hague: W. van Hoeve.

Boserup, E. (1981) *Population and Technology*, University of Chicago Press.

Clague, C. and S. Grossbard-Shechtman (eds.) (2001) *Culture and Development: International Perspectives, Special Issue of the Annals of the American Academy of Political and Social Science*, 573 (January).

Cochrane, G. (1979) *The Cultural Appraisal of Development Projects*, New York: Praeger.

Dia, M. (1994) 'Indigenous Management Practices: Lessons for Africa's Management in the 90s', in I. Serageldin and J. Taboroff (eds.), *Culture and Development in Africa*, Washington, DC: World Bank, pp. 165–91.

Diamond, J. (1998) *Guns, Germs and Steel: The Fates of Human Societies*, New York: Norton.

Dore, R.P. (1987) *Taking Japan Seriously: A Confucian Perspective on Leading Economic Issues*, Stanford University Press.

Dumont, R. (1962) *L'Afrique Noire est Mal Partie* [False Start in Black Africa], Paris: Editions du Seuil.

Elias, N. (1969) 'Zur Soziogenese des Begriffs "Civilisation" in Frankreich', in N. Elias, *Über den Prozess der Zivilisation*, Erster Band, Bern und München: Franke Verlag, pp. 43–64.

Evers, H.D. and H. Schraders (eds.) (1994) *The Moral Economy of Trade: Ethnicity and Developing Markets*, London: Routledge.

Fang, T. (2003) 'A Critique of Hofstede's Fifth National Culture Dimension', *International Journal of Cross Cultural Management*, 3(3), pp. 351–72.

Geertz, C. (1963) *Peddlers and Princes: Social Change and Economic Modernization in Two Indonesian Towns*, University of Chicago Press, 1963.

Goodell, G. (1995/6) 'Another Way to Skin a Cat, The Spirit of Capitalism and the Confucian Ethic', *The National Interest*, Winter, pp. 66–71.

Harrison, L.E. (1985) *Underdevelopment Is a State of Mind: The Latin American Case*, Boston, MA: Madison Books.

Harrison, L.E. and S.P. Huntington (eds.) (2000) *Culture Matters: How Values Shape Human Progress*, New York: Basic Books.

Hartz, L. (1964) *The Founding of New Societies*, New York: Harcourt Brace and World Inc.

Hirschman, A.O. (1967) *Development Projects Observed*, Washington, DC: Brookings Institution, 1967 (qtd in R. Klitgaard, 1994).

Hoetink, H. (1984) 'Culture vs. Progress? Notes on the Cultural Aspects of the US–Latin American Relations', in C.A.D. van Nieuwenhuijze (ed.), *Development Regardless of Culture*, Leiden: Brill.

Hofstede, G. (1991) *Cultures and Organisations: Software of the Mind*, London: McGraw-Hill, 1991.

Hofstede, G. (2001) *Culture's Consequences: Comparing Values, Behaviors, Institutions and Organizations Across Nations*, 2nd edn, London: Sage Publications (first published 1980).

Hofstede, G. and M.H. Bond (1988), 'The Confucius Connection: From Cultural Roots to Economic Growth', *Organization Dynamics*, 16(4), pp. 5–21.

Huntington, S.P. (2000) 'Cultures Count' in L.E. Harrison and S. P. Huntington (eds.), *Culture Matters: How Values Shape Human Progress*, New York: Basic Books, pp. xiii–xvi.

Inkeles, A. and D.H. Smith (1974) *Becoming Modern: Individual Change in Six Developing Countries*, Cambridge, MA: Harvard University Press.

Kerr, C. et al. (1962) *Industrialism and Industrial Man: The problems of Labour and Management in Economic Growth*, London, Heinemann.

Klitgaard, R. (1994) 'Taking Culture into Account: From "Let's" to "How"' in I. Sarageldin and J. Taboroff (eds.), *Culture and Development in Africa*, Washington, DC: World Bank, pp. 75–120.

Kottak, C.P. (1986) 'Dimensions of Culture in Development', in UNESCO, *The Cultural Dimension of Development*, The Hague: UNESCO 1986.

Kottak, C.P. (1991) 'When People Don't Come First: Some Sociological lessons from Completed Projects', in M. Cernea (ed.), *Putting People First: Sociological Variables in Rural Development*, 2nd edn., New York: Oxford University Press.

Kuper, A.J. (1984) 'African Culture and African Development', in C.A.O. van Nieuwenhuijze (ed.), *Development Regardless of Culture*, Brill: Leiden.

Lal, D. (1988) *The Hindu Equilibrium*, Vol. I: *Cultural Stability and Economic Stagnation: India, c. 1500 BC–AD, 1980*, Oxford University Press.

Landes, D. (2000) 'Culture Makes Almost All the Difference', in L.E. Harrison and S.P. Huntington (eds.), *Culture Matters: How Values Shape Human Progress*, New York: Basic Books, pp. 2–13.

Levy, M. and K. Shih (1949) *The Rise of Modern Chinese Business Class: Two Introductory Essays*, New York: Institute of Pacific Relations.

Lewis, M.K. and L.M. Algaoud (2001) *Islamic Banking*, Cheltenham: Edward Elgar.

McClelland, D. (1961) *The Achieving Society*, Princeton, NJ: Van Nostrand.

Maddison, A. (1974) *Class Structure and Economic Growth in India and Pakistan*, London: Allen and Unwin.

Moore, B. Jr (1967) *Social Origins of Dictatorship and Democracy: Lord and Peasant in the Making of the Modern World*, Harmondsworth: The Penguin Press.

Naipaul, V.S. (1982) *Among the Believers. An Islamic Journey*, New York: Vintage Books.

North, D.C. (1990) *Institutions, Institutional Change and Economic Performance*, Cambridge University Press.

North, D.C. and R.P. Thomas (1973) *The Rise of the Western World*, Cambridge University Press.

Nyang, S.S. (1994) 'The Cultural Consequences of Development in Africa', in I. Serageldin and J. Taboroff (eds.), *Culture and Development in Africa*, Washington, DC: World Bank, pp. 429–46.

Patterson, O. (2000) 'Taking Culture Seriously: A Framework and an Afro-American Illustration', in L.E. Harrison and S.P. Huntington (eds.), *Culture Matters: How Values Shape Human Progress*, New York: Basic Books, pp. 202–18.

Perkins, D. (2000) 'Law, Family Ties and the East Asian Way of Business', in L.E. Harrison and S.P. Huntington (eds.), *Culture Matters: How Values Shape Human Progress*, New York: Basic Books, pp. 232–43.

Plattner, S. (ed.) (1989) *Economic Anthropology*, Stanford University Press.

Putnam, R.D. (with R. Leonardi and R.Y. Nanetti) (1993) *Making Democracy Work: Civic Traditions in Modern Italy*, Princeton University Press.

Putnam, R.D. (1994) 'Democracy, Development and the Civic Community: Evidence from an Italian Experiment', in I. Serageldin and J. Taboroff (eds.), *Culture and Development in Africa*, Washington, DC: World Bank, pp. 33–73.

Pye, L. (2000) 'Asian Values: From Dynamos to Dominoes', in L.E. Harrison and S.P. Huntington (eds.), *Culture Matters: How Values Shape Human Progress*, New York: Basic Books, pp. 244–54.

Rao, V. (2001) Poverty and Public Celebrations in Rural India', in C. Clague, and S. Grossbard-Shechtman (eds.), *Culture and Development: International Perspectives, Special Issue of the Annals of the American Academy of Political and Social Science*, 573 (January) p. 85–104.

Sachs, J. (2000) 'Notes on a New Sociology of Economic Development', in L.E. Harrison and S.P. Huntington (eds.), *Culture Matters*, pp. 29–43.

Salim, S.A. (1994) 'Opening Remarks', in I. Serageldin and J. Taboroff (eds.), *Culture and Development in Africa*, Washington, DC: World Bank, pp. 9–14.

Schech, S. and J. Haggis (2000) *Culture and Development. A Critical Introduction*, Oxford: Basil Blackwell.

Schönhut, M. (ed.) (1991) *The Socio-Cultural Dimension of Development: The Contribution of Sociologists and Social Anthropologists to the Work of Development Agencies*, Eschborn: Deutsche Gesellschaft für Technische Wissenschaften.

Schumpeter, J.A. (1976) *Capitalism, Socialism and Democracy*, London: Allen and Unwin (first published 1943).

Sen, A.K. (1999) *Development as Freedom*, New York: Anchor Books.

Senghaas, D. (1984) 'Kultur und Entwicklung. Überlegungen zur aktuellen Entwicklungspolitischen Diskussion [Culture and Development: Reflections on Current Issues in the Politics of Development]', *Zeitschrift für Kultur* [Journal for Culture], no. 4, pp. 417–24.

Serageldin, I. (1994) The Challenge of a Holistic Vision: Culture, Empowerment and the Development Paradigm', in I. Serageldin and J. Taboroff (eds.), *Culture and Development in Africa*, Washington, DC: World Bank, pp. 15–32.

Serageldin, I. and J. Taboroff (eds.) (1994) *Culture and Development in Africa*, Washington, DC: World Bank.

Shweder, R.A. (2000) 'Moral Maps, "First World" Conceits and the New Evangelists', in L.E. Harrison and S.P. Huntington (eds.), *Culture Matters: How Values Shape Human Progress*, New York: Basic Books, pp. 158–72.

Tawney, R.H. (1947) *Religion and the Rise of Capitalism: A Historical Study*: New York: Penguin (first published 1926).

Trevor-Roper, H. (1972) *Religion, The Reformation and Social Change, and Other Essays*, London: Macmillan.

UNDP (2002) *Arab Human Development Report 2002: Creating Opportunities for Future Generations*, New York: UNDP.

Weber, M. (1969) 'Die Protestantische Ethik und der Geist des Kapitalismus' [The Protestant Ethic and the Spirit of Capitalism], in *Die Protestantische Ethik*, ed. J. Winckelmann, Munich: Siebenstern (first published 1905).

Weber, M. (1920) *Gesammelte Aufsätze zur Religions-soziologie* [Collected Essays on the Sociology of Religion], vol. I, Tübingen: Mohr.

Weisner, T.S. (2000) 'Culture, Childhood and Progress in Sub-Saharan Africa', in L.E. Harrison and S.P. Huntington (eds.), *Culture Matters: How Values Shape Human Progress*, New York: Basic Books, pp. 141–57.

Wilk, R. (1996) *Economies and Cultures: Foundations of Economic Anthropology*, Boulder, CD: Westview.

Worsley, P. (1957) *The Trumpet Shall Sound: A Study of 'Cargo Cults' in Melanesia*, London: McGibbon and Kee.

Chapter 13 The international economic and political order since 1945

Adelman, I. (2000) 'Editor's Introduction', Special Issue on Architecture of Global Financial Systems, *World Development*, 28(6), pp. 1053–60.

Adelman, A. and E. Yeldan (2000) 'The Minimal Conditions for A Financial Crisis: A Multi-regional Intertemporal CGE Model of the Asian Crisis', *World Development*, 28(6), pp. 1087–100.

Athukorala, P. (2001) *Crisis and Recovery in Malaysia: The Role of Capital Controls*, Cheltenham: Edward Elgar.

Baehr, P.R. (1992) 'De rol van internationale organisaties sinds 1945 [The Role of International Organisations since 1945]', in D.F.J. Bosscher, H. Renner, R.B. Soetendorp and R. Wagenaar (eds.), *De wereld na 1945* [The World since 1945], Utrecht: Het Spectrum, Aula.

Bhagwati, J.N. (1977) *The New International Order: The North–South Debate*, Cambridge, MA: MIT.

Bhagwati, J.N. (1988) *Protectionism*, Cambridge, MA: MIT Press.

Boote, A.R. and K. Thugge (1997) *Debt Relief for Low-Income Countries and the HIPC initiative*, Working Paper of the International Monetary Fund, IMF, March.

Brandt, W. *et al.* (1980) *North-South: A Programme for Survival*, London, Sydney: Pan Books.

Buiter, W.H. and T.N. Srinivasan (1987) 'Rewarding the Profligate and Punishing the Prudent and Poor: Some Recent Proposals for Debt Relief', *World Development*, 15(3), pp. 411–17.

Burk, K. (1990) 'The International Environment', in A. Graham and A. Seldon (eds.), *Government and Economies in the Postwar World*, London: Routledge.

Caballero, R.J. (2003) 'The Future of the IMF', *The American Economic Review*, 93(2), May, pp. 31–8.

Chenery, H. et al. (1974) *Redistribution with Growth*, London: Oxford University Press.

Citrin, D. and S. Fischer (2000) 'Strengthening the International Financial System: Key Issues', *World Development*, 28(6), pp. 1133–42.

Corden, W. (1979) *The NIEO Proposals: A Cool Look*, London: Trade Policy Research Centre.

Cornia, G.A., R. van der Hoeven and T. Mkandawire (eds.), *Africa's Recovery in the 1990s: From Stagnation and Adjustment to Human Development*, UNICEF, New York: St. Martin's Press.

Cornia, G.A., R. Jolly and F. Stewart (eds.) (1987) *Adjustment with a Human Face*, Oxford: Clarendon.

Dicken, P. (2003) *Global Shift: Reshaping the Global Map in the 21st Century*, 4th edn, London: Sage Publications.

Dijkstra, A.G. (2000) 'Trade Liberalization and Industrial Development in Latin America', *World Development*, 28(9), pp. 1567–82.

Dijkstra, A.G. and J.K. van Donge (2001) 'What Does the "Show Case" Show? Evidence of and Lessons from Adjustment in Uganda", *World Development*, 20(5), pp. 841–63.

Doroodian, K. (1993) 'Macroeconomic Performance and Adjustment under Policies Commonly Supported by the International Monetary Fund', *Economic Development and Cultural Change*, 41(4), July, pp. 349–64.

Dunning, J. (1988) 'Trade, Location of Economic Activity and the Multinational Enterprise: A Search for an Eclectic Approach, in J. Dunning, *Explaining International Production*, London: Unwin Hyman, pp. 13–40.

Easterly, W. (2000) *How did Highly Indebted Poor Countries Become Highly Indebted? Reviewing two Decades of Debt Relief*, Washington, DC: World Bank, mimeograph.

Easterly, W. (2001a) *The Elusive Quest for Growth*, Cambridge, MA: MIT Press.

Edwards, S. (1990) 'The Sequencing of Economic Reform: Analytical Issues and Lessons from Latin America', *The World Economy*, 13, pp. 1–14.

Eichengreen, B. (2000) 'Taming Capital Flows', *World Development*, 28(6), pp. 1105–116.

Elbadawi, I.A. (1992) *Have World Bank-Supported Adjustment Programs Improved Economic Performance in Sub-Saharan Africa?*, World Bank, Policy Research Working Papers, WPS 1001, October.

Elbadawi, I.A., D. Ghura and G. Uwugaren (1992) *Why Structural Adjustment Has Not Succeeded in Sub-Saharan Africa*, World Bank, Policy Research Working Papers, WPS 1000, October.

Emmer, P.C. (1992) 'De contractie van het Westen: de dekolonisatie na 1945 [Contraction of the West: Decolonisation after 1945]', in D.F.J. Bosscher, H. Renner, R.B. Soetendorp and R. Wagenaar (eds.), *De Wereld na 1945*, Utrecht: Het Spectrum, Aula.

Fey, J.N. (1985) 'GATT – Een vlucht naar voren? [GATT – An Escape Forwards?]', *Internationale Spectator*, 39(11), November, pp. 670–8.

Fischer, S. (2003) 'Globalization and its Challenges', Richard T. Ely Lecture, *American Economic Review*, 93(2), May, pp. 1–30.

Fitzpatrick, J. (1983) *Trade and the Lomé Convention*, Lomé briefing, No. 9.

Franck, T.M. and M.M. Munansangu (1982) *The New International Economic Order: International Law in the Making*, New York: United Nations Institute for Training and Research.

Gillis, M., D.H. Perkins, M. Roemer and D.R. Snodgrass (1992) *Economics of Development*, 3rd edn, New York: W.W. Norton and Co.

Gore, C. (2000) 'The Rise and Fall of the Washington Consensus as a Paradigm for Developing Countries', *World Development*, 28(5), pp. 789–804.

Grassman, S. and E. Lundberg (eds.) (1981) *The World Economic Order: Past and Present*, London: Macmillan.

Greenaway, D. and O. Morrissey (1993) 'Structural Adjustment and Liberalisation in Developing Countries: What Lessons Have We Learned?', *Kyklos*, 46, pp. 241–61.

Griffin, K. (1988) 'Toward a Cooperative Settlement of the Debt Problem', *Finance and Development*, June, pp. 12–14.

Grilli, E.R. and C.Y. Maw (1998) 'Primary Commodity Prices, Manufactured Goods Prices, and the Terms of Trade of Developing Countries: What the Long Run Shows', *The World Bank Economic Review*, 2(1), pp. 1–47.

Grimal, H. (1978) *Decolonization: The British, French, Dutch and Belgian Empires, 1919–1963*, London: Routledge and Kegan Paul.

Gunning, J.W. (1988) 'Structurele aanpassing en armoedebestrijding: de rol van de Wereldbank [Structural Adjustment and Poverty Prevention: The Role of the World Bank]', *Internationale Spectator*, December, pp. 751–5.

Helleiner, G.K. (1989) 'Transnational Corporations and Direct Foreign Investment', in H. Chenery and T.N. Srinivasan (eds.), *Handbook of Development Economics*, Vol. II, Chapter 28, Amsterdam: North Holland, pp. 1387–1439.

Helleiner, G.K. (1992a) 'The IMF, the World Bank and Africa's Adjustment and External Debt Problems: An Unofficial View', *World Development*, 20(June), pp. 779–92.

Helleiner, G.K. (1992b) 'Structural Adjustment and Long-Term Development in Sub-Saharan Africa', in F. Stewart, S. Lall and S. Wangwe (eds.), *Alternative Development Strategies in Sub-Saharan Africa*, Basingstoke: Macmillan Press.

Hermes, C.L.M. (1992) *De internationale schuldencrisis* [The International Debt Crisis], Groningen: Wolters-Noordhoff.

Hill, H. (1999) *The Indonesian Economy in Crisis: Causes, Consequences and Lessons*, Singapore: Institute of South East Asian Studies.

Hofman, A. (1993) 'Economic Development in Latin America in the 20th Century', in A. Szirmai, B. van Ark and D. Pilat (1993), *Explaining Economic Growth*, pp. 241–66.

Husain, I. (1993) 'Structural Adjustment and the Long-Term Development of Sub-Saharan Africa', Paper presented at the International Seminar of Structural Adjustment and Long-Term Development in Sub-Saharan Africa: Research and Policy Issues, DGIS, The Hague, 1–3 June, 1993.

IDA/IMF (2003) *Heavily Indebted Poor Countries (HIPC) Initiative – Statistical Update*, International Development Association, IMF, IDA/R2003–0042/2, 11, April.

IMF (1992) *International Financial Statistics Yearbook*, Washington, DC, 1992.

IMF (1995) *International Financial Statistics*, Washington, DC, February, 1995.

IMF (2001) *International Financial Statistics Yearbook 2001*, Washington, DC: IMF.

Johnson, H.G. (1967) *Economic Policies towards Less Developed Countries*, Washington, DC: Brookings.

Knack, S. (2001) 'Aid Dependence and the Quality of Governance: A Cross-Country Empirical Analysis', *Southern Economic Journal*, 68(2), pp. 310–29.

Krueger, A.O. (1990) *Theory and Practice of Commercial Policy 1945–90*, Cambridge, MA: NBER, Working Paper, No. 3569, December.

Krueger, A.O. (1992) *Economic Policy Reform in Developing Countries*, Cambridge, MA/Oxford: Blackwell.

Krueger, A.O. (1993) *Free Trade Agreements as Protectionist Devices: Rules of Origin*, Cambridge, MA: NBER.

Krueger, A.O. and R. Duncan (1993) *The Political Economy of Controls: Complexity*, Cambridge, MA: NBER.

Lensink, R., (1993) *External Finance and Development*, Groningen: Wolters-Noordhoff.

Lensink, R. (1995) *Structural Adjustment in Sub-Saharan Africa*, London: Longman.

Lewis, A. (1978) *The Evolution of the International Economic Order*, Princeton University Press.

Maddison, A. (1982) *International Economic Orders Past and Present: The West and the Rest since 1500*, in Syllabus Leergang Ontwikkelingsproblematiek [Syllabus for Development Studies], Groningen, pp. 23–38.

Maddison, A. (1985) *Two Crises: Latin America and Asia 1929–38 and 1973–83*, Paris: OECD.

Maddison, A. (1989) *The World Economy in the Twentieth Century*, Paris: OECD.

Maddison, A. (1995) *Monitoring the World Economy*, OECD Development Centre, Paris: OECD.

Maddison, A. (2001) *The World Economy: A Millennial Perspective*, Development Centre Studies, Paris: OECD.

Maddison, A. (2003) *The World Economy: Historical Statistics*, Development Centre Studies, Paris: OECD.

Marshall, M.G. and T.R. Gurr (2003) *Peace and Conflict, 2003: A Global Survey of Armed Conflicts, Self-Determination Movements and Democracy*, Centre for International Development and Conflict Resolution, University of Maryland.

Meier, G. (1984) *Emerging from Poverty: The Economics that Really Matters*, New York: Oxford University Press.

Meltzer, A.H. (2000) *Report of the International Financial Institution Advisory Commission*, Washington, DC, International Financial Institution Advisory Commission US, Government Printing Office, March.

Menshikov, S., 'The Socialist Experiment' and Transition towards the Market', in A. Szirmai, B. van Ark and D. Pilat (1993), *Explaining Economic Growth*, pp. 467–84.

Morris-Jones, W.H. and G. Fischer (1980) *Decolonisation and After: The British and French Experience*, London: Frank Cass and Co.

Mosley, P. (1991) 'Structural Adjustment: A General Overview 1980–89', in V.N. Balasubramanyam and S. Lall (eds.), *Current Issues in Development Economics*, London: Macmillan.

Mosley, P., J. Harrigan and J. Toye (1991) *Aid and Power: The World Bank and Policy Based Lending*, Vol. I, *Analysis and Policy Proposals*, Vol. II, *Case Studies*, London: Routledge.

Mosley, P. and J. Weeks (1992) *Has Recovery Begun? Africa's Adjustment in the 1980s Revisited*, Department of Economics, School of Oriental and African Studies, Working Paper, No. 29, November.

Mosley, P., T. Subasat and J. Weeks (1995) 'Assessing Adjustment in Africa', *World Development*, 23(9), pp. 1459–73.

Myint, H. (1980) *The Economics of the Developing Countries*, 5th edn, London: Hutchinson.

Nerfin, M. (1985) 'The Future of the United Nations System: Some Questions on the Occasion of an Anniversary', *Development Dialogue*, No. 1, pp. 1–23.

Neumayer, E. (2002) 'Is Good Governance Rewarded? A Cross-National Analysis of Debt Forgiveness', *World Development*, 30(6), pp. 913–30.

OECD (1979) *The Impact of the Newly Industrializing Countries*, Paris: OECD.

OECD (2003) Development Assistance Committee, *Geographical Distribution of Financial Flows to Aid Recipients, 1960–2001,* CD-Rom, International Development Statistics (IDS), Paris: OECD.

Perez, C. and L.L. Soete (1988), 'Catching up in Technology: Entry Barriers and Windows of Opportunity', in G. Dosi, C. Freeman, R.R. Nelson, G. Silverberg and L.L. Soete (eds.), *Technical Change and Economic Theory*, London: Pinter Publishers Ltd, pp. 458–79.

Raffer, K. and H.W. Singer (2001) *The Economic North South Divide: Six Decades of Unequal Development*, Cheltenham: Edward Elgar.

Sachs, J.D. and Woo, W.T. (1997) *Understanding China's Economic Performance*, NBER Working Papers 5935, Cambridge MA: National Bureau of Economic Research, Inc.

Sanford, J.E. (2002) 'World Bank: IDA Loans or IDA Grants', *World Development*, 30(5), pp. 741–62.

Sapsford, D. (1985) 'The Statistical Debate on the Net Barter Terms of Trade between Primary Commodities and Manufactures: A Comment and Some Statistical Evidence', *The Economic Journal*, 95(September), pp. 781–8.

Sapsford, D. (1988) 'The Debate over Trends in the Terms of Trade', in D. Greenaway (ed.), *Economic Development and International Trade*, London: Macmillan, pp. 117–30.

Sapsford, D. and V.N. Balasubramanyam (2003) 'Globalization and the Terms of Trade: The Glass Ceiling Hypothesis', in H. Bloch (ed.), *Growth and Development in the Global Economy*, Cheltenham: Edward Elgar, pp. 157–69.

Sarkar, P. (1986) 'The Singer–Prebisch Hypothesis: A Statistical Evaluation', *Cambridge Journal of Economics*, 10, pp. 355–71.

Sarkar, P. (2001) 'The Long-term Behaviour of the North–South Terms of Trade: A Review of the Statistical Debate', *Progress in Development Studies*, 1, pp. 309–27.

Schrijver, N. (1985) 'De Verenigde Naties, de internationale economische organisaties en ontwikkelingssamenwerking [The United Nations, International Economic Organisations and Development Cooperation]', in *Leergang Ontwikkelingsproblematiek* [Syllabus for Development Studies], Groningen.

Seers, D. (1979) 'The Meaning of Development', in D. Lehman (eds.), *Development Theory: Four Critical Studies*, London: Frank Cass, pp. 9–30.

Selowsky, M. (1987) 'Adjustment in the 1980s: An Overview of the Issues', *Finance and Development*, June, pp. 11–13.

Singer, H.W. (2001) *International Development Co-operation: Selected Essays by H.W. Singer on Aid and the United Nations System*, ed., with contributions, D. John Shaw, Basingstoke, Palgrave.

Soros, G. (2000) *Open Society: Reforming Global Capitalism*, New York: Public Affairs.

Soros, G. (2002) *On Globalisation*, Oxford: Public Affairs Limited.

Spraos, J. (1980) 'The Statistical Debate on the Net Barter Terms of Trade between Primary Commodities and Manufactures', *The Economic Journal*, 90 (March), pp. 107–28.

Stiglitz, J. (2000) 'Capital Market Liberalization, Economic Growth, and Instability', *World Development*, 28(6), pp. 1075–86.

Stiglitz, J. (2002) *Globalization and Its Discontents*, New York/London: Norton.

Streeten, P. (1984) 'Approaches to a New International Economic Order', in C.K. Wilber (ed.), *The Political Economy of Development and Underdevelopment*, 3rd edn, New York: Random House, pp. 473–97.

Sunkel, O. and G. Zuleta (1990) 'Neo-Structuralism Versus Neo-Liberalism in the 1990s', *CEPAL Review*, 42, pp. 36–51.

Sunkel, O. (1993) *Development from within: Toward a Neostructuralist Approach for Latin America*, Boulder, Co: Lynne Reiner Publishers.

Szirmai, A., B. van Ark and D. Pilat (eds.) (1993) *Explaining Economic Growth: Essays in Honour of Angus Maddison*, Amsterdam: North Holland.

Tarp, F. (1993) *Stabilization and Structural Adjustment: Macro-economic Frameworks for Analysing the Crisis in Sub-Saharan Africa*, London: Routledge.

Teunissen, P.J. (1990) 'Een ambigue wereld: Compendium: Sociologie van de interna-
    tionale betrekkingen [An Ambiguous World: Compendium: Sociology of Interna-
    tional Relations], photocopy, Groningen.
Thoburn, J.T. (1997) *Primary Commodity Exports and Economic Development: Theory, Evidence
    and a Study of Malaysia*, New York: Wiley.
Tobin, J. (2000) 'Financial Globalization', *World Development*, 28(6), pp. 1101–04.
Toye, J. (1993) 'Structural Adjustment: Context, Assumptions, Origin and Diversity', Paper
    presented at the International Seminar of Structural Adjustment and Long-Term
    Development in Sub-Saharan Africa: Research and Policy Issues, The Hague: DGIS,
    1–3 June.
UIA (2003/4) *Yearbook of International Organizations 1999–2000*, Vol. I, 40th edn, Munich:
    Union of International Associations, Saur Verlag.
ul Haq, M. (1976) *The Poverty Curtain: Choices for the Third World*, New York: Columbia
    University Press.
UNCTAD (2000) *The Competitiveness Challenge: Transnational Corporations and Industrial Re-
    structuring in Developing Countries*, New York/Geneva United Nations.
UNCTAD (2002) *Handbook of Statistics 2002*, New York/Geneva: United Nations.
UNIDO (2002) *Industrial Development Report, 2002/3: Competing through Innovation and Learn-
    ing*, Vienna: UNIDO.
United Nations (1993a) *Statesman's Yearbook*, New York: UN.
United Nations (1993b) *Monthly Bulletin of Statistics*, March.
Urquidi, V. (1993) 'The Developmentalist View', in Szirmai, van Ark and Pilat, *Explaining
    Economic Growth*, pp. 447–65.
van Dam, F. (1984) 'Honderd jaar ontwikkelingsvraagstuk [The Issue of Development:
    One Hundred Years]', *Economisch Statistische Berichten*, pp. 162–8.
van der Hoeven, R. and L. Taylor (2000) 'Introduction: Structural Adjustment, Labour
    Markets and Employment: Some Considerations for Sensible People', *The Journal of
    Development Studies*, Special Section on Structural Adjustment and the Labour Market,
    36(4), April, pp. 57–65.
Vernon, R. (1966) 'International Investment and International Trade in the Product Cycle',
    Quarterly Journal of Economics, 80, pp. 246–63.
Vernon, R. (1974) 'The Location of Economic Activity', in J.H. Dunning (ed.), *Economic
    Analysis and the Multinational Enterprise*, London: Allen and Unwin.
Vernon, R. (1977) *Storm over Multinationals: The Real Issues*, Cambridge MA: Harvard
    University Press.
Westphal, L.E. (2002) 'Technology Strategies for Economic Development in a Fast
    Changing Global Economy', *Economics of Innovation and New Technology*, 11(4/5),
    August/October, pp. 275–320.
Williamson, J. (1990) 'What Washington Means by Policy Reform', in J. Williamson, ed.,
    Latin American Adjustment: How Much Has Happened?, Washington, DC, Institute for
    International Economics.
Williamson, J. (1993) 'Democracy and the Washington Consensus', *World Development*,
    21(8), 1329–36.
Williamson, J. (1997) 'The Washington Consensus Revisited', in L. Emmerij (ed.), *Economic
    and Social Development into the XXI century*, Washington, DC: Inter-American Develop-
    ment Bank/Baltimore: Johns Hopkins University Press, pp. 48–61.
Woo, W.T., J.D. Sachs and K. Schwab (eds.) (2000) *The Asian Financial Crisis: Lessons for a
    Resilient Asia*, Cambridge, MA: MIT Press.
Wood, R. (1985) 'The Aid Regime and International Debt: Crisis and Structural Adjust-
    ment', *Development and Change*, 16, pp. 179–212.
World Bank (1985) *World Development Report 1985*, Oxford University Press.
World Bank (1987) *World Development Report 1987*, Oxford University Press.
World Bank (1989) *Sub-Saharan Africa: From Crisis to Sustainable Growth*, Washington, DC,
    World Bank.
World Bank and UNDP (1989) *Africa's Adjustment and Growth in the 1980s*, Washington/New
    York: World Bank/UNDP.

World Bank (1993) *The East Asian Miracle: Economic Growth and Public Policy*, New York: Oxford University Press.

World Bank (1995) *World Debt Tables 1994/95*, Washington, DC, and previous issues.

World Bank (2002) *World Development Indicators 2002*, CD-Rom, Washington, DC: World Bank.

World Bank (2003) *Global Development Finance: Striving for Stability in Development Finance*, Washington, DC: World Bank. (successor to the series *World Debt Tables*).

Chapter 14   Foreign aid and development

Alesina, A. and D. Dollar (2000) 'Who Gives Foreign Aid to Whom and Why?', *Journal of Economic Growth*, 5(1), March, pp. 33–63.

Balassa, B. (1978) 'Exports and Economics Growth: Further Evidence' *Journal of Development Economics*, 5(June), pp. 181–9.

Bauer, P.T. (1976) *Dissent on Development*, London, Weidenfeld and Nicolson.

Bauer, P.T. (1981) *Equality, the Third World and Economic Delusion*, London: Weidenfeld and Nicolson.

Bauer, P.T. (1984) *Reality and Rhetoric*, London: Weidenfeld and Nicolson.

Bauer, P.T. (1988) 'Comment on R.A. Cassen, Aid Evaluation. Its Scope and Limits', in C.J. Jepma (1988), *North–South Cooperation in Retrospect and Prospect*, 1988, pp. 182–6.

Bauer, P.T. and B. Yamey (1981) 'The Political Economy of Foreign Aid', *Lloyds Bank Review*, October, pp. 1–15.

Bauer, P.T. and B. Yamey (1986) *Development Forum*, 14, (3), Geneva: United Nations, April.

Berlage, L. and R. Renard (1993) 'Evaluatie van Ontwikkelingshulp in België en Neder-land [Evaluation of development aid in Belgium and the Netherlands], Research Paper in Economic Development, No. 24, Centrum voor Economische Studieën, Leuven.

Bhagwati, J.N. (1985) 'Foreign Trade Regimes', in J.N. Bhagwati, *Dependence and Interdependence: Essays in Development Economics*, Vol. 2, ed. G. Grossman, Oxford: Basil Blackwell, pp. 123–38.

Bol, D. (1983) *Economen en armoede, Moedwil en misverstand in de ontwikkelingshulp* [Economists and Poverty: Malice and Misunderstanding in Development Aid], Amsterdam: Van Gennep.

Bos, H.C. (1990) 'Ontwikkelingseconomie [Development economics]', *Economisch Statistische Berichten*, 5-12-1990, pp. 1160–7.

Boserup, E. (1983) 'The Impact of Scarcity and Plenty on Development', *Journal of Interdisciplinary History*, 14(2), pp. 383–407.

Brandt, W. *et al.* (1980) *North–South: A Programme for Survival*, London: Pan Books.

Brandt, W. *et al.* (1983) *Common Crisis: North–South Cooperation for World Recovery*, London/Paris.

Breman, J. (1986) 'Over hobbies en lobbies: de uitbesteding van de Nederlandse ont-wikkelingshulp [On Hobbies and Lobbies: Farming out Dutch Development Aid]', *Internationale Spectator*, 40(6), June, pp. 353–63.

Brundtland, G.H. et al. (1987) *Our Common Future*, The World Commission on Environment and Development, Oxford University Press.

Bruno, M., M. Ravallion and L. Squire (1998), 'Equity and Growth in Developing Countries: Old and New Perspectives on the Policy Issues', in V. Tanzi and K. Chu (eds.), *Income Distribution and High-Quality Growth*, Cambridge, MA: MIT Press.

Bruton, H.J. (1969) 'The Two-Gap Approach to Aid and Development: Comment', *The American Economic Review*, 59(June), pp. 439–46.

Burki, S.J. and Ayres, R. (1986) 'A Fresh look at Development Aid', *Finance and Development*, 23(1), March, pp. 6–10.

Burnside C. and D. Dollar (1997) *Aid, Policies and Growth*, Policy Research Working Paper, 1777, Washington, DC: World Bank.

Burnside C. and D. Dollar (2000) 'Aid, Policies and Growth', *American Economic Review*, 90(4), pp. 847–68.

Cassen, R.A. (1986) *Does Aid Work?*, Oxford: Clarendon Press.

Cassen, R.A. (1988) 'Aid Evaluation – Its Scope and Limits', in C.J. Jepma (ed.), *North–South Cooperation in Retrospect and Prospect*, London: Routledge and Kegan Paul, 1988, pp. 167–81.

Chenery, H. (1979) *Structural Change and Development Policy*, New York: Oxford University Press.

Chenery, H. and I. Adelman (1966) 'Foreign Aid and Economic Development: the Case of Greece', *Review of Economics and Statistics*, February.

Chenery, H., M.S. Ahluwalia, C.L.G. Bell, J.H. Duloy and R. Jolly (1974) *Redistribution with Growth*, New York/Oxford: Oxford University Press.

Chenery, H. and A. MacEwan (1966) 'Optimal Patterns of Growth and Aid: The Case of Pakistan', *Pakistan Development Review*, Summer.

Chenery, H. and A.M. Strout (1966), 'Foreign Assistance and Economic Development', *American Economic Review*, 56, September, pp. 679–733.

Cochrane, G. (1979) *The Cultural Appraisal of Development Projects*, New York/London: Praeger.

Cracknell, B.E. (2000) *Evaluating Development Aid*, New Delhi/London: Sage Publications.

Dalgaard, C. and H. Hansen (2001) 'On Aid, Growth and Good Policies', *The Journal of Development Studies*, 37(6), August, pp. 17–41.

Dijkstra, G. and H. White (eds.) (2003) *Programme Aid and Development: Beyond Conditionality*, London: Routledge.

Dollar, D. and L. Pritchett (1998) *Assessing Aid: What Works, What Doesn't and Why*, A World Bank Policy Research Report, New York: Oxford University Press.

Doornbos, M. (2001) '"Good Governance": The Rise and Decline of a Policy Metaphor', *The Journal of Development Studies*, 37(6), August, pp. 93–108.

Easterly, W. (1997) *The Ghost of the Financing Gap*, Policy Research Working Paper 1807, World Bank, Development Research Group, Washington, DC: World Bank.

Emmerij, L.J. (1984) 'Ontwikkelingssamenwerking op een kruispunt? Noodzaak tot omvorming van het Nederlandse beleid en Apparaat [Development Cooperation at Crossroads? The Need to Change Dutch Policy and Apparatus]', *Internationale Spectator*, 38, March, p. 121 ff.

Frankel, F.R. (1978) *India's Political Economy, 1947–77*, Princeton University Press.

Fukuyama, F. (1992) *The End of History and the Last Man*, New York: The Free Press.

George, S. (1988) *A Fate Worse than Debt*, London/New York: Penguin.

Griffin, K. (1970) 'Foreign Capital, Domestic Savings and Economic Development', *Bulletin of the Oxford Institute of Economics and Statistics*, 32(2), May, 1970 and 'reply' 33(2), May.

Griffin, K. (1987) 'Doubts about Aid', in K. Griffin, *World Hunger and the World Economy*, London: Macmillan, pp. 235–54.

Griffin, K. and J.L. Enos (1970) 'Foreign Assistance: Objectives and Consequences', *Economic Development and Cultural Change*, 18(April).

Griffin, K. and J. Gurley (1985) 'Radical Analyses of Imperialism, the Third World and the Transition to Socialism', *Journal of Economic Literature*, 23(3), September, pp. 1089–1144.

Guillaumont, P. and L. Chauvet (2001) 'Aid and Performance: A Reassessment', *The Journal of Development Studies*, 37(60), August, pp. 66–92.

Gupta, K.L. and M.A. Islam (1983) *Foreign Capital, Savings and Growth*, Boston: Reidel.

Haan, L.J. (1989) 'Over de kwaliteit van de ontwikkelingssamenwerking [On the Quality of Development Cooperation]', *Internationale Spectator*, 43(6), June, pp. 374–75.

Hancock, G. (1991) *Lords of Poverty*, London: Mandarin Paperbacks.

Hansen H. and F. Tarp (2000a) 'Aid Effectiveness Disputed', *Journal of International Development*, 12(3), pp. 275–398.

Hansen, H, and F. Tarp (2000b) 'The Effectiveness of Foreign Aid', in F. Tarp and P. Hjertholm (eds.) (2000) *Foreign Aid and Development*, London: Routledge.

Hayami, Y. and V.W. Ruttan (1985) *Agricultural Development: An International Perspective*, rev. edn, Baltimore: Johns Hopkins Press.

Hayter, T. (1971) *Aid as Imperialism*, London: Penguin.

Hayter, T. (1981) *The Creation of World Poverty: An Alternative View to the Brandt Report*, London: Pluto.

Hayter, T. (1989) *Exploited Earth: British Aid and the Environment*, London: Earthscan Publications.

Hayter, T. and C. Watson (1985) *Aid: Rhetoric and Reality*, London: Pluto.

Heller, P.S. (1975) 'A Model of Public Fiscal Behavior in Developing Countries: Aid, Investment and Taxation', *American Economic Review*, 65(June), pp. 429–45.

Hermes, N. and R. Lensink (2001a) 'Changing the Conditions for Development Aid: A New Paradigm?', *Journal of Development Studies*, 37(6), pp. 1–16.

Hermes, N. and R. Lensink (eds.) (2001b) *Changing the Conditions for Development Aid: A New Paradigm?* London: Frank Cass.

Hertz, N. (2001) *The Silent Takeover: Global Capitalism and the Death of Democracy*, London: Heineman.

Hoebink, P. (1988) *Geven en Nemen: De Nederlandse ontwikkelingshulp aan Tanzania en Sri Lanka* [Giving or Taking: Dutch Development aid to Tanzania and Sri Lanka], Nijmegen: Stichting Derde Wereld Publikaties.

Hoebink, P. (1990a) 'Tussen militair, dominee en koopman: hulpbeleid van westerse landen [Between Soldier, Clergyman and Merchant: Aid Policies in Western Countries]', *Internationale Spectator*, 44, March, pp. 126–39.

Hoebink, P. (1990b) 'De Nederlandse ontwikkelingshulp [Dutch Development Aid]', in R. Doom, *Derde wereld handboek: Deel I, Noord-Zuid en Zuid-Zuid in politiek perspectief*, Brussels/The Hague, pp. 197–218.

Hoeven, R. van der (2001) 'Assessing Aid and Global Governance', *Journal of Development Studies*, 37(6), August, pp. 109–117.

ILO (1976) *Employment, Growth and Basic Needs: A One-World Problem*, Geneva: ILO.

IMF (1993) *Statistical Yearbook*, Washington, DC, IMF.

Jackson, T. (1982) *Against the Grain: The Dilemma of Project Food Aid*, Oxford: Oxfam.

Jay, K. and C. Michalopoulos (1989) 'Donor Policies, Donor Interests, and Aid Effectiveness', in A.O. Krueger et al. (1989) *Aid and Development*, pp. 68–88.

Jepma, C.J. (1984) 'Ontwikkelingssamenwerking op het nieuwe spoor [Development 'Cooperation on a New Track]', *Internationale Spectator*, 38, September, p. 504 ff.

Jepma, C.J. (ed.) (1988) *North–South Cooperation in Retrospect and Prospect*, London: Routledge and Kegan Paul.

Jepma, C.J. (1992) *EC-Wide Untying*, Development and Security, No. 37, Groningen: Centre for Development Studies, October.

Jepma, C.J. (1997) 'On the Effectiveness of Aid', World Bank, unpublished.

Klein, N. (1999) *No Logo: Taking Aim at the Brand Bullies*, New York: Picador.

Knack, S. (2001) 'Aid Dependence and the Quality of Governance: A Cross-Country Empirical Analysis', *Southern Economic Journal*, 68(2), pp. 310–29.

Krauss, M. (1983a) *Development without Aid*, New York: McGraw-Hill.

Krauss, M. (1983b) *Transferring Incomes Versus Transferring Prosperity*, Report, New York: Manhattan Institute for Policy Research, January.

Krueger, A.O. (1978) *Foreign Trade Regimes and Economic Development: Liberalization Attempts and Consequences*, NBER, Cambridge, MA: Ballinger.

Krueger, A.O., C. Michalopoulos and V. Ruttan, (1989) *Aid and Development*, Baltimore/London: Johns Hopkins University Press.

Kruyt, D. (1988) 'De Sociologie van ontwikkelingsbureaucratieën [The Sociology of Development Bureaucracies]', in D. Kruyt and K. Koonings (eds.), *Ontwikkelingsvraagstukken: Theorie, beleid en methoden*, Muiderberg: Coutinho, pp. 57–73.

Kruyt, D. and K. Koonings (eds.) (1988) *Ontwikkelingsvraagstukken: Theorie, beleid en methoden* [Development Issues: Theory, Policy, and Methods], Muiderberg: Coutinho.

Kruyt, D. and M. Vellinga (1983) *Ontwikkelingshulp getest: Resultaten onder de loep* [Development Aid Examined: A Closer Look at the Results], Muiderberg: Coutinho.

Kuznets, S. (1955) 'Economic Growth and Income Inequality', *American Economic Review*, 45(1), pp. 1–28.

Lal, D. (1978) *Poverty, Power and Prejudice: The North–South Confrontation*, London: Fabian Society.

Lal, D. (1983) *The Poverty of Development Economics*, London: Institute of Economic Affairs.

Lal, D. (2000) *The Poverty of Development Economics*, 2nd rev. and exp. US edn, Cambridge, MA/London: The MIT Press.

Lappé, F.M., J. Collins, and D. Kinley (1980) *Aid as Obstacle: Twenty Questions about our Foreign Aid and the Hungry*, San Francisco: Institute for Food and Development Policy.

Lensink, R. (1993a) *External Finance and Development*, Groningen: Wolters Noordhoff.

Lensink, R. (1993b) 'Recipient Government Behavior and the Effectiveness of Development Aid', *De Economist*, 141(4), pp. 543–62.

Lensink, R. and H. White (2001) 'Are there Negative Returns to Aid?', *The Journal of Development Studies*, 37(6), August, pp. 42–65.

Lewis, W.A. (1954) 'Economic Development with Unlimited Supplies of Labour', *Manchester School of Economic and Social Studies*, 22, pp. 139–91.

Lumsdaine, D.H. (1993) *Moral Vision in International Politics*, Princeton University Press.

Lundvall, B.A. (1992) *National Systems of Innovation: Towards a Theory of Innovation and Interactive Learning*, London: Pinter.

Maddison, A. (1989) *The World Economy in the 20th Century*, Paris: OECD.

Maizels, A. and M.K. Nissanke (1984) 'Motivations for Aid to Developing Countries', *World Development*, 12(9), September, pp. 879–900.

Maren, M. (1997) *The Road to Hell: The Ravaging Effects of Foreign Aid and International Charity*, New York: The Free Press.

Meltzer, A. (2000) *Report of the International Financial Institutions Advisory Commission*, Washington, DC, International Financial Institutions Advisory Committee, March.

Mende, T. (1973) *From Aid to Recolonisation: Lessons of a Failure*, London: Harrap.

Millikan, M.F. and W.E. Rostow (1957) *A Proposal: A Key to Effective Foreign Policy*, New York: Harper and Row.

Mosley, P. (1980) 'Aid, Savings and Growth Revisited', *Oxford Bulletin of Economics and Statistics*, 42(2), May, pp. 79–95.

Mosley, P. (1987) *Overseas Aid: Its Defence and Reform*, Brighton, Sussex: Wheatsheaf Books.

Myrdal, G. (1971) *The Challenge of World Poverty*, New York: Vintage Books.

OECD (1985) *Twenty Five Years of Development Cooperation. A Review*, Paris: OECD.

OECD (1986) *Financing and External Debt of Developing Countries 1985*, Paris: OECD.

OECD (1993a) *Financing and External Debt of Developing Countries 1992*, Paris: OECD.

OECD (1993b) *Development Cooperation 1992*, Paris: OECD.

OECD (1994) *Development Cooperation 1994*, Paris: OECD.

OECD (1998) *Development Cooperation 1997*, Paris: OECD.

OECD (2000) *Development Cooperation 1999*, Paris: OECD.

OECD (1995) *Geographical Distribution of Financial Flows to Developing Countries 1989–1993*, Paris: OECD, and various earlier issues.

OECD (2003a) Development Assistance Committee, *Geographical Distribution of Financial Flows to Aid Recipients, 1960–2001*, CD-Rom, International Development Statistics (IDS).

OECD (2003b) Development Assistance Committee, *Development Co-operation Report 2002, Statistical Annex*, CD-Rom, International Development Statistics (IDS).

Pack, H. and J.R. Pack (1993) 'Foreign Aid and the Question of Fungibility', *Review of Economics and Statistics*, 75(2), pp. 258–65.

Pack, H. and C. Paxson (2001) 'Is African Manufacturing Skill Constrained?', in A. Szirmai and P. Lapperre (eds.), *The Industrial Experience of Tanzania*, Basingstoke: Palgrave, pp. 50–72.

Papanek, G.F. (1972) 'The Effect of Aid and Other Resource Transfers on Savings and Growth in Less Developed Countries', *The Economic Journal*, 82 (327), September, pp. 934–50.

Papanek, G.F. (1973) 'Aid, Foreign Private Investment, Saving and Growth in Less Developed Countries', *The Journal of Political Economy*, 81, pp. 120–30.

Papanek, G.F. (1983) 'Aid, Equity and Growth in South Asia', in J. Parkinson (ed.), *Poverty and Aid*, Oxford: Blackwell.

Prince, G.H.A. (1976) 'Ontwikkelingssamenwerking; als voortzetting van koloniaal beleid [Development Cooperation as a Continuation of Colonial Policies]' *Internationale Spectator*, 30(3), March, pp. 173–80.

Quarles van Ufford, P., D. Kruijt and T. Downing (eds.) (1988) *The Hidden Crisis in Development: Development Bureaucracies*, Amsterdam: Free University Press.

Raffer, K. and H.W. Singer (2001) *The Economic North–South Divide: Six Decades of Unequal Development*, Cheltenham: Edward Elgar.

Rana, P.B. and J.M. Dowling (1988) 'The Impact of Foreign Capital on Growth: Evidence from Asian Developing Countries', *The Developing Economies*, 36(1), pp. 3–11.

Rana, P.B. and J.M. Dowling (1990) 'Foreign Capital and Asian Economic Growth', *Asian Development Review*, 8, pp. 77–102.

Riddell, R.C. (1987) *Foreign Aid Reconsidered*, Baltimore/London: Johns Hopkins/Curry.

Rosenstein-Rodan, P. (1961) 'International Aid for Underdeveloped Countries', *Review of Economics and Statistics*, 43, May, pp. 107–38.

Rostow, W.W. (1971) *The Stages of Economic Growth*, Second edition, Cambridge, MA: Cambridge University Press (first published 1960).

Roth, D. (1993) 'Ontwikkelingshulp ter discussie: Kwaliteitsdecreet of kwaliteitsdebat? [Development Aid in Discussion: Quality Decree or Quality Debate]', *Internationale Spectator*, 47(5), May, No. 5, pp. 274–80.

Ruttan, V.W. (1989a) 'Improving the Quality of Life in Rural Areas', in A.O. Krueger, C. Michalopoulos and V. Ruttan (eds.), *Aid and Development*, Baltimore/London: Johns Hopkins University Press.

Ruttan, V.W. (1989b) 'Why Foreign Economic Assistance?', *Economic Development and Cultural Change*, 37(2), January.

Sachs, J. and A. Warner (1995) *Economic Reform and the Process of Global Integration*, Brookings Papers on Economic Activity, 1, pp. 1–118.

Schraeder, P., S. Hook and B. Taylor (1998) 'Clarifying the Foreign Aid Puzzle: A Comparison of American, Japanese, French and Swedish Aid Flows', *World Politics*, pp. 294–320.

Schultz, T.W. (1964) *Transforming Traditional Agriculture*, New Haven and London: Yale University Press.

Sen, A.K. (1960) *Choice of Techniques*, Oxford: Basil Blackwell.

Soest, J. van (1975) 'Het begin van de ontwikkelingshulp in de Verenigde Naties en in Nederland 1945–1952' [Early Development Aid in the United Nations and the Netherlands, 1945–1952]. University of Nijmegen.

Stern, N. (2002) 'Making the Case for Aid', in World Bank, *A Case for Aid: Building a Consensus for Development Assistance*, The World Bank, Washington, DC: pp. 15–24.

Stiglitz, J. (1999) 'The World Bank at the Millennium', *Economic Journal*, 109(November), pp. 577–97.

Stiglitz, J. (2002) *Globalization and Its Discontents*, New York/London: Norton.

Szirmai, A. (1988) *Inequality Observed: A Study of Attitudes towards Income Inequality*, Aldershot: Avebury Press.

Tarp, F. and P. Hjertholm (eds.) (2000) *Foreign Aid and Development*, London: Routledge.

Teszler, R.K., 'Nederlandse samenwerking met ontwikkelingslanden [Dutch Cooperation with Developing Countries]', in E.H. v.d. Beugel et al., *Nederlandse buitenlandse politiek; Heden en verleden* [Dutch Foreign Policies; Past and Present], Baarn: In en Toren.

Tims, W. (1985) 'Commentaar: Organisatie en doeltreffendheid van de Nederlandse ontwikkelingssamenwerking [Comment: Organisation and Effectiveness of Dutch Development Cooperation]', *Internationale Spectator*, 39(12), December, p. 759 ff.

Tims, W. (1989) 'Development Cooperation: a Dutch Preoccupation', *Internationale Spectator*, 43(11), November, pp. 714–17.

UNDP (2003) *Human Development Report 2003, Millennium Development Goals: A Compact among Nations to End Human Poverty*, New York: Oxford University Press.

van Dam, F. (1978) 'Mode in het ontwikkelingsvraagstuk [Trends in the Issue of Development]', *Economisch Statistische Berichten*, 17-5-1978, pp. 496–500.

van Dam, F. (1989a) 'Het ontwikkelingsvraagstuk op hoofdpunten bezien [Main Issues in Development]', *Economisch Statistische Berichten*, 31–5–1989, pp. 529–33.

van Dam, F. (1989b) 'Zin en onzin over projecthulp [Sense and Nonsense in Project Aid]', *Internationale Spectator*, 43(6), June, pp. 372–3.

Vingerhoets, J. (1986) 'Het "nieuwe" hulpbeleid van minister Schoo [The 'New' Aid Policies of Minister School', *Internationale Spectator*, 40(3), March, pp. 149–57.

White, H. (1992) 'The Macroeconomic Impact of Development Aid: A Critical Survey', *The Journal of Development Studies*, 28(2), pp. 163–240.

Williamson, J. (1990) 'What Washington Means by Policy Reform', in J. Williamson (ed.), *Latin American Adjustment: How Much Has Happened?*, Washington, DC: Institute for International Economics.

World Bank (1980) *World Tables 1980*, Baltimore: Johns Hopkins University.

World Bank (1985) *World Tables 1985*, Baltimore, Johns Hopkins University Press.

World Bank (1993) *World Tables 1993*, Baltimore, Johns Hopkins University Press.

World Bank (1995) *World Tables 1995*, Baltimore: Johns Hopkins University Press.

World Bank (2002a) *A Case for Aid. Building a Consensus for Development Assistance*, Washington, DC: World Bank.

World Bank (2002b) *World Development Indicators 2002*, World Bank, CD-Rom.

World Bank (2003) *Global Development Finance: Striving for Stability in Development Finance, Vol. 2: Summary and Country Tables*, Washington, DC: World Bank.

Zeylstra, W.G. (1975) *Aid or Development: The Relevance of Development Aid to Problems of Developing Countries*, Leiden: A.W. Sijthoff.

Zoomers, E.B. (1992) 'Effectiviteit van Nederlands ontwikkelingsbeleid: Suggesties tot verbetering van de projectcyclus [Effectiveness of Dutch Development Policy: Suggestions for Improvements in the Project Cycle]', *Internationale Spectator*, 41, March, pp. 114–19.

Author index

Subject index

abortion   166–7, 173
accumulation function of the state   444
acephalous political units   442
Africa
  costs of education   234–7
  culture and fertility rates   170–1
  data on production   360
  decolonisation   522
  GDP and agriculture   300
  importance of social obligations   500–1
  one-party states   480–3
  scramble for   52–3, 441–2
  structural adjustment policies   571
    investment in infrastructure   572–3
  traditional versus modern culture
    496
  see also AIDS; deforestation; enrolment
    ratios; food production; foreign
    aid, low income countries; slave
    trade
agricultural development models
  conservation model   376
  diffusion model   377–8
  high-payoff input model   378–9
  resource exploitation model   375–6
  urban–industrial impact model   376–7
  see also green revolution
agricultural and mining exports 5; *see also*
    primary exports
agricultural multinationals   386, 387
agricultural production   111
  efficiency of traditional farmers
    409–10
    significance of risk   410–11
  growth of   355–7
  labour outflow from   273, 297, 307–8,
    319
  and population growth   164, 355–9,
    384
  and price policies   395
  share of   30–1
    in national income   396–9
  see also agricultural sector; expansion of
    cultivated area; increased yields;

intensification of land use; green
    revolution; modernisation theory
agricultural research institutes and new
    technology   385
agricultural revolution   369
agricultural sector   269–71
  contributions to economic development
    40, 272–4, 296–8, 310
  contributions from manufacturing
    298
  and development   40
  exports and source of currency   274
  inputs for industrial sector   297–8
  investment in   378–9
    in infrastructure   293, 299, 371
  irrigation and growth   273–4
  labour force   40
  as market for
    consumer and producer goods
      297–8
    industrial products   273, 298
  profitability of   280
  seasonal (disguised) unemployment
    319, 371
  structural adjustment policy measures
    567
  see also closed model of economy
agricultural technology
  diffusion   377
  ecological consequences of   385
  inequality   383–4
  policy   386
  population density   367, 369, 384–5
  see also green revolution; high-payoff
    input model; induced
    technological development theory
agriculture
  educational shortcomings   241
  farm size   414
  and foreign aid   622
  employment in   110, 156–8
  and industrialisation   271, 294, 319,
    325
  price incentives   299

698